D1326760

THE VICTORIA HISTORY
OF THE
COUNTIES OF ENGLAND

———

A HISTORY OF
OXFORDSHIRE
VOLUME VI

THE VICTORIA HISTORY
OF THE
COUNTIES OF ENGLAND

EDITED BY R. B. PUGH

THE UNIVERSITY OF LONDON
INSTITUTE OF
HISTORICAL RESEARCH

Oxford University Press, Amen House, London, E.C.4

GLASGOW NEW YORK TORONTO MELBOURNE WELLINGTON
BOMBAY CALCUTTA MADRAS KARACHI KUALA LUMPUR
CAPE TOWN IBADAN NAIROBI ACCRA

© *University of London 1959*

PRINTED IN GREAT BRITAIN

INSCRIBED TO THE
MEMORY OF HER LATE MAJESTY
QUEEN VICTORIA
WHO GRACIOUSLY GAVE THE TITLE TO
AND ACCEPTED THE DEDICATION
OF THIS HISTORY

View of Market Hill in about 1860

BICESTER

A HISTORY OF THE COUNTY OF

OXFORD

EDITED BY MARY D. LOBEL

VOLUME VI

PLOUGHLEY HUNDRED

PUBLISHED FOR

THE INSTITUTE OF HISTORICAL RESEARCH

BY THE

OXFORD UNIVERSITY PRESS

AMEN HOUSE, LONDON

1959

CONTENTS OF VOLUME SIX

CONTENTS OF VOLUME SIX

LIST OF ILLUSTRATIONS

LIST OF ILLUSTRATIONS

LIST OF MAPS AND PLANS

The maps of Ploughley Hundred, Bicester, Bletchingdon, Islip, Lower and Upper Heyford are partly based on the Ordnance Survey, and are published with the sanction of the Controller of H.M. Stationery Office, Crown Copyright reserved.

The historical work on the maps was done by Mary D. Lobel, R. F. Walker, and Mary Barran. All the maps were drawn by Mary E. Potter. The church plans and the plan of Hampton Gay Manor House are the joint work of P. J. P. Boby, H. M. Colvin, R. Smith, and J. Stevens.

EDITORIAL NOTE

THIS volume, the sixth of the series of Victoria Histories of Oxfordshire, is a further outcome of the partnership between Oxfordshire and the University of London. The local committee under the chairmanship of Sir Charles Ponsonby has been responsible for the preparation of the text, and the University of London has borne the cost of its publication. In this case the local committee has also taken responsibility for the final editing of the volume, which, with the agreement of the Institute of Historical Research, was entrusted to an editorial committee consisting of Professor V. H. Galbraith (Chairman), Mr. H. M. Colvin, Professor H. J. Habakkuk, Dr. W. G. Hoskins, Miss K. Major, Principal of St. Hilda's College, and Mr. L. Stone.

For financial support of the editorial and research staff the committee is indebted to the generous subsidies of the University and City of Oxford and of the Oxfordshire County Council: also to the Borough of Henley, the Oxford colleges, and to many private subscribers, whose names are printed below.

As much property in Ploughley Hundred was held by corporate bodies, their archives have provided an abundance of material for the agrarian history of many of the parishes. A number of private collections have also proved of value, and the records of the diocese and archdeaconry of Oxford, now easily accessible in the Bodleian Library, have enabled the ecclesiastical history of the parishes to be written with greater fullness and certainty.

The volume owes much to the kindness of governing bodies of many Oxford colleges, to the incumbents of Oxfordshire parishes, and to others who have given permission to use documents in their care. Particular mention may be made of Mr. J. N. L. Myres, Bodley's Librarian, of Dr. W. O. Hassall and other members of the Bodleian staff, of Mr. H. M. Walton, the County archivist, and his assistant, Mr. S. G. Baker, who have assisted the History in every way in their power. Thanks are due to the Governors of St. Bartholomew's Hospital, to Mr. G. Elliott, Provost of Eton, and to the Dean and Chapter of Westminster for their kindness in allowing access to their archives, and to their respective archivists, Mrs. G. Whitteridge, Mr. T. Lyon, and Dr. L. E. Tanner, for their courteous help. Among private owners especial thanks are due to Mr. T. Cottrell-Dormer and Mrs. Stanley Barry for the trouble they have so willingly taken.

Valuable help has been given in architectural matters by Mr. H. M. Colvin and on heraldry by Mr. P. S. Spokes. Mr. A. R. Charlton, Director of Education for Oxfordshire, and Mr. J. Garne, Chief Education Officer for the City of Oxford, have kindly supplied notes on the Oxfordshire schools. Mr. A. Cossons has allowed the use of his unpublished paper on the Oxfordshire turnpikes, and Mr. W. L. Brown has made an index of recent archaeological finds especially for the Victoria Histories of Oxfordshire. Mr. W. H. Godfrey put at the committee's disposal the photographs in the collection of the National Buildings Record, and the Revd. B. F. L. Clarke lent his notes on church buildings. To all these and to many others who have given general help sincere thanks are expressed. To others who have given specific information or help acknowledgement is made in the footnotes.

EDITORIAL NOTE

The illustrations owe much to Miss D. B. Dew's generosity in lending pen drawings from the late Mr. G. J. Dew's collection, and to the Revd. W. H. Trebble, Vicar of Bicester, in lending a lithograph of the interior of the church. Much general assistance, often of a laborious kind, has been voluntarily given by the Revd. E. P. Baker, Mrs. H. M. Colvin, Miss K. FitzGerald, Miss C. L. M. Hawtrey, Mr. and Mrs. J. L. Kirby, Miss K. E. Moore, Miss Katharine Price, Miss Ethel Savill, Miss Mary Savill, Mrs. Arthur Selwyn, and above all by Miss Mary Barran, a part-time honorary assistant.

OXFORDSHIRE
VICTORIA COUNTY HISTORY
COMMITTEE
1949—JUNE 1958

President

THE RT. HON. LORD BICESTER, Her Majesty's Lieutenant and Custos Rotulorum for the County (died 1956)

†*COL. SIR CHARLES PONSONBY, BT., T.D., D.L. (since 1956)

Vice-Presidents

THE RT. REVD. THE LORD BISHOP OF OXFORD

THE VICE-CHANCELLOR OF THE UNIVERSITY OF OXFORD

THE RT. WORSHIPFUL THE MAYOR OF OXFORD ex officio

THE RT. HON. THE EARL OF MACCLESFIELD (Lord Lieutenant since 1954), Chairman of the Oxfordshire County Council

Chairman

†*COL. SIR CHARLES PONSONBY, BT., T.D., D.L.

Representatives of the Oxfordshire County Council

MRS. R. H. GRETTON

C. J. PEERS, ESQ.

LT.-COL. SIR ALGERNON PEYTON, BT., D.L. (resigned 1952)

MAJOR THE HON. S. STONOR (resigned 1955)

MISS J. M. SHELMERDINE (since 1955)

Representatives of the University of Oxford

†*A. L. POOLE, ESQ., D.LITT., F.B.A., President of St. John's College (resigned 1956)

*V. H. GALBRAITH, ESQ., LITT.D., F.B.A., Regius Professor of Modern History

E. F. JACOB, ESQ., F.B.A., Chichele Professor of Modern History

†MISS L. S. SUTHERLAND, C.B.E., D.LITT., F.B.A., Principal of Lady Margaret Hall (since 1956)

Representatives of the City of Oxford

COUNCILLOR M. MACLAGAN

COUNCILLOR P. S. SPOKES

COUNCILLOR N. WHATLEY

Representatives of District Councils in Oxfordshire

Banbury	THE WORSHIPFUL THE MAYOR OF BANBURY ex officio
Chipping Norton	G. J. C. PRIESTLEY, ESQ. (until 1956)
	COUNCILLOR S. O. WYKES (since 1956)
Henley	COUNCILLOR G. H. J. TOMALIN
Woodstock	COUNCILLOR R. B. RAMSBOTHAM, M.B.E.

Urban Districts

Bicester	COUNCILLOR I. G. McD. GOBLE (resigned 1957)
	COMMANDER E. T. CLOTHIER (since 1957)
Thame	COUNCILLOR MISS J. E. M. FANSHAWE
Witney	COUNCILLOR E. S. WOOD

Rural Districts

Banbury	MRS. J. M. BERKELEY
Bullingdon	LT.-COL. C. R. C. BOYLE, D.S.O.
Chipping Norton	J. S. ROSS, ESQ. (until 1952)
	G. J. C. PRIESTLEY, ESQ. (since 1952)
Henley	THE HON. MRS. S. STONOR
Ploughley	MAJOR A. G. C. FANE, M.C.
Witney	THE REVD. J. L. LOPES, D.D.

Representatives of Learned Societies

Oxfordshire Archaeological Society
R. T. LATTEY, ESQ.

Oxford Record Society
L. G. WICKHAM LEGG, ESQ. (until 1956)
R. V. LENNARD, ESQ. (since 1956)

Oxford Historical Society
W. A. PANTIN, ESQ., F.B.A.

Oxford Architectural and Historical Society
P. S. SPOKES, ESQ.

Co-opted Members

CANON R. F. BALE

E. R. C. BRINKWORTH, ESQ.

SIR GEORGE N. CLARK, D.LITT., F.B.A., Provost of Oriel College

THOMAS LOVEDAY, ESQ., LL.D.

*MISS K. MAJOR, Principal of St. Hilda's College

*J. N. L. MYRES, ESQ., Bodley's Librarian

*SIR MICHAEL OPPENHEIMER, BT.

*R. B. PUGH, ESQ., Editor, Victoria History of the Counties of England (since 1950)

H. A. SMITH, ESQ. (d. 1957)

MISS G. SMITH (since 1957)

OXFORDSHIRE V.C.H. COMMITTEE

Finance and Working Committees

†Sir Basil Blackwell

*H. M. Colvin, Esq.

*H. J. Habakkuk, Esq., Chichele Professor of Economic History in the University of Oxford

*W. O. Hassall, Esq.

*W. G. Hoskins, Esq.

†J. W. Shilson, Esq.

*Lawrence Stone, Esq.

*Miss M. V. Taylor, c.b.e.

†*Col. the Hon. E. H. Wyndham, m.c.

together with the persons marked with an asterisk and/or dagger.

Hon. Treasurer: †*Lt.-Col. H. T. Birch Reynardson, c.m.g., The High Sheriff of Oxfordshire

Secretary: †*Mrs. M. D. Lobel

* A member of the Working Committee.
† A member of the Finance Committee.

LIST OF SUBSCRIBERS

JANUARY 1949—JUNE 1958

UNIVERSITY, COUNTY, CITY, AND COLLEGES

Oxford University Chest
Oxfordshire County Council
Corporation of Oxford
Henley Borough Council
All Souls College
Balliol College
Brasenose College
Christ Church
Corpus Christi College

Exeter College
Hertford College
Jesus College
Keble College
Lincoln College
Magdalen College
Merton College
New College
Oriel College

Pembroke College
The Queen's College
St. Edmund Hall
St. John's College
Somerville College
Trinity College
University College
Wadham College
Worcester College

PRIVATE SUBSCRIBERS

OXFORD CITY

Miss Cecilia Ady, D.Litt.
Mrs. Percy Allen
The Ancient and Modern Club
Barclays Bank, Ltd.
Basil Blackwell, Ltd.
Mrs. G. G. Buckler
Mrs. E. W. Burney
Miss C. V. Butler
Sir George N. Clark, D.Litt.,
    F.B.A.
A. D. M. Cox, Esq.
The Dragon School
A. B. Emden, Esq.
Mrs. E. Ettlinger
Sir Charles Fawcett

Miss H. E. Fiedler
Miss H. E. Fitzrandolph
Sir Alan Gardiner, D.Litt., F.B.A.
W. R. Gowers, Esq.
Mrs. Sturge Gretton
Miss C. L. Hawtrey
Miss D. C. S. Hole
Mrs. Arthur Hunt
Professor E. F. Jacob, F.B.A.
H. R. Leech, Esq.
Miss W. Lickes
Mrs. Edgar Lobel
Miss M. McKisack
Miss K. Major
Miss J. de Lacy Mann

Canon R. R. Martin
N. R. Murphy, Esq.
W. A. Pantin, Esq., F.B.A.
K. T. Parker, Esq., C.B.E., F.B.A.
L. C. W. Phillips, Esq.
A. L. Poole, Esq., D.Litt., F.B.A.
Miss E. E. S. Procter
G. D. Ramsay, Esq.
Miss V. I. Ruffer
Mrs. C. M. Snow
P. S. Spokes, Esq.
A. L. B. Stevens, Esq.
G. H. Stevenson, Esq.
L. Stone, Esq.
H. D. Wilson, Esq.

BANBURY BOROUGH

Banbury Co-operative Industrial
    Society, Ltd.
Mrs. Mary Cheney

Messrs. Cheney & Sons, Ltd.
Messrs. Hunt, Edmunds & Co.,
    Ltd.

Miss C. H. Mackay
Northern Aluminium Co., Ltd.
Messrs. Thornton & Thornton

HENLEY BOROUGH

A. J. Crocker, Esq.
Professor A. M. Hind, O.B.E.

C. Luker, Esq.

C. Cecil Roberts, Esq.

WOODSTOCK BOROUGH WITH BLADON AND BEGBROKE

Miss M. Barnett
F. A. Bevan, Esq.
Miss F. N. Budd
A. J. Henman, Esq.
Mrs. N. M. Lambourn, M.B.E.

The Revd. H. A. McCann
The Marlborough Arms Hotel
R. C. Morley, Esq.
R. B. Ramsbotham, Esq., M.B.E.
Sir John Russell, O.B.E., F.R.S.

The Rt. Revd. Bishop Shedden,
    D.D.
Miss J. M. Shelmerdine

BICESTER URBAN DISTRICT

Bicester Local History Circle
Mrs. M. R. Coker

N. Collisson, Esq.
R. A. Evans, Esq.

F. T. Hudson, Esq.
Dr. G. N. Montgomery

THAME URBAN DISTRICT

Col. S. E. Ashton, O.B.E.
F. Bowden, Esq.
Arthur G. Enock, Esq.

Miss J. E. M. Fanshawe
The Four Horseshoes (Mrs. A.
    Baverstock)

Messrs. Jenner, Blackburn & Co.
Mrs. A. A. Lester
Sir Ralph Pearson, C.I.E., LL.D.

WITNEY URBAN DISTRICT

Canon R. F. Bale
Dr. W. Dalgliesh
Messrs. Charles Early & Co., Ltd.

R. E. Early, Esq.
F. W. Marriott, Esq.
Capt. Sydney Smith

E. S. Wood, Esq.

LIST OF SUBSCRIBERS

BANBURY RURAL DISTRICT

Mrs. J. Berkeley
Miss Monica Bradford
Mrs. A. Browning
Capt. and Mrs. W. H. Carter
H. F. Chamberlayne, Esq.
Lady Dugan of Victoria
Lord Elton
L. C. M. Gibbs, Esq.

R. P. T. Gibson, Esq.
Lady Hohler
Thomas Loveday, Esq., LL.D.
A. J. Morris, Esq.
Lt.-Col. H. E. du C. Norris, D.L.
W. L. Pilkington, Esq.
G. B. Randolph, Esq.
Lord Saye and Sele, M.C., D.L.

Lady Saye and Sele
Lt.-Col. A. D. Taylor
R. S. Thompson, Esq.
A. W. C. Thursby, Esq.
Lady Wardington
Major S. P. Yates

BULLINGDON RURAL DISTRICT

B. G. K. Allsop, Esq., M.C.
Mrs. L. A. R. Anstruther
Capt. L. H. Bell, R.N.
Miss Bell
Lt.-Col. H. T. Birch Reynardson, C.M.G.
F. G. Bonham Carter, Esq.
Miss Edith Bousfield
Lt.-Col. E. C. Bowes
Lt.-Col. C. R. C. Boyle, D.S.O.
N. M. Clark, Esq.
Miss Clerke Brown
Lord Conesford, Q.C.
Cuddesdon College
E. Hayes Dashwood, Esq.
Col. A. V. G. Dower, T.D.
Mrs. S. C. Evans
F. J. Fane, Esq.
Mrs. M. J. Fisher
Mrs. E. E. H. Gallia
The Hon. Sir Geoffrey Gibbs, K.C.M.G.
H. Gilbert, Esq.
Major John Glyn
Brigadier-General C. A. L. Graham, D.S.O., O.B.E., D.L.

Brigadier Lord Malise Graham, C.B., D.S.O., M.C.
G. Hastwell Grayson, Esq.
Capt. G. S. Greene
Clarence Hailey, Esq.
Mrs. Ducat Hamersley
Lt.-Col. R. Hardcastle, D.S.O.
W. O. Hassall, Esq.
The Hon. Mrs. W. Holland-Hibbert
Mr. and Mrs. A. D. Hough
Dr. Leo Jacobi
Capt. R. F. Kershaw
Major Alastair G. Mann
Philip B. Mansel, Esq.
Major A. A. Miller
Mrs. Ethel M. Miller
Miss F. C. Mitchell
Professor D. Mitrany
E. B. Montesole, Esq.
Lt.-Col. C. L. Mould
S. Nowell Smith, Esq.
Herbert Orpwood, Esq.
J. A. C. Osborne, Esq.
J. W. G. Payne, Esq.
Col. H. S. Pearson

C. J. Peers, Esq.
Mrs. D. G. Pott
Sir Stanley Pott
C. H. Priestley, Esq.
J. S. Puttock, Esq.
R. N. Richmond-Watson, Esq.
R. Roadnight, Esq.
K. E. Robinson, Esq.
Bernard C. Rowles, Esq.
Mrs. E. Shepley Shepley
The Rt. Hon. Lord Somervell of Harrow, O.B.E.
F. Speakman, Esq.
Lt.-Col. A. V. Spencer, D.S.O., D.L.
H. V. Stammers, Esq.
Mrs. G. B. Starky
H. H. Stevens, Esq.
J. Stewart Thomson, Esq.
R. C. Surman, Esq.
Lt.-Col. John Thomson, T.D.
Susan, Lady Tweedsmuir
J. W. Wheeler-Bennett, Esq., C.M.G., O.B.E.
Major Cecil C. Whitaker
Lady Wilson

CHIPPING NORTON RURAL DISTRICT

The Hon. Michael Astor
Miss H. L. Bailey
A. Balfour, Esq.
Col. J. A. Ballard, D.L.
Capt. R. N. Bevan, R.N.
Miss G. Boulton
Major N. Brooks, M.C., and Mrs. Brooks
Miss J. E. Bruce
J. Bullocke, Esq.
H. D. Campbell, Esq.
Mrs. J. A. Chaffers
Mrs. D. H. Chamberlayne
H. F. Chamberlayne, Esq.
Mrs. H. Clutterbuck
Col. G. M. Cooper
Major R. W. Cooper, O.B.E., M.C.
The Hon. Elsie Corbett
T. Cottrell-Dormer, Esq.
Sir Henry Dashwood, Bt.
R. Dodds, Esq.
A. D. Dodds-Parker, Esq., M.P.
E. F. Evetts, Esq.

Major P. Fleming
H. M. Gaskell, Esq.
A. P. Good, Esq.
W. C. Green, Esq.
Messrs. A. Groves & Sons, Ltd.
Heythrop College
Cdr. E. G. Heywood-Lonsdale, R.N., D.S.C.
Bernard Hunt, Esq.
Miss J. Hutchinson
Miss L. M. Jenkinson
Major E. N. F. Loyd, D.L.
N. Mavrogordato, Esq.
Mrs. T. More
F. P. Nicholson, Esq.
C. H. Norris, Esq.
M. P. Parker, Esq.
Harald and Dame Felicity Peake, D.B.E.
Mrs. F. H. Peel
Stephen Peel, Esq.
Col. Sir Charles Ponsonby, Bt., T.D., D.L.
G. B. Randolph, Esq.

J. W. Robertson Scott, Esq.
L. W. Robson, Esq.
The Rt. Hon. Lord Roche
Mrs. E. Rose
J. S. Ross, Esq.
The Hon. A. G. Samuel
Miss N. Sanders
Lord Sandford, D.L.
J. B. Schuster, Esq.
J. W. Shilson, Esq.
Messrs. S. G. Shilson & Sons, Ltd.
Mrs. H. M. Sitwell
Miss O. M. Snowden, O.B.E.
Lord Strang, G.C.B., G.C.M.G., M.B.E.
Mrs. E. M. Stubbs
A. N. Sword, Esq.
M. B. Watts, Esq.
E. D. Welford, Esq.
B. Whitaker, Esq.
Mrs. V. Wickham Steed
H. D. H. Wills, Esq.
Lady Wyfold

HENLEY RURAL DISTRICT

J. P. C. Bridge, Esq.
Sir Felix Brunner, Bt.
C. W. Christie-Miller, Esq.
Lt.-Col. F. A. L. Cooper
The Viscount Esher, G.B.E.
Col. Peter Fleming, O.B.E.
Mrs. R. B. Goyder
Mrs. George Hamilton

The Rt. Hon. Lord Justice Hodson, M.C.
Lt.-Col. Lord John Hope, M.P.
Col. E. Janes, O.B.E.
Mrs. Eric Kennington
Mrs. Melville
Sir Everard Meynell, O.B.E., M.C.
Miss L. R. Mitchell

Col. Guy de Pass, D.S.O., O.B.E.
G. F. Peel, Esq.
The Dowager Lady Rathcreedan
Miss A. Riddell Blount
W. N. Roe, Esq.
Daphne, Lady Rose
Evan John Simpson, Esq.
Sir John Stainton, K.B.E., Q.C.
The Hon. Mrs. S. Stonor

LIST OF SUBSCRIBERS

PLOUGHLEY RURAL DISTRICT

Lord Bicester
The late Lord Bicester, Lord Lieutenant
The Hon. Mrs. L. Bowlby
Lady Brooke-Popham
Mrs. H. M. Budgett
The Revd. C. L. Chavasse
Mrs. Ellis Chinnery
T. G. Curtis, Esq.
Major A. G. C. Fane, M.C.
Miss P. R. Gosling
Brigadier W. T. Hodgson, D.S.O., M.C.
G. A. Kolkhorst, Esq.

Brigadier and Mrs. Lake
Lt.-Col. P. J. Luard, D.S.O., O.B.E.
Lt.-Col. A. G. Lyttelton
The Revd. H. A. MacCann
Canon H. D. A. Major, D.D.
G. T. Morton, Esq.
Major M. Lloyd Mostyn
Dr. G. D. Parkes
J. Pennybacker, Esq., F.R.C.S.
Lt.-Col. Sir Algernon Peyton, Bt., D.L.
Mr. and Mrs. C. F. L. Piggott
Mrs. E. P. Pinching

Miss M. Pollard
John S. Purbrick, Esq.
Mrs. Douglas Stewart
Major H. G. Temple
Col. Sir P. Vickery, C.I.E., O.B.E.
A. C. Wall, Esq.
J. Warner, Esq.
Dr. A. Q. Wells
Professor and Mrs. J. H. C. White-head
Mrs. A. B. Whiteley
Col. The Hon. E. H. Wyndham, M.C.

WITNEY RURAL DISTRICT

Harold Abraham, Esq.
Major-General W. E. V. Abraham, C.B.E.
Major B. G. Barnett, O.B.E.
The Bay Tree Hotel, Burford (Miss S. M. Gray)
Miss H. B. Bryce
Lt.-Col. Sir John Burder
R. A. P. Butler, Esq.
Dr. C. T. Cheatle
H. E. Conway, Esq.
The Countryman
John Cripps, Esq.

Mrs. M. F. Davey
W. Freund, Esq.
J. S. Furley, Esq.
Sir William Goodenough, Bt., D.L.
Brigadier J. H. Gradidge
F. A. Gray, Esq.
Lt.-Col. W. H. Green
The Viscount Harcourt, K.C.M.G., O.B.E.
Capt. D. Mackinnon
Michael Mason, Esq.
Mrs. M. Montague

The Hon. Henry Parker
Major P. H. Parker
H. Phillimore, Esq., O.B.E., Q.C.
Lord Piercy, C.B.E.
Miss M. Pollard
Lt.-Col. J. J. Powell
Captain The Lord Redesdale, D.S.O., R.N.
C. H. Scott, Esq.
G. F. Smith, Esq.
H. A. Smith, Esq.
Witney Historical Club

SUBSCRIBERS FROM OUTSIDE THE COUNTY

Miss M. K. Ashby
D. T. Bailey, Esq.
A. E. Bye, Esq. (U.S.A.)
W. C. Clark, Esq.

J. Firth, Esq.
C. Foster, Esq.
John Hay, Esq., M.P.
Miss M. C. Howell

W. Keigwin, Esq.
The Revd. G. Tyndale-Biscoe
Mrs. Hugh Walker
P. J. H. Whiteley, Esq.

LIST OF THE CLASSES OF PUBLIC RECORDS
USED IN THIS VOLUME
WITH THEIR CLASS NUMBERS

Chancery

C 1 Proceedings, Early
C 2 Proceedings, Series I
C 3 Proceedings, Series II
C 5 Proceedings, Six Clerks' Series, Bridges
C 33 Decrees and Orders, Entry Books
C 43 Pleadings on Common Law Side, Rolls Chapel Series
C 47 Miscellanea
C 54 Close Rolls
C 60 Fine Rolls
C 66 Patent Rolls
C 78 Decree Rolls
C 93 Proceedings of Commissioners for Charitable Uses, Inquisitions and Decrees
C 132 Inquisitions post mortem, Series I: Hen. III
C 133   Edw. I
C 134   Edw. II
C 135   Edw. III
C 136   Ric. II
C 137   Hen. IV
C 139   Hen. VI
C 140   Edw. IV and Edw. V
C 141   Ric. III
C 142 Inquisitions post mortem, Series II
C 145 Miscellaneous Inquisitions
C 146 Ancient Deeds, Series C

Court of Common Pleas

C.P. 25 (1) Feet of Fines, Series I
C.P. 25 (2) Feet of Fines, Series II
C.P. 26 (1) Notes of Fines
C.P. 40 Plea Rolls
C.P. 43 Recovery Rolls

Exchequer, Treasury of the Receipt

E 32 Forest Proceedings
E 40 Ancient Deeds, Series A
E 41 Ancient Deeds, Series AA
E 106 Extents of Alien Priories
E 134 Depositions by Commission
E 150 Inquisitions post mortem, Series II
E 164 Miscellaneous Books, Series I
E 178 Special Commissions of Enquiry
E 179 Subsidy Rolls, &c.
E 210 Ancient Deeds, Series D

Exchequer, Augmentation Office

E 308 Fee Farm Rents, Particulars of sale
E 315 Miscellaneous Books
E 318 Particulars for Grants of Crown Lands
E 326 Ancient Deeds, Series B

Exchequer, Lord Treasurer's Remembrancer

E 368 Memoranda Rolls
E 372 Pipe Rolls

Exchequer, Office of the Auditors of Land Revenue

L.R. 2 Miscellaneous Books

Home Office

H.O. 107 Census, Population Returns
H.O. 129 Census, Ecclesiastical Returns

Justices Itinerant

Just. Itin. 1 Assize Rolls, Eyre Rolls, &c.

Duchy of Lancaster

D.L. 7 Inquisitions post mortem
D.L. 29 Ministers' Accounts
D.L. 30 Court Rolls
D.L. 42 Miscellaneous Books
D.L. 43 Rentals and Surveys

Court of Queen's Bench

K.B. 27 Coram Rege Rolls

Special Collections

S.C. 2 Court Rolls
S.C. 6 Ministers' Accounts
S.C. 11 Rentals and Surveys, Rolls

Court of Requests

Req. 2 Proceedings

Court of Star Chamber

Sta. Cha. 2 Proceedings

State Paper Office

S.P. 16 State Papers Domestic, Chas. I

LIST OF PRINCIPAL
BODLEIAN LIBRARY MANUSCRIPTS
USED IN THIS VOLUME

d.d. Dashwood (Oxon.) Dashwood family papers about Bicester and Kirtlington

d.d. Valentia Valentia family papers about Bletchingdon and Hampton Poyle

Oxon. Dioc. Pp.

b 6–18 Parochial returns to bishop's queries, 1793–1824

b 21–23 Oxford diocesan registers, 1737–1868

b 29–36 Parochial returns to bishop's queries, 1814–27

b 37 Bishops' visitations, 1778–87

b 38, 39, 41 Bishops' visitations, 1831, 1834, 1838

b 70 Returns of church, rectory, and school buildings, 1860

c 21–31 Attestations and depositions in ecclesiastical courts, 1570–1694

c 66–76 Presentations to livings, 17th–19th centuries

c 155 Value of livings, 1675–1874

c 264 Oxford diocesan register, 1604–23

c 266 Oxford diocesan register, 1699–1736

c 273 Churchwardens' presentments, 1842–8

c 327 Diocese book, 1778–1808

c 332, 341, 344 Bishop's visitations, 1866, 1875, 1878

c 430–2 Return of recusants, 1682–1706, 1767–80

c 433 Return of schools, 1815

c 434–5 Register of faculties, 1737–1827

c 446 Papers about Queen Anne's Bounty

c 448–9 Terriers, early 19th century

c 454–6 Faculty papers, c. 1660–1850

c 643–7 Certificates of dissenting meeting houses, 1731–1852

c 650–64 Episcopal correspondence, 1635–1854

d 14–16 Depositions and attestations in ecclesiastical courts, 1543–93

d 105–6 Oxford diocesan register, 1543–69, 1660–1702

d 178 Bishop Wilberforce's diocese book, 1854–64

d 179 Bishop's visitation, 1857

d 549 Diocese book, 1807–12

d 552–65 Bishop's visitations, 1738–74 (that of 1738, d 552–5, now printed in Oxon. Record Soc.)

d 566–81 Bishop's visitations, 1802–23

d 707 Return of schools, 1808

d 708 Bishop Fell's diocese book, c. 1685

Oxf. Archd. Pp. Oxon.

b 22–27 Miscellaneous papers about Oxfordshire parishes

b 40–41 Terriers, 17th century

c 2–27 Liber actorum of archdeacon's court, 1566–1761

c 35–44 Archdeacon's articles of enquiry, 1837–68

c 46–115 Churchwardens' presentments, 1730–1844

c 118 Depositions in ecclesiastical courts, 1616-20

c 141–2 Terriers

c 153 Archdeacon's visitation book, 1792–1802

d 13 Archdeacon's visitation book, 1756–9

MS. Top. Oxon.

a 37–39 Oxfordshire drawings, 18th and 19th centuries

a 42 Oxfordshire sketches, 18th and 19th centuries

a 64–69 Drawings by J. C. Buckler and J. Buckler

b 75 Historical notes on Oxfordshire churches and parishes

b 86–87 Papers about Hampton Poyle, 16th–17th centuries

b 121, 178–91, 210 Papers about the Earl of Abingdon's estates, 18th–19th centuries

b 220 Descriptions and drawings of Oxfordshire churches, c. 1808

c 42–68 Historical collections relating to Oxfordshire by W. H. Turner, c. 1865–70

c 103–5 Papers about Oxfordshire church restorations, mainly 1860–70

c 112 Memoranda about Islip by W. Vincent, rector, 1807

c 165–7 Oxfordshire monumental inscriptions and extracts from parish registers, by Col. J. L. Chester, c. 1880

c 307 Collections of Sir John Peshall, mid-18th century

c 328/1–4 Papers about Hampton Gay manor, 16th-20th centuries

c 381 Survey of the Earl of Abingdon's estates, 1728

c 398 Transcripts of charters of Bicester, Clattercote, Littlemore, and Studley Priories

d 90 Notes on church restorations, c. 1892

d 171 Collections of C. Richardson, early 19th century

d 351 Enquiry into lands of Oxfordshire recusants, 1700

d 460 List of medieval incumbents and presentations from the Lincoln registers and other sources prepared by Florence E. Thurlby and the Oxfordshire V.C.H. staff

MS. Top. Gen.

e 23 Tours of R. Gough, c. 1760–80

MS. Wills Oxon. Oxfordshire wills, 1543–19th century

NOTE ON ABBREVIATIONS

Among the abbreviations and short titles used the following may require elucidation:

Manuscript Sources

C.C.C. Mun.	Muniments of Corpus Christi College, Oxford
Cal. Q. Sess.	Calendar of Quarter Sessions
Compton Census	William Salt Library, Stafford, MS. 33, 'The census taken in 1676 in the province of Canterbury giving an account of inhabitants, papists and other dissenters in the various dioceses'
Dashwood D.	Bodleian MS. d.d. Dashwood (Oxon.)
Dunkin MS.	Collections of John Dunkin (London Guildhall MSS. temporarily deposited in the Bodleian Library)
E.C.R.	Records of Eton College
MS. Top. Oxon.	Bodleian Library, MS. Top. Oxon.
Oldfield, Clerus	Bodleian Library, MS. index to clergy by W. J. Oldfield, 'Clerus Diocesis Oxoniensis, 1542–1908'
O.R.O.	Oxfordshire County Record Office, Oxford
Oxf. Archd.	Bodleian Library, Oxfordshire Archdeaconry Papers
Oxf. Dioc.	Bodleian Library, Oxfordshire Diocesan Papers
Par. Rec.	Parish Records
Val. D.	Bodleian Library, MS. d.d. Valentia
W.A.M.	Westminster Abbey Muniments

Printed Sources

Archdeacon's Ct.	*The Archdeacon's Court, Liber Actorum 1584*, ed. E. R. Brinkworth (O.R.S. xxiii, xxiv, 1941, 1942)
Arkell, *Oxf. Stone*	W. J. Arkell, *Oxford Stone* (Oxford, 1947)
Bacon, *Lib. Reg.*	John Bacon, *Liber Regis* (London, 1786)
Baker, *Northants.*	George Baker, *History and Antiquities of the County of Northampton* (2 vols. London, 1822–41)
Berks. Arch. Jnl.	*Berkshire, Buckinghamshire and Oxfordshire Archaeological Journals*, 1895–1930, and *Berkshire Archaeological Journal*, 1930–

J. C. Blomfield, *History of the Deanery of Bicester*, containing:

Blo. *Bic.*	Part ii, *History of Bicester* (Bicester, 1884)
Blo. *Cot., Hard., Tus.*	Part iii, *History of Cottisford, Hardwick, and Tusmore* (Bristol, 1887)
Blo. *Mid., Som.*	Part iv, *History of Middleton and Somerton* (Bristol, 1888)
Blo. *Fring., Hethe, Mix., Newt., Shel.*	Part v, *History of Fringford, Hethe, Mixbury, Newton Purcell, and Shelswell* (London, 1890)
Blo. *U. Heyf., L. Heyf.*	Part vi, *History of Upper and Lower Heyford* (London, 1892)
Blo. *Frit., Sould.*	Part vii, *History of Fritwell and Souldern* (London, 1893)
Blo. *Ard., Buck., Cav., Stoke*	Part viii, *History of Ardley, Bucknell, Caversfield, and Stoke Lyne* (London, 1894)
Blo. *Fin.*	J. C. Blomfield, *History of Finmere* (Buckingham, 1887)
Boarstall Cart.	*The Boarstall Cartulary*, ed. H. E. Salter (O.H.S. lxxviii, 1930)
Brewer, *Oxon.*	J. N. Brewer, *A Topographical and Historical Description of the County of Oxford* (London, 1819)
Bridges, *Northants.*	John Bridges, *History and Antiquities of Northamptonshire*, ed. Peter Whalley (2 vols. Oxford, 1791)
C.R.S.	Catholic Record Society
Calamy Rev.	A. G. Matthews, *Calamy Revised* (Oxford, 1934)
Ch. Bells Oxon.	F. Sharpe, *The Church Bells of Oxfordshire* (O.R.S. xxviii, xxx, xxxii, xxxiv, 1949–53)

Ch. Ch. Arch.	*Cartulary of the Medieval Archives of Christ Church*, ed. N. Denholm-Young (O.H.S. xcii, 1931)
Chant. Cert.	*The Chantry Certificates and the Edwardian Inventories of Church Goods*, ed. Rose Graham (O.R.S. i, 1919)
Char. Don.	*Abstract of the Returns of Charitable Donations made by the Ministers and Churchwardens, 1786–8*, H.C. 511 (1816)
Chron. Abingdon	*Chronicon Monasterii de Abingdon*, ed. J. Stevenson (2 vols., Rolls Series, 1858)
Clutterbuck, *Herts.*	Robert Clutterbuck, *History and Antiquities of the County of Hertford* (3 vols. London, 1815–27)
Davenport, *Oxon. Sheriffs*	J. M. Davenport, *Lords Lieutenant and High Sheriffs of Oxfordshire, 1086–1868* (Oxford, 1868)
Davis, *Oxon. Map*	Richard Davis, *Map of the County of Oxford* (1797)
Dom. of Incl.	*The Domesday of Inclosures, 1517–1518*, ed. I. S. Leadam (2 vols. London, 1897)
Dunkin, *Bic.*	John Dunkin, *History and Antiquities of Bicester* (London, 1816)
Dunkin, *Oxon.*	John Dunkin, *History and Antiquities of the Hundreds of Bullingdon and Ploughley* (2 vols. London, 1823)
E.E.T.S.	Early English Text Society
Educ. Enq. Abstract	*Education Enquiry Abstract*, H.C. 62 (1835), xlii
Educ. of Poor	*Education of the Poor*, H.C. 224 (1819), ix (B)
Elem. Educ. Ret.	*Elementary Education Returns*, H.C. 201 (1871), lv
Emden, *O.U. Reg.*	A. B. Emden, *A Biographical Register of the University of Oxford to A.D. 1500* (Oxford, 1957–)
Evans, *Ch. Plate*	J. T. Evans, *The Church Plate of Oxfordshire* (Oxford, 1928)
Eynsham Cart.	*The Eynsham Cartulary*, ed. H. E. Salter (O.H.S. xlix, li, 1906–8)
Eyton, *Salop.*	R. W. Eyton, *Antiquities of Shropshire* (12 vols. London, 1854–60)
Farrer, *Honors*	William Farrer, *Honors and Knights' Fees* (3 vols. London, 1923–5)
Fines Oxon.	*The Feet of Fines for Oxfordshire, 1195–1291*, ed. H. E. Salter (O.R.S. xii, 1930)
Fosbrooke, *Glos.*	T. D. Fosbrooke, *History of Gloucestershire* (2 vols. Gloucester, 1807)
Foss, *Judges*	Edward Foss, *The Judges of England* (9 vols. London, 1848–64)
Foster, *Alumni*	J. Foster, *Alumni Oxonienses, 1500–1886* (8 vols. Oxford, 1887–92)
Gardner, *Dir. Oxon.*	R. Gardner, *History, Gazetteer and Directory of Oxfordshire* (Peterborough, 1852)
Gen. Digest Char.	*General Digest of Charities*, H.C. 292 (2) (1871), lv
Godstow Reg.	*The English Register of Godstow Nunnery*, ed. A. Clark (E.E.T.S. orig. ser. 129, 130, 142, 1905–11)
Hasted, *Kent*	Edward Hasted, *History and Topographical Survey of Kent* (4 vols. Canterbury, 1778–99)
Hearne, *Remarks*	*Remarks and Collections of Thomas Hearne*, ed. C. E. Doble and others (11 vols. O.H.S. ii, &c. 1884–1918)
Hearth Tax Oxon.	*Hearth Tax Returns for Oxfordshire, 1665*, ed. Maureen Weinstock (O.R.S. xxi, 1940)
Kelly's Handbk.	*Kelly's Handbook to the Titled, Landed and Official Classes*
Kennett, *Paroch. Antiq.*	White Kennett, *Parochial Antiquities attempted in the History of Ambrosden, Burcester and other adjacent parts in the Counties of Oxford and Bucks.* (2 vols. 2nd edn. Oxford, 1818)
L.R.S.	Lincoln Record Society
Lamborn, *Arm. Glass*	E. A. Greening Lamborn, *Armorial Glass of the Oxford Diocese, 1250–1850* (London, 1949)
Lipscomb, *Bucks.*	George Lipscomb, *History and Antiquities of the County of Buckingham* (4 vols. London, 1847)
List of Sch.	*List of Public Elementary Schools*, C. 3182, H.C. (1906), lxxxvi
Luke, *Jnl.*	*Journal of Sir Samuel Luke*, ed. I. G. Philip (O.R.S. xxix, xxxi, xxxiii, 1947–53)

Lunt, *Val. Norw.*	*The Valuation of Norwich*, ed. W. E. Lunt (Oxford, 1926)
Macray, *Magd. Reg.*	*Register of Magdalen College, Oxford*, N.S. ed. W. D. Macray (8 vols. London, 1894–1915)
Nichols, *Leics.*	John Nichols, *History and Antiquities of the County of Leicester* (4 vols. in 8 parts, London, 1795–1811)
O.A.H.S. *Proc.*	*Proceedings* of the Oxford Society for Promoting the Study of Gothic Architecture, 1839–47
	Proceedings of the Oxford Architectural Society, 1847–60
	Proceedings of the Oxford Architectural and Historical Society, 1860–93
O.A.S. *Rep., Trans.*	*Reports* and *Transactions* of the North Oxfordshire Archaeological Society, 1853–86, and of the Oxfordshire Archaeological Society, 1887–
O.H.S.	Oxford Historical Society
O.R.S.	Oxfordshire Record Society
Oseney Cart.	*The Cartulary of the Abbey of Oseney*, ed. H. E. Salter (O.H.S. lxxxix–xci, xcvii, xcviii, ci, 1929–36)
Oxf. Jnl.	*Jackson's Oxford Journal*
Oxon. Chart.	*Facsimiles of Early Charters in Oxford Muniment Rooms*, ed. H. E. Salter (Oxford, 1929)
Oxon. Poll, 1754	*Poll of the Freeholders of Oxfordshire taken at Oxford on 17th April, 1754* (Bodl. G.A. Oxon. 4° 346)
Oxon. Visit.	*The Visitations of the County of Oxfordshire taken in the Years 1566, 1574, and 1634*, ed. W. H. Turner (Harl. Soc. v, 1871)
Par. Coll.	*Parochial Collections made by Anthony Wood and Richard Rawlinson*, ed. F. N. Davis (O.R.S. ii, iv, xi, 1920–9)
Parker, *Eccles. Top.*	J. H. Parker, *Ecclesiastical and Architectural Topography of England: Oxfordshire* (Oxford, 1850)
Parker, *Guide*	J. H. Parker, *A Guide to the Architectural Antiquities in the Neighbourhood of Oxford* (Oxford, 1846)
Plot, *Nat. Hist. Oxon.*	R. Plot, *The Natural History of Oxfordshire* (Oxford, 1677)
P.N. Oxon. (E.P.N.S.)	Margaret Gelling, *The Place-Names of Oxfordshire*, pt. i (English Place-Name Soc. xxiii, 1953)
Poor Abstract	*Abstract of the Answers and Returns relative to the Expense and Maintenance of the Poor*, H.C. 175 (1804), i
R.C. Families	*Genealogical Collections Illustrating the History of Roman Catholic Families*, ed. J. J. Howard and H. F. Burke (4 parts, priv. printed, 1887–95)
Reg. Antiquiss.	*The Registrum Antiquissimum of the Cathedral Church of Lincoln*, ed. C. W. Foster and Kathleen Major (7 vols. L.R.S. 1931–53)
Reg. Chich.	*The Register of Henry Chichele*, ed. E. F. Jacob (Cant. and York Soc. xlii, xlv, xlvi, xlvii, 1937–47)
Reg. Univ.	*Register of the University of Oxford, 1449–63, 1505–71, 1571–1622*, ed. C. W. Boase and A. Clark (O.H.S. i, x, xi, xii, xiv, 1884–9)
12th Rep. Com. Char.	*12th Report of the Commissioners for Charities*, H.C. 348 (1825), x
Ret. of Sch.	*Return for Public Elementary Schools*, H.C. 403 (1890), lvi
Rot. Graves.	*Rotuli Ricardi Gravesend, 1258–79*, ed. F. N. Davis (Cant. and York Soc. xxxi, 1925, and L.R.S. xx, 1925)
Rot. Grosse.	*Rotuli Roberti Grosseteste, 1235–53*, ed. F. N. Davis (Cant. and York Soc. x, 1913, and L.R.S. xi, 1914)
Rot. Welles	*Rotuli Hugonis de Welles, 1209–35*, ed. W. P. W. Phillimore (Cant. and York Soc. i, ii, iv, 1905–8, and L.R.S. iii, vi, ix, 1912–14)
St. Frides. Cart.	*The Cartulary of the Monastery of St. Frideswide at Oxford*, ed. S. R. Wigram (O.H.S. xxviii, xxxi, 1895–6)
St. John's Hosp. Cart.	*A Cartulary of the Hospital of St. John the Baptist*, ed. H. E. Salter (O.H.S. lxvi, lxviii, lxix, 1914–16)
Salter, *Oxon. Recusants*	'Recusants in Oxfordshire, 1602–33', ed. H. E. Salter, O.A.S. *Rep.* 1924
Sandford Cart.	*The Sandford Cartulary*, ed. Agnes M. Leys (O.R.S. xix, xxii, 1937–41)
Saxon Oxon.	G. B. Grundy, *Saxon Oxfordshire* (O.R.S. xv, 1933)
Schools Enq.	*Schools Enquiry Commission Reports* [3966–XI], H.C. (1867–8), xxviii (10)

Skelton, *Oxon.*	Joseph Skelton, *Illustrations of Principal Antiquities of Oxfordshire* (Oxford, 1823)
Stapleton, *Cath. Miss.*	Mrs. Bryan Stapleton, *Oxfordshire Post-Reformation Catholic Missions* (London, 1906)
Subsidy 1526	*A Subsidy Collected in the Diocese of Lincoln in 1526*, ed. H. E. Salter (O.H.S. lxiii, 1909)
Summers, *Congreg. Chs.*	W. H. Summers, *History of the Congregational Churches in the Berkshire, South Oxfordshire and South Buckinghamshire Association* (Newbury, 1905)
Thame Cart.	*The Thame Cartulary*, ed. H. E. Salter (O.R.S. xxv, xxvi, 1947–8)
Thoroton, *Notts.*	Robert Thoroton, *History of Nottinghamshire*, ed. J. Throsby (3 vols. Nottingham, 1790–6)
Venn, *Alumni*	J. and J. A. Venn, *Alumni Cantabrigienses* (10 vols. Cambridge, 1922–54)
Visit. Dioc. Linc. (1420–49)	*Visitations of the Religious Houses in the Diocese of Lincoln*, ed. A. Hamilton Thompson (L.R.S. vii, xiv, xxi, 1914–29)
Visit. Dioc. Linc. 1517–31	*Visitations in the Diocese of Lincoln 1517–31*, ed. A. Hamilton Thompson (L.R.S. xxxiii, xxxv, xxxvii, 1940–7)
Vol. Sch. Ret.	*Voluntary Schools Returns*, H.C. 178–xxiv (1906), lxxxviii
Walker Rev.	A. G. Matthews, *Walker Revised* (Oxford, 1948)
Wilb. Visit.	*Bishop Wilberforce's Visitation Returns for the Archdeaconry of Oxford, 1854*, ed. E. P. Baker (O.R.S. xxxv, 1954)
Wing, *Annals*	William Wing, *Brief Annals of Bicester Poor Law Union* (5 parts, Bicester, 1877–81)
Wood, *Athenae*	*Athenae Oxonienses, to which are added the Fasti*, ed. P. Bliss (5 vols. London, 1813–20)
Wood, *Life*	*The Life and Times of Anthony Wood, Antiquary, of Oxford, 1632–95, described by Himself*, ed. A. Clark (O.H.S. xix, xxi, xxvi, xxx, xl, 1891–1900)
Woodward's Progress	*The Progress Notes of Warden Woodward Round the Oxfordshire Estates of New College, Oxford, 1659–75*, ed. R. L. Rickard (O.R.S. xxvii, 1945)
Young, *Oxon. Agric.*	Arthur Young, *General View of the Agriculture of Oxfordshire* (London, 1809 and 1813)

PLOUGHLEY
HUNDRED

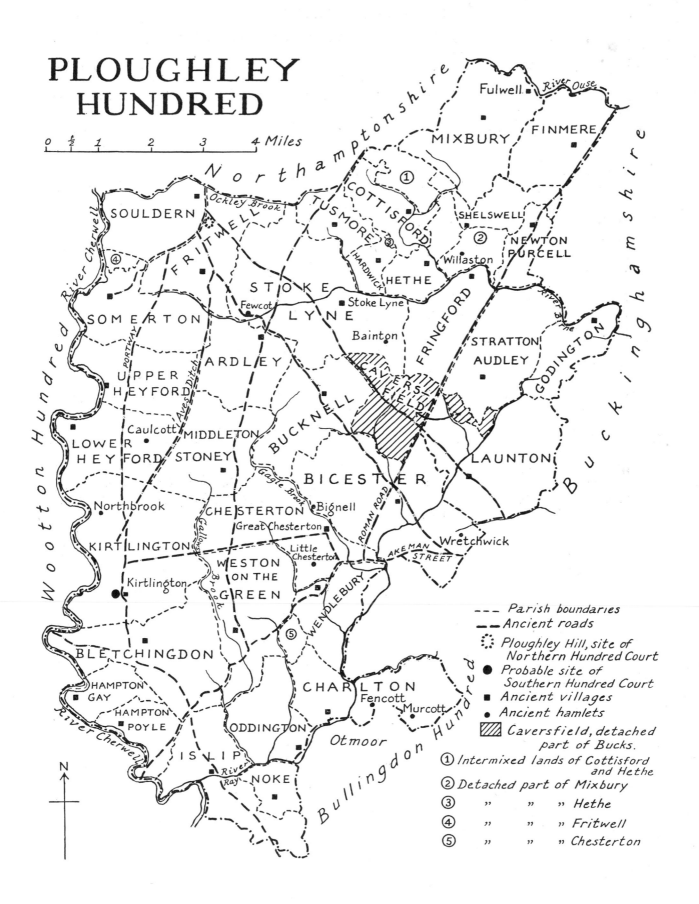

0 ½ 1   2   3   4 Miles

Northamptonshire

Fulwell · *River Ouse*

MIXBURY   FINMERE

① COTTISFORD

SOULDERN   *Ockley Brook*   TUSMORE   SHELSWELL

FRITWELL   ②   NEWTON PURCELL

④   ③   Willaston

STOKE   HARDWICK   HETHE

SOMERTON   *Fewcot*   LYNE   Stoke Lyne   FRINGFORD

PORTWAY   Bainton   STRATTON AUDLEY   GODINGTON

ARDLEY   CAVERSFIELD   *River Bire*

UPPER HEYFORD   *Aves Ditch*

Caulcott   MIDDLETON   BUCKNELL   LAUNTON

LOWER HEYFORD   STONEY   *Gagle Brook*   BICESTER

Northbrook   CHESTERTON   Bignell   *ROMAN ROAD*   Wretchwick

Great Chesterton   *AKEMAN STREET*

KIRTLINGTON   Little Chesterton

Galloss Brook   WESTON ON THE GREEN

Kirtlington   WENDLEBURY

⑤

BLETCHINGDON

HAMPTON GAY   CHARLTON

Fencott

HAMPTON POYLE   Murcott

ODDINGTON

River Cherwell   ISLIP   *Otmoor*   *Bullingdon Hundred*

River Ray   NOKE

N

- - - *Parish boundaries*

— — *Ancient roads*

⦂ *Ploughley Hill, site of Northern Hundred Court*

● *Probable site of Southern Hundred Court*

■ *Ancient villages*

• *Ancient hamlets*

▨ *Caversfield, detached part of Bucks.*

① *Intermixed lands of Cottisford and Hethe*

② *Detached part of Mixbury*

③   "   "   " *Hethe*

④   "   "   " *Fritwell*

⑤   "   "   " *Chesterton*

Wootton Hundred

Buckinghamshire

THE HUNDRED OF PLOUGHLEY

I N 1831, before the 19th-century alterations in parish boundaries, the hundred contained about 59,520 acres and 33 parishes, of which one was in Buckinghamshire, as well as a hamlet in the parish of Stowe in the same county. It had a population of 14,050.[1] Its aspect was described by a contemporary topographer as 'in general flat or relieved only by downy expanses little conducive to pictorial effect'.[2] This description does less than justice to the scenery: the Cherwell valley with its rich meadowland has a quiet beauty and the many parks, mainly laid out in the 18th century, at Bletchingdon, Kirtlington, Middleton Stoney, Shelswell, and Tusmore, to name the largest, are notable features of the landscape. Until modern times the area, with its predominantly stonebrash soil, has been wholly devoted to agriculture and has produced some experimental farmers of note. Since the mid-18th century, when this part of the county became the centre of the first organized fox-hunting in England, much wealth has been attracted to the district. Among the resident hunting families were the Annesleys at Bletchingdon, the Peytons at Stoke Lyne, and in more recent times the earls of Jersey at Middleton and Lord Bicester's family at Tusmore.

In the 20th century the flat nature of the country and its central position have made it an ideal site for use by the army and air force. The R.A.F. has stations at Upper Heyford (leased since 1951 to the United States Air Force) and Bicester, with a subsidiary station at Weston-on-the-Green and a dormitory site at Stratton Audley. The army's large ordnance depot is mainly in the neighbouring hundred of Bullingdon, but its influence has spread into many Ploughley villages, and the market-town of Bicester, once mainly noted as a hunting centre, has been transformed into a garrison town.

The boundaries of the hundred were largely natural ones. Bryant's map of 1824, the first accurate delineation, shows the River Cherwell bounding the whole of the hundred's western extent.[3] On the north the River Ouse and a tributary of the Cherwell separate it from Northamptonshire except for a short stretch by Cottisford heath where the medieval highway from Oxford to Brackley and a branch road to Tingewick (Bucks.) formed the boundary. The line separating Ploughley from Buckinghamshire on the east was almost purely artificial, while on the south-east tributaries of the Ray and the Ray itself largely separated the hundred from that of Bullingdon. The highly artificial loop made by the boundary line so as to include Fencott and Murcott is an interesting feature and probably represents a later change after these hamlets had been colonized by the mother village of Charlton.[4] Earlier maps, such as that of Jan Blaeu in 1663, Robert Morden in 1695, and Richard Davis in 1797, do in fact erroneously show them as lying in Bullingdon hundred. The history of landownership also led to some other peculiarities. Caversfield, though physically in the hundred, has always been administratively outside it, while Lillingstone Lovell and Boycott have been administratively in the hundred though lying in the county of Buckinghamshire.

Unlike most of the other Oxfordshire hundreds, which were named after vills,

---

[1] *Census*, 1831.
[2] Brewer, *Oxon.* 533.
[3] A. Bryant, *Map of the County of Oxford from Actual Survey.*
[4] See below, p. 83.

Ploughley took its name from a barrow in Fritwell parish in the extreme north-west of the hundred.[5] The first element of the name may be *pohhede*, meaning baggy, or *Pohhede*, a personal name derived from *Pohha*. The second element is *hlaw*, a tumulus.[6] Plot noted this tumulus and William Stukeley described it in 1776 as 'a curious barrow, neatly turned like a bell, small and high'.[7] It lay just inside the county and the hundred, beside the Portway, a pre-Roman trackway, running northwards into Northamptonshire. The barrow was levelled before 1845, but in that year, according to Blomfield, bones dug up on its supposed site were transferred to a new mound about 50 yards away, which was partly in the garden of the Bear Inn.[8]

A second meeting-place for this large hundred may have been at 'Speech Hill' (*Spelleburge*) in Bletchingdon parish.[9] There is little doubt that this hill is the modern Enslow Hill, a notable landmark and also near the Portway, but eight miles south of Ploughley Hill.[10] The site of Speech Hill not only had natural advantages, but it lay about a mile south of Kirtlington, the royal estate to which the 2½ hundreds of Ploughley (though not so named) were attached in 1065.[11] Bletchingdon itself, moreover, was a royal vill, and it may perhaps be significant that in 1086 Alwi the Sheriff held 2½ hides of the king in the vill.[12] Indeed, as Northbrook in Kirtlington was stated in Domesday Book to be in the hundred of 'First Gadre', it is reasonable to suppose that this southern part of Ploughley was originally called the hundred of 'First Gadre', a hundred which was apparently absorbed by Ploughley soon after 1086.[13]

The name Ploughley does not occur in Domesday, which gives few hundredal rubrics for Oxfordshire. It is first mentioned in the form *Pokedelawa* hundred in the Pipe Roll of 1169,[14] and little is known of its composition until the early 13th century. It is, however, indirectly referred to in the Domesday survey, which states that the soke of 2½ hundreds belonged to Kirtlington except for 2½ hides in Launton (given by the Confessor to Westminster Abbey) which used to belong to it.[15]

The first complete list of villages and hamlets in the hundred occurs in the Hundred Rolls of 1279.[16] It includes the 32 Oxfordshire parishes and the Buckinghamshire parish of Lillingstone Lovell, which continued to make up the hundred until the mid-19th century.[17] In addition there is Fulwell, at that time a parish.[18] With the exception of Newton Purcell and Souldern, all the parishes were Domesday vills. Twelve hamlets, including the Buckinghamshire Boycott, are also described.[19]

Although this is the earliest complete list, there are a number of earlier references, direct or indirect, which point to the inclusion of many of these villages in Ploughley in the 12th or early 13th century. The appearance on the Pipe Rolls of 1169, 1178, 1184 and 1185 under Ploughley hundred of the monks of Bec and Thame, of the brothers of the hospital (i.e. St. Bartholomew's Hospital, London), of the nuns of Godstow, and of the Knights Templars are the earliest indications that their Oxfordshire properties were in the hundred.[20] The lands of the first four were respectively at Cottisford, Otley

---

[5] See below, p. 135.

[6] *P.N. Oxon.* (E.P.N.S.), i. 196. There is a great variety of spellings. The most common medieval forms are *Poghedele*, *Powedelowe*, and *Ploudlegh*. In the 17th cent. *Poughley alias Poofly* occurs: Oxf. E 317.

[7] Plot, *Nat. Hist. Oxon.* ch. 10, para. 48; W. Stukeley, *Itinerarium Curiosum* (1724), 40.

[8] Blo. *Frit.* 4.

[9] *Godstow Reg.* i. 214, 220. This site is suggested in *P.N. Oxon.* (E.P.N.S.), i. 196.

[10] Part of the parish's arable lands lay on Enslow Hill (see below, p. 63), and the references in the charters to *Spelleburge* are consistent with its identification with Enslow Hill.

[11] For the system by which groups of manors were annexed to royal manors, see Helen Cam, 'The Hundred and the Hundredal Manor', *E.H.R.* xlvii. 353–76.

[12] *V.C.H. Oxon.* i. 424.

[13] Cf. A. Morley Davies, 'The Hundreds of Bucks. and Oxon.', *Records of Bucks.* xv. pt. 4, 236.

[14] *Pipe R.* 1169 (P.R.S. xiii), 86.

[15] *V.C.H. Oxon.* i. 400.

[16] *Rot. Hund.* (Rec. Com.), ii. 822–39.

[17] *Hearth Tax Oxon.* 235–6; *Census*, 1801, &c.

[18] See below, p. 252.

[19] For their names, see below, p. 354.

[20] *Pipe R.* 1169 (P.R.S. xiii), 86; ibid. 1178 (P.R.S. xxvii), 118; ibid. 1184 (P.R.S. xxxiii), 72; ibid. 1185 (P.R.S. xxxiv), 108.

in Oddington, Hethe, and Bletchingdon.[21] The Templars had property at Bletchingdon, Hampton Gay, and Fewcot in Stoke Lyne by 1185, and all or any one of these holdings may have accounted for the Templars' being mentioned on the Pipe Roll.[22] As many as 22 parishes and a number of hamlets—Bainton, Bignell, Northbrook in Somerton, and Willaston—were listed for the carucage of 1220.[23] The absence from this list of Bicester, Chesterton, and Upper Heyford is accounted for by their inclusion in the honor of Wallingford,[24] and other parishes, such as Cottisford, Islip, and Launton, the property of the abbeys of Bec and Westminster, were no doubt exempted from payment. There can be little doubt that all had been in the hundred from early times.[25]

The inclusion of the outlying Buckinghamshire district of Boycott and Lillingstone Lovell may be of ancient origin. Both were royal manors at an early date and may therefore have always been a part of the district dependent on Kirtlington: in 1065 Boycott was held by Reinbald, chief of the Confessor's clerks and perhaps his chancellor, and it later claimed to be ancient demesne;[26] Lillingstone, a 10-hide vill, was divided between Azor and Syric, both Queen Edith's men, and later evidence shows that its church was under royal patronage.[27] After the Conquest Azor's 5 hides at Lillingstone were given half to Richard Ingania, the king's chief huntsman, and half to Benzelin, a royal usher.[28] These 5 hides (later known as Lillingstone Lovell), which were listed in 1086 among the Oxfordshire entries, were no doubt already attached to Ploughley hundred. The other 5 hides later known as Lillingstone Dayrell were given to Walter Giffard. They were described in the Buckinghamshire Domesday and became or perhaps remained a part of Stodfald hundred, in which they lay.[29] A reference on the Pipe Roll of 1188 under Ploughley hundred to the monks of Biddlesden (Bucks.) is the earliest indication that Boycott was in Ploughley:[30] it had originally been given to Cirencester Abbey by Henry I, but was later given to Biddlesden Abbey.[31]

Caversfield (5 hides), though lying physically within the hundred,[32] was attached by 1086 at least to the Buckinghamshire hundred of Rovelai, which was then assessed at 105 hides.[33] Before the Conquest, when Caversfield was held by Edward, a man of Earl Tostig, it was no doubt in Ploughley hundred along with Stoke Lyne, another of Tostig's possessions.[34] It remained in Rovelai hundred until it was transferred to Ploughley and Oxfordshire in 1834 and 1844.[35]

The inclusion of Noke in Ploughley hundred may also have been the result of feudal ties. The Ray forms the natural dividing line between the hundreds of Bullingdon and Ploughley, and it is possible that Noke, which lay on the Bullingdon side of the Ray, may have been drawn into Ploughley hundred, as Westminster Abbey held ½ fee in it and was also lord of the neighbouring vill of Islip, which was in Ploughley hundred.[36]

The total hidage of the vills found in the hundred in 1279 amounts to 293⅝ hides. This figure excludes Souldern, which has not yet been identified with any Domesday vill, and includes Charlton, Cottisford, Finmere, Hethe, and Shelswell, which were listed by the Domesday scribes under Northamptonshire. If the hidage of the last five vills, which amounts to a total of 42 hides, is subtracted from the Ploughley

[21] For these, see below under their respective parishes.
[22] Ibid.
[23] *Bk. of Fees*, 318–19.
[24] Ibid. 313.
[25] It may be noted that Chesterton occurs on the eyre rolls of 1267–8 and the Abbot of Westminster was a suitor of the hundred court: Just. Itin. 1/696; ibid. 703.
[26] *V.C.H. Oxon.* i. 421; *V.C.H. Bucks.* iv. 235.
[27] *V.C.H. Oxon.* i. 410, 421, 424; *V.C.H. Bucks.* i. 227, 250, 258, 268; iv. 197, &c.
[28] *V.C.H. Oxon.* i. 386, 421, 422.

[29] In 1086 the hidage of Stodfald was 101 hides: *V.C.H. Bucks.* iv. 135. See also hundred map: ibid. i. 227.
[30] *Pipe R.* 1188 (P.R.S. xxxviii), 153.
[31] For its history see *V.C.H. Bucks.* i. 365; Dugd. *Mon.* v. 364.
[32] See map facing p. 1.
[33] *V.C.H. Oxon.* i. 426; *V.C.H. Bucks.* iv. 135.
[34] *V.C.H. Oxon.* i. 411.
[35] 2 & 3 Wm. IV, c. 64; 7 & 8 Vict. c. 61. For Caversfield see also *V.C.H. Bucks.* iv. 157.
[36] See below, pp. 269–70.

total, the figure of 251⅝ hides is obtained for the 2½ Domesday hundreds attached to Kirtlington.[37]

The annual value of the hundred was said to be £5 0s. 6d. a year in 1255, of which £2 1s. was derived from hidage and £2 19s. 6d. from the view of frankpledge,[38] a sum which was still derived from the courts in 1652.[39] The 'rents called certainty money' then amounted to £4 13s. 3½d. with 2 quarters of oats (or 30s.) from Wendlebury and a bushel of oats with a fat goose (or 3s. 6d.) from Ardley. The total revenue was £11 6s. 9½d. The Hundred Rolls and the eyre rolls show how difficult it might be to collect even this small sum and to exact services and other customary payments. It was reported, for instance, that the 1s. which the king used to have from Boycott at the sheriff's tourn had been withdrawn; and that the payments from Finmere, Shelswell, Hethe, and Stoke Lyne had been withheld through the might of the earls of Gloucester.[40] Similarly at Lower Heyford Gilbert, Earl of Gloucester, had usurped the king's rights and had held the view from the time of the Battle of Evesham up to 1279.[41] Earl Richard was also accused of preventing suit being done by five men and taking all amercements.[42] The Abbot of Westminster was another of those guilty of usurpation: he had prevented the payment of 2s. or a quarter of hay from Hampton Gay for the king's holding at Northbrook in Kirtlington and had prevented Adam de Gay from doing suit,[43] while the Abbot of Oseney had opposed the enforcement of the king's rights. He forbade his men of Newton to follow the hue when John FitzNigel, who was distrained to make his suit, seized the distraint.[44]

The small value of the hundred was due to the number of lords of manors who were either partly or wholly exempt from its jurisdiction. From time immemorial Souldern, for example, had enjoyed exceptional rights. It was described on the Hundred Rolls as a 'free manor' to which bailiffs had no entry save by the king's writ. Its lord could come if he wished to the two great courts of Ploughley hundred to claim 'his liberty for his men,' and also the profits of justice, for they could depart, it is stated, without being amerced.[45] Members of the honor of Wallingford were other places to claim exemption. The jurors of 1279 stated that the Earl of Cornwall and his predecessors before him had had view of frankpledge 'since the Conquest' at Great and Little Chesterton;[46] that the earl's lands at Caulcott in Lower Heyford, at Bicester Market End and at Stratton Audley all owed suit to the honor court once a year, while at Mixbury the Abbot of Oseney held the view under the earl[47] and at Willaston the Abbot of Rewley, as a tenant of the honor, was declared by a jury in 1293 to owe 'no suit or service' to the king's hundred court.[48] So privileged an abbey as Westminster was naturally exempt.[49] The abbot held his court at Islip, to which the men of Fencott and Murcott owed suit twice a year, and also had the view at Launton.[50] In 1316 indeed not only Fencott and Murcott, but also Noke (i.e. half of Noke) and Oddington with Northbrook are listed apart from the rest of the vills of Ploughley hundred as being in the Abbot of Westminster's liberty of Islip.[51] Such was the abbot's pre-eminence that his court was called the 'hundred of Islip' and its officer bore the title of seneschal.[52] Other lords who had view of frankpledge were the Damorys at Bucknell[53] and the lords of Ardley, but only

[37] V.C.H. Oxon. i. 427–8.
[38] Rot. Hund. (Rec. Com.), ii. 45. Cf. Just. Itin. 1/700, m. 9.   [39] Oxf. E 317.
[40] Rot. Hund. (Rec. Com.), ii. 31; Just. Itin. 1/703.
[41] Rot. Hund. ii. 826–7.
[42] Ibid. 31.   [43] Ibid.
[44] Just. Itin. 1/703.
[45] Rot. Hund. (Rec. Com.), ii. 823.
[46] Ibid. 826.
[47] Ibid. 827, 828, 832, and for Bicester see below, p. 36.
[48] Kennett, Paroch. Antiq. i. 455–6.
[49] For the abbey's manors in the hundred, see below, pp. 208, 234, 269–70.
[50] Rot. Hund. (Rec. Com.), ii. 832.
[51] Feud. Aids, iv. 170; cf. Rot. Hund. ii. 45, where Launton is included in the liberty.
[52] Balliol Coll. Arch. A 23. For hundreds of this kind see Helen Cam, E.H.R. xlvii. 358.
[53] Rot. Hund. ii. 826. The lord went to the sheriff's tourn twice a year to claim his liberty.

in the presence of the sheriff and the king's bailiffs and on payment of 10s.[54] The sheriff also went once a year to Middleton, where he took 4s., and to Wendlebury, where he received two quarters of oats.[55] The Abbot of St. Évroul also claimed exemption for his half of Charlton and claimed his liberty when the sheriff impounded one of his tenants because he lived in a house from which it was alleged suit was owed to the sheriff's tourn twice a year.[56]

One account of the hundred in action has survived. When a dispute between Oseney Abbey and the lord of Hampton Gay arose over boundaries in 1280, a writ was obtained and the court ordered twelve jurors to set stones and pales between the fields of Hampton Gay and Hampton Stephen (or Poyle) before the hundred. This order was followed by an action begun by a writ of novel disseisin against the Abbot of Oseney and the twelve jurors.[57]

Ploughley remained in royal hands throughout the Middle Ages. In the Confessor's time the soke of the 2½ hundreds was attached to the vill of Kirtlington, then a royal manor, but when Kirtlington was given away the hundred apparently remained with the Crown.[58] It was described as the king's hundred in 1255, 1293, and 1316.[59] In 1594 it was granted by Queen Elizabeth I for 21 years to Sir William Spencer of Yarnton.[60] He was in possession in about 1606, when his court, held every three weeks at Islip, was called 'curia baronis of the hundred of Ploughley'.[61] In 1629 the Crown granted the hundred to Gilbert North and others,[62] but by 1648 Sir Robert Croke held it. He sold it in December 1649 with the office of bailiff and the bailiwick to John West of Hampton Poyle.[63] The parliamentary survey of 1652 recorded that John West held the courts in fee farm, but that the rents belonging to the hundred had been bought by Col. Henry Martin, M.P.[64]

In 1697 John West and his wife Elizabeth mortgaged the hundred and the manor to Christopher Clitheroe and John Stevens.[65] In 1699 the mortgages were taken over by William Lord Digby and in 1702 by the executors of Sir Edward Sebright, Bt. (d. 1702).[66] In 1714 the hundred was mortgaged along with the manor-house of Hampton Poyle and lands in the parish by Sir Thomas Sebright to Arthur, 7th Earl of Anglesey.[67] On John West's death in 1717 his widow and the Sebrights sold the mortgage to the earl.[68] In 1723 the hundred and manor were sold to Christopher Tilson and descended in the Tilson family for several generations.[69] John Henry Tilson of Watlington Park succeeded to the property in 1774 and in 1795 sold the whole to Arthur Annesley for £25,000.[70] The Annesleys were still in possession of the hundred and manor in 1808,[71] and probably later, for Dunkin, writing in 1820, stated that they were holding courts leet at Wendlebury.[72]

At this time the hundred was composed of the parishes named in the hundred rolls of 1279 with the exception of Fulwell. Most of the hamlets had long disappeared as separate administrative units, and in the 19th century Boycott hamlet alone continued to figure on the list of the constituents of the hundred.[73] An unsuccessful attempt was

[54] Ibid. 833.
[55] Ibid. 833, 834.
[56] *Cal. Close*, 1341–3, 252; *Bk. of Fees*, 831.
[57] *Oseney Cart.* vi. 66.
[58] *V.C.H. Oxon.* i. 400; and see below, p. 221.
[59] *Rot. Hund.* (Rec. Com.), ii. 45; Kennett, *Paroch. Antiq.* i. 455–6; *Feud. Aids*, iv. 169.
[60] C 66/1423, m. 8.
[61] E.C.R. no. 184; cf. MS. Top. Oxon. b 87, f. 217.
[62] C 66/2497, no. 4.
[63] MS. Top. Oxon. b 87, ff. 46–49.
[64] Oxf. E 317.
[65] C.P. 25(2)/865/Mich. 9 Wm. III.

[66] MS. Top. Oxon. b 87, f. 91.
[67] O.R.O. SB 17.
[68] Ibid. 18; MS. Top. Oxon. b 87, ff. 233–4: schedule of title deeds.
[69] Bodl. MS. D.D. Valentia a 1: abstract of title.
[70] See below, p. 162.
[71] C.P. 43/899/407.
[72] Dunkin, *Hist. Oxon.* ii. 197.
[73] *Census*, 1831, &c. The 19th-cent. boundary changes resulted in Caversfield's transference to Ploughley and the exclusion of Lillingstone and Boycott. See 1932 jury lists in O.R.O.

made in 1833 to transfer the two Hamptons, Islip, and Noke to Bullingdon hundred on the ground that Oxford, the centre for Bullingdon, was nearer to these places than was Bicester.[74] In the 19th century Bicester was the centre for the hundred, but there is no evidence about when it became so.[75] In 1652 the courts leet were usually held at Ardley, Fringford and Wendlebury and the three-week court at Islip.[76] By 1607 if not earlier the hundred was divided into two high or chief constable's divisions, the north and south divisions. A taxation return of that date gives eighteen parishes with Boycott, Fulwell and Willaston in the north division and fifteen with Bicester King's End in the south division. It omits Lillingstone, but the parish was presumably normally in the northern division.[77] These divisions were abolished in 1848 when Ploughley became a petty-sessional division.

No court rolls for the hundred have been found and there is little documentary record of the hundred's business in the post-medieval period. Its use for military purposes is seen in 1539, when the returns for the muster of the king's subjects were made,[78] and for dealing with rogues and vagabonds in the reign of Elizabeth I.[79] The chief constables were responsible for seeing that the petty constables of the parishes made their returns to quarter sessions on such matters as the good repair of the stocks and pound, the upkeep of bridges and highways, the due observation of watch and ward, proper provision for the poor; and that they generally carried out their duties as the guardians of law and order. To report regularly on recusants was another of their functions, or, as in 1722, to make a special summons to all papists and non-jurors to appear at Bicester to take the oaths of allegiance and supremacy.[80]

[74] MS. Dunkin 438/7, f. 107d (b), citing *Jackson's Oxford Journal.*

[75] The high constable was resident in Bicester in 1864: *Kelly's Dir. Oxon.* (1864). For a list of chief constables and bailiffs, 1687–1830, see O.R.O. Cal. Q. Sess. iii. Jurors' lists for the hundred, 1764–1932, are also in the O.R.O.

[76] Oxf. E 317.

[77] E 179/164/515.

[78] *L. & P. Hen. VIII*, xiv (2), pp. 362–3.

[79] *Cal. S.P. Dom.* 1547–80, 418; cf. ibid. 423, 428.

[80] O.R.O. Cal. Q. Sess. iii, ix.

ARDLEY

THE parish lies on either side of the Oxford–Brackley road, roughly mid-way between the market-towns of Bicester and Brackley (Northants). In the early 18th century it was described as of 'not many more than a 1,000 acres',[1] but the improved surveying of the 19th century showed it to cover 1,493 acres, and in 1948 it was increased to 2,178 acres by the addition of Fewcot hamlet and that part of Stoke Lyne parish which lay west of the Oxford road.[2] The old northern boundary used to skirt Ardley village until it joined a stream flowing eastwards, which still forms the western part of the northern boundary.[3] Part of the eastern boundary is also a natural one, the Gagle Brook or the Saxon *Sexig Broc*, and on the west it is the ancient pre-Roman dyke, Ashbank or Aves Ditch.[4] A late 10th-century charter granted by Ethelred II shows that the Saxon boundaries corresponded closely with those of the 19th century.[5]

The present parish is about a mile broad and two miles long. It is a flat tableland, lying between the 300- and 400-foot contour lines, and forming a part of the Great Oolite belt which crosses the country. The Lower Oolite is exposed in the railway cuttings.[6] The soil is stonebrash and field-names indicate that much of the land was once rough pasture: the part near Aves Ditch was known as the 'great moor' in 1685[7] and in the 19th century as the Great Heath.[8] Here also were Church Furze and Heath Ground, while Pearson's Heath lay in the south, west of the Brackley road, and Margrett's Heath and Little Heath lay in the south-east corner.[9] But by the early 19th century this land had been reclaimed and was growing good corn crops.[10] The soil is well watered, for apart from the boundary streams, a third stream rises in the centre of the parish and flows southwards.

Ardley Wood (40 a.) and Ballard's Copse (called Chilgrove in the 17th century, Child Grove in 1797,[11] and probably to be identified with the 'lytle Ciltene' of a 10th-century charter)[12] are the remains of more extensive woodland. Ardley Wood was partly cut down in the early 19th century to facilitate quarrying,[13] but as late as 1881 the parish still had nearly 60 acres of wood.[14]

From early times the parish was traversed by an important highway—the road from Oxford into Northamptonshire; it is the *via regia* of an early 13th-century record[15] and the Oxford Way of 1679.[16] It was made a turnpike in 1757.[17] Today it is crossed by branch roads to Fritwell and Bucknell, which follow the line of older roads: the Bucknell road was already hedged in 1797.[18] The course of the present branch road to Upper Heyford, however, has been straightened since Davis's survey of 1797. The old road was probably the 10th-century 'green way to Heyford'.[19]

The former G.W.R. main line from Birmingham to London crosses the parish and Ardley station was opened in 1910.[20]

In the south-west of the parish 86 acres were taken over by Upper Heyford R.A.F. station after 1925.[21]

Ardley village lies at the extreme northern edge of the ancient parish, near a good spring and cross-roads.[22] There is no evidence for any Roman settlement here, although Roman remains have been found in the parish at Ballard's Copse,[23] and at least in the early Middle Ages there was evidence for still earlier settlement. The tumulus, called *Cwichelmes Hlæw* in a 10th-century charter, is thought to have stood near the present Ashgrove Farm.[24] The Saxons called the settlement *Eardulfes lea* or 'Eardwulf's wood or clearing', and the remains of the wood still lie just west of the village.[25] The village seems never to have been very large or rich and in 1662 and 1665 only eleven and nine houses, most of which were humble dwellings, were listed for the hearth tax.[26] Twenty houses were recorded in 1768 and 35 in 1821.[27] The 19th-century village was reputed to be a mile long; its thatched two-story cottages built of rubble with brick dressings or only of rubble were scattered along the main road, while the church and more houses lay on a branch road to the west.[28]

Blomfield thought that the triangular field on the north side of the churchyard, called the Park, marked the site of the medieval manor-house[29]—the *curia* of Ralph son of Robert mentioned in the early 13th century.[30] But it is more probable that it was in the precincts of the 12th-century castle. Of the latter there remains in Ardley Wood just west of the village an almost circular moat with a diameter of 100 yards. In 1823 the antiquary Skelton recorded the existence

[1] Oxf. Dioc. d 552.
[2] O.S. Map 6", xvi (1885); *Census*, 1951.
[3] O.S. Map 6", xvi (1885); ibid. 2½", 42/52 (1951).
[4] For Aves Ditch see *V.C.H. Oxon.* i. 275–6; *Oxoniensia*, ii. 202; ibid. xi. 162.
[5] *Cod. Dipl.* ed. Kemble, vi, no. 1289.
[6] W. J. Arkell, L. Richardson and J. Pringle, *Proc. Geol. Assoc.* xliv. 340; G.S. Map 1", xlv NE.
[7] Oxf. Archd. Oxon. b 40, f. 12.
[8] Bodl. Tithe award map (1839).
[9] Ibid.
[10] Blo. *Ard.* 14; Wing, *Annals*, 14.
[11] Oxf. Archd. Oxon. b 40, ff. 10, 12; Davis, *Oxon. Map*. The Child Grove shown by Davis actually lies on the Upper Heyford side of the parish boundary. Cf. field map below, p. 202.
[12] *Saxon Oxon.* 3; *P.N. Oxon.* (E.P.N.S.), i. 197.
[13] *Oxf. Jnl.* 23 Jan. 1830: sale of 560 trees.
[14] O.S. *Area Bk.* (1876).

[15] MS. Top. Oxon. c 398, f. 97.
[16] Terrier: Blo. *Ard.* 31.
[17] 30 Geo. II, c. 48.
[18] Davis, *Oxon. Map*.
[19] *Saxon Oxon.* 3.
[20] E. T. MacDermot, *Hist. G.W.R.* ii. 448–9.
[21] Local inf. For Heyford see below, p. 197.
[22] O.S. Map 25", xvi. 12 (1881).
[23] *V.C.H. Oxon.* i. 330; O.S. *Map of Roman Britain* (1956): found in a line with Aves Ditch which was used as a road by the Romans.
[24] *Saxon Oxon.* 2.
[25] *P.N. Oxon.* (E.P.N.S.), i. 197.
[26] *Hearth Tax Oxon.* 204, 235; see below, p. 10 for the medieval village.
[27] Oxf. Dioc. d 558; *Census*, 1821.
[28] Blo. *Ard.* 14; O.S. Map 25", xvi. 12 (1881).
[29] Blo. *Ard.* 7.
[30] e.g. *Oseney Cart.* vi. 37.

of subterranean passages on the site.[31] There is no record of any resident lord of the manor after the Reformation, and no manor-house is marked on Plot's map of 1676.[32]

Some 17th-century houses remain: there is the Old Rectory, now Ardley House, and Ralph Ford's house to the west of the church, both taxed on four hearths in 1665, and the Manor Farm, taxed on six hearths.[33] In 1679 the Rectory was described as a house of four bays with a barn and stables attached. In a later terrier the house was said to have six bays[34] with a kitchen and malt-house of five bays in addition to the barn and stables. It was enlarged in 1860 and entirely remodelled in 1874 by the architect E. G. Bruton at a cost of £1,200.[35] It was then refronted, although one of the original windows was retained.

The Fox and Hounds Inn, standing at the crossroads at the northern end of the village, was probably built or rebuilt at the end of the 18th century as a result of the turnpike traffic. By 1852 a second inn, the 'Horse and Jockey', had opened and in 1861 a school was built.[36]

Of the outlying farm-houses, Ashgrove is marked on Davis's map of 1797, and Neville's Farm, Hall's Barn and Scotland Barn were all built by 1839.[37] Ardley Fields Farm dates from the end of the 19th century.[38]

The only well-known person connected with Ardley was Master John London, rector (1521–4) and later Warden of New College. He acquired notoriety as 'the most terrible of all the monastic spoilers'.[39]

MANOR. In the late 10th century 5 hides in Ardley were held by three brothers. Two of them were slain in resisting the arrest of one of their men as a thief, and the third fled to sanctuary. Their estate fell to the king, Ethelred II, who in 995 granted it in perpetuity to Æthelwig, the reeve (*praepositus*) of Buckingham.[40] In 1243 *ARDLEY* manor consisted of 1 knight's fee held of the honor of Pontefract: ½ fee in Ardley parish and ½ fee lying in Somerton parish.[41] The latter was described in 1279 as a part of the vill of Somerton called Northbrook.[42] This *Northbroc iuxta Somerthonam*[43] should not be confused with Northbrook in Kirtlington which was held of the honor of Stafford.[44] In the assessment of 1220, Northbrook was included in the 12 carucates of Somerton,[45] and a fine of 1244 shows that some part of it belonged to the barony of Arsic and became part of the De Grey manor of Somerton.[46]

Hugh d'Avranches, Earl of Chester, held Ardley at the time of the Domesday survey,[47] and the overlordship of the fee descended with the Earldom of Chester until the death of Earl Ranulf de Blundeville in 1232.[48] Earl Ranulf's vast possessions were then partitioned between his coheirs and their descendants, and the overlordship of Ardley fell to the share of Hugh d'Aubigny, Earl of Arundel, the son and heir of Mabel, Earl Ranulf's second sister.[49] Of the manors which Hugh received the chief was Coventry, which became the *caput* of a new honor;[50] hence in 1236 Ardley was said to be held 'de feudo Hugonis de Auben' de Coventre'.[51] Hugh died in 1243, and his lands were divided between his four sisters and coheiresses.[52] Ardley passed to Hugh's fourth sister Cecile and her husband Roger de Montalt, Steward of Chester.[53] Roger died in 1260, and his son Robert held the overlordship of the manor at his death in 1275.[54] Robert was succeeded by his sons Roger (d. 1296) and Robert, who in 1327, two years before his death, settled all his estates on himself and his wife for life, with reversion to Queen Isabel, and successively to her son John of Eltham and his heirs, and to the king, if he, Robert, left no male issue. In 1331 his widow surrendered her life interest to Queen Isabel, and in 1335 Robert de Morley, Robert de Montalt's heir, granted her the rents and services due from Ardley manor.[55] John of Eltham died without heirs in 1336, so that after Isabel's death in 1358 Edward III was the overlord. As early as 1285, however, the mesne tenants, the De Plescy family, were thought to hold Ardley in chief.[56]

In 1086 Ardley was held of the Earl of Chester by Robert d'Oilly,[57] and the mesne lordship of the manor followed the same descent as the overlordship of Bucknell, passing from the D'Oillys in 1232 to the De Plescy family and in the 15th century to the dukes of Suffolk. The tenant of Ardley under Robert (I) d'Oilly was Drew d'Aundeley, who also held Hardwick and Shirburn of Robert's own honor.[58] About 1100 Drew became a monk of Abingdon, and gave the abbey some of his land at South Weston. He was succeeded by his son-in-law, Roger son of Ralph, a nephew of Nigel d'Oilly, his lord.[59] Roger was followed by Ralph son of Roger, probably his son, who witnessed Robert (II) d'Oilly's charter to Oseney Abbey about 1130.[60] In 1156 Ralph was pardoned the payment of Danegeld in Oxfordshire,[61] and in 1166 he was the tenant of one of Henry (I) d'Oilly's three fees of the honor of Stafford.[62] His

[31] Skelton, *Oxon.* (Ploughley), 1; *V.C.H. Oxon.* ii. 327. For an illustration see MS. Top. Oxon. c 6, f. 133.
[32] Plot, *Nat. Hist. Oxon.* frontispiece.
[33] *Hearth Tax Oxon.* 204.
[34] Blo. *Ard.* 31; Oxf. Archd. Oxon. c 141, p. 277 (1679); ibid. p. 281.
[35] Blo. *Ard.* 33.
[36] Ibid. 17; Gardner, *Dir. Oxon.*; see below, p. 13.
[37] Davis, *Oxon. Map*; Bodl. Tithe award map.
[38] Blo. *Ard.* 13 citing *Sale Cat.* 1894; cf. O.S. Map 6", xvi (1885) which does not mark it.
[39] *D.N.B.*
[40] *Cod. Dipl.* ed Kemble, vi. no. 1289.
[41] *Bk. of Fees*, 825.
[42] *Rot. Hund.* (Rec. Com.), ii. 833.
[43] *Oseney Cart.* iv. 3, 26.
[44] Farrer, *Honors*, ii. 245, wrongly identifies the Northbrook held of the Earl of Chester with the Northbrook held by Rainald in Domesday survey, i.e. Northbrook in Kirtlington; see below, p. 223.

[45] *Bk. of Fees*, 319.
[46] *Fines Oxon.* 237; see below, p. 291.
[47] *V.C.H. Oxon.* i. 409.
[48] *Complete Peerage*, iii. 164–9.
[49] Farrer, *Honors*, ii. 9.
[50] Ibid. 11; *Complete Peerage*, iii. 169 note a.
[51] *Bk. of Fees*, 447.
[52] *Complete Peerage*, iii. 169 note a.
[53] Ibid. i. 239 note b; Farrer, *Honors*, ii. 10.
[54] *Complete Peerage*, ix. 13–14; *Cal. Inq. p m.* ii, p. 84.
[55] *Complete Peerage*, ix. 15–17; *Cal. Pat. 1334–8*, 130; *Cat. Anct. D.* v. A 10947–8.
[56] *Feud. Aids*, iv. 158.
[57] *V.C.H. Oxon.* i. 409.
[58] Ibid. 382, 409; see below, p. 169.
[59] Farrer, *Honors*, ii. 244–5; *Chron. Abingdon*, ii. 67, 69, 74, 103.
[60] *Oseney Cart.* i. 2; iii. 352, n. 3; Farrer, *Honors*, ii. 245.
[61] *Pipe R. 1156–8* (Rec. Com.), 37.
[62] *Red Bk. Exch.* (Rolls Ser.), 265.

wife was named Adelize[63] and their son Robert had succeeded his father by 1201.[64] He temporarily forfeited his lands in 1215 when he joined the baronial party opposed to King John.[65] The date of his death is uncertain, but his son Ralph son of Robert presented to Ardley church before 1218 and in 1221,[66] and Ralph's brother Guy had succeeded him at Ardley by 1235 when he granted 9 virgates in the manor to Oseney Abbey.[67]

Guy also held ½ knight's fee of the Earl of Winchester at Shipton-on-Cherwell, besides estates in Warwickshire.[68] He was escheator for Oxfordshire from 1246 to 1253,[69] and sheriff of the county in 1248.[70] In 1243 Guy held ½ fee in Ardley, while his other ½ fee in Northbrook appears to have been held of him by Stephen Simeon and Thomas de la Haye.[71] Guy was still in possession of Ardley in 1255[72], but had been succeeded by his son John by 1268.[73] If John son of Guy is 'Johannes, heres de Arde de Ardul',[74] then he was one of the twelve jurors whose returns for Ploughley hundred are embodied in the Hundred Rolls. John son of Guy took part in the Welsh and Scottish wars of Edward I[75] and was succeeded by 1309 by his son Robert.[76] Fitzguy, in the form 'Fitzwyth', now became established as the family surname. Robert Fitzwyth died in 1316, and his son Guy, who inherited Ardley, died later the same year, leaving a widow Joan, and an infant daughter Elizabeth.[77] Ardley may have been held in dower by Joan, who presented to the church in 1318.[78] By 1326 the manor of Shotteswell (Warws.) was held by John Fitzwyth, possibly a cousin of Guy, who was succeeded there by his son Robert,[79] who also held Ardley in 1346[80] and in 1352 conveyed part of his Warwickshire estates to his nephew Robert and his wife Agnes.[81] It was this younger Robert who died seized of Ardley in 1362.[82] The manner of his death was revealed in 1369 when his widow, his second wife Joan, and her second husband claimed her dower in the Fitzwyth manors. He had died as the result of an attack by an armed band led by Roger de Careswell which had carried off Joan to St. Thomas's Hospital, Southwark. Later, she successfully refuted the allegations of Joan, Robert's daughter by his first wife, and her husband John de Beauchamp, that she had willingly lived in adultery with Roger de Careswell, and her claims to dower were upheld.[83] In 1370, however, she granted her dower in Ardley manor and elsewhere to John de Beauchamp in return for £20 a year in rents.[84] In 1375 John had his wife's Oxford-

shire manors including Ardley settled upon himself and his wife and their heirs in fee tail.[85]

John, who was the son of Richard de Beauchamp of Holt (Worcs.), fought in the French wars, was appointed Steward of the King's household in 1387 and was created Lord de Beauchamp, Baron of Kidderminster. In 1388 when the Lords Appellant seized power he was attainted and finally beheaded.[86] Ardley was taken into the king's hand,[87] but in 1389 Philip de la Vache, during the minority of the heir, successfully claimed the wardship of the manor as overlord on the grounds that it was held in tail, not in fee simple.[88] Joan de Beauchamp had died a few months before her husband's execution,[89] and in 1390 Philip de la Vache placed Ardley in the hands of trustees for the duration of the minority of her son John.[90] In 1398, his father's attainder and forfeiture having been reversed, John obtained his titles and estates, but in 1400 the atainder was reaffirmed and he lost the peerage. He died in 1420, leaving a widow Alice and a daughter Margaret, widow of John Pauncefoot.[91] Alice received Ardley for life, but was dead by 1428, when Margaret and her second husband John Wysham were in possession.[92] Margaret had three daughters: Alice, who married John Guise; Joan, who married John Croft; and Elizabeth, who married firstly Thomas Croft, a ranger of Woodstock (d. 1488), and secondly Nicholas Crowemer.[93] Margaret and her third husband Sir Walter Skull were dead by 1472, and the manor was divided between the three co-heiresses.[94] After the death of Elizabeth without issue, the third of Ardley which she and Nicholas Crowemer had held[95] was divided between her surviving sisters, for whereas in 1499 John and Joan Croft held a third of the manor, in 1501 they held a half,[96] and in the same year John Guise died holding the other half.[97] In 1513 John Croft conveyed his portion to William Billing of Deddington,[98] and four years later William acquired the other half from John Guise's son John.[99] In 1533 William died in possession of the whole manor.[1]

In a letter to Thomas Cromwell written in 1538 Sir Thomas Pope, the future founder of Trinity College, Oxford, referred to his having bought land in Ardley of the value of £8 a year from 'one Billyng' —presumably William Billing's son John. Though Billing challenged the legality of the sale,[2] Pope appears to have kept him to his bargain. In 1540 Sir Thomas received a grant of the lands in Ardley which had belonged to Oseney Abbey and Studley

[63] *Thame Cart.* i. 47.
[64] Ibid. 6, 74, 75; *Rot. de Ob. et Fin.* (Rec. Com.), 155.
[65] *Rot. Litt. Claus.* (Rec. Com.), i. 239 b.
[66] *Rot. Welles,* i. 68; ii. 7; Farrer, *Honors,* ii. 245.
[67] *Bk. of Fees,* 447; *Fines Oxon.* 94.
[68] *Bk. of Fees,* 448; for the Warws. estates see *V.C.H. Warws.* v. 148; vi. 46–47; Dugd. *Warws.* (1656), 32.
[69] *Cal. Pat. 1232–47,* 483; *Close R. 1251–3,* 303.
[70] P.R.O. *L. & I.* ix.
[71] *Bk. of Fees,* 825, 836; Farrer, *Honors,* ii. 246; see below, p. 291.
[72] *Rot. Hund.* (Rec. Com.), ii. 44.
[73] *V.C.H. Warws.* v. 148; Farrer, *Honors,* ii. 246.
[74] *Rot. Hund.* (Rec. Com.), ii. 822.
[75] Dugd. *Warws.* 32.
[76] *V.C.H. Warws.* v. 148.
[77] Ibid.; *Feud Aids,* iv. 169.
[78] Blo. *Ard.* 22.
[79] *V.C.H. Warws.* v. 148; cf. Dugd. *Warws.* 32.
[80] *Feud. Aids,* iv. 180; cf. *Cal. Inq. p.m.* ix, p. 184.
[81] *Cat. Anct. D.* iv. A 6888.
[82] *Cal. Inq. p.m.* xi, p. 260.
[83] *Hist. Collect. Staffs.* xiii. 76.
[84] *Cat. Anct. D.* iv. A 9265.
[85] C.P. 25(1)/288/50/121.
[86] *Complete Peerage,* ii. 46.
[87] *Cal. Close, 1389–92,* 74.
[88] C 145/241/91, 151; C 47/74/155; K.B. 27/515, m. 18.
[89] C 145/241/91.
[90] *Cal. Close, 1389–92,* 301; *Cat. Anct. D,* iii. D 390.
[91] *Complete Peerage,* ii. 46; *V.C.H. Warws.* v. 148; vi. 47; *V.C.H. Worcs.* iii. 404.
[92] C.P. 25(1)/291/65/9; cf. *Feud. Aids,* iv. 190.
[93] *V.C.H. Warws.* v. 148; vi. 47; *V.C.H. Worcs.* iii. 404.
[94] *V.C.H. Worcs.* iii. 404; C.P. 25(1)/294/76/87.
[95] C.P. 40/933, m. 141.
[96] C.P. 25(1)/294/80/78, 102; C.P. 40/957, m. 21.
[97] E 150/783/11.
[98] C.P. 25(2)/34/225, East. 4 & 5 Hen. VIII.
[99] Ibid. Trin. 9 Hen. VIII; C.P. 40/1018, m. 419.
[1] C 142/56/5.
[2] *L. & P. Hen. VIII,* xiii (1), p. 404.

Priory before the Dissolution, and five years later he was granted certain rents previously reserved in his grant.[3] By 1555 he appears to have obtained the manor,[4] and it formed part of his considerable possessions at his death in 1559.[5] Sir Thomas was succeeded by his brother, John Pope of Wroxton, who died in 1584.[6] In accordance with a settlement made by Sir Thomas, Ardley next passed to his nephew, Edmund Hochens, and on the latter's death in 1602 it reverted to William, son of John Pope,[7] then Sheriff of Oxfordshire and later created Earl of Downe (1628). On his death in 1631 his title and lands, including Ardley, passed to his grandson Thomas Pope.[8] In June 1646 his estates between Oxford and Banbury, presumably including Ardley, were reported to be 'consumed by the King's garrisons', and in 1650 they were sequestered. Ardley, together with the earl's other estates in Oxfordshire, was let by the Oxford County Committee to Edward Twiford.[9]

Thomas died without male issue in 1660[10] and was succeeded by his uncle Thomas who conveyed Ardley manor to Philip Holman in the same year.[11] Philip was succeeded by George Holman, and in 1698 his widow Anastasia conveyed the manor to George Townsend, who was still lord of the manor in 1718.[12] In 1753 Ardley was purchased by Charles, Duke of Marlborough, whose descendants held the manor until 1894, when the Ardley estates of the 9th duke were sold by auction.[13] The manorial rights were offered for sale, but were withdrawn, a bid of £100 being rejected. By 1903, however, C. W. Perryman, who had purchased the advowson, had acquired the manorial rights.[14]

LESSER ESTATES. In 1235 Guy son of Robert granted 9 virgates in Ardley to Oseney Abbey, for a yearly payment of 1s. or a pair of gilt spurs for all services.[15] This estate, which was administered as part of the bailiwick of Weston-on-the-Green, was held by Oseney until the Dissolution.[16] It still consisted of 9 virgates in the early 16th century,[17] when the lord of Ardley manor was receiving 1s. a year from the abbey.[18] Studley Priory had acquired 3 virgates in Ardley by 1279[19] and had 5s. rents there at the Dissolution.[20] In the 1230's Ralph son of Robert granted Bicester Priory about 11 acres of land,[21] and at some time the priory must have received more land in Ardley, for it is later known to have held more than 3 virgates. In 1267 it exchanged 2 virgates and 5 acres of this property with William and Joan Paute for property in Grimsbury (Northants).[22]

Although in 1279 the priory still held one virgate in Ardley in free alms of the lord of the manor,[23] no more is known of this land, and Bicester had no property in Ardley at the Dissolution.[24]

ECONOMIC HISTORY. At the time of the Domesday survey there was said to be sufficient land for 11 ploughs, although 10 were at work, of which 4 were in demesne and 6 belonged to 8 villeins (villani) and 15 bordars.[25] In view of the comparatively small area of the later parish, these figures are surprisingly high, more especially as there is 13th-century evidence for the clearance of new land. For when Ralph son of Robert granted Bicester Priory in the early 1230's pasture for 200 sheep on the common land, whether it belonged to the demesne or to the villeins, he made an exception of Stockmead and a new assart near his manor-house. These were to be fenced in from Easter to Michaelmas.[26]

Ralph's charter and a grant of land to Oseney made by Guy son of Robert in 1235 add further details about agrarian arrangements. The 9 virgates which Guy gave to the abbey were held by villein virgaters, who were also granted with their land and families;[27] there were two fields, North and South Fields, since the 11 acres given to Bicester by Ralph were divided equally between these two fields; there were already small inclosures. Bicester, for example, was given an inclosed (fossatum) piece of ground called 'Southleye' near the manor woods, where a sheepfold was to be made.

The account in the Hundred Rolls of 1279 shows that the lord's demesne had been much reduced. He had 4 virgates in demesne and nine villein virgaters paying a rent of 5s. each and working at will. More than half the recorded land was now held freely; Oseney held its 9 virgates for 12d.; the Prioress of Studley held 3 virgates which were occupied by a free tenant; the Prior of Bicester held a virgate;[28] and the rector another.[29] The only lay free tenant was an unidentified Ralph of Chesterton, who held 4 virgates.[30] Only 31 virgates are accounted for in this survey compared with the 42 recorded in the 17th century.[31] The 1279 survey is incomplete, however, since Oseney's tenants, for instance, are not recorded.

Fourteenth-century tax assessments[32] show that Ardley was among the poorer communities in Ploughley hundred. It seems certain that the village was comparatively small then and had dwindled in size by the 15th century, when it was returned as

³ L. & P. Hen. VIII, xv, p. 169; xx (1), p. 216.
⁴ C.P. 40/1162, m. 158.
⁵ C 142/124/153.
⁶ Ibid. 205/191; for Pope pedigree see Oxon. Visit. 151–2; Baker, Northants, i. 707.
⁷ C 142/124/153; ibid. 271/178.
⁸ C 142/472/103; Complete Peerage, iv. 449–50.
⁹ Cal. Cttee. for Compounding, 407, 934–5.
¹⁰ Complete Peerage, iv. 450–1.
¹¹ C.P. 25(2)/588, East. 1660.
¹² Par. Coll. i. 8; C.P. 25(2)/865, Mich. & Hil. 10 Wm. III.
¹³ Blo. Ard. 13; Sale Cat.: Bodl. G.A. Oxon. b 90(12).
¹⁴ Blo. Ard. 13; Kelly's Dir. Oxon. (1903).
¹⁵ Oseney Cart. vi. 36; Fines Oxon. 94.
¹⁶ Rot. Hund. (Rec. Com.), ii. 833; Tax. Eccl. (Rec. Com.), 45; Valor Eccl. (Rec. Com.), ii. 216.
¹⁷ Oseney Cart. vi. 230.
¹⁸ Ibid. 248.
¹⁹ Rot. Hund. (Rec. Com.), ii. 833.

²⁰ Valor Eccl. (Rec. Com.), ii. 186.
²¹ MS. Top. Oxon. c 398, f. 97: transcript of E 326/ B 8537.
²² Fines Oxon. 243.
²³ Rot. Hund. (Rec. Com.), ii. 833.
²⁴ Valor Eccl. (Rec. Com.), ii. 187.
²⁵ V.C.H. Oxon. i. 409.
²⁶ MS. Top. Oxon. c 398, f. 97: transcript of E 326/ B 8537; see above, p. 7.
²⁷ Oseney Cart. vi. 36; cf. Fines Oxon. 94.
²⁸ Rot. Hund. (Rec. Com.), ii. 833. In 1267 he was said to hold 2 virgates and 5 a.: Fines Oxon. 243.
²⁹ This was apparently not the glebe.
³⁰ Rot. Hund. (Rec. Com.), ii. 833. Ralph, the lord of Chesterton, died in 1272.
³¹ Ibid.; Blo. Ard. 31.
³² E 179/161/10 (incomplete), 17. In 1316 Ardley was assessed with Hardwick and Tusmore: ibid. 161/8. There were 20 contributors in 1327 (ibid. 161/9).

having fewer than ten households.[33] Early 16th-century subsidy lists also point to a small and poor population, 10 persons being assessed at a low figure in 1523 and 7 in 1524 compared with 39 at the large neighbouring village of Somerton.[34] Decreasing population was accompanied it seems by a growth in the size of farms: Oseney's 9 virgates were farmed in the 16th century to 3 tenants instead of nine. One held as much as 4 virgates.[35] Inclosure too was on the increase. Meadow closes had probably long existed, but in the early 16th century and perhaps before there had been inclosure of the arable. Thomas Prior was accused of inclosing 30 acres worth 10s. and converting it into pasture in 1505, thus depriving six men of occupation.[36] The movement was checked, for 17th-century terriers of the rectory show that the glebe at any rate was still in strips in the open fields.[37] The population may have increased by 1676, when the Compton Census recorded 51 adults.

The terriers give other indications of conservative farming practice. There were still only two fields, now called East and West Fields;[38] meadowland was assigned by lot; much of the land was given up to grazing sheep and cattle. The usual number of sheep to the yardland was 30,[39] but the rector was allowed commons for 6 beasts and 80 sheep for his two yardlands.[40] General inclosure must have taken place after 1685 and before 1770 when the whole parish, except for 100 acres, was said to be inclosed.[41] Davis's map of 1797 shows the inclosed fields with the arable lying mostly to the south of the village and east of the Brackley road. Four of the farms were already fairly large, as they continued to be. In 1839 there were three of between 50 and 100 acres and three of over 250 acres. Of these, a freehold farm, which had once belonged to the Youngs, and two others, now belonged to the Duke of Marlborough.[42] He had put in good heart the exceptionally large Ashgrove farm (522 a.) and in 1870 its tenant Mrs. Millington won a Royal Agricultural Society cup for the best-cultivated farm in the Midlands. At this time the land of the parish was fairly equally divided between arable (608 a.) and grass (683 a.), and the main crops grown were wheat, barley, oats, and turnips.[43]

In 1956 there were nine farms, 762½ acres were grassland, 1,083½ arable, and 10 rough grazing.[44]

In the 18th century all the inhabitants of Ardley parish were said to be farmers or day labourers,[45] but with the sudden growth of population in the early 19th century, when numbers rose from 109 in 1801 to 191 in 1821,[46] a few turned to trade or crafts. In the mid-19th century there were two journeymen masons,[47] a lacemaker, a dressmaker, a carpenter, a shoemaker, a brewer, a baker, a blacksmith, and two innkeepers.[48] The population declined in the second half of the century and by 1901 there were only the Rectory, two farm-houses and about 30 houses and cottages for the parish's 130 inhabitants. By 1951, owing to the inclusion of Fewcot in the parish, the number of the inhabitants had increased to 318 and of houses to 87.[49] A wheelwright's works was opened in the 20th century,[50] and since the Second World War many of the villagers have found employment at the Bicester Ordnance Depot.

CHURCH. There was a church in Ardley by 1074, when a grant of its tithes was made (see below). The first recorded presentation occurs in the early 13th century,[51] and since then the advowson has, with a few exceptions, followed the descent of the manor. An exception occurred in 1318 when Hugh de Plescy, who perhaps had custody of the manor during the minority of Elizabeth Fitzwyth, tried to present to the church. Joan, the widow of Guy Fitzwyth (d. 1316), contested this claim and the king's court upheld her right.[52] Other exceptions occurred when the king presented in 1363 after the death of Robert Fitzwyth, and again in 1389 and 1390 because of the attainder of John de Beauchamp. In 1396 Philip de la Vache presented as guardian of John de Beauchamp; in 1435 an unidentified John Blount did so; and in 1441 Walker Skull, the third husband of John de Beauchamp's daughter Margaret. After 1472, when the manor was divided among coheiresses, the advowson was apparently also divided, for the husbands of two of them, Thomas Croft and John Guise, presented in 1484 and in 1497 respectively. In 1510 the bishop collated by lapse and by 1521 William Billing, then lord of the united manor, held the whole advowson.

For some time after 1540, when the manor and advowson were acquired by Sir Thomas Pope, the advowson seems to have been usually leased separately.[53] From at least 1559 to 1584 the patron was Edward Love of Aynho (Northants), who had also been patron of Stoke Lyne.[54] He twice sold his right of presentation.[55] In the early 17th century Nicholas Blount (1622) and Ralph Drope, mercer of Banbury (1629), were patrons.[56] In 1645 the king presented because Thomas Pope, Earl of Downe, had not taken legal possession of his lands.[57] The advowson passed with the manor to Philip Holman in 1661, and in 1682 and 1683 George Holman

---

[33] *Feud. Aids*, vi. 379.
[34] E 179/161/176, 198.
[35] *Oseney Cart.* vi. 230.
[36] *Dom. Incl.* i. 350.
[37] See Oxf. Archd. Oxon. c 141, pp. 281–3 for an undated 17th-cent. terrier; ibid., pp. 273–80: terriers 1679 and 1685. These are partly printed in Blo. *Ard.* 31–33.
[38] Ibid.
[39] Blo. *Ard.* 32 n. (terrier of 1685).
[40] Ibid. 31.
[41] MS. Top. Oxon. c 307, f. 126.
[42] Bodl. Tithe award. For the Youngs' farm see Blo. *Ard.* 11–12, but there is no proof that it had been the Oseney estate.
[43] Wing, *Annals*, 14; Bodl. G.A. Oxon. b 90(12): *Sale Cat.* 1894.
[44] Inf. Oxon. Agric. Executive Cttee.
[45] Oxf. Dioc. d 555.

[46] *V.C.H. Oxon.* ii. 221.
[47] Stone was still being quarried in Ardley wood.
[48] H.O. 107/1729; *Kelly's Dir. Oxon.* (1854, 1864).
[49] *Census*, 1901, 1951. Between 1945 and 1954 24 council houses were built: inf. Ploughley R.D.C.
[50] *Kelly's Dir. Oxon.* (1939).
[51] *Rot. Welles*, i. 68.
[52] For references to medieval presentations see MS. Top. Oxon. d 460.
[53] C.P. 40/1162, m. 158 (1555); C 142/124/153 (1559); C 142/205/191 (1584); C 142/472/103 (1631).
[54] See below, p. 321.
[55] *O.A.S. Rep.* 1914, 216–17. Howe, given there once, is a misreading for Love: Oxf. Dioc. d 105, p. 189.
[56] Blo. *Ard.* 24.
[57] Oxf. Dioc. c 66, f. 38. The phrase used is *per defectum liberationis*.

presented to Ardley church.[58] In 1894, when the Duke of Marlborough's estates in the parish were sold by auction, the advowson was sold for £470 to C. W. Perryman of Farnborough (Hants),[59] who later bought the manorial rights.

In 1921 the living of Fewcot and in 1933 that of Stoke Lyne were united to Ardley.[60] Colonel the Hon. E. H. Wyndham, lord of the manor of Caversfield and patron of Stoke Lyne, presents for two turns, and the executors of Mrs. Perryman for one turn.

In the Middle Ages Ardley was one of the poorest parishes in the deanery. In 1254 it was valued at £2, in 1291 at £4 6s. 8d., and in 1535 at £5 12s. 8d.[61] Its value was thus generally slightly above the minimum level of 5 marks considered necessary for the maintenance of a parish priest. In addition to the glebe, the rector held a virgate of land from the lord of the manor for 6d. a year.[62]

Robert d'Oilly in the late 11th century granted two-thirds of his demesne tithes at Ardley to the church of St. George in Oxford castle,[63] which in 1149 was given, with all its possessions, to Oseney Abbey.[64] A late 13th-century rector, Roger de Schulton (c. 1260–1300), objected to this deduction from his income, and the case was taken to the Court of Arches. There, Oseney's proxy declared that the abbey had been continuously and peacefully in possession of two-thirds of the tithes of the ancient demesne, which lay around the park and grove of the lord John Fitzwyth.[65] The court's decision has not been found, but by 1291 the Rector of Ardley was paying a pension of 10s. to Oseney;[66] this continued into the 15th century, but had stopped in the next century.[67]

The earliest post-Reformation valuation to be found is that of 1751, when the church was worth £80.[68] In 1839 the tithes were commuted for £285.[69] There were then 60 acres of glebe which had been allotted instead of the 2 yardlands formerly held in the open fields.[70] They lay in three arable fields along the road to Bucknell, and were rented for about £30.[71] They have since been mostly sold.[72] The rector also had the right to a third of the tithes on a field in Somerton, which were commuted with the tithes of Somerton for 30s.[73]

None of the medieval rectors was remarkable, and few were university graduates.[74] An early exception was Master Helias, a physician, presented in 1221 before he was even an acolyte by Ralph, son of Robert.[75] His successors were rather on the level of vicars, and most of the exchanges of Ardley were for nearby vicarages: for the vicarage of Fritwell, for example, or that of Dinton (Bucks.), but in 1419 it was for a chantry.[76]

All but one of the 16th-century rectors were graduates. Among the early ones was Master John London (1521–4), probably Ardley's most famous rector.[77] He was succeeded by Edward Heydon (1524–37), a student who received his degree three years after becoming rector.[78] The living brought him little immediate profit, as in 1526 out of his income of £8 he paid a curate over £5 and spent, among other things, £1 13s. in repairs.[79] A few years before there had been complaints that the walls of the church were dilapidated and the churchyard not enclosed.[80]

There was a tendency for post-Reformation rectors to be absentees: Richard Love (1615–18), a Fellow of Magdalen College, was also Vicar of Stoke Lyne, and in 1615 was chaplain to Sir Ralph Winwood, the Secretary of State;[81] John Hull (1622–9) was another resident Fellow of Magdalen;[82] Thomas Drope (1629–45) was Vicar of Cumnor (Berks.), where he lived and was buried.[83] But Lionel Piggott (1645–82), presented by the king in 1645[84] and evidently a royalist, resided in his parish. He may have been dispossessed during the Commonwealth, for there were two nonconformist ministers in Ardley in the 1650's.[85] He was living there, however, after the Restoration,[86] when it was recorded that in return for his common pasture rights he had to provide a 'drinking' for the parishioners at Easter. It cost 20s. and took place in the parsonage.[87]

Eighteenth-century rectors, such as John Percival (1707–53), were likewise often resident. A relative of the lord of the manor,[88] he resided 'constantly' and in 1738 reported that none was absent from church, that there were two services on Sundays, and usually fifteen or sixteen communicants at the four yearly sacraments.[89] His successor, however, Benjamin Holloway (1753–78), the first rector presented by the Duke of Marlborough, was also Rector of Bladon with Woodstock,[90] and in his time Ardley was served by curates, who usually lived in the Rectory and received a stipend of £30. One of these was the rector's son, who was allowed 'more than is generally given to curates'.[91] It was said that churchgoing had decreased by the early 19th century, but the influence of John Lowe, rector for more than half the century (1815–73) and described in 1864 by Bishop Wilberforce as 'hearty and good as ever',[92] led to a revival. He instituted monthly communion services and in one year preached about 95 sermons

[58] See above, p. 10; P.R.O. Inst. Bks.
[59] *Kelly's Dir. Oxon.* (1903); Blo. *Ard.* 13.
[60] Bodl. Par. Box (uncat.), Orders in Council.
[61] Lunt, *Val. Norw.* 312; *Tax. Eccl.* (Rec. Com.), 31; *Valor Eccl.* (Rec. Com.), ii. 161.
[62] *Rot. Hund.* (Rec. Com.), ii. 833.
[63] *Oxon. Chart.* no. 58; *Oseney Cart.* iv. 26.
[64] *V.C.H. Oxon.* ii. 90.
[65] *Oseney Cart.* vi. 35–36.
[66] *Tax. Eccl.* 31.
[67] *Feud. Aids*, vi. 379; *Valor Eccl.* ii. 222.
[68] Oxf. Dioc. c 653, f. 84.
[69] Bodl. Tithe award.
[70] Blo. *Ard.* 31.
[71] Par. Rec. 1814 terrier; Blo. *Ard.* 33.
[72] *Kelly's Dir. Oxon.* (1939).
[73] Blo. *Ard.* 31, 33.
[74] See list of medieval rectors in MS. Top. Oxon. d 460.
[75] *Rot. Welles*, ii. 7.
[76] Linc. Reg. x, f. 335; xi, f. 312; xiv, f. 422.

[77] *D.N.B.*; see above, p. 8.
[78] *Reg. Univ.* i. 149.
[79] *Subsidy 1526*, 274.
[80] *Visit. Dioc. Linc. 1517–31*, i. 122.
[81] Macray, *Magd. Reg.* iii. 106.
[82] J. R. Bloxam, *Magd. Reg. Demies*, ii. 20.
[83] Blo. *Ard.* 24; Macray, *Magd. Reg.* ii. 188–9. For pedigree see Wood, *Life*, i. 285. Thomas Drope's daughter married Wood's brother Robert: ibid. 284.
[84] Oxf. Dioc. c 66, f. 38.
[85] *Walker Rev.* 299, where his name is given as Edmund Piggott.
[86] Blo. *Ard.* 25; *Hearth Tax Oxon.* 204; for Rectory see above, p. 8.
[87] Blo. *Ard.* 32.
[88] Ibid. 25.
[89] Oxf. Dioc. d 552.
[90] Ibid. c 653, f. 84.
[91] Ibid. d 555, d 558.
[92] Ibid. c 327, p. 42; ibid. d 570.

to congregations of 50 to 60 in the mornings and 70 to 80 in the afternoons. Nothing special impeded his ministry, Lowe once reported, except 'unbelief and hardness of heart. These are my great hindrances, and, in a few cases, the love of drinking.'[93] Another difficulty, however, was the growing hamlet of Fewcot which, although in Stoke Lyne parish, lay much nearer to Ardley church than to Stoke church. In 1846 Lowe offered to take it into his parish if he were paid £10 from the vicarage of Stoke, but the patron refused the offer.[94] Lowe later complained of the influence on his parishioners of Fewcot's increasing Methodist population.[95] At about this time Ardley was unusual in having a woman churchwarden, Mrs. Millington of Ashgrove Farm.[96]

Although the Old Rectory was converted into a large modern house at the end of the 19th century,[97] it was sold in 1923, as after Fewcot had been united to Ardley the rector went to live in Fewcot.[98]

The present church, dedicated to *ST. MARY*[99] and largely rebuilt at the end of the 18th century, is a stone building consisting of chancel, nave, and western tower. The saddle-backed tower has two stages and dates from the 14th century, though the tower arch appears to be earlier.

The present chancel arch and piscina are part of a 13th-century church, but the chancel windows are 14th century. The south wall has a double piscina and a low side window, now walled up, which was formerly covered by a shutter. The elaborate 14th-century recess on the north wall may have been a benefactor's tomb and was later used as an Easter sepulchre; it has a shield on each cusp, one bearing two bends, perhaps for Oseney Abbey, which had part of the tithes.[1]

In the early 18th century Rawlinson found the church 'but ordinary'.[2] A number of minor repairs were later carried out,[3] but by 1791 the building was in urgent need of restoration.[4] In 1792 the original nave with its two aisles and porch were pulled down and the present plain nave with five windows was erected under the direction of the 3rd Duchess of Marlborough.[5] In 1834 a western gallery was built for the inhabitants of Fewcot.[6] In 1865 a further restoration was carried out, largely at the expense of Miss Anne Hind,[7] which was said to remedy the 'vile architectural taste' of the duchess.[8] A sum of £600 was spent. A new roof was put on the chancel; a new altar, seats, and a heating system were installed; the floor was relaid and the step between the nave and chancel removed.[9] The organ, once in an Oxford college chapel, was installed in 1874, and in 1888 the roof of the nave and the tower were repaired at a cost of £73.[10]

The circular font is probably 13th century.[11] Memorial inscriptions to the following are in the church: Nicholas Marshall (d. 1729) and family; John Percival, rector (d. 1753), and family; Richard Young (d. 1778) and family.[12] There are marble tablets to Lady Elizabeth Spencer (d. 1812), 2nd daughter of George, Duke of Marlborough; to Thomas Hind, rector (d. 1815),[13] and to the Revd. Robert Downes (d. 1816). Rawlinson noted a monumental inscription in the chancel to John Norman (d. 1674), Rector of Ickford (Bucks.), but this cannot now be traced.[14]

The church was poorly furnished in 1552 with one chalice and only one cope, two bells and a 'sakering' bell.[15] In 1955 the plate included an early-18th-century pewter plate;[16] the tower had a 17th-century and an 18th-century bell.[17]

The registers date from 1758, but there are incomplete transcripts from 1681.[18] Churchwardens' accounts (1757–1892), from which Blomfield made abstracts, have disappeared.[19]

NONCONFORMITY. A few Roman Catholics were recorded in the 18th century: in 1738 a carpenter, in 1759 a woman servant, and in 1771 two 'of low condition'.[20]

Protestant dissent appeared in the 1820's, and in 1829 a private house was licensed as a place of worship.[21] Later in the century there were a few Methodists, who sometimes attended church but occasionally went to chapel at Fritwell.[22]

SCHOOLS. In 1808 a few children were looked after and instructed by a 'poor woman'.[23] In 1815 21 children attended a school where they were taught the principles of religion at their parents' expense;[24] there was an attendance of 16 infants and 6 older girls in 1833.[25] By 1854 there was a day school supported by the Rector of Ardley and the Vicar of Stoke Lyne, and by the weekly pence of 30 pupils.[26]

In 1861 a school with accommodation for 60 children was built at the expense of the Duke of Marlborough; it was enlarged shortly afterwards with the aid of a donation from Miss Anne Hind.[27] Although affiliated to the National Society in 1862,

---

[93] *Wilb. Visit.*; Blo. *Ard.* 28. For his sister-in-law Anne Hind see below, p. 322.
[94] Blo. *Stoke*, 38.
[95] Oxf. Dioc. d 179.
[96] Blo. *Ard.* 37; see above, p. 11.
[97] Blo. *Ard.* 33.
[98] Par. Rec.
[99] This is the traditional dedication: Bacon, *Lib. Reg.* 790. The O.S. 25″ Map xvi. 12 (1881) marks it as St. Thomas, and *Crockford* (1953–4) gives this as an alternative dedication.
[1] Bodl. G.A. Oxon. 16° 217, p. 48; ibid. 4° 685, p. 8; G.A. Oxon. b 180, Ploughley, p. 1a; see above, p. 12.
[2] *Par. Coll.* i. 8.
[3] Oxf. Archd. Oxon. d 13, f. 33: e.g. the tower was repointed in 1757.
[4] Ibid. c 48, f. 53.
[5] Ibid. c 153, f. 14; Blo. *Ard.* 1936; see above, p. 10.
[6] Blo. *Ard.* 20; see below, p. 322.
[7] See below, p. 322.
[8] Wing, *Annals*, 14.

[9] Blo. *Ard.* 20.
[10] Ibid. 20–21; Clarke MS. Drawings (1810) showing the church before restoration are in MS. Top. Oxon. b 220, f. 168 and a drawing (1823) by J. Buckler is ibid. a 65, f. 42.
[11] Buckler drawing ibid. a 65, f. 43.
[12] See above, p. 11.
[13] Storey of London *fecit*.
[14] *Par. Coll.* i. 8.
[15] *Chant. Cert.* 81.
[16] Evans, *Ch. Plate*.
[17] *Ch. Bells Oxon.* i. 17.
[18] Oxf. Dioc. c 478.
[19] Blo. *Ard.* 34–37.
[20] Oxf. Dioc. d 522, d 555, d 561.
[21] Ibid. c 645, f. 123; Brackley Circuit Plan, 1833.
[22] Oxf. Dioc. c 332, c 344.
[23] Ibid. d 707.
[24] Ibid. c 433; cf. *Educ. of Poor*, 717.
[25] *Educ. Enq. Abstract*, 738.
[26] *Wilb. Visit.*
[27] Blo. *Ard.* 17; cf. ibid. 20; see below, p. 322.

it gave religious instruction when required to children who were not members of the Church of England.[28] The attendance was 65 in 1871, and 29 in 1906.[29] The school was closed in 1914, when the children were transferred to Middleton Stoney school.[30]

CHARITIES. None known.

THE MARKET-TOWN OF BICESTER

THE medieval parish covered a wide area, possibly over 5,800 acres, as Stratton Audley (2,088 a.) was included in its boundaries as well as the hamlets of Bicester King's End, Bignell, and Wretchwick.[1] The parish was first reduced in size in 1454, when Stratton Audley became a separate parish.[2] In 1901 the Urban and Rural Districts of Bicester, comprising the two civil parishes of Bicester Market End (2,282 a.) and Bicester King's End (1,457 a.), covered 3,739 acres.[3] The civil parishes were identical in area with the ancient townships, and their boundaries may be regarded as historic ones.[4] The Gagle Brook formed the boundary on the south-west; on the north and east the parish was separated from Bucknell, Caversfield and Launton by an irregular line with a number of right-angled bends, which indicate that it was fixed after the field furlongs had been laid out. For a short distance in the north the Roman road formed the boundary. In 1932 these ancient boundaries were radically changed and a new civil parish, co-extensive with the urban district, was formed. It comprised parts of the 19th-century civil parish of King's End (472 a.), of Market End (1,060 a.), and of Caversfield (147 a.), and covered in all 1,679 acres. The rest of Market End was transferred to Ambrosden and Bucknell and the rest of King's End to Chesterton. Thus Bicester's two 19th-century civil parishes were abolished and with them Bicester Rural District.[5]

The ancient parish was crossed by a network of roads. One, the Stratton road, was a Roman road, running from Alchester to Towcester.[6] The Launton, Caversfield, Bucknell, and Denton (Bucks.) roads were ordered to be made 40 feet wide by the Market End inclosure award of 1758.[7] The state of the roads about that time may be judged from Sir Harbottle Grimston's observation that the road between Bicester and Buckingham was 'very bad, almost impassable for a carriage'.[8] The turnpike acts, however, transformed this situation. Stratton road was turnpiked in 1768–9; the Caversfield road, a part of the coach road from London to Birmingham, was turnpiked in 1790–1 along with the Bicester–Aynho section of this road. The Bicester–Aylesbury section of it had already been turnpiked

in 1770.[9] When this road entered the parish in the south it followed the line of Akeman Street. Coaches began to run from Bicester to London in 1752[10] and by 1795 the 'Old Banbury' coach went through Bicester to London six days a week and there was a weekly wagon passing through from Birmingham to London.[11] A weekly coach to Oxford for the Saturday market began to run in 1794 and a mail cart in 1798.[12] The turnpike from Aylesbury to Aynho via Bicester (i.e. the London road) was freed from toll by acts of 1875 and 1876.[13] The toll-house on the London road was still standing in 1956.

A new arterial road to by-pass the centre of Bicester was built in 1939; it followed the line of the old road through King's End to Crockwell; it was named Queen's Avenue and planted with trees in 1953 in commemoration of the coronation of Queen Elizabeth II.[14]

The railway first came to Bicester in 1850, when the Bletchley to Oxford line was completed and the London Road station on the L.N.W.R.'s Birmingham line was opened. Bicester North station was opened by the G.W.R. in 1906.[15] Co-operation between the rival companies was so good after the First World War that until 1940 both stations shared one stationmaster.

The Bicester district was inhabited at an early date: traces have been found of an Iron Age and Romano-British settlement beside the Roman road just inside the southern border of the later parish.[16] The Anglo-Saxons, however, settled farther to the north. The village was well sited near the Roman road and by a ford over the Bure; it lay on the Cornbrash, just off the Oxford Clay which composes the southern half of the parish, and about 240 feet up.[17] Its name—originally *Bernecestre*—means 'the fort of the warriors' or 'of Beorna', some Anglo-Saxon war-lord.[18] The form of the name indicates early settlement, though there is nothing else to substantiate the tradition that the village was founded by Birinus, the 7th-century Bishop of Dorchester. There may be more truth in the tradition that the 'burg' or 'bury', as it was called throughout the Middle Ages, was first intended as a frontier garrison of the West Saxons against the

[28] *Vol. Sch. Ret.* 35.
[29] *Elem. Educ. Ret.*; *List of Sch.* 524.
[30] Inf. Oxon. Educ. Cttee.
[1] The author wishes to thank Miss G. Dannatt of Bicester for constant help, and Mrs. M. Coker and Col. the Hon. E. H. Wyndham for reading and commenting on this article.
[2] See below, p. 330.
[3] *Census*, 1901.
[4] O.S. *Area Bk.* (1876). The discrepancy between the 1901 acreage and the 2,580 a. given in *Census*, 1851 is inexplicably large. The ancient parish is on O.S. Map 2½", 42/52, 62 (1951).
[5] *Oxon. Review Order* (1932).
[6] O.S. *Map of Roman Britain*.
[7] O.R.O. Incl. award.
[8] Hist. MSS. Com. *Verulam*, 244.

[9] 9 Geo. III, c. 88; 10 Geo. III, c. 72; 31 Geo. III, c. 101. For acts repairing these roads until 1876 see nos. 516, 526, 534 of E. H. Cordeaux and D. H. Merry, *Oxon. Bibliography* (O.H.S. N.S. xi).
[10] J. Hodges, *A New Description of all Counties in England and Wales* (1752).
[11] *Rusher's Banbury List* (1795). Cf. *Pigot's Dir. Oxon.* (1823). Two coaches then ran three times a week to London.
[12] Blo. *Bic.* 42, citing advertisements.
[13] 38 & 39 Vict. c. 194; 39 & 40 Vict. c. 39.
[14] Local inf.
[15] Blo. *Bic.* 54. See 9 & 10 Vict. c. 82 (loc. and pub. act) for railway act of 1846.
[16] *O.A.S. Rep.* 1937, 23 sqq.
[17] G.S. Map, 1". 45 SE (old series).
[18] *P.N. Oxon.* (E.P.N.S.), i. 198.

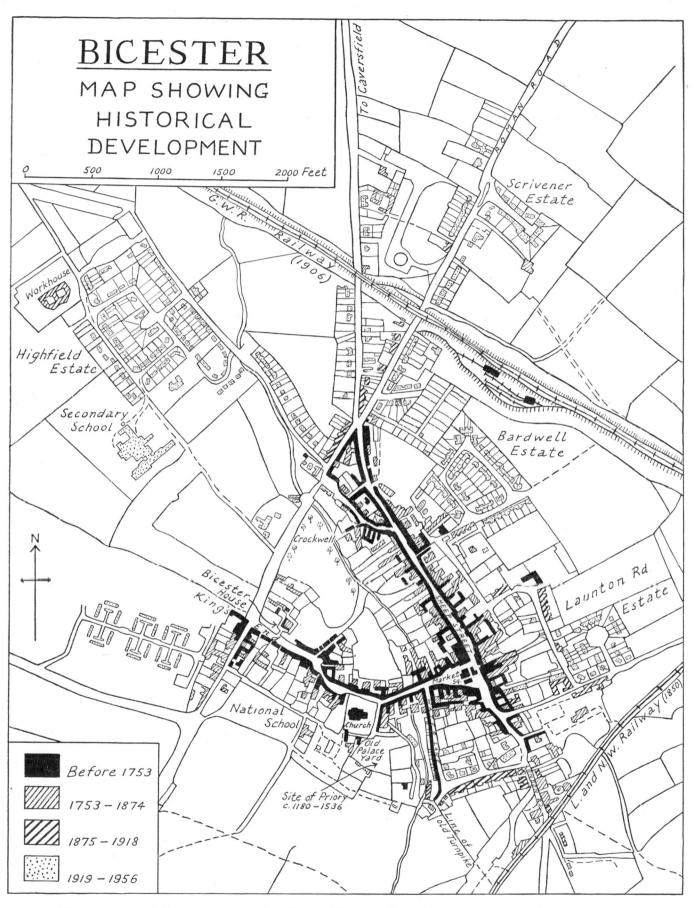

BICESTER

MAP SHOWING HISTORICAL DEVELOPMENT

0   500   1000   1500   2000 Feet

To Caversfield

ROMAN ROAD

Scrivener Estate

G.W.R. Railway (1906)

Workhouse

Highfield Estate

Secondary School

Bardwell Estate

N

Crockwell

Bicester House

King's End

Launton Rd Estate

National School

Market Sq.

STREET

Church

Old Palace Yard

Site of Priory c. 1180–1536

Line of old Turnpike

L. and N.W. Railway (1850)

Before 1753

1753 – 1874

1875 – 1918

1919 – 1956

The above map is from one of 1753 by Thomas Williams, the ordnance survey map of 1876 and a map of 1956 by the Surveyor of the Bicester U.D.C.

Mercians.[19] According to tradition the original town was on the site of King's End and was destroyed by the Danes. It is possible that Bury End, the older name for Market End, lying on the other side of the Bure, was fortified by Edward the Elder, for its church was dedicated to St. Edburga, probably to be identified with one of the king's saintly daughters.[20]

Water was plentiful. Apart from the Bure, a feeder of the Ray, there were a number of springs, which kept the town wells constantly supplied. The well of St. Edburg, for instance, early gained a miraculous reputation. It was reached from the village from the late 13th century at latest by St. Edburg's Way.[21] Another well, Crockwell, described by White Kennett as a 'lively spring . . . arched and vaulted', gave its name to the northern extension of the medieval town.[22]

The core of the modern street plan has probably altered little since medieval times. The main streets were St. John the Baptist's Street (the later Sheep Street), the Market Square at its southern end, Church Way and the Causeway, running westwards from the square across the ford[23] and past the parish church and Vicarage. The western end of this street was called le Kynges End at least by 1345 as there lay the manor-house and township of King's End.[24] The northern limit of the town in the 14th century was probably some way to the south of the present New Buildings. On the site of one of these houses was a hermitage and chapel dedicated to St. John the Baptist, and a field survey of 1399 makes it clear that it lay in open country.[25] The Crockwell area was also mainly in the fields: the priory had a grange and a sheepfold there with some poor tenants living near.[26]

The site of the 12th-century manor-house and chapel of the Bassets, lords of Bury End (or Market End as it was later called), was not known even in Leland's time, but it was probably, as tradition had it, near or on the site of the priory, for in the 1180's Gilbert Basset gave crofts and messuages near his fishpond and the free chapel of his *curia* as a site for a house of Augustinian canons.[27] There are 13th-century charter references to other medieval houses which show that they were of two stories with a cellar and solar and were built contiguously. Some lay on the Causeway next to the cemetery of the parish church.[28] In the 14th century there was an inn called the 'Bell', which belonged to the priory and was let in 1395 for £1 16s. a year,[29] but its site cannot be determined.

Although almost nothing has survived above ground of the priory buildings, their plan can be partly restored from documentary and archaeological evidence. The main entrance to the priory, which was standing in about 1800, adjoined the churchyard of the parish church. Excavations undertaken in 1819 show that the principal buildings lay between the present 17th-century dovecote and the upper garden wall of Old Palace Yard.[30] The convent had the usual offices—chapter house, sacristy, locutory, refectory, lavatory, and dormitory.[31] The last was repaired in 1425 at a cost of £34 17s. 4½d. In 1424 the prior had spent over £20 on materials: timber was obtained from the Breach and Gravenhill (both in the parish), Bernwood, and farther afield; stone from a quarry in Crockwell.[32] The kitchen wing comprised the kitchen, slaughterhouse, bakehouse, brew-house, dairy, and laundry.[33] There were also a cellar, a treasury and infirmary.[34] The cloisters connected the conventual buildings with the priory church.

The guest house may have been detached from the main building. It has been suggested that it was the same as the existing building called Old Priory House. The latter is a two-storied house (41 ft. by 16½ ft.), which appears to have been largely rebuilt in the early 16th century, but retains traces of medieval work in its west gable.[35]

The prior had his own hall and chamber, garden and stables.[36] In 1397 his lodgings were enlarged by the insertion of a second chamber between the hall and the upper chamber.[37] In Henry VI's reign 1,000 bricks were bought to make a chimney for his chamber.[38]

The conventual church, dedicated to the Virgin Mary and St. Edburg, had been built by about 1200.[39] Early in the next century there are references to its altars to St. Nicholas and St. John as well as to the high altar.[40] At the turn of the 13th century the church was enlarged: payments by the bursar in 1296 for craftsmen's stipends and for bringing stone from Bloxham for the seats of the church suggest that the work was already in full swing.[41] A loan raised from Florentine merchants in 1300 may well have been connected with this enterprise,[42] and in 1304 an indulgence of twenty days was granted

[19] Kennett, *Paroch. Antiq.* i. 36–38.
[20] For the dedication see below, p. 44, n. 16.
[21] Kennett, *Paroch. Antiq.* i. 192; cf. ibid. ii. 187 where it is said to divide the fields of King's End and Market End. The name *Edburg-balk* survived in the 17th cent.: ibid. i. 192.
[22] Ibid. ii. 427.
[23] Sheep St. was an alternative name for St. John the Baptist's St. at least by 1660: O.R.O. Misc. Bea. 1/2. The ford does not appear to have been bridged except for foot passengers until the 19th cent. See Davis, *Oxon. Map*, and H. Wyndham, *A Backward Glance*, 46.
[24] Dunkin, *Bic.* 241 (*In vico vocato le Kynges End*).
[25] Ibid. 115–17; Kennett, *Paroch. Antiq.* ii. 195.
[26] e.g. Dunkin, *Bic.* 242; Blo. *Bic.* 126; Trin. Coll. Arch. MS. Bicester Roll, 1397–8.
[27] Kennett, *Paroch. Antiq.* i. 186–9; Leland, *Itin.* ed. Toulmin Smith, ii, pt. v, 34.
[28] e.g. Kennett, *Paroch. Antiq.* i. 461.
[29] Dunkin, *Oxon.* ii. 239.
[30] Ibid. 250–2.
[31] See plan in Blo. *Bic.* opp. 112 and priory accounts *passim*. Accounts survive for 23 years between 5 Ed. I

and 20 Ed. IV. They have been mostly printed in whole or in part in Kennett, *Paroch. Antiq.* i. 405–6; ii. 247–59; Blo. *Bic.* 136–91; Dunkin, *Oxon.* ii. 220–48. The originals are in the P.R.O. and Trin. Coll. Archives, Oxford. For a list compiled by Mr. H. M. Colvin, see MS. Top. Oxon. c 482.
[32] Dunkin, *Bic.* 241; ibid. *Oxon.* ii. 253.
[33] e.g. see accounts 1295–6 (Blo. *Bic.* 138), 1407–8 (ibid. 163–4, where it is wrongly dated).
[34] Accts. *passim*, e.g. Blo. *Bic.* 163, 179–80, 189.
[35] Dunkin, *Bic.* 81–82; Blo. *Bic.* 111. For the retiling of the roof in 1408–9, see ibid. 163.
[36] e.g. Blo. *Bic.* 137, 157, 163, 169, 189–90; Dunkin, *Oxon.* ii. 229 (1395–6 acct.).
[37] Trin. Coll. Arch. MS. Bic. Roll, 1397–8.
[38] Blo. *Bic.* 189.
[39] Kennett, *Paroch. Antiq.* i. 225; B.M. Add. ch. 10607.
[40] Blo. *Bic.* 107.
[41] Ibid. 136–40: 1295–6 acct.
[42] Ibid. 107; cf. Kennett, *Paroch. Antiq.* i. 487, where he erroneously connects it with a controversy with Aulnay Abbey.

to all persons who would give towards the fabric and maintenance of the church.[43] In 1312 it was reconsecrated by the Irish Bishop of Annaghdown, acting as suffragan to the Bishop of Lincoln. He consecrated three new altars, and a second indulgence was granted.[44] A few years later a chantry was founded by Master Walter of Fotheringay, who left £40 for a mass. The indulgence obtained in 1323 for those who prayed for his soul may have been sought with the object of obtaining alms to help defray the cost of building alterations.[45] A window inserted in the 'new chapel' is recorded on a surviving account roll of 1317.[46]

To this period also belongs the construction of the shrine of St. Edburg, which is now in the church at Stanton Harcourt. It can be dated from heraldic evidence between 1294 and 1317 and may have been a gift from Henry de Lacy, Earl of Lincoln, the priory's patron, on the marriage of his daughter to Thomas, Earl of Lancaster. It is one of the last surviving pieces of figure sculpture in Purbeck marble.[47] The beautification of the church was still being carried out in 1320. Roger the painter was then paid £2 for painting an image of the Virgin for the high altar, and £2 14s. was paid for white and coloured glass.[48] In 1327 and 1333 two more chantries were founded.[49]

At the end of the 14th century a 'new choir' was constructed. It is not clear from the surviving accounts if this entailed a lengthening of the original church or only interior alterations. Work had begun at least by 1393 for in the account roll for 1395–6 Robert Dryffeld was paid £10 in addition to the £10 paid in each of the two preceding years for his work on the new choir. A smith from Bedford was paid for making the hinges (*gemellae*) for the stall seats, while Robert Dryffeld received an extra 33s. 4d. for making 30 finials for them.[50] Work was still being paid for in the account of 1397–8. John Stacy was paid £20 for finishing the end of the choir; sawyers for three weeks' work sawing the boards for the floor which was supported on walls. The masons worked on these for four weeks. John Smyth was employed to mend the hinges (*gemewes*), and the boards under the 'crestying' of the walls were varnished.[51] At the same time the old choir was removed and the floor levelled and some unspecified work, described as 'novum opus ultra vestiarium', was carried out.[52] Work was still going on in 1411–12, when a new roof was placed over the high altar. The roll refers to purchases of timber and expenses of sawing and carting, which were sufficiently large to be accounted for separately. Carpenters, including one from Brackley, and masons, including a freemason and his mate from Eynsham, were hired; Peter the painter of Banbury and John the painter

of Thame were brought in to colour the roof with oil colours supplied by the latter. Gold leaf was bought in Oxford, and 'divers colours' in London.[53] William Hayle founded a fourth chantry about this time.[54]

The church was pulled down in 1537; its site and the priory buildings and the medieval hostelry called the 'Bell' were granted to the Duke of Suffolk and in 1537 to Roger Moore.[55] Various small alterations were made to the house by Moore's son Thomas to fit it for the visit of Elizabeth I.[56] In the late 16th century the Roman Catholic family of Blount resided there. Sir Richard was followed by Sir Charles Blount, whose children were baptized in the church, and later by Welsbourne Blount.[57] After 1656 Lord Chief Justice Glynne made it his home. In 1673 his son removed to Ambrosden and the priory mansion was pulled down.[58]

There was rebuilding generally in the town in the late 16th and 17th centuries. The Town House itself, erected at the south end of the market-place before 1599, was repaired in 1622.[59] Other houses were evidently built about this time on the open space of the market-place, for it was laid down in 1605 that no one should be allowed to build there, and the removal of a butcher's shop was ordered.[60] Dwellings were also being put on the lord's waste at Crockwell at the north end of the town,[61] but the main evidence for the building activity of this period comes from the many surviving houses. They are mostly built of coursed rubble, though brick and timber are also used, and many are concealed behind 18th-century fronts of stucco or variegated brick. Tysul House (now nos. 1 and 3 Church Street), for example, is substantially a 17th-century building with a contemporary newel staircase. Of the same period are nos. 9 and 11, which were originally one building and are inscribed TNI 1676, the Six Bells Inn and the Swan Inn. The last is inscribed EME 1681.[62] But the oldest building in this part of Bicester is probably the Vicarage. The original late-16th-century house appears to have been L-shaped. It is two-storied and is built of coursed rubble. The north–south wing still retains three ancient stone window-frames with square moulded labels. Sash windows were later inserted in the other wing, and a large bay window was added when the house was enlarged in 1882. At that date the front porch, the corridor, running the whole length of the street front, and the ground- and first-floor rooms at the north-east corner were built. The kitchen wing at the south-west end seems to have been an earlier addition.[63] The rooms of the old house all led into one another and there was no connecting passage. A Stonesfield-slate roof on one wing was removed in 1955, when the house was

---

[43] Blo. *Bic.* 107.

[44] Ibid.

[45] Ibid. 128.

[46] Ibid. 153.

[47] L. Stone, *Sculpture in Britain: the Middle Ages*, 134 and pl. 110a. For the Harcourt connexion with Bicester see below, p. 43.

[48] Blo. *Bic.* 153.

[49] See Blo. *Bic.* 128–31 for a translation of the deed of foundation of one; Linc. Reg. iv, Burghersh, f. 266b.

[50] Trin. Coll. Arch. Bic. roll, 1395–6.

[51] Dunkin (*Oxon.* ii. 252) translated *gemewes* as 'jewels'.

[52] Trin. Coll. Arch. Bic. roll, 1396–7. Cf. Dunkin, *Oxon.* ii. 229–52.

[53] Blo. *Bic.* 169.

[54] Ibid. 167.

[55] Ibid. 14; see below, p. 22.

[56] Bodl. MS. Rawl. A 195 c, f. 265.

[57] See below, pp. 22, 47; Par. Reg.

[58] Below, p. 23; *V.C.H. Oxon.* v. 15–16.

[59] *12th Rep. Com. Char.* 286. Dunkin states that there was documentary evidence for its erection in 1622, but repairs were probably undertaken at that date. It was repaired again in 1686: Dunkin, *Bic.* 18 and n.

[60] Bic. U.D.C. docs.

[61] Dunkin, *Bic.* 172; cf. ibid. 17 for the lord's waste.

[62] This Swan Inn is not to be confused with the Market Square 'Swan': see below, pp. 18, 36.

[63] Bodl. Bic. Par. Box. (uncat.), specification and plan.

modernized inside and divided into two at a cost of over £3,000.[64]

The greatest number of early houses, however, are to be found in Market Square and Sheep Street: among the oldest are Nos. 46, 48, and 51, which constitute a block of three gabled houses standing with others in a detached group at the north end of the market-place. Nos. 48 and 51 were probably built as one two-storied house with attics in the mid-16th century. No. 51 is timber-framed with brick and plaster fillings. In one of the gables on its north side are the remains of two projecting casement windows of three lights. They have in part the original leaded lights and glass, and side pilasters with enriched carving and plain brackets. The gables have carved barge boards. In the late 17th century or possibly a little later no. 46, a timber-framed house of lath and plaster (now rough-cast), was added to the east side of the 16th-century block. Other houses of 17th-century origin are no. 44, built with an overhang; Waverley House, partly built of brick and timber, and refronted in the 18th century;[65] and no. 39, the gabled house next door, which has a massive rubble-stone chimney-stack. In the London Road the most interesting early houses are nos. 2, 10, and 17. The first, which has a coachway and so may have been a 16th-century inn, is now the King's Arms Garage. It has two stories and three gables on the street front, and in the centre a massive chimney-stack of moulded stone with three ancient brick shafts set diagonally. Three four-light windows with wooden transoms survive. The Hermitage (no. 17) was originally built in the 17th century, but was remodelled in the 19th century and is now two cottages. It is distinguished by its five small two-light attic dormers and its three-light casement windows in square frames of heavy moulded stone. At the back is a gabled projecting staircase which is lit by casement windows in wooden frames.

Disastrous fires in 1718, 1724, and 1730[66] were the occasion of much 18th-century rebuilding, but fashion and prosperity also led many inhabitants to reface their ancient houses of coursed rubble with stucco or, less often, with variegated brick; to put in sash windows, add classic porticoes to their front entrances, and modernize the interiors. No. 10 London Road, for example, though originally an L-shaped 16th-century house, was given a brick dentilled cornice, its front door was embellished with a carved and bracketed hood (recently removed), and a new staircase was inserted. The east wing, which projects to the road frontage, was extended by a rounded bay of two stories. Inside, the rooms were panelled, and the two first-floor ones were decorated with four painted corinthian columns, which are said locally to have come from Ambrosden Park, destroyed in 1768. The south wing of this house bears the inscription GKE 1770. The 18th-century bay window was removed during the Second

World War, but the 16th-century overhang supported by massive beams with carved ends is still a striking feature of the house. No. 16, inscribed JSI 1773, and no. 14, which appear to have been originally one house, were evidently modernized at about the same time as no. 10. There are many similar examples in Market Square and Sheep Street. No. 44 the Market Square acquired a stucco front, sash windows, a moulded cornice, and iron balustrade railings. No. 30 was refronted with variegated brick: it is dated RNL 1751. The present offices of the Midland Mart were also largely rebuilt: it is a striking three-storied house of stucco and rusticated stone quoins. Its porch of three stories with an ogee-shaped roof of red tiles is surmounted by a lead ball and weather vane. Its roof is hipped with attic dormers and a stone, inscribed B I M 1698, probably records earlier repairs. Possibly the best house in the square is no. 28, which was refronted in about 1800 with brick. It was the 'Swan', one of the principal inns in the mid-18th century, but later became the private residence of George King, a brazier. To this century too belong in the main the present buildings of the 'King's Arms', one of Bicester's many ancient inns and today its principal hotel. It is a three-story building of stucco. Its main doorway has fluted pilasters, a moulded entablature, and another characteristic feature of the period is its two three-light Venetian windows with moulded wooden frames, one fronting the London Road and one the courtyard.[67]

New three-storied houses were erected in the less crowded parts, particularly on Market Hill and in the Causeway,[68] which were the fashionable parts of the town in the 18th and 19th centuries. No. 4 Market Hill is an instance. Its street front is partly of stucco and partly of variegated brick. It has painted stone bands at the first and second floors. The stone architraves and bracketed sills of the windows and the wooden hood of the front doorway with a dentilled cornice on carved brackets are typical of the work of the period. Claremont House, now a part of the Grammar school, is a comparatively elegant specimen of Regency work. There was also new building in Water Lane (now Chapel Street) where the houses were destroyed in the fire of 1724.[69] Here the Congregational church was erected in 1728.[70] It is of variegated brick on a stone base; the arched entrance is decorated with rusticated stone and the four long upright windows have stone jambs and bracketted sills. It is likely that New Buildings also (the modern North Street) were erected for the poorer part of the population in the 18th century. White Kennett does not mention them and Dunkin, writing in 1816, observes that they formed the newest part of the town. He noted too that the north end was a poor quarter and that the old houses had been divided by speculators and let at high rents. Sheep Street dwellings generally he described as 'very respectable'.[71]

64 Inf. the Revd. W. H. Trebble.
65 Its leases go back to at least 1705: Bic. U.D.C.
66 Dunkin, *Bic.* 181.
67 For a view of the 'King's Arms' and market-place see frontispiece.
68 See *Lascelles' Oxon. Dir.* (1853): e.g. there were 2 surgeons and 2 solicitors in Market Hill and its continuation, London Rd.
69 Dunkin, *Bic.* 19; see below, p. 33.

70 Cal. Q. Sess. viii. It was restored *c.* 1840 at a cost of £300 and again in 1873 at a cost of £400: Congregat. Min. Bk. ii; W. Ferguson, *Facts 300 years Ago, and Facts Now; or the Trials and Triumphs of Nonconformists* (Oxf. 1855), 28. For an illustration see MS. Top. Oxon. a 37, f. 103.
71 Dunkin, *Bic.* 17 n. 2, 18. For a reconstruction of the appearance of the town in 1793 see H. Wyndham, *A Backward Glance*, 46, 47, 51–52. For views of New Buildings and Water Lane see plates facing p. 47.

The appearance of the town was considerably altered in the 19th century by the loss of the Town Hall and Shambles, destroyed by rioters in 1826,[72] by the erection of a number of new public and private buildings, and the extension of its streets.[73] Among the new buildings were the Girls' school (c. 1835), the Wesleyan Methodist church in Sheep Street (c. 1841),[74] the National school for Boys, designed in gothic style in 1858 by the architect Thomas Nicholson of Hereford,[75] the Court House (1864) in Sheep Street, the Infant school (1869), the Police House and Magistrates' Chamber (1873) in the Causeway, and finally St. Edburg's Hall (1882) in London Road, which was designed by the architect E. G. Bruton and erected at a cost of £1,200.[76] Bicester Hall, now the Grammar school, was also built in this century for the Earl of Cottenham as a hunting-box.

There were two 19th-century improvements of note. The town, once notorious amongst hunting men for not having 'ten yards of flagging in its streets', was paved and its streets 'cleared of filth' in the 1860's. In 1845 it had been first lit by gas.[77] Another change was the covering in of the Bure in the Causeway, which had become foul from misuse.[78] This 'pretty brook', as a 17th-century visitor called it, had once been one of the town's most attractive features.[79] Nevertheless, Bicester was still very rural. The local board in 1864 ordered a new gate for the pound, and forbade the washing of pigs on the footpath.[80]

During the 20th century Bicester has developed considerably. The old town has been little changed and is chiefly remarkable for the variety of styles and materials displayed in its streets, where houses dating from the 16th to the 19th century stand side by side. But there has been much public and private building on the outskirts. Priory Road, for example, dates from the first decade of the 20th century, the council houses on the Buckingham Road from after the First World War, the Highfield estate mostly from the 1930's, but partly, together with the Bardwell estate, from after the Second World War. Between 1947 and 1956 over 600 council houses in all have been erected, of which 300 were especially made to house civilian workers at the Ordnance Depot.[81]

Among the chief individual works of the century are the Methodist church (1927), the County Secondary Modern school at Highfield, constructed principally of aluminium by B.A.C., Bristol (1952), and the new Police Station. Notable changes occurred in 1910, when the Sheep Street cattle market was transferred to the new market near Victoria Road, and in 1929, when electricity was introduced.[82]

The ancient parish had three hamlets besides Stratton Audley. They were Wretchwick, Bignell, and Bicester King's End, which was really always geographically an extension of Bicester Market End. Today the first is represented only by Middle Wretchwick Farm, in part a 17th-century house, and the second by Bignell House, a 19th-century mansion, for both hamlets were already in full decline in the 16th century.[83] Bignell Farm-house, which was regarded locally in the 17th century as the remnant of the ancient manor-house, and a nearby medieval chapel, once a private chapel attached to the manor-house,[84] survived until 1866, when the present Bignell House was built by the architect W. Wilkinson for the Misses Tyrwhitt-Drake at a cost of £5,500.[85] The chapel was then pulled down and the farm-house was converted into a gardener's house. Enough of the chapel, though already a ruin in 1695, was standing in about 1816 for Dunkin to say that it was a 14th-century building.[86] It must have once been used by the Langley family, the resident lords of Bignell from the 13th to the 14th century,[87] and later by the families of Stokes and Staveley, who also lived at Bignell.[88] In the 17th century the manor-house was inhabited for some years after 1660 by Samuel Lee, the Puritan divine, who was lord of the manor.[89] Later residents of note were the progressive farmer William Forster, the Revd. Griff Lloyd, the hunting parson of Newton Purcell,[90] and in the second half of the 19th century the Tyrwhitt-Drake and Hoare families, who were both well known in the hunting field and in local government.[91] Mounds and depressions in the field between Middle Wretchwick Farm-house and the main road indicate clearly the site of Wretchwick village and its green,[92] but no traces of Bignell village have been found so far.

Bicester King's End, though administered as a separate township for most of its history, was divided from Bicester Market End only by the Bure Brook.[93] The name occurs at least as early as 1316.[94] It was presumably so named in the 11th century when Kirtlington, of which it was a member, was a royal manor. White Kennett and other historians have erroneously identified Bignell near Chesterton with King's End, a confusion which probably arose from the fact that the names Bignell Field and King's End Field were used alternatively in the Middle Ages for the common field of the two townships.[95]

[72] Blo. Bic. 52. For an illustration see plate facing p. 20.
[73] Fullarton's Imperial Gazetteer (1866).
[74] Now the Freemasons' Hall, North St.
[75] For a 19th-cent. view see MS. Top. Oxon. a 37, f. 83; see below, p. 52.
[76] Kelly's Dir. Oxon. (1869, 1887). For St. Edburg's Hall, schools and church, see below, pp. 44, 51, 52.
[77] G. P. Crawfurd, Recollections of Bicester 1894–1907 (Reading), 50; Hunt's Oxford Dir. (1846); U.D.C. Local Gov. Board Min. Bk. 1866, 1871 for paving and sanitation.
[78] The date is uncertain, but was perhaps in the 1860's. All the Bicester brooks became polluted as a result of the sewerage scheme of 1863.
[79] Hist. MSS. Com. Portland, ii. 289.
[80] Bic. U.D.C. Local Govt. Board Min. bk.
[81] Inf. Bic. U.D.C.
[82] Bicester Guide and Dir. (1953).
[83] See below, p. 28.
[84] Kennett, Paroch. Antiq. ii. 156.

[85] W. Wilkinson, English Country Houses (1875), pls. v and vi; Blo. Bic. 73. See also infra plate facing p. 325.
[86] Dunkin, Bic. 139–40.
[87] See below, p. 23. For a Langley charter 1316–17 given at Bignell see B.M. Add. Ch. 10628.
[88] See below, pp. 23, 43.
[89] Wood, Athenae, iv. 345–8. See below, p. 23.
[90] Blo. Newt. 17; for Forster see below, p. 30.
[91] Mr. C. T. Hoare was High Sheriff in 1893 and for many years a J.P.: inf. Major A. G. C. Fane.
[92] Cf. M. Beresford, Lost Villages of England, 295.
[93] See below, p. 36 and map, p. 29.
[94] Feudal Aids, iv. 158.
[95] Kennett, Paroch. Antiq. ii. 185–99, passim. It is possible that the name Bignell gave way to King's End after 1421 (not 1399 as Rawlinson states), when the possessions of the honor of Lancaster were merged in the Crown: Bodl. MS. Rawl. B 180, f. 124; and cf. below, p. 222, for the date when Kirtlington was included in the Duchy.

The hamlet then consisted mainly of the nuns' grange and the cottages of their tenants. The north side of its green, on which the annual King's End fair was customarily held, was inclosed by John Coker in the 1790's when he was rebuilding his house, the former 'Nonnes Place'.[96] He put up the row of cottages which still stands on the main Oxford road (once the King's End turnpike) to replace those on the green, which he had demolished. The oldest surviving cottages in King's End today are nos. 41–47, which may perhaps date from the end of the 17th century.[97] They are all built of coursed rubble with brick chimney-stacks and are mostly thatched. Among the oldest houses are the L-shaped Manor and Home Farms, and Stow House, which may also date from the late 17th century.

Bicester House (known as Burcester Hall in the 17th century) is on the site of the manor-house of the nuns of Markyate and lies a little back from the main street of King's End.[98] Its history is almost undocumented owing to the destruction of the Coker archives in a fire, but the main developments can be traced from prints and a study of the building itself. The present house comprises 18th- and 19th-century additions to a 17th-century and possibly older structure. The nuns are known to have leased their estate to a John Griffith in 1530, but in 1584 it was purchased with the house by John Coker, and he settled in Bicester.[99] In 1665 Burcester Hall was a fairly substantial house for which six hearths were returned, but it was probably enlarged soon after by John Coker (d. 1710), the grandson of the first John Coker.[1] A contemporary print, depicting what is now the north-west range, shows a two-storied building of four bays, with an extension at the north end.[2] The date 1682 appears over the porch, which evidently then formed the main entrance to the house. The stable buildings shown at right angles to the front of the house still remain. The northern extension was later destroyed by fire, the position of the entrance way was moved, and the roof raised, probably in the 1780's when the house was reconstructed. It appears from internal evidence that this 17th-century house was half H-shaped with two wings projecting to the south-east from each end of the main north-west range. In two rooms good contemporary panelling and grey marble fire-places of the William and Mary period survive. White Kennett described the house as a 'commodious seat'.

In the 1780's the old house was considerably enlarged and the pleasure gardens were extended by the inclusion of land which had once formed the village green. The court between the two wings of the 17th-century house was filled up. The new façade can be seen in an engraving of about 1800.[3] It had a range of ten windows surmounted by a

pediment containing an armorial shield.[4] Work on the house was left uncompleted through the death of John Coker's wife early in 1794, but his seat had already been transformed, as Dunkin put it, into 'the chief ornament of the town'. In about 1820, in the time of Captain Thomas Lewis Coker (d. 1849), there was a further substantial rebuilding after a fire which destroyed two bays of the north-east side of the building. The central porch was removed, and the main staircase was moved to its present position at the south-west end of the building, where the main entrance was made and a large portico in the classical style constructed. The extensive alterations carried out at this date led Gardner's *Directory of Oxfordshire* to describe the house in 1852 as a 'large modern building'.[5] Possibly just before the captain's death, but probably at some later date in the 19th century, the rooms on the south-west front were enlarged by the addition of a central three-sided bay of two stories.

The main 20th-century alteration has been the replacement of the regency iron balusters and mahogany handrail of the staircase by oak ones. The original oak treads remain.[6]

Of the nine outlying farm-houses now in the ancient parish, most date from after the inclosure of the open fields in the late 18th century, but Langford Farm, called after the ford recorded as early as the 13th century, and the three Wretchwick Farms were originally 17th-century buildings.[7]

As a market-town lying on important roads, Bicester has often been brought into touch with national events and persons. Throughout its existence the priory entertained dignitaries of the church, including an Archbishop of Canterbury, and members of the feudal nobility as well as royal officials.[8] Many persons of rank were buried in the priory church: Gilbert Basset and his wife Egeline, Philippa Basset, Countess of Warwick, a Lord Lestrange, and members of the Damory family.[9] In the 16th century the town had three royal visitors: Henry VIII in 1526, Princess Mary in 1543, and Elizabeth I, when on her way to Rycote, was entertained by Thomas Moore in 1568 at his home at the Priory.[10]

In the 17th century the town was often the headquarters of the contending armies in the Civil War.[11] In 1643 and 1644 royalist forces were constantly in and about it: there was a skirmish there, for instance, on 6 May 1643; on 21 June the king lay the night in the town;[12] on the 27th, 4,000 of the king's forces were reported to be there; Prince Rupert had also been in the town on 14 June with 1,000 horses. His men were encamped there for some time, and were said to be scouting up and down and causing the country to bring in victuals daily.[13] Early the next year Prince Maurice with horse and foot soldiers

[96] Dunkin, *Bic.* 20; Kennett, *Paroch. Antiq.* ii. 156.
[97] They are now (1956) scheduled for demolition, an attempt to preserve them having failed.
[98] See below, p. 24; Blo. *Bic.* 76 n. 1.
[99] See below, p. 24.
[1] *Hearth Tax Oxon.* 189.
[2] See plate opposite (reproduced in Kennett, *Paroch. Antiq.* ii, opp. p. 156, and in Blo. *Bic.* opp. p. 76).
[3] See plate facing p. 21 (reproduced in Dunkin, *Bic.* opp. p. 133).
[4] A drawing *penes* Mrs. M. Coker, Bicester House, of about this date shows the house without a pediment, but with a balustrade.
[5] Gardner, *Dir. Oxon.*

[6] Inf. Mrs. M. Coker.
[7] For farms see O.S. *Area Bk.* (1876).
[8] Priory Accts. *passim* (see above, p. 16, n. 31); *Visit. Dioc. Linc.* 1420–49, i, pp. xxvi, xxix, xxx.
[9] Leland, *Itin.* ed. Toulmin Smith, ii. 34.
[10] *L. & P. Hen. VIII*, iv (2), p. 1079; Bodl. MS. Rawl. A 195 c, f. 265. For Thomas Moore see below, p. 22, and inscription on his brass in Bicester church. Bicester lay on one of the proposed routes for the queen's progress to Kenilworth in 1575: Hist. MSS. Com. *Pepys*, 179.
[11] Luke, *Jnl.* 78, 100, 104, 109, 112, 121–2, 133, 143, 257.
[12] *Cal. S.P. Dom.* 1644, 266.
[13] Luke, *Jnl.* 96, 97, 106, 115; MS. Dunkin 438/4, f. 42*b*.

The Shambles and Town House before 1826

Bicester House in 1695

BICESTER

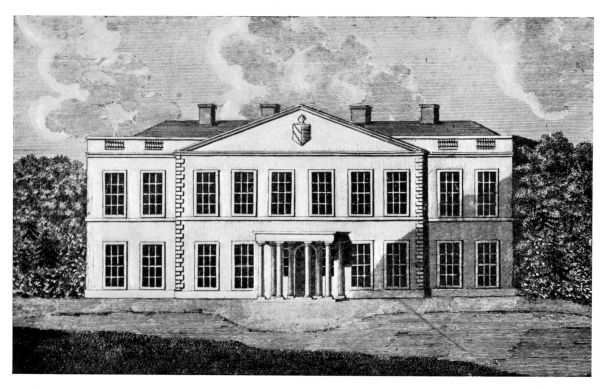

Bicester House before the fire of *c.* 1820

Bicester House after the fire of *c.* 1820

arrived, and in August men of the parliamentary army under Essex passed through on their way to Gloucester.[14] By July 1644 Parliament was in control of the neighbourhood; Sir William Waller made Bicester his headquarters and Parliament levied £60 on the town.[15] It was there that Captain Abercromby is alleged to have said that he would make Oxfordshire so poor that the very children would curse him.[16] In 1645 Parliament was considering making Bicester 'horse quarters' for the siege of Oxford.[17]

In 1710 national affairs impinged on the town when Dr. Sacheverell visited it and received a tumultuous welcome.[18] Later, the Napoleonic war gave rise to the formation of the Independent Company of Infantry (1804–9).[19] It was in the late 18th century, furthermore, that Bicester became a centre for horse-racing and hunting.[20] In the next century, the Bicester and Warden Hill Hunt made the town and its fine sporting country widely known. 'Mr. Drake's hounds' (i.e. the Bicester pack) and 'Deakin's' (i.e. the 'King's Arms') have been immortalized by Surtees.

The world wars of the 20th century turned the hunting town into a cosmopolitan and garrison town. Belgian refugees were housed at the George Inn during the First World War and in 1948 a camp for 1,000 European Voluntary Workers was established. The Second World War resulted in the establishment in 1940 at Arncot, three miles away, of Southern Command's Bicester Base Ordnance Depot, which has since been made permanent.[21]

Among Bicester's most distinguished sons was Sir Thomas Grantham, a naval commander in the service of the East India Company, whose father Thomas Grantham of Bicester was killed fighting for the king at Oxford in 1645.[22] A contemporary of his was Samuel Blackwell (vicar 1670–91), who was Dean of Bicester Deanery and founder of the town's noted 17th-century grammar school.[23] His curate and assistant master was White Kennett, the future Bishop of Peterborough and author of many learned works. Many documents in the Coker archives, since destroyed, were transcribed by him, and preserved in his *Parochial Antiquities*, published in 1695.[24] In the late 18th century John Dunkin (1782–1846), author of a *History of Bicester* (1816) and of the *History and Antiquities of the Hundreds of Bullingdon and Ploughley* (1823), was born and educated in the town.[25] Another well-known local figure was Francis Penrose, a Bicester 'surgeon' (1718–98), who was one of the first to excavate at Alchester.[26]

Although not resident at Bicester, the Turners (afterwards Page-Turners) of Ambrosden were closely associated with it for several generations

after 1728, when they acquired land in the parish.[27] Sir Edward Turner was 'one of the best friends to the parish' and his heir received his early education at the Bicester grammar school.[28] Yet at the great election contest of 1754 the town, whose freeholders had cast a decisive vote for Sir Edward and Lord Parker, and whose vicar was a prominent Whig, was wholeheartedly for the Wenman and Dashwood interest, and the bells were rung backwards when Sir Edward and Lord Parker were reported victors.[29] It was the Coker family, however, that had the longest and closest association with the town. Since 1584 Cokers have been lords of King's End manor and, except for a period of 70 years after 1849, were resident at Bicester House. They were active in local government and benefactors to the neighbourhood. A John Coker was sheriff in 1749 and another John Coker (d. 1819) was chairman of Quarter Sessions and 'an especial friend to Bicester'. He is particularly remembered for putting an end to bull-baiting in the town.[30] In recent times Major Lewis Aubrey Coker also played a leading part in local affairs until his death in 1953.

MANORS.[31] Before the Conquest Bicester was probably part of the possessions of Wigod of Wallingford, but after it land assessed at 15½ hides was held by Robert d'Oilly as two manors[32]—represented in the 12th century by the manors of *BICESTER* and *WRETCHWICK*. Like other D'Oilly estates Bicester appears to have passed to Miles Crispin as the marriage portion of Robert d'Oilly's daughter Maud;[33] it subsequently formed part of the honor of Wallingford and was later merged in the new honor of Ewelme.[34] Early in the 12th century the demesne tenant of Bicester was Gilbert Basset, a brother or perhaps a younger son of Ralph Basset the justiciar.[35] Gilbert, who was dead by 1154, was succeeded by his son Thomas, a sheriff of Oxfordshire who married Alice, daughter of Walter Dunstanville. Thomas died in 1180, and a few years later his eldest son and successor Gilbert founded Bicester Priory and endowed it with part of his demesnes.[36] Gilbert died in 1205 and his widow Egeline received Bicester in dower. She married Richard Burdun as her second husband, but was a widow again by 1219, when her marriage was in the king's gift.[37] Eustachia Basset, only child of Gilbert and Egeline, had married firstly Thomas de Verdun, and secondly Richard de Camville, son of Gerard de Camville of Middleton Stoney.[38] Eustachia was dead by 1215, when as a consequence of Richard's taking part in the baronial rebellion her daughter and heiress Idoine, her only surviving child by Richard,

[14] Luke, *Jnl.* 243; Dunkin, *Oxon.* ii. 257.
[15] MS. Dunkin 438/4, ff. 53, 57*b*; *Cal. S.P. Dom.* 1644, 266–7, 362; ibid. 1644–5, 176.
[16] MS. Dunkin 438/4, f. 64.
[17] *Cal. S.P. Dom.* 1645–7, 251, 311; for troop movements in 1645 see MS. Dunkin 438/4, f. 80.
[18] MS. Diary of J. Rolls *penes* Mr. S. G. Hedges, Bicester.
[19] MS. Top. Oxon. c 223.
[20] See below, p. 35.
[21] Inf. Bic. U.D.C.
[22] See monumental inscription in church and *D.N.B.*
[23] White Kennett, *Paroch. Antiq.* ii. 370; *V.C.H. Oxon.* i. 463.
[24] *D.N.B.* and *V.C.H. Oxon.* v. 25–26.
[25] *D.N.B.* For an account of the family see J. Dunkin, *Biographical Sketches* (Bromley, 1816) with MS. notes in Bodl. G.A. Oxon. 8° 257.

[26] *D.N.B.* and see below, p. 339.
[27] Below, p. 23. For the family see *V.C.H. Oxon.* v. 18.
[28] Dunkin, *Oxon.* i. 54 n., 56; *V.C.H. Oxon.* i. 463.
[29] For a full account see Dunkin, *Oxon.* i. 54–55 and notes; R. J. Robson, *The Oxon. Election of 1754*, 155.
[30] Dunkin, *Oxon.* i. 259; idem, *Bic.* 133; local inf.
[31] This section is based largely on material supplied by Mary and Ethel Savill, and was written by R. F. Walker.
[32] *V.C.H. Oxon.* i. 413.
[33] Ibid. 383; *Boarstall Cart.* 323.
[34] Dunkin, *Bic.* 34.
[35] *Boarstall Cart.* 324; cf. J. H. Round in *D.N.B.*
[36] *Boarstall Cart.* 324; *Rot. de Dominabus* (P.R.S. xxxv), 8 and n. 2; *V.C.H. Oxon.* ii. 94.
[37] *Boarstall Cart.* 324; *Cat. Anct. D.* ii, C 1872; *Bk. of Fees*, 253.
[38] See below, p. 245.

was taken into the king's custody. Idoine's wardship was subsequently granted to William, Earl of Salisbury, and she married his son, William Longespée.[39] Richard de Camville died about 1219,[40] and his mother-in-law Egeline may have been dead by 1225, when William Longespée had a house in Bicester.[41] It was not until the following year, however, when Idoine had come of age, that William was formally granted her inheritance. From 1226 to 1597 Bicester manor followed the same descent as Middleton Stoney.[42] In 1577 Henry Stanley, Earl of Derby, leased the manor for 21 years to Thomas Wygyns (or Wykyns) of Bicester, and in 1597 William Stanley, Earl of Derby, conveyed it to 31 of his tenants for £750 on a lease for 9,999 years.[43] The earl later sold the reversion of the manor to trustees of the leaseholders, and in 1605, after Thomas Clements, one of the two nominal purchasers,[44] and his sons, who held the capital messuage,[45] had claimed the manorial rights and profits, it was decided that these belonged to the leaseholders. The manor was henceforth administered by a bailiff on behalf of the leaseholders and was consequently known as the bailiwick of Bicester Market End. In the 18th century the estates of the Clements family passed in turn to Thomas Coker of King's End and to Sir Edward Turner, who is said to have attempted to turn some of the leaseholds, or 'Derby holds' as they were called, into freeholds, in order to obtain more votes in the county election of 1754.[46] By 1816 the Page-Turners and Cokers were the largest lessees of the bailiwick, but the Page-Turners' claim to be lords of the manor of Market End was unfounded, since no single lessee could claim the lordship unless he gained possession of the whole of the original Derby estate.[47] In 1902 and 1913, however, the Bicester Urban District Council purchased the manorial rights with all the shares in the bailiwick from F. A. Page-Turner and other lessees.[48]

WRETCHWICK first appears as a separate manor in 1194, when half of it was given in marriage with his daughter Eustachia by Gilbert Basset to Thomas de Verdun. Gilbert retained the other half, which on his death in 1205 passed with Bicester manor to his widow Egeline.[49] In 1208 Egeline claimed that she had not received a full third part of Gilbert's estate in dower. Egeline subsequently received certain additional estates from her daughter Eustachia and her second husband Richard de Camville. In the calculation of Egeline's third part Wretchwick was treated as part of Bicester manor.

She had possession of the half which Eustachia had held, and successfully defended her right to it in 1211.[50] Shortly afterwards Egeline granted the half of Wretchwick she had originally held to Bicester Priory, a gift confirmed by Eustachia and Richard.[51] The second half of Wretchwick passed on Egeline's death to William Longespée and his wife Idoine, heiress of Richard de Camville. William gave part of his portion of Wretchwick to Bicester Priory about 1234,[52] and in 1244 gave the remainder to his daughter Ela on her marriage to James Audley.[53] James received a grant of free warren in his Wretchwick demesnes in 1252.[54] Soon after James's death in 1272 Ela gave all her lands in Wretchwick to Bicester Priory and in 1274 confirmed her gift.[55] In 1279, therefore, the Prior of Bicester held the whole manor of Wretchwick in free alms of Henry de Lacy, Earl of Lincoln, who held in turn of Edmund of Cornwall's honor of Wallingford.[56] In Bicester manor at the same time the prior held 1½ hides—Gilbert Basset's original endowment plus later acquisitions—as a tenant of the Earl of Lincoln.[57]

After the dissolution of Bicester Priory in 1536 the site of the monastery and its demesne lands in Bicester and Wretchwick were granted to Charles Brandon, Duke of Suffolk, at fee farm.[58] In 1537 the duke granted the site of the monastery to Roger Moore and his wife Agnes and sold him nearly 400 acres of demesne for £505.[59] A number of royal grants followed, including in 1539 that of the reversion of five estates in Wretchwick held on leases from the former prior.[60] Roger Moore died in 1551[61] and his only son, Thomas, who came of age in 1558 or 1559, succeeded to the manor; he was killed in Ireland in 1574.[62] Roger Moore's widow Agnes married as her second husband Sir Edward Saunders, Lord Chief Baron, who died in 1576.[63] Agnes was dead by 1583 and the estates which she had held jointly with Roger were divided between her daughters Mary wife of Sir Michael Blount of Mapledurham and Elizabeth wife of Gabriel Fowler of Tilsworth (Beds.). Gabriel Fowler had died in 1582,[64] and in 1583 Elizabeth conveyed her moiety of what was called the manor of Bicester to Sir John Brockett,[65] whom she married. In 1589 Sir John conveyed it to Sir Michael Blount and his wife Mary.[66] Mary died in 1592, and when Livia Ellen Moore, the widow of Thomas Moore, died in 1597 part of her property reverted to Mary's son Sir Richard Blount.[67] Thus when Sir Richard succeeded his father in 1610 he was in possession of nearly all

[39] Rot. Litt. Pat. (Rec. Com.), 170, 178.
[40] H. E. Salter says he died in 1216 (Boarstall Cart 324); Bk. of Fees, 253; see below, p. 245.
[41] Rot. Litt. Claus. (Rec. Com.), ii. 62.
[42] See below, p. 245-6.
[43] Bic. U.D.C. deed no. 7; C 2 Jas. I B 41/42; Dunkin, Bic. 170-1; Blo. Bic. 22-23 citing list of purchasers in Par. Rec.
[44] C.P. 25(2)/198/Trin. 39 Eliz. Thomas Wygyns (or Wykyns) was the other nominal purchaser.
[45] C 142/403/96: inq. p.m. of Ralph Clements, 1624; Dunkin, Bic. 170-1.
[46] R. J. Robson, The Oxon. Election of 1754, 63, 118, 146 n.; Dunkin, Bic. 175.
[47] Dunkin, Bic. 170-3.
[48] Bic. U.D.C. deeds nos. 5, 10, 29.
[49] MS. Top. Oxon. c 398, f. 113: transcript by H. E. Salter from B.M. Add. MSS.; Boarstall Cart. 324.
[50] Cur. Reg. R. v. 157-8, 226, 235; ibid. vi. 123.
[51] MS. Top. Oxon. c 398, ff. 113-14; MSS. at Rec. Office, Shire Hall, Bed., bdle. 8, no. 1.

[52] Cal. Pat. 1313-17, 359; Kennett, Paroch. Antiq. i. 305.
[53] Fines Oxon. 129.   [54] Cal. Chart. R. 1226-57, 409.
[55] Cal. Inq. p.m. i, p. 261; MS. Top. Oxon. c 398, ff. 127, 129.
[56] Rot. Hund. (Rec. Com.), ii. 827; cf. Cal. Inq. p.m. v, p. 156; Feud. Aids, iv. 158.
[57] Rot. Hund. ii. 828.
[58] Dunkin, Bic. (author's copy, Bodl. G.A. Oxon. 8°257), 84-85 with MS. notes; C 66/681.
[59] L. & P. Hen. VIII, xiii(2), p. 492.
[60] Dunkin MS. 438/1, Originalia, ff. 176, 187; L. & P. Hen. VIII, xiv(1), pp. 251-2.
[61] Par. Coll. i. 37; he left part of his Bicester estates to his daughters Mary and Elizabeth: C 142/96/57.
[62] C 142/257/60.
[63] D.N.B.; Foss, Judges, v. 537; Blo. Bic. 17.
[64] V.C.H. Beds. iii. 433.
[65] C.P. 25(2)/197/Trin. 25 Eliz.; V.C.H. Herts. ii. 434.
[66] Cal. S.P. Dom. 1581-90, 606; C 66/1336; Cal. Chan. Proc. Eliz. (Rec. Com.), i. 126.
[67] C 142/257/60.

the original Moore estate, and in 1621 he settled his Bicester lands on his son Sir Charles and his wife Dorothy Clerk.[68] Sir Richard died in 1628, [69] and in 1644 Sir Charles, who was with the king's forces at Oxford, was accidentally killed by a sentry.[70] The family estates were sequestrated in 1646, and in 1649 Sir Charles's elder son Michael died while still a minor. In the following year Sir Charles's second son Walter appealed for the discharge of his lands. Other claims against Sir Charles's estates reveal that his Bicester property was burdened with mortgages,[71] and though Walter's appeal was eventually successful he was compelled to sell the former priory lands to Chief Justice John Glynne.[72] From the latter the property, called in the 17th century 'the manors of Bicester and Wretchwick',[73] descended on his death in 1666 to his son Sir William Glynne, Bt.[74] Sir William died in 1690, and was succeeded by his sons Sir William (d. 1721) and Sir Stephen (d. 1729).[75] Shortly before his death Sir Stephen sold his Bicester property to Edward Turner.[76] The priory estates subsequently followed the same descent in the Turner family as the manor of Ambrosden,[77] and by the beginning of the 19th century were confused with the bailiwick of Bicester Market End, in which the Page-Turners were among the principal shareholders.[78]

BIGNELL, though in the parish of Bicester, was a member of Kirtlington manor. Its overlordship followed the same descent as Kirtlington.[79] In the early 13th century the tenant of Bignell was James le Bret, who made a number of grants to Bicester Priory of lands in Bignell.[80] In 1279 the tenant holding Bignell as a $\frac{1}{4}$ knight's fee of the lord of Kirtlington was Walter de Langley, son of Geoffrey de Langley, the notorious justice of the forest.[81] Walter died in 1280[82] and Bignell was then held in dower by his widow Alice.[83] By 1316 the manor had passed to Walter's son John de Langley,[84] who about 1325 gave it to his younger son Geoffrey. Geoffrey died leaving a son, also Geoffrey, under age, and the manor was then said to have been alienated by Thomas de Langley, the child's uncle, to William de Bohun, Earl of Northampton[85]—who as lord of Kirtlington would have been entitled to the custody of Bignell during Geoffrey's minority. By 1354 the earl had granted Bignell for life to Peter Favelore,[86] on whose death in 1360 it reverted to the earl's son and successor, Humphrey de Bohun.[87] After holding

Bignell for some time Humphrey restored it to the heirs of Geoffrey de Langley. The younger Geoffrey, his only child Joan, and his uncle Thomas were all dead by 1375, when the right heir to the manor was found to be Sir John de Worthe, a great-grandson of John de Langley's sister Christine.[88] Sir John had obtained possession by 1377,[89] and died childless about 1390.[90] In 1409 a Robert Worthe conveyed the manor to a number of feoffees[91] of whom one, Robert James, was the tenant in 1428.[92] In 1439 Bignell was held by Humphrey, Earl of Stafford, and John Felmersham,[93] having perhaps fallen in to the earl as son and heir of the Countess Anne who had succeeded to Kirtlington manor in 1399. By 1446 Bignell had been acquired by John Stokes,[94] but as he and his wife Alice had no surviving children they arranged in 1465 that after their deaths Bignell should pass to William Staveley, John's friend and, like him, a trusted servant of Edward IV.[95] John died in 1476 and Alice in 1479.[96] William Staveley succeeded and settled the manor on his wife Alice for life, with remainder to his son George. By a later settlement, however, the manor was to pass on Alice's death to their sons William and John.[97] William the father died in 1498 and was buried in the parish church. Alice held the manor until her death two years later,[98] but in accordance with the earlier settlement it passed to George, the eldest son,[99] who held it at his death in 1525.[1] George's son and successor John came of age about 1530, and was resident at Bignell in 1539.[2] From John, who is said to have sold many of his lands (probably to the Cokers) and who died in 1569, Bignell descended to his son Thomas (d. 1582) and his grandson Thomas (d. 1631). The younger Thomas went to reside on the Leicestershire estate which the Staveleys had inherited through Isabel Strelley, wife of George Staveley,[3] and Thomas's son Arthur sold what was left of Bignell in 1651, a few years before his death in 1655.[4] After passing through a number of hands the manor was purchased in 1655 by Samuel Lee,[5] a Puritan divine who after the Restoration retired from London to live at Bicester and who was probably the last resident lord of Bignell manor. He left Bicester in 1678, migrated to New England in 1686, and died a prisoner in France in 1691.[6] Bignell manor was divided between his four daughters Anne, Elizabeth, Rebecca, and Lydia and their husbands.[7] Two moieties were conveyed in 1702 and 1721 by

[68] A. H. Cooke, *Early Hist. of Mapledurham* (O.R.S. vii), 209; C.P. 25(2)/340/Mich. 19 Jas. I.
[69] C 142/440/83.
[70] Cooke, *Mapledurham*, 116.
[71] Ibid. 146; *Cal. Cttee for Compounding*, 2245–6.
[72] Blo. *Bic.* 35; *D.N.B.*
[73] e.g. C.P. 43/295/200; ibid. 422/179.
[74] G.E.C. *Baronetage*, iii. 199; Blo. *Bic.* 35.
[75] G.E.C. *Baronetage*, iii. 199–200.
[76] Blo. *Bic.* 38.
[77] *V.C.H. Oxon.* v. 18.
[78] e.g. C.P. 43/496/390.
[79] *Cal. Doc. France*, ed. Round, 185, and see below, pp. 221–3.
[80] *Bk. of Fees*, 319; Kennett, *Paroch. Antiq.* i. 245, 254–5; MS. Top. Oxon. c 398, f. 111.
[81] *Rot. Hund.* (Rec. Com.), ii. 839; for the Langleys see Dugd. *Warws.* 135; *Misc. Gen. et Her.* 2nd ser. ii. 273 sqq.
[82] *Cal. Inq. p.m.* ii, p. 200.
[83] Kennett, *Paroch. Antiq.* i. 417–18; MS. Top. Oxon. c 398, f. 118.
[84] *Feud. Aids*, iv. 169.
[85] *Cal. Inq. p.m.* xiv, p. 74.

[86] *Cal. Pat.* 1354–8, 104.
[87] *Cal. Inq. p.m.* x, p. 555.
[88] Ibid. xiv, p. 74.
[89] *Cal Chart. R.* 1341–1417, 235.
[90] C 136/67/18; Dugd. *Warws.* 530.
[91] C.P. 25(1)/191/25/41.
[92] *Feud. Aids*, iv. 191.
[93] *Cal. Pat.* 1436–41, 288.
[94] J. C. Wedgwood, *Hist. Parl.: Biogs.* 812.
[95] Wedgwood, op. cit. 806; cf. *V.C.H. Berks.* iii. 322.
[96] C 140/537/68; ibid. 551/66.
[97] *Cal. Inq. p.m. Hen. VII*, ii, p. 240.
[98] Ibid.; *Par. Coll.* i. 38.
[99] *L. & P. Hen. VIII*, i(1), p. 256.
[1] E 150/796/4.
[2] *L. & P. Hen. VIII*, xiv(2), p. 363.
[3] C 142/152/108; ibid. 201/132; for the Staveley pedigree see Nichols, *Leics.* ii(2). 664, 667, 676; Blo. *Bic.* 71.
[4] C.P. 25(2)/587/East. 1651; Nichols, *Leics.* ii(2). 664.
[5] C.P. 25(2)/588/Trin. 1655.
[6] *D.N.B.*; Dunkin, *Bic.* 139.
[7] C.P. 25(2)/865/Hil. 8 Wm. III; ibid. 956/Trin. 1 Anne.

three of these daughters and their respective husbands to John and Samuel Bishop and to Samuel Clarke.[8] In 1723 the whole manor was bought by Sir Robert Dashwood, who as lord of Kirtlington was already entitled to suit of court once a year.[9] Towards the end of the century John Coker purchased Bignell farm. His family had already acquired most of the land of the original manor and the fair.[10] William Forster was a tenant at the end of the century.[11]

NUN'S PLACE or *KING'S END* manor was originally part of Bignell and therefore of Kirtlington. It is not known when or from whom the Bedfordshire nunnery of Markyate Priory obtained lands in Bignell, but it acquired property in Oxfordshire soon after its foundation in 1145[12] and about the beginning of the 13th century made an exchange of lands at Bicester with Bicester Priory.[13] In 1279 Markyate Priory held $2\frac{1}{2}$ carucates in Bignell in free alms under Walter de Langley,[14] an estate valued in 1291 at £2 16s. 10d. a year.[15] By 1316 the manor was known as King's End.[16] In 1530 the priory leased the estate to John Griffith, a servant of Cardinal Wolsey, for 21 years at a rent of 10 marks a year.[17] Markyate Priory was suppressed in 1536, and in 1542 what was called 'the manor of Nun's Place in Bicester King's End' and the reversion of Griffith's leasehold estate were sold by the Crown to John Denton of Blackthorn (d. 1576).[18] In 1584 John's son Edward conveyed the manor to John Coker.[19] The Cokers were a West Country family in origin, said to have taken their name from West Coker (Som.),[20] and were to play a leading part in the affairs of Bicester for more than three and a half centuries. John, who in 1605 acquired a part of the former priory estate from Sir Richard Blount,[21] died in 1607[22] and was succeeded by his son Cadwallader,[23] who in 1646 compounded for £290 for his delinquency in having contributed to the maintenance of the king's forces.[24] From Cadwallader (d. 1653) King's End passed to his son John (d. 1710) and his grandson Thomas, canon of Salisbury (d. 1741). In the early 18th century Sir Robert Dashwood, lord of Kirtlington and of Bignell, unsuccessfully claimed the lordship of King's End against the Cokers.[25] The lord and inhabitants of King's End, however, on account of the ancient connexion of King's End with Bignell and Kirtlington manor continued to owe suit to the manorial court of Kirtlington on into the 19th century.[26] Thomas Coker's son and successor John died childless in 1767, and King's End descended to his brother Thomas (d. 1798), who, probably because of his age at the death of his brother, made over the property to his nephew John, son of Cadwallader Coker (d.

1780). John died in 1819 leaving an only daughter Charlotte, but the manor, having been entailed on his heirs male by Thomas Coker,[27] passed to John's nephew Thomas Lewis Coker. The Coker estate of over 888 acres was sold in 1918 and manorial rights lapsed. Bicester House and estates in King's End were in 1957 still in the possession of Mrs. Margaret Coker, widow of Major Lewis Aubrey Coker (d. 1953).[28]

AGRARIAN HISTORY. By the time of Domesday it is likely that cultivation had reached the boundaries of Bicester's *territorium*, and that the hamlets of Wretchwick and Bignell, although not mentioned, were like Stratton already in existence.[29] The name *Wrec-wic* means 'shelter of the exiles' and was probably originally used by men looking after the cattle in the summer months. Bignell—Biga's hill—is derived from a personal name and so is likely to have been settled at an early date.[30] Something of the struggle of the early settlers to reclaim the land from scrub and marsh is indicated by the field names recorded in later documents: such names as Crocwellmor, Reidemor, Overdemerschelonde, Kyngesmere, Brademor, and Thoftwellmor abound.

The Domesday account of Bicester states that there was land for 22 ploughs in the two D'Oilly manors of Bicester (i.e. Wretchwick and Bicester).[31] There were 6 plough-teams at work on the demesne, where 5 serfs were employed, while 28 villeins (*villani*) and 14 bordars owned 16 ploughs. Thus all the available land seems to have been cultivated. Twelve acres of meadow are recorded. There may have been devastation at the Conquest as elsewhere in this area, for the value of the estates in contrast to most estates in the hundred only rose from £15 to £16 in the following twenty years.[32] But this account does not include the whole of the medieval parish. Stratton, though described in Domesday Book, is omitted here as it later became a separate parish; it had its own field system and manorial courts and its early agrarian history will be found below in the account of Stratton Audley parish. Bignell is also omitted, as Domesday gives no details about the hamlet, which was probably included in the account of Kirtlington.[33]

The Hundred Rolls survey of 1279 records a number of developments. Bicester Priory, by then lord of Wretchwick manor, had 10 virgates in demesne and $18\frac{1}{2}$ virgates held by 25 villein virgaters and half-virgaters. The rents and works of each were worth 10s. or 5s. There were also 2 cotlanders, each owing rents and works worth 4s., and 5 cottagers with rents of 1s. to 2s., who may have owned a few

---

[8] C. P. 25 (2)/956/Trin. 1 Anne; ibid. 1050/Hil. 7 Geo. I.
[9] Ibid. 1051/East. 9 Geo. I; C.P. 43/881/10; for the descent of the site of the manor-house see *Bicester Par. Mag.*, Feb. 1902.
[10] Dunkin, *Bic.* 136–7; Blo. *Bic.* 72; C.P. 25(2)/340/East. 9 Jas. I.
[11] See below, p. 30.
[12] *V.C.H. Beds.* i. 358–60.
[13] Dugd. *Mon.* iii. 373.
[14] *Rot. Hund.* (Rec. Com.), ii. 839.
[15] *Tax. Eccl.* (Rec. Com.), 45.
[16] *Feud. Aids*, iv. 169.
[17] *L. & P. Hen. VIII*, xvii, p. 568; cf. *Valor Eccl.* (Rec. Com.), iv. 209.
[18] *L. & P. Hen. VIII*, xvii, p. 568; C 142/178/61; for Denton see *V.C.H. Oxon.* v. 17, 18.
[19] C.P. 25(2)/197/Trin. 26 Eliz.
[20] Blo. *Bic.* 76–77.
[21] C.P. 25(2)/339/East. 3 Jas. I.

[22] *Par. Coll.* i. 39; C 142/296/107.
[23] C 60/449/21.
[24] *Cal. Cttee for Compounding*, 1536.
[25] Dunkin, *Bic.* 139.
[26] Ibid. 136–7.
[27] Ibid. 133.
[28] For Coker pedigree see Burke, *Land. Gent.* (1937), and corrected MS. pedigree by Mr. R. de la Lanne Mirrlees, Rouge Dragon Poursuivant *penes* Mrs. M. Coker.
[29] The word *territorium* (meaning parish) is used in a 12th-cent. Aulnay deed: St. John's Coll.
[30] *P.N. Oxon.* (E.P.N.S.), i. 198–9. There is no sign of any hill or tumulus now.
[31] See above, p. 21.
[32] *V.C.H. Oxon.* i. 413. For devastation in Northants see *V.C.H. Northants*, i. 260–1.
[33] Ibid. 400. For Bignell in Kirtlington see above, p. 23, and below, p. 227.

acres as well. In Bicester Market End the Earl of Lincoln had 3 carucates in demesne and had 7 villein virgaters, a half-virgater, and 6 tenants with 5 acres each. The prior held 1½ hides in free alms of this manor, and there were two other recorded free tenants: Robert Clerk with a virgate, and Robert Puff the miller, who paid a rent of 5s. to the prior.[34] The earl's villein tenants may have been rather better off than the prior's: only payment of rent is mentioned and this was 2s. lower than that exacted on the prior's manor.[35]

In the south-west of the parish, Bignell manor was remarkable for the number of its free tenants, a consequence no doubt of its status as ancient demesne. Walter de Langley held 2 carucates in demesne with meadow and pasture. He had 12 villein virgaters, who each paid a rent of 2s. 2d. and owed works and tallage at the lord's will. Beside these there were 3 free virgaters and 3 free half-virgaters, paying rents of 10s. the virgate and 5s. the ½-virgate. In addition the Prior of Bicester had 16 acres and the Prioress of Markyate (Beds.) had a small manor. She held a carucate of land in demesne and had 11 villeins, who held 6 virgates between them. They paid rent at the rate of 5s. the virgate, owed works and tallage at will, and were bound to pay fines if their sons left the manor (*redimere pueros*).[36] This is the earliest account of the settlement, which is later known as Bicester King's End, though the nunnery must have been granted its estate here before 1212, and may have held it since its foundation in 1145.[37] Its grange and the hamlet of King's End might, therefore, date from the mid-12th century.

There were about 35 recorded virgates on the Kirtlington fee (i.e. in Bignell), and 56 in the Market End and Wretchwick manors, assuming that the prior's 1½ hides in Market End can be equated with 6 virgates. Thus 91 arable virgates were recorded. As the virgate on at least one of the manors equalled 28 or 30 acres, it is possible that roughly 2,730 field acres were under cultivation at this time.[38]

The Hundred Rolls account of the tenants is incomplete. Domesday records 47 peasants on the Market End and Wretchwick manors, the Hundred Rolls only one more, although numbers elsewhere in Ploughley hundred had risen considerably since 1086. A comparison of the figures given in the 1279 survey with those given in an extent of Market End manor in 1310 shows that most of the free tenants, probably free craftsmen and traders living on the market, were omitted from the 1279 survey of the estate.[39]

Early charters, 14th-century extents and custumals, court rolls, and tax lists provide miscellaneous information about the topography of the fields and the manorial organization of the estates. The number of persons taxed and the amounts paid in the first half of the 14th century give a clue to the relative wealth and at least a minimum figure for the size of the town and its hamlets. In 1316 at Market End 122 contributors paid £9 1s. 7d., 35 at King's End paid £4 18s. 10d., and at Bignell 11 paid £2 0s. 11d.[40] On this and other occasions Wretchwick appears to have been included in Market End.[41] After the reassessment of tax payments in 1334 Market End paid £10 19s. 10d., King's End £5 5s. 2d., and Bignell £2 3s. 11d.[42]

A manorial extent of 1310 shows that the Earl of Lincoln's Market End manor contained a messuage with fishpond worth 10s. a year, a dovecot worth 2s., 160 acres of arable valued at 3d. the acre, 16 acres of meadow valued at the high price of 3s. the acre, and 'several' pasture worth 2s. The earl's 22 free tenants rendered £3 15s. 8d.;[43] the 20 villeins £5 0s. 10d., while their summer and autumn works were valued at £1. Their annual tallage was £1 6s. The total value including the profit of the market was given as £17 16s. 10d.[44] The prior's manor of Wretchwick was worth £20, but he also held 4 carucates of arable of the earl, 20 acres of meadow and a water-mill, which were valued at £40.[45] Thus, since 1279 it appears that the earl's demesne had decreased and the prior's holding had increased from 1½ to 4 carucates.[46]

The Prioress of Markyate's King's End manor, comprising 10 virgates[47] or about 300 field acres, was valued in c. 1325 at £7 11s. 8¼d. Of this £1 14s. 6d. came from the rents and services of the customary tenants and £3 4s. 6¾d. from leaseholders.[48]

When Bignell manor was extended in 1361 it had 120 acres of arable, each acre being worth 2d.; 7 acres of meadow, worth 1s. 6d. an acre; separate pasture worth 2s.; and common pasture for 2 cart-horses, 8 oxen, and 120 sheep. The rents of free tenants amounted to £2 5s. 2d.; those of 3 virgaters and 6 half-virgaters to £1 4s. 9d. The customary tenants also owed an aid of 9s. at Michaelmas. Five cottagers paid a rent of 13s., but 4 villein cottages and 2½ virgates of land were tenantless and their produce had been sold for 8s. 1d.[49]

It is clear that the ancient parish, excluding Stratton,[50] originally had two sets of fields: one for Bicester Bury End, or Market End as the town came to be called, although the fields were always described as in Bury End throughout the Middle Ages; and another set for the townships of Bignell and Bicester King's End.

One of Gilbert Basset's foundation charters implies that there were two fields on his Market End estate in the 12th century, and a survey of c. 1325 shows that Bignell had two fields, a North and a

[34] For the free tenants' charters see Kennett, *Paroch. Antiq.* index of persons. He has printed the charters now B.M. Add. Ch. 10593–10633. There are transcripts by H. E. Salter in Bodl. MS. Top. Oxon. c 398, ff. 104–141.

[35] *Rot. Hund.* (Rec. Com.), ii. 827–8.

[36] Ibid. 839. The Prioress *de Cella* is the Prioress of Markyate or Market Cell: Dugd. *Mon.* iii. 368.

[37] There is no Markyate cartulary, but James le Bret (see above, p. 23) is a likely donor.

[38] The virgate = 28 a. in 1349 on the Market End manor: C 135/101/6. In 1535 the virgate = 30 a. on the prior's land at Wretchwick and 26 a. at Market End: *Valor Eccl.* (Rec. Com.), ii. 189.

[39] C 134/22 (partly printed in Kennett, *Paroch. Antiq.* i. 514–15). Cf. below, p. 32.

[40] E 179/161/8; cf. E 179/161/39 for poll-tax figures of 73 and 19 for King's End and Bignell, and E 179/161/40 for 140 persons at Market End.

[41] In 1306 it was listed separately: E 179/161/10.

[42] e.g. E 179/161/12; E 164/7.

[43] C 134/22; see below, p. 32.

[44] C 134/22. The value £25 14s. 2d. given at later inquest (1328) includes 70 a. at Arncot: C 135/108/2.

[45] Kennett, *Paroch. Antiq.* i. 514–15.

[46] See below, n. 87, for grant made to the priory.

[47] *Rot. Hund.* (Rec. Com.), ii. 839.

[48] Kennett, *Paroch. Antiq.* i. 575, 577.

[49] C 135/155/19.

[50] For Stratton see below, p. 324.

South Field,[51] which were shared by Bignell manor and the nuns' King's End manor. The survey's mention of 'Oldfield' suggests that the ancient two-field system had undergone some reorganization, but a Bignell extent of 1361 describes the demesne arable as half sown and half fallow, and so indicates that there was still a simple two-course rotation.[52] On the Market End demesne, however, two parts of the arable were stated in 1349 to be sown each year.[53]

By 1399 there were certainly three fields in Market End as well as signs of variations in the normal three-course rotation. A number of furlongs could be sown each year 'if it was so agreed', and another furlong could be sown only with the consent of the tenants.[54] The prior's land was unequally distributed among the three fields: he had 153½ acres and 3 butts in North Field, 60 acres in Langford Field, and about 110 in East Field. Each acre is said to contain 2 selions, while 4 and sometimes more roods made an acre and 5 to 8 butts according to their size went to the acre.[55]

The main crops grown were wheat, barley, beans, and peas, with barley taking an easy lead on at least part of the priory lands. The grange account of 1397, for instance, shows that 301 quarters of barley were threshed, 178 of wheat, and 57 of beans and peas.[56]

There is some evidence about manorial organization and customs. The survey of the Markyate manor records that the prioress had seven hereditary free tenants and six who held for life. The latter appear to form a class of especially privileged craftsmen and women, among them Maud the tailoress and John the baker and his wife. The demesne was leased on various terms: some tenants held for life by copy, some by indenture, and some at will.[57] Full details are given about the customary services of the villeins. A villein tenant owed one ploughing service in winter, one mowing service, and a 'we[e]d bedrip' with food at the lady's will and a half-day's mowing. He was entitled to 'evenyngs', i.e. a virgater or a half-virgater with a companion could carry home as much hay as he could lift on his scythe, and also to a breakfast (*jentaculum*) at the lady's expense. All the customary tenants had to turn, lift, and cock the hay in 'Gilberdesham' meadow. Each had to cart four cart-loads of hay to the lady's court. A virgater also owed three boon-works in autumn—one boon-work without food with three men, one boon-work without food with one man, and a third with his whole family except for his wife. If he was a binder he was entitled to a sheaf of corn when the last sheaf was bound; if he had food he was not to have a sheaf. He had to carry four cartloads of corn in autumn to the lady's manor and was given breakfast. He could

be tallaged annually at will, he might not sell a male horse or an ox of his own breeding, nor put his son to learning, nor marry his daughter without licence. If the prioress was in residence the customary tenant had to supply her with food and drink at her will for as long as she stayed in the county. In addition the half-virgater owed an annual rent of 2s. 6d.[58]

On the prior's manor of Wretchwick it was customary for a widow to keep her husband's holding as long as she remained unmarried.[59] But this was contingent on her being able to pay the heriot and having sufficient capital to carry on. In the case of a villein virgater, whose heriot was an ox and a cow, priced at 13s., the jurors reported in 1344 that his widow could not hold the messuage and land on account of poverty.[60] Another Wretchwick custom was that if the land was sown on the death of a tenant and his widow could not find sufficient pledges to support her claim to the land they had jointly held, then the lord should choose who should be invested with the land.[61] Fines on entry were probably of varying amounts, but a fine of £3 6s. 8d. was exacted on at least two occasions for entering a villein messuage and virgate.[62] A fine of 10s. was paid by a virgater for licence to marry a widow.[63]

From an early date there was a marked tendency to inclose pasture and meadow, although lot meadows also persisted.[64] Apart from the inclosed crofts attached to each messuage, which were commonly found in most villages, the demesne pasture of the Bassets was inclosed in the late 12th century, as the foundation charter of Bicester Priory shows. Gilbert Basset granted the priory both demesne and common pasture for 400 sheep, and also the right to depasture three teams of oxen in his demesne.[65] Then early in the next century William Longespée, the successor of the Bassets, made a grant of land in Wretchwick (*tota cultura . . . quae vocatur Horscroft*) with the adjoining demesne meadow so that the canons might inclose it.[66] In 1309 there was a dispute over this or another inclosure with the tenants of Market End manor, who claimed common of pasture for their cattle in the prior's field in Wretchwick called the Breach.[67] Another dispute over pasture rights, this time with the canons of Ashridge, had ended a few years earlier with Bicester Priory being allowed to appropriate and inclose 3 acres of common in Wretchwick.[68]

Fourteenth-century records also show that there was much inclosed land, particularly in Wretchwick. Court rolls of 1343 and 1348 for Wretchwick, for instance, contain many fines for trespass in the lord's separate pasture,[69] and there is evidence that in addition to the Breach, there was a large 'New

---

51 Kennett, *Paroch. Antiq.* i. 188–9; ibid. 565–78 (translated in Dunkin, *Bic.* 215–29).

52 C 135/155/19.

53 C 135/101/6.

54 e.g. Kennett, *Paroch. Antiq.* ii. 186, 187. The ridges seem to have been divided by green balks if 17th-cent. evidence is valid for an earlier date, e.g. St. Edburg's balk was a green balk between plough-ridges on each side: ibid. i. 192.

55 Ibid. ii. 185–99, *passim*. No total for East Field is given but the number of acres, &c. in each furlong is stated. In the 18th-cent. these fields were called Home, Middle, and Further Fields: U.D.C. Market End map (1753) by Thos. Williams, and sketch-map, below, p. 29.

56 Blo. *Bic.* 204.

57 Kennett, *Paroch. Antiq.* i. 569–73.

58 Ibid. 575–6.

59 Ibid. ii. 85, 101.

60 Ibid. 85.

61 Ibid. 86.

62 Ibid. 83, 86.

63 Ibid. 101.

64 e.g. ibid. i. 575.

65 e.g. B.M. Add. Ch. 10613, printed in Kennett, *Paroch. Antiq.* i. 186–7.

66 B.M. Add. Ch. 10608, printed in Kennett, *Paroch. Antiq.* i. 333–4.

67 *Cal. Pat.* 1307–13, 131; for the Breach farm see below, p. 28.

68 B.M. Add. Ch. 10626; Kennett, *Paroch. Antiq.* i. 478–9. Cf. *V.C.H. Oxon.* v. 22.

69 Kennett, *Paroch. Antiq.* ii. 82, 100–1. The text is corrupt.

Close' which was later (1425) being farmed for as much as £3 6s. 8d.[70] There are also many references to closes on the Market End manor. The lord allowed the priory and also the lords of Caversfield's two manors rights in his separate pastures beyond Bucknell Bridge and the 'old ford'; in exchange he and the priory had pasture rights in Caversfield. In two other separate pasture grounds, called Twyfold More and Langford Hawes, the priory had had rights since its foundation.[71] In the early 15th century it was probably a shortage of pasture which led to the priory's being deprived of these rights, but in 1405 after protest it was given a demesne meadow, Cowbridge Mead, in exchange.[72]

There are signs that economic decline had already begun before the economy of the parish was disorganized by a very severe visitation of the Black Death in 1349. Rents from customary tenants on the Wretchwick manor amounted only to £3 6s. 8d. in 1345,[73] a good deal less than in 1296 or 1303, when the annual rent was over £4 3s. in addition to an aid each year of about £4.[74] The priory, indeed, may have been inclosing because of the difficulty of finding tenants: in 1345 vacant land was being leased for 23s. 5d. to men of Blackthorn in the neighbouring parish of Ambrosden.[75] Nevertheless, the decline must have been accelerated after 1349. The death-roll was clearly high: two priors and the parish priest died,[76] and Roger Lestrange's inquisition *post mortem* shows that the rents from the free tenants of his Market End manor had dropped from £5 12s. 5d. to £3 12s. owing to deaths in the pestilence.[77] Their lands lay 'fallow and uncultivated' and were valueless. The rents from villein tenants had dropped even more catastrophically; they were worth £1 instead of £4 2s. No new tenants could be found to take up the holdings of the dead men, 'for almost all the men in these parts are dead in this pestilence'. Cultivation of the demesne land suffered: only 5s. was forthcoming for the autumn works of the tenants. Both the toll from the market and the receipts from the court had diminished on account of the depopulation.

The first clear intimation of the disaster which had overtaken the whole parish, however, is the comparatively large tax abatements allowed in 1354. Wretchwick was remitted 4s., King's End (including Bignell) 3s., and Market End 2s. Only to Tusmore and Kirtlington in Ploughley hundred were larger sums remitted.[78] In 1356 and in later bursars' accounts of the priory there are references to the repayment of sums paid for the 15th,[79] and in 1412 part of Wretchwick's 15th for the 'prior's gift' was remitted.[80] The details given in the account for the year 1433–4 show that this hamlet had failed to recover its former prosperity: several tofts and

crofts had not been taken up that year and were in the lord's hand; only £2 3s. 4d. had been received from vacant lands, meadows, and pastures in Wretchwick fields, owing to the poverty of the tenants and because much land (*multe et quamplurime*) lay untilled. Fines levied in the manorial court were remitted and 3s. 4d. was given by the priory towards the payment of the 15th to the king.[81] A rental of 1432–7 giving the names of men renting tenements and crofts in Wretchwick shows that the community was small. Never more than ten names a year are listed. Moreover, vacant tenements are again in evidence. The rental for Michaelmas 1432 under the heading 'tofts and vacant crofts' lists 12 of which 10 were rented by other Wretchwick tenants and 2 were still vacant. It is significant that the rents of some of the 'vacant' tofts show a progressive decline. One, for instance, which was let for 4s. in Michaelmas 1432 was let for 2s. in Epiphany 1433.[82] Vacant land was again recorded in 1447, and in 1452 customary rents only amounted to £2 19s. 8d., while £1 15s. 5½d. was received from vacant land leased to men of Blackthorn 'to be sown'.[83] Part of this poverty was evidently due to murrain among the sheep and cattle, which was probably worse on the heavy clay soil of Wretchwick with its many streams than on the Cornbrash in the rest of the parish. It was recorded as 'grievous' in 1409, and 1446 and 1452 were other exceptionally bad agricultural years.[84] In 1412 there had been floods.[85]

Bignell also suffered from economic difficulties. In 1361 2½ virgates of villein land and four cottages were in the lord's hand for lack of tenants.[86]

It is likely that the lack of tenants in the 14th century encouraged an increase in sheep-farming. Sheep flocks had long been an important part of the economy on the priory lands. The priory's sheepfolds at Crockwell to the north of Bicester and at Wretchwick in the south are recorded in the 13th century,[87] and the prior had been among the religious from whom a loan, mainly on wool, had been demanded for the war with France in 1347.[88] In 1409 a new sheepcote and shepherd's house were built at Wretchwick, but it is not clear if this was an extension or merely a modernization of the old buildings.[89] At least by 1447 the priory had a grange near its Crockwell fold.[90] The surviving 15th-century accounts of the priory contain regular entries concerning the care of the sheep and the disposal of their products.[91] The guest house was supplied with mutton and lamb; skins and wool were sold. In 1424–5 the receipts from the sale of wool amounted to £11 10s. 6d. The chief purchaser was an Oxford merchant, who bought 23 tods of pure wool at 9s. 6d. the tod.[92] In 1447 as many as 28 men

[70] Dunkin, *Bic.* 235.
[71] Kennett, *Paroch. Antiq.* ii. 192, 197–9.
[72] Ibid. 220–1.
[73] Dunkin, *Oxon.* ii. 238.
[74] Blo. *Bic.* 136, 146. (The 1303 acct. was for 9 months and only the ½-yearly rents are entered.)
[75] Dunkin, *Bic.* 239.
[76] *V.C.H. Oxon.* ii. 95. Nicholas Brode, pst., admitted Dec. 1348, was dead by June 1349: MS. Top. Oxon. d 460.
[77] C 135/101/6.
[78] E 179/161/30.
[79] Blo. *Bic.* 159. See also ibid. 160; Dunkin, *Oxon.* ii. 236.
[80] Blo. *Bic.* 168.
[81] Ibid. 172–3.

[82] E 315/408, ff. 78–87. This is partly printed in M. Beresford, *Lost Villages of England*, 295–6.
[83] Blo. *Bic.* 182, 184.
[84] Ibid. 12 (1409 acct.); ibid. 181–7 (1447 and 1452 accts. *passim*).
[85] Ibid. 171.
[86] C 135/155/19. For 'old inclosures' at Bignell see Thos. Williams's map (1753), *infra* p. 29.
[87] The priory was given land in Crockwell for a sheepfold in *c.* 1220: Kennett, *Paroch. Antiq.* i. 260–1.
[88] *Cal. Close, 1345–9,* 268.
[89] Blo. *Bic.* 163.
[90] Ibid. 182.
[91] e.g. ibid. 164, 172, 180.
[92] Kennett, *Paroch. Antiq.* ii. 250.

and women were hired for sheep-washing at Wretchwick.[93]

Cattle as well as sheep were pastured in the Wretchwick closes. By the 15th century and probably earlier the Breach (an inclosure of 40 acres)[94] was being used as a dairy farm. An account of 1406–7 kept by Henry and Joan Dey, the dairyman and woman, gives details of the farm. The payment of 17s. 9d. to ploughmen shows that it was a mixed farm; cheese and butter worth £3 7s. 6d. were sold to the priory, and calves and old cows to the butchers of Bicester and Launton. The Deys' receipts were £4 13s. 7½d., and their expenses £7 7s. 5d.[95] In the year 1424–5 the bursars' account records the receipt of £1 15s. 6d. from the Deys, but by 1433–4 the system of running the farm with paid servants—the Deys' stipend was 13s. 4d.—had been abandoned and it was leased for £6 a year.[96]

A decision to inclose more land at Wretchwick appears to have been taken at the end of the 15th century. In 1517 the prior was accused of having pulled down five houses in the hamlet in the year 1489; it was said that he had inclosed 200 acres of arable there, and that he had converted to pasture the lands of the messuages, each messuage having at least 30 acres of arable land. Three plough-teams had thus been put out of work and eighteen persons had lost their livelihood; they were obliged to wander wretchedly (dolorose) and seek their bread elsewhere.[97] The alleged value of the land was £6 13s. 4d. A worse disaster overtook the canons themselves between 1520 and 1530. The community was mortally attacked by the sweating sickness. The sheep also died off and it was reported that there were few or none, and that the prior intended to buy as many as he could afford.[98] But demesne farming was by this time on a small scale. In 1535 the priory had only 49 acres of inclosed pasture and meadow, mostly in Wretchwick, in hand, and had leased for a term of years to a Bicester draper and others a number of closes, which had formerly been demesne land. The land in hand brought in £6 17s. 7d. The receipts from leased land were £22 4s.[99]

The process of inclosure may have continued during the second half of the century, but the evidence is contradictory. In 1608 the vicar complained in Chancery 'that whereas Wretchwick had been heretofore well manured and inhabited with at least 30 several tenants . . . whose small tithes would be worth 100 marks', the manor was depopulated owing to the misdeeds of the Blounts.[1] The defendants replied that any conversion to pasture, if any there was, was done before the dissolution of the priory.[2] Wretchwick, however, was certainly all inclosed long before the Parliamentary inclosure in the second half of the 18th century of Market End and King's End fields. A pre-inclosure map of 1753

of Bicester Fields shows that there were also already extensive inclosures, named King's End Mead and King's End Inclosure, in the Bignell or King's End Field. The present Bignell House, the supposed site of Bignell hamlet, was also surrounded by inclosed land. Indeed, the hamlet's final decline seems to have occurred during the 16th century. The evidence of the court rolls and the subsidy lists points to this. Until at least 1549 a Bignell tithing seems to have attended the Kirtlington leet court. In Henry VII's reign the hamlet's name appears on the roll. On the next surviving roll of 1515 it was presented that George Staveley and the inhabitants of his vill of Bignell had defaulted in their suit and there was a similar presentment in 1520.[3] Nevertheless Bignell though no longer separately entered appears to be included in the two tithings of King's End until the end of Henry VIII's reign, when a return was made to the old form of entry.[4] In Elizabethan times and later only two King's End tithings are ever represented instead of the former four.[5] By Elizabeth I's reign, too, the hamlet of Bignell had become too small to be assessed separately for taxation,[6] and by 1695 White Kennett wrote that there was only one farm left.[7]

The treatment of the common arable land seems to have been conservative. There are indications that some tenants on the Markyate manor had accumulated by sale or exchange numbers of contiguous strips by 1325, but for the most part holdings remained minutely subdivided, and in 1579 an account of Michael Blount's lands in King's End fields shows that his 29 acres were still almost all divided into ½-acre strips.[8] The court rolls of Kirtlington for the Tudor period and later also show that the open fields of King's End were being managed in the traditional way. The stint of sheep and horses was a common subject for regulation, and presentments for pasturing animals on prohibited grounds were frequent. In the first half of the 17th century Cadwallader Coker was several times presented for making small inclosures.[9] A roll of 1609 throws light on how the regulations, enrolled from time to time by the courts, were drawn up. It was then agreed that all the inhabitants of Bicester King's End and Bignell should meet at King's End cross on New Year's eve and agree 'upon some good orders', which were to be delivered to the steward.[10] An observation of Robert Plot's, however, shows that 17th-century farmers at Bicester could sometimes be inventive. He says that dry land was commonly broken with a beetle after harrowing, but that at Bicester they had a much quicker way and used a weighty octangular roll, 'the edges whereof meeting with the clods would break them effectually'.[11]

In 1758 the agricultural scene and practice were transformed by inclosure. Sir Edward Turner and

[93] Blo. Bic. 183.
[94] This was its 16th-cent. extent: MS. Top. Oxon. b 42, ff. 53–62.
[95] Kennett, Paroch. Antiq. ii. 211–14. Cf. acct. 1407–8: ibid. 214–15.
[96] Ibid. 248; Blo. Bic. 172.
[97] Domesday of Incl. i. 340.
[98] Visit. Dioc. Linc. 1517–31, ii. 81.
[99] Valor Eccl. (Rec. Com.), ii. 187, 189. The details of the closes and their lessees are given in L. & P. Hen. VIII, xiv(1), p. 251; MS. Top. Oxon. b 42, ff. 53–62 (e.g. Winter Pasture (44 a.), Weston Heyes (40½ a.)).
[1] The Blounts had obtained 11 yardlands in Market End and King's End in 1586–7: MS. Top. Oxon. b 42, f. 53.

[2] Kennett, Paroch. Antiq. ii. 224–32.
[3] Bodl. MS. D.D. Dashwood (Oxon.) a 1.
[4] e.g. in 35, 36, and 38 Hen. VIII: ibid.
[5] Ibid. and ibid. c 1.
[6] E 179/162/33. Only 3 persons (the lord and 2 peasants) were taxed in Bignell in 1524: E 179/161/198.
[7] Kennett, Paroch. Antiq. ii. 156.
[8] Ibid. i. 565 sqq.; Bodl. MS. ch. Oxon. 4005. Little change had been made in the holdings in King's End Field by 1753: see Bic. U.D.C. map by Thos. Williams.
[9] e.g. Oct. ct. 1631: Bodl. MS. D.D. Dashwood (Oxon.) c 1.
[10] Oct. ct. 1609: ibid.
[11] Plot, Nat. Hist. Oxon. 248.

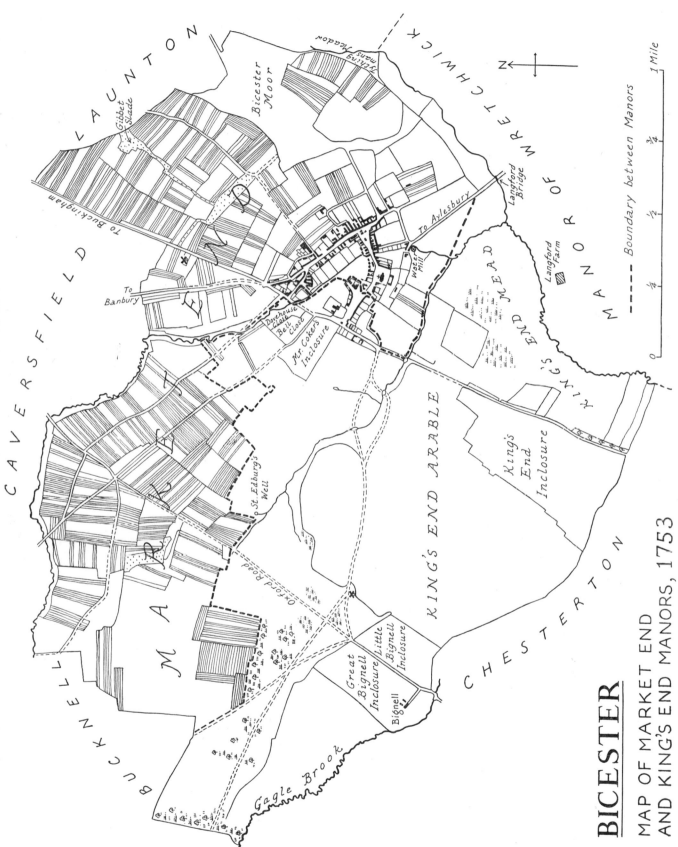

BICESTER

MAP OF MARKET END
AND KING'S END MANORS, 1753

The above map is from a survey by Thomas Williams made before the inclosure of Market End fields. King's End fields were not surveyed

---- Boundary between Manors

0 ¼ ½ ¾ 1 Mile

Map labels: LAUNTON, CAVERSFIELD, BUCKNELL, MARKET END, KING'S END ARABLE, KING'S END MEAD, MANOR OF WRETCHWICK, CHESTERTON, Bicester Moor, Wretchmans Meadow, Gibbet Slade, To Buckingham, To Banbury, To Aylesbury, Langford Bridge, Langford Farm, King's End Inclosure, Water Mill, Dovehouse Close, Bell Close, Mr. Coker's Inclosure, St. Edburg's Well, Oxford Road, Great Bignell Inclosure, Little Bignell Inclosure, Bignell, Gagle Brook

others had obtained an act for inclosing the field and commons of Market End in 1757.[12] By the award Sir Edward received about 230 acres and Christopher Metcalfe about 236 acres out of a total of some 1,200 acres. There were four allotments of between 99 and 62 acres; four of 30 to 20 acres, and 27 allottees received smaller allotments, some of a few rods only. Nine men were given 2 rods in the Moor as compensation for loss of common rights for a horse and cow.[13]

It was not until 1793 that an act was obtained for inclosing the common land at King's End, on the grounds that the land of the proprietors was so dispersed in small parcels as 'to be incapable of any considerable improvement'.[14] The award was made in 1794. The area inclosed was 1,302 acres; the chief allottees were John Coker, who as lord of the manor was entitled to the waste and common pasture 'by determinate stints' (631 a.); Sir Gregory Page-Turner, the lay rector (168 a.); the vicar (54 a.), and Dame Elizabeth Dashwood, who held the residue of the open land (433 a.). Some small allotments of 10 acres and under were made to Richard Pates, the churchwardens, the constable, and the tithingmen.[15]

At the turn of the century Bicester fields were on the whole exceptionally well farmed. John Coker, with land at neighbouring Wendlebury as well as at Bicester, had large-scale dairy farms. He kept a breed of long-horned cattle, which was considered particularly suitable for the poorish soil, and was noted for his butter and cheese production.[16] The whole district was in fact reputed for its butter, and Arthur Young recorded that weekly wagons of butter were sent to London. William Forster at Bignell was another successful farmer; Young considered him 'one of the best cultivators in the country'. His long-horned cattle fetched high prices; his cross-bred sheep were successful; and he was exceptional in using heifers for ploughing. He experimented in grass seeds—white clover, hay seeds, and sainfoin. The last he valued highly and grew much of it. He used the Norfolk four-course rotation of turnips, barley or oats, clover, and wheat. Young especially admired him for sinking so much capital in the thorough drainage of his land: he dug drains 4 feet deep, by blasting with gunpowder.[17]

After inclosure the arable was normally divided into seven parts, $\frac{1}{7}$th under sainfoin, $\frac{2}{7}$ths under seeds, $\frac{3}{7}$ths under corn, and $\frac{1}{7}$th under turnips.[18] The new crops most commonly used were turnips and clover, though some continued with the old rotation of wheat, beans, and barley, common on the strong land before inclosure.[19] Rents of farm land at Bicester trebled at the end of the 18th century, but nevertheless by the 1820's agriculture in the parish was suffering from a severe depression.[20] The national need in the Napoleonic War had led to a great expansion of arable farming, and population had greatly increased. Now the market had collapsed

and in 1822 owners and occupiers of land met at the 'Cross Keys' and passed a number of resolutions on the distressed state of agriculture. They regretted their inability to employ their increasing number of labourers, 'whose miserable and degraded subsistence is now derived from parochial contributions, tending to make them dangerous members in society and disloyal subjects'. Meanwhile the committee of the Bicester Agricultural Association was preparing petitions to both Houses opposing the free importation of agricultural goods from Ireland.[21] Later in the century, in the 1860's, it was reported that Bicester was predominantly a grazing parish and 'a great many men' were out of work and that some left their homes altogether to seek employment elsewhere during the summer months.[22]

The pattern of land-holding in the late 18th and early 19th centuries showed little change. The influence of the town and bailiwick in Market End fields was noticeable. In 1786 there were about 140 owners, of which 64 were owner-occupiers. The only big landowner was Sir Gregory Page-Turner; out of a total land tax of £411 16s. 11d. (of which £20 came from Excise duty), he paid over £171. He leased his land to eleven tenants. The return for 1800 gives details about some of the small town owners: typical of them was Sarah Penrose with her tax of £2 12s. for her house and 10s. for the surrounding land, which was let to two tenants. By 1816 owner-occupiers had increased to about 85, and in 1832 it is stated that 'all the estates and property in this township consist of about 62 freeholds and the remainder is held by leases for long terms of years at peppercorn rents (if demanded)' of 1d. a year, dating originally from 1597. In King's End there were 18 owners of whom 7 were owner-occupiers. There were 19 tenants and the total land tax amounted to about £92. The largest landowners were the Revd. Mr. Coker, paying over £42, Sir Henry Dashwood, paying over £29, and Sir Gregory Page-Turner, paying £11 odd. By 1816 Dashwood had sold his land to John Coker and others.[23]

By 1851 there were some largish farms: Langford farm in Wretchwick, for instance, comprised 500 acres and employed 14 men; King's End Field farm in Bignell comprised 400 acres and employed 13 men and another King's End farm was over 400 acres. There were at least ten other farms of between 100 and 260 acres.[24] Mr. C. T. Hoare, who bought Bignell House and park in 1884, was a well-known farmer. By 1929 he farmed about 1,460 acres and kept a fine stud of shire horses and a large flock of Hampshire Down sheep. He laid down extensive plantations in and around the park.[25]

In 1881 the Ordnance Survey map marked nine farms. In 1955 there were still nine, but most of the land belonging to Home farm had been taken for the Western Development Scheme, and the War Office had bought land from Manor, Langford, and Wretchwick farms for the Arncot Depot.[26]

[12] O.R.O. Incl. award, Market End. There had been 35 resident freeholders in 1754: *Oxon. Poll, 1754.*
[13] 30 Geo II, c. 7 (priv. act): copy in Bodl. G.A. Oxon. a 117.
[14] 33 Geo. III, c. 45 (priv. act): copy in Bodl. L. Engl. C 13 c 1 (1793. ii. 4).
[15] O.R.O. Incl. award, King's End.
[16] Young, *Oxon. Agric.* 274, 278.
[17] Ibid. 50, 97, 114, 198, 218, 244, 275, 306.
[18] For a discussion of the layout of the new farms in

this district see H. Wyndham, *A Backward Glance* (1950), 17.
[19] Young, *Oxon. Agric.* 127.
[20] Ibid. 91.
[21] *Oxf. Jnl.* 12 Jan. 1822.
[22] *Agric. Rep.* 358.
[23] O.R.O. Land tax assess.
[24] H.O. 107/1729.
[25] Inf. Major A. G. C. Fane.
[26] Local inf.

MILLS. In 1086 two mills together valued at £2 were recorded as part of the D'Oilly holding.[27] These mills are later found attached to Wretchwick and Market End manors.

In about 1180 Gilbert Basset gave a little meadow and a mill-pond to Bicester Priory so that it might make a mill on the site of the old one or near by. The flow of water had been recently increased.[28] Later Basset consented to an agreement made between the prior and Basset's men of Wretchwick whereby the men were granted 2 acres of meadow at the head of their crofts beside the stream, so that they might make a mill-pond and a way to the mill. It was agreed that if the mill should be abandoned the acres were to be returned to the canons, who undertook to level the ground as before.[29] The agreement was confirmed in 1315 by the king.[30] The mill continued in the canons' possession until the Dissolution.[31] It was afterwards granted to Roger Moore with the priory buildings and estate. It was then valued with the Bell Inn at £6 14s.[32] It followed the descent of the manor of the Moore family and passed to the Blounts, the Glynnes and Turners.[33] In 1609 when the Blounts were in possession it was valued at £4 14s.[34] It was situated in Water Lane (later Chapel Street), where the mill stream can still (1956) be seen.

The other Domesday mill was given by William Longespée to the priory in c. 1245.[35] It was then held of him by a free tenant Robert Puff, whose family was to continue as millers for several generations.[36] The grant to the priory reserved free multure to Puff and his heirs.[37] A confirmatory charter by the overlord in 1286 reveals that there had been some evasion of suit to this mill by the tenants of Wretchwick manor. A fine of two 'sous' was ordered to be imposed on those who carried corn elsewhere.[38] In 1279 the Puffs were paying a rent of 5s.,[39] a rent which exceeded any in the district, probably because the custom of the townsmen made the mill valuable. This mill lay on the stream near Langford Bridge on the Aylesbury road, and traces of it could be seen in the 1880's.[40]

The priory accounts contain numerous references to a water-mill, but whether they are to both mills or only to the Water Lane one is uncertain. In 1326–7, for instance, freestone, lime, and iron were purchased for the mill-gate; in Richard II's reign a great wheel and a cog-wheel were renewed; in 1424–5 and again in 1432–3, 26s. 8d. was received for the lease of the Water Lane mill.[41]

Besides the water-mills, there was a horse-mill within the priory grounds for the convent's own special use. This was farmed in 1407–8 for £4 13s. 4d. and in 1411–12 for £4.[42] In 1424–5 only 36s. was obtained for the farm on account of the falsity of the miller, who after occupying it for a half-year and more fled without making any payment.[43] In 1432–3 the bursar recorded the receipt of £6 4s. 4d. from the horse-mill, then in the priory's hands.[44] It was last recorded in 1545.[45] It must have been one of these mills which the prior leased to the Couplands (or Coplands) at some date before 1535, when Margery Coupland was imprisoned in Wallingford jail for sedition.[46]

There was also a windmill. It is first recorded in 1285–6, when Henry de Lacy gave his Bicester windmill to the priory.[47] In 1396–7 this mill was either renewed or a new one was erected at a cost of £20 14s.[48] It was made by a carpenter named William Thompson and full details of its construction are given on the account roll. The following points may be noted here: 'Estrygebord' and canvas for the sails had to be bought in London; two millstones were bought at Islip; iron came from Banbury; keys were made at Woodstock and Bicester.[49] The mill was farmed this year for 26s. 8d., but in the year 1411–12 nothing was received because the mill had been assigned with the prior's consent as an endowment for William Hayle's chantry.[50] It may have been on the site of the one shown in a map of 1753, which lies to the north-east of the town.[51]

Another windmill belonged to Bignell manor. It is first recorded in 1279 when it was worth 13s. 4d.[52] In about 1280 Alice de Langley, lady of Bignell, granted a building site in the town, but reserved suit of court and of mill with all wheat and barley.[53] The descent of this mill followed that of Bignell manor.[54] The surviving court rolls of the Tudor period often refer to the Staveleys' miller. In 1521–2, for example, he was presented for taking excessive toll.[55] The mill is known to have been in use in the 1570's, when Thomas Staveley was lord.[56] It appears to have passed with other land in Bignell manor to the Cokers: in 1819 they were stated to have two windmills, one possibly Bignell mill and the other the onetime priory mill.[57] A 'post windmill', which was at work and up for sale in 1836, may have been one of these two.[58] A windmill near the Middleton road in King's End (or Bignell) field was finally blown down in 1881.[59] It was clearly the one depicted by Thomas Williams on his map of 1753.

MARKETS AND FAIRS. William de Longespée obtained from the king in 1239 the grant of a market

[27] V.C.H. Oxon. i. 413.
[28] Kennett, Paroch. Antiq. i. 186. The miller's name was Gilbert: B.M. Add. Ch. 10593.
[29] Kennett, Paroch. Antiq. i. 188–9.
[30] Cal. Pat. 1313–17, 359.
[31] Valor Eccl. (Rec. Com.), ii. 187. Margery Copland was leasing the 'Bell' and the priory mill for £6 8s.
[32] E 318/772/4.
[33] See above, pp. 22, 23.
[34] L.R. 2/197.
[35] Kennett, Paroch. Antiq. i. 333–4.
[36] White Kennett prints a number of charters relating to this family: see ibid. ii, index of persons.
[37] Ibid. i. 333–4.
[38] B.M. Add. Ch. 10624 (transcribed in MS. Top. Oxon. c 398, ff. 132–3).
[39] Rot. Hund. (Rec. Com.), ii. 828.
[40] Blo. Bic. 2 n. 1.
[41] Ibid. 154, 155, 161, 172; Dunkin, Bic. 234.

[42] Blo. Bic. 162, 167. The same sum was received in 1429–30: Bodl. G.A. Oxon. a 117, f. 16 (11 b).
[43] Kennett, Paroch. Antiq. ii. 248.
[44] Blo. Bic. 172.
[45] C.P. 25(2)/34/230/East. 37 Hen. VIII.
[46] L. & P. Hen. VIII, viii, p. 323.
[47] E 210/5533.
[48] Dunkin, Oxon. ii. 229–30.
[49] Blo. Bic. 162–3.
[50] Ibid. 167.
[51] See map on p. 29.
[52] Rot. Hund. (Rec. Com.), ii. 839.
[53] Kennett, Paroch. Antiq. i. 417–18.
[54] See above, p. 23.
[55] Bodl. MS. D.D. Dashwood (Oxon.) a 1, f. 25; cf. ff. 4, 23.
[56] C 3/160/72.
[57] C.P. 43/944/234.
[58] Oxf. Jnl. 23 Jan. 1836.
[59] Blo. Bic. 66.

for his Bicester manor.[60] As the jurors stated at the inquiry of 1279 that Henry III had granted the market, it is probable that this was the original grant and not a confirmation.[61] De Longespée like other founders of market-towns no doubt hoped to profit from the market dues and an increase in rents. The vill already enjoyed certain advantages which might be expected to assist its development: it lay at the meeting of two of the main lines of communication between the south and the Midlands;[62] as a part of the honor of Wallingford it shared in the privileges of the honor, and its tenants were free from toll and other dues normally exacted from traders in 'foreign markets' as well as from many royal taxes.[63] The presence of the monastery, moreover, and the maintenance of a household not only for the canons themselves but for visitors of all ranks, guaranteed a constant demand.

The grant of the market was followed in 1252 by a licence to hold a fair for three days on and about the feast of St. Edburg (18 July).[64] There is no direct evidence that the earl offered traders any special privileges beyond the free market, but it is more than likely that he tried to attract settlement by offering building sites in return for money rents only. Indeed, early charters show that some of the inhabitants enjoyed a privileged form of tenure resembling burgess tenure; they might give or sell their tenements freely to anyone (religious men and Jews are sometimes excepted); they owed no service beyond an annual rent, which was sometimes one of 12d., an amount common in newly founded towns of this period.[65] In some cases houses were granted with the right to bequeath freely, and there is also at least one instance of a grant with a clause, often found in charters relating to urban property, which stipulates that if the grantee should wish to sell then he must first offer the property to the grantor or his heirs at a lower price than to others.[66]

The venture was successful. A community developed which was far larger than that of the ordinary agrarian village and which must have depended to some extent on trade. The Hundred Rolls apparently omit all record of the market community, but it is significant that among the villein tenants of the earl and the prior were three called Chapman, who held only $\frac{1}{2}$ or $\frac{1}{4}$ virgate each, and that one of the five cottars of Wretchwick, who paid rent only, was Philip the Merchant. One of the few free tenants recorded was Robert Clerk, the local scribe,[67] whose brother, William the Shipman, was apprenticed in London.[68] Other surnames show that families from the neighbouring villages of Cottisford, Stratton, Wendlebury, and Drayton (Bucks.) had been attracted to Bicester. But the first definite evidence for the

growth of the market comes from an extent of 1310, which records the comparatively large number of 22 free tenants, rendering £3 15s. 8d. and probably 'living on the market', and a Friday market worth £1.[69] The early 14th-century tax lists, with a high number of contributors in Bicester Market End compared with those in Bignell or King's End, and the relatively large sum at which the parish as a whole was assessed, are, however, the best evidence for the progress which had been made. In 1316 the total tax was over £16 and in 1344 £18 8s. 11d., compared with £11 17s. 9d. paid by Charlton and its two hamlets, which was the heaviest-taxed rural parish in the hundred.[70] But the community remained too humble a one to make any effort to obtain self-government. In 1327 the largest contribution from a townsman was 3s., except for that of Jacob Daniel, who was surely a Jew.[71] Many of Bicester's traders were also partly dependent on agriculture, for their charters show that some had 'great gates' to their town houses, which probably opened on to yards for cattle and horses, and that they had many acres in the fields. Even so they were less well off than many of the inhabitants of rural villages.[72] The limited scope of the market at this time is, moreover, indirectly revealed by the priory accounts. They make few specific references to it, and though probably more was bought and sold in Bicester than appears, it is clear that for all luxuries and for most necessities the priory went regularly to other markets and fairs in Oxfordshire, Buckinghamshire, or Northamptonshire as well as to the annual Stourbridge fair.[73]

Notable among the trade names recorded in the 14th century are the following: barker, currier, skinner, glover, fuller, dyer, webber.[74] There are some references to individual tradesmen such as Richard Skinner, who purchased skins; Thomas Tanner and 'other merchants in the market', who bought ox-hides; Robert Brasier, who sold red wine, and Thomas Draper, who sold cloth hoods.[75] At least one foreigner was settled in the town by the early 15th century—the Brabanter Hans Taillour of 'Merebek', and it is possible that the Gilbert Janekyns taxed in 1316 may have been an earlier immigrant.[76]

The severity of the Black Death of 1349 both in Bicester parish and the surrounding villages considerably reduced Market End's prosperity.[77] The toll from the market fell off and was stated to be 'no more than 30s. on account of the pestilence'.[78] It is possible that the market suffered further loss after 1377, when the king granted Sir John de Worthe of Bignell a Monday market and a three-day fair about the feast of St. James (25 July),[79] but although it was customary for markets not to be set up within

60 See above, p. 22; *Cal. Chart. R.* 1226–57, 247.
61 *Rot. Hund.* (Rec. Com.), ii. 828.
62 See above, p. 14.
63 Blo. *Bic.* 3.
64 *Cal. Chart. R.* 1226–57, 413.
65 e.g. Kennett, *Paroch. Antiq.* i. 364, 373–4, 380, 417; B.M. Add. Ch. 10632. In 1739 the phrase 'a burgage or tenement' occurs in the lease of a house in Water Lane: O.R.O. Misc. Pe IV/19.
66 Kennett, *Paroch. Antiq.* i. 364, 373–4, 377–8.
67 *Rot. Hund.* (Rec. Com.), ii. 827–8. For Robert Clerk see Kennett, ii, index of persons.
68 Kennett, *Paroch. Antiq.* ii. 72–73, 133.
69 C 134/22.
70 See below, p. 358.
71 E 179/161/9.

72 e.g. Kennett, *Paroch. Antiq.* ii. 105, 108–9. In 1340–1 it was stated that there were no men or merchants without land and farm stock: Blo. *Bic.* 98. For comparative wealth see E 179/161/8 and 9 for contributions paid by rural tenants in other parishes in 1316 and 1327.
73 Priory accts. *passim*, e.g. Blo. *Bic.* 110 n. 6, 137, 140, 141, 157, 169, 174.
74 e.g. Kennett, *Paroch. Antiq.* ii. 70–71, 93, 95, 112–13.
75 Blo. *Bic.* 168, 203; Kennett, *Paroch. Antiq.* ii. 254; *Cal. Close*, 1409–13, 195.
76 *Cal. Pat.* 1429–36, 577; E 179/161/8.
77 Cf. above, p. 27, and below, p. 247.
78 C 135/101/6.
79 *Cal. Chart. R.* 1341–1417, 235. As no poll-tax figures have survived for Market End, there is no clue to the number of inhabitants at this date.

five miles of one another, there is no record that the lord of Market End protested against the infringement of his market rights. The Bignell market was confirmed to its lords in 1439 and 1463–4, but is not heard of later.[80] In 1441 a 'new' Friday market in Bicester Market End was granted to the king's servant Robert Brooke for life. He was to have picage, stallage, boothage, and toll with the assize of bread and ale and all the profits therefrom for an annual 6s. 8d. to the king.[81] There is no recorded explanation of this 'new market'. It is possible that it refers to the beginning of the Sheep Street Market for sheep and cattle (see below), the old market continuing as a general market in Market Square. The lordship of the market continued in the possession of the lords of Market End manor.

Evidence from the 16th and 17th centuries indicates that the town was prospering. Out of the 108 contributors in the parish to the subsidy of 1524, 84 were listed under Market End and 21 under King's End. Many farmers and peasants, of course, lived in both ends of Bicester, but the majority of contributors in both parts must have been traders and craftsmen.[82] Indeed, when Leland visited Bicester about this time, he especially commented on the 'common market', and in 1622 an anonymous writer described Bicester as a 'very good market for all manner of cattle and well supplied with all kinds of trades'.[83] By this time the market was no longer controlled by the lord of the manor, but by a bailiff appointed by the various purchasers, some of them tradesmen, of the Earl of Derby's manorial rights. The owners of the bailiwick, as it was called, did not enjoy corporate rights and the absence of incorporation was said to be an advantage to traders.[84] Towards the end of the 17th century White Kennett, who had lived in Bicester, wrote that the Friday market was 'a great resort and a good vend for all country commodities, especially all sorts of cattle', which were sold in Sheep Street.[85]

The market's prosperity, however, was seriously checked in the 18th century, when the smallpox epidemic of 1704 nearly ruined it. Grass grew in the market-place so that it looked like 'a meadow'.[86] This disaster was followed by the great fire of 1724, which destroyed quantities of stores of malt, barley, beans, oats, tobacco, flax, hemp, hay, candles, household and other goods. The loss was computed at £2,231.[87] In the middle of the century Sir Edward Turner's Horned Cattle Bill inflicted another blow. In 1752 he wrote that Bicester 'hath suffered more than any other in the county by the prohibition of markets'.[88] In 1790, however, the market could still be described as large, and the spring and autumn markets for the sale of sheep as 'very large', with graziers coming from distances of 20 miles.[89] In the early 19th century 300 to 500 sheep and 40 to 50 cattle were still brought to the market each fortnight, but as a general market for butter, cheese, and other commodities it had declined.[90] The decline was accelerated by the severe cholera outbreak of 1832, which inflicted lasting damage. It cost over £700 to overcome and resulted 'in a total stagnation of trade'.[91]

Bicester's industries were the product of the custom attracted to the town by the market. Local produce—wool, skins, barley—encouraged particular trades such as glove-making, saddle-making, tanning, and malting, while those dependent on wool were many.[92] The clothworker, fuller, weaver, woolman, woollen draper, and clothier are found in 17th-century records.[93] The following tradesmen are among the many others also recorded in this period: draper, linendraper, collarmaker, fellmonger, cordwainer, joiner, bodicemaker, slatter, plumber, mason, chandler, hempdresser, mercer, grocer, and grazier.[94] Two mercers, it may be noted, a vintner, a glover, and a tanner were among the town's aristocracy at the beginning of the 17th century.[95] Many townsmen were, of course, poor men, who left at their death chattels worth £6 and less,[96] but the feltmaker, whose stock of hats, hatbands, and household goods was valued at about £55 in 1637, was representative of a substantial number of lower-middle-class men.[97] Some like Thomas Paxton, haberdasher, left goods valued at over £260, and in 1688 when a Bicester collarmaker petitioned the justices for help, because of the destruction of his house and stock by fire, his property was valued at £195.[98] A minor indication of trading activity is the special 'tokens' which were issued by some tradesmen in the second half of the century. Two of the influential Clements family—one a grocer and the other a draper—were among those to do so.[99] This family had tried to acquire sole control of the market and other manorial rights, and though defeated theirs must have been a predominant influence in the town.[1] In 1665 Richard Clements and William Potter paid tax on nine and twelve hearths, the highest numbers recorded except for those of the lord of the manor, Sir John Glynn, and two gentlemen.

A large proportion of the town's inhabitants who were taxed had houses with three hearths or less and

[80] *Cal. Pat.* 1436–41, 288; ibid. 1461–7, 276.
[81] *Cal. Pat.* 1436–41, 550. It is assumed that the market was in Market End as payment was made to the receiver of the Duchy of Cornwall. It was still being called the 'new market' in 1628: C 66/2472.
[82] E 179/161/204. Market End included Wretchwick, then depopulated. There were three contributors at Bignell. Cf. E 179/162/222 for King's End including Bignell.
[83] Leland, *Itin.* ed. Toulmin Smith, ii. 34; Kennett, *Paroch. Antiq.* ii. 424.
[84] Blo. *Bic.* 23. For the bailiwick see above, p. 22, and below, p. 36.
[85] Kennett, *Paroch. Antiq.* ii. 156.
[86] Dunkin, *Bic.* 128.
[87] Ibid. 181.
[88] L. Dickins and M. Stanton, *An 18th Century Correspondence* (1910), 211.
[89] *Universal British Dir. of Trade, Commerce, and Merchandise* (London 1790), ii. 471.
[90] Blo. *Bic.* 53; cf. Dunkin, *Bic.* 128 n.

[91] *Oxf. Jnl.* 11 Aug. 1832; cf. Oxf. Dioc. c 454, ff. 63, 64, for the postponement of the bishop's visitation.
[92] e.g. O.R.O. Misc. Pe IV/12; ibid. II/6; ibid. IV/1; Bodl. MS. Wills Oxon. 204, f. 18; ibid. 205, f. 19; ibid. 18 (Jas. Dodd, 1671); ibid. 107, f. 130; ibid. 199, f. 193; ibid. 193, f. 248; ibid. 106, f. 119; ibid. 196, f. 175.
[93] e.g. Bodl. MS. Wills Oxon. 1 (H. Alexander, 1631); ibid. 196, f. 94; ibid. 107, f. 211; ibid. 107, f. 140; ibid. 205, f. 274; O.R.O. Misc. Bea I/2.
[94] e.g. O.R.O. Misc. Pe IV/13; ibid. Be I/9; ibid. Bea I/7; ibid. Pe IV/8; ibid. Pe II/4; Bodl. MS. Wills Oxon. 204, f. 124; ibid. 13 (J. Cooper, 1661); ibid. 106, f. 82; ibid. 208, f. 172; ibid. 93, f. 367; ibid. 208, f. 71; ibid. 205, f. 307; ibid. 93, f. 253.
[95] Bic. U.D.C. deed.
[96] e.g. Bodl. MS. Wills Oxon. 84 (T. Page, 1698).
[97] Ibid. 107, f. 46.
[98] Ibid. 199, f. 7; O.R.O. Cal. Q. Sess. iii. 294.
[99] Blo. *Bic.* 24.
[1] See above, p. 22, and below, p. 37.

so were less well housed than many a yeoman farmer. Of the 88 householders listed in Market End, sixteen were discharged on account of poverty. Six were listed in King's End.[2] In 1662 the tax had been paid by 124 in Market End and King's End together.[3] Of the real poor, who would certainly be more numerous in a town than in a village, there is no record. The value of the hearth-tax returns for the population of Bicester is dubious. A list of suitors of King's End to the Kirtlington court of 1592 gives 27 persons of which 26 bear different surnames; a list of about 1750 gives 41 names, 37 having different surnames. The hearth tax of 1662 lists only 12 names.[4] The figure of 844 adults given by the Compton Census of 1676 probably represents the total population of Bicester rather than the adult population, but as no nonconformists were recorded in this stronghold of nonconformity, the number is almost certainly an under-estimate.[5] A calculation based on Blomfield's analysis of the parish registers shows that the population increased little between 1670 and 1750. There were 3,440 baptisms as against 3,298 burials. Epidemics and infantile diseases (the number of monumental tablets in the church to young children is noticeable) helped to prevent growth until the last decades of the 18th century, when there was a definite advance. Between 1770 and 1800 there were 1,674 baptisms and 1,253 burials.[6] The incumbents' returns during the 18th century also indicate that there was an upward trend: they reported 200 houses in the 'town' in 1759; 400 or 500 in 1771; and 423 families and 2,046 souls in 1808.[7] The official census figures for 1801 had been 1,946.

With the 18th century new trades such as the peruke-maker's appeared and some exponents of old crafts acquired a more than local fame.[8] John Warcus, carpenter, who was employed at the Fermors' house at Tusmore in about 1789, should be noted.[9] His family was well established in Bicester at least by 1747, when William Warcus had a 'handsome dwelling house' and sought licence to make a small gallery for himself in the church.[10] The Hemins family should also be noted. At the end of the 17th century Edward Hemins, senior, made Islip's church clock and others.[11] His son Edward (d. 1744), who made lantern, long-case, and turret clocks, added bellfounding to the family business and supplied bells to Oriel College, All Saints' and St. Clement's churches in Oxford as well as to Ardley and a number of other villages in Oxfordshire, Buckinghamshire, and Northamptonshire. The

market bell, which once hung in Bicester shambles and is now at the Garth, was also made by him. The business closed in 1743 after casting a bell for Ambrosden,[12] but Bell Lane, where the business was, remains. Another notable clockmaker was William Ball, who was working round about 1760.[13] The family continued in the trade into the 19th century.[14] William Musselwhite was another late-18th-century clockmaker and Thomas Tomlinson was working at the end of the 18th century and in the early 19th century.[15]

The town derived great benefit from improved communications. The construction of turnpikes was followed by that of the Oxford canal in 1790 with a wharf at Lower Heyford, six miles away. This was particularly valuable as it brought Bicester into direct connexion with the Wednesbury collieries and ensured a supply of cheap coal.[16] The railway followed in 1850. Minor manufactories in the 18th century were concerned with clothing, sacking, and leather slippers. The manufacture of sackcloth and the combing of jersey, which had been important, were declining by 1790, when most of the poor were being employed in the lace trade.[17] At this time the manufacture of the common leather slipper was the town's most important business. *The Universal British Directory of Trade* noted that it is supposed that at Bicester 'more are made than in any other place in the kingdom'. The directory's list of Bicester trades includes lacemen, sackcloth-makers, soap-boilers, breeches-makers, stay-makers, hemp-dressers, a flaxdresser, a wool-sorter, a mantua-maker, a basket-maker, a cabinet-maker and all the common trades.[18]

Many of the town's traditional crafts suffered from the industrial revolution, otherwise the town was only indirectly affected. Its population in 1801 was under 2,000, and nearly half those gainfully employed were agricultural workers. By 1891 the peak figure for the century of 3,343 was reached.[19] Agriculture continued to be Bicester's chief occupation. The census of 1851 revealed that it employed the largest number of workers; the next largest group consisted of carpenters and masons. The mason's was an old trade: the priory had used a quarry at Crockwell throughout the Middle Ages, and in 1700 'Bissiter paving' was used in building the offices of Winslow Hall (Bucks.).[20] In the mid-19th century the women of the poorer classes were mainly employed in the home industries of lacemaking, dressmaking, tailoring, and millinery.[21] Lacemaking, however, is said to have declined somewhat in the

[2] E 179/164/513. Another roll for 1665 (E 179/164/514) omits those entered as 'discharged' in the preceding roll, otherwise its total of names would be higher.

[3] E. 179/255/4. For purposes of taxation Market End was assessed at about three times as much as King's End, e.g. in 1667 Market End paid £60 18s. 4d. and King's End £19 11s. 8d.: E 179/164/515.

[4] Bodl. MS. D.D. Dashwood (Oxon.) a 1; ibid. c 1; E 179/164/504. The Kirtlington figures show a similar discrepancy: 47 householders were listed in 1665 and a list of 'parishioners' of 1753, who were also suitors to the court, gives 88 names of which 69 have different surnames.

[5] Compton Census.

[6] Blo. *Bic.* 45.

[7] Oxf. Dioc. d 555, d 561, d 570; *Census,* 1801.

[8] Bodl. MS. Wills Oxon. 205, f. 274 (a periwig-maker and a woollen draper are witnesses). For other trades see O.R.O. Cal. Q. Sess. ii, parish index; ibid. Bic. deeds, e.g. Misc. Pe IV/17, 18, 19; ibid. Be I/6, 46; ibid. Be II/1

(mantle-maker); *Universal Brit. Dir.* (1790); and list of volunteers (1803) in MS. Top. Oxon. c 223.

[9] John Dunkin's MS. Diary cited in *Bic. Advertiser,* 12 Apr. 1901.   [10] Oxf. Dioc. c 434, f. 20.

[11] For him see F. J. Britten, *Old Clocks and Watches* (5th edn.), 708.

[12] Article by F. Sharpe, *Bic. Advertiser,* 11 May 1951.

[13] Britten, *Old Clocks,* 544, 638, where there is an illustration of his work.

[14] MS. Top. Oxon. c 223.

[15] Inf. Dr. C. Beeson, Adderbury, who has three clocks by W. Ball and E. Hemins in his collection. Another clock by Hemins is in the Painted Room, Oxford.

[16] See below, p. 182.

[17] *Universal Brit. Dir.* (1790), ii. 471.   [18] Ibid.

[19] *Census,* 1801, 1891.

[20] e.g. Kennett, *Paroch. Antiq.* ii. 254: acct. roll (1424–5); and see priory accts. *passim;* Wren Soc. xvii. 60–61.

[21] H.O. 107/1729.

early part of the century and to have been replaced by the new business of straw-plaiting, a subsidiary to the manufacture of straw hats.[22] This represented a social improvement, for lacemaking was regarded by enlightened persons as detrimental to the health of women and children. The ancient craft of brewing was by now conducted on a fairly large scale. Two brewers and seven maltsters were listed early in the century and by 1846 Shillingford's brewery, which acquired a considerable reputation, had been established.[23] In 1866 the manufacture of pale ale along with clothing and sacking were mentioned as Bicester's three chief manufactures by Fullarton's *Imperial Gazetteer*.

As an antidote to beer the 19th century encouraged popular reading. In 1846 Bicester had eleven booksellers and stationers, one of whom had 'news and reading rooms', while there was also a Depository for Christian Knowledge.[24] A small printing business had been in existence since 1790 and its owner, George Smith, had published the first *Bicester Directory* in 1819. The first local newspaper, the *Bicester Advertiser*, appeared in 1855 and the *Bicester Herald* four months later. The first was discontinued in 1866, but restarted in 1879; the other, published for most of its existence by George Hewiett or his son, came to an end in 1917. Two more papers were published in the town in the 19th century: the *Illustrated Oxfordshire Telegraph*, later called the *Oxfordshire Telegraph*, which ran from June 1859 to June 1894; and the *Midland Mail*, later called the *South Midland Mail*, which ran from 9 June to 5 October 1900.[25]

Among the minor industries were tanning, ropespinning, patten and clogmaking, the making of wooden ploughs and harrows, milling, coach-making (in spite of the new railway), and brickmaking. The railway introduced new employments: in the middle of the century well over 30 persons were directly occupied on railway work, most of them as labourers, while many like the coal merchants were indirectly dependent on it.[26]

Like other 19th-century market-towns Bicester had the usual group of professional men and civil servants. Chief among them were William and Thomas Tubb with Messrs. Kirby and Wooten, who had opened their bank in 1793. Tubb's bank issued its own notes until 1918, when it was taken over by Barclays bank. Until the 20th century it was without a rival; the Oxford and Buckinghamshire bank then opened a small sub-branch; in 1919 Lloyds and the Midland bank opened branches.[27]

Much of the town's prosperity in the 18th and 19th centuries was due to the local horse-races and to the Bicester and Warden Hill Hunt. The races

were being run at least as early as 1718.[28] They were said to have been held then in King's End Field, but later they were held at Northbrook in Kirtlington parish, on Bucknell Cow Common, or on Cottisford Heath.[29] They were an important social event and brought much trade to the town. Erasmus Philipps wrote in 1721 of the 'Plate Balls' in the Black Boy Inn and of the distinguished company there, which included leading members of London society, 'Martha of the Cocoa Tree' among them, as well as Oxfordshire gentry.[30] In 1755 it was the races on the 'adjacent plain' together with its excellent 'malt-liquors' which were the only two points of interest about Bicester thought worthy of record by the *Universal Magazine*. In the early 19th century the Bicester Hunt organized races which were the first hunt races in the county; the 1837 meeting also made sporting history by opening two races to horses of the Bicester Troop.[31]

The Bicester and Warden Hill Hunt goes back to 1778, when John Warde kept a pack of hounds at Weston-on-the-Green and hunted the Bicester country. The hunt became known as the Bicester when the kennels were moved to Bicester in the early 19th century.[32] A number of trades—saddlers, harness-makers, farriers, horseclippers, breeches-makers, sporting tailors, ostlers and grooms—were in some cases almost entirely dependent on the work the hunt provided.[33] The hunt's reputation was maintained well into the 20th century, and since about 1930 the Boxing Day meet in the Market Square has become an outstanding event in the Bicester year.[34]

Another popular feature of 19th-century Bicester was its seven annual fairs. St. Edburg's three-day fair originated in 1252 and the King's End fair in 1377.[35] The last was granted to the lord of Bignell manor and was held 'in the manor of Bignell'. As he had property in King's End, the fair may always have been held in the main street of King's End and on the green, as it was in White Kennett's day.[36] Kennett stated that formerly it was of 'great note'.[37] It was still one of the best in the country in the early 19th century, according to Dunkin, although it had declined in importance during the Napoleonic wars. He states that it had been noted for its sales of leather, and that on account of the great numbers attending, watches had had to be appointed in Bicester and the surrounding villages to keep order.[38] Sheep and pony sales were still an important part of the fair in the early 20th century, but it has since degenerated into an amusement fair.[39] It was sold with the greater part of the Coker estate in 1918.[40]

In 1769 the steward of Market End appointed three additional fairs, to be held in Easter week, June,

[22] *Hewiett's Bic. Dir.* (1846).
[23] *Pigot's Dir.* (1823); *Hunt's Oxford Dir.* (1846); *V.C.H. Oxon.* ii. 265. For a 17th-cent. King's End maltster see Bodl. MS. ch. Oxon. 2914. The wills of other early maltsters may be found in Bodl. MS. Wills Oxon.
[24] Inf. Mr. F. Smith, printer, Bicester.
[25] Letter from Mr. A. Keith Falconer, *The Oxford Times*, 8 June 1953. The Brit. Mus. has complete sets.
[26] *Hewiett's Companion to Bic. Dir.* (1847); *V.C.H. Oxon.* ii. 274; H.O. 107/1729 (census 1851).
[27] Inf. Barclays, Lloyds, and Midland Banks. For the Tubbs see below, pp. 47, 54.
[28] Dunkin, *Bic.* 181.
[29] Blo. *Buck.* 32; see below, pp. 71, 105.

[30] Blo. *Buck.* 32, 33. The Cocoa Tree was Sir James Dashwood's London club.
[31] *V.C.H. Oxon.* ii. 367.
[32] Ibid. 356–7. By 1855 the kennels had been moved to Stratton Audley.
[33] *Hewiett's Bic. Dir. passim.* For trades in 1851 see H.O. 107/1729.
[34] Bic. U.D.C. *Guide and Dir.* (1953).
[35] See above, p. 32. The grant of St. James's fair is attributed to Richard I by a misprint in Kennett, *Paroch. Antiq.* ii. 409.   [36] C.P. 25(2)/340/East. 9 Jas. I.
[37] Kennett, *Paroch. Antiq.* ii. 156.
[38] Dunkin, *Bic.* 126 n. 3.
[39] Inf. Mr. F. Smith, Bicester.
[40] Bodl. MS. D.D. Coker, c 1.

and December.[41] However, by the early 19th century only the Easter fair, which was noted as a cattle fair, and the autumn fairs were much attended.[42] Towards the end of the century Blomfield notes that an October fair was held for hiring servants.[43] There were nine fair days in 1939.[44]

As might be expected in a market-town, Bicester, since the days of the medieval 'Bell', has had many inns.[45] The market and fairs had always provided them with plenty of rough custom, but in the 18th century the races and coaching brought them a better-class clientele. The 'Swan', for example, was a prosperous inn with 'the greatest rent . . . in the parish'. Its innkeeper claimed that it was a 'well accustomed inn and that often times travellers of good custom and condition pass their Sundays there' and that he, therefore, ought to have a certain pew in the church, which had long been regarded as the inn's private property.[46] It later lost its custom because of the 'insolent remonstrances' of the landlord to Lord Abingdon and others, who brought their own wine when they came to the King's End races.[47] In 1847, in addition to the two leading inns, the 'King's Arms' and the 'Crown' (described in 1790 as 'capital'), there were eighteen others.[48] The decline of the market and of road traffic in the 19th century did not result in ruin, as the Bicester Hunt and the Heythrop Hunt, for which the town was within easy reach, provided new custom. The fame of the hunt under a succession of celebrated masters brought many visitors during the hunting season: Bicester stables were then full, inns were hard-pressed, and the wine-merchants flourished.[49]

In 1921 in the Urban District 141 men were engaged in commerce and finance, 120 in transport, 77 as builders and bricklayers, 49 as metal workers, and 186 in agriculture. Of women, 159 were employed in personal service. This pattern of employment has since been considerably altered. Bicester's business has been expanded by the development of the R.A.F. station. It was first constructed in 1917, when it was a training-depot station for the Southern Army Command. It was closed in 1920 and reopened as a bomber station in 1928. A Station Headquarters was formed at Bicester in 1938. In 1939 it was being used as an operational training station and after 1945 as a supply centre for the British air forces in Germany. In post-war years agriculture, particularly the breeding of pigs and the cultivation of root crops, has been practised on an extensive scale at the station.[50]

Another great change has resulted from the estab-lishment in 1941 of the Ordnance Depot at Arncot. It was completed shortly before 'D Day' in 1944 and in 1950 the War Office decided to make Bicester a peace-time garrison town, and barracks were built.[51] A camp for European Voluntary Workers was also established in 1948. These developments and the existence of the United States Air Force at Upper Heyford have had a noticeable effect on business. The café is now as conspicuous as the inn, a cinema flourishes, the taxicab-hire-service has been expanded, and motor and electrical engineers appear in Bicester's list of traders.

The Model Laundry, opened in 1938 and employing 50 persons, is one of the chief new businesses. The newest arrival is the firm of Norman Collisson (Contractors) Ltd. It was established in 1951 by Mr. N. Collisson, formerly of Banbury and the descendant of a family of masons, who have been master men in the trade in Northamptonshire or Oxfordshire since at least the early 17th century. The firm has an average of 160 employees and specializes in the restoration of historic buildings.[52]

Population has increased rapidly in recent years. The decline which followed 1891, the peak year for the 19th century, was arrested after 1918 and numbers rose rapidly after 1945. The population in 1951 of the Urban District, which is much smaller in area than the ancient parish, was 4,171.[53]

LOCAL GOVERNMENT. Throughout the medieval period the main organs of local government were the manorial courts of Bicester's four manors.[54] Few records of these have survived: a number of priory rolls for courts held at Bicester exist for the years beginning in 1286, 1308, 1340–3, 1356, 1360, 1403–5, and for 1431–3.[55] A few excerpts from rolls, now lost, of courts held at Wretchwick have been printed,[56] and a number of rolls of courts held at Kirtlington, to which Bignell and King's End owed suit, from the time of Henry VI are among the records of the Duchy of Lancaster and the Dashwood archives.[57] Leet jurisdiction was divided between the honor of Wallingford (later Ewelme) and Kirtlington. The steward of the honor held an annual view at Bicester, one of the six places in Oxfordshire where the honor's views were held. In Henry VIII's reign the 'bailiwick of Bicester' was one of the divisions of the honor.[58] The manors of Wretchwick and Bicester each paid 6s. 8d. certainty money.[59] Bignell and King's End, which included the nuns' manor, owed suit twice a year at Kirtlington and paid 13s. 4d. certainty money.[60] A constable and four tithings

[41] Dunkin, *Bic.* 128–9.
[42] Ibid. 129; *Brit. Traveller*, iv (1819); *Pigot's Dir.* (1823).
[43] Blo. *Bic.* 126–7.
[44] *Kelly's Dir. Oxon.* (1939).
[45] For the 'Bell' see *Valor Eccl.* (Rec. Com.), ii. 187, and above, p. 17.
[46] Oxf. Archd. Oxon. c 31, f. 163.
[47] Dunkin, *Oxon.* ii. 258.
[48] *Hewiett's Bic. Dir.* (1847); *Universal Brit. Dir.* (1790). In 1784 there had been 23 inns: O.R.O. Cal. Q. Sess. Cf. Dunkin, *Oxon.* ii. 258–9.
[49] *Hunt's Oxford Dir.* (1846).
[50] Inf. Wing-Cdr. R. C. Rotheram.
[51] Inf. Officer Commanding, Royal Ordnance Depot.
[52] Bic. U.D.C. *Guide* (1953).
[53] *Census,* 1891, 1921, 1951.
[54] See above, pp. 21–24 sqq. For Wretchwick ct. see *Rot. Hund.* (Rec. Com.), ii. 827. A lease of 1530 reserves to the

Prioress of Markyate half the profits of wards, reliefs, and cts. at her Bicester manor: Dunkin, *Bic.* 247.
[55] S.C. 2/197/6, 7, 8, 10.
[56] Dunkin, *Bic.* 33–34 (Dunkin states that the 1343 ct. was for Bicester, but the names of the tenants mentioned are those of Wretchwick manor); Kennett, *Paroch. Antiq.* ii. 85, 100–1. See also references to cts. for Bicester and Wretchwick manors in the priory acct. rolls, e.g. Blo. *Bic.* 162, 173.
[57] Bodl. MS. D.D. Dashwood (Oxon.) a 1, c 1; D.L. 30/108/1594.
[58] *Rot. Hund.* (Rec. Com.), ii. 828; and see ibid. 864 for the suit of a Rousham tenant at Bicester; *Cal. inq. p.m.* iii, p. 467. For the great ct. held in 1327 see Blo. *Bic.* 155. For cts. in 1408–9 and the reign of Henry VIII see S.C. 2/212/2, 16, 17, 19, 20.
[59] e.g. S.C. 2/212/2: court of March 1421/2; Blo. *Bic.* 155.
[60] In 1279 Bignell was said to owe suit every three weeks at Kirtlington: *Rot. Hund.* (Rec. Com.), ii. 839.

(two from Bignell, one from the nuns' manor, and one from King's End), attended the court; after the Reformation the number of Bicester tithings decreased and in the 17th century only two King's End tithings attended.[61] As early as 1517 the lord of Bignell had been presented in the court for sending no tithingmen.[62] In the Tudor period presentments concerned the usual breaches of the assize of bread and ale, including the selling of ale with unsealed measures. Millers were occasionally charged with taking excessive toll; others were charged by the verderers with offences in the king's park (i.e. at Kirtlington), or with breaking the common pound of King's End, or with assault. Pleas of debt and covenant were also heard. Among the orders of the court was one to remove from King's End a man of evil fame who had lately come to the village, another was to see that the archery butts were made, and numerous regulations about the management of the open fields were drawn up.[63]

A hayward and fieldsmen (two *supervisores camporum* and two *enumeratores pecorum*) were elected in the Elizabethan period;[64] in the early 18th century the tithingmen were called 'Third Boroughs'.[65] The court leet and baron was being held as late as 1819. Out of the fine of 13s. 4d. the lord of King's End paid 1s. 8d., Bignell Farm (the old manor house) 1s. 8d., and each cottager 4d.[66] After the Reformation the town's affairs continued to be conducted in the various manorial courts, and by the vicar and churchwardens, but the charity feoffees were by then another body which played an important part.[67] A suit brought in 1529 by John Bodicote, Benedict Wygyns, Richard Sherman, Nicholas Rowell, John More senior, William Walker, and Henry More, who were apparently acting on behalf of the charity, is the earliest example of their joint action.[68] Of these men Bodicote was by far the wealthiest, but Wygyns, probably one of the founders of the charity, Walker, and Sherman were also men of substance.[69] The management of the fund provided the townsmen with a measure of experience in self-government. In 1551 in an apparent attempt to increase efficiency the feoffees agreed to elect Thomas Bodicote, Humphrey Hunt, and two others for the coming year to be the 'rulers and governors of all the said lands and tenements . . . and the issues and profits thereof to receive and the same to distribute'.[70] Nevertheless abuses occurred. A commission of inquiry in 1598 found that much of the fund had been used to build the town hall, and to pay the wages of the mole-catcher and the sexton.[71]

The purposes of the fund were set out anew by the commissioners, who laid down that the poor and impotent, whose relief was the first charge on it, were to be relieved by the feoffees with the consent of the vicar, the churchwardens, and the overseers of the poor and with the consent of four inhabitants that were rated highest in the subsidy book. The feoffees also had to submit an annual account to the vicar and his associates. Their records were kept in a coffer in the church porch.[72] The charity account book of 1682 shows that by that date the vicar was himself acting as one of the feoffees along with John Coker, Ralph Clements, and the two collectors of town rents. The management of the fund involved the sale and purchase of land from time to time, and in the 18th century the building (presumably) of the workhouse, which was let to the overseers of Market End.[73]

The influence of the townsmen was considerably increased in 1597, when the Earl of Derby granted a 9,999 years' lease of Market End manor to his 31 tenants.[74] The manorial rights included the control of the markets and fairs with all the profits arising from toll, picage, and stallage, and rights over the waste of the manor. The profits were said to be worth as much as £50 a year and in 1752 were still worth over £35 in spite of the decline of the popularity of the Bicester market.[75] Among the biggest leaseholders in 1596 were John Lacy (yeoman), Thomas Wilson, Walter Hunt (glover), Edmund Bodicote, Ralph Hunt, Humphrey More (vintner), and Thomas Clements (yeoman).[76] Edmund Bodicote was the biggest leaseholder and was almost certainly wealthier than most of the others. It was alleged in a Chancery suit in 1623 that Bodicote, then dead, had lands and tenements in Bicester worth £1,500 a year.[77] But the other leaseholders mentioned above were substantial men and there is little doubt that they became the ruling oligarchy in Bicester. When the powerful Clements family, of which the head was then Thomas Clements, tried to secure the manorial rights for themselves they were opposed by other members of the oligarchy, including two members of their own family, one a tanner and the other a mercer.[78]

A contemporary opinion was that the town profited by having no corporation: 'it is the richer thereby for such as be in debt and danger need not shun it, neither are there any polling officers to draw fees and sconcing money to enrich themselves and impoverish others, which maketh a market town to flourish so much the more.'[79] The purchasers of the bailiwick, or the liberty as it was sometimes called,[80] normally appointed the bailiff, but the first known bailiff, John Lacy, one of the largest shareholders, was made bailiff by a Chancery decree in 1605 'so as to avoid all disputes' and was empowered to act for one year.[81] The bailiff's duty was to receive the profits of

[61] e.g. D.L. 30/108/1593–5; Bodl. M.S. D.D. Dashwood (Oxon.) a 1, Jan. ct. 15 Hen. VII, undated ct. temp. Hen. VII; there were commonly three tithingmen at the cts. in Hen. VIII's reign.
[62] Bodl. MS. D.D. Dashwood (Oxon.) a 1; cf. 1521 ct.
[63] Ibid. rolls *passim*.
[64] e.g. ibid. Oct. ct. 1587.
[65] Ibid. 1749 ct.
[66] Blo. *Bic.* 74.
[67] See below, p. 54.
[68] Blo. *Bic.* 56, n. 2.
[69] See subsidy assessments: E 179/161/204. For wills of John Bodicote (1541) and John More (1543) see Blo. *Bic.* 80.
[70] Blo. *Bic.* 56–57.
[71] *12th Rep. Com. Char.* 286–7.

[72] Barclays Bank, Bic., Char. Feoff. box: copy (1723) of indenture of 1598; Dunkin, *Bic.* 141–2.
[73] Barclays Bank, Bic., Char. Feoff. box, acct. bk. 1682–1797.
[74] See above, p. 22.
[75] Barclays Bank, Bic., Char. Feoff. box; see above, p. 33.
[76] Blo. *Bic.* 22 for list of leaseholders. Their occupations have been obtained from their wills and other sources.
[77] C 3/372/35. The trustees of his estate were Cadwallader Coker and the Maundes of Chesterton: ibid.
[78] U.D.C. Decree 1605.
[79] Blo. *Bic.* 23. Blomfield's original source has not been found.
[80] Bodl. MS. ch. Oxon. 2914 (1672).
[81] U.D.C. Decree 1605.

the bailiwick and distribute them to the shareholders in proportion to their respective holdings. The property included the town house, the guardhouse, or lock-up, all shops and houses built on the waste, all shops and sheds in the market-place, and the profits of the courts and market. The court baron of 'the manor and town' was held by a steward. The title-deeds of the bailiwick and the court rolls were ordered by Chancery to be kept in a chest with three locks in the church porch.[82] By the same decree the tithingmen of Market End were to have the grass from the 'Yield Mead' and were to pay the bailiff £1 6s. 8d. half-yearly for it. At the inclosure of Market End in 1758 the tithingman was allotted land for which £1 was being paid in the 19th century. By the 18th century the shareholders were reduced to ten in number, including John Coker, lord of King's End manor, besides the trustees of the poor who had by then acquired two shares. The shareholders leased the bailiwick in 1752 to Jacob Thomas, ironmonger, and George King, brasier, for seven years for £250 10s.[83] Thus, these two leading tradesmen acquired the valuable right of controlling the market and fixing the stallage charges.

Following the Local Government Act of 1858 Bicester became a Local Government District in 1859. King's End and Wretchwick, though the latter had always been associated with Bicester, objected and were at first exempted from the operation of the act.[84] Since time immemorial King's End had been separately administered. It had its own churchwardens and contributed a fifth to the necessary sum for church repairs; it maintained its own poor and highways.[85] The Local Government Act was adopted by King's End in February 1859 and by Market End in October 1862. Each district continued to maintain its own poor and highways, elected its own overseers, churchwardens, and guardians. There were separate boards of health for each township and some charities were kept separate.[86] The Burial Board and the Turnpike Trustees acted for both areas.

Market End's Local Board consisted of twelve members. Its first chairman was a Bicester chemist, R. B. Sandiland; its clerk W. Foster, a solicitor, was paid a salary of £30 a year; its first meeting was held in October 1862 in the clerk's office. The board's chief business was public health and arrangements for improving sanitation, but it had a variety of other responsibilities. Among them was the lighting of the town and keeping the highways, the pavements, and the market square in repair. Towards the upkeep of the last a request for a contribution was made in 1866 to the bailiwick. In 1869 the Board decided to afford facilities for carrying a telegraph line to the Post Office. One of its failures was the decision not to make a recreation ground, for which the vestry had made a grant of money in 1867. The money was said to have been spent on other 'interests of the

ratepayers', and with a rate of 1s. 6d. and often one as low as 1s. in the £ it was clearly impossible to satisfy all interests.[87] The functioning of the Board was in fact not entirely satisfactory: in the course of seven years, 27 meetings had had to be abandoned because fewer than three members were present.

In 1875 the King's End Board was amalgamated with the Board for Market End, and the hamlet of Wretchwick was also included, under the name of the Bicester District.[88]

Under the Local Government Act of 1894 the Board gave place to the Urban District Council, which still rules Bicester.[89] It consists of twelve councillors including the chairman, of which one-third are elected each year. Its activities are limited by the low product of the penny rate: in 1945 it produced just under £80; by 1953 it had risen to £87.[90] Since 1946, when the town was given the Garth, formerly the residence of the Keith-Falconer family, the Council offices have been established there. Since 1888 the County Council has gradually been absorbing the functions of the old boards, which were numerous even in so small a place as Bicester. The Bicester Turnpike Trusts ceased to function in 1867 and 1877; the Highway Board and the Burial Board in 1896 and 1899; the Board of Guardians in 1939—the old workhouse was later converted into flats.[91] Until 1941 there was a Joint Fire Brigade Committee for the Bicester Urban and Rural District Council. Education and the care of the old and children are now the business of the County Council. The U.D.C.'s chief remaining business is housing. At present (1956) it has in hand the Western Development Scheme, a joint scheme with the War Department, for housing Arncot workers. A new sewerage scheme was begun in 1953.[92]

The justices of the peace for the Ploughley area still meet in Bicester, but the town is no longer the head of a county-court district. The court used to meet monthly at the 'King's Arms', until the Court House was erected in 1864. It ceased to meet in about 1926.[93] Throughout the 19th century a court of summary jurisdiction for the Ploughley Division met at the 'King's Arms'. Petty Sessions were held fortnightly on Fridays with a number of special sittings to deal with applications for remands and other urgent business. Since 1950 Petty Sessions have been held weekly, but are called the Magistrates' Court of the Bicester Division. In the 19th century the landed gentry, including the Earl of Jersey, and the clergy formed the majority on the bench. Now eight active magistrates on the commission for the County and two ex-officio magistrates are allocated to the Bicester bench. Businessmen and housewives are prominent.[94]

Bicester became a sub-division of the Banbury Constabulary, one of the three Oxfordshire divisions formed in 1857 when the Oxfordshire Constabulary was formed.[95] The members of its present force are

---

[82] U.D.C. doc. no. 26: copy (1762) of Chancery decree of Mar. 1607/8.

[83] U.D.C. lease.

[84] Wing, *Annals*, 21.

[85] For two surveyors in 1683 and a churchwarden in 1684 see Barclays Bank, Bic., Char. Feoff. box, acct. bk. 1682–1797.

[86] U.D.C. Bic. King's End Board of Health min. bk. 1859–74.

[87] U.D.C. Bic. Market End Local Board min. bk. 1862–78. The recreation ground was only provided in 1946

through the gift of the Garth.

[88] U.D.C. Local Bd. min. bk. 1862–78; Local Board for the Bic. District min. bk. 1878–90.

[89] U.D.C. Local Bd. for Bic. District and Bic. U.D.C. min. bks. 1890–6; Bic. U.D.C. min. bks. 1896–1956.

[90] Inf. U.D.C.

[91] Ibid.; U.D.C. Burial Bd. min. bk. 1859–99; notices of interment to 1949; fees 1862–98.

[92] Inf. U.D.C.

[93] Magistrates' bks. *penes* Mr. E. K. Truman, Bicester.

[94] Ibid.   [95] *Kelly's Dir. Oxon.* (1864).

the successors of the medieval constables regularly elected in the manorial courts. In 1827 the Vestry had appointed a parish bedel whose duty was to watch the precincts of the market-place and generally keep order. He had a blue coat and staff.[96] In 1837 there were at least two constables and the old lock-up may still be seen in the London Road, near the Hermitage.[97] In 1857 one inspector and five subordinates were appointed for Bicester. In the 20th century Oxfordshire was a pioneer in the use of women special constables and Bicester regularly employs them. In 1953 the need to look after 1,200 aliens in the Bicester district led to the opening of a new police station.[98]

From an early date many voluntary societies have supplemented the work of the local government officers. In 1813 the Bicester Benevolent Society for the Relief of Poor Lying-in Women was founded and continued in existence until 1911. A Sick Visiting Society and Dorcas Society had been organized by 1869 and its work of supplying soup and clothing to the aged and poor also went on until 1911. The recreation of Bicester's inhabitants has been looked after by numerous active local organizations. A Rifle Range, one of the best known in the country, was founded in 1906. The Unemployment Relief Committee of 1933 was responsible for the provision of a public swimming-pool. Other sports were organized by the Bicester Bowling Club, the Cricket Club (founded in 1871), and the Football, Hockey, and Tennis Clubs. The clubs have a fine sports ground provided by private enterprise. Dr. G. N. Montgomery initiated the scheme in 1922 and was supported by a number of local men. In 1929 the trustees of the Bicester Sports Association bought for £900 the ground formerly rented from Major Aubrey Coker. The club has no paid officials.

PUBLIC HEALTH. The earliest information about measures taken to deal with public health appears in 1752, when as a result of a virulent outbreak of smallpox the pest-house was built.[99] The cholera outbreak in 1832 led to the formation of a Board of Health under Viscount Chetwynd, who was then residing at Bicester House. Sixty-four deaths occurred, a higher number in proportion to the population than in any other town in England. Fortunately, Bicester had in Chetwynd a man of intelligence and energy to cope with the situation. Relief was organized, the affected areas cleansed (the crowded quarters of Crockwell and New Buildings were the worst), and the dead buried.[1]

In 1853 the Sanitary Committee, after a careful survey of the town and especially of the quarters inhabited by the poor, reported that it was in a 'very unsatisfactory state' and that there was a general disregard for the 'existence of filth'. In 1854 there were letters of complaint about sanitary conditions, about the bad state of the Brook and the drains, and

there were reports of typhus fever. In 1855 several cases of smallpox occurred in the workhouse.[2]

An act of 1848 had ordered the drainage of large towns, but it was not until an amending act (1858–9) extended the order to towns like Bicester that the root cause of epidemics was tackled. At its first meeting in October 1868 the new Market End Board initiated a drainage scheme. By July 1863 work in Market Place and Water Lane (i.e. Chapel Street) was in hand. The scheme was later extended throughout the town at a total cost of £2,827. Plans by Mr. Selby of Oxford and the tender of Messrs. Hartland and Bloomfield of London for the first scheme were accepted by the Board in 1863.[3] The Board provided the main sewers but the householders had to provide the drains leading into them. These were supplied at cost price. Smallpox, nevertheless, continued to be a scourge, particularly in Crockwell, and the Board coped with it by sending families to the pest-house and ordering the purification of their homes. It was for health reasons too that in 1867 it ordered the collection of refuse and in 1891–2 the emptying of earth closets once a week. Horses and carts for these purposes were provided at the public expense.[4] Outbreaks of typhoid led to an agitation about the water-supply. Piped water finally came in about 1905 and waterworks were built.[5] Plans for building a fever hospital near the workhouse were made after 1872 and tenders were being received in 1881.[6]

POOR RELIEF. In the Middle Ages the priory made some provision for the sick and indigent. £6 1s. 8d. was distributed annually among the poor on the anniversary of Gilbert Basset and there was an annual distribution of 13s. 4d. to the poor and lepers on Shrove Tuesday.[7] After the Reformation the overseers of the poor were responsible for relief, though the charity feoffees, acting under the overseers, evidently played an important part in relieving poverty.[8] By the mid-18th century, when growing population and the strain of war had aggravated the problem, a workhouse for 40 paupers was built, probably by the charity feoffees.[9] In 1761 a rent of £10 was being paid to them; in 1826 £16.[10] In 1782 the poor were set to work there on spinning wool, jersey, and coarse linen for the Witney 'manufactory'.[11] In 1809 Henry Chandler, a plumber and glazier, undertook to look after the poor in the workhouse for a year. He agreed to supply them with food, clothing, and proper attention in health and sickness, though 'surgery and physick in all casualties, distemper and illnesses' were excepted. He also agreed to live in the workhouse and teach the children to read. His salary was £3 10s. a week for 20 paupers or less and 3s. 6d. a week for each extra pauper. He was to benefit from the labour performed by the poor in his charge.[12]

The inexperienced attempts of the Vestry to deal with increasing poverty during the Napoleonic war

[96] Blo. *Bic.* 52–53.
[97] Barclays Bank, Bic., Char. Feoff. box.
[98] Inf. Inspector Smith, Bicester.
[99] Dunkin, *Bic.* 181.
[1] U.D.C. Board of Health Mins.; *Kelly's Dir. Oxon.* (1864); Blo. *Bic.* 51; ibid. n. 4.
[2] U.D.C. Local Govt. Bd. min. bks.
[3] Ibid. 1862–78.
[4] Ibid. 1878–1890 &c.
[5] Ibid.
[6] U.D.C. Local Bd. min. bks. for the infectious diseases

hosp. for 1893; min. bks. for Bic. Rural Sanitary Auth. exist from 1884.
[7] *Valor Eccl.* (Rec. Com.), ii. 187.
[8] Barclays Bank, Bic., Char. Feoff. box. For an acct. of the charity see below, p. 54.
[9] Blo. *Bic.* 49 and char. acct. bks. for payments of rent to the feoffees.
[10] Barclays Bank, Bic., Char. Feoff. box, acct. bks. 1682–1797; 1798–1857.
[11] *Oxf. Jnl.* 31 May 1782.
[12] Bodl. MS. D.D. Oxon. c 7: Articles.

had led to the introduction at Bicester of the Speen-hamland system with the result, as the Poor Law commissioner later observed, that 'the evils, which result from a system which destroys the connexion between work and wages, flourish more vigorously in Oxfordshire than in its original home in Berkshire'. Nowhere, he declared, had he seen the relation between employer and employed so disturbed as round Bicester. The opinion of the farmers was that unless some change was made labourers, who derived under the system no benefit from industry and good character, would cease to work altogether. At a special Vestry meeting in 1821 Sir Gregory O. Page-Turner proposed to end the practice of employing 'roundsmen' and making up their wages from the rates in proportion to the size of their families. He offered to extend his stone quarry and brick field at Blackthorn and employ there all labourers for whom the farmers could not find piece-work. This scheme reduced the rates by half.[13] Local distress came to a head on 15 December 1827, when the labourers on the roads assaulted their foreman for withholding part of their wages and were supported by a 'great part of the labouring population' of Bicester. The leaders of the riot were taken to Oxford jail, 28 special constables were sworn in to preserve the peace, and 300 'respectable persons' were stated to have patrolled the town all night. A nightly patrol of ten was afterwards set up.[14] In 1830 the disastrous but common expedient of farming the poor was adopted. £1,000 was paid by the Vestry for the employment and maintenance of the poor in the workhouse and elsewhere, and in 1831 £1,200. Lord Chetwynd, who considered that more harm had been caused by this expedient than by 'five years of ordinary mis-management', used his influence to end the system both in Bicester and in the country generally.[15] Another method of dealing with the problem, though not as it turned out an entirely successful one, was the free emigration scheme to the U.S.A. organized in 1830 by the Bicester Emigration Committee. In May, 71 adults and 40 children were conveyed in wagons to Liverpool, £1,000 having been borrowed from the rates to finance the scheme. But some lost heart and worked their way back to Bicester to become once more a burden to the Vestry. It set them to work fetching coals from Heyford wharf.[16] It is not surprising to find that in 1832, the year of the cholera outbreak, outdoor and permanent relief reached its height. A fifth part of the residents was declared paupers and expenditure on poor relief rose to £3,752,[17] compared with £332 in 1776.

More efficient management began in 1835 when the first Bicester Union Board of Guardians was formed.[18] It held weekly meetings at the Black Boy Inn under the chairmanship of Viscount Chetwynd.

The chief business was first to build a new work-house for '350 paupers' for the new Bicester Union, which included 38 parishes or townships,[19] and then to control its management. The architect John Plowman, junior, of Oxford, was appointed at a fee of £50; the contractor was James Long of Witney, whose tender was for £4,140. Local stone was used and he undertook to employ as much pauper labour as he could. The work was completed by the end of 1836. A governor and matron at a salary of £70 and £30 respectively were appointed and also a school-master and schoolmistress. The guardians desired to have either a tailor or shoemaker as master so that the children might be taught a trade. The governor was to see that they were later apprenticed to trades. The guardians were farmers, clergymen, the land-lord of the 'Crown', and Shillingford, the owner of the Bicester Brewery. The clerk was a Bicester solicitor with a salary of £100 a year.[20] The magnitude of their task is revealed by the fact that in time of peace in 1868 the proportion of paupers to population was stated to be one in eighteen in the Bicester Union.[21] In Bicester itself 161 persons were receiving outdoor or indoor relief by 1879, compared with 437 in 1816.[22]

The Bicester Union area since 1928 has been under the Guardians Committee of the Ploughley area.

CHURCH. The tradition that the church dated from the 7th century may be exaggerated, and the archi-tectural evidence for a late Saxon building cannot be accepted without question.[23] That there was a church before the Conquest cannot, however, be doubted, and like the town it probably belonged to Wigod of Wallingford and after him to Robert d'Oilly.[24] The church's early importance is indicated by its relations with the dependent chapels of Stratton and Launton, and particularly with the latter. Until 1435 the parishioners of Launton were obliged to take their dead to Bicester for burial. The mother church is unlikely to have secured this privi-lege after the grant of Launton to Westminster Abbey by the Confessor.[25] Moreover, by the end of the 12th century at latest Bicester had given its name to a deanery comprising 33 churches.[26]

Soon after 1182 Gilbert Basset, then lord of Bicester and Stratton, gave the church with its dependent chapel at Stratton to his newly founded priory of Austin canons at Bicester.[27] The priory appropriated the church before 1226[28] and retained the rectory and advowson of the vicarage until its dissolution in 1536.[29] The Crown then granted the rectory to Charles Brandon, Duke of Suffolk,[30] who in turn granted it to Roger Moore and his wife Agnes.[31] The advowson was granted by the king to Roger Moore alone.[32] On Roger's death in 1551 the

[13] Dunkin, *Oxon.* ii. 260; rep. of 1835 cited in Blo. *Bic.* 48–49.   [14] Dunkin MS. 439/3, ff. 103–4.
[15] Ibid. ff. 104–5; Blo. *Bic.* 50 n. 1, citing vestry min. Sept. 1831; ibid. 50.
[16] Ibid. 50 and nn. 1–4; papers *penes* Mr. Reginald Haynes, Bicester.
[17] *Poor Abstract*; Blo. *Bic.* 48.
[18] See U.D.C. Bic. Union min. bks. 1835–6, 1847–1928.
[19] The union was roughly equivalent to the rural district plus Market End and King's End: see *Kelly's Dir. Oxon.* (1903, 1920). The R.D. also contained Mixbury and Finmere.
[20] Gwen Dannatt, 'Market End House', in *Festival of Britain Bk.* (Bic. 1951); Blo. *Bic.* 195; U.D.C. Bd. of Guardians min. bk. 1835–6.

[21] *Agric. Rep.* 364.
[22] Blo. *Bic.* 48 n. 2.
[23] See above, p. 14, and below, p. 44.
[24] See above, p. 21.
[25] Kennett, *Paroch. Antiq.* ii. 321, and see below, p. 234.
[26] *Eynsham Cart.* i. 14; *V.C.H. Oxon.* ii. 63.
[27] Kennet, *Paroch. Antiq.* i. 186–7, 188; *V.C.H. Oxon.* ii. 94.
[28] Robert de Sparkford was instituted vicar in 1226: *Rot. Welles,* ii. 23.
[29] *Valor Eccl.* (Rec. Com.), ii. 162.
[30] Dunkin, *Bic.* (author's copy, Bodl. G.A. Oxon. 8° 257), 84–85 with MS. notes; C 66/681.
[31] C 142/174/58.
[32] *L. & P. Hen. VIII*, xv, p. 408.

rectory remained in the possession of his widow Agnes and the advowson passed with Roger's Bicester manors to his son Thomas. The latter was killed in 1574 before his mother's death, so he never obtained the rectory.[33] After her death in 1583 it passed to her daughters, Mary wife of Sir Michael Blount of Mapledurham, and Elizabeth wife of Gabriel Fowler of Tilsworth (Beds.). In 1583 Elizabeth Fowler, by then a widow, conveyed her moiety of the rectory, and that of the advowson, which she had inherited from her brother, to Sir John Brockett, whom she subsequently married.[34] In 1589 Brockett conveyed this moiety to Sir Michael Blount of Mapledurham, his brother-in-law, and the holder of the other moiety.[35] The rectory and advowson descended with the Bicester manor to Sir Michael Blount's descendants and were sequestrated in 1646.[36] After the family had recovered its estates the rectory and advowson followed the descent of its Bicester manor, passing from the Blounts to the Glynnes and later to the Turners and Page-Turners.[37] When the Page-Turner family sold its Bicester property in 1930 the advowson was not sold; in 1941 the patrons were the trustees of the estate, Mrs. M. F. Strode and E. C. Charleton, Esq.[38] In 1953 Mrs. Strode of Shere (Surr.) was sole patron.[39]

The patrons have not always presented. After Bicester's dissolution and the death of the incumbent in 1537 the Crown failed to exercise its right and the Bishop of Lincoln collated.[40] Later, the right to present was occasionally sold. Benedict Wygyns and Thomas Shoer presented John Wykyns in 1541; Agnes Wentworth presented in 1559; Ann Chamberlain in 1564 and 1565.[41] In 1605 the patron, Sir Michael Blount, presented.[42] His son and daughter-in-law were recusants, but he seems to have conformed. In 1654 the Parliamentary Commissioners 'put in' William Hall.[43] Thereafter the patrons always presented except in 1835 when the Crown did so on account of the lunacy of Sir Gregory Page-Turner.[44]

Although the rectory was burdened with the payment of various pensions, it was worth more than most others in the neighbourhood: in about 1220 it was worth £13 6s. 10d.; in 1254 and in 1291 it was valued at £8 and £12 respectively, after the various deductions had been made.[45] No separate valuation of the rectory was made in 1535 when it was included in the valuation of the priory's other Bicester property.[46]

A part of the parish's tithes was given away at an early date. Robert d'Oilly gave two parts of his demesne tithes in Bicester and Wretchwick in 1074 to his church of St. George in Oxford castle.[47] These later passed to Oseney Abbey, but in 1300 after long litigation they were transferred for an annual pension of £3 to Bicester Priory.[48] The pension was still being paid in 1535.[49] Other tithes were also given away in the early 12th century. Gilbert Basset (1100–35) gave the tithe of colts reared in his demesnes to Abingdon Abbey, where his brother was a monk.[50] To Eynsham Abbey he gave two parts of the tithe of Stratton, then in Bicester parish, and the tithe of wool and cheese in all his lands;[51] in 1228 these were commuted for a pension of 12s.[52] Furthermore, the tithe of the demesne of Bignell was given by Jordan de Sai and his wife to Aulnay Abbey when they gave it Kirtlington church.[53] By 1291 Bicester Priory appears to have purchased these tithes in return for a pension of £1 6s. 8d. to Aulnay.[54] In 1304 Aulnay agreed that Bicester should have the tithes of sheaves in Bignell at a perpetual farm of £2 a year.[55]

Little is known about the rectory estate. In the reign of Edward III it comprised 50 field acres and when the open fields were inclosed in 1758 (Market End Award) and in 1794 (King's End Award) the rectorial glebe was consolidated, and the tithes commuted.[56] In 1758 Sir Edward Turner as rector impropriate received 158 acres and the vicar received over 39 acres for small and vicarial tithes due from Sir Edward's property; in 1794 Sir Gregory Page-Turner received 33 acres for rectorial glebe and he and John Coker, the lord of the manor of King's End, received 135 acres and 87 acres respectively for tithes.[57]

When the vicarage was ordained in or before 1226 the following arrangements were made: the vicar was to have a stipend of £2 for himself, his chaplain and clerks, and sufficient food. The priory was also to give the vicar provender for a horse; the offerings (i.e. 1d. for a burial, a marriage, and a purification; 3d. on Christmas Day; 2d. on Easter day, and at each of the other two principal feasts 1d.). It was also to allow him the offerings at confession or from bequests up to 6d.; any surplus receipts were to be divided between the vicar and the canons. The priory further undertook to provide a suitable house outside the priory and bear all the 'burdens' of the church except those belonging to the parish.[58] Later evidence

[33] C 142/174/58.
[34] C.P. 25(2)/197/Trin. 25 Eliz.; see above, p. 22.
[35] C 66/1336.
[36] Cal. Cttee. for Compounding, 2245–6.
[37] See above, p. 23. For the Glynnes and Turners, &c., see V.C.H. Oxon. v. 18.
[38] See above, p. 22. Bodl. Bic. Par. Box (uncat.): Solicitor's letter.
[39] Ibid.
[40] Linc. Reg. xxvii, Longland, f. 196.
[41] Kennett, Paroch. Antiq. ii. 319. For the Wykyns or Wygyns family, see above, pp. 22, 37.
[42] Kennett, Paroch. Antiq. ii. 319.
[43] Blo. Bic. 104. Dunkin (Bic. 89) errs in stating that a Mr. Basnet was ejected in 1666.
[44] P.R.O. Institution Bks.
[45] Rot. Welles, i. 177; Lunt, Val. Norw. 311; Tax. Eccl. (Rec. Com.), 31.
[46] Valor Eccl. (Rec. Com.), ii. 162, 187.
[47] Oseney Cart. iv. 2–3: forged charter. For the date see ibid. 1; H. E. Salter, Medieval Oxford, 114. There is a confirmation in Cal. Chart. R. 1257–1300, 69.

[48] Kennett, Paroch. Antiq. i. 81, 83; Cal. Chart. R. 1300–26, 424; Oseney Cart. vi. 26–28. The tithes had been valued at £2 in 1291: Tax. Eccl. 31. Another dispute, possibly over tithes, occurred in c. 1316. The priory accounts record the expenses in London and Lincoln for a 'decree touching the muniments and privileges of the church of Bicester' before the Bishop of Lincoln: Blo. Bic. 152.
[49] Valor Eccl. ii. 187.
[50] Chron. Abingdon, ii. 145–6.
[51] Eynsham Cart. i. 36–37.
[52] Ibid. 71–72; cf. Tax. Eccl. (Rec. Com.), 31. Payment was still being made in 1539; Eynsham Cart. ii. 251.
[53] Confirmed 1157: Cal. Doc. France, ed. Round, 185. For the original grant see below, p. 222.
[54] Tax. Eccl. (Rec. Com.), 31.
[55] St. John's Coll. Aulnay Deed. See below, p. 229.
[56] Inq. Non. (Rec. Com.), 132; O.R.O. Market End incl. award; King's End incl. award.
[57] John Coker (d. 1606/7) had acquired rectorial tithes of 276 a. which he purchased from Sir Richard Blount: C 142/296/107.
[58] Rot. Welles, i. 177.

shows that it became the custom for the priory to provide two cart-loads of hay a year and four of wood.[59]

Particularly early accounts of the vicarage and its dependent chapel at Stratton Audley have been preserved. The receipts were £14 15s. 8d. in 1340, of which over £10 went to the prior and convent. The vicar and his chaplain received £2. The money was derived from dues, from offerings, and from small tithes. The vicar's stipend, which had remained unaltered since the early 13th century, was increased in 1357, probably as a result of the Black Death and the subsequent impossibility of finding a chaplain to undertake the church at the old stipend. Thereafter the vicar, his chaplain, and clerk received a payment of £11 6s. 8d. a year. In the financial year 1362–3 the priory's total receipts were £24 7s. 5¼d. and its expenses £17 1s. 3d.[60] Some time later, possibly as a measure of economy, the practice of boarding the vicar in the priory instead of providing him with food and drink was adopted. It was condemned at the visitation of 1445.[61]

A new arrangement over the vicarage was made in 1455.[62] The direct money payment to the vicar was abandoned and he was relieved of the duty of serving the chapel at Stratton, the parishioners of which had long desired independence. In future the vicar was to have all small tithes and offerings from Bicester and its two hamlets of Bignell and Wretchwick. The convent reserved all the great tithes in Bicester and its hamlets, and all tithes in Stratton, as well as the small tithes from closes in its own hand.

From later evidence it appears that the priory provided the bread and wine for the parish church: at the visitation of 1520 the delivery of wafers at Easter was said to have been withheld, and after the dissolution a payment of 30s. a year was made out of the county revenue for bread and wine. In 1631 John Bird claimed that he was owed £10 by the Exchequer on this account,[63] and in 1635 an order was made to pay him £12 for his pension of 30s. a year, due for the past seven years.[64] This Exchequer payment was being made as late as 1782.[65]

In about 1608 John Bird brought a chancery suit against Sir Michael Blount and his son Sir Richard for not carrying out the composition of 1455.[66] The case was partly a result of the confusion which inevitably arose about payment of tithe after land had been inclosed.[67] Bird alleged that the defendants had not only refused to pay tithes themselves but had required their leasehold and customary tenants not to do so; that they had withheld the customary grants of wood and hay and had prevented their lessees from paying tithe of 400 sheep. Moreover, he declared that through the depopulation of Wretchwick he had lost tithes worth 100 marks at least. The Blounts' answer was that since the Dissolution tithe had been retained first by the king, then by Roger

Moore, and that no tithe had been paid from Wretchwick since before the Dissolution. They further disputed the vicar's right to any tithe from inclosed land. Early in 1609 the court decreed that Sir Richard Blount ought to pay tithe of mills, woods, furzes, orchards, hemp in the fields, and small tithes, and that a rate of £20 should be paid for the closes, then rented for nearly £600 a year. The vicar was assigned various closes of his own. The dispute dragged on, however, until May 1609. The vicar complained *inter alia* that the defendants' tenants defrauded him of his tithe of lambs and calves by moving their animals out of the common field into the closes just before their young were born and that they also pretended that the closes were tithe-free, so doing him a 'double wrong'.

Although the court issued a decree in the vicar's favour, the vicarage remained a poor one. In 1254 it had been valued at £1 10s.; in 1291 at £2 13s. 4d.; in 1535 at the comparatively large sum of £16; but by 1656 it was worth no more than £40 a year.[68] During the Commonwealth the vicarage was further damaged by the sequestration of Sir Charles Blount's estates as the vicar used to receive 1s. 6d. in the pound in lieu of Sir Charles's tithes. The county commissioners, therefore, requested in 1654 that £18 a year should be paid to him out of the Blount estate, but the Committee for Compounding was unable to accede to the request.[69] In 1657, however, the trustees for the maintenance of ministers ordered that the vicar's stipend should be increased by £50 to be paid out of the profits of the impropriated rectory.[70] Even so, in Queen Anne's reign the vicarage was discharged from the payment of first fruits and tenths.[71] Their small value may well have induced Sir Stephen Glynne to drop the claim, which he had revived in 1727, to a part of the endowments of the vicarage.[72] In 1758 the vicarage was worth £120 a year. The vicar's small tithes were commuted in 1758 and 1794 for some 125 acres, and by 1815 glebe and some remaining small tithes produced an annual income of £308 10s.[73] About 38 acres of glebe were sold to the G.W.R. company in 1905–6 for £2,000, when the railway was built, and the rest was sold later at an unknown date.[74] In 1882 Blomfield gave the gross value of the vicarage as about £320.[75] A part of this sum (£25) was derived from rents of lands at Langford farm bequeathed to the vicar in perpetuity in 1868 by Sir Edward Page-Turner.[76]

In 1957 Bicester and Caversfield were held in plurality. Between 1920 and 1924 the Vicar of Bicester was curate-in-charge of Caversfield. He has been vicar since 1924. Since 1955 he has also been curate-in-charge of Bucknell. Thus three parishes are served by a vicar and curate who are both resident in Bicester.[77]

As a result possibly of the poor endowment of the

59 Blo. *Bic.* 102.
60 Ibid. 100–1.
61 *Visit. Dioc. Linc. 1420–49*, ii. 35.
62 Kennett, *Paroch. Antiq.* ii. 393–5.
63 MS. Top. Oxon. c 56, f. 66; *Visit. Dioc. Linc. 1517–31*, i. 125.
64 *Cal. S.P. Dom. 1634–5*, 520.
65 Oxf. Dioc. b 3, f. 15.
66 Kennett, *Paroch. Antiq.* ii. 224–32.
67 For a tithe dispute in 1572 see Oxf. Dioc. c 26, ff. 286, 289, 295. It may be noted that it was alleged that tithe wool was paid after wool was wound.

68 Lunt, *Val. Norw.* 311; *Tax. Eccl.* (Rec. Com.), 31; *Valor Eccl.* (Rec. Com.), ii. 162; Blo. *Bic.* 104.
69 *Cal. Cttee. for Compounding*, 698, 2246–7.
70 *Cal. S.P. Dom. 1656–7*, 244.
71 Bacon, *Lib. Reg.* 792.
72 Dunkin, *Bic.* 89–90.
73 Blo. *Bic.* 104; O.R.O. Market End and King's End incl. awards.
74 Oxf. Dioc. b 32; inf. the vicar.
75 Blo. *Bic.* 104.
76 Inf. the vicar.
77 Idem.

vicarage, Bicester's vicars were seldom well-educated men in the Middle Ages and resignations after short periods of office to take better cures were common.[78] In 1412 a proposed exchange was opposed by the prior, who journeyed to London to prevent the institution of Master Geoffrey Dankeport of Oxford, accused by the prior's friends of 'many misdoings'.[79] No vicar served Bicester for longer than fifteen years before John Adam's long incumbency, which lasted from 1434 until his death in 1479,[80] a circumstance which may probably be accounted for by the fact that he was the first to benefit from the increase in endowment made in 1455. Nor were there any graduate vicars until 1481, when Master Thomas Kirkeby was presented, and after him Master John Stanley (1512–at least 1526) and Master Florence Volusen' (post 1526–1530). Both Kirkeby and Volusen', it may be noted, received on their resignations annual pensions from their successors of £17 and £5 respectively.[81]

The medieval incumbents had a chaplain to assist them: one is recorded as early as c. 1152.[82] The original ordination of the vicarage (c. 1226) refers also to clerks, but in 1357 it appears that the vicar had a chaplain and one clerk only.[83] Some of the vicars were clearly not poor men: Robert de Burton, for example, gave 5½ acres to the priory; another vicar gave £5 towards the expenses of rebuilding the canons' dormitory in 1425, and another £5 in 1430 for the rebuilding of the bakehouse.[84]

In 1423 the vicar was threatened with a loss of income when his Stratton parishioners began to bury their dead at Stratton. The priory took the affair seriously: the prior himself spent a week in London taking counsel and after much expenditure judgement was given by the Bishop of Worcester at Bicester. It ended with the exhumation of two corpses buried at Stratton and their reburial at Bicester.[85] But discontent evidently did not end, for in 1455 Stratton seems to have been given parochial status.[86] There is evidence at this date that the vicar sometimes supplemented his income by acting as private chaplain to the lord of Bignell: in 1454 he was licensed to solemnize the marriage between William Harcourt of Stanton Harcourt and Elizabeth Stokes, daughter of John and Alice Stokes.[87] He does not appear to have had any connexion with the chapel of St. John the Baptist at the north end of the town, which was tended by a hermit when it was first recorded in 1355.[88]

At the visitation of 1520 it was found that a canon, William Billington, was serving the cure, and the bishop enjoined that he should remain in the monastery until the prior had shown by what authority he sent brothers to serve cures.[89] As a secular priest, John Stanley, had been admitted as vicar in 1512 and was still in office in 1526, the canon must have been acting as his assistant. In 1526 Stanley had two assistants, Thomas with a stipend of £6 13s. 4d. and Richard Worthing with a stipend of £2 13s. 4d for the half-year, but neither was a canon.[90]

It was in 1520 also that another irregularity was recorded: both the canons and certain of the parishioners were stated to have withdrawn land and contributions of barley which belonged to the church.[91] It is likely that these irregularities were the result of the priory's weak financial position, which is also indicated by the ruinous state of their buildings at this date.[92]

After the Dissolution the spiritual life of the parish appears to have been troubled. Between 1537 and 1584 there were at least six different vicars and by the 1580's serious differences had arisen between the vicar, Robert Phipps, and his flock.[93] Doctrinal matters were apparently the cause of the trouble, for it was the vicar's association with a 'preacher' which made a parishioner call him a 'plagye knave' in 1584.[94] In 1593 the churchwardens complained that Phipps had held no services for over a month and more, and that he had refused to do so or to let anyone else do so, as no one would guarantee his safety in going to and coming from the church. In the following year he was suspended and his church sequestered because he still refused to hold services. Later he was again presented for encouraging the parishioners to refuse payment of oblations to the sequestrators, for 'disordered speeches', for deriding the minister sent to replace him during his suspension, and for libelling one of his parishioners.[95]

His successor John Bird (1605–53) was a pluralist, holding Bicester with the neighbouring village of Wendlebury, where he lived.[96] He had a curate at Bicester, William Hall, 'a godly and painful preacher', who was made vicar in 1654 by the Cromwellian Commissioners. Hall appears to have resided until his death in 1670.[97] His successors until 1768 were all resident, and like Hall they often had resident curates; one was White Kennett, the future bishop of Peterborough and the historian of the neighbourhood.[98] The vicars of this period were all scholarly men and notable for the grammar school which they conducted, and for the excellent classical library which they formed and housed in the church.[99] They also subscribed to and encouraged

[78] See list of medieval incumbents in MS. Top. Oxon. d 460.

[79] Blo. Bic. 170–1.

[80] Linc. Reg. xvii, Gray, f. 63; xxi, Rotherham, f. 88b.

[81] Ibid. xxiii, Smith, f. 306b; xxvii, Longland, f. 186b; Subsidy 1526, 273.

[82] Boarstall Cart. 101, 103. The earliest recorded priest, William, occurs in the same year.

[83] Blo. Bic. 100–1. For Ric. atte Grene (oc. 1392), probably the vicar's chaplain, see Kennett, Paroch. Antiq. ii. 174.

[84] MS. Top. Oxon. c 398, f. 104; Dunkin, Oxon. ii. 253, 254; MS. Top. Oxon. d 460.

[85] Kennett, Paroch. Antiq. ii. 258.

[86] Ibid. 395.

[87] Linc. Mem. Chedworth, f. 14, cited Blo. Bic. 70 n. 2. The vicar is described as vicarius ecclesie de Bygnell. For the Stokes see above, p. 23.

[88] Cal. Pat. 1354–8, 218.

[89] Linc. Reg. xxiii, Smith, f. 306b; Visit. Dioc. Linc. 1517–31, ii. 80.

[90] Subsidy 1526, 273.

[91] Visit. Dioc. Linc. 1517–31, i. 125.

[92] Ibid. ii. 81.

[93] See list of incumbents in Blo. Bic. 89–90. Cf. Kennett, Paroch. Antiq. ii, plate facing p. 224.

[94] MS. Top. Oxon. c 55, f. 262.

[95] Ibid. c 56, ff. 11–14; Oxf. Dioc. c 22, f. 234.

[96] For Bird, see below, p. 345.

[97] Par. Reg. sub annis 1658, 1663, 1670; Cal. Cttee. for Compounding, 1654, 2246.

[98] Oxf. Dioc. d 552, d 555; Blo. Bic. 92–94. For Kennett, cf. above, p. 21.

[99] For their school see V.C.H. Oxon. i. 463–4. In 1757 the library consisted of 130 books: Oxf. Archd. Oxon. b 22, ff. 249–52. They were sold in the early 20th cent. by the vicar: G. P. Crawford, Recollections (Reading), 53.

the charity school.[1] Their office in a town where dissent was so strong called for tact and vigilance and they undoubtedly considered their educational work as a means of combating nonconformity. Thomas Airson, for instance, reported in 1738 that the good influence of the charity school was a cause of the decline of Presbyterianism.[2] He was active in carrying out his spiritual duties: he preached two sermons on Sundays for most of the year; catechized every Sunday and twice a week in Lent; administered the sacrament once a month and on the main festivals. He had no regular curate, but a Mr. Penrose of Christ Church came out when required.[3] His successor John Princep reported in 1759 that the monthly number of communicants was about 40 and that there were about 140 at Easter and Christmas.[4] He was the last resident vicar until the 19th century and by 1771, after three years of non-residence, his curate's return shows that the number of communicants was already falling off,[5] although the curate was attentive to his duties, holding services three times a week and on holidays, and administering the sacrament once a month. By 1808 communicants, in spite of an increase in the population, numbered only 60 or 70 on festivals and about 30 at other times.[6] At this date there was once again a resident vicar. John Smith, instituted in 1800, began to reside in 1805. In 1816, however, he obtained leave of absence and the parish was served by a licensed curate, who lived at the Vicarage and received an annual stipend of £100.[7]

By 1817 there were signs that a revival of religious life had begun: there were 130 communicants on festivals and a Sunday school had been started.[8] In 1835 absenteeism ended.[9] Significant of the new spirit was the establishment of the Bicester Bible Society in 1822 and of a 'depository' of the S.P.C.K.[10] soon after. The long incumbency of J. W. Watts, vicar from 1843 to 1881, was particularly fruitful. The church building was restored and the cost of restoration was paid for partly by local contributions. Congregations grew, as Watts was a 'powerful preacher of the Evangelical school'—a school of thought long favoured by Bicester people and adhered to in spite of Bishop Wilberforce's influence.[11] It may be noted here that Wilberforce conducted an ordination at Bicester in 1869. Watts held three services on Sundays, attended by average congregations of 800, 1,000, and 400; catechized weekly, and held monthly communion services as well as on the four great festivals. There were generally 100 or more communicants. He was fully alive to the importance of education: he wanted to get an infant school opened and reported to his bishop that the state of his schools was a source of 'constant anxiety'.[12] Watt's successor, J. B. Kane, did good work in getting St. Edburg's Hall built. It comprised

reading, refreshment, and assembly rooms.[13] He was also active in the poverty-stricken Crockwell district, where there was a mission room. But his high church doctrine led to bitter divisions in the congregation in the 1890's. These, however, were quickly healed by G. P. Crawfurd (1894–1907), a moderate and devoted man. He held two services daily; had two choirs in addition to the ordinary male choir, one for men and women and one for girls, and a Church Lads' Brigade, while his wife organized the St. Edburg's Guild—a missionary guild and working party. There was a weekly children's service for about 300 children and two Sunday schools. His efforts to influence the teaching in the local schools was opposed by the dissenters, but he was ultimately successful.[14] Owing to his initiative Bicester had a Church Council of 25 members. It was nominated by the vicar and was useful in raising funds, particularly for the curate's stipend.[15]

The parish church of *ST. EDBURG*[16] now consists of a chancel, clerestoried nave and transepts with north and south aisles, a vestry (the former north chapel), a western tower and a north porch.[17] At the eastern end of the north arcade there is a small arch with a roughly built triangular head which has often been regarded as a relic of the pre-Conquest church. This may be the case, but the ascription of the arch to the Saxon period cannot be regarded as established, and it may well be of later date. In the 12th century the building consisted of chancel, nave, transepts, and central tower. Of this Romanesque church there survive three of the tower arches, parts of the transepts, and portions of a stringcourse with chevron moulding between the arches on the north side of the nave arcade. During the next century the chancel was enlarged and a priest's door was made in its south wall. A south aisle was also added: its four arches supported on clustered pillars are characteristic examples of the period.

In the 14th century octagonal pillars with moulded capitals were inserted in the north wall of the nave when the north aisle and chapel were added. The chapel (now the vestry) is entered through a wide arch in the north wall of the chancel. It once had an upper chamber, perhaps intended to lodge the sexton, which was later used as the vicars' grammar school. The doorway and external stair turret by which the upper room was reached still remain; so also does the perpendicular window in the east wall. The wooden screen, now dividing the vestry from the transept, is of the same date as the original chapel. A doorway in the north wall of the chapel has been blocked up.

Extensive alterations to the church were carried out in the 15th century. The central tower was taken down, its western arch was removed, and the space formerly occupied by the crossing was thrown into

[1] See below, p. 52.
[2] Oxf. Dioc. d 552.
[3] Ibid.
[4] Ibid. d 555.
[5] Ibid. d 561.
[6] Ibid. d 570.
[7] Oxf. Archd. Oxon. b 22, f. 297; ibid. b 21, ff. 33, 71.
[8] Oxf. Dioc. d 576.
[9] Blo. Bic. 95.
[10] Lascelles Dir. Oxon. (1853).
[11] Crawfurd, Recollections, 50–51; Oxf. Dioc. c 332, c 344.
[12] Wilb. Visit.

[13] Kelly's Dir. Oxon. (1887). It was sold in c. 1955 and became a furniture storehouse.
[14] See below, p. 52.
[15] Crawfurd, Recollections, passim.
[16] St. Edburga (d. 924) was the daughter of Edward the Elder. For a discussion of the dedication see Kennett, Paroch. Antiq. i. 189–91; K. E. Kirk, Church Dedications, 54–57. See above, pp. 16, 32.
[17] For accounts of the church building see Parker, Guide, 23–26; Blo. Bic. 78–85. There are no grounds for White Kennett's suggestion that the original dedication was to St. James or that the church was built at the end of the 14th cent.: Kennett, Paroch. Antiq. ii. 156–7.

the nave. The clerestory was added and the prolonged nave was reroofed with the existing low-pitched timber roof, supported on stone corbels.[18] The external walls of the building were surmounted by a parapet, and the western tower (75 ft. high) and its graceful interior arch were built. Its upper story is battlemented and it has panelled and crocketed pinnacles of similar design to those at New College, Oxford. In this century also a large Perpendicular window was added in both the north and south transepts, and a north porch with crenellated parapet and a chamber above, the last destroyed in 1863,[19] were built.

certainly being taken in the furniture of the church. In 1685 Sir William Glynne gave a large carpet of purple velvet with gold and silver fringe, a purple velvet cushion with gold and silk tassels for the communion table, and a similar cloth for the pulpit. At the same time the chancel was decorated with the hatchments and banners of the Glynne family.[24]

At the end of the century, during the incumbency of Thomas Shewring (1691–6), a faculty was sought for 'erecting' a vestry (16 ft. by 16 ft.) and for the removal of the font. The petition stated that the position of the pulpit and clerk's seat had been

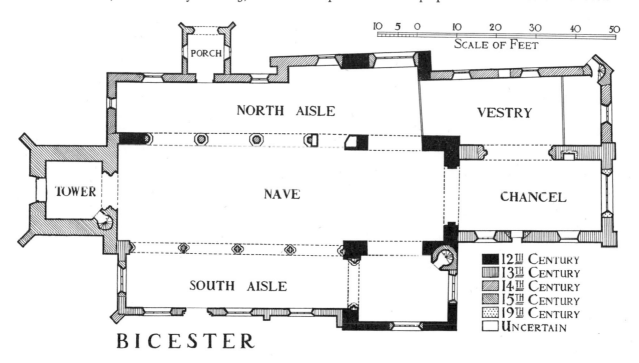

BICESTER

There is documentary evidence that some repairs, though perhaps only minor ones, were undertaken in the 1630's, since church vessels were sold in 1634 to defray the expense.[20] Later repairs included the provision of the rainwater pipes, one of whose heads, bearing the date 1655, survives on the north side of the nave. Two adjoining heads are dated 1704.

The wainscoting and black and white marble paving in the chancel, which were removed at the restoration of 1863, were probably added in the 17th century.[21] It may have been this beautification which led the vicar, Samuel Blackwell (1670–91), and others to complain that the churchwardens had spent 'great sums of money', with the result that the wardens undertook not to spend more than £5 in future without the consent of the parishioners.[22] The I H S 'within a splendid glory of red and yellow', which was once painted over the communion table,[23] may also have dated from this period, for interest was

already altered.[25] In 1693 a west gallery (25 ft. by 16 ft.), which was largely paid for by Sir William Glynne, Ralph Holt, and the vicar, was erected. A gallery warden was appointed to look after it.[26]

The ever-growing congregation and the desire of the better-off for more comfort led to the transformation of the interior of the church in the 18th and early 19th centuries by the addition of galleries. Faculties for two private galleries between the pillars of the north aisle were sought in 1739 and 1747; a third was erected over the north door, a fourth at the east end of the south transept, a fifth was constructed in 1810 across the chancel arch, and a sixth was added to the south aisle.[27] Two of the galleries were used by the singers and the charity-school children,[28] but the others were for the private use of various tradesmen.

Another change was the removal of the tracery in the medieval windows in order to lighten the church.

[18] A print of 1849 (see plate facing p. 46) shows that the roof was once more elaborate than now. It must have been much 'restored' in 1862–3.
[19] Blo. *Bic.* 79 n. 5. This room housed the grammar-school library and parish muniments. It was customary for rents to be paid to the Trustees of the Town Stock here: Char. Feoff. box, Barclays Bank, Bicester.
[20] Oxf. Archd. Oxon. c 12.
[21] [Sir Thomas Phillipps], *Paroch. Coll. of Co. of Oxf.* (1825): Bodl. copy is Manning, fol. 6.
[22] Oxf. Dioc. c 454, f. 56.

[23] Recorded in [Sir T. Phillipps], *Paroch. Coll. of Co. of Oxford* (1825).   [24] *Par. Coll.* i. 41.
[25] Oxf. Dioc. c 454, f. 60. For the school in the vestry see below, p. 52.
[26] Dunkin, *Bic.* 94 n. 8, citing gallery wardens' bk. (now lost). For a 17th-cent. view of the church see engraving by M. Burghers in Kennett, *Paroch. Antiq.* ii, facing p. 224.
[27] Oxf. Dioc. c 454, ff. 63, 64, 66, 68; Oxf. Archd. Oxon. c 36, f. 204; Blo. *Bic.* 84, citing faculties. For other faculties see Bodl. Oldfield's Paroch. Index, pp. 57–58.
[28] Oxf. Archd. Oxon. b 22, f. 293.

The windows in the south aisle were damaged in the great storm of 1765 and the occasion of their repair may well have been taken to remove their mullions and tracery.[29] By 1820 the tracery of the east window had also been cut out and a semicircular arch had been turned on the outside. The tracery of the clerestory windows had similarly been removed.[30] The lighting in the church had already been improved early in the 18th century by the gift of a brass chandelier, which was hung in the nave in memory of Robert Jemmett (d. 1736).[31] It was removed in 1862–3.

Rising standards led the parish to buy in 1770 for £50 from Sir Gregory Turner a fine organ, which had been at Ambrosden House. It was placed in the west gallery and superseded the bassoon bought in 1744.[32]

A thorough restoration took place in 1862–3. A beginning had been made in 1842, when the box pews had been cut down and the seating increased.[33] (Many of these high-backed pews had been installed in the 18th and early 19th centuries and had been appropriated to particular tradesmen's houses.)[34] But the church remained in 'a sadly dilapidated state' and a discredit to the parish.[35] The restoration, undertaken by the architect C. N. Beazley in consultation with G. E. Street, cost £3,214.[36] The builder was Fassnidge of Uxbridge.[37] The work consisted of the repair of the roofs, walls, and flooring of the body of the church; the chancel was completely rerooofed and new tiled. The tracery of all the windows in the chancel and the north and south aisles was restored in 'Geometrical' Gothic style. The galleries, 'a chaos of uplifted boxes',[38] were removed and the whole church was reseated. Heating and gas lighting were installed. The vestry was beautified later with a wooden screen with painted panels, dated 1882. In 1896 an iron chancel screen, which must also have been installed at this time, was removed on the advice of G. F. Bodley and T. Garner.[39]

The church is large and impressive but is not richly furnished. A 15th-century piscina in the south transept marks the site of a demolished altar; a loft to St. George, recorded in the 16th century,[40] and the roodloft over the chancel screen, to which access was gained by a staircase in the south transept, together with the screen have also gone;[41] so has the stained-glass window in memory of John Wykyns, vicar (1541–59), recorded in 1660.[42] Rawlinson mentioned coats of arms, painted on wainscoting in the north aisle, commemorating the local families of Staveley, Moore, and others, which are no longer in

situ.[43] A fragment of medieval glass, a figure blowing a trumpet, remains over the priest's door in the chancel.

The font, a plain polygonal one, probably dates from the 13th century. Early in the 20th century it was raised on two steps and the baptistery was panelled in oak in memory of the Revd. G. P. Crawfurd (vicar 1894–1907) and of his family.[44] The church once had a wooden three-decker pulpit, which was removed at the restoration in 1862, when the present stone and marble pulpit was installed.[45]

Recent stained-glass windows commemorate the death of Major Lewis Coker (d. 1858), Sir Gregory Page-Turner, Bt., and other members of the family, the Revd. John Watts (vicar 1843–81), Thomas Tubb and family, General Gordon (d. 1885), and C. A. Keith-Falconer (d. 1920).

Some fragments of medieval sculpture have been preserved. Built into the wall over the south nave arcade are two panels from a 14th-century tomb-chest with figures of knights for 'weepers', illustrated by Dunkin, and the effigy of a medieval lady stands against the west respond of the north aisle.[46] These are reputed to have been removed from the priory church at the time of the Dissolution. An unidentified Elias of Bicester and his wife were buried in the church and an indulgence was granted in 1302 to those who prayed for their souls,[47] but no memorial has survived.

There are brass inscriptions to the following: William Staveley (d. 1498), lord of Bignell, and his wife Alice (d. 1500); Roger Moore, Esq. (d. 1551), lord of the priory's manor, his wife Agnes Hussey (Husye) and son Thomas (d. 1574), with coats of arms; William Hartt or Hortt, gent. (d. 1584); Humphrey Hunt (d. 1601) and his wife Elizabeth; Rafe Hunt (d. 1602) and his two wives; John Coker (d. 1606/7) and wife Joane (d. 1618); John Lewes (d. 1612) of Lyn in Carnarvonshire who desired to be buried near John Coker 'for the love he bare' him; Richard Clarke (d. 1624/5), and Cadwallader Coker (d. 1653) and his two wives.[48] There are a large number of other memorials of which the most imposing are those to Robert Carver (d. 1698), the father of White Kennett's wife; to Sir Thomas Grantham (d. 1718), by Delvaux and Scheemakers;[49] to Sir Edward Turner (d. 1766) and his wife Cassandra (d. 1770).[50] The last, a large marble monument by J. Wilton with medallion portraits and an urn, was once in the chancel, but is now in the vestry. There is also a wall tablet to Sir Edward G. T. Page-Turner, 5th Bt. (d. 1846).

Seventeenth-century and later inscriptions to the

[29] Dunkin, *Bic.* 95, citing Par. Reg.; Blo *Bic.* 84–85. The initials and date W T 1750 cut in the moulding of the west window may date the mutilation of its tracery.
[30] Parker, *Guide*, 24.   [31] Ibid.
[32] Dunkin, *Bic.* 94–95, citing churchwardens' bk. (now lost).
[33] Blo. *Bic.* 85 n. 3, citing churchwardens' bk.
[34] e.g. Oxf. Archd. Oxon. b 22, ff. 293–6, 301–2, 311.
[35] MS. Top. Oxon. c 103, ff. 74, 78. There is a pre-restoration drawing (1800) ibid. b 220, f. 190; a drawing (1820) by J. Buckler ibid. a 65, f. 88. See also plate opposite.
[36] MS. Top. Oxon. c 103, ff. 63, 68, 82–84.
[37] Oxf. Dioc. b 70.   [38] Blo. *Bic.* 84.
[39] Faculty (Bodl. Bic. Par. Box).
[40] Blo. *Bic.* 80: bequest of 1543.
[41] The wooden chancel screen remained until the 19th cent.: ibid.

[42] Ibid. 81; Blomfield places in Bicester memorials to the Clements, Freemans ('Threman' in Wood), and others, but a compilation of 1662 (B.M. Harl. MS. 4170, p. 29) and Wood (*Par. Coll.* i. 64) assign them probably correctly to Bucknell, although the Clements and Freemans mentioned certainly resided in Bicester. For the Clements, see above, p. 37; for Wykyns, see above, p. 37, and *O.A.S. Rep.* 1914, 203.
[43] Blo. *Bic.* 81–82; *Par. Coll.* i. 38–39. See also *Topographer*, ii (1790), 306–9.
[44] G. P. Crawfurd, *Recollections* (Reading), 84. For an illustration of the font see Dunkin, *Oxon.* ii, between pp. 252–3.   [45] See plate opposite.
[46] Some are illustrated in Dunkin, *Oxon.* ii, opp. p. 252.
[47] Blo. *Bic.* 82, citing Linc. Reg. Dalderby.
[48] For these families see index.
[49] R. Gunnis, *Dictionary of British Sculptors* (1952), 126.
[50] For Sir E. Turner see *V.C.H. Oxon.* v. 16, 18.

The interior of the church from the east in 1849

BICESTER

New Buildings

Water Lane

BICESTER IN THE MID-19TH CENTURY

Cokers include the following: Catherine Coker (d. 1682), John Coker, gent. (d. 1710); Hearst Coker (d. 1719); Cadwallader Coker, citizen of London (d. 1780); an undated memorial to another John Coker and his wife Catherine and their elder sons Cadwallader and John;[51] John Coker (d. 1819); Thomas Lewis Coker (d. 1849); John Cadwallader Coker (killed in action 1914); Lewis Edmund Coker (d. 1924); and Major Lewis Aubrey Coker (d. 1953).

There were once tablets to three vicars: William Hall (d. 1670); Thomas Forbes (d. 1715); Thomas Airson (d. 1752); there is still one to the five children (d. 1677–84) of a fourth vicar, Samuel Blackwell, and his wife. Among the inhabitants of Bicester who are commemorated are Anne wife of Richard Clements (d. 1652); Ralph Clements (d. 1683); Gabriel Burrows (d. 1676/7), who shares a memorial with William Finch (d. 1692) and John Finch, grocer of London (d. 1707/8); Sarah Kennett (d. 1693/4), daughter of Robert Carver and wife of White Kennett;[52] William, son of Stephen Glynne of Merton (d. 1704); Mary, wife of John Burrowes (d. 1706); Mary, wife of John Burrowes, jr. (d. 1724); John Walker (d. 1783), and his son John (d. 1810). George and Susannah Tubb, well-known benefactors of the town, have a memorial erected in 1887 by 'the poor of this parish'.

There is a monument to Thomas Russell (d. 1718/19), 'late of St. James's, Westminster'. His connexion with Bicester has not been established. A 20th-century memorial commemorates Commander R. G. Fane (d. 1917), Capt. H. A. Fane, M.C. (d. 1918), and Major O. E. Fane, M.C. (d. 1918) of Wormsley (Bucks.), whose family were the tenants of Bicester House. They were killed in action.[53]

In 1552 the church was reported to have 2 silver chalices, 2 latten candlesticks, a latten censer, 5 copes, and 8 vestments.[54] In 1956 there was a silver-gilt Elizabethan chalice (1571); a service of silver comprising an enormous chalice and paten-cover, a large paten with foot, and a pair of large tankard flagons all hallmarked 1684. The flagons were given by Sir William Glynne. There were also a pair of silver chalices and a flagon inscribed 'Bicester Church 1873'.[55]

In 1552 there were four bells and a sanctus bell.[56] There is a local tradition that a ring of bells, probably the four at Ambrosden in 1552, was removed there because too heavy for Bicester's tower. If true, the bells must have gone before the erection of the present tower in the mid-15th-century.[57] In 1956 there was a ring of eight: four of the bells were made in the 18th century, three by the Whitechapel foundry, and one in 1715 by Richard Chandler of Drayton Parslow, Bucks. The churchwardens' accounts record recasting bells in 1708 and 1714 and 'mending the chimes' at a cost of £14 in 1766; they also show that there were six bells by 1714.[58]

In the Middle Ages a 'lampe light' (to burn perpetually before the Blessed Sacrament) had been endowed with lands valued in 1552 at 4s. 8d. The donor was not then known.[59]

The registers begin in 1539, the year in which Cromwell ordered the keeping of registers, and are among the earliest in the country.[60]

There was a medieval cross in the churchyard; it was removed in 1863. There is a memorial there to the 64 victims of the cholera epidemic of 1832.

ROMAN CATHOLICISM. There is little record of any Roman Catholicism in the parish until the 19th century. A certain John Butler of Bicester was fined £60 for recusancy in 1582[61] and in the early 17th century many of the Blount family were prominent Catholics.[62] Elizabeth, wife of Richard Blount, was returned as a recusant in 1605, and their son, Sir Charles Blount (d. 1644), paid heavy fines between 1623 and 1626.[63] His son Walter claimed that he was not a Roman Catholic, but in 1650 his estates at Mapledurham and Bicester were sequestered for his supposed recusancy, and in 1651 two-thirds of his woods there were ordered to be felled and sold.[64] His brother Lister also had great difficulty in clearing himself from the charge of recusancy, but was eventually discharged from sequestration for his lands in Bicester in 1654.[65] Four papists were recorded by the Compton Census of 1676; two papist families by the incumbent in 1738 and a third where the wife and children only were papists.[66] In 1768 there were said to be only two families—a farmer's and a brazier's—and in the early 19th century 'a few papists', who used the Tusmore chapel.[67] In 1869 the Hon. William North of Wroxton Abbey, later Lord North, a convert, endeavoured to revive the Roman Catholic mission in Bicester. Through his initiative Father Robson of Hethe started to celebrate mass in a cottage in Sheep Street. His successor Dr. Philip Sweeney built in King's End in 1883 St. Mary's School, which was also used as a chapel. The total cost was £900. Sweeney was followed by Father Glossop, who for twelve years served Bicester from Souldern.

In 1902 'South View' in the Oxford Road was lent to some Benedictine Olivetan nuns, exiled from France. In 1907 they moved to a new site near the Priory and opened a school. Their chapel, the present (1956) church, was opened to the public in 1908.

At the beginning of the 19th century the few Bicester Roman Catholics were served from

[51] This must be John Coker who died in 1767: Burke, *Land. Gent.*

[52] For details of a charity providing for the upkeep of her monument see Par. Rec.: indenture of 28 Nov. 1717, and below, p. 55.

[53] For blazons of arms and inscriptions in the church, see Bodl. G. A. Oxon. 4° 685, pp. 37–42; ibid. 688, pp. 37–40; ibid. 16° 217, pp. 64–66.   [54] *Chant. Cert.* 80.

[55] Evans, *Ch. Plate*; inf. the vicar.

[56] *Chant. Cert.* 80.

[57] *Ch. Bells Oxon.* i. 17, 43–46.   [58] Ibid. 44.

[59] *Chant. Cert.* 34.

[60] There are modern transcripts of marriages for 1539 to 1811: MS. Top. Oxon. e 264, 265.

[61] Hist. MSS. Com. *Salisbury MSS. XIII.* 212.

[62] For the family's connexion with Bicester, see above, p. 22.

[63] Salter, *Oxon. Recusants*, 22, 37, and *passim*.

[64] *Cal. Cttee. for Compounding*, 2245.

[65] Ibid. 2246. For the sequestration of Joan Busby's lands at Bicester, see ibid. 3239; Stapleton, *Cath. Miss.* 107–8. Her husband was John Busby of Addington (Bucks.) and she does not seem to have been resident at Bicester. No papists were recorded in the Compton Census.

[66] Oxf. Dioc. d 552.

[67] Ibid. d 555, d 558, d 570, d 574, d 576. Cf. return of 1767: ibid. c 431, which gives 4 papists.

Begbroke by fathers[68] of the Servite monastery there. In 1904 a Basque priest settled in the town[69] and was later joined by French Fathers of the Sacred Heart. In 1920, when the religious persecution in France had subsided, the French nuns and priests returned to France. The nuns' chapel continued to be used as a parish church.

The mission was again served mainly by priests from Begbroke until 1931, when Bicester began to share a parish priest with Hethe, Father Ignatius McHugh. In 1937 he was succeeded by Father Stephen Webb, who moved to Bicester in 1942 to a house bequeathed to the mission. In 1943 Bicester became a Roman Catholic parish.[70]

In 1948 the work of the mission was immensely increased by the arrival of 1,000 European Voluntary Workers, mostly Polish. By 1949, when General Anders visited his compatriots and presented to the church of the Immaculate Conception a painting of 'Our Lady of Czestochowa', they had a Polish chaplain. The Roman Catholic parish was still growing in numbers in 1955 owing to the influx of workers from Ireland and elsewhere to meet the local demand for labour.[71]

SERBO-ORTHODOX CHURCH. St George's Chapel at the garrison, just outside Bicester, is used for worship by the Jugoslav community (20 civilian families and 130 Jugoslavs from the camp for European Voluntary Workers). Services conducted by their own priest are held there every four or six weeks, and burial services are sometimes held there. For the great festivals the community attends services in London, but there is a special celebration of the Orthodox Christmas Eve in Bicester.[72]

PROTESTANT NONCONFORMITY. The history of Protestant dissent in Bicester seems to go back to the reign of Elizabeth I, when trouble, apparently over doctrinal matters, broke out between the vicar and his parishioners.[73] Order was restored, and the next record of nonconformity occurs in 1654, when the Cromwellian commissioners appointed vicar the 'godly and painful' preacher William Hall, who had been curate in Bicester for some years.[74] After the Act of Uniformity of 1662 an 'illegal' conventicle was set up: in 1669 'separa-

tists', numbering one or two hundred, are said to have met in the barn of a baker, Thomas Harris. A pulpit, seats, and a gallery were erected, and the incumbent reported that numbers were increasing 'by reason of their (i.e. the separatists') impunity'.[75] Dr. Thomas Lamplugh, Rector of Charlton-on-Otmoor, wrote in alarm at the boldness and daring of the 'sectarians' and of this public meeting-place, where 'there is a greater number every Sunday than in the church'. He also complained that sectarian influence from Bicester had infected most of the neighbouring parishes.[76] Nevertheless, it is noteworthy that the Compton Census of 1676 and Bishop Fell in about 1685 recorded no dissenters.[77] The preachers at Bicester were the ministers ejected from neighbouring churches—Edward Bagshawe, Samuel Wells, George Swinnock, John Dod, John Troughton, and Thomas Whateley.[78] Samuel Lee, the eminent Puritan divine who was resident at Bignell between 1664 and 1678, also 'sometimes kept conventicles at Bicester'.[79] Troughton, a learned Oxford theologian, respected for his moderation even by the Anglican clergy, was licensed as a Presbyterian preacher in 1672, and his house as a meeting-place; he died in 1681 and was buried in Bicester parish church.[80] Henry Bornish, another well-known Puritan preacher, became in 1690 the first pastor of the Bicester congregation.[81] A contemporary pamphlet says he preached 'for profit's sake (his salary was £30 a year) to silly women and other obstinate people'.[82] Less prejudiced observers remarked on the community's intelligence and vital religion.[83] Cornish lived 'very loveingly' with his flock, until his death in 1698.[84] John Troughton the younger followed him.[85] He had occasionally assisted Cornish and was later responsible for building the new chapel. It was licensed in 1728 in place of the old house 'now ruinous'.[86] He was buried in its cemetery in 1739.

The denominational history of the Bicester congregation is of exceptional interest. After the Toleration Act of 1689, Presbyterians and Independents in the country generally formed the 'Happy Union', which terminated in acrimony in 1694.[87] In Bicester, on the contrary, the records show clearly that late into the 18th century Presbyterians and Independents continued to work together, and sometimes brought preachers of other denominations

---

[68] The above account from 1869 is based on an 'Account of the Bicester Catholic Mission' by Fr. S. F. Webb, S.J.: *Bicester Advertiser*, 11 Jan. 1946.

[69] Stapleton, *Cath. Miss.* 95.

[70] Fr. Webb's account: *Bic. Advertiser*.

[71] Inf. Fr. Thomas Foynes, Bicester.

[72] Inf. Mr. and Miss Janković; *Oxf. Mail*, 7 Jan. 1957.

[73] See above, p. 43.

[74] Ibid.

[75] *Early Nonconformity Records*, ed. G. L. Turner, iii. 69, 827. An inscription on the outside of the church claims that it was founded in 1662.

Calamy probably erred in saying that a certain Mr. Basnet was ejected from the vicarage, but as Bird died in Sept. 1653 it has been suggested that Samuel Basnet filled his place for a time before Hall: *Freedom after Ejection*, ed. A. Gordon, 214.

[76] *Cal. S. P. Dom.* 1668-9, 151.

[77] Compton Census; Oxf. Dioc. d 708, f. 137.

[78] *Early Nonconformity Recs.*, ed. Turner, iii. 827, 829-30.

[79] Wood, *Athenae*, iv. 345-8.

[80] *Early Nonconformity Recs.* iii. 827, 830; *Cal. S. P. Dom.* 1672, 236; Dunkin, *Bic.* 119; Wood, *Athenae*, iv. 9-12. In 1724 and 1727 Hearne wrote about a local wheelwright who

was 'zealous for predestination' and preached in his own house and had printed a pamphlet or two: Hearne, *Remarks*, viii. 234; ix. 265.

[81] *Freedom after Ejection*, ed. Gordon, 85, 242.

[82] [? White Kennett], *Some remarks on the life, death and burial of Mr. Henry Cornish B.D. an eminent dissenting teacher . . .* '1698'.

[83] The Vicar of Dinton (Bucks.), cited in Dunkin, *Bic.* 121. He preached the funeral sermon: G. P. Crawfurd, *Recollections* (Reading), 88.

[84] *Freedom after Ejection*, ed. Gordon, 242.

[85] Dunkin, *Bic.* 121-2; John Rolls, *Some Account of the Bicester Dissenters*, p. 11. This MS. (*penes* Mr. S. G. Hedges, Bicester) was completed in 1827, but was continued by the author's nephew Samuel Rolls during the years 1831-3. There is a transcript in the Cong. Ch. Chest. It will be referred to hereafter as Rolls MS. It is not a reliable source. Troughton's name first appears on the list of officiating ministers in 1695 and 1696: Reg. of Marriages and Baptisms at the Cong. Ch. For the inscription on his tombstone in the Cong. Ch., now almost illegible, see Rolls MS. p. 30. A list of ministers from 1690 to 1952 corrected and added to by Miss G. Dannatt is in Cong. Ch. Chest.

[86] Cal. Q. Sess. viii.

[87] *Freedom after Ejection*, ed. Gordon, 154-7.

into their fellowship. The bond of union was their common aversion to the Established Church. Local opinion was uncertain how to designate the nonconformists; in 1738 and 1759 the vicar described them as Presbyterians; in 1808 he said they described themselves as Independents.[88] The earliest surviving minute-book, under the date 1771, speaks of 'the Congregation or Society of Protestant Dissenters from the Church of England commonly called Presbyterians'.[89] In Cornish's time the church's income was derived from the Presbyterian and Congregational (i.e. Independent) Common Fund, and at least as late as 1827 it came partly from the Presbyterian Fund and partly from the Independent Board, as well as from private benefactions.[90]

The congregation was even more catholic in the choice of its ministers and preachers. John Ludd Fenner, pastor from 1771 to about 1774, was a Unitarian; that 'dear man of God', Edward Hickman (d. 1781), 'was quite Calvinistical in principle, but of a truly catholic spirit';[91] and another minister was of the Countess of Huntingdon's Connexion.[92] As for preachers, 'they had all sorts . . . Calvinistic, Arminians, Arians, Socinians, Baptists, and Methodists'.[93] In the 19th century the church was served by Independents or Congregationalists, as they were beginning to be called locally. Yet between 1810 and 1855, of seven young men[94] who entered the ministry from Bicester chapel, three became Baptists, and as late as 1903 the deacons of the chapel would have appointed a Baptist as their regular pastor, had not the Congregational Union refused permission. The chapel, however, did not tolerate the Antinomians, who seceded from it in 1812, or the Antipaedobaptists.[95]

A study of the earliest baptismal register suggests that Bicester was a centre for Nonconformists in a wide area; children were brought from Buckingham, Tingewick (Bucks.), Fritwell, Charlton, and other villages.[96] In spite of a decline after Troughton's death in 1739 the church became in time the founder of other congregations. In 1789 John Rolls withdrew to form a church at Aylesbury; in 1807 Richard Fletcher's influence led to the founding of a church at Launton; a church at Blackthorn followed in 1825 and one at Merton in 1890.[97] Open-air preaching in neighbouring villages, begun by John Fenner in Buckinghamshire villages in about 1772, was revived in the 1830's by Henry Davis, assistant to Richard Fletcher.[98] But its principal exponent was Davis's

successor, William Ferguson. He preached himself and tried the method of sending out 'lay agents' to evangelize.[99] Revival prayer meetings were another characteristic of his work; they were initiated in September 1859 and held six days a week.[1]

Through Ferguson's energy the Water Lane chapel was enlarged and modernized.[2] In the face of strong opposition he got it licensed for the solemnization of marriages, only a few years after it had been permitted by law to conduct marriage services in nonconformist chapels.[3] He collected some £200 towards the upkeep of the chapel, and increased its effective membership from about 27 to 70.[4] He claimed to have added 111 new members, but some emigrated and some were expelled as unsatisfactory. Under the year 1860, for example, he notes: 'Jessie Carter gone back to sin'.[5] He was also active in good works in Bicester and the surrounding villages, and founded a missionary and other societies, libraries, Sunday and evening schools, and a clothing club.[6] His wife kept a young ladies' boarding-school. Such an energetic crusader against the 'fearful and blasting immorality of the town and neighbourhood' —his own description to a select committee of the House of Commons—was bound to meet with opposition.[7] He was consequently obliged to leave Bicester temporarily. After his return, though he found some of his 'crew very unmanageable', he stayed until 1860.[8] Another important pastor of the 19th century was W. H. Dickenson (1864–74 and 1887–8). His ministry was especially notable for its Good Friday anniversary gatherings, for good relations with the Anglicans, and for the building of a schoolroom and the restoration of the chapel building.[9]

A few of the pastors were less worthy: Samuel Park (1739–c. 1766) was 'gay and light in his practices, fond of convivial company';[10] David Davis (1768–71) was 'a slave to his ale and pipe', and finally absconded with his debts unpaid.[11] T. H. Norton (1899–1902), who abandoned his wife for the wife of one of his deacons, caused a scandal from which the church did not fully recover until the stable ministry of Thomas Smith (1915–25).[12] Later, there was another set-back when the church was without a regular minister for about eight years, a period which ended with the part-time appointment in 1952 of the Revd. S. G. Burden, who was also pastor of Launton.[13]

The congregation fluctuated both in numbers and

[88] Oxf. Dioc. d 552; ibid. d 555; ibid. d 507.
[89] Cong. Ch. Min. bk. i. (Feb. 1780–1865): see heading to list of bequests at back of volume.
[90] Rolls MS. p. 42.
[91] Cong. Ch. Min. bk. i; account written by Wm. Rolls, father of John Rolls: Rolls MS. p. 47.
[92] Rolls MS. pp. 45, 47.
[93] Ibid. p. 50.
[94] W. Ferguson, *Facts 300 Years Ago and Facts Now: or the Trials and Triumphs of Nonconformists* (priv. print. Oxf. 1855), 31–32 n., for six of them. The seventh was the younger Richard Fletcher, who preached in Bicester in 1865: Cong. Ch. Min. bk. i; Cong. Ch. Deacons' mins. (1901–15).
[95] Rolls MS. continuation, p. 7; Cong. Ch. Min. bk. i, 28 Aug. 1800.
[96] Cong. Ch. The register contains 1 marriage and 434 baptisms 1696–1745. For its loss and recovery, see correspondence in Deacons' minutes. Later registers include burials 1894–1929, marriages 1889–1929, baptisms 1890–1929.
[97] Cong. Ch. Min. bk. i; Ferguson, *Trials*, 34.

[98] Rolls MS. p. 45 and continuation. The MS. states that Davis did not apparently become minister until 1833.
[99] Ferguson, *Trials*, 39, and Ferguson, *Our Rural Churches* (Bic. 1819), *passim*.
[1] Oxf. Dioc. b 70: letter from J. Fogg of Winslow (Bucks.), an independent minister, whose preaching in Bicester had roused 'great emotional scenes'.
[2] See above, p. 18.
[3] For whole story see Ferguson, *Trials*, 44–46.
[4] Ibid. 28, 31–32.
[5] Cong. Ch. Min. bk. ii (1866–74).
[6] Ferguson, *Trials*, 31–33, 51–52.
[7] Ibid. 53.
[8] Ibid. 51, 57–60.
[9] Cong. Ch. Min. bk. ii, 10 Apr. 1868 and *passim*; ibid., enclosed draft of testimonial.
[10] Rolls MS. p. 36; cf. also his neglect of the baptismal register. There are only 9 entries signed by him, the last dated 1745. [11] Rolls MS. p. 45.
[12] See Cong. Ch. Deacons' min. 1901–3, *passim*, for whole case.
[13] Inf. the Revd. S. G. Burden.

influence during the centuries. In the late 17th century and throughout the 18th century the dissenters were influential and respected: they included several gentlemen, such as Metcalfe, Wilson, and Jonathan Sayer, the son-in-law of the elder Troughton.[14] They were 'a little company of true disciples', which was joined for a time by Col. Gardiner, the commander of troops quartered in the town before the Jacobite Rebellion of 1745.[15] A list of chapel trustees of 1749 includes bakers, glovers, a hempdresser, and a mason.[16] William Rolls, a currier, to take another example, was a deacon and church secretary for many years in the mid-18th century; his son wrote an account of the early history of the church and formed a church at Aylesbury, and his grandson Samuel Rolls, a pawnbroker, was a deacon in Ferguson's time.[17] Another notable family was the Gurdens: father and son taught for a long period in the Sunday school, which the elder Gurden (d. 1830), a deacon, helped to establish in 1792.[18]

Nonconformity declined in the mid-18th century. The vicar reported in 1759 that the Presbyterians were 'so reduced in numbers and property that they could not support a teacher had he not a fortune of his own'.[19] In 1767 the congregation petitioned for outside help with the payment of their minister's salary. They declared that even with help from the funds at London it was a heavy burden, and that they were now unable to raise £130 needed for the repair of the meeting-house and the purchase of a house for a Latin school, which is 'proposed as the only possible way of continuing the interest amongst us'.[20] The vicars' returns to episcopal visitations repeatedly refer to diminishing numbers: in the early 19th century there were said to be no more than about 100 Independents.[21] This information is supported by Rolls, who accounted for his church's apathy by the dying out of the families once prominent in the movement, by the lack of manufacturing employment in the town, which led many of the younger men to leave the district; but chiefly by the indifference of generations which had not known persecution and were too often obliged to endure poor preachers.[22] Nevertheless in 1793, when war with revolutionary France was imminent, the Bicester Independents were sufficiently alive to draw up a 'Loyalist Address' of their own rather than co-operate with the 'Gentry, Clergy, and Citizens of the Town'.[23] And in 1794 they forestalled the Anglican church in giving support to a Sunday school.[24]

Although numbers were small throughout the 19th century and later,[25] the congregation included many who played an important part in the life of the town.[26] Especially notable among them were G. R. Hewiett, editor of the *Bicester Herald* and a member of the Market End Local Government Board,[27] and A. F. Lambourne (d. 1949), who was also prominent in local government.[28]

THE SOCIETY OF FRIENDS. The earliest reference to Quakers at Bicester occurs in 1676.[29] Two years later permission was given by the Witney Quarterly Meeting for a monthly meeting to be held in turn at the houses of Edward Thomas and John Harper. In 1679 it was being held regularly in Harper's barn. It was placed in the Banbury Division.[30] The meeting soon seems to have lapsed, for in 1709 a 'new' meeting was set up,[31] and it is likely that Jeremy Lepper, labourer, of Bicester, and William Giles of Winslow (Bucks.), a woollen-draper, who were both heavily fined at Quarter Sessions in 1708 and 1709, were connected with the revival. One was fined for having an illegal conventicle in his house, the other for preaching.[32] In 1738 there were six families of Quakers (of which some members were churchgoers), who met twice a week. All refused legal dues and the incumbents had had recourse five times to the justices.[33] In 1749 John Griffith of Pennsylvania visited this 'small poor meeting' and found 'little of the life of religion among them'.[34] Their decline continued: in 1757 the Quarterly Meeting noted that no weekday meetings were held at Bicester, and in 1759, according to the vicar's return to the bishop, the fortnightly meeting was composed of only five families and ten other persons.[35] Bishop Butler's reference of 1779 to the 'peaceable' and law-abiding characteristics of the Quakers at Bicester are probably less of a compliment than would appear on the surface, for in 1796 the Quakers were said to meet seldom or not at all.[36] John Dunkin, writing in 1816, said their meeting-house was in a yard off Sheep Street nearly opposite the 'White Lion', but that the meeting had ceased to exist.[37] It has never been revived.

THE METHODISTS. John Wesley's preaching in Brackley (Northants) in 1748 was indirectly responsible for the origin of the Bicester Methodist church.

[14] Rolls notes (Rolls MS. p. 21) 'that Metcalfe had great possessions in and about Bister', and it is likely that he is the Christopher Metcalfe who figures in the Market End inclosure award (see above, p. 30). The cousins of a Samuel Wilson, Mary Shepley (d. 1770) and Joanna Hodges (d. 1772), each left £100 to the Bicester dissenters, to be invested in 3 per cent. govt. stock: Cong. Ch. Min. bk. i, note at back; Rolls MS. p. 10 n. For Sayer, see ibid. p. 15.

[15] Rolls MS. pp. 21 n., 40.

[16] Listed in chapel trust deed 1874 in Cong. Ch. Min. bk. ii.

[17] Wm. Ferguson, *Trials*, 53 n. and Cong. Ch. Min. bk. i. Some of the Rolls family now live in Bedford and are members of the Bunyan Meeting: inf. Beds. County Archivist, Shire Hall, Bedford.

[18] Rolls MS. continuation, p. 2; Gurden's tablet in Cong. Ch.; Min. bk. i.

[19] Oxf. Dioc. d 555.

[20] Cong. Ch. Petition of 31 Aug. 1767. It did not succeed: Rolls MS. p. 45.

[21] Oxf. Dioc. d 570; ibid. d 576.

[22] Rolls MS. pp. 35, 50.

[23] *Oxf. Jnl.* 19 Jan. 1793.

[24] See below, p. 54.

[25] Oxf. Dioc. d 570, d 576; Ferguson, *Trials*, 30. In 1951 there were 24 church members, 18 scholars in the schools: *Cong. Handb. of N. Bucks Union*, 1951.

[26] Cong. Ch. Min. bk. ii: chapel trust deed 1874.

[27] For his local govt. activities see Bic. U.D.C. Market End Local Govt. Board Min. bks. (late 1860's and 1870's, especially vol. ii, 1874–5, and last vol.); Cong. Ch. Financial mins.

[28] Inf. Bic. U.D.C. office.

[29] Witney Q. Meeting, Min. bk. 1671–1746: Berks. Record Office, Reading.

[30] Ibid.

[31] Ibid.

[32] Cal. Q. Sess. viii.

[33] Oxf. Dioc. d 552.

[34] John Griffith, *Journal of Life, Travels and Labours in Work of Ministry* (London 1779), 187.

[35] Witney Q. Meeting, Min. bk. 1747–80; Oxf. Dioc. d 555.

[36] Oxf. Dioc. c 327, p. 45; *Returns of Places of Worship of Protestant Dissenters*, H.C. 156, pp. 83 sqq. (1852–3), lxxviii.

[37] Dunkin, *Bic.* 124.

While there he 'awakened' a certain Mrs. Bowerman, and when she and her husband moved to Bicester they invited the Brackley Methodist minister to preach in the town.[38] In 1815 a room in a farm-house in Sheep Street was licensed for worship, and in 1816 a building in Sheep Street was licensed as a chapel.[39] The vicar reported in 1817 that the Wesleyans had no resident preacher and seldom the same one.[40] The sect prospered and in 1841 a new chapel was built in North Street.[41] In 1885 a school-room was added, in 1892 the chapel was enlarged at a cost of £438, and in 1904 an organ was installed for £270. Early in the 20th century the property in Sheep Street, now called Wesley Hall, together with Wesley cottages, was purchased at a cost of £1,650. In 1927 the church in Sheep Street was opened, the North Street chapel having been sold two years previously. The new red brick building seated 420 and cost £7,921.[42] Wesley Hall was sold to Messrs. F. W. Woolworth in 1955.[43]

The Sunday school has long been an important feature of Methodist life in Bicester. For instance, during the Sunday school anniversary of 1860, 'the communion rail was crowded with penitents',[44] and at the present time (1956) the school's religious and social life has a strong influence on the youth of the town.

As the Methodist movement grew in Bicester, it was threatened with schism. In May 1843 preachers of the Primitive Methodist group from Oxford—'Ranters'—began to preach in the Market Square. The magistrates complained to the Secretary of State that attempts by Bicester people to stop them preaching had created 'a very great disturbance', and they asked if any legal steps could be taken to prevent this open-air preaching. The group persisted in its visits for eleven weeks, but appears to have been finally deterred by the threat of violence.[45] Two houses, however, were licensed for dissenting meeting-places in 1843 which may have been connected with this revival, and in 1846 a licence was certainly issued for a meeting-place for the sect.[46] A much more serious threat to the Methodist movement came in about 1860 from the United Methodist Free Church led by W. A. Ryder, a Bicester grocer.[47] The group built its own chapel in Sheep Street in 1863, but after about 40 years of separate existence its chapel was taken over by the Wesleyans, and has since been known as Wesley Hall.[48] In 1883 Ryder had prosecuted several persons for disturbing his congregation.[49]

The activities of the reunited Bicester Methodists have included special evangelistic services, a sister-hood, a guild, a ladies' working-party and a boys'

brigade.[50] In 1955 the Methodists were the largest of the nonconformist societies in Bicester.[51]

PLYMOUTH BRETHREN. This society had a chapel in New Buildings in July 1904.[52] In the 1950's it met in Gospel Hall in North Street, but ceased to do so in 1956. A rival branch of the society has met in a building in Victoria Road at least since 1938. In both cases membership was small.

THE SALVATION ARMY. The Army has been active in Bicester since 1886 at least, and in August 1955 was visited by General Booth.[53] By 1939, however, its numbers had fallen considerably. In the early days of the Second World War the meeting-hall in Victoria Road was given up and the Bicester branch ceased to exist. Since then members of the Buckingham branch have visited the town annually to make house-to-house collections in their self-denial week.

THE UNITED CHURCH. In March 1954 the first known United Church for Christians of all denominations to be set up in Great Britain was established. The church began with an invitation to the Congregational minister, the Revd. S. G. Burden, to hold a service on the premises of the social club of Highfield estate, a newly developed suburb of Bicester. Regular Sunday services followed, conducted by clergy and laymen from the Church of England, the Congregational, the Baptist and Methodist churches, and others. A Sunday school, attended by 100 children, was opened. The experiment has been so successful that the church committee opened a fund in 1955 to purchase land and pay for the erection of a permanent building.[54]

SCHOOLS. There may well have been some provision for the education of Bicester boys in the early Middle Ages, but the first indication of it occurs in 1445, when it was reported at an episcopal visitation that the schoolmaster was taking his meals with the canons in their refectory, and that two sons of neighbouring gentry, one a Purcell of Newton Purcell, were being boarded in the priory.[55] The schoolmaster was probably a chantry priest of the parish church, and his admission to the refectory was considered irregular.[56]

There is no evidence about what steps, if any, were taken to provide schooling for the children of the town and neighbourhood after the dissolution of the chantries. A private grammar school in the town is first recorded about 1669. The school, preferred by the Verneys of Claydon to Eton, was well supported by the local gentry and tradesmen, and apparently continued until at least 1768.[57] An endowed elementary school may have been founded

[38] *Birthday Booklet, Wesleyan Methodist Ch. Bicester* (1928); *John Wesley's Jnl.*, ed. N. Curnock.

[39] Oxf. Dioc. c 644, f. 172.

[40] Ibid. d 576.

[41] H.O. 121/158. Rooms in houses were licensed as dissenting meeting-places in 1781, 1810, 1813, and 1831. These may have been for Methodists: Oxf. Dioc. c 644, ff. 66, 112, 159, 179. The North Street chapel is now Weyland Hall.

[42] The above inf. comes from the *Birthday Booklet* (1928). For a detailed description of the new church see F. Smith, *Bic. Guide and Dir.* (Bic. U.D.C. 1953).

[43] Local inf.

[44] *Birthday Booklet* (1928).

[45] Ferguson, *Trials*, 41–43. He wrongly dates these events May 1842; Magistrates' Bk. (1843–46) *penes* Mr. E. K. Truman, Bicester.

[46] Oxf. Dioc. c 646, ff. 193, 203; c 647, f. 41. Cf. H.O. 129/158 (the census of 1951 records an independent 'preaching room' opened in 1846).

[47] Inf. the Revd. P. H. Foster, High Wycombe (Bucks.).

[48] *Cassey's Dir. of Berks. and Oxon.* (1868).

[49] Reg. of Court of Summary Jurisdiction (1880–2), Magistrates' mins. (1834–9), Magistrates' meetings (1853–7) *penes* Mr. E. K. Truman.

[50] *Birthday Booklet* (see above, n. 38).

[51] Inf. the Revd. A. S. Valle, Bicester.

[52] *Bic. Advertiser*, 8 July 1904.

[53] Ibid. 31 Dec. 1886.

[54] *Oxf. Times*, 7 Jan. 1955.

[55] *Visit. Dioc. Linc. 1420–49*, ii. 35.

[56] Ibid.

[57] For the history of the grammar school see *V.C.H. Oxon.* i. 463.

earlier than the grammar school. It must have existed before 1688 when George Wickham, mercer of Oxford, left £50 by will 'to the trustees of the charity school of Bicester for the benefit of poor children'.[58]

As elsewhere the war of the Spanish succession was followed at Bicester by a renewed interest in education. The inhabitants and the local gentry subscribed in 1721 to set up a Church school to teach reading and the knowledge and practice of the Christian religion, since 'profaneness and debauchery are greatly increased owing to . . . want of an early and pious education in youth'.[59] The charity school which opened in the 'Free School House' adjoining the church was evidently an enlargement of the old school, for it was supported by investments as well as subscriptions.[60] Like many other schools founded at this period the charity school was called a Blue Coat school, since its boys were provided annually with blue coats, leather breeches, and cap.[61] In 1725, after a subscriber had declared that he would withdraw his subscription unless the children were employed in some kind of work, a short-lived experiment was made of setting the children to spin jersey.[62] By 1738 the school was in financial difficulties owing to the deaths of many of the original supporters and it was feared that it might come to an end. Thirty boys were then being educated, and 24 of them clothed; on leaving they went into husbandry or service.[63] New subscribers, including the bishop, were obtained and the school was flourishing in 1745.[64]

The number of boys in the school was usually about 30. Those receiving clothes varied in number —in 1748 24 were being clothed, while in 1752 all 30 boys received clothes. In 1748 John Dunkin, who was to become a noted local historian, had been elected a probationer by the trustees and in the following year part of the school was moved to rooms under the Town Hall.[65] It was later moved to a room over the 'Cage and Engine House' and then to the vestry.[66] When Dunkin wrote his diary he said that the master of the school in his day, James Jones, was 'an excellent writer and arithmatician, who keeps the best school in Bicester', and that all the tradesmen's and farmers' sons were educated there.[67] The chief subscribers at this period were the Earl of Abingdon, and members of the Dashwood, Turner, and Coker families. In 1761 they subscribed sums varying from £12 10s. to £4 4s. A charity sermon provided £3 17s. out of the income of £32 4s. received in 1783. By 1836 receipts had risen to £87 19s. 11d.[68] Part of this increase came after 1811 from £16 a year from the Walker charity.[69] Nevertheless, in 1825 it was recorded that the master's salary of £25 a year had been recently reduced from £30 a year.[70] In the 1820's the number of boys was fixed at 30, since the schoolroom was incapable of holding a larger number.[71] The school had presumably been moved by 1833, when it was officially stated that there were 60 boys at a school, which was partly supported by an endowment of £22 a year and partly by voluntary subscriptions.[72] The high numbers are probably to be explained by the attendance of fee-paying pupils as well as the 30 charity boys. In 1854 a school, described as the Blue Coat school, was being held in the vestry.[73]

NATIONAL SCHOOLS. Early in the 19th century efforts were made to convert the charity school into a National school. In 1815 it was reported that 'peculiar circumstances prevent the adoption of the National System at present'.[74] The difficulties were due to differences between the church and the large nonconformist element in the town. The system was introduced for girls, however, in 1835, when T. L. Coker, the lord of the manor and a strong Anglican, gave ground opposite the church for the school building.[75] The new school was financed by local subscriptions and a government grant.[76] This success was followed in 1858 by the opening of a National school for boys and girls. Due chiefly to the efforts of Charles Fowler, a tenant farmer, and the vicar, the Revd. J. W. Watts, over £1,000 was raised and a government grant of £800 was obtained. The building comprised two classrooms, one for boys and one for girls, and a master's house. It cost nearly £2,000.[77]

In 1861 the Blue Coat School was amalgamated with the new National school.[78] According to the Deed of Trust the school's Board of Management was to be elected by the subscribers. The nonconformist strength in the town resulted in an annual struggle with the church's supporters to obtain a majority on the board. The nonconformists were doubtless responsible for the stipulation that 'the Bible was to be read daily but that no child was to be required to learn the catechism or other religious formulary'.[79] They were also strong enough to prevent the clergy teaching in the National schools until the Education Act of 1902 abolished the School Board and they lost their influence. Since the vicar had been designated as the chairman of the Board of Management by the Deed of Trust of 1858, he was able to induce the Board of Education to classify the school as a Church school,[80] and henceforward the school was managed in accordance with the form prescribed for such schools. Church influence had already gained a victory when the infant school was opened in 1869 in Spring Close off the Bucknell Road. The land was again leased by the Coker family and the vicar and his successor were authorized 'to superintend

[58] MS. Top. Oxon. c 45, f. 207.
[59] Dunkin, Bic. 111.
[60] Ibid. 112.
[61] Ibid. 113; for the earliest use of the name found see Oxf. Dioc. d 564 (1774).
[62] Dunkin, Bic. 112.
[63] Oxf. Dioc. d 552.
[64] See Char. Sch. Acct. Bk. 1745–83: Char. Feoff. box, Barclays Bank, Bicester.
[65] Ibid.
[66] Dunkin, Bic. 18. Elsewhere Dunkin refers to the Cage, &c., as the Guardroom: ibid. 112; P.O. Dir. Oxon. (1854).
[67] Dunkin's MS. Diary cited Bic. Advertiser, 12 Apr. 1901.
[68] Char. Sch. Acct. Bk. 1745–83. For reports in 1759, 1768, and 1771 see Oxf. Dioc. d 555, d 558, d 561.
[69] See below, p. 55.
[70] 12th Rep. Com. Char. 285.
[71] Ibid.
[72] Educ. Inq. Abstract, 741.
[73] P.O. Dir. Oxon. (1854).
[74] Oxf. Dioc. c 433.
[75] P.O. Dir. Oxon. (1854).
[76] Educ. Inq. Abstract, 741.
[77] P.O. Dir. Oxon. (1864).
[78] Hewiett's Almanack and Bic. Dir. (1861).
[79] Deed of Trust (1858) penes the vicar.
[80] G. P. Crawfurd, Recollections of Bicester (Reading), 72.

the religious and moral instruction of all the children'.[81]

The three 'Rs', geography, history and scripture, and needlework for the girls were taught in the National school.[82] Fees in 1869 were 1d. to 3d. a week for each pupil, according to the rateable value of the houses in which they lived; by 1882 they had doubled, but in 1891 an Act of Parliament abolished all fees.[83] Numbers had risen from about 300 in 1862 to an average attendance of 372 in 1890.[84] By 1906, in spite of there being accommodation for over 500 and no fees, numbers had dropped to 283.[85] These had so increased again, however, by 1924 that Standard I in the boys' school was moved to the Infant school because of overcrowding.[86] At this time the Walker Charity was paying £30 a year to the school. Twenty pounds of the charity money was spent on clothing five boys as a reward.[87]

As a result of the Hadow Report the boys' and girls' departments were amalgamated in 1933 into a new senior school with 146 pupils, and the Bucknell Road premises became the junior school with 268 children.[88] After the Butler Act of 1944 the Oxfordshire Education Committee assumed full responsibility for the infant and secondary schools, but the junior school continued as a Church school with the status of an 'aided' junior mixed school.[89] When the Highfield secondary modern school (see below) was built in 1952, the junior school was divided. There has since been a county primary school in the Bucknell Road buildings with 252 pupils in 1955, and a Church of England primary school in the old senior school premises with capacity for 320 pupils. The town was divided into zones allotted to each school.[90]

COUNTY GRAMMAR SCHOOL. A group of local business men persuaded the Oxfordshire Education Committee to establish at Bicester the co-educational County Grammar school for children who had hitherto travelled daily to Oxford. It opened in 1924 with 42 pupils at Bicester Hall, formerly a hunting-box of the Earl of Cottenham. The number had risen to 113 by 1928, to 247 by 1946 after Claremont House had been brought into use,[91] and to 277 by 1956. By then the headmaster had a staff of 13 full-time and 2 part-time teachers, and a sixth form with 17 pupils. There were 9 classrooms, a gymnasium, 2 laboratories, a woodwork-room, dining-room, and kitchen. The pupils came from an area of 80 square miles between Buckinghamshire and the Cherwell and from Kidlington to the Northamptonshire border.[92]

HIGHFIELD SECONDARY MODERN SCHOOL. This school was built in 1952 with accommodation for 510 boys and girls between the ages of 11 and 15. The increased population in Bicester and the neighbourhood, mainly a consequence of the Ordnance Depot,

made a new school essential. The children came from Bicester itself and from about 26 villages and hamlets. Highfield opened with 381 pupils and by 1955 there were 460. The original three-form entry had increased to a four-form one by 1955, when the headmaster had a staff of eighteen.

There are 13 classrooms, 8 rooms for various crafts, a canteen, showers, and 2 drying-rooms, an administrative block, and 7 to 8 acres of playing-fields and gardens.[93]

ROMAN CATHOLIC SCHOOLS. As a result of the movement to revive the Roman Catholic mission in Bicester a Catholic private school had been opened in King's End by 1871,[94] and in 1882 a new school was built there and was opened as St. Mary's School in 1883. By 1894 the average attendance was 86.[95] Although the school was reported in 1890 to have annual government grants of £42 15s. 2d. and in 1894 to have received increased grants of £61 17s. 6d., it was being carried on at a considerable annual deficit.[96] After the Education Act of 1902 its financial position was eased as the Board of Education paid the teachers' salaries. At first only a small proportion of the children attending this school was Roman Catholic; in 1930 there were still only 13 Catholics amongst its 50 or 60 pupils, but by 1953, owing to the Irish and continental influx into Bicester, there were 114 Catholic children out of a total of 120, and many children from non-Catholic families had to be turned away because of overcrowding.[97] Yet the buildings had been twice expanded, once in 1939 when two classrooms were added and central heating installed so as to conform with the requirements of the local education authorities, and again in the 1950's, when the senior school used St. Mary's Hall.[98] In 1953 the school was taken over by the Presentation Order of Sisters.[99]

OTHER SCHOOLS. There have been a great variety of other small private schools in Bicester. Among them was the Revd. Mr. Wood's grammar school for young gentlemen opened in 1773. The terms for board and instruction were 16 guineas.[1] John Dunkin's account of his early education records several other instructors: he learnt his letters at 'old Betty Thornton's in Sheep Street', and 'Master Tooley' taught him 'writing and summing'.[2] In the early 19th century there were said to be two day schools for dissenters and ten schools kept by women who taught reading to 100 children, who were too young to be taught to make lace.[3] But the private schools were also concerned with older children. In 1823 two academies for ladies and one for gentlemen were advertised.[4] In 1829 Mrs. Farnell's seminary is mentioned, in 1839 a Diocesan school for boys was opened in the London Road, and several other

[81] C 54/16931, m. 18.
[82] Deed of Trust.
[83] Hewiett's Alm. and Bic. Dir. (1869, 1882).
[84] Ibid. (1862); see also ibid. (1882) for an unofficial figure of c. 400 pupils; Ret. of Sch.
[85] Vol. Sch. Ret.
[86] Min. Bk. of Managers of Nat. Schls. penes the vicar.
[87] Gen. Digest Char.; Schools Inq.; Hewiett's Alm. and Bic. Dir. (1884); Kelly's Dir. Oxon. (1920). In 1954 the Charity paid £8 8s. for clothing four boys and the rest to two Sunday schools: inf. the vicar.
[88] Min. Bk. penes the vicar. An extension was added to the senior school after the Second World War.
[89] Min. Bk. penes the vicar.
[90] Ibid.; inf. the headmistresses.
[91] Min. Educ. Reports, 1939 and 1951.

[92] Ibid.
[93] Inf. Mr. G. W. Price, headmaster.
[94] Elem. Educ. Ret.
[95] Ret. of Sch. In 1890 the attendance was said to be 59: ibid.
[96] Ibid.
[97] Inf. Mrs. Mary Morpeth, headmistress 1930–52.
[98] Bic. Advertiser, 11 Jan. 1946: 'Short History of Bicester Catholic Mission' by Fr. S. F. Webb.
[99] Inf. Father Foynes, priest at Bicester.
[1] Oxf. Jnl. 27 Nov. 1773.
[2] Dunkin's MS. Diary, cited Bic. Advertiser, 12 Apr. 1901.
[3] Oxf. Dioc. d 707 (1808).
[4] Pigot's Dir. (1823).

establishments were advertised, one kept by Elizabeth Easton, and two by clergymen.[5] In 1869 Hewiett's *Almanack* says there were 8 private schools of which 6 were boarding-schools. They included 3 'seminaries' and 2 'commercial schools'.[6] In the 1870's the Misses Simmons established the Ladies' Collegiate School at Oxford House, where the boarders 'enjoy every home comfort combined with careful training'. A little later, in 1882,[7] Miss Collis of Sheep Street was receiving 'a select number of young ladies and gentlemen to educate in all branches of a superior education with accomplishments'. She claimed a 'happy method of imparting knowledge' and offered private lessons in music, drawing, and fretwork.[8] At the same time Miss Kirby at the 'Limes' in Church Street was issuing elegantly printed advertisements for a similar school. Cambridge House Academy was a middle-class boarding and day school for boys.[9] Schools such as these testify to the growing refinement of manners.

Carlton House, the most successful of Bicester's private schools in the 20th century, was established in the Causeway in 1915. The headmistress in 1955 took boys and girls to the age of eleven. There were 59 pupils.[10]

SUNDAY SCHOOLS. Bicester took an active part in the movement at the end of the 18th century to provide schools to keep the children off the streets on Sundays. James Jones, who taught Dunkin, is said to have started the first Sunday school and evening school. He taught the 'three Rs'. His appeal to the parish for financial help was refused on the grounds that only scripture should be taught. The Independents, however, offered their help and the school was transferred to their meeting-house.[11]

After this challenge offered by the dissenters the vicar, Joseph Eyre (1779–97), was able to raise subscriptions for another school. It was held in the building adjoining the church and took about 100 pupils.[12] In 1808 there were 55 boys and 55 girls attending the Church sunday school and 20 boys and 30 girls at the dissenters' school. Fifteen boys and girls also attended a night school to learn to write.[13] In 1815 the Church school had 74 boys and 62 girls, and the incumbent reported 'none are refused'.[14]

In 1819 the schools were said to be capable of accommodating all the children of the labouring classes; each had 150 children in 1833 and was in receipt of £7 a year from the Walker Charity. By this time the Wesleyan Methodists also had a Sunday school for 54 children; it was supported by voluntary subscriptions and the children's pence.[15]

CHARITIES. The Feoffee Charity, as it was later called, was probably founded in 1529 by John Wygyns (or Wykyns) and Henry More. In that year they conveyed to feoffees property described as land of 'their inheritance', which later sources give as the endowment of the charity. Wygyns gave property in Bicester, Bucknell, Souldern, Stratton Audley, Wendlebury, Woodstock, Wallingford (Berks.) and Brackley (Northants), and More[16] gave lands in Potterspury, Cosgrove, and Yardley (Northants). The income of these properties was to be applied to the relief of the poor, the marriage of poor girls, the mending of the common highways, and the payment of poor people's taxes. The gift of lands in Bucknell and Wendlebury may not have had effect, for they were not included in a rental of 1553, when the annual income was £8 7s. 8d.[17] A commission for charitable uses discovered in 1599 that some of the charity money had been used to build a Town House and to pay the sexton and the mole-catcher. The commissioners ordered that in future it should be used primarily to relieve the poor; when this had been done surplus funds might be employed in the other ways envisaged by the founders. The poor were not to be relieved by being allowed to occupy any part of the estate rent free, but might only be assisted out of its income.[18]

Thereafter the charity appears to have been conscientiously administered:[19] in 1738 it was reported that the income had lately increased from £80 to £100 a year through the care of the feoffees, and was well applied.[20] Part of the Wallingford property was sold in 1670, and the Brackley and Stratton Audley estates in 1677 and 1707. In 1755 the income was £268 10s. 6d. a year.[21] The remainder of the Wallingford property was sold in 1772, and the Woodstock property between 1762 and 1782. The proceeds were partly invested in stock, and partly used to buy an estate in Ludgershall (Bucks.). In 1824 the feoffees still held lands in Bicester, Souldern,[22] Potterspury, Cosgrove, and Yardley, and a large building in Bicester used as a workhouse. The annual income was then £210 8s. and money was distributed weekly, four-fifths of it to the poor of Market End, and a fifth to those of King's End. In 1823–4, when the payments amounted to £4 a week, there were 37 recipients. No one receiving parish relief might benefit from the charity.[23] In 1826 the gross income was £271 8s.[24]

Between 1846 and 1907 the fund administered by the feoffees was increased by the foundation of six new charities. John Shirley by will dated 1846 left £90. This charity seems to have been first paid in 1851, and in 1870 its annual income was £2 14s. By deed dated 1876 George Tubb endowed Tubb's Bicester Charity with £1,000 in stock, giving an income of £30 in 1870. By will proved 1878 Richard Painter left £500; by will proved 1883 Richard Phillips left £50; by deed dated 1886 Henry Tubb

[5] *Oxf. Jnl.* 17 Jan. 1829; *Kelly's Dir. Oxon.* (1854).
[6] *Hewiett's Alm. and Bic. Dir.* (1869).
[7] Ibid. (1882) (advertisement).
[8] Ibid.
[9] Ibid.
[10] Local inf.
[11] Dunkin, *Bic.* 114–15.
[12] Ibid. 115.
[13] Oxf. Dioc. d 707.
[14] Ibid. c 433.
[15] *12th Rep. Com. Char.* 285; *Educ. of Poor*; *Educ. Inq. Abstract*, 471.
[16] When Dunkin wrote the original deeds were in the parish chest (*Bic.* 140). They cannot now be found. For the More and Wygyns families see above, p. 37. There

appears to be no connexion between the More family and the important Moore family which obtained a grant of the priory after the Dissolution.
[17] Blo. *Bic.* 56–58.
[18] C 93/1/36; *12th Rep. Com. Char.* 286. See above, p. 37. A copy of the order of 1599 made in 1723 is in the Char. Feoff. box, Barclays Bank, Bicester.
[19] e.g. see Char. Feoff. box, indenture 19 Jan. 1723: conveyance to new feoffee.
[20] Oxf. Dioc. d 552.
[21] Char. Feoff. box, Charity acct. bk. 1755–1797.
[22] In 1842 the Bicester poor owned 28½ acres in Souldern: Bodl. Souldern Tithe award.
[23] *12th Rep. Com. Char.* 287–91.
[24] Char. Feoff. box, Charity Acct. bk. 1798–1903.

gave £1,000; by will proved 1886 Susannah Tubb left £100;[25] and by will proved 1907 Mary Ann Greenwood left £412.[26] The gross income of the Charity Feoffees' fund thus rose to £294 11s. 8d. in 1903.[27]

Bailiwick Rent. In 1824 it was found that the poor were entitled to four shares out of the 34 in the profits of the manor and bailiwick of Bicester.[28] The date when this grant to the poor was made or the name of the donor are not known. The profits from the bailiwick had amounted to £50 in the 18th century, but had declined by 1824, when it was let for £21. Once every five or six years the poor's shares were distributed in clothing, four-fifths to Market End and a fifth to King's End. At Christmas 1819 about 20 poor women received calico and cloth for gowns worth £5 17s.[29] The collection of tolls, the chief remaining source of the bailiwick's fund, was abandoned later in the century, and by 1864 distribution of the small remnant of the profits had ceased.[30]

Poor's Stock. A cottage, possibly a Church House, appears to have been sold by 1767 by the church-wardens. The churchwarden of Market End eventually received £50 in 1792, and it was invested in stock. The dividends were distributed among nineteen poor people of Market End in 1824.[31]

Weekly Bread. The origin of this charity is unknown, but it was being distributed for many years before 1796 by the owners of property in St. John's Street (i.e. Sheep Street). In 1824 the owner nominated six poor widows of Market End to receive a 2d. loaf each every Sunday.[32]

Wilson's Gift. By will dated 1735 Mary Wilson gave £1 10s. a year, charged upon property in Bicester and Caversfield, to be distributed in bread to poor widows every year upon St. Thomas's Day. In 1824 60 poor people, most of them widows, received a 6d. loaf each.[33]

In 1913, by order of the Charity Commission, all those of the above charities which survived were amalgamated under the title of the Feoffee Charity. Since then most of the land of the original charity has been sold and the money invested in stock. The charity is advertised annually and poor people submit applications to a body of eleven trustees, who meet twice a year at least. It was ordered by the feoffees in 1874 that no one outside Bicester should benefit by the charity,[34] and preference is still given to old residents of the town. In 1956 there were 27 recipients in Market End and £1 10s. was distributed to the poor of King's End. The gross income was £324 6s. 4d.[35]

Walker's Charity. By deed dated 1811 William Walker gave £1,000 in stock to fulfil the intention of his father John Walker of Hackney (Mdx.) to found a charity for the support of three schools in Bicester,

although no provision for this had been made in the latter's will. Of the annual income of £30, £16 was to contribute towards the support of a Church of England charity school, and the remaining £14 was to be divided equally between a Church of England Sunday school and the Congregational Sunday school of the Water Lane chapel.[36] From the terms of his deed Walker seems to have envisaged the foundation of a new school, but the £16 was paid to the Blue Coat school already established in the town.[37] In 1952 the annual income of the charity was £29 10s. 8d., of which £8 8s. was paid to four boys, members of the Church of England, recommended by the headmaster of the Church of England secondary school. Formerly the recipients were bought a blue uniform suit; now the parents select clothes to the value of £2 2s. The Church of England and the Congregational Sunday schools each receive £10 11s. 4d.[38]

Mary Carlton's Charity. By deed dated 1717 Mary Carlton, mother-in-law of White Kennett, gave a rent-charge of £2 12s. 6d. on land in Brill (Bucks.), of which £1 was to be paid each year to the minister of Bicester church for a sermon preached on 2 March in memory of her daughter, Sarah Kennett, and 2s. 6d. to the clerk for ringing the bell that day and keeping the family monuments clean; £1 was to be distributed in 6d. loaves to 40 poor widows after the sermon. In the 1820's the churchwardens added 10s. for bread, since more than 40 widows usually attended.[39] The charity was distributed annually until 1946 when bread-rationing was introduced, and it had not been revived by 1957.[40]

Lost Charities. John Hart, lessee of Cottisford manor, by will dated 1664, gave a rent-charge of £10 on the manor for apprenticing poor boys of Bicester. The charity never appears to have been paid.[41] Richard Burroughs by will of unknown date left £10 a year to the poor. In 1738 it was reported that the charity money was £6 or £6 10s. a year, distributed in clothing to seven poor men and women every year on All Saints day. There were eight recipients in 1750, but no more is known of the charity.[42] Sir Thomas Grantham (d. 1718)[43] left £50, the interest to be distributed at Christmas to poor widows. In 1738 the charity produced £2 10s. a year, which was used to buy a Christmas dinner for widows. In 1750 £1 19s. was distributed, but the charity was subsequently lost through the insolvency of the holder of the principal.[44] At an unknown date Drusilla Bowell left £5 a year for apprenticing poor boys of Chesterton, Bicester and Wendlebury. In 1738 it was reported from Chesterton that the charity had been neglected for several years, and from Bicester that the town could not take its turn unless the villages took theirs.[45] Neglect evidently continued and the charity was lost.

[25] Ibid.; Gen. Digest Char.
[26] Kelly's Dir. Oxon. (1903).
[27] Char. Acct. bk. 1798–1903.
[28] For the bailiwick, see above, p. 38.
[29] 12th Rep. Com. Char. 291.
[30] Blo. Bic. 60.
[31] Ibid. 59; 12th Rep. Com. Char. 291–2.
[32] 12th Rep. Com. Char. 292.
[33] Ibid. 293.
[34] Char. Acct. bk. 1798–1903.
[35] Inf. Barclays Bank.
[36] See above, p. 54.
[37] 12th Rep. Com. Char. 284–5.

[38] Inf. Miss G. H. Dannatt. After the reorganization of the school in 1952 the headmistress of the Church of England primary school chose the four boys.
[39] 12th Rep. Com. Char. 292–3; Oxf. Dioc. d 552. Mary Carlton's first husband was Robert Carver: see above, p. 46.
[40] Inf. Miss G. H. Dannatt.
[41] 12th Rep. Com. Char. 293–4; see also E. C. R. nos. 194, 276–7, 288, and Oxf. Dioc. c 650, ff. 50–54b.
[42] 12th Rep. Com. Char. 294; Oxf. Dioc. d 552.
[43] Blo. Bic. 61.
[44] 12th Rep. Com. Char. 294; Oxf. Dioc. d 552.
[45] Oxf. Dioc. d 552.

In 1908 the Cottage Hospital at King's End was built on ground leased at £1 a year by Colonel L. E. Coker at a cost of approximately £1,100. In 1918

Major Lewis Aubrey Coker gave the ground, and in 1927 an extension was added in memory of Henry Tubb through the generosity of his widow.[46]

BLETCHINGDON

THIS parish of 2,654 acres lies roughly mid-way between Oxford and Bicester.[1] Its long and narrow shape, twice as long as it is broad, has been dictated by the need to divide the frontage of the River Cherwell with its neighbours and to obtain a variety of soils. There have been no recorded changes of boundary.[2]

The ground rises from about 220 feet at river level to 328 feet on the central plateau; it drops again to 212 feet on the eastern and south-eastern boundary. The plateau is capped with Hanborough terrace gravel, but save for the alluvial valleys most of the south and east of the parish lies on the Oxford Clay. To the west the clay is bordered successively by Cornbrash, Forest Marble, and Great Oolite,[3] which can be clearly seen where quarrying and the railway cuttings have laid bare the lower strata.[4] Until the early 19th century much of the eastern part of the parish was uncultivated heathland. The high-quality meadowland lay along the banks of the Cherwell and other meadows bordered the brooks in the north[5] and east.[6] At the end of the 18th century Davis's map shows two largish woods, one west of the Brackley road and Blackleys, the only modern survivor.[7]

The principal road is that from Chipping Norton to London, which enters by Enslow Bridge over the Cherwell[8] and used to leave the parish by Islip Gate. Locally it was important as the way to the nearest market town at Islip, but it was also the chief route for traffic from Worcester to London and in the 17th century at least was regularly called London Way.[9] It was made a turnpike in 1718.[10] In the Middle Ages the present by-road, which runs north to join the Brackley road and was known as Brackley Way,[11] was important locally on account of the trade between the Oxford region and the midland and eastern regions of England. The present by-road to Weston-on-the-Green, once no more than a field path, was the 'New Road' constructed in 1789.[12]

The completion of the Oxford canal in 1790 brought cheap coal to the village, but ruined some of

the best meadowland, as the engineers failed to provide an adequate drainage system to prevent flooding.[13] Communications were still further improved in the 19th century: Enslow Bridge was largely rebuilt and nearly doubled in width in 1814 at a cost of £1,900,[14] and the section of the G.W.R. line from Oxford to Banbury, with a station at Enslow, was completed in 1850.[15]

The village, unlike Kirtlington and the Hamptons, lies on high land nearly a couple of miles from the river-bridge and at the junction of the London road with three by-roads. It was built originally round a green, but the houses on the north side were pulled down when Bletchingdon park was extended in the 16th century.[16] The parish church is inclosed within the park, now covering some 70 acres,[17] and can only be approached by a footpath, which after a struggle in 1795 was declared a right of way. The parishioners still retain this right.[18]

The village buildings skirting the park wall and near the church are still predominantly 17th- or 18th-century in character. Many are built of coursed rubble and have roofs of stone slates.

On the south side of the green there was a row of thirteen rubble-stone cottages with slate roofs, built in 1794,[19] and condemned in 1952 by the local housing authority. In 1954 this row, an interesting survival of an 18th-century housing scheme, was reconditioned and converted into seven cottages at a cost of £9,000, after a public appeal and donations of £2,000 each from the Pilgrim and Dulverton Trusts.[20] Near by is 'The Black's Head', a late 18th-century house of two stories,[21] which probably took its original name of 'The Blackamoor Head' from the Dashwoods' black man-servant.[22] The 'Red Lion', which lost its licence in 1951, lies on the opposite side of the green and is probably of a rather earlier date, along with the adjoining cottages. It was recorded in 1793 as one of three village inns—the other two being the 'Green Man' and the 'Swan'.[23] The earliest known reference to an ale-house occurs in 1616;[24] in the 1670's there was one called the 'Angel and Crown'.[25]

[46] U.D.C. *Bic. Guide and Dir.* (1953).
[1] O.S. Map 6″, xxvii NE., NW. (1900); ibid. 2½″, 42/41, 51 (1951).
[2] *Census*, 1881, 1951.
[3] G.S. Map 1″, N.S. 236; *G.S. Memoir* (1946), 116.
[4] W. Wing, *Bletchingdon Annals* (1872), 4.
[5] For the 13th-cent. Curtleford Brook see *Oseney Cart.* vi. 95.
[6] See map on p. 63.
[7] Davis, *Oxon. Map* (1797).
[8] Perhaps the 13th-cent. Kirmannes Bridge: *Oseney Cart.* vi. 91.
[9] e.g. Par. Rec. indenture of 1623; ibid. Mill's Bk. *passim* (a vellum bk. containing Dr. Mill's transcripts of records relating to the Bletchingdon tithe suits in Queen's Coll. muniments and other notes of his own. He was instituted rector in 1681).
[10] 5 Geo. I, c. 2 (priv. act).
[11] Par. Rec. indenture 1623.
[12] Bodl. Tithe award map.

[13] Wing, *Bletch. Annals*, 2.
[14] Ibid. 36; *Oxon Co. Bridges* (1878), 48.
[15] E. T. MacDermot, *Hist. G.W.R.* i. 300.
[16] See below, p. 64.
[17] *V.C.H. Oxon.* ii. 301; Par. Rec. Tithe award.
[18] The diverted road (reserving footway to church) was completed in 1805: O.R.O. Cal. Q. Sess. viii. 645. The right of way was safeguarded in 1948 by agreement with the Hon. W. Astor, Bletchingdon Park: inf. the rector.
[19] See dated stone.
[20] *Oxf. Times*, 18 June 1954; *Twenty-Third Annual Report* (1953) of the Pilgrim Trust has a pre-restoration photograph.
[21] The date 1791 can be seen in the kitchen.
[22] *Oxf. Jnl.* 11 Nov. 1780; see below, p. 230.
[23] Par. Rec. Overseers' acct bk.; title-deeds of the 'Swan': Bodl. MS. D.D. Valentia (uncat.), cited below as Val. D.
[24] Par. Rec. Mill's Bk., f. 21.
[25] Plot, *Nat. Hist. Oxon.* 160.

Between 1918 and 1939 the village spread out along the Oxford Road, and between 1945 and 1954 58 council houses were built, including a new estate of 40 houses—Valentia Close—on the Chipping Norton road.[26]

Bletchingdon Park is a Georgian mansion built of stone with a pedimented portico projecting from the south front. It was rebuilt by Arthur Annesley[27] in 1783–5 to the designs of the architect James Lewis, who published engravings of it in the second volume of his *Original Designs in Architecture* (1797). It is notable for its fine views and well-timbered park. The latter is recorded as early as 1322,[28] but it was greatly enlarged in the 16th century.[29] The history of the earlier house which Annesley's house replaced is obscure. The medieval manor-house of the Poures seems to have been on or near its site. When Francis Poure[30] lived there at the end of the 16th century it was described as lying on the village street. It was lived in by Sir John Lenthall in the 1620's,[31] and was presumably the 'house and lodge in the park', which Sir Thomas Coghill rebuilt in about 1630 after obtaining the manor from Lenthall. The cost no doubt contributed to the financial difficulties which later compelled him to sell his 'new house' to William Lewes.[32] It was clearly on a large scale, for during the Civil War it was fortified and garrisoned by 200 men. It is said to have been partly destroyed in 1644, but as its defenders surrendered without making any resistance, it is doubtful if the damage was extensive.[33] In any case, when the Earl of Anglesey occupied it in 1665 it was one of the largest houses in the county: he returned 30 hearths for the hearth tax.[34] Robert Plot, writing in 1676, commented on the rare and ingenious style of the staircase, leading to a gallery overlooking the entrance hall, by which all the rooms were approached.[35]

There were other gentlemen's houses in Bletchingdon in the 17th century, but it is difficult to identify them now with certainty. In 1623 a 'mansion house called Old House' was part of Lady Lenthall's jointure[36] and may have been the house to which Sir Thomas Coghill and his wife retired after selling the 'Great House'.[37] Their new home stood near the church, had once been occupied by a yeoman farmer, and was a substantial building for which Lady Coghill returned ten hearths in 1665.[38]

Another 17th-century house was Adderbury's manor-house, which had been rebuilt by Richard Poure before 1623. It stood opposite Sir Thomas Coghill's 'new mansion' in the 1630's.[39] It was later occupied by Thomas Edgerley, who returned seven hearths for the tax of 1665.[40]

Among the 17th-century houses which certainly survive is the Rectory. In 1634 it consisted of hall, parlour and buttery with chambers above, kitchen, larder, and dairy.[41] It was repaired in 1637 and 1681,[42] and the present south-west front with its casement windows and slate roof was added in 1752.[43] Extensive repairs were carried out in 1788; these were perhaps mainly internal improvements, as the rector's bill of £146 was mostly for the carpenter's work.[44] The Laurels, on the fringe of the village, is an L-shaped 17th-century house of two stories. Although much modernized it still retains some of its original stone-mullioned windows. Manor and Home Farms are other houses of the same period. Manor Farm has two stories and its eastern front is decorated with a medallion with a bust, which is traditionally supposed to represent Cromwell. In the 18th century Home Farm was a posting-house on the London road called the 'Swan'.[45]

Owing to the early inclosure of the open fields[46] the parish has an unusual number of outlying 17th-century farm-houses, such as Stonehouse Farm, Grove Farm, and Diamond Farm. They are all two-storied houses with attics, are built of coursed rubble and retain many of their original features. Stonehouse, for example, has a stone spiral staircase, while Grove House has early casement windows. Underdowns Farm, rebuilt in the 19th century, was originally built at least by the 1680's.[47] Staplehurst Farm, College Farm, Dolly's Barn, Greenhill Farm, and Frogsnest Farm[48] seem to be 18th-century houses, and Heathfield was built in 1814 by the Oxford banker Richard Walker. The last was bought by Viscount Valentia in 1889 for a dower house.[49]

The hamlet of Enslow grew up as a result of the construction of the canal and the railway. In 1788 a wharf and wharfinger's house were built and early in the next century the 'Rock of Gibraltar' public house.[50] The mill and the mill house at Enslow, however, have a much longer history. A mill was recorded in Domesday;[51] by 1340[52] it seems to have been already a double mill as it was in the 17th and 18th centuries.[53]

Both in the 16th and 17th centuries the parish figured in events of national importance—in the projected agrarian rising of 1596[54] and during the Civil War. The king's forces lay in and around the village in July 1643, and in October Sir Samuel Luke reported that '200 hurt men lie at Bletchingdon and Islip'.[55] In 1644 the strategically important point, Bletchingdon House, was surrendered to Cromwell without a fight by Colonel Windebank, who was court-martialled and shot. The house was

---

26 Inf. Ploughley R.D.C.
27 See below, p. 59.
28 *Cal. Close*, 1318–23, 596.
29 See below, p. 64. In 1664 it covered 60 a.: lease in Val. D.
30 See below, p. 59; Par. Rec. Mill's Bk., f. 72; marriage settlement 1623: Val. D.
31 e.g. MS. Top. Oxon. c 56, f. 37.
32 Par. Rec. Mill's Bk., f. 9; evidence in suit Coghill *v.* Potter: E 134, 14 Chas. I, Trin. 5.
33 For Bletchingdon and the Civil War see F. J. Varley, *Siege of Oxf.* 85–86.
34 *Hearth Tax Oxon.* 196.
35 Plot, *Nat. Hist. Oxon.* 267–8.
36 Marriage settlement: Val. D.   37 Lease: Val. D.
38 *Hearth Tax Oxon.* 196.
39 Marriage settlement: Val. D.; Queen's Coll. Mun. 4 H. 20 c, f. 26; cf. ibid. 20*b*.

40 *Hearth Tax Oxon.* 196.
41 Oxf. Archd. Oxon. c 141, p. 285.
42 Queen's Coll. Mun. 4 H. 10. The bill was *c.* £71, the mason Wm. Hankes: Par. Rec. Mill's Bk., ff. 67–68.
43 Oxf. Archd. Oxon. c 54, f. 15; see also dated stone on house.
44 Par. Rec. Mill's Bk. (no folio number).
45 Leases: Val. D.
46 See below, p. 64.
47 Par. Rec. Rector's tithe bk.
48 Ibid.: the rector built stables at Frogsnest in 1780.
49 Wing, *Bletch. Annals*, 54.
50 Ibid. 2.
51 *V.C.H. Oxon.* i. 424.
52 C 135/59/22.
53 e.g. C.P. 25(2)/340/East. 9 Jas. I.
54 See below, p. 157.
55 Luke, *Jnl.* 118, 161.

then garrisoned for the Parliament. From here, no doubt, Cromwell wrote his dispatch of 25 April 1644, reporting his success.[56]

In the 14th century Bletchingdon manor-house was the chief seat of Roger Damory and his wife Elizabeth de Clare (d. 1360), the foundress of Clare College, Cambridge.[57] Later, the village was the birthplace of the Puritan John Nixon (1589–1662), son of a Bletchingdon husbandman, three times mayor of Oxford and founder of Nixon's school.[58] It has also been associated with an unusual number of other well-known men. Many of its rectors, notably Henry Airay (? 1560–1616), Christopher Potter (1591–1646), and John Mill (1645–1707), were distinguished scholars and divines,[59] and one, Dr. William Holder (1616–98), was the inventor of a method to teach deaf mutes to speak.[60] As Holder married Sir Christopher Wren's sister, the future architect was much at Bletchingdon Rectory as a young man, was grounded in mathematics by the rector, and later married the daughter of the squire, Sir Thomas Coghill.[61] From 1682 until his death in 1686 the Earl of Anglesey, at one time President of the Council of State, Vice-Treasurer for Ireland, and Lord Privy Seal, lived at his Bletchingdon house, where he collected a magnificent library, and was much visited by his London friends.[62] Later, the house was well known as the home of Arthur Annesley (d. 1841), one of the four celebrated four-in-hand gentleman whips of the county, and famed for his victory at the Oxford election of 1796.[63] He resided more than half a century, 'distributing bountifully to the comfort and necessities of his poorer brethren'. His son Arthur, who became the 10th Viscount Valentia in 1844, was born at Bletchingdon Park in 1785, and until 1948 his descendants, the Lords Valentia, were generous and influential residents.

MANORS. In 1086 an estate assessed at 8 hides in Bletchingdon, later known as *POURE'S MANOR*, was held by Gilbert of Robert d'Oilly.[64] Robert is said to have 'bought back' (*redemit*) the estate from the king. The overlordship followed the same descent as that of Bucknell,[65] for Gilbert appears to have been the ancestor of the Damory family, tenants of that manor. Bletchingdon manor was held by Robert Damory in 1139,[66] and passed to his son Roger,[67] and his grandson Ralph.[68] Ralph's eldest

son Robert succeeded him about 1187[69] and died about 1205. Robert's son Robert died in 1236,[70] and in 1243 his son Roger Damory held Bletchingdon as 1 knight's fee.[71] In 1279, however, the manor was held as ½ fee of Roger by his son Robert, who succeeded him about 1281[72] and died in 1285. In 1312 Robert's son Sir Richard granted the manor to his younger brother Roger for life.[73] Roger Damory had married Elizabeth de Burgh, Edward II's niece,[74] and later actively opposed the king's favourite, Sir Hugh Despenser. Although he was pardoned in 1321, his estates were seized and he himself died in prison in 1322.[75] Sir Richard Damory recovered Bletchingdon manor in accordance with the terms of his grant to his brother,[76] and held it at his death in 1330.[77] It appears, however, that his sister-in-law Elizabeth held the manor as his tenant: she was certainly in possession in 1346 and 1349.[78] It is uncertain whether she retained Bletchingdon at her death in 1360,[79] and whether it passed to Sir Richard's son, Sir Richard the younger. It was not listed among the latter's Oxfordshire lands in 1375[80] and so may have already passed to the Poure family.

In 1376 Hugh Poure was described as 'of Bletchingdon'.[81] Since his grandfather Walter Poure of Oddington had married Katherine, a sister of Sir Richard Damory the elder,[82] it is possible that Hugh had obtained Bletchingdon by inheritance. But he had an elder brother, who had inherited Oddington,[83] and in view of the financial straits of the younger Sir Richard Damory[84] it is equally possible that Hugh had obtained Bletchingdon by purchase from his needy kinsman. Hugh was dead by 1385[85] and by 1395 his son Roger had inherited the manor from an elder brother Ralph.[86] Roger had been succeeded by 1408[87] by his son Roger, who appears to have acquired Adderbury's manor in Bletchingdon.[88] Roger was still alive in 1478.[89] His son Thomas died in 1482[90] and Thomas's son John either predeceased him, or died shortly after, since in 1483 John Poure, son of John and grandson of Thomas Poure, was described as a minor.[91] He married Mary, daughter of Walter Curson of Waterperry, and died in 1526.[92]

Vincent Poure, who succeeded his father, married Dorothy, daughter of Sir John Brome of Holton.[93] He died in 1558, having settled a third of his estates on his wife during the minority of his son Francis, then aged fourteen.[94] About 1566 she married her

[56] F. J. Varley, *Siege of Oxf.* 85–86.
[57] See below.
[58] Wood, *City of Oxford*, i. 155; iii. 118.
[59] See below, p. 68.
[60] *D.N.B.*
[61] Ibid.; for his lawsuits over property in Bletchingdon see below, p. 59.
[62] Hist. MSS. Com. *13th Rep. App. VI*, 266.
[63] Wing, *Bletch. Annals*, 29.
[64] *V.C.H. Oxon.* i. 414. This section is largely based on material supplied by Patricia Hyde.
[65] See below, p. 72.
[66] *Godstow Reg.* i. 214; for further details of Damory descent see below, p. 73.
[67] *Godstow Reg.* i. 215.
[68] Ibid. 216.
[69] *Thame Cart.* i. 68; cf. *Oseney Cart.* v. 63.
[70] Blo. *Buck.* 4; see below, p. 73.
[71] *Bk. of Fees*, 824.
[72] *Rot. Hund.* (Rec. Com.), ii. 830; *Complete Peerage*, iv. 46 and n. 3; *V.C.H. Oxon.* v. 286.
[73] *Complete Peerage*, iv. 46 and n. 3; *Cal. Inq. Misc.* ii, p. 126.
[74] For her see *D.N.B.* under Elizabeth de Clare.

[75] *Complete Peerage*, iv. 44–48.
[76] *Cal. Close*, 1318–23, 596.
[77] *Cal. Inq. p.m.* vii, p. 203.
[78] *Feud. Aids*, iv. 181; *Cal. Inq. p.m.* ix, p. 183.
[79] *Cal. Inq. p.m.* x, pp. 507 sqq.: there are no Oxfordshire returns.
[80] Ibid. xiv, p. 115.
[81] *Misc. Gen. et Her.* 5th ser. vi. 370.
[82] Ibid. 364, 368; *Oxon. Visit.* 210; see below, p. 278.
[83] *Misc. Gen. et Her.* 5th ser. vi. 364; see below, p. 278.
[84] *Complete Peerage*, iv. 47–48; see below, p. 73.
[85] *Misc. Gen. et Her.* 5th ser. vi. 364, 368.
[86] *Cal. Close*, 1392–6, 412.
[87] *Misc. Gen. et Her.* 5th ser. vi. 364, 368.
[88] See below, p. 60.
[89] Kennett, *Paroch. Antiq.* i. 496; see below, p. 69.
[90] *Par. Coll.* i. 47.
[91] Kennett, *Paroch. Antiq.* i. 496.
[92] C 142/45/25; *Oxon. Visit.* 211; the date is erroneously given as 1525 in *Oxon. Visit.* 36, and as 1426 in *Par. Coll.* i. 47.
[93] *Oxon. Visit.* 211; see *V.C.H. Oxon.* v. 171.
[94] C 142/121/146.

second husband Alexander Horden and a few years later Francis Poure contested their right to Bletchingdon.[95] Francis married firstly Prudence, daughter of Sir George Gifford of Middle Claydon (Bucks.), and secondly Ann, daughter of Julius Ferrers of Margetsell (Herts.), whose daughter Margaret married Edward Ewer of Bucknell.[96]

About 1596 Francis[97] settled Bletchingdon and Oddington[98] on Richard, his son by his first wife, reserving a life interest for himself, and in 1610 conveyed them to trustees for Richard, to secure the estate against his children by his second wife.[99] In 1612 Richard mortgaged the manors to Sir Michael Dormer and others,[1] who in 1613 sold their interest to Sir John Lenthall.[2] Francis Poure then settled Bletchingdon on the children of his second marriage, but left Oddington to Richard so that he might redeem the mortgage.[3] In 1614 Richard's brother-in-law Edward Ewer lent him £3,000 to redeem the manors from Lenthall.[4] It was later alleged that Richard was forced to sell Bletchingdon to Lenthall for £14,000, which the latter did not pay,[5] and it is possible that Lenthall obtained possession through Richard's failure to redeem the mortgage despite Ewer's loan.

Sir John, son of William Lenthall of Lachford (Great Haseley), belonged to an old Oxfordshire family and was an elder brother of the Speaker, William Lenthall. Although in 1623 Lenthall settled his Bletchingdon estates on his wife Bridget,[6] in 1624 he conveyed his right to the manor to Thomas Coghill,[7] and in 1627 granted him an 80-year lease of the estate.[8] Richard Poure finally surrendered his rights to Coghill in 1639.[9] Coghill, younger son of a London merchant, John Coghill, married Elizabeth Sutton[10] of Aldenham (Herts.), was knighted in 1633 and was Sheriff of Oxfordshire in 1632.[11] In 1656 he sold a large part of his Bletchingdon estates to William Lewes of Boarstall (Bucks.) for £10,000.[12] By his will dated 1659 Coghill left his property to his wife for life, with reversion of Bletchingdon manor to his second son John, and of lands in Bletchingdon to his son Sutton.[13] Nevertheless, after his death in the same year the manor passed to his eldest son Thomas.[14] Thomas and John died in 1694 and 1695,[15] after Thomas had settled the manor in 1692 on his nephew Thomas,[16] third son of Sutton.[17] The younger Thomas died in 1706[18] and the manor passed

to his eldest brother Sutton,[19] who died in 1708 leaving it to his younger brother John.[20] During the following years John got into debt and mortgaged the estate. In 1716 he sold the manor to Arthur, the 7th Earl of Anglesey, for £7,000, receiving for himself an annuity of £200, which was never paid as he died within a year.[21]

The Angleseys had been the chief landowners in the parish since 1666 when Arthur, the 3rd Earl of Anglesey, had bought Bletchingdon House and estate for £3,864 from Charles, Duke of Richmond.[22] The latter had acquired them in 1661 through a marriage settlement with his wife Margaret, the widow of William Lewes.[23] Lord Anglesey had been created earl in 1661 and had held many important political posts before his death in 1686.[24] A marriage settlement between the earl's son James and Elizabeth, daughter of the Earl of Rutland, settled the Bletchingdon estates on James, and after his death on his wife for her lifetime.[25] Elizabeth took possession of these lands after her husband's death in 1690, and probably lived there until her own death in 1700.[26] In 1694 the architect Sir Christopher Wren brought a lawsuit laying claim to the Anglesey estates in Bletchingdon on the pretence that they had been mortgaged to him by the third earl; his claim was, however, dismissed as an invention.[27]

James, the 4th Earl of Anglesey, left three sons, James (d. 1702), John (d. 1710), and Arthur (d. 1737), who all died without male issue. In 1737 the title passed to Richard,[28] a cousin of the 7th earl, and Bletchingdon manor was sold by him for £6,000 to Francis Annesley, M.P., of the Inner Temple and of Thorganby (Yorks.),[29] to whom the estate had previously been mortgaged. He belonged to a younger branch of the Annesley family, and his son the Revd. Francis Annesley, Rector of Winwick (Lancs.), was related to the earls of Anglesey through his marriage in 1728[30] to Anne Gayer, whose mother Elizabeth was the daughter and eventual heiress of James, 2nd Earl of Anglesey. Francis Annesley the elder died in 1750 and was succeeded by his grandson Arthur, the Revd. Francis Annesley having died in 1740.[31]

In 1765 Arthur Annesley was High Sheriff of Oxfordshire. He died in 1773 and was followed by his son Arthur, who was elected in 1796 M.P. for Oxford.[32] In 1785, at the time of Arthur's marriage to Catherine Hardy, the estate was settled on her.

[95] C 3/172/32.
[96] Oxon. Visit. 211.
[97] C 3/349/4: case Sir Edw. Frere v. Rich. Poure for debt of £5,000.
[98] Ibid. 283/6.
[99] Ibid. 349/4.
[1] C.P. 25(2)/340/East. 9 Jas. I.
[2] C 2 Jas. I, E 2/40 gives details.
[3] C 3/349/4 gives details; cf. C.P. 25(2)/340/East. 17 Jas I.
[4] C 2 Jas. I, C 21/20.
[5] C 3/349/4; ibid. 400/113; C 2 Jas. I, C 21/20.
[6] Bodl. MS. D.D. Valentia a 3 and a 4 (uncat., and cited below as Val. D) for details of this and subsequent conveyances.
[7] C.P. 25(2)/340/Mich. 22 Jas. I.
[8] Val. D.: indenture of 1631. In 1630 Lenthall and Coghill were described as the principal landowners in Bletchingdon: Par. Rec. For Lenthall see D.N.B.
[9] C.P. 25(2)/474/Trin. 15 Chas. I.
[10] J. H. Coghill, Hist. of Coghill Family, 38–39. Thomas's elder brother Henry also lived at Bletchingdon but inherited Aldenham (Herts.) through his wife, the sister of Thomas's wife: ibid. 43–44.

[11] Davenport, Oxon. Sheriffs.
[12] Val. D.
[13] Will printed in Coghill Family, 57–59.
[14] e.g. Val. D.: indenture 1662.
[15] Par. Reg.
[16] Val. D.: indenture 1692.
[17] It is unlikely that Sutton senr. ever held the manor: ibid. his will, 1707.
[18] Par. Reg.
[19] Val. D.: indenture 1706.
[20] Ibid.: will of Sutton junr. 1708.
[21] Ibid.: indenture 1716.
[22] Ibid.: sale 1666.
[23] Ibid.; Par. Coll. i. 46.
[24] D.N.B.; see above, p. 58.
[25] C 5/111/2.
[26] Complete Peerage, i. 135.
[27] C 5/111/2; see above, p. 58.
[28] Complete Peerage, i. 136; Burke, Peerage and Baronetage (1931).
[29] Val. D.
[30] Ibid.
[31] Complete Peerage (orig. ed.), viii. 16.
[32] W. Wing, Bletch. Annals, 29.

The trustees under this settlement applied sums derived from the sale in 1786 of the Annesleys' Irish estates to the purchase of freehold land in Bletchingdon.[33] Arthur Annesley was succeeded in 1841 by his son Arthur, who inherited the title of Lord Valentia from a cousin, who was a great-grandson of Richard Annesley (d. 1761).[34] Bletchingdon continued to be owned by this family until 1948, when Lord Valentia sold it to the Hon. William Astor, who resold it in 1953 to the Hon. Robin Cayzer.

In 1086 Alwi the sheriff, perhaps the same Alwi who held lands in one of the Wortons in North Oxfordshire, held 2½ hides in Bletchingdon of the king, which he had, however, sold to a certain Manasses without the king's licence.[35] The son of Manasses had a house in Oxford attached to this estate.[36] The property must have reverted to the Crown or been forfeited, for by the 12th century it was divided into a sergeanty held of the king and ½ knight's fee held of the barony of Stafford.[37] The two were reunited in the 15th century to form what was thereafter called *ADDERBURY'S MANOR* and the distinction between them was lost. The sergeanty[38] seems to have consisted originally of the service of providing a spit for roasting the king's dinner when he hunted in Cornbury Forest.[39] In some 13th- and 14th-century records the service was interpreted as the provision of a roast dinner.[40] Later evidence makes it clear that the Richard Fitzneil, who granted land in Bletchingdon to the Templars before 1151,[41] must have then been holding the sergeanty. In about 1190 Robert Fitzniel of Tackley seems to have been in possession, for he then granted land in Bletchingdon to Godstow Nunnery.[42] In about 1210 his gift was confirmed by William Poure, Walter Prescote, and William Grenevile.[43] As William Poure married Alice, one of the four daughters and coheiresses of Robert Fitzniel,[44] it is likely that Walter Prescote and William Grenevile, both members of local families, may have been other sons-in-law. One Grenevile family is found in close association with the Fitzniels of Boarstall (Bucks.), and the Prescotes had ties with the Poures.[45] At all events, the heirs of a Richard Grenevile were holding the sergeanty in 1219.[46] In 1238, however, Richard Prescote was in possession,[47] and it appears that the sergeanty had escheated to Henry III because Richard Grenevile had alienated it to his brother

William without licence.[48] The inquisition on the death of Richard Prescote was not held until 1251,[49] but his brother and heir Walter had succeeded him by 1247.[50] Walter had perhaps died without a known heir by 1256, when Henry III granted the sergeanty, with the reservations 'quantum ad eum pertinet . . . salvo jure cujuslibet', to Master John of Gloucester, the king's mason.[51] After John's death in 1260[52] it was granted to Henry Wade, the king's cook, who held another sergeanty at Stanton Harcourt. He was holding the Bletchingdon sergeanty in 1279[53] and died in 1287,[54] to be succeeded by his son John, who died in 1309, leaving his brother Henry as his heir.[55] In 1320 Henry sold the estate to Thomas de Musgrave and his wife Joan,[56] who survived her husband and died in possession in 1339, when her heir was her son Thomas.[57] By 1345 Thomas had conveyed the estate to his son William and his wife Elizabeth.[58] In 1354 Elizabeth, by then a widow, conveyed what was called the 'manor of Bletchingdon' to Sir Roger de Cotesford: this may have been a confirmation of a previous sale, for Sir Roger had demesne lands in Bletchingdon in 1349.[59] Sir Roger was sheriff of the county from 1363 to 1365 and again in 1369, and died in 1375 in possession of the Bletchingdon sergeanty.[60] The subsequent history of the estate is not clear. It eventually formed part of the Poures' estates, and may have passed to that family in about 1430 by the marriage of Roger Poure to Juliana, said to be the daughter and heiress of a Robert de Cotesford.[61]

It is not clear when the Stafford family acquired the Stafford fee in Bletchingdon. It has been wrongly stated[62] that Robert de Stafford held a fee there in 1086, a fee assumed to have been included in that held by the undertenant Henry d'Oilly in 1166.[63] Later evidence shows that this Bletchingdon ½ knight's fee was one of the small fees of Mortain held by the barony of Stafford—fees which owed only ⅔ of the knight service of an ordinary fee.[64] If the barony of Stafford acquired the privileges of the honor of Mortain when King Stephen was Count of Mortain and lord of the honor of Lancaster,[65] the Bletchingdon fee was possibly granted to the Staffords in that period, but it was first specifically included in the honor of Hervey de Stafford in 1211–12.[66] Hervey died about 1214; his son Hervey about 1237; and his grandson Hervey in 1241. The

[33] Val. D. a 1, Abstract of Title.
[34] *Complete Peerage* (orig. ed.), viii. 16.
[35] *V.C.H. Oxon.* i. 424.
[36] Ibid. 397.
[37] Occasionally the sergeanty was described as a sergeanty of Stafford, e.g. *Rot. Hund.* (Rec. Com.), ii. 830.
[38] A. L. Poole, *Obligations of Society in 12th and 13th centuries*, 69–70, gives some of its history.
[39] *Bk. of Fees*, 253, 1374; cf. C 135/59/22.
[40] *Cal. Inq. p.m.* i, pp. 53, 294; *Cal. Inq. Misc.* iii, p. 387.
[41] *Sandford Cart.* ii. 301; see below, p. 61.
[42] *Godstow Reg.* i. 217. [43] Ibid. 218.
[44] *Misc. Gen. et Her.* 5th ser. vi. 373, citing Farrer, *Honors*, ii. 242; *Feet of F.* 1197 (P.R.S. xx), 16; *Rot. Cur. Reg.* (Rec. Com.), ii. 200.
[45] For the Greneviles see *Boarstall Cart.* 82, 97, 98, 341; cf. Poole, op. cit., who connects them with the West Country family, and J. H. Round, *Family Origins*, 130; for the Prescotes see *Thame Cart.* i. 8, 18.
[46] *Bk. of Fees*, 253.
[47] Ibid. 1374; Richard Prescote presented to Bletchingdon church in 1231: *Rot. Welles*, ii. 36.
[48] Queen's Coll. Mun. 4 H. 1; cf. *Rot. Hund.* (Rec. Com.), ii. 45; *Close R.* 1254–6, 352.

[49] *Cal. Inq. p.m.* i, p. 294.
[50] *Bk. of Fees*, 1397; *Cal. Inq. p.m.* i, p. 53; cf. *Rot. Hund.* (Rec. Com.), ii. 45.
[51] *Close R.* 1254–6, 352; *Cal. Pat.* 1247–58, 495.
[52] *Ex. e Rot. Fin.* (Rec. Com.), ii. 339.
[53] *Rot. Hund.* (Rec. Com.), ii. 830.
[54] *Cal. Inq. p.m.* ii, p. 376.
[55] Ibid. v, p. 98.
[56] *Cal. Pat.* 1317–21, 524. Musgrave already held ½ knight's fee of the Stafford barony (see below).
[57] *Cal. Inq. p.m.* viii, p. 163; *Cal. Fine R.* 1337–47, 135.
[58] *Cal. Pat.* 1343–5, 452.
[59] C.P. 25(1)/190/20/69; cf. *Cal. Chart. R.* 1341–1417, 109.
[60] *Cal. Inq. Misc.* iii, p. 387; *Blo. Cot.* 12; *Cal. Fine R.* 1369–77, 327.
[61] C.P. 25(1)/191/27/37; *Oxon. Visit.* 210.
[62] G. Wrottesley, *Hist. Collect. Staffs.* i. 168; cf. *V.C.H. Oxon.* i. 412.
[63] *Hist. Collect. Staffs.* i. 168.
[64] Ibid. 160.
[65] Ibid.
[66] *Red. Bk. Exch.* (Rolls Ser.), 613.

latter was succeeded by his brother Robert, who died before 1261,[67] and Robert's son Nicholas was overlord of the Stafford fee in Bletchingdon in 1279.[68] Nicholas died about 1287.

The tenant of the Staffords in 1235 and 1243[69] was Richard Prescote, who had land at Whitehill and who held the Bletchingdon sergeanty. Richard Grenevile (see above) was mesne lord between Richard Prescote and Robert de Stafford.[70] In 1279 the fee was held by Hugh de Musgrave and his wife Maud.[71] The latter was in possession in 1311, but her son Thomas had succeeded her by 1316,[72] and in 1320 he purchased the Bletchingdon sergeanty.[73] His grandson William held the Stafford fee in 1346,[74] and in 1349 William's wife Elizabeth was given judgement in a suit against Roger de Stafford,[75] which may have been concerned with the overlordship, although there was no Roger in the direct line of the barony.[76] By 1387 the fee appears to have been acquired by Sir Richard Abberbury or Adderbury,[77] who in 1390 received a grant of free warren in his Bletchingdon lands.[78] Sir Richard was dead by 1401,[79] but he seems previously to have conveyed his Bletchingdon estate to Thomas Chaucer and other feoffees.[80] In 1428 the Stafford fee was held by Walter Cotton,[81] second husband of Joan Poure, whose first husband Roger Poure had died by 1408.[82] It is not clear who had purchased the estate, but it was subsequently held by Joan's son Roger[83] and followed the same descent as Poure's manor (see above).

LESSER ESTATES. About 1139 Robert Damory and his son Roger gave some 50 acres, and Walter Pery gave a yardland and 10 acres in Bletchingdon to Godstow Abbey. Roger's gift was confirmed by his son Ralph about 1150.[84] Robert Fitzniel gave a yardland about 1190, possibly as the dower of his mother Anneys and his daughter Margery, who may have become nuns.[85] His tenant Geoffrey Bodyn was to receive a rent of 4s. a year from the abbey. Geoffrey's successor Martin Bodyn, and Robert's successors William Poure, Walter Prescote, and William Grenevile, confirmed the grant about 1210.[86] About 1250 Godstow acquired more lands and rents, partly in Bletchingdon and partly in Hampton Gay, by purchase from small freeholders, of whom one was obliged to sell on account of his debts to Oxford Jews.[87] By 1279 its possessions were probably greater than the 3 virgates recorded in the Hundred

Rolls.[88] Godstow retained its estate until the Dissolution.[89]

Before 1151 Richard Fitzniel and his mother Agnes gave ½ hide in Bletchingdon to the Templars of Cowley (later of Sandford).[90] In 1194 the Templars' tenant was Richard, younger brother of Robert Damory.[91] The Hospitallers held the ½ hide in 1513 as an appurtenance of their manor of Merton.[92] Oseney Abbey was granted 2 virgates in Bletchingdon by Ralph Damory before 1187,[93] and about 1240 it received lands from John Pileth, clerk of Oxford, with the consent of his lord Robert de Marny.[94] Further gifts of lands and rents were added later in the century.[95] In 1291 Oseney's possessions were assessed as part of its Hampton Gay estate.[96] The abbey retained its Bletchingdon lands until the Dissolution,[97] and in 1543 they, together with the Godstow and Hospital lands, were granted to Arthur Longfield of Wolverton (Bucks.).[98] In 1279 Cirencester Abbey and Littlemore Priory held 2 virgates and 1 virgate respectively of the Damory fee,[99] but the subsequent history of these lands is unknown.

ECONOMIC AND SOCIAL HISTORY. At the time of Domesday and for many centuries after a large part of the parish was rough pasture. But the pre-Conquest plough-land was fully cultivated: on Gilbert Damory's 6 plough-lands there were 2 teams at work on the demesne and 4 on the villeins' land; the other small estate belonging to Alwi the sheriff was all demesne and had 1½ plough-team working on it. Fourteen acres of meadow are recorded and there is an unusual reference to pasture land—6 by 3 furlongs. There had been some increase in prosperity: although the value of the small estate remained £2 as before, the other had risen in value from £4 in 1065 to £5.[1]

As for the inhabitants, the demesne land of both estates was cultivated by serfs—Gilbert's by five and Alwi's by two. In addition there were 9 villeins (villani) and 7 bordars and presumably a miller, since a watermill worth 7s. 6d. was already in existence.[2] Thus, the community consisted of at least 17 peasant families with the addition of serfs. By 1279 the Hundred Rolls record some degree of economic development and considerable changes in the tenurial pattern.[3] Instead of the demesne serfs, one manor now had 3 villein virgaters paying rents

[67] Complete Peerage, xii(1). 168–72.
[68] Rot. Hund. (Rec. Com.), ii. 830.
[69] Bk. of Fees, 447, 824.
[70] Cal. Inq. p.m. i, p. 294.
[71] Rot. Hund. (Rec. Com.), ii. 830; see below, p. 66.
[72] Feud. Aids, iv. 170.
[73] Cal. Pat. 1317–21, 524.
[74] Feud. Aids, iv. 181.
[75] C.P. 40/358, m. 5.
[76] Complete Peerage, xii (1). 168 sqq.
[77] Kennett, Paroch. Antiq. ii. 73–74.
[78] Cal. Chart. R. 1341–1417, 319; cf. F. N. Macnamara, 'Donnington Castle', Berks. Arch. Jnl. iv. 48–60; C. C. Brookes, Hist. of Steeple Aston, 51; Blo. Sould. 12.
[79] Cal. Pat. 1399–1401, 486; for his descendants see below, p. 304.
[80] Kennett, Paroch. Antiq. ii. 73–74. They presented to Bletchingdon church in 1409.
[81] Feud. Aids, iv. 191.
[82] C.P. 25(1)/191/27/37; see above, p. 58.
[83] Kennett, Paroch. Antiq. ii. 73–74.
[84] Godstow Reg. i. 214–16.
[85] Ibid. 217.

[86] Ibid. 217–19.
[87] Ibid. 219 sqq.
[88] Rot. Hund. (Rec. Com.), ii. 830.
[89] Tax. Eccl. (Rec. Com.), 45; Valor Eccl. (Rec. Com.), ii. 192.
[90] Sandford Cart. ii. 301. 'Blegedun' in the inquest of 1185 has been wrongly identified as Bladon: Records of the Templars in England in the 12th Century, ed. Beatrice A. Lees (Brit. Acad. Rec. of Soc. and Econ. Hist. ix), 45.
[91] Kennett, Paroch. Antiq. i. 213.
[92] Bodl. MS. C.C.C. 320, f. 16b.
[93] Oseney Cart. vi. 90 (dated too late, cf. above, p. 58).
[94] Ibid. vi. 90–91.
[95] Ibid. 92–96.
[96] Tax. Eccl. (Rec. Com.), 45; see below, p. 155.
[97] Oseney Cart. vi. 233; Valor Eccl. (Rec. Com.), ii. 216.
[98] L. & P. Hen. VIII, xviii (1), p. 197; V.C.H. Bucks. iv. 507.
[99] Rot. Hund. (Rec. Com.), ii. 830; cf. Tax. Eccl. (Rec. Com.), 45.
[1] V.C.H. Oxon. i. 414, 424.
[2] Ibid. 424.
[3] Rot. Hund. (Rec. Com.), ii. 830.

of 8s. each and 2 half-virgaters paying 4s. and 4s. 6d. respectively. These tenants also owed works and tallage, and had to pay fines if their sons left the manor (*redimere pueros*). The other manor had 5 virgaters and 10 half-virgaters. But the most striking change was the growth in the number of free tenants: the Damory manor now held 6, of whom 4 had other tenants holding of them. Richard de Henred, for example, occupied no land himself, but had 3 tenants, each holding a virgate; of William Rolf's 4 virgates, a virgate and 12 acres were held by 2 tenants, while the Prioress of Littlemore had enfeoffed Adam the Clerk with a virgate. The Stafford fee had a similarly complex tenurial pattern; 4 free tenants held 7 virgates of Hugh de Musgrave and 2 held a ½-virgate and ⅓ a messuage of Master Henry Wade.[4] As on so many other Oxfordshire estates the religious houses were outstanding among the free tenants: there were Cirencester Abbey, the Templars of Sandford, Godstow Abbey, and Oseney Abbey.[5]

The tax assessments of the early 14th century[6] indicate that Bletchingdon was still not a particularly prosperous village. Of the 35 inhabitants who contributed in 1316 none was outstandingly rich, and the village's total tax was a good deal less than that paid by its neighbours Weston and Kirtlington. Two of the largest contributors were Robert the Shepherd and William le Schepman, and in view of the parish's wide stretches of heathland, it is not unlikely that Walter of Bicester, who paid nearly half the village's total tax in 1327, also owed his wealth to sheep. Bletchingdon's later material progress cannot be accurately judged from the increased tax paid after the reassessment of 1334 as it was combined with Hampton Gay for the purposes of taxation. Both together, however, were relatively highly taxed for Ploughley hundred, and in 1377 the 100 persons listed for the poll tax suggests that at least there had been no decline in population since the early 14th century.[7] An increase in sheep-grazing during the 15th century and the high profits accruing from it probably account for the village's high contribution of £9 4s. 6d. compared with Weston's £1 18s. 6d. to the subsidy of 1523.[8] Of the 37 contributors, there were three substantial men besides the lord, John Poure, whose contribution was outstanding, and a number of men of moderate wealth.

The arable land of the parish in the 13th and 14th centuries lay in the West and East Fields, on either side of the village.[9] At some unrecorded date before 1539 a third field, the South Field, was made.[10] This seems to have been done by bringing Breadcroft,[11] which was certainly arable land in the early 17th century, into cultivation, and by the division of the old East Field. The detailed terrier of the whole parish made in 1539 shows that with some notable exceptions the land was still divided up in accordance with the traditional strip system. Godstow, for example, had mostly acre and ½-acre strips in 63

furlongs, divided between the three fields. Similarly the parson's glebe of 71½ acres was held in acre and ½-acre strips in 42 different furlongs.[12]

The meadowland lay along the banks of the Cherwell and is minutely described in the 'Meadow Book made . . . by lords and tenants' in 1544.[13] It amounted to 99 acres and except for a 7-acre close belonging to the Lady Denham, the parson's 2-acre close, and some demesne closes, the meadow was still mostly distributed by lot. The lots were commonly divided into 12-acre fields and the normal 'lot' was an acre. Freeholders and copyholders of the manor were as a rule alone entitled to lots: the men of Kirtlington and Weston who held acres in the fields had no meadow and no common,[14] but the church of Weston was an exception. It held a ½-acre of mead. The meadowland's value was very high compared with the poor-quality arable: Poure's demesne arable and leys were valued at 2d. an acre and the mead at 3s. 4d. an acre.[15]

The extensive heathland encouraged sheep breeding in the 15th and 16th centuries. The normal stint was 50 sheep and 15 other animals for each yardland; the farmer of the 8 yardlands of Adderbury manor in 1544 could thus keep 400 sheep and 92 other animals on the common, and Vincent Poure could keep 700 sheep and 168 other animals for his 14 yardlands.[16]

Although the tenants' land was still held in small parcels in 1539,[17] there are signs of considerable consolidation of the lord's demesne. In the East and South Fields Poure had acquired blocks of 22, 20, 19½, and 15 acres and several others of from 12 to 10 acres, as well as smaller accumulations, while in Long Marsh Furlong he held all its 54 acres.[18] In West Field, except for 12 acres, the whole of Mill Furlong (126 a.) belonged to Adderbury's farm, while in the other fields it had blocks of 22, 20, and 17½ acres. Mill Furlong[19] and some other open-field land[20] had been inclosed and converted to pasture, but it is impossible to say with certainty whether all the extensive demesne closes which existed in 1544[21] had been inclosed from the arable or whether some had been inclosed from the waste. A survey made for the year 1543–4 shows that apart from the 42 closes attached to the tenants' holdings, which were no more than the hay closes normally found in most villages, Poure's demesne had a number of closes of exceptional size and value. The total acreage of the demesne arable and leys, for instance, was valued at £4 4s. 10d. a year, but the park and other closes in its area were valued at £34 9s.[22]

There is no evidence to show how far inclosure had gone in the 15th century, but it is clear that much of the pre-1544 inclosure may be attributed to Vincent Poure, who succeeded to the manor in 1526 and took advantage of the favourable conditions of the time to increase his demesne lands, alter the conditions of tenancy in his own favour, and convert

4 See above, p. 61.
5 See above, p. 61.
6 See below, p. 358; E 179/161/8, 9.
7 E 179/161/39.
8 See below, pp. 358–9.
9 *Oseney Cart.* vi. 91; C 135/59/22.
10 See terrier (1539): Par. Rec. Mill's Bk. (see above, p. 56, n. 9), ff. 29–55; for a field-map see below, p. 63.
11 By 1597 the names of East and South Fields were Stone and Heath Fields: Par. Rec. Mill's Bk. f. 20.
12 Ibid. ff. 29–55.

13 Ibid. ff. 55–59.
14 Ibid. f. 63.
15 Ibid. ff. 63–64.
16 Ibid. ff. 18, 60.
17 Terrier of arable and leys, 1538–9: ibid. ff. 29–55.
18 Ibid. f. 53.
19 Ibid. f. 29.
20 e.g. Bean Hill: ibid. f. 17; Long Furlong: E 134, 14 Chas I, Trin. 5.
21 Mill's Bk. ff. 60–64: bk. of yardlands, 1543–4.
22 Ibid. f. 64.

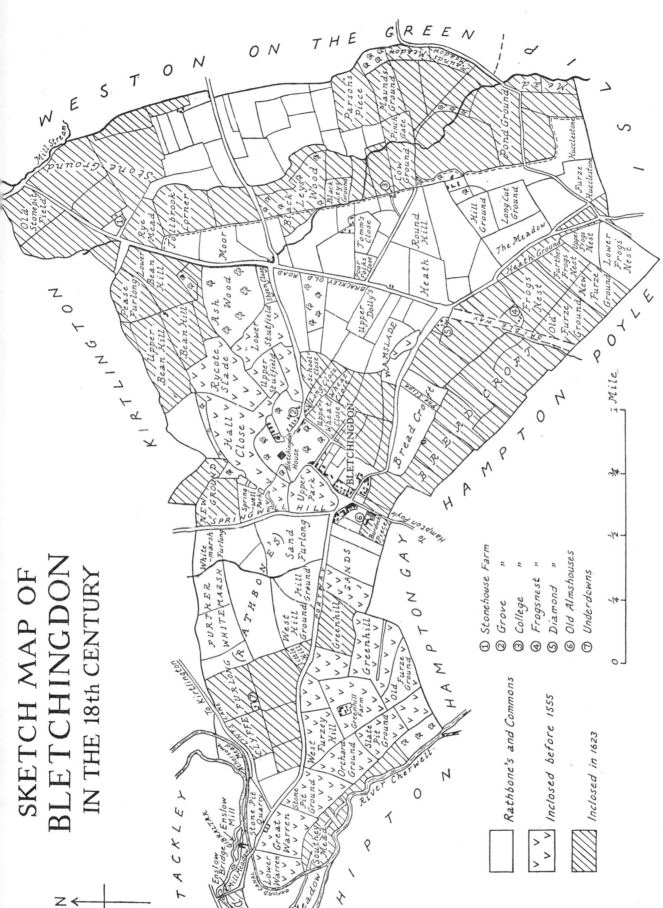

SKETCH MAP OF BLETCHINGDON
IN THE 18th CENTURY

N

The above map shows the probable areas inclosed before 1555 and in 1623. The sources are the 16th- and 17th-century documents cited in the text and the tithe award map of 1839.

① Stonehouse Farm
② Grove   "
③ College   "
④ Frogsnest   "
⑤ Diamond   "
⑥ Old Almshouses
⑦ Underdowns

Rathbone's and Commons

Inclosed before 1555

Inclosed in 1623

½ Mile

0   ¼   ½   ¾

WESTON ON THE GREEN

KIRTLINGTON

HAMPTON POYLE

HAMPTON GAY

SHIPTON

TACKLEY

River Cherwell

Dornford Meadow

Oxford Canal

Enslow Mill

Enslow Bridge

GIBRALTAR

Stone Pit Quarry

Lower Warren

Great Warren

Mill Meadow

Southey Mead

Stone Pit Ground

West Furzey Hill

Orchard Ground

Slate Pit Ground

Greenhill Farm

Old Furze Ground

CLIFFE FURLONG

LINE FURLONG

To Kirtlington

FURTHER WHITEMARSH

RATHBONE'S

Whitemarsh Furlong

West Hill Ground

Little Hill Ground

Sand Furlong

Greenhill

SANDS

PORTWAY

Buckland Piece

To Hampton Poyle

NEW GROUND

SPRING

Springwell Park

Spring Well

Upper Park

WELL HILL

Hall Close

Rycote Slade

Lower

Upper Stuffield

Sheri Close

Stuffield Close

School Close

Mill Hill

Wheatley Close

Upper Park Close

BLETCHINGDON

Bletchingdon House

Bean Furlong

Pease Furlong

Upper Bean Hill

Lower Bean Hill

Bean Hill

Ash Wood

Moor

Rye Mead

Tollbrook Corner

Old Stonepit Field

Stone Ground

Mill Streams

WEASLADE

Upper Dolly's

Books Piece

Tomm's Close

Heath

Round Hill

Black Leys Wood

Black Leys Ground

Parsons Piece

Maunds Meadow

Pinch Ground

Cow Ground Gate

Maunds Meadow

Hands Meadow

POW

Pond Ground

Hucclestone

Furze Hucclestone

Hucclestone

Hill Ground

Long Cut Ground

The Meadow

Heath Ground

RED CROFT

Bread Croft

Frogs Nest

Further Frogs Nest

Old Furze Ground

New Ground

Upper Furze

Upper Frogs Nest

Lower Frogs Nest

Lower Furze Ground

BRACKLEY OLD ROAD

ROAD

from arable to pasture farming. The beginnings of the process are indicated in the 1544 survey. Besides his demesne land he is said to hold 45 acres, once the holding of certain 'decayed' cottages.[23] Copyholders, it may be noted, were benefiting too. One Bailley had increased his holding by ¼-yardland, once the land of a 'decayed' cottage.[24] References in the 1544 survey to 'late tenants' show how much land was coming into the market, mainly as a result of the dissolution of the monasteries. Godstow, for instance, had held about 214 acres and Oseney about 77, besides closes, while another freehold of over 48 acres was also vacant. The evidence collected for the rector's tithe suit in 1555 also shows that much of the inclosed land, if not all the land for which a rate had been substituted instead of tithe in kind, had been inclosed by 1544.[25]

Vincent Poure evidently continued to increase the amount of inclosed land until his death in 1558. By 1552 Bailley's copyhold and another had come into his hands;[26] their closes, the sites of their houses, and gardens had been added to the park, which was inclosed pasture ground.[27] Some idea of the extent of his inclosures can be obtained from an examination of the documents relating to the tithe disputes.[28] Later evidence shows that he attempted to substitute the payment of a fixed rent in lieu of tithes in the case of certain meadow and pasture lands,[29] and their extent can be gauged from the tithe map of 1839,[30] where the lands still paying the fixed rate or modus amounted to 377 acres. These acres can be identified for the most part with those closes from which the tithe was in dispute in the 17th century, and there can be little doubt that the modus lands of 1839 represent fairly exactly the lands which Poure had inclosed before 1555, when the trouble over tithes first began.[31] It is true that 17th-century rectors alleged that there had been a tendency for the 'rateable to encroach on the titheable', but their vigilance and that of the law courts probably saw to it that there was little real alteration in the area.

Dorothy Poure, Vincent's widow, and her second husband Alexander Horden, and later her son Francis Poure, continued the process of piecemeal inclosure. There are no terriers to give an exact picture of the rate of progress but there is evidence to show that it was continuous. A particularly big inclosure was made by Francis Poure soon after 1596, when he secured Thomas Rathbone's large freehold of 96 acres.[32] The total amount of land inclosed in the second half of the 16th century can be estimated from a lost terrier of 1596–7, cited in 17th-century notes.[33] The land in the three fields, both arable and leys, was then reckoned as over 1,123 acres, whereas in 1539 it had been about 1,905 acres.[34] Thus, over 780 acres had been taken out of the fields. The

common heath and meadow were not included in this figure, although the meadow was all inclosed when the lot system was abolished by 'a composition' with the tenants. The exact date of their inclosure is uncertain, but a witness in 1610 said that there had been lot meadows within living memory.[35] Lea Furlong, comprising about 360 acres, was also excluded. It was divided severally among the tenants, who could take their fuel there 'on their own ground'.[36]

The social upheaval naturally resulting from these changes is substantiated by documentary evidence. The 'decayed' cottages point to rural depopulation and the enforced abandonment of holdings; statements by the rectors stress the evil effects of the dispossession of the yeoman farmer. Provost Dennyson, for instance, stated that Vincent Poure turned out tenants as soon as the lease expired and let the tenements at rack rents to new tenants; and that by allowing to the houses which had formerly kept good plough-teams only 3 acres of land apiece he had depopulated the town. Worst of all, as the yeoman farmer had been dispossessed, the town now consisted of 'nothing but poor people'.[37]

The rector, though not an unprejudiced witness, was probably right in his view that Alexander Horden was more ruthless; he described him as 'a covetous, greedy and insatiable worldling' seeking his private profit, and declared that, as 'a stranger to the county and without pity for the losses of his tenants, he practised against them the extremity and rigour of law'.[38] On one occasion Horden was accused of trying to evict seven tenants, including Francis Poure, as a result of an alleged agreement to give up the interest in that part of their holdings which was 'fallow, mead, and sheep common'. Horden's defence was that they had seemed pleased with the arrangement.[39] The pace of the inclosure, together with the fact that the men who were being forced to sell were substantial men with much to lose, was no doubt the reason for Bletchingdon's playing a leading part in the abortive agrarian revolt of 1596.[40] It is significant of the strength of local discontent that Enslow Hill (i.e. the high ground east of the bridge) was to be the meeting-place for 300 or more men of the neighbourhood. They threatened to sack Francis Poure's house and to 'throw his hedges and those that made them into the ditches'.[41]

Inclosure was completed early in the next century. In spite of opposition from the Queen's College, Sir John Lenthall persuaded the rector and the fifteen tenants of the manor, who had land in the fields, to agree to the tripartite indenture of 1623, which completed the inclosure of the open fields and the heathland.[42] The total acreage then inclosed was 785½ acres. The only uninclosed part of the parish left was

23 Mill's Bk. f. 60. 24 Ibid.
25 Ibid. f. 20 and *passim*.
26 Ibid. f. 18.
27 Ibid. f. 13.
28 These are as follows: Queen's Coll. Mun. 4 H. 20; E 134, 14 Chas. I, Mich. 37; ibid. Trin. 5; ibid. 14–15 Chas I, Hil. 21; Par. Rec. Mill's Bk. *passim*, which contains many excerpts from documents no longer at Queen's Coll.
29 Par. Rec. Mill's Bk. f. 19; sources cited in n. 28 above, *passim*.
30 Bodl. Tithe map.
31 Par. Rec. Mill's Bk. f. 18.
32 Lord of Shipton-on-Cherwell, d. 1596: C 142/350/59.

Thomas Rathbone died possessed of 96 a. but notes in Mill's Bk. suggest that Poure had already purchased another 40 a. of his land.
33 Par. Rec. Mill's Bk. f. 20.
34 Ibid. f. 55.
35 Ibid. f. 15.
36 Ibid. f. 20.
37 Ibid. f. 17.
38 C 3/172/32.
39 Ibid.
40 See below, p. 157.
41 *Cal. S.P. Dom.* 1595–7, 319.
42 Par. Rec. Mill's Bk. ff. 4, 77–102. For a field-map see above, p. 63.

a few acres of grazing along the verges of the roads—the Cow Common of the tenants and a few acres of the lord. By the award Lenthall received 478 acres, the rector 192 acres, two tenants 60 and 56 acres each, and the other thirteen tenants smaller awards, five of them under 10 acres.

There is contemporary evidence that the land was surveyed and measured; this is reinforced by the fact that the 43 acres allotted to the rector for tithe of the heath was an exact tenth of the acreage of the heath in the early 19th century.[43] The economic advantages of inclosure were indisputable. In 1544 the rents of the pasture closes were already one of the most valuable parts of the manor: demesne rents, pasture and the mills brought in altogether £47 7s. 6d., but of this one close (Greenhill) alone produced £13 6s. 8d. rent, while the park and Hall Close produced £10 together. The rents of customary tenants and Adderbury's farm brought in the comparatively small sum of £21 odd, and freeholders' quitrents only 4s. 6d.[44] Owing to the spectacular rise in land values in the 16th century, the park and Hall Close were worth £30 each by the early 17th century; Ricott's slade, Stutfolds, and others near the park were worth £63, while Greenhill in the old West Field was worth £90, whereas the two corn mills with the fishing rights, always a valuable part of a manor, were valued at £30.[45]

The changes in the pattern of landholding are also of interest. In 1544 there were 17 copyholds comprising about 704 acres and 21 freehold tenements, including the four which had been held by Godstow and Oseney, comprising about 645 acres. There were over 646 acres in the hands of the Poures, more or less equally divided between Adderbury's farm and Poure's manor. Most holdings were about a yardland in extent, although some consisted only of a few acres and some, notably Rathbone's freehold and those of four copyholders, were much larger. The four last had accumulated holdings of 60 to over 100 acres.[46] By the time of the 1623[47] inclosure the freeholders had been reduced to fifteen. When a list of the annual value of the lands in Bletchingdon was drawn up in 1684[48] there were six large estates together valued at £1,153 and 21 small ones worth about £480. Seven of the latter were no more than smallholdings, each valued at under £20. The large estates belonged to the gentry—the largest, valued at £375 10s., to the Earl of Anglesey, the next largest, valued at £231 11s., to Thomas Coghill, the lord of the manor. The remaining four, valued respectively at £150, £104, £75 18s., and £63, belonged to the rector, a Mr. Barber, and to John and Sutton Coghill. Thus, the misfortunes of the Coghill family had led to a temporary splitting up of the large property accumulated by the Poures, while at the same time the number of resident freeholders was being reduced

by death and other causes. Of the fifteen there in 1623 only five were left and one was a widow, and some 60 years later there was only one more. By the end of the 18th century more than half the land of the parish belonged to Arthur Annesley; of the 24 other owners the parson, assessed for the land tax at a fifth of the squire's rate, and Sir John Arundell were the only ones with substantial properties. Most of the land was occupied by tenant farmers.[49] By 1839 the Annesleys had still further increased the extent of their property by buying up some of the smaller estates.[50]

The tithe disputes provide some interesting scraps of evidence for farming practice in the late 16th and 17th centuries. There was a clear falling off of sheep-grazing. In 1611, for example, the rector claimed tithe from Francis Poure on only 200 ewes,[51] and in 1634 another rector claimed more tithes from the squire's closes because now 'much tilled'.[52] To take one case, Underdown was usually worth in tithe £3 10s., but in 1635 the rector claimed that being sown it was worth at least £14 or £15.[53]

Rye, oats, wheat, barley, peas and beans were grown, and some changes in cropping practice before the inclosure of 1623 may perhaps be indicated by the division of the Heath Field into quarters.[54] Excessive cropping, however, might lead to impoverishment of the soil, and in the late 17th century leases frequently contain the clause that land was not to be ploughed up.[55] The rector complained in 1681 that land which he had leased was so out of heart that when the lease terminated the living was likely to be worth £40 less a year.[56] Rather earlier in the 1630's some land was sown three times in the year, and some twice with oats.[57] At the end of the century, in 1683, in an effort to restore fertility a new crop, sainfoin, was introduced.[58] Turnips are first recorded in 1719.[59]

In the 1770's on the manor estate rather more than half the land was still being used for pasture,[60] but a change took place in the 19th century. In 1839 there were still only about 836 acres of arable in the whole parish compared with about 1,350 acres of meadow and pasture,[61] but by the middle of the century, when agricultural prices were booming, the proportion of arable to pasture had risen to as much as two to one. Farms were larger than elsewhere: in 1851 there were ten farms of over 100 acres, of which six were between 200 and 400 acres.[62] Although some advance had been made in reclaiming the heathland by drainage, particularly on the Heathfield estate,[63] the general standard of farming does not appear to have been high. Arthur Young found nothing of note to record in the opening years of the century, and later at least one small farm (40 a.), although said to have some excellent dairy land, was reported to be disgracefully cultivated and without a

---

[43] Par. Rec. Mill's Bk. f. 3.
[44] Ibid. f. 64.
[45] Ibid.; E 134, 14 Chas. I, Trin. 5.
[46] Par. Rec. Mill's Bk. ff. 60–64.
[47] Ibid. ff. 77–102.
[48] Ibid. ff. 3–6: valuation made by Dr. Mill, the church-wardens and two parishioners, appointed by the Earl of Anglesey and the parishioners, 1684. Thos. Coghill's estate included closes, meadow and mill; his 'manor' was not rated.
[49] O.R.O. Land tax assess.
[50] Bodl. Tithe award.
[51] Par. Rec. Mill's Bk. f. 15.

[52] Ibid. f. 25.
[53] Ibid. f. 27.
[54] Par. Rec. 1623 indenture.
[55] Ibid. Mill's Bk. ff. 27, 68, 72.
[56] Ibid. f. 68.
[57] Ibid. f. 25.
[58] Ibid. f. 72.
[59] Par. Rec. Rector's tithe bk.
[60] Val. D.: Lord Valentia's Estate Bk.
[61] Bodl. Tithe award.
[62] H.O. 107/1729.
[63] Wing, Bletch. Annals, 54.

four-course rotation.[64] But in the 1870's the parish boasted a prize-winning breed of long-woolled sheep.[65] In the 1950's sheep, mostly South Down or Clun Forest, were still kept on four farms; there were pedigree herds of cattle on two, and mechanized farming was generally practised. Out of fourteen farms mostly devoted to mixed farming, four had 300 acres or more and the rest were under 150 acres.[66]

Information about local trades is scarce: among the 17th-century tradesmen recorded were the miller, a master stone-mason, Robert Springhall,[67] a tailor, carpenters, and blacksmiths. It is noteworthy, however, that when the Rectory was repaired in 1633, the rector had to get a second carpenter from Oxford, a plasterer from Shipton, and a mason from Hampton Gay.[68] There must have been quarrymen, for both marble and stone quarries were well known at this period.[69] The quarries were perhaps one of the chief reasons for the increasing population in the first half of the 18th century. The Compton Census of 1676 had recorded 160 adults; by 1750 the estimated population was 355,[70] and the settlement papers suggest that there had been some immigration from the neighbouring villages.[71] There was a certain measure of prosperity, for out of 75 families eleven were well-to-do enough to keep one or more servants. In 1795 the reputed population of 524 included four masons, two each of carpenters, shoemakers, blacksmiths, butchers, bakers, and millers. There were also a tailor and nine farmers.[72]

The steep rise in the cost of poor relief at the end of the 18th century reflects the poverty and unrest of the period. The surviving overseers' accounts (1787–99)[73] show that in 1787 the total expenditure was £174 3s. 3d.; in 1797 it rose to £350 3s. and in 1803 was £496 10s. 5d.[74] with a rate of 6s. in the £, the second highest in the hundred. In 1794 the roundsmen system, as a means of dealing with the unemployed, was introduced, and in the following year, when as many as 67 families were receiving some kind of relief, bread payments began. The account books show that the administration of the poor law was entrusted to two overseers, who were locally elected and confirmed by the justices. The usual entries for clothes, funeral expenses, and faggots occur; no parish doctor was employed but the poor received occasional medical assistance at home in the way of extra delicacies such as tea, sugar, or mutton, or were sent to the new infirmary at Oxford; in 1790 the apothecary's bill was £38 8s. 9d. Poor-law expenditure continued to rise in the early 19th century and by 1832–5 the average annual expenditure was £802.[75] In 1835 Bletchingdon became part of the Bicester poor-law union, returning one guardian.[76]

At the end of the 18th century, in 1789, monthly parish meetings were held at the two local inns, absentees being fined 6d. In 1872 there were said to be two Friendly Societies. One established in Bletchingdon over a century had 94 members and a capital of £300. It had been converted into a seven-years club about ten years previously. The school club had a capital of over £300 and about 107 members.[77]

Population continued to rise in the 19th century. In 1801, at the first official census, there were 503 inhabitants, and this figure rose, with some fluctuations, to a peak of 693 in 1871. It had declined to 549 by 1901, a trend which continued in the 20th century. In 1951 the population was 478.[78]

CHURCH. The earliest evidence for the existence of a church at Bletchingdon is the grant of tithes made by Robert d'Oilly in 1074 (see below). In the 11th century, however, the church apparently belonged to the estate of Alwi the sheriff and not to the D'Oilly manor, for in the 13th century the patronage is known to have been divided between the two fees into which Alwi's estate had been divided, the royal sergeanty and the fee of the honor of Stafford.[79] When these two fees were in different hands, the holders should have presented alternately, but confusion arose, particularly as there were periods when the two fees were united and the question of alternate presentation did not arise. Richard Prescote, for example, held both sergeanty and fee in the early 13th century after the Grenevile moiety of the advowson had been forfeited to the Crown and regranted.[80] Richard presented in 1231 and 1234,[81] and it was stated at his death that the advowson belonged to the sergeanty and the fee.[82] But in 1279, when sergeanty and fee were in different hands, the king presented a chancery clerk, Thomas de Capella.[83] In 1289 it was stated that the king held half the advowson and Hugh de Musgrave, lord of the Stafford fee, the other half, as they each held a half of the manor.[84] Thus, it appears that the king, at least on occasions, did not grant the moiety of the advowson with the sergeanty.

The division caused great confusion: in 1298 when Hugh de Musgrave exercised his right of alternate presentation, his right was disputed on unknown grounds by Nicholas Trimenal and his wife;[85] and again in 1311 the king's presentation was opposed by both Henry Wade and Maud de Musgrave.[86] The court, however, recognized the king's right for this turn and his nominee was admitted as rector.[87]

In 1337 no opposition was made to the king's presentation[88] and in 1343, at the request of Queen Philippa, the royal moiety was granted to the Queen's

64 St. John's Coll. Arch. VIII, 65.
65 Wing, op. cit. 53.
66 Inf. the Revd. D. G. Davies.
67 For him see MS. note by H. E. Salter: Bodl. Univ. Arch. (uncat.) of the Vice-Chancellor's court papers.
68 Par. Rec. Mill's Bk.
69 Plot, *Nat. Hist. Oxon.* 267–8; C 5/111/2.
70 Compton Census; cf. the 1662 hearth tax which lists only 31 householders: *Hearth Tax Oxon.* 235; Par. Rec. Misc. papers.
71 Par. Rec. Misc. papers.
72 Ibid.
73 Ibid. Overseers' accts.
74 *Poor Abstract*, 404.
75 Wing, *Bletch. Annals*, 56.
76 Ibid.

77 Ibid. 59.
78 *Census*, 1801–1951.
79 See above, p. 60.
80 *Cal. Cat. 1343–5*, 103.
81 *Rot. Welles*, ii. 36; *Rot. Grosse.* 464.
82 *Cal. inq. p.m.* i, p. 294.
83 See above, pp. 60, 61; *Rot. Graves*, 235.
84 *Abbrev. Plac.* (Rec. Com.), 197.
85 Linc. Reg. i, Sutton, f. 347b.
86 Ibid. ii, Dalderby, f. 160b. The third party in this suit, John de Croxford, may have been Maud's second husband. A relative, Thomas de Croxford, was presented at the Musgraves' next turn.
87 Ibid.
88 *Cal. Pat. 1334–8*, 421.

College at Oxford.[89] The college presented for the first time in 1395.[90] In 1343 it had also been granted the right to acquire the other half of the advowson and to appropriate the church. No steps were taken about appropriation and the moiety of the advowson was not acquired until 1621.

In 1355 Elizabeth, widow of William de Musgrave, had sold her moiety to Sir Roger de Cotesford[91] and it had passed with the manor successively to the Abberburys and Poures,[92] and finally to Sir John Lenthall. He sold it to the college in 1621,[93] which was still patron in 1955.

The rectory was moderately well endowed: in 1254 it was valued at £4 13s. 4d.; in 1291 at £10; in 1535 at £12 9s. 4d.[94] The rectors alleged in the 16th century and later that its value had been diminished by the inclosure of the open fields and by the acceptance of a modus in lieu of a part of the tithes.[95] Nevertheless, in 1803 it was still a comfortable living worth £492.[96] It was one of the churches in the hundred to be transferred from Bicester deanery to the new Islip deanery by 1854.[97]

In the Middle Ages the rector enjoyed a fair-sized glebe. The earliest description of it, dated 1539, shows that it consisted of 67 acres and 6 butts of arable strips scattered in the open fields. A good proportion of the strips were in the West Field where the best-quality land lay.[98] Besides the arable the rector had 5½ acres of meadow, a close, and the right to keep 100 sheep and 23 cattle and horses on the common land. He also had the great and small tithes from the whole parish apart from ⅔ of the demesne tithes of the Damory manor, which had been given at an early date to the church of St. George in Oxford castle and passed in 1149 to Oseney Abbey.[99] In 1535 Oseney's share of the tithes was valued at 6s. 8d.[1]

After the Dissolution the rector received all the tithes until 1555 when Vincent Poure, lord of the two manors,[2] withheld payment. Provost Denysson, who was then rector, began a suit for their recovery.[3] The outcome of this dispute appears to have been the indenture of 1568, by which the incumbent of the day accepted a modus of 58s. 4d. on certain lands for 81 years—an arrangement which Provost Airay later described as 'sacriligious'.[4] However, no objection was made during the rest of the century, probably because, so long as the land for which the modus was paid remained pasture, the arrangement was equitable. It was only in the 17th century when the land was improved by tillage[5] that the parsons found how bad a bargain they had made.

Dr. Aglionby (rector 1601–10) seems to have been the first to attempt to abolish the modus, but he was 'quietened' by Francis Poure, who compensated him for his losses from tithes with the gift of two advowsons and other favours.[6] His two successors both went to law,[7] but it was Dr. Potter who finally obtained a decision in the Exchequer court in the church's favour in 1638.[8] His previous offer to close the dispute, if Sir Thomas Coghill would set out and hedge for the church a piece of land worth £50,[9] had been rejected.

The depositions in all these cases throw light on the difficulties of tithe-owners arising from changes of landownership and piecemeal inclosure. The case of the rectors may be summed up as follows: the modus or the 'rate' as it was called had no support in custom or equity; it was an 'evil, growing and infinite', for where there were no hedges or boundary marks tithable land could easily be confused with the rateable land, especially as the names of ancient furlongs were changed after inclosure. Furthermore, temporary compositions made by the parsons tended to be regarded by the villagers as permanent 'rates', and thus made the possibility of future loss to the rectory likely. The confusion arising from inclosure is demonstrated by the fact that one of the main points of dispute was whether the modus had ever applied to land belonging to Adderbury's manor or not. The rectors contended that it only applied to Poure's manor and that before the final inclosure of 1623 Adderbury's manor as well as Rathbone's freehold had always paid tithes.[10]

Apart from the question of the modus, the rectors further complained that tithes from those grounds which were admitted to be tithable were adversely affected. Corn-tithes were lost, as the greatest portion of corn was grown on the 'rateable' land. Tithe lambs and calves were lost: in 1634, for instance, the rector had one tithe lamb out of two or three hundred lambs, because although Coghill's sheep were fed on the tithable land care was taken to see that lambs were born on the 'rateable'. It was similarly the case with cattle which were pastured on both kinds of land. Furthermore, small tithes of fruit, pigeons, and so on were lost when Adderbury's manor-house was allowed to fall into decay.[11] Potter, indeed, maintained that the value of the rectory had been reduced from £400 to at least £340 and that tithe on the 'rateable' land should be £40 instead of under £3, the amount received from the modus.[12]

The quarrel flared up again in Dr. Mill's time, 1682 to 1707. In the 'bad times' of the Civil War the

---

[89] Ibid. 1343–45, 103–4; J. R. Magrath, *Queen's Coll.* i. 18.

[90] Linc. Reg. xi, Buckingham, f. 330.

[91] C.P. 25(1)190/20/69.

[92] See above, p. 61 : Sir Roger de Cotesford presented in 1368, Sir Richard Abberbury in 1387, the feoffees of Sir John Abberbury in 1409, Roger Poure in 1460, and John Poure in 1507: MS. Top. Oxon. d 460.

[93] C.P. 25(2)/340/Trin. 19 Jas. I.

[94] Lunt, *Val. Norw.* 312; *Tax. Eccl.* (Rec. Com.), 31; *Valor Eccl.* (Rec. Com.), ii. 160.

[95] See below.

[96] Par. Rec.

[97] There is some confusion about the exact date of the formation of Islip rural deanery. Bishop Wilberforce appointed the first dean in 1847 (Oxf. Dioc. d 109, p. 200). In the *Clergy List* the deanery is first recorded in 1852 (*Clergy List*, 1851, 1852), while in the episcopal visitations it is first found in Nov. 1854 (Oxf. Dioc. c 437, p. 300). It

does not occur in May 1854 (ibid. p. 163). (Refs. supplied by Dr. Molly Barratt.)

[98] Par. Rec. Mill's Bk. ff. 29–55.

[99] *Oseney Cart.* iv. 3, 7, &c. For the dispute of 1324 see ibid. vi. 96–98.

[1] *Valor Eccl.* (Rec. Com.), ii. 160.

[2] See above, pp. 58, 61.

[3] Par. Rec. Mill's Bk. ff. 15, 16.

[4] Ibid. f. 1.

[5] Ibid. f. 21.

[6] Ibid. f. 6.

[7] Ibid. ff. 1, 22.

[8] For the original record of this suit see E 134, 14 Chas. I, Trin. 5; and Queen's Coll. Mun. 4 H. 20 a–e; for transcripts see Par. Rec. Mill's Bk. ff. 21–22.

[9] Par. Rec. Mill's Bk. f. 26.

[10] Ibid.; see above, p. 64.

[11] Par. Rec. Mill's Bk. ff. 6, 13.

[12] Ibid. f. 26.

'rate' had been accepted out of fear,[13] and had become customary. Moreover, Mill had an additional grievance about the state of the glebe. As a result of inclosure in 1622 his glebe lay in inclosed fields. He made no complaint about the quality or quantity of land allotted in lieu of the ancient glebe, but complained of insufficient compensation for the loss of tithes on the land inclosed.[14] An early 19th-century rector, however, considered that the rectory had been damaged by being allotted land which lay as far as two miles away from the parsonage, and could only be approached by a lane which was often impassable.[15]

Though Mill made exhaustive transcripts of the evidence in the Potter case with a view to bringing a new action, he finally had to content himself with advising his successors never to make any compositions for tithes as they were always prejudicial to the rectory.

At the first inclosure of 1623 the rector was allotted 60 acres of arable for his glebe and 43 acres in lieu of tithe plus 89 acres of heath.[16] At the date of the tithe award in 1839 out of 2,654 acres in the parish 1,032 acres still paid a tithe and 356 acres a modus of £2 18s. 4d. These were both commuted for £332 8s. 4d., including tithe on the glebe which then amounted to 209 acres.[17] Of this, part was ancient glebe and part was the rector's allotment of 1623. The glebe was sold to the Ecclesiastical Commissioners in 1935 and the annual interest derived from the investment of the proceeds of the sale amounted thereafter to £89 15s.[18]

The 13th-century incumbents were all in minor orders.[19] The earliest recorded was a subdeacon, admitted in 1231 on condition that he attended the schools of Oxford.[20] Another incumbent was a Chancery clerk and a pluralist, presented by the king.[21] In the 14th century two parsons were priests and in 1395 the first graduate was instituted. This precedent was followed in 1409 and henceforth, whenever the Queen's College exercised its alternate right of presentation, graduates were the rule. Members of the college were presented in 1421, 1443, 1457, and 1493.[22]

As a result of this connexion the parish got a number of distinguished rectors. Edward Rigge (1493–1507), for example, resigned in 1507 to become provost.[23] William Denysson, who began the hundred-year struggle over tithes, was another provost.[24] The learned John Aglionby, Principal of St. Edmund Hall, held the cure from 1604 to 1610, but for part of his incumbency had a curate at Bletchingdon.[25] Provost Airay, a constant preacher and opponent of 'scurril jesting, carousing and dancing about the maypole', was rector in 1615.[26] The Laudian Provost Potter (rector 1631–42), a believer

in order and discipline, immediately saw to the restoration of the chancel and parsonage, which had been much neglected, and was active in defence of the church's rights.[27] Another equally vigorous rector was John Mill (1682–1707), Principal of St. Edmund Hall and a scholar of repute.[28]

During the 18th century the rectors, all fellows of Queen's, were resident for much of the year and after 1759 were assisted by a curate.[29] They held the normal number of Sunday services and attracted an unusually large number of communicants—between 50 and 60—at the four communion services. They claimed that attendance at church was on the whole good, though in 1759 it was complained that 40 parishioners, mostly farmers or day labourers, were constantly absentees from an 'unconcernedness about religion'.[30] But at this date the rector was old and too blind to read the services, and his curate was unlicensed, resident in Oxford, and paid only £25 a year. As elsewhere there was a great falling off in the second half of the century. In 1803 only 26 communicants were reported.[31] A new spirit in the early 19th century is shown in the setting up of a Sunday school, in the fair congregation of 200 reported in 1851, and the 36 monthly communicants recorded in 1866.[32] By 1875, however, the number of communicants had dropped to twenty.[33]

The church of *ST. GILES* comprises a chancel, nave with south door and porch, a western tower and north aisle.[34] It is in the main a 15th-century building, but it has been much restored. Traces of earlier work can be seen in a blocked window on the north side of the chancel, and in a fragment of Romanesque carving (probably the lintel of a former south doorway) built into the south wall of the nave. The lower stage of the tower probably dates from the 13th century. The belfry is surmounted by a small square 15th-century turret with a pyramidal roof and a weather-vane.

Two special rates were levied in 1630[35] for church repairs and by 1634 the restoration of the chancel had been completed at a cost of over £33.[36] The south porch is thought to date from 1695, the date above the sundial over the doorway. When visited by Rawlinson some years later the church was in good condition and the chancel 'very neat'.[37] Two galleries were erected in the 18th century, one at the western end for the children[38] and the other near the chancel. The last, the Annesleys' pew, built in 1761 and approached by an external staircase leading through a window, was later described as 'a hideous square gallery pew with battlements'.[39] In the same year the church was 'rufcasted'[40] and the tower repaired.

In 1814 a vestry meeting ordered the nave and

13 Par. Rec. Mill's Bk. f. 72.
14 Ibid. f. 68.
15 Ibid. Dr. Bacon's notes.
16 Ibid. Mill's Bk. ff. 77–102.
17 Bodl. Tithe award.
18 Par. Rec. Misc. notes; inf. the Revd. R. H. Daubney.
19 See list of presentations in MS. Top. Oxon. d 460.
20 *Rot. Welles*, ii. 36.
21 *Cal. Pat.* 1272–81, 323, 328.
22 MS. Top. Oxon. d 460.
23 J. R. Magrath, *Queen's Coll.* i. 163; ii. 282. For his successor Edw. Hilton, who was guilty of some minor irregularities, see *Visit. Dioc. Linc.* 1517–31, i. 125. For an earlier provost, Walter Ball (1421–?), see Emden, *O.U. Reg.* i.
24 See above, p. 67.

25 *V.C.H. Oxon.* iii. 327; Wood, *Athenae*, ii. 60–61.
26 Cf. R. H. Hodgkin, *Six Centuries of an Oxf. Coll.* 81.
27 Cf. ibid. 92.
28 *D.N.B.*; see above, p. 67.
29 Oxf. Dioc. d 555.   30 Ibid.
31 Ibid. d 570.
32 Ibid. c 332.   33 Ibid. c 341.
34 For an account see Parker, *Guide*, 51–52.
35 Par. Rec.
36 Queen's Coll. Mun. 4 H. 10.
37 *Par. Coll.* i. 46.
38 This may have been for the 'singers', for whom a bassoon was purchased in 1808: Par. Rec.
39 Oxf. Archd. Oxon. c 54, ff. 25 sqq.
40 Wing, *Bletch. Annals*, 48. The date 1761 on the tower can be seen in J. Buckler's drawing.

porch to be 'new slated and ceiled and otherwise repaired' at a cost of £295.[41] In 1870 the dilapidated chancel was reroofed,[42] and an estimate of £1,015 was obtained for a thorough restoration of the whole church by the architect Charles Buckeridge.[43] Financial difficulties prevented the work being undertaken until 1878, although the building was in a 'most discreditable condition' with crumbling walls and rotten beams.[44] The north aisle was then added, the square-headed east window of two lights in the chancel was replaced by one in the 14th-century style,[45] the galleries and the plaster ceiling of the nave were removed, and other minor repairs were carried out. Lord Valentia bore a large part of the cost.

In 1928 electric light was installed by Lord Valentia's son; in 1946 the church was reroofed with Stonesfield slates as before, and in 1948 an electric organ was installed.[46]

The pulpit and the pews in the north aisle are Jacobean. It is recorded that in 1630 the pulpit and reading-desk were moved to the south side of the church, an unusual position, so as to make way for the installation of new pews in the chancel. This was the result of a dispute between Sir John Lenthall and Sir Thomas Coghill, in which each claimed precedence and refused to sit one behind the other.[47] More family pews were erected in 1671 by Sutton Coghill, but in 1682 Dr. Mill[48] declared these unusable. He also said that the reading-desk and the parson's seat were decayed, the pulpit in danger of collapse and the floor-boards of nave and chancel uneven; that the communion table had no railings and was 'mean', that the font was broken and the belfry loft 'much decayed'. Mill himself did something to restore decency. In 1701 he put up new wainscoting (now gone) in the chancel, set up two new pews, and perhaps installed the octagonal font of grey marble, which appears to belong to this period.[49]

Rawlinson noted some armorial glass in the chancel, including an inscription to 'Roger Cotesford Miles';[50] but by 1955 there was only modern stained glass. It included memorial windows to members of the Annesley family and to Thomas Dand, rector (d. 1868). The painting of St. Peter and the cock (school of Ribera) was given by the rector, the Revd. D. G. Davies, in 1946. The medieval church had a number of brasses which had been torn up before Rawlinson visited it, but he noted four, which have since been lost. The first was to Roger Poure (d. 1479 ?) and his wife, the second to Thomas Poure (d. 1481/2) and his wife, the third to John Poure (d. 1526) and his two wives, on which

was the figure of God seated with the Child Christ between his knees, and the fourth was to the rector, Edward Hilton, a Fellow of the Queen's College.[51]

There is a fine monument in the chancel to Elizabeth Collins, only daughter of Sutton Coghill (d. 1713), and her brother John (d. 1716), and an elaborate monument to the four children of Henry and Thomas Coghill, who died in 1628 and 1630. A cartouche ornamented with swags of fruit, cherubs' heads, and shields of arms (signed by J. Piddington, Oxon.) commemorates Sir Thomas Coghill (d. 1659) and his family, which included the following: Thomas (d. 1694), John (d. 1694/5), Sutton (d. 1707), and his sons Thomas (d. 1706), and Sutton (d. 1708).[52] There are inscriptions to Elizabeth Brown (d. 1631), to John Knapp, gent. (d. 1727), and to a number of rectors: the 'pious and laborious minister' George Birkhead (d. 1631); John Hooke (d. 1673/4); John Mill (d. 1707) and his wife Priscilla (d. 1685); William Scott (d. 1742); and James Coward (d. 1807).

There are many 19th- and 20th-century memorials to the Annesley family. The war memorial (1939–45) was designed by T. Rayson of Oxford.

In the 16th century, the church was comparatively rich in goods: besides a chalice of silver-gilt it had two copes of crimson velvet and '9 paires of sutes of vestments'.[53] In the 17th century John Mill gave an altar cloth and a crimson cushion.[54] In 1955 the church owned two silver chalices, one dated 1786 with a plate-paten of 1782 and the other a 19th-century one.[55] There was a ring of five bells, of which one was partly the gift of the squire John Coghill. Three were cast in the 18th century: one in 1738 and another about 1776 by Matthew Bagley, who was paid £18 5s. in that year for his work.[56] The 18th-century oak frame is of an unusual and ingenious design.

The registers begin in 1559 and are complete.

NONCONFORMITY. In the late 16th century Ralph Coxe, a member of a well-known yeoman family, was a recusant,[57] and in the early 17th century there was a comparatively large Roman Catholic community, including five members of the Poure family,[58] and several people of the yeoman class.[59] No papists were reported in 1676[60] or in any 18th-century episcopal visitations, except for one woman in 1738 and a poor widow in 1767.[61] In 1854 there were two Roman Catholics.[62]

The influence of nearby Bicester may once have encouraged dissent:[63] in 1676 the Compton Census recorded seven dissenters.[64] But apart from a

---

[41] Ibid. 62.
[42] MS. Top. Oxon. c. 103, ff. 89–92.
[43] Ibid.
[44] Wing, *Bletch. Annals*, 10.
[45] Drawings by J. Buckler (1825) in MS. Top. Oxon. a 65, ff. 98–99, show the church before restoration.
[46] Inf. the Revd. D. G. Davies.
[47] MS. Top. Oxon. c 56, f. 37; see above, p. 59.
[48] For him see above, p. 68.
[49] Par. Rec. Mill's Bk. f. 67. For Buckler's drawing of font see MS. Top. Oxon. a 65, f. 97.
[50] *Par. Coll.* i. 48.
[51] Ibid. 47. Rawlinson could only read 'MCCCCLXX . . .', but Roger was alive in 1478 (see above, p. 58). He also wrote '1425' in error for 1525, the date of John Poure's death, and gives 1530 as the date of Hilton's death. Hilton, however, made his will in 1533, and probably died in 1545, when his successor was presented to Bletchingdon (*Liber*

Obituarius Aulae Reginae in Oxonia, ed. J. R. Magrath, 80; Oxf. Dioc. d 105, pp. 15–16.
[52] For blazons of arms in the church see Bodl. G.A. Oxon. 16° 217, pp. 60a, 68–69; ibid. 4° 685, pp. 46–49; ibid. 688, p. 48.
[53] *Chant. Cert.* 86.
[54] Par. Rec. Mill's Bk. f. 67.
[55] Evans, *Ch. Plate*.
[56] Wing, *Bletch. Annals*, 48, citing the churchwardens' accounts, which have since been lost; *Ch. Bells Oxon.* i. 49.
[57] C.R.S. xviii, 259.
[58] See above, p. 59.
[59] Salter, *Oxon. Recusants, passim*.
[60] Compton Census.
[61] Oxf. Dioc. d 552, c 431.
[62] *Wilb. Visit.*
[63] See above, p. 48.
[64] Compton Census.

Presbyterian mentioned in 1738,[65] there is no further mention of dissent until the 19th century, when Methodism became important. There seem to have been two groups at the beginning, for in 1830 two places, one a shop, were licensed for worship.[66] In the 1830's Bletchingdon was on the Oxford Methodist Circuit,[67] but later the Bletchingdon Methodists became Primitive Methodists. In 1851 a granary was licensed for meetings;[68] it was bought in 1855 for £70 and converted into a chapel.[69] The group was an active one, for in the 1870's there were said to be between 50 and 100 dissenters in the parish.[70] Later a new chapel was built,[71] which continued in use until the winter of 1946–7. It was demolished in 1954.[72]

SCHOOLS. Leonard Poure left money in 1621 for the maintenance of almshouses and a school,[73] but although the house which he had erected[74] was known as a 'schole-house' it always seems to have been used as an almshouse. When Rawlinson visited Bletchingdon in about 1719 there was talk of using part of the charity money for a free school,[75] but there was no school in 1738 or in 1759.[76] In 1769 a charity school supported by the Annesleys and other subscribers was opened for 10 boys and girls.[77] In the early 19th century 15 to 30 children were being taught reading, writing, and the catechism in a house lent by Arthur Annesley (d. 1841).[78] The official report of 1818 records a total of 70 pupils, of whom 10 were charity-school children, being taught in 4 schools.[79] By 1833 there were 75 fee-paying pupils and 10 who were paid for out of an allowance of £10 made by Annesley.[80] Two schools survived in 1864, one supported by Lord Valentia and one by the rector.[81]

Bletchingdon Parochial school was built in 1870 on land conveyed to the united charities, and was partly supported by the charity funds.[82] In 1871 there were two teachers, two departments, mixed and infants, and 103 pupils.[83] By 1906 the average attendance was 120.[84] In 1928 the school was reorganized for juniors, and senior pupils were transferred to Kirtlington. In 1954 the school was controlled and had 63 pupils, compared with an average attendance of 28 in 1937.[85]

CHARITIES. By his will, proved in 1621[86], Leonard Poure bequeathed £200 for the maintenance of four almshouses and a school (see above), which he had built in Bletchingdon, provided that the owners of Constable's Close (4 a.) and Painter's Hill Close (6 a.) endowed his foundation with these lands.[87] The almshouses or 'Hospitall Houses', as they were

called in 1687,[88] consisted of four ground-floor rooms in one building; a room above them, called the 'school room', was approached by an outside staircase.[89] The legacy was confirmed by the inclosure agreement of 1623,[90] and in 1631 the building and the closes were conveyed by Sir William Temple and other feoffees to trustees for the benefit of four almspeople, who were to be appointed by Sir John Lenthall or his heirs.[91] In 1685 William Lenthall, grandson and heir of Sir John, was found to have failed either to appoint almspeople, or to employ the income of the charity or to appoint new feoffees. Accordingly in 1686 a commission for charitable uses ordered Lenthall to convey the premises to James, Earl of Anglesey, and six others, including the rector, who in future was always to be a feoffee.[92]

In the same year it was ordered that a trust should be formed to administer the Poor's land, which then consisted of Burdock Piece (bequeathed in 1619 by a parishioner of that name), Poor Folk's Close, Heath Close, the Poor's Eight Acres, and a tenement and close (c. 22 a. in all) and the sum of £105, then put out at interest by the overseers. The income from the Poor's Land had previously been distributed by the overseers, but had been recently misapplied.[93] In 1738 the incumbent knew nothing of the £105,[94] but it had possibly been used to purchase land in Kidlington which was included with the Poor's Land by 1724. The yearly income of the Poor's Land with Constable's Close and School (formerly Painter's Hill) Close, was £29 17s.[95] During the 18th century the charity money was distributed regularly, part being paid to the overseers, and the remainder—£10 in 1738, £12 10s. in 1742[96]—being divided among the four almswomen.

In 1792 four new almshouses were built on part of the Poor's Land to the south of the village green at a cost of £200, and the old ones were pulled down. Each new almshouse had a living-room, a pantry and two bedrooms above.[97] The income from rents had risen to £44 by 1808[98] and was about £45 in 1824. It was then found that although pensions of 14s. a month were being paid to four widows, only two of them lived in the almshouses, three of which were entirely occupied by families of paupers. Each almshouse received an allowance of about half a ton of coal every year. The Charity Commissioners recommended that each almshouse should be assigned to one poor person or family, and that part of the income of the Poor's Land might be used to assist other poor people.

In 1793 the charity land in Kidlington had been

[65] Oxf. Dioc. d 552.
[66] Ibid. c 643, p. 2; c 645, f. 146. Another place belonging to the same group was licensed later in 1830: ibid. f. 155.
[67] *Lord's Day Plan, 1835.*
[68] Oxf. Dioc. c 643, p. 192.
[69] Bletch. chapel deeds dep. with A. H. Franklin & Sons, 14 King Edward St., Oxford.
[70] Oxf. Dioc. c 344.
[71] *Kelly's Dir. Oxon.* (1887).
[72] Inf. the Revd. R. H. Daubney.
[73] See below.
[74] Mill's Bk. (see above, p. 56, n. 9), f. 108.
[75] *Par. Coll.* i. 46.
[76] Oxf. Dioc. d 553, d 556.
[77] Ibid. d 561, d 707; see above, p. 59.
[78] Ibid. d 707, c 327, p. 362.
[79] *Educ. of Poor*, 719.
[80] *Educ. Enq. Abstract*, 741.

[81] *Kelly's Dir. Oxon.* (1864).
[82] *Vol. Sch. Ret.; Kelly's Dir. Oxon.* (1887).
[83] *Kelly's Dir. Oxon.* (1887); *List of sch.; Elem. Educ. Ret.*
[84] *Vol. Sch. Ret.*
[85] Inf. Oxon. Educ. Cttee.
[86] P.C.C. 93 Dale.
[87] *12th Rep. Com. Char.* 294–5.
[88] Par. Rec. Mill's Bk. (see above, p. 56, n. 9), f. 112.
[89] *12th Rep. Com. Char.* 295.
[90] See above, p. 64.
[91] *12th Rep. Com. Char.* 294; *Char. Don.* ii. 989.
[92] C 93/42/19; *12th Rep. Com. Char.* 294–5.
[93] C 93/42/22; *12th Rep. Com. Char.* 296.
[94] Oxf. Dioc. d 552.
[95] Par. Rec. Rector's tithe bk.
[96] Ibid.; Oxf. Dioc. d 552.
[97] *12th Rep. Com. Char.* 295; Par. Rec.
[98] Par. Rec. Rector's tithe bk.; ibid. Overseers' acct. bk.

sold and the money invested. In 1817, because of the shortage of houses, the money (£188 1s. 6d.) was spent on building two houses in Burdock's Piece. These were later subdivided and inhabited by six families of paupers put in by the overseers. In 1824 the latter agreed to pay £10 rent to the charity trustees.[99]

The income of the charity was about £50 in 1852,[1]

and in 1870, when there were 12 cottages as well as 33 acres of land, it was £79 19s. Of this £17 19s. was used to support the Parochial school, £33 4s. was paid to the almspeople, and £27 16s. was spent on fuel for the poor.[2] Under a scheme of the Charity Commission made in 1934 the income was to be used to keep 4 cottages in repair, and to pay 3s. 6d. a week to 4 almspeople. In 1955 the income was £75.[3]

BUCKNELL

THIS parish, roughly rectangular in shape, lies 2½ miles north-west of the market-town of Bicester. The ancient parish covered 1,894 acres, but it was enlarged in 1932 to 2,152 acres, when land from Bicester Market End was added.[1] The Gagle Brook, as it flows southwards to join the Ray, forms the parish's western boundary and a part of its southern one. The brook has two fords in the parish, one of them near Trow Pool.[2] Bucknell lies mostly on the Cornbrash, but is bounded on the west by the Forest Marble and the Great Oolite;[3] it lies between the 300-foot and 350-foot contour lines and its soil is chiefly stonebrash. Several small plantations and copses but no woodland were marked on Davis's map of 1797. Domesday Book recorded a wood of 1 by ½ furlong.[4] The park of the medieval lords of the manor was believed in the mid-18th century to have been south-west of the village near Bucknell Lodge.[5]

The main Banbury to Bicester road, an important highway since medieval times, runs along part of the parish's eastern boundary (the Bucknell section was made a turnpike in 1791);[6] a road from Middleton Stoney to Bicester skirts the southern boundary and roads radiate from the village to Ardley, the Banbury road, Bicester itself, and Middleton. Farm tracks and foot-paths still mark the line of the road by Trow Pool towards Somerton, which was one of the principal roads in the parish in 1797.[7]

A number of new roads were 'set forth' after the inclosure of 1780, including a road over Bucknell Cow Pasture to Caversfield. This pasture was well known as one of the courses for the Bicester horse races in the 18th century.[8] It was much improved by Joseph Bullock of Caversfield, who removed many hawthorn bushes in 1764 and planted trees both then and in 1780.[9]

The Aynho and Ashendon section of the former G.W.R.'s main line from London to Birmingham crosses the centre of the parish, but the nearest station is the former L.M.S. station at Bicester.

Bucknell village lies in the northern part of the parish at the source of a small stream, a feeder of the Gagle Brook, which flows eastwards and south of the village street. The village is named 'Bucca's hill' after some early settler.[10] The medieval village appears to have been larger than it was in later centuries.[11] In the 16th century there were 26 messuages in the manor and these, with the manor-house and Rectory, probably made up almost the entire village, for there were few, if any, freeholders.[12] At the time of the hearth tax of 1665, apart from the Trotmans' large manor-house and a comfortable Rectory, the village had only fourteen other dwellings listed for the tax. Of these thirteen were humble with only one hearth.[13] In the 18th century there were said to be about 30 houses:[14] these were mainly spread out on either side of the road running east from the village green past the church and the manor-house. A small group of cottages lay south of the triangular green, which lay at the cross-roads.[15] Some twenty years later Dunkin described the village as consisting of 'one crooked street, thinly studded with cottages, and some two or three farm houses'.[16] These farms were Rectory Farm opposite the church, Manor and Lower Farms at the eastern end of the street, and Home Farm. The smithy and the pound were by the green.[17] Increasing population in the 19th century led to a growth in the size of the village. By 1851 there were 58 houses.[18] A group of 19th-century cottages, built of stone and brick, still stand opposite the church, but the school, built in 1861, is now derelict.

Much of the old village has been rebuilt since 1945 and modern council houses have replaced the old two-storied cottages of rubble with thatched roofs. Post-war building, which is all at the west end near Home Farm, brought the number of houses up to 60 by 1951 compared with 53 in 1901.[19]

The present manor-house stands behind the church on the site of a medieval house, once the home of the Damory family[20] and perhaps built by

[99] 12th Rep. Com. Char. 295, 297.
[1] Gardner, Dir. Oxon.
[2] Gen. Digest Char.
[3] Inf. the Revd. R. H. Daubney.
[1] Census, 1881, 1931; Oxon. Review Order (1932): copy in O.R.O.
[2] O.S. Map 6″, xvi SE., xvii SW.; xxii. NE., xxiii NW. (1900); ibid. 2½″ 42/52 (1951).
[3] G.S. Map 1″, xlv NE. and SE.; G.S. Memoir (1864), 26.
[4] V.C.H. Oxon. i. 414; Davis, Oxon. Map.
[5] MS. Top. Oxon. c 307, f. 156b.
[6] 31 Geo. III, c. 103.   [7] Davis, Oxon. Map.
[8] O.R.O. Incl. award; Blo. Buck. 32.
[9] Joseph Bullock's diary, penes Col. the Hon. E. H. Wyndham, Caversfield.

[10] P.N. Oxon. (E.P.N.S.), i. 203.
[11] See below, p. 75.
[12] See below, p. 76.
[13] Hearth Tax Oxon. 201. Cf. 23 houses listed in 1662: ibid. 235.
[14] Oxf. Dioc. d 552, d 558; MS. Top. Oxon. c 307, f. 147.
[15] Davis, Oxon. Map.
[16] Dunkin, Oxon. i. 180.
[17] O.S. Map 25″, xvii. 13 (1881); Bucknell Lodge, Upper Farm, and Crowmarsh Farm are the only outlying farmhouses in the ancient parish: O.S. Map 2½″, 42/52.
[18] Census, 1851.
[19] Census, 1901, 1951. Fourteen Council houses were built 1945–54: inf. Ploughley R.D.C.
[20] See below, p. 73.

Richard Damory, who was often an honoured guest at Bicester Priory.[21] Traces remain of the moat by which it was formerly surrounded. The 17th-century manor-house was a large one for which nineteen hearths were returned for the tax of 1665.[22] The present building of two stories with attics is built of ashlar and coursed rubble and although it has been completely modernized appears to date largely from about 1700. Lenthall Trotman, lord of the manor from 1685 to 1710, is said to have been the builder and the date 1702 was once over the south doorway.[23] One of the bedrooms, however, contains a plaster ceiling of late 16th-century design with seven roundels, on each of which is the head of some mythical or Biblical character—such as Julius Caesar, Fama, Proserpine, Bellona, and Joshua.[24] The last of the Trotmans to reside died in 1775.[25] In the 1820's, when Thomas Tyrwhitt-Drake was leasing the house and park, the house had a low wall and railing in front of it. It still preserved its original H-shaped plan.[26] In about 1830 Tyrwhitt-Drake added a southern wing and further additions and alterations were made later in the century by Lt.-Col. F. D. Hibbert.[27] In 1949 it was bought for use as an Old People's Home by the Oxfordshire County Council from the B.B.C., who had occupied it during the Second World War.[28]

The Old Rectory stands to the north-east of the churchyard and probably dates from about 1600. A description of the house and farm buildings in 1614 speaks of 'two courts'.[29] A detailed description of 1634 gives the hall two bays, the parlour three bays, and mentions a gallery and a little chamber, and other rooms totalling eleven bays.[30] With its outhouses, the whole property comprised 48 bays of building. In 1665 the rector returned six hearths for the tax;[31] today the house is an L-shaped building of coursed rubble with a roof of stone slates. It consists of two stories with attic dormers. Its 18th-century windows were put in perhaps when the house was divided into two, half being let to the glebe farmer and half reserved for visiting rectors.[32] Early in the 19th century part of the house was pulled down and the rest partly rebuilt and modernized.[33]

The new Rectory, which was built in 1833 and enlarged in 1878, stands on the opposite side of the road next to a row of four ancient thatched cottages and a house.[34] All are built of the local rubble stone. Manor Farm is a two-storied 17th-century house, but has been modernized. The Trigger Pond Inn at the other end of the village is a stone L-shaped building with casement windows and thatched roof,

and has become a public house comparatively recently. Blomfield, writing in 1894, says there was no inn in his day. The Trotmans would not allow one as they feared it would lead to drunkenness.[35]

The water-supply and sewerage system, installed in the village by Capt. P. Hunloke before 1918, were still in use in 1951. The water tower, near Trow Pool, was built of local stone.[36]

The site of the lost hamlet of Saxenton has not yet been discovered. According to Dunkin it was to be identified with the numerous foundations of houses visible in the 1820's in a copse at a short distance from Bucknell church,[37] but there seems no reason to suppose that these were not once part of Bucknell itself. A more probable site would be near the boundary of the parish on the Gagle Brook, particularly as the Gagle may probably be identified with the *Sexig Broc* of a charter of 995.[38] This brook, like the Gagle now, was said to divide Ardley from Bucknell, and it has been suggested that its name is an early back-formation from the name Saxenton or 'Seaxa's farm'.[39] At least one house remained in the 15th century,[40] and White Kennett writing in 1695 says that there were foundations visible on ground called Ball-yards,[41] but this place cannot now be traced. It is possible that the hamlet lay near the site of Bucknell Lodge, a 17th-century farm-house which lies on high ground on the road running just above Trow Pool and the Gagle.

Bucknell was a centre of fox-hunting at an early date: Samuel Trotman, squire from 1751 to 1775, kept a pack and in the first half of the 19th century the village was closely associated with the Bicester Hunt. Sir Henry Peyton, a well-known hunting man, was followed at the manor-house by T. Tyrwhitt-Drake, master of the Bicester Hunt in 1830, who brought the kennels to Bucknell.[42]

Bucknell is also distinguished for its vigorous Morris Dancing tradition and a number of well-known dances such as the 'Princess Royal' and the 'Blue-Eyed Stranger' and the jigs 'Bonnets so Blue' and 'Shepherd's Hey' were collected there at the beginning of the 20th century. The last traditional pipe and tabor player in England, Joseph Powell, lived in the village from about 1846 to 1937.[43]

MANOR. *BUCKNELL* was one of the many manors which were granted by William I to Robert d'Oilly, and it is possible that before the Conquest it had formed part of the possessions of Wigod of Wallingford.[44] Robert d'Oilly's manors were eventually divided into three groups, one of which, the

[21] Kennett, *Paroch. Antiq.* i. 510, 564.
[22] *Hearth Tax Oxon.* 201.
[23] Blo. *Buck.* 21, 35 n.
[24] The tradition that the room with this ceiling was made by Samuel Trotman (d. 1749) is impossible, but he may perhaps have altered it: Dunkin, *Oxon.* i. 181, 200 n. There is similar plaster-work at Home Farm, Wendlebury, and at Hardwick House, Whitchurch.
[25] Ibid. 183.
[26] Dunkin, *Oxon.* i. 180–1, and illustration of early 19th-cent. house; cf. MS. Top. Oxon. a 38, f. 27.
[27] Blo. *Buck.* 36.
[28] Inf. Clerk Oxon. C.C.
[29] Oxf. Archd. Oxon. c 141, p. 297.
[30] Ibid. p. 298.
[31] *Hearth Tax Oxon.* 201. For case (1671–3) about dilapidations to Rectory see Lambeth Libr. Ct. of Arches Bbb 250; Eee 4, ff. 352–4; Eee 3, ff. 631b–633, 687b–691, 724b–725; Sentence bk. B 8/136.

[32] See below, p. 78.
[33] Blo. *Buck.* 37.
[34] Ibid.
[35] Ibid. 38; Dunkin, *Oxon.* i. 181.
[36] Par. Rec. Minute Bk. entry Aug. 1918; *Kelly's Dir. Oxon.* (1920).
[37] Dunkin, *Oxon.* i. 203–4.
[38] *P.N. Oxon.* (E.P.N.S.), i. 203.
[39] Ibid.; *Cod. Dipl.* ed Kemble, vi. no. 1289.
[40] Kennett, *Paroch. Antiq.* ii. 375.
[41] Ibid. i. 55.
[42] Wing, *Annals*, 50; Dunkin, *Oxon.* i. 180; *V.C.H. Oxon.* ii. 356–7.
[43] Clare Coll. (Cambridge), Sharp MS.: Folk Dance Notes (2). 161–8; Bodl. Manning MS. Top. Oxon. d 200, p. 85.
[44] *V.C.H. Oxon.* i. 383, 414; Kennett, *Paroch. Antiq.* i. 75.

honor of D'Oilly or of Hook Norton, remained in the hands of the D'Oilly family. Bucknell belonged to this honor, and its overlordship therefore descended in the D'Oilly family until the death of Henry (II) in 1232.[45] The honor then passed to Henry's nephew Thomas de Newburgh, Earl of Warwick, and on his death in 1242 to his sister Margaret and her husband John de Plescy, styled Earl of Warwick.[46] John had no children by Margaret, and after his death in 1263 the overlordship of Bucknell should have followed the descent of the earldom of Warwick. But John had succeeded in settling Hook Norton on his son by his first wife, Hugh de Plescy, and he and his descendants were overlords of Bucknell until the end of the 14th century.[47] Hugh's great-grandson John died in 1354, and was succeeded by his nephew John Lenveysy, who took the name of Plescy.[48] After his death in 1379 or 1380 Hook Norton passed to his widow Elizabeth, and to her second husband Philip de la Vache, who survived her and who gave the manor to Thomas Chaucer. Thomas's daughter Alice married the Earl of Suffolk; Hook Norton was formally granted to her by the Crown in 1438, and the overlordship of Bucknell thereafter followed the descent of the earldom and dukedom of Suffolk.[49]

At the time of the Domesday survey Robert d'Oilly's lands in Bucknell assessed at 7 hides were held of him by a certain Gilbert,[50] probably the ancestor of the Damory or de Damori family.[51] He may have come from Amars or Amory near Caen, and was perhaps identical with the Gilbert de Almereio who gave a house near Oxford to Eynsham Abbey[52] and, it should be noted, held other manors—Bletchingdon and Weston-on-the-Green for instance—which also descended to the Damorys.[53] Gilbert was probably succeeded by Robert Damory,[54] who was followed by his son Roger, a frequent witness to the charters of Oxfordshire religious houses between 1130 and 1145,[55] and who like his father was a benefactor of Godstow. Roger's son Ralph had three sons, Robert, Richard, and Ralph, by his wife Hawise,[56] and was succeeded by his eldest son by about 1187.[57] It is uncertain when this Robert died: he and his son, also named Robert, are frequently mentioned between 1180 and 1205; and it appears probable that he died in or soon after the latter year.[58] The younger Robert was under-sheriff of

Oxfordshire in 1207, served frequently as a justice in the county in the early years of Henry III's reign, and was one of the collectors of the 15th in 1225 shortly before his death in 1236 he was appointed Sheriff of Oxfordshire and Constable of Oxford castle.[59] Robert was succeeded by his eldest son Roger, who was recorded as holding Bucknell of the honor of D'Oilly in 1243.[60] Roger later mortgaged the manor to Oseney Abbey, but in 1271 he paid off his debt and recovered 'scripturas obligatorias et feoffamenta de manerio de Bukenhull'.[61] He died in or soon after 1281, and Bucknell passed in quick succession to his son Robert, who died about 1285, and his grandson Richard.[62]

In both local and national affairs Richard took an active part, and on the whole he enjoyed the favour of Edward II, who granted him free warren in his demesnes at Bucknell in 1312 and again in 1317.[63] He was Sheriff of Oxfordshire from 1308 to 1310, Constable of Oxford castle from 1311 to 1321,[64] and the holder of other important posts. He died in 1330.[65] His son and heir Richard was a minor, and his mother Margaret was granted his wardship and the custody of his lands. After he came of age in 1337[66] Margaret continued to hold Bucknell in dower until her death in 1354.[67] Her son Richard had meanwhile become burdened with heavy debts largely because of the expenses he had incurred in the king's service in France; he sold most of his property,[68] and in 1354, shortly after Margaret's death, he surrendered Bucknell and other manors to Edward III and received them back for his life at an annual rent of £10.[69] In 1366 the king granted the reversion of Bucknell after Richard's death to his squire John Beverley and his wife Amice and in 1373 granted them free warren at Bucknell.[70] Richard had complicated matters by granting parts of the manor to tenants for life, but it was eventually arranged to the king's satisfaction that the parts should be reunited and that John and Amice should receive the whole manor.[71] John presumably obtained possession on Richard's death in 1375, and in 1378 he obtained a quitclaim of the Cranford family's right to £2 a year rent for lands in Bucknell and Saxenton which had belonged to their fee.[72] Amice held jointly with John, and continued to hold the manor after his death in 1380.[73] She married as her

---

[45] *Ex. e Rot. Fin.* (Rec. Com.), i. 231; for the descent of Hook Norton see Margaret Dickins, *Hist. Hook Norton*, 6–20.

[46] *Complete Peerage* (orig. edn.), viii. 54–55.

[47] Ibid. x. 548–50; cf. *Rot. Hund.* (Rec. Com.), ii. 826; *Feud. Aids*, iv. 158, 181; *Cal. Inq. p.m.* xi, p. 354.

[48] *Complete Peerage*, x. 551; the Plescy-Lenveysy descent in Dickins, *Hook Norton*, 13–14, is inaccurate.

[49] *Cal. Close*, 1377–81, 299; *Cal. Pat.* 1436–41, 166; Dickins, *Hook Norton*, 15 sqq.; *Complete Peerage*, xii (1), 477 sqq.

[50] *V.C.H. Oxon.* i. 414.

[51] Cf. *V.C.H. Bucks.* iv. 240.

[52] Blo. *Buck.* 3; *Eynsham Cart.* i. 37; ii. 158.

[53] *V.C.H. Oxon.* i. 414; see above, p. 58; below, p. 348.

[54] *Godstow Reg.* i. 214; cf. *Oseney Cart.* i. 2. Robert was alive *c.* 1139.

[55] *Godstow Reg.* i. 215; *Thame Cart.* 2, 77; *Oseney Cart.* i. 2; iv. 18; v. 89; see above, p. 58.

[56] *Godstow Reg.* i. 216–17; *Oseney Cart.* i. 6; vi. 90. Ralph's relationship to the Gilbert Damory who held Woodperry in 1167 has not been determined: *Pipe R.* 1167 (P.R.S. xi), 14; cf. *V.C.H. Oxon.* v. 286.

[57] *Thame Cart.* 68; *Oseney Cart.* v. 63.

[58] *Oseney Cart.* iv. 463, v. 207, 213; *Thame Cart.* 6–7, 133; *V.C.H. Bucks.* iv. 240.

[59] *Pipe R.* 1207 (P.R.S. N.S. xxii), 42; *Pat. R.* 1216–25, 395, 567; ibid. 1225–32, 85, 280, 301, 367; *Cal. Pat.* 1232–47, 126, 141.

[60] *Oseney Cart.* ii. 559; *Bk. of Fees*, 824; cf. *Rot. Hund.* (Rec. Com.), ii. 45.

[61] *Oseney Cart.* vi. 35.

[62] *Complete Peerage*, iv. 46 and note c; *Rot. Hund.* (Rec. Com.), ii. 826; *Feud. Aids*, iv. 158.

[63] *Cal. Chart. R.* 1300–26, 194, 334.

[64] His imprisonment in 1322 was probably due to his brother Roger's opposition to the Despensers: *Complete Peerage*, iv. 46; for Roger Damory see above, p. 58.

[65] *Complete Peerage*, iv. 46–47; *Cal. Inq. p.m.* vii, p. 203.

[66] *Cal. Fine R.* 1327–37, 192; *Complete Peerage*, iv. 47.

[67] *Cal. Inq. p.m.* ix, p. 183; ibid. x, p. 145; Kennett, *Paroch. Antiq.* ii. 10; Blo. *Bic.* 158: ref. to Margaret as 'the lady of Bucknell' in 1346.

[68] *Complete Peerage*, iv. 47; Kennett, *Paroch. Antiq.* ii. 106.

[69] C.P. 25(1)/190/20/75, 76; cf. *V.C.H. Oxon.* v. 286.

[70] *Cal. Pat.* 1364–7, 225; *Cal. Chart. R.* 1341–1417, 228.

[71] *Cal. Pat.* 1370–4, 359.

[72] *Cal. Inq. p.m.* xiv, p. 115; *Cal. Close*, 1377–81, 121; see below, p. 75.

[73] C 136/12/10; *Cal. Close*, 1381–5, 19; A. H. Cooke, *Early Hist. of Mapledurham* (O.R.S. vii), 34.

second husband Sir Robert Bardolf of Mapledurham, another squire of Edward III and a friend
of John Beverley.[74] Sir Robert died in 1395, and
Amice in 1416, when her heirs were found to be her
grandchildren Robert Langford and Walter Dauntesy, the sons of Anne and Elizabeth, her daughters
by John Beverley.[75] Although Bucknell manor was
divided into two portions, both seem to have passed
almost immediately to Walter Dauntesy, who granted
them to Sir William Hankeford and a number of
other feoffees.[76] Sir William Hankeford died in 1423
and his share of both moieties of the manor passed
to his grandson Richard.[77] The other feoffees dropped
out of the picture, since it had been provided that the
whole manor should revert to Sir William's heirs.[78]
Richard Hankeford enfeoffed trustees who eventually
arranged the conveyance of the manor to John
Langston of Caversfield and his wife Elizabeth.[79]
Bucknell was to remain in the Langston family until
1558. John Langston died in 1435,[80] leaving a son
and heir John who later married Amice, daughter
of John Danvers, one of the trustees. John seems to
have come of age in 1449 when the manor was settled
on himself and his wife,[81] and he lived until 1506.[82]
His son and heir Richard, who succeeded at the age
of 40, died in 1526,[83] and Richard's son John died
in 1558 leaving Bucknell to his wife Jane for life;
after her death it was to pass to John's nephew and
heir Thomas Moyle.[84]

Although John Langston had left Bucknell manor
to Thomas Moyle, the latter's right was challenged
by the Denton family, who claimed that by another
will John had left Bucknell to Thomas Denton and
his heirs.[85] The will on which Moyle's opponents
principally relied was of doubtful validity and he
continued to hold the manor,[86] but he did not reside
and by 1574 had let the manor to Thomas Ashe.[87]
When Thomas Moyle died in 1594 his estates passed
to his grandson Thomas, son of Ralph Moyle of
Moleash (Kent).[88] Shortly before his death in 1622
Thomas the younger settled Bucknell as well as
Caversfield upon his second son Thomas,[89] and it
was he and not his elder brother John who received
the manor and sold it soon afterwards to Edward
Ewer.

By his marriage to Margaret, daughter of Francis
Poure of Bletchingdon, Edward became involved in
the suits concerning that manor and Oddington.[90]
When he died in 1638 he left his son Francis an
estate burdened with debts taken over from the
Moyles. Francis Ewer in spite of all manner of
attempts to pay off the debts got steadily into greater
difficulties. He leased Bucknell manor-house to

Capt. William Rawlinson; mortgaged both Bucknell
and Oddington to Samuel Trotman, his father's
'loving friend';[91] and in 1647 borrowed £1,550 from
John Penrice on the security of the manor. Francis
failed, however, to pay his debt to Samuel Trotman,
who took possession of Bucknell in 1652. There followed a series of lawsuits between Francis, Samuel
Trotman, John Penrice, and the heirs of William
Rawlinson, which lasted until 1675.[92] While the
course of these suits is difficult to follow it is clear
that they completed the utter ruin of the Ewer
family. There is a tradition that Francis's descendants were 'reduced to the situation of drovers or
cattle dealers', which may well have been true, for
when the antiquary Rawlinson visited Bucknell in
1718 he noticed that there was 'a son of Ewers now
kept by the parish of Stoke Lyne'.[93] Samuel Trotman
retained Bucknell and the heirs of John Penrice
finally abandoned their claims in 1687.[94] Samuel
Trotman may well have favoured the parliamentary
side in the Civil War, for his second wife was the
niece of Speaker Lenthall and one of his sons was
named after him.[95] The case for Francis Ewer having
done so is not strong. Blomfield wrote that he 'joined
the side of the opposition' and there is evidence that
he incurred the king's displeasure in 1639, but some
of the Ewers were recusants.[96] In 1685 Samuel was
succeeded by his third son Lenthall Trotman (d.
1710), whose son Samuel settled Bucknell on his
younger brother Thomas.[97] Samuel, who was M.P.
for Woodstock from 1724 to 1730, died in 1749.
Two years later, when Thomas died, Bucknell passed
to his son Samuel, who was Sheriff of Oxfordshire
in 1760, and who died in 1775.[98] His cousin and
successor Fiennes, son of Edward Trotman of
Shelswell and lord of Shelswell manor, did not
marry, and settled Bucknell on a nephew, Fiennes,
who succeeded him in 1782, and who died in 1823.
With the death of his son, a third Fiennes, in 1835
the male line of the Trotman family came to an end.[99]
Bucknell then passed to Hester Louisa, the second
daughter of the last lord, and her husband Lt.-Col.
F. D. Hibbert. Lt.-Colonel Hibbert died in 1897 and
his son and heir Robert Fiennes Hibbert sold Bucknell to Anthony Babington, whose widow was lady of
the manor in 1939.[1]

LESSER ESTATES. Besides Robert d'Oilly's lands
in Bucknell there were two smaller estates in the lost
hamlet of *SAXENTON* in 1086.[2] Odo, Bishop of
Bayeux, was lord of both of them, and his tenants
Adam and Alfred held 2 hides and 1½ hide respectively.[3] Nothing is known of the subsequent history

[74] Cooke, *Mapledurham*, 31, 34.
[75] Ibid. 32, 40; C 138/21; Mary Stapleton, *Three Oxon. Parishes* (O.H.S. xxiv), 22.
[76] C 139/12; C 140/557/94; C.P. 25(1)/291/63, 64.
[77] C 139/12; *Cal. Close*, 1422–9, 111.
[78] *Cal. Close*, 1422–9, 111–12.
[79] C 140/557/94.
[80] C 139/78.
[81] C 140/557/94; *Cal. Pat.* 1446–52, 214; Kennett, *Paroch. Antiq.* ii. 376.
[82] Blo. *Buck.* 14; *V.C.H. Bucks.* iv. 158.
[83] C 142/45/46.
[84] Ibid. 121/145; *V.C.H. Bucks.* iv. 159.
[85] C 142/122/12; C 3/130/6, 7.
[86] C.P. 40/1380, m. 939; Blo. *Buck.* 14.
[87] Blo. *Buck.* 15; Blo. *Cav.* 18; *Oxon. Visit.* 199; see below, p. 79.
[88] Dunkin, *Oxon.* i. 199; C 142/238/78.
[89] C.P. 25(2)/340/East. 20 Jas. I; C 142/419/35.

[90] C 5/408/117; cf. Dunkin, *Oxon.* i. 200; *Oxon. Visit.* 211; see above, p. 59; below, p. 278.
[91] Blo. *Buck.* 15–16, 19; *Glos. Visit. 1623* (Harl. Soc. xxi), 168; Fosbrooke, *Glos.* ii. 55–56.
[92] C 3/464/48; C 5/43/86; ibid. 408/117; C.P. 25(2)/473/ Hil. 3 Chas. I; Hist. MSS. Com. *7th Rep. App.* 118; ibid. *9th Rep. App. II*, 45, 60; Blo. *Buck.* 16–18.
[93] Dunkin, *Oxon.* i. 200; *Par. Coll.* i. 63.
[94] C.P. 25(2)/792/Mich. 3 Jas. II.
[95] Blo. *Buck.* 21.
[96] Ibid. 16; *Cal. S.P. Dom.* 1639, 121.
[97] Blo. *Buck.* 22–23; C.P. 25(2)/1049/Trin. 1 Geo. I.
[98] Blo. *Buck.* 23.
[99] Ibid. 24.
[1] Ibid.; Burke, *Land. Gent.* (1937); *Kelly's Dir. Oxon.* (1920, 1939).
[2] See above, p. 72.
[3] *V.C.H. Oxon.* i. 404 and n.

of these estates until the 13th century, when they reappear in the possession of the Boffin and De Ivaus families. The Boffins' Oxfordshire lands were not extensive and were assessed at only ¼ knight's fee in the 13th century.[4] William was probably succeeded after 1233[5] by Thomas Boffin, of whom William de Blakevill held ⅛ knight's fee in Saxenton in 1243.[6] In 1279 John of Saxenton held a hide in the hamlet 'of the fee of Boffin' and paid 12s. a year to the Prior of Chetwode (Bucks.).[7] By 1257 Thomas Boffin had endowed the priory, founded twelve years earlier,[8] with all his land in Nethercot, in Steeple Aston parish,[9] and it is likely that he gave the priory his Saxenton lands about the same time. Chetwode Priory was annexed to Notley Abbey (Bucks.) in 1460,[10] and the rent of 12s. a year, which the abbey held in Bucknell at the Dissolution,[11] must represent the former Boffin estate in Saxenton. Its subsequent history is unknown.

In the mid-13th century the second *SAXENTON* estate was held by Ralph de Ivaus, the lord of two fees in South Newington.[12] In 1259, however, Ralph granted his Saxenton estate to Nicholas de Cranford, on the condition that he and his wife Agnes should hold it of Nicholas, and that it should revert to Nicholas if they died without issue.[13] Ralph was still living in 1264,[14] but he had evidently died childless by 1279, when Roger Damory held the ⅛ knight's fee in Bucknell of Robert de Cranford, presumably Nicholas's heir, of the fee of 'Inwes', i.e. Ivwes or Ivaus.[15] Robert was said to hold of the Abbot of Abingdon, but in fact held of the De Ivaus family. Robert de Cranford had also succeeded to South Newington,[16] and the overlordship of the ½ fee of Ivaus in Saxenton followed the descent of that manor. In 1307 Richard, brother of Ralph de Ivaus, released his rights in Saxenton to Robert, son of Robert de Cranford.[17] The Damorys and their successor John Beverley (see above) continued to hold as tenants of the Cranfords, and the Ivaus land was virtually merged in Bucknell manor. In 1316, for instance, Richard Damory was said to hold Bucknell 'cum membro de Sexinton'.[18] The union was completed in 1378 when Richard de Cranford of South Newington quitclaimed to John Beverley the 40s. rent which was his inheritance in 'Bucknell or Saxinton'.[19]

ECONOMIC HISTORY. Domesday records two settlements in Bucknell: Bucknell itself and the smaller one of Saxenton. The main manor at Bucknell had probably suffered from the Conquest, for its value had declined from £10 to £7.[20] Although there was land for 10 ploughs, there were in fact only 7 ploughs, 2 of them in demesne with 3 serfs, while outside 6 villeins (*villani*) and 3 bordars shared

5 ploughs. In one of the two small estates at Saxenton there was land for 3 plough-teams, which were shared between 6 villeins. This estate's value had risen from 40s. to 60s. On the other estate, valued as formerly at 30s., there was said to be land for 1½ plough-team although in fact 3½ were in use: the lord had 1½, while his 3 villeins and 4 bordars had 2 ploughs.[21] Thus there was a recorded working population of 25.

The account in the Hundred Rolls of 1279 reveals a number of changes.[22] On the large Damory manor of Bucknell there were 4 cottars paying rents varying from 1s. 6d. to 3s., and 13 villeins holding a virgate each for which each paid a rent of 5s. They worked, were tallaged at the lord's will, and had to pay fines if their sons left the manor. At Saxenton there were 9 villein virgaters, once tenants of the De Ivaus fee, but now tenants of the Damorys.

The extensive demesne consisted of 8 virgates in Bucknell and 4 in Saxenton. The most significant change is the appearance of four freeholders: John of Saxenton with 4 virgates, who paid 12s. rent to Chetwode Priory (Bucks.) and did suit at the hundred court; another holding a ½ virgate; Walter the Smith, who held 1 virgate of the fee of Hardwick, and Thomas of the Church holding 2 virgates of Richard Damory.

The survey accounts for only about 40 virgates— say 1,000 field acres out of the 1,894 statute acres of the 19th-century parish. One explanation may be that as the Damorys lived at Bucknell and had free warren there much of the parish may have been uncultivated and preserved for hunting.[23]

Later evidence for the medieval history of Bucknell is scant. From a grant of land made in the 1370's it appears that the virgate was still the average holding.[24] Fourteenth-century tax lists also suggest that there had been little accumulation of property, 26 people being assessed in 1316 of whom only Richard Damory and his bailiff had goods worth more than 4s.[25] Saxenton never appears to have been taxed separately and the 92 adults in Bucknell listed for the poll tax of 1377 almost certainly include Saxenton.[26] The hamlet seems to have declined early. In 1379 its lands were described as in 'Bucknell or Saxenton'[27] and except for a mid-15th-century reference to a house in Saxenton, there is no later record of the place.[28]

The fact that all the land in the parish except the glebe and Notley Abbey's holding belonged to the manor assisted early inclosure. The movement may have been well under way by the late 16th century, when there was said to be 220 acres of meadow and 700 of pasture,[29] and certainly by the mid 17th century, when there was a 'great inclosed ground' of about 300 acres called Bicester Ground.[30] By the

⁴ *Pipe R.* 1202 (P.R.S. N.S. xv), 209; ibid. 1203 (N.S. xvi), 191; *Red Bk. Exch.* (Rolls Ser.), 176; *Pipe R.* 1230 (P.R.S. N.S. iv), 256.
⁵ *Oseney Cart.* iv. 174.
⁶ *Bk. of Fees*, 825.
⁷ *Rot. Hund.* (Rec. Com.), ii. 826.
⁸ *V.C.H. Bucks.* i. 380.
⁹ *Cal. Pat.* 1247–58, 575; cf. *Oseney Cart.* iv. 189.
¹⁰ *V.C.H. Bucks.* i. 381; Dugd. *Mon.* vi (1), 498.
¹¹ *Valor Eccl.* (Rec. Com.), iv. 232.
¹² *Bk. of Fees*, 834, 835.
¹³ *Fines Oxon.* 177.
¹⁴ *Close R.* 1261–4, 380.
¹⁵ *Rot. Hund.* (Rec. Com.), ii. 826.
¹⁶ Ibid. 848.

¹⁷ Bodl. MS. ch. Oxon. 408.
¹⁸ *Feud. Aids*, iv. 169.
¹⁹ *Cal. Close*, 1377–81, 121.
²⁰ *V.C.H. Oxon.* i. 414.
²¹ Ibid. 404.
²² *Rot. Hund.* (Rec. Com.), ii. 826.
²³ *Cal. Chart. R.* 1300–26, 194, 334.
²⁴ *Cal. Pat.* 1370–4, 359–60.
²⁵ E 179/161/8. The hamlet does not appear on any 14th-cent. tax list: see below, p. 358.
²⁶ E179/161/39.
²⁷ For its site, see above, p. 72.
²⁸ Kennett. *Paroch. Antiq.* ii. 375.
²⁹ Dunkin, *Oxon.* i. 198.
³⁰ C 3/464/48.

time of the parliamentary inclosure in 1780, slightly more than half the parish was already inclosed.[31] By the award the rector received 336 acres of the 870 acres of land involved, and the rest went to the Trotmans. The arable strips, so far as is known, still lay in the three fields recorded in 1700—North, West, and South Fields.[32]

The general effect of inclosure in the neighbourhood was to increase the amount of arable and to treble at least the rent of land.[33] At Bucknell the wheat-growing land increased by 40 acres in the first 30 years after inclosure,[34] and the pattern of landholding was altered. A few comparatively large farms were created and so continued throughout the 19th century.[35] In 1888, when the manor lands were sold, besides the glebe or Rectory farm there were four farms of over 200 acres: Home farm, Lower farm, Manor farm, and Bucknell Lodge farm.[36] At this date the parish was still a 'closed' one, all the land belonging to the manor except for the glebe.[37] Another consequence of inclosure was the building of outlying farm-houses: Davis's map of 1797 shows only Bucknell Lodge, but in the 19th century there were four more.[38]

In the early 20th century, through the initiative of William Barrett (d. 1943) of Lower farm, self-binding machines were sent to the Bucknell district from the United States by an American, Walter Woods. Demonstrations were given in Bucknell, particularly on Bucknell Lodge farm, with the result that the parish took the lead in the introduction of the machine. In the 1950's Bucknell's nine farms were in the hands of owner-occupiers, of whom four farmed between 225 and 300 acres each. Mixed farming was the rule. Wheat, barley, and oats were the main crops grown; the cultivation of sugar-beet was discontinued after the Second World War. There were several pedigree stocks of pigs (Large White and others), Guernsey cows, and Hampshire sheep.[39]

Post-Reformation figures suggest that Bucknell had a relatively poor population: for the subsidy of 1524, for example, only twelve people were assessed, one of the lowest numbers in the hundred;[40] in the late 17th century there is mention of day-labourers[41] and the hearth-tax returns of the 1660's, with a relatively small number of hearths listed, indicate an absence of prosperity.[42] By 1801 the population had risen to 218 and continued to rise steadily to 343 in 1851. Thereafter a decline set in. It was noted in the 1890's that on account of the agricultural depression many were leaving the village.[43] During the 20th

century numbers have risen from 205 in 1901 to 259 in 1951.[44]

Until recent years the villagers have nearly all been occupied in agriculture. A miller presumably existed in the late 13th century, when a mill was recorded, but there is no later reference to either.[45] In the mid-19th century there were a butcher, baker, carpenter, and blacksmith, and a large establishment of nineteen servants at the manor-house.[46] Every cottager, however, was also a gardener. A 19th-century account of the village states that each of the 46 cottages had its garden, that most farms allowed their labourers potato ground, and that the rector let off part of the glebe as allotments.[47]

CHURCH. The earliest evidence yet found for the existence of a church at Bucknell dates from 1074, when a grant of the tithes was made (see below). From the first recorded presentation to the rectory in 1243–4[48] the advowson descended with the manor until 1348, when Sir Richard Damory, no doubt because of his financial difficulties, sold it to the rector William Peek (probably acting as agent for Oseney Abbey) for £66 6s. 8d.[49] In 1350 Peek conveyed it to Oseney, who immediately attempted but failed to exchange the advowson and that of Swerford for Mixbury advowson.[50] A similar attempt was made in 1396 to exchange Bucknell and Cornwell advowsons for that of Mixbury, which was said to be much more convenient to them, being near their manor Fulwell.[51]

Oseney held the advowson until its dissolution in 1539; it at least twice sold the right of presentation and once was guilty of simony.[52] In 1547 the advowson was granted to Thomas, Lord Seymour;[53] in 1551 to Walter Mildmay, a prominent civil servant,[54] but by 1552 it was in the hands of a Richard Weston.[55] In 1574 Jeremiah Weston of Essex sold it to Mrs. Alice Ball of Lichfield, who gave it in 1578 to her son Robert, a Fellow of New College. He gave it to his college in 1611, on condition that it always presented a scholar of the college, and preferably one of his own relatives.[56] New College is still patron.

In the Middle Ages the rectory was of medium value. In 1254 it was worth £6 13s. 4d.[57] and in 1291 £10, plus the pension of 10s. to Oseney (see below).[58] In 1535 it was valued at £13 16s. net.[59] Around 1600 it was said to be worth £60,[60] and in the early 18th-century £120.[61] By the mid-19th century its value had risen to £350.[62]

In addition to the tithes, there was glebe consist-

---

[31] O.R.O. Incl. award. There is no map. The act, 19 Geo. III, c. 59 (priv. act), was initiated by Fiennes Trotman: copy in Bodl. L. Eng. C 13 c I (1779, i. 17).

[32] Oxon. Archd. Pp. Oxon. b 40, f. 79: rectory terrier.

[33] Young, *Oxon. Agric.* 91.

[34] Ibid. 89.

[35] O.R.O. Land tax assess.; H.O. 107/1729.

[36] Bodl. G.A. Oxon. b 85a (24): *Sale Cat.* 1888. Part of Hawkwell farm was in the parish, but the house and much of its land lay in Caversfield.

[37] E. Miller, 'Confessions of a Village Tyrant', *19th Century*, 1893, 955–66.

[38] Davis, *Oxon. Map*; Bodl. G.A. Oxon. b 85a (24).

[39] Local inf.

[40] E 179/161/176.

[41] Blo. *Buck.* 57.

[42] *Hearth Tax Oxon.* 201; cf. above, p. 71.

[43] *19th Century*, 1893, 955–66.

[44] *Census*, 1901, 1951.

[45] *Rot. Hund.* (Rec. Com.) ii. 826.

[46] H.O. 107/1729; Gardner, *Dir. Oxon.*

[47] *19th Century*, 1893, 955–66.

[48] *Rot. Grosse.* 483. For references to medieval presentations see MS. Top. Oxon. d 460.

[49] *Oseney Cart.* vi. 34–35; *Cal. Pat.* 1348–50, 290.

[50] *Cal. Pat.* 1348–50, 573; ibid. 1350–4, 227.

[51] Ibid. 1396–9, 19; *Cal. Papal L.* iv. 376; see below, p. 253.

[52] Linc. Reg. xxiii, Smith, f. 271b; xxvii, Longland, ff. 178–178b, 185b.

[53] *Cal. Pat.* 1547–8, 29. For Seymour see *Complete Peerage*, xi. 637–9.

[54] *Cal. Pat.* 1550–3, 102. For Mildmay see *D.N.B.*

[55] *O.A.S. Rep.* 1914, 204.

[56] Blo. *Buck.* 54–55.

[57] Lunt, *Val. Norw.* 312.

[58] *Tax. Eccl.* (Rec. Com.), 31.

[59] *Valor Eccl.* (Rec. Com.), ii. 160.

[60] Blo. *Buck.* 63.

[61] *Par. Coll.* i. 63.

[62] *Kelly's Dir. Oxon.* (1864). By 1894 the rectory was worth less than half this: Blo. *Buck.* 64.

ing of 4 yardlands with common for three.[63] At the inclosure in 1780 the glebe was exchanged for 82 acres and the tithes were commuted for 254 acres, about a seventh of the land in the parish.[64] In 1956 only 5 acres of glebe remained.[65] Tithe was paid on 6 acres near the Middleton Stoney border until 1850, when it was commuted for £1 16s.[66]

In 1074 Robert d'Oilly granted two-thirds of the demesne tithes of Bucknell, along with those of some 70 other manors, to the church of St. George in Oxford castle.[67] In 1149 the church and all its possessions were given to Oseney Abbey.[68] In the 13th century Oseney was receiving 10s. a year for these tithes[69] and in the 15th century it used to lease them to the rector for 13s. 4d. In 1502 the abbot successfully sued the rector Edmund Croston for eight years' arrears of this sum.[70] The sum continued to be paid until Oseney's dissolution.[71]

A tithe case of 1615 shows that it had been customary for 50 years past for every landowner to pay each year a bushel of malt, or its equivalent in money, on every yardland to repair the church or supply necessaries for it. Sometimes the malt was used for the Whitsun Ales, from which £4 or £3 10s. were afterwards received for the church.

Some of the medieval rectors were distinguished men. Such a one was Master John de Cheam (rector 1243–64), who was also papal chaplain and Archdeacon of Bath. In 1259 he became Bishop of Glasgow, but continued to hold Bucknell, perhaps because he was unable to get recognition in his Scottish diocese.[72] According to the Lanercost chronicler, he always preached piety but never practised it.[73] Another rector, Roger (1264–92), was a member of the local Damory family and may have been responsible for the beautiful 13th-century chancel. A later one, Ichel de Kerwent (1291–1335), perhaps a Welshman, Ithel from Caerwent, for several years disrupted the church life of the parish. In his first year there, the tax assessment on his church was raised from £6 13s. 1d. to £10, and he refused to pay the clerical subsidy. The church was accordingly put under an interdict; he was summoned before the Exchequer, and his living put into the hands of trustees.[74] When in 1298 he finally made submission and the interdict was revoked, the trustees refused to give the church back. The rector appealed to the bishop, who excommunicated the intruders and forbade the ministers of surrounding churches to admit them to their services. The rector was reinstated[75] and remained in office until his death in 1335.[76]

The frequent exchanges at the end of the 14th and in the 15th century show that by this time the church was regarded by its rectors principally as a source of additional income. Several are known to have had

other occupations: Master Alexander Sparwe alias Herbard (1415–19), an illegitimate son, was Archdeacon of Salisbury;[77] Master William Symonds (?–1431) was Official of the Archdeacon of Oxford;[78] Thomas Darcy (c. 1437–69), who had papal dispensation to hold another church, was allowed to rent his benefices for seven years, even to laymen, while studying at a university.[79]

Two early-16th-century rectors were outstanding men: Edmund Croston (1498–1503),[80] later Principal of Brasenose Hall in Oxford, and Bryan Higden (1505–24), Principal of Broadgates Hall, who in 1516 became Dean of York.[81] At the visitation of about 1520 it was noted that he was non-resident and that the chancel windows were broken.[82]

Throughout the second half of the 16th century (1552–92) the living was held by Richard Bennett, a graduate of Christ Church; he survived all the religious changes of this period, and the inscription on his brass, once in the church, said that he had lived in the parish for 40 years.[83]

After New College got the advowson, the living was held until the 19th century by successive fellows. They lived in comfort: their house, called a manor-house, was the second largest in the parish in the 17th century, and had a dovecote, pigsties, stables, and other outhouses attached to it.[84]

The religious life of the parish was disrupted by the Civil War. John Gardner, rector from 1643, was ejected in 1654; replaced by Giles Woolley, the brother of a prominent Worcestershire nonconformist, and restored in broken health in 1660.[85] His successor, William Morehead,[86] a nephew of General Monck, caused great dissatisfaction in 1678 by living at his other cure at Whitfield (Northants), and leaving Bucknell in the charge of young non-resident curates. The parishioners, headed by the churchwardens, protested to the bishop that their rich and ancient parish, worth £100 a year, had always supported a resident minister, 'who hath not only performed the duty of his ministry, but also afforded great relief to the poor, by good hospitality and by setting them on work'. The deficiencies of the young curates from Oxford, who neither did these things, nor visited the sick, nor punished vagrants nor sent them out of the parish, were listed; they only rode over on Sundays, neglected to catechize and to read prayers on holidays, and held services at dinner-time. The parishioners' plea for a resident minister of at least 24 years old was evidently not granted, for Morehead seems to have continued to live mostly at Whitfield.[87] In 1687 he was the only Oxfordshire minister who subscribed to the address thanking James II for his declaration about liberty of conscience;[88] and in 1688, when he read the king's

[63] Terriers of 1614, 1634, and 1700 in Oxf. Archd. Oxon. b 40, ff. 78–79a.
[64] O.R.O. Incl. award.
[65] Inf. the Revd. W. H. Trebble.
[66] Bodl. Tithe award.
[67] Oseney Cart. iv. 26; Oxon. Chart. no. 58.
[68] V.C.H. Oxon. ii. 90.
[69] Tax. Eccl. (Rec. Com.), 31b.
[70] Oseney Cart. vi. 34–35.
[71] Valor Eccl. (Rec. Com.), ii. 160.
[72] Rot. Graves, pp. xxiv, 218. The earliest recorded priest is Hugh, chpl. before 1196: Oseney Cart. vi. 90. For a list of medieval presentations see MS. Top. Oxon. d 460.
[73] For him see J. Dowden, Bishops of Scotland, ed. J. M. Thomson, 304–5.
[74] Kennett, Paroch. Antiq. i. 467–8, 471.

[75] Ibid. 476–8; Linc. Reg. i, Sutton, f. 277b.
[76] Blo. Buck. 48.
[77] Cal. Papal L. viii. 139.
[78] Reg. Chich. i. 336.
[79] Cal. Papal L. ix. 280, 185; Emden, Biog. Dict.
[80] For him see Brasenose Coll. Monographs (O.H.S. lii), i. 15; ix (ibid. liii), 46.
[81] For him see D.N.B.
[82] Visit. Dioc. Linc. 1517–31, i. 124.
[83] O.A.S. Rep. 1914, 204–5.
[84] See above, p. 72.
[85] Walker Rev. 26, 297; Calamy Rev. 546; Blo. Buck. 56.
[86] See D.N.B. and Wood, Athenae, iv. 353.
[87] Blo. Buck. 57–58.
[88] Wood, Life, iii. 220.

declaration on this question in Bucknell church, was one of the few ministers in the county to do so.[89] He died at Bucknell in 1692.[90]

Morehead's successor, John Coxed (1692–1709), was resident with his family and was clearly a conscientious pastor. He improved the parsonage; gave communion on four instead of the more customary two great festivals; kept lists of his communicants,[91] of whom there were usually between 20 and 30, and a record of the alms given.[92] Rectors resided throughout the 18th century, but after the inclosure award, when the new Rectory estate with the Rectory house, by now described as 'very indifferent',[93] was granted to a farmer, non-residence became customary.[94] James Yelden (1801–22), for example, whose brother-in-law bequeathed the Gauntlett charity,[95] was Vicar of Weston-on-the-Green, where he lived. He gave the absence of a house and his gout as reasons for not residing at or serving Bucknell, which was once again left to a curate.[96] With William Master (1833–78), a supporter of the Oxford Movement, there was a change for the better. He built the present Rectory on a new site,[97] he restored the church building and had a school built. He had been Dean of Civil Law in the University and his interest in education led him in 1840 to start with others a middle-class school in Bicester, where he occasionally taught.[98] This and his refusal to follow Bishop Wilberforce's suggestion that he should preach twice on Sundays account for the bishop's comment: 'Master no preacher but shines in school-room.'[99]

Edward Miller, his successor, was another outstanding parish priest. Although a distinguished Biblical scholar, his 'heart had always been in parish work'. He came to Bucknell from Butler's Marston (Warws.), and found his new parish comparatively backward in education and church matters, but not in general civilization.[1] With some difficulty, he started a village library and reading-room; he catechized the children in church on one day a week, and visited the school every other morning. He alleviated poverty by letting out the glebe in $\frac{1}{4}$-acre allotments.

The church dedicated to *ST. PETER* is a stone building comprising a chancel, clerestoried nave, south porch, and central tower. The church is a fine example of 13th-century architecture, but the massive tower, placed between chancel and nave, is 12th-century and belongs to an earlier church; another story with windows and battlements was added in the 15th century. The tower stands on plain Romanesque arches; the north and south ones have filled-in arches with small 12th-century windows under them, but the eastern arch was rebuilt in the 14th century. On the north side of the tower there is a 12th-century stair turret, and on the south side a door leading into the Victorian vestry.

The chancel, which is exceptionally long (35 ft. by 19 ft.), is a fine specimen of early-13th-century work.[2] At the east end there are three lancet windows with elegant shafts and deeply cut arch mouldings. On the north and south sides are lancet windows and two low windows, lancet outside and square-headed inside. In the north wall of the chancel is a blocked doorway and (externally) the piscina of a vanished vestry; the barrel roof of wood was formerly (1846) concealed by plaster.

The 13th-century nave has a lancet window at the west end, with shafts and moulded rear-arch. The striking south door is carved with unusual mouldings, and supported by clustered shafts; the northern door is also of early-13th-century workmanship. On the south side of the nave there is a 13th-century holy-water stoup, and there are the remains of a piscina and altar at the north-east corner of the nave. The absence of aisles is singular, and it is possible that the blocked arches on the north and south sides of the nave were intended to open into the transepts. The nave roof and a clerestory with square-headed two-light windows were added in the 15th century. The flat plastered ceiling which concealed the roof in the 19th century has been removed.

The church, described by Rawlinson in 1718 as beautiful and in good repair, has preserved its distinctive medieval character, in spite of later alterations.[3] It was ordered to be painted in 1633; was beautified in 1706; was again ordered to be repaired in 1757; and in 1829 the old seats were replaced by high deal pews and a western gallery was built, both of which have since been removed.[4] In 1855 the parish spent £50 on repairing the inside of the church,[5] and in the following year the rector spent £220 on repairing and partially rebuilding the chancel walls. More thorough restoration was undertaken in 1893 (architect A. Mardon Mowbray). The nave was refloored and a new oak roof was inserted; the top story of the tower was rebuilt; a new arch put in the south porch; new choir seats were installed in the chancel and a vestry and a heating system were added, at a total cost of £740.[6] In 1955 the church retained its 19th-century oil lamps.

There is a plain octagonal font on an octagonal base of two tiers,[7] and a fine pulpit of carved oak, probably of Jacobean date. The organ is early 19th-century. An oak altar table was given in 1872.[8]

In the chancel there is a brass tablet to Edward Ewer (d. 1638) and Margaret Poure his wife, daughter of Francis Poure of Bletchingdon, and another to their eldest son Francis Ewer. There are also a number of memorial slabs on the chancel floor, now mostly indecipherable or partially concealed under pews. Rawlinson mentions memorials to William Rawlinson (d. 1643); Richard Bennett, rector (d.

---

[89] Wood, *Life*, iii. 267.
[90] Ibid. 381. Blomfield says he died at Whitfield.
[91] It is MS. Top. Oxon. e 11.
[92] Blo. *Buck.* 27–30, 59.
[93] Oxf. Archd. Oxon. c 57, ff. 87–88, 109.
[94] Oxf. Dioc. c 659, ff. 150–1.
[95] See below, p. 80.
[96] Oxf. Dioc. c 659, ff. 150–1.
[97] Blo. *Buck.* 37; Oxf. Dioc. b 39.
[98] Blo. *Buck.* 61.　　　　[99] Oxf. Dioc. d 178.
[1] 'Confessions of a Village Tyrant', *19th Century*, 1893, 955–66; Blo. *Buck.* 62.

[2] Parker, *Guide*, 34–35.
[3] *Par. Coll.* i. 63.
[4] MS. Top. Oxon. c 55, f. 276; *Par. Coll.* i. 63; Oxf. Archd. Oxon. d 13, f. 35; ibid. c 57, f. 115; Blo. *Buck.* 44.
[5] Blo *Buck.* 44; see Oxf. Dioc. d 179. For pre-restoration drawings by J. Buckler see MS. Top. Oxon. a 65, f. 131 and reproduction opposite.
[6] Blo. *Buck.* 44; Faculty (Bodl. Buck. Par. Box).
[7] See Buckler drawing in MS. Top. Oxon. a 65 f. 129.
[8] Blo. *Buck.* 44.

South-east view of the church in 1824

BUCKNELL

Interior of the church from the west in 1823

CHARLTON-ON-OTMOOR

1591/2); John Gardner, rector (d. 1670); John Coxed, rector (d. 1709) and others to his family.[9] In the nave there are a number of well-carved marble monuments to the Trotman family;[10] to Samuel Trotman (d. 1684/5) and Mary his wife (d. 1667); to Lenthall Trotman (d. 1709/10); to Samuel Trotman (d. 1719/20); to another Samuel Trotman (d. 1748/9); to Thomas Trotman (d. 1751) and his son Samuel (d. 1775);[11] and a modern brass to Lt.-Col. Frederick Drummond Hibbert (d. 1897) and his wife (née Trotman).

The armorial glass in the chancel mentioned by Wood has disappeared, as have also the windows

Ewer, the daughter of Francis Poure and wife of Edward Ewer, two more Ewers, and two other persons were fined.[18] By 1643 there seems to have been only one Roman Catholic,[19] and in 1706 there was still only one, a shepherd.[20]

There was apparently no Protestant dissent in the parish except for an early-19th-century Quaker schoolmistress.[21]

SCHOOLS. 'Goody Poel the school dame' is mentioned in 1708,[22] and by 1738 most of the village children were being taught reading, writing, and the

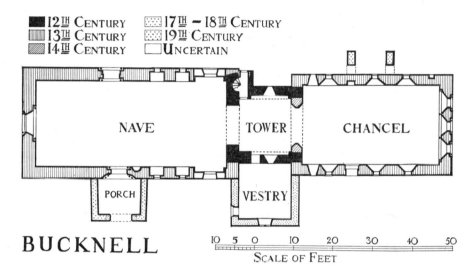

■ 12TH CENTURY   ▦ 17TH – 18TH CENTURY
▥ 13TH CENTURY   ▦ 19TH CENTURY
▨ 14TH CENTURY   ☐ UNCERTAIN

NAVE   TOWER   CHANCEL

PORCH   VESTRY

BUCKNELL

10 5 0   10   20   30   40   50
SCALE OF FEET

containing figures and inscriptions to the Larwoldes, the Freemans, and to Robert and Thomas Clement and their wives.[12]

In 1552 it was recorded that the church was furnished with one silver chalice, four pairs of vestments, a pall of blue damask and four copes. It had three great bells and a sanctus bell.[13] The church's post-Reformation plate was acquired in the 18th century during the incumbency of John Woodford (1710–45) and includes a silver chalice and flagon (1723) and a paten, all inscribed 'Bucknell'.[14] In 1955 the earliest of the three bells dated from 1597, but the bell frame was medieval.[15]

The registers date from 1653.

The ancient base of a cross, restored in the 19th century, is in the churchyard.

NONCONFORMITY. A few Roman Catholics are recorded in the late 16th and early 17th centuries.[16] Among the gentry, Thomas Ashe, the lessee of the manor, was noted in 1592.[17] In the 1620's Margaret

catechism by a 'poor woman' paid by the lord of the manor.[23] The latter's successors continued to support a dame school. In 1808 the dame was a Quaker, and the children were taught reading and knitting. There were then 12 pupils, 20 in 1854, and 12 in 1869—the last record of this school.[24]

A Sunday school, opened in 1802, was supported by the parishioners and was conducted partly on National Society lines. In 1808, 35 children were learning to read and write,[25] and 46 in 1833.

By 1833 there was also a day school attended by 30 children of whom 20 were paid for by Mrs. T. Tyrwhitt-Drake, wife of the tenant of the manorhouse, and 10 by their parents.[26] There were 40 pupils in 1854.[27]

Bucknell Church of England school, which replaced Mrs. Tyrwhitt-Drake's school, was built in 1861 on land given by Lt.-Col. F. D. Hibbert, at a cost of £450 paid by the Revd. William Master, whose nephew Master White designed the plans.[28] The school first received a National Society grant in 1865, and about 1867 evening classes in the winter

[9] Par. Coll. i. 63–65.
[10] See above, p. 74. For blazons of arms in church see Bod. G.A. Oxon. 4° 685, pp. 63–65; ibid. 688, pp. 63–64; ibid. 16° 217, pp. 80, 80b.
[11] James Lovell fecit 1777.
[12] B.M. Harl. MS. 4170, p. 29, cited in Dunkin, Oxon. i. 183. Wood read 'Thremon' for 'Ffreeman' (Par. Coll. i. 64).   [13] Chant. Cert. 88.
[14] Evans, Ch. Plate.
[15] Ch. Bells, Oxon. i. 64.
[16] C.R.S. xviii, 258; Salter, Oxon. Recusants, passim.
[17] Hist. MSS. Com. Salisbury MSS. IV, 270.

[18] Salter, Oxon. Recusants, 32, 34, 56. The Ewers had come from Cottisford.
[19] E 179/164/496A.
[20] Oxoniensia, xiii. 78.
[21] Oxf. Dioc. d 570; see below.
[22] MS. Top. Oxon. e 11.
[23] Oxf. Dioc. d 552.
[24] Ibid. d 707; Wilb. Visit.; Oxf. Dioc. c 335.
[25] Oxf. Dioc. c 327, p. 293; ibid. d 707.
[26] Educ. Enq. Abstract, 743.
[27] Wilb. Visit.
[28] Blo. Buck. 38.

were started for adults and the older boys.[29] There were 41 pupils in 1871 and 26 in 1906,[30] and the school never had more than one teacher. It was re-organized as a junior school in 1926, when senior pupils were sent to Bicester. In 1937 there were 14 children on the books, and in 1948 the school was closed, the pupils being transferred to Bicester Church of England primary school.[31]

CHARITIES. Samuel Trotman by will dated 1684 left £20, Lenthall Trotman by will dated 1691 left £10, and Mary Trotman by will dated 1710 left £10, forming a poor's stock of £40 which in the 18th and early 19th centuries was held by the lord of the manor, who paid £2 10s. a year interest. In 1824 this income was used in buying meat distributed to the poor at Christmas.[32] Later in the century the £2 10s. appears as a rent-charge on the manorial estate.[33]

This income, which remains unchanged, was expended in coal and clothing in 1887, in meat and clothing in 1939,[34] and in money distributed to eight poor people in 1954.[35]

By his will dated 1820, with a codicil dated 1822, the Revd. Samuel Gauntlett, Warden of New College, left £300 in stock, the income from which was to be applied to the purchase in December of eight woollen cloaks or gowns for wives of labourers with one or more legitimate children, or of eight pairs of stout shoes for the men, in alternate years. The cloaks and shoes were to be marked with the initials 'D. G.' in honour of Dr. Gauntlett's late wife, Deborah. The charity was first distributed at Christmas, 1823.[36] The annual income of £7 10s. was distributed in money to eight poor people not receiving the Trotman Charity in 1954.[37]

CHARLTON-ON-OTMOOR

THE ancient parish consisted of 1,961 acres and was roughly two miles wide and one mile long. In the 19th century Charlton civil parish had an area of 822 acres and the hamlets of Fencott and Murcott formed a separate civil parish of 1,139 acres.[1] In 1932 Fencott and Murcott parish was enlarged to 3,333 acres, when 2,194 acres of Otmoor were transferred from Beckley. Thus the ecclesiastical parish of Charlton (which still included Fencott and Murcott) was increased to 4,155 acres.[2] Most of the northern boundary of the ancient parish followed the River Ray and one of its feeders; the southern boundary skirted the northern edge of Otmoor.[3] The southern part of the eastern boundary, along Boarstall Lane, was also the county boundary between Oxfordshire and Buckinghamshire. In the 18th century the parish's circumference was said to be six miles.[4]

The major part of the ancient parish lies on the Oxford Clay, though Charlton village, like the near-by Ambrosden and Merton, lies on a domed 'island' of Cornbrash with the Forest Marble outcropping in the centre.[5] The whole parish is low-lying, only rising much above 200 feet above sea-level at Charlton village. The main arm of the River Ray runs through the centre of the parish, between Charlton and Fencott villages; part of the New River Ray, dug in 1815 to drain Otmoor, runs parallel with the parish's southern boundary. The Islip–Merton road crosses the western part of the parish and has a branch to Charlton village. A road skirting the edge of Otmoor connects Oddington, Charlton, Fencott, and Murcott. Between Charlton and Fencott this road follows the line of the Church Way mentioned

in 1469,[6] and crosses the Ray by a three-arched bridge built about 1820.[7] There was a bridge here in 1483.[8] Between Fencott and Murcott the present line of the road was defined by the Otmoor inclosure award in 1815; a causeway connecting Fencott and Murcott existed in the 15th century.[9] The Roman road which crosses Otmoor passes to the west of Fencott village and farther north gives its name to Street Hill. Roman remains have been found just south of Fencott.[10]

A branch of the former L.M.S. railway touches the western end of the parish, but the nearest station is at Islip three miles away.[11]

Charlton and its hamlets of Fencott and Murcott lie in the south of the parish, along the northern edge of Otmoor. Charlton stands on a slight rocky eminence (223 ft.); its church at the western end is a landmark for the surrounding countryside, and a local poem records how the tolling of the curfew, a custom which is still kept up, saved a traveller lost on Otmoor.[12]

The village, though never a very prosperous one, was once more populated than it is now.[13] In the 17th century besides the Rectory there were 24 houses listed for the hearth tax of 1662 and in 1665 there were 16, of which 4 were substantial farm-houses for which 4 or 3 hearths were returned.[14] Today (1956) Charlton consists of one long street with a loop on the north-west. Apart from the Rectory, the village[15] never seems to have had any house of note and there is no record of the existence of a manor-house.[16] It is distinguished by its numerous small farm-houses—ten in number. A large number of old

[29] *Vol. Sch. Ret.*; Oxf. Dioc. c 335.
[30] *Elem. Educ. Ret.*; *Vol. Sch. Ret.*
[31] Inf. Oxon. Educ. Cttee.
[32] *Char. Don.* ii. 989; *12th Rep. Com. Char.* 297.
[33] Wing, *Annals*, 49.
[34] *Kelly's Dir. Oxon.* (1887, 1939).
[35] Local inf.
[36] *12th Rep. Com. Char.* 298.
[37] Local inf.
[1] *Census*, 1881; O.S. Map 6", xxvii (1884); 2½", 42/51, 61 (1951).
[2] *Kelly's Dir. Oxon.* (1939); *Oxon. Review Order* (1932): copy in O.R.O.
[3] O.S. Map 6", xxvii, xxviii (1884).

[4] Oxf. Dioc. d 558.
[5] G.S. Map 1" xlv SE.
[6] S.C. 2/197/48.
[7] Dunkin, *Oxon.* i. 236.
[8] S.C. 2/197/48.
[9] Ibid.
[10] *V.C.H. Oxon.* i. 337.
[11] Completed 1851: W. L. Steel, *Hist. L.N.W.R.* 185.
[12] Par. Rec. 'An Oxfordshire Legend', by Thomas Tryte.
[13] See below, p. 83.
[14] *Hearth Tax Oxon.* 194, 235.
[15] O.S. Map 25", xxviii, 5, 9 (1876).
[16] See e.g. Oxf. Dioc. d 552, d 555, d 558.

farm-houses and cottages, built of the local stone, have survived: most of the houses are roofed with tiles or Welsh slate, but owing to the skill of local thatchers, thatch still predominates among the cottages.[17]

Among the 17th-century houses is Yew Tree Farm, a two-storied rectangular house, with two-light casement windows with wooden lintels and frames. There is a staircase projection at the back, and a few old ceiling beams with fleur-de-lis stop chamfers remain inside. The 'George and Dragon' at the eastern end of the village is a two-storied house with a stone dated 1691 on the north-east gable. It originally consisted of one room up and one down, but two more rooms have been added at the back. It was here that the moor-men resolved to form an Otmoor Association in 1830.[18] There seems to have been much rebuilding in the 18th century: Cumberland House has a stone inscribed with the date 1708 and the initials S.C.E., and a two-storied cottage is dated 1751. Indeed most of the surviving ancient cottages probably date from that century or the first quarter of the 19th century. The local anti-quary Dunkin described the village dwellings in the 1820's as 'neat and commodious' and published a contemporary drawing of the village street showing the stocks near the church and the Crown Inn standing opposite.[19] Both the 'Crown' and the 'George and Dragon' were known by those names in 1785, but they were probably inns very much earlier.[20] An innkeeper of Charlton is mentioned in 1618.[21]

The most imposing house in the village is the Rectory, enlarged by the rector John Knipe in about 1805:[22] it is an L-shaped house of three stories. The old Rectory, part of which still survives, was also in its day a substantial 'gentleman's residence'. In 1634 it was described as 'the manor house of the rectory'.[23] It then seems to have been a long build-ing of two stories with a cock-loft over two of the rooms. There were at least thirteen rooms, five of which are said to have had chimneys. Several rooms had boarded floors, wainscoted walls and plastered ceilings. It was separated from the 'comon street' by a walled garden and had another garden and orchard to the south-east. The rector returned six hearths for this house for the hearth tax of 1665.[24]

Knipe's new house is built of coursed rubble. It has a pedimented porch on the north front; a high wall separates it from the street. Dunkin thought it a pleasant residence 'calculated to convey to posterity the rector's superior taste and public spirit'.[25] After the Second World War it was divided into two: the older half serves as a Rectory and the newer half as a private residence.[26]

Later 19th-century additions to the village were the Baptist chapel, built in 1835; the school with a schoolmistress's house, built in 1866; and the parish room.[27] The last was a building adjoining the Rectory, which was converted with the aid of a dona-tion from the Revd. George Hayton, rector 1884–95. Among the 20th-century additions are eighteen council houses, fourteen of them built between 1945 and 1954,[28] a petrol-pump and motor mechanic's shop. There have been some losses: the windmill, which lay to the north-east of the village and was at work about 40 years ago, has gone;[29] so has the Star Inn, which went in the early 1920's.[30] But on the whole there has been remarkably little change in the appearance of the village since the early 19th century.

Fencott, a small straggling hamlet on the eastern side of the Ray, lies less than a mile away from its parent village. With its neighbour Murcott, over a mile farther east, it has suffered much from floods. Fifteenth-century court rolls frequently mention overflowing ditches and flooded roads.[31] For the hearth tax of 1665 three farm-houses returned two hearths each.[32] Today Fencott's few farm-houses and cottages are mostly built of local stone, and one, a two-storied house with a gabled attic dormer, bears the date 1737 and the initials TWE. Murcott hamlet is rather larger than Fencott. Many of its cottages are stone built and have thatched roofs, but most of the small farm-houses were rebuilt in red brick or variegated brick during the 19th century. A Method-ist chapel was erected in 1845.[33] The 'Nut Tree' at the east end of the hamlet is a one-storied inn with attics and a thatched roof. There were three inns in the hamlets in the mid-18th century, of which the 'Black Bull' in Fencott and the 'Marlake House' in Murcott survived into the 20th century. Both had closed by 1939.[34] The 'Marlake House' was near the site of the house of that name shown on a 17th-century map of the adjoining manor of Studley.[35]

The parish has only produced one 'worthy' of note: Daniel Featley, the celebrated Anglican contro-versialist and preacher, was born at Charlton in 1582.[36] The village's other most distinguished resi-dents are to be found among its rectors.[37]

At the time of the inclosure of Otmoor, it was alleged that in 1830 two Charlton men led some of the bands who, believing they had the law on their side, broke down the fences, and that Charlton men threatened to 'fetch' the Horton men if they did not join them voluntarily.[38] Many of the villagers were subsequently concerned in the events of St. Giles' Fair day, and in the formation of the Otmoor Association.[39]

MANOR. Before the Conquest Baldwin held freely 10 hides in *CHARLTON*;[40] in 1086 Roger d'Ivry held them of Hugh de Grantmesnil, whose daughter Adeline he had married.[41] With Hugh's consent Adeline and her daughter Adelize granted the manor

[17] The Shirley family have long been notable thatchers.
[18] Dunkin MS. 438/6, f. 26b.
[19] Dunkin, *Oxon.* i. 206.
[20] O.R.O. Victlrs' recog.: 3 victuallers were licensed in 1735.
[21] Oxf. Archd. Oxon. c 118, ff. 110–110b.
[22] See below, p. 90.
[23] Oxf. Archd. Oxon. b 40, f. 91.
[24] *Hearth Tax Oxon.* 194.
[25] Dunkin, *Oxon.* i. 206.
[26] Inf. the rector.
[27] See below, pp. 91, 92.
[28] Inf. Ploughley R.D.C.
[29] A windmill in 'ruins' in 1551 was situated at 'Towns-end'. It was probably rebuilt as suggested by the royal surveyors: L.R. 2/189, f. 48.
[30] Local inf.
[31] S.C. 2/197/48–9.
[32] *Hearth Tax Oxon.* 195–6.
[33] See below, p. 91.
[34] O.R.O. Victlrs' recog.; *Kelly's Dir. Oxon.* (1939).
[35] O.S. Map 6″, xxviii (1884); George Sargeant, Map of Studley (1641): Bodl. MS. map C 17: 49(92).
[36] Dunkin, *Oxon.* i. 228 sqq.
[37] See below, pp. 89, 90.
[38] Dunkin MS. 438/6, f. 49b; *O.A.S. Trans.* 1900, 10; see below, p. 273; *V.C.H. Oxon.* v. 71.
[39] Dunkin MS. 438/6, f. 26b; *O.A.S. Trans.* 1900, 11. For the Otmoor riots see *V.C.H. Oxon.* v. 70–71.
[40] *V.C.H. Oxon.* i. 427.
[41] T. Banks, *Dormant and Extinct Baronage*, i. 90; cf. *Complete Peerage*, vii. 532–3, note h.

to St. Évroul Abbey in Normandy. Between 1190 and 1204[42] Robert, Earl of Leicester, son of Pernel, the great-granddaughter of Hugh de Grantmesnil,[43] confirmed the grant. The overlordship of Charlton descended to Margaret, sister and coheiress of Robert Fitz Pernel, who married Saer de Quincy, Earl of Winchester,[44] and to their son Roger. In 1242 10 marks a year from the revenues of Charlton church were reserved to Roger, son of Earl Roger, 'so long as he should demean himself honestly as a clerk, not take a wife, nor receive the habit of the religious nor be endowed with any other ecclesiastical benefice'.[45] In 1279 the Earl of Leicester was erroneously said to be overlord.[46] Earl Roger de Quincy (d. 1264) left three daughters, one of whom, Ela, had married Alan la Zouche (d. 1270).[47] The overlordship then descended to their grandson Alan, who died in 1314 leaving three daughters.[48] One of them, Maud, married Robert de Holland,[49] and her great-granddaughter Maud married Sir John Lovel, second son of John, Lord Lovel of Titchmarsh, about 1372.[50] Charlton was included in the possessions of Sir John's grandson William at his death in 1455,[51] the last occasion on which the overlordship was mentioned.

The alien priory of Ware, a cell of St. Évroul and a foundation of Hugh de Grantmesnil, held Charlton until it was suppressed in 1414.[52] The manor was granted by Henry V to his new foundation at Sheen (Surr.) in the following year,[53] and Sheen held it until the Dissolution.[54] The Poure family[55] were tenants of Charlton under Ware from the 12th to the 15th century. Walter Poure, a brother of William Poure of Oddington, was alive about 1175, and his son Hugh granted his meadow of 'Le Dene' in Charlton to Thame Abbey about 1190.[56] Hugh was succeeded by his son John, who also held land at Garford (Berks.), and his grandson Richard, who held Charlton,[57] Garford, and Wendlebury in 1279. Richard's son William had succeeded him by 1284. He died in 1316 or 1317, leaving a son Richard,[58] who was dead by 1338, when another William Poure held Charlton.[59] William was succeeded by Sir Thomas Poure of Black Bourton, who was dead by 1398, leaving as his heir a son Thomas.[60] Thomas died a minor in 1407,[61] and was succeeded by his sister Agnes, who married firstly William Winslow of Ramsbury (Wilts.), who died in 1414, and secondly Robert Andrew, who died in 1437.[62]

Sheen Priory was dissolved in 1539 and in 1552 Charlton manor was still in the king's hands.[63] In 1558[64] and again in 1560 it was conveyed to groups of London citizens as security for loans to Elizabeth I, who recovered it in 1562.[65] In 1574 Charlton manor was granted to Lord Cheney of Toddington,[66] at whose request it passed in 1575 to Sir John Dudley and John Ayscough.[67] They sold it in the following year to William Shillingford alias Izard,[68] who died in 1589. The manor was granted by letters patent to his son Edmund in 1612,[69] but it was charged with so many legacies by him that his son John was forced to mortgage it in 1668 to Mary Hatton, widow of Sir Thomas Hatton. In 1671 she claimed that she had lent John Shillingford £1,500 on the security of Charlton and half the manor and rectory of Beckley. The money had not been repaid, but Francis Hall of Noke claimed an earlier title to the manor. John Shillingford, then a prisoner in the Fleet, replied that there were numerous other mortgages and securities and that he had been imprisoned just when he was about to make a good marriage. Francis Hall had assigned a judgement for £400 that he had received against Shillingford in 1670 to George Scudamore,[70] and in 1680 Hatton's mortgage of Charlton was assigned to Hall and Scudamore. The manor was afterwards sold to Gregory Geering, who in 1688 sold it to John Pope of East Ginge (Berks.).[71] In 1717 the latter gave it to his son Gregory Pope.

In 1732 Gregory Pope's widow and son sold Charlton to Thomas Cooper, who also secured from Matthew Biggs, John Shillingford's heir, his reversionary interest in the estate. Cooper at once mortgaged the manor to John Coker of Bicester and finally sold it in 1753 to Sir Edward Turner of Ambrosden,[72] whose descendants remained lords of the manor until 1874.[73] The new lords owned very little land in Charlton, but they were still holding manorial courts there in the 1820's.[74] Soon after the death of Sir Edward Page-Turner in 1874,[75] the family lands in Charlton were purchased by John Rowland, who was described as lord of the manor in 1887.[76] Any claim to manorial rights seems to have lapsed after another sale of the former Turner property in 1902.[77]

LESSER ESTATES. Westminster Abbey held almost all the land in the hamlets of Fencott and Murcott as part of its Islip manor.[78] The estate was

42 *Cal. Doc. France*, ed. Round, 229, where the manor is called Fencott and Murcott; *Cal. Pat.* 1338–46, 156.
43 *Complete Peerage*, vii. 532.
44 Ibid. (orig. edn.), viii. 168–70.
45 *Rot. Grosse.* 477.
46 *Rot. Hund.* (Rec. Com.), ii. 829.
47 *Complete Peerage* (orig. edn.), viii. 170, note a.
48 *Cal. Inq. p.m.* v, p. 258.
49 *Complete Peerage*, vi. 530; *Cal. Close*, 1313–18, 154.
50 *Complete Peerage*, vi. 532; viii. 219.
51 *Cal. Inq. p.m.* (Rec. Com.), iv, p. 264; C 139/158.
52 e.g. *Rot. Hund.* (Rec. Com.), ii. 45, 829; *Bk. of Fees*, 831.
53 *V.C.H. Surr.* ii. 89–94.
54 *Valor Eccl.* (Rec. Com.), ii. 52.
55 G. A. Moriarty, 'Poure Family of Oxon.', *Misc. Gen. et Her.* 5th ser. vi. 363–75 for full details.
56 *Thame Cart.* i. 6; see also *Cal. Close*, 1337–9, 235.
57 *Rot. Hund.* (Rec. Com.), ii. 829.
58 E 179/161/9; *Cal. Close*, 1327–30, 235.
59 *Cal. Close*, 1337–9, 420.
60 *Misc. Gen. et Her.* 5th ser. vi. 369–70 citing C.P. 40/582, m. 136.

61 C 138/59/51; cf. *Cal. Close*, 1405–9, 299.
62 For Agnes's descendants see below, p. 340.
63 *V.C.H. Surr.* ii. 93; L.R. 2/189, f. 48; cf. S.C. 6, Hen. VIII 3464.
64 *Cal. Pat.* 1557–8, 408.
65 Ibid. 1558–60, 431, 435–7.
66 *Complete Peerage*, iii. 192–3; E 318/2310.
67 C 66/1127, m. 12.
68 Dunkin, *Oxon.* i. 100, 223; cf. *Oxon. Visit.* 303; Req. 2/59/7; see below, p. 88.
69 C 66/1949/15; C 142/220/77.
70 C 5/496/65, 66.
71 *Par. Coll.* i. 83; Dunkin, *Oxon.* i. 224–5.
72 Dunkin, *Oxon.* i. 225; Wing, *Annals*, 46.
73 For the Turners see G. E. C. *Baronetage*, v. 77–79; O.R.O. Gamekprs' deps.; *V.C.H. Oxon.* v. 18.
74 O.R.O. Land tax assess.; Dunkin, *Oxon.* i. 226.
75 G. E. C. *Baronetage*, v. 79; Wing, *Annals*, 45.
76 *Kelly's Dir. Oxon.* (1887).
77 Ibid. (1903); *Sale Cat.*: Bodl. G.A. Oxon. b 90 (20).
78 The hamlets are not mentioned in the Domesday survey. For the Westm. estate see below, pp. 83, 84.

granted to the Dean and Chapter of Westminster in 1542, and save for the years 1556–60 when the abbey, refounded by Queen Mary, was lord of the manor,[79] it was held by them until the end of the 19th century. The Ecclesiastical Commissioners were lords of the manor in 1939.[80] Between 1786 and 1845 the estate was leased to the Queen's College, Oxford, at a rent of 7s. a year.[81]

On her deathbed, Adeline d'Ivry granted a hide in Charlton to Abingdon Abbey.[82] In about 1180 Abbot Roger granted this land, which was in Fencott township, to William Turpin, *camerarius regis*, in exchange for lands in Dumbleton (Berks.): it was to be held for a quit-rent of 2s.[83] About 1200 William granted the land to his son Geoffrey, subject to the quit-rent,[84] and by 1218 it had passed to Osbert Turpin,[85] who also held land at North Moreton (Berks.).[86] About 1230 Osbert sold the hide in Fencott to Godstow Abbey for £17 6s. 8d., still subject to the 2s. quit-rent: Abingdon Abbey confirmed the grant, but increased the quit-rent to 5s.[87] The hide was held of Godstow in 1247 by John Bereworth[88] and in 1279 by John 'Bere-wike',[89] perhaps the same man or his son. In 1314 the tenant of Godstow was William de la Hide[90] and in 1318 it was granted to Sir Richard Bere for a quit-rent of 8s. a year and a casualty of 50s. for heriot and relief.[91] Sir Richard, who appears to have been in possession two years earlier,[92] was Sheriff of Oxford-shire in 1318,[93] and the Ralph de la Bere said to hold ½ knight's fee in Fencott and Murcott in 1455 may perhaps have been his descendant.[94] At the Dissolution the Fencott property yielded to Godstow £1 17s. 4d. a year, and the abbey still paid the 5s. quit-rent to Abingdon.[95] In 1553 the estate was granted to George Owen, the king's physician, and to William Martyn together with other Godstow lands.[96] In 1645 it was being held in fee farm of the Crown by Sir William Spencer and others for £2 13s. 10d. a year.[97]

In the 13th century two virgates in Charlton were granted to Catesby Priory (Northants) by Hugh Russel and the grant was confirmed by Gilbert de Hyda.[98] In 1283 Hugh son of Margery de Hynton granted to the priory all the land in Charlton that he had acquired from Hugh Russel for a rent of 2s. a year, and agreed to pay a similar sum in settlement of a rent granted to the priory by Nicholas de Crevleton.[99] At the Dissolution the priory was receiving 14s. a year in rents from Charlton.[1] In 1540 its lands were granted by Henry VIII to Sir Michael Dormer, who in 1543 conveyed them to his brother Peter Dormer of Shipton Lee (Bucks.).[2]

ECONOMIC HISTORY. Early settlement of the parish is unlikely since most of it lies either on the Oxford Clay, which carried thick oak forest, or on the alluvial deposits of Otmoor.[3] There is no evidence of Roman settlement, and the place-names Charlton, 'the tūn of the ceorls', and Fencott and Murcott, both meaning 'cottages on marshy ground'. are all of Anglo-Saxon origin.[4] In 1086 Roger d'Ivry's estate in Charlton probably included the hamlets. All the available arable, land for 15 ploughs, was probably under cultivation, for Roger's tenants had 11 ploughs and there were 4 on the demesne. There was meadow-land (4×2 furls.) and pasture (3×2 furls.), and a rise in the value of the estate from £8 to £10 since 1066 may indicate that woodland had recently been cleared. The peasant population possibly numbered 32 families, for there were 15 villeins (*villani*), 11 bordars, and 6 serfs.[5]

The Hundred Rolls of 1279 show considerable changes: in Charlton the Prior of Ware had 3 virgates in demesne, while under him Richard Poure held 4 virgates for 6d. a year and another free tenant, whose servants had to do 2 *precaria* in autumn on the prior's demesne, held 1 virgate. Of the 26 villeins on the manor 6 held half-virgates of Richard for 6s. 8d. a year. Under the prior 20 half-virgaters paid 2s. 6d. and 6¾d. in lieu of works, 1 virgater paid 5s. and 1s. 2½d. and 2 cottagers paid 2s. 4½d. each. In all there were about 22 virgates of arable land, each consisting, in Charlton, of 30 customary acres.[6] In 1294 the 3 virgates of arable in the prior's demesne were worth £1 2s. 6d. a year and his 15 acres of meadow £1 10s. The whole demesne was then worth £9 4s. 4d. a year, including 10s. for the common oven and £2 6s. 8d. for the windmill.[7]

On the Abbot of Westminster's estates in Fencott and Murcott, which formed part of his manor of Islip, there were in 1279 27 half-virgaters rendering 2s. 6d. a year and 1s. in lieu of works. Five cottars paid a total of 4s. 7d., and the only free tenant paid 11s. 8d. for a virgate and a quarter share of a cottage. Of the Abbess of Godstow's lands in Fencott a free tenant held 1 virgate for 8s. 4d. a year and 3 villeins paying 5s. each held half a virgate.[8] Altogether about 20 virgates in the hamlets were cultivated by 2 free tenants and 35 villeins and cottars. A total of 61 villeins and cottars in Charlton and its hamlets shows that the population may perhaps have doubled since 1086, and a possible increase in the extent of arable land is suggested by the mention about 1230 of a 'Newebreche' in Charlton.[9]

In the early 14th century Charlton was both more populous and more prosperous than its hamlets.

[79] *L. & P. Hen. VIII*, xvii, p. 392; *Cal. Pat.* 1555–7, 349; ibid. 1558–60, 398.
[80] *Kelly's Dir. Oxon.* (1939).
[81] Queen's Coll. deeds Q 14, Q 17.
[82] *Chron. Abingdon*, ii. 72–73; cf. *V.C.H. Berks.* ii. 151–62.
[83] *Godstow Reg.* i. 327.
[84] Ibid. 327–8.
[85] Ibid. 328.
[86] Ibid. 40; *V.C.H. Berks.* iii. 494.
[87] *Godstow Reg.* i. 328–9.
[88] Ibid. 329–30.
[89] Ibid. 330; *Rot. Hund.* (Rec. Com.), ii. 832.
[90] *Godstow Reg.* i. 330.
[91] Ibid. 332–3.
[92] *Feud. Aids*, iv. 170.
[93] *Cal. Fine R.* 1307–19, 360, 391.
[94] C 139/158.

[95] Dugd. *Mon.* iv. 373.
[96] *Cal. Pat.* 1553, 260; *D.N.B.*
[97] E 308/3/26, rot. 23, no. 142; cf. S.C. 6, Hen. VIII 2927.
[98] E 326/B 11444–5.
[99] Ibid. B 11443, 11446.
[1] *Valor Eccl.* (Rec. Com.), iv. 339.
[2] *L. & P. Hen. VIII*, xvi, p. 173; xviii, p. 282; *Visit. Bucks.* (Harl. Soc. lviii), 40–42.
[3] Mary Marshall, *Land Utilization Survey Oxon.* 211.
[4] *V.C.H. Oxon.* i. 337; *P.N. Oxon.* (E.P.N.S.), i. 205, 207.
[5] *V.C.H. Oxon.* i. 427.
[6] *Rot. Hund.* (Rec. Com.), ii. 829–30.
[7] Dunkin, *Oxon.* i. 222, citing B.M. Add. MS. 6164; E 106/2/6.
[8] *Rot. Hund.* ii. 831–2.
[9] *Cat. Anct. D.* ii. C 2700.

Charlton's assessment for the 15th from 1334 onwards was £6 10s. 7d., the highest in Ploughley hundred except Bicester, while the hamlets' joint assessment was £5 7s. 2d.[10] The decrease in the Prior of Ware's annual revenue from Charlton to £5 0s. 6d. by 1324 is largely accounted for by the leasing of the demesne. Week-works had already been commuted by 1279, and a subsequent commutation of boon-works may be indicated by a slight rise in rents of customary lands by 1324.[11] At the Dissolution Charlton manor was worth £15 2s. 3d. a year.[12] In 1551 there were 21 copyholders holding some 14¼ virgates for rents which averaged 12s. a virgate and which totalled £10 7s. 3½d. a year. The demesnes, 4 virgates and 6 acres of meadow,[13] were leased for £4 a year, and the mill and the common bakehouse brought in 15s. There was very little good timber available, for of about 350 trees on the manor all but a few were 'dotterells', 'wranglinges', and 'slyppes'.[14] In relative prosperity Charlton had declined greatly in 200 years: its assessment for the lay subsidy of 1523 was 10s. 6d., nearly the lowest in Ploughley hundred, while Fencott and Murcott were each to pay as much.[15] The reason for its decline may well be that after 1300 further extension of tillage was not possible save on to unrewarding Otmoor. In fact the area under cultivation in 1551 was much the same as it had been in 1279.

In 1390 in Fencott and Murcott Westminster's customary tenants were cultivating one more virgate than in 1279. In 1390 there were 11 half-virgaters and 1 tenant with 11 acres in Fencott, and 1 virgater, 18 half-virgaters, 5 cottagers, and 1 small freeholder in Murcott. All the half-virgaters owed heriot, merchet, and tallage. Most of them paid 4s. 6d. a year, rents having risen through the 14th century, and owed 3 days' autumn works and 2 boon-works, while some of the cottagers owed a boon-work.[16] Week-works had been commuted in the hamlets by 1279 and were not reimposed in the 14th century, whereas in the parent manor of Islip they were exacted till 1349.[17] The earlier commutation of works in Fencott and Murcott may be accounted for by the distance of the hamlets from Islip and the smallness of the demesne lands.[18] There is evidence that in the late 14th and early 15th centuries the lord was finding it difficult to enforce services in the hamlets, and in 1433 all labour services were finally commuted.[19]

The population of Fencott and Murcott may have remained much the same between 1279 when there were 35 half-virgaters and cottars and 1390 when there were 36. The Black Death took a much lighter

toll than it did at Islip, and when holdings did fall into the lord's hands they were quickly taken up by new tenants.[20] A fall in population in the 15th century, however, may be indicated by a decrease in the number of tithings in the hamlets from 7 in 1387 to 5 in 1438. The flight of villeins is first mentioned in 1430,[21] and a number of customary tenants abandoned their holdings after 1450. The lord's grant in 1463 of a joint lease of their lands to all his customary tenants failed to check the exodus from the manor.[22] The number of tithings fell to 3 by 1482, one each for Fencott, Murcott, and Godstow's lands.[23] This decline may have been partly caused by the rise of some tenants from villein status and by evasion of the system of frankpledge.

The acreage of arable at Fencott and Murcott increased slightly between 1279 and 1540, for in the latter year Godstow's estate in Fencott comprised at least 6 virgates—compared with 4 at the earlier date—held by 5 customary tenants.[24] Nevertheless by 1523 the hamlets were among the poorest places in the hundred.[25]

There were four open fields in Charlton in 1622[26] and these remained virtually unchanged until their inclosure in 1858. The distribution of the glebe arable in 1634 was: North Field 14 lands, Middle Field 13 lands, Field next Fencott 17 lands, and Field next Oddington 20 lands.[27] In 1844 the distribution in statute acres in the same fields was 10:9:11:12.[28] A belt of old inclosures, the Woodside and Mansmoor Closes, occupied about 160 acres, a fifth of the township; their shape suggests that they had once been arable land. In 1622 they are called the closes 'in North Field', and in 1634 the rector held one (11 a.) 'in leewe of soe many acres in Northfield'.[29] The artificial appearance of Close Hedge and Middle Fields on the map may be explained by the drastic rearrangement of furlongs which must have followed the inclosure, perhaps not long before 1622, of much of North Field.[30] It is likely that there were originally only two fields, North and South.[31] The lot meadows of Charlton lay in two groups—to the east and west of the township. There were also the Lammas lands.

It is uncertain how many open fields Fencott and Murcott had originally. *Campus vocatus Corneffeld* is mentioned in 1419 and 'le stubblefyld' in 1539. But, also in 1419, there is a reference to *Campi bladales*.[32] In the 15th century there were occasional attempts by tenants to consolidate holdings, and there are numerous references to Westcroft as a close and to 'le lunge close'.[33] By 1844 there were five open fields, but it is possible that there was only

[10] E 179/161/17. The poll-tax returns except for Fencott are missing: see below, p. 358.
[11] E 106/8/5; cf. S.C. 6/1126/16.
[12] S.C. 6, Hen. VIII 3464; cf. E 318/2310.
[13] *Misc. Gen. et Her.* 5th ser. vi. 369.
[14] L.R. 2/189, ff. 48–50.
[15] E 179/161/176, 189.
[16] W.A.M. 15200, transcribed in Barbara Harvey, 'Islip Manor' (Bodl. MS. B.Litt. d 53), pp. 249–52; ibid. 95, 101, 108–9 for rents.
[17] *Rot. Hund.* (Rec. Com.), ii. 831–2; Bodl. MS. B.Litt. d 53, pp. 124, 225.
[18] For the demesnes see W.A.M. 15200; *Fines Oxon.* 83; S.C. 2/197/48; Bodl. Tithe award.
[19] Bodl. MS. B.Litt. d 53, pp. 108–9, 281, 288.
[20] Ibid. 111, 198–9.
[21] Ibid. 115, 200.
[22] Ibid. 108–9, 116.
[23] S.C. 2/197/48, 49.

[24] S.C. 6, Hen. VIII 2927.
[25] E 179/161/176, 198.
[26] Oriel Coll. Mun. Charl. deeds, drawer 9, no. 1.
[27] Queen's Coll. Mun. Q 4; the fields were called Close Hedge F., Middle F., Windmill F., and Oddington Hedge F. by 1693: Oriel Coll. Mun. Charl. deeds, drawer 7, mortgage.   [28] Bodl. Tithe award and map.
[29] Queen's Coll. Mun. Q 4. They remained pasture closes in 1858.
[30] Close Hedge Field and Close Hedge Furlong still retained their old names of North Field and Lancates Furlong in 1634: ibid.; cf. 'Lamchoteforlung' (c. 1230); *Cat. Anct. D.* ii. C 2700.
[31] See map opposite for their probable extent.
[32] Bodl. MS. B.Litt. d 53, pp. 281, 283.
[33] Ibid. 283; S.C. 2/197/48, 49; *Fines Oxon.* 83; *Godstow Reg.* i. 331, 332; *Cat. Anct. D.* ii. C 2700; *Cal. Close, 1343–6*, 515; S.C. 6, Hen. VIII 2927.

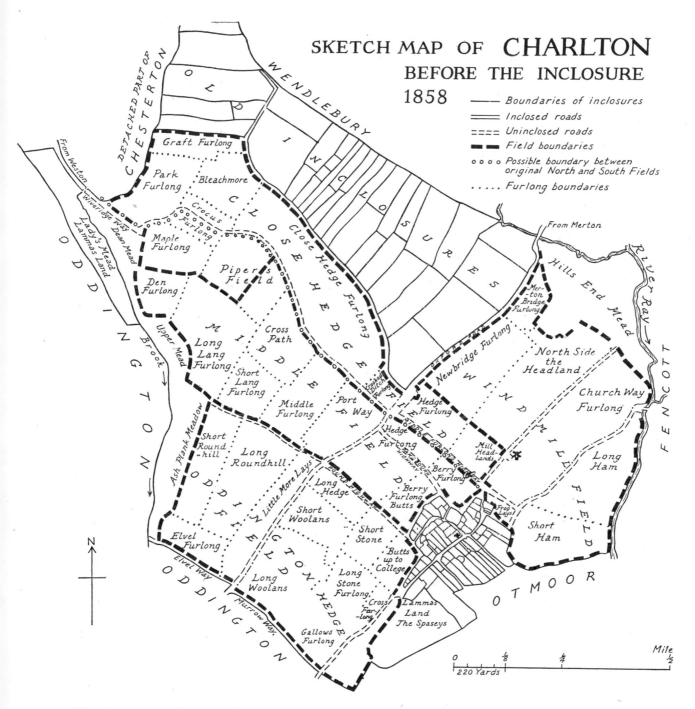

SKETCH MAP OF CHARLTON
BEFORE THE INCLOSURE
1858

Boundaries of inclosures
Inclosed roads
Uninclosed roads
Field boundaries
Possible boundary between original North and South Fields
Furlong boundaries

DETACHED PART OF CHESTERTON

OLD INCLOSURES

WENDLEBURY

From Weston

From Merton

River Ray

Hills End Mead

FENCOTT

Graft Furlong

Park Furlong

Bleachmore

Crocus Furlong

Maple Furlong

Den Furlong

Piper's Field

ODDINGTON

Riveridge Way

Lady's Mead Dean Mead

Lammas Land

Upper Mead

Brook

CLOSE HEDGE

Close Hedge Furlong

Mer-ton Bridge Furlong

North Side the Headland

Church Way Furlong

MIDDLE FIELD

Long Lang Furlong

Short Lang Furlong

Cross Path

Newbridge Furlong

WINDMILL FIELD

Long Ham

Middle Furlong

Port Way

Crooked Ditch

Hedge Furlong

Hedge Furlong

Mill Head-lands

Berry Furlong

Short Round-hill

Ash Plank Meadow

Long Roundhill

Little More Lays

Long Hedge

Short Woolans

Short Stone

Berry Furlong Butts

Frog Lays

Short Ham

ODDINGTON

Elvel Furlong

Elvel Way

Long Woolans

Murrow Way

Long Stone Furlong

Cross Far-long

Gallows Furlong

Butts up to College

Lammas Land The Spaseys

OTMOOR

ODDINGTON HEDGE

N

0   ⅛   ¼   Mile ½

220 Yards

The above map is based on documents cited in the text, and the tithe and inclosure award maps of
1844 and 1857 respectively

a four-course rotation, the furlongs of the small Fencott Field being worked in groups with the four larger fields. A study of the field boundaries and furlong names of 1844 rather suggests that the four fields had once been three. The meadow and pasture lands were nearly all beside the River Ray, and in 1844 the only inclosures of any size were four in the Croft, about 33 acres in all.[34]

Whereas the land of Fencott and Murcott was still predominantly held by copyholders at the beginning of the 19th century, Charlton's land was largely freehold. In the course of the 17th century the Shillingford family had sold much of their lands to their tenants:[35] the demesne lands which had been leased in the late 16th century were a freehold estate by the end of the 17th century.[36] Thirty Charlton freeholders voted in the county election of 1754,[37] and 27 received awards under the Otmoor inclosure of 1815—though perhaps only a third of these was then resident in Charlton. In Fencott and Murcott in 1815 there were only 5 entirely freehold estates to 23 copyholds.[38]

A slight increase in prosperity in Charlton in the late 16th and early 17th centuries may have been the result of the rise of a few yeoman families;[39] in the 17th and 18th centuries the Alley or Leveret family, the Kirbys, Coopers, and Priests were particularly prominent in the life of the parish. They were already established in Charlton in the 16th century and were still there in the 19th.[40]

To the cottagers and even to many of the parish's small farmers their rights of common on Otmoor were important.[41] The parish, like others, suffered from the effects of the Napoleonic Wars. The burden of the poor rates increased by about eight times between 1776 and 1815.[42] Distress was increased after 1815 by the inclosure of Otmoor, which deprived the poorer cottagers of their livelihood and involved many of the smaller farmers in losses.[43] By the award of 1815, 214 acres were allotted to Charlton township and 266 acres to the hamlets; about 138 acres of Otmoor adjoining these allotments were purchased by a few rich landowners.[44] Many of the smaller proprietors out of the 59 to receive awards were too poor to fence them and sold them, some for as little as £5.[45] After the floods of 1829, nineteen farmers from the parish were among those who cut the banks of the New River Ray and flooded Otmoor to save their own lands.[46]

By 1830 the formation of larger farms in Charlton had begun, and by 1844 out of 62 holdings, 6 were of over 50 acres.[47] Oriel College had acquired about 140 acres by 1850, lands which the Alleys and Coopers had once held.[48] In Fencott and Murcott the small copyholder had virtually disappeared by 1849, when of 980 acres allotted under the inclosure award five farms occupied about 700 acres. There were ten small farms of between 15 and 50 acres and only six smallholdings.[49] Evidently through the poverty of the old tenants' families many small copyholds had fallen in to the lords of the manor in the past quarter-century and had been granted to comparatively few new tenants. Charlton fields finally inclosed in 1858. A total of 585 acres was inclosed, the largest allotment (147 a.) going to Oriel College. The amalgamation of estates was still going on: the three largest proprietors between them held what had been eight separate holdings. Twenty-two proprietors received awards, fourteen of them freeholders, but perhaps twice that number of cottagers got nothing.[50] Inclosure led to better drainage and better cultivation.[51]

In the second half of the 19th century the number of farms continued to decrease: there were 33 farmers in Charlton and the hamlets in 1864, and 17 in 1903. By 1887 John Rowland had become the principal landowner,[52] and Oriel College, which added some small purchases to its estate after 1850, remained a prominent landowner until 1921–2 when the college estates were sold.[53] In 1844 there had been over 1,500 acres of arable land in the parish,[54] but by 1914 the farms had gone over to dairying, a change confirmed by the increased demand for milk in the present century. By 1939 most of the land was permanent grass and there were only two small patches of arable left—one of them on and around the Cornbrash 'island'.[55]

The population figures recorded in the census of 1676 and in 18th-century visitation returns are for the parish as a whole, apparently, and so no precise picture of the growth of each place can be obtained. The hearth-tax returns of 1662, however, listed 24 householders in Charlton and 29 in the hamlets.[56] In 1676 there were said to be 228 adults altogether.[57] In 1738 it was estimated that there were 99 houses and 450 persons including children, 'which are very numerous', but later 18th-century estimates sometimes put the houses at 80.[58] The first official census of 1801 gave the population as 478; it reached its peak of 687 in 1861, and thereafter declined, particularly at Fencott and Murcott, and by 1901 the figure was 464 for the whole parish. The trend continued in the 20th century, and in 1951 there were 424 inhabitants.[59]

[34] Bodl. Tithe award map (1844): Fencott Field *furlongs* are given same conventional boundary as the 4 other *fields*.
[35] Dunkin, *Oxon.* i. 225; e.g. Oriel Coll. Mun. Charl. deeds, drawer 9, no. 1: sale by Edmund Shillingford 1622.
[36] L.R. 2/189, f. 50, E 318/2310; Oriel Coll. Mun. Charl. deeds, drawer 7: mortgage of manor 1693.
[37] Wing, *Annals*, 45.
[38] O.R.O. Otmoor incl. award.
[39] E 179/162/319; ibid. 164/476.
[40] For these families see particularly S.C. 6, Hen. VIII 2927; L.R. 2/189, f. 50; E 179/162/319; ibid. 164/476; *Hearth Tax Oxon.* 194; O.R.O. Victlrs' recog.; ibid. Land tax assess.; ibid. Otmoor incl. award; Oriel Coll. Mun. Charl. deeds, drawer 7, Curtis estate deeds.
[41] MS. Top. Oxon. b 121, ff. 7–8.
[42] Dunkin, *Oxon.* i. 206.
[43] See C. E. Prior, 'Account of Otmoor', *O.A.S. Trans.* 1900, 3–13; *V.C.H. Oxon.* v. 71.
[44] O.R.O. Otmoor incl. award.
[45] Dunkin, *Oxon.* i. 124.
[46] Dunkin MS. 438/6, f. 14.
[47] Bodl. Tithe award.
[48] Oriel Coll. Mun. Charl. deeds, drawers 7, 9, 16.
[49] O.R.O. Fencott and Murcott incl. award.
[50] Ibid. Charl. incl. award.
[51] C. E. Prior, 'Charlton Open Fields', *O.A.S. Trans.* 1907, 3–10; Oriel Coll. Mun. Charl. deeds, drawer 7, valuation 1858.
[52] *Kelly's Dir. Oxon.* (1864, 1887, 1903).
[53] Inf. the treasurer, Oriel Coll.
[54] Bodl. Tithe award.
[55] M. Marshall, *Land Util. Survey Oxon.* 216, 225, 235; O.S. Land Util. Map 1", sheet 94 (1939).
[56] *Hearth Tax Oxon.* 235.
[57] Compton Census.
[58] Oxf. Dioc. d 552; d 555 (1759); d 558 (1768); d 561 (1771).
[59] *Census*, 1801–1951.

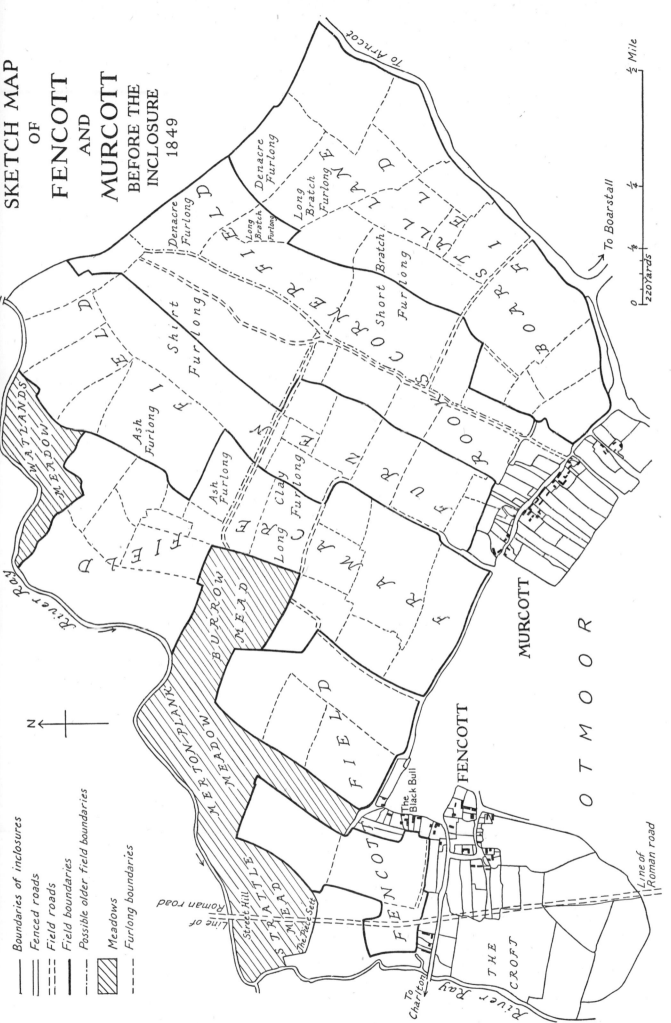

SKETCH MAP
OF
FENCOTT
AND
MURCOTT
BEFORE THE
INCLOSURE
1849

Boundaries of inclosures
Fenced roads
Field roads
Field boundaries
Possible older field boundaries
Meadows
Furlong boundaries

N

To Arncot

Denacre Furlong

Denacre Furlong

Long Bratch Furlong

Long Bratch Furlong

FENCOTT FIELD

Short Bratch Furlong

BORSTALL FIELD

Shirt Furlong

Ash Furlong

Ash Furlong

Long Clay Furlong

MURCOTT FIELD

WATLANDS MEADOW

River Ray

BURROW MEAD

MERTON-PLANK MEADOW

STRATTLE MEAD

Street Hill

The Peel Sett

Line of Roman road

FENCOTT FIELD

To Chariton

River Ray

THE CROFT

FENCOTT

The Black Bull

MURCOTT

OTMOOR

Line of Roman road

To Boarstall

0   220Yards
⅛   ¼   ½ Mile

The above map is based on documents cited in the text, and the tithe and inclosure award maps of 1844 and 1847 respectively

In 1811 57 families out of 75 in Charlton and 55 out of 59 in Fencott and Murcott had been engaged in agriculture.[60] There were about 20 tradesmen in the parish in the 1850's.[61] Population declined in the second half of the century;[62] inclosure and the adoption of a more economic system of husbandry no doubt contributed to the decline, which, like inclosure, came later at Charlton than in the hamlets.

The traditional trades of the parish were closely connected with agriculture, and the millers and innkeepers had often been farmers as well. Charlton windmill is first mentioned in 1294, when it was worth £2 6s. 8d. a year.[63] In 1551, however, it was 'cleane downe' and worth but 5s., though it had been working as recently as 1545.[64] Fencott and Murcott probably had their own mill up to the 16th century at least.[65] In the early 19th century the Charlton millers ran a meal and bakery business.[66] The mill had ceased working by 1920.[67] Good barley can be grown on the Cornbrash and the descent of a maltster's business in Charlton can be traced from 1737 into the second half of the 19th century.[68] There were stonemasons in the village into the 20th century, but nothing is known of the later history of a quarry of *lapis vermiculatus* noted by Plot in 1673.[69] A brickworks using local clay was disused by 1876.[70] Other village craftsmen in the mid-19th century were carpenters, wheelwrights, blacksmiths, shoemakers and tailors, and in 1864 there were two carriers. The number of tradesmen did not fall off noticeably until the 20th century. A significant newcomer in 1903 was the 'threshing machine owner'.[71]

CHURCH. There was an 11th-century church at Charlton: after the Conquest Hugh de Grantmesnil granted the advowson with the tithes, 5 virgates of land and a villein to the Benedictine monastery of St. Évroul in Normandy. His grant was confirmed by the king in 1081.[72] The abbey never appropriated the church and it left the right of presentation in the hands of the Prior of Ware.[73] This alien priory in Hertfordshire did all St. Évroul's English business and is consequently found in 1291 with a pension of £2 from Charlton living.[74] From 1324 it was in difficulties with its property, which was subsequently taken into the king's hands. In 1348, at the queen's request, the king returned its advowsons on payment of 100 marks. Thus, the prior was able to present to Charlton in 1349. The presentation by the king in 1351 is probably to be explained by the prior's death from the plague,[75] and royal presentations between 1369 and 1451 by the wars with France.

In 1398, after the confiscation of alien priories, the king granted Charlton's advowson with licence to appropriate the revenues to Henwood Nunnery (Warws.).[76] The grant was made on condition that the nunnery allowed suitable maintenance for a priest and for the poor; although confirmed by the pope, and by the king in 1403,[77] it never came into effect. In 1405[78] the king granted Ware Priory with its lands and advowsons to the queen, and she consequently presented to Charlton in 1406 and 1408.

In 1409 there is evidence that the Prioress of Henwood did not abandon her claim without a struggle.[79] A Walter Walkstede, clerk, then gave a recognizance to the prioress to abide by an award made in a dispute over the possession of Charlton. However, the matter was settled in 1414, when the king gave the advowson with the manor and the rest of the possessions of Ware Priory to his new foundations at Sheen in Surrey.[80] In 1416 the Abbot of St. Évroul begged Sheen for the return of his property, and after years of struggle the abbey carried the case in 1427 to the papal court, where it was defeated. Sheen Priory retained the advowson and received the pension formerly paid to Ware until its dissolution in 1539.[81] In 1535 the prior granted the right of patronage and first voidance of the church to William Parre and others.[82] In 1543 the king granted the advowson, subject to the annual payment of £2, formerly due to Sheen and now to the patron, to the agents of the Queen's College, Oxford.[83] The feoffees presented the Provost, William Dennyson, in 1543;[84] he held the living until his death in 1559. The next incumbent, Alan Scot, was presented by the college and not by the surviving feoffee.[85] The college still (1955) holds the advowson, and the living is held with Wood Eaton.

The rectory was one of the richest in Bicester deanery, valued at £13 6s. 8d. in 1254[86] and at £20 in 1291.[87] By 1535 its net value was £21 9s. 4d., not as great an increase in value as was usual. The benefice was charged with a pension of £2, payable first to Ware Priory and then to Sheen Priory.[88]

The rectory was impoverished in the second half of the 16th century by a lease for 81 years at £20 or £30 a year, which Provost Scot of the Queen's College and rector from 1559 to 1578 made to William Izard of Beckley for £280.[89] Even at the time this lease appears to have been injudicious—a later provost said that Scot should have been hanged for it—and rising prices made it increasingly so. It is probable that attempts to break the lease were made as early as 1579, when a rector was paid £6 13s. 4d. by the

[60] Dunkin, *Oxon.* i. 206, 236.
[61] Gardner, *Dir. Oxon.*
[62] *V.C.H. Oxon.* ii. 221.
[63] Dunkin, *Oxon.* i. 222.
[64] L.R. 2/189, f. 50; S.C. 2/197/24.
[65] Bodl. MS. B.Litt. d 53, p. 288; S.C. 2/197/48.
[66] Dunkin MS. 438/5, p. 184.
[67] *Kelly's Dir. Oxon.* (1864–1920).
[68] O.R.O. Dodwell deeds, D I d/2–6.
[69] Bodl. MS. Hearne's Diaries 158, pp. 17, 102.
[70] O.S. Map 25″, xxviii. 5 (1876).
[71] Gardner, *Dir. Oxon.*; *Kelly's Dir. Oxon.* (1864, 1887, 1903).
[72] Ordericus Vitalis, *Historia Ecclesiastica*, ed. A. Le Prévost (Soc. de l'Histoire de France, 1845), iii. 22–24. For Grantmesnil, see above, p. 81.
[73] For list of medieval presentations see MS. Top. Oxon. d 460.   [74] *Tax. Eccl.* (Rec. Com.), 31.

[75] *V.C.H. Herts.* iv. 456.
[76] *Cal. Pat.* 1396–9, 414; *V.C.H. Warws.* ii. 65.
[77] Dugd. *Mon.* iv. 212–13; *Cal. Pat.* 1401–5, 345.
[78] Ibid. 1405–8, 48, 414; *V.C.H. Herts.* iv. 456.
[79] *Cal. Close*, 1405–9, 520–1.
[80] *V.C.H. Surrey*, ii. 89.
[81] *Subsidy 1526*, 273; *Valor Eccl.* (Rec. Com.), ii. 161.
[82] E 315/96/6/187b.
[83] *L. & P. Hen. VIII*, xviii (1), pp. 529–30; E 318/24.
[84] Foster, *Alumni*. The date of presentation has not been found in either the appropriate Linc. or Oxf. register. It may have been 1545. Cf. above, p. 69, n. 51.
[85] Oxf. Dioc. d 105, p. 195.
[86] Lunt, *Val. Norw.* 313.
[87] *Tax. Eccl.* (Rec. Com.), 31.
[88] *Valor Eccl.* (Rec. Com.), ii. 161.
[89] Oxf. Dioc. d 105, pp. 251–5; H. Airay, *The Just and Necessary Apologie* (1621), 21–23.

college 'ad prosecucionem circa rectoriam de Charl-ton'.[90] Finally in 1606 Provost Airay, then Vice-Chancellor, accepted the living in order to restore the church's rights.[91] After failing to get the lessor to accept an independent arbitration, Airay, supported by the college, went to law.[92] The suit proved extremely costly, being heard intermittently from 1609 to 1615.[93] In the end it was ruled in the King's Bench that the lease was invalid,[94] the decision being based on a law of 1571, which declared such leases illegal for more than 21 years.[95]

About this time the rectory was worth £200 a year.[96] It was entitled to tithe from the whole parish, except for 44 acres in Fencott and Murcott belonging to the Dean and Chapter of Westminster, and it had 66 field acres of glebe.[97] In 1844 the tithe was commuted for £603,[98] and in 1858 at the inclosure award the rectory was allotted 49 statute acres in four lots.[99] On the inclosure of Otmoor the rector had received another 11 acres of glebe.[1] In 1956 no glebe was left.[2] The parish was in Bicester deanery until the 19th century, but by 1854 it had been transferred to the new deanery of Islip.[3]

In spite of the richness of the living, the rectors were not usually university graduates until after Sheen Priory obtained the advowson. The priory presented a series of distinguished academic rectors: Master Robert Thwaites, Master of Balliol and a former Chancellor of the University;[4] Thomas Key, who was a canon of Lincoln;[5] and Master Martin Joyner, once prominent in Oxford University, who became Chancellor of Lincoln Cathedral in 1481.[6] How much of their time, if any, these men spent in the parish, it is impossible to say. The highly connected Master James Fitzjames, who was a canon of St. Paul's and a pluralist,[7] was certainly non-resident in the early 16th century and his church in consequence was somewhat neglected. It was reported in about 1520 that the door of the chancel (*ostium cancelli*) was insufficient, the windows and sedilia in both chancel and nave dilapidated, the Rectory out of repair, and the cemetery not enclosed.[8]

In 1522, when a Fellow of Queen's became rector, began the close connexion between Charlton and the college. There were initial troubles, but on the whole it had the beneficial result of the parish's having rectors of more than average ability and often men of considerable eminence, for example, Master Edward Hilton (1522–?)[9] and Provost Dennyson (see above). Provost Scot, the first rector to be presented by the college, though able, impoverished the living by leasing the rectory on a long lease. By its terms no

more than a room in the parsonage house was reserved to the rector and £20 a year, or £30 if he should serve the cure.[10] If he did not, the lessor was to hire a curate. One rector, John Sheppard (1581–1605), who resided with his family for part of the year, condemned the lease as wholly detrimental to the parish, particularly as the glebe was being alienated and exchanged on inclosure.[11] In the circumstances, though many contemporaries criticized Provost Airay for the years of litigation, it is difficult not to recognize the justice of the arguments advanced in the *Just and Necessary Apologie of Henry Airay . . . touching his suite in law for the rectorie of Charleton*.[12] It was argued that not only had a rich living been bringing in only about a fifth of its value to the rector, but that the needs of the parish, 'where there are three villages and much people', were being completely disregarded. The allowance of £30, specified in the lease, had been insufficient to maintain 'any fit Minister' for the instruction of so many people.

Unfortunately Thomas Garth (1615–43), who reaped the financial reward of the recent years of struggle, was at best an unsuccessful pastor.[13] In 1618 he was summoned before the church court on various charges, one of which was clearly malicious, and several of his parishioners were witnesses against him.[14] One yeoman witness said he was 'exceedingly negligent in the discharge of his cure here' and had read no prayers in the church on fourteen Sundays in the last year; another witness remembered occasions when there were no prayers except for twice in the evening. It was also alleged that one of the parishioners had brought a child to be christened, but there being no minister had taken it to another church, and all were said to be 'offended at being disappointed of their prayers' and at the minister's refusal to christen, church, and bury. On the other hand, it was stated that once during morning prayers the rector left the church in his surplice, to the 'admiration of all or most of the congregation', and went from house to house to collect absent parishioners, among them the ale-house keeper. It seems clear from this case and from the fact that Garth leased the Rectory house that he was non-resident and served the church from Oxford. His lease led him into further trouble with the parish: in 1634 he accused Allen Roberts, a husbandman of Fencott and for many years the lessee of the rectory, of neglecting to keep the house in repair. He described it as gone 'to decaye, the outhouses quite ruined, the gardens layde open and other edifices . . .

[90] J. R. Magrath, *The Queen's College*, i. 209, n. 2.

[91] Airay, *Apologie*, 11.

[92] The lease had been inherited by John Alcock, son of William Alcock, to whom Izard had sold it for £400: ibid. 8–9, 21. For later litigation among the Alcocks see C 2/Eliz./S 18/38; C 2/A 9/10/; C 2/P 12/26; Req. 2/107/13.

[93] Magrath, *Queen's*, i. 234.

[94] Airay, *Apologie: Attestation*, 4. For earlier cases see *English Reports*, vol. 145, 261–2 (Lane 16), and 276–8 (Lane 33–36); ibid. vol. 77, 1168–73 (Coke's 11th Rep. 18*b*); 2nd *Dep. Kpr's. Rep.* App II, 256.

[95] An Acte against Fraudes, 13 Eliz. c. 10.

[96] Airay, *Apologie*, 40.

[97] See above, p. 82.

[98] Bodl. Tithe award; terrier of 1634 in Oxf. Archd. Oxon. c 141, pp. 305–9. The award was adjusted in 1850 and again in 1859: Bodl. Altered awards.

[99] O.R.O. Charlton incl. award.

[1] Ibid. Otmoor incl. award.

[2] Inf. the Revd. J. R. Coulthard.

[3] For date of formation of Islip deanery see above, p. 67, n. 97.

[4] *V.C.H. Oxon.* iii. 39, 89; *Cal. Papal L.* x. 100. For a 14th-century master, John of Belvoir, see Emden, *Biog. Dict.*

[5] *Par. Coll.* i. 84; see below, p. 91.

[6] *Reg. Univ.* i. 4; *Reg. Cancelarii*, ed. H. E. Salter (O.H.S. xciv), ii, *passim*; J. Le Neve, *Fasti*, ii. 93.

[7] Wood, *Fasti*, i. 4, 27, 33, 44.

[8] *Visit Dioc. Linc.* 1517–31, i. 124.

[9] For Hilton see above, pp. 68, 69, nn. 23, 51.

[10] Dunkin, *Oxon.* i. 212–13, quoting lease from Oxf. Dioc. d 105, pp. 251–5.

[11] Airay, *Apologie: Attestation*, 2–3; *Apologie*, 19.

[12] See above, n. 89. It is followed by an *Attestation*, signed by T. W. For Airay see *D.N.B.* and Magrath, *Queen's*, i. 231–4.

[13] Foster, *Alumni*; Oxf. Dioc. c 68, f. 94.

[14] Oxf. Archd. Oxon. c 118, ff. 108–108*b*, 109*b*–110*b*, 119*b*–120*b*.

demolished'.[15] Two years later Garth was in prison for a debt to another lessee of the rectory, who he alleged had a 'pretended lease', and he petitioned both the king and the archbishop on the matter.[16]

During the second half of the 17th century Charlton had two other distinguished rectors. One, Thomas Lamplugh (c. 1658–85), was a future Bishop of Exeter and Archbishop of York.[17] After 1664, when he became Principal of Alban Hall in Oxford, he seems to have lived for a part of the year at the Rectory and to have occupied himself with his charge.[18] Although appointed to Charlton under the Commonwealth, he survived the Restoration, having, as Wood puts it, 'cringed' to the Presbyterians and then to the Royalists.[19] He was succeeded in 1685 by Provost Halton of the Queen's College, who spent 'near £2,000' on rebuilding 'a noble parsonage' for his own and the church's benefit.[20]

Eighteenth-century rectors were all Fellows of Queen's and except for John Hill (1721–45) and John Lowry (1753–84), who lived in the parish out of term until 1768, did not reside. Some, however, it may be noted, remembered the parish in their wills,[21] and at least some kept a resident curate. One curate, a Fellow of Queen's, at a salary of 40 guineas, did good work in the 1730's.[22] He held two services on Sundays, read daily prayers in Passion Week, and administered the sacrament five times a year: his zeal was reflected in the very fair number of communicants, 150 at Easter and 80 at other times.[23] By 1759 the number had dropped to between 40 and 80, but attendance at church was considered good and few persons of the 'lower rank' were reported absent.[24] Towards the end of the century conditions worsened. Elderly and sick non-resident rectors[25] could do little for the parish, and curates were badly paid. The number of communicants fell from about 40 in 1778 to between six and eight in 1805;[26] the contrast with the figures in the early 18th century is still sharper.

A change took place with the arrival of the energetic John Knipe, a former chaplain to the British Embassy in Hamburg.[27] He found the people 'sunk into a strange state of demoralization', but about 1823 he told the local historian Dunkin that he considered them then 'as orderly and devout as any in the county'.[28] He had not been afraid to fight the prevailing vice of drunkenness and to use his powers as magistrate to prevent the renewal of the licence to the local innkeeper, whom he considered unsuitable.[29] By 1830, however, he was over £2,000 in debt as a result of rebuilding the Rectory and was given two years' leave of absence by the bishop, on condition that he hired a resident curate.[30]

The backward moral and spiritual state of the parish caused general concern for the rest of the century. It was unfortunate that for many years it was without an able rector. Knipe never returned to Charlton, and until his death in 1845 the parish was in charge of a curate. He was followed by George Riggs (1846–55), whom Bishop Wilberforce summed up in the words 'inactive—drone—bee in a bottle'.[31] It is therefore not surprising to find that congregations were small and had diminished since the institution of two sermons, and that the bishop found 'no warmth or enthusiasm' when he confirmed at Charlton in 1855.[32] Henry Gough, who became rector in 1856, was so depressed by the lamentable state of the parish with its 'drunkenness, indifference and dissent', that he thought the institution of monthly communions would be welcomed by none and that the great majority of communicants would be absent.[33] Thomas Falcon (1862–83) was the first to make much impression. He was active, an excellent scholar, and he greatly improved the Rectory.[34] He built the school[35] and doubled the numbers of his congregations and communicants. Considering the wide prevalence of nonconformity in the parish, he thought that church members bore a fair proportion to the population.[36] The mission room built at Murcott in about 1890 in his successor's time is a witness to the increasing activity of the church.[37]

The church of ST. MARY THE VIRGIN is a stone building, dating mainly from the 13th and 14th centuries and comprising a chancel, clerestoried nave, north and south aisles, western tower, and south porch.[38] The 13th-century nave is separated from the aisles by arcades of three arches. The northern arcade has remains of contemporary painted decoration on both arches and pillars. The three windows with quatrefoil tracery on the north side of the clerestory are probably of the same date. The tower arch is a good example of early-13th-century work. Also of the 13th century is the lower part of the tower with a lancet window in the west wall, the south aisle with its plain doorway and porch, and the walls of the north aisle.

The church was extensively altered in the 14th century. New windows were inserted in the north aisle and on the west and south sides of the south aisle. In both aisles traces of an altar and piscina are to be found. An embattled upper story with crocketed pinnacles at the angles was added to the tower. The chancel was rebuilt towards the end of the 14th century, perhaps by the rector John de Craneforde (see below). The east window has four lights and reticulated tracery; the three sedilia and piscina on the south side are 14th-century as well as the plain

[15] MS. Top. Oxon. c 55, ff. 287–8; Oxf. Archd. Oxon. c 12, f. 170.
[16] Bodl. N. Denholm-Young, Cal. of Queen's Arch. iii. 61 (deeds Q 5–6).
[17] D.N.B.; Wood, Athenae, iv. 878–80; Magrath, Queen's, passim.
[18] Hearth Tax Oxon. 194, 251; Flemings in Oxf. ed. J. R. Magrath (O.H.S. xliv), i. 169–70, n. 4; Cal. S.P. Dom. 1668–9, 49.
[19] Wood, Athenae, iv. 878.
[20] Par. Coll. i. 83; Magrath, Queen's, ii. 71. For Halton see D.N.B.; Magrath, Queen's, passim.
[21] See below, p. 92.
[22] Letters of Radcliffe and James, ed. M. Evans (O.H.S. ix), 119 n.
[23] Oxf. Dioc. d 552.
[24] Ibid. d 555.

[25] Letters of Radcliffe and James, pp. xxvii, 231, 182.
[26] Oxf. Dioc. c 327, pp. 46, 293. The curate in 1805 was receiving only £30.
[27] Dunkin, Oxon. i. 214 n.; Foster, Alumni.
[28] Dunkin, Oxon. i. 206.
[29] MS. Dunkin 438/5, f. 265.
[30] All the correspondence is in Oxf. Dioc. c 664, ff. 46–66.
[31] Ibid. d 550, f. 17b.
[32] Wilb. Visit.; Oxf. Dioc. d 178.
[33] Oxf. Dioc. d 178.
[34] Ibid.; Magrath, Queen's, ii. 169, 324.
[35] See below, p. 92.
[36] Oxf. Dioc. c 332.
[37] Kelly's Dir. Oxon. (1939).
[38] There is a drawing by J. Buckler from SE. (1825) in MS. Top. Oxon. a 66, f. 153.

recess opposite, which was perhaps an Easter sepulchre. In the 15th or early 16th century a new window was inserted in the south aisle, and the two-light clerestory windows on the south side may be also 16th-century.

The church has been little restored. In 1757 the roof was repaired, in 1771 a gallery was erected (since removed), and in 1807 the roof was again repaired.[39] In 1857 the roof and north wall, then in a bad state, were restored (architect G. E. Street); the flat plaster ceiling in the chancel, there in 1846, may have been removed then, and the rafters of the nave partially uncovered.[40] New seats and flooring were also installed.[41] The tower was repaired in 1954, and in 1955 the church was reroofed and the plaster ceiling of the nave was totally removed so as to expose the medieval roof-timbers.

The chief glory of the church is the richly carved rood-loft and screen, dating probably from the beginning of the 16th century and thoroughly restored in 1889.[42] The gallery (about 3 ft. wide) rises from slender carved pillars and is supported by intersecting ribs with elaborate tracery. The screen is surmounted by a cross, which stands some 3 feet high, and is decorated with box shrub and flowers on 1 May, the feast of the dedication of the church, and again for the harvest festival. It is an immemorial custom to carry it round the parish in a May-day procession.[43]

There are some fragments of glass in the chancel windows, including a medieval figure of the Virgin and child, and a shield to Joseph Williamson of the Queen's College in the east window.[44] There are still some medieval tiles.[45] During the 1955 restoration some wall-paintings were uncovered on the north and south walls of the nave.

The stone font is plain and round with a pyramid-shaped cover of wood.[46] The 17th-century oak altar rails are carved in the style of Grinling Gibbons, and the pulpit of panelled oak is dated 1616.

In the chancel there are stone slabs to John de Craneforde, rector (1369–?), with fleurie cross and an indecipherable inscription, to Adam Airay, to K. L. (Katherine Lamplugh), and Thomas Yates, rector (d. 1721). There are a brass with the figure of a priest in a cope to Thomas Key, rector (1467–75); monuments to Adam Airay, rector (d. 1658); Katherine (d. 1671), wife of Thomas Lamplugh, rector; Robert Benn, rector (d. 1752); and tablets to William Westcar (d. 1806); to John Knipe, rector (d. 1845), and to George Riggs, rector (d. 1855).[47]

It is recorded in 1552 that the church owned among other things one silver and one gilt chalice, and there were four great bells and a sanctus bell.[48] The

plate now (1956) includes a large gilt chalice and paten cover (1670) given by Thomas Lamplugh.[49] The present tower has a ring of five bells, of which two are 17th-century and two 18th-century. The sanctus bell is dated 1793.[50]

The registers date from 1577. There are churchwardens' accounts from 1747.

In the churchyard are the pediment and shaft of an early cross, raised on three steps.[51]

NONCONFORMITY. No record has been found of Roman Catholicism.

No Protestant dissenters are recorded in the Compton Census of 1676, although in 1668 the rector, Thomas Lamplugh, had written that there was scarcely a parish around Charlton which was not infected by the sectarian influence from Bicester. 'Unless speedily suppressed', dissenters would grow so numerous 'that I dread the event'.[52]

There is no further record of dissent until the beginning of the 19th century, when both the Baptists and the Methodists acquired a considerable following. In 1802 the Methodists had a meeting-place at Fencott; there was no resident teacher, but some 'low mechanic' was reported to come and 'arayne men', and sometimes the meetings were addressed by James Hinton, the well-known preacher who was descended from a family long established in Charlton, which had turned to dissent in the mid-18th century.[53]

The Baptists opened their first meeting-house in 1810,[54] and the present stone chapel in the village street was built in 1835; by 1851 the congregation numbered 55.[55] The chapel is still in use and is a member of the Oxford Fellowship.[56]

The Methodists registered a meeting-place in Charlton in 1829[57] and in 1840 a chapel was built. The congregation was small, only about 30 in 1851, and the chapel ceased being used towards the end of the century.[58] In 1920 it was sold for £30 to the rector for a club room. It is still standing, but now unused.[59]

In 1829 a barn in Murcott and in 1834 a barn in Fencott, the latter belonging to Thomas Wainwright, publican, were registered for worship.[60] In 1845 a Primitive Methodist chapel was built in Murcott.[61] The trust deeds date from 1843, and the trustees included a shoemaker and three Murcott labourers.[62] This chapel, now Methodist, is in the Oxford Circuit and has twenty members.[63]

With these three chapels, in the mid-19th century Charlton was a nonconformist centre, and people from other parishes, such as Oddington, used to

[39] Oxf. Archd. Oxon. d 13, f. 36; Dunkin, *Oxon.* i. 208; Oxf. Archd. Oxon. c 59, f. 333.
[40] Parker, *Guide*, 10, 12.
[41] MS. Top. Oxon. c 103, ff. 225–7. The estimate was £270.
[42] *Kelly's Dir. Oxon.* (1891); ibid. (1939) is incorrect.
[43] For screen see O.A.S. *Rep.* 1900, 19; *Arch. Jnl.* lxvii. 180–2, with two photographs, and *intra*, plate facing p. 78.
[44] E. S. Bouchier, *Notes on Stained Glass of Oxford District*, 66; Bodl. G.A. Oxon. 4° 685, p. 83.
[45] For them see L. Haberly, *Mediaeval English Paving-tiles*, pl. 40, &c.
[46] Buckler drawing in MS. Top. Oxon. a 66, f. 152.
[47] For arms on monuments see Bodl. G.A. Oxon. 16° 217, pp. 94a, 94b; ibid. 4° 685, pp. 83–84.
[48] *Chant. Cert.* 79.

[49] Evans, *Ch. Plate.*
[50] *Ch. Bells Oxon.* i. 84.
[51] For illustration see MS. Top. Oxon. a 38, f. 44.
[52] *Cal. S.P. Dom.* 1668–9, 151.
[53] Oxf. Dioc. c 327, p. 293; Dunkin, *Oxon.* i. 230–5.
[54] Regent's Park Coll. Libr.: Pamphlet by W. Bottoms and W. Stevens, *New Inn Road Chapel.*
[55] Oxf. Dioc. c 643, p. 6; H.O. 129/158.
[56] *Baptist Handbk. 1955*, p. 146.
[57] Oxf. Dioc. c 645, f. 130.
[58] Ibid. c 643, p. 80; H.O. 129/158; *Kelly's Dir. Oxon.* (1887 and 1903).
[59] Inf. Chairman Oxf. District.
[60] Oxf. Dioc. c 645, ff. 129, 131.
[61] Ibid. c 647, f. 28.
[62] Cowley Road Methodist Ch.
[63] *Methodist Ch. Oxf. Circuit Plan*, no. 273 (1954).

come there. Towards the end of the century there was still a fairly large nonconformist community.[64]

SCHOOLS. In 1759 it was reported that the rector was teaching a few children reading and writing at his own expense, but no further teaching is recorded until 1815, when about fifteen children were taught reading during the winter months, and when the farmers were said to be too poor to pay for a school.[65] There was no elementary school in 1819,[66] but by 1833 there were four day schools with 70 pupils in all, paid for by their parents.[67] In 1854 the rector reported that he supported two dame schools, but that the parish was unwilling to pay for a proper school: some farmers sent their sons to Dr. South's School at Islip.[68]

The inclosure award of 1858 set aside a plot of land for a school,[69] and in 1866 Charlton Parochial School and a master's house were built, mainly at the expense of the rector.[70] In 1871 there were 55 children attending, drawn from Fencott and Murcott as well as Charlton.[71] Numbers had risen to 81 by 1889, and in 1892 an additional classroom was built.[72] Occasional grants were received from the National Society. The school had 133 pupils in 1906,[73] and in 1937, after its reorganization as a junior school, 46. It became a controlled school in 1951, and had 60 pupils in 1954.[74]

CHARITIES. Alice Coales (d. 1616) left by her will £1 for the poor of Charlton: of the annual interest 1s. 6d. was to be given to the poor, and 6d. to the bellringers on Coronation Day. John Poole (d. 1688) bequeathed £5, the interest on which was to be distributed to the poor on St. Thomas's Day.

By his will, of unknown date, William Halton, Vicar of Probus (Cornw.) from 1679,[75] left £20 as a poor stock. Thomas Lamplugh, Archbishop of York and a former Rector of Charlton, by will dated 1691, left £5 to the poor of Charlton. Dr. Thomas Yates, Rector of Charlton, by will dated 1721 left £10, the interest on which was to be distributed to the poor of Charlton each Ascension Day. These bequests were held as a poor stock of £41 until 1724, when £38 was spent on the purchase of property, which later appears as three cottages. They were occupied rent-free by poor people until about 1810, when a rent of £5 5s. was paid out of the poor rates.[76]

To the £3 left in 1724 was added £10 left by Dr. Yates's widow, by a will dated 1746, and £10 left by John Lowry, Rector of Charlton, by his will dated 1784. Of this £23 all but 10s.—which was unaccounted for—was spent on road repairs at some time after 1786. In 1810 it was acknowledged that the parish owed the poor £22 10s., and in the following year £3 10s. 7d. was paid for repairs to the cottages and £18 11s. 5d. was put to pay for the erection of a coal-house for the poor—the parish paying 18s. 9d. interest each year to the charity funds.

Between 1811 and 1817 the rent of the cottages and the interest on the £18 11s. 5d., together with liberal contributions from the rector, John Knipe, were used to supply the poor with cheap coal. Under the Otmoor inclosure award of 1815 an allotment of about ¾ acre was made to the poor of Charlton in right of the cottages. The draining and fencing of the allotment cost nearly £30, paid off by 1824, and the funds were thereafter again used to provide cheap coal. The allotment was let at £1 10s. a year.[77] In the late 19th century there were four cottages, and the rents paid into the fuel fund amounted to about £8 a year.[78]

Besides their bequests to the poor of Charlton, Archbishop Lamplugh left £5 and Dr. Yates, Mrs. Yates, and John Lowry left £10 each to the poor of Fencott and Murcott. Richard Phillips, by will dated 1781, bequeathed £3, and before 1786 further sums of £10 and £7 10s. came from unknown donors. By 1824, however, £23 15s. had been lost. In 1818 an acre of land on Otmoor costing £60 was bought and later paid for out of the charity money. The acre was let at £2 10s. a year, which was spent on coal for the poor at Christmas.[79]

George Hayton, rector 1884–95, is said to have augmented the parish charities. By 1954 the poor's cottages were under a demolition order. The poor's field was let annually by auction at the parish meeting. The annual income of all the charities, now united as 'the charity of Hayton and others', was about £10, which was distributed from time to time at the discretion of the trustees.[80]

CHESTERTON

THE parish formerly covered an area of about 2,527 acres, of which 188 were detached from the rest and lay between Charlton and Weston-on-the-Green.[1] In 1932 the detached portion was transferred to Weston parish, while to Chesterton were added 986 acres from Bicester King's End, enlarging it to 3,325 acres.[2] The ancient parish was curiously shaped, for a narrow arm of land projected southwards from Akeman Street almost to Wendlebury village. In the 18th century its extent was said to be about six miles.[3] A feeder of the Ray formed the boundary on the extreme east, the Gallows Brook part of the western boundary, and the Gagle Brook used to separate the parish on the north-east from the former

64 Wilb. Visit.; Oxf. Dioc. c 344.
65 Oxf. Dioc. d 555; ibid. d 707.
66 Educ. of Poor, 721.
67 Educ. Enq. Abstract, 743.
68 Wilb. Visit.
69 O.R.O. Incl. award.
70 Kelly's Dir. Oxon. (1887).
71 Elem. Educ. Ret.
72 Ret. of Sch.; Kelly's Dir. Oxon. (1920).
73 Vol. Sch. Ret.
74 Inf. Oxon. Educ. Cttee.
75 Foster, Alumni.

76 12th Rep. Com. Char. 298–9; Char. Don. ii. 989.
77 12th Rep. Com. Char. 299–300.
78 Gen. Digest Char.
79 12th Rep. Com. Char. 300–1; Char. Don. ii. 989.
80 Inf. the Revd. J. F. B. Chitty.
1 This detached portion is on O.S. Map 6″, xxvii (1885) but it is not clear how or when it became part of Chesterton: it is not on map of c. 1760 in O.R.O.
2 Census, 1931; Oxon. Review Order (1932): copy in O.R.O. For ancient par. see O.S. Map 6″, xxii, xxiii, xxvii, xxviii (1900); cf. ibid. 2½″, 42/51, 52 (1951).
3 Oxf. Dioc. d 552.

hamlet of Bignell in the parish of Bicester King's End.[4]

The land rises gradually from just over 200 feet in the south-east to over 300 feet in the north-east. The greater part lies on the Cornbrash, but the Forest Marble, Great Oolite, and Oxford Clay are exposed in places.[5] The soil is mainly stony limestone. Woodland, three furlongs square, was recorded in Domesday.[6] A carucate called 'le Shortwood' in the 13th century was then partly pasture, but at the end of that century there were at least 80 acres of woodland, which may have been the manor park.[7] The deer here were killed in about 1590, when the woodland was mostly cleared and divided into closes; by 1760 there were only 12 acres of wood,[8] and in 1955 there was none apart from a couple of recently planted coppices.

The main road from Oxford to Brackley, a road of considerable importance throughout the Middle Ages, crosses the parish as does the Roman Akeman Street, which is now a modern road connecting Kirtlington with Bicester.

The site of the village is interesting: it lies close to the parish boundary, and its houses are mainly along a line parallel with the Gagle Brook.[9] The name Chesterton suggests that the Saxons named it after the nearby Roman settlement of Alchester.[10] The medieval village may have been grouped round a green, since taken into the grounds of the present Chesterton Lodge; its nucleus at all events was clearly the church and the manor-house, now Manor Farm, which lie between the brook and the mill on the east and the village street on the west.

Judging from the early 14th-century tax assessments,[11] it seems to have been fairly large and prosperous, and in the 17th century there were a number of substantial farm-houses besides the manor-house and the Vicarage. One was taxed in 1665 on five hearths and seven on three or four.[12] By the beginning of the 19th century there were 73 houses in Chesterton and its hamlet Little Chesterton, and 99 by the middle of the century.[13] Correspondence between the vicar and New College in 1859 reveals that some of the cottages which had been built on the waste were 'more like pig styes' at this time, but much was later done by the Earl of Jersey to improve the cottages on the manor estate.[14] Increasing population was accompanied by the opening of new public houses: the 'Ball', formerly the 'Blue Ball', the 'Red Cow', and the 'Fox and Hounds' are mentioned in 1853.[15] Only one had been licensed in 1774. In the 19th and 20th centuries the village spread northwards along the main road. There stand the 19th-century school and reading-room, and the sixteen cheerfully coloured council houses, constructed since 1945.[16]

The older cottages, one bearing the date 1769, are rubble-built; many have casement windows and thatched or stone-slated roofs. The 'Red Cow' dates mainly from the late 17th or early 18th century: it is of two stories with ashlar quoins and has an attic dormer. The date 1790 with the initials J.C. is inscribed over the doorway. Home Farm in the main street is probably also 17th-century in origin; the extension at the back with its stone slates is the oldest part. Manor Farm, a two-storied house with attic dormers, stands on the site of the original manor-house. It is built of coursed rubble, is roofed with brown tiles, and has brick chimney-stacks. Although much restored, it probably dates from about 1700. In the 16th century it was the home of the Maundes,[17] but by 1665 seems to have been reduced in size, for the Earl of Lindsey, who then owned it, returned only two hearths for the tax.[18] In the 1680's it was occupied by James Bertie, the 1st Earl of Abingdon,[19] and early in the 18th century was restored and modernized, according to Dunkin, when it became the home of some of the younger members of the Abingdon family. It is no doubt the 'gentleman's house' marked on a map of 1705.[20] Soon after the death in 1734 of the Hon. Captain Henry Bertie, M.P., the manor-house was let as a hunting-box. Before the end of the century part of the house was pulled down and the rest was turned into a farm. In Dunkin's day the large tithe barn was still standing and had been roofed by the Berties with the ancient roof of the hall of Notley Abbey (Bucks.).[21] In 1630 it measured 20 feet by 70 feet.[22]

The Old Vicarage to the north of the manor-house was enlarged by John Burton, vicar between 1720 and 1726, but it has been much restored and had a new south-east wing added in 1859.[23] It is a two-storied house of coursed rubble with a roof of stone slates; its north-west side is the oldest.

Dunkin states that in the early 18th century there was a mansion house at the south-east end of the village.[24] The building and its pleasure-grounds were improved in the middle of the century by Francis Penrose,[25] and still further at the end of the century, when George Clarke, Sheriff of Oxfordshire in 1801, obtained permission to turn the line of the road (i.e. Akeman Street) and so extend his grounds. By 1823 the house was the principal mansion in the village.[26] Clarke's son, George Rochfort Clarke, lived there for many years, but it was unoccupied in 1887 and was replaced by the present house, built in 1889–90 for Henry Tubb, the Bicester banker; by 1939 Chesterton Lodge, as it was called, had become the property of the Royal Exchange Assurance Corporation,[27] and by 1955 it was a preparatory school for boys and girls called Audley House.

[4] See above, p. 19.   [5] G.S. Map 1″, xlv SE.
[6] V.C.H. Oxon. i. 418.
[7] Fines Oxon. 200, 220; C 133/97.
[8] New Coll. Arch. Chesterton deeds (1641); O.R.O. J VII/1.
[9] O.S. Map 25″, xxiii. 9 (1875).
[10] P.N. Oxon. (E.P.N.S.), i, pp. xvii, 206.
[11] See below, p. 96.
[12] Hearth Tax Oxon. 198. The vicar Philip French had a house with 3 hearths.
[13] Census, 1811, 1851, 1901.
[14] New Coll. Arch.; Wing, Annals, 54.
[15] O.R.O. Victlrs.' recog.; Lascelles' Oxf. Dir. (1853), 109.
[16] Inf. Ploughley R.D.C.
[17] See below, p. 97.

[18] Hearth Tax Oxon. 198.
[19] Cal. S.P. Dom. 1684–5, 184, 186, 203; Hist. MSS. Com. 9th Rep. App. II, 457.
[20] Dunkin, Oxon. i. 244, 271; Benjamin Cole, Map of 20 Miles Round Oxf. (1705).
[21] Dunkin, Oxon. i. 244. The roof timbers are now in the hall of the Manor House Hotel, Weston-on-the-Green. For Capt. Bertie, see W. R. Williams, Parl Hist. of Oxford, 123–4.
[22] New Coll. Arch. Bk. of Evidence, ff. 345–6.
[23] Ibid.; Oxf. Dioc. d 178.
[24] Dunkin, Oxon. i. 273.
[25] See below, p. 94.
[26] Dunkin, Oxon. i. 273.
[27] Gardner, Dir. Oxon.; Kelly's Dir. Oxon. (1869, 1887, 1895, 1939).

Little Chesterton hamlet grew up along the stream at the southern extremity of the parish and about half a mile from Chesterton. In the 18th century it was called 'Little Town' and had eleven houses.[28] By 1955 it was almost a 'lost' hamlet: out of its fifteen cottages nine, stone-built in the late 18th century, were empty, their former inhabitants having moved to the new council houses in Great Chesterton; Grange Farm, a two-storied house built of coursed rubble in about 1700, had been derelict since 1946 and had recently been replaced by a new farm-house on a different site; the 19th-century Tower Farm still survived.[29]

The parish as it was before the recent boundary changes had nine outlying farm-houses, all apparently built after the inclosure of the open fields in 1768. Except for Chestertonfields Farm (College Farm), none is shown on Davis's map of 1797[30] and their buildings appear to date from the 19th century.

The parish is distinguished for its many outstanding incumbents, notably the famous 12th-century writer Gerald de Barry (c. 1146–c. 1223);[31] for its association in the 17th and 18th centuries with the Bertie family and the earls of Abingdon, and in the 18th and 19th centuries with the earls of Jersey.[32] An 18th-century resident, Francis Penrose (1718–98), was an archaeologist and a medical and scientific writer of some repute.[33] More celebrated was the Chesterton oak, which was said to contain 700 cubic feet of timber; it was purchased in about 1840 and converted into church furniture by the Revd. W. C. Risley of Deddington.[34]

MANORS. An estate at Chesterton may have belonged to the Anglo-Saxon alderman Æthelmar. Among the lands which he gave to his new foundation of Eynsham Abbey in 1005 were some which he had obtained from his kinsman Godwin in exchange for 5 *mansae* at 'Stodleye' and 10 at 'Cestertune'. It is possible, however, that this 'Cestertune' was Chesterton in Warwickshire, or Chastleton, often confused with Chesterton.[35] Immediately before the Conquest the Oxfordshire *CHESTERTON* was held by Wigod; by 1086 it was part of the possessions of Miles Crispin,[36] and it belonged to the honor of Wallingford until the end of the 13th century when it was no longer listed among the fees of the honor.[37] Miles Crispin's tenant at the time of the Domesday survey was the same William who held under him

at Adwell and Henton, at Betterton and Sulham (Berks.), and at Bradwell (Bucks.)[38], and who as 'William de Suleham' granted certain tithes to Abingdon Abbey.[39] William's lands passed to Aumary, the Domesday tenant of Britwell Salome, who may either have married William's daughter or have been William's younger brother.[40] Aumary was dead by 1130 and his lands were divided between his sons Ralph and Robert, Chesterton and Betterton falling to the latter's share.[41] Ralph seems to have been the elder son, and his descendants from time to time confirmed the various gifts made to religious houses by the junior branch of the family.[42] Although at the end of the 12th century the lord of the honor of Wallingford had the custody of Chesterton and the wardship of its heir during a minority (see below), the senior branch may not have given up all claim to mesne lordship in Chesterton, for in 1247 William of Sulham recognized Ralph of Chesterton's lawful possession of lands in the manor.[43]

Robert son of Aumary, tenant of Chesterton manor, gave lands to the monks of Otley at Oddington in 1137, and in about 1151–4, after the removal of their house to Thame, he granted them a large estate in his manor. By his wife Yvice, Robert had at least four sons, William, Robert, Ralph, and Henry. Yvice and William were dead by the date of Robert's grant to Thame,[44] and he was succeeded, perhaps about 1166, by his son Robert, who confirmed his gifts to the abbey and himself gave more lands in the manor about 1170.[45] Robert the younger may have been dead by 1173,[46] and Chesterton passed to his brother Ralph, a benefactor of Oseney Abbey as well as of Thame.[47] Ralph died about 1189 leaving as his heir a son Robert, who was a minor. In 1193 Chesterton was in the custody of Gerard de Camville, Count John's keeper of the honor of Wallingford,[48] but in the following year King Richard entrusted the wardship of Robert and the custody of his fees to William de Ste Mère Église, later to become Bishop of London.[49] Robert was of age by 1207[50] and in 1212 held 3 fees in the honor of Wallingford—2 at Chesterton and 1 at Betterton.[51] Robert held Chesterton until 1222 when he entered religion and when the wardship of his son Ralph was granted to William, Archdeacon of London.[52] By 1229 Ralph had been transferred to the custody of Henry Foliot,[53] and by 1235 he was of age and in

---

28 Oxf. Dioc. d 552.
29 Local inf.
30 Oxf. Dioc. d 558; Davis, *Oxon. Map.*
31 See below, p. 101.
32 Below, p. 95.
33 *D.N.B.*; see below, p. 339.
34 Wing, *Annals*, 57.
35 *Eynsham Cart.* i, pp. vii, 21–22. White Kennett (*Paroch. Antiq.* i. 46) identifies 'Stodleye' with Studley in Beckley and Chesterton with the Oxon. Chesterton. H. E. Salter has suggested Studley and Chesterton in Warwickshire as the places intended. The Oxfordshire Studley was not a Domesday village and the identification with Studley (Warws.) is therefore more likely, and the identification with Chesterton (Warws.) is not impossible, though it was given in 1043 by Earl Leofric to Coventry Abbey (*V.C.H. Warws.* v. 42). Chastleton is another possible identification. Henry d'Oilly's grant of land there (c. 1152–4) to Eynsham may have been by way of restitution (*Eynsham Cart.* i. 74).
36 *V.C.H. Oxon.* i. 418.
37 *Boarstall Cart.* 325.
38 Ibid.; *V.C.H. Oxon.* i 383, 418. A charter, dated

1087(?) by H. E. Salter (*E.H.R.* xl. 75), says that Chesterton was held by Hugh, whereas in Domesday all 3 manors were held by William. Salter (ibid. 74) says this Hugh was son of Miles, alive in 1116 or 1117 and a knight of Brian FitzCount.
39 *Chron. Abingdon*, ii. 141.
40 *Boarstall Cart.* 325; Farrer, *Honors*, i. 215.
41 *Boarstall Cart.* 325; *Red. Bk. Exch.* (Rolls Ser.), 309.
42 e.g. *Thame Cart.* 129–30; *Oseney Cart.* vi. 32–33.
43 *Fines Oxon.* 144.
44 *Thame Cart.* 122, 128–9; for Otley, see below, p. 279.
45 *Thame Cart.* 129; *Oseney Cart.* vi. 30–32.
46 Farrer, *Honors*, i. 215.
47 *Oseney Cart.* vi. 33; *Thame Cart.* 130–1.
48 Farrer, *Honors*, i. 216; *Giraldi Cambrensis Opera* (Rolls Ser.), i. 262.
49 *Giraldi Camb. Op.* i. 263; *Rot. de Ob et Fin.* (Rec. Com.), 169, 309; *Pipe R.* 1204 (P.R.S. N.S. xviii), 12.
50 *Fines*, ed. J. Hunter (Rec. Com.), i. 141.
51 *Red. Bk. Exch.* 146; *Bk. of Fees*, 118.
52 *Fines Oxon.* 51–53, 55; *Boarstall Cart.* 325; *Rot. Lit. Claus.* (Rec. Com.), i. 489.
53 *Ex. e Rot. Fin.* (Rec. Com.), i. 188.

possession of Chesterton.[54] Ralph died in 1268, leaving a widow Iseult,[55] and was succeeded by another Ralph, probably his son, who was holding Chesterton in 1271.[56] The younger Ralph died in 1273, leaving as his heir a daughter Sarah, wife of John le Bret,[57] but some time in the year before his death he had sold Chesterton to Edmund, Earl of Cornwall.[58]

In 1283 Edmund founded Ashridge College (Herts.)[59] and between 1285[60] and 1291 he added Chesterton to his original endowment of that house.[61] In the latter year the possessions of Ashridge in Chesterton were valued at £12 14s. 7d. a year.[62] For some years after the death of Edmund of Cornwall in 1300 his widow Margaret claimed a third of the manor in dower against Ashridge, but apparently without success.[63] In 1309 Ashridge was granted free warren in Chesterton[64] and in 1320 the college was permitted to purchase lands in the manor which had previously been held of it in fee.[65] Ashridge College held the manor, valued at £27 13s. 2½d. a year in 1535,[66] until its dissolution in 1539.

In 1279 Edmund of Cornwall's manor had comprised the two villages of Great and Little Chesterton.[67] Although the manor held by Ashridge was called simply 'Chesterton' it did not include Little Chesterton, and in 1316 the college shared the parish with Rewley Abbey.[68] Rewley's manor of *LITTLE CHESTERTON* had its origin in the estates acquired from 1137 onwards by Thame Abbey from Robert son of Aumary and his descendants. The abbey had a grange at Chesterton and its possessions were rated as 1 hide.[69] Robert of Chesterton exchanged some lands in the manor with the abbot in 1219,[70] and although the abbey lands were not specifically mentioned in the hundredal returns of 1279, they were probably among the free holdings recorded.[71] In 1291, however, Thame had no possessions in Chesterton, whereas Rewley held lands and rents there worth £1 16s. a year.[72] Rewley was founded by Edmund of Cornwall in 1281,[73] and although no record of the transfer of the estate to the new abbey has survived, it is probable that Little Chesterton passed from the one Cistercian house to the other with Edmund's approval.[74] Rewley held Little Chesterton or Chesterton Grange until the Dissolution, when it was worth £7 16s. 8d. a year in rents.[75]

In 1537 Henry VIII granted the former possessions of Rewley Abbey in Little Chesterton to Sir Thomas Pope,[76] who reunited Chesterton manor by obtaining in 1540 the lands which had belonged to Ashridge College, and to three Oxfordshire houses —Oseney Abbey, Bicestor Priory, and Studley Priory.[77] At some time between 1546 and 1557[78] the manor passed from Sir Thomas Pope to John, Lord Williams of Thame, who held it until his death in 1559.[79] By the terms of Lord Williams's will Chesterton passed to his younger daughter Margery and her husband Henry, later Lord Norreys.[80] Henry died in 1601 and was succeeded by his grandson Francis, created Earl of Berkshire in 1621, on whose death in 1622 Chesterton passed to Elizabeth, his daughter and heiress.[81] The manor was eventually brought to the Bertie family by the marriage about 1653 of Bridget, only daughter of Elizabeth Norreys and her husband Edward Wray, to Montagu Bertie, Earl of Lindsey.[82] Bridget's son James Bertie, a boy of four at the time of her death in 1657, succeeded her, and in 1682 was created Earl of Abingdon.[83]

In 1764 the manor was sold by the trustees of Willoughby, 3rd Earl of Abingdon, who had died in 1760, to George, Duke of Marlborough, for £13,000.[84] In 1808 the duke sold it to George Villiers, Earl of Jersey, for £51,000.[85] The manor then followed the descent of the Earldom of Jersey.[86] Manorial rights finally lapsed when the Jersey estates in Chesterton were split up and sold in 1920–1.

LESSER ESTATES. About 1166 Robert son of Aumary granted a hide in Chesterton to Amfridus, son of Richard of Oxford, to be held as $\frac{1}{5}$ knight's fee. Within a few years Amfridus, with the assent of his lord Robert son of Robert, granted this estate to Oseney Abbey. Ralph of Chesterton added a small piece of ground[87] and by 1280, when it was being administered as part of the abbey's bailiwick of Weston, the estate was bringing in a rent of £1 4s. a year.[88] In the early 16th century the Oseney lands were rented for £2 a year,[89] which was their recorded value at the Dissolution.[90] Studley Priory had lands in Chesterton by 1227,[91] and may have later acquired others—possibly from its patron Edmund of Cornwall—for at the Dissolution it had £1 6s. 8d. a year in rents in Chesterton.[92] In 1291 Bicester Priory held lands worth 5s. a year,[93] which it may

[54] *Fines Oxon.* 100; *Bk. of Fees*, 445.
[55] *Ex. e Rot. Fin.* (Rec. Com.), ii. 405, 586.
[56] *Fines Oxon.* 200.
[57] *Cal. Inq. p.m.* ii, p. 25.
[58] *Rot. Hund.* (Rec. Com.), ii. 826; cf. *Fines Oxon.* 204, 220.
[59] *V.C.H. Bucks.* i. 386.
[60] *Fines Oxon.* 220; *Cal. Chart. R. 1257–1300,* 325; *Feud. Aids,* iv. 158.
[61] *Cal. Chart. R. 1257–1300,* 405–6; *Dugd. Mon.* vi (1), 515.
[62] *Tax. Eccl.* (Rec. Com.), 45.
[63] *Cal. Inq. p.m.* iii, pp. 484, 487, 488; *Cal. Pat. 1301–7,* 197.
[64] *Cal. Chart. R. 1300–26,* 131.
[65] *Cal. Pat. 1317–21,* 522.
[66] *Valor Eccl.* (Rec. Com.), iv. 225.
[67] *Rot. Hund.* (Rec. Com.), ii. 826.
[68] *Feud. Aids,* iv. 169.
[69] *Thame Cart.* 128–9, 130–1.
[70] *Fines Oxon.* 51–53.
[71] *Rot. Hund.* (Rec. Com.), ii. 826.
[72] *Tax. Eccl.* 45.
[73] *V.C.H. Oxon.* ii. 82.

[74] See below, p. 341.
[75] *Valor Eccl.* (Rec. Com.), ii. 255.
[76] *L. & P. Hen. VIII,* xii (2), p. 350.
[77] Ibid. xv, p. 169; C 54/420/41, 42. See below, Lesser Estates.
[78] *L. & P. Hen. VIII,* xxi (1), p. 92; *Cal. Pat. 1555–7,* 238.
[79] C 142/126/150; *Complete Peerage* (orig. edn.), viii. 140–1.
[80] Dunkin, *Oxon.* i. 269.
[81] C.P. 43/72/9; C 142/399/153; for Norreys family see *Complete Peerage,* ix. 645–9.
[82] *Hearth Tax Oxon.* 168; Dunkin, *Oxon.* i. 270.
[83] For earls of Abingdon see *Complete Peerage,* i. 45 sqq.
[84] O.R.O. J II a/27–30.
[85] Ibid. a/35–37.
[86] *Complete Peerage,* vii. 91 sqq.; Burke, *Peerage* (1953).
[87] *Oseney Cart.* vi. 29–33.
[88] Ibid. 192; cf. *Tax. Eccl.* 45.
[89] *Oseney Cart.* vi. 230, 258.
[90] *Valor Eccl.* (Rec. Com.), ii. 216.
[91] *Fines Oxon.* 82.
[92] *Valor Eccl.* ii. 186.
[93] *Tax. Eccl.* (Rec. Com.), 45.

have been given by Ralph of Chesterton about 1244.[94] At the Dissolution they were still worth 5s. a year.[95]

ECONOMIC HISTORY. The Anglo-Saxons, attracted by the Roman road, Akeman Street, and the excellent water-supply, probably settled at Chesterton at an early date.[96] By the time of Domesday, 12 plough-lands were said to be in use, although there was land for 16 ploughs.[97] The demesne had 2 ploughs and 2 serfs working on it, while outside 22 villeins (villani) and 10 bordars shared 10 ploughs. The manor also had 39 acres of meadow and a wood, 3 furlongs square. The whole estate, with a mill worth 10s., was valued at £10 as it had been before the Conquest.

The deeds of two religious houses add further information about the early agrarian history of Chesterton. A charter of 1137 shows Robert son of Aumary, the lord of the manor, giving the monks of Otley (later Thame) Abbey a part of his demesne by Curtlicgrave;[98] about fifteen years later he granted more of his demesne (70 a. of 'inland' in all); 20 acres of common land ('warland') by Akeman Street; the meadow near the bridge to Weston; and 10 acres of his demesne meadow. He also gave common for 300 sheep, 16 oxen, and 6 cows; and 20 cartloads of wood.[99] Robert's second grant, it may be noted, was made with the consent of his family, that of the parish priest and his son, and also with the consent of all the villeins. A few years later Robert's son Robert gave another 69 acres of arable (rated at ½ hide), and meadow land as well.[1] Thame's property in Chesterton was finally stabilized in about 1178, when Ralph, the brother of Robert (II), allowed the monks a small meadow opposite the door of their grange in exchange for other meadow, and permitted them to keep their sheepfold there provided they took steps to prevent the sheep from damaging his land.[2] The abbey's grange was probably on the site of the present-day Grange Farm. Its inclosed meadow covered 12 acres; it also had 10 acres in the common meadow and 169 acres of arable. Careful regulations were laid down in a fine of 1219 about the abbot's pasture rights. He was allowed to keep 360 sheep, 19 rams, and 16 cattle in the common pasture, but he renounced all rights in the great meadow, the later Asthills, which was a part of Robert's demesne.[3]

Of the land which Oseney acquired in about 1170 2 virgates had been held in villeinage in the 1160's and there were 64 acres of demesne, with 16 acres of meadow.[4] When Oseney received its holding of 4 virgates, the land was all held in villeinage,[5] but the abbey seems to have turned the former demesne virgates back into demesne.[6]

Information about the progress of these two monastic estates is missing from the survey of 1279.

The whole account is sketchy compared with those of other parishes, perhaps because Chesterton was part of the Earl of Cornwall's honor. There were 70 virgates in the manor, 48 in Great Chesterton and 22 in Little Chesterton. In the former the earl held 12 in demesne, an unusually large amount, while 24 were held in villeinage, 8 were held freely and 4 belonged to the church. In Little Chesterton 8 virgates were held in villeinage and 14 freely, partly no doubt by Oseney and Thame. There were also 28 villein cottagers in Great Chesterton, while the smith was a free cottager, holding 7 acres of land, of which one was meadow.[7]

An extent of the main manor, made in 1304 soon after it had been given to Ashridge, shows that it was large and valuable.[8] Valued at £42 13s. 4d., it contained over 50 virgates, and had perhaps between 60 and 70 tenants. The demesne, where the convent had a grange, produced about a quarter of the whole sum.[9] It consisted of 13 virgates, each valued at 10s.; 20 acres of meadow worth 2s. 6d. an acre or £2 10s. in all; inclosed meadow, partly in Shortwood, worth £2 9s.; 2 mills and 2 dovehouses. On the other hand 7 small free tenants held 7 virgates for rents amounting to £1 2s. 7d., and over half the income from the manor (£22 6s. 8d.) came from the 33½ virgates held in villeinage, each virgate, including rents and services, being valued at 13s. 4d. There were also 29 cottages, worth £2 17s. in all.

There are no similar extents for the Rewley[10] (formerly Thame) and Oseney estates, but there is evidence that these too had granted away a part of their demesne land before the end of the 13th century. In 1280 Oseney was leasing a part for £1 4s., while the rest was kept in demesne and farmed with the grange of Weston.[11] By 1291 Rewley had land and rent in Chesterton worth £1 16s., while the produce and stock from its demesne was worth £2 10s.[12] Later both houses followed the common practice of leasing all the demesne. At the end of the 14th century Rewley's land was already all leased out.[13] By 1535 it was receiving £7 16s. 8d. from a tenant for Grange Farm. Oseney's 4 virgates were leased for £2 at the same date.[14]

Early-14th-century tax assessment lists point to a large and prosperous community. Forty-four householders were assessed in 1316, the fourth largest number in the hundred; of these 26 had goods taxed at over 3s., an unusually high proportion.[15] The figures for 1327, and for 1344 when there had been a reassessment, bear out this impression of prosperity.[16] After Bicester and Bletchingdon, Chesterton with an assessment of £6 6s. 2d. in 1344 was taxed the highest in the hundred. For the poll tax of 1377 Chesterton's return of 79 taxpayers was comparatively high.[17]

The system of landholding changed greatly

[94] Kennett, Paroch. Antiq. i. 329–31; Dunkin, Oxon. i. 261.
[95] Valor Eccl. ii. 188.
[96] P.N. Oxon. (E.P.N.S.), i, pp. xvii, 206; see above, p. 92.
[97] V.C.H. Oxon. i. 418.
[98] Thame Cart. ii. 128.
[99] Ibid. 128–9. The 'warland' rated at ½ hide had certain services attached; the demesne was free of services.
[1] Ibid. 128–9.
[2] Ibid. 130–1.
[3] Fines Oxon. 51–53.
[4] See above, p. 95; Oseney Cart. vi. 31.
[5] Oseney Cart. vi. 30.
[6] Ibid. 29.
[7] Rot. Hund. (Rec. Com.), ii. 826.
[8] C 133/97.
[9] E 179/161/10.
[10] See above, p. 95.
[11] Oseney Cart. vi. 192–3.
[12] Tax. Eccl. (Rec. Com.), 45.
[13] Cal. Papal L. v. 161, 393.
[14] Oseney Cart. vi. 230; Valor Eccl. (Rec. Com.), ii. 216, 254.
[15] E 179/161/8.
[16] Ibid. 9, 17; E 164/7.
[17] E 179/161/39.

between the 14th and 16th centuries. In the 16th century, for example, Oseney Abbey's 4 virgates which had once been held by 4 villeins were rented by one tenant.[18] A survey of the manor made in 1589 shows that the average holding was larger than the normal medieval holding of a virgate.[19] Twelve copyholders held 37 virgates divided into two holdings of 4 virgates each, eight of about 3 virgates and two of 2 virgates each. Only six tenants had small holdings of mostly a few acres each. The copy usually ran for the life of the holder and his son, and the rent was roughly at the rate of 8s. a virgate. Fines paid on entry varied from about £1 10s. to £10.

Two important leaseholders at this time were John Bourne,[20] the tenant of Grange farm, and William Maunde, the tenant of the manor. The latter's property consisted of the house now called Manor Farm, the fishponds and water-mill, 170 acres of common field land, about 100 acres of meadow including the Asthills, and common for 280 sheep.[21] In addition, he usually farmed the tithes.[22] The Maundes had been in the parish since the late 13th century, when a William Maunde held a virgate freely.[23] By the early 16th century John Maunde with taxable goods worth over £6 was the richest man in the parish; he probably acted as bailiff for Ashridge as his son certainly did.[24] During the 16th century the family rose in social position: Simon Maunde could still be styled a yeoman in 1559, but at his death in 1578 when he left goods valued at £290, he was styled a gentleman,[25] and his son William (d. 1612) also had a coat of arms.[26] The Maundes continued to hold the leading position in the parish in the first half of the 17th century:[27] a vicar said that all their 'generation' was buried in the chancel and that without their consent no one else could be.[28] In the second half of the century they died out or left; the last Maunde in Chesterton died in 1692.[29]

The large number of surviving 17th-century court rolls show about fourteen of the leading farmers governing the parish.[30] Each year the court elected two overseers of the fields, a tithingman for both Great and Little Chesterton, and the hayward and constable. The last two were paid £4 and £1 respectively by the tenants, including widows, who contributed in proportion to the amount of land held.[31]

The rolls also throw some light on farming customs. The yardland consisted of 34 computed acres or 20 statute acres, and 5 computed or 2 statute acres of meadow. Each yardland had right of common for 30 sheep, 3 cattle (later reduced to 2),[32] and a horse, although if needed for ploughing another horse could be substituted for 2 cows; part of the fields was to be broken at Michaelmas, the rest on 1 November; no cattle were to be kept in the lot meadows or any

ploughed ground until the land was quite clear; no oxen were to be kept in the cow pasture or the balks until Lammas; hogs were to be ringed at Michaelmas, and none was to be kept in the common fields until after harvest.

A complete terrier of the parish made in the 1760's shows only 275 inclosed acres.[33] They were nearly all meadow or pasture land and had probably been inclosed since the Middle Ages. Of the 2,300 acres surveyed, 1,088 were arable land in the open fields; 112 were common meadow; and 742 were common land, roads, and lanes, the greatest part of which consisted of the unusually large common, the Old Field Leys (571 a.). At this time there were eight fields, each substantial tenant's land being divided among them, although somewhat unevenly.[34] This complicated system may have resulted from an amalgamation of separate fields belonging to Great and Little Chesterton. The name of the common, Old Field Leys, and its unusually large size, together with the fact that the number of virgates decreased from 70 in 1279[35] to 62 in the 18th century, seems to indicate that the amount of arable had decreased.

There had been remarkably little change in the pattern of landholding since the 16th century. Rather less than a third of the land was held by 18 copyholders. Of these, nine held 10 acres or less and there were eight substantial farms of over 60 acres, the largest being 130 acres. Thus, the size of the average copyhold farm had slightly increased since earlier in the century, when the average was 3 yardlands.[36] The leasehold farms of 1760 were larger: Grange farm consisted of 195 acres and some 500 other acres were divided mostly between three tenants, whereas in 1728 there had been four farms of 4 yardlands each. Only 154 acres, including the Vicarage farm of 82 acres, were held by freeholders. Thirteen cottagers with their dwellings on the waste, four of them at Little Chesterton, complete the list of inhabitants.

Manorial courts were still held, but as elsewhere they were now mainly concerned with admissions.[37] Heriots of small value were taken from copyholders, in cash rather than in kind, whereas fines on entry had become very heavy, amounting sometimes to several hundred pounds.[38] Among the tenant families there had been great changes: a comparison of lists of tenants of 1589, 1728, and 1760 shows that, as in many other Oxfordshire villages, families did not usually last for more than a hundred years.[39] Of the tenant families of 1589, only two, each holding a half-yardland, survived until 1728. And of the leading tenants of 1728, only two families were still property-holders in 1760. One of these, the Tanners, was still at Manor farm in 1955, and until shortly

[18] Oseney Cart. vi. 230.
[19] Bodl. MS. D.D. Bertie c 15.
[20] Oxon. Visit. 183, 316; cf. C 3/196/7; see below, p. 103.
[21] MS. Top. Oxon. c 381; Bodl. MS. Top. Gen. c 43–44 passim.
[22] See below, p. 100.
[23] C 133/97. See also Kennett, Paroch. Antiq. i. 491; Cal. Pat. 1313–17, 416.
[24] E 179/161/198; Valor Eccl. (Rec. Com.), iv. 226.
[25] New Coll. Arch. Bk. of Evidence, ff. 337–40; Bodl. MS. Wills Oxon. 185, f. 540.
[26] Brass in church. The Maundes were summoned to the visitation of 1634 but were not granted arms: Oxon. Visit. 334.
[27] Bodl. MS. Top. Gen. c 43–44, passim.

[28] New Coll. Arch. undated memo. by Philip French.
[29] Bodl. MS. Wills Oxon. 290 (index).
[30] Bodl. MS. D.D. Bertie c 13: Ct. R. 1623–5; Bodl. MS. Top. Gen. c 43–44 passim: Ct. R. 1631–49.
[31] Bodl. MS. Top. Gen. c 43: Ct. R. 1631, 1633.
[32] MS. Top. Oxon. c 381, f. 102.
[33] O.R.O. J IV/1: map and see reproduction on p. 98; J VII/1: terrier.
[34] See map on p. 98.
[35] Rot. Hund. (Rec. Com.), ii. 826.
[36] e.g. in 1728: MS. Top. Oxon. c 381, ff. 98–101.
[37] There are a few 18th-cent. court docs. in O.R.O. J II b/1–3.
[38] MS. Top. Oxon. b 129, ff. 8b–9.
[39] Bodl. MS. D.D. Bertie c 15; MS. Top. Oxon. c 381 ff. 98–101; O.R.O. J VII/1.

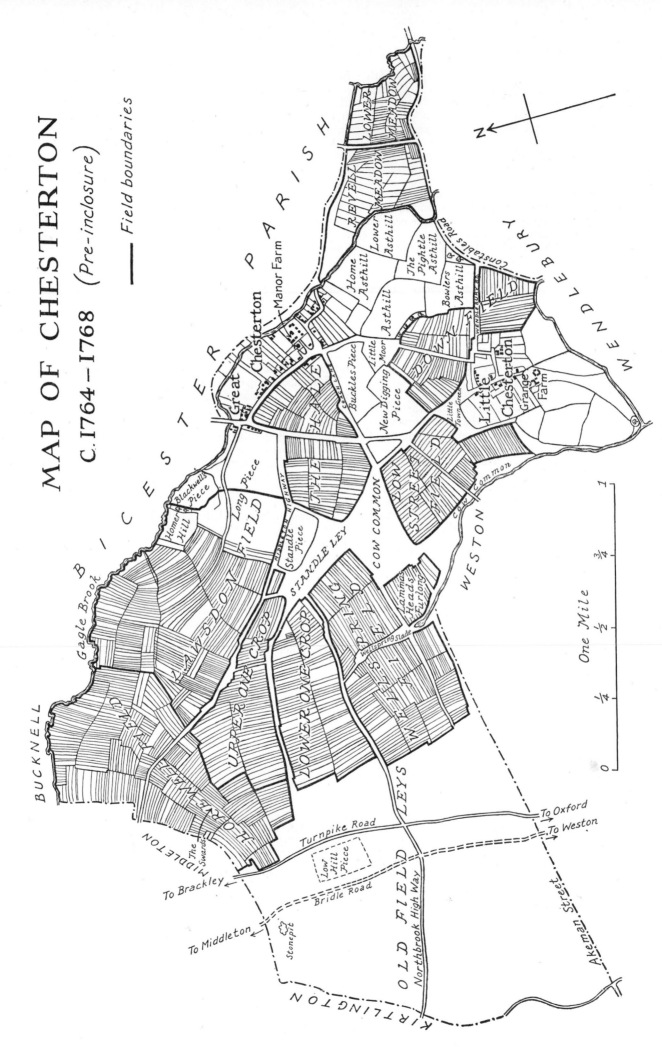

MAP OF CHESTERTON

C.1764–1768 (Pre-inclosure)

—— Field boundaries

The above map is a copy of an estate map by an unknown mapmaker

BICESTER PARISH

LOWER MEADOW

REVELY MEADOW

Manor Farm

Chesterton

Home Asthill

Lower Asthill

The Pightle Asthill

Asthill

Bowlers Asthill

Great Chesterton

Little Asthill

TOWN FIELD

KINDLE WAY

Little Chesterton

Grange Farm

Little Town Green

Buckles Piece

Little Asthill

New Digging Moor Asthill

BUCKLES PIECE

Homer Hill

Blackwells Piece

Long Piece

THE HALE

FIELD

LOW STREET FIELD

Standle Piece

MIDDLETON HIGHWAY

Standle Ley

STANDLE LEY

COW COMMON

Cow Common

WESTON WENDLEBURY

HOME CLOSE FIELD

UPPER ONE CROP

LOWER ONE CROP

WELLSPRING FIELD

Wellspring Slade

Lammas Heads Furlong

BUCKNELL

Gagle Brook

HORNWELL FIELD

The Swards

To Brackley

To Middleton

Stonepit

Turnpike Road

Low Hill Piece

Bridle Road

Northbrook High Way

OLD FIELD LEYS

To Oxford

To Weston

Akeman Street

KIRTLINGTON

MIDDLETON

One Mile
0   ¼   ½   ¾   1

before Tredwells were tenants of Grange farm as they were in 1760.

In 1768 the open fields, which were reckoned as 62 yardlands, were inclosed.[40] Out of the 1,975 acres allotted, 1,173 went to the Duke of Marlborough for his holding of 44¾ yardlands; New College got 355 acres for the great tithes and the vicar 173 for the small tithes and 4 yardlands of glebe; about 200 went to the Tanner family for land held by lease and copy; and some 50 acres went to freeholders.

As elsewhere one of the effects of inclosure was to raise rents and another to improve methods of cultivation. The total rental of the manor in 1728 had been a little over £500; this had been increased by a half by 1771 and tripled by 1807, when some 1,500 acres brought in a rent of about £1,550.[41] As for changes in cultivation, one of the chief difficulties had always been the poor, badly-drained soil. An estate agent had complained in 1728 that except for about 60 acres, the field land was 'poor loam, red, and great part of it very wett'. He also complained of insufficient meadow land and advised laying down a third of the arable with grass.[42] By 1807 the following rotation was in use: fallow for turnips; wheat; barley or oats with seeds; beans, peas, or vetches; at the end of the course a fifth of the land was to be left in seeds.[43] When New College farm (c. 350 a.) was leased in 1823, it was a condition that a quarter of the arable was to lie fallow every year, and that the tenant must lay down 30 acres yearly in seed.[44] There were still complaints about the quality of the land and bad drainage, and even as late as the 20th century Chesterton has had drainage trouble.[45] The proportion of pasture and meadow to arable has been often affected by the demands of war-time economy, but the proportion of roughly 63 per cent. pasture to 37 per cent. arable found in 1760 and in 1914 is probably what is best suited to the soil.[46]

Since inclosure the tendency has been for farms to increase in size. In 1807 there were ten farms of over 60 acres, the largest being 475 acres, and by 1850 there were eight of 100 acres and over, of which two were over 400 acres.[47] There are now (1955) nine farms in the parish as it was before recent boundary changes, of which three have more than 200 acres in Chesterton, while the rest have between 60 and about 150 acres. Mainly mixed and dairy farming is carried on, but there is considerable production of beef cattle and other fat stock.[48]

Copyholding died out and manorial courts ceased to be held after 1763. The only business of the courts held in 1761–3 was admissions and surrenders; heriots were still exacted.[49] In November 1832 a court leet was revived, which fourteen tenants attended. A tithingman and hayward were elected for the following year, and orders were made for the removal of dunghills by the roadside and for the impounding of a cow if its owner persisted in allowing it to trespass on the waste.[50] This revival was probably due to Lord Jersey's interest in his Chesterton estate, as it lay near to his home at Middleton Stoney.[51]

Population did not increase rapidly until the 19th century. In 1676 the Compton Census had recorded 82 adults in Chesterton, and there may have been an expanding population in the mid-18th century: incumbents recorded 43 houses in Chesterton and its hamlet in 1738 and about 50 in 1768. The sharp rise from 330 inhabitants in 1801 to 435 in 1851 was accompanied by poverty and overcrowding.[52] In 1820 the parish was 'much in distress for want of cottages', and the vicar feared the arrival of new labourers, 'who are already become frightfully numerous and expensive'.[53] Thirty poor families were given bedding, and coal was distributed free to the poor, but such was their poverty that they pulled down the hedges to get wood with which to light it.[54] Later in the century Lord Jersey built new cottages and by the 1870's Chesterton's housing record was one of the best in the hundred.[55] By 1901 the population had decreased to 352. Since the addition of part of Bicester parish in 1932, and particularly since the establishment of the Arncot Depot, the population has risen sharply. In 1951 it numbered 784 compared with 384 in 1931.[56]

Apart from scattered references to the miller, no record of village tradesmen has survived before the mid-18th century. In 1760 there was one publican;[57] in 1807 there were two, one at the 'Blue Ball' and the other at the 'Cow', later named the 'Red Cow'. At this time there was also a village shop, a carpenter, and a maltster.[58] A few years later seven out of 85 families were in trade or business,[59] and by 1851 besides the general shopkeeper there were nine people engaged in non-agricultural occupations. These included two dressmakers, a cordwainer, and a railmaker.[60] Today (1955) the village still has an inn, the 'Red Cow', a general shop, a shoemaker, and a blacksmith.

In 1086 the mill was worth 10s.,[61] and by 1279 a second had been constructed.[62] In 1294 they were together valued at £1 16s.[63] One remained until the early 19th century, when it was let for £16 7s.,[64] and was the cause of friction between Lord Jersey and the vicar. The latter claimed that the artificial raising of the volume of water in the stream had caused the flooding of his glebe and the ruin of good grassland.[65]

[40] 7 Geo. III, c. 7 (priv. act): copy in Bodl. L. Eng. C 13 c 1 (1767); O.R.O. Incl. award (2 copies but no map). There was a map: New Coll. Arch. Chest. deeds, notebk. of 1821. Figures for yardlands in text taken from award.
[41] MS. Top. Oxon. c 381, f. 102; O.R.O. J II k/68; ibid. 71.
[42] MS. Top. Oxon. c 381, f. 102.
[43] O.R.O. J II k/39.
[44] Ibid. i/95.
[45] Ibid. k/39, 73.
[46] J. Orr, Agric. in Oxon. maps facing pp. 161, 201.
[47] O.R.O. J II k/71; H.O. 107/1727.
[48] Inf. Miss G. E. Townsend.
[49] Courts for Oct. 1761–3 only are recorded in MS. Top. Oxon. e 302, although the volume goes to 1770.
[50] O.R.O. J II b/6.
[51] Ibid. II i, passim.

[52] Compton Census. The 1662 hearth-tax return (the fullest) gives only 28 householders: Hearth Tax Oxon. 235; Oxf. Dioc. d 552, d 558; Census 1801–51.
[53] O.R.O. J II i/21, 51.
[54] Ibid. i/54, 67; k/37.
[55] Wing, Annals, 54.
[56] Census, 1931–51.
[57] O.R.O. J VII/1.
[58] Ibid. J II k/71.
[59] Dunkin, Oxon. i. 244.
[60] H.O. 107/1727.
[61] V.C.H. Oxon. i. 418.
[62] Rot. Hund. (Rec. Com.), ii. 826.
[63] C 133/97.
[64] O.R.O. J II k/71.
[65] New Coll. Arch. Chest. deeds, where the mill is often mentioned.

He further asserted that more money had been spent on it than it was worth: the Duke of Marlborough had tried to supply it from a reservoir at a cost of £500; it had once been converted into a hemp mill at a cost of £200; and recently £300 had been spent on it,[66] a reference very probably to the installation of the 'elaborate hydraulic machine' mentioned by Dunkin,[67] and yet it would not grind, or so the vicar said, as much as it did in its original state. Moreover, it was little used, as the miller was fraudulent.[68] The vicar's complaints were apparently justified: in 1822 the mill was closed and was not replaced.[69]

CHURCH. The earliest evidence for the existence of a church at Chesterton dates from the grant of its tithes to Bec Abbey in Normandy probably in 1087.[70] A priest, Osmund the clerk, and his son are mentioned in a mid-12th-century charter,[71] and architectural evidence indicates that the church was rebuilt in that century. The first record of the advowson occurs in about 1193, when there was a disputed presentation during a minority.[72] There was a second dispute during another minority in 1223, when William, Archdeacon of London and custodian of the manor, presented.[73] In the 13th century the lords of the manor, the De Chesterton family, were patrons until Edmund Earl of Cornwall bought the advowson for 80 marks in 1274.[74] He gave it with the manor to his new foundation of canons at Ashridge.[75]

This house of Bonshommes presented throughout the 14th century except during a vacancy in 1396,[76] when the college was in the king's hands, and there was a disputed presentation. It occurred on the death at the papal court of Robert Belage, rector since 1375.[77] The Pope, according to long-established custom in such cases, claimed the right of providing,[78] despite the recent Statute of Provisors.[79] He provided two litigious pluralists, Lewis de Byford and John Bremor.[80] The latter was actually instituted in 1398,[81] having been first pardoned by the king for accepting the provision[82] and then given a royal presenta-

tion.[83] Byford, however, successfully appealed to the papal court against his rival[84] and by 1401 after some difficulty[85] had gained possession of the rectory.[86] Bremor, having failed in two counter-appeals to Rome,[87] had presumably given way on being offered a pension of £5, which he later received from Ashridge.[88]

In 1401 and 1402 royal[89] and papal[90] permission was given to Ashridge to appropriate Chesterton; the college had pleaded its sufferings from the Peasants' Revolt[91] and paid £40. It held both rectory and advowson until its dissolution in 1539. In 1545[92] the king granted them to Walter Hendle, attorney for the Court of Augmentations, and to Sir John Williams of Thame,[93] later lord of the manor; and in 1558 New College bought them for £144.[94] The college, however, was at law in 1563 over the title[95] and may not have had clear possession until after 1575, when the queen presented to the church.[96] Until 1923, when the livings of Chesterton and Wendlebury were united,[97] New College was sole patron, but it has since presented in turn with Christ Church.

The church was a moderately rich one. In 1254 it was valued at £6 13s. 4d.,[98] and in 1291 at £10 13s. 4d.[99] When it was appropriated by Ashridge, the college got the great tithes,[1] and although 16th-century evidence shows that there was some land belonging to the rectory,[2] in the early 17th century it appears to have had only the great tithes and the tithe barn.[3] From the early 16th century until the mid-17th the rectory was usually leased by the Maundes, the lessees of the manor, for about £8.[4] They were followed as lessees in 1662 by William Bayly, a mercer and later a mayor of Oxford,[5] and in the first half of the 18th century by John Rutton, Vicar of Sandwich.[6] The latter paid the old rent of £8 plus a heavy fine, and then sublet the tithes, probably to a local farmer, for £80 or £85.[7]

At the inclosure of 1768 the great tithes were commuted for 355 acres, the land of the newly formed College farm.[8] In 1829 this farm was

---

[66] O.R.O. J II i/23.
[67] Dunkin, *Oxon.* i. 244.
[68] O.R.O. J II i/23.
[69] Ibid. i/76, 78; k/62–64.
[70] See below, n. 1.
[71] *Thame Cart.* ii. 128.
[72] See below.
[73] *Rot. Welles*, ii. 9–10.
[74] *Fines Oxon.* 204. This followed a double case before the king's court, in which William de Lisle recovered the right against John le Bret, and the Earl of Cornwall against de Lisle: *Rot. Graves.* 225–6.
[75] Dugd. *Mon.* vi (i), 517. For its history see *V.C.H. Bucks.* i. 386–70. It was originally in Bucks.
[76] *V.C.H. Bucks.* i. 390. For list of medieval presentations see MS. Top. Oxon. d 460.
[77] *Cal. Pat.* 1396–9, 46.
[78] *Cal. Papal L.* iv. 531–2.
[79] 12 Rich. II, c. 15.
[80] *Cal. Pat.* 1396–9, 46, 420. For them see *Cal. Papal L.* v, *passim.*
[81] Linc. Reg. xi, Buckingham, f. 377b. His estate was ratified in 1399: *Cal. Pat.* 1399–1401, 6.
[82] Ibid. 1396–9, 46.
[83] Ibid. 266.
[84] *Cal. Papal L.* v. 70.
[85] *Cal. Close*, 1399–1402, 199, 205; C 1/3/125.
[86] *Cal. Papal L.* v. 393.
[87] Ibid. 70.
[88] Ibid. 413.
[89] *Cal. Pat.* 1401–5, 50.
[90] *Cal. Papal L.* v. 432.
[91] *V.C.H. Bucks.* i. 387.

[92] Ashridge had sold the right of next presentation, i.e. that of 1544, before its dissolution: Oxf. Dioc. d 105, p. 10.
[93] *L. & P. Hen. VIII*, xx (1), p. 670. See also ibid. xxi (1), p. 318.
[94] *V.C.H. Oxon.* iii. 159; *Cal. Pat.* 1558–60, 130; New Coll. Arch. Bk. of Evidence, ff. 337–40.
[95] Ibid. ff. 342–4.
[96] *O.A.S. Rep.* 1914, 209.
[97] Bodl. Par. Box (uncat.), Order in Council.
[98] Lunt, *Val. Norw.* 311.
[99] *Tax. Eccl.* (Rec. Com.), 31.
[1] Kennett, *Paroch. Antiq.* ii. 203.
Miles Crispin granted a virgate and the small tithes from the demesne to Bec Abbey probably in 1087 (H. E. Salter, 'Two deeds about the Abbey of Bec,' *E.H.R.* xl. 75, 78). From the 13th cent. on the Rector of Chesterton paid 15s. a year, probably for both land and tithes, to the keeper of Bec's manor of Cottisford (e.g. *Select Docs. of English Lands of Bec*, ed. Marjorie Chibnall (Camden Soc. 3rd ser. lxxiii), 99). In 1252 a papal mandate of 1249 was cited, which had ordered the hearing of a complaint by Bec against the Rector of Chesterton and others about the non-payment of tithes: E.C.R. no. 37.
[2] New Coll. Arch. Bk. of Evid. f. 335. Part of this land was granted to the church in 1271: *Fines Oxon.* 200.
[3] New Coll. Arch. Bk. of Evid. ff. 345–6.
[4] Ibid. f. 335; Bodl. MS. ch. Oxon. 1149–50, 1169–70; *Valor Eccl.* (Rec. Com.), iv. 226.
[5] Bodl. MS. ch. Oxon. 1178–80.
[6] Ibid. 1196–7, 1216; Foster, *Alumni.*
[7] New Coll. Arch. Chest. deeds.
[8] O.R.O. Incl. award.

exchanged with Lord Jersey for two farms worth between £400 and £500.[9] In 1894 New College sold the smaller one.[10]

In the 12th century, judging from a dispute over the living, the parish was evidently considered rich and important. It is probable that it was the mother church of a chapelry at Wendlebury, for the rector received a pension of 13s. 4d. from the early 13th century[11] until at least the 15th century.[12] In any case, Gerald de Barry, the famous Welsh writer,[13] whose presentation to Chesterton by Gerard de Camville, probably in 1193,[14] was disputed, thought the living worth a struggle. The bishop of Lincoln had doubts about the legality of the presentation, especially as William de Ste Mère Eglise, one of Richard I's trusted officials,[15] was trying to get possession of both manor and church. After long negotiations, a compromise was reached which Gerald considered most unjust: a vicarage was ordained and the vicar was assigned over £13 of the revenue (probably an exaggerated estimate on Gerald's part), while Gerald as rector was to be paid only £3. He died in 1222 or 1223 and the new rector was assigned a pension of £3 13s. 4d.[16] There is no further record of the vicarage in the 13th century and it probably came to an end with the vicar's death.

Another distinguished medieval rector was Master William de Ardern (1361–75), a pluralist and Fellow of Merton College.[17] But after 1403 when the living again became a vicarage it was too poor to attract such men. According to the ordination of 1403,[18] the vicar was to have the Rectory house with its grounds; the glebe of 4 virgates; the revenue from the altar and the small tithes except those from the manor; and the pension from Wendlebury. On his side he had to bear all the expenses of the church, including the repair of the chancel, an unusual feature which was to cause trouble later. Ashridge had permission to serve the church with one of its own brethren,[19] but the names of the known incumbents suggest that it never did. Although before the Reformation all vicars were ordinarily bound to reside and from the 13th century took an oath to do so, one early-16th-century incumbent, who paid a curate £5 6s. 8d., appears to have been non-resident,[20] and got only about £2 for himself.[21] It is, therefore, not surprising to find complaints that the chancel needed repair, the

entry to the cemetery wanted attention, and the glebe was let to a layman.[22]

In 1535 the vicarage was valued at £7 8s. 8d.,[23] but after the Reformation it did not benefit from the general rise in prices. Thus, whereas the vicarage had once been more valuable than the rectory, by the early 17th century the rectory was double the value of the vicarage, partly because the profits of the altar had ceased to be of any value.[24] This poverty led to disputes between New College, the lessee of the rectory, and the vicar, despite the fact that almost all post-Reformation vicars have been Fellows or graduates of the College.

One of the chief causes of dissension was the vicar's responsibility for the repair of the chancel. New College bore the cost in the time of Edward Evans (1604–10), a noted university preacher and a relation of the Maundes,[25] as it probably did in the 16th century.[26] But Evans's successor Hudson was said to have paid for the repairs at the request of the Maundes, to whom he was heavily in debt.[27] Partly as a consequence Hudson ended by being imprisoned for debt and letting the vicarage.[28] The matter came to a head when a storm damaged the chancel in 1637,[29] and Philip French (1625–75) was later forced to admit that the repairs were his responsibility.[30] Relations with the college were further embittered by one of those disputes, so common in the county at this date, over the commutation of tithes. French refused to accept a composition of 7s. 2d. for the tithes of the manor park, valued at £8, and only accepted after a struggle a modus of about 12s. for other tithes valued at £14.[31]

Although French was a Fellow of New College and also Rector of Shipton-on-Cherwell,[32] he spent much of his time in Chesterton, where he enlarged the Vicarage.[33] He was 'outed' during the Commonwealth and replaced in 1654 by the college chaplain,[34] but was probably restored at the Restoration.[35] After his death in 1675 the living changed hands frequently —eighteen times in a hundred years.[36] A few vicars such as John Coxed (1728–30), later Warden of New College,[37] and John Burton (1720–6)[38] were men of distinction. In the second half of the century non-residence became common and the vicars usually let the fine Vicarage[39] so as to supplement their income.[40] Nevertheless by 18th-century standards the church appears to have been well served up to 1770. It had

⁹ 10 Geo. IV, c. 47 (priv. act): copy in Bodl. L. Eng. C 13 c 1 (1829); New Coll. Arch. Chest. deeds; O.R.O. J II i.
¹⁰ New Coll. Arch. Estate bk.
¹¹ Rot. Welles, i. 151.
¹² Kennett, Paroch. Antiq. ii. 203, gives the pension as 6s. 8d.
¹³ D.N.B.; F. M. Powicke, Christian Life in the Middle Ages, 107–29; J. C. Russell, Dict. of Writers of 13th Century England (Bull. Inst. Hist. Res. Special Supp. 3).
¹⁴ The only account is from a long letter from him to Bishop Hugh of Lincoln (1186–1200) in Giraldi Cambrensis Opera (Rolls Ser.), i. 259–68.
¹⁵ D.N.B.
¹⁶ Rot. Welles, ii. 9–10. This is the only information there is about his death: Autobiography of Giraldus, ed. H. E. Butler, 360.
¹⁷ See A. H. Thompson, 'Pluralism in the Medieval Church', Assoc. Archit. Soc. Rep. and Papers, xxxiv. 6–7.
¹⁸ Kennett, Paroch. Antiq. ii. 203.
¹⁹ Cal. Papal L. v. 432.
²⁰ Subsidy 1526, 273.
²¹ Valor Eccl. (Rec. Com.), ii. 159.
²² Visit Dioc. Linc. 1517–31, i. 123–4.

²³ Valor Eccl. ii. 159.
²⁴ New Coll. Arch. Chest. deeds (undated memo. by Philip French).
²⁵ Ibid.; D.N.B.
²⁶ Archd. Ct. 161.
²⁷ See above, n. 24.
²⁸ New Coll. Arch. Chest. deeds (1641). He left everything out of repair: as n. 24.
²⁹ As n. 24; Oxf. Archd. Oxon. c 13, f. 76.
³⁰ New Coll. Arch. Chest. deeds (1639).
³¹ Ibid. (1641) and (1664). Sir Francis Norreys summoned him to Chancery to see why he refused to accept it as former vicars had done. For an earlier dispute see Oxf. Dioc. d 14, ff. 108b–109.
³² Wood, Life, ii. 27; tablet in church.
³³ As n. 24.
³⁴ New Coll. Arch. Sewell's coll. livings.
³⁵ He was buried in the chancel: tablet once in church.
³⁶ For these vicars see Dunkin, Oxon. i. 255.
³⁷ V.C.H. Oxon. iii. 162.
³⁸ Dunkin, Oxon. i. 255. Foster, Alumni, confuses him with a Brasenose man.
³⁹ See above, p. 93.
⁴⁰ Oxf. Dioc. c 657, f. 115.

two services and a sermon on Sunday, a service on the great feasts, catechism for the children in Lent, and more than the four celebrations of the sacrament a year common at that period.[41]

From about the end of the century the poverty of the living gave grounds for frequent complaint and anxiety. The main support of the vicars came from Glebe farm (173 a.), which had been created at the inclosure of 1768 when the scattered strips of the glebe were exchanged and the small tithes commuted.[42] In 1771 this farm let for £111 and in 1805 for £150, but taxes and repairs reduced the vicar's receipts.[43] The consequence of this meagre endowment was that the vicarage was sequestrated in the 1770's so that the profits might be used to pay off the vicar's debts,[44] and that later another vicar, Aubrey Price (1826–48), had to be removed for debt, although an 'exemplary pastor and a worthy man'. After a petition from the parishioners he was allowed to remain as curate.[45] His immediate predecessor Joseph Hollis, who as Rector of Godington was in a better financial position, admitted that if he had known the bishop would require residence, he would not have accepted so poor a living.[46] Even in the second half of the 19th century, when the value of the farm rose and New College gave the vicar part of the income from the rectorial estate, there was thought to be little 'to tempt a Fellow to accept Chesterton living'.[47]

Probably partly through Price's influence, the spiritual life of the parish was in a sound state in the 19th century. The number of communicants more than trebled in the first half of the century[48] and continued to increase in the second half under William Fortescue (1849–89), who even attracted ten non-parishioners to his church.[49] The fabric was restored in his time and he built the present Vicarage.[50] He considered that the chief hindrances to his ministry were drinking, 'the neighbourhood of Bicester and Bicester (i.e. nonconformist) influence',[51] and the very early age at which children, especially boys, started work.[52] To meet the last challenge, he held during the winter a very successful evening school for boys.[53]

The church of *ST. MARY* is a stone building comprising a chancel, clerestoried nave, north and south aisles, western tower, and south porch with an ancient wooden door. The nave has three 12th-century arches on the north side, supported on round pillars with scalloped capitals. The rest of the church was rebuilt in the 13th century; the loftier southern arcade, which also has round pillars but with plain capitals, and the chancel arch date from this period. In the chancel there are three elegant early-14th-century sedilia with detached shafts and three cinquefoiled arches with ball-flower decoration; a double piscina with aumbry above, and two 14th-century windows on the south side. The five-light 15th-century east window was replaced in 1852.[54] The fine timber roof is supported on carved corbels. The tower built early in the 14th century has a parapet ornamented with quatrefoils. The clerestory was added in the 15th century. The square-headed windows in the south aisle, in which there are two stone brackets for images, were also inserted in the 14th or 15th century. There is a piscina in the north aisle.

Little record of post-Reformation alterations has survived. The chancel was damaged by a storm in 1637;[55] early in the 18th century the church was said to be 'in tolerable repair';[56] in 1757 repairs including a new north door were ordered.[57] In 1819 the stone screen between the chancel and nave was recorded as decayed;[58] it has since been removed. In the mid-19th century the east window was rebuilt and in 1854 the gallery was removed and the chancel arch restored.[59] But in spite of this the rural dean, J. C. Blomfield, wrote to the churchwardens in 1865, stating that the church required 'immediate and serious attention' and should be thoroughly restored. The restoration was undertaken by the architect F. C. Penrose. It cost about £1,000. A new pavement was laid down, the east and west windows in the north aisle and the windows in the south aisle were restored, the north door was blocked up and new seating installed.[60] One box pew was left. A turret-staircase bearing the date 1866 was added to the tower. Later, in 1884, a clock was given by Miss Tyrwhitt-Drake of Bignell.

The plain 12th-century font, surrounded by Jacobean altar rails, is cylindrical, and has an elaborate wrought-iron framework for lifting the lid.[61] There is a Jacobean altar table. The 17th-century carved oak reredos came from Brittany,[62] as did the panelling in the chancel and probably the pulpit. The organ was presented in 1898 by the banker Henry Tubb and his wife.[63]

A brass to John Maunde (d. 1630/1) and his wife, which had figures of seven boys, was mentioned by Rawlinson when he visited the church in the 18th century,[64] but has now disappeared. There are still brasses to William Maunde, gentleman (d. 1612), and his wife Ann with effigies and shield of arms. In the chancel are inscriptions to Thomas Prior, steward of New College (d. 1777), and to Joseph Hollis, vicar (d. 1826). The following inscriptions cannot now be traced: to Richard Maunde (d. 1615), the son of George; to George Maunde (d. 1628); to Philip French, vicar (d. 1675); to Robert Snow (d. 1708/9) and Ann, his wife.[65]

[41] Oxf. Dioc. d 552, d 555.
[42] O.R.O. Incl. award. It was sold in 1898: New Coll. Arch. Estate bk.
[43] Oxf. Dioc. c 155, f. 58; c 657, ff. 114–15.
[44] Oxf. Archd. Oxon. b 23, f. 197; Oxf. Dioc. c 155, f. 58.
[45] Oxf. Dioc. c 664, ff. 100–7.
[46] Ibid. c 657, f. 118.
[47] Ibid. c 664, f. 106b; New Coll. Arch. Chest. deeds, where there is correspondence.
[48] Oxf. Dioc. d 570; *Wilb. Visit.*
[49] Oxf. Dioc. c 344.
[50] Ibid. d 178.
[51] Ibid. c 332.
[52] *Wilb. Visit.*
[53] Oxf. Dioc. c 332.
[54] A drawing by J. Buckler in MS. Top. Oxon. a 66, f. 159, shows the unrestored church. The marks of an earlier high-pitched roof of the nave can be seen on the east face of the tower.
[55] Oxf. Archd. Oxon. c 13, f. 76; see above, p. 101.
[56] *Par. Coll.* i. 88.
[57] Oxf. Archd. Oxon. d 13, f. 35.
[58] Dunkin, *Oxon.* i. 247.
[59] Par. Rec.
[60] Ibid.; MS. Top. Oxon. c 103, ff. 235–9; New Coll. Arch. Chest. corresp.
[61] See Buckler drawing in MS. Top. Oxon. a 66, f. 158.
[62] *Kelly's Dir. Oxon.* (1920).
[63] Ibid. See above, p. 35.
[64] *Par. Coll.* i. 88. It had gone by Dunkin's time: *Oxon.* i. 246.
[65] For blazons of arms see Bodl. G.A. Oxon. 4° 685, p. 88; ibid. 16° 217, p. 99; ibid. 4° 688, p. 88.

In 1552 the church owned, among other things, a chalice, two copes and two vestments, three bells, a sanctus bell, and two handbells.[66] Today it has a silver chalice (1712) and paten (1732), inscribed as the gift of Katherine Bertie, and a silver flagon (1753), the gift of Bridget Launder.[67] The tower has a ring of three bells: the tenor is inscribed with the initials of William Watts of Bedford and dates from about 1590; the second and treble, also inscribed, were made in 1623 by Henry Farmer and James Keene, an unusual combination. The sanctus bell dates from 1715.[68]

The registers date from 1539, but there are gaps from 1595–1603 and 1645–62.

NONCONFORMITY. In the Elizabethan period John Bourne of Chesterton Grange was a leading Roman Catholic. He was noted as a recusant in 1577,[69] and in 1583 was accused of having harboured five priests.[70] William Bourne, of the Wendlebury branch of the family,[71] living then at Chesterton Grange, was noted as a recusant in 1599.[72] There is no further record of recusancy.

Protestant dissent was never important. In 1676 there were two dissenters;[73] in 1738 there was a Presbyterian farmer and one other dissenter,[74] and in the 1850's two dissenting families went to chapel at Bicester and possibly more later.[75]

SCHOOLS. About 1800 a school was opened for 10 to 20 children and in 1815, after the opening of another, about 51 children between the ages of four and ten received some instruction in reading.[76] In 1819 there were 36 pupils, most of whom were paid for by Lady Jersey (d. 1867),[77] who by 1833 was contributing £12 a year to the support of a single school with 41 pupils.[78] Lady Jersey appears to have built by 1854 a school which was subsequently leased to managers by successive Lords Jersey.[79] There were 56 pupils in 1871[80] and 74 in 1906.[81] The school was reorganized in 1933 as a junior school, and senior pupils were moved to Bicester. The numbers on the books were 31 in 1937 and 33 in 1954.[82]

CHARITIES. It was reported in 1738[83] that at some unknown date Miss Drusilla Bowell of Bicester had left two-thirds of her estate to provide for the apprenticing of two poor boys every year. Great Chesterton—which shared the charity with Bicester and Wendlebury[84]—was to nominate one boy every other year. Five pounds a year was to be used to assist boys, who had finished their apprenticeship, to set up in trade. The charity had been neglected for some years before 1738 and no more is heard of it.

By 1768 £30 had been given to the poor of Chesterton apparently by one of the Bertie family. The principal was then held by Peregrine Bertie of Weston-on-the-Green, and the interest was regularly distributed to the poor.[85] In 1786 the principal was said to have been £25 and the interest £1, but payments had then ceased for some years,[86] and inquiries made in 1824 failed to reveal any record of the charity.[87]

In 1864 a certain person of unknown sex called Tredwell left stock worth £284 9s. 11d. to the poor of Little Chesterton. The interest amounted to £8 10s. 8d. in 1870.[88]

COTTISFORD

THIS parish[1] lies about six miles north of Bicester and four miles south of Brackley in the north-eastern corner of Oxfordshire, which is enclosed by Northamptonshire and Buckinghamshire.[2] In the 19th century it covered 1,506 acres of which 438 were part of 634 acres of 'intermixed lands' shared with Hethe. In 1932 the whole of these lands was awarded to Cottisford, increasing its area to 1,702 acres.[3] The parish boundaries form an irregular parallelogram, tipped from north-west to south-east. Its southern boundary separating it from Hethe, Hardwick, and Tusmore is noticeably artificial and must have been drawn after the fields had been laid out: Cottisford's history has been closely connected with these parishes

from early times. The Northamptonshire border bounds it on the north-west. The parish forms a part of the Great Oolite belt (covered by fine drift gravel in the south) and lies mostly at 400 feet above sea-level; its soil is gravelly, with a stone subsoil.[4] Much of the land was once heath, particularly on Cottisford Heath in the north and Hardwick Heath in the south.[5]

Apart from the Oxford–Brackley road which partly bounds it on the north-west the parish has no main roads. Minor roads connect the village of Cottisford with the Buckingham–Deddington road to the north, the Bicester–Buckingham road to the south-east, and the Oxford–Brackley road to the west. This last is

[66] Chant. Cert. 90.
[67] Evans, Ch. Plate.
[68] Ch. Bells Oxon. i. 88–89.
[69] C.R.S. xxii, 109 and n. 4.
[70] H. Foley, Records of the English Province, vi. 719; see also Hist. MSS. Com. Salisbury MSS. IV. 270.
[71] C.R.S. xviii. 254. For family see Oxon. Visit. 316.
[72] Acts of P.C. 1599–1600, 53.
[73] Compton Census.
[74] Oxf. Dioc. d 552.
[75] Wilb. Visit.; see above, p. 102.
[76] Oxf. Dioc. d 707, c 433.
[77] Educ. of Poor, 721.
[78] Educ. Enq. Abstract, 743.
[79] Wilb. Visit.; Wing, Annals, 54; Vol. Sch. Ret.
[80] Elem. Educ. Ret.
[81] Vol. Sch. Ret.
[82] Inf. Oxon. Educ. Cttee.

[83] Oxf. Dioc. d 552.
[84] See above, p. 55; below, p. 346.
[85] Oxf. Dioc. d 558.
[86] Char. Don. ii. 989; cf. below, p. 352.
[87] 12th Rep. Com. Char. 301.
[88] Gen. Digest Char. For the Tredwell family see above, p. 99.
[1] The author wishes to thank Mrs. Marjorie Chibnall for lending her transcripts of the manorial accounts of Bec Abbey, Mrs. Gweneth Whitteridge for transcripts of documents of St. Bartholomew's Hospital, and Mr. N. Blakiston for his typescript of the Eton College Record.
[2] O.S. Map 6", xi, xvii (1884); 25", xi. 13, 14, 15 (1881); xviii. 1, 2, 3, 6; Census, 1881.
[3] Census, 1931; Oxon. Review Order (1932).
[4] G.S. Map 1", xlv NE.; Kelly's Dir. Oxon. (1939).
[5] Davis, Oxon. Map (1797).

described in a 13th-century deed as 'the royal way leading from Oxford to Brackele', while the first appears as the 'way leading from Cotesford to Brackele'.[6] The road west from the village was described in 1358, when its course was changed, as 'a way leading from Coteford to Sulthorn' (i.e. Souldern).[7]

The village of Cottisford lies towards the south-east on the banks of the Crowell stream, where there was once a ford: hence the name Cotts-ford. In early 13th-century charters it is named 'Wolfheysford' or 'Urlfesford'.[8] The village was described by Peshall in the 18th century as 'lying in the form of a street from e(ast) to w(est)', and this layout is shown in Davis's map of 1797.[9] The church and manor-house (now Cottisford House) are depicted lying, as they do today, north of the road, but divided by a lane running north and south with a number of cottages standing to the north of both. Both lane and houses to the north have now gone as the result of alterations in the line of the roads made in the late 1820's by William Turner, the tenant of Cottisford House, when he was laying out pleasure-grounds. At the same time he pulled down all the houses which stood round the church and planted the site with the trees still growing there.[10] The incumbent's return of 1831 notes that 'the village once stood round the church and that the cottages are now removed to a distance'.[11] A drawing of 1825 of the church from the south-east shows cottages lying west of the church,[12] and Blomfield records that the churchyard was closed in by cottages on three sides.[13] He adds that the road which Turner stopped used to continue in a southerly direction towards Hethe and that traces of it could be seen in dry weather in the field in front of the Rectory. If this was so Davis did not show it on his map. Blomfield's further statement that Turner substituted an east to west road for the old north to south one seems clearly an exaggeration.[14] What Turner evidently did was to build new cottages to replace those he had pulled down along the already existing village street.

The old village lay mainly west of the ford. Here is the Rectory and College Farm (formerly Manor Farm), a stone 18th-century house of two low stories facing on to the road. East of the stream, now crossed by the road, is Manor Farm, a medieval house. Numerous fishponds to the south are shown on the Ordnance Survey map of 1881. Opposite, on the north of the village street, was the village pond and stocks.[15] In the 17th century the hearth-tax returns of 1665 show that besides the Rectory, with 4 hearths, there were 2 substantial houses with 6 and 7 hearths.[16] There was some expansion in the 18th century and the first half of the 19th century. In 1738 twelve cottages, a farm-house, and a gentleman's house (i.e. Cottisford House) were recorded.[17] In the 19th century the comparatively new hamlet in the north-west

of the parish at Juniper Hill developed, and Cottisford itself spread up the hill to the east.[18] The village school was built there in 1856,[19] and on the road to Hethe to the south there is a row of six semi-detached model 19th-century cottages. Farther south still is another row of early 19th-century ones. The water-tower near the school is of unknown origin, but must belong to this period. In 1868 Cottisford's cottages were described as 'very bad to very good' and some were said to be 'not fit for human habitation'.[20] Six semi-detached council houses have been built since 1946.[21]

The village has two houses of considerable interest. One is Manor Farm, possibly the De Cotesfords',[22] which used to be assigned to the 13th century, but is now considered to be a 'very doubtful example of the period'.[23] It more probably dates from the 14th century. The house, composed of uncoursed rubble, consists of an oblong block lying north–south, subdivided into two compartments, probably a first-floor hall and a solar, with two smaller blocks of unequal size projecting from the west wall, with a lean-to between them. There is also a later south wing added when the original building was remodelled in the 16th century. Most of the windows have been modernized, except two in the north wall of the solar, each of one trefoil-headed light, which were probably inserted in the 15th century. In the north gable above is a two-light attic window of c. 1200, but this does not appear to be in its original position. The most interesting part of the house is the north-west projection, which contains what was probably a garde-robe opening from the solar. Within there is a projecting semicircular stone trough with a drain. Above the gable rises an octagonal chimney shaft, which has been assigned to the 14th century, but which may be of later date. Sixteenth-century roof timbers can be seen in the north gable; the roof is of Welsh slate. The interior has been much modernized, but the fittings include a 16th-century fireplace in a ground-floor room. In the early 18th century the farm-house was leased by the Fermors to William Topping for £51 10s.[24] Its farmer tenant and economy in the 1880's have been described in Flora Thompson's *Lark Rise*. The house was owned by the Ramsays until 1857, when it was bought by Lord Effingham.[25] It changed hands again in 1898 and in 1944 when Col. M. L. Mostyn purchased it. It is now leased to Twyford Mills Ltd. and used as a hostel for their apprentices.[26]

As Cottisford manor between 1100 and 1885 was first in the hands of Bec Abbey and later in those of Eton College, there was no resident lord of the manor.[27] The abbey's lands were administered by the Prior of Ogbourne (Wilts.), who had a bailiff at Cottisford. There was a grange there at least as early as 1306.[28] An indenture of 1325 gives details of what was evidently a substantial building: a hall, chamber,

6 E.C.R. no. 29.
7 *Cal. Pat.* 1358–61, 4.
8 *P.N. Oxon.* (E.P.N.S.), i. 207; E.C.R. nos. 10, 20.
9 MS. Top. Oxon. c 307, f. 119.
10 Blo. *Cot.* 23, 39.
11 Oxf. Dioc. b 38.
12 See plate opposite.
13 Blo. *Cot.* 26.
14 Ibid. 39.
15 O.S. Map 25″, xvii. 2 (1881).
16 *Hearth Tax Oxon.* 208.
17 Oxf. Dioc. d 552.
18 *Census*, 1851.

19 See below, p. 115.
20 *Agric. Rep.* (1868–9), 352.
21 Inf. Ploughley R.D.C.
22 See below, p. 106.
23 For an account of this house see M. E. Wood, *Arch. Jnl.* cv (1950), *Supplement*, 57–58. For an illustration see plate opposite.
24 O.R.O. Reg. of Papists' estates.
25 O.R.O. Land tax assess.; Bodl. G.A. Oxon. b 85b (57).
26 Inf. Col. Mostyn.
27 See below, pp. 105, 106
28 E 179/161/8.

View of Manor Farm in 1823

South-east view of the church in 1825

COTTISFORD

kitchen, and granary. There was a close and garden attached, a fishery worth 1s. and a dovecote worth 3s.[29] When the property passed to Eton in the middle of the 15th century, the college's lessee probably took over the house.

At the end of the 16th century or at latest before 1606 the college built a new house for its tenants, which is variously designated the manor-house or the mansion house.[30] About a century later, the tenant Laurence Lord, junior, built another house, described in the renewal of his lease in 1707 as a 'good house'.[31] This house, now called Cottisford House, is built of coursed rubble with ashlar quoins; it is of two stories with attic dormers in a hipped roof. The south front has a doorway with a broken pediment and a modillioned eaves-cornice. Early 19th-century alterations and additions were made by William Turner, who obtained the lease in 1825,[32] and the house has since been well restored. In the garden, to the north-east, are the remains of a large brick dovecote, which was mentioned when the estate was sold in 1773. It was square and is now roofless.

It has been stated that Cottisford House was on the site of Barsis Place, which was once the home of the De Bar family.[33] The house was let by Ogbourne in 1375 and 1400 to Edward Metteley; it later came into the possession of the Copes of Hanwell, who sold it in 1620 to Eton College.[34]

The parish has long been noted as good hunting country, and there is a fine painting by Ben Marshall (1767?–1835)[35] of Mr. Fermor's hounds on Cottisford Heath. Annual horse-races were held there at the close of the hunting season in the early part of the 19th century.[36]

The parish has had interesting associations. The priors of Ogbourne who acted as agents for the Norman Abbey of Bec, the lord of the manor, were frequent visitors to their grange in the village, and so were the priors of Goldcliff (Mon.) and Steventon (Berks.). After the manor had passed to Eton College several Oxfordshire families of lesser gentry were lessees or freeholders, notably the Samwells, Ardens, and Pettys.[37] In the 18th century the Eyres were another resident family of note. James Eyre (1734–99) was Recorder of London and finally Chief Justice of the Common Pleas. The Copes of Hanwell and the important Roman Catholic family of Fermor were also landowners in the 17th and 18th centuries, though never resident.[38] Sir Henry Savile, Provost of Eton, appears to have taken a particular interest in the college estate and much correspondence between him and Sir Anthony Cope (1548?–1615) of Hanwell has survived.[39] Robert Petty, Anthony Wood's grandfather, and also his nephew Maximilian were Eton College's tenants.[40] Charnell Petty of Tets-

worth and later of Stoke Lyne was the lessee of Barsis Place.[41]

A memorable 19th-century resident was Flora Thompson, the daughter of a stonemason of Juniper Hill and the author of *Lark Rise* (1939) and its sequels, *Over to Candleford* (1941) and *Candleford Green* (1943). She was born in the hamlet in 1877 and educated at Cottisford village school. Her books are important social documents for life at Juniper ('Lark Rise') and Cottisford ('Fordlow') in the 19th century.[42] In the 20th century Air Chief Marshal Sir Robert Brooke-Popham, who so much influenced the formative years of the R.A.F., resided at Cottisford House for some years before his death in 1953.[43]

Juniper Hill, the hamlet in the north-west of the parish, dates from the second half of the 18th century and mainly developed in the 19th century. The name is derived from the prevalence on the surrounding heath in the past of the common juniper shrub.[44] Two cottages were built there in 1754, but the hamlet mainly developed after the inclosure of the common fields in 1854. By the end of the 19th century there were about 30 cottages, mostly built on lands ceded as 'squatters' rights'.[45] Its inn, the 'Fox', came into existence between 1852 and 1864 and figures in Flora Thompson's *Lark Rise* as 'The Waggon and Horses'.

There are a number of outlying farm-houses in the parish: the Warren, which was a 17th-century house built for the warrener and used in the early 19th century as a hunting-box by Sir Edward Lloyd, Bt.,[46] has recently been pulled down; Heath Farm, Glebe Farm, and Coneygre Farm are 19th-century buildings, probably erected after the inclosure in 1854. The 'Conygree' Farm mentioned in 17th-century records was in the village.

MANOR. In 1086 *COTTISFORD*, assessed at 6 hides, was held of Hugh de Grantmesnil by Roger d'Ivry,[47] who had married Hugh's eldest daughter Adeline. He died in exile a few years later, having forfeited his English lands.[48] Adeline, who survived until about 1110,[49] gave Cottisford to Bec Abbey in Normandy.[50] Later evidence shows that her grant included all the land of the township with the exception of two small estates. One of these was held by Adeline's sister Rohais, wife of Robert de Courcy, the son of Richard de Courcy and an important landowner in Oxfordshire. In about 1125, with Robert's consent, she gave it to Bec.[51] The other, a hide of land, had been given before 1081 by Hugh de Grantmesnil with Cottisford church to St. Évroul Abbey in Normandy,[52] but in 1167 this too was acquired by Bec.[53] Many of Bec's English manors, including Cottisford, were administered from its cell at Greater Ogbourne (Wilts.),[54] and it became

[29] E.C.R. no. 40.
[30] Blo. *Cot.* 19–20.
[31] MS. Dunkin 439/3, f. 126.
[32] Blo. *Cot.* 23.
[33] Ibid. 22; see below, p. 107.
[34] E.C.R. nos. 42, 45, 64–68.
[35] Reproduced in H. Wyndham, *A Backward Glance* (1950), opp. p. 73.
[36] e.g. MS. Dunkin 438/7, f. 99.
[37] See below, p. 106; cf. below, p. 316.
[38] See below, p. 107.
[39] e.g. see E.C.R. no. 181.
[40] Wood, *Life*, i. 50; E.C.R. no. 256.
[41] See below, p. 107.
[42] For a letter from Flora Thompson to Greening Lamborn see Bodl. 247126 e. 250(a).

[43] 21 Oct. 1953, *The Times*.
[44] Blo. *Cot.* 37.
[45] See below, p. 113, and Flora Thompson, *Lark Rise*.
[46] For the warrener see below, p. 111.
[47] *V.C.H. Oxon.* i. 427.
[48] Ordericus Vitalis, *Historia Ecclesiastica*, ed. Le Prévost, iii. 25 n. 1; for Roger see *V.C.H. Oxon.* v. 60.
[49] *Chron. Abingdon*, ii. 72.
[50] *Bk. of Fees*, 831; *Rot. Hund.* (Rec. Com.), ii. 44, 837.
[51] Ordericus, *Hist. Eccl.* iii. 25 n. 1, 359, 361.
[52] Ibid. iii. 22, 24: charter of Wm. I to St. Évroul.
[53] *Select Doc. of Eng. Lands of Bec*, ed. Marjorie Chibnall (Camden Soc. 3rd ser. lxxiii), 17.
[54] Marjorie Morgan, *Eng. Lands of Bec* (1946), 1, 43, 45.

customary to regard the Prior of Ogbourne, the effective administrator of Cottisford, as the lord of the manor.[55]

It has been conjectured that there was a second manor in Cottisford, held in the second half of the 14th century by Sir Roger de Cotesford.[56] Thirteenth-century records, however, show that there was only one manor, the whole of which was held by Bec.[57] The surname 'De Cotesford' was borne, though not consistently, by a number of families living in the parish from the late 12th century onwards, who were tenants of the abbey and not lords of the manor.[58] In 1279 Bec held 'Manerium de Coteford cum tota villata'.[59]

The last Prior of Ogbourne to hold Cottisford was William de St. Vaast, nominated in 1364.[60] In 1404 Ogbourne, an alien priory, with its manors was granted by Henry IV to his son John, later Duke of Bedford, Thomas Langley, later Bishop of Durham, and William de St. Vaast for the duration of the war with France.[61] The prior died soon afterwards and by 1422 Thomas Langley had surrendered his rights to the Duke of Bedford, who continued to farm the manors of the priory, which had been suppressed in 1414.[62] The duke died in 1435 and in 1438 Henry VI granted Cottisford to his uncle Humphrey, Duke of Gloucester.[63] In 1441, however, the king gave Cottisford to his new foundation of Eton College.[64] Edward IV confirmed his predecessor's grant in 1462.[65]

In the late 14th century the Prior of Ogbourne had adopted the practice of leasing Cottisford manor. Edward Metteley, who held a lease of land[66] in Cottisford as early as 1375, obtained a lease of the manor for nine years in 1391.[67] This was renewed in 1400, for the lives of himself and his wife Margaret.[68] Eton College continued the practice, and its leaseholders came to be termed lords of the manor. In 1450 the estate was leased to Robert Arden for a term of 20 years and in 1469 for 60 years to John Samwell. He was apparently Arden's brother-in-law and the bailiff of Cottisford and Fringford (where Eton also owned a small property). John Samwell died before 1505, since from that year until 1512 his son Roger paid rent to the college. Roger Samwell's widow Eleanor was the leaseholder in 1513–14, and her second husband Thomas Danvers of Banbury paid the rent from 1515 to 1521.[69] Thomas and Eleanor Danvers then quitclaimed their rights in the manor of Cottisford, and in 1522 the lease returned to the Arden family in the person of John Arden (d. 1535), grandson of Robert Arden. In 1542

the leaseholder was his son, John Arden (d. 1556), who in his turn was succeeded by his son, a third John Arden, who obtained a renewal of the lease.

Some time after 1570 Arden sold the remainder of his lease to (Sir) Thomas Ridley, who became headmaster of Eton in 1580 and to whom the college granted a new lease for 21 years in 1587.[70] In the following year, however, the manor was leased by the college to Robert Calcot of Byfield (Northants), to hold for the lives in survivorship of John and James Arden, sons of John Arden, and of John Calcot his own son.[71] Calcot was dead by 1606, and in that year a lease of 21 years was granted to Robert Wilcox of Hilmorton (Warws.).[72] The next leaseholder was Richard Stephens, who was tenant from 1627 to 1641,[73] when George Austin of Coleman Street, London, became the lessee.[74] Austin devised the lease to his wife Frideswide, who married as her second husband Valentine Walton of Great Stoughton and Somersharn (Hunts.). In 1650 he sub-let to John Hart of Chilton (Bucks.), for nine years from 1651. Walton and his wife surrendered the lease of the manor to Eton in 1658,[75] and Hart obtained a lease in 1660 for the customary 21 years.[76] In 1664 Hart's widow married Edward Andrews of Lathbury (Bucks.), and they obtained a new lease in 1671.[77] In 1675 Andrews surrendered his rights and those of his wife in Cottisford to Laurence Lord of Fritwell, who received a new lease in 1676:[78] he died at Fritwell in 1708. His eldest son Laurence resided at Cottisford during his father's lifetime, and continued renewals of the lease of the manor until 1731. He died in 1743.

In 1739 the manor was leased to Richard Eyre, who was 'a power in the village life, and even after his death it was long before he was forgotten'.[79] He was a son of the Revd. Richard Eyre, Prebendary of Salisbury, undoubtedly a member of a younger branch of the well-known Wiltshire family, and had spent 28 years in the East India Company's service.[80] His lease was renewed in 1752 for 20 years,[81] but in 1760, the year before his death, a lease of 20 years was granted to Thomas Berney Bramston of the Middle Temple and Skreens (Essex), and Sir James Eyre (1734–99) of Gray's Inn.[82] James Eyre, a Chief Justice of the Common Pleas, was a nephew of Richard Eyre, being the son of his elder brother Thomas, also a Prebendary of Salisbury.[83] Bramston's and Eyre's lease was renewed in 1766 for 20 years.[84] But Richard Eyre's widow, Martha, daughter of Christopher Clitherow of Boston House, Brentford, continued to live at Cottisford until her death in

[55] e.g. *Feud. Aids*, iv. 169; *Tax. Eccl.* (Rec. Com.), 45; for details of the organization and administration of the bailiwick of Ogbourne see Morgan, *Eng. Lands of Bec*, 38–73.
[56] Blo. *Cot.* 19–20; for the family, see above, p. 60; below, p. 336.
[57] *Bk. of Fees*, 831; *Rot. Hund.* (Rec. Com.), ii. 837.
[58] e.g. *Bracton's Note Bk.* ed. Maitland, iii. 45; *Fines Oxon.* 72, 86; E.C.R. box 8: Cottisford ch.
[59] *Rot. Hund.* (Rec. Com.), ii. 837–8.
[60] Morgan, op. cit. 126.
[61] *Cal. Pat.* 1401–5, 466.
[62] Ibid. 1416–22, 441; Morgan, op. cit. 131; Dugd. *Mon.* vi (2). 1016.
[63] *Cal. Pat.* 1436–41, 189, 304.
[64] *Rot. Parl.* v. 47.
[65] *Cal. Pat.* 1461–7, 73.
[66] E.C.R. no. 42.
[67] Ibid. no. 43.

[68] Ibid. no. 44.
[69] Blo. *Cot.* 15.
[70] E.C.R. no. 46; Blo. *Cot.* 15–17; for the Ardens see *Oxon. Visit.* 207.
[71] E.C.R. no. 56.
[72] Ibid. nos. 62, 70, 71.
[73] Ibid. nos. 72–74.
[74] Ibid. no. 75.
[75] Ibid. no. 76.
[76] Ibid. no 79; cf. *Hearth Tax Oxon.* 208.
[77] E.C.R. no. 81.
[78] Ibid. nos. 84, 86, 88.
[79] Blo. *Cot.* 22 n. 1.
[80] M.I. in Cottisford church; for the elder Richard see Foster, *Alumni*.
[81] E.C.R. no. 89.
[82] Ibid. no. 90.
[83] *D.N.B.*
[84] E.C.R. no. 91.

1772, and in 1773 the lease was sold by auction by order of her executors.[85]

The Cottisford lease was bought for £7,300 by the Revd. John Russell Greenhill, the Rector of Fringford (d. 1813). He was succeeded by his son, Robert Russell Greenhill, M.P., of Lincoln's Inn,[86] who held the estate until 1825, when William Turner, a member of the Irish bar, obtained a lease from Eton College for 17 years and renewed in 1829 for 20 years.[87] Turner, however, became involved in money difficulties, sold the remainder of his lease, and went abroad.[88] In 1836 Eton leased the manor to Susanna Ingram of Warminster, widow of Christopher Ingram of Stapleford (Wilts.).[89] The lease was transferred in 1842 to James Edwards Rousby.[90] Rousby died in 1848, and in 1850 Eton granted a lease to his son Edwards Rousby and John Kendall of Towton Hall, near Tadcaster, his executors.[91] Edwards Rousby died in 1875, and his son Edwards Richard Kendal Rousby succeeded to the lease. In 1885 he bought from Eton College the manor-house and Warren farm. He was succeeded by his son, F. R. Rousby, who later sold his family property to Sir Robert Brooke-Popham.[92] The rest of the college's estate was sold in 1921 and 1922.[93]

LESSER ESTATES—In the early 13th century a hide in Cottisford belonged to the abbey of St. Pierre-sur-Dives (Calvados), which had enfeoffed William le Bar.[94] William gave his houses and at least two virgates to Biddlesden Abbey (Bucks.),[95] and in 1232 leased another virgate to Bec.[96] In 1237 St. Pierre granted Biddlesden William's whole estate, with his homage and service.[97] William's son Ralph had succeeded him as Biddlesden's tenant of the hide by 1247.[98] Some time after 1266[99] Biddlesden quitclaimed Ralph's estate to Bec for 13½ marks,[1] and in 1279[2] and in 1289 Ralph was holding the hide of Bec for a rent of 13s. 5d. a year.[3] A Robert le Bar, perhaps his son, occurs in 1282 and 1295,[4] and a John le Bar in 1310 and 1345.[5] The last contributed to the tax of 1327 for his Cottisford lands.[6]

The Arden family held a freehold estate of 4 yardlands in the 16th century, which appears to have been once Bar's holding.[7] It probably descended in the family with its leasehold property from the reign of Henry VIII until the end of the 16th century.[8] It was doubtless this 4 yardlands which was leased in 1619 with Barsis Place to Charnell Petty of Tetsworth.[9]

Another freehold estate of 6 yardlands, held by John Samwell, was sold to the Fermors of Somerton in 1527 and was later conveyed to John Arden,[10] but Thomas Fermor (d. 1580), lord of Hardwick manor, had pasture rights and an estate in Cottisford after this sale.[11] The Arden estate was purchased by Sir Anthony Cope of Hanwell in or before 1606.[12] An estate of 360 acres was held by Sir Humphrey Ferrers in the 16th century, for which it was said 'he acknowledgeth nothing but to the king'.[13] Ferrers was lord of Hethe and there can be little doubt that this estate followed the descent of that manor. Both were bought by Sir Rowland Lytton and sold to Sir Anthony Cope before 1606.[14] It is possible that when the Copes alienated Hethe manor some time after 1637, the Cottisford estate was acquired by the Fermors. At all events the family, then established at Tusmore, was holding 23 yardlands in Cottisford by the early 18th century.[15] The Fermor estate followed the descent of Tusmore from at least 1717 until 1857, when it was sold to the Earl of Effingham.[16] After inclosure the estate covered 616 statute acres.[17] Between 1898 and 1920 it was split up and sold.[18] Although the Fermor estate covered nearly half the parish and their farm-house was called Manor Farm there is no other evidence for the existence of a second manor in Cottisford. It is probable that from early times much of Cottisford's land had always been attached to Hethe manor or to Hardwick, where the Ardens were lords of the manor in the 15th century, and the Fermors in the 16th century. Herein probably lies the explanation of the 635 acres of 'intermixed lands' of which 196 acres were shared with Hethe.

ECONOMIC AND SOCIAL HISTORY.[19] A clue to the character of Cottisford's land is given by its field names, first recorded in the early 13th century. Heath and fen predominate. For instance, there is Widemor, Mareweye, Nordmoresende, Nordesortheth, Cotesthorn, Blakelond (used elsewhere in this part of Oxfordshire of poor soil), and Eylesbrech. La Brueria presumably refers to the area later known as Cottisford Heath.[20]

Domesday Book states that there was land for 10 ploughs: in demesne there were 3 plough-teams, but

[85] Ibid. no. 172 and see below, p. 112.
[86] Ibid. nos. 100, 101.
[87] Ibid. nos. 104, 106.
[88] Blo. Cot. 23.
[89] E.C.R. no. 108.
[90] Ibid. no. 110.
[91] Ibid. no. 114.
[92] Inf. Lady Brooke-Popham, Cottisford.
[93] Inf. Eton Coll.
[94] E.C.R. no. 36.
[95] Ibid. nos. 24, 25, 38; Fines Oxon. 139.
[96] E.C.R. no. 26.
[97] Hist. MSS. Com. 9th Rep. App. I, 357: abstract of doc. not in E.C.R.
[98] Fines Oxon. 139, 149; E.C.R. no. 36.
[99] E.C.R. no. 38.
[1] Ibid. no. 35.
[2] Rot. Hund. (Rec. Com.), ii. 838, where he appears as Ralph 'de Thar'.
[3] Doc. Bec Lands, ed. Chibnall, 125; for the rent of a mark and a penny cf. E.C.R. no 38.
[4] St. Bart.'s Hosp. deed no. 1378; E.C.R. no. 39.
[5] St. Bart.'s Hosp. deeds nos. 1383, 1381.
[6] E 179/161/9.
[7] E.C.R. no. 294.

[8] Blo. Cot. 16–18.
[9] E.C.R. no. 66.
[10] Ibid. nos. 54, 55.
[11] See below, p. 111. No lands in Cottisford are mentioned in his will: R.C. Families, i. 26.
[12] E.C.R. no. 179.
[13] Ibid. no. 294.
[14] E.C.R. nos. 176, 179; and see below, p. 175.
[15] O.R.O. Reg. of Papists' estates, pp. 47, 92; see below, p. 336.
[16] O.R.O. Reg. of Papists' estates, p. 47; Bodl. G.A. Oxon. b 85b (57); Kelly's Dir. Oxon. (1864).
[17] Bodl. G.A. Oxon. b 85b (57).
[18] Ibid. c 317 (7): Sale Cat. 1898; Kelly's Dir. Oxon. (1920).
[19] This section is contributed by Mary Lobel. It is based on material supplied by Miss Margaret Toynbee (see above, p. 103, n. 1.) and on material at Eton College examined by permission of the Provost.
[20] E.C.R. nos. 25, 26, 30, &c. The following names also occur: Wowelond, N(H?)uperhinland, Oppingland, Walchamstede, Fuwelesdene, Lutleslade, Sortebrodelond, Gorefurlong, Hakesdefurlong, Fulridi, Ulfesford, Lilliesfurlong, Portwei, Stocwei (these place names from E.C.R. have not been printed in P.N. Oxon. i. 207).

land for four. The 10 villeins (*villani*) and 5 bordars presumably shared some plough-teams, though no figure is stated. Forty acres of pasture are recorded. The value of the estate had risen steeply from £5 to £8 since 1066.[21]

By the end of the 12th century, if not earlier, the parent village must have thrown off a colony at Cotes—'apud Cotes in parochia de Cotesford'[22]— possibly on the east side of the Crowell Brook, for there are several references in the records to its land and to a family of De Cotes. A William de Cotes, for example, was granted ½ hide of land in Cotes between 1194 and 1197,[23] and in 1279 the Abbot of Bec was said to hold 3 virgates there.[24] The early 14th-century bailiffs' accounts also mention separate meadow in Cote and 'Cotefeld'.[25]

During the 13th century there were many other developments. Progress on the abbey's manor is recorded in a custumal of about 1245[26] and in the Hundred Rolls survey of 1279.[27] In both records the number of customary virgaters and half-virgaters is 13 and 2 respectively, but in 1279 one cottar instead of 5 is recorded.[28] A category of tenant unknown to the Domesday account appears at both dates: there were 5 free tenants. One, William le Bar, was a member of a family which was to be of local importance for some generations. Before 1232 he had granted land (29 a.), houses, and pasture for 240 sheep to Biddlesden Abbey.[29] Another was Roger le Blunt (or *Blundus*), who in 1226 had granted the abbey over 5 virgates of land.[30] His son John in 1279 held 4 virgates of the abbey by the service of holding the court twice a year. The usual practice on Ogbourne's manors was for the prior, or his steward, or an itinerant bailiff to go the rounds of the manors, holding courts after Easter and again after Martinmas.[31] In 1245 all the free tenants had held of the abbot, but by 1279 only three were doing so or four including Richard Poure, whose position is uncertain; the abbot was himself a sub-tenant for half a virgate. At least 48 virgates were under cultivation compared with 40 (land for 10 ploughs) in 1086. The Cottisford virgate was 20 field acres,[32] so at least 1,060 field acres or perhaps about 700 statute acres were being cultivated. Actually as the Hundred Rolls account appears to be incomplete the extent was probably greater.

According to the custumal of 1245 the virgater owed a rent of 5s. and a number of works in addition. He must plough an acre at the feast of St. Martin for 'garsherth', whether with his own plough or another's. He must also plough an acre for 'cherset'.

At the spring sowing, he had to do a day's harrowing and a day's weeding; he had to mow the lord's meadow, lift and cart the hay. Between Lammas and Michaelmas he had to find a man for whatever work the lord needed. For the great boon-works of the lord he had to appear with his whole family and for three *precariae* he had to find two men. Usually food was provided and on one day hay for his horse. When he mowed he was allowed to take bundles of hay, i.e. as much as he could lift on the handle (*manubrium*) of the scythe. The half-virgater's services differed slightly: in particular if need arose he had to drive sheep, oxen, or other animals.

The smith's virgate was held on rather different terms. He paid 2s. and had to make the iron of three ploughs. He had to plough at 'garsherth' and find a man for the four autumn boon-works.[33] With the exception of four out of the six free tenants, all had to obtain licence to marry their daughters and to sell an ox or stallion of their own breeding. They had to pay all 'gifts' and common aids, give their best beast as a heriot, and if they died intestate all their chattels were to be at the disposition of the lord. For anything sold within the manor they had to pay toll; if they brewed for sale they must give ale money or a penny for *tolsextarium*.[34]

Some additional customs have been preserved on the early court rolls.[35] The abbot's tallage was regularly 20s. Fines were levied for leave to contract marriage with a widow, and for leave to give a daughter in marriage.

A series of account rolls beginning with an incomplete Pipe Roll of 1288–9 provide details of the manor's economy.[36] This account was audited by the prior's steward at Cottisford on 7 October 1289, and the court was held on the following day. Total receipts amounted to over £29.[37] By far the largest items were those resulting from the sheep flock: e.g. £19 18s. 8½d. was received for wool and skins. A fairly full corn account shows that the yield was over 34 qrs. of wheat, 70 qrs. of rye, 51½ of dredge, and 50 of oats.[38] Nearly all this was consumed on the manor by the *famuli* and their animals or used for seed.[39]

An account roll of 1292[40] shows that at the end of the year the animal stock consisted of 12 horses, 14 oxen, 13 other cattle, 68 pigs, 865 sheep and lambs, and 19 'busch'. £19 16s. was received for 73 stones of wool at 5s. 6d. a qr. and £6 16s. for other wool. Small quantities of cheese and butter, 22 qrs. of wheat, 15 qrs. of dredge, and 6 bus. of lentils were sold. The bailiff was resident at the grange and the *famuli* consisted of a carter, a miller, a reaper,

[21] *V.C.H. Oxon.* i. 427.
[22] E.C.R. no. 33.
[23] Ibid. no. 1. For the family, which can be traced down to 1266, see also ibid. nos. 28, 32, 38. For refs. to land in Cotes or 'le Cote', see ibid. nos. 28, 29, 31–33; *Bracton's Note Bk.* ed. Maitland, iii. 45–46; *Fines Oxon.* 80.
[24] *Rot. Hund.* (Rec. Com.), ii. 837–8.
[25] e.g. E.C.R. nos. 145–8, 150. Cf. references to Cote Field in the 17th cent.: see below, p. 110.
[26] *Select Doc. of Eng. Lands of Bec*, ed. Marjorie Chibnall (Camd. Soc. 3rd ser. lxxiii), 97–99.
[27] *Rot. Hund.* (Rec. Com.), ii. 837.
[28] Cf. extent of 1324 when 3 cottars paid rents of 1s. each; 13 villeins 5s. each; half-virgaters were not recorded and free tenants paid 23s. 5d.: E 106/8/5.
[29] E.C.R. no. 25.
[30] *Fines Oxon.* 76.
[31] Marjorie Morgan, *Eng. Lands of Bec*, 60.
[32] E.C.R. no. 256.
[33] Cf. John Smith, whose works were worth 7s. a year,

[33 cont.] who paid rent and made the iron of one plough (E.C.R. no. 144).
[34] *Doc. Bec Lands*, ed. Chibnall, 97–99.
[35] These are dated 1249, 1275, 1289, 1290: *Select Pleas in Manorial Courts*, ed. F. W. Maitland (Selden Soc. ii), 22, 23, 32, 37.
[36] *Doc. Bec Lands*, ed. Chibnall, 125–7. There are composite rolls for the Bec manors for 13 years between 1246 and 1320–1; separate accts. for Cottisford exist for 10 years between 1292 and 1360: E.C.R. nos. 144–51. For list see Morgan, *Bec Lands*, 6. For the Eton period there are 4 rolls: E.C.R. nos. 152–5.
[37] *Doc. Bec Lands*, ed. Chibnall, 125. Cf. *Tax. Eccl.* (Rec. Com.), 45, where fruits, flocks, and cattle are recorded as worth £8 14s. 4d.; lands, mills, rents, and court £10.
[38] 'Dredge' means a mixture of various kinds of grain, especially oats and barley sown together (*O.E.D.*).
[39] *Doc. Bec Lands*, ed. Chibnall, 125, 137.
[40] E.C.R. no. 144.

3 shepherds, a cowman and pigkeeper, 3 plough-leaders, 3 ploughmen, a dairymaid, a woman who collected herbage for the oxen and cows and harvested in autumn, a miller's boy, a boy to watch the animals in autumn, and a boy to help the shepherd. Among the payments made were £37 to the lord, 35s. 2d. to the king for the 15th,[41] and 3s. as a gift to the assessor of taxes.

In common with other Bec manors,[42] Cottisford manor had a separate bailiff or reeve, who was resident at the grange. Extents of 1294 and 1324 complete the evidence for the economy of the manor in this period. Cottisford, it has been said, was primarily an arable manor, with very light labour services.[43] The arable acres in 1294, not including the fallow, amounted to 128, of which 126 were sown.[44] In 1324 the arable had increased to 150 acres, of which 80 were separate and 70 were in the common fields. The latter were worth 1d. an acre—half the value of the separate arable. Sixty more common-field acres were fallow and of no value to the lord. There were 12 acres of meadow compared with 5 in 1294.[45]

In January 1325 the farm goods and stock consisted of over 22 qrs. of wheat at 5s. a qr., over 13 qrs. of rye at 3s. 4d. a qr., 60 qrs. of dredge at 2s. a qr., 10 qrs. of oats at 20d. a qr., 7 qrs. of mixed pease and vetches at 2s. a qr. There were 2 cart-horses (value 5s. each), 3 farm horses (value 4s. each), 6 oxen (value 6s. 8d. a head), 529 sheep, of which 194 were ewes and 140 two-year-old sheep (price 12d. to 1s. 2d. a head), and 21 head of poultry at 1½d. to 3d. a head.[46]

The prosperity of Cottisford was at its height at the end of the 13th century. In 1292 a flock of 765 sheep was recorded,[47] a figure never approached in the 14th century. A decline set in during the reign of Edward II, when part of the manor may have been let.[48] The number of *famuli* in 1318–19 was eleven with a 'repe-reeve' and a clerk for the accounts in the autumn, but in 1319–21 there were only eight *famuli*.[49] The decreased activity on the manor in the early 14th century is particularly noticeable in the smaller numbers of sheep kept. The flock, as far as the surviving accounts record, generally varied between 400 and 500 sheep.[50] It may be noted that the death-rate among them was often high: in 1321 more than half the lambs died. For the shearing and washing of the 260 to 370 sheep an extra boy was taken on. The wool was sold to merchants, who came to Cottisford to inspect it, and it was then carried to Bledlow (Bucks.), Henley, or Ruislip (Mdx.).[51]

Precise details about the customary services in the early 14th century are lacking. The bailiff stated: 'of the ploughings and works . . . all the ploughings were used in cultivating the lord's land. And the works were expended in the lord's services within the court and outside it, by tallies between the reeve and the customary tenants.' The tenants still performed some weeding and mowing services in addition to ploughing and harvest boons; in 1344–5 they were responsible for about 21 per cent. of the harvest work.[52] In 1324 the works of 13 villeins had been worth £3 6s. 7½d. and the autumn works of 3 cottars 1s. 1½d.[53]

There is little evidence for the topography of the fields beyond the fact that there were an East and a West Field in the early Middle Ages. Early 13th-century charters show that land was then equally divided between the two fields,[54] and the bailiff's account of 1319-20 records that the whole of one field was still being left fallow.[55] It is of interest in this connexion that in 1391, when Metteley (see below) leased the demesne, it was stated that there were '20 acres of fallow land of which 12 are being ploughed for the third time and manured with the fold'.[56] Pasture was clearly much prized and some was inclosed at an early date. In 1288, for instance, Bec's steward accused a man of trying to deprive the lord and his men of their common pasture, presumably by inclosing,[57] and it is known that the demesne had at least 86 acres of separate pasture at Cote.[58] Some, if not all, of the meadow was assigned by lot.[59]

Early 14th-century tax assessments show that the community was relatively small and far from rich: 15 persons were assessed in 1306, 16 in 1316, and 15 in 1327.[60] The total tax of £2 5s. paid in 1316 was only about a third of that paid by the larger villages in the hundred, such as Chesterton and Somerton. The abbey's contribution was naturally the highest, but it is worth noting that the amount paid by its grange in 1306 was unusually high—more than three times as much again as the next highest contributor —whereas in 1316 it was less than twice as much.

The break in the series of accounts between 1343 and 1360 is in itself significant of the dislocation caused by the Black Death. The badly written roll of 1360,[61] apparently the first since the disaster, begins by stating that no accounts have been kept for many years. The pardon, issued to John Hardyng in 1355, of his outlawry for non-appearance before the justices to answer a plea of the prior that he render an account of his bailiwick at Cottisford, affords an explanation, and throws light on the economic difficulties of men in responsible positions in these disastrous years.[62]

A comparison of the accounts of 1343 and 1360 well illustrates the severity of the economic consequences. In 1343 the amount realized for the sale of corn and stock, for instance, was £11; in 1360 it was £2 18s. 2d. The number of the *famuli* had dropped from 13, including 8 ploughmen, to 4, including the bailiff and only 2 ploughmen. Instead of the permanent shepherd once employed a shepherd was paid to fold his own sheep on the lord's land. Rents of

[41] This payment is not otherwise known: no tax list before 1306 has survived for Cottisford.
[42] See Morgan, *Bec Lands*, 54–55.
[43] Ibid. 87.
[44] E 106/2/6.
[45] Ibid. 8/5.
[46] E.C.R. no. 40.
[47] Ibid. no. 144.
[48] Morgan, *Bec Lands*, 100.
[49] E.C.R. nos. 146–8.
[50] e.g. ibid. nos. 145 (1316–17), 148 (1320–1).
[51] Ibid. nos. 145–9 (1316–22).

[52] Morgan, *Bec Lands*, 100.
[53] E 106/8/5.
[54] e.g. E.C.R. nos. 6, 8, 19.
[55] Ibid. no. 147.
[56] Ibid. no. 44.
[57] *Select Pleas*, ed. Maitland, 32, 37.
[58] See above, n. 36.
[59] See E.C.R. no. 8 for 'Dolmede'.
[60] E 179/161/8, 9, 10.
[61] E.C.R. no. 151. There were only 27 contributors to the poll tax of 1377: E 179/161/39.
[62] *Cal. Pat.* 1354–8, 212.

assize had dropped to less than half. A note adds that villein rents were not more because the tenements were in the lord's hand for lack of tenants. Furthermore, 9s. had been remitted so that they might pay the king's 15th. The rent of 13s. 4d. from one of the chief freehold tenements—John Bar's—was owing because 'it could not be raised'. The total receipts in 1343 had been £21 8s. 6¼d. and in 1360 they were £12 15s. 9½d.

The mills and the miller appear also to have been victims of the declining economic activity. There is a reference in about 1230 to the erection of a mill and to its water-power;[63] one is mentioned in 1291,[64] and in 1292 the exits of the manor mill were 30s. for maslin and malt sold.[65] At this period there were both a water and a windmill. The heading *custos molend(inorum)* occurs on the 1341–2 account roll, but not on the 1360 account.[66]

Another consequence of the Black Death may have been the final disappearance of the small hamlet of Cote, which seems to have been already in decline by 1343.[67] In this connexion an entry on the 1360 account roll stating that 3s. 4d. had not been paid to William de Audley (lord of Hardwick) for suit to the hundred done for the lord each year 'pro terra de Coteland' may be of significance.

Some measure of prosperity had returned to the manor by the end of the century, but judging from the tax assessments it seems that the decline noted on the manor in the early 14th century was a permanent feature and was probably true of the whole parish. Cottisford's earlier expansion could not be sustained in view of its comparatively small area. After the reassessment of 1334 its tax—in comparison with Chesterton's or Somerton's—was a good deal lower than it had been before,[68] and in 1428, as a village with fewer than 'ten inhabitants', it escaped taxation.[69] However, although the system of demesne farming had been abandoned as unprofitable,[70] the manor farm was fairly prosperous and well stocked at the end of the 14th century. Leasing had become the rule, and when it was leased in 1391 to Edward Metteley, a small country gentleman, there were 400 sheep and lambs, 3 horses, 8 oxen, 28 head of poultry, and a little boar. The crops grown were wheat, barley, maslin, peas, and oats.[71] Rye and dredge, regularly grown at an earlier date, seem to have been given up.[72]

The changes of ownership in the 15th century must have disorganized the economy of the manor. Although granted to Eton College in 1441, after having been farmed by various laymen since the dissolution of the alien priories in 1414, Eton did not immediately obtain possession. In 1454 the provost complained that the manor was unjustly detained by the Sheriff of Oxfordshire, and only obtained a decision in his favour in 1458.[73] Eton continued the system of leasing. The dangers attendant on this practice in

the 15th century may be illustrated by the history of 'Pygot's' freehold. It was leased by John Bar (Barres) from the college, but on the victory of Edward IV over Henry VI, relying on the king's hostility to the college, he planned to keep it permanently. When the two were reconciled Bar sold 'Pygot's', and it eventually came by way of the Samwells and Ardens to Thomas Langston of Tusmore. The last was 'aferde of hys tytle and would have gyven the college the patronage of Tusmore to have byn at a poynte with theyme'.[74] Throughout the 16th century the Arden family, members of the class of lesser gentry and lessees of the Eton manor, were the chief family in the parish.[75] John Arden held a freehold of four yardlands as well[76] and contributed five-sixths of the Cottisford tax in 1524. The village paid £13 4s. 4d. compared with Somerton's £27 1s. 1d. and Chesterton's £18 8s.[77]

The field system in the absence of any pre-inclosure maps cannot be satisfactorily made out. A 1612 terrier of Eton College's estate mentions a West and a North Field; in another terrier of 1675 the college's property is said to lie in North and South Fields; in a late-17th-century glebe terrier the glebe is described as lying in two fields, of which one lay eastwards and the other westwards.[78] In a terrier of 1700 and another 18th-century terrier of uncertain date the arable land is given as lying in East and West Fields.[79] It is doubtful if there were more than two fields. Considering the position of the village it would be possible to describe the arable as lying either north and south, or east and west. There are frequent references to Cote Field in the terriers, but this was a close of 100 acres which belonged to the college. So also did Winter Field (80 a.),[80] which may perhaps be identified with the Dry Great Ground (80 a.) mentioned in 1675. At this last date closes and meadows amounted to about 172 acres. Dry Great Ground and Poole Dry Ground (30 a.) may have been arable closes.[81]

The open-field system as so often elsewhere led to boundary disputes. A number of 17th-century records about these have survived. The fact that Arden's freehold was 'intermingled' with his 9 yardlands leased from the college gave rise to litigation, even though in the 16th century at least the boundaries of the two holdings and of others were clearly distinguished. A college memorandum of that period states that Arden's 6 yardlands are known by 'a balk in the middle of the land', Pygot's property 'by balks in the middle of the acre', and the college property by 'a balk in the middle of the land'.[82] Nevertheless, when Sir Anthony Cope bought 6 yardlands from the Ardens in 1606, he appears to have been sold some of Eton College's leasehold along with the Arden freehold, and protracted disputes followed, which were only ended by a Chancery decree in 1618 by which the college recovered its demesne.[83]

[63] E.C.R. no. 28.
[64] *Tax. Eccl.* (Rec. Com.), 45.
[65] E.C.R. no. 144.
[66] E.C.R. nos. 150, 151.
[67] The entries refering to Cote on earlier accts. do not occur in the 1343 acct.: ibid. 150.
[68] See below, p. 358.
[69] *Feud. Aids*, iv. 201.
[70] Morgan, *Bec Lands*, 113 sqq.
[71] E.C.R. no. 44, which also lists in detail the farm implements.   [72] Ibid. nos. 144–51 *passim*.
[73] E 368/227/32.
[74] E.C.R. no. 245. For the Bar family see above, p. 107. For Langston (Langeton) see below, p. 336.
[75] Eton Coll. leases. For the Arden pedigree see *Oxon. Visit.* 207.
[76] E.C.R. no. 256.
[77] E 179/161/176, 198.
[78] E.C.R. nos. 156, 164, 166.
[79] Ibid. nos. 167, 174.
[80] Ibid. no. 294, ff. 19–21.
[81] Ibid. no. 164.
[82] Ibid. no. 294, f. 23.
[83] Ibid. nos. 255–71.

At the beginning of the dispute Eton complained in 1606 of the encroachments of Robert Petty of Tetsworth, who held a 'very good farm' at Cottisford.[84] The provost complained that Petty and other tenants had allowed 'divers wrongs' to be done. In particular Petty had ploughed up and sown with corn 'Cuckolds Burrowe', and in order to deprive the parson of his tithes had declared that it belonged to Hethe parish, the tithes of which Petty farmed.[85] A crude contemporary map of 'Cuckolds Burrowe' shows that Cottisford and Hethe land was here intermixed, the furlongs of each parish being separated by grass balks.[86] In a terrier of 1700 the burrow was said to cover about 8 acres of heath land near Cote Field, which is known to have been in the south of the parish near the Hethe boundary.[87]

Sir Anthony Cope's tenants in Hethe also caused trouble after 1606 by pasturing their sheep in Cottisford fields.[88] The Cottisford tenants retaliated by cutting down Sir Anthony's corn in Hethe and making 'a great garboile there'.[89] Cope offered to discuss the boundary question with the college,[90] but the quarrel was still going on in 1607, when a college tenant complained that Cope had put 200 sheep on Cottisford common and was seeking 'his own private gain and the undoing of your poor tenants', who were unable to pay their rent.[91] Cope responded later by accusing the provost's servants of unjustly detaining his sheep at Cottisford.[92] Sir Rowland Lytton, Sir Anthony's brother-in-law, who afterwards sold his land to him, was also involved in this dispute. It was recorded in 1606 that Lytton had ploughed up and sown with oats above 100 acres of land, formerly used as pasture by the college's tenants.[93] This may have been the land in the south of Cottisford parish, on the Hethe border. It is uncertain whether this land was restored to pasture, but records in the late 17th century state that closes covering about 31 acres were customarily shared with Hethe from Michaelmas to Martlemas, and there may have once been a larger area of common land here.[94]

There might have been similar trouble at this time with the Fermors of Tusmore and Hardwick, who held property in Cottisford, had not the college and Thomas Fermor made a partition as early as 1576 of their pasture and heath in Cottisford.[95] In 1573 Fermor had gone to law with the college because of its refusal to divide 300 acres of arable, 10 acres of meadow, 100 acres each of pasture and heath, and 40 of moor in Hardwick and Cottisford (which they held together) so that each could have and inclose his moiety 'according to the statute'.[96] Rights of intercommoning between the two parishes are likely to have dated from early times and were no doubt encouraged by landowners holding land in both parishes. The Ardens, for instance, had been lords of Hardwick for most of the 15th century and may also have already owned land in Cottisford.[97]

The increasing interest in arable land is shown by references to the ploughing up of pasture. The college's tenant at Barsis Place was in trouble in the 1630's on this account and the matter was referred to the Archbishop of Canterbury.[98] There are references in 1700 also to 8 acres ploughed for the college on Juniper Hill, which was part of the heath, when the tenant of Sir John Holman of Ardley ploughed Sir John's 'heath piece' there.[99]

In about 1690 the Eton estate in Cottisford was valued at £176 10s. a year. Of this the closes and meadows were worth £126 10s. and the arable in the common field £50. It is uncertain if all the closes were meadow, but those so named were worth £70.[1] Another 17th-century valuation gives the total value as £164, but states that the bailiff in 1648 had said that the farms were worth about £200 besides the college rent. The rents in kind in 1690 included 60 couple of fat rabbits, valued at £3, and payments of wheat and malt valued at £57 16s. The entertainment provided for the college when on progress was valued at £16.[2] After 1587 all leases contained a clause obliging the tenant to provide entertainment for a day and two nights for the Provost and the college officers up to the number of ten.[3]

There is some evidence in the 17th century for the economic value of the rabbit warren, the history of which dates back to the Middle Ages, and of the need to control a potential pest. A warrener of Hardwick was leasing the warren in 1606, when trouble arose from poachers.[4] The rights of the villagers to protect their corn from the rabbits were carefully preserved, and the warrener was bound to see that there was no excessive increase in the number of rabbits. Further proof of the warren's importance comes from Ogilby's map, where 'Cottesford or a great Coney warren' is marked.[5] The college had 'free game of hunting and free warren'.[6] As bucks were a common present to the college from its tenant in the 17th century, the heath was clearly the home of large game as well as small.[7] A terrier of the manor in 1700, when Laurence Lord, gent., was tenant and there were five undertenants living in the parish, shows that Dove House Close and other closes covered about 88 acres and that there were 56 acres of meadow, including 31 acres shared with Hethe. It is probable from their position on the ground that all the 31 acres were meadowland, though only 10 acres were actually called meadow. The arable still consisted of 18 yardlands of dispersed strips. There were 40 sheep commons, 4 cow, and 2 horse commons to each yardland.[8]

[84] Wood, *Life*, i. 50. Cf. E.C.R. nos. 57, 59, 61, 63 for his tenancy of lands called the Warren and the Flats.

[85] E.C.R. no. 178.

[86] Ibid. no. 289.

[87] Ibid. no. 167: a terrier of 1700. For position of Cote Field see also ibid. no. 164: a terrier of 1675.

[88] Ibid. no. 178.

[89] Ibid. no. 179.

[90] Ibid. no. 183.

[91] Ibid. no. 187.

[92] Ibid. nos. 232–40.

[93] Ibid. no. 176.

[94] Ibid. no. 167. The land in dispute may, however, have been a part of the land in the north-west of the parish, later known as the 'intermixed' lands, which was shared with Hethe. See map above, facing p. 1, and below, p. 177.

[95] Ibid. nos. 54, 55.

[96] Ibid. no. 230.

[97] See below, p. 170.

[98] Blo. *Cot.* 21.

[99] E.C.R. no. 167. For the Holmans see above, p. 10.

[1] E.C.R. no. 166.

[2] Ibid. no. 165.

[3] Blo. *Cot.* 17.

[4] E.C.R. no. 250. For a Chancery case in *c.* 1500 about the warren, which was then rented for 10 marks p.a., see C 1/136/55.

[5] John Ogilby, *Britannia*, 1675 (London to Bucks. section).

[6] E.C.R. no. 164: terrier of 1675.

[7] Blo. *Cot.* 21.

[8] E.C.R. no. 167.

In the 18th century 54 acres of meadow and closes were let for £59 19s. 9d. The grounds 'lying open' to Hethe for six weeks were reckoned as 52½ acres and were let for £19 8s. Three grounds lying together in several amounted to 138 acres and were let for £47 16s. The warren was let for £10.[9]

During the first half of the 18th century Eton College's estate was neglected, and when Richard Eyre took the lease in 1739 he found it in a 'miserable condition'.[10] An account of 1759 shows that the estate then consisted of two farms in Cottisford worth £90 and £34 a year, the warren worth £8, Mr. Eyre's own farm and 'very good house' worth £97, besides the Fringford farm and mill, which were worth £55 a year. The total gross value was £284. The average rental of the estate was £8 and the fine on entry had been set at £250, though it was stated that it should have been £270. Eyre pleaded for an abatement on account of his great expenses, which as the accountant observed 'do indeed appear to have been very considerable'.[11] Although Eyre had spent a great deal on building and repairs, when J. R. Greenhill, the purchaser of the lease in 1773, paid £7,300 for it at an auction, he considered that he had paid 'a very extravagant price' and at least £1,300 too much. In 1776 he wrote that he had so far not made 3 per cent. on his money.[12]

In 1776 the Eton estate consisted of three farms, the tenant's (the Revd. J. R. Greenhill), and two let for £130 and £53 respectively. The warren was let for £8 and some meadow to a butcher of Hethe for £10—a rent double its real value.[13] When the lease of the manor was sold in 1773 it was said to consist of 240 acres of inclosed land and 800 acres of common field land, with a water-mill and a mill-house at Fringford.[14] Some of this land, however, must have been at Fringford, for the college had 4¼ yardlands there.

Apart from Eton College, the only proprietors in the parish in the 18th century were the rector and the non-resident Fermor family. Together these two held rather less than half the land.[15] James Fermor's property was described in about 1720 as the 'manor of Cottisford' with a manor-house, several closes, and 23 yardlands and four tenements. It was leased to William Topping at a yearly rent of £51 10s.[16] He resided and farmed his property himself. Evidence for his sheep-breeding comes from entries in the parish register: in 1715 'William Topping . . . shore 600 sheep' and 460 in 1716.[17] From 1725 to 1733 the family was at law with the college over fishing rights in Cottisford Great Pond.[18] When the Ramsays became proprietors they continued to lease the estate.[19] By 1832 a small part of it had been sold to the rector and the remainder was put on the market at the Tusmore sale of 1857.[20] It then consisted of 616 acres, chiefly arable, and was described as a fine stock farm, suitable for the production of turnips and barley of the first quality.

Before the inclosure of the open fields in 1854 farming practice had been very conservative. In 1761 Mrs. Martha Eyre and William Fermor of Tusmore[21] had taken unsuccessful steps to secure inclosure of the common fields and obtain an act of Parliament.[22] The matter was raised again unsuccessfully in 1777 after Mrs. Eyre's death and again in 1809 by the college's tenant, the Revd. J. R. Greenhill, Rector of Fringford. On the second occasion his efforts were frustrated by the alleged unreasonable demands of the Rector of Cottisford.[23] In 1848 an act was finally obtained, but the award was not made until 1854.[24] The chief allottees were the Provost of Eton and his lessees Edwards Rousby and John Kendal (489 a.), Sir Henry Dryden and Harriette Eliza Ramsay (592 a.), and the rector C. S. Harrison.[25]

When the tithe award was made in September 1855 Eton College had in hand about 30 acres of plantation and wood, and the manor-house and grounds, out of its whole estate of 865 acres. Its tenants William Mansfield at Manor farm and John Mansfield at Coneygre farm held about 370 and 137 acres respectively. Two other tenants with no houses in the parish held about 270 and 41 acres respectively. The college also had nine comparatively new cottages in the south-east corner of the parish. The cottages in the village and at Juniper Hill were owned by the Fermor trustee or by their occupiers. The chief tenant on the Fermor estate, Richard Woods, held three holdings of over 332 acres, 255 acres, and 27 acres, amounting to about 615 acres. There were two closes of about 30 acres (Home and Dove Home closes), which were exempt from tithe. The parson's glebe was about 70 acres. There were 676½ acres of arable at this time and about 82 acres of meadow and pasture including the non-tithable closes. A large part of the parish (350 a. 1 r.) was still uncultivated heathland held in common.[26] The tithe map marks some land as sainfoin ground, but there is no evidence about when the crop was first introduced.

In 1881 the Ordnance Survey map shows that Heath Farm had been built in the north of the parish and that there were five farms in all. In 1951 there were also five farms, including the experimental farm of Twyford Mills Ltd., the seed merchants of Banbury,[27] but much of their land lay outside the parish boundaries.

No constables' or overseers' books have survived, and the vestry minutes (1854–1928) and highway surveyors' books (1828–49), as might be expected in a small rural parish, are uninformative.[28] With some exceptions a vestry was held annually. In 1856–7, at the time of a dispute with Hethe over rates and boundaries, of which no details have survived, there were eight meetings. Until 1872, when constables ceased to be appointed, the village had two. There were 2 churchwardens, 2 overseers of the poor, and 4 allotment wardens until the last were reduced to 2 in the 1880's. In addition a guardian and two sur-

[9] E.C.R. no. 174.
[10] Ibid. no. 196.
[11] Ibid. no. 169. For Fringford see below, p. 130.
[12] E.C.R. no. 208.
[13] Ibid. no. 175.
[14] Ibid. no. 172.
[15] O.R.O. Land tax assess. 1760–1832; Oxf. Dioc. d 552.
[16] O.R.O. Reg. of Papists' estates, p. 92.
[17] Par. Rec.
[18] E.C.R. nos. 278–82. In 1773 the college leased it as part of its estate: ibid. no. 172.

[19] O.R.O. Land tax assess.
[20] Bodl. G.A. Oxon. b 85b (57): *Sale Cat.* 1857.
[21] Mrs. Eyre was the widow of Richard Eyre and aunt of Eton College's tenant in 1761. See above, p. 106.
[22] E.C.R. no. 197.
[23] Ibid. nos. 216–29.
[24] Incl. act: 11 & 12 Vict. c. 109.
[25] O.R.O. Incl. award.
[26] Bodl. Tithe award.
[27] *Kelly's Dir. Oxon.* (1939).
[28] Par. Rec.

veyors of the roads were annually appointed, and after 1865 a way-warden. From 1893 the vestry only appointed the churchwardens. Attendance at meetings dropped from 6 or 7 men to 2 or 3 in the 1870's during the agricultural depression and thereafter remained mostly at two. On one occasion in 1922 no one attended.

The first record of the parish's concern for the poor occurs in 1754 when two cottages were built on Juniper Hill for the use of the poor. They cost £28 7s. 6d. and the money was raised by a rate charged on the landholders.[29] The poor rate in Cottisford, as elsewhere in the county, rose rapidly in the late 18th century. In 1776 it was £32 10s. and in 1803 nearly £78. The rate of 4s. in the £ was rather higher than the average and was unusually high for a thinly populated parish.[30]

In the early 19th century the poor were accustomed to keep their cattle on the heath and had the right to cut furze and brushwood, but later the farmers 'usurped and sold the privilege'.[31] Flora Thompson has described in *Lark Rise* how towards the end of the century landless labourers had to keep their families on 10s. a week, but that the community was healthy and happy.[32]

Apart from an occasional groom or mason recorded in the parish registers, the inhabitants of Cottisford were nearly all farmers and agricultural labourers in the 18th and 19th centuries. There was a considerable increase in numbers since the 17th century. The nine householders recorded in the hearth tax return of 1662 and the six recorded in 1665 represent the richer inhabitants, though two of them were ultimately discharged from payment on the grounds of poverty.[33] In fact there were many more householders. The Eton estate alone had ten tenants with houses or cottages in the parish in 1675:[34] in addition there was the rector and the tenants of the Fermor manor. In 1676 the Compton Census recorded 46 adults in the parish. The Fermor farm-house still survives, but there is no record of its cottages until 1855, when the tithe award shows that there were then ten on the estate.[35] In 1738 the incumbent recorded twelve cottages, a farm-house, and a gentleman's house (i.e. Eton College's house and the present Cottisford House).[36] No Rectory was recorded throughout the century. There was some increase by 1768, when 18 families and 99 inhabitants were returned. The decade 1710–20 had the highest number of baptisms in the century.[37] There was a rapid rise in the 19th century. Numbers increased from 105 in 1801 to 187 in 1841 and to 263 in 1851.[38] The village then had a blacksmith and a baker.[39] Some of the new inhabitants were immigrants from outside: in 1841 there were 47 of these.[40] The peak was reached in 1871 with 327 persons. Thereafter on account of the agricultural depression numbers dropped to 240 in 1881. Mechanization encouraged the decline: in 1931 there were 169 inhabitants, mostly at Juniper Hill, and only 154 in 1951.[41]

CHURCH. Before 1081 Hugh de Grantmesnil had given the church with the tithes and a hide of land to the abbey of St. Évroul in Normandy.[42] In 1167 St. Évroul transferred its Cottisford property to the Norman abbey of Bec, which already held the manor, in return for an annual pension of 13s. 4d.[43] Although the patronage of the church is not mentioned, it was undoubtedly included in the grant, for from the early 13th century the Proctor of Bec, usually the Prior of Ogbourne, presented.[44] When the lands of the alien priories were confiscated by the king during the Hundred Years War, Ogbourne's property, including the advowson of Cottisford, passed to the Crown. The king, therefore, presented in 1370, 1374, 1375, and 1403. Henry IV granted away the manor in 1404, and thereafter the advowson followed the descent of the manor. Thus Eton College became patron in 1441, and retained the advowson until 1923, when it was transferred to the Bishop of Oxford. Since 1867 it had been held with Tusmore-with-Hardwick.

Bec never appropriated Cottisford, but from the early 13th century received a pension from the rector of 13s. 4d.,[45] which went to St. Évroul according to the arrangement of 1167.[46] This pension, which was paid to the Prior of Ogbourne,[47] was taken over by the king with the advowson, and by him granted to Eton College.[48] It was not infrequently in arrears, and is not mentioned in 1535.

Cottisford in the Middle Ages was a very poor church, worth £2 in 1254, and £2 13s. 4d. at the new valuation of 1291.[49] By 1535 it was worth £6 13s. 4d.[50]

During the next 200 years the value first rose rapidly to £66 net in 1611 (as recorded by the rector), and then dropped to £48 by the beginning of the 18th century, when it was discharged from the payment of tenths.[51] In 1723 it was helped by a gift of £200 from Queen Anne's Bounty and the same amount from the Dean of St. Paul's.[52] The greatest part of the income came from the tithes, which were commuted in 1856 for £321.[53] It is to be noted that a few acres in Hethe and Hardwick were tithable to the Rector of Cottisford.[54]

According to an imperfect terrier dated 1686, the glebe consisted of about 60 acres.[55] At about this time Bishop Fell noted—'The glebe much embezled, some akers quite lost, others lessend'.[56] The church

[29] Blo. *Cot.* 37–38.
[30] *Poor Abstract*, 404.
[31] MS. Top. Oxon. d 171, f. 303.
[32] For F. Thompson see above, p. 105.
[33] *Hearth Tax Oxon.* 208, 235.
[34] E.C.R. no. 164.
[35] Bodl. Tithe award.
[36] Oxf. Dioc. d 552.
[37] Ibid. d 558; Blo. *Cot.* 36.
[38] *Census*, 1801, 1841, 1851.
[39] Gardner, *Dir. Oxon.*
[40] Blo. *Cot.* 37 n. 1.
[41] *Census*, 1871, 1881, 1931, 1951.
[42] Orderic Vitalis, *Hist. Ecclesiastica*, ed. A. Le Prévost (Soc. de l'Hist. de France, 1845), iii. 22, 24.
[43] *Select Docs. of English Lands of Bec*, ed. M. Chibnall (Camden Soc. 3rd. ser. lxxiii), 17.

[44] For list of medieval presentations see MS. Top. Oxon. d 460.
[45] *Rot. Welles*, i. 28.
[46] Chibnall, op. cit. 17, 99.
[47] *Tax. Eccl.* (Rec. Com.), 31.
[48] Blo. *Cot.* 32.
[49] Lunt, *Val. Norw.* 312; *Inq. Non.* (Rec. Com.), 133. It is not included in the *Tax. Eccl.*, being worth less than 5 marks.
[50] *Valor Eccl.* (Rec. Com.), ii. 161.
[51] Blo. *Cot.* 33; Bacon, *Lib. Reg.* 792.
[52] Blo. *Cot.* 33; *Papers Rel. to Q.A.B. 1703–1815*, H.C. 115 (1814–15), xii.
[53] Bodl. Tithe award.
[54] Blo. *Cot.* 33.
[55] Oxf. Archd. Oxon. b 40, f. 106.
[56] Oxf. Dioc. d 708, f. 139b.

registers of this period and later also contain memoranda regarding the glebe. In 1848 it consisted of 50 acres.[57]

The first known documentary record of the parsonage house comes from the terrier of 1606,[58] which mentions 'an orchard, garden, little close, homestall and meadow adjacent to the parsonage house', and states that the rector may have furze to burn at his house at Cottisford. However, the date 1618 or 1619 can be made out at the back of the present Rectory house, and the tithe barn bears the date 1651, when it was restored. The house, its outbuildings[59] and barn[60] were in a bad state in the second half of the 18th century, and though repaired[61] by 1810, the rector, Samuel Cooke, complained to Eton about the house.[62] As a result the old Rectory was pulled down in 1821 and a new house was built for about £450 (builder, Peake of Fringford) at the expense of the rector, T. W. Champneys.[63] He, however, continued to live at Fulmer (Bucks.).[64] Non-residence in fact did not cease until the presentation of C. S. Harrison in 1853, when he enlarged the Rectory house at the then considerable cost of £400.[65]

No connexion has been found between the medieval rectors and the patrons, Ogbourne Priory and Eton College. Cottisford was no doubt too poor a living to attract Eton graduates.[66] James Arden (rector 1521–46) was probably a relative of the Arden family, the lessees of the manor. While he was rector John Arden (d. 1535), besides leaving bequests to the church, made elaborate provision for memorial services there. For a year after his death five priests were to keep his 'month's mind'; during the same year a priest was to say services for him, probably every day; and for seven years five priests were to say a yearly dirge and five masses for him.[67]

Non-resident rectors did not become usual until the 18th century, but an exception was Robert Clay (1609–24), a Fellow of Merton and a pluralist,[68] from whom the living was sequestered in 1616 for non-residence.[69] None of the resident rectors is worthy of note except William Paxton, who was a shining example of devotion to his cure, since the registers are consistently kept in his handwriting throughout the 29 years (1691–1720) of his incumbency. By contrast, the visitation return of 1738,[70] made by James Smith (1727–68), discloses an unsatisfactory state of affairs. To begin with, Smith was a pluralist: 'I constantly supply my vicarage of Hurley in Berks . . . tho' my family lives at a small Hospital (at Stoke) in Bucks. of which I am Master.' Smith paid for a resident curate, John Lord by name, though apparently not related to the family at the manor-house. Lord conducted two services on Sundays, read prayers on Holy Days, and celebrated Holy Communion three times a year. But there were very few communicants and children were not sent by their parents to be catechized, though, as Lord assured the bishop, he did his best for them. Lord also told the bishop that as the parish consisted 'of but few inhabitants and those chiefly illiterate and indigent labourers', the children's parents 'had it not in their power to instruct them themselves nor the means of procuring the instruction of a common school-master'.[71]

Unfortunately, John Prinsep, who succeeded Smith and who, in the return of 1768,[72] declared that he constantly resided at the Rectory house, was already an old man and died after a year at Cottisford. He had no time to improve what he found—'lukewarmness superabundant'. Prinsep's successor, Samuel Cooke, held the living for 51 years, but he is chiefly remembered as an opponent of inclosure and as a non-resident for at least part of his incumbency. He declared that the Rectory was 'so confined as not to admit of any clergyman's residence, however desirable in the neighbourhood of so many Roman Catholics belonging to the Fermor estates'.[73] For a time Cottisford was served by the Rector of Hethe: in 1793 he reported that the people attended church well and that a Sunday school was supported by private subscription.[74] Later (1814) the parish was served by a curate, living at Hethe.[75] Matters did not begin to improve until the advent in 1853 of C. S. Harrison, who followed Francis Hodgson, Provost of Eton and rector from 1842 to 1852. Harrison resided constantly in his parish until his death in 1896. He restored the church and keenly supported the day school.[76] As 'Mr. Ellison' he figures in *Lark Rise*, where he is unsympathetically portrayed by Flora Thompson as an old-fashioned, if kindly, autocrat.

The church of *ST. MARY* is a small building dating from the 13th century. It was described in the early 19th century as a 'low mean structure consisting of a tower covered with slate, a nave and chancel'.[77] The 'tower' was, however, no more than a bell-cote contrived by raising the pitch of the roof at the west end of the nave. The roof was made uniform in the 19th century, and the church now consists of a chancel, an aisleless nave, and a south porch. The three-light east window of the chancel seems to be late 13th century: a recess on the north side contains a stone tomb-slab decorated with the stem of a cross. The remains of the original rood-screen steps, rough stones about 2 feet high, were formerly visible under the pulpit. The south porch has a 13th-century doorway and two mass-clocks on the west side of the porch; there is also a priest's door.

When Rawlinson visited the church in 1718, he found it very much out of repair and 'very nastily kept by reason of holes and a pigeon house at the west end of it.'[78] The only 18th-century work recorded is the pointing of the walls and relaying of the pavement of the porch in 1757,[79] but the imposts of

[57] Bodl. Tithe award.
[58] Oxf. Archd. Oxon. b 40, f. 106.
[59] Ibid. c 62, f. 384.
[60] Ibid. f. 412.   [61] Ibid. f. 413.
[62] E.C.R. no. 223.
[63] Oxf. Dioc. c 454, ff. 170–1; ibid. c 435, pp. 350–6; Oxf. Archd. Oxon. c 62, ff. 460–1.
[64] Oxf. Dioc. b 38.
[65] Blo. *Cot.* 31.
[66] For Guy and Gilbert, two chaplains of Cottisford (c. 1200), see E.C.R. nos. 2, 4, 24. For Roscelinus de Andria (rector 1242/3–1277) see ibid. 29.
[67] Blo. *Cot.* 15–16: John Arden's will.

[68] See Foster, *Alumni*, and Wood, *Fasti*, i. 335.
[69] Bodl. MS. D.Phil. d 692 (thesis by Miss D. M. Barratt), p. 168; see also ibid. 57.
[70] Oxf. Dioc. d 552.
[71] Ibid. c 651, ff. 9–10.
[72] Ibid. d 558.
[73] E.C.R. no. 222.
[74] Oxf. Dioc. b 9.
[75] Ibid. d 574.
[76] Blo. *Cot.* 31; *Wilb. Visit.*; Oxf. Dioc. c 332, c 344.
[77] MS. Top. Oxon. d 171, f. 299.
[78] *Par. Coll.* i. 102; *Oxoniensia*, xvi. 60.
[79] Oxf. Archd. Oxon. d 13, f. 34*b*.

the chancel arch have crudely cut classical mouldings which suggest that the arch was reconstructed in the late 17th or 18th centuries. The parishioners re-seated the north side with open sittings in 1849 and the south side in 1854. In 1860 the rector, C. S. Harrison, reported that the fabric was in a very dilapidated condition, the roof not weatherproof, the windows unsightly, and the accommodation insufficient. Hopes of enlarging the church came to nothing, but restoration was carried out in 1861 by Charles Buckeridge at a cost of £365, largely raised by private subscription.[80] Most of the square-headed windows were gothicized,[81] and the small belfry shown in Buckler's drawing of 1825 was taken down. The church was retiled with Daneshill tiles in 1933.

The font was given in 1861 by John Mansfield of Hethe. There is a carved royal coat of arms of Georgian date (1714–1801), and an oak screen, dating from the 17th century, which was given by the rector, S. M. Statham, in 1935. The 18th-century organ, from the chapel in Steane Park, was installed in about 1940 as a memorial to him. It was made by Samuel Parsons of London: it has a sliding keyboard and an elegant mahogany case of Gothic design.[82]

There is a mutilated brass without inscription depicting a man in armour and his wife, both kneeling, and thirteen children. It bears the arms of Samwell and probably commemorates John Samwell (d. c. 1500), leaseholder of Eton's manor.[83] There was once a memorial inscription to Robert Petty (d. 1612), a Cottisford landowner, but it cannot now be traced.[84] There are wall monuments to the following: Richard Eyre (d. 1761) and his wife Martha Eyre (d. 1772);[85] James Edwards Rousby (d. 1848); Edwards Rousby (d. 1875); and C. S. Harrison (rector 1853–96). There is a tablet commemorating John Mansfield's charity.[86]

At the Reformation the church owned a parcel-gilt chalice, two sets of vestments, two copes, and a censer.[87] In the Commonwealth period there were a silver chalice, a carpet, and two chests.[88] There are now two Elizabethan chairs from Cottisford House in the sanctuary, and an old iron chest brought in 1953 from Fringford church. The present Elizabethan chalice and paten cover (1585) are respectively inscribed 'Cotsford Church Cup' and 'Cotsford'. Another chalice and paten, purchased in Spain, were presented by the 4th Earl of Effingham of Tusmore Park.[89]

The timber belfry in the apex of the roof contains two bells, dated 1710 and 1858, there were also two in the 16th century. A small late-17th-century sanctus bell is in the church.[90]

The earliest register contains baptisms from 1611, marriages from 1651, and burials from 1610. Those for baptisms 1760–1811 and burials 1762–1812 contain notes on the parish.

The base and part of the shaft of an ancient cross still stand in the churchyard near the south porch.

NONCONFORMITY. In the late 16th and early 17th centuries the Arden family, lessees of the manor, were recusants.[91] John Arden, his wife, and Ann Arden were fined as such in 1603, and his widow was again fined in 1605.[92] In 1610 Margaret Ewer was fined.[93] In spite of the fact that Cottisford was close to the Fermor estate at Tusmore, and that the Fermors held land in Cottisford, there were few Roman Catholics. One was recorded in 1685;[94] perhaps another, Thomas Pape, 'a Papist and carpenter', in 1701;[95] and in 1738 the rector wrote a full account of a papist farmer's daughter to the bishop.[96] In the early 19th century one family was visited by a priest from Tusmore.[97]

Protestant dissent has never been strong. A Methodist meeting-house was opened in 1844,[98] but there were only a few members,[99] and in 1860 the rector could write that 'the greatest unity prevails from almost the absence of dissent'.[1] In *Lark Rise* Flora Thompson[2] mentions a small group of Methodists, who met in a cottage in Juniper Hill in the 1880's.

SCHOOLS. In 1808 a dame school supported by subscriptions taught 12 children to read.[3] It had closed by 1815 when a few children attended Hethe school.[4] A Sunday school was established by 1819 and had 30 pupils in 1833.[5] There was a dame school again, supported by the rector, by 1852, and by the inclosure award of 1854 a plot was set aside for a village school. The rector said that it was impossible to raise the necessary money in the neighbourhood,[6] but with the help of Eton College a National school consisting of one large room was built in 1856 to accommodate 50 children. A two-roomed cottage adjoining it was built for the schoolmistress.[7] There were 30 pupils in 1860[8] and 42 in 1906.[9] Flora Thompson has described the school in the 1880's in *Lark Rise*. It was closed in 1920, but in 1924 it was leased to the County Council and reopened as a Council school. It was reorganized as a junior school in 1929 when the senior pupils were transferred to Fringford. There were 17 pupils in 1937 and 22 in 1954.[10]

[80] MS. Top. Oxon. c 103, ff. 292–8; Blo. *Cot.* 26.
[81] For the church before restoration see plate facing p. 104.
[82] *Church Guide.*
[83] Blo. *Cot.* 6.
[84] MS. Dunkin 439/3, f. 128 n.; see above, p. 111.
[85] See above, pp. 106, 112.
[86] See below, p. 116. For arms on monuments see Bodl. G.A. Oxon. 16° 217, pp. 106a, 110–11; ibid. 4° 685, p. 102.
[87] *Chant. Cert.* 84.
[88] Blo. *Cot.* 25.
[89] Evans, *Ch. Plate,* where there is a photograph; Par. Rec.
[90] Par. Rec. Inventory; *Ch. Bells Oxon.*
[91] See above, p. 110; C.R.S. xviii. 256, 260.
[92] Salter, *Oxon. Recusants,* 16, 22.
[93] Ibid. 26; for her see also above, p. 59.
[94] Oxf. Dioc. d 708, f. 139b.

[95] Par. Reg. Baptisms, sub anno 1701.
[96] Oxf. Dioc. d 552; ibid. c 651, ff. 9–10.
[97] Ibid. c 327, p. 294.
[98] H.O. 129/158. The meeting-house had 50 sittings but was not a separate building.
[99] It was on the Brackley Circuit in 1851; *Wilb. Visit.*
[1] MS. Top. Oxon. c 103, f. 292.
[2] See above, p. 105.
[3] Oxf. Dioc. d 707.
[4] Ibid. c 433.
[5] *Educ. of Poor,* 721; *Educ. Enq. Abstract,* 744.
[6] Gardner, *Dir. Oxon.; Wilb. Visit.*
[7] Blo. *Cot.* 39.
[8] MS. Top. Oxon. c 103, f. 295. There is a school report for 1897–9 among the parish documents.
[9] *Vol. Sch. Ret.*
[10] Inf. Oxon. Educ. Cttee.

CHARITIES. By will proved 1869 John Mansfield of Hethe left £100 in stock in trust for the poor, the yearly dividend to be distributed at Christmas to six of the oldest deserving poor of the parish.[11] At Christmas 1954 six old people received 9s. each.

Louisa Catherine Rousby of Cottisford House, by will proved 1917, left £100, the interest to be divided between the four oldest and most deserving in-habitants each year at Christmas. In 1954 four recipients were given 18s. 6d. each.

Grace Margaret Harrison bequeathed £100 in 1923 for the benefit of six of the oldest and most deserving poor. Six old people received 11s. 8d. each in 1954. It is permissible for one person to share in more than one charity, and the number of recipients of the three charities in 1954 was fourteen.[12]

FINMERE

FINMERE lies in the extreme north-east corner of Oxfordshire which is enclosed between Buckingham-shire and Northamptonshire. The River Ouse, which separates Oxfordshire from Buckinghamshire, forms its northern boundary, and the line of the Roman road from Bicester to Towcester separates it from Buckinghamshire on the east.[1] There have been no recorded changes in its boundaries or its area of 1,570 acres.[2] Geologically, the parish lies on the Great Oolite but is nearly all covered by drift gravel;[3] the soil is stiff clay, gravel, and stonebrash. The height above sea-level nowhere exceeds about 400 feet and falls to about 300 at the Ouse. Except in the south, where there are several plantations, Finmere, Grassy, Widmore, and Diggings Wood, the parish is remarkably bare of trees. It is traversed by the Buckingham–Banbury road, which was made a turnpike in 1744. The Roman road was then left as a bridle-way only.[4] In 1813 the branch turnpike road from Bicester was formed.[5] Two lesser roads connect Finmere and Water Stratford, over the Buckinghamshire border, crossing the Ouse by Fulwell Bridge.[6]

The parish is also crossed by two stretches of rail-way: one made in 1845–6, and formerly part of the London and North-Western Railway, and the other a branch of the Great Central Railway opened in 1899.[7] The nearest stations are at Buckingham and Westbury.

The village lies almost on the Buckinghamshire border, just off the main road from Buckingham and less than half a mile from the Roman road which marks the county boundary. Its name Finmere means 'pool frequented by woodpeckers'.[8] The chief part of the ancient and modern village lies to the north of a small brook, which was covered over in 1872.[9] The village is unusual in being sited at some distance from its manor-house, which used to lie in the ex-treme north-east corner of the parish, on land sloping down to the Ouse.

Finmere was among the larger villages in the hundred in the Middle Ages,[10] and in the 17th century it was among those of medium size: for the hearth tax of 1665, besides the manor and the Rectory, there were nineteen listed houses of which ten were farm-houses, returning mostly three or two hearths.[11] There seems to have been a steady growth in the size of the village during most of the 18th century, with a sharp increase in the last quarter.[12] Finmere continued to expand until 1851, when the census recorded 89 houses, but by 1901 had shrunk to 65 inhabited houses. There has been much re-building since the Second World War: by 1951 there were 72 houses.[13]

The present village straggles up the hill from the covered brook to the church.[14] Below the church, there is also a steep lane which runs down past the old schoolhouse,[15] built in 1824, to the drive of the 19th-century Rectory. The Rectory, a private house by 1955, was built in 1867[16] on a new site when the old one was pulled down. This last house is first described in detail in 1634, when it was a house of four bays, thatched and in good repair. Attached to it was a new barn, thatched and walled, as well as an old pease barn.[17] In 1662 a violent storm destroyed ten bays of building, perhaps part of the farm build-ings, of which the rector re-erected five.[18] In 1665 the house was taxed on six hearths, but three years later it was partly destroyed by fire.[19] The terrier of 1685 consequently notes that the rectory consisted of only three bays with barn and stable of four bays.[20] It had been again enlarged by 1738 when there were six bays and two stables: the terrier of 1805 adds the information that the house was built of stone and was thatched.[21] Its beautiful garden was described by Lord Selborne. It was laid out or rather improved by 'Capability' Brown at a time when he was working on the grounds of Stowe House (Bucks.), perhaps in the 1740's.[22] His grouping of trees gave 'the effect of a long perspective and considerable space . . . where there was really little'.

At the point where the street to Fulwell, with a number of cottages and houses on either side, branches off westwards from the main village street, a natural centre is formed, and here are the stump of what is known as the 'cross' tree, and the post

[11] Blo. *Cot.* 39; *Kelly's Dir. Oxon.* (1887).
[12] Inf. the Revd. C. Rayner-Smith.
[1] O.S. Map 6", xi (1885); ibid. 2½", 42/63 (1951).
[2] *Census*, 1881, 1951.
[3] G.S. Map 1", xlv NE.
[4] Blo. *Fin.* 23; 17 Geo. II, c. 43.
[5] Blo. *Fin.* 23.
[6] See below, p. 251.
[7] W. L. Steel, *Hist. L.N.W.R.* 185; R. Bucknall, *Railway Hist.* 69. For Finmere station see below, p. 285.
[8] *P.N. Oxon.* (E.P.N.S.), i. 209.
[9] Blo. *Fin.* 28.
[10] See below, p. 358.
[11] *Hearth Tax Oxon.* 204.

[12] Oxf. Dioc. d 552, d 558; ibid. c 327, p. 49.
[13] *Census*, 1811, 1851, 1901, 1951. Between 1945 and 1954 22 council houses were built: inf. Ploughley R.D.C.
[14] O.S. Map 25", xi, 16 (1881).
[15] See below, p. 124.
[16] Blo. *Fin.* 81–82: W. Ashwell, the patron, paid for it. It was sold in 1937.
[17] Oxf. Archd. Oxon. b 40, f. 129.
[18] Blo. *Fin.* 80–81.
[19] *Hearth Tax Oxon.* 204; Blo. *Fin.* 81.
[20] Blo. *Fin.* 81.
[21] Oxf. Archd. Oxon. b 40, f. 134; Oxf. Dioc. c 448, f. 63.
[22] Blo. *Fin.* 62, 81; illustrations of old and new rectories ibid. 52, 54; Dorothy Stroud, *Capability Brown*, 34.

office. In the 1880's there was a small green there and the stocks stood beneath the elm.[23] Many of the old cottages still (1955) have thatched roofs; they are built, some of red or vitreous brick, timber and rubble, others of brick and rubble only. A group of 20th-century council houses borders the Tingewick road to the south.

Two houses on the outskirts of the village are of special note:[24] Lepper's House, a stone-built house, dated 1638 with the initials 'I.Y.'(ates) and 'E.Y.'(ates), was rebuilt or altered in 1879. This date appears on the east porch with the monogram 'A.T.L.'(epper). When Lepper bought the house it was one story high and covered with a long thatched roof: he raised the walls and turned it into a two-story building. Finmere House with its 18th-century south front of brick dates from about 1600 and is T-shaped. The date 1739 appears on rain-water heads with the crest of a gazing stag, the crest of John Pollard, who bought the house, probably in 1739, from the James family, inheritors of a third of Finmere manor.[25]

There are several outlying farm-houses: Widmore Farm in the south-west of the parish, Warren Farm to the west of the village, Finmere Grounds to the north, probably built soon after the inclosure,[26] and Bacon's House in the extreme north-east corner. The last was the former manor-house or Court House, but takes its name from its early 18th-century owners. In 1887 Blomfield, possibly echoing local tradition, wrote that it had been a house 'of considerable size and pretensions, with . . . a court-yard . . . fishponds . . . a bowling green, garden, and pleasure grounds'.[27]

In the first half of the 19th century the Duke of Buckingham, lord of the manor, pulled down the greater part of the old house and reduced it to its present proportions, a pleasant small farm-house of stone. At the same time he destroyed the water-mill on the Ouse and built the existing farm buildings.[28] In 1853 Merton College, Oxford, purchased part of the farm and in 1858 the remainder.[29] Finmere Grounds is also an ancient house, probably built immediately after the inclosure of the common fields in 1667. It too was bought by Merton College in 1853, whose land in Finmere covers the whole of the north-eastern part of the parish and extends almost to the church.[30]

For a few years in the early 13th century a house in Finmere was occasionally used by King John. It was built in 1207 at a recorded cost of less than £50[31] by the king's carpenters.[32] As the work was supervised by Hugh de Neville, the king's chief forester,[33] and the house lay within easy reach of the forests of Bernwood and Whittlewood, there can be little doubt

that it was constructed as a hunting-lodge. It was ready by January 1208, when the king ordered wine to be sent there.[34] He subsequently stayed in it four times.[35] The overlordship of the manor was in the king's hands at the time,[36] and the house was built on land belonging to a hermit,[37] who had a hermitage there. As compensation he was assigned a penny a day for life.[38] After the king's death, however, he recovered his property, and in 1218 it was described as 'the place where the house of King John was situated'.[39]

The only other striking event connected with Finmere occurred in 1645, when a party of eighteen royalists, stationed here, was surprised by a force of parliamentarians from the garrison at Newport Pagnell and driven out.[40] Parliament troops were then quartered in the village. The local tradition that the troopers' horses were stabled in the Rectory was confirmed in 1867, when a quantity of oat-husks was found under the flooring.[41]

In 1840 the church bells were rung for the Dowager Queen Adelaide as she passed through the village on her way to Stowe,[42] and two brothers, Dr. James and Dr. Charles Clark, resident at Finmere House at the time, may be mentioned for their services to the community, particularly for the improvement of the sanitary conditions.[43] But several of the rectors were more outstanding, notably William Cleaver (1742–1815), successively Bishop of Chester, Bangor, and St. Asaph, and the saintly rector, W. J. Palmer (rector 1814–52),[44] the father of Roundell Palmer, Lord Selborne, and William Palmer, theologian and archaeologist.[45]

The following old customs survived until modern times: the pancake bell was rung on Shrove Tuesday at 11.30 a.m. and the curfew bell was rung each night from 4 October to 5 April.[46]

MANOR. Before the Conquest and for nearly twenty years after it the larger of two estates in FINMERE, assessed at 8 hides, was held by Wulfward the White, a thegn of Queen Edith. By 1086, however, like part of Wulfward's Buckinghamshire lands, it had been granted to Geoffrey, Bishop of Coutances.[47] On Geoffrey's death in 1093 his lands passed to his nephew, Robert de Mowbray, Earl of Northumberland, who forfeited them by his rebellion in 1095. A smaller estate of 2 hides was held after the Conquest by Odo, Bishop of Bayeux,[48] but was later joined to the larger estate, for the whole of Finmere became part of the honor of Gloucester, possibly as the result of a grant by William II to Robert FitzHamon of some of Robert de Mowbray's lands,[49] or perhaps by a grant by Henry I to his illegitimate son Robert of Gloucester.

[23] See illustration in Blo. *Fin.* 20.
[24] Inf. Mr. P. S. Spokes; Blo. *Fin.* 25.
[25] See below, p. 119; Blo. *Fin.* 24.
[26] Blo. *Fin.* 24.
[27] Ibid. 14; see illustration ibid. facing p. 8.
[28] Blo. *Fin.* 25–26.
[29] Inf. Merton Coll. Bursary.
[30] Blo. *Fin.* 26.
[31] Mr. H. M. Colvin supplied the facts in this paragraph. *Pipe R.* 1207 (P.R.S. N.S. xxii), 209; ibid. 1211 (P.R.S. N.S. xxviii), 84.
[32] *Rot. Lit. Claus.* (Rec. Com.), i. 80, 100b.
[33] *Pipe R.* 1207 (P.R.S. N.S. xxii), 209; cf. C 47/3/46/1: account of money 'liberata carpentariis Regis ad operacionem de Finemer' per manus Radulphi de Nevill apud Finemer' '.

[34] *Rot. Litt. Claus.* i. 100b.
[35] Itinerary prefixed to *Rot. Litt. Pat.* (Rec. Com.).
[36] As part of the honor of Gloucester, see below.
[37] See below, p. 122.
[38] *Rot. Litt. Claus.* i. 155.
[39] Ibid. 362.
[40] Blo. *Bic.* 29–30.
[41] Blo. *Fin.* 20.
[42] Ibid. 28.
[43] Ibid. 25.
[44] See below, pp. 121, 123.
[45] *D.N.B.*
[46] Inf. the rector.
[47] *V.C.H. Oxon.* i. 379, 427; *V.C.H. Bucks.* i. 216–17.
[48] *V.C.H. Oxon.* i. 404.
[49] See below, pp. 175, 286.

The overlordship of Finmere followed the descent of the Earldom of Gloucester,[50] and after the death of Gilbert de Clare in 1314 passed to Hugh Audley, who married Gilbert's sister Margaret. Hugh's only daughter and heiress Margaret married Ralph, Earl of Stafford, and after Hugh's death in 1347 the overlordship followed the descent of the Earldom of Stafford.[51]

The tenant of both Finmere estates in 1086 was a certain Robert.[52] By the mid-12th century Finmere was held by the De Turri family, who were tenants of the nearby Buckinghamshire manor of Tingewick, and were closely associated with the Earls of Gloucester in their lordship of Glamorgan.[53] Gregory son of Robert de Turri, who may have held Tingewick as early as 1135,[54] had lands in Oxfordshire in 1158: about 10 hides, which may well have been Finmere.[55] Gregory had been succeeded by his eldest son William by 1176.[56] Some time in the reign of Richard I, William son of Gregory remitted to Biddlesden Abbey (Bucks.) the rent of £2 which it owed him for Finmere mill, the abbey undertaking to pay the £4 a year William owed to a Jewess of Oxford. Later, William granted lands in the manor to the abbey in return for the discharge of a debt of 8 marks owed to the Jews.[57] Gilbert of Finmere, William's elder son, succeeded his father in about 1205;[58] he was one of the collectors of the carucage in Oxfordshire in 1220,[59] and died soon after 1225,[60] leaving three daughters by his wife Emma: Philippa, wife of William de Bois, Alice, wife of Robert de Chandos, and Cecily, wife of David de Bovenden.[61] The three husbands held Finmere as 1 knight's fee in 1243, but in 1247 Robert de Chandos's portion and in 1251 William de Bois's portion were purchased by Laurence de Broke.[62] The latter received a grant of free warren in his Finmere demesnes in 1251,[63] and appears to have acquired the whole manor by 1255.[64]

On Laurence de Broke's death in 1274 Finmere passed to his son Hugh,[65] who was holding the manor in 1285.[66] In 1295, however, the Earl of Gloucester's tenant was said to be 'the heir of Robert of Finmere', presumably the Osbert of Finmere who was named as tenant in 1314.[67] Robert and Osbert were in fact probably sub-tenants, and Robert may be identical with Robert Peronele who

had held ½ hide under Hugh de Broke in 1279 and who was perhaps a son of Pernel of Finmere,[68] who had been granted 2 virgates by Gilbert of Finmere in 1222.[69] Hugh de Broke, who was dead by 1300,[70] was succeeded at Finmere by his son Laurence, but the latter, as he afterwards asserted, was unlawfully dispossessed by Walter de Langton, Bishop of Coventry and Lichfield.[71] The bishop was in possession in 1300,[72] but in 1301 he alienated the manor to Sir William Tuchet.[73] In 1312 Tuchet granted Finmere to Bartholomew Badlesmere; it was regranted to him in part with the provision that it should revert to Badlesmere if Tuchet died without issue.[74] Both Tuchet and Badlesmere took part in Thomas of Lancaster's rebellion and were hanged in 1322 after the battle of Boroughbridge.[75] Finmere was claimed by Laurence de Broke soon afterwards,[76] but the manor probably remained in the king's hands until 1333. William Tuchet had died childless and under the settlement of 1312 the manor was claimed for Giles, son and heir of Bartholomew Badlesmere.[77] Giles received his father's lands in 1333 and at his death in 1338 held two-thirds of Finmere.[78] A compromise had evidently been reached with the De Brokes, for Laurence's widow Ellen held the remaining third of the manor until her death in about 1341.[79] Giles's widow Elizabeth was given his part of Finmere in dower,[80] and she and her successive husbands, Hugh Despenser (d. 1349) and Guy de Brian, held it until her death in 1359.[81] By a partition made in 1341 the reversion of Finmere had been allotted to Giles Badlesmere's third sister and coheiress Elizabeth,[82] who had married firstly Edmund Mortimer (d. 1332), by whom she had a son Roger, Earl of March, and secondly William de Bohun, Earl of Northampton. In 1346 Elizabeth and William held the third of the manor which had been Ellen de Broke's dower:[83] this part William retained after his wife's death in 1356 until his own death in 1360.[84] Roger Mortimer inherited two-thirds of the manor on the death of Giles Badlesmere's widow in 1359, but also died in 1360,[85] a few months before William de Bohun. Roger's heir Edmund was a minor, and in 1361 his wardship and the custody of the manor of Finmere were granted by Edward III to his daughter Isabel.[86]

Edmund was granted his father's lands in 1373

[50] e.g. *Red Bk. Exch.* (Rolls Ser.), 288; *Cal. Inq. p.m.* iii, p. 248; ibid. iv, p. 344.
[51] *Complete Peerage*, v. 719; C 135/230/1.
[52] *V.C.H. Oxon.* i. 404, 427.
[53] *V.C.H. Bucks.* iv. 249–50; *Cur. Reg. R.* Ric. I (P.R.S. xxiv), 221; W. de Gray Birch, *Hist. of Margam Abbey*, 42–44.
[54] *Cur. Reg. R.* Ric. I (P.R.S. xxiv), 221.
[55] *Pipe R.* 1156–8 (Rec. Com.), 150; cf. *Red Bk. Exch.* (Rolls Ser.), 288 where 'Gregory' is perhaps Gregory son of Robert.
[56] *Pipe R.* 1176 (P.R.S. xxv), 177; cf. Birch, *Margam Abbey*, 44.
[57] *Collectanea*, ii. (O.H.S. xvi), 291; B.M. Harl. Ch. 84, D 15; 86, C 24.
[58] *Pipe R.* 1204 (P.R.S. N.S. xviii), 232; ibid. 1205 (N.S. xix), 105; *Oseney Cart.* v. 142, 407.
[59] *Bk. of Fees*, 315.
[60] *Oseney Cart.* v. 422, 464.
[61] Ibid. 188; *Fines Oxon.* 142, 163; E 210/D 3451.
[62] *Bk. of Fees*, 824; *Fines Oxon.* 151, 157, 163.
[63] *Cal. Chart. R.* 1226–57, 372.
[64] *Rot. Hund.* (Rec. Com.), ii. 44. For De Broke's ancestry and his other Oxon. lands see *Cal. Inq. p.m.* ii, p. 75; E. Hasted, *Kent*, i. 253; *Fines Oxon. passim*.
[65] *Cal. Inq. p.m.* ii, p. 75.

[66] *Feud. Aids*, iv. 157.
[67] *Cal. Inq. p.m.* iii, p. 248; ibid. v, p. 344.
[68] *Rot. Hund.* ii. 837, where other members of the family are mentioned.
[69] Pernel does not appear to have been Gilbert's kinswoman: *Bracton's Note Bk.* ed. Maitland, iii. 425, 707; *Cur. Reg. R.* x. 71, 349; *Fines Oxon.* 65.
[70] *V.C.H. Bucks.* ii. 333.
[71] *Cal. Inq. Misc.* ii, p. 143. For Langton see *D.N.B.*
[72] *Cal. Chart. R.* 1257–1300, 481.
[73] C.P. 25(1)/285/25; cf. *V.C.H. Bucks*, iv. 216 for the De Broke manor in Preston Bissett which followed a similar descent.
[74] *Cal. Inq. p.m.* vii, p. 240; cf. *Feud. Aids*, iv. 169.
[75] *Complete Peerage*, ii. 598–9.
[76] *Cal. Inq. Misc.* ii, p. 143.
[77] *Cal. Inq. p.m.* vii, p. 240.
[78] Ibid. viii, pp. 130, 141; *Complete Peerage*, i. 372–3.
[79] *Cal. Inq. p.m.* viii, p. 141; *Cal. Close*, 1341–3, 149.
[80] *Cal. Close*, 1337–9, 499.
[81] *Feud. Aids*, iv. 179; *Cal. Inq. p.m.* x, pp. 416–17.
[82] *Cal. Close*, 1341–3, 149.
[83] *Feud. Aids*, iv. 179.
[84] *Cal. Inq. p.m.* x, pp. 248, 525.
[85] Ibid. p. 530.
[86] *Cal. Pat.* 1358–61, 552.

and Finmere then followed the descent of the Earl-dom of March until the death of Edmund, the 5th earl, in 1425.[87] Edmund's nephew and heir Richard, Duke of York, son of Richard, Earl of Cambridge, and Anne Mortimer, was a minor and in 1428 Fin-mere was in the custody of Sir Richard Neville.[88] Richard, Duke of York, was attainted in 1459 and killed at Wakefield in 1460, but shortly after his attainder Henry VI granted Finmere with other lands to his duchess, Cecily, for her support.[89] After his accession as King Edward IV in 1461 Richard's son confirmed the grant to his mother, and it was again confirmed by Richard III in 1484.[90] After Cecily's death in 1495 Finmere reverted to the Crown.

Henry VIII granted Finmere to four of his queens, to Katherine of Aragon in 1509, to Jane Seymour in 1536, to Anne of Cleves in 1540, and to Katherine Howard in 1541.[91] In 1546 the manor was granted to Leonard Chamberlayne of Shirburn and John Blundell, mercer, of London.[92] Blundell acquired the whole manor in 1547 and died in possession in 1559.[93] Finmere was then divided between his three daughters, Elizabeth, wife of Edmund Hogan; Mary, who married firstly Gerard Croker and secondly Richard Lee; and Theodora, who married firstly John Denton and secondly Justinian Champneys.[94] In 1602 Theodora's son Richard Champneys sold his third part of the manor to John Temple of Stowe (Bucks.).[95] Mary's son John Lee conveyed his third part to John Croker and others, who sold it in 1614 to John Temple's son, Sir Thomas Temple, Bt. Two-thirds of the manor thereafter followed the same descent as Stowe,[96] and the Temples held the manorial rights.[97] In the late 16th century this included the privilege of proving in the court baron the wills of people who died within the manor.[98] The remaining third of Finmere remained with the descendants of Elizabeth and Edmund Hogan for four generations. Her granddaughter Elizabeth Hogan married Sergeant Thomas Waller, who was in possession in 1667.[99] Their daughter Dorothy married John James, a barrister and a member of an Essex family. The Jameses were buried in Finmere church, as was their son Hogan James, who died without children in 1725. He bequeathed his share of the manor to his aunt Frances James, who on her death in 1739 left it to Nathaniel Bacon, a kinsman by marriage, who had inherited another part. Nathaniel died in 1746 and his brother Edward sold his share to Richard, Earl Temple, soon afterwards.[1] Earl Temple's descendant Richard Grenville, 2nd Duke of Buckingham and Chandos, sold the manor in 1848, when the chief purchasers were Merton College, John Warner, and John Painter, and manorial rights lapsed.[2]

ECONOMIC AND SOCIAL HISTORY. Domes-day Book records that on the Bishop of Bayeux's

small estate there was land for 2 ploughs, but that the tenant's men had only one at work. On the larger estate of the Bishop of Coutances[3] there was land for 9 ploughs, although only 8 (2 being on the demesne) were employed. No labourers are recorded for the small estate, but as both estates were held by a cer-tain Robert it is likely that the 4 demesne serfs, 10 villeins (*villani*), and 5 bordars recorded for the large estate covered the total labour supply. The value of the small estate had sunk to 40s., half of its pre-Conquest value; while the other remained stationary at £8. A hundred acres of pasture are mentioned, also woodland a furlong square and a mill rendering 14s.

The only evidence for economic conditions in the early 13th century comes from a charter of about 1200, which indicates that the canons of St. Augus-tine's, Bristol, were keeping sheep on their land in Finmere.[4]

By the end of the 13th century there had been tenurial changes and a considerable growth in popula-tion. In 1279 there were 4 free tenants and 29 villein virgaters. The free tenants held 8½ virgates between them and owed scutage and rent, with the exception of one who held his 4 virgates by military service as $\frac{1}{10}$ knight's fee. The villeins each paid 4s. and owed works, paid tallage, and were fined if their sons left the manor. Their names suggest a population of comparatively recent growth, many families having come from neighbouring villages such as Hethe, Fringford, Fritwell, and Willaston and being still called after them. An unusual number of them are named after parts of the village: 'ate Tunesende', 'ate Welle', 'ate Broke', and 'ate Church'.[5]

Two 14th-century extents, of 1338 and 1359, cover two-thirds of Finmere manor, the part held in turn by Giles Badlesmere and his widow Eliza-beth.[6] Their demesne contained some 200 acres of arable, valued at 4d. an acre in 1338 and 2d. an acre in 1359, 5¼ acres of meadow at 2s. an acre, and 4 acres of pasture at 6d. an acre. A park of 80 acres, partly wooded, was worth £1 a year, but the rabbit warren was worth only 2s. as pasture because it had been destroyed before Giles's death. The number of customary tenants in 1338 is not explicitly stated, but there were certainly 9 cottars and possibly 16 villeins. The villeins owed each year 48 ploughing works valued at 1½d. each, 16 harrowing works at 1d., 48 weeding works at ½d., 16 lifting and carrying works at 1d., 16 mowing works at 2d., 306 autumn works at 2d., 16 works collecting stubble at ½d., and 16 works carrying wood at 1d. each. The cottars owed 30 weeding works at ½d., 81 autumn reaping works at 1½d. and 9 works collecting stubble at ½d. each. No indication is given of how many of these works were exacted, if any. Besides these labour services the customaries owed £1 6s. 8d. 'Martin-mesgeld', 12s. 11¼d. in loaves and poultry at Christ-mas, and 9d. Peter's pence on 1 August. The total annual value of the estate was £16 16s. 5d. By 1359

[87] *Complete Peerage*, viii. 446 sqq.
[88] *Feud. Aids*, iv. 189.
[89] *Cal. Pat.* 1452–61, 131.
[90] Ibid. 1461–7, 131; ibid. 1476–85, 459.
[91] *L. & P. Hen. VIII*, i, p. 50; ibid. xv, p. 52; ibid. xvi, p. 241.
[92] Ibid. xxi (2), p. 160.
[93] Blo. *Fin.* 13; C 142/121/143.
[94] Blo. *Fin.* pedigree between pp. 12 and 13 illustrates the descent from 1559 to 1746.
[95] C 142/575/142.

[96] Ibid.; G. E. C. *Baronetage*, i. 82–83; *V.C.H. Bucks.* iv. 232–4.
[97] *Par. Coll.* ii. 145–6.
[98] Blo. *Fin.* 18.
[99] See below, p. 120.
[1] Blo. *Fin.* pedigree and pp. 13, 15, 82.
[2] Ibid. 24; *Complete Peerage*, ii. 406–10; xii (1), 657–9.
[3] *V.C.H. Oxon.* i. 404, 427.
[4] Magd. Coll. Arch., Brackley Cart. i, B. 234.
[5] *Rot. Hund.* (Rec. Com.), ii. 837.
[6] C 135/56–57; ibid. 145.

this had fallen to £13 11s. 2d. The mill and dovecote brought in 10s. and 2s. 6d. instead of 13s. 4d. and 4s. 5¾d.; the demesne arable, although increased to 234 acres, was valued at 39s. instead of 44s. 8d. for two-thirds of the arable in 1338. But the most striking difference appears in the receipts from rents and customary works. Rents were worth £6 18s. 8d. compared with £5 18s. 2d. in 1338 and works £1 16s. compared with £5 15s. 3¾d. In 1359 the customaries were holding 18 virgates, a little less than two-thirds of the recorded 29 virgates of 1279; no vacant holdings are noted in the extent, but the decline in the value of the customary payments indicates that Finmere had suffered from the effects of plague, though not so catastrophically as elsewhere.

The only evidence for the medieval field system comes from the extent of 1338. As two-thirds of the lord's arable was then sown it seems that there were three fields.[7]

Fourteenth-century tax lists show that Finmere was one of the fairly prosperous communities in the hundred.[8] The names of 21 persons appear on the subsidy roll for 1523, but the smallness of the total contribution[9] in comparison with other villages and with previous payments in the 14th century suggests that there had been a considerable decline in prosperity and population since the first half of the 14th century. Part of this may have been due to the Black Death.[10]

The division of the manor into five separate estates in 1574 meant that in the post-Reformation period the village continued to suffer from absentee landowners. In the second half of the 17th century, however, the manor-house was let to three families in succession, the Keats, the Gardiners, and the Payntons, who may have supplied in some measure the place of the owners.[11] In the latter half of the 18th century the Pollards of Finmere House were the only family of any standing;[12] their name occurs in the land-tax assessments until 1807, when the Halls supersede them as the leading family.[13]

The Paxtons, whose name appears in the registers from 1561 onwards, were the chief yeoman family. John, who died in 1615, had a substantial holding which his son William inherited.[14] The family was prominent throughout the 17th century,[15] and the rector described Peter Paxton at his death in 1677 as 'the head of the people of our place'.[16] As late as 1808 a Paxton was serving as a churchwarden and the name occurs on the land-tax list for 1832.[17]

The small extent of the parish and the comparatively small number of freeholders encouraged early inclosure. It was effected in the 1660's by agreement between the principal owners and occupiers on the grounds of the inconvenience of the existing 'intermediary' which produced 'involuntary trespass'. A survey was made in 1661, and in 1663 the rector, Richard Horn, noted in the register that the field had been inclosed and allotments awarded,

Sir Richard Temple and Thomas Waller receiving lands worth £220 and £112 a year respectively.[18] The rector was accused by Temple and Waller of having made difficulties, and of refusing to comply with the surveyors' award, and a collusive suit followed in Chancery so as to get the agreement formally ratified. In 1667 an inclosure agreement was finally drawn up and ratified in Chancery in 1668.[19] Of about 1,300 acres inclosed Temple received 556 acres and Waller 414 acres, the former's arable being in 10 inclosures of an average size of 35 acres, and the latter's in 16 inclosures of about 23 acres average size.[20] Between them they received 19 acres of meadow, at least 17 acres of closes including the mill and its close, and 99 acres of woodland— Finmere Park. Temple received the whole of Finmere Warren, 125 acres. The largest of the resident holders was Peter Paxton with 117 acres, and there were smaller awards to six others including the rector and the trustees of the poor's land.[21] All proprietors were allowed to kill rabbits on their own land, and the fern on the Warren was to be divided proportionally between them, being allotted by 1 September and carried away by 18 October each year. The fern was not to be destroyed save by ploughing.

The Temples acquired the Waller estate of 1667 in the 18th century,[22] and in 1786 the Marquess of Buckingham's estate was by far the largest in Finmere, and was assessed for land tax at £66 compared with the £20 and £16 paid by the two next largest of a total of seven estates. There were then 11 occupiers. There had been little change by 1832, when there were 8 estates and 14 occupiers, 7 of them tenants of the Duke of Buckingham.[23]

The Vestry Books (1815–33) give much information about conditions after the Napoleonic War.[24] In 1818, 2s. a week was enough to keep a girl of under ten years. In 1817 labourers were to get 17s. a week in haytime; in 1826 this was reduced to 8s. a week, although the Duke of Buckingham paid his men 9s., in his view the minimum subsistence wage. The lowness of wages in general is evident from the fact that in 1821 23 persons were forced to apply for relief because of the rise in the price of bread. The vestry's chief business was to cope with the severe unemployment in the parish, and the methods adopted show the advantage to the village of having a good landlord and a conscientious rector. The Duke of Buckingham, as 'open hearted' as he was wealthy, and the Revd. William Palmer were most active.

Details of the 'roundsmen system'—an effort to give work to the many able-bodied men living on parish relief—are first recorded in 1818, when there were 24 such men. The men and boys were divided into four groups according to their age and were allocated to employers in proportion to the value of their land. The overseers gave applicants for relief

---

[7] C 135/56–57. In the 17th cent. there were South Field, Mill Field, and the Field next Fulwell: Oxf. Archd. Oxon. c 141, pp. 317, 321.

[8] See below, p. 358. [9] E 179/161/198.

[10] See above.

[11] Blo. *Fin.* 14–15.

[12] Oxf. Dioc. d 555; Blo. *Fin.* 16.

[13] O.R.O. Land tax assess. [14] C 142/358/92.

[15] They had a 3-hearth house in 1665: *Hearth Tax Oxon.* 204.

[16] Par. Reg.

[17] Blo. *Fin.* 69; O.R.O. Land tax assess.

[18] Blo. *Fin.* 20–21.

[19] O.R.O. Incl. deed and a copy of proceedings in Chancery.

[20] Blo. *Fin.* 82–91: abstract of incl. deed.

[21] See below, p. 121.

[22] See above, p. 119.

[23] O.R.O. Land tax assess.

[24] Par. Rec.

work, either on the highways or in the Duke of Buckingham's woods. The number of unemployed increased rapidly: in 1820 there were 33 men on the rounds and 55 in 1822. By 1826 nearly the whole village was living on relief; out of 90 able-bodied men with families only 19 were in regular employment—of these 5 were in trade and 7 in service, and women and girls were obliged to do lace-making. The average expenditure on the poor in the 1820's was £473. In September 1826 the vestry submitted to the Duke of Buckingham a number of resolutions dealing with the problem. In spite of great overcrowding the vestry, for fear of encouraging increases in the population, refused to recommend the building of new cottages. It recommended, however, letting land to the poor. The plan of letting small allotments of land to agricultural labourers for spade husbandry was, therefore, tried here at a comparatively early date. From 1826 to 1833 the Duke of Buckingham rented Poor's Plot from the churchwardens and let it to the poor at cheap rates with the aim of eradicating pauperism. Then in 1834 he subdivided a farm into allotments, but this scheme was not very successful, as the allotments were too large for spade husbandry and too small to be successful as smallholdings. Meanwhile the rector, William Palmer, had drawn up a new code of rules for the management of Poor's Plot. His scheme was still working in 1887.[25]

Another remedy recommended in 1826 was to use money from the rates to apprentice children, £15 to be spent in the first year, £75 and £90 in the two following years. Ten children were apprenticed between 1826 and 1831 to men outside the parish, but in 1832 an attempt to apprentice nine boys, mainly to Northampton cordwainers, failed as the parents were unwilling to part with their children. Only three were sent. The vestry also agreed in 1826 that no new-comer should be given legal settlement in the village; that no relief should be paid to persons living outside the parish; that a premium of £2 should be paid to any man finding work outside the parish, and that the overseers should not give relief to anyone who refused work.

A proposal made in 1829 to adopt the workhouse system was abandoned on account of the too great expense of building a workhouse. In 1831 money from the rates was paid to help families to emigrate. The first family to go was that of Paxton, one of the leading farmers, and in 1832 four more families left for New York. In 1832 there were still 54 able-bodied men out of work as well as 43 boys under 21, and 12 older men. The vestry, therefore, agreed that farmers should employ two labourers for every 100 acres owned, and that the parish should employ one man to every mile of road, two men on the turnpike, and two older men to keep the village streets and paths tidy.

Other questions dealt with by the vestry included the administration of the parish's charities and ap-

plications for special help. These seem to have been treated sympathetically: for instance, in 1823 £2 15s. was spent on sending a man to London to have his eyes cured. The overseers paid a surgeon to look after the village poor and also sent a subscription to the Oxford infirmary.

The vestry normally consisted of 2 to 8 members; an attendance of 33 in 1830 was quite exceptional. The rector or his curate was always present. In 1815 and 1832 a professional valuer was employed to survey the parish for the poor rate. In 1828 a salary of £15 was offered to the overseer.[26] The rector's work was outstanding. Palmer owned at least eighteen cottages himself, which he let at uneconomic rents but at the same time enforced strict rules of conduct on the tenants. He also looked after the health of the villagers and saw to it that they had sufficient heating and food. He organized a coal society and sold faggots at cost price. There were free dinners on rent day for the parents and children; there was a school-tea on 1 May and a school-dinner at Christmas. Soup-dinners were also provided twice a week for six weeks in the year. There was a Finmere Provident Clothing Club and the schoolchildren's clothing was provided. The hair of boys and girls alike was cut short once every six weeks. Lace-making was discouraged and finally forbidden because of its ill effects on health.[27]

Milling was for long the chief village trade. A mill is mentioned in Domesday Book and in the 14th century, and one was working in the 17th century when the inclosure agreement contained provisions safeguarding its flow of water in summer.[28] There may have been a blacksmith in the 13th century: a Robert *filius Fabri* is mentioned in 1279.[29] In the mid-19th century there were two in the village, when other tradesmen included seven butchers, carpenters, and shoemakers, a cattledealer, a cooper, a brickmaker employing three labourers, and an innkeeper-brewer.[30] In 1826 98 women and 48 girls above the age of ten had been engaged in lace-making, which was carried on in almost every cottage. It was still being carried on in 1851 by eighteen women.[31] Clay was dug and bricks were made in Finmere in the 19th and early 20th centuries;[32] two coal merchants' businesses were established after the coming of the Great Central Railway.[33] There were seven farmers in the parish in 1853[34] and in 1920, when five of them held farms of over 150 acres.[35]

There seems to have been a steady growth in population from the late 17th to the first half of the 19th century. The Compton Census of 1676 recorded 81 adults, while the rector returned 34 houses in 1738, about 40 with 219 inhabitants in 1768, and 46 families in 1778.[36] In 1801 there were 308 inhabitants and this increased to a peak figure of 399 in 1851. During the second half of the century as the consequence of the agricultural depression there was a steady decline, and by 1901 the population was 226. In 1951 it had risen to 265 and was beginning to increase fairly rapidly.[37]

[25] Blo. *Fin.* 27, 30.
[26] Par. Rec. Vestry Bk.
[27] Blo. *Fin.* 63–66.
[28] *V.C.H. Oxon.* i. 427; Blo. *Fin.* 85, 90–91.
[29] *Rot. Hund.* ii. 837.   [30] H.O. 107/1735.
[31] Ibid.; Par. Rec. Vestry Bk.
[32] *V.C.H. Oxon.* ii. 274; Kelly's *Dir. Oxon.* (1903).
[33] Kelly's *Dir. Oxon.* (1903, 1920).

[34] *Lascelles' Dir. Oxon.* (1853), p. 113.
[35] Kelly's *Dir. Oxon.* (1920).
[36] For the hearth tax returns of 1662 see below, p. 360; Compton Census; Oxf. Dioc. d 552, d 558; ibid. c 327, p. 49. Cf. Blo. *Fin.* 24, where a list of 1778 is cited giving 53 families and 238 persons.
[37] *Census*, 1801–1951. The estimated population in 1954 was 294: inf. Ploughley R.D.C.

CHURCH. The first evidence for the existence of a church at Finmere dates from the late 12th century. The advowson was granted before 1189 by William, son of Gregory, to the abbey of Augustinian canons at Bristol.[38] The abbey's plan to transfer the church in 1200 to the Hospital of St. John and St. James at Brackley (Northants) never materialized,[39] and it held Finmere until its dissolution in 1539.[40] In 1546 the king sold it with the manor to John Blundell.

After Blundell's death in 1559 there was a long period of confusion about the advowson. His heirs failed to present, for in 1560 the Archbishop of Canterbury presented after a vacancy of several months,[41] and in 1576 there was again a presentation through lapse, this time by the queen.[42] The next year the three owners of the three thirds of the manor presented, as they did again in 1592, when Robert Higgins became rector.[43] On his death the situation was more complicated: by this time two-thirds of the manor belonged to Sir Thomas Temple, and the other third to the two Hogan coheiresses, who were wards of the king. In 1632 the king presented Lewis Wemys,[44] but a few months later, after a case before the royal court, the right to present was recovered by Thomas Fowkes of Buckingham,[45] who seems to have been acting for Sir Thomas Temple, for Richard Horn, who then became rector, called Temple his patron,[46] and Sir Thomas held two-thirds of the advowson at his death.[47]

The advowson, like the manor, continued to be divided into a third and two-thirds, but the owners do not seem to have presented in turn, and there were several sales of presentations. In 1678 Pope Danvers and Ambrose Holbech were patrons, after having bought the right from both Sir Richard Temple and the Wallers, who owned the other third of the manor.[48] William Chaplin, who in 1704 presented his son, probably acquired his right in the same way.[49] Richard Temple, Viscount Cobham, presented in 1726, and Francis Edwards of Tingewick (Bucks.) in 1734.[50] From 1771 until 1848 the Earls Temple and the Marquess of Buckingham were patrons.[51] The advowson was then bought by John Walker, who in 1853 presented his son. In about 1865 it was sold to W. Ashwell, who presented his son in 1866.[52] In 1931 the livings of Finmere and Mixbury were united,[53] and the Misses Ashwell now (1955) present for two turns and the Bishop of Oxford for one.

In 1254 the rectory was valued at £5 6s. 8d[54] and in 1291 at £8.[55] By 1535 its value had only risen to £8 9s. 4d.,[56] but in the second half of the 16th century it rose sharply, for in 1595 the rector was leasing most of the tithes for £34,[57] while perhaps farming the glebe himself. In 1667 the tithes were commuted at the inclosure for a rent charge of £80.[58] When prices rose in the 18th century this fixed sum was very disadvantageous to the rector. In 1808 the value of the living was only £126,[59] but as the result of a new valuation of the tithes in 1814,[60] the value of the rectory was nearly trebled.[61] In 1842, after a third valuation, the rent charge was fixed at £457,[62] and this with the glebe made the living worth about £500.

A terrier of 1601 shows that the glebe then consisted of 80 separate pieces of arable land in the open fields, three plots of meadow, and common for 8 beasts, 5 horses, and 60 sheep;[63] a terrier of 1634 lists an even larger number of strips;[64] but by the inclosure award of 1667[65] all were exchanged for a compact area of 45 acres adjoining the rectory and 'distinctly mounded'.[66] In 1760 the rector, Thomas Long, gave the church half a yardland in Tingewick (Bucks.), thus increasing the size of the glebe to the 56 acres mentioned in 1808.[67] There was no glebe in 1955.[68]

There is a detailed 17th-century record of the tithe payments.[69] It was the custom to give a shoulder when a lamb was killed, the tenth penny if it was sold, and a halfpenny when it was weaned. At Easter the rector received a penny offering, and a penny from every garden; tithe eggs on Good Friday; tithe wool at shearing time; cream at a christening, and a mortuary at a death. His small tithes included the tithe of hemp, pigs, bees, rabbits, fruit, tithe milk, and tithe lambs. Some parts of Finmere Field were free of hay tithes and it was thought that the parson had been allotted in lieu of these lands by the riverside called Tythe Meadow and Parsons Holmes (2 a.).

The living changed hands very frequently in the Middle Ages: there were 24 pre-Reformation incumbents of whom only four are known to have died in office.[70] The first known rector, Roger de Cherlecote (oc. 1200), was a graduate with a son.[71] In about his time Finmere also had a hermit, a monk called William, who had been granted the hermitage by King Richard.[72] In 1213 the king ordered that he should have 1d. a day for life in exchange for land on which the royal hunting-lodge had been built.[73] In the next year it was proposed to give the hermitage, if William had died, to Roger, a former Prior

[38] V.C.H. Glos. ii. 75; Dugd. Mon. vi (1), 367.
[39] Magd. Coll. Arch., Brackley Cart. i, B 232, 234.
[40] Bristol Rec. Soc. ix. 42 n. For list of medieval presentations see MS. Top. Oxon. d 460.
[41] O.A.S. Rep. 1914, 230; Blo. Fin. 45–46 has a list, taken from parish records, of presentations of this period.
[42] O.A.S. Rep. 1914, 231.
[43] Ibid.; Blo. Fin. 45.
[44] Blo. Fin. 46; Oxf. Dioc. c 70, no. 30.
[45] Oxf. Dioc. c 70, no. 31; ibid. c 264, f. 123.
[46] Par. Reg.
[47] C 142/487/142.
[48] Oxf. Dioc. c 70, nos. 32, 33; C.P. 25(2)/709/Hil. 29 Chas. II.
[49] Blo. Fin. 51; Oxf. Dioc. c 70, no. 34.
[50] Oxf. Dioc. c 266, ff. 160b, 140b.
[51] Blo. Fin. 53, 55–58; P.R.O. Inst. Bks.
[52] Blo. Fin. 58; Bodl. Par. Box (uncat.).
[53] Bodl. Par. Box, Order in Council.
[54] Lunt, Val. Norw. 311.
[55] Tax. Eccl. (Rec. Com.), 31.
[56] Valor Eccl. (Rec. Com.), ii. 159.
[57] Blo. Fin. 77.
[58] Ibid. 78–79, 83–84.
[59] Oxf. Dioc. c 446, ff. 91–92.
[60] Blo. Fin. 79. The original has not been found.
[61] Report of Comm. to Inquire into Eccl. Rev. H.C. 54 (1835), xxii.
[62] Bodl. Tithe award.
[63] Oxf. Archd. Oxon. b 40, f. 133.
[64] Ibid. f. 129.
[65] Abstract in Blo. Fin. 83.
[66] Oxf. Archd. Oxon. b 40, ff. 130, 131; Blo. Fin. 77–78. 83.
[67] Blo. Fin. 79; Oxf. Dioc. c 446, f. 92.
[68] Inf. the Revd. M. G. Sheldon.
[69] Blo. Fin. 77–78.
[70] Ibid. 42–43; MS. Top. Oxon. d 460: list of medieval rectors.
[71] Magd. Coll. Arch., Brackley Cart. i, B 234.
[72] Rot. Litt. Claus. (Rec. Com.), i. 169b.
[73] Ibid. 155a; see above, p. 117.

of Wallingford Priory.[74] In 1216 another monk called William was installed at the hermitage, now called the chapel of Finmere, on condition that he provided with necessaries the hermit (William or Roger presumably) who was already there but by now decrepit with age.[75] In 1218 the king gave instructions to pay 1*d.* a day to William 'our chaplain of Finmere' for serving the chapel,[76] and in 1228 William was enjoined to return to his monastery, the Benedictine priory of Bradwell (Bucks.). The king's forester was to take the chapel into the king's hands and see that services were continued there.[77]

A rare piece of evidence about an early 13th-century parson, probably John de Langton (1299–1306), occurs in a letter from Bishop Langton to the Abbot and Convent of Bristol, saying that his clerk wanted to resign Finmere because of its poverty and asking that they would present someone chosen by himself. Langton's successor was Richard de Abingdon, a former Fellow of Merton, and another graduate, Geoffrey Damport, was instituted in the early 15th century.[78]

In the post-Reformation period Finmere was fortunate in being spared the evil of absenteeism: during three centuries, out of twenty incumbents fourteen resided from their institutions to their deaths.[79]

One of the most notable rectors in the 17th century was Richard Horn (or Horne) of Hart Hall, Oxford (1632–77). It was his practice to record in Latin in the registers the chief contemporary events both national and local.[80] Typical of his irregular entries are the opening of the Civil War (1642); the intrusion of a Presbyterian, Richard Warr, into his office (1647); and the deaths of Oliver Cromwell (1658), Thomas Appletree, *Horneromastix*, the magistrate resident at Deddington, who had taken an active part in the rector's ejection (1666), and Henrietta, Duchess of Orleans (1670). The comments are often trenchant. Horn continued to reside at Finmere during the Commonwealth and regained his rectory after the Restoration.[81]

Thomas Long (1734–71), 'a man of the most exemplary piety and charity',[82] is the most interesting of the 18th-century rectors and a marked contrast to the better known and less desirable type of 18th-century parish priest. The memorial to his sister Mary Turner and her husband in Finmere church shows that he was a man of good family, one 'of the Longs of Wiltshire'. Like Richard Horn, Long believed in keeping records, and instituted the Rector's Book for notes on matters of local importance: his first entry is a useful abstract of the deed of inclosure. It is characteristic of him that his answers to the episcopal visitation questionnaires,

unlike those of many of his colleagues, are extremely full and careful. He resided constantly at his parsonage, held two services every Sunday, celebrated Holy Communion five times a year, and duly observed festival days, as also Lent and 'the passion week'.[83] Long's special concern seems to have been for the children of Finmere. He kept a school,[84] and excelled as a catechizer. In 1759 he claimed that he catechized every Sunday and every other day of the week except in the harvest season, and he gave details of his system.[85] In his latter years, owing to illness, he was obliged to have a curate and substituted for his own catechitical method Crossman's *Introduction to the Christian Religion*. In 1762 he printed *The Holy Scripture the best Teacher of Good Manners and Civility*, his last lecture on the catechism, which he presented to the youth of Finmere and their elders as a permanent memorial of his teaching.[86] Happily, his work at Finmere was followed up by that of the younger William Cleaver, rector from 1783 to 1787 and afterwards a bishop.[87] Among other things, Cleaver instituted eight celebrations of Holy Communion, introduced musical instruments into the church services, and patronized a resident schoolmaster.[88] Finally, mention must be made of William Joscelyne Palmer, of whose devoted cure (1814–52) Dean J. W. Burgon wrote a vivid sketch.[89]

The church of *ST. MICHAEL*, which has been much restored, comprises a nave and chancel, separated by a chancel arch, a western tower, south porch, and north aisle. The north wall of the chancel, the battlemented tower of three stages and most of the windows are the only survivals of the 14th-century church. By the mid-17th century the fabric was in a precarious condition, for an entry of 1651 in the registers records that the walls 'were propt with timber'. In 1664 the churchwardens reported that their church was 'in decay and ready to fall', and that the two lords of the manor had covenanted with the parishioners to rebuild it.[90] In 1668 the churchwardens stated that they 'had been at extraordinary charges (wth ye whole towne) about repairing their church which is now done'.[91] A stone with the date 1666 and the name of a mason (?) formerly in the south porch may commemorate this work.[92] In 1695 further work was carried out, according to Blomfield, and was commemorated by an inscription with the date 1695 and the names of the two churchwardens.[93] Blomfield states that at this time the roof of the chancel was covered with a low plaster ceiling, which concealed the upper part of the east window, and the walls were covered with plain painted woodwork.[94] But this may have been done in the 1760's when a considerable amount of work was in progress, for the rector refers to a period 'when no Duty could be done by reason of being

[74] *Rot. Litt. Claus.* (Rec. Com.), i. 169*b*.
[75] Ibid. 258*b*.
[76] Ibid. 362*a*.
[77] *Close R.* 1227–31, 19–20.
[78] *Liber Epistolaris of Richard de Bury*, ed. N. Denholm-Young (Roxburghe Club, 1950), 295–6; Emden, *O.U. Reg.* i.
[79] Blo. *Fin.* 43–58.
[80] Listed in *Genealogist*, N.S. ii. 48–49.
[81] Blo. *Fin.* 48; Hist. MSS. Com. *7th Rep. App.* 106; *Walker Rev.* 297–8.
[82] Par. Reg. 13 Apr. 1771.
[83] Oxf. Dioc. d 558.
[84] Ibid. d 552.

[85] Ibid. d 555.
[86] Ibid. d 558.
[87] *D.N.B.*; see above, p. 117.
[88] Blo. *Fin.* 52–54.
[89] Printed ibid. 58–68; see above, p. 117, and below, pp. 253, 260.
[90] MS. Top. Oxon. c 56, f. 71; Blo. *Fin.* 74.
[91] Oxf. Archd. Oxon. c 17, f. 126*b*.
[92] Blo. *Fin.* 34 and note. This stone was removed when the porch was rebuilt in 1876.
[93] Blomfield may have taken his information from a churchwardens' book now lost.
[94] Blo. *Fin.* 34–35.

embarrassed by much scaffolding employed in repairing and ornamenting my church and chancel'.[95] It was probably at this time that the western gallery was built. Some years earlier the north door of the nave had been blocked up.[96]

Repairs to the fabric were executed in 1833 and 1840, those in the latter year costing £70.[97] But the great restoration of the 19th century was begun in 1856; the south and east walls of the chancel were then rebuilt, a new south-west window inserted[98] and the east window restored. The plaster ceiling was removed. In 1858, following the plans of G. E. Street, the south wall of the nave and the chancel arch were rebuilt, a new nave roof was erected, a north aisle was built, and the western gallery was removed; new seating was also provided.[99] A vestry was added in 1868 and the south porch rebuilt in 1876.[1]

The plain circular font may date from the 12th century.[2] The clock, placed in the tower in 1697, was altered and re-erected in 1859.[3] A new mahogany communion table was put in in 1755.[4] The organ, pulpit, reredos, and tower screen are late-19th-century work.[5] The statue of St. Michael in the gable of the south porch was placed there in 1894.

There is a series of 18th- and 19th-century mural tablets and gravestones commemorating members of the manorial families.[6] They include Mrs. Frances James (d. 1739), Nathaniel Bacon (d. 1746), Francis Turner (d. 1752) and his wife Mary, who have a cartouche with coat of arms, and William Long (d. 1780) and family. A number of rectors have inscriptions: William Chaplin (d. 1726), William Cleaver (d. 1783), W. L. Bennett (d. 1790), and Robert Holt (d. 1802). There are 20th-century memorials to Capt. C. Symes-Thompson (killed 1914) and to H. E. Symes-Thompson (d. 1952), father of R. E. Symes-Thompson (killed 1941).[7]

At the Reformation the church had the minimum of plate.[8] In 1955 the plate included a silver chalice, inscribed 'Finmere, Oxfordshire' (1699), and a paten (1840) given by the Right Hon. Thomas Grenville.[9] Besides this chalice the church had a pewter flagon in the 18th century, and in 1758 a flagon and paten of French plate were given. Other possessions of the church recorded at that time were a carpet, and table and pulpit cloths, dated 1699, and a damask napkin, dated 1737. In 1757 these were replaced by a further gift of furnishings costing over £13, and made of 'very fine purple cloth, and ornamented with yellow silk fringe', the gift of John Pollard.[10] The old parish chest was destroyed about this time.[11]

As at the Reformation, there was a ring of three bells in 1955. The inscribed tenor is a fine example of a 15th-century bell; the treble, which is also inscribed, is 16th century, and the second was recast in 1754.[12]

The registers date from 1662, with four pages of entries from an earlier book, which began in 1560.[13]

The churchwardens' book from which Blomfield quotes has been lost.

NONCONFORMITY. William Keat (d. 1667) and his family are the only Roman Catholics known to have lived in the parish.[14]

The diocesan returns of the 18th century record the absence of Protestant dissent, but an Anabaptist was excommunicated in 1685,[15] and in 1738 there was a family of poor Quakers.[16] In the 1830's two houses were licensed for worship,[17] and in 1854 there were about seven dissenters in the parish.[18] By 1866 dissent had disappeared.[19]

SCHOOLS. There was a schoolmaster living in Finmere in 1784, but there is no record of his school. There was a Sunday school by 1806,[20] and in 1808 the parish clerk was teaching 24 children reading and the catechism, in a house provided rent free by the Marquess of Buckingham.[21] This school had 25 pupils—the rector paying for 8—in 1815,[22] and 30 in 1819.[23]

In 1824 a National school was built by the Duke of Buckingham on a piece of waste ground. The rector and churchwardens accepted responsibility for its upkeep. A cottage near by was rented from the duke for the schoolmistress, and was bought in 1848.[24] There were 42 pupils in 1833,[25] and 60 in 1854, when it was reported that evening classes to teach boys writing held in the spring had been unsuccessful: Sunday evening classes for girls were being tried with better results.[26] Attendance figures were 43 in 1889, 40 in 1906,[27] and in 1937 there were 20 pupils. In 1926 pupils over 11 years old had been transferred to Fringford school; in 1948 Finmere school was closed, the infants being transferred to Mixbury and the juniors to Fringford.[28]

CHARITIES. By his will dated 1666 William Keat[29] left a rent-charge of 45s. a year on about 10 acres of land in Breach Furlong, of which 25s. was to be distributed annually to five poor people of Finmere. This charity has been regularly distributed[30] and five people received 'Keat's Crowns' at Christmas 1954.

[95] Oxf. Dioc. d 558. There is a drawing of the interior dated 1766 in Blo. *Fin.*, facing p. 30.
[96] Blo. *Fin.* 38, 36.
[97] Oxf. Archd. Oxon. c 68, ff. 343, 359; ibid. c 38, f. 282.
[98] Blo. *Fin.* 39.
[99] MS. Top. Oxon. c 103, ff. 468–70.
[1] Blo. *Fin.* 40. For a drawing (1824) by J. Buckler of the unrestored church see plate facing p. 133.
[2] See Buckler drawing in MS. Top. Oxon. a 66, f. 264.
[3] Blo. *Fin.* 35, 39.
[4] Ibid. 36.   [5] Ibid. 40.
[6] They are listed in *Genealogist*, N.S. ii. 103–4.
[7] For arms on monuments see Bodl. G.A. Oxon. 16° 217, p. 140; ibid. 4° 686, p. 146.
[8] *Chant. Cert.* 85.
[9] Evans, *Ch. Plate.*
[10] Blo. *Fin.* 36–37.
[11] Ibid. 36.
[12] *Ch. Bells Oxon.* ii. 135–6.
[13] *Par. Coll.* ii. 145. Extracts from Richard Horn's

register are in *Genealogist*, N.S. ii. 48–49.
[14] Blo. *Fin.* 14, citing Par. Reg. records the secret baptism of a baby from London in 1665.
[15] Oxf. Dioc. d 708, f. 140.
[16] Ibid. d 552.
[17] Ibid. c 643, pp. 12, 42. It is not mentioned on Methodist circuit plans.
[18] *Wilb. Visit.*
[19] Oxf. Dioc. c 332.
[20] Blo. *Fin.* 26.
[21] Oxf. Dioc. d 707.
[22] Ibid. c 433.
[23] *Educ. of Poor*, 723.
[24] Blo. *Fin.* 26.
[25] *Educ. Enq. Abstract*, 746.
[26] *Wilb. Visit.*
[27] *Ret. of Sch.*; *Vol. Sch. Ret.*
[28] Inf. Oxon. Educ. Cttee.
[29] See above.
[30] *12th Rep. Com. Char.*; Blo. *Fin.* 28.

At the inclosure of 1667 12 acres of furze, set aside at some earlier date for the use of the poor, were assigned to trustees. The plot was producing a yearly rent of £3 in 1786, and of £7 2s. 6d. in 1823, when the income was used to enable poor families to buy 1 cwt. of coal a week at a reduced price from Christmas to Easter.[31] From 1827 to 1834 the Duke of Buckingham rented the Poor's Plot and sub-let it as allotments at 3s. the chain. The duke's allotment scheme broke down, but was successfully revived by the rector, who paid the rent—£16 in the mid-19th century—into the village coal club funds.[32] In 1954 the rent was £10 12s., and after the payment of expenses the balance was paid to the coal and clothing clubs.

The Revd. Richard Ells, by his will dated 1701, left Rickyard Close (1 a.) in trust, the rents[33] to be used for apprenticing one poor boy or girl of Finmere whenever a sufficient sum had accumulated. From 1715 onwards the close was leased to the rector for £2 10s. a year and became part of the rectory garden.[34] In 1867 it was purchased from the Charity Commissioners and was added to the glebe. The proceeds were invested in stock,[35] which in 1954 produced an annual income of £3 5s. 4d. The charity is still applied when needed for putting out apprentices. William Baker of Rousham, by a codicil to his will dated 1770, left £100 in trust for the payment

of an annuity, and after the death of the annuitant for such poor people of Finmere as were not receiving alms. Baker's executors transferred £100 in stock to the rector and churchwardens in 1782. It proved impracticable to limit the distribution of the charity as intended by the founder, and by 1824 the income was being used in the same way as the rents from the Poor's Plot.[36] The annual income was £3 9s. 6d. in 1954. Stephen Painter bequeathed £100 to the Sunday schools of the parish in 1834.[37] In 1954 an income of £2 13s. 4d. was paid into the Sunday school funds.

Roundell Palmer, Lord Selborne, by deed dated 1872 gave the interest on stock then amounting to £1 17s. 6d. a year to the parochial clothing club, or to be divided among five old men.[38] In 1954 the stock produced £1 11s. 4d. which was paid to the clothing club.

Corbett Charles Barrett by his will proved in 1928 left three cottages in Finmere to be converted into almshouses, and £500 in stock the income of which was to be spent on the cottages. The latter proved unfit for the founder's purpose, and were reclaimed by his executors after an order made in 1929 had transferred the stock to the Official Trustees. The annual income of £20 has since been distributed in quarterly payments to three poor people towards their rent.[39]

FRINGFORD

THIS small rectangular parish of 1,460 acres lies nearly three miles to the north-east of Bicester.[1] There have been no recorded changes of boundary.[1] A tributary of the River Ouse separates it from Hethe and Newton Purcell on the north; the old Roman road from Alchester, now the main Buckingham–Bicester road, forms the eastern boundary, and a small brook divides Fringford from Stratton Audley on the south.

Most of the parish is a high tableland standing within the 300-foot contour, and rising to 368 feet at Fringford Hill in the east. It lies mostly on the Cornbrash with an outcrop of limestone on the north-western boundary, while around Fringford Hill the Cornbrash is covered with drift gravel.[2] It is naturally a treeless region but in 1881 there were two small coverts and a third has since been planted.[3] The ancient moor-like character of the country is indicated by many of its field names: Popes meare, Dodmoore, Whitemore, and Coatmore, for example.[4]

The parish is still (1955) roughly quartered, as it was in the 18th century, by two secondary roads, one running from Cottisford through Fringford village to Caversfield, and the other from Stoke Lyne to Stratton Audley.[5]

Fringford village lies on sloping ground in a loop of the river close to the parish boundary, with Fringford Bridge on the north-west and the corn mill and Fringford Mill Bridge to the east.[6] Blomfield noted traces of a ford in the late 19th century and says that once a road ran from the village green west of the Rectory down to the stream and that a stone-paved way went on to Willaston.[7] His suggestion that there was a second ford where the road to Hethe is now bridged, which was used after the hamlet of Willaston had become depopulated and its traffic diverted to Hethe and Cottisford, is credible. Towards the middle of the 19th century a narrow bridge with a single arch was replaced by the present Fringford Bridge.[8]

The Mill Bridge, which is built of Hornton and local stone, is 44 feet long and was repaired by the Bicester and Enstone Turnpike Trust until 1877, when it became the liability of the Bicester Highway Board.[9]

The 17th-century village was of a medium size for Ploughley hundred, as it had been in the Middle Ages.[10] It had 35 and 24 houses listed for the hearth taxes of 1662 and 1665.[11] There was no large manor-house, but a good Rectory,[12] two more than

[31] Char. Don. ii. 989; 12th Rep. Com. Char. 303.
[32] Blo. Fin. 30; Gardner, Dir. Oxon.
[33] Except 8s. to be paid to the ringer of the curfew bell.
[34] Char. Don. ii. 989; 12th Rep. Com. Char. 302.
[35] Blo. Fin. 31–32.
[36] Char. Don. ii. 989; 12th Rep. Com. Char. 303.
[37] Blo. Fin. 33.
[38] Ibid.
[39] Inf. the Revd. P. A. Parrott on state of all charities in 1954.
[1] Census, 1881, 1951.
[2] G.S. Map 1″, xlv NE.

[3] O.S. Map 25″, xvii. 11, 14 (1881); ibid. 2½″, 42/52, 62 (1951).
[4] P.N. Oxon. (E.P.N.S.), i. 210–11; Blo. Fring. 40–41.
[5] Davis, Oxon. Map.
[6] O.S. Map 25″, xvii. 7 (1881).
[7] Blo. Fring. 8; the ford is marked on O.S. Map 2½″, 42/62.
[8] Blo. Fring. 9.
[9] Oxon. Co. Bridges (1878), 52–53.
[10] See below, p. 129.
[11] Hearth Tax Oxon. 206, 235.
[12] See terrier: Oxf. Archd. Oxon. c 141, p. 329.

usually large farm-houses with six and five hearths apiece, and two farm-houses belonging to the Addington family with four hearths each. In the early 18th century incumbents recorded 34 houses, four of them farm-houses and the rest cottages: by 1768 there were 42 houses, but of them, one farm-house, the mill, and a cottage lay outside the village.[13] Houses continued to increase and numbered 52 by 1811.[14] By 1851 new building had raised the number of dwellings to 80 and there were as many as 94 in 1901.[15] The 20th century has seen an equally startling housing development. Thirty-four houses were built between 1945 and 1954.[16]

The village was originally built round a large green, mostly inclosed in 1760.[17] The church and former manor-house lie at its northern end, and until the end of the 19th century the pound was here also.[18] Many old cottages of one or two stories survive: they are built of rubble and have thatched roofs or stone slates. The 'Butchers' Arms', although refronted in the 19th century, is a survivor from the 17th century, and was possibly the ale-house that was licensed in 1735.[19] In 1774 it or another inn was called the 'Bricklayers' Arms'.[20] At the western edge of the ancient green is a large pond and a 17th-century house, for many years a bakery.[21] Across the road a 19th-century school building stands on the site of the 16th-century house of the Wenmans. A part of this house was used in the 19th century as a parish house, known as the 'Barracks': it was inhabited by four or five families and also used as a school. It was pulled down in 1830.[22] In 1851 the number of 'good farm-houses' in the village impressed the visitor.[23] In 1955 it was the concrete council houses on the outskirts of the ancient village which struck the eye.

The only old house of any size now surviving is Hall Farm, formerly the home of the Addington family.[24] It is a rectangular-shaped building of about the year 1600, but much altered at later periods. The main part of the house is built of rubble and rough-cast; it has three stories and casement windows, and is roofed partly with Welsh slate; the two-storied addition on the south-west side has a tiled roof and is probably of late-17th-century date; a pigeon loft is built into the house. Inside the house there is a 17th-century (?) plaster carving of a royal coat of arms, and an oak staircase. The present Rectory is mainly a 19th-century house, though the kitchen wing belongs to an earlier building. In 1598[25] the kitchen was reported to be 'decayed'; in 1665[26] the house was listed with five hearths for the hearth tax but by the end of the 18th century was described as only a thatched cottage. Additional rooms were added in 1818, when the house was refaced,[27] and in 1873.

There are three out-lying farms: Glebe and Waterloo Farms (built in the 19th century)[28] in the centre of the parish and Cotmore Farm near the southern boundary, where there are the remains of a medieval moat,[29] probably denoting the site of the manor-house of the De Greys. There are also two other houses of note: Fringford Lodge, built before 1814[30] near the Roman road at the south-eastern end of the parish, and standing on the site of a Roman villa,[31] and Cotmore House, built in 1857[32] and lying in its own park north of Fringford Lodge.

In 1645 a small force of royalist troops retreating from Finmere was overtaken and forced to surrender at Fringford.[33]

Anthony Addington (1713–90), a doctor to William Pitt the elder, was born and buried in Fringford.[34] His son Henry, the first Lord Sidmouth and Prime Minister in 1801–4, kept up his family's long connexion with the village.[35] Their descendant the 6th Lord Sidmouth still owned Hall farm in 1955.

In the 1890's Flora Thompson was an assistant in the village post office. She has described her life there in *Candleford Green*.[36]

MANORS. After the Conquest the two Saxon settlements at Fringford, assessed at $10\frac{1}{2}$ hides in all, were granted to Odo, Bishop of Bayeux, and were held of him in 1086 by his retainer Wadard.[37] When Odo was exiled many of his fees were redistributed by William II and were henceforth held by the service of doing castle guard at Dover. FRINGFORD was among the $18\frac{1}{2}$ of the bishop's fees granted to William Arsic,[38] and until the death of John Arsic in 1205 followed the descent of the Arsic barony of Cogges.[39] The manor was then assigned in dower to John's widow, Margery de Vernon.[40] Margery was remarried in the same year to Thomas de Stok, and after his death in 1213[41] she took as her third and fourth husbands Robert Picher[42] and then William Buzun.[43] In 1233 and again in 1243 William was recorded to be holding Fringford as his wife's dower.[44]

In the meantime the male line of the Arsic family had come to an end with the death in 1230 of Robert, John's brother and successor. Robert left as his co-heiresses two daughters, Joan, wife of Eustace de Grenevile, and Alexandra, wife of Thomas de la

[13] Oxf. Dioc. d 552, d 558.
[14] *Census*, 1811.
[15] Ibid. 1851, 1871, 1901.
[16] Inf. Ploughley R.D.C.
[17] See below, p. 130.
[18] Bodl. Tithe award map; Blo. *Fring.* 26. The present manor-house was built 1899–1900, and was converted into six separate dwellings in about 1950: inf. the rector.
[19] O.R.O. Victlrs' recog.   [20] Ibid.
[21] Deeds in possession of Mr. J. H. Crook, baker.
[22] Blo. *Fring.* 16.
[23] Gardner, *Dir. Oxon.*
[24] See below, p. 129.
[25] Blo. *Fring.* 34.
[26] *Hearth Tax Oxon.* 206.
[27] Oxf. Dioc. d 564; Blo. *Fring.* 44.
[28] Blo. *Fring.* 25.
[29] O.S. Map 6″, xvii (1885); *V.C.H. Oxon.* ii. 329.
[30] It was enlarged in the 1870's: Wing, *Annals*, 63.

[31] *V.C.H. Oxon.* i. 320, 343; Blo. *Fring.* 25. Roman remains have also been discovered on Fringford Hill and near Glebe Farm.
[32] Blo. *Fring.* 25.
[33] Blo. *Bic.* 29–30.
[34] *D.N.B.*; Blo. *Fring.* 19; see below, p. 130.
[35] *D.N.B.*; see below, pp. 130, 134.
[36] See also above, p. 105.
[37] *V.C.H. Oxon.* i. 404.
[38] Blo. *Fring.* 10; *V.C.H. Oxon.* i. 440; but cf. Blo. *Som.* 92 for a different account.
[39] Blo. *Som.* 92.
[40] *Rot. de Ob. et Fin.* (Rec. Com.), 261, 270.
[41] Ibid. 322, 513.
[42] *Bracton's Note Bk.* ed. Maitland, ii. 612–13; see below, p. 131.
[43] *V.C.H. Hants.* v. 241.
[44] *Bracton's Note Bk.* ed. Maitland, ii. 612; *Bk. of Fees*, 824.

Haye.[45] While the greater part of the Arsic possessions was partitioned between Joan and Alexandra, Margery de Vernon continued to hold Fringford for life. In 1245 Walter de Grey, son of Robert de Grey of Rotherfield and nephew of Walter de Grey, Archbishop of York, purchased from Joan Arsic and her second husband Stephen Simeon their right to half of Fringford after Margery's death.[46] Margery was still alive in 1251, and the date of her death is unknown.[47] In 1255 the manor was still described as her dower, and the whole of it was held at farm by Walter de Grey[48] of William de Lille—possibly a kinsman of Margery, possibly William de Chabbeneys who had been granted the reversion of Margery's manor of Freshwater in the Isle of Wight in 1249.[49] By 1263 Alexandra, wife of William de Gardinis and daughter of Alexandra Arsic and Thomas de la Haye, was suing Walter de Grey, presumably for the half-portion of Fringford, which legally should have gone to her.[50] By 1279 the manor had been divided into two parts, one held by the Greys and one by the De Gardinis family.[51]

Walter de Grey had married Isabel de Duston, the ward of his uncle the archbishop,[52] and was succeeded in 1268 by his son Robert,[53] who in 1279 held the half of Fringford purchased by his father.[54] Robert married Joan de Valoines, and on his death in 1295[55] was succeeded by his son John (d. 1311).[56] The Grey portion of Fringford, however, was held in dower by Joan until her death in 1312. Her heir, her grandson John (II), was a minor,[57] and until 1322 the manor was in the custody of Hugh Despenser the elder.[58] In 1330 John received a grant of free warren in all his demesnes, including Fringford.[59] In 1338 he became the first Lord Grey of Rotherfield; after a distinguished career he died in 1359.[60] He had been married twice, firstly to Catherine Fitzalan, by whom he had a son John (III), who became his heir, and secondly to Avice Marmion, who received Fringford in dower.[61] Avice was still living in 1379, having survived her step-son, John (III), and his two eldest sons John (IV) and Bartholomew, all of whom had died by 1375. In 1380 a third son, Robert, got Fringford settled upon himself and his wife Joan[62] and their heirs. Shortly before his death in 1388 Robert took a second wife Elizabeth, widow of John de Bermingham, but left as his heiress an only daughter Joan, the child of his first wife.[63] Fringford was assigned in dower to

Robert's widow Elizabeth, who within the same year was married a third time to John de Clinton.[64] Joan Grey had married Sir John Deincourt by 1401, but died in 1408 leaving a son William (d. 1422) and two daughters, Alice and Margaret.[65] When Elizabeth died in 1423 the Grey lands she had held in dower were partitioned between Alice and her husband William, Lord Lovel, and Margaret and her husband, Sir Ralph Cromwell.[66] The Grey manor of Fringford was therefore divided into two portions[67] until 1455, when Margaret died without issue and Alice as her heiress[68] reunited it. After the death of her husband William Lovel, also in 1455,[69] Alice married Sir Ralph Butler,[70] later Lord Sudeley. Alice's son by William, John, Lord Lovel, died in 1465, so that when Alice died in 1474 the heir to the Grey and Deincourt estates, including Fringford, was her grandson Francis, Lord Lovel.[71] Francis, one of the Yorkist lords who opposed Henry VII to the last, was probably killed in 1487 at the battle of Stoke.[72] He had been attainted in 1485, and in the following year some of his Oxfordshire estates, including Fringford, were granted to Thomas Lovel,[73] son of Sir Ralph Lovel of Barton Bendish (Norf.). Thomas, although possibly a kinsman of Francis, fought on the Lancastrian side at both Bosworth and Stoke, and was Chancellor of the Exchequer under Henry VII and Henry VIII.[74] Thomas died childless in 1524 and in accordance with the terms of his grant Fringford reverted to the Crown.[75] It was subsequently granted to Sir Thomas More, and after his attainder and execution in 1535 to Henry Norreys, a Gentleman of the Privy Chamber.[76] In the following year Henry was beheaded on a charge of adultery with Queen Anne Boleyn, and the manor came once more into the king's hands.[77] It may be noted that Thomas Lawless or Lawley, who was appointed bailiff of Fringford by Thomas Lovel in 1524,[78] was still holding his office in 1541.[79] In 1545 the manor was granted to Christopher Edmondes and Sir Richard Long,[80] and in 1548 to Sir John Williams, later Lord Williams of Thame.[81]

On Lord Williams's death in 1559 his possessions were divided between his two daughters, Isabel and Margaret, and their husbands Richard Wenman and Henry Norreys the younger. Fringford fell to Isabel's share. Although Henry had succeeded in recovering most of his father's estates, an exception had been made of all the former possessions of Francis, Lord

[45] *Ex. e Rot. Fin.* (Rec. Com.), i. 193.
[46] *Cal. Chart. R.* 1226–57, 285; *Complete Peerage*, vi, between pp. 128–9: pedigree of Grey of Rotherfield.
[47] *V.C.H. Hants.* v. 241.
[48] *Rot. Hund.* (Rec. Com.), ii. 44.
[49] 'Wm. de Lille' may be a mistake, as the name does not occur elsewhere in *Rot. Hund.*; cf. *Cal. Chart. R.* 1226–57, 340.
[50] *Close R.* 1261–4, 312.
[51] *Rot. Hund.* (Rec. Com.), ii. 829.
[52] *Cal. Inq. p.m.* i, p. 246.
[53] *Ex. e Rot. Fin.* (Rec. Com.), ii. 464.
[54] *Rot. Hund.* (Rec. Com.), ii. 829; cf. *Feud. Aids*, iv. 157.
[55] *Cal. Inq. p.m.* iii, pp. 182–3; Blo. *Fring.* 13; *Complete Peerage*, vi. 144.
[56] *Complete Peerage*, vi. 144–5; *Cal. Inq. p.m.* v, p. 193.
[57] *Cal. Inq. p.m.* v, pp. 220–1.
[58] *Cal. Fine R.* 1307–19, 151; cf. *Feud. Aids*, iv. 169.
[59] *Cal. Chart. R.* 1327–41, 189.
[60] *Complete Peerage*, vi. 145–6; *Cal. Inq. p.m.* x, p. 406.
[61] *Complete Peerage*, vi. 146–7; *Cal. Close*, 1354–60, 602.
[62] *Complete Peerage*, vi. 147–9; *Cal. Pat.* 1377–81, 334; C.P. 25(1)/289/52/28.

[63] C 136/52/2.
[64] *Complete Peerage*, vi. 150; *Cal. Close*, 1385–92, 544.
[65] *Complete Peerage*, iv. 124–7; ibid. vi. 150.
[66] C 139/12; *Complete Peerage*, iv. 129.
[67] P.R.O. Harrison, Extracts, vi. 975; C.P. 25(1)/292/67/8 (Margaret); ibid. 292/68/56 (Alice).
[68] C 139/159; *Complete Peerage*, iv. 128.
[69] C 139/158.
[70] *Complete Peerage*, iv. 129; ibid. viii. 222–3.
[71] Ibid. iv. 130; ibid. viii. 223–4; C 140/47.
[72] *Complete Peerage*, viii. 225.
[73] *Rot. Parl.* vi. 275–8; *Cal. Pat.* 1485–94, 25.
[74] *D.N.B.*
[75] Ibid.; *Cal. Pat.* 1485–94, 25: grant in tail male.
[76] Blo. *Fring.* 14; *D.N.B.*; *L. & P. Hen. VIII*, viii, p. 47.
[77] *Complete Peerage*, ix. 643; *L. & P. Hen. VIII*, x, p. 364.
[78] *L. & P. Hen. VIII*, Addenda, i, p. 148; E 40/A 14607.
[79] *L. & P. Hen. VIII*, xvi, p. 350.
[80] Ibid. xx (2), p. 117.
[81] C.P. 40/1139, mm. 5, 7d.

Lovel.[82] Henry and Margaret finally gave up all claims to Fringford in 1561.[83]

By 1279 the De Gardinis family had gained possession of the half of *FRINGFORD* which they inherited from Alexandra, the second daughter of Robert Arsic, but though the manor is recorded as part of the possessions of William de Gardinis in the inquest taken after his death in 1287,[84] it was held by his son Thomas both in 1279 and in 1285.[85] Thomas held Fringford at his death in 1328, and it then passed to John Giffard the younger of Twyford (Bucks.), son of John the elder and Thomas's daughter Alexandra.[86] In 1361 John and his wife Lucy settled the reversion of the manors of Fringford and Somerton on their son Thomas[87] and in 1368 obtained a licence to enfeoff him and his wife Margery with Fringford.[88] When John died in the following year Thomas succeeded him in all his estates.[89] In 1383 Thomas arranged to hold Fringford jointly with his wife Sybil.[90] Thomas died in 1394[91] and Sybil then enjoyed sole possession[92] until her death in 1429, surviving her eldest son Roger by ten years. She was succeeded by another Thomas Giffard, Roger's son by his second wife, Isabel Stretele.[93] This Thomas died in 1469 and the manor then passed from father to son for a further three generations—to John (d. 1492), Thomas (d. 1511), and Thomas (d. 1550).[94] This last Thomas Giffard left a daughter Ursula, the wife of Thomas Wenman, a member of a notable family of Witney merchants.[95] Their son Richard succeeded his mother in 1558. He had married Isabel, the elder daughter of Lord Williams of Thame, and on her father's death in 1559 Fringford manor was reunited after a lapse of more than three centuries. Richard had received the Giffard manor from his mother, while Isabel inherited the Grey manor from her father.[96]

By 1567, however, Sir Richard Wenman seems to have conveyed the former Giffard manor to his younger brother William,[97] or it is possible that his mother, Ursula, had settled it on him; William, who certainly lived at Fringford,[98] in turn settled his portion of the manor on his eldest son Richard. William died at Fringford in 1586 and Richard duly succeeded him.[99] After the death of the elder Richard in 1572, his widow Isabel seems to have retained the Grey portion of the manor, and to have conveyed it in 1574 to William Risley,[1] possibly as part of a marriage settlement, since her grandson

Ferdinand married a Risley.[2] This part of the manor passed on William's death in 1603 to his son Paul,[3] but had come back to the Wenmans by 1624. The William who had died in 1586 had left at least two sons living, Richard and Giles. William's nephew Thomas, Sir Richard's eldest son, had died in 1577, leaving three sons, Richard, who was raised to the peerage as Viscount Wenman of Tuam in 1628, Thomas, and the Ferdinand mentioned above, who seems to have been dead by 1624.[4] In this year the whole of Fringford was purchased by Fulke Greville, 1st Lord Brooke,[5] from Richard and Giles Wenman and their kinsmen Sir Richard and his son Thomas Wenman.[6] From Lord Brooke, who was murdered in 1628, Fringford passed to his cousin and heir Robert Greville.[7] Robert fought at Edgehill in 1642, on the parliamentarian side, and was killed early in the following year.[8] He was succeeded in turn by his eldest son Francis (d. 1658) and by his second son Robert (d. 1677), but his widow Catherine held half the manor as her jointure until her death in 1676.[9] A conveyance of part of the manor to Francis Dashwood in 1664 was probably connected with a marriage settlement, as Fulke Greville, Robert's youngest son, married Sarah Dashwood in the following year.[10] He succeeded his elder brother Robert in 1677 and died in 1710, when his title passed to his grandson Fulke,[11] his eldest son Francis having died a few days previously. The Fringford estate was left to the Hon. Dodington Greville, a younger son.[12] Dodington died in 1738 and the manor descended to his nephew Sir Fulke, son of Algernon Greville. In 1763 Sir Fulke sold it to Henry, Lord Holland,[13] father of Charles James Fox.[14] Henry, 3rd Baron Holland, sold Fringford to John Harrison of Shelswell in 1815, and it descended on his death in 1834 to his nephew John Harrison Slater-Harrison (d. 1874). Edward Slater-Harrison, John's only son, then succeeded and on his death without issue in 1911 his nephew Arthur William Dewar-Harrison, son of Augusta Slater-Harrison and William Dewar of Cotmore House, inherited his estates. In 1955 the lord of the manor was John Francis Dewar-Harrison, Esq.[15]

ECONOMIC HISTORY. Judging from the Old English name, which means 'the ford of the people of Fēra', Fringford was among the earlier settlements made by the Anglo-Saxons.[16] By 1086 there

[82] *Complete Peerage* (orig. edn.), viii. 140 and note g; *Complete Peerage*, ix. 644.
[83] C.P. 25(2)/196/East. 3 Eliz.
[84] *Cal. Inq. p.m.* ii, p. 411.
[85] *Rot. Hund.* (Rec. Com.), ii. 829; *Feud. Aids*, iv. 157.
[86] *Cal. Inq. p.m.* vii, p. 107; cf. *Feud. Aids*, iv. 169; for pedigree of Giffards of Twyford see G. A. Moriarty, *Genealogist*, N.S. xxxviii. 134; G. Wrottesley, *Hist. Collect. Staffs.* N.S. v. 44–50.
[87] *Cal. Pat.* 1358–61, 571.
[88] Ibid. 1367–70, 81.
[89] *Cal. Inq. p.m.* xii, p. 340; *Cal. Close*, 1369–74, 22.
[90] *Cal. Pat.* 1381–5, 295–6.
[91] C 136/83.
[92] *Cal. Close*, 1392–6, 347.
[93] C 139/45.
[94] *V.C.H. Bucks.* iv. 255–6; C 142/26/24; ibid. 94/44.
[95] C 142/94/44; Blo. *Fring.* 15.
[96] *V.C.H. Bucks.* iv. 255; *Complete Peerage* (orig. edn.), viii. 91, 140.
[97] C.P. 25(2)/196/Trin. 9 Eliz.
[98] *Oxon. Visit.* 175.
[99] C 142/214/195; C 60/410/31.

[1] C.P. 25(2)/196/Hil. 16 Eliz.
[2] *Oxon. Visit.* pedigree p. 179.
[3] C 142/280/47.
[4] *Oxon. Visit.* 179, 307–8; *Complete Peerage* (orig. edn.), viii. 91–92, 92 note g. The descent given in Blo. *Fring.* 15–16 is incorrect.
[5] *Complete Peerage*, ii. 331–2.
[6] C.P. 25(2)/340/Hil. 21 Jas. I; ibid. East. 22 Jas I; cf. Wards 7/49/213.
[7] *Complete Peerage*, ii. 332; cf. C.P. 25(2)/527/Trin. 12 Chas. I; C.P. 43/214/46.
[8] *Complete Peerage*, ii. 333.
[9] Ibid. 333–4; C 142/624/63.
[10] *Complete Peerage*, ii. 334; C.P. 25(2)/707/Mich. 16 Chas. II.
[11] *Complete Peerage*, ii. 334; *Cal. Cttee. for Compounding*, 79.
[12] *Par. Coll.* ii. 146; Lipscomb, *Bucks.* i. 268: pedigree.
[13] Lipscomb, *Bucks.* i. 268; Blo. *Fring.* 24–25; C.P. 25(2)/1388/Trin. 4 Geo. III.
[14] *Complete Peerage*, vi. 543.
[15] Burke, *Land. Gent.* (1937); *Kelly's Handbk.* (1954).
[16] *P.N. Oxon.* (E.P.N.S.), i. 209–10.

were two estates. One had land for 8 ploughs and was worth £8 as it had been before the Conquest. There were 2 plough-teams and 4 serfs on the demesne and 18 villeins (*villani*), and 8 bordars shared 6 plough-teams. Two mills rendered 10s. The smaller estate consisted entirely of demesne land; it had 1 plough-land and 1 plough-team with 3 bordars at work on it. Its value had increased from 30s. to 40s. There were thus 33 recorded male workers.[17]

By 1279 there had been a number of changes:[18] the two manors, which were not the same as the two estates of 1086, were roughly equal in size and each had a hide of land in demesne. Robert de Grey had 14 villein tenants; 6 virgaters paying 5s. 10½d. each, 4 half-virgaters paying 2s. each, and 4 holders of cottages or cotlands with 4 acres of land in each case, who each paid 1s. 5½d. rent. All owed works and paid fines at the lord's will if their sons left the manor; all except the cottars owed tallage. Thomas de Gardinis had 13 villein tenants holding on almost the same terms: there were 6 virgaters, 3 half-virgaters, and 4 cottars. In addition there were 3 free tenants at Fringford: Elias the Clerk[19] held a virgate of Thomas de Gardinis for a rent of 6s. a year and suit twice a year at the county and hundred courts; Juliana de Wappole and Robert de Piry each held a virgate of Robert de Grey for a rent of ½d. a year, one being sub-let for 10s. a year. These virgates had been acquired by Philip de Wappele in 1243 for £13 6s. 8d.[20]

Extents of 1288 and 1313 add further details about the two manorial estates. The De Gardinis's demesne comprised a house and garden, 120 acres of arable worth £2 (i.e. 4d. an acre), and 2 acres of meadow worth 2s. an acre.[21] The customary tenants paid £2 8s. rents and owed works, valued at 9s., from 1 August to 29 September. The rents of cottages brought in 20s. 6d. In addition each tenant paid twice a year 2 cocks and 6 hens. On the De Grey manor, there were 9 villeins paying £2 18s. 11½d. in rent and owing works worth £1 10s. 1½d. The demesne consisted of 80 acres of arable worth 4d. an acre and 5 acres of meadow worth 2s. an acre. The gross value of the manor was £19 10s. 6d.

There were two more pieces of property freely held by Cogges and Bicester Priories, which are not mentioned in the Hundred Rolls. In 1103 Manasses Arsic had granted Cogges 2 mills and 2 carucates in Fringford;[22] the mills they apparently still held with probably about 100 acres of land in 1291, when they were valued at £2 1s.[23] There is no record of how this land was administered: possibly Walter le Monk, taxed on property worth 4s. in 1316,[24] was in charge

of it, and there is earlier evidence for a connexion in 1241 between Cogges and one of the millers.[25] After Cogges had been dissolved and its possessions given in 1441 to Eton College,[26] this land was let to Eton's tenant of its Cottisford manor.

Bicester Priory's property, valued at 1s. in 1291[27] and at 2s. in 1434,[28] appears to have consisted of a mill only. Its site was probably near Poplar Spinney, where foundations of a mill were found in the 19th century.[29] In the 1560's this property also went to Eton.[30]

Although the Hundred Rolls only record 30 tenants,[31] rather less than the recorded Domesday population, there can be little doubt that the population increased during the 12th and 13th centuries, although apparently not so much as in many villages in the hundred. Thirty-one property-holders were taxed in 1316[32] including Thomas de Gardinis, and these taxpayers almost certainly do not represent the total number of householders. Ten were fairly substantial men. The tax list of 1525 shows greater concentration of wealth: of the 25 property-holders taxed, by far the richest was John Arden, the tenant of the Eton College estate, who lived at Cottisford.[33] He was assessed at £16, while the four next richest men were assessed at £6 or £3. Families here as elsewhere seldom throve for more than a hundred years. Not one of the substantial families of the 16th century made a return for the hearth tax of 1665,[34] and the Addingtons are the only family whose name appears on the 1665 list and the land-tax assessment list of 1786.[35]

The vicissitudes of the Crosse family will serve to illustrate the history of a family of the yeoman class. They were leaseholders of the manor at least as early as 1618.[36] During the Civil War John Crosse was 'keeper of the ammunition' in Oxford and a scout for the royalist army, but later fell 'into exceeding great distress'.[37] Towards the end of the century, another John Crosse, a son perhaps, was forced to mortgage and then sell land to the Addingtons.[38] The family, nevertheless, remained in the village until the 1760's.[39]

The Addingtons were living in the village in the 16th century. In 1597 William, yeoman (d. 1600), and Henry, a husbandman and probably his son (d. 1610), acquired 2,000-year leases of 2½ yardlands from the manor.[40] In the 1660's two members of the family were affluent householders.[41] Henry Addington was constable in 1662 and churchwarden in 1664; his son William, the first member of the family to be called a gentleman, had a private family pew in the church and described himself as 'one of the principal inhabitants of Fringford'.[42] He and his

[17] V.C.H. Oxon. i. 404.
[18] Rot. Hund. (Rec. Com.), ii. 829.
[19] He does not seem to have been the rector.
[20] Fines Oxon. 127.
[21] Blo. Fring. 12–13; Cal. Inq. p.m. ii, p. 411; ibid. v, p. 221.
[22] O.A.S. Rep. 1930, 321, has a better text than Dugd. Mon. vi (2), 1003a; see below, pp. 131, 132.
[23] Tax. Eccl. (Rec. Com.), 45. 100 acres was the approximate size of the later Eton College estate: Blo. Fring. 21.
[24] E 179/161/8.
[25] Fines Oxon. 111. A William molendinarius held half a virgate in 1279: Rot. Hund. (Rec. Com.), ii. 829.
[26] V.C.H. Oxon. ii. 162.
[27] Tax. Eccl. 45.
[28] Blo. Bic. 172; see also E 210/3472.
[29] Blo. Fring. 10.

[30] E.C.R. nos. 50–51. In 1796 3 mills are mentioned: C.P. 43/854/532.
[31] Rot. Hund. (Rec. Com.), ii. 829.
[32] E 179/161/8.
[33] Ibid. 176.
[34] Hearth Tax Oxon. 206.
[35] O.R.O. Land tax assess.
[36] E.C.R. no. 272.
[37] Blo. Fring. 18; Cal. S.P. Dom. 1660–1, 169.
[38] Bodl. MS. ch. Oxon. 3641.
[39] Par. Reg.
[40] Devon R.O. Sidmouth and Addington Trust Pps.; cf. E.C.R. no. 272.
[41] Hearth Tax Oxon. 206.
[42] Oxf. Dioc. c 455, f. 19; Devon R.O. Sidmouth Pps. For pedigree see Blo. Fring. 20.

brother Richard, who was Rector of Newton Purcell, acquired further small amounts of land in Fringford. William's son Henry, who was buried in the church in 1730, succeeded to the property, and by the early 18th century the family also owned property in Bicester and Bainton.[43] Henry Addington's son Anthony left the village and became a fashionable London doctor, and his son was the first Lord Sidmouth.[44] The family long exercised an active interest in the village,[45] and still retained Hall Farm[46] and their estate of over 100 acres in 1955.[47]

No outline of landownership exists before about 1760, when inclosure was being discussed. At that time, out of 1,400 to 1,500 acres in the parish, the manor comprised about 1,000 acres; the Addington and Eton College estates over 100 acres each; and there were a few smaller properties.[48] There were hardly any resident owners: in 1754, for example, out of seven 40s. freeholders, including the rector, only one lived in the parish.[49] Although about two-thirds of the parish was divided in small parcels in the common fields, it was all held by a few large farmers, three of whom were tenants of the manor.[50]

This system of landholding continued into the 19th century. There were the three manor farms, each over 150 acres, known as Manor, Waterloo, and Cotmore farms;[51] glebe farm of over 200 acres, which had been awarded to the rector at inclosure; and the smaller Addington, Fringford Lodge, and Eton College estates.

Since the 15th century the Eton College estate of 4¼ yardlands with the mill and the meadow around it had been let to the tenant of its Cottisford manor, who in his turn sub-let the Fringford land.[52] In the mid-15th century the rent for it was about 50s. to 55s., and in the early 16th century about 45s.[53] The mill, with watercourse and fishing, and the meadows called Milne Hame and Milne Leyes, were an important part of the property. In 1595 they were in the possession of Charles Stookes, miller, and in the late 18th century the Stimson family were millers.[54] The whole estate typifies the tendency for farms to grow larger. In the 15th century it had five houses, no doubt each with its own land; in the late 17th century it was divided into three farms; and by the 1770's it was rented to one farmer only and the miller.[55]

Almost the only evidence of agricultural practice in the parish before inclosure comes from records of the Eton College estate and the glebe. Late 17th-century terriers mention only furlongs, and there is no sign of any division into three or more regular fields. There had been little consolidation of strips. The Eton estate, for example, consisted of about 260, so that there were some 60 strips to a yardland.[56]

The yardlands were of varying sizes; one of Eton's consisted of 15 acres, but the average size of its 4¼ yardlands was about 17 acres, with commons for 2 cows, 2 horses, and 40 sheep.[57] By the mid-18th century yardlands had grown larger. The open fields of the parish, computed at about 800 acres, consisted of 33½ yardlands, 'which make 23 a. 3 r. 20 p. to the yardland'. The commons for cows and horses remained the same, but only 30 sheep were allowed for a yardland.[58] It seems possible, therefore, that part of the pasture had been converted into arable. It may be noted, however, that Stephen Mercer, woolmonger, lived at Fringford in 1726.[59]

Between 400 and 500 acres had been inclosed before the inclosure award of 1762. Of this nearly 400 acres was part of the manor lands, about 45 acres belonged to the Addingtons and 20 to the mill.[60] The early inclosure lay in three parts of the parish: land, mostly meadow and pasture, bounded by the river, the Buckingham–Bicester road, and the road leading off from it to Cottisford; fields, for the most part arable, in the centre of the parish, on both sides of the road from Caversfield to the village; and the fields in the south-eastern corner of the parish, partly arable and partly grass, lying around Cotmore Farm. There remained 33½ yardlands or, as the yardland was computed at nearly 24 acres, about 800 acres uninclosed. Common for 2 horses, 2 cows, and 30 sheep went with each yardland.[61] By the award[62] the open fields were divided up and the lord of the manor received 385 acres, the rector for tithe and glebe 227 acres, Eton College 71 acres, Anthony Addington 89 acres, and two others 39 acres and 59 acres respectively. Three smallholders, only one of whom lived in Fringford, received awards of under 10 acres.

Arthur Young, writing in 1809, considered that inclosure had been 'very beneficial', and that the value of rents and procedure had at least trebled. Although much of the land was pasture, he noted the absence of dairies.[63] On the arable land he found turnips, barley, clover, wheat, and oats being grown in rotation, the same system as at Stoke Lyne, and one that was very suitable for stonebrash soil.[64] In the late 19th century these crops, with the addition of peas, were still being grown, and about half of the parish was grassland.[65] In 1956 there were 742 acres of grassland and 639¾ acres of arable.[66]

As early as 1676, when the Compton Census recorded 105 adults, the parish was fairly populous. The increase in the number of houses during the 18th century indicates an expanding population.[67] In 1801 there were 252 inhabitants and this rose to a peak figure of 479 in 1871. The estimated population in 1954 was 356.[68]

43 Devon R.O. Sidmouth Pps.
44 D.N.B.
45 See below, p. 134.
46 See above, p. 126.
47 Bodl. Tithe award; local inf.
48 Blo. *Fring.* 21.
49 *Oxon. Poll, 1754.*
50 Blo. *Fring.* 24, quoting advertisement of sale of manor in 1763.
51 Ibid. 25.
52 See above, p. 106.
53 E.C.R. nos. 153, 154: accts. of 1446–7, 1460–1; ibid. no. 294, f. 20: coll. of 16th-cent. deeds.
54 Ibid. no. 60; Par. Reg.
55 E.C.R. no. 154; ibid. no. 164: 1675 terrier; ibid. no. 175: particulars of estate, 1776.

56 Ibid. no. 164; ibid. no. 167: 1700 terrier; Blo. *Fring.* 41–43: 1685 rectory terrier.
57 E.C.R. no. 167.
58 Ibid. no. 164.
59 Blo. *Fring.* 21: memo. in Par. Rec.
60 Bodl. Tithe award, which applies only to land inclosed before the incl. award.
61 Blo. *Fring.* 21.
62 Ibid. 22, quoting from incl. award, since lost. The act is 1 Geo. III, c. 35 (priv. act) (copy in O.R.O.).
63 Young, *Oxon. Agric.* 91.
64 Ibid. 114.   65 Blo. *Fring.* 26.
66 Inf. Oxon. Agric. Executive Cttee.
67 See above, p. 126.
68 *Census*, 1801–71; inf. Ploughley R.D.C. In 1951 the population was 331: *Census*.

For most of this late period the inhabitants have been farmers and farm labourers with a handful of craftsmen and small traders. The census of 1851 recorded some 15 tradesmen, of whom two were masons and two millers.[69] Late in the century a brickworks was opened near the claypit on the Bicester–Buckingham road.[70] In 1955 there were still a number of tradesmen and the mill, run partly by water and partly by steam, was still in use.

CHURCH. The earliest evidence yet found for a church at Fringford dates from 1103, when Manasses Arsic, lord of Fringford, granted it to the alien Priory of Cogges, which he had founded near Witney.[71] It is uncertain whether Cogges ever exercised the right to present, but in an assize of darrein presentment in 1233 the prior claimed that he had presented the last parson, a certain Robert Lovel, and that a Robert Picher, who had just died, was presented in time of war (i.e. 1215–17) by William and Margery Buzun.[72] It is implied that the presentation was irregular and that Robert had never been admitted. The Buzuns claimed that they had presented Robert after the war, in fact in the time of the general council at Oxford (i.e. 1222). The evidence of the jury was that Margery, who held Fringford in dower,[73] presented Robert Lovel 40 years ago and after the death of her husband Robert Picher. Margery brought an action against Robert Lovel, who agreed to grant her son, Robert Picher, a pension of 2s. On Lovel's death Margery and William Buzun (who was her fourth husband) presented Robert Picher. It was decided that William Buzun had recovered his seisin.[74] No more is heard of Cogges's claim. After Margery's death some time after 1251, the advowson like the manor was divided.[75] Walter de Grey had acquired the reversion of the moiety of the advowson as early as 1245 when he purchased Joan Arsic's inheritance in Fringford.[76] The other moiety eventually went to the Giffards who are found presenting alternately with the Greys.[77] Sir Thomas Giffard presented in 1377, but in 1391 the king presented on the grounds that he had the custody of Joan de Grey, heiress of Robert de Grey, who had died in 1388,[78] although in fact the Grey portion of Fringford with its share of the advowson was held in dower by Robert's widow Elizabeth until her death in 1423.[79] Again, in 1406, at the next vacancy but one, Henry IV presented to Fringford although Joan had received livery of her lands five years before.[80] By 1444, however, the advowson had been recovered by the successor of the Greys, for in

that year William Lord Lovel presented. The system of alternate presentation by the two manorial lords was still functioning, for the Giffards presented in 1460 and 1523, and Francis Lord Lovel in 1480.[81] Sir Thomas More as successor to the Lovels presented in 1528, but in 1549 John Arden[82] took the turn of Thomas Giffard, who died in possession of the advowson in 1550.[83] The former Grey manor had been forfeited to the Crown on the attainder of Sir Thomas More in 1535, and in subsequent grants to Henry Norreys and Sir John Williams no mention was made of the advowson: in 1554 the Crown presented,[84] and the advowson with the manors was in the hands of the Wenman family by 1559,[85] and in 1561 Henry Norreys the younger gave up any claim he might have to the advowson.[86] It passed with the manor from the Wenmans to Fulke Greville, Lord Brooke.[87] In 1635 the king presented through lapse[88] but in 1697 Fulke Lord Brooke[89] did so, thereby recovering a right which his family had possessed for over 70 years, but had not exercised. His successors[90] presented until 1756, when Fulke Greville offered the presentation for sale, but Bishop Secker 'so strictly examined and threatened' those who thought of buying it that the church remained without a rector for seven months and the bishop was able to collate.[91] In 1763, when Fulke Greville sold the manor to Lord Holland, he apparently sold the advowson also.[92] A few years later the advowson was bought by Lady Shaftesbury and exchanged with the Crown for Hinton Martell (Dorset).[93] The Grevilles were evidently uncertain about what had happened, for in 1814 Greville was planning to present 'some person' to the living until one of his younger sons came of age to take it.[94] Since the exchange, the rectory has been in the patronage of the Lord Chancellor.[95] In 1924 the living was combined with that of Hethe, also in the patronage of the Lord Chancellor.[96]

In the Middle Ages Fringford was rather a poor living. In 1254 it was valued at £3 6s. 8d.;[97] in 1291 at £6, plus a pension to Cogges[98] (see below); in 1535 the net value was £12 16s.[99] After the Reformation the rectory increased considerably in value, and by 1685 was worth £188.[1]

In addition to his glebe, the rector was entitled to all the tithes in the parish, except for those on one acre called Newell's Close. During the 18th century the tithes were being farmed for about £100.[2] At the inclosure award in 1761 the rector was awarded 209 acres in lieu of tithe from the open fields,[3] but tithes on the 481 acres of inclosed land continued to be

[69] H.O. 107/1729.
[70] O.S. Map 25″, xvii. 11 (1881); Kelly's Dir. Oxon. (1903).
[71] V.C.H. Oxon. ii. 161; Dugd. Mon. vi (2), 1003; O.A.S. Rep. 1930, 321.
[72] Bracton's Note Bk. ed. Maitland, ii. 612–13.
[73] See above, p. 126.
[74] Bracton's Note Bk. ii. 612–13.
[75] See above, p. 127.
[76] Cal. Chart. R. 1226–57, 285.
[77] e.g. Cal. Inq. p.m. x, p. 406; ibid. vii, p. 107. For a list of medieval presentations see MS. Top. Oxon. d 460; Blo. Fring. 33.
[78] Cal. Pat. 1391–6, 13.
[79] C 139/12.
[80] Cal. Pat. 1405–8, 289; Complete Peerage, vi. 150.
[81] Blo. Fring. 34.
[82] Ibid.
[83] C 142/94/44.

[84] L. & P. Hen. VIII, viii, p. 47; Blo. Fring. 34.
[85] O.A.S. Rep. 1914, 223.
[86] C.P. 25(2)/196/East. 3 Eliz.
[87] Blo. Fring. 37.
[88] Foedera (1732), xix. 778.
[89] P.R.O. Inst. Bks.
[90] Ibid.
[91] Oxf. Dioc. c 659, ff. 213–14.
[92] C.P. 25(2)/1388/Trin. 4 Geo. III.
[93] Oxf. Dioc. c 659, ff. 213–14; ibid. c 662, ff. 54–56.
[94] Ibid. c 662, ff. 54–56.
[95] P.R.O. Inst. Bks.; Blo. Fring. 38.
[96] Bodl. Par. Box (uncat.): Order in Council.
[97] Lunt, Val. Norw. 312.
[98] Tax. Eccl. (Rec. Com.), 31.
[99] Valor Eccl. (Rec. Com.), ii. 162.
[1] Oxf. Dioc. d 708, f. 140.
[2] Blo. Fring. 21, 43.
[3] Ibid. 22, 43, citing Incl. award.

paid until 1848, when they were commuted for £137.[4] By the early 19th century Fringford had thus become a rich living, considered worth £441 in 1818.[5]

When Manasses Arsic granted the church to Cogges Priory in 1103, he also gave its land, the tithe on the 'vill', and two mills.[6] The tithes were evidently commuted for a pension of £1 6s. 8d., which was paid until the dissolution of the priory in 1441.[7] The church's land did not go to Cogges, but remained as part of Fringford rectory.[8] In 1341 there was glebe valued at 26s. 8d.,[9] probably the same as the yard-land of glebe described in the 17th-century terriers.[10] This was exchanged for 18 acres of land at the inclosure[11] and became part of the new rectory estate of about 220 acres. It was agreed then that the lord of the manor should build a house, barn, and stables on the land at a cost of £200, receiving land equal in value in return.[12] This was the origin of the farm now known as Glebe farm.[13]

Probably because the living was poor none of the medieval Rectors of Fringford was a university graduate until the end of the 15th century. Several of the 14th- and 15th-century ones kept the living for many years. But long residence might have its disadvantages: Master Thomas Kirby, rector from 1480 to 1523, was found to have neglected the church. It was said that the cemetery was not well closed, the font and chrism were not kept locked, and several people owed money to the church.[14] On the other hand wills of this period show that parishioners were pious and often made bequests to the church: Roger Copeland, for example, who died in 1532, left in all twelve bushels of barley to the high altar, the altars of St. Catherine and St. Thomas, the bells and the 'torches'.[15]

The best-known 16th-century rector was Richard Aldrich (1565–1604),[16] prebendary of Hereford:[17] in 1590 he was ordered to reside in Fringford and explain to the bishop why he had been absent.[18] In the last years of his life he had as curate Emmanuel Scott, who succeeded him as rector. As Scott was married and died in Fringford, he presumably resided.

The Civil War saw considerable changes in the village: early in the 1640's[19] the rector William Overton was sequestered from his living and was succeeded by John Bayley.[20] Shortly after 1649, having abandoned his earlier Puritan views Bayley was removed from his living,[21] but at the Restoration he regained possession.[22]

The early-18th-century rectors have left few records. At least one was non-resident; he paid his curate Daniel Wardle £35 a year.[23] Wardle, who was also Vicar of Caversfield, became rector in 1735.[24] John Russell Greenhill (1756–1813), although he never lived in the parish, took an active interest in it. The 17th-century parsonage with a barn and a stable,[25] which in 1665 had been the largest house in the village,[26] was described by him as a mere thatched cottage and too small for his family.[27] After 1767 he lived at Finmere, and later in Cottisford.[28] He found his parishioners in general 'very good frequenters' of the church; he made a practice of counting them and found there were about 100 and more in summer. In 1768, when the unusually large number of 56 people wanted to be confirmed, he had visited every house and spoken widely on the subject. He catechized every Sunday in summer, but found that after the age of 12 or 13 the children considered themselves too old to say their catechism in public; servants also refused to repeat it. He expounded, as he said, 'by a composition of my own drawing up'.[29] By 1808, when he was 77 years old and had a curate, receiving £45 and living in the parsonage house, he no longer read the services, but he attended regularly and always visited the sick himself.[30]

His successor Henry Roundell (1815–52),[31] who was already curate, was 'possessed of ample means and genial temperament'. He did much for the parish[32] and earned great personal devotion.[33] He enlarged the Rectory, was responsible for the rebuilding of the chancel and much of the other restoration;[34] and he let out part of the glebe in small allotments to the labourers. He was followed by Henry Fane de Salis (1852–73), another man of means and influence, who also did a great deal for the parish. De Salis obtained the living through the influence of his father-in-law, the Rt. Hon. J. W. Henley, a member of the Cabinet.[35] He completed the restoration of the church, built the schoolroom, and increased the allotment of land for labourers. He attracted a large congregation—an average of 150, with about 50 communicants usually.[36] Besides the Sunday services there were services on Wednesday and Friday evenings, and prayers every morning. Bishop Wilberforce held several confirmations at Fringford. In 1855 he confirmed for Shelswell, Newton Purcell, Cottisford, and Godington: 'the most attentive set of perhaps any', he wrote.[37]

[4] Bodl. Tithe award.
[5] Oxf. Dioc. c 435, p. 93.
[6] Dugd. *Mon.* vi (2), 1003; *O.A.S. Rep.* 1930, 321; see above, p. 129.
[7] *Tax. Eccl.* (Rec. Com.), 31; *Feud. Aids*, vi. 379; *V.C.H. Oxon.* ii. 161.
[8] Dugd. *Mon.* vi (2), 1003. Although Cogges did not get the land belonging to the church, it got some land in Fringford.
[9] *Inq. Non.* (Rec. Com.), 133.
[10] Blo. *Fring.* 41–43.
[11] Ibid. 22, 43.   [12] Ibid. 43.
[13] Gardner, *Dir. Oxon.*
[14] *Visit. Dioc. Linc. 1517–31*, i. 121–2.
[15] MS. Top. Oxon. c 47, f. 107. There are other wills ibid.
[16] *O.A.S. Rep.* 1914, 223. Blo. *Fring.* 34 is wrong in saying Richard Wenman was rector.
[17] Foster, *Alumni.*
[18] Oxf. Dioc. c 38, f. 2.
[19] Blo. *Fring.* 35. His writing in the register ceases in Sept. 1640.
[20] Hist. MSS. Com. *6th Rep.* 173. He was not instituted

until 1647: Blo. *Fring.* 35. For Overton see *Calamy Rev.* 376.
[21] Blo. *Fring.* 36; for Bayley see *Walker Rev.* 30. For his later attempts to convert dissenters see Oxf. Dioc. c 430, f. 20; Blo. *Fring.* 53.
[22] Blo. *Fring.* 36; Hist. MSS. Com. *7th Rep.* 106b, 115a.
[23] Oxf. Dioc. d 552.
[24] Blo. *Fring.* 37.
[25] Ibid. 41.
[26] *Hearth Tax Oxon.* 206.
[27] Oxf. Dioc. d 561.
[28] Ibid.; Blo. *Fring.* 37–38.
[29] Oxf. Dioc. d 558.
[30] Ibid. d 570. For family memorials in church of Ellesborough see Lipscomb, *Bucks.* ii. 185, 194–5.
[31] For him see Macray, *Magdalen Reg.* v. 154–5.
[32] Blo. *Fring.* 38.
[33] Oxf. Dioc. d 178.
[34] See below.
[35] Blo. *Fring.* 39; see *V.C.H. Oxon.* v. 299.
[36] Oxf. Dioc. d 179, c 332.
[37] Ibid. d 178.

South-east view of the church in 1820

FRINGFORD

South-east view of the church in 1824

FINMERE

The church, dedicated to *ST. MICHAEL AND ALL ANGELS*, is a stone building comprising a chancel, clerestoried nave with three bays, two aisles, and a western tower.[38] The only remains of the 12th-century church are a much restored south door and the two northern arches of the nave. The three-arched south arcade, of which two of the pillars are decorated with curiously carved grotesque female heads, probably dates from the 13th century.[39] The south aisle (see below) may have been rebuilt in the 14th century.[40] At the north-west end of the nave is a blocked-up arch. In the 16th century there were altars to Sts. Catherine and Thomas.[41] The roughly carved medieval screen has been preserved.

Small repairs are recorded at several dates in the 18th century: in 1739; between 1765 and 1792, when sums ranging from £1 to £9 were paid to local craftsmen; and in 1788 when £14 odd was spent on replastering and painting the interior and retiling the roof.[42] In the 19th century the church was largely rebuilt: in 1804 and 1809 a total of £60 was paid for work on the fabric; in 1812 £38 on the tower;[43] in 1821 a new chancel was built at the rector's expense and the parish spent £34 on the main body of the church. In 1829 the north aisle was rebuilt, and in 1831 £237 was spent on replacing the wooden belfry by the present stone tower. The mason was Daniel Mansfield of Hethe.[44] In 1838 and 1841 the church was reseated;[45] in 1856 and 1857 the original Early English porch[46] was taken down and replaced and the south aisle was rebuilt and enlarged by the architect G. E. Street at a cost of £650.[47]

In 1905 the north aisle was enlarged and rebuilt at the expense of H. J. Chinnery (architect T. B. Carter) and two clerestoried windows on the north were opened. The altar was removed from the chancel to the north aisle to form a chapel and a new altar erected in the chancel.[48] In 1909 the roof was restored.[49]

The church has had three fonts in recent times. In the early 19th century there was a plain circular one.[50] The origin of the fine octagonal font, decorated with four heraldic stone shields, which was presented in the late 19th century, is uncertain.[51] In 1880 a new font, in memory of Mrs. Anne King, replaced the latter,[52] but both are now in the south aisle.

In 1842 the church was beautified at the expense of the rector Henry Roundell and Miss Roundell. The clerk's desk was altered and a new pulpit was erected. The pulpit's finely carved 17th-century panels are said to have been bought from the manor-house at Hardwick. Crimson furnishings for the communion table, pulpit, and reading-desk, and kneeling-cushions were provided. A vestry was made in the same year and additional open sittings were provided in 1842 and 1847. In 1855 the Roundell family paid for fitting two of the chancel windows with stained glass. The rector Henry de Salis gave a new organ in 1859; its case was made by John Rogers of Fringford, a local carpenter, who was also responsible for the carved seats in the nave and was church organist for many years. The clock in the tower dates from 1876.[53]

There is a stone tablet in the chancel to Richard Wenman (d. 1637/8), and two fine marble monuments on the north side of the nave to the Addington family: one to Anthony Addington (d. 1790) and his wife Mary (d. 1778) is signed by Richard Westmacott and is surmounted by arms; the other is to Henry Addington (d. 1729/30) and his wife Elizabeth (d. 1746).[54]

There are also memorials to Daniel Wardle, rector (d. 1756), John Russell Greenhill, rector (d. 1813), Elizabeth Greenhill, his wife (d. 1807), Richard Gibbs, gent. (d. 1807) and family, Henry Dawson Roundell, rector (d. 1852), Cadwallader Coker, rector (d. 1894), and H. J. Chinnery, J.P. of Fringford Manor (d. 1914). Tablets commemorate the charitable bequests by Elizabeth de Salis and John Mansfield.

In 1552 the church owned a silver chalice and some vestments. There was also a light, the donor of which was unknown, supported by lands worth 6d. a year and five sheep and two lambs valued at 10s.[55] The church now possesses an Elizabethan chalice and some Victorian silver given by Eleanor Roundell.[56]

At the Reformation there were three bells, a sanctus bell and two handbells; the present tower has a ring of three bells, one dating from the early 16th and two from the early 17th century. There is an 18th-century saunce. The bells were repaired and a new bell-frame was erected by John Waters in 1832.[57]

No trace remains of the medieval cross once in the grave yard. As early as 1633 a Fringford man stated that he could not remember any cross there but only a heap of 'rubbidge stone'.[58]

The registers begin in 1586 for marriages, in 1588 for burials, and in 1596 for baptisms. From 1640 to 1660 they are irregular, and there is a gap 1736–51.[59] There is a book of churchwardens' accounts from 1751 to 1921.

NONCONFORMITY. No recusants are recorded in the early 17th century, but in 1676 there were

---

[38] Cf. C. Rayner-Smith, *Cottisford and its church* (1955).
[39] *N. & Q.* 7th ser. iv. 208, 333.
[40] A drawing by J. Buckler shows the S. aisle with a 2-light E. window with simple tracery and a square S. window. For a reproduction, see plate opposite.
[41] MS. Top. Oxon. c 77, f. 107.
[42] Par. Rec. Churchwardens' Accts.
[43] Ibid.; Oxf. Archd. Oxon. c 69, f. 209.
[44] Par. Rec. Churchwardens' accts.; Blo. *Fring.* 27. The Buckler drawing shows the old chancel with a square-headed window, and a lancet, a 2-light 14th-cent. window, and priest's door on S. side.
[45] Blo. *Fring.* 28.
[46] Parker, *Eccles. Top.* no. 37.
[47] Blo. *Fring.* 28; MS. Top. Oxon. c 103, ff. 486–7.
[48] Faculty (Bodl. Fring. Par. Box); *Kelly's Dir. Oxon.* (1939).
[49] Par. Rec. Churchwardens' accts.

[50] Buckler drawing in MS. Top. Oxon. a 66, f. 264.
[51] See E. A. G. Lamborn, *Berks. Arch. Jnl.* xlv. 115–17, for description and discussion on heraldic font. He considers Blomfield's story (*Fring.* 30), that it came from Coleorton (Leics.), unlikely. For arms see Bodl. G.A. Oxon. 16° 217, p. 142; ibid. 4° 686, pp. 146–7; Bodl. 137 e 169/1, pp. 115–17.
[52] Blo. *Fring.* 30.
[53] Ibid. 28–30; Par. Rec. Churchwardens' accts.
[54] Bodl. G.A. Oxon. 16° 217, p. 142; ibid. 4° 686, pp. 146–7.
[55] *Chant. Cert.* 82, 32.
[56] Evans, *Ch. Plate.*
[57] *Ch. Bells Oxon.* ii. 138–9; Par. Rec. Churchwardens' accts.
[58] Blo. *Fring.* 30.
[59] For description see ibid. 44.

three.[60] From this time on occasional recusants are recorded: in 1682 the rector said one man was a reputed papist, 'but unwilling to admit as much';[61] in 1706 a Welshman was returned as one;[62] and in 1738 the millwright's wife was a papist.[63] In 1780 a Roman Catholic family was living in the village, and in 1808 there was one old woman.[64]

Protestant dissent is recorded in 1682, when a Quaker from London and an anabaptist lived in the parish.[65] In 1759 three or four Presbyterians were recorded,[66] but although only one, a mason, was left in 1768,[67] in 1772 Daniel Mansfield's house was licensed for Presbyterian meetings.[68] Presbyterianism died out in the first decade of the 19th century.[69]

In 1840 some Methodists met in a private house,[70] in 1854 three dissenting families met occasionally for services,[71] and this was probably the case during the rest of the century.[72]

According to the 1851 census, a small Independent chapel was opened in 1844,[73] but no other record of this has been found.

SCHOOLS. In 1768 a small school was started by the rector and Dr. Addington,[74] who provided the house, to teach the children the catechism and reading and writing. In 1808 Lord Sidmouth and the rector still paid for eight children to be educated at the dame school, where the other children were paid for by their parents.[75] In 1815 the boys and girls were reported to be leaving school at an early age so as to start work on the farms or at lace-making.[76] In 1833 two day schools with an average attendance of 24 were partly supported by donations from Lord Sidmouth and the rector.[77] In 1854 there were 35 children at one day school, which was mainly paid for by the rector and held in his barn, and 20 children at an infant school.[78] A National school was

built in 1866 by the rector Henry de Salis.[79] There was one master and the average attendance was 73 in 1871[80] and 51 in 1906.[81] By 1929 Fringford school was receiving senior pupils from Cottisford, Finmere, Hethe, Mixbury, Newton Purcell, and Stratton Audley. There were 92 pupils on the books in 1943 besides 32 evacuees. After a reorganization in 1948 the school retained its pupils aged 5 to 11, and 13 to 15, while those aged 11 to 12 were transferred to Bicester Voluntary Secondary School. The school was controlled in 1951. It had 84 children in 1954.[82]

CHARITIES. At an unknown date a Mrs. Addington and an Ann Richards, both apparently members of the Addington family,[83] left £15 for poor widows of the parish.[84] By 1768 the principal was held by the leading farmers, and 12s. a year interest was distributed by the overseers.[85] In 1793 Henry Addington, then Speaker of the House of Commons, was holding the £15 and another £25 left to the poor by a certain William Thonger.[86] Later donations appear to have increased the fund to £55 in all by 1805,[87] but by the 1820's only the original £15 could still be accounted for.[88] In 1853 the Revd. Henry Roundell, son of a former rector, augmented the charity fund, bringing it up to £50; in 1870 it yielded £1 10s. a year.[89]

In 1869 John Mansfield, a member of a family long established in Fringford, left £100 in stock, the interest to be divided between six poor people,[90] and in 1877 Martha Ann Symonds left £200 for the benefit of poor widows. In 1888 the funds of all the charities were invested in stock.[91] In 1898 Grace Elizabeth de Salis, widow of a rector of Fringford, left £100 to be distributed in coal to poor widows.[92] The annual income of the charities was £14 5s. in 1939.[93]

FRITWELL

FRITWELL lies roughly mid-way between two market towns—Banbury nine miles to the north-west and Bicester six miles to the south-east.[1] In 1888 a detached part of the parish[2] (135 a.) on the eastern bank of the Cherwell, between Souldern and Somerton parishes, was transferred to Somerton, reducing the area of Fritwell from 1,878 to 1,743 acres.[3] In 1953 about 506 acres lying north

of the Bicester–Banbury road was transferred to Souldern.[4] On the east and in the south-west corner the boundaries of the main body of the ancient parish, with their many right-angled bends, evidently followed open-field furlongs. Two of its boundaries were natural ones, the Ockley Brook (the county boundary between Oxfordshire and Northamptonshire) on the north, and a small stream, a

[60] Compton Census.
[61] Oxf. Dioc. c 430.
[62] *Oxoniensia*, xiii. 78.
[63] Oxf. Dioc. d 552.
[64] Ibid. c 432 and d 570.
[65] Ibid. c 430.
[66] Ibid. d 555.
[67] Ibid. d 558.
[68] Ibid. c 644, f. 10.
[69] Ibid. c 327, p. 295, and d 570.
[70] Ibid. c 646, f. 116. Another house was licensed in 1845: ibid. c 647, f. 33.
[71] *Wilb. Visit.*
[72] Oxf. Dioc. c 332, c 344.
[73] H.O. 129/158.
[74] Oxf. Dioc. d 558; see above, p. 126.
[75] Oxf. Dioc. d 707.
[76] Ibid. c 433.
[77] *Educ. Enq. Abstract*, 746.
[78] *Wilb. Visit.*; cf. Oxf. Dioc. b 70, f. 335.
[79] *Kelly's Dir. Oxon.* (1887); Blo. *Fring.* 39.
[80] *Elem. Educ. Ret.*

[81] *Vol. Sch. Ret.*
[82] Inf. Oxon. Educ. Cttee.
[83] See above, p. 129.
[84] Oxf. Dioc. c 327, p. 50.
[85] Ibid. d 558.
[86] Ibid. c 327, p. 50.
[87] Ibid. p. 362.
[88] *12th Rep. Com. Char.* 304.
[89] *Gen. Digest Char.*; Blo. *Fring.* 50–51 states that Roundell gave a further £50 for the poor.
[90] *Gen. Digest Char.* register; Blo. *Fring.* 51.
[91] Par. Reg.; tablet in church. Both register and tablet state that trust deeds are in custody of churchwardens in par. chest: they were not there in 1954.
[92] Tablet in church.
[93] *Kelly's Dir. Oxon.* (1939).
[1] O.S. Map 6″, x (1886); xvi (1885); ibid. 2½″, 42/52, 53 (1951).
[2] Ibid. 6″, xvi (1885).
[3] *O.A.S. Rep.* 1907, 20; *Local Govt. Bd. Order 21435* (copy in O.R.O.).
[4] *Oxon. Confirm. Order* (copy in O.R.O.).

tributary of the Great Ouse, on the south, while the Souldern–Somerton road formed the boundary on the north-west.

The parish lies between 400 and 450 feet above sea-level on a plateau forming part of the Great Oolite escarpment. The soil is stonebrash with a sub-soil of clay and marl, and railway cuttings have exposed greenish clay beds, characteristic of the Upper Estuarine series of Northamptonshire.[5] Local quarries supplied the stone for Tusmore House in the 1760's[6] and freestone was quarried in the 19th century.[7] No woodland was recorded in Domesday Book and the plateau is bare except for a small fir plantation on the north-eastern boundary.

On Ploughley Hill (466 ft.) was a round barrow, at one time the meeting-place of the hundred. The barrow was levelled in the early 19th century, but in 1845 human bones were found on its site.[8] Numerous roads converge on the hill: the pre-Roman Portway, a grass lane which crosses the west of the parish, joins the road from Somerton less than a mile to the south, while the roads from Somerton, Souldern, and Tusmore meet the main Bicester–Banbury road near by. All very probably follow the line of ancient tracks. So does the road between Fritwell village and Middleton Stoney. It runs along the line of Aves Ditch,[9] but the stretch near the village is called Raghouse Lane, after the rag-house built in the 18th century to serve the Deddington paper mill.[10] Before the inclosure in 1807 all these roads were gated: Troy Gate and other names are recorded by Blomfield.[11]

The London–Birmingham line of the former G.W.R., completed in 1910,[12] crosses the south of the parish.

Fritwell village,[13] standing about 400 feet up, lies in the south of the ancient parish. By 1086 and throughout the Middle Ages there were two settlements dependent on the two manorial estates in Fritwell, and the village is still divided into a western part on the Somerton road and a southern part on the Middleton road.[14] The latter, in the former Ormond manor, was perhaps the original settlement: it lay beside Aves Ditch and close to a spring which no doubt gave the village its name of *Fyrht-w(i)elle* or 'wishing well'.[15] This spring, with others in the village, feeds the southern boundary stream, and was thought by Plot to be the source of the Great Ouse.[16] In the 19th century it was known as the Townwell.[17] The church was built between the two settlements. Its dedication to St. Olave, the early-11th-century king of Norway, suggests that there was Danish influence before the Conquest.

For the hearth tax of 1665, besides the 2 manor-houses and 16 other listed houses there were 8 substantial farm-houses paying tax on 3 or 4 hearths.[18]

In the 18th century incumbents recorded that there were about 66 houses in the parish,[19] and by 1811 there were 85. Increasing population led to more building after the Napoleonic War, but in 1821 there was still overcrowding, with only 95 houses for 100 families. Since the First World War there has been much new building, including 38 council houses.[20]

Today the village is still remarkable for the number of its well-preserved 17th-century houses. They are mostly two-story houses, built of the local rubble stone, and many have stone-slate roofs. The Vicarage, enlarged in 1933,[21] is a good example: it is built on an L-shaped plan, and on the first floor retains its original windows with wooden mullions. It may have been built at two dates, the earlier 16th-century part being the southern wing. This consists of two ground-floor rooms and three bedrooms above.[22] Its ancient tithe barn still stands. 'The Hollies', with the date 1636 on its high-pitched gable and the initials N. K.(ilby), is another example. 'The Limes' has attic dormers, a stone-slate roof, brick chimney shafts, and a spiral newel staircase in the square stair projection on the north-west of the building. The Wheatsheaf Inn, built on a T-shaped plan, and the 'King's Head' are other 17th-century houses, although both have been much restored.[23] These, and the 'George and Dragon', mentioned by name in 1784, were probably the three inns licensed in 1735.[24] The last, however, is now a modern building. Seventeenth-century cottages also survive, some with thatched and some with stone-slate or Welsh slate roofs. One is dated 1637 with the initials I.W. Hazel Cottages, which are L-shaped in plan, may date from the 16th century; they are thatched and rubble built and have two-light windows with stone mullions and square labels.

There was much rebuilding in the 18th century, and today the main village street with its many derelict cottages and cheap brick accretions is redeemed by the plain dignity of its small stone 18th-century houses.[25] In striking contrast are the three-story raghouse, built in 1885, now used as a general store, and the late 19th-century block of two semi-detached houses, also three stories high, and built of incongruous red brick with stone facings to the windows. In the mid-19th century the village was described as 'expensive and respectable'. By 1864, two Methodist chapels had been built—one at each end of the street.[26] A well-built school was erected in 1872[27] and in 1919 two cottages were converted into a reading-room by Lord Jersey.[28] The number of small 19th-century houses is to be accounted for by Fritwell's convenient position for tradesmen: Bicester, Brackley, Deddington, and Banbury are all within easy reach.[29] A crescent of well-designed

[5] *V.C.H. Oxon.* i. 12; G.S. Map 1″, xlv NE.
[6] See below, p. 334.
[7] *G.S. Memoir* (1864), 16–18.
[8] Blo. *Frit.* 4; see above, p. 2; for archaeological refs. see *Archaeologia*, lxxi. 243.
[9] For the Portway and Aves Ditch see above, map facing p. 1; pp. 2, 7. Roman coins have been found NE. of the village: *V.C.H. Oxon.* i. 337, 342.
[10] Blo. *Frit.* 22.   [11] Ibid. 23.
[12] E. T. MacDermot, *Hist. G.W.R.* ii. 448.
[13] O.S. Map 25″, xvi. 7, 8 (1881).
[14] See below, pp. 136, 139.
[15] *P.N. Oxon.* (E.P.N.S.), i. 211.
[16] Plot, *Nat. Hist. Oxon.* 30.
[17] Blo. *Frit.* 2.

[18] *Hearth Tax. Oxon.* 202.
[19] Oxf. Dioc. d 552, d 555, d 558.
[20] *Census*, 1811, 1851, 1901, 1951.
[21] Local inf.
[22] Blo. *Frit.* 51.
[23] 'Wheatsheaf' mentioned in 1776 and 'King's Head' in 1784: O.R.O. Victlrs' recog.; deeds of 'King's Head' date back to 1816.
[24] O.R.O. Victlrs' recog.
[25] Brick, when used, was probably of local manufacture: see below, p. 142.
[26] *Kelly's Dir. Oxon.* (1864); see below, p. 145.
[27] See below, p. 145.
[28] O.R.O. J XIV a.
[29] Blo. *Frit.* 31.

council houses opposite the school is the chief 20th-century addition to the village.

Dovehouse Farm (called Lodge Farm by 1955), at the southern end of the village street,[30] apparently stands on the site of the Ormonds' manor-house and incorporates fragments of it. The old house may still have been standing in 1665 when two houses in Fritwell each paid tax on ten hearths,[31] but it is not marked on Plot's map of 1677,[32] and had presumably been partly pulled down and converted into a farm-house. A farm-house on the Ormond estate, at all events, was rented by Samuel Cox in the early 18th century, and later let to Sir Edward Longueville. In 1702 Cox had built a large dovecote there,[33] which was still standing in 1897[34] but had gone by 1955.

The De Lisle manor-house in the west end of Fritwell, on the other hand, has had a continuous history. It is a fine E-shaped house originally of 16th-century date, but probably rebuilt in 1619 by George Yorke.[35] His initials and this date were once carved over a chimney-piece. The house is built of coursed rubble, has two stories with three projecting gables on the southern front and a stone-slate roof. The main entrance is on the south side through a fine porch with two Corinthian columns, and there is a contemporary oak door. In the 1660's the royalist Colonel Sandys had the house and re-turned ten hearths for it in 1665.[36] In the 18th century it was occupied by Sir Baldwin Wake,[37] and later by Captain Barclay. In 1893 the house was extensively restored by the architect Thomas Garner; it was further modernized in 1910 and a west wing added in 1921 by Sir John Simon, who had bought it in 1911 and held it until 1933. Nearly all the casement windows have stone mullions, and a number of the rooms have stone-carved open fire-places and oak panelling. There is a fine oak staircase, and the state bedroom has a plaster ceiling and oak panelling with carved Corinthian columns on either side of the fireplace.

The main appearance of the west end of the village is neat, though few of its houses have any aesthetic merit. Two 17th-century farm-houses are situated here: Court Farm,[38] built on an L-shaped plan, and a neighbouring farm-house which has preserved its original windows with their stone mullions. There is also a farm-house dated H.B. 1835, a Temperance Hall (1892), several modern houses built of stone, and some 20th-century cottages of rough-cast.

The village used to be known in the 19th century as Fritwell in the Elms, on account of its fine trees,[39] and this description still applies to the west end of the village, which is surrounded by fields.

At one time there were both a water-mill and a windmill. The water-mill, probably on the Cherwell, is mentioned in 1235, and was valued at 6s. 8d. in the 14th century.[40] In the early 19th century the windmill still stood in Windmill Ground Field, near the turnpike on the Souldern–Fritwell road.[41]

The three outlying farms, Inland, The Tower, and Inkerman, probably date from after the inclosure;[42] Inkerman was built about 1863.[43] The Bear Inn, on the north-west boundary at Souldern Gate, dates from at least the 1850's,[44] and was a well-known meet for the Bicester hounds.

Fritwell played a small part in the Civil War: parliamentary foot were quartered in the village during Essex's advance to relieve Gloucester.[45]

The village has had two notable residents: Robert Barclay Allardice (1779–1854), usually known as Capt. Barclay and renowned for his pedestrian feats and interest in the Bicester Hunt and in prize-fighting;[46] and Sir John Simon (1873–1954), later created 1st Viscount Simon, who was a distinguished public servant and Lord Chancellor from 1940 to 1945.[47]

MANORS. After the Conquest William Fitz-Osbern, Earl of Hereford, held an estate assessed at 10 hides in Fritwell.[48] On his death in 1071 his estates passed to his son Roger of Breteuil, who probably died in prison after the rebellion of 1075.[49] A large part of his lands was later granted to the De Riviers, Earls of Devon,[50] but FRITWELL manor seems to have been given to Roger de Chesney, the founder of a notable Oxfordshire family.[51] While the genealogy of the De Chesney family has not been worked out completely, it is clear that Fritwell, like Albury[52] and Noke,[53] which also belonged to William FitzOsbern, descended from Roger, who was dead by about 1109, to his granddaughter Maud.[54] By 1160 she had married Henry Fitz-Gerold, chamberlain to Henry II,[55] and had been succeeded by 1198 by her son Warin FitzGerold (d. 1216). Warin was followed by his daughter Margaret, wife of Baldwin de Riviers.[56] Baldwin died in 1216, a year before his father, William, Earl of Devon, leaving a young son Baldwin as heir to the earldom. As Margaret married the notorious Fawkes de Bréauté, it is likely that the latter possessed the overlordship of Fritwell until his exile in 1224.[57] Although Margaret's son was not invested with his earldom until 1239, in 1236 Fritwell was said to be held 'de feudo comitis de Lill' de Cristischurck'.[58] The overlordship descended with the earldom until the death of Isabel, Countess of Aumale and Devon, in

[30] P. Hookins, *Fritwell* (O.A.S. 1888), ii. 10.
[31] *Hearth Tax Oxon.* 202.
[32] Plot, *Nat. Hist. Oxon.* frontispiece.
[33] Blo. *Frit.* 19–20.
[34] Ibid. The shell of the older house was also standing.
[35] T. Garner and A. Stratton, *Tudor Domestic Architecture*, ii. 180–1, pl. cxvi for illustration; Blo. *Frit.* 10–11; see also *Sale Cat.* (1911): Bodl. G.A. Oxon. b 90 (53).
[36] *Hearth Tax Oxon.* 202.
[37] For tenants of the manor-house and the murders connected with it see Blo. *Frit.* 11–14.
[38] See below, p. 141.
[39] Blo. *Frit.* 2.
[40] *Fines Oxon.* 101; Blo. *Frit.* 22.
[41] Blo. *Frit.* 22–23.
[42] None is on Davis, *Oxon. Map* (1797).
[43] Blo. *Frit.* 14; Wing, *Annals*, 65.

[44] *Kelly's Dir. Oxon.* (1854); deeds in Bodl. MS. D.D. Hall's Brewery c 11.
[45] Dunkin MS. 438/4, f. 45b.
[46] *D.N.B.*; *Gent. Mag.* 1854, N.S. xlii. 80–82; Blo. *Frit.* 14.
[47] Obituary in *The Times*, 12 Jan. 1954, p. 8.
[48] *V.C.H. Oxon.* i. 425.
[49] *Complete Peerage*, vi. 449.
[50] Ibid. iv. 310.
[51] *Eynsham Cart.* i. 412.
[52] *V.C.H. Oxon.* v. 9.
[53] See below, p. 269.
[54] Farrer, *Honors*, iii. 227, 234.
[55] *Eynsham Cart.* i. 422; *Boarstall Cart.* 309.
[56] *Eynsham Cart.* i. 423; *Boarstall Cart.* 309; *Complete Peerage*, iv. 316.
[57] *Complete Peerage*, iv. 316.
[58] Ibid. 318; *Bk. of Fees*, 447.

1293.[59] One of her heirs was Warin de Lisle, a descendant of Henry, younger son of Maud de Chesney,[60] and through him the overlordship of Fritwell passed to the De Lisles of Rougemont. It was incorrectly reported in 1307 that the manor was held of the Earldom of Aumale: confusion had no doubt arisen from Isabel de Riviers having held two carldoms after the deaths of her husband William de Forz and her brother Baldwin de Riviers, and because part of Warin's inheritance was kept, like the Earldom of Aumale, in the king's hands. Warin's son Robert became the first Lord Lisle of Rougemont, and his successors were recognized as overlords of Fritwell[61] until 1368, when Robert de Lisle surrendered all his fees to Edward III, including 1½ fee in Fritwell. Although in 1428, when the Earl of Warwick held Fritwell, his overlord was stated to be unknown, tenants of the manor after 1368 did in fact hold in chief.[62]

In 1086 the tenant of the FitzOsbern manor of Fritwell was Rainald,[63] son of Croc, the Conqueror's huntsman, and an ancestor of the Foliot family,[64] one branch of which held Fritwell in the 12th century of the De Chesneys. The genealogy of the Foliots, a family with many branches in Oxfordshire,[65] is difficult to establish. A Ralph Foliot was definitely connected with Fritwell before 1166[66] and was the successor of Robert, probably a brother of Gilbert Foliot, Bishop of Hereford and later of London.[67] As the bishop's mother was a De Chesney, the Foliots of Fritwell were kinsmen of their overlords.[68] The 1½ knight's fee in Oxfordshire held in 1199 by Ralph Foliot (d. c. 1204), perhaps one of the first Ralph, may have been at Fritwell.[69] He was succeeded by Henry, the eldest of his three brothers,[70] who died about 1233, when the wardship of his son Sampson was given to Andrew de Chaunceus.[71] In 1236 Sampson held 1 knight's fee in Fritwell of the Earl of Devon,[72] but in 1243 1 fee there was held by Roger Foliot and ½ fee of Roger by Laurence de Broke.[73] Roger may have been Sampson's uncle, and he presumably held the 1½ fee of Sampson. By 1255 Fritwell was back in Sampson's own hands,[74] but by 1279 he had given the manor to his son Ralph.[75] Sampson was Sheriff of Oxfordshire in 1267.[76] In 1265, after the battle of Evesham, his lands at Fritwell had been seized by the victorious royalists, but it does not appear that he had supported the Montfortians.[77] Ralph Foliot and another son Roger[78] died before their father, who was succeeded at Fritwell between 1281 and 1285[79] by Henry Teyes, whose precise relationship to Sampson has not been determined.[80]

Laurence de Broke's ½ fee, held of the Foliots in 1243, had possibly originally belonged to the Fritwell family, which is frequently mentioned in the early 13th century. Miles of Fritwell, who was a tenant of Maud de Chesney at Deddington,[81] quitclaimed ¼ knight's fee in Wood Eaton to Eynsham Abbey in 1199, in return for a hide of land at Fritwell.[82] By 1209 Miles had been succeeded by his son Stephen,[83] who also held 2½ hides and the mill in Fritwell. He was at law over them with one Robert Wolf as early as 1209,[84] and appears to have lost this suit by 1219, when the Abbot of Eynsham promised to help him recover his lands in Fritwell.[85] Stephen was dead by 1231,[86] and in 1235 his widow Sarah quitclaimed to Robert Wolf the third part of the 2¼ hides and the mill which she had claimed as dower.[87] By 1239 Stephen of Fritwell, presumably Sarah's son, was claiming the same 2½ hides and the mill but this time against Laurence de Broke, Roger Foliot, and Matthew le Bedel, who had apparently succeeded Robert Wolf.[88] Stephen was still pursuing his claims two years later,[89] but it is likely that in 1243 Laurence's ½ fee represented the original holding of Miles and the elder Stephen of Fritwell. Another Laurence de Broke was holding this ½ fee in 1368.[90] It is not mentioned separately in later records, but may be presumed to be included in the 1½ knight's fee held by the successors of the Foliots.

Henry Teyes, Sampson Foliot's successor, died in 1307[91] and Fritwell passed to his son Henry, who was one of the rebels captured at Boroughbridge in 1322 and later hanged. His lands were seized by the king, and in 1326 his Oxfordshire manors including Fritwell were placed in the custody of Nicholas de la Beche.[92] His heir was his sister Alice,[93] whose husband Warin de Lisle (of Kingston Lisle) had suffered the same fate as her brother.[94] Alice recovered Henry's lands, and some time before her death in 1347[95] gave Fritwell to her son and heir Gerard de Lisle, who was in possession in 1346.[96] By a settlement made in 1359, Fritwell was to be held by Gerard for life and then by his younger son Richard for life:[97] at Gerard's death in 1360 he and

[59] Rot. Hund. (Rec. Com.), ii. 44, 824.
[60] Cal. Inq. p.m. iii, p. 98; Complete Peerage, viii, pedigree between pp. 48–49. Warin (d. 1296) is to be distinguished from his cousin Warin (d. 1322) who married Alice de Teyes: see below, p. 269.
[61] Complete Peerage, viii. 71–78; Cal. Inq. p.m. x, p. 472.
[62] Complete Peerage, viii. 76; Cal. Close, 1364–8, 493–8; Feud. Aids, iv. 190.
[63] V.C.H. Oxon. i. 425.
[64] Farrer, Honors, iii. 234.
[65] Ibid. 234–6; Boarstall Cart. 313; F. N. Macnamara, Memorials of Danvers Family, 218–19.
[66] St. Frides. Cart. ii. 95, 221; see below, p. 142.
[67] Farrer, Honors, iii. 234–5.
[68] Eynsham Cart. i. 412.
[69] Red. Bk. Exch. (Rolls Ser.), 124.
[70] Farrer, Honors, iii. 235.
[71] Ex. e Rot. Fin. (Rec. Com.), i. 239.
[72] Bk. of Fees, 446.
[73] Ibid. 825.
[74] Rot. Hund. (Rec. Com.), ii. 44.
[75] Ibid. 824; Ex. e Rot. Fin. ii. 260.
[76] C. Moor, Knights of Edw. I (Harl. Soc. lxxxi), 78.
[77] Cal. Inq. Misc. i, p. 262.
[78] Cal. Pat. 1272–81, 441.

[79] See below, p. 269.
[80] Farrer, Honors, iii. 236.
[81] Chanc. R. 1196 (P.R.S. N.S. vii), 202; Pipe R. 1197 (P.R.S. N.S. viii), 36.
[82] Eynsham Cart. i. 132; see below, p. 308.
[83] Eynsham Cart. i. 137.
[84] Pipe R. 1209 (P.R.S. N.S. xxiv), 155; cf. Fines Oxon. 101.
[85] Fines Oxon. 57.
[86] Ibid. 88.
[87] Ibid. 101.
[88] Ex. e Rot. Fin. i. 329.
[89] Fines Oxon. 112.
[90] Cal. Close, 1364–8, 496; for the De Broke family see above, p. 118.
[91] Feud. Aids, iv. 169; Complete Peerage (orig. edn.), vii. 380; Cal. Inq. p.m. v, p. 26.
[92] Complete Peerage (orig. edn.), vii. 381; Cal. Fine R. 1319–27, 427.
[93] Cal. Inq. p.m. vii, p. 24.
[94] Complete Peerage, viii. 49.
[95] Cal. Fine R. 1347–56, 277; Cal. Inq. p.m. ix, p. 395.
[96] Feud. Aids, iv. 180.
[97] C.P. 25(1)/190/21/37.

his son held the manor jointly.[98] Gerard's heir was his elder son Warin, who married firstly Margaret, daughter of Sir William Pipard, and secondly Joan, widow of John Wynnow,[99] and since he was recorded as sole lord of Fritwell in 1368,[1] his brother Richard may have died by this date. Warin died in 1382 holding Fritwell jointly with his wife,[2] who does not, however, appear to have continued to hold it.[3]

By his first wife Warin had a son, Gerard, who died in 1381, and a daughter Margaret, the wife of Thomas, Lord Berkeley. They inherited all Warin's lands, and in 1383 had possession of Fritwell.[4] Margaret died in 1392, and Thomas in 1417, leaving an only daughter Elizabeth, wife of Richard de Beauchamp, Earl of Warwick.[5] Thomas held Fritwell at his death,[6] and after Elizabeth's death in 1422 her husband retained the manor.[7] Richard and Elizabeth had three daughters, Margaret, Eleanor, and Elizabeth, and after Richard's death in 1439[8] Fritwell passed to Eleanor. Eleanor's first husband, Thomas, Lord Ros, by whom she had a son Thomas, had died in 1430, and by 1436 she had married Edmund Beaufort, Earl and later Duke of Somerset.[9] By a settlement made in 1447, Fritwell was to pass to the male heirs of Edmund and Eleanor, with remainder to Eleanor's heirs.[10] Edmund was killed at the first battle of St. Albans in 1455, and his eldest son by Eleanor, Henry, Duke of Somerset, was attainted in 1461 and executed in 1464.[11] Fritwell had already been granted by Edward IV in 1462 to James Hyett.[12] Eleanor, who had married Walter Rokesley as her third husband, died in 1467, when her heir was found to be her grandson Edmund Ros.[13] But Edmund's father Thomas, Eleanor's son by her first husband, had been attainted after Towton and executed in 1464;[14] all his estates had been forfeited. According to the settlement of 1447, Fritwell should have gone to Edmund, Eleanor's second son by Edmund, Duke of Somerset, but he, the last of the house of Beaufort, also lay under attainder, and was beheaded in 1471.[15] Meanwhile Fritwell had been granted in 1467 to Edward IV's secretary, Master William Hatcliff.[16] In 1480, after his death, it was granted for life to Nicholas Southeworthe,[17] clerk of the king's kitchen,[17] who probably held it until the accession of Henry VII.

In 1529 it was found that Fritwell had been occupied, presumably in 1485, by Edward, Duke of Buckingham, Mary, Countess Rivers, and Joan, Lady Howth.[18] Edward Stafford, Duke of Buckingham, aged seven in 1485, was grandson of Humphrey

Stafford, who had married Margaret, one of the daughters of Edmund and Eleanor Beaufort.[19] Lady Rivers was the daughter of Elizabeth, another daughter of Eleanor, while Lady Howth was probably Eleanor's only surviving daughter.[20] In 1506 these claimants handed over the manor to Sir Robert Spencer,[21] of Spencercombe (Devon), who must have based his claim on the right of his wife Eleanor, eldest daughter of Edmund and Eleanor Beaufort and widow of James Butler, Earl of Ormond and Wiltshire (see below). Since she had died in 1501, Sir Robert presumably sought the manor for her daughters.[22] In 1513, however, Henry VIII granted the manor to Walter Harper, Yeoman of the Male, and William Holmes for their lives.[23] Sir Robert duly gave up the manor.[24] It is clear that the king did not recognize any claim of the female line of the Beauforts. Although the attainder of the Ros family had been reversed in 1485, Edmund, the true heir of Fritwell, was found to be 'not of sufficient discretion to guide himself',[25] and his lands were reserved during the king's pleasure.[26] Edmund died without issue in 1508, and his title passed to his nephew George Manners, son of Thomas de Ros's daughter Eleanor. The family's claim to Fritwell was eventually recognized, for by 1571 Edward Manners, Earl of Rutland, was lord of the manor.[27]

In effect the earl seems to have been overlord, while the successors of Harper and Holmes remained the tenants of the manor. In 1530 Henry VIII granted the reversion of Fritwell to William Gunson or Gonson, whose son Christopher received the manor after the death of Harper and Holmes. Christopher died in 1553, leaving a son Benjamin, then aged about two, who eventually inherited Fritwell.[28] His son Anthony was baptized at Fritwell in 1575.[29] Within two years both father and son were dead, and in 1580 Benjamin's younger brother Anthony was found to be his heir.[30] William Andrews, who married Benjamin's widow Jane, claimed Fritwell from Anthony as her jointure,[31] but in 1587 Anthony's claims were upheld.[32] Soon after the manor passed to Edward, son of the George Yorke who had purchased the advowson of Fritwell in 1562.[33] Edward was living at Fritwell by 1584.[34] It is uncertain when he acquired the manor, but he appears by a series of conveyances to have purchased the overlordship from the Earl of Rutland and the lands from the Gonsons.[35]

Edward Yorke died in 1613. His son George succeeded to the manor[36] but sold it to Dr. Hugh Barker in 1626.[37] Barker died in 1632, and the

[98] *Cal. Inq. p.m.* x, p. 472.
[99] *Complete Peerage*, viii. 52.
[1] *Cal. Close*, 1364–8, 496.
[2] C 136/26/47.
[3] C 136/72/7.
[4] *Complete Peerage*, viii. 54; C.P. 25(1)/289/53/72.
[5] *Complete Peerage*, ii. 131.
[6] C 138/259/50.
[7] *Complete Peerage*, viii. 54; *Feud. Aids*, iv. 190.
[8] C 139/94.
[9] *Complete Peerage*, xi. 104; xii (1). 53.
[10] C.P. 25(1)/293/71/52.
[11] *Complete Peerage*, xii (1). 53, 57.
[12] *Cal. Pat.* 1461–7, 117, 434.
[13] *Complete Peerage*, xii (1). 53; C 140/502/24.
[14] *Complete Peerage*, xi. 105.
[15] Ibid. xii (1). 57.
[16] *Cal. Pat.* 1467–77, 36.
[17] Ibid. 1476–85, 222, 242.
[18] C 142/50/133.

[19] *Complete Peerage*, ii. 389.
[20] Ibid. vi. 605; xi. 24.
[21] C 142/50/133.
[22] *Complete Peerage*, x. 128.
[23] *L. & P. Hen. VIII*, i (1), p. 435; i (2), p. 966.
[24] C 142/50/133.
[25] *Rot. Parl.* vi. 452.
[26] Ibid. 310, 452.
[27] Hist. MSS. Com. *Pepys*, 177; ibid. *Rutland, I*, 96.
[28] C 142/142/94; C 60/382/19.
[29] Par. Reg.
[30] C 142/190/64.
[31] *Cal. Chan. Proc.* (Rec. Com.), i. 22; C 60/398/39.
[32] C.P. 25 (2)/197/East. 29 Eliz. I.
[33] Ibid. 196/East. 4 Eliz. I; Blo. *Frit.* 42.
[34] Par. Reg.
[35] *Cal. Chan. Proc.* (Rec. Com.), i. 321; Blo. *Frit.* 10.
[36] C.P. 43/135/37; C 60/476/16.
[37] C.P. 25(2)/473/East. 2 Chas. I.

manor was purchased from his widow Mary by Samuel Sandys about 1639.[38] Between 1647 and 1651 there was considerable litigation over it, apparently to establish Sandys' title.[39] It is uncertain at what date he sold Fritwell to Sir Samuel Danvers of Culworth (Warws.): Sir Samuel is said[40] to have come into residence at Fritwell in the early 1650's, but members of the Sandys family were still there in 1665.[41] Sir Samuel died in 1683, and was succeeded by his son Sir Pope Danvers.[42] He appears to have sold the manor to Sir Baldwin Wake, Bt., who already held the advowson.[43] The Wake family held the manor until 1770, when Sir William Wake sold it to John Freke Willes of Astrop (Northants).[44] Like his predecessors Willes was not continuously resident in Fritwell, but his daughter Frances, who married one of the Fermors (see below), lived in the manor-house after 1784. On Willes's death in 1802 the manor passed to his cousin, the Revd. William Shippen Willes.[45] The latter died in 1822,[46] and William, second son of John Freke Willes, who was occasionally resident, was lord of the manor[47] until 1863. He then sold it to Isaac Berridge, who in turn sold it to Samuel Yorke of Penzance, the holder of the advowson. In 1876 the manor was bought by William Remington, whose son the Revd. Reginald Remington came into residence in that year,[48] but the original estates of the De Lisle manor had long been split up and manorial rights seem to have lapsed after the time of Samuel Yorke.[49]

A Fritwell estate, assessed at 6 hides and held in 1086 by Odo, Bishop of Bayeux,[50] passed after his exile to the Arsic family, who remained overlords of the manor until 1230, when Robert, last of the male line, died.[51] Robert's possessions were divided between his daughters, Joan and Alexandra, and their husbands, Eustace de Grenville and Thomas de la Haye.[52] Fritwell seems to have fallen to Joan's portion, and by 1245 she and her second husband Stephen Simeon had granted the manor to Walter de Grey of Rotherfield.[53] The overlordship of this Fritwell manor, later known as *ORMONDES-COURT*, then followed the same descent in the Grey family[54] as one of the Fringford manors[55] until the early 14th century. Edmund Butler, the tenant of the manor, held it of John de Grey at his death in 1321,[56] but Edmund's successors, the Earls of Ormond, held the manor in chief and no more is heard of the Grey overlordship.

In 1086 Odo of Bayeux's tenant was his retainer Wadard,[57] who held many of his Oxfordshire manors. This manor next appears in the possession of Gilbert Pipard[58] of Rotherfield Peppard, a descendant of another Gilbert who had been steward to Miles Crispin in 1106–7.[59] Gilbert died on his way to the Holy Land in 1191 or 1192, and his brother and successor William died about 1195. He was succeeded in turn by his sons Walter (d. 1214) and Roger, who inherited the family lands in Ireland from his uncle Roger. He died in 1225, and his son William survived him by only two years, leaving a young daughter Alice as his heiress. Alice became the ward of Ralph FitzNicholas, who by 1242 married her to his younger son Ralph.[60] In 1243 Ralph held Fritwell of the honor of Arsic as $\frac{1}{4}$ knight's fee.[61] He died about 1265,[62] but the date of Alice's death is not known. Her son Ralph took the name of Pipard, and inherited Fritwell, where he was in possession in 1279.[63] On his death in 1303 he was succeeded by his grandson John, a minor, whose father Ralph had died by 1302.[64] By 1306 John too was dead, and was succeeded in 1309 by his uncle John. The latter married Maud, daughter of Theobald Butler,[65] and in 1310 granted the reversion of his English lands after his death to his brother-in-law, Edmund Butler.[66] Although Edmund was said to be lord of the Arsic fee in Fritwell in 1316,[67] and although he received a grant of free warren in his demesnes at Fritwell in the same year,[68] John by the terms of his agreement with Edmund remained in possession until his death in 1331.[69]

Edmund Butler, twice Justiciar of Ireland, died in 1321,[70] and was succeeded by his son James, the future Earl of Ormond,[71] but then a minor. In 1328 he received a new grant of free warren at Fritwell,[72] although John Pipard was still alive. James died in 1338, leaving as his heir his second son James (II), aged seven, who eventually received his father's estates in 1347. Fritwell was held of James and his father by John de Alveton,[73] who was Sheriff of Oxfordshire for several terms between 1335 and 1354.[74] Since John died without known heirs in 1361[75] his holding must have fallen in to his lord. James (II) Butler died in 1382,[76] and Fritwell was then held in dower by his widow Elizabeth until her death in 1390.[77] Her son James (III) succeeded her, and held 'Ormondescourt' manor until his death in 1405.[78] His son and successor James (IV) died in

[38] C 142/467/184; C 60/544/29.
[39] C.P. 43/265/10; ibid. 275/139; C.P. 25(2)/474/Hil. 23 Chas. I; for Sandys' royalist sympathies see *Cal. S.P. Dom.* 1651, 207.
[40] F. N. Macnamara, *Memorials of Danvers Family*, 475.
[41] *Hearth Tax Oxon.* 202.
[42] G. E. C. *Baronetage*, ii. 210.
[43] See below, p. 142; cf. Blo. *Frit.* 12.
[44] Blo. *Frit.* 12; G. E. C. *Baronetage*, i. 180.
[45] Blo. *Frit.* 14; O.R.O. Land tax assess.; ibid. Incl. award.
[46] Dunkin MS. 438/5, f. 207.
[47] Blo. *Frit.* 14; Gardner, *Dir. Oxon.*
[48] Blo. *Frit.* 14; *Kelly's Dir. Oxon.* (1864).
[49] *Kelly's Dir. Oxon.* (1864, &c.).
[50] *V.C.H. Oxon.* i. 404.
[51] See above, p. 126.
[52] *Ex. e Rot. Fin.* (Rec. Com.), i. 193.
[53] *Cal. Chart. R.* 1226–57, 285.
[54] For the De Greys see *Complete Peerage*, vi, pedigree between pp. 128–9.
[55] See above, p. 127.
[56] *Cal. Close*, 1324–7, 23.

[57] *V.C.H. Oxon.* i. 404.
[58] *St. Frides. Cart.* ii. 222.
[59] *Complete Peerage*, x. 526.
[60] Ibid. 527 sqq.
[61] *Bk. of Fees*, 825.
[62] *Complete Peerage*, x. 531; *Rot. Hund.* (Rec. Com.), ii. 44.
[63] *Rot. Hund.* ii. 824.
[64] *Complete Peerage*, x. 532; *Cal. Inq. p.m.* v, p. 98.
[65] *Complete Peerage*, x. 533; *Cal. Fine R.* 1307–19, 53.
[66] *Cal. Pat.* 1307–13, 207.
[67] *Feud. Aids*, iv. 169.
[68] *Cal. Chart. R.* 1300–26, 307.
[69] *Cal. Close*, 1323–7, 23; cf. *Cal. Inq. p.m.* vi, p. 274.
[70] *Complete Peerage*, ii. 449.
[71] Ibid. x. 116.
[72] *Cal. Chart. R.* 1327–41, 95.
[73] *Feud. Aids*, iv. 180.
[74] P.R.O. *L. & I.* ix.
[75] *Cal. Inq. p.m.* xi, p. 216.
[76] *Complete Peerage*, x. 121.
[77] C 136/58/4.
[78] C 138/39.

1452; his grandson James (V), who had been created Earl of Wiltshire in 1449, married as his second wife Eleanor Beaufort, daughter of Edmund, Duke of Somerset, who held the former De Lisle manor in Fritwell in his wife's right (see above). Like his father-in-law, James was one of the leaders of the Lancastrian faction, and was beheaded after the battle of Towton in 1461.[79] 'Ormondescourt' was forfeited to the Crown, and between 1462 and 1485 it shared the history of the De Lisle manor, being held in turn by James Hyett, William Hatcliff, and Nicholas Southeworthe.[80]

James Butler's brother and heir, John, died in 1477, but his younger brother Thomas, after the reversal of his attainder by Henry VII,[81] seems to have recovered Fritwell. It passed on his death in 1515 to his daughter and coheiress Margaret, the widow of Sir William Boleyn and the mother of Sir Thomas, later Lord Rochford.[82] By 1519 Margaret and Sir Thomas had alienated the manor to Richard Fermor, merchant of the Staple at Calais.[83] Richard continued to live at Easton Neston (Northants) and Fritwell was held by his younger brother William, who also acquired Somerton. On his death in 1552 William was succeeded by his nephew Thomas, younger son of Richard.[84] By his will, made in 1580, Thomas left Fritwell to his son Richard Fermor of Somerton,[85] who died in 1643.

The 'Ormond' manor remained in the possession of the Fermor family, which lived at Tusmore after 1643, until the death of William Fermor in 1828. He left the manor to his illegitimate daughter Maria, the wife of Capt. John Turner Ramsay.[86]

The Ramsays divided all their property between their children. In 1857 Fritwell manor was bought by Henry Howard, Earl of Effingham,[87] who sold the estate within a few years in several lots. By 1867 the greater part of the original manor had been bought by Pembroke College, Oxford, which held it until 1923,[88] but manorial rights lapsed when the estate was broken up.

ECONOMIC AND SOCIAL HISTORY. In 1086 there were two manorial estates:[89] the larger, which was to become the De Lisle manor, had 8 plough-lands, but only 6 plough-teams. The demesne had 2 plough-teams and 2 serfs at work, while 8 villeins (villani), and 6 bordars shared 4 plough-teams. There had been a drop in value since the Conquest from £7 to £6.

The smaller manor, the later Ormond manor, had 4 plough-teams and was worth £3 as before the conquest. Only 1 plough-team and 1 serf are recorded on the demesne and there were 4 villeins and 1 bordar with 1½ plough-teams. There were 32 acres of meadow, 20 on one manor and 12 on the other.[90] Thus on both the estates, neither of which was fully cultivated, there was a recorded working population of 22, a number which had almost doubled by 1279, when 40 tenants are mentioned for the two manors.[91] At that time there were 58 virgates under cultivation: 16 were in demesne, 12½ were held by freeholders, and the rest by customary tenants. Since at the time of the inclosure award[92] the open fields were reckoned as 68 yard-lands, it would appear that 10 virgates were as yet uncultivated.

On the De Lisle manor in 1279, where there were 8 virgates in demesne, 14 peasants (servi) held a virgate each for a rent of 6s. the virgate, and worked, paid tallages at will, and fines if their sons left the manor. Three cottagers with a few acres each paid 5s. rent and did no labour services. Of the 6 free tenants, the most important was Philip Stiward, who held 3 virgates at a rent of 9s. and for suit at the hundred and county courts. The 5 other free tenants had holdings of various sizes, ranging from 2 acres to a virgate. St. Frideswide's Priory, the only religious house to hold land in the parish, had 1½ virgate.[93]

The Ormond manor had by now expanded its demesne to 8 virgates. As on the other manor, there were 14 villein virgaters owing the same services and paying rent. Five paid 4s. and nine 6s. There were also 2 cottagers, with 2 acres apiece, who each paid 2s. The free tenant with the largest holding was the Rector of Souldern,[94] with 1 hide, while of the others one held 2 virgates for 12s. and the other, John son of Guy, held a virgate and as much meadow as belonged to 3 hides of land.[95]

An early-14th-century extent of the De Lisle manor gives further information about these tenants.[96] There were five classes: free tenants who paid only a money rent; free tenants holding in free socage, who paid a money rent and worked for the lord when the meadow was mown; villeins, who paid rent and worked one day in autumn—certainly no more than the free tenants; and villein sokemen and cottars, both of whom worked in autumn. The total value of the manor then was about £20, and the greater part of the revenue, more than £15, came from the rent of villeins. This had more than doubled since 1279, each villein paying about 13s. Other developments were that the size of the demesne had decreased, and the number of tenants, especially cottagers, had increased. A less detailed extent of the other manor, taken the next year, shows that this manor, valued at £7 4s. 8d., was considerably less rich.[97]

Many of the inhabitants were moderately prosperous. Thirty-four were assessed for taxation in 1316.[98] By far the richest was William of Tingewick, assessed at 15s. 8d., who may have been a tenant of one of the manors; eleven others were fairly substantial men. The subsidy list of 1524 with 21 names listed shows that wealth continued to be fairly widely distributed.[99]

[79] Complete Peerage, x. 123–9.
[80] Cal. Pat. 1461–7, 117, 434; ibid. 1467–77, 36; ibid. 1477–85, 222, 242.
[81] Complete Peerage, x. 129–33; Rot. Parl. vi. 26, 296.
[82] Complete Peerage, x. 137.
[83] C 54/386/45; L. & P. Hen. VIII, iii (1), p. 996.
[84] C 142/98/54; see below, p. 293.
[85] Ibid. 190/66; C 66/1258, mm. 9–10.
[86] See below, p. 336; Gardner, Dir. Oxon.
[87] Blo. Frit. 20.
[88] Ibid.; inf. Revd. E. Glanfield.
[89] See above, pp. 136, 139.

[90] V.C.H. Oxon. i. 404, 425.
[91] Rot. Hund. (Rec. Com.), ii. 824.
[92] O.R.O. Incl. award (1808).
[93] See below, p. 142.
[94] Below, p. 308.
[95] John, son of Guy, was lord of Ardley and John de Ladwell held his Fritwell virgate.
[96] Blo. Frit. 17; Cal. Inq. p.m. v, p. 26.
[97] Blo. Frit. 7–8; Cal. Inq. p.m. v, p. 98.
[98] E 179/161/8. For poll tax returns see below, p. 358.
[99] E 179/161/176.

From this point until the 18th century the history of Fritwell is a blank. The earliest indication of the field system dates from about 1700. There were then seven fields, and deeds relating to several small pieces of property ($\frac{1}{4}$, $\frac{1}{2}$, and $\frac{3}{4}$ yardland in extent) show that each holding was divided among these seven fields. Holders of arable strips had been entitled to common for 5 beasts and 30 sheep for each yardland, but at the end of the 17th century this was reduced to 4 beasts and 25 sheep.[1]

From the inclosure map of 1808 it is possible to work out the approximate position of the fields.[2] In the west of the parish there were three fields: Meadway Field, in the western corner; next to it Wheatland Field, running from the northern to the southern boundary; and east of that, bounded on the north by the Souldern Hedge road and on the east by the road from Souldern to Fritwell, lay Darlow Field. The eastern part of the parish was divided into four fields, whose positions are not so easy to define, since furlong rather than field names are commonly used. The south-east corner of the parish, to the east of Raghouse Lane, was South Field; north of that, along the eastern boundary on both sides of the Souldern–Bicester road, lay Lindon Field; Horwell Field was in the north of the parish towards Ockley Brook; and between the Souldern Hedge road and the Souldern–Bicester road, south of the Bear Inn, lay Souldern Field. South of the village, on the west of Raghouse Lane, was the cow common, sometimes also called Fritwell Moor, and in the north-east corner were the Leys.

Except for the cow common, almost the whole parish, as might be expected in the middle of the Napoleonic War, was arable.[3] Fritwell was noticeably lacking in meadow-land, probably the reason why it had a detached portion of 135 acres on the east bank of the Cherwell—the meadow mentioned in Domesday Book[4] and in the 14th century.[5] Before inclosure each land-holder was entitled to a certain proportion of this meadow-land, known as Fritwell Meadow, the exact location to be decided by lot before the hay was cut. Every yardland also had a certain allotment of fuel from the 'meadlands',[6] which must have been more wooded than now (1955).

Fritwell was notable in the 18th century for its large number of freeholders. While the smaller manor consisted of about 600 acres,[7] and was thus virtually intact, the lands of the larger manor had been sold, only 236 acres remaining. Much of this land had probably been bought by yeoman farmers, and in 1754 there were twenty-nine 40s. freeholders in Fritwell, the largest number in Ploughley hundred except for Bicester.[8] Twenty-one of these lived in the parish.

A churchwardens' rate of 1746 shows how the land was held.[9] Of the 24 people who paid the rate, eleven, excluding the lord of the manor, had a yardland or more. Farms had started to grow larger, for there were six farms of from 5 to 6 yardlands. Nine of the larger farmers were freeholders,[10] but they may have also rented part of the Fermor land. In the early 18th century the land of this manor, consisting of about 28 yardlands, was divided among seven tenant farmers and a few cottagers, and let on a yearly tenancy of about £5 a yardland.[11]

Because Fritwell yeoman families owned their own land they show an unusual continuity. Of the eleven farmers who held a yardland or more in 1746, Kilby and Wise were from families which had been in the parish since the 16th century,[12] and Colley, Rand, and Hickock were from families which had been there since the 17th. In 1665 these were the families which had the largest houses in the village,[13] but about 100 years later they neither owned nor rented any of the principal farms, although several of their members remained in the parish.[14] The Kilby farm, for example, was sold to the Fermors, and the Hickock farm, once the property of William Hickock (d. 1638),[15] had become the Court Farm.[16]

The yeoman family of Hopcroft had the longest connexion with Fritwell. In 1279 Philip de Oppercroft was a villein virgater;[17] by the early 16th century there were five Hopcroft households, some of them fairly prosperous.[18] The family throve throughout the 17th and 18th centuries. In 1754 two Hopcrofts were freeholders,[19] but by the early 19th century the Hopcrofts were smallholders or cottagers[20] and soon disappeared altogether.

The subdivision of the land undoubtedly delayed inclosure. In the 1570's the tenant of the manor appears to have attempted to inclose. A number of 'poore men' petitioned the Earl of Rutland, the lord, against their threatened eviction and offered to purchase their land.[21] Inclosure was evidently prevented, for in 1790 and 1791 another attempt was made. Some of the landowners petitioned Parliament for an inclosure bill, but William Fermor, by far the largest landowner, successfully opposed it on the grounds, it is said,[22] that it was proposed to commute the tithes beyond their value.[23]

When inclosure finally came in 1808, only 100 acres out of 68$\frac{1}{2}$ yardlands or 1,850–1,900 acres had been inclosed.[24] By the award, William Fermor received 715 acres; W. S. Willes 236 acres, and 252 as commutation for the great tithes; the vicar 85 as commutation for the small tithes; the Rector of Souldern 122; three proprietors received from about 50 to 100 acres; twelve under 20 acres and 23 cottagers received under an acre each.[25]

[1] A. Ballard, 'Open Fields of Fritwell', O.A.S. Rep. 1907, 16–22.
[2] O.R.O. Incl. award.
[3] Davis, Oxon Map. (1797), agrees with this conclusion.
[4] V.C.H. Oxon. i. 404, 425.
[5] Blo. Frit. 17.
[6] O.A.S. Rep. 1907, 20–22; O.R.O. Reg. of Papists' Estates, p. 81.
[7] O.R.O. Incl. award.
[8] Oxon. Poll, 1754.
[9] Blo. Frit. 58–59.
[10] Oxon. Poll, 1754.
[11] O.R.O. Reg. Pap. Estates, pp. 81–82, 92–93.
[12] Blo. Frit. 53–56; Bodl. MS. Wills Oxon. 290 (index).
[13] Hearth Tax Oxon. 202.
[14] O.R.O. Land tax assess. (1832).

[15] See below, p. 145.
[16] See Blo. Frit. 32 for Wm. Hickock; Matthew Kilby was later a prominent tenant farmer: Bodl. G.A. Oxon. b 85b (57).
[17] Rot. Hund. (Rec. Com.), ii. 824.
[18] E 179/161/176; for 16 wills of Hopcroft men between 1558 and 1700 see Bodl. MS. Wills Oxon. 289 (index).
[19] Oxon. Poll, 1754.
[20] O.R.O. Incl. award.
[21] Hist. MSS. Com. Rutland I, 96; ibid. Pepys, 177; Blo. Frit. 8–9.
[22] C.J. xlv. 215; xlvi. 235, 413, 553; Blo. Frit. 24.
[23] Oxf. Archd. Oxon. b 24, f. 94.
[24] O.A.S. Rep. 1907, 22.
[25] O.R.O. Incl. award; Blo. Frit. 25–26.

After inclosure the greater part of the land was divided into medium-sized farms, let to tenants. The Fermor manor consisted of four such farms of 140 to 220 acres: two were Fritwell and Dovehouse farms, and one formed part of Roundhill farm in Stoke Lyne.[26] To the other manor belonged two farms: one of 298 acres, with a farm-house near the church,[27] part of the land of which later became Inkerman farm,[28] and the Great Tithe farm.[29] In the mid-19th century the land belonging to both the manors was broken up and sold to various owners.[30] Other farms were Inland farm, belonging to the Rector of Souldern,[31] and Court farm, the only large freehold farm.[32] In 1956 there were 12 farms. Out of their 1,298 acres, 786 acres were grassland and 512 arable.[33]

Apart from the usual village craftsmen Fritwell has had a succession of clockmakers. In the 17th century there was George Harris (1614–94),[34] a clockmaker of repute,[35] who made among others the clock of Hanwell church; in the mid-18th century and early 19th century there was Thomas Jennings, followed by William Jennings.[36] Quarrying and brick-making were also local occupations.[37] The size of the village encouraged an increase in craftsmen and tradesmen. In the 1850's there were three public houses[38] and a number of shops. Craftsmen included a straw-bonnet maker, a harness-maker, a cordwainer, a maltster, and a brazier. Lace-making was a considerable home industry and several lace-makers were recorded in the 1851 census.[39] At the end of the century Blomfield commented on the high number of resident tradesmen.

Since at least the 17th century Fritwell has had a comparatively large population. Forty houses were listed for the hearth tax of 1662 and these can hardly have been more than a portion for in 1676 the adult population numbered 252, the fourth highest figure in the Bicester deanery. At the first official census in 1801 there were 396 inhabitants. The number increased until 1891 when it reached 560. It had dropped to 468 by 1931, but rose again to 497 in 1951.[40]

CHURCH. The dedication to the Norwegian saint, Olave, suggests that Fritwell's church was dedicated in the 11th century.[41] In 1103 a grant was made of its tithes (see below). By 1166 Ralph Foliot, the tenant of the De Chesney manor in Fritwell, had given the church to St. Frideswide's Priory.[42] The gift was many times confirmed: by Pope Alexander III, by King John, and by Ralph Foliot, probably the donor's son, around 1200.[43] In 1219 a final concord was made between Henry Foliot and the priory whereby he quitclaimed all right to the advowson in return for his association in its prayers and almsgiving.[44]

Although the advowson was granted by Edward IV with the manor to James Hyett in 1462,[45] this was evidently a mistake: the Hyetts never claimed the church, and St. Frideswide's held the advowson until its dissolution in 1524.[46] Fritwell was then granted to Cardinal Wolsey, who gave it to his Oxford college.[47] On the Cardinal's disgrace, Henry VIII became patron and in 1532 granted the advowson to his own foundation at Oxford.[48] Nevertheless in 1552 it was bought from the Crown for 'ready money' by Thomas Cecil, gentleman, and Philip Bolde, cloth-worker of London, and in 1562 by George Yorke.[49] After Yorke's son Edward had purchased the manor, the descent of the advowson followed that of the manor until the late 17th century.[50] The Sandys family then sold the manor. The advowson was sold separately to Sir Samuel Jones, a rich London merchant.[51] He died in 1672 leaving as heir his sister's grandson Samuel Wake (d. 1713) of Waltham Abbey (Herts.).[52] His descendants continued to hold the advowson until it was sold with the manor in 1770 to John Freke Willes.[53] In the mid-18th century on account of the slender endowments of their vicarages the patrons of Fritwell and North Aston made an informal arrangement, lasting until 1833, to hold the vicarages together. They presented alternately.[54]

In 1862 the sale of the advowson gave rise to a legal problem which puzzled Bishop Wilberforce. It was bought by friends of the Revd. Samuel Yorke[55] with the purpose of presenting him to the vicarage. The law was that if an advowson were sold while a benefice was vacant, the former patron still had the right to present; if the patron had received an unusually high price for the sale and presented as the agent of the purchaser, the presentation would be simoniacal and therefore void. After legal consultation, it was decided that the presentation should stand, although the case was not 'free from doubt'. The advowson passed with the manor from the Yorkes to the Remingtons[56] and in 1911 to Lord Simon, who gave it in 1934 to the present patron, Wadham College.[57]

[26] Bodl. G.A. Oxon. b 85b (57).
[27] Ibid. b 85a (31).
[28] Ibid. b 6 (60).
[29] Blo. Frit. 52; see below, p. 143.
[30] See above, p. 140.
[31] Wing, Annals, 65. See below, p. 309.
[32] O.R.O. Land tax assess.
[33] Inf. Oxon. Agric. Executive Cttee. 61 acres lay outside the parish.
[34] Bodl. MS. D.D. Glanfield.
[35] Blo. Frit. 23; cf. Hearth Tax Oxon. 202.
[36] Oxf. Jnl. 11 Sept. 1773.
[37] Oxf. Dioc. d 555.
[38] Gardner, Dir. Oxon. The number of tradesmen probably accounts for the unusually large number of small properties in the parish: O.R.O. Land tax assess.
[39] H.O. 107/1729.
[40] Hearth Tax Oxon. 235; Compton Census; Census, 1801–1951.
[41] K. E. Kirk, Ch. Dedications of the Oxf. Diocese, 14. It is said to be the only one of the 14 English churches dedicated to St. Olave which is not near the sea.

[42] St. Frides. Cart. ii. 221. The dating here is wrong, as the confirmation must have been by Robert de Chesney, Bishop of Lincoln 1148–66: Boarstall Cart. 313.
[43] St. Frides. Cart. i. 43; ii. 95–96, 219.
[44] Ibid. ii. 220; Fines Oxon. 53.
[45] Cal. Pat. 1461–7, 117.
[46] V.C.H. Oxon. ii. 100. For a list of medieval presentations see MS. Top. Oxon. d 460.
[47] Visit. Dioc. Linc. 1517–31, ii. 33.
[48] L. & P. Hen. VIII, v, p. 587.
[49] Cal. Pat. 1550–3, 442; C.P. 25(2)/196/East. 4 Eliz. I.
[50] Mary Barker presented in 1642: Oxf. Dioc. c 70, no. 42.
[51] Ibid. no. 43.
[52] For him see V.C.H. Northants. iv. 243; ibid. Families, 330.
[53] See above, p. 139.
[54] Blo. Frit. 44–45.
[55] Ibid. 46; Oxf. Dioc. d 178.
[56] See above, p. 139.
[57] Wadham College MSS., Fritwell 17.

According to the ordination of the vicarage, St. Frideswide's as appropriator was entitled to most of the great tithes and the land belonging to the church.[58] In 1254 the rectory was worth £5 6s. 8d.; in 1291 £8 13s. 4d.; but by the 16th century its value had decreased to £4 13s. 4d.[59] By the inclosure award of 1808 the lay rector of Fritwell received 251 acres in exchange for the land formerly held by St. Frideswide's, and the tithes.[60] Later, probably in about 1860, when the lay rectory was separated from the advowson, most of this land, which carried with it the obligation to repair the chancel, was sold to Henry Crook of Souldern. In 1935 the owner of the property, which was sometimes known as the Great Tithe farm,[61] questioned his responsibility, and the case was heard in 1936. The Parochial Church Council was plaintiff and judgement was given for it.[62]

In the Middle Ages St. Frideswide's took part in a number of tithe disputes. The earliest was with Cogges Priory, founded in 1103 by Manasses Arsic, lord of one of the Fritwell manors. At its foundation he had granted it two-thirds of his demesne tithes.[63] In about 1166, after some controversy, the priory gave up its claim in return for a pension of 2s.[64] No later record has been found of this payment either to the priory or to Eton College, its successor at Cogges. Another controversy was with Walter Foliot, Rector of Noke, who in 1229 claimed a third of the tithes, both great and small, of the demesne of Roger Foliot in Fritwell. He was evidently a relative of the Foliots, but it is not clear on what he based his claim, and after the case was heard by papal commissioners he renounced it.[65] At about the same time there was a somewhat similar dispute with Elias, Rector of Ardley, who claimed certain tithes of sheaves (*garbarum*), and of hay in Fritwell meadow, from the lord of Ardley. The rector agreed after an inquiry by papal commissioners to pay a pension of 2s. a year for life to St. Frideswide's in return for these tithes.[66] A more protracted dispute occurred over the tithes on a hide of land in Fritwell called *Sulthorn* (i.e. Souldern), which was the glebe of Souldern church.[67] St. Frideswide's held at least 1½ virgates which had once belonged to Fritwell church:[68] a virgate had been given in about 1200, and the grant of another 10½ acres was confirmed in the mid-13th century by Fulk de Banville for the gift of a knife and a weekly mass from Ralph the priest.[69] In 1341 Fritwell glebe was valued at 26s. 8d.[70]

When the vicarage was first ordained by Bishop Hugh de Welles (1209–35),[71] it was arranged for the vicar to get the obventions from the altar, the small tithes,[72] and all tithes on 3 virgates of land. He was also to have a croft and messuage, the other church land going to St. Frideswide's Priory. His income was supposed to be £3 6s. 8d., a half of the church's value; in 1254[73] the vicarage was valued at 13s. 4d. and in 1291 at less than £5.[74] In 1535 it was worth £7 9s. 4d.[75]

After the Reformation Fritwell was considered a poor living, worth no more than £40 in 1718,[76] and freed from paying tenths because of poverty.[77] The sources of its income, described in a terrier of 1584,[78] were an annual payment of £2 13s. 4d. from the rectory the small tithes from the whole parish and the tithes of corn and hay on 3 yardlands (i.e. the 3 virgates of the original ordination), and on all closes in Fritwell 'town'. At the inclosure award of 1808 the vicar's tithes were commuted for 85 acres of land[79] and the rent of this land, usually a little over £100,[80] formed almost the only income of the living. There were about 80 acres of glebe.[81]

The medieval vicars were undistinguished. The only university graduate connected with the church before the 16th century was Master Richard de Hunsingore, official of the Archdeacon of Oxford[82] and a benefactor of two Oxford colleges.[83] He was not vicar, but in 1317 the bishop licensed St. Frideswide's to farm the church to him on condition that the cure of souls was not neglected.[84]

During the 15th century the priory frequently served its appropriated churches with its own canons, but only two seem to have been vicars of Fritwell. It is doubtful, however, how far they performed their duties. One, Master Robert Brice (1520–4), was absent from the visitation of St. Frideswide's in 1520 on the grounds that he was serving Fritwell,[85] but a few years later he is known to have been paying a curate £6 out of his income of £7 9s. 4d.[86] Furthermore, at an episcopal visitation of this period, Fritwell was found to be in much the same state of neglect as other churches: the vicar was non-resident, the chancel and Vicarage were ruinous, the vestry had not been repaired, the seats in the choir and the windows of the chancel were broken, and the churchwardens were unjustly detaining an altar vestment lent them by the wardens of Ardley.[87]

An unusually long series of churchwardens' accounts, beginning in 1568,[88] throws light on church life (there was a library, for instance, of ten books) and shows the important part in church administration played by the wardens. They were chosen in turn from among the chief householders of the parish until John Palmer, vicar from 1711 to 1729, nominated one in spite of protests; they regularly

[58] *St. Frides. Cart.* ii. 219.
[59] Lunt, *Val. Norw.* 313; *Tax. Eccl.* (Rec. Com.), 31; *St. Frides. Cart.* ii. 386.
[60] O.R.O. Incl. award.
[61] Blo. *Frit.* 52. The farm is now called Tower farm.
[62] *Banbury Guardian*, 10 Dec. 1936, p. 10; inf. the Revd. H. G. Benson.
[63] *V.C.H. Oxon.* ii. 161.
[64] *St. Frides. Cart.* ii. 222.
[65] Ibid. 223.
[66] Ibid. 224–5.
[67] See below, p. 308.
[68] *Rot. Hund.* (Rec. Com.), ii. 824.
[69] *St. Frides. Cart.* ii. 221, 222.
[70] *Inq. Non.* (Rec. Com.), 133.
[71] *St. Frides. Cart.* ii. 219; *Rot. Welles*, i. 180–1.
[72] A later ruling was that tithes on hay and mills were not included among small tithes: *St. Frides. Cart.* ii. 39.

[73] Lunt, *Val. Norw.* 313.
[74] Because it is not included in the *Tax. Eccl.*
[75] *Valor Eccl.* (Rec. Com.), ii. 159.
[76] *Par. Coll.* ii. 147.
[77] Bacon, *Lib. Reg.* 792.
[78] Blo. *Frit.* 49.
[79] O.R.O. Incl. award; cf. Blo. *Frit.* 50–51.
[80] Ibid. 51; Gardner, *Dir. Oxon.*
[81] Inf. the Revd. H. G. Benson.
[82] *Oseney Cart.* iv. 370; vi. 97.
[83] *Cal. Pat.* 1317–21, 43, 407.
[84] Blo. *Frit.* 40, quoting Linc. Reg.
[85] *V.C.H. Oxon.* ii. 99. For him see also ibid. 95; *V.C.H. Bucks.* i. 379–80.
[86] MS. Top. Oxon. c 394, f. 148.
[87] *Visit. Dioc. Linc. 1517–31*, i. 122, 124.
[88] Extracts are in Blo. *Frit.* 53–59.

attended the archdeacon's visitation, one held at Bicester or Oxford in May or June, the other at Islip in October. In 1659, during the troubled period of the Commonwealth, they had to appear in Oxford 'upon business concerning our minister', perhaps the Job Dashfield who appears as minister in 1654.

In the 17th and 18th centuries the parish had the advantage of having a number of well-educated and learned men as vicars. There was John Hunt (1608–39),[89] a 'preacher', who seems to have resided for some years at Fritwell; Theophilus Tilden (1668–90), principal of Magdalen Hall and a frequent preacher at St. Mary's;[90] and John Davies (1703–11), who was considered a good scholar and preacher by Hearne, and became Vice-Principal of Hart Hall.[91] But most was done for the parish by Davies's predecessor Robert Wake (1691–1703), a brother of the patron. He had the church repaired, increased the number of communion services from two to four, preached sermons (two of which were published), and kept the register and church accounts carefully.[92] William Vaughan (1729–40)[93] began the custom of holding North Aston and Fritwell together; he lived at Fritwell, had one service in each of his parishes on Sundays, and administered the sacrament five times a year.[94]

The union of the parishes ended in 1833, when Henry Linton (1799–1833), who had never lived on either of his Oxfordshire livings and had little interest in them, resigned Fritwell.[95] The neglect of the parish continued during the unfortunate ministry of William Rawlings (1836–62),[96] the 'great weakness' of whose intellect, according to Bishop Wilberforce, 'was one cause of his useless life and sins'.[97] After his suspension in 1852, it was reported that in spite of the thorough neglect of the parish the congregations, averaging about 200, were increasing;[98] that on the other hand there were many dissenters, 'who sometimes go to one place, sometimes to another'; 'that there was drunkenness among the farmers'; that there was a 'great want of eloquent preaching'; and that the church was too damp for most of the congregation to kneel if they wished.[99] The church and Vicarage were later put in order by Samuel Yorke (1863–74), who lived at the manor-house and did much good work in the parish.[1]

The church of *ST. OLAVE* is a stone building comprising chancel, nave, north and south aisles, western tower, and south porch. The Romanesque chancel arch, now inserted in the north wall of the chancel, the nave arcades, and the north and south doorways are the oldest parts of the church. The north door has cable mouldings on the dripstone terminating in two grotesque animal heads, and the south door is surmounted by a tympanum with a carving representing two monsters on either side of a tree.[2] The chancel was rebuilt early in the 13th century, when the south aisle and tower were added. Some lancet windows remain in the chancel and south aisle. The north aisle was added early in the 14th century. In the 15th century a good deal of work was done to the building: the former clerestory with its square-headed windows was probably built then; some new windows were inserted in the aisles; and a battlemented top story was added to the tower.

Work costing £22 was done to the church in 1694,[3] and in 1718 Rawlinson described the building as 'very neat' and 'in good repair'.[4] Minor repairs were carried out in the second half of the 18th century and in the early 19th century.[5] But a period of neglect followed, and in 1852 and 1853 the roofs of the chancel and the nave were said to be in a bad condition.[6] In 1854 the curate thought the church 'in the most disgraceful possible condition and unsafe to minister in'.[7] The lay rector promised to repair the chancel.[8] In 1864, largely owing to the vicar, Samuel Yorke, a drastic restoration costing £2,000 was undertaken (architect G. E. Street).[9] As the medieval tower was cracked, it was rebuilt with a pyramidal roof covered with shingles; both chancel walls, the north wall of the nave, and the south porch were also rebuilt; the clerestory was removed and replaced by a new high-pitched roof; a new chancel arch was built, and the original one, being considered too narrow, was moved to its present position; a new east window was inserted and the former square-headed one was moved to the north aisle; the western gallery was taken down; new seating was put in, in imitation of the seats found during restoration work; and heating was installed.[10]

The font is octagonal, with carving in low relief.[11] There is a 13th-century holy-water stoup in the chancel and a medieval oak bench in the nave. The organ loft has Jacobean panels taken from an old pew.[12] The woodwork of a finely carved pew, erected by Edward Yorke, was taken to the manor-house during the restoration of 1864.[13] Part of the rood loft was still in position in 1823.[14]

There is a brass inscription to William Hickock (d. 1638).[15] Inscriptions to Richard Hickock (d. 1708/9), William Vaughan, vicar (d. 1740), James Hakewill, vicar (d. 1798), two daughters of Laurence Lord (early 18th cent.), and Mary Court (d. 1824), a descendant of the Hickocks, have disappeared.

In 1552 the plate consisted of a chalice, censer, and brass 'holywater stooke' and candlesticks.[16] By 1593 there were a communion cup, a pewter ewer and

[89] See Macray, *Magd. Reg.* iii. 135; J. R. Bloxam, *Magd. Reg.* (*Choristers*), i. 27.
[90] Wood, *Life*, iii. 232.
[91] Blo. *Frit.* 43; Hearne, *Remarks*, vi. 14, 169.
[92] *V.C.H. Northants. Families*, 330–1; Blo. *Frit.* 42–43.
[93] Blo. *Frit.* 44.
[94] Oxf. Dioc. d 552.
[95] Blo. *Frit.* 45.
[96] Ibid.
[97] Oxf. Dioc. d 178.
[98] *Wilb. Visit.*
[99] Oxf. Dioc. d 179.
[1] Blo. *Frit.* 46; Oxf. Dioc. c 332, c 344; see below.
[2] Skelton, *Oxon.* (Ploughley), 5, has an engraving of S. door. See also P. Hookins, *Fritwell* (O.A.S. 1884), i, for drawings and description of church.
[3] Blo. *Frit.* 59.

[4] *Par. Coll.* ii. 147.
[5] Oxf. Archd. Oxon. d 13, f. 33; Blo. *Frit.* 61.
[6] Blo. *Frit.* 37.
[7] *Wilb. Visit.*
[8] Blo. *Frit.* 37.
[9] For a pre-restoration drawing by J. Buckler see plate opposite.
[10] For restoration see Blo. *Frit.* 37; MS. Top. Oxon. c 103, ff. 490–1; and *O.A.S. Rep.* 1903, 17–19 with a sketch of the church in 1863.
[11] Cf. Buckler drawing in MS. Top. Oxon. a 66, f. 266.
[12] *Kelly's Dir. Oxon.* (1939).
[13] Blo. *Frit.* 36. Skelton, *Oxon.* (Ploughley), 4, describes it.
[14] Skelton, op. cit. 4.
[15] See below, p. 145.
[16] *Chant. Cert.* 83.

South-east view of the church in 1823

FRITWELL

South-east view of the church in 1823

SOMERTON

dish, and a brass pan.[17] In 1722 the plate was still pewter, except for a silver cup which had been given by Mary Barker.[18] This was probably the silver chalice, dated 1637, the only pre-19th-century plate which the church had in 1955.[19]

In 1955 there were four bells instead of the three bells of 1552. The second and tenor were made in 1612 and 1618, the third, recast in 1665, may be of 16th-century or earlier date, and the sanctus bell probably dates from the 16th century.[20]

The registers begin in 1558. The churchwardens' accounts, beginning in 1568, from which Blomfield quotes, have disappeared.

In the churchyard in 1955 was the remains of a cross, restored in 1913.[21]

NONCONFORMITY. In the late 16th and early 17th century five recusant women were several times fined.[22] In 1644 Elizabeth Hatton was the only recusant assessed for the subsidy levied in that year, and in 1676 two others were listed.[23] Throughout the 18th century there was a moderately large community. In 1706 Samuel Cox and his wife, the daughter of Richard Kilby of Souldern,[24] were returned as papists, together with the yeoman family of Hore, a maltster, and a few others.[25] The Coxes were succeeded as tenants of the Fermor manor-house by Sir Edward Longueville (d. 1718), a prominent Roman Catholic.[26] The number of papists increased towards the end of the century: in 1738 there were said to be only 5, but by 1767 there were 21, including a maltster and a wheelwright with their families.[27] Some were tenants of the Fermors, and a priest from Tusmore visited the parish.[28] By 1808 a Roman Catholic school had been opened, and 37 Roman Catholics were reported to be living in the parish in 1817.[29] The community, however, declined rapidly in the next 40 years, and no Roman Catholics were recorded in 1854, or at later visitations.[30] At the end of the century there was a revival, when Thomas Garner,[31] who was converted in 1897, obtained permission to have mass said at the manor-house.[32] Peter Collingridge (1757–1829), Roman Catholic Bishop of Thespiae and a prominent Franciscan, was connected with Fritwell,[33] for his father lived there when an old man.

Two Protestant dissenters are recorded in the 1680's,[34] but in the 18th century there is no report of dissent. The early 19th century saw the growth of Methodism. In 1808 the two schoolmasters were nonconformists,[35] in 1823 six Methodists were returned,[36] and in 1829 a house was licensed as a Methodist meeting-place.[37] This may have been the first Methodist chapel, which was built about that time.[38] In 1853 it was described as a plain stone building; it was visited by local preachers and by a circuit preacher on the first Monday of each month;[39] its congregation was nearly a hundred.[40] In 1874 a new chapel was built at a cost of £281,[41] and this was still in use early in the 20th century.[42]

There was also a Reformed Methodist congregation, and in 1853 a 'neat' stone chapel, served by local preachers, was reported to be nearly finished.[43] By 1878 the nonconformists were said to form about a third of the population.[44] Their numbers later decreased, and by 1920 the two Methodist societies had amalgamated.[45] The Reformed chapel was still in use in 1955 and was a member of the Wesleyan Reform Union.[46]

SCHOOLS. About 1685 a few children were being taught in the church.[47] A school, opened about 1795, was held in the vicarage barn and was supported by the children's parents.[48] In 1808 there were two schools, both kept by dissenters, with 30 children, while four Roman Catholic children were taught by a co-religionist.[49] Only one school survived in 1815[50] and that had closed by 1818.[51] In 1833 there was a school for 30 children;[52] in the 1850's it was held in the Vicarage and was supported by voluntary contributions and the children's pence.[53] There were 67 pupils in 1871.[54]

In 1872 a new school affiliated to the National Society and a mistress's house were completed at a cost of £700. Two teachers were appointed for 64 pupils. The school was supported by a voluntary rate of 4d. in the pound in 1878.[55] In 1928 £1,500 was raised by public subscription, and in 1930, when a new classroom was opened, children from Ardley, Fewcot, Somerton, Souldern, and Stoke Lyne were admitted. The average attendance, which had been 87 in 1893,[56] was 119 in 1937, and in 1939 77 evacuees were received. In 1948 the school was reorganized as a junior school and the older children were sent to Steeple Aston. The school was controlled in 1953. There were 77 pupils in 1954.[57]

CHARITIES. William Hickock (d. 1638)[58] gave to the poor an annual rent charge of £2 on lands in the parish.[59] In the 18th century this was distributed at

[17] Blo. *Frit.* 56.
[18] Ibid. 58. She was lady of the manor in the 1630's.
[19] Evans, *Ch. Plate.*
[20] *Ch. Bells Oxon.* ii. 139–40.
[21] *Kelly's Dir. Oxon.* (1939).
[22] C.R.S. xviii. 256; Salter, *Oxon. Recusants, passim.*
[23] E 179/164/496A; Compton Census.
[24] See below, p. 305.
[25] *Oxoniensia*, xiii. 78.
[26] Stapleton, *Cath. Miss.* 97.
[27] Oxf. Dioc. d 552; c 431, f. 6b.
[28] Ibid. d 555.
[29] Ibid. d 707, d 576.
[30] *Wilb. Visit.*; Oxf. Dioc. c 332; c 344.
[31] See above, p. 136.
[32] Stapleton, *Cath. Miss.* 98.
[33] *D.N.B.*; Stapleton, *Cath. Miss.* 98.
[34] Oxf. Dioc. d 708, f. 140b.
[35] Ibid. d 707.
[36] Ibid. d 580.
[37] Ibid. c 645, f. 136.
[38] H.O. 129/158.

[39] *Lascelles' Oxf. Dir.* (1853), 386.
[40] H.O. 129/158.
[41] 'Bicester 50 Years Ago', *Bicester Herald*, 1924.
[42] *Kelly's Dir. Oxon.* (1903).
[43] *Lascelles' Oxf. Dir.* 386.
[44] Oxf. Dioc. c 344.
[45] *Kelly's Dir. Oxon.* (1920).
[46] *Deddington Circuit Plan* (1955).
[47] Oxf. Dioc. d 708.
[48] Ibid. c 433.
[49] Ibid. d 707.
[50] Ibid. c 433.
[51] *Educ. of Poor*, 724.
[52] *Educ. Enq. Abstract*, 747.
[53] Gardner, *Dir. Oxon.*; *Wilb. Visit.*
[54] *Elem. Educ. Ret.*
[55] Oxf. Dioc. c 338; ibid. c 344; Blo. *Frit.* 31.
[56] *Ret. of Sch.*
[57] Inf. Revd. E. Glanfield; inf. Oxon. Educ. Cttee.
[58] Cf. *Char. Don.* ii. 989, which gives the donor as Richard Hickock, by will 1635.
[59] *12th Rep. Com. Char.* 304.

Easter and Christmas, and by 1824 at Christmas only, either in bread or coal.[60] Between 1935 and 1952 the charity was regularly applied to buy coal for ten widows at Christmas.[61]

An unknown donor gave a rent charge of £1 on South Field Farm before 1786. It was distributed with Hickock's Charity in 1824[62] and appears to have still been paid in 1852,[63] but in 1935 it was said to have been in abeyance for many years.[64]

The Town Stock of £20 is mentioned from 1737 onwards. It was thought lost in 1750, but was recovered in 1755. Up to 1793 it was held by local landowners, and the interest at 10 per cent. was distributed to the poor each year.[65] In 1824 it was again reported lost[66]—but in 1872 £20 'town stock' was given to the school building fund.[67]

In 1859 an unknown donor paid £20 into Bicester Savings Bank for the poor of Fritwell.[68]

GODINGTON

THIS isolated parish (1,019 a.) is elongated in shape and projects into Buckinghamshire: the county and parish boundaries are therefore for the most part the same. On the north and east the parish is bounded by the Birne, a tributary of the River Ouse, which here divides into several parallel streams.[1] There have been no recorded changes of boundary.[2] The centre of the parish lies on drift gravel, bordered by Cornbrash in the valley on the north-west and by the Oxford Clay in the south-east.[3] The greater part of it is a bleak almost treeless table-land, mostly above the 300-foot contour line. The highest point of 356 feet is reached in the centre of the parish near Godington Hall. The south-west of the parish is crossed by the Stratton Audley–Poundon road, from which a branch, called the Stratton Audley–Buckingham road in 1817, runs north-eastwards to the village.[4] The nearest station is the former L.M.S. one at Marsh Gibbon and Poundon, two miles distant.

The village, standing about 290 feet up, lies at the northern end of the parish.[5] The medieval village was never large and may have declined in numbers in the late Middle Ages.[6] In 1665 there were two gentlemen's houses, one of them the Rectory, which each returned six hearths for the hearth tax. There were only five other houses listed, and none had more than two hearths. In the fuller list of 1662 there were nine houses.[7] During the 18th century incumbents estimated that there were sixteen houses in the parish.[8] In 1951 the village had only twelve dwellings, some of which were red-brick cottages dating from the 19th century.[9] They were spread out on either side of the road running from Moat Farm, past the church and the Old Rectory, to Grange Farm and the new Rectory, half a mile away.

Moat Farm stands a short distance to the north of the church. It is surrounded by a rectangular moat of medieval date.[10] The present farm-house was built in the 17th century, and the date 1672 with the

initials C B appears on a weather-vane on the roof. The sash windows were inserted in 1782 by William Fermor,[11] whose initials are carved on a date-stone on the south side. It may have been the house occupied by one Davis in 1738, who had a resident priest and made the house a centre for the Roman Catholics of the neighbourhood.[12] It was later occupied by another yeoman family of well-known Catholics—the Collingridges.

In 1787 the old Rectory was 'in so ruinous and decayed a state' that it was rebuilt at a cost of £200 with the help of a loan from Corpus Christi College. The new house (37 ft. wide by 16 ft. high) was of brick, and consisted of parlour, kitchen, dairy, brew-house, three bedrooms, and two garrets.[13] In 1867 a new Rectory on a different site was built at a cost of £1,200 (architect W. Wilkinson of Oxford),[14] but in the 1930's it was sold for use as a private house.[15]

Formerly there were a blacksmith's shop near the Rectory and a number of mud cottages, which have been pulled down within living memory. There is no record of any public house in the village.[16]

Poodle Farm at the southern end of the parish has a history going back to the 13th century and stands on the site of a grange belonging to Missenden Abbey.[17] The name is possibly derived from Old English pōl-dæl, 'the stream valley',[18] and no doubt refers to the never-failing spring of water which still supplies the farm. The present house is stone-built with walls of great thickness, but has been refronted with blue vitreous bricks said to have been made in the local brick works.[19] The house is of two stories with attic dormers; a west wing was added in the 19th century, possibly in 1822 when the stables were rebuilt.[20]

Godington Hall is a well-built house dating from the early 19th century.[21] Grange Farm, formerly Manor Farm, has been rebuilt, but still retains parts of an earlier 17th-century house.

The only family of note connected with Godington

---

[60] 12th Rep. Com. Char. 304.
[61] Inf. the Revd. E. Glanfield.
[62] Char. Don. ii. 989; 12th Rep. Com. Char. 304.
[63] Gardner, Dir. Oxon.
[64] Inf. the vicar.
[65] Par. Rec.
[66] 12th Rep. Com. Char. 304.
[67] Blo. Frit. 33.
[68] Kelly's Dir. Oxon. (1887).
[1] O.S. Map 6″, xvii (1884); 2½″, 42/62 (1951).
[2] Census, 1881, 1951.
[3] G.S. Map 1″, xlv NE.
[4] O.R.O. Incl. map.
[5] O.S. Map 25″, xvii. 12 (1881).
[6] See below, p. 358.
[7] Hearth Tax Oxon. 203, 235.

[8] Oxf. Dioc. d 552 (1738), d 555 (1759).
[9] Census, 1951.
[10] V.C.H. Oxon. ii. 329.
[11] See below, p. 148.
[12] Oxf. Dioc. d 552.
[13] Ibid. c 434, ff. 101b–102; Oxf. Archd. Oxon. b 24, f. 103.
[14] MS. Top. Oxon. c 103, ff. 494, 503.
[15] See below, p. 151.
[16] Local inf.
[17] See below, p. 149.
[18] Ekwall, Dict. Eng. P.N.
[19] Local inf.
[20] See dated stone.
[21] For Godington Hall Farm and Moat Farm see Sale Cat. 1857: Bodl. G.A. Oxon. b 85b (57).

was the medieval one of the De Camvilles. A 12th-century charter of Hugh de Camville suggests that he then lived in the village. It is witnessed by his wife and brother, by Regnerus the painter and others, who appear to be members of Hugh's household, together with the halimot of Godington.[22] The parish has, however, been well known for generations as an outpost of Roman Catholicism.[23] In more recent times its coverts have been renowned in connexion with the Bicester Hunt.[24]

MANOR. *GODINGTON*, which before the Norman Conquest had been held by Siward and Siwate, was held in chief as 7 hides by Richard Puingiant in 1086, while a tenant, William, held it of Richard.[25] Until the early 14th century the overlordship of Godington followed the same descent as Richard Puingiant's Domesday manor of Middleton Stoney, of which it was regarded as a dependent member.[26] In the mid-12th century Godington appears in the possession of the De Camville family, who until the loss of Normandy in King John's reign still held Canville-les-Deux-Eglises (Seine-Inférieure), from which they took their name.[27] Richard de Camville held 1 knight's fee in Oxfordshire in 1166,[28] of which Godington no doubt formed part, for Richard and his brother Roger granted lands in Godington to Missenden Abbey (Bucks.) about that time.[29] Richard died in 1176.[30] His eldest son Gerard married Nichole, daughter and heiress of Richard de la Hay, hereditary Sheriff of Lincolnshire and Constable of Lincoln castle, and held these offices in his wife's right.[31] He supported Count John against King Richard and so lost his lands,[32] and in 1194 had to pay 2,000 marks for their recovery.[33] He died about the end of 1214, leaving his son Richard, the husband of a daughter of Gilbert Basset, as his heir.[34] Unlike his mother Nichole, Richard seems to have sided with the barons in the civil war, and suffered for his opposition. He recovered some of his confiscated manors early in 1217, but died a few years later.[35]

His heir was his daughter Idoine, and the right to arrange for her marriage had been given to William Longespée, Earl of Salisbury, in 1216.[36] The earl's eldest son William married her and received her inheritance when she came of age in 1226.[37] He held Godington as ¼ knight's fee in 1243,[38] but was killed on crusade in 1250, a year or two before Idoine died.[39] Her son William succeeded[40] in 1252, but died in 1257, leaving an infant daughter,

Margaret, as his heiress.[41] In 1268 her husband Henry de Lacy, Earl of Lincoln, received his wife's inheritance.[42] In 1279 and 1285 he was said to be holding Godington in chief.[43] Henry, one of the most loyal and capable of the earls of Edward I's reign, died in 1311, leaving his large possessions, including Godington,[44] to his only surviving child, Alice de Lacy, who inherited two earldoms. At his inquest *post mortem* Godington was said to be held of Middleton Stoney of the honor of Pontefract. Alice married Thomas, later Earl of Lancaster, in 1294, and he was recorded as lord of Godington in 1316.[45] Thomas was beheaded in 1322 after the failure of his rebellion against Edward II, and all his possessions were taken into the king's hands. His widow Alice never recovered Godington.[46]

Richard de Camville (d. 1176) appears to have enfeoffed first his younger brother Roger, and later, presumably on Roger's death, another brother Hugh with the manor of Godington. Hugh, who was in possession about 1160,[47] was succeeded by his son Thomas, who about 1206 enfeoffed William Falconer with a carucate of land in Godington as $\frac{1}{12}$ knight's fee[48] and undertook to perform the service due to Gerard de Camville, the chief lord of the fee. Thomas died in 1235,[49] and in 1243 Roger de Witchester held Godington, presumably of Robert de Camville, Thomas's son.[50] Robert was of age by 1246, and in 1255 the tenant of the manor, Philip Lovel, held of Robert, who held of the younger William Longespée.[51] There had been another change of tenants by 1279 when William de Havere held the principal estate in Godington as $\frac{1}{8}$ fee.[52] Robert de Camville does not appear as mesne lord of Godington in 1279 for in that year he surrendered the manor to the king and queen.[53] In 1281 Queen Eleanor granted the manor, 'late of Sir Robert de Camville', to Guy Ferre, to be held for a nominal rent and the services due to the chief lord of the fee[54]—the Earl of Lincoln. Robert clearly acquiesced in this arrangement, for a few months later he promoted a grant to Guy Ferre of lands and rents in Godington by Godfrey and Joan Fitzpeter.[55] Guy died childless in 1323 and the manor reverted to the Crown,[56] which had already acquired the overlordship by Thomas of Lancaster's forfeiture.

In 1325 Edward II granted the manor to Richard Damory of Bucknell at fee farm. During the lifetime of Eleanor, Guy Ferre's widow, Richard was to hold two-thirds of the manor for 10 marks a year. On Eleanor's death the remaining third would revert

[22] *Oxon Chart.* no. 54.
[23] See below, p. 152.
[24] Wing, *Annals*, 61.
[25] *V.C.H. Oxon.* i. 417.
[26] *Cal. Inq. p.m.* v, p. 157; see below, p. 244.
[27] L. C. Loyd, *Anglo-Norman Families* (Harl. Soc. ciii), 24.
[28] *Red Bk. Exch.* (Rolls Ser.), 304.
[29] *Missenden Cart.* ed J. G. Jenkins (Bucks. Arch. Soc. Rec. Branch ii), i. 17.
[30] Loyd, *Anglo-Norman Families*, 24; R. W. Eyton, *Itin. of Henry II*, 204.
[31] Farrer, *Honors*, ii. 221.
[32] See Kate Norgate, *John Lackland*, 31, 33, 35.
[33] *Pipe R.* 1194 (P.R.S. N.S. v), 118.
[34] See below, p. 245.
[35] Farrer, *Honors*, ii. 221; for the date of his death, see below, p. 245.
[36] *Rot. Litt. Claus.* (Rec. Com.), i. 265.
[37] Ibid. ii. 110, 123.
[38] *Bk. of Fees*, 825.
[39] *Complete Peerage*, xi. 383.

[40] *Rot. Hund.* (Rec. Com.), ii. 45.
[41] *Complete Peerage*, xi. 384.
[42] Ibid. vii. 682.
[43] *Rot. Hund.* (Rec. Com.), ii. 833; *Feud. Aids*, iv. 157.
[44] *Complete Peerage*, vii. 682–6; *Cal. Inq. p.m.* v, p. 157.
[45] *Complete Peerage*, vii. 687; *Feud. Aids*, iv. 169.
[46] *Cal. Pat.* 1321–4, 180; see below, p. 245.
[47] *Oxon. Chart.* no. 54; *Sir Chris. Hatton's Bk. of Seals*, ed. L. C. Loyd and Doris M. Stenton (Northants Rec. Soc. xv), p. 8.
[48] *Fines Oxon.* 36, 55, 66.
[49] *Close R.* 1234–7, 47.
[50] *Bk. of Fees*, 825.
[51] *Ex. e Rot. Fin.* (Rec. Com.), ii. 2; *Rot. Hund.* (Rec. Com.), ii. 45.
[52] *Rot. Hund.* ii. 833.
[53] C.P. 25(1)/284/21/90.
[54] *Cal. Chart. R.* 1257–1300, 248; *Feud. Aids*, iv. 157, 169.
[55] *Fines Oxon.* 212.
[56] *Cal. Inq. p.m.* vi, pp. 248, 249

to him, and his farm would be increased by £10.[57] Eleanor was still alive in 1330 when Richard died[58] leaving his son Richard, who was still a minor, as his heir. The wardship of the younger Richard was granted to his mother, and he came of age in 1337.[59] In 1347 Richard was permitted to entail the manor on himself and his male heirs.[60] The reversion of Eleanor's dower in Godington seems to have fallen in by 1354,[61] but by then Richard was heavily in debt.[62] In 1354, when he owed Edward III £2,000, he surrendered Godington to the king, who re-granted it to him for life at the farm of £10 a year.[63] In 1373 the farm was made payable to John de Beverley, who with his wife Amice was granted the reversion of the manor in the same year.[64] In 1374 Richard was allowed to let the manor to John for £2 a year;[65] in 1375 he died without issue and without known heirs,[66] and Godington duly reverted to the De Beverleys.

John de Beverley died in 1380, and Godington was delivered by the escheator to his widow Amice, since they had held the manor jointly.[67] On Amice's death in 1416 Godington, like Bucknell, passed to Robert Langford and Walter Dauntesy, John de Beverley's grandsons.[68] The manor continued to be held of the Crown at a farm of £10 a year, and in the course of the 15th century a number of grants of the farm were made by successive sovereigns. Richard Bedford, an auditor of the Exchequer, received a grant of the farm of Godington for ten years in 1439, and in 1447 he and Edmund Hampden were granted it for life.[69] In 1466—the Lancastrian Hampden having been attainted—Edward IV gave the farm of Godington to his queen, Elizabeth. During his brief restoration in 1471, Henry VI granted it to George, Duke of Clarence, but Elizabeth probably regained it when Edward IV recovered his kingdom.[70] Richard III seems to have taken the revenue from Godington for himself, but Henry VII restored it to Elizabeth in 1486.[71] Unfortunately this series of grants refers to those who were responsible for paying the farm as 'Richard Damory and his heirs', without giving any indication of who were the tenants of the manor. In 1428 William Parkins held the manor, but it was not known of whom he held it.[72] Robert Langford and Walter Dauntesy may well have alienated the manor as they did Bucknell but with the exception of Parkins subsequent tenants in the 15th century are not known.

The Fermor family seems to have acquired its first possessions in Godington shortly after the Dissolution (see below), and by his death in 1552 William Fermor held Godington manor,[73] although his will mentions only his lands in 'Poodle'[74] (i.e. Missenden Abbey's former estate).[75] William Fermor's nephew and heir Thomas succeeded to Godington, and held the manor, with appurtenances in Hardwick, of the queen in fee farm, paying the £10 a year which the successors of Richard Damory had paid.[76] Thomas died in 1580 and by the terms of his will left Godington manor in trust for sixteen years until his son Richard came of age.[77] Like Somerton Godington was held by Richard's eldest son John and his wife Cicely Compton. John died before his father, and Cicely and her second husband Lord Arundell of Wardour continued to hold the manor in dower. Lord Arundell's estates were sequestered during the Civil War and he petitioned to compound for them in 1646. But it was not until 1653 that Godington manor was purchased for £2,131 from the Treason Trustees by his brother-in-law, Humphrey Weld, for the duration of the lives of Arundell and his wife.[78] In 1665, as the house was being leased by a Mr. Croker, a member of a well-known local family, it is possible that the estate was also leased to him.[79] Henry Fermor (d. 1673) left lands in Godington to his wife Ursula,[80] and from his son Richard (d. 1684) Godington descended to Henry (d. 1703) and James (d. 1722). When Rawlinson visited Godington early in the 18th century he recorded that the lord of the manor was Sir Edmund Denton,[81] not James Fermor. The Dentons of Hillesden (Bucks.) held land in Godington,[82] but based their claim to the lordship of the manor with view of frankpledge on their possession of the manor of Middleton Stoney which they held until 1712,[83] although Godington had been separated from Middleton since 1322. Proof of the reality of the claim to lordship by the lords of Middleton lies in the fact that their steward was holding the Godington court leet at Middleton in the 1650's.[84]

Godington remained in the Fermor family, following the same descent as Somerton until the death of the last of the direct line, William Fermor, in 1828.[85] William left his property to his illegitimate daughter Maria Ramsay, and after her death it was split up among her children, who sold Godington to Henry, 2nd Earl of Effingham, in 1857.[86] The lordship of the manor descended with the Earldom of Effingham[87] until 1927, when the estates were sold.[88] Manorial rights have now lapsed.[89]

[57] Cal. Fine R. 1319–27, 347; Cal. Pat. 1370–4, 360; for the Damorys see above, p. 73.
[58] Cal. Inq. p.m. vii, p. 203.
[59] Cal. Fine R. 1327–37, 192; Complete Peerage, iv. 47–48.   [60] Cal. Pat. 1345–8, 329.
[61] Ibid. 1370–4, 360.
[62] Cal. Close, 1346–9, 415, 546, 610; ibid. 1349–54, 483.
[63] Cal. Pat. 1367–70, 220; ibid. 1370–4, 360; Cal. Close, 1354–60, 56; C.P. 25(1)/190/20/76.
[64] Cal. Pat. 1370–4, 360, 377; for the De Beverleys see above, p. 73.
[65] Cal. Pat. 1374–7, 30.
[66] Cal. Inq. p.m. xiv, p. 115.
[67] C 136/12/10; Cal. Close, 1377–81, 417.
[68] A. H. Cooke, Early History of Mapledurham (O.R.S. vii), 32, 34, 40; Cal. Close, 1392–6, 156; C 138/21.
[69] Cal. Pat. 1436–41, 305; ibid. 1446–52, 84.
[70] Ibid. 1461–7, 480; ibid. 1467–77, 241; Cal. Close, 1461–8, 282.
[71] Cal. Pat. 1476–85, 452; ibid. 1485–94, 76.
[72] Feud. Aids, iv. 190.

[73] C 142/98/54; for the Fermors see below, pp. 293, 336.
[74] R.C. Families, i. 25.
[75] See below.   [76] C 142/190/66.
[77] R.C. Families, i. 26.
[78] Cal. Cttee. for Compounding, ii. 1223; C 54/3734/12; cf. below, p. 293.
[79] E 179/164/513.
[80] R.C. Families, i. 27.
[81] Par. Coll. ii. 151.
[82] O.R.O. J I a/8, 10.
[83] Ibid. a/15, 19; cf. C.P. 25(2)/710/Trin. 31 Chas. II; see below, p. 246.
[84] Wilts. Arch. Soc. Libr. (Devizes), Antrobus deeds: court leets held 17 Apr. 1651, 4 Oct. 1652, 6 Oct. 1656.
[85] O.R.O. J VIII a/4, 5, 6, 8, 10, 23; see below, p. 336.
[86] R.C. Families, i. 8; Sale Cat.: Bodl. G.A. Oxon. b 85, b (57).
[87] Kelly's Dir. Oxon. (1864, 1920); Complete Peerage, v. 15–16; Burke, Peerage (1953), 710.
[88] Local inf.
[89] Kelly's Dir. Oxon. (1939).

LESSER ESTATES. Missenden Abbey acquired 2 hides, the Poodle estate, in Godington from the De Camvilles in the 12th century[90] and held it until the Dissolution.[91] By 1541 the estate had been purchased by William Fermor[92] and it again became part of the manor. A virgate in Godington was held by Chetwode Priory (Bucks.) in 1279[93] and passed with the priory's possessions to Notley Abbey (Bucks.) in 1461.[94] Notley held it at the Dissolution,[95] and in 1554 it was held by the Risley family.[96] The later history of 2 virgates held by Elstow Abbey (Beds.) in 1279[97] is unrecorded.

ECONOMIC HISTORY. Godington was probably first settled by the Saxons; the place-name is derived from *Gōdan dūn* or perhaps *Gōdinga dūn*, 'the hill of Goda' or of 'Goda's people'.[98] In the Domesday survey the village had land for 7 ploughs and was worth £5, as it had been at the Conquest. There were 2 plough-teams with a serf on the demesne, and 6½ worked by the 16 villeins (*villani*) and 2 bordars, who made up the recorded working population.[99] In 1279 William de Havere, tenant of the manor under the Earl of Lincoln, held 6 virgates in demesne; the only other free tenants were probably the Abbess of Elstow and the Prior of Chetwode, with 3 virgates between them. Holding of William de Havere were 25 villeins—2 virgaters and 23 half-virgaters—paying rents of 5s. a year on a virgate, 2 cottars and 6 tenants, who each held a messuage and a few acres of land for an average rent of 1s. a year.[1] This survey of the village does not include the estate given to Missenden Abbey by Richard de Camville about the middle of the 12th century;[2] it lay in the lower south-western part of the parish called Poodle.

In 1291 the abbey's lands in Godington were worth £2 8s. 8d. a year, and its stock and crops £1 10s. 8d.[3] The labour services owed by the villeins of the Camville manor had apparently been commuted by the late 13th century: no services are specified in 1279 when rents probably included payments in lieu of works. In 1323 these payments came to £4 14s. 6d. a year.[4] For a comparatively small parish Godington was fairly prosperous in the early 14th century, judging by its assessments for taxation.[5] In 1327 as many as 23 individuals were assessed, and it may be noted that in 1316 Missenden's grange of Poodle was the highest contributor.[6] At the end of Edward III's reign there were 43 contributors to the poll tax in Godington.[7]

At the Dissolution Missenden Abbey's estate was bringing in rents of £2 6s. 8d. a year[8] and it is prob-

able that much of it was then used for grazing, for of an estate of 120 acres in Poodle in 1541 all but 20 acres were pasture.[9] By the end of the 16th century the whole parish, with the exception of the glebe lands and a ½-yardland held by Nicholas Jackman, had been bought by the Fermors, the lords of the manor.[10] In 1524 two Jackmans, Robert senior and junior, had been among Godington's subsidymen, and another Robert had contributed to the subsidies of 1559 and 1569. But by 1603 these and other substantial yeoman families, the Allens and the Lambournes,[11] had evidently given up their holdings, and in about 1615 Nicholas Jackman sold his lands to Sir Richard Fermor.[12]

There had no doubt been a number of small closes in Godington dating from the Middle Ages; the acre of land with appurtenant meadow lying between two houses in Godington and granted by Hugh de Camville in about 1160 to Regnerus the painter may have been one,[13] and an inclosure, 'Garscroft', is mentioned in about 1208.[14] But very nearly the whole of the parish was inclosed in or shortly after 1603 by agreement between Sir Richard Fermor, James Benskyn, the rector, and Nicholas Jackman.[15] By the early 18th century the Fermors' estate was split up into five farms each let at over £40 a year, and three smaller ones let at between £20 and £40 each, the total annual rents amounting to about £347.[16] There were six farms at the beginning of the 19th century, but rents had more than doubled, having risen very steeply in the last decade of the 18th century.[17] Godington Cow Pasture, nearly 100 acres in the south-west of the parish, remained uninclosed[18] until 1817 when the tithes were commuted,[19] and Magdalen College, which had held three small meadows in the parish in 1535,[20] was awarded 2 acres in lieu of its right to the first crop of hay from certain lands.[21]

In the 19th century two of the farms belonged to the rector: Glebe farm (about 50 acres), 'one of the most compact glebe farms in the kingdom',[22] was in the early part of the century let as a dairy farm;[23] the other, consisting of the 130 acres the rector received at inclosure, was known as Tithe farm.[24] In 1918 both these farms were sold to Thomas Markham of Hall Farm.[25] In 1956 there were five farms in the parish. There were 360 acres of arable and 744 acres of grassland.[26]

Although the population was probably always comparatively small, it has considerably declined in recent years. In 1676 there were 65 adults, and the population may have been static for most of the 18th

---

[90] See above, p. 147.
[91] *Valor Eccl.* (Rec. Com.), iv. 246.
[92] *L. & P. Hen. VIII*, xvi, p. 246.
[93] *Rot. Hund.* (Rec. Com.), ii. 833.
[94] *V.C.H. Bucks.* i. 378.
[95] Dugd. *Mon.* vi (i), 280.
[96] *Cal. Pat.* 1558–60, 8.
[97] *Rot. Hund.* (Rec. Com.), ii. 833.
[98] *P.N. Oxon.* (E.P.N.S.), i. 212.
[99] *V.C.H. Oxon.* i. 417.
[1] *Rot. Hund.* (Rec. Com.), ii. 833–4.
[2] *Oxon. Chart.* no. 54.
[3] *Tax. Eccl.* (Rec. Com.), 45. The abbey was granted free warren in Poodle in 1302: *Cal. Chart. R.* 1300–26, 24.
[4] C 134/76/11.
[5] See table, p. 358.
[6] E 179/161/8, 9.
[7] Ibid. 161/39.
[8] *Valor Eccl.* (Rec. Com.), iv. 246.

[9] *L. & P. Hen. VIII*, xvi, p. 246.
[10] C 2 Jas. I, F 12/8.
[11] E 179/161/176; ibid. 162/319, 331.
[12] C 2 Jas. I, F 12/8.
[13] *Oxon. Chart.* no. 54.
[14] *Fines Oxon.* 37.
[15] C 2 Jas. I, F 12/8.
[16] O.R.O. Reg. Papists' Estates.
[17] Ibid. Land tax assess.
[18] Oxon. Dioc. c 448, f. 67: terrier 1806; cf. Davis, *Oxon. Map*.
[19] See below, p. 150.
[20] *Valor Eccl.* ii. 276.
[21] O.R.O. Incl. award.
[22] C.C.C. Mun. Godington corresp.
[23] Gardner, *Dir. Oxon.*; Oxf. Dioc. c 661, f. 139.
[24] Gardner, *Dir. Oxon.*
[25] MS. notes by the Revd. D. G. Peck.
[26] Inf. Oxon. Agric. Executive Cttee.

century, when the incumbents constantly returned 16 houses and 100 inhabitants. By 1801 the population was 99, and it reached a peak of 118 in 1831. Thereafter the number of inhabitants has steadily declined. It was 57 in 1901 and had fallen to 45 by 1951.[27]

In 1086 the mill was worth 3s.:[28] it is mentioned in 1279, when it was held by William de Havere. Another is recorded in 1323, worth £1, and on the estate of Missenden Abbey. It was held of the abbey by the Prior of Chetwode.[29] No more is heard of it and it had evidently fallen into disuse by 1535, when it was not included in the survey of the abbey's and priory's possessions. Twyford mill, two miles away and reached by a footpath,[30] was commonly used by the people of Godington until the late 19th century.

CHURCH. It is likely that there was a church at Godington at least by about 1160, when Hugh de Camville and his wife Christina held the manor and probably lived in the parish. A charter of this date is witnessed by the halimot and Humphrey the clerk, who was perhaps the parish priest.[31]

The earliest evidence about the advowson comes from a case of 1221 between Thomas de Camville, lord of the manor, and the Abbess of Elstow (Beds.), a rich Benedictine nunnery. It was agreed that Thomas's mother Christina had presented the last rector, but the abbess claimed that after his mother's death Thomas had granted the church to her convent in free alms, and she produced his charter and a confirmation by St. Hugh, Bishop of Lincoln (1186–1200). Thomas denied the gift and said that neither the charter nor the seal was his.[32] Next year, however, Thomas de Camville quitclaimed the advowson to the abbess and was received with his heirs into the abbey's prayers.[33]

Elstow held the advowson until its dissolution in 1539.[34] Thereafter, the Crown was patron[35] until 1608, when it granted the advowson, with that of four other churches, to Sir Henry Fowkes,[36] who at once sold it for £320 to Corpus Christi College, Oxford.[37] In 1928[38] the rectory was annexed to the vicarage of Stratton Audley, in the patronage of Christ Church, and the two colleges have since presented in turn.[39]

The church was valued at only £2 in 1254,[40] but by 1291 it had risen in value to £4 6s. 8d.,[41] and by 1535 to £7 18s. 10d. net.[42] Eighteenth-century valuations vary: in the early years it was worth 'near £200',[43] but in 1787 the gross value of the living, before the deduction of £16 land tax, was about £150. This consisted of £71 for the rent of about 50

acres of glebe and £79 from the lease of tithes and Easter offerings. By 1814 the glebe was let for £250 and the tithes for £415.[44] In that year the rector complained that since there was no resident curate or bailiff the farmers were witholding part of their tithes.[45] In 1817 the tithes were commuted for 124 acres of land, plus 7 acres in lieu of common for 4 cows.[46] The scattered strips of glebe in the open fields had been exchanged for about 50 acres near the parsonage as early as about 1603.[47] Although the rector later became dissatisfied with the exchange, his efforts to recover his old glebe were unsuccessful. The value of the rectory declined in the course of the 19th century and in 1867 was valued at £361.[48] In 1918 all the land was sold.[49]

One of Godington's earliest rectors was a prominent civil servant, Eustace de Fauconberg, who became rector before 1200.[50] He had had a vicar, William de Esseburn, but when Eustace became Bishop of London in 1221, William was collated to the rectory, thus uniting it with the vicarage.[51] In the later 13th century the living was usually held by university graduates;[52] some rectors stayed for many years, but in the later middle ages the church, on account of its poverty, no doubt, was frequently exchanged. Between 1400 and 1420, for instance, it was exchanged at least eight times, sometimes for neighbouring livings, such as Westbury (Bucks.), sometimes for distant ones, such as Butterwick (Lincs.). The main evidence about the rectors in the early 16th century comes from a visitation of about 1517. It was then reported that the rector was living in the parish and keeping a woman and a girl in his house.[53]

Almost no records of the post-Reformation church survive before the late 17th century: even the parish register does not begin until then. After Corpus Christi College had acquired the advowson, it presented its own Fellows or scholars. Of one, John Kerswell (1643–68),[54] it may be noted that he was resident[55] and was buried in the church.[56] Another, Theodore Fletcher (1673–1706), was the last resident rector for 150 years. He too, with many of his family, was buried in the church.

Eighteenth-century rectors were rather more distinguished, but were non-resident. William Buckeridge (1707–14) was the author of a pamphlet attacking occasional conformity;[57] William Tilly (1714–40) was well known for his sermons and was also Rector of Albury;[58] Francis Ayscough (1741–63), said to be of Bangorian principles,[59] held many offices including those of Dean of Bristol and tutor to George III and his brother;[60] and Timothy Neve

[27] Compton Census; Oxf. Dioc. d 552, d 555; *Census*, 1801–1951.
[28] *V.C.H. Oxon.* i. 417.
[29] *Rot. Hund.* (Rec. Com.), ii. 833; C 134/76/11.
[30] O.R.O. Incl. award map.
[31] See above, p. 147.
[32] *Cur. Reg. R.* x. 250–1.
[33] *Fines Oxon.* 66.
[34] For Elstow see *V.C.H. Beds.* i. 353–7. For list of medieval presentations see MS. Top. Oxon. d 460.
[35] *O.A.S. Rep.* 1914, 210.
[36] *Cal. S.P. Dom.* 1603–10, 418.
[37] C.C.C. Bursary transcripts, xiv. 2. [38] Par. Rec.
[39] Kelly's *Dir. Oxon.* (1939).
[40] Lunt, *Val. Norw.* 312.
[41] *Tax. Eccl.* (Rec. Com.), 31.
[42] *Valor Eccl.* (Rec. Com.), ii. 161.
[43] *Par. Coll.* ii. 151.
[44] Oxf. Dioc. c 434, f. 102; ibid. c 662, f. 62a: C.C.C. Mun. Godington corresp.

[45] Oxf. Dioc. c 662, f. 62a.
[46] O.R.O. Incl. award.
[47] For inclosure see above, p. 149. There is a terrier of 1679 in Oxf. Archd. Oxon. b 40, f. 141.
[48] MS. Top. Oxon. c 103, f. 494.
[49] See above, p. 149.
[50] *D.N.B.*
[51] *Rot. Welles*, ii. 7.
[52] For list of medieval rectors see MS. Top. Oxon. d 460.
[53] *Visit. Dioc. Linc. 1517–31*, i. 124.
[54] Oxf. Dioc. c 70, nos. 63, 65.
[55] *Hearth Tax Oxon.* 203.
[56] *Par. Coll.* ii. 151.
[57] Hearne, *Remarks*, i. 11.
[58] For him see ibid. *passim*.
[59] Ibid. x. 243.
[60] *D.N.B.*; for his suit against Corpus Christi, see T. Fowler, *Hist. of Corpus Christi College* (O.H.S. xxv), 278–9.

(1763–98), also rector of Middleton Stoney, where he lived, was a noted theologian.[61]

During this time the parish was served by a curate. For many years in the middle of the century Stephen Richardson held the office for a salary of £35 a year.[62] Although for at least part of the time he was also curate of Stoke Lyne, he lived in Godington, held services there twice on Sundays, when he preached one sermon,[63] and administered the sacrament three times or more a year. When in 1739 the Roman Catholicism of the parish was causing concern, he assured the bishop that he took 'as particular care of the parish of Godington as any curate in your diocese'.[64] In 1812 the poor state of the Rectory, recently rebuilt,[65] was given as a reason for his non-residence by the rector, H. J. Beaver (1798–1815).[66] To make it 'barely convenient', he said, would cost at least £1,500. The situation was 'low and wet in the extreme' and among other disadvantages, although two horses could stand in the stable, only one could lie down. His other reasons throw an equally interesting light on the social position of the clergy: there was no society within eight or nine miles; the roads were too bad for travelling; and as the farmers were Roman Catholics, there would not be 'that ease and freedom of communication' with them which was desirable.[67]

Beaver's poor opinion of the parish was reciprocated. In 1814 the churchwarden presented that the church was not well served and the children not catechized.[68] He also wrote to the bishop asking for a resident minister, who would 'instruct the lower class men in their duty' and hold two services on Sunday.[69] The parishioners of Godington fared no better under Beaver's successor Joseph Hollis (1815–26), Vicar of Chesterton. He did not reside and would not enlarge the Rectory for a curate. 'There is hardly a parish in your Lordship's diocese where the presence of a curate is so little wanted',[70] he wrote. The congregation seldom exceeded twenty, and the whole Protestant population amounted to fifty-one.[71] Its smallness accounted for there being only one churchwarden, and its humble and illiterate character is demonstrated by the fact that Thomas Turner, who was warden from 1745 to 1790, made his mark each year on the presentments.[72]

During most of the 19th century the parish was served by the curates, the William Perkinses, father and son, who came over from Twyford (Bucks.). Services were held regularly, but only once on Sundays in winter.[73] By 1854 the congregation had reached its peak of about forty.[74] On the death of the rector, Thomas Haverfield (1826–66), who had lived

at his London cure, it was decided to get a resident rector. One urgent reason for this was the need to have someone to superintend the education of the children.[75] Consequently a new Rectory was built,[76] but since the living was combined in 1928 with Stratton Audley the rector has lived there.

The church of *HOLY TRINITY* is a small Georgian building with seating for only 50 persons. It consists of a rectangular body without structural division between nave and chancel, and has a small western tower and a south porch. The original rectangular casement windows were converted into lancets in the 19th century.

The only relic of the medieval church is the circular font. The old building was considered 'very indifferent' by Rawlinson;[77] it had already been reported 'out of repair' in the late 17th century;[78] in 1757 the chancel screen among other things needed rebuilding,[79] and by 1790 the church was in danger of falling down.[80] In 1792 a new one was built at the expense of William Fermor, the Roman Catholic lord of the manor, who employed a co-religionist as builder.[81]

In the 19th century the roof caused trouble[82] and around 1850 the rector, T. T. Haverfield, planned to rebuild the church in a 12th-century style, but was unable to raise the money.[83] He did, however, in 1852 install pointed windows in the chancel in place of the 'old shabby ones', a new pulpit, open seats, and an altar at a cost of about £100.[84] The church was restored and the south porch added in 1905.[85]

When the church was rebuilt, some of the monumental inscriptions from the old church were transferred to it. These include stone slabs to James Benskyn, rector (d. 1643); to the family of Theodore Fletcher, rector (d. 1706); to Frances Busby, daughter of Charles Busby, gent.[86] (d. 1679, aged 4); and an interesting inscription, formerly in the chancel but now on the floor of the tower, to George Sargeante of Brill (d. 1668), a surveyor 'known in most parts of England, Ireland and Wales'. Those to Ralph Coker (d. 1648), son of John Coker of Bicester, John Kerswell, rector (d. 1668), and Charles Howse (d. 1705), have not survived.[87]

At the Reformation the church possessed two sets of vestments, two copes, a silver-gilt chalice, and a brass cross. There was a light supported by lands worth 1s. 6d. a year.[88] In 1955 the church owned a silver chalice and paten cover of 1674. The former was inscribed: 'enlarged for the use of the church of Godington by Mr. Mew, late Rector, 1674.'[89]

In the 16th century there were three bells and a

[61] *D.N.B.*
[62] Oxf. Dioc. d 552.
[63] Ibid. d 552, d 555.
[64] Ibid. c 652, ff. 42–43.
[65] See above, p. 146.
[66] See Blo. *Hethe*, 27.
[67] Oxf. Dioc. c 661, ff. 139–41.
[68] Oxf. Archd. Oxon. c 71, f. 212.
[69] Oxf. Dioc. c 662, f. 62a.
[70] Ibid. ff. 84–85.
[71] Ibid. ff. 96–97.
[72] Oxf. Archd. Oxon. c 71.
[73] *Wilb. Visit.*; MS. Top. Oxon. c 103, f. 494.
[74] *Wilb. Visit.*; Oxf. Dioc. c 332, c 344.
[75] MS. Top. Oxon. c 103, f. 496.
[76] See above, p. 146.
[77] *Par. Coll.* ii. 151.
[78] Oxf. Dioc. d 708, f. 90.

[79] Oxf. Archd. Oxon. d 13, ff. 35, 38.
[80] Oxf. Dioc. c 327, p. 52.
[81] Oxf. Archd. Oxon. c 153, f. 14b; ibid. c 71, ff. 177–8; Oxf. Dioc. b 70, f. 352.
[82] Oxf. Archd. Oxon. c 153, ff. 55, 59; ibid. c 39, f. 56.
[83] There is a drawing of the proposed church in MS. Top. Oxon. a 38, f. 120. The architect was J. C. Sharpe.
[84] Oxf. Dioc. b 70; *Wilb. Visit.* A drawing of the church (1813) in MS. Top. Oxon. b 220, f. 122, and a drawing by J. Buckler (1825), ibid. a 67, f. 279, show the square-headed 18th-cent. windows in the chancel.
[85] Par. Rec.
[86] See below.
[87] *Par. Coll.* ii. 152. For 'Coke' read Coker.
[88] *Chant. Cert.* 33, 78.
[89] Evans, *Ch. Plate.* This was Nathaniel Mew, who probably died in 1673: Foster, *Alumni.*

sanctus bell. Rawlinson noted 'three new bells'. One of these, cast in 1717, was in use in 1955,[90] and the other two were sold to help rebuild the church in 1792.[91] The sanctus bell is of 1793.

The register of baptisms and burials dates from 1672, that of marriages from 1679.

There are many Roman Catholic gravestones in the churchyard.[92]

ROMAN CATHOLICISM. For several centuries after the Reformation this parish was an important Roman Catholic stronghold. During the Elizabethan persecution four local farmers, one a Paxton, were accused in 1583 of sheltering priests;[93] members of their families were later fined for their religious beliefs. The gentry were also recusants: in the early part of the 17th century the Godbeheres and Halls,[94] and towards the end the Busbys, who were originally a Bicester family.[95] The persistence of the old faith was encouraged by the fact that the manor was owned by the Fermors of Somerton and Tusmore.[96] Sixteen papists were returned in 1676 and fifteen in 1706, the largest Catholic family at that time being the Paxtons.[97] The community grew throughout the 18th century. In 1739 the rector, writing to his bishop for advice about his 'Popish parish', said 'the distemper grows and requires a pretty rough remedy'.[98] A list of a few years later shows that there were 40 Papists and 36 Protestants: there were two branches of Paxtons, and the large Davis family had 15 members.[99] At this time a priest named Whitcraft lived in the parish and held Sunday services,[1] but in 1759 the Papists were said to go to church at Tusmore.[2]

At the beginning of the 19th century there was still a large congregation, consisting of five farming families: the labourers were Protestants.[3] By 1834, owing perhaps to the disappearance of the Fermors, the numbers had decreased, though the two chief families of the parish were still Roman Catholic.[4] As late as 1840 there were still Roman Catholic members of the important yeoman family of Collingridge which had been established in Godington and adjoining parishes for several centuries.[5] In 1854 there was one Roman Catholic family[6] and by 1866 none.[7]

It is said that mass used to be said at Moat Farm, where a branch of the Collingridge family lived. The chapel in the roof, served in the 18th and 19th centuries by a priest from Hethe, was only dismantled in about 1900.[8]

SCHOOLS. In 1744, when the number of Roman Catholics was causing concern, the curate said that not more than four or five Protestant families could read or write and all were very neglectful of the education of their children.[9] Soon after, a small school was started and the schoolmaster received £3 or £4 a year from the rector and the Fermors, lords of the manor.[10] By 1800 it had been found unnecessary, as there was a good school at Twyford (Bucks.).[11] There has been no day school in the parish since. In 1854 there was a Sunday school with about ten pupils.[12] In 1871 Godington children went to school at Stratton Audley,[13] but from about 1929 the juniors went to Fringford and the seniors to Bicester.[14]

CHARITIES. None known.

HAMPTON GAY

THE 19th-century parish, covering 684 acres, was bounded on the south by the parish of Hampton Poyle to which it was united in 1932.[1] The River Cherwell bounds it on the west and Bletchingdon parish on the north and east. The river here meanders through an alluvial flood-plain that is seldom less than 200 yards wide and in some parts well over twice that width. This has prevented the building of roads direct to the lands on the west bank of the Cherwell, which today are connected with Hampton Gay only by a footbridge. The only metalled roads are that from Hampton Poyle to Bletchingdon, which crosses the east end of the parish, and its branch, nearly a mile long, that runs westward to the Manor

Farm and the cottages near the church. From this nucleus footpaths lead to Shipton-on-Cherwell church as well as to Bletchingdon village.

In 1709 the inhabitants were indicted for the bad state of their highway; and in 1758 the rector was empowered to levy a tax of $3\frac{1}{2}d.$ in the £1 on holdings and $3\frac{1}{2}d.$ on £20 of personal estates for the repair of the roads.[2]

The geology and relief of the parish are simple. From the flat riverine alluvium the land rises gently through a narrow band of Cornbrash to a wide, flat terrace, which is floored by gravels in the west and elsewhere by Oxford Clay with occasional thin patches of downwash soils. In the north-east this

90 Ch. Bells Oxon. ii. 144.
91 Bodl. Blomfield MS. hist. of Godington (uncat.).
92 MS. Top. Oxon. b 220, f. 122.
93 H. Foley, Records of the English Province, vi. 719.
94 C.R.S. xviii. 256, 259, 260; Salter, Oxon. Recusants, passim. For Hugh Godbehert [sic] see Bucks. Visitation (Harl. Soc. lxiii), 102.
95 For them see Stapleton, Cath. Miss. 107–9.
96 See below, pp. 293, 299, 338.
97 Compton Census; Oxoniensia, xiii. 78. Three Paxtons were reported in 1694: O.R.O. Cal. Q. Sess. ix.
98 Oxf. Dioc. c 651, ff. 68–69.
99 Ibid. c 652, f. 42.
1 Ibid. d 552.
2 Ibid. d 555.
3 Ibid. c 327, p. 296.
4 Ibid. b 39.

5 Oxf. Archd. Oxon. c 71, f. 198 (1806).
6 Wilb. Visit.
7 Oxf. Dioc. c 332.
8 Stapleton, Cath. Miss. 106–7.
9 Oxf. Dioc. c 652, f. 42.
10 Ibid. f. 73; ibid. d 555.
11 Ibid. d 555; c 327, p. 296.
12 Wilb. Visit.
13 Elem. Educ. Ret.; Kelly's Dir. Oxon. (1920).
14 Inf. Oxon. Educ. Cttee.
1 O.S. Map 6″, xxvii (1884); Census, 1931; Oxon. Review Order (1932) (copy in O.R.O.). The author wishes to acknowledge the courtesy of Mrs. Stanley Barry of Long Crendon Manor (Bucks.) for allowing access to the late Col. Barry's MSS.
2 O.R.O. Cal. Q. Sess. viii. 557, 605.

Manor house in 1822

South-west view of church and manor house in 1822

HAMPTON GAY

undulating plateau slopes up to a higher patch of gravel.[3] On the side facing Hampton Gay hamlet this patch has been deeply cut by a small stream. Whereas the meadows lie at about 208 feet above sea-level and the main terrace at 230 to 260 feet, this higher gravel patch rises to 326 feet. On the hill slope near Bletchingdon lies Knapp's acre, formerly an arable strip but now grassland. It was once clearly marked by two rows of stones, which have since been mostly replaced by two lines of trees. The acre therefore remains a remarkable, if not unique, feature of the Oxfordshire landscape.

The Oxford canal does not enter the parish, but the level of the canalized stretch of the Cherwell, which it uses, is controlled by the weirs of Hampton Gay mill. The London and Western canal or the Hampton Gay canal, planned in 1792 to connect the Oxford canal and London, was never cut.[4]

The hamlet stands on the northern edge of a patch of gravel and, as A. D. Godley noted, within a large meander of the Cherwell:

'Cherwell winds with devious coil
Round Hampton Gay and Hampton Poyle.'

The Old English name Hampton means village or farm, and the distinctive name Gay comes from the De Gay family, the 12th-century lords of the manor.[5]

Hampton once had a larger population than it has today. In the 17th century there were seven taxable houses for the hearth tax of 1665[6]—the manor-house, two largish farm-houses or gentlemen's houses for which twelve hearths were returned, a small farm-house with three hearths, and three cottages. No estimate of the number of houses survives for the 18th century as no returns were made to episcopal visitations, but Davis's map of 1797 shows at least ten houses in the village and two a little way off. It marks Mill Lane parallel with the northern loop of the river.[7] A victualler had been licensed in 1735, but there is no further record of one.[8] By 1811 there were thirteen houses and by 1851 there were seventeen. By 1901 the village had shrunk to six houses.[9] In 1955 there were two isolated cottages, another isolated dwelling, Watkin's Farm, which had recently been converted into a cottage, while the Manor Farm and a group of five cottages made up the hamlet.[10]

The farm-house is a substantial building of two stories with gables, and probably dates from the 17th century. It is built of coursed rubble and roofed with Stonesfield slate. The end stacks of the main block are surmounted by brick shafts. The entrance to the forecourt is between a pair of ashlar gate-piers with stone ball finials. The house was enlarged in the 19th century by a two-story wing.

To the west is the ruin of the manor-house: most of its outer walls are still standing. This residence was erected by the Barry family[11] in the second half of the 16th century. When Vincent Barry's daughter married Edward Fenner in 1598 provision was made for her father to live on at the manor-house. By an agreement of 1612 Barry was to have board and lodging for himself and two servants, and stabling for two geldings.[12] The house retained its original Elizabethan plan and features almost unaltered up to the destruction of its roofs and interior by fire in 1887. It was three-storied and constructed throughout of coursed rubble with freestone dressings. E-shaped in plan, it has a battlemented central porch with a doorway with moulded jambs and a four-centred arch with blank shields in the spandrels. The south window of the hall has eight lights with stone mullions and transoms and a moulded course running along the whole façade.[13] All the other windows were stone-mullioned and square-headed, with moulded dripstones. When it was sold to William Wilson in 1809 it was described as 'a venerable Gothic mansion, which has been very substantially built of stone'. Several of the rooms were then said to be in 'an unfinished state' and the whole much neglected. The amenities included 'a garden, surrounded on three sides with brick and stone walls, lately built and planted'.[14] About 1870, when the first extant photographs were taken, the interior retained many handsome chimney-pieces, and several of the rooms were nearly in their original state with some excellent oak panelling.[15] The house was subdivided into two tenements shortly before it was gutted by fire in April 1887. It was then jointly occupied by a farmer and Messrs. J. and B. New, paper manufacturers.[16] The mansion was never repaired, but the stone exterior has withstood the weather well, and together with the nearby site of the former paper-mill it formed in 1955 one of the most picturesque ruins in Oxfordshire.

The village is memorable for its part in the abortive agrarian rising of 1596.[17]

MANOR. In 1086 there were two estates in *HAMPTON GAY*, one of 3 hides held by Roger d'Ivry, and one of 2 hides which ought to have been royal demesne, but which was held by Rainald, Roger d'Ivry's tenant of his estate.[18] Roger's lands were part of the honor which had been given to him by Robert (I) d'Oilly,[19] and which ultimately passed as the honor of St. Valery to Richard, Earl of Cornwall.[20] Edmund, Earl of Cornwall, claimed his rights as overlord in 1292, and the $\frac{1}{2}$ fee became merged in the Duchy of Cornwall.[21] The king's estate in Hampton became part of the honor of Gloucester, and together with lands at Otley in Oddington formed $\frac{1}{2}$ knight's fee.[22] The overlordship of the estate followed the same descent as that of Finmere.[23] By the 13th century the Champernowne family were

[3] G.S. Map 1″, N.S. 236; *G.S. Memoir* (1946).
[4] *Statement of Facts in favour of the intended London and Western Canal, lately called the Hampton Gay Canal* (1792).
[5] *P.N. Oxon.* (E.P.N.S.), i. 213; see below, p. 155.
[6] *Hearth Tax Oxon.* 208.
[7] Davis, *Oxon. Map.*
[8] O.R.O. Victlrs' recog.
[9] *Census*, 1811, 1821, 1851, 1901.
[10] The population of the two Hamptons in 1951 was 140: *Census.*   [11] See below, p. 155.
[12] Barry MSS. *penes* Mrs. Stanley Barry, Long Crendon Manor (Bucks.).
[13] See plates opposite.

[14] MS. Top. Oxon. c 328/4, f. 52.
[15] Photographs *penes* Mr. R. P. Beckinsale, School of Geography, Oxford.
[16] See below, p. 158.   [17] Below, p. 157.
[18] *V.C.H. Oxon.* i. 416.
[19] *Oxon. Chart.* no. 58.
[20] *Oseney Cart.* vi. 53, 56, 60; *Bk. of Fees*, 825; for the descent of the honor see *V.C.H. Oxon.* v. 60.
[21] *Oseney Cart.* v. 398; *Feud. Aids*, iv. 158, 181.
[22] *Oseney Cart.* vi. 55; see below, p. 279.
[23] *Bk. of Fees*, 825; *Rot. Hund.* (Rec. Com.), ii. 45; *Cal. Inq. p.m.* v, p. 344; ibid. ix, p. 55; *Cal. Inq. p.m.* (Rec. Com.), iii, pp. 152, 251; ibid. iv, p. 290.

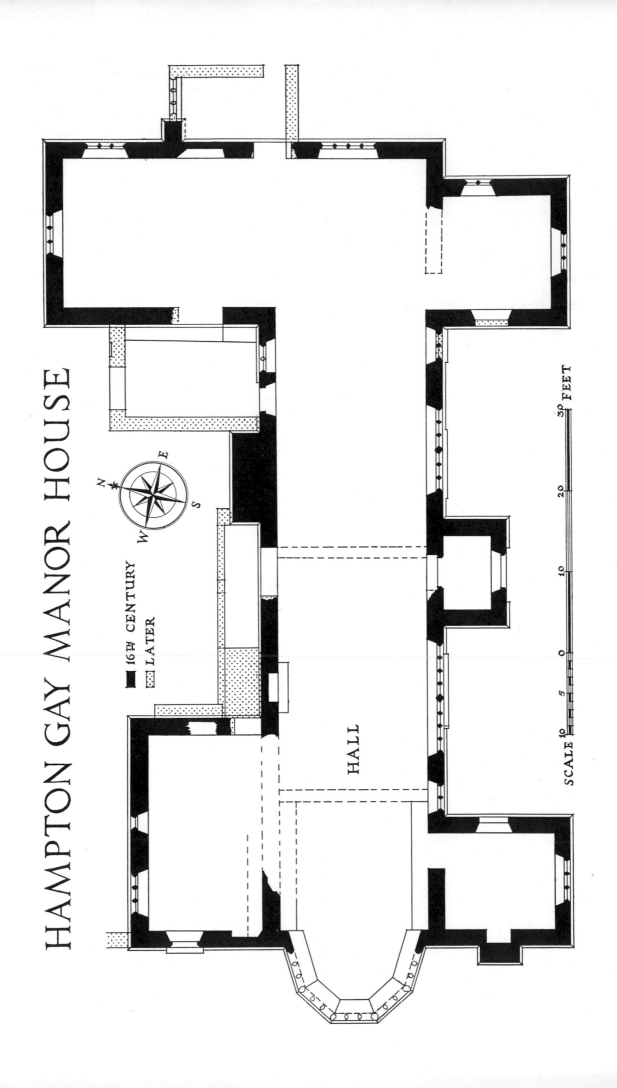

HAMPTON GAY MANOR HOUSE

■ 16TH CENTURY
▫ LATER

HALL

SCALE
10 5 0 10 20 30 FEET

mesne lords of the Gloucester fee,[24] as they were of the Gloucester fee in Lower Heyford. William de Champernowne was succeeded by his daughter Joan by about 1260, and the mesne lordship probably descended through Joan's son John de Willington (d. 1339) to her grandson Henry, who was mesne lord at his death in 1349:[25] it is not subsequently mentioned.

About 1137 Robert de Gay was tenant of both the Hampton estates, as his predecessor Rainald had been in 1086. Robert, the founder of the monastery at Otley, was succeeded in 1138 or very soon afterwards by his son Reginald.[26] Reginald died between 1173 and 1177 and survived his son Robert, being succeeded by his grandson Robert, a minor who was placed with his land in the ward of William le Poure of Oddington.[27] Robert's wife Maud le Poure was no doubt William's daughter.[28] Between about 1195 and 1205 Oseney Abbey acquired 2 virgates in Hampton Gay from Robert's nephew, Reginald son of Norman,[29] and about 1210 Robert himself started a series of gifts to the abbey, which by 1218 held nearly all the ½ fee of St. Valery. In 1219 Robert let his whole demesne in Hampton at farm to Oseney, and finally, between 1220 and 1222, gave the abbey the whole manor for a nominal rent. Oseney became responsible for the forinsec service of the two ½ fees, and Robert's gift was confirmed by his sons Philip and Robert, and later by his immediate lords Richard of Cornwall and William de Champernowne.[30] In 1292 Edmund of Cornwall released the abbey from the payment of homage and relief due to him and his successors, but retained the service of ½ knight.[31] William and Joan de Champernowne, however, acquitted the abbey of half the service of the ½ fee held of the Earl of Gloucester.[32]

Within the manor of Hampton, which was held by Oseney Abbey until the Dissolution,[33] were two small estates belonging to the Templars and Godstow Abbey respectively. About 1170 Reginald de Gay, with the consent of his son Robert, gave a virgate in Hampton to the Templars of Cowley. Reginald's grandson confirmed the gift about 1190,[34] and the Templars held the estate[35] until 1311, when it passed to the Hospitallers. In 1512 it was held under the Hospital by John Kempster and was worth 13s. 4d. a year.[36] Godstow received ½ hide in Hampton Gay, part of the St. Valery fee, from Robert de Gay about 1218.[37] A Bletchingdon

under-tenant of the manor gave the abbey a few acres in about 1220 and 1250; and another Bletchingdon man added some adjoining land about 1250.[38] Godstow held this property until the Dissolution, when it seems to have been included in their Bletchingdon estate.[39]

In 1542, after the suppression of Oseney, Hampton Gay manor and the Hospitallers' lands there were sold by the Crown to Leonard Chamberlayne of Shirburn.[40] In 1544 Leonard Chamberlayne sold Hampton Gay manor to John Barry of Eynsham for £1,100.[41] Barry died in 1546 and left Hampton to his son Lawrence,[42] who was succeeded in 1577 by his son Vincent.[43] In 1598, on the marriage of his daughter and heiress Katherine to Edward Fenner, Vincent Barry conveyed the manor to Edward Fenner's father Edward and to Henry Collier, to his own use for his life, and then to his son and his daughter-in-law Katherine and their heirs.[44] In 1613, however, he surrendered the manor to Katherine and Edward in return for annuities, totalling £63 6s. 8d., for himself and his wife Anne, and for their maintenance in the manor-house for life.[45] Vincent died in 1615,[46] Edward in 1625, and Katherine in 1663.[47] In 1657 Katherine had settled the reversion of Hampton Gay at her death on her cousin Vincent Barry of Thame.[48] Vincent died in 1666, and the manor descended to his son Vincent (d. 1680) and his grandson Vincent. The estate was mortgaged in 1671; and in 1682 the last Vincent Barry first mortgaged it again for £4,500 to Robert Jennings of Abingdon and then sold it outright to Sir Richard Wenman of Caswell for £6,400.[49] Sir Richard, who succeeded to the viscountcy of Wenman of Tuam in 1686, died in 1690,[50] and in 1691 his widow Katherine sold the manor to William Hindes of Priors Marston (Warws.).[51]

By his will William Hindes (d. 1706) left Hampton Gay to trustees, with the provision that if it were not sold to pay his debts it should pass to his son Thomas when he married or came of age.[52] Thomas received the manor from the trustees in 1715,[53] but died in 1718, leaving it to his elder son John, although his widow Elizabeth continued to hold a part of the estate as her jointure.[54] John died childless in 1743 and was succeeded by his brother the Revd. Thomas Hindes, who in 1761 settled the manor jointly on himself and his intended wife Susannah Ryves, daughter of Edward Ryves of

[24] *Oseney Cart.* vi. 55, 61.
[25] *Feud. Aids*, iv. 158, 181; *Cal. Inq. p.m.* ix, pp. 197, 199; see below, p. 185.
[26] *Oseney Cart.* vi. 39; *Thame Cart.* i. 2, 4; *Sandford Cart.* i. 50.
[27] *Oseney Cart.* vi. 39, 48; *Pipe R.* 1177 (P.R.S. xxvi), 13; *Cur. Reg. R.* 1194–5 (P.R.S. xiv), 68.
[28] *Oseney Cart.* vi. 56.
[29] Ibid. 40–41, 43.
[30] Ibid. 43–47, 51–61; *Fines Oxon.* 67.
[31] *Oseney Cart.* v. 398.
[32] Ibid. vi. 50–51, 55–56.
[33] *Valor Eccl.* (Rec. Com.), ii. 216.
[34] *Sandford Cart.* ii. 300, 301.
[35] *Rot. Hund.* (Rec. Com.), ii. 836.
[36] Bodl. MS. C.C.C. 320, f. 16.
[37] *Oseney Cart.* vi. 66; *Godstow Reg.* i. 338.
[38] *Godstow Reg.* i. 221, 225, 338.
[39] *Rot. Hund.* ii. 836; *Valor Eccl.* ii. 192.
[40] *L. & P. Hen. VIII*, xvi, p. 423; for the Chamberlaynes see *Oxon. Visit.* 236; Chamberlayne paid £534 11s. 8d. for these properties and lands in Hampton Poyle: MS. Top. Oxon. c 328/1, f. 10; see Bodl. MS. D.D. Barry a 1–2 (P)

for Hampton Gay deeds 1544–1928 (typescript abstracts or transcripts in MS. Top. Oxon. c 328/1–4).
[41] *L. & P. Hen. VIII*, xix (1), p. 385; C 54/436/4; MS. Top. Oxon c 328/1, f. 13.
[42] C 142/74/64.
[43] C 142/182/44; *Oxon. Visit.* 326; for the Barrys see S. L. Barry, *Pedigree of Barrys of Eynsham* (1928); below, p. 157.
[44] MS. Top. Oxon. c 328/1, f. 44; C.P. 25(2)/339/East. 1 Jas. I.
[45] For details see MS. Top. Oxon. c 328/1, f. 49.
[46] C 142/355/83.
[47] Barry, op. cit. 9; *Par. Coll.* ii. 156.
[48] Barry, op. cit. 12; MS. Top. Oxon. c 328/1, ff. 70, 73.
[49] Barry, op. cit. 14–15; MS. Top. Oxon. c 328/1, ff. 87–100.
[50] *Complete Peerage* (orig. ed.), viii. 92.
[51] MS. Top. Oxon. c 328/1, f. 101.
[52] Ibid. c 328/2, f. 41; the Hindes's descent is based on the Barry MSS. at Long Crendon Manor (Bucks.).
[53] MS. Top. Oxon. c 328/2, f. 55.
[54] Ibid. f. 114: probate of will; Elizabeth died 1761: ibid. c 328/3, f. 108.

Woodstock.[55] Thomas died in 1768 and his widow in 1798, when the manor passed to Ann Hindes, only child of Richard Hindes (d. 1776), a cousin of the Revd. Thomas Hindes.[56] Ann married first Henry Hill (d. 1803) and then Henry Huguenin. The Huguenins won a long Chancery case against the Revd. Thomas Bazeley, a kinsman of the Revd. Thomas Hindes, who had got possession of the deeds relating to Hampton Gay.[57] The estate had become heavily mortgaged, however, and in 1809 it was sold by the Huguenins' creditors to William Wilson for £16,500.[58] William Wilson died in 1821 and was succeeded by his son the Revd. William Wilson the elder,[59] who in 1848 surrendered his interest in Hampton Gay to his son, the Revd. William Wilson the younger.[60] In 1849 the latter sold the manor to Charles Venables, the sitting tenant, for £12,850.[61] In 1862 Venables sold it to Wadham College for £17,500.[62] The college rounded off the estate by purchasing a small piece of meadow land from Tyrrell Knapp of Hampton Poyle in 1867,[63] some 8 acres from the Duke of Marlborough in 1868,[64] and about 11 acres from Arthur Annesley, Viscount Valentia, in 1902.[65] In 1928 Col. S. L. Barry of Long Crendon manor (Bucks.) bought the estate from Wadham College for £6,500, thus re-acquiring it for the family which had held it from 1544 to 1682.[66] On Col. Barry's death in 1943 the estate passed to his daughter Jeanne Irene, wife of the Hon. James Angus McDonnell.[67]

LESSER ESTATE. The manorial estate covers 228 acres: the remainder of the parish, 447 acres, was part of the land purchased by John Barry in 1544 and shortly before 1637 passed to Christopher, a younger brother of Vincent Barry (d. 1666).[68] By 1700 this estate was being administered by John and Sutton Coghill of Bletchingdon, and in that year it was bought by William, Lord Digby, who in 1719 sold it to Christopher Tilson, a clerk of the Treasury (d. 1742).[69] It remained in the Tilson family until 1795, when John Henry Tilson sold it to Arthur Annesley. It has since followed the descent of Bletchingdon manor.[70]

ECONOMIC HISTORY. The Domesday survey gives details for 3 of the 5 hides of Hampton, the D'Ivry estate.[71] Here there was land for 3 ploughs, and there were 3 ploughs at work, all on the demesne. The meadowland was 3 by 1½ furlongs in extent, and the estate, on which a single villein (*villanus*) lived, had increased in value from £2 10s. to £3 since the Conquest. In the late 12th century husbandry was organized on a two-field system,[72] although the fields are not named. The virgates of arable—of which there were about 30[73]—each consisted of 24 or 25 field acres and were divided more or less equally between the two fields.[74] The selion or ridge was commonly reckoned as a ½ acre.[75] To each virgate of arable pertained 2 acres of meadow, and in one instance the acre of meadow is known to have been 4 perches in breadth.[76] 'Brodemede' at least was a lot-meadow in the late 13th century.[77] Much of the demesne arable lay in compact blocks in about 1185, when it included at least 7 complete furlongs.[78] By 1219 the demesne arable was unequally divided, 74 acres in one field and 18 in the other,[79] but this may be accounted for by the alienation of much of the demesne by the De Gay family by this date. The pastures of 'Hulliwaldene' and 'Colowelle' and the meadow of 'Depeham' were among demesne lands granted to Oseney Abbey about 1218,[80] and the abbey finally acquired the remaining demesne meadows, the isle of Petham, 'Hulmede', and the meadow 'at the head of the croft', by Robert de Gay's gift of the whole manor.[81] The manor-house had gardens and a dovecote by 1219,[82] and about the same time Oseney acquired the water-mill, to which pertained 2 acres of arable, two hams in the Cherwell, and the fishery of the whole river from Shipton weir to 'the meeting of three waters' below the mill, and of half the river from Thrupp mill to 'Goldebroc'.[83]

By 1279 Oseney Abbey held almost the whole manor in demesne.[84] The Abbess of Godstow held a ½ hide granted by Robert de Gay about 1220,[85] and the Templars of Cowley held a virgate given to them by Reginald de Gay about 1170,[86] but besides these there were only six free tenants with about 4 virgates in all.[87] The commonest rent was 6s. a year for a virgate. Two villeins with ½-virgates worked at the lord's will, owed tallage and were bound to pay fines if their sons left the manor.[88] Oseney Abbey was keeping sheep on the manor in the 1220's when by a reciprocal agreement with the lord of Hampton Poyle it secured pasture for a flock of 200 in the fields and meadows of the adjacent manor after the corn and hay harvests. A gap near Hampton Poyle church gave access to Hampton Poyle North Field when it lay fallow.[89] The crops grown, wheat, barley,

[55] MS. Top. Oxon. c 328/3, f. 53: probate of will; ibid. f. 76.
[56] Ibid. f. 134; ibid. c 328/4, ff. 48–49; Barry MSS. at Long Crendon.
[57] Details in Bodl. dep. b 47 and Barry MSS.
[58] MS. Top. Oxon. c 328/4, f. 52.
[59] Ibid. f. 80.   [60] Ibid. f. 106.
[61] Ibid. f. 117.
[62] Ibid. ff. 141, 144.
[63] Ibid. f. 148.
[64] Wadham Coll. Mun. Estates, p. 157; Bodl. dep. c 125.
[65] MS. Top. Oxon. c 328/4, f. 152.
[66] Barry MSS. at Long Crendon; for Col. Barry's descent from Vincent Barry see S. L. Barry, *Pedigree of Barrys of Eynsham*, 48.
[67] *Kelly's Handbk.*
[68] Barry, op. cit. 10.
[69] See monument in Hampton Poyle church.
[70] For details see MS. Top. Oxon. b 87, f. 233 (1691–1798); Bodl. MS. D.D. Valentia a 5; c 14 (1660–1933).
[71] *V.C.H. Oxon.* i. 416; see above, p. 153.
[72] Cf. H. L. Gray, *Eng. Field Systems*, 487.

[73] *Oseney Cart.* vi. 55–56.
[74] Ibid. 41, 43, 51; *Godstow Reg.* i. 338–9.
[75] e.g. *Oseney Cart.* vi. 43.
[76] *Godstow Reg.* i. 338–9.
[77] *Oseney Cart.* vi. 62.
[78] Ibid. 49.
[79] Ibid. 54.
[80] Ibid. 52.
[81] Ibid. 54; see above, p. 155.
[82] *Oseney Cart.* vi. 54.
[83] Ibid. 70–72.
[84] *Rot. Hund.* (Rec. Com.), ii. 836. The 2 carucates in Otley held by the Abbot of Thame of the fee of Hampton were in Oddington.
[85] *Godstow Reg.* i. 338.
[86] *Sandford Cart.* ii. 300–1.
[87] *Rot. Hund.* ii. 836 gives 8 lesser free tenants, but 2 and perhaps 3 entries appear to be repetitions.
[88] In 1357 a customary tenant taking up a messuage and 2½ a. owed 2s. a year, 2 days lifting hay and 'bedrepes' as the other customaries do: Bodl. MS. ch. Oseney 365.
[89] *Oseney Cart.* vi. 82–84.

rye, and beans, had given their names by the late 12th century to 'Whethulle', 'Berefurlong', 'Ruifurlong', and 'Beanlonde'.[90] Oats and peas were being grown in 1280 and malt was evidently being produced from the barley. At this time a canon of Oseney was resident at Hampton Gay as bailiff of the abbey's land there and in adjoining parishes. At Michaelmas 1280 his return of stock included 314 sheep in the whole bailiwick, 69 cattle, and 71 pigs.[91]

In the early 14th century Hampton Gay was one of the smallest communities in Ploughley hundred.[92] There were only nine taxpayers in 1306, including Oseney Abbey, whose assessment was more than half the total, and only twelve in 1316 and 1327.[93] By 1344 Hampton had been combined with Bletchingdon for purposes of taxation, and in 1428 it was exempted from taxation because there were fewer than ten resident householders.[94] In 1509–10 Oseney received from its estate a revenue of £13 16s., but reserved to itself pasture for 240 sheep.[95] The manor was leased for 40 years in 1518 and in 1535 it brought in a farm of £11 and £6 2s. from the rents of customary tenants.[96] Some arable land had by this time gone back to waste: in 1512 in the former Templars' (now the Hospitallers') virgate there were 6 acres uncultivated and covered with furze.[97] In 1524 there were seven contributors to the lay subsidy,[98] and inclosure, with some consequent depopulation,[99] may have already begun. The acquisition of the manor in 1544 by John Barry, who had made his money from wool,[1] may have accelerated the work, which was evidently carried on by his successors Lawrence and Vincent Barry. Inclosure was probably facilitated by the natural division of the parish into two, part lying within the meander of the Cherwell, which could easily be inclosed by a ring fence, and part without. Christopher Barry's will (1670) suggests that inclosure had been long accomplished. It states that a parcel of land and pasture called the Great Leas had formerly been 'one inclosure', but is now divided into several inclosures.[2]

Late Elizabethan inclosure of lands in Hampton Gay and the neighbourhood involved most of the male inhabitants of the village in an agrarian revolt in 1596.[3] The originator and driving force of the plot was Bartholomew Steere of Hampton Poyle, but Richard Bradshaw of Hampton Gay spread the discontent as he travelled on his rounds as a miller's man. The conspirators first met at John Steere's house at Hampton Poyle and eventually involved people as far afield as Rycote and Witney. They aimed at destroying inclosures and the inclosers and incidentally at helping the poor, who had suffered

from them. They planned to meet on Enslow Hill in Bletchingdon and, if necessary, to go towards London where the apprentices might help them. Among the chief proposed victims was Vincent Barry, who was to be murdered as well as his daughter. Many of the would-be rioters worked for Barry.

The plot proved abortive. Only 'some ten persons with pikes and swords' assembled on Enslow Hill. But official action was taken against the rioters, as a Hampton Gay carpenter, Roger Symonds,[4] warned Vincent Barry of the plot,[5] and Lord Norreys was notified. When asking the government for instructions, he asked that some 'order should be taken about inclosures . . . that the poor may be able to live'.[6] Five Hampton Gay men were among those arrested and sent to London; one was sentenced to be hanged and quartered as a ringleader.[7] The revolt undoubtedly affected parliamentary opinion, and helped to secure the re-enactment of the Tillage Acts in 1597, which included the order that lands in Oxfordshire converted to pasture since the accession of Elizabeth should be restored to tillage.

The population and pattern of land-holding altered little between 1560 and 1665. There were still the main estate, held by the Barry family, and five leasehold tenements. Edward Belson, taxed on five hearths for the tax of 1665,[8] had a leasehold of Kempster's house and three closes of meadow adjoining for which he paid 5s. yearly, having paid £160 for the original copyhold in 1633. John Dennet, carpenter, taxed on one hearth, held for 99 years at 5s. annual rent and an initial payment of £30 a dwelling, a plot of ground, and a pasture called Gouldhill containing 11 acres. He had to pay £5 yearly for every acre of pasture converted into tillage but was not to plough Gouldhill for six years from his new lease (1654). He also had to pay 10s. for every apple or pear tree lopped or felled. Robert Springall, taxed on one hearth, had a tenement in reversion; Anne Gilkes, discharged from payment on one hearth on account of poverty, had a cottage and small plot at a rent of 5s. a year. William Tomson, taxed on three hearths, may have held the tenement formerly in the possession of one Paul Triplett.[9]

The parish was mainly under pasture and large tracts were often leased to outside graziers, such as Oxford butchers.[10] Sainfoin, mentioned in 1691,[11] was introduced early, as at Bletchingdon: its cultivation emphasizes the stock-fattening aspect of farming at this date. Yet the predominance of this pastoral economy was greatly altered in 1681 when the grist mill was leased by Vincent Barry to John

[90] P.N. Oxon. (E.P.N.S.), i. 214–15.
[91] Oseney Cart, vi. 189–90.
[92] For comparisons, see below, p. 358.
[93] E 179/161/8, 9, 10.
[94] Ibid. 161/17; Feud. Aids, vi. 379.
[95] Oseney Cart. vi. 233.
[96] Ibid. 265; Valor Eccl. (Rec. Com.), ii. 216.
[97] Bodl. MS. C.C.C. 320, f. 16.
[98] E 179/161/198.
[99] Cf. M. Beresford, Lost Villages of Eng. 381.
[1] Bodl. MS. Wills Oxon. 180, ff. 37b–39. Among Barry's bequests were 12 sacks of wool or £100; £20 to be delivered to a clothier of Burford; 600 ewes with their lambs.
[2] Bodl. MS. Wills Oxon. 6.
[3] The revolt has been briefly mentioned in V.C.H. Oxon. ii. 194–5; E. F. Gay, 'Midland Revolt', Trans.

R.H.S. n.s. xviii, 212, 238–9. A fuller account appears in E. P. Cheyney, History of England, 1588–1603, ii. 3, 24, 32–34, 262–4, 266–7, and in the MS. account by Mr. W. E. Tate.
[4] He was Barry's tenant: Barry MSS. at Long Crendon.
[5] Cal. S.P. Dom. 1595–7, 316–18, 319–20, 323–4, 325, 342–5.
[6] Ibid. 316.
[7] For this and later events see also Acts of P.C. 1596–7, 364, 365, 373, 383, 398, 412, 455; Hist. MSS. Com. Salisbury MSS. VII. 49–50, 236; 4th Dep. Kpr's Rep. App. II, 289–90; B.M. Add. MS. 41257; K.B. 8/53, mm. 1–16.
[8] Hearth Tax Oxon. 208.
[9] MS. Top. Oxon. c 328/1, ff. 60, 62, 65–66; Barry MSS. at Long Crendon.
[10] MS. Top. Oxon. c 328/1, f. 10.
[11] Ibid. f. 31.

Allen of Hampton, paper-maker, at a rent of £9 a year. The lessors were to pay £10 for rebuilding or supply rough timber of elm or ash to that value, if the dwelling-house should be burnt down. The mill was to be used only for paper-making.[12] So began an industry which flourished until the early 19th century and continued until 1887, although its condition was now less prosperous partly on account of the uncertain state of the paper trade and partly because of disastrous fires at the paper-mill. In 1863–73 the mill was reconstructed and James Lee, iron-founder of Oxford and Millbank Iron Works, erected a gas-works and a steam-engine and other machinery, but the new works were destroyed by fire in 1875. In 1876 the main building was reroofed by St. Vincent's Corrugated Iron Works of Bristol, the sheets coming by canal and costing all told £610. By July 1880 the machinery was in good order and a considerable amount of paper had been made. The fittings included an iron water-wheel, 2 iron pit-wheels, 4 iron rag-washing and heating engines, a 60-inch paper-making machine, a 30 h.p. Cornish steam-boiler, a new 8 h.p. high-pressure steam-engine, and various other machinery 'capable of making about one ton of paper per day'.[13] Yet within a few years the tenant had gone bankrupt and the same fate overtook subsequent tenants. In April 1887 the stock in trade was sold under a distress for rent. It consisted of about 15 tons of rags, waste paper, &c., 8 tons of white and brown mineral alum, resin, face-blue, oil, a quantity of paper bags, colouring, string, &c.[14] Today only the site and a few portions of the walls and the water-falls remain.

Hampton Gay was little more than a hamlet in the late 17th century, when the Compton Census (1676) recorded 28 adults. There appears to have been an increase in population during the late 18th century, for by 1811 there were 17 families crowded into 13 houses. The peak was reached in 1821, with 86 inhabitants, and numbers had declined to 67 by 1861. After the destruction of the manor-house in 1887 the population fell to 30. The decline continued during the 20th century until in 1955 there were only 14 parishioners, probably the lowest total since Anglo-Saxon times.[15]

The agricultural economy has changed almost as much in the 19th and 20th centuries as the number of farm-workers. On the manor estate of 210 acres in 1809, the arable occupied 70 acres; in 1848 about 55 acres; in 1862 about 30; in 1928 there was no arable;[16] in 1955 over 100 acres were ploughed by tractor.[17] The non-manorial part of the parish also has a high proportion of arable land, and, as has been usual since 1630, part is farmed from Hampton Poyle and rather more from Bletchingdon. The manorial holding still differs in economy from the non-manorial estates. Its grassland is used mainly for

fattening, especially of bullocks, while the pastures of the remainder of the parish are devoted almost entirely to dairy cattle.

CHURCH. The earliest evidence that has been found about a church at Hampton Gay is a grant of tithes in 1074 (see below). In the late 12th century the advowson belonged to the lord of the manor, for by a charter dated before 1173 Reginald de Gay presented his clerk Gilbert to the church with a ½ hide of land, free of all service except the royal service.[18] Soon after, he granted the church to Oseney Abbey, and in the 1180's Robert de Gay made a similar grant with the provision that the abbey should not take possession until after Gilbert's death.[19] Gilbert must have died in about 1190, when Hugh, Bishop of Lincoln, allowed the canons to appropriate the church, and Urban III allowed them to serve it with three or four canons. One was to be responsible for cure of souls and to be presented to the bishop.[20] The absence of institutions in the Lincoln registers shows that this last provision was not complied with. It is in any case unlikely that Oseney served the church with its own canons,[21] but as the church was valued at only £2 in 1254 and 1291, it may not have been rich enough to support a resident priest.[22]

Its 16th-century value is not known, since in 1535 the rectory was being farmed with the manor. The church was then served by a chaplain who received only £2 a year from Oseney.[23] An episcopal visitation found the chancel and nave dilapidated, the chancel windows broken, and no distributions being made to the poor—a reference perhaps to the 10s. which Oseney was supposed to distribute for the soul of its founder Robert d'Oilly.[24]

In the 11th century Robert d'Oilly granted two-thirds of his demesne tithes in Hampton to the church of St. George in Oxford castle.[25] When St. George's and its possessions became part of Oseney in 1149,[26] the abbey tried to collect these tithes in spite of the opposition of Hampton's rector, Gilbert. Oseney won its case, and in a general synod at Oxford, probably that of about 1166,[27] Reginald de Gay confirmed the abbey's claims.[28] When Oseney appropriated the church, obtaining all the tithes in the parish, this portion came to an end.

St. Frideswide's also had some rights in the church, its claim to 16d. and 2 chaldrons (coddos) of grain a year being confirmed by the Pope in 1158.[29] In a property settlement of 1388 between Oseney and St. Frideswide's this income was awarded to Oseney.[30]

After Oseney's dissolution in 1539, the rectory estate continued as an indistinguishable part of the manor, and Hampton Gay was considered as an extra-parochial free chapel, exempt from the bishop's jurisdiction.[31] As the church then had no endow-

[12] MS. Top. Oxon. c 328/1, f. 87.
[13] The whole correspondence on the state of the mill for many years is in the Barry MSS. at Long Crendon.
[14] Oxf. Jnl. 16 Apr. 1887.
[15] Census, 1801–1951; local inf.
[16] Barry MSS.
[17] Local inf.
[18] Oseney Cart. vi. 48. Oseney kept the deed because it mentioned an exchange of land.
[19] Ibid. 40.
[20] Ibid. 47–48; iii. 374.
[21] V.C.H. Oxon. ii. 91.
[22] Lunt, Val. Norw. 313; Tax. Eccl. (Rec. Com.), 31.

[23] Valor Eccl. (Rec. Com.), ii. 216, 223; Subsidy 1526, 282. The chaplain is said to receive £4: ibid. 276.
[24] Visit. Dioc. Linc. 1517–31, i. 123; Valor Eccl. ii. 216.
[25] V.C.H. Oxon. ii. 160; Oseney Cart. iv. 7.
[26] Oseney Cart. iv. 25.
[27] Handbk. of Chron. ed. F. M. Powicke, 356. Robert Foliot, Archdeacon of Oxford 1151–73, was present.
[28] Oseney Cart. vi. 48. For Oseney's claim to the tithes of Northbrook see below, p. 228.
[29] St. Frides. Cart. ii. 28.
[30] Cal. Pat. 1385–8, 534–5, where 16s. is mistakenly given. The original is in Balliol Coll. Arch.
[31] Oxf. Dioc. c 651, f. 47; Bacon, Lib. Reg. 793.

ment, the lords of the manor, 'out of their generosity', paid a minister.[32] A rector of Shipton-on-Cherwell is known to have served it in the 16th century,[33] and occasionally it was served from Blenheim or Charlbury. Early in the 18th century a curate from Kidlington was receiving £10.[34]

The living was again endowed in 1768, when the Revd. Thomas Hindes, who rebuilt the church, left £700 to buy government securities to provide £20 annually for a minister. He was to be nominated by the owner of the manor, with preference for a Fellow of the Queen's College, Oxford. The bequest was to be void if the bishop insisted on licensing the minister, or if he or any ecclesiastical court meddled with him, or if any attempt were made to make Hampton into a parish or to help it with Queen Anne's Bounty.[35]

During the 19th century there was much uncertainty about the ecclesiastical status of Hampton. The patronage of the church remained with the lord of the manor, but from 1809 the bishop began to license the curates in spite of the provisions of Thomas Hindes's will, and in the 1830's acquired the right to subject the parish to his visitations.[36] By then it had been decided that although Thomas Hindes's bequest was valid, the provisions attached to it were not, and during the 1850's Hampton was treated as an ordinary parish.[37] It was transferred from Bicester deanery by 1854 to the new deanery of Islip.[38]

After Wadham College bought the manor in 1862, it provided a minister, usually the Rector of Shipton-on-Cherwell; paid him partly from Hindes's bequest; and refused to nominate him to the bishop.[39] During this period the church was sometimes considered a donative, sometimes a chapelry attached to the manor-house.[40] It was finally decided in the 1920's that Hampton was an ancient ecclesiastical parish and not extra-parochial, and that the church was not a donative but a perpetual curacy in the gift of the lord of the manor.[41] Its endowment remained £20 a year, and it was served by the Rector of Shipton-on-Cherwell in 1955.

The church of *ST. GILES*, built in 1767–72, comprises a nave, south porch, and western tower. Of the medieval building nothing remains except the cross on the eastern gable and the reused battlements of the tower. During the 19th-century restoration, remains were found inside the walls of a 13th-century stiff-leaf capital and fragments of windows, which were probably parts of the original church.[42] It is recorded that it was in need of repair in the early 16th century, and that it was in 'tolerable repair' in 1717, while the next year Thomas Hindes (d. 1718) left £50 to repair and beautify it.[43]

The Revd. Thomas Hindes (d. 1768) provided

money to rebuild the church, and it was opened for services in 1772.[44] The original foundations were used but the fabric of the medieval church was ruthlessly destroyed. The new Georgian building was considered by 19th-century admirers of gothic architecture 'a very bad specimen of the meeting-house style'.[45]

In 1859 the curate F. C. Hingeston had the church restored according to his own plans, at a cost of £154.[46] He replaced the four round-headed Georgian windows and south doorway with new ones in the Early English style, built a south porch, notched the surround of the external doorway to the tower in the Norman style, and replaced the old high seats.[47]

The most noticeable Georgian features left are the gallery at the west end, the coved and panelled plaster ceiling, and the stone ball finial and weather vane surmounting the pyramidal roof of the tower. There was another restoration in 1929.[48]

There is an elaborate alabaster monument with kneeling effigies to Vincent Barry (d. 1615) and his wife Anne Denton, with a later inscription at the bottom to their daughter, Lady Katherine Fenner (d. 1663).[49] It bears the arms of Barry, Brome, Baldington, and Rous, and two crests, one being that of Brome of Holton, Anne Barry's grandfather.

There are several memorials to the Hindes family: to William Hindes (d. 1706), lord of Hampton Gay, to Thomas Hindes (d. 1718) and his eldest son John Hindes (d. 1754), and to the Revd. Thomas Hindes (d. 1768). Other inscriptions are to Elizabeth Lydall (d. 1662), Vincent Oakley (d. 1723), Sarah Venables (d. 1858) and her two daughters, Sir Francis Barry, Bt. (d. 1907), and his son Col. Stanley Barry (d. 1943).

The font, which originally belonged to the church of Shipton-on-Cherwell, is modern.[50] The church is lit by candle light.

In 1552 the church owned, among other things, chalice and two brass candlesticks.[51] In 1955 the plate included a small silver chalice of 1768.[52] The church possesses a barrel organ made in the 1830's and restored in 1929: it has three barrels, each containing ten tunes, and a mahogany case designed in the Gothic style. As in the 16th century, there were in 1955 two bells: the treble, of mid-13th-century date and shrill in tone, is one of the oldest bells in the country; the tenor is of 1782.[53]

The registers date from 1621 for baptisms and burials, and from 1657 for marriages.

NONCONFORMITY. None known.

SCHOOLS. None known.

CHARITIES. None known.

[32] Oxf. Dioc. c 651, f. 52.
[33] O.A.S. Rep. 1914, 229–30.   [34] Par. Coll. ii. 156.
[35] Barry MSS. at Long Crendon Manor (Bucks.); Oxf. Dioc. c 446, f. 101; Clerus Oxon.: Bodl. Par. Box (uncat.).
[36] Hampton was first visited in 1838: Oxf. Dioc. b 41. In 1846, by Order in Council, all churches and chapels in the diocese were put under the bishop's control.
[37] Bodl. Par. Box, 1928 letter; Wilb. Visit.; Oxf. Dioc. d 178.
[38] For the formation of the deanery see above, p. 67, n. 97.
[39] Bodl. dep. b 47.
[40] Bodl. Par. Box.   [41] Ibid. 1928 letter.
[42] The 18th-cent. church is described in the Building News, Nov. 25, 1859 (copy in Bodl. G.A. Oxon. 4° 697, opp. p. 56).

[43] Visit. Dioc. Linc. 1517–31, i. 123; Par. Coll. ii. 156; MS. Top. Oxon. c 382/2, f. 113.
[44] Par. Reg.   [45] Parker, Guide, 56.
[46] MS. Top. Oxon. c 103, ff. 524–6. The builder was Geo. Wyatt, Oxford.
[47] Ibid. The unrestored church is shown in an uncompleted drawing (1800) in MS. Top. Oxon. b 220, f. 156, and a drawing (1822) by J. Buckler; see plate facing p. 153.
[48] Kelly's Dir. Oxon. (1939).
[49] See Par. Coll. ii. 156–7, for inscriptions; Bodl. G.A. Oxon. 4° 686, p. 156.
[50] MS. Top. Oxon. d 90, f. 39.
[51] Chant. Cert. 81.
[52] Evans, Ch. Plate.
[53] Ch. Bells Oxon. ii. 119, with a photograph of both bells.

HAMPTON POYLE

THIS small parish lies on the east bank of the Cherwell some six miles north of Oxford. It is opposite the old part of Kidlington village, the churches of the two parishes being separated only by the river, which forms the civil boundary, and half a mile of flat, floodable alluvium. Hampton had an area of 807 acres until 1932.[1] It was then joined with Hampton Gay (684 a.) and together with 18 acres from Gosford parish, 3 acres from Kidlington, and 9 acres from Thrupp—all uninhabited riverine land—today (1955) forms the civil parish of Hampton Gay and Poyle with an area of 1,521 acres.[2]

At Hampton Poyle the Cherwell enters upon the wide, flat flood-plain of its lower course, and all but the northern one-sixth of the parish is floored by fine alluvium which, in the lowest parts, is liable to occasional inundation. The land varies in height above sea-level from 200 feet near Gosford Bridge in the south to 238 feet in the north, where the alluvium gives way to Oxford Clay.[3] In 1948–9 extensive dredging of the Cherwell greatly decreased the danger of flooding.[4]

The south part of the parish is crossed by the Oxford–Bicester highway, which bridges the Cherwell at Gosford, five miles from Oxford. From this the village of Hampton got its names of 'Hampton *ad pontem*', first recorded in 1255,[5] 'Hampton atte bridge'[6] or sometimes '*juxta pontem de Gosford*'.[7] All three were used concurrently in the reign of Edward III. In later years when the parishioners had to repair the eastern half of the bridge and the causeway to it they found the repairs a constant burden.[8] In 1797 the inclosure award set aside a stone-pit (Surveyor's Piece) of over five roods for providing material for the repair of the roads.[9]

The present-day hamlet of Hampton Poyle is reached by a mile of minor road that branches northward from the main highway and continues to Bletchingdon. From the hamlet footpaths converge southward on a footbridge over the Cherwell, which at this point has a gravel bed. This bridge, formerly of wood, was in 1947 rebuilt in reinforced concrete[10] and continues to form the parishioners' main connexion on foot with outside amenities.

Hampton Poyle, unlike most of the villages in the Cherwell valley, stands on alluvium and not on gravel. Its few buildings are spaced at uneven intervals along the road to the church and Manor Farm, both of which stand near the former mill stream.[11] Their alignment and situation in the north-west corner of the parish were clearly a response to the need for water-power and water-supply, as here the Cherwell flows close to the junction of the Oxford Clay and the riverine deposits: along this zone the claybeds hold up water in shallow wells dug in the overlying alluvium. Before its inclosure in 1797 there was a large green of nearly 9 acres.[12]

The hamlet's first name means a 'village' and its suffix commemorates its 13th-century lords.[13] Until at least 1267, when Walter de la Poyle became lord, the village was called 'Philipeshamton' or 'Hampton Stephani' after its 12th-century lord and his descendants.[14] It was also sometimes called Great Hampton to distinguish it from its smaller neighbour, Hampton Gay. Compared with other villages in Ploughley hundred, however, it never seems to have been large and may have decreased in size in the late Middle Ages.[15]

In 1625 ten farm-houses, a Rectory, and a manor-house were recorded;[16] in 1662 seventeen householders were listed for the hearth tax. There were a number of fair-sized houses: in 1665 the manor returned fourteen hearths, the Rectory six,[17] and ten other houses from three to one hearths.[18]

Several of the present (1955) dwellings date from the 16th and early 17th centuries.[19] Among the oldest is the former Rectory: it is partly an early 16th-century building, but by 1754 was seriously decayed.[20] A description of it in 1685[21] says that it had a courtyard, orchard, and garden besides a barn and stable. The main block now dates from about 1802, when the Revd. W. Benson, finding the house 'too small and mean', had it repaired and had four new rooms added by the builder John Hudson of Oxford.[22] Soon after 1840 £500 was spent on enlarging the new addition.[23]

Manor Farm, the successor to the mansion house called Hampton Poyle Place in 1625,[24] dates from about this time, except for its early 19th-century windows. It is L-shaped in plan, has two stories with attics, and is built of local limestone with a stone band at the first floor on the south. Until 1954 it had a Stonesfield-slate roof. As late as 1949 there were traces in the manor meadow of what were apparently the fishponds of the medieval manor-house.[25]

Between the farm and the Cherwell is the site of the mill. In 1086 Hampton's mill rendered 15s.[26] and it appears constantly in the records until it was burnt down in 1771.[27]

Poyle Court, the Old Manor House, and Knapp's

[1] *Census*, 1881, 1931; O.S. Map 6", xxvii (1884).
[2] *Census*, 1951; O.S. Map 2½", 42/51, 42/41 (1951).
[3] G.S. Map 1", N.S. 236.   [4] Local inf.
[5] e.g. *Rot. Hund.* (Rec. Com.), ii. 31; C.P. 25(1)/190/19/57.
[6] C 135/151/8; C.P. 25(1)/190/18/7.
[7] e.g. C.P. 25(1)/189/16/4.
[8] O.R.O. Cal. Q. Sess. viii. 513, 523, 537, 545, 549.
[9] O.R.O. Incl. award. By 1873 the patch had long been exhausted and was sold to Lord Valentia for £100: Par. Rec. Minute bk. 1859–92.
[10] Local inf.
[11] O.S. Map 25", xxvii. 6, 10.
[12] It covered 8½ a. in 1625: MS. Top. Oxon. b 87, ff. 123 sqq.; cf. O.R.O. Incl. award (1797).
[13] See below, p. 161; *P.N. Oxon.* (E.P.N.S.), ii. 450.
[14] *P.N. Oxon.* (E.P.N.S.), i. 213–14.

[15] See below, pp. 164, 358.   [16] C 146/C 8926.
[17] Identified as Rectory because Skinner was rector in 1665.
[18] *Hearth Tax Oxon.* 193, 235.
[19] The following descriptions are based on personal observation and inf. Mr. P. S. Spokes.
[20] Oxf. Archd. Oxon. c 72, f. 112.
[21] Ibid. c 141, p. 341.
[22] Oxf. Dioc. c 434, ff. 143b–149; ibid. c 70, f. 74. Estimated cost was £525.
[23] Par. Rec. Min. bk. under 1875.
[24] MS. Top. Oxon. b 87, ff. 123 sqq.
[25] Obliterated by dredging the river. See O.S. Map 25", xxvii. 10 (1876).
[26] *V.C.H. Oxon.* i. 423.
[27] The site of a second mill mentioned in 1589 and 1625 is not known: C.P. 25(2)/197/Hil. 31 Eliz.; C 146/C 8926.

Farm all date in part from the early 17th century, when the manor was sub-divided.[28] Poyle Court retains its L-shaped plan and has two ancient stone stacks on each end gable, but was refronted in about 1800, when a battlemented parapet and wooden casements in 'gothic' style with square stone frames were inserted.

The Old Manor House, built of limestone with a Stonesfield-slate roof, was formerly called Moat Farm and adjoins 'Moat Cottage', which was its former stable. Its 'moate' is recorded in 1625.[29] Knapp's Farm, built of limestone rubble, was originally rectangular in plan with a staircase projection at the back, but has been refashioned. A part of it was the building bought by Merton College in 1512[30] as a refuge in time of plague. Lincoln College also took refuge in the village both in 1512 and 1526.[31]

The parish has been associated with some noteworthy events and persons. In 1949 a fine Viking spearhead was found in the Cherwell near the bridge.[32] The battle of Gosford Bridge was fought on the borders of the parish in 1644. In 1654 Anthony Wood and a party of friends disguised as country musicians played at John West's manorhouse, where they 'had some money but more drink' given them.[33]

Bartholomew Steere, leader of the abortive agrarian revolt[34] of 1596, was born in Hampton Poyle in 1568.[35] Anthony Hall, an antiquary of some standing although Hearne though him 'a dull, stupid, sleepy fellow', was Rector of Hampton Poyle (1720–3). He wrote the introduction to Thomas Cox's *Magna Britannia*.[36] Throughout the 19th century and up to 1929 the Viscounts Valentia and other members of the Annesley family were closely connected with Hampton, which greatly benefited from their generosity.

MANOR. At the time of the Domesday survey 'Hamtone' (10 hides) was held of the king by Jernio or Gernio. Five thegns had held it as five manors before the Conquest.[37] In 1166 *HAMPTON* manor was held in chief as 1 knight's fee by Philip of Hampton (*de Hanton'*), who was succeeded in 1182 by his son Stephen,[38] in 1220 by his grandson William, and in 1246 by his great-grandson Stephen. Stephen died in 1252 leaving an estate held in chief as ½ knight's fee.[39] His heir was his daughter Alice, an infant

whose wardship, after passing through several hands, was granted to Walter de la Poyle, who had married her by 1267.[40] After Walter's death in 1298 Alice continued to hold the manor of 'Hamptone Stevene' as her own inheritance.[41] The date of her death is uncertain, but she survived her son John, who inherited Walter's Surrey estates and died in 1317.[42] John's elder son and successor John died in 1332.[43] By 1335 Henry de la Poyle, brother and heir of the younger John, was in possession of Hampton Poyle.[44]

His son Thomas de la Poyle succeeded in 1360[45] and died in 1402. His widow Katherine held the manor until her death in 1407.[46] Thomas's brother John succeeded and survived his own son Henry, who married Elizabeth, daughter of Robert Warner. It seems that well over a year before his death in 1423 John had leased the manor to Robert Warner, John Gaynesford, and others. He afterwards released it without licence to the same persons, who were probably feoffees to uses, and after his death they had to pay a fine of £15 before they obtained possession.[47]

In 1438 they released their rights to Robert Warner for life, with remainder to John Gaynesford and his eldest son John.[48] Robert died in 1439, leaving property in Surrey and Sussex as well as Hampton. His daughter and heiress Elizabeth, widow of Henry de la Poyle, had become the second wife of Sir Walter Grene of Theobalds (Herts.), who had by his first wife two daughters, Joan and Katherine.[49] This Katherine had married John Gaynesford the younger. In 1440 John Gaynesford the elder acquired all the former properties of the De la Poyles and in 1447 he granted Hampton to his son John, his wife Katherine and their issue.[50] John the elder died in 1450, and after the death of John the younger in 1460 Katherine married Sir Edmund Rede of Boarstall (Bucks.).[51] In 1471 Edmund and Katherine settled the reversion of Hampton on George Gaynesford, Katherine's son, and his wife Isabel Croxford,[52] and in the following year they conveyed it to trustees to the use of George and Isabel. In 1496 George reconveyed the manor to his mother Katherine,[53] whose husband Sir Edmund had died in 1489, but it reverted to him on her death in 1498.[54] Four years later he sold his Hampton properties to Richard Hungerford.[55]

When Hungerford died in 1510, his executors sold

---

[28] See below, p. 162.

[29] C 146/C 8926; Queen's Coll. Mun. box 2a, f. 2.

[30] *Reg. Annalium Coll. Merton.* ed. H. E. Salter (O.H.S. lxxvi), 429, 434, 518.

[31] *Linc. Dioc. Doc.* (E.E.T.S. cxlix), 28.

[32] *Oxoniensa,* xiv. 76.

[33] Wood, *Life,* i. 190.   [34] See above, p. 157.

[35] Par. Reg.: Bodl. dep. b 40, f. 3; the Steere family continued in the village for many generations, cf. Steere Close: O.R.O. Incl. award.

[36] *D.N.B.*; Hearne, *Remarks,* ii. 164, 171.

[37] *V.C.H. Oxon.* i. 423.

[38] E 210/3260; *Red Bk. Exch.* (Rolls Ser.), 304; *Pipe R.* 1163 (P.R.S. vi), 49; ibid. 1177 (P.R.S. xxvi), 14; ibid. 1182 (P.R.S. xxxi), 85.

[39] *Oseney Cart.* vi. 76; *Gent. Mag.* 1806, lxxvi(2), 809–11: an attempt at a history of Hampton before 1422 (probably by Sir Henry Ellis); see also MS. Top. Oxon. b 87, ff. 218 sqq.: transcripts of deeds about title of Hampton up to 1513.

[40] *Cal. Inq. p.m.* i, p. 209.   [41] Ibid. iii, p. 405.

[42] Alice contributed to the tax of 1327: E 179/161/9; *Cal. Inq. p.m.* vi, p. 64.

[43] Ibid. vii, p. 307; *V.C.H. Surr.* ii. 617.

[44] *Cal. Pat.* 1334–8, 84; *Cal. Fine R.* 1327–37, 331, 336; C.P. 25 (1)/190/18/7; ibid. 190/19/57.

[45] *Cal. Inq. p.m.* x, p. 488.

[46] C 137/3; ibid. 57.

[47] C 139/10; *Cal. Pat.* 1422–9, 164.

[48] *Cal. Pat.* 1436–41, 151; C.P. 25(1)/292/69/13; *Herald and Genealogist,* i. 209–24, 321–4; iii. 296–307: detailed descent of manor 1422–1860, partly based on papers now in MS. Top. Oxon. b 87.

[49] C 139/90; for another connexion between the Gaynesfords and the Poyles see *Her. and Gen.* i. 211–12.

[50] MS. Top. Oxon. b 87, f. 220: summary of Gaynesford title to manor; *Cal. Pat.* 1446–52, 66; *Her. and Gen.* i. 210–11.

[51] *Boarstall Cart.* p. ix.

[52] *Cal. Pat.* 1467–77, 295.

[53] *Her. and Gen.* i. 213–14.

[54] C 142/13/131: the date (1489) given in Kennett, *Paroch. Antiq.* ii. 407, is wrong; for Katherine's will see *Boarstall Cart.* 295.

[55] MS. Top. Oxon. b 87, ff. 221–3; C.P. 25(1)/191/31 East. 18 Hen. VII; C 142/25/61.

the manor and advowson to Henry Smyth of Shirford (Warws.) and William Fermor of Somerton, who in the following year conveyed them to Edmund Bury.[56] Edmund died in 1512 leaving as his heir a son James, aged ten.[57] His widow Jane, who in 1513 bought the remaining Gaynesford property in Hampton, later married Thomas Lovett, and her step-daughter Elizabeth Lovett eventually married James Bury. On James's death in 1558 his property was divided between his three daughters—Jane, wife of Ambrose Dormer of Ascot, Elizabeth, and Ursula. Hampton fell to Jane's share.[58]

Dormer died in 1566[59] leaving three children by Jane—Michael, Ambrose, and Winifred. Jane remarried in 1574,[60] and after her death in 1594 her second husband William Hawtrey held the manor. In 1597 he settled it for life on his step-son Michael Dormer (later Sir Michael), who subsequently married William Hawtrey's daughter Dorothy. Sir Michael was succeeded on his death in 1624 by his sister Winifred's four daughters,[61] Mary, Bridget, and Anne—her children by her first husband, William Hawtrey's son William—and Katherine, her daughter by her second husband John Pigott. Hampton was partitioned in 1625,[62] Mary and Katherine receiving a quarter share each. Bridget and her husband Sir Henry Croke received two quarters, Anne having sold her interest to her sister before her death in the previous year. Bridget obtained the capital messuage and the manorial rights.

Bridget's sister Mary, wife of Sir Francis Wolley, died childless in 1638. She left two conflicting deeds. By the first of 1626 her lands, a quarter of the manor, were settled to her use for life and afterwards to that of her half-sister, Katherine Pigott. The second deed, dated 1629, settled them on herself and on her heirs. After some dispute it was held that the second deed and the fine which had been levied thereon was a sufficient revocation of the uses limited in the earlier one. The rents were therefore adjudged to belong to Sir Henry Croke and Sir Walter Pye, by right of their wives Bridget and Elizabeth, the daughter of Anne, but they were to repay them if Pigott recovered the lands at Common Law. In this way the Crokes acquired another eighth part of the manor.[63] Henry's son, Robert Croke, knighted in 1641, was a member of the king's parliament at Oxford in 1644, and in 1646 he had to compound for his estates in Hampton Poyle and elsewhere.[64] On their own showing the Crokes were much impoverished by the Civil War, and in 1648 Sir Henry and Sir Robert sold their shares of the manor to John West for £5,000.[65] Katherine, daughter of Katherine Pigott,

was still claiming a quarter of the manor in 1653; moreover, the Crokes appear to have broken their sale contract, so that it was not until 1662, after a series of expensive lawsuits, that John West enjoyed undisturbed possession and a clear title.[66]

In 1665 John West's son John married Katherine Seaman, who died without issue in 1669. By the terms of their marriage settlement John West the elder retained his estates in Hampton Poyle for life. After his death they were to be held by trustees to raise £1,300 for the purposes of his will.[67] John died in 1696, leaving Hampton to his son but making no specific disposition of the £1,300, which was eventually awarded to his second daughter Mary.[68] Legacies amounting to £3,000 had to be paid, and in 1697 John the younger mortgaged Hampton for £1,600 to Christopher Clitheroe.[69] The mortgage was assigned to Lord Digby in 1699, and in 1702 to the executors of Sir Edward Sebright,[70] from whom West borrowed further sums. He was unable to redeem the manor and after his death in 1717 his widow, Elizabeth, and Sir Edward's heir, Sir Thomas Sebright, who had by then come of age, sold it with other properties to Arthur Annesley, Earl of Anglesey.[71]

In 1723 the earl sold his Hampton estates to Christopher Tilson, who bequeathed them to his nephew John Tilson of Watlington Park.[72] In 1767, on John Tilson's marriage to Maria Lushington, they were the subject of a marriage settlement. By this she received a jointure of £500 from the manor on his death in 1774. In 1795 John Tilson's eldest son, John Henry, sold the estate to Arthur Annesley for £25,000, £7,000 of which remained on mortgage.[73] Throughout the 19th century Hampton Poyle followed the same descent as Bletchingdon. The connexion with the Annesley family was broken in 1929, when the farms and holdings on Viscount Valentia's estate were sold to the various tenants.[74]

LESSER ESTATES. About 1222 William de Hampton sold Oseney Abbey his mill in Hampton with a croft and arable and meadow land. Within the next few years the abbey received other gifts of lands and rents from William and his tenants,[75] and in 1279 possessed two water-mills and over 4 virgates of land.[76] At the Dissolution the abbey's estate was bringing in £1 0s. 8d. in annual rents.[77] In 1541 the greater part of the former Oseney lands was granted by the Crown to Leonard Chamberlayne of Shirburn.[78] Chamberlayne succeeded his father as keeper of Woodstock Park about this time[79] and he may have sold his estate in Hampton soon after-

---

[56] C 54/378, m. 36.   [57] C 142/27/127.
[58] Ibid. 115/31; MS. Top. Oxon. b 86: Ct. R. 1559, 1563, 1565. For James Bury's will see R. E. C. Waters, *Genealogical Memoirs of Chester*, i. 64.
[59] C 142/143/49.
[60] C.P. 25(2)/196/Mich. 16–17 Eliz. I.
[61] C 146/8670.
[62] Ibid. 8926; Queen's Coll. Mun. Box 2A: copy of partition with full details of manor. At this date it was said to be held in free socage of the heir of Sir Thomas Spencer as of his manor of Wendlebury at a rent of 6s. 8d.: MS. Top. Oxon. b 87, f. 217.
[63] MS. Top. Oxon. b 87, ff. 1–25: deeds, letters, and details of lawsuits 1626–39.
[64] Ibid. ff. 26–29.
[65] Ibid. ff. 32–33, 37–38, 40, 46–49, 79b–c.
[66] Ibid. ff. 35, 41–80: documents relating to all these proceedings; cf. C 5/387/64; ibid. 17/179.

[67] C.P. 25(2)/707/16 Chas. II.
[68] MS. Top. Oxon. b 87, ff. 81c–90, 94–122, 154–6: briefs, abstracts of title, &c.; cf. C 5/576/34; ibid. 287/16.
[69] C.P. 25(2)/865/Mich. 9 Wm. III.
[70] MS. Top. Oxon. b 87, ff. 91–93: assignment of mortgage, will of Sir Edw. Sebright.
[71] Ibid. ff. 233–4: schedule of title-deeds of Annesley estates in Hampton Poyle, &c. 1691–1798; C.P. 25(2)/1049/East. 4 Geo. I: sale of 1718.
[72] MS. Top. Oxon. b 87, ff. 233–4.
[73] See Bodl. MS. D.D. Valentia a 1, Abstract of title, for full details; C.P. 43/843/422.
[74] Bodl. MS. D.D. Valentia a 1, Abstract of title.
[75] *Oseney Cart.* iv. 140; vi. 77–87.
[76] *Rot. Hund.* (Rec. Com.), ii. 831.
[77] *Valor Eccl.* (Rec. Com.), ii. 216.
[78] *L. & P. Hen. VIII*, xvi, p. 423.
[79] *D.N.B.*

wards. Most of it was later united with the manorial estate, but a small parcel of it may be represented by lands mortgaged by John Brotherton to the borough of New Woodstock in 1714. Woodstock had acquired a small estate in 1578, the gift of Thomas Rydge, and the borough still owns (1955) a few acres in the parish.[80]

In 1512 Merton College leased a ruinous tenement from James Bury.[81] In 1535 it was worth 6s. 8d. a year,[82] and later leases show that it was adjacent to another tenement and lands granted to Merton after the dissolution of Oseney Abbey.[83] In 1797 Merton held about 7 acres in the parish, but in 1818 they were acquired by the Knapp family in exchange for land in Kidlington.[84]

The quarter of the manor allotted to Katherine Pigott in 1625 passed to her daughter Katherine, wife of William Plaistowe. By 1766 this holding was in the possession of Joseph Tyrrel, and in 1797 it was held by George and Joseph Knapp of Abingdon.[85] This estate—consisting of Model Farm and about 230 acres in 1869—remained in the Knapp family until 1910, when it was sold by F. G. Knapp to Viscount Valentia.[86]

ECONOMIC HISTORY. The place name Hampton (O.E. *hamtun*)[87] indicates early settlement by the Anglo-Saxons. At the time of Domesday there was land for 6 ploughs, all of which was fully cultivated. In the demesne were 3 ploughs and 2 serfs; and 7 villeins (*villani*) and 2 bordars had 3 ploughs. Sixty acres of meadow are recorded. Since the Conquest the value of the estate had risen from £6 to £10,[88] perhaps as a consequence of an increase in the rich meadow-land along the river. There was also woodland ($\frac{1}{2}$ league × 16 furls.) and a water-mill worth 15s.

Early in the 13th century William of Hampton on account of his debts to the Jews was obliged to part with some of his valuable meadow-land, his mill, and fishery as well as arable land and the miller's cottage.[89] His grant to Oseney and other Oseney charters dated between 1220 and 1234 throw some light on economic affairs at Hampton at this time. The water-mill, for instance, served not only the lord's *curia* and the village but outsiders as well; there was no lack of work for it, as provision was made for the erection of a second mill if the abbot so wished.[90] There were two main fields[91] which it seems were divided mostly into $\frac{1}{2}$-acre strips;[92] one was called North Field[93] and the other very probably South Field.[94] There was also a third much smaller field called Colworth.[95] As for the pasture, there is evidence that there had long been intercommoning between the villages of Hampton Gay and Hampton Poyle.[96] Sheep-rearing may well have been generally

important here, as it certainly was to the abbot, who had rights of common in Hampton Poyle for 200 sheep.[97] Some meadow-land was assigned by lot annually; but some was inclosed and held in severalty.[98] The simple tenurial picture of Domesday had by now given way to more complicated arrangements, and there is evidence of the existence of free tenants and of buying and selling of land.[99]

By 1279[1] it seems clear that the area of cultivated land in the parish had been extended: Walter de la Poyle's manor contained about 31 virgates of land of which 8 were in demesne, a smaller proportion than in 1086. Of the 6 free tenants, the Abbot of Oseney held 8 acres in free alms, 2 water-mills and the fishery in the Cherwell besides a virgate of land for 6d. to the lord. Thus advantage had been taken of William of Hampton's concession about a second mill. Another tenant, Walter de Crokesford, held $2\frac{1}{2}$ virgates of the lord for 6s. 1d., and 2 virgates for a rent of 4s. to Oseney—a rent which William de Crokesford had paid to William of Hampton before the latter gave it to Oseney in about 1230.[2] Three other free tenants held 4 virgates between them for rents ranging from 1d. to 2s., while a sixth held a virgate of Oseney for 6s. and suit at the hundred and county. There were 15 villeins, all virgaters, who each paid 6s. a year rent, owed works and tallage, and had to pay fines at the lord's will if their sons left the manor (*redimere pueros*). Seven cottars each held a messuage and 2 acres of land for 2s. a year and owed the same autumn works as the virgaters, but were privileged in so far as they received their food from the lord. As a miller and a fisherman are numbered among the villeins and cottars, it seems clear that Walter de la Poyle's and the abbot's unfree tenants were listed together in the Hundred Rolls.

It is likely that it was during this period of expansion that the two main fields gave way to a three-field system. Later evidence shows that at some date before the early 16th century there were three fields—West Field, North-east Field, and South-east Field—beside the small Colworth Field.[3]

There is an unusual record of a boundary dispute in 1280 between the two Hamptons.[4] On receipt of a royal writ obtained at the instance of Oseney twelve jurors of the hundred court demarcated the boundary with stones and pales. The Poyles then claimed that they had been disseised of a part of their land, and the justices of assize at Henley, who heard the suit, ordered another jury to go to Hampton Poyle, remove the boundary marks, and replace them at their discretion in their proper places. In the next year difficulties arose over intercommoning. The parson of Hampton Poyle and a parishioner claimed that they had right of pasture in Hampton Gay

[80] Woodstock Borough Arch.
[81] *Reg. Annalium Coll. Merton*, ed. H. E. Salter (O.H.S. lxxvi), 429, 434, 518; cf. Merton Coll. MS. Cal. of Rec. iii (Oxon.), 149–62.
[82] *Valor Eccl.* ii. 224.
[83] Merton Coll. Mun.: leases 1550–1792.
[84] Ibid.: leases 1700–1800, 1820; ibid. Reg. of Leases 1796–1815, ff. 321–4.
[85] O.R.O. Incl. award.
[86] Bodl. MS. D.D. Valentia a 1.
[87] *P.N. Oxon.* (E.P.N.S.), i. 213–14.
[88] *V.C.H. Oxon.* i. 423.
[89] *Oseney Cart.* vi. 77–78.
[90] Ibid.
[91] Ibid. 78; cf. ibid. 83.
[92] Ibid. 81.
[93] Ibid. 83.
[94] The earliest detailed extant survey (1547) mentions North-east and South-east Fields: MS. Top. Oxon. b 86, ff. 1–7.
[95] *Oseney Cart.* vi. 86, 87. In 1797 it was 64 acres: see below.
[96] *Oseney Cart.* vi. 67–68.
[97] Ibid. 82–83.
[98] Ibid. 85.
[99] e.g. ibid. 82, 84.
[1] *Rot. Hund.* (Rec. Com.), ii. 831.
[2] *Oseney Cart.* vi. 82–83.
[3] See terrier of 1547: MS. Top. Oxon. b 86, ff. 1–7b.
[4] *Oseney Cart.* vi. 66.

belonging to their two free tenements in Hampton Poyle. It was decided that they had no such right.[5]

In 1298–9 the value of the manor was £12 18*s.* 5¼*d.* An extent records that there were 120 acres in demesne and 8 of meadow. The arable was worth 3*d.* an acre and the meadow 2*s.* an acre. The free tenants were six in number as in 1279; there were only thirteen villein virgaters, but three half-virgaters. Their rents as in 1279 were 6*s.* the virgate, and the virgate was said to equal 16 acres. Their works, which are set out in detail, had been commuted. From each virgate, for instance, a day's weeding, price ½*d.*, was due and a day's carriage of corn with one horse, price 1*d.* The total value of the works was 9*s.* 2¼*d.* Seven cottars with a cottage and two acres each paid rent of 1*s.*[6] In 1360 the value of the manor was £13 6*s.* 8*d.*,[7] compared with £10 in 1268.[8]

Early 14th-century tax lists show 25 contributors with the lady of the manor paying the highest sum.[9] Although not among the richer villages in the hundred, Hampton Poyle was a larger and more prosperous community than its neighbour Hampton Gay—which was taxed at 19*s.* 10*d.* for the 20th of 1327, for example, compared with Hampton Poyle's tax of £2 13*s.* 6*d.* After the revision of assessments in 1334, its payment was fixed at £5 2*s.* 8*d.* and there were 67 contributors to the poll tax of 1377.[10]

There are indications of depopulation by the early 16th century. In 1510 it was recorded in the bailiff's accounts that fulling mills at Hampton had fallen down and the rent of 30*s.* 8*d.* had not been paid.[11] This was still the case in 1521.[12] Moreover, there had been some conversion of arable land into sheep and cattle pasture. Two men were accused in 1517 of converting 60 acres and putting two ploughs out of use, while Edmund Bury was alleged to have had 80 acres sown with grain in 1511, which he had since converted and had thus deprived twelve people of their livelihood.[13] Whatever the truth about these particular charges it was stated clearly in 1547 that the West Field had been inclosed.[14] Payments, moreover, to the subsidy of 1523 show a considerable change since the early 14th century in the pattern of landholding and the distribution of wealth. There were thirteen contributors, but Henry Rathbone paid £2 out of the total of £2 15*s.* 8*d.*[15]

Manor court rolls for 1549–92 have survived. The homage consisted of ten or twelve persons and proceedings mainly concerned fences, bridle paths, interference with boundaries, the straying of cattle and hogs, and the clearing of ditches.[16]

The most complete of the many surviving terriers is dated 1625.[17] It shows that the demesne covered just over 285 acres and included a rabbit-warren ('coneygree') of 5⅓ acres. The lord also possessed the fishing in the Cherwell, the mill, and the parcel of meadow called Flat Hamm between the old river and the new (2¼ a.). As the demesne was counted as 4 yardlands it had grazing for sixteen beasts (valued at 6*s.* 8*d.* a gate), a bull and 'a breeder', and 80 sheep-walks at 1*d.* each. The lord had the right to hold a court baron, but not a court leet. The profits of the court hardly equalled the outlay. Six leaseholders for a term of two or three lives held 137 acres in all. Four of them held substantial holdings of between 22 and 44 acres. Besides their rents they were bound to supply one or two beasts in 'name of two heriots whensoever they shall happen'.[18] In addition, there were five customary tenants holding nearly 176 acres, mostly for one or two lives only and paying the usual heriots; four tenants at will, whose small plots with attached cottages had been carved out of the waste; the glebe (32 a.) and parsonage house; a tenement and ½ yardland held by Merton College; and two freeholders—Widow Kempe (32¾ a.) and John Lumber (1½ a.). The wastes and common lands included the cow pastures of Abbott Marsh (21 a.) and Broad Marsh (3 a.), the Town Green (8½ a.), and the 'ways' (16 a.). The rents from the demesne amounted to £214 and those from the tenants and freeholders to £12 2*s.* 10*d.*

At this time, of the 783 acres available for agricultural purposes about 368 acres were arable, 233 acres were pasture of various kinds, 105 acres were meadow and nearly 32 acres were furze. There was also the lord's osier bed of 28 poles. It is noticeable that of the demesne only 31 per cent. (89 a.) was given over to arable whereas the tenants mostly kept from 70 per cent. up to 83 per cent. of their holdings under the plough. Moreover, almost all the demesne ploughland was leased to four tenants so that the Mr. Fyndale, who rented the main part of the demesne, was in practice a large-scale sheep or cattle farmer.

In the first half of the 17th century Hampton's prosperity was affected first by the Civil War and later by the neglect of John West, the lord of the manor. In 1646 Sir Robert Croke declared that his part of Hampton was worth only £122 10*s.* but this, so John West alleged, was only an attempt to hoodwink the compounding authorities.[19] In 1649 the annual value of the rents and tithes was £367 0*s.* 10*d.* and the parish was subsequently rated on £350 a year.[20] In the latter half of the century John West's son averred that the decay and neglect was such that his part of the manor did not yield £200 a year.[21] There was poverty too among the smaller farmers, for in 1665 four were discharged from payment of the hearth tax.[22] One of these farmed 45½ acres and the other 22 acres and rented a yardland in the demesne. By 1717 the selling price of the manor increased to £6,000 and within a few decades to £10,000.[23]

The main interest of the history of the parish at

[5] *Oseney Cart.* 67–68.
[6] C 133/89/5. The total value given in this extent (1298–9) is £8 18*s.* 5¼*d.* but the individual items add up to more.
[7] C 135/151/8.
[8] C 132/35/4.
[9] E 179/161/8, 9, 10.
[10] e.g. E 164/7; E 179/161/39.
[11] *Oseney Cart.* vi. 233.
[12] Ibid. 265.
[13] *Dom. of Incl.* 329, 348.
[14] MS. Top. Oxon. b 86, f. 2; ibid. b 87, f. 176. The position of the old inclosures on the inclosure map of 1797 makes it probable that West Field had been bounded on the east by the road to Bletchingdon: O.R.O. Incl. map.
[15] E 179/161/198; ibid. 176.
[16] MS. Top. Oxon. b 86, ff. 9–17.
[17] Ibid. b 87: the main part of the terrier is ff. 123–49; the first pages are inserted separately as ff. 215–17.
[18] Ibid. ff. 125*b*, 128, 130.
[19] Ibid. f. 26; see above, p. 162.
[20] MS. Top. Oxon. b 87, ff. 39, 40.
[21] Ibid. f. 87. Part of the manor was settled on West on his marriage in 1665.
[22] *Hearth Tax Oxon.* 193.
[23] MS. Top. Oxon. b 87, f. 91.

the turn of the century was the growing demand for inclosure. In 1685 the glebe of 2 yardlands lay scattered in 58 strips,[24] but this may have been exceptional and may not prove that little advance had been made over medieval practice on the uninclosed land. In 1729 a document was drawn up which stated that the distribution of the meadows by lots 'was so perplexed and confused' a method 'that none of the possessors know any foot of land in the said meadows to be their own'. The chief landowners agreed to abolish 'lotting' and have the meadows measured and justly assigned.[25] For some reason this attempt seems to have been unsuccessful and the system of assigning the meadows by lot prevailed for another 70 years. When a survey of the manor was made in 1789,[26] it was stated that 'the method and manner of lotting is one year above the middle stone and the other year below it with a pole of 14 feet. One draught answers six acres.'

At this time, out of a total of about 770 acres, over 355 acres were held by the lord, 272 were freehold, 119 were common land, $16\frac{1}{2}$ were taken up by roads and ways, and 8 acres 3 roods made up the Town green. In 1766[27] the lord's land had been valued at £320, more than half the total valuation of £629. This is in marked contrast with the valuation of 1649, when the lord's land was valued at about a quarter of the whole estate.

The open fields were finally inclosed by the award of 1797,[28] under which the main grants amounting to over 593 acres were as follows: Arthur Annesley and Charles Warde (6 parcels and a small manorial allotment) 408 acres, George Knapp, gent. (7 parcels and a small manorial allotment) 88 acres, and George Knapp, merchant (4 parcels) 43 acres. The remaining odd 52 acres were assigned to the rector, Woodstock Corporation, Islip and Hampton Poyle poor, Merton College, a cottager, and for roads and stonepits. Assuming that the parish's total area was 830 acres, it appears that over 200 acres had previously been inclosed. A part of this probably consisted of small inclosures of orchards and closes dating back to the medieval period, but most originated in Tudor times.

By the time of the award there were five fields, the three recorded in 1547[29] having been redivided. There had then been two large fields, the North-east and South-east Fields, and a third small field, Colworth. By 1797 these had become Lower, Bletchingdon, Grettingdon, Collet (Colworth), and Friezeman's (Freezeman's Well), but the last was small and the parish had in fact almost a typical four-field system, with a four-course rotation. The survey of 1789 had recorded that the arable fields, covering nearly 367 acres, were fallowed every fourth year,

except Colworth (64 a.), which was cropped every year.[30]

The most tangible result of the inclosure was the great improvement in the tract that had been lot meadows.[31] This and the improvement in tillage generally was partly responsible for a considerable increase in the population of the parish. Inclosure may also have encouraged the amalgamation of farms. By about 1850 there were four largish ones.[32]

As the manor-house was never large the parishioners were tenant farmers and farm labourers rather than domestic servants or craftsmen. In 1811 out of 24 families only one was not employed in agriculture.[33] Later the following craftsmen occur: a shoe-maker, carpenter, and blacksmith,[34] and in 1926 one inhabitant was occupied as a 'motor-driver'. Within the next decade the influence of Morris Motor Works becomes increasingly apparent in the registers.

There have been many fluctuations in population since 1676 when the Compton Census recorded 63 adults. In 1738 the parish was said to have few inhabitants, and in 1759 about 19 families lived there.[35] Towards the end of the century baptisms rarely exceeded burials:[36] the population had dropped to 100 persons by 1801.[37] The tide had turned before 1811 when there were 24 families and 128 persons, and by 1851 the population had reached 156. Families decreased in size in the last decades of the century and by 1901, on account of the drift of the villagers away from agriculture, there were only 105 inhabitants. This trend was continued in the early part of the 20th century, but numbers rose from 80 in 1931 to 91 in 1951.[38]

CHURCH. No record of the church at Hampton Poyle has been found before about 1225, when the rector Simon witnessed a charter for the lord of the manor, William de Hampton.[39] From the first recorded presentation in 1247 or 1248 until the 17th century the descent of the advowson usually followed that of the manor.[40] In 1347, however, Sir William Shareshull, the father of Henry de la Poyle's wife Elizabeth, was patron, and in 1361 Sir John de Pyrton, her second husband, presented.[41] When the manor was sold in 1648 to John West, the Crokes retained the advowson,[42] but Sir Robert Croke sold it in 1670 for £275 to William Morrell,[43] vintner and later mayor of Oxford.[44] Morrell in 1676 sold the next presentation for £150 to Robert Mayott of Fawler,[45] who in 1680 presented William Mayott,[46] and in 1677 Morrell sold the advowson for only £150 to the Queen's College, Oxford.[47] William Mayott died almost immediately, and from 1680[48] until the end of the 19th century the college presented. In 1897

[24] Queen's Coll. Mun. box 2, A 6.
[25] Ibid. box 2, A 7.
[26] Ibid. box 18, day bk.   [27] Ibid.
[28] O.R.O. Incl. award.
[29] MS. Top. Oxon. b 86, ff. 1–7b.
[30] Queen's Coll. Mun. box 18, day bk.
[31] Young, Oxon. Agric. 91.
[32] H.O. 107/1727.
[33] Census, 1811.
[34] Bodl. dep. b 40: Par. Reg.
[35] Oxf. Dioc. d 553, d 556.
[36] Par. Reg., Bodl. dep. b 40: between 1550 and 1559 there were 41 baptisms and 28 burials; Oxf. Dioc. d 562: the return of 15 or 16 houses in 1771 seems too low to be trustworthy.
[37] Census, 1801.

[38] Ibid. 1811–1951.
[39] Oseney Cart. vi. 86.
[40] Rot. Grosse. 492. For list of medieval presentations see MS. Top. Oxon. d 460.
[41] For genealogy see Gent. Mag. 1806, lxxvi (2), 810. M. John de Shareshull and John Trymenel, chpl., had been enfeoffed in 1335 with the manor: Cal. Pat. 1334–8, 84; C.P. 25(1)/190/18/7.
[42] C.P. 25(2)/474/Mich. 24 Chas. I.
[43] Ibid. 708/Trin. 22 Chas. II. The original is in Queen's Coll. Mun. box 2, A 1.
[44] A. Wood, City of Oxf. (O.H.S. xxxvii), iii. 39, 40.
[45] Queen's Coll. Mun. box 2, A 3.
[46] Oxf. Dioc. c 70, f. 72.
[47] Queen's Coll. Mun. box 2, A 4.
[48] Oxf. Dioc. c 70, f. 73.

the Revd. H. W. Yule of Shipton-on-Cherwell bought the advowson for £300, but in the following spring sold it to the Revd. S. T. Gwilliam, the Rector of Hampton Poyle. Gwilliam's widow presented the next two rectors, and on her death in 1933 the advowson passed, in accordance with the provisions of her husband's will, to King's College, London. In 1946, at the suggestion of the bishop, Exeter College, Oxford, obtained the patronage in exchange for that of Bolney (Sussex), thereby allowing the Vicar of Kidlington (an Exeter College living) to hold Hampton Poyle and Kidlington conjointly.[49]

The benefice of Hampton Poyle was rated annually at £2 in 1254,[50] at £3 13s. 4d. in 1291,[51] and at £6 2s. 8d. in 1535.[52] It was therefore a very poor living. The next known valuation is of 1649, when the rectory was worth £45: £29 for tithes and £16 for glebe.[53] In the mid-18th century the rectory was let for £85,[54] and in 1766 for £100, although the rector claimed only to receive an average of £60.[55] But the main grievance of 18th-century rectors was that some tithes[56] had been commuted by a modus of £5 10s., while their real value was £17 10s. William Atkinson (1723-8) tried to break this modus, but was non-suited for non-residence.[57] In 1797, at the inclosure, most of the tithes were commuted for £135, but the fate of the tithes on which a modus had been paid was left in abeyance to be settled at law.[58] By 1831 the income of the living, which came partly from the glebe, had risen to £250.[59]

The parsonage lands are mentioned in 1281.[60] Many summarized accounts and a few detailed surveys survive. The first is of 1547,[61] when the glebe consisted of 2 yardlands or 33 acres, mixed up with a yardland of the rector's private property. Another terrier of 1625[62] lists the following possessions: parsonage house with courtyard, barn, stable, orchard, garden and close, 27 (field) acres of arable, 1 of furze, and 2 of meadow, and common for 4 fodder beasts and 20 sheep.[63] Detailed surveys of 1789-90 reveal slight changes. The total glebe was then nearly 35 acres, of which 8 acres were meadow.[64] At the inclosure award in 1797 this land was exchanged for over 27 acres.[65] By 1927 all but 3 acres of the glebe had been sold.[66]

The parish, which until the 19th century was in Bicester deanery, had been transferred by 1854 to the new deanery of Islip.[67]

In the Middle Ages there was frequently a close relationship between the rectors and the lords of the manor. Thomas de la Poyle, John de Shareshull, and John de la Poyle were doubtless related to the De la Poyle lords, and at a later date Thomas and John Rede were certainly related to the Redes of Boarstall.[68] On the point of residence, all that is known is that John Nason or Mason, rector for 40 years in the early 16th century, was at least sometimes resident, for he was accused in about 1520 of keeping two women in his house, one of them pregnant.[69]

In the post-reformation period the parish was one of those which suffered from the doctrinal changes. During Mary's reign, the Protestant Richard Plumpton was temporarily replaced by Richard Thomason, very possibly the Catholic priest of that name who had been condemned to hang in chains from Duns Tew steeple for his opposition to the first prayer book of Edward VI.[70] Plumpton was apparently in the parish early in 1557, however, when he witnessed the will of his patron James Bury, who called him 'my ghostly father'.[71] In the following century, although the parish had been fortunate enough to have the able John Tolson, Provost of Oriel College,[72] as its pastor for a quarter of a century, it again suffered from the controversial views of the day. This time its rector, Edward Fulham, who had succeeded Tilson in 1645, was forced to resign Hampton and flee abroad on account of his strong royalist views and his opposition to Puritanism.[73]

After the Queen's College became patron, the rectors were often non-resident: Anthony Addison (1693-1719), for instance, already a pluralist,[74] was said only to have taken the poor living of Hampton because of a poor marriage.[75]

From 1728 to 1801 the living was usually held with South Weston, where the rector lived, while Hampton was served for £20 a year by a curate, living in Oxford or a nearby village.[76] In the middle of the century the religious life of the parish was disturbed by open discord between the rector and his parishioners. Jonathan Dennis (1752-66), a resident Fellow of Queen's,[77] presented them all (except two old women) at the archdeacon's visitation for absenting themselves from church, and also presented the churchwardens for failing to obtain a new bible and prayer books. In 1754, the year after, the churchwardens presented that the church and chancel and parsonage house were out of repair, the minister

49 Exeter Coll. Mun. Title-deeds and correspondence 1897-1946; inf. the Bursar, King's College, London.
50 Lunt, Val. Norw. 312.
51 Inq. Non. (Rec. Com.), 133. It is not in Tax. Eccl.
52 Valor Eccl. (Rec. Com.), ii. 159.
53 MS. Top. Oxon. b 87, f. 39.
54 Oxf. Dioc. c 653, f. 152.
55 Queen's Coll. Mun. box 18, day bk.
56 Some 42 acres according to the inclosure estimate.
57 As n. 55.
58 O.R.O. Incl. award.
59 Rep. of Comm. on Eccl. Revenue, H.C. 54 (1835), xxii.
60 See above, p. 163; they were valued at 6s. 8d. in 1341: Inq. Non. (Rec. Com.), 133.
61 MS. Top. Oxon. b 86, ff. 7-7b.
62 Ibid. b 87, ff. 140b-141b.
63 This seems to have been commons for one yardland. See above, p. 164. According to a terrier of 1685, he had commons for two yardlands: Oxf. Archd. Oxon. b 40, f. 147.
64 Queen's Coll. Mun. box 18, day bk. The rector computed the acreage to 4 decimal places, pointing out that he gained a few pence by his elaborate calculations.

65 O.R.O. Incl. award.
66 Par. Rec. Terrier 1926-7.
67 For date of formation of Islip deanery, see above, p. 67, n. 97.
68 For references see MS. Top. Oxon. d 460.
69 Visit. Dioc. Linc. 1517-31, i. 122.
70 O.A.S. Rep. 1914, 232-3.
71 R. E. C. Waters, Genealogical Memoirs of Chester, i. 64, quoting Bury's will. Plumpton was buried in the church in 1598: Par. Reg.
72 For him see G. C. Richards and C. L. Shadwell, Provosts of Oriel, 85-86.
73 Oxf. Dioc. c 70, f. 69. For him see Walker Rev. 297.
74 Flemings in Oxf. ed. J. R. Magrath, ii (O.H.S. lxii), 38 n. 1.
75 Hearne, Remarks, i. 120.
76 Oxf. Dioc. d 553, d 559. William Thompson, who is said to have written poetry while Rector of Hampton (D.N.B.), never seems to have held this living, although he was Rector of Weston.
77 Letters of Radcliffe & James, ed. M. Evans (O.H.S. ix), p. xxiii.

absent, and Sunday tippling allowed in two houses.[78] From early in 1763 to the spring of 1768 no services were held in the church because it needed repair, and the parishioners went to Weston-on-the-Green.[79] The late 18th century was also an unsatisfactory period. The curate's stipend was too small to secure a qualified person, and it was reported that, not being in priest's orders, he knew 'nothing of the sacrament' and even neglected to catechize the children on the grounds that they were too ignorant.[80] Improvements began with the 19th century: William Benson (1801–39), although he continued to hold Hampton with South Weston, rebuilt Hampton Rectory,[81] and his successor Joseph Dodd (1840–74) was permanently resident after the separation of the two livings. In his day congregations increased in numbers in spite of the presence of 'long rooted dissent, the apathy of the farmers, poor education and the feeling against the church, which has been strong in the minds of the people'.[82]

The small church of *ST. MARY* consists of chancel, short nave, north and south aisles, and a double bellcote at the west end. Built mainly of limestone rubble with freestone dressings, it is roofed with Stonesfield slates except for the nave, which is covered with lead.[83]

Much of the church dates from the 13th century. There is a plain lancet window on the south side of the chancel, and the three-light east window, probably late 13th century, has Geometrical tracery. There are brackets for figures of saints on either side of this window.

The church was considerably altered in the 14th century, when the west window was inserted and the north aisle either added or rebuilt. The north nave arcade consists of two arches springing from a pier whose capital bears the north Oxfordshire decoration of half-figures with interlocking arms. The arches on the south side spring from a flat pier and may be slightly earlier. The chancel arch is also 14th century.

Early in the 18th century the church was considered 'very ordinary and in bad repair'.[84] By the 1750's the decay was serious. A plan of 1756 to repair the church by taking down the south aisle and using the material for the rest of the building at a cost of £56 came to nothing, because John Tilson, the principal landowner, refused to contribute £30.[85] By 1759 it was 'exceedingly dangerous in stormy weather to assemble in church, and at other times far from safe'.[86] From 1763 to 1768 no services could be held,[87] but temporary repairs, including work on the roof, made the building usable until the 19th century.

An extensive restoration began in 1844 with the reroofing of the chancel for £25 14s.; in 1847 the nave roof was repaired; in 1859 the north aisle was reroofed for £46, and work was begun on the south aisle. About 1870 there was a more general restoration (architect G. E. Street), during which the south doorway was rebuilt, the chancel floor was laid with Minton tiles, and new seats, stone pulpit, reading-desk, and alabaster reredos were installed. The carved panelling at the back of the old pulpit was retained, and many of the finely carved panels of the old seats, dating from the early 16th century, were incorporated in the new seating. Between 1844 and 1875 over £1,500 was spent on the church.[88] The bellcote, described in 1806 as 'a small open gable',[89] was also rebuilt during the 19th century. In 1951 the south aisle was restored at the expense of Dr. G. D. Parkes.

In 1952 the stone pulpit was covered in oak panelling to match the linen-fold of one of the old bench-ends and an oak altar table, copied from the 17th-century one at Kidlington, was set up.

There is a small piscina in the north aisle, with its basin resting on a human head. The font is low and circular, with an octagonal base. There are late-14th-century fragments of stained glass, bearing the symbols of the four evangelists, in a chancel window.[90] A rood-screen, there in 1806, had disappeared by the late 19th century.[91]

There are three medieval monuments. There is a stone effigy of a knight in armour with crossed legs (datable to c. 1330–40). It bears traces of colour.[92] There is a brass with figures of John de la Poyle (d. 1423, although the inscription says 1424) and Elizabeth his wife. There is an elaborate late-14th-century tomb recess with crocketed canopy supported by angels with shields, bearing the arms of Poyle and Elmerugg (?) impaling Poyle.[93] Beneath is a 14th-century effigy of a female placed there in the 19th century.

A monument by Peter Scheemakers to Christopher Tilson (d. 1742), a clerk of the Treasury,[94] consists of a pyramid of grey marble, with arms, surmounted by an urn. There are tablets to John Blake (d. 1788), the Revd. Thomas Breeks (d. 1800), Rector of South Weston and Hampton Poyle, Thomas Goodall (d. 1814), and the Revd. William Benson (d. 1839). There was once a stone to Humphrey Turton, rector (d. 1678/9).[95]

In 1552 the church owned a chalice and several copes and vestments.[96] In 1955 the only old plate was a silver chalice with paten cover of 1575.[97] As at the Reformation, there were two bells, but both were of later date. One is 17th century.[98]

The registers date from 1540 for baptisms, 1544 for burials, and 1545 for marriages.[99] There are also

---

[78] Oxf. Archd. Oxon. c 72, ff. 111–12; ibid. d 13, f. 32.
[79] Ibid. c 72, f. 120; Oxf. Dioc. d 559.
[80] Oxf. Dioc. c 327, p. 53.
[81] Ibid. b 39; see above, p. 160.
[82] Oxf. Dioc. d 179, c 332; *Wilb. Visit.*
[83] Cf. Parker, *Guide*, 53–55, and an article in *Gent. Mag.* 1806, lxxvi (1), 524–6. There are early 19th-cent. drawings in MS. Top. Oxon. b 220, ff. 65, 67, and a Buckler drawing (1820), ibid. a 67, f. 291.
[84] *Par. Coll.* ii. 157.
[85] Oxf. Dioc. c 653, ff. 150–7.
[86] Ibid. d 556.
[87] Ibid. d 559.
[88] Details of the restoration are from Par. Rec. Churchwardens' accts. and Par. minute bk.
[89] *Gent. Mag.* 1806, lxxvi (1). 525.

[90] In 1844 a stained-glass window made by Mr. Wailes of Newcastle upon Tyne was given.
[91] MS. Top. Oxon. d 90, f. 51.
[92] It was for some time in the churchyard. In 1804 it was in the south aisle, but by 1806 had been placed beside that of the lady.
[93] See above, p. 161. For photographs of angels with shields, see Bodl. G.A. Oxon. 4° 686, p. 156.
[94] See above, p. 162.
[95] *Par. Coll.* ii. 157; for tricks of arms, see Bodl. G.A. Oxon. 4° 688, p. 157.
[96] *Chant. Cert.* 88–89.
[97] Evans, *Ch. Plate.*
[98] *Ch. Bells Oxon.* ii. 152.
[99] Those up to 1764 are deposited in the Bodl.: dep. b 40.

churchwardens' accounts from 1816 and vestry minutes from 1859.

NONCONFORMITY. No record has been found of Roman Catholicism.

In 1835 a private house was licensed for Protestant worship,[1] and at least until the 1870's there were a few dissenters who gathered together sometimes on Sunday evenings.[2]

SCHOOLS. In 1759 the absence from church of many labourers' families was attributed partly to 'their inability to read, occasioned perhaps by want of a school at a proper distance from them'.[3] There was still no school in 1819[4] but in 1833 there was one for 20 children supported by the rector and landowners,[5] notably Arthur Annesley.[6] In 1837 the school was united to the National Society.[7] Thereafter the rector seems to have been the main support of the school,[8] which occupied a small cottage. In 1854 there were also an infant school for children under five and a winter school held once a week for the older boys.[9] The National school had 19 pupils in 1871,[10] but in that year owing to its inadequacy it was decided to send children over six to Bletchingdon school. Their instruction cost £5, half being found by the rector and half by the Hampton farmers according to the size of their farms.

The schoolmistress's salary of £14 11s. 8d. a year in 1875–6 was later reduced to £8 9s. 6d. when a cottage next to the school was provided for her. The school closed soon after 1890 and the children then went to Bletchingdon, and later to Kidlington, as most of them did in 1955.[11]

CHARITIES. Among early charitable bequests were £5 left to the poor in 1664 by Edward Fulham, a former rector, and distributable on Good Friday; and £5 left for the same purpose by John West the elder in 1696. Both charities were lost by being put in the hands of Anthony Addison, a rector who died insolvent in 1719.[12]

Poor's Land. From early times the lord of the manor allowed the churchwardens certain lands free of rent for the provision of Whitsun ale. In 1625 these lands comprised over 6½ acres.[13] In the 18th century it was customary for the rectors to spend £1 1s. a year, derived from the lands, on bread and cheese for the poor at Easter.[14] The inclosure award of 1797 granted 4 a. 1 r. 3 p. in trust for the poor, and at that time there were also three small cottages and gardens in the care of the churchwardens and overseers. In 1808 an income of £7 7s. from the poor's land was said to be properly applied. In the 19th century the benefits were, however, sporadic and varied much in nature. In 1817 the poor received their share of 26 cwt. of coal at 1s. 5d. a cwt.; in 1875 the rent of £13 10s. for Poor's Piece was divided equally among the cottagers at 12s. 6d. a house, except for two needy women who received £1 each. In 1875 it was agreed to split Poor's Piece into allotments for the cottagers, and it was exchanged for land nearer the village.[15] In the 20th century the cottagers ceased to cultivate the allotments, and they were subsequently rented from the parish by Mr. F. Kerwood of Manor Farm. In 1954 the income, about £4 10s. a year, was distributed at Michaelmas by the rector among the cottagers, each receiving about 5s.[16]

HARDWICK

This small parish of 385 acres[1] was united with Tusmore in 1932 to form the modern parish of Hardwick-with-Tusmore.[2] The ancient parish lay in the north-east corner of Oxfordshire, near the Northants border, midway between the market-towns of Brackley and Bicester. A stream, crossed by Hardwick ford, marks the southern boundary and Stoke Bushes, its only other natural boundary, separates Hardwick from Stoke Lyne on the south-west. This wood was named Stoke Spinney in 1797.[3] The parish lies on the Great Oolite, here overlain by fine flint gravel.[4] The ground falls from 381 feet in the north to 337 feet in the south. Minor roads connect Hardwick with Stoke Lyne and the Oxford–Brackley road, and with Hethe and the Bicester–

Aynho road. A map of 1797 shows a well-defined road to Cottisford, but today (1955) there is only a bridle track. The nearest railway station is at Ardley, three miles distant.

The name Hardwick[5] means in Old English a sheep farm or perhaps a cattle farm, or dwelling-place for flocks and herds, and indicates that a settlement was made here because the drift gravel of the uplands provides fine pasture. As its church was a chapelry of Stoke Lyne in the mid-12th century it is possible that it was the 'herdwick' of a Saxon estate there. In the 13th century the village became known as Hardwick Audley[6] after its manorial lord and was so described as late as the 15th century.[7]

The village lies roughly in the centre of the parish.

[1] Oxf. Dioc. c 646, f. 4; *Oxf. Circuit Plan* (1835).
[2] *Wilb. Visit.*; Oxf. Dioc. c 332, c 344.
[3] Oxf. Dioc. d 556.   [4] *Educ. of Poor.*
[5] *Educ. Enq. Abstract*, 747.
[6] Par. Rec. Minute bk.
[7] Queen's Coll. Mun. box 2, A 8: certificate.
[8] Gardner, *Dir. Oxon.*
[9] *Wilb. Visit.*   [10] *Elem. Educ. Ret.*
[11] All details from Par. Rec. Minute bk. 1859–1956.
[12] Oxf. Dioc. d 556.
[13] MS. Top. Oxon. b 87, ff. 123–49: Church Ham meadow, near Gosford bridge (3 r. 15 p.), Church Mere under Lumber Hedge (30 p.), 2 leys of furze in Heath Furlong (1 a.), 1 ley of furze, belonging to the town (1 a.), 8 leys of furze in Syna Pye (3 a. 0 r. 20 p.), and 1 ley butt in Friezeman's Well (1 r. 39 p.). Total, 6 a. 2 r. 24 p.

[14] Queen's Coll. Mun. box 18, day bk.
[15] Par. Rec. Minute bk.
[16] Inf. Revd. C. L. Chavasse. J. P. Dodd's benefactions, 1894 and 1925 (£145 stock: dividend £5 11s. in 1954), are for the upkeep of the churchyard.
[1] O.S. Map 6″, xvii (1884); a detached portion (4 a.) of Hethe was added to Hardwick in 1888: *Local Govt. Bd. Order* 21435 (copy in O.R.O.).
[2] *Oxon. Review Order* (1932); O.S. Map 2½″, 42/52, 53, (1951).
[3] Davis, *Oxon. Map.*
[4] G.S. Map 1″, xlv, NE.; *G.S. Memoir* (1864), 53.
[5] *P.N. Oxon.* (E.P.N.S.), ii. 452. Cf. H. Alexander, *Oxfordshire Place Names*, 121.
[6] See below, p. 169.
[7] C 142/190/66.

The Manor Farm and the church stand on relatively high ground, which falls away to a stream on the west: this forms pools and a pond and makes the whole ground marshy as far as the ford to the south-west.[8] The one-time school (dated 1873), now a private house; a few semi-detached cottages built of stone with brick trimmings, which are dated 1869 and 1870, and lie on both sides of the road to Hethe; and two rather later semi-detached brick cottages make up the rest of the village. These cottages are due to the 2nd Earl of Effingham, who purchased Tusmore and Hardwick in 1857, and pulled down the dilapidated old ones, built of local stone.[9]

The village was probably one of the smallest in Ploughley hundred in the 14th century and continued to be so.[10] In 1327 it had seventeen taxpayers, in 1524 seven,[11] and in 1665 there was only one house listed, besides the small Rectory and Richard Fermor's manor-house, for the hearth tax.[12] The Rectory had evidently gone by 1682,[13] when there is a reference to its site. It had been described as 'ruinous' in 1679.[14]

The only building of note left in the parish is the former manor-house, now the Manor Farm. The house dates from the late 16th century and must have been built between 1580 and 1643 when Sir Richard Fermor was lord of the manor.[15] His father Thomas Fermor had resided at Somerton and leased the Hardwick house to a servant.[16] The heads of the Fermor family never resided in the new manor-house, but it is known that in the reign of Charles II the house was the residence of the eldest son. The will of Richard Fermor Esq. (proved 1684) mentions 'such goods as I brought from thence [i.e. Hardwick] when I came to live at Tusmore'.[17] Throughout the 18th century the house was let by the Fermors. The Day family occupied the farm until 1793,[18] Robert Day (d. 1712) and later Days being buried in the chancel of the church. They were succeeded by their relatives the Collingridges, who remained until 1812.[19] The house is rectangular in plan, and has two stories with cellars and attic dormers. The walls are of coursed rubble, over 2 feet thick at the ground floor; the roof has been retiled with asbestos tiling; the west gable was restored in 1946. The most interesting feature of the interior is the staircase, which has no balusters remaining, but a heavy moulded projecting hand-rail and massive fleur-de-lis shaped finials: there are shallow oak treads, of which parts have been renewed.

MANOR. Walter Giffard, Lord of Longueville, held *HARDWICK* after the Conquest, but by 1086 he had given it to Robert d'Oilly in an exchange of lands.[20] Of the 7½ hides at which Hardwick was then assessed, 2½ later became part of the manor of Tusmore.[21] The overlordship of Hardwick descended in the D'Oilly family[22] until the death of Henry (II) d'Oilly in 1232. It then passed to Thomas de Newburgh, Earl of Warwick, and subsequently followed the same descent as the overlordship of Bucknell.[23] Robert d'Oilly's tenant of Hardwick in 1086 was Drew d'Aundeley, whose descendants the Fitzwyths of Ardley held a mesne lordship of Hardwick in the 13th century.[24]

A certain Maud of Hardwick was tenant of the manor before 1225, when she confirmed her gift of a knight's fee there to William d'Aundeley,[25] who appears to have belonged to a junior branch of the D'Aundeleys of Tusmore. Maurice d'Aundeley of Tusmore, and his successors Hugh and John, were mesne lords between the tenants of Hardwick and the Fitzwyths in 1272, 1285, and 1346 respectively.[26] William d'Aundeley was still in possession in 1243,[27] and was succeeded by Ralph d'Aundeley. In 1265, after the battle of Evesham, although Ralph had never supported Simon de Montfort, his manor of Hardwick was seized and he himself was imprisoned and held to ransom by James de Audley of Stratton Audley.[28] By 1272, perhaps under compulsion, Ralph had sold the manor to Alice de Beauchamp. In that year it was taken into the king's hand on the death of James de Audley on the assumption that it had been one of his possessions.[29] Alice recovered the manor and was the tenant in 1279.[30] While her identity is not certain, Alice was probably a daughter of Alice de Clinton of Aston Clinton (Bucks.) and her second husband Robert de Beauchamp, and sister of the John de Beauchamp who married James de Audley's daughter Joan.[31] James de Audley acquired Aston Clinton from the Beauchamps, and on the other hand Alice de Beauchamp held Horseheath (Cambs.) of his gift.[32] Alice was still alive in 1282,[33] but by 1285 Hardwick manor had passed to Anthony de Bek, Bishop of Durham,[34] whose friendly relations with the Audleys are illustrated by his gift to another James de Audley of the manor of Ashby Magna (Leics.).[35]

After Anthony de Bek's death in 1310 Hardwick evidently passed to the Audleys of Aston Clinton. The 'Alice of Hoke' who held the manor in 1316[36] may be identified as Alice de Audley, whose possessions at her death in 1342 included the manor of

---

[8] Description of village based on O.S. Map 25″, xviii. 6; personal observation, local inf. and inf. Mr. P. S. Spokes.

[9] Blo. *Hard.* 58; see below, p. 336.

[10] See below, p. 358.

[11] E 179/161/9; ibid. 176.

[12] *Hearth Tax Oxon.* 205. The list for 1662, usually fuller, has only 2 householders: ibid. 235; cf. M. Beresford, *Lost Villages of Eng.* 383, who says there are clear signs of former houses at O.S. Nat. Grid 576297.

[13] Oxf. Archd. Oxon. b 40, f. 157; cf. Bishop Fell's bk. (1685): Oxf. Dioc. d 708, f. 143.

[14] Blo. *Hard.* 55.

[15] See below, p. 293.

[16] P.C.C. 30 Arundell.

[17] Ibid. 40 Hare.

[18] O.R.O. Land tax assess.; Stapleton, *Cath. Miss.* 84.

[19] O.R.O. Land tax assess.

[20] *V.C.H. Oxon.* i. 414.

[21] See below, p. 335.

[22] e.g. *Fines Oxon.* 31.

[23] *Cal. Inq. p.m.* ix, p. 183; xi, p. 353; xii, p. 1; see above, p. 73.

[24] *Rot. Hund.* (Rec. Com.), ii. 838; *Feud. Aids*, iv. 158; see above, p. 9.

[25] *Fines Oxon.* 73.

[26] *Close R.* 1268–72; cf. *Feud. Aids*, iv. 158, 169, 180.

[27] *Bk. of Fees*, 824.

[28] *Cal. Inq. Misc.* i, p. 261; see below, p. 326.

[29] *Cal. Inq. p.m.* i, p. 261; *Close R.* 1268–72, 582.

[30] *Rot. Hund.* ii. 838.

[31] *V.C.H. Bucks.* ii. 314; Eyton, *Salop.* vii. 187.

[32] *Rot. Hund.* (Rec. Com.), ii. 420; W. Farrer, *Feudal Cambs.* 65.

[33] *Cal. Inq. p.m.* ii, p. 220.

[34] *Feud. Aids*, iv. 158.

[35] Nichols. *Leics.* iv. 17.

[36] *Feud. Aids*, iv. 169.

'Oke' in Aston Clinton.[37] This Alice was the widow of a James who may have been an illegitimate son of James de Audley (d. 1272).[38] She was succeeded at Hardwick and Aston by her son William de Audley,[39] who at his death in 1365 held Hardwick jointly with his wife Joan.[40] The manor was taken into the king's hands in error, but Joan recovered possession in 1366,[41] and held Hardwick until her death in 1382. In 1383 the manor was placed in the custody of Sir William de Drayton during the minority of Elizabeth, daughter of William de Audley's brother Thomas.[42] Elizabeth and her husband John Rose (d. 1410) held the Audley lands in Aston Clinton,[43] but the descent of Hardwick is unknown until 1428, when it appears in the possession of the Arden family.

William Arden held Hardwick in 1428,[44] and either he or a successor of the same name entailed the manor to his heirs male. In 1468, however, after the death of John, son and successor of William Arden, the entail was broken by John's son William, who conveyed the manor to himself and a number of feoffees to the use of himself and his heirs general.[45] William left four daughters, but William Rede, grandson and heir of Edmund Rede,[46] one of the feoffees of 1468, held Hardwick and allowed John Arden's widow Margery, and William's brother and heir male Robert, to have possession. In 1492 after a Chancery suit William Rede was ordered to surrender the manor to William Arden's daughters, Margery, wife of William Gygour, Juliana, wife of William Pope, Eleanor and Elizabeth.[47] One of the daughters seems to have died by 1496, when Juliana and her husband[48] held a third of Hardwick.[49]

In 1514 William Fermor of Somerton purchased a third part of Hardwick from Thomas Colyer and his wife Margery[50]—perhaps the Margery who had previously married William Gygour—and in 1523 William Spencer, son of Robert Spencer and Elizabeth Arden, released to Fermor his right to a share of the manor.[51] The remaining third part seems to have been held in 1511 by Edmund Bury, who conveyed it to Edward Chamberlain,[52] but William Fermor evidently acquired this share also by 1548, when he made a settlement of the whole manor. William was succeeded in 1552[53] by his nephew Thomas, who died in 1580.[54] When in 1606 Thomas's son Sir Richard Fermor acquired the manor of Tusmore, the two estates of Hardwick and Tusmore were united, and have since followed the same descent.[55]

LESSER ESTATES. A virgate of land in Hardwick was given by Ralph d'Aundeley to Oseney Abbey, which in turn granted it to the Hospitallers.[56] This may have been either the virgate held in 1279 by Robert le Newman of Gosford Hospital,[57] or land then held by Richard Bartlett of Hogshaw Hospital (Bucks.), which in 1279 was said to hold the advowson.[58] The later history of these small estates is not known, but it was probably the former connexion of the Hospitallers with Hardwick which led to the erroneous statement in 1580 that Thomas Fermor had held the manor of Thomas Pigott,[59] then lord of the manor of Hogshaw.[60]

ECONOMIC HISTORY. In the Domesday estate of $7\frac{1}{2}$ hides in Hardwick, part of which became attached to Tusmore,[61] there was land for 6 ploughs. But as the place was probably primarily a pastoral settlement there were only $3\frac{1}{2}$ plough-teams, one in demesne and $2\frac{1}{2}$ held by 5 villeins (villani), and 2 bordars. The value of the estate, £5, had not changed since the Conquest.[62] In 1279 Alice de Beauchamp held 2 carucates in demesne, and a water-mill worth 10s. a year.[63] Eight villeins held a virgate each, and worked and were tallaged at the lady's will. Two free tenants held the Gosford and Hogshaw properties,[64] perhaps a virgate each, for rents of 3s. and 8s. respectively. The total extent of the arable land was then perhaps 18 virgates. In 1272 the annual value of Hardwick had been £7,[65] and it changed little in the 14th century: £6 13s. 4d. in 1349 and in 1355.[66] In 1316 the village was combined with Ardley and Tusmore for purposes of taxation, but in 1327, when it was taxed independently, seventeen contributors paid £2 0s. 8d., and the parish was among the poorest in Ploughley hundred.[67] Its contribution to the 15th was raised in 1334 to £2 9s. 10d.,[68] and in 1347 the men of Hardwick petitioned the king, pleading that there were only nine poor tenants in the village and that the new assessment was far too heavy for them to bear. They asked that the village might be reassessed, and that they might receive a rebate on the 15th granted in 1344. If they received no redress, they would be forced to leave their holdings and to abandon the village.[69] The petition evidently failed, for Hardwick's assessment remained unchanged.[70]

Although the village was less severely ravaged by the Black Death than the neighbouring village of Tusmore it suffered sufficiently badly to be allowed an abatement of 3s. in 1354 out of its total tax of 49s. 10d., a comparatively high relief for the

37 Cal. Inq. p.m. viii, p. 217; V.C.H. Bucks. ii. 316.
38 V.C.H. Bucks. ii. 314; for the identities of five contemporary James de Audleys see Hist. Collect. Staffs. N.S. ix. 245 sqq.
39 Feud. Aids, iv. 190; Cal. Inq. p.m. ix, p. 183.
40 Cal. Inq. p.m. xii, p. 1.
41 Cal. Close, 1364–8, 582.
42 Cal. Fine R. 1377–83, 352.
43 V.C.H. Bucks. ii. 314.
44 Feud. Aids, iv. 190.
45 C 1/314/57. The recovery was by writ of right.
46 Boarstall Cart. p. x.
47 C 1/314/57.
48 Wm. Pope of Deddington: Oxon. Visit. 151.
49 C.P. 40/938, m. 160; cf. ibid. 963, m. 124.
50 C 1/311/31.
51 C 54/391/17.
52 C.P. 25(2)/34/225, Mich. 3 Hen. VIII.
53 C 142/98/54; P.C.C. F 29 Powell: Wm. Fermor's will.
54 For the Fermors see below, p. 293; P.C.C. 30 Arundell.

55 See below, p. 336.
56 Oseney Cart. v. 449.
57 Rot. Hund. (Rec. Com.), ii. 838. For Gosford Hospital (not in V.C.H. Oxon. ii) see Dugd. Mon. vi (2). 802; Mary Stapleton, Three Oxon Parishes (O.H.S. xxiv), 125–6.
58 Rot. Hund. (Rec. Com.), ii. 838; for Hogshaw Hospital see V.C.H. Bucks. i. 390.
59 C 142/190/66.
60 V.C.H. Bucks. iv. 55.
61 See above, p. 169.
62 V.C.H. Oxon. i. 414.
63 Rot. Hund. (Rec. Com.), ii. 838.
64 See above.
65 C 132/41/2.
66 C 135/96/10; ibid. 184/1.
67 E 179/161/8, 9.
68 E 179/161/17.
69 Rot. Parl. ii. 184. The assessment according to the petition was £2 9s. 11d.
70 e.g. E 164/7.

hundred.[71] In 1377 its adult population was only 37,[72] and by 1428 there were fewer than ten resident householders in the village.[73] Sixteenth-century subsidy lists reflect the consolidation of estates in the hands of the Fermor family: there were seven contributors in 1524, two of them men of considerable means.[74]

Inclosure probably started early in Hardwick. In 1515 a tenant of William Fermor and Richard Samwell was alleged to have allowed the decay of a messuage, and to have converted 40 acres of arable to pasture.[75] By 1520, however, the house had been rebuilt.[76] Sheep were evidently being kept, for in 1533 William Mortimer of Hardwick made several bequests in sheep[77] and in 1606 Sir Richard Fermor exercised his right to graze 400 sheep from Hardwick on lands in Cottisford.[78] In 1573 Thomas Fermor unsuccessfully tried to induce Eton College to divide 300 acres of arable, 10 acres of meadow, 100 acres of heath, and 30 acres of moor in Hardwick and Cottisford, which he said they held jointly with him, so that they might be inclosed.[79] Nevertheless there had been some inclosure by 1601, when Rye Close, New Close, and others are mentioned.[80]

From two 17th-century glebe terriers and two 19th-century maps something of the topography of Hardwick before inclosure had gone very far can be reconstructed.[81] There were still three open fields in 1601:[82] Heath Field in the north-east of the parish, bounded by Hardwick Heath; Tinker's Field in the north-west, and Mill Field in the south-west. Posey meadow lay on the southern boundary, and east of the stream flowing south from the fishponds was Stoney Holms pasture. In the arable fields were 'powles' or strips of mowing ground, 18 feet wide in one instance. Woodland lay along the boundary with Tusmore,[83] while the Heath occupied the extreme north-east of the parish. There was a cow pasture called Bayard's Green—evidently part of the large stretch of waste ground of that name which extended into several neighbouring parishes.[84] Between 1601 and 1682 closes were taken out of Mill Field and Heath Field[85] and by about 1717 the latter appears to have been entirely inclosed.[86] The inclosure of Mill Field and Tinker's Field seems to have been completed early in the 18th century, for in 1784 the parish was described as inclosed 'from time immemorial'.[87]

In the 18th century the Fermors kept only the woods and a few closes in hand: the manor farm and the greater part of the parish was let to the Day

family, and at the beginning of the century there was one other very small farm.[88] In 1857 Manor farm occupied some 430 acres out of the 452 acres of the Hardwick estate, and there was still only one farm in the parish in 1939.[89] The later inclosures in the parish remained arable land in the 19th century: in 1849 there were 253 acres of arable to 96 acres of meadow and pasture in the lands covered by the tithe award.[90] The land was particularly suitable for wheat, barley, and turnips[91]—Hardwick lies just within that part of Oxfordshire noted for its barley and for its sheep. By 1939, however, there only remained a little over 80 acres of arable, and in the north-east of the parish land formerly cultivated had gone back to the heath from which it had been won.[92]

Hardwick has always been one of the least populous places in the hundred. The Compton Census (1676) recorded 23 adults. In the 18th century incumbents reported that there were 2 houses and 3 cottages in 1738; 6 cottages and the farm-house in 1759, and 11 houses in 1771.[93] There was the usual increase in population in the early 19th century and by 1821, the peak year, there were 17 houses and 98 inhabitants, an increase of 37 over the figure for 1801. Thereafter numbers declined, and by 1901 there were only 11 inhabited houses for 46 people. In 1951 the population was forty-one.[94]

CHURCH. A grant was made of Hardwick tithes in the late 11th century (see below), but as Hardwick was a chapelry of Stoke Lyne in the mid-12th century, the grant is not certain evidence for the existence of a church other than that of Stoke Lyne. Hardwick chapel is first mentioned in the mid-12th century, when it was granted with Stoke Lyne by Walter Giffard to Notley Abbey.[95] This grant does not seem to have taken effect, and by 1249 or 1250 when the lord of the manor, William d'Aundeley, presented, Hardwick was a separate church.[96] Two years later the advowson was in the hands of the Knights Hospitallers, although no record of any grant has been found.[97] The Prior of St. John's, Clerkenwell, the English head of the order, presented throughout the Middle Ages,[98] with one exception in 1482, when the bishop collated by lapse. An attempt by a clerk in 1344 to get possession of the living with a fraudulent royal presentation had been unsuccessful.[99] After the suppression of the Hospitallers in 1540, Henry VIII in 1545 sold the advowson to John Pope of London,[1] with whom the lord of the manor, William Fermor, was associated.[2] The latter

[71] See below, p. 358; E 179/161/30; E 164/7. (This is an assessment for 1415, but after 1334 assessments remained fixed.)
[72] E 179/161/39.
[73] *Feud. Aids*, iv. 201.
[74] E 179/161/176.
[75] *Dom. of Incl.* i. 367. The editor's suggestion that Hardwick near Bicester is intended is supported by the fact that Samwell held land in the neighbouring parish of Cottisford.
[76] C 43/28/58.
[77] Blo. *Hard.* 46.
[78] E.C.R. no. 176.
[79] Ibid. no. 230.
[80] Oxf. Archd. Oxon. c 141, p. 345.
[81] Ibid. pp. 345, 349; Bodl. Tithe award map; plan in *Sale Cat.* (1857): Bodl. G.A. Oxon. b 85*b* (57).
[82] Cf. H. L. Gray, *Eng. Field Systems*, 492.
[83] Cf. Davis, *Oxon. Map* (1797).
[84] e.g. see below, pp. 314, 319.
[85] Oxf. Archd. Oxon. c 141, pp. 345, 349.

[86] Inference from comparison of field names in O.R.O. Reg. of Papists' Estates, pp. 86–87, and sources cited in n. 81 above.
[87] Oxf. Dioc. c 434, f. 96.
[88] O.R.O. Reg. Papists' estates, pp. 86–87, 93–94.
[89] Bodl. G.A. Oxon. b 85*b* (57).
[90] Bodl. Tithe award map.
[91] Bodl. G.A. Oxon. b 85*b* (57).
[92] O.S. land utilization map 1″, sht. 94.
[93] Oxf. Dioc. d 553, d 556, d 562.
[94] *Census*, 1801–1951.
[95] Dugd. *Mon.* vi (1), 278.
[96] Rot. *Grosse.* 497.   [97] Ibid. 501.
[98] In 1279 the advowson was said to belong to the house of the Hospitallers at Hogshaw (Bucks.) (*Rot. Hund.* (Rec. Com.), ii. 838), but it never presented. For a list of medieval presentations see MS. Top. Oxon. d 460.
[99] Linc. Reg. vi, Beke, f. 84*b*.
[1] *L. & P. Hen. VIII*, xx (1), p. 123, where it is mistakenly said to belong to Plympton Priory.
[2] C 54/436/29.

had in fact already presented in 1532 by reason of a grant from the Hospitallers. The advowson then descended with the manor, the Fermors presenting until the mid-19th century.[3] Since 1841 the living has been held with Tusmore, and in 1932 the two parishes were united. Since 1867 Hardwick and Tusmore have been held with Cottisford.[4] The patron in 1955 was the Hon. R. H. Vivian Smith, son of Lord Bicester.

In 1254, when the rectory was valued at 10s., it was the poorest in the deanery.[5] In 1291 it was valued at 33s. 4d. and in 1535 at £5.[6] Until the late 17th century the rector continued to get his income from tithes and glebe,[7] but by 1706 these had been commuted for an annual sum of £20, to be paid by the lord of the manor; the net value of the living was only about £15.[8] In 1784 a new arrangement was made by which the £20 was increased to £27 9s., estimated as the equivalent of 3s. in the pound on the rent of the land. The rector was in addition promised the sinecure of the living at Tusmore.[9] In 1780 the value of the living was further augmented with £200 from Queen Anne's Bounty,[10] and in 1849 the tithes were again commuted for £101 10s.[11]

The glebe in the 17th century consisted of a yard-land in the common fields,[12] but efforts made in the 1780's to locate it were unavailing, the two 17th-century terriers 'very much contradicting each other'.[13] The rector's claims to glebe were extinguished by the agreement of 1784.[14] He also had glebe, three 'lands' in Hardwick Field in Hethe, which was commuted at the Hethe inclosure in 1772.[15]

Robert d'Oilly gave two-thirds of his demesne tithes in Hardwick to the church of St. George in Oxford castle,[16] and these in 1149 were transferred with St. George's to Oseney Abbey.[17] In 1291 and 1428 they were valued at 6s. 8d., but by the 16th century at 3s. 4d.[18] In 1502 the abbot successfully sued the rector, Thomas Wright, for twelve years' arrears of this sum.[19] In 1542 this pension was granted to Christ Church.[20]

Hardwick was always too poor a living to support properly a resident priest, and the very large number, nearly 40, of medieval rectors implies that the living was very difficult to fill. However, services were said to be held regularly in the late 16th century,[21] although the parish was so poor that it could not provide a bible in the church. The rector himself promised to give one.[22] At this time there was a Rectory House, and rectors were living there as late as 1665, though by 1679 it was a ruin.[23]

By the 18th century weekly services were no longer held: Rawlinson noted that divine service was read once a month 'if there be any auditors'.[24] During the early part of the century the rector paid curates a crown a Sunday to hold these monthly services.[25] George Sheppard (1739-84), for instance, who held the living 'for a young gentleman now at Oxford', vainly besought neighbouring incumbents to take the duty for this sum.[26] A Mr. Fletcher, whom he finally secured, proved not to be in priest's orders, and was forbidden by the bishop to officiate further.[27] The bishop had already in 1739 written a 'sharp letter' to Sheppard, urging him to hold weekly services.[28] Although Sheppard promised to do so, a service once a fortnight seems to have been the usual practice until the early 19th century.[29] This unusual situation was due to the fact that the patron and most of the parishioners were Roman Catholics;[30] for many years even the churchwardens (there was only one at a time) belonged to the Roman Catholic families of Day and Collingridge.[31] In 1746 it was said that seldom could more than three or four church members, and never more than six, be assembled;[32] and in the early 19th century there were seven. These were said never to have expressed dissatisfaction with the services.[33] By the mid-19th century regular services were being held for a small congregation: in 1854 about twenty was the average number.[34]

The church of *ST. MARY* comprises a chancel, nave, and south aisle, with a south porch and western bell-turret. A late 12th- or early 13th-century doorway forms the main (south) entrance to the church and an ancient stoup, discovered built into some masonry, has been placed inside it. The chancel is 14th century with three original windows including a three-light east window and a low side window. There is a priest's door and piscina. The nave, also originally 14th century, is now mainly 15th century, with a fine west window.[35] The South aisle and its arcade, the porch and bell-turret are 19th century.

When Rawlinson visited the church in about 1718 he noted it as a 'small chapel going to decay'.[36] In 1757 some minor repairs to the fabric were ordered;[37] in 1812 it was declared to be 'out of repair';[38] in 1847 the rural dean reported the state of the church as 'moderately decent'.[39] In 1877 the 2nd Earl of Effingham[40] undertook at his sole charge a thorough restoration and also the enlargement of the church

³ For list of presentations see Blo. *Hard.* 52–53.
⁴ See above, p. 170; Oldfield, Clerus Oxon.
⁵ Lunt, *Val. Norw.* 312.
⁶ *Inq. Non.* (Rec. Com.), 133; *Valor Eccl.* (Rec. Com.), ii. 161.
⁷ Blo. *Hard.* 54–56: terriers of 1601, 1682.
⁸ Oxf. Dioc. c 155, f. 30.
⁹ Ibid. c 434, ff. 96–96b; ibid. c 327, p. 56.
¹⁰ *Papers Rel. to Queen Anne's Bounty, 1703–1815*, H.C. 115 (1814–15), xii.
¹¹ Bodl. Tithe award.
¹² Blo. *Hard.* 54–56: terriers of 1601, 1682.
¹³ Oxf. Dioc. c 327, p. 56; ibid. c 434, f. 96.
¹⁴ Blo. *Hard.* 56.
¹⁵ Ibid. (terrier of 1682); Blo. *Hethe*, 31–32 (terrier of 1679).
¹⁶ *Oseney Cart.* iv. 26; *Oxon. Charters*, no 58.
¹⁷ *V.C.H. Oxon.* ii. 160.
¹⁸ *Tax. Eccl.* (Rec. Com.), 31; *Feud. Aids*, vi. 380; *Oseney Cart.* vi. 242.
¹⁹ *Oseney Cart.* v. 450; C.P. 40/962, m. 423.
²⁰ *L. & P. Hen. VIII*, xvii, p. 491.

²¹ *Archd. Ct.* 142.
²² Ibid. 102.
²³ Blo. *Hard.* 54–55; *Hearth Tax Oxon.* 205; see above, p. 169.
²⁴ *Par. Coll.* ii. 164.
²⁵ Oxf. Dioc. c 651, f. 41.
²⁶ Ibid. ff. 27, 41.
²⁷ Ibid. f. 82.   ²⁸ Ibid. f. 40.
²⁹ Ibid. c 327, pp. 56, 298; ibid. b 11.
³⁰ See below, p. 173.
³¹ Blo. *Hard.* 56–57.
³² Oxf. Dioc. c 652, ff. 105–6.
³³ Ibid. c 659, f. 99.
³⁴ *Wilb. Visit.*
³⁵ On the NW. wall of the nave is a corbel shield of the Sydenham arms. For blazons of other arms see Bodl. G.A. Oxon. 16⁰ 217, p. 153.
³⁶ *Par. Coll.* ii. 64.
³⁷ Oxf. Archd. Oxon. d 13, f. 33b.
³⁸ Ibid. c 73, f. 206.
³⁹ Blo. *Hard.* 49–50.
⁴⁰ See below, p. 336.

in accordance with the plans of Sir George Gilbert Scott. The work was carried out on the death of Sir George by his son G. G. Scott between 1878 and 1879 at a cost of £2,000. The completed building was a notable example of mid-Victorian restoration. The chancel walls were scarcely touched, but the nave was largely rebuilt: as far as possible the timbers of the old roof were preserved and the west window, the greater part of which had been blocked up, was restored to its original size.[41] The south aisle, porch, and bell-turret were added. A new altar, font (from Fringford church), pulpit, and lectern were provided: the woodwork is good. An organ was added in 1900.

There are two panels of medieval glass (Christ in majesty and the Crucifixion) in the west window, and there is ancient glass in the three top lights of the east window.[42]

There are inscriptions to Capt. Francis Hereman (d. 1687); Ralph Hatton (d. 1694/5) and Mary his wife (d. 1717); Ann, wife of Nicholas Saers of London (d. 1721); Samuel Tooley (d. 1721/2); and three to members of the Freeman family: Ursula (d. 1726/7), her son Basil (d. 1722), and his wife Winifred (d. 1751). There is a brass to Henry Howard, 2nd Earl of Effingham (d. 1889), and a brass and memorial window to Eliza, Countess of Effingham (d. 1894). Inscriptions to Ann, wife of William Lyne (d. 1622/3), John Pennington (d. 1680), and Pascha Bat (d. 1672) are no longer visible,[43] nor are those to the 18th-century Roman Catholic Days,[44] though there are floor slabs to other Roman Catholic families.

In 1552 the church possessed a small silver chalice and paten.[45] In 1955 it had some fine plate, given by the earls of Effingham in the late 19th and 20th centuries: a beautiful Elizabethan silver chalice (1562) and paten cover; a silver tankard flagon (1704), from a London church; a large early 18th-century paten; and a tray and two cruets, the latter apparently of Spanish workmanship.[46]

There were in 1552 two bells and a sanctus bell, the last provided by a bequest from William Baker (1533). In 1955 one bell hung in the turret: probably originally an early 14th-century bell, it was recast in 1873.[47]

The registers begin in 1760, and there are incomplete transcripts from 1739.

NONCONFORMITY. Hardwick is an interesting example of an out-of-the-way village in which propitious circumstances permitted a small Roman Catholic community to flourish throughout much of the post-Reformation period. The lords of the manor, the Roman Catholic family of Fermor, settled at Tusmore since the first half of the 17th century, naturally favoured tenants of their own faith. In the late 16th and early 17th centuries few recusants, besides the Smiths, a family of husbandmen, were recorded,[48] but members of four families were noted in 1706;[49] and by the 1760's there were over 30 Roman Catholics, more than half the population.[50] The proportion remained high: in 1796 the 'greatest part' of the inhabitants were Roman Catholics;[51] in 1802 there were 53 out of 61;[52] in 1823 78 out of 98.[53] The proportion later declined, and in 1854 under half the population was said to be Roman Catholic.[54]

In the 18th century the Hardwick community probably attended the Fermors' chapel at Tusmore, but in 1768, while Tusmore House was being rebuilt, the local centre for worship became 'Farmer Day's', i.e. Hardwick Manor Farm.[55] From this time at least until 1790, there seems to have been a resident priest there, as the Days, and after them the Collingridges, the tenants of the farm, were well-known Catholic families.[56] In 1772 a large group of people was confirmed at Hardwick.[57]

When William Fermor left Tusmore in 1810, the chapel in Hardwick Manor Farm, a long attic running the length of the house, fitted with furnishings from Tusmore, was the Roman Catholic centre for the neighbourhood.[58] From 1810 until his death in 1830 the Revd. Samuel Corbishley was in charge of the mission; he ran a school and began to keep careful registers. His death was a blow to the local community and led to the building of the church at Hethe,[59] for although Fermor had died in 1828, it was understood that his non-Catholic heirs would not disturb the chapel at Hardwick during Corbishley's lifetime.[60]

The church and graveyard of the parish church were used by the Roman Catholics of Somerton and Tusmore as their burying-ground:[61] they have many gravestones there, on some of which there is undisguisedly Roman Catholic phraseology.

There is no record of Protestant dissent.[62]

SCHOOL. A free school which taught children to read in 1818 had disappeared by 1833.[63] The mistress of a school mentioned in 1854 was paid by the Hon. P. Barrington of Tusmore Park.[64] In 1870 the Earl of Effingham financed the building of a new school, and continued to maintain it.[65] It had 24 pupils in 1887, but never appears to have been recognized as a public elementary school.[66] It closed at some date between 1895 and 1903 and the children were sent to the schools at Hethe and Cottisford.[67]

CHARITIES. None known.

[41] Blo. *Hard.* 51. Drawings by J. C. Buckler (1824–5) in MS. Top. Oxon. a 67, ff. 299, 300, show the church before restoration, with only nave and chancel, and the west window partly blocked.

[42] For medieval glass in the chancel windows in 1660 see Blo. *Hard.* 46–47. Rawlinson describes the heraldic glass in 1718: *Par. Coll.* ii. 164–5; Bodl. G.A. Oxon. 4° 685, p. 165.   [43] *Par. Coll.* ii. 165.

[44] Members of the family are said to have been buried in the chancel: Stapleton, *Cath. Miss.* 84.

[45] *Chant. Cert.* 79   [46] Evans, *Ch. Plate.*

[47] *Ch. Bells Oxon.* ii. 155.

[48] C.R.S. xxii. 111; Salter, *Oxon. Recusants*, 16, 21, 26, 37.   [49] *Oxoniensia*, xiii. 79.

[50] Oxf. Dioc. c 431; ibid. d 562, d 564.

[51] Ibid. b 11.   [52] Ibid. d 566.

[53] Ibid. d 580.   [54] *Wilb. Visit.*

[55] Oxf. Dioc. d 559.

[56] Ibid. d 562; d 564; ibid. b 37; ibid. c 327, p. 298.

[57] Stapleton, *Cath. Miss.* 41.   [58] Ibid. 81.

[59] See below, p. 181.

[60] Stapleton, *Cath. Miss.* 81–83, 85.

[61] Ibid. 84.

[62] The Compton Census of 1676 records 17 conformists and 6 Protestant nonconformists. It seems likely that 6 papists is meant.

[63] *Educ. of Poor*, 725; *Educ. Enq. Abstract*, 747.

[64] *Wilb. Visit.*; *Kelly's Dir. Oxon.* (1854).

[65] *Kelly's Dir. Oxon.* (1887).

[66] Ibid.; the official figure of 52 pupils in 1871 can hardly be correct: *Elem. Educ. Ret.*

[67] *Kelly's Dir. Oxon.* (1895, 1903).

HETHE

THE ancient parish covered 1,102 acres of which 4 were a detached part lying in Hardwick and 196 were part of the intermixed lands (634 a.) shared with Cottisford, which were also detached and lay to the north of Cottisford.[1] In 1888 523 acres including Willaston hamlet were transferred to Hethe from Mixbury parish, but Hethe lost the 4 detached acres to Hardwick.[2] In 1932 all the intermixed lands were given to Cottisford,[3] so that the present (1955) area of the parish is 1,425 acres.[4] It lies about five miles north of Bicester and just west of the Bicester–Buckingham road, with which it is indirectly connected by two minor roads. In 1738 it was said that the parish's 'greatest length is not above a tolerable mile, the greatest breadth not half a mile, in some parts not a quarter'.[5] Geologically it lies partly on the Great Oolite and partly on the Cornbrash, both covered except in the south-east by drift gravel.[6] A small stream, which is crossed by a bridge in the village, crosses the parish and joins a tributary of the Ouse which forms its southern boundary. The ground rises sharply from the bridge on the west and less steeply on the east to a plateau a little under 400 feet above sea-level.

The position of the village,[7] somewhat on the eastern side of the parish, is determined by the stream which divides it into two distinct parts, and a well, St. George's well, which very possibly gave its name to the 13th-century family of *ad Fontem*,[8] and was still noted in 1718. The name Hethe means 'uncultivated ground' (OE *hæþ*)[9] and the earliest settlement may have been on the eastern side of the stream, where there are still a small number of houses. When, however, the first church was erected in the 12th century,[10] it was placed a good distance back on the upland ridge, to the west of the stream. The names of 13th-century inhabitants,[11] Henry Ate Streme, Geoffrey Bywundedbrok, Roger Ate Brugge, attest that there were houses by the stream side and the bridge, although there was at least one villager, Roger Ate Hulle, who was living by the church. Gradually the church became linked up with the original settlement by a chain of dwellings which today (1955) form a continuous street almost to the old bridge of two arches.[12] The returns for the hearth tax of 1662 listed 25 houses, but few were of any size. In 1665 only one house returned four hearths and the rest only two or one.[13] In 1738 there were said to be about 49 houses, occupied by small farmers, day labourers, and craftsmen.[14] Eighteenth- and early 19th-century building increased the number of houses to 67 in 1811 and 94 in 1851. In 1901

there were only 84 inhabited houses.[15] Since then rebuilding, particularly after the Second World War, has brought the number of houses up to well over a hundred.[16]

Most of the buildings are two-storied cottages, built of rubble, with thatch or Welsh slate roofs. The so-called Round House, the newer part of which dates from 1752, is unusual, but the only houses of any note are the Old Rectory and Hethe House. The former is first mentioned in 1679 as 'one mansion house together with the yard, garden and one pightle or little close thereunto annexed'.[17] In 1813 the churchwardens reported that the house was under repair.[18] It stands just west of the church and is built of coursed rubble; it was burnt out in 1928 and restored and refitted internally. Hethe House, the former dower house of Shelswell, also built of rubble, with a Welsh slate roof, was built in the 18th century. Part of its premises are today used for village meetings. The fact that Hethe was owned by the lords of Shelswell in the 18th century also accounts for the fact that part of Shelswell Park and Shelswell Plantation lies in the parish. Beyond the Old Rectory stands the 'Whitmore Arms', named after Thomas Whitmore, a member of a Shropshire family, who resided at Hethe House from 1808 to 1811. Before that it was called the 'Maltster's Arms'.[19] The chief 19th-century additions were the village school, the stone-built Roman Catholic church, with its presbytery and school, and the Methodist chapel.[20]

The village is surrounded by a cluster of farms: Nestleton (or Wesselden in *c.* 1575),[21] Mansfield, and Hospital Farm. The last is named from the hide of land in Hethe owned by St. Bartholomew's Hospital since the 12th century.[22] It was described in 1617 as a building measuring 40 by 18 feet. It had a hall, 'a chamber therein', a buttery, and a garret above, divided into three rooms and reached by a pair of stairs. Its barn measured 40 by 20 feet and its stable 60 by 12 feet.[23] Glebe Farm lies away from the village near the western boundary, and Willaston Farm, now on the eastern boundary, marks the site of a lost hamlet which was once in Mixbury parish.[24]

Perhaps the chief interest of the parish's history has been its long connexion with St. Bartholomew's Hospital in London,[25] and with a distinguished medieval scholar, Master Adam de Senestan.[26]

MANOR. At the time of the Conquest and for some years afterwards *HETHE* was held by the thegn

---

[1] O.S. Map 6", xi, xvii (1885); *Census*, 1881. See map above, facing p. 1.
[2] *Census*, 1891; *Local Govt. Bd. Orders 21435–6*: copies in O.R.O.
[3] *Census*, 1931; *Oxon. Review Order* (1932): copy in O.R.O.
[4] O.S. Map 2½", 42/52, 53, 62 (1951).
[5] Oxf. Dioc. d 553.
[6] G.S. Map 1", xlv NE.
[7] O.S. Map 25", xvii. 6 (1881).
[8] St. Bart.'s Hosp. deeds, *passim*.
[9] *P.N. Oxon.* (E.P.N.S.), i. 217.
[10] See below, p. 179.
[11] *Rot. Hund.* (Rec. Com.), ii. 837.
[12] Architectural evidence.

[13] *Hearth Tax Oxon.* 193, 235.
[14] Oxf. Dioc. d 553.
[15] *Census*, 1811, 1851, 1901.
[16] Inf. Ploughley R.D.C.: 22 houses were built 1947–54. In 1951 there were 96 houses: *Census*.
[17] Oxf. Archd. Oxon. b 40, f. 161.
[18] Ibid. c 75, f. 90.
[19] Blo. *Hethe*, 16–17.
[20] *Kelly's Dir. Oxon.* (1920).
[21] *P.N. Oxon.* (E.P.N.S.), i. 218.
[22] See below, p. 176.
[23] St. Bart.'s Hosp. Repertory bk. f. 74.
[24] *P.N. Oxon.* (E.P.N.S.), i. 218; see below, p. 252.
[25] See below, p. 176.
[26] Ibid. p. 179.

Wulfward the White, who also held Finmere. By 1086, however, when it was assessed at 8 hides, it was in the possession of Geoffrey, Bishop of Coutances.[27] On the death of Geoffrey in 1093 his estates passed to his nephew Robert de Mowbray, Earl of Northumberland, who was deprived of his possessions in 1095. Hethe may have been subsequently granted either by William II to Robert FitzHamon or by Henry I to his natural son Robert, Earl of Gloucester (d. 1147), for in the 13th century the manor was part of the honor of Gloucester.[28] From Gilbert de Clare, Earl of Gloucester (d. 1314), the overlordship of Hethe passed to his sister and coheiress Margaret and her second husband Hugh Audley, later Earl of Gloucester.[29] Hugh died in 1347; his daughter and heiress Margaret married Ralph Stafford, and the overlordship of Hethe then followed the descent of the Earldom of Stafford and Dukedom of Buckingham,[30] until the attainder and forfeiture of Edward, Duke of Buckingham, in 1521, when it reverted to the Crown. In 1576 the manor was said to be held of Queen Elizabeth as of her Duchy of Buckingham.[31]

In 1086 Geoffrey of Coutances's tenant of Hethe was a certain Roger.[32] Early in the 12th century the manor appears to have been the property of the wife of Geoffrey de Clinton of Glympton, Henry I's chamberlain. She gave the whole village as a marriage portion to her daughter Lesceline, wife of Norman de Verdun.[33] Norman, the son of Bertram de Verdun the Domesday tenant of Farnham Royal (Bucks.),[34] who probably came from Verdun in Vessey (Manche),[35] died about the beginning of Henry II's reign[36] and was survived by Lesceline, who gave a hide of land in Hethe to St. Bartholomew's Hospital, London.[37] Norman de Verdun's son and heir Bertram died on the Third Crusade in 1192 and was succeeded by his son Thomas, who confirmed Lesceline's gift to St. Bartholomew's.[38] On Thomas's death in 1199 his estates passed to his brother Nicholas, from whom Thomas's widow Eustachia and her second husband Richard de Camville claimed dower in 1200.[39] In 1204 Nicholas conceded Hethe to Eustachia as part of her dower.[40] Eustachia was dead by 1216, and the manor reverted to Nicholas,[41] who was succeeded in 1231 by his only daughter Rose,[42] widow of Theobald Butler and foundress of Grace Dieu Abbey (Leics.). Rose

died in 1247,[43] and her son and heir John took De Verdun as his surname. John was granted free warren at Hethe in 1258[44] and was succeeded in 1274 by his son Theobald,[45] who forfeited his estates for treason in 1291, but recovered them for a fine of 500 marks.[46] Theobald died in 1309[47] and his son Theobald in 1316.[48] During the minority of the latter's heirs his lands were placed in the custody of Roger Damory, who in 1317 married his widow, Elizabeth, a sister and coheiress of Gilbert de Clare, Earl of Gloucester (d. 1314).[49]

By his first wife, Maud Mortimer (d. 1312), the younger Theobald de Verdun left three daughters, Joan, Elizabeth and Margery, and in 1327 Hethe was put in the keeping of Bartholomew Burghersh, husband of Elizabeth.[50] A partition of the Verdun estates in 1328 awarded Hethe to Margery and her husband William Blount,[51] but in 1331 a fourth daughter Isabel, Theobald's posthumous child by his second wife, came of age and claimed her portion of the inheritance. By a new partition in 1332 Hethe fell to Isabel and her husband Henry, Lord Ferrers of Groby (d. 1343).[52] At Isabel's death in 1349, her son William was still a minor,[53] but he was granted Hethe with other manors for his maintenance.[54] William died in 1371,[55] and his son and successor Henry in 1388. A third part of Hethe was then held in dower by Henry's widow Joan until her death in 1394.[56] Henry's son William came of age in that year, and in 1442, three years before his death, he settled Hethe upon his younger son Thomas, and his heirs male.[57] Hethe then descended in the family of Ferrers of Tamworth,[58] passing from Thomas (d. 1459)[59] to his son Sir Thomas (d. 1498), who was succeeded by his grandson Sir John (d. 1512).[60] Sir John's grandson John Ferrers, son of Sir Humphrey Ferrers, held Hethe at his death in 1576.[61] In 1578 Humphrey may have mortgaged the manor to William Colmore,[62] and in 1595 there was a similar transaction by fine between Ferrers and John Chamberlayne and Rowland Lytton of Knebworth (Herts.).[63] This time the manor permanently left Ferrers' possession, and by 1606 had been acquired by Sir Rowland's brother-in-law, Sir Anthony Cope of Hanwell (d. 1615).[64] Sir Anthony's son, Sir William, held Hethe at his death in 1637,[65] but it is uncertain how long the Copes retained the manor, which by 1652 was in the hands of a London

[27] V.C.H. Oxon. i. 379, 427.
[28] e.g. Bk. of Fees, 824; Rot. Hund. (Rec. Com.), ii. 837; Feud. Aids, iv. 157.
[29] Cal. Inq. p.m. vi, p. 36; ibid. vii, p. 71.
[30] e.g. C 139/119.
[31] C 142/174/62.
[32] V.C.H. Oxon. i. 427.
[33] St. Bart.'s Hosp. deed, 1389.
[34] V.C.H. Bucks. i. 268.
[35] L. C. Loyd, Anglo-Norman Families (Harl. Soc. ciii), 109.
[36] Hist. Collect. Staffs. (1933), ii. 126.
[37] St. Bart.'s Hosp. deed, 1389.
[38] Hist. Collect. Staffs. (1933), ii. 126; N. Moore, Hist. St. Bartholomew's Hosp. i. 222.
[39] Cur. Reg. R. i. 261.
[40] Fines Oxon. 230.
[41] Rot. Litt. Claus. (Rec. Com.), i. 265; Close R. 1227–31, 412.
[42] Ex. e Rot. Fin. (Rec. Com.), i. 217, 218; Bk. of Fees, 449, 824.
[43] Ex. e Rot. Fin. ii. 7, 11.
[44] Cal. Chart. R. 1257–1300, 12; cf. Rot. Hund. (Rec. Com.), ii. 44.

[45] Cal. Inq. p.m. ii, p. 60; Rot. Hund. (Rec. Com.), ii. 837; Feud. Aids, iv. 157.
[46] Complete Peerage (orig. edn.), viii. 24.
[47] Cal. Inq. p.m. v, p. 96.
[48] Ibid. vi, p. 36; cf. Feud. Aids, iv. 169.
[49] Cal. Fine R. 1307–19, 294; Complete Peerage, iv. 43; see above, p. 58.
[50] Cal. Pat. 1327–30, 183.
[51] Cal. Inq. p.m. vii, p. 77.
[52] Ibid. pp. 78, 283 sqq.; Feud. Aids, iv. 180.
[53] Cal. Inq. p.m. ix, p. 299.
[54] Cal. Pat. 1348–50, 411.
[55] C 135/219.
[56] C 136/50, 51; ibid. 81/1; for the Ferrers descent see Complete Peerage, v. 344 sqq.
[57] C 139/119.
[58] See pedigree, Complete Peerage, v. 333.
[59] C 139/174.
[60] Cal. Inq. p.m. Hen. VII, ii, p. 85; C 142/27/109.
[61] C 142/174/62; cf. C 3/65/22.
[62] C.P. 25(2)/197/Mich. 20 Eliz.; cf. C 66/1267.
[63] C.P. 25(2)/198/Mich. 37 Eliz.
[64] E.C.R. nos. 178–9.
[65] C 142/486/148.

family, the Blakes,[66] who do not appear to have resided on their estate.[67] William Blake was lord of the manor in 1682, and in 1692 a Daniel Blake conveyed it to Joseph Biscoe, a London apothecary.[68] About 1719 Biscoe conveyed Hethe to Samuel Trotman of Bucknell,[69] from whom it appears to have passed to his brother Edward and to have subsequently followed the descent of Shelswell.[70] The present (1956) lord of the manor is John Francis Dewar-Harrison, Esq., of Willaston.[71]

LESSER ESTATE. At some date after 1167[72] Lesceline de Clinton granted in frankalmoign to St. Bartholomew's Hospital, Smithfield, a hide of land in Hethe. Her mother had bought it from a certain Baldric, who held by free tenure, and had given it to Lesceline as her marriage portion.[73] Thomas de Verdun (d. 1199), Lesceline's grandson, confirmed the grant to the hospital, reserving the homestead, as in the original grant, to the donor's use.[74] Henry III's charter of 1254 confirming the possession of its property to the hospital[75] does not mention Hethe or any other estates, but in 1279 it was recorded that a freeman, William de la Hyde,[76] held the St. Bartholomew's hide for 20s. and payment of scutage. The Master of the Hospital held of Theobald de Verdun in free alms. A few of the 14th-century leases made by the hospital have been preserved: in 1366, for instance, the master leased William 'atte Hide's' land to Rewley Abbey for 50 years at a rent of 20s. a year.[77] In 1397 John Baker 'of Oxfordshire' obtained a lease,[78] and later acquired other land in Hethe belonging to the Skynners.[79] Finally in 1439 John Derye became lessee at a rent of 10s. a year.[80]

St. Bartholomew's Hospital was dissolved in 1537 and all its property, including Hethe, seized by the Crown. In January 1547 the king returned all these lands to the hospital, which had been refounded.[81] It is probable that the tenancy of the hospital's property in Hethe was undisturbed by the Dissolution. Andrew Smith had obtained a lease of 31 years in 1520,[82] and he heads the subsidy list of 1525 for which he was one of the two sub-collectors.[83] His relations probably succeeded him: in 1551 Thomas Smythe was the tenant, and in 1561 Alice Smythe.[84] Alice was followed in 1563 by Henry Sprawson of Hethe, who remained the tenant until 1583.[85] Since 1439 the annual rent named was 10s., but there is no evidence for the size of the fine paid on entry.

In 1583 when Richard Rivers, servant to Sir John Rivers, took on the lease, the rent was raised to 40s., without a fine.[86] Rivers's successor, Oliver Pang-

bourne, yeoman, paid 40s. annual rent and a fine of £10 in 1603; in 1604 Robert Goodson, a husbandman, became the tenant, but two years later the lease was taken over by Sir Anthony Cope,[87] who about this time also acquired the manor. Goodson may have remained as Cope's tenant, however, for he was occupying the farm in 1617.[88] Cope died in 1615 before the expiry of his lease and his son, Sir William Cope, succeeded to it.[89]

In 1631 John Beaumond, husbandman, became the tenant, and paid an increased fine of £30.[90] Later tenants are listed by Blomfield. After 1720 the lords of the manor, first the Trotmans, then the Harrisons, were tenants. Before inclosure the estate consisted of about 59 acres. In 1648 the rent was raised to £4 and continued at this sum until the inclosure in 1773. Entry fines varied from £20 in 1648 to £60 in 1665, £105 in 1732 and £160 in 1754. After inclosure fines were abolished, but the rent was raised to £14 in 1773, £28 in the 1790's, £92 in 1810 as a result of the Napoleonic War, and £70 in 1831. In 1842 Richard Jones became tenant and was followed by William Bonner in 1872 and David Dagley in 1884. They paid rents of £100 in 1842, £70 in 1852, £90 in 1862, £110 in 1872, and £75 in 1884.[91]

ECONOMIC HISTORY. In 1086 there was land for 8 ploughs, although there were only 3 at work. Two were in demesne with one serf, and the other belonged to 8 villeins (villani) and 5 bordars.[92] There were 20 acres of pasture and the value of the estate was £8, as it had been in 1066.

In 1279 there were 2 carucates in demesne with adjacent meadow and pasture. There were 26 or 27 villein virgaters (servi), each of whom paid 9s. rent and owed work and tallage at will.[93] There were also two cottars, each holding a cotland for 12d. rent a year and work at will. The only two free tenants were William de la Hyde, who held of the Master of St. Bartholomew's Hospital,[94] and the Prior of Kenilworth, who held 1 virgate.[95] This may not have been a complete return of all the landholders in the parish, for in 1316 29 people were assessed for taxation. By that time Hethe, which paid £2 18s. 6d., was one of the more prosperous parishes in the hundred.[96] Its assessment for taxation after 1334 was still well above the average.[97]

In 1274 the manor was estimated to be worth £24 a year in all,[98] but extents made in 1327 and 1331 gave totals of £19 1s. and £18 13s. 3½d. respectively.[99] Early 14th-century estimates of the demesne lands varied from 80 to 140 acres of arable and 3 to 12

[66] C.P. 25(2)/587/Mich. 1652.
[67] Hearth Tax Oxon. 193.
[68] St. Bart.'s Hosp. deed, 1388; C.P. 43/437/49; O.R.O. Misc. Far. VIII/I.
[69] Par. Coll. ii. 173; C.P. 43/545/65.
[70] O.R.O. Gamekprs'. dep.; ibid. Land tax assess.
[71] Burke, Land. Gent. (1937), under Slater-Harrison; Kelly's Handbk. (1954).
[72] Among those mentioned in the grant who were to be prayed for was the Empress Matilda, who died in 1167.
[73] St. Bart.'s Hosp. deed, 1389.
[74] Ibid. 67.
[75] Cal. Chart. R. 1257–1300, 368–70.
[76] Rot. Hund. (Rec. Com.), ii. 837.
[77] St. Bart.'s Hosp. deed, 1382.
[78] Ibid. 1386.
[79] Ibid. 1385.
[80] Ibid. 1387.
[81] N. Moore, Hist. St. Bartholomew's Hosp. ii. 159.

[82] St. Bart.'s Hosp. Repertory bk. f. 33b.
[83] E 179/161/176.
[84] Blo. Hethe, 9.
[85] Ibid.
[86] Ibid. 10.
[87] Ibid. 10–11.
[88] A survey with map was made in 1617: St. Bart.'s Hosp. Repertory bk. f. 74.
[89] Ibid.
[90] Blo. Hethe, 11.
[91] Ibid. 11–15.
[92] V.C.H. Oxon. i. 427.
[93] The two 'Hugh Bachelers' may be a scribal error.
[94] See above.
[95] Rot. Hund. (Rec. Com.), ii. 837.
[96] E 179/161/8.
[97] e.g. E 164/7.
[98] C 133/7/1.
[99] C 135/7; ibid. 29/7.

acres of meadow, besides pasture. Arable was worth 4*d.* an acre, and meadow 3*s.* an acre in 1331 compared with 2*d.* and 1*s.* in 1309. The capital messuage with its dovecote and garden was worth 10*s.* in 1331.[1] In 1327 there were still 27 villeins, each holding a messuage and a virgate and paying a total of £12 13*s.* rent, and £1 2*s.* 6*d.* for labour services, evidently commuted since 1279. Seven cottagers paid 7*s.* 4*d.* rent and 5*s.* 10*d.* for works, and two free tenants owed only suit of court and the labour of eight men for one day at corn harvest, commuted for 8*d.* The principal works of the villeins had been reaping corn, and of the cottagers weeding and reaping corn, and lifting and tedding hay.[2]

The increase in population which had taken place since 1279 was sharply checked by the Black Death. In September 1349 it was reported that of 27 villeins 21 were dead and their lands lying untilled.[3] In 1371 the manor was said to be worth only £8 a year. The dower assigned to Margaret, widow of William de Ferrers, in that year included £2 0*s.* 8*d.* in rents from four free tenants paying from 4*s.* 10*d.* to 16*s.* 6*d.* each, and £2 5*s.* 8*d.* from three villeins.[4] There is no evidence of how many tenants there were whose rents were not assigned to Margaret, but it may be deduced that free tenants had replaced some of the dead villeins, that the number of tenants was lower than before 1349, and that holdings were probably larger. The value of the manor remained £8 a year into the first half of the 15th century,[5] but was only £5 in 1459.[6] In the 16th century it rose again to £9 10*s.* in 1513 and was over £10 by 1576.[7] The capital messuage is mentioned in 1349, but not in 1371, when only a toft is recorded,[8] and it is probable that the manor-house was abandoned by the lord after the death of Isabel Ferrers in 1349. In the 16th century the manor was held by lessees of the Ferrers family,[9] and in 1524 with thirteen people assessed for taxation Hethe was one of the villages with the lowest number of contributors, and the third smallest in taxable value in Ploughley hundred.[10]

In the 13th century the parish had two fields, the 'Home Field' and 'the field on the north of Hethe and Cottisford'. The last appears to be an early reference to the 'intermixed lands' shared by the two villages—an arrangement which one would expect to have originated at an early date.[11]

In the 14th century Hethe evidently still had two open fields, for in 1349 it was said that half the demesne arable was worth 3*d.* an acre when sown, while the other half which lay fallow was used as common pasture and was worth nothing to the lord.[12] About the beginning of the 17th century there were three fields called Berry Field, 'the second field', and 'the third field', of which the last appears to

have been much larger than the others.[13] A change seems to have been made before the survey made of the St. Bartholomew's Hospital estate in 1617, which shows that there were then four fields, 'the field on the west parte of the house', Hardwick Field (north-west of the village), Brede Field,[14] and 'Nast feilde'. The hospital had 10, 20, 9, and 9 acres of arable in the four fields, besides 11 acres of pasture and ¼ acre of meadow.[15] A terrier of 1679 shows that Brede Field comprised most of the first or Berry Field of the earlier terrier, that Hardwick Field represented the 'second field', and that the 'third field' had been divided into Nasthill Field and Leete Field, the latter being no doubt the field 'on the west part' of the hospital's farm-house. Part of the first field had retained the name Berry Field, so that there were five fields mentioned in 1679: Berry Field may, however, have been comparatively small.[16]

Part of the arable lands were detached and intermixed with Cottisford land lying to the north of Cottisford. In 1606 Sir Henry Savile complained that Sir Anthony Cope's Hethe tenants had encroached on land which formerly belonged to his Cottisford tenants—Hethe men had recently been going 'when and where they will in Cotsforde field to mark ground at their pleasure'. They had also taken advantage of this intermingling of land to pasture their sheep in Cottisford field 'contrary to all right'.[17] In the 18th century, however, Hethe people had right of common in a piece of land in Cottisford called 'Conigree' (60 a.) belonging to Eton College, perhaps the site of the post-inclosure Coneygre farm in Cottisford.[18]

In the late 16th century there was a large warren attached to some property called the Flats (360 a.), which adjoined Cottisford and belonged to Hethe manor. In a lease of 1594 Hethe tenants were allowed to 'hunt and hay' in their corn fields and to kill rabbits on the 'near' (probably the south) side of the brook in order to protect their corn, while the tenant of the warren undertook not to allow the rabbits to multiply to the excessive damage of the corn field, and to kill those that bred near the corn fields.[19] By the time of inclosure in the 18th century the warren had been divided. It was reported in 1682 that more than 40 years before Sir William Cope had taken 80 acres 'from the town of Heath' and turned it into a warren, on which he allowed the hospital's tenant to keep 80 sheep.[20] At the time of parliamentary inclosure in 1773 Hethe Warren, belonging to Fiennes Trotman, still consisted of 80 acres, and there was another piece of inclosed heath, nearly equal in size (75 a.), belonging to William Fermor and called Courtfield or Cottisfield, on which the landholders of Hethe had rights of common

[1] C 134/14/19; ibid. 56/1; C 135/7; ibid. 29/7.
[2] C 135/7.
[3] Ibid. 103/27.   [4] Ibid. 219.
[5] C 136/50; C 139/119.
[6] C 139/174.
[7] C 142/27/109; ibid. 174/62.
[8] C 135/103/27; C 135/219.
[9] C 3/65/11.
[10] E 179/161/176.
[11] St. Bart.'s Hosp. deed, 1377. See map above, facing p. 1.
[12] C 135/103/27. East Field which also occurs in 13th-cent. charters may have been an alternative name for

'le Homfeld'. Among other field names mentioned are 'Cotemannedich', 'Coppethornedich', and 'Akermanne-dich': St. Bart.'s Hosp. deeds, 1377, 1378, 1380.
[13] Oxf. Arch. Oxon. b 40, f. 162.
[14] Cf. Hethe Brede farm (in Stoke Lyne parish).
[15] St. Bart.'s Hosp. Repertory Bk. f. 74. Cf. ibid. C 19/1/1 (The plan Bk.).
[16] Oxf. Archd. Oxon. b 40, f. 161.
[17] E.C.R. nos. 178, 180; see above, p. 111.
[18] Incl. act (see below, n. 22), p. 13; O.S. Map 25″, xvii. 6 (1881).
[19] E.C.R. nos. 57, 59.
[20] St. Bart.'s Hosp. deeds 1388.

(extinguished at inclosure) and the poor had the right to cut fuel.[21] There was, however, comparatively little inclosure before the act of 1772, when there remained about 804 acres (39¼ yardlands) of open field and pasture. The preparation of the inclosure award was complicated by the rectors of Cottisford and Hardwick as well as the rector of Hethe having glebe lands and tithes in the parish. Under the award made in 1773 the largest allotment, 262 acres, went to Fiennes Trotman, the lord of the manor. The Rector of Hethe received 172 acres in all, but surrendered 4 acres which were sold for £80 towards the cost of his fences. St. Bartholomew's received 45 acres of which 3 acres were in lieu of its sheep commons on the Warren. The rectors of Cottisford and Hardwick got 3 and 5 acres; and of the ten other allotments there were three over 60 acres and three less than 5 acres.[22]

In 1760 the highest assessments for land tax had been of a Mr. Harden's land (£8) and the rector's (£5 16s.). Of 23 other occupiers of land nine were assessed at over £1. Thomas Trotman's assessment was only £1 16s., but in 1786 the then lord of the manor, Gilbert Harrison, was assessed at £8 15s., second only to the former Harden estate (£10).[23] In the county election of 1754 seventeen freeholders of Hethe, eleven of them resident, had voted.[24] In 1796 out of 20 occupiers assessed at under £1 seventeen owned their land. At that time the Harrison estate was by far the largest, assessed at £15 10s., and there were six estates assessed at between £1 10s. and £6. In the early 19th century the Harrison estate continued to grow, and the number of small owner-occupiers slowly decreased, falling to fourteen in the 1820's and to nine in 1832.[25] In 1939 Kelly listed five farms of which only one was over 150 acres. In 1956 there were seven farms and out of 1,142 acres of agricultural land 558 acres were grassland and 584 arable.[26]

Agriculture has always been the predominant occupation of the villagers. In 1738 it was reported that there were a few farmers and smallholders, 'the rest day labourers, and some handicrafts'.[27] In the 1630's there was a smith's forge belonging to the Webb family;[28] there was still one in the late 19th century.[29] In the late 16th century there was a mill belonging to the manor, but no later record of a mill has been found.[30] The early 19th-century parish registers record an innkeeper, a schoolmaster, a post boy, and the usual village craftsmen.[31] One female straw-hat-maker appears in 1852.[32] Throughout the century there were a number of small shopkeepers,[33] but by 1935 there were only four.[34] The parish registers show that many surnames which occur regularly during the 18th century persist well into the 19th century; others which appear in the 19th

century were still found in the village in 1955. But some, such as Mansfield, Heydon, Laurence, and Dagley, have been known in the parish for more than two centuries.

The population must have been comparatively large in the late 17th century if the figure of 203 adults recorded in the Compton Census of 1676 is accurate. The hearth tax returns of 1662 and 1665 show that the village was in comparison with the rest of the hundred so outstandingly poor that it seems as if it may have suffered from some recent disaster. The constables returned 21 persons in 1662 as 'poor people of whom no distress may be had'. Twenty-five others paid the tax, but of fifteen householders listed in 1665, six were exempted on grounds of poverty. There were less than 50 houses in 1738 and at the first official census in 1801 the population was 262. Numbers increased, and a peak figure of 442 was reached in 1861. A steady decline then set in and by 1901 there were 311 inhabitants. The population in 1921 was 283, but after the Second World War it increased and in 1954 was estimated to be 338.[35]

CHURCH. The church of Hethe was in existence during the lifetime of Norman de Verdun (d. c. 1154), if not earlier, and was given by his widow Lesceline to the priory (afterwards abbey) of Augustinian canons at Kenilworth, which had been founded by her father, Geoffrey de Clinton, in 1122.[36] This grant was confirmed by Lesceline's son Bertram de Verdun.[37] In 1206 Eustachia de Camville, who held Hethe manor in dower, and her second husband, Richard de Camville, tried unsuccessfully to recover the advowson, but had to admit it belonged to Kenilworth,[38] which presented throughout the Middle Ages. The abbey was dissolved in 1538, when the advowson came into the hands of Henry VIII. It has remained in the possession of the Crown ever since, but since the living was valued at under £20 in the King's Book, the Lord Chancellor had the right of presentation.[39] In 1924 the living was united to that of Fringford, also in the gift of the Lord Chancellor.[40]

The value of the church was £4 in 1254 and £6 13s. 4d. in 1291, while in 1535 its net value was £7 9s. 4½d.[41] When it was valued in 1716 it was worth £54.[42] When the parish was inclosed in 1773 the rector was awarded £120 for the tithes of Hethe Warren and about 172 acres of land, of which 121 acres were for the tithes, 4½ acres for the tithes on ancient inclosures, 25 acres for the tithes on William Fermor's land in Hethe and his 12 yardlands in Cottisford and an acre of glebe in Cottisford, and 22 acres for the rector's Hethe glebe.[43] At the same time the rector was freed from the obliga-

[21] Incl. act, pp. 10–12. The poor were provided with a charity in place of their right to fuel: see below, p. 181.
[22] O.R.O. Incl. award. The act is 12 Geo. III, c. 103 (priv. act) (copy in Bodl. L. Eng. C 13 c 1 (1772. i. 54)).
[23] O.R.O. Land tax assess.
[24] Oxon. Poll, 1754.
[25] O.R.O. Land tax assess.
[26] Kelly's Dir. Oxon. (1939); Inf. Oxon. Agric. Executive Cttee.
[27] Oxf. Dioc. d 553.
[28] C 142/761/113; ibid. 763/195.
[29] O.S. Map 25", xvii. 6 (1881).
[30] C.P. 25(2)/197/Mich. 20 Eliz.
[31] Par. Reg.
[32] Gardner, Dir. Oxon.
[33] Par. Reg.; Kelly's Dir. Oxon. (1854–1903).

[34] Kelly's Dir. Oxon. (1935).
[35] Hearth Tax Oxon. 193; E 179/255/4, no. 37; Oxf. Dioc. d 553; Census, 1801–1951; inf. Ploughley R.D.C.
[36] V.C.H. Warws. ii. 86.
[37] Dugd. Mon. vi (1), 222.
[38] Cur. Reg. R. iv. 146; ibid. v. 54. For list of medieval presentations see MS. Top. Oxon. d 460.
[39] E. Gibson, Codex Juris Ecclesiastici Anglicani (2nd ed. 1761), ii. 763–4; Clergy List (1852), 295.
[40] Bodl. Fringford Par. Box (uncat.): Order in Council.
[41] Lunt, Val. Norw. 311; Tax. Eccl. (Rec. Com.), 31; Valor Eccl. (Rec. Com.), ii. 160.
[42] Oxf. Dioc. c 155, f. 55Ab.
[43] O.R.O. Incl. award; 12 Geo. III, c. 103 (priv. act), pp. 10–11: copy in Bodl. L. Eng. C 13 c 1 (1772, i. 54).

tion of keeping a bull and a boar for the use of the inhabitants.[44] From that time the income of the living came from the land awarded at the inclosure, which was called Glebe farm. When it was surveyed in 1857 it was valued at £175.[45]

In the 14th century the glebe was valued at 6s. 8d.;[46] in the earliest terrier of 1601 it consisted of about 30 strips of land, scattered over the three open fields; in a later terrier of 1679, when there were four fields, the number of strips had slightly risen, and the rector had land in Cottisford.[47] At the time of the inclosure the glebe was reckoned as a yardland.[48]

There was a close connexion between Hethe, Cottisford, and Hardwick. The Rector of Hethe had two 'lands' or an acre of glebe in Cottisford, and there were twelve yardlands in Cottisford, belonging to William Fermor, which paid tithes to Hethe.[49] The Rector of Cottisford had two acres of glebe in Hethe, and was entitled to receive tithes from about eighteen 'lands' in Hethe,[50] the land of Eton College. There were also eight 'lands' in Hardwick which paid tithes to Cottisford,[51] while the Rector of Hardwick had three 'lands' of glebe in the field 'that joins to Hethe field', which may be the Hardwick Field in Hethe.[52] The confusion which might arise is illustrated by a dispute of about 1600 between Robert Petty of Tetsworth, who was farming the Hethe tithes, and the Rector of Cottisford.[53] At the inclosure some of these anomalies were straightened out, but the Rector of Hardwick later had trouble over his Hethe glebe.[54]

There was a priest at Hethe in the first half of the 12th century. His name is not known, but he had a son named Ralph who lived in the parish. Later in the century William the clerk of Hethe also had a son, who with his father witnessed a charter of Lescelinc de Clinton.[55] The most distinguished medieval rector was Master Adam de Senestan (1233–68), who was probably studying in Paris when he was presented to Hethe.[56] Said to be a good theologian and a man of great knowledge and abstinence, he was a benefactor of Oseney Abbey, to which he left his books and where he was buried.[57] No other medieval rector held the living for such a long period; indeed in the 15th century changes were very frequent. It is worth noting that Master John Sharp (1484–92) was a regular canon and possibly from Kenilworth Abbey.[58]

Of the post-Reformation clergy, mention must be made of Richard Evans (1646–99). Although he is said to have had royalist sympathies, he seems to have remained undisturbed throughout the Commonwealth period, for Anthony Wood saw him in Hethe in 1659.[59] His long incumbency of 52 years was distinguished for his constant residence.[60] The next five rectors followed Evans's good example,

but with the appointment in 1732 of James Edgecumbe, Rector of Exeter College, Oxford, from 1737 to 1750, a considerable period of non-residence opened. Fortunately for Hethe, however, John Warren, Edgecumbe's predecessor (1725–32), continued to reside in Hethe for another twenty years as curate to the absent rectors.[61] He was allowed the use of the parsonage house and received £20 a year salary. Warren was followed by a succession of curates-in-charge, but in 1769, with the institution of George Lamb, who remained rector until his death in 1801, Hethe again enjoyed a resident rector.[62] The rectors from 1801 to 1850 were again non-resident, with curates-in-charge: the curate in 1820 received £100.[63] After that until 1927, when the living was united to that of Fringford, residence once more prevailed.

In 1738[64] two services were held every Sunday, and the rector complained that there were 'very few holidays which will produce a congregation'. Holy Communion was celebrated four times a year for about twenty communicants. Lent catechizing was 'tolerably well' attended by the children. The few people (other than the handful of dissenters) who did not attend church were thought to absent themselves from 'poorness of dress and laziness'. In 1771[65] there was only one Sunday service; as the living was so small, Lamb said that he must serve two parishes, and for long he acted as curate of Cottisford. Holy Communion was still celebrated four times a year, with twenty to thirty communicants each time: in 1808[66] the number had fallen to fifteen. By 1820[67] matters had somewhat improved: two services were held every Sunday and the number of communicants had more than doubled. By 1854[68] there was a monthly celebration.

The small church of ST. EDMUND AND ST. GEORGE comprises a nave, north and south aisles, chancel, a western open belfry of wood surmounted by a spire, and a south porch. The church is in origin a 12th-century structure. Of this Romanesque church there survive the west wall of the nave and the south wall of the chancel, with a window and priest's doorway. The original chancel probably terminated in an apse, but early in the 13th century this was replaced by the existing square east end, with pilaster buttresses. A south aisle was added in the 14th century, and a new window with Decorated tracery was inserted in the east wall of the chancel. In 1859 this window was removed to the newly erected north aisle. The clerestory is an addition of the 15th century.

In 1634 the churchwardens reported the church to be in bad condition, but there is no record of structural repairs.[69] When Rawlinson visited the church in 1718 he noted the names of John Dagley

[44] Incl. act, p. 20.
[45] Bodl. Par. Box (uncat.): map.
[46] Inq. Non. (Rec. Com.), 133.
[47] Blo. Hethe, 29–32; Oxf. Archd. Oxon. b 40, ff. 161–2b. A third terrier, dated 1771, said to be in Bodl., has not been found.
[48] 12 Geo. III, c. 103 (priv. act), p. 2.
[49] Ibid.; Blo. Hethe, 32.
[50] Blo. Cot. 33; O.R.O. Hethe incl. award.
[51] Blo. Cot. 33.
[52] Blo. Hethe, 31; Blo. Hard. 56.
[53] See above, p. 111.
[54] Above, p. 172.
[55] St. Bart.'s Hosp. deed, 1389.
[56] Rot. Welles, ii. 42.

[57] Oseney Cart. i, p. xxi; Annales Monastici (Rolls Ser.), iv. 215.
[58] Reg. Univ. i. 35.
[59] Wood, Life, i. 277.
[60] Blo. Hethe, 25. He was again presented in 1649 by the parliamentary govt.: Oxf. Dioc. c 71, no. 20.
[61] Blo. Hethe, 26; Oxf. Dioc. d 553.
[62] Oxf. Dioc. c 327, p. 57.
[63] Ibid. d 578.
[64] Ibid. d 553.
[65] Ibid. d 562.
[66] Ibid. d 570.
[67] Ibid. d 578.
[68] Wilb. Visit.
[69] Blo. Hethe, 34.

and Alexander Peny (i.e. Petty), churchwardens, and the date 1708 painted on the west wall: this inscription (no longer in existence) suggests that the church was repaired then, since Rawlinson found it in good condition.[70] In 1757 the churchwardens reported that substantial repairs were contemplated.[71] But by 1810 the fabric was reported to be in 'a ruinous and dilapidated' condition and over £300 were spent on it.[72] Shortly afterwards a licence was obtained to reseat the church with pews for the richer families

and members of the Petty family (c. 1700)[81] are now illegible. There are inscriptions to members of the Lamb family (18th cent.) and to John Westcar (d.1784), George Lamb, rector (d. 1801), Richard Dutton (d. 1802), Henry Westcar of Southwark (d. 1805), William Mansfield of Bainton (d. 1846), Frederick Salter, rector (d. 1881), and four benefactors:[82] John Mansfield (d. 1869), Thomas Mansfield (d. 1874), Mary Waddington (d. 1876), and George Mansfield (d. 1946).

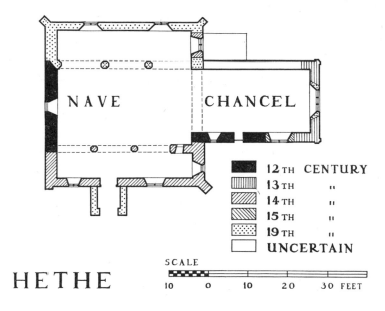

NAVE   CHANCEL

12TH CENTURY
13TH   ''
14TH   ''
15TH   ''
19TH   ''
UNCERTAIN

HETHE

SCALE
10   0   10   20   30 FEET

and open seats for the poor.[73] A drawing by J. Buckler shows the church as it was at this date, with a square bellcote surmounted by a raised roof with stone ball finial and vane.[74]

In 1833 the church was again under repair,[75] yet in 1854 Bishop Wilberforce could say that the church was 'in most miserable order' and 'utterly too small for the population'.[76] In 1859 the Revd. Frederick Salter undertook a thorough restoration.[77] At a cost of £800, and to the plans of G. E. Street, a new roof was placed over the nave and chancel; a north aisle (said in 1848 by the rural dean to be needed for the poor) was added; new windows were put in; the whole church was reseated and new furniture provided. Salter made a further bequest (1881) of a painted glass window for the east end.[78]

The plain font was perhaps part of an earlier church. Rawlinson noted a fragment of armorial glass, which has now disappeared.[79] At one time the church owned a statue of one of its patron saints, for in 1659 Wood noted that the 'effigies of St. George killing the dragon cut in stone' had been found in the churchyard.[80]

Inscriptions to Richard Evans, rector (d. 1698/9),

The church goods inventoried in 1552, including a chalice, were of little value.[83] The present plate includes an early 17th-century chalice, inscribed '... Heath ... 1716', and another silver chalice and paten, both 18th century, but given to the church in the 19th century.[84] At the Reformation there were two bells as well as two handbells and a 'sakeringe bell'. Today there is only one bell of 1886. A former bell, dated 1755, hangs in the school.[85] The registers date from 1678. Rawlinson noted that the earlier ones had been lost.[86] The Vestry Book begins in 1738 and the Churchwardens' Accounts in 1803.

ROMAN CATHOLICISM. The first notice of recusants at Hethe appears to be in the Compton Census of 1676, when ten Roman Catholics were returned.[87] In 1682 the rector reported that there were nine or ten Catholics, four of whom were excommunicated: they were all labouring people who were or had been employed by the Fermors of Tusmore.[88] Throughout the 18th century there was a small Catholic population. In a return of 1706 six were listed, including two carpenters and two poor widows.[89] In 1738 there were five, one man and four

[70] Par. Coll. ii. 173. Rawlinson wrote 'Peny' (Bodl. Rawl. B 400 c, f. 122) but there can be little doubt that it was Alexander Petty who was churchwarden.
[71] Oxf. Archd. Oxon. d 13, f. 34.
[72] Blo. Hethe, 21, 35.
[73] Ibid. 20–21; Oxf. Archd. Oxon. c 75, f. 88; ibid. b 24, ff. 285–96.
[74] MS. Top. Oxon. a 67, f. 322.
[75] Oxf. Archd. Oxon. c 75, f. 121.
[76] Wilb. Visit. 70 n. 2.
[77] Blo. Hethe, 22; MS. Top. Oxon. c 103, ff. 561–3.
[78] Blo. Hethe, 22; Kelly's Dir. Oxon. (1939).

[79] Par. Coll. ii. 173; Bodl. G.A. Oxon. 4⁰ 686, p. 173; Lamborn, Arm. Glass, 131. Blomfield (p. 19) was mistaken in connecting these with the Heaths of Shelswell.
[80] Wood, Life, i. 277.
[81] Par. Coll. ii. 173.
[82] See below, p. 181.
[83] Chant. Cert. 79–80.
[84] Evans, Ch. Plate.
[85] Ch. Bells Oxon. ii. 162.
[86] Par. Coll. ii. 173.
[87] Compton Census.
[88] Blo. Fring. 54.
[89] Oxoniensia, xiii. 78.

women, and a handful of children.[90] In three cases, as might be expected, there was a connexion with the Fermor estate. A Roman Catholic priest sometimes visited this small flock.

Late 18th and early 19th-century visitation returns report between two and eight Catholics, who first went to services in the Fermor chapel at Tusmore, and later to Hardwick.[91] The closing of the chapel at Hardwick in 1830[92] produced a difficult situation for the Roman Catholic population of the neighbourhood, said to number 350. Mass was said in different houses, until the priest from Hardwick, Alfred McGuire, bought a piece of land and built the present chapel (see below), opened in 1832.[93] It has been served by secular priests, and the congregation in 1948 numbered about sixty. In the 1950's it was serving the R.A.F. station at Bicester.[94]

The church of the *HOLY TRINITY* is a small stone building in the Gothic style. It cost £800. Some of its lancet windows have stained glass in memory of the Collingridge family.[95] A visitor in 1838 considered it of 'tolerable Gothic, though much too wide for its length', and suggested that the 'horrible' altar should be replaced by one designed by Pugin.[96] The registers date from 1832.[97]

PROTESTANT NONCONFORMITY. The visitation return of 1738 reported four Presbyterians (two shoemakers and their wives).[98] In 1794 the house of a shoemaker named Heydon was licensed for worship.[99] The members, who also attended church, called themselves Arminian or Wesleyan Methodists and had various teachers.[1] Two other houses were licensed in 1810 and 1816,[2] of which the second was described by the rector as a small hovel. An occasional teacher came over from Brackley.[3] Another licence was issued in 1829,[4] and by 1854 a Wesleyan Methodist chapel had been built.[5] In the 1860's and 1870's there were between 30 and 40 Wesleyans.[6] In 1876 the present chapel was built;[7] in 1955 it had eight members.[8]

SCHOOLS. In 1808 20 children were being taught in two dame schools.[9] These had closed by 1815[10] and in 1819 the only education was provided by a Sunday school, which was attended by children from Cottisford as well as Hethe.[11] By 1833, however, there were two day schools, one with an average attendance of 26 boys, and the other with 9 boys and 31 girls.[12] In 1854 a dame school was preparing children for the National school.[13]

A National school, projected in 1815,[14] was eventually built in 1852[15] and enlarged in 1874,[16] as the average attendance had risen from 40 in 1854[17] to 50 in 1871.[18] There was only one teacher in the 19th century.[19] The average attendance was 58 in 1906[20] and 29 in 1937. This Church of England school was reorganized in 1924, when senior pupils were sent to Fringford, and in 1948 was again reorganized as an infants' school. Juniors aged eight and over were then transferred to Fringford. The school was controlled in 1951, and was temporarily closed in 1952. In 1954 there were 19 pupils.[21]

Land for St. Philip's Roman Catholic school was purchased in 1831, and a building was then begun.[22] It was not completed until 1870, when the school opened[23] with accommodation for 50 children. It had an average attendance of 8 in 1889,[24] and 29 in 1906.[25] By 1920 it appears to have taken infants only,[26] and it was closed in 1924.[27]

CHARITIES. By his will proved in 1664 John Hart left £10 to the parish of Hethe,[28] but like his other benefactions it does not appear to have been paid. In the 19th century the parish officers of Hethe received £4 a year charged on a farm of the Fermors in Hardwick, said to be in lieu of a right to cut fuel on part of Hardwick Heath.[29] The payment dated from the inclosure of Hethe in 1773, when the right of the poor to cut furze on a heath of William Fermor's called Courtfield or Cottisfield (75 acres) was extinguished.[30] The £4 was distributed to the poor each year about Christmas either in fuel or in money.[31] In 1954 it was still being used to provide fuel.

In 1869 John Mansfield of Fringford bequeathed £100 in stock, the interest, then £3 4s. 4d., to be distributed annually to six of the eldest and deserving poor of Hethe.[32] Thomas Mansfield left £150 in 1874, providing for distributions to eight poor people, and in 1876 Mary Waddington, formerly housekeeper at Shelswell, left £532 6s., the interest to be divided among 30 of the poor each January.[33]

[90] Oxf. Dioc. d 553.
[91] Ibid. d 559, d 562, d 564; c 327, pp. 57, 299; d 570, d 578.
[92] See above, p. 173.
[93] Stapleton, *Cath. Miss.* 85–86.
[94] *Catholic Dir.* (1955), 111.
[95] Stapleton, *Cath. Miss.* 85–87.
[96] Ibid. 86.
[97] They have been edited with an historical introduction by Brig. T. B. Trappes-Lomax. A copy is at the office of the Catholic Record Society, 33 Wilfred St., London, S.W. 1.
[98] Oxf. Dioc. d 553.
[99] O.R.O. Cal. Q. Sess. viii.
[1] Oxf. Dioc. c 327, p. 299.
[2] Ibid. c 644, ff. 107, 170.
[3] Ibid. d 578.
[4] Ibid. c 645, f. 122.
[5] *Wilb. Visit.*
[6] Oxf. Dioc. c 332, c 344.
[7] *Kelly's Dir. Oxon.* (1903).
[8] *Buckingham and Brackley Methodist Circuit Plan, 1955–6.*
[9] Oxf. Dioc. d 707.
[10] Ibid. c 433.

[11] *Educ. of Poor*, 721, 725.
[12] *Educ. Enq. Abstract*, 748.
[13] *Wilb. Visit.*
[14] Oxf. Dioc. c 433.
[15] *Kelly's Dir. Oxon.* (1895).
[16] Wing, *Annals*, 70.
[17] *Wilb. Visit.*
[18] *Elem. Educ. Ret.*
[19] *Kelly's Dir. Oxon.* (1864, 1887).
[20] *Vol. Sch. Ret.*
[21] Inf. Oxon. Educ. Cttee.
[22] *Vol. Sch. Ret.*
[23] *Kelly's Dir. Oxon.* (1887).
[24] *Ret. of Sch.*
[25] *Vol. Sch. Ret.*
[26] *Kelly's Dir. Oxon.* (1920).
[27] Inf. Oxon. Educ. Cttee.
[28] P.C.C. 102 Bruce; Oxf. Dioc. c 650, f. 54b.
[29] Oxf. Dioc. c 327, p. 362; *12th Rep. Com. Char.* 304–5; *Gen. Digest Char.*
[30] 12 Geo. III, c. 103 (priv. act), pp. 11–12.
[31] Gardner, *Dir. Oxon.*; Wing, *Annals*, 70.
[32] Blo. *Hethe*, 39; *Gen. Digest Char.*
[33] Blo. *Hethe*, 39; Wing, *Annals*, 68.

LOWER HEYFORD or HEYFORD BRIDGE

THIS parish of 1,765 acres[1] lies midway between Oxford and Banbury and 4½ miles from the ancient market-town of Deddington. It is bounded on the west by the Cherwell[2] and on the east by the Romano-British earthwork, Aves Ditch.[3] Until about 1545, when the mills were moved and the course of the Cherwell was diverted to the east, the main river, and not a subsidiary stream as now, formed the parish's north-western boundary.[4] From the river the ground rises sharply to the plateau of the Great Oolite:[5] the parish is mostly within the 300-foot contour, but in the centre reaches nearly 400 feet. The low hedges and the comparative scarcity of trees add to the plateau's upland character. While the Cherwell meadows suffer from flooding[6] the plateau with its one small stream suffers from drought.[7] The stonebrash soil, however, is suitable for both pasture and arable. There is little woodland: Coopers Spinney is the main survivor of woods in the south-west of the parish which were cut down in the mid-19th century.[8]

The main Bicester–Enstone road, which became a turnpike in 1793,[9] crosses the river and enters the parish by Heyford Bridge. Part of the bridge, notably the chamfered vaulting-ribs of the arches at the eastern end, probably dates from the late 13th century; there are 19th-century additions on the north side. Records of numerous bequests for its upkeep in the 16th century have survived. In 1544, for instance, William Carter gave 2 bushels of malt towards its 'mending and reparation', and in 1564 the Rector of Rousham bequeathed 3s. 4d.[10] Levies on the parish were also made for its upkeep. In 1840, partly as the result of the heavy traffic on the turnpike, the bridge was in ruins and the county sued the parish for neglect. Judgement was given against the county, which accordingly became liable for the upkeep of the bridge, and in 1842 had it repaired by William Fisher of Oxford at a cost of £209. The county was also responsible for the upkeep of the causeway which crossed the low-lying land between the bridge and the village.[11] A second road, which crosses the parish from north to south, follows the line of the Portway,[12] and a third connects Heyford village with Upper Heyford and Somerton. The course of these roads has changed little since they were mapped by Thomas Langdon in 1606,[13] but

the pattern of the other old roads and tracks was greatly altered by the inclosure of the open fields in 1802.[14] Church Way vanished and the courses of Southway and 'Fordrowe Way' were changed.[15]

The Heyford section of the Oxford Canal was completed in 1790 and a wharf was built on it.[16] The British Transport Commission acquired them in 1946 and by 1954 traffic had practically ceased, although the wharf was still used as a coal-yard and the canal continued to be the resort of anglers. The Oxford and Banbury branch of the old G.W.R., opened in 1850, runs parallel to the canal for some way.[17] Unfortunately the engineers failed to provide sufficient culverts beneath the embankment so as to prevent an increase in flooding.[18] One of the three original intermediate stations was built at Lower Heyford.

The village lies above the river in the north-west of the parish, and just off the main Bicester–Enstone road.[19] Until the mid-13th century it was called Heyford, 'the ford used at hay harvest'. After the construction of the bridge, first recorded in 1255, it was commonly called Heyford *ad pontem* or Heyford Bridge, although Lower Heyford and even Little or *Parva* Heyford were sometimes used.[20] No explanation has been found of the use of 'Heyforde Porcells' by the rector in 1634.[21] The village appears on Plot's map of 1677 as Heyford Purcell and was frequently called that in the 19th century.[22]

A small square used as a market-place in the mid-19th century forms the centre of the old part of the village. Here are the Bell Inn, mentioned in 1819,[23] and the school. The manor-house, now a farm-house, the church and the old Rectory lie along a lane to the west. The stocks and the pound (removed in 1878) once stood on the west side of the churchyard.[24]

Langdon's map of 1606 shows houses round and in the middle of the square, with the 'Town House' and other houses along the main village street which runs eastwards.[25] The largest of the 18 houses listed in the hearth-tax returns of 1665 were the Rectory (7 hearths), the manor-house (6 hearths), the house of Gabriel Merry, one of the tenants of the demesne (5 hearths), and the mill house (4 hearths).[26] In 1742 the total number of houses was reported to be forty.[27] Three of them had been licensed as ale-houses in 1735, of which one may have been the 'Red Lion',

---

[1] *Census*, 1951; no boundary changes have been recorded: cf. *Census*, 1881.

[2] The construction of the railway altered the course of the river for a short distance on the SW.: the boundary follows the old course.

[3] *V.C.H. Oxon.* ii. 342; *Oxoniensia*, ii. 202.

[4] See below, p. 191.

[5] O.S. Map 6", xvi (1885), xxii (1884); ibid. 2½", 42/42, 52 (1951); G.S. Map 1", xlv SW.

[6] See Wing, *Annals*, 76.

[7] C.C.C. Mun. Ao 10.

[8] Ibid.: correspondence about Heyford 1846–7; Blo. *L. Heyf.* 34.

[9] Blo. *L. Heyf.* 27; 33 Geo. III, c. 180.

[10] Blo. *L. Heyf.* 5.

[11] *Oxon. Co. Bridges* (1878); J. M. Davenport, *Oxon. Bridges*, 5.

[12] *V.C.H. Oxon.* i. 109–10. For Roman and pre-Roman discoveries in the parish see ibid. 340.

[13] *Sixteen Old Maps of Properties in Oxon.* ed J. L. G. Mowat, plates i–iv: reproduction of Thomas Langdon's

map of L. Heyf. (1606) in C.C.C. Mun. cited below as *Langdon's Map*.

[14] See sketch map p. 189; cf. Bryant, *Oxon. Map* (1824).

[15] A Robert le Fordrowe was a villein tenant in Caulcott in 1279: *Rot. Hund.* (Rec. Com.), ii. 827.

[16] 10 & 11 Geo. III, c. 49, sch. iii, pt. 2. For Grantham's wharf see plate facing p. 276.

[17] E. T. MacDermot, *Hist. G.W.R.* i. 178, 294, 300.

[18] C.C.C. Mun.: correspondence about Heyf.; Wing, *Annals*, 163.

[19] O.S. Map 25", xxii. 2 (1875).

[20] *P.N. Oxon.* (E.P.N.S.), i. 218–19; *Fines Oxon.* 119; C.C.C. Mun. *passim*; *Woodward's Progress*, 43.

[21] Wing, *Annals*, 79.

[22] e.g. on J. Buckler's drawing of the church: MS. Top. Oxon. a 67, f. 323; Gardner, *Dir. Oxon.*

[23] C.C.C. Mun. Ao 8.

[24] Wing, *Annals*, 76.

[25] *Langdon's Map*.

[26] *Hearth Tax Oxon.* 191–2.

[27] Blo. *L. Heyf.* 23.

first mentioned by that name in 1784[28] and subsequently used in 1801 as the meeting-place of the Heyford landowners, when they resolved to inclose the open fields.[29] By 1800 at least seven new cottages had been built, and others had been divided.[30] With the coming of the turnpike, toll gates had been erected at each end of the village,[31] and it was along the road to the eastern toll-gate and along the turnpike itself that the main early 19th-century building took place. By 1841 there were 87 inhabited houses.[32] Among the chief 19th-century additions were a Methodist chapel (replaced in 1906), the school, and the railway station. In 1888 the Deddington, Heyford, and Aston Permanent Building Society was established,[33] and though population was falling there was much new building to replace old cottages. In the 20th century the village continued to extend eastwards. Between 1939 and 1954 38 council houses were completed.[34] A noteworthy addition to the social life of the village was the combined club room and library, built in 1926 to house the War Memorial Library which had been founded after the First World War.[35]

Caulcott, first mentioned in 1199,[36] lies about a mile to the east. Almost all the houses, including Caulcott Farm, lie along one side of the village street. There is an inn, the 'Horse and Groom', and the former Methodist chapel, now a garage. The incumbent estimated 14 houses in 1742 and in 1771, and in 1841 the census recorded twenty-nine[37].

In about 1900 a piped water-supply was brought to Heyford village and three farms. In 1926 many houses in Heyford and the whole of Caulcott still depended on wells.[38] A main water-supply was laid to the village and Caulcott in 1954, and electricity supplies were made available in about 1932.[39]

The old houses and cottages in the village are mainly of two stories and are built of the local ironstone. The better ones such as the manor and Rectory have ashlar quoins; some are thatched and others are roofed with stone slates, or Welsh slate. Among the oldest is the manor-house, rebuilt in 1669 on an L-shaped plan with two stories and an attic dormer.[40] It apparently stands on the same site as its predecessor, which is shown on Langdon's map of 1606, but is said to be less extensive. Its many original features include a 17th-century window of three lights with a moulded wooden frame; and a stone with the date of rebuilding, 1669, and the initials W.E.B.—William and Elizabeth Bruce. A part of the former Rectory—the east side—dates back to the 16th century,[41] but most of the oldest parts were pulled down in 1867, when extensive modernization was undertaken. A

relic of the medieval house is still preserved in the form of a small wooden carving of a shield, inscribed I H S within a crown of thorns,[42] perhaps from the oratory built in the Rectory in 1337.[43] Before the house was enlarged by Thomas Greenway in the second half of the 16th century, it was said to consist of a panelled hall with a chamber above. A piece of stained glass with Greenway's initials together with the figure of a pelican (the crest of Corpus Christi College) and the words 'Gracia Dei mecum (15)69' was removed from the Rectory in 1867 and is now in a window of the vestry.[44] The house fell into disrepair during the Civil War,[45] but by 1679 it was said to have eight or nine bays.[46] In 1731 the rector added the present northern wing.[47] The house was sold in 1949 when the present Rectory was built.[48]

Other substantially 17th-century houses are the Bell Inn, originally rectangular in plan, Glebe Farm with its thatched roof, and Knapton's Farm. An interesting feature of the 'Bell' is the staircase projection on the east side, which rises to the attic level and contains an ancient newel staircase lighted by a single rectangular window. The Mill house with its three stories and original rectangular plan may also date from the late 17th century, though its sash windows and inside shutters were 18th-century insertions.

There are several outlying farm-houses, but none of them appears to have been built before the inclosure of the open fields in 1802.

Despite its position near one of the crossings of the Cherwell, Heyford has been scarcely touched by events of national importance. During the Civil War it is recorded that royalist troops went over the bridge en route for Banbury in 1643, but no skirmishes in the parish have been recorded.[49] Heyford's historian William Wing listed six Heyford worthies in 1877,[50] but none save William Filmer, the early 19th-century 'experimental farmer', had more than local fame.[51]

Heyford men had their own version of a Mumming Play, figuring King George and Bonaparte, at least until 1885, and John Fathers of Heyford was one of the last players of the 'whittle and dub', the traditional Oxfordshire instruments for dancing.[52]

MANORS. In 1086 a certain Ralph held 5 hides of Miles Crispin in *LOWER HEYFORD*, which had been freely held by Besi before the Conquest.[53] The overlordship of this estate followed that of the honor of Wallingford.[54] In the 12th century the De la Mares of Steeple Lavington (Wilts.)[55] appear as tenants of the manor. In 1166 Peter de la Mare was

[28] O.R.O. Victlrs'. recog.
[29] C.C.C. Mun. Ao 8.
[30] Ibid. Ao 6.
[31] Blo. *L. Heyf.* 27.
[32] Ibid. 28–29.
[33] *Rules of Deddington . . . Building Soc.* (Bodl. G.A. Oxon. 8° 567).
[34] Inf. Ploughley R.D.C. One group of council houses is called Bromeswell Close—the name of the site on *Langdon's Map.*
[35] Inf. Mr. R. V. Lennard. The donor was anonymous.
[36] *Fines Oxon.* 7; cf. St. John's Coll. Mun. xx for an early 13th-cent. charter which refers to the 'boundary of the people of Caulcott'; cf. *P.N. Oxon.* (E.P.N.S.), i. 219.
[37] Blo. *L. Heyf.* 23, 25, 29.
[38] C. V. Butler, *Village Survey Making,* 18 and map II.
[39] Local inf.
[40] Blo. *L. Heyf.* 13; architectural evidence.

[41] A 16th-cent. inner door frame of moulded wood, with four-centred head and chamfered jambs, survives.
[42] *Penes* the rector and churchwardens.
[43] Blo. *L. Heyf.* 89, citing Linc. Reg.
[44] Ibid. 90.   [45] Ibid. 71.
[46] Oxf. Archd. Oxon. c 141, p. 353.
[47] Oxf. Dioc. c 455, f. 56; Blo. *L. Heyf.* 91.
[48] Inf. Miss D. B. Dew, Lower Heyford.
[49] Luke, *Jnl.* 106.
[50] Wing, *Annals,* 29–30.
[51] See below, pp. 190, 193. For Humphrey Keene, yeoman and bellfounder, see *Ch. Bells. Oxon.* iv. 475.
[52] MS. Top. Oxon. d 200, p. 74; R. J. E. Tiddy, *The Mummers' Play,* 219.
[53] *V.C.H. Oxon.* i. 418.
[54] For the honor see *Boarstall Cart.* App.
[55] Ibid. 321, where the early history of the family is discussed; see also *V.C.H. Oxon.* v. 33.

holding 3 fees in Oxfordshire of the honor of Wallingford,[56] one of which was in Heyford.[57] By 1173 he had been succeeded by his son Robert,[58] who was Sheriff of Oxfordshire from 1187 to 1190,[59] and served King John overseas before 1205.[60] He is known to have been still in possession of his Heyford manor in 1201,[61] but was dead by 1211 when his lands were in the hands of Warin Fitzgerold of Fritwell, presumably the guardian of Robert's son Peter, to whom Fitzgerold surrendered the property in the following year.[62] Peter (II) was followed after his death in 1254 by his son Robert, then aged 40,[63] a partisan of Simon de Montfort.[64] Robert died in 1272 and was succeeded by his son Peter (III),[65] who could not do homage for his lands because of Edward I's absence on crusade, but who was allowed to exploit them until Edward's return.[66]

In 1291 Heyford and Marsh Baldon were included among the lands which Roger de Somery, lord of Dudley, had held;[67] the reason for this is not apparent, for Peter de la Mare held both manors on his death in 1292,[68] when he was succeeded by his son Robert, who was given seisin of his father's estates in 1296 when he attained his majority.[69] In 1306 Robert was given licence to lease £20 worth of land in Heyford (i.e. the manor) to Walter of Aylesbury, then keeper of the honor of Wallingford,[70] since he was going to the Scottish wars.[71] Robert died in 1308 when his son Peter was still a minor;[72] in the same year a rent of 6s. 8d. a year in Heyford was granted to Robert's widow Lucy, as part of her dower.[73] Peter's wardship was committed to Hugh Despenser the elder.[74] He was of age by 1318 when he was granted free warren at Heyford.[75] During the troubles of Edward II's reign Peter twice forfeited his lands for armed opposition to the Despensers and their allies,[76] but he obtained a final pardon for his rebellion in 1324, when his lands were again restored.[77] Thereafter he rose steadily in importance and held a number of royal offices.[78] He married Joan Achard of Aldermaston (Berks.), and the reversion of that manor was settled upon him in 1342.[79] By 1345 he had acquired the Lisle manor (see below) in Heyford,[80] and by 1348 had been rewarded for his services to the house of Lancaster[81] by the office of steward of the Earldom of Lancaster.[82]

Peter died in 1349[83] and was succeeded by his son Robert,[84] who like his father was an important official of Henry, Duke of Lancaster.[85] On Robert's death in 1382[86] both Heyford manors were assigned to his widow in dower,[87] but on her death in 1405[88] they were once more divided. The De la Mare manor passed to Robert's heir male, his nephew Robert, son of Thomas de la Mare of Aldermaston and Sparsholt (Berks.), who had died in 1404.[89] In 1431 Robert de la Mare died in possession of the manor. He had previously settled it on his eldest son William and Katherine his wife, but they were dead by 1431 and the manor passed to Robert's grandson, Thomas,[90] who was probably the son of Richard de la Mare.[91] Thomas came of age in 1448.[92] Although he was at first a Lancastrian, he was pardoned by Edward IV, under whom he was three times Sheriff of Oxfordshire and Berkshire.[93] He was attainted after his rebellion in 1483, but his estates were restored to him in 1485.[94] When he died in 1490[95] he had been predeceased by his son John, and was therefore succeeded by his grandson Thomas, who was still a minor on his own death in 1493.[96] His heirs were his sisters, Elizabeth, the wife of George Foster, and Frideswide (later the wife of John Moreton), who died in 1497.[97] Heyford had been assigned in dower to Thomas's mother, Joan, and was held by her until her death in 1517.[98] Elizabeth and George Foster then succeeded, and before the death of his wife in 1526 Foster had settled the manor on himself and his son Humphrey.[99] In 1527 Edward Baynton, the tenant of the Lisle manor, claimed the manor on the ground of descent from the Peter de la Mare who held it in fee tail in 1340.[1] In 1528 judgement was given in Baynton's favour and he reunited the manors.[2]

Before the Conquest an estate had been held in *LOWER HEYFORD* by Edwin, son of the thegn Burred,[3] who also held Barton Seagrave and other lands in Northamptonshire.[4] In 1086, assessed at 5 hides, it was in the hands of Geoffrey, Bishop of Coutances.[5] It subsequently passed to the earls of Gloucester, perhaps through Robert FitzHamon,

[56] *Red Bk. Exch.* (Rolls Ser.), 309.
[57] *Eynsham Cart.* i. 109.
[58] *Pipe R.* 1173 (P.R.S. xix), 78.
[59] Ibid. 1187 (P.R.S. xxxvii), 45; ibid. 1188 (P.R.S. xxxviii), 149; ibid. 1189 (Rec. Com.), 104; ibid. 1190 (P.R.S. N.S. i), 10.
[60] *Rot. Litt. Claus.* (Rec. Com.), i. 34.
[61] *Pipe R.* 1201 (P.R.S. N.S. xiv), 203.
[62] *Boarstall Cart.* 321.
[63] *Cal. Inq. p.m.* i, p. 311; *Ex. e Rot. Fin.* (Rec. Com.), ii. 178.
[64] *Close R.* 1261–4, 381; ibid. 1264–8, 6, 169.
[65] *Cal. Inq. p.m.* i, p. 260.
[66] *Close R.* 1268–72, 533; *Cal. Close,* 1272–9, 7, 27, 38.
[67] *Cal. Inq. p.m.* ii, p. 497.
[68] Ibid. iii, p. 31.
[69] *Cal. Close,* 1288–96, 485.
[70] *Cal. Fine R.* 1272–1307, 437; for Walter see *Earldom of Cornwall Accts.* ed. I. M. Midgeley (Camd. Soc. 3rd ser. lxvi), i, p. xxxiii.
[71] *Cal. Pat.* 1301–7, 443; cf. C 134/10/5.
[72] *Cal. Inq. p.m.* v, p. 62.
[73] *Cal. Close,* 1307–13, 86.
[74] *Cal. Chanc. R. Var.* 134.
[75] *Cal. Chart. R.* 1300–26, 391.
[76] *Cal. Pat.* 1321–4, 19, 162; *Cal. Close,* 1318–23, 420.
[77] *Cal. Pat.* 1321–4, 394.
[78] Ibid. 1330–4, 294; ibid. 1343–5, 413, 424, 430, 590.

[79] *V.C.H. Berks.* iii. 389.
[80] See below.
[81] *Cal. Pat.* 1340–3, 176; see *Complete Peerage,* vii. 404.
[82] R. Somerville, *Duchy of Lancaster,* i. 359. His identity is proved by *Cal. Pat.* 1348–50, 261.
[83] *Cal. Inq. p.m.* ix, p. 310.
[84] For his marriage see *Cal. Close,* 1396–9, 83.
[85] Somerville, op. cit. 360. He was one of the duke's executors.
[86] *Cal. Fine R.* 1377–83, 302.
[87] *Cal. Close,* 1381–5, 148.
[88] C 137/46; cf. *V.C.H. Herts.* iii. 39.
[89] *V.C.H. Berks.* iii. 389.
[90] C 139/53.
[91] J. V. Wedgwood, *Hist. of Parl.: Biogs.* 572 citing *Cal. Pat.* 1467–77, 425.
[92] C 139/153.
[93] Wedgwood, op. cit. 572–3.
[94] *Rot. Parl.* vi. 246, 273.
[95] *Cal. Inq. p.m. Hen. VII,* i, p. 325.
[96] Pedigree in C.C.C. Bursary Transcripts, iv, p. 277.
[97] *Cal. Inq. p.m. Hen. VII,* i, p. 562.
[98] C 142/78/102.   [99] Ibid. 46/12.
[1] P.R.O. P. Harrison, Extracts, ix. 342.
[2] C.C.C. Bursary Transcripts, iv. 281–4.
[3] *V.C.H. Oxon.* i. 427.
[4] *V.C.H. Northants.* i. 287–8.
[5] *V.C.H. Oxon.* i. 427.

to whom William II may have granted certain lands forfeited by Geoffrey's nephew and heir, Robert de Mowbray.[6] Richard de Clare died seised of the overlordship in 1262,[7] and it descended with the Earldom of Gloucester to the last male of the line, Gilbert, on whose death at Bannockburn in 1314 it was given in dower to his widow Maud.[8] From the Clares the overlordship passed through Hugh Audley to Ralph Stafford,[9] thereafter following the descent of the Earldom of Stafford.[10] The overlordship was last mentioned in 1460 when it was held by Humphrey, Duke of Buckingham and Earl of Stafford, at his death.[11]

By 1262 the Champernowne family, whose main estates were in Devon, were the tenants of Heyford under the Clares,[12] to whom they were related.[13] William de Champernowne was the mesne lord of Hampton Gay in 1235[14] and his heir was the Clare tenant at Heyford in 1262.[15] Presumably this was Joan, his daughter, who was mesne tenant in 1275 and 1284,[16] and was apparently still alive in 1314.[17] Joan married Sir Ralph de Willington,[18] and the mesne lordship of Heyford descended to John de Willington, probably their son, who held lands in Cornwall in 1302[19] and died in 1339,[20] when he was succeeded by his sons, Ralph (d. 1348) and Henry (d. 1349).[21] Henry's son and heir John came of age in 1361,[22] but was never mentioned in connexion with Heyford. To judge from the vague reference to 'the heirs of William Champernoun' in 1392 and 1398,[23] the mesne lordship had by then become extinct.

In 1086 a certain Robert held under the Bishop of Coutances[24] the 5 hides in Heyford which had formerly belonged to Edwin, but until the 13th century no tenant of this manor is mentioned. In 1218 William de Moreton conveyed to Richard Henred ½ fee in Heyford and Caulcott, receiving in exchange 1 hide of land in Caulcott.[25] The Henreds appear in West Hendred (Berks.) early in the 12th century,[26] and in Northamptonshire, where they later held a manor at Barton Seagrave, in the mid-12th century.[27] The history of Heyford follows closely that of Barton Seagrave from the late Anglo-

Saxon period until the end of the 13th century, so it is likely that the Henreds had been under-tenants of Heyford before 1218. Richard Henred[28] was dead by 1242 when his widow Lucy was holding the manor in dower.[29] She was apparently succeeded by their son Richard, who was imprisoned at Northampton for murder in 1264,[30] and was a royalist in the baronial wars.[31] In 1274 Richard exchanged Heyford with William de Lisle for North Brampton manor (Northants).[32] He died in 1275 seised of a mesne lordship over William de Lisle in Heyford,[33] leaving a son William, who obtained seisin later in the same year.[34] The Henred mesne lordship became extinct in 1293 when William was hanged for the murder of the parson of North Brampton.[35] William de Lisle, who had been custodian of Oxford castle in 1270,[36] died in 1277[37] and his son Roger was given seisin in the next year.[38] In 1297 he settled the manor on his son John and his wife Amice, the daughter of Richard de Shulton,[39] and they conveyed the manor to Peter de la Mare in 1330.[40] In 1345 Katherine de Lisle confirmed the transaction.[41] The manor then followed the descent of the De la Mare manor, being assigned in dower to Maud, the wife of Robert de la Mare, on the latter's death in 1382. When Maud died in 1405 it was again separated from the De la Mare manor and passed to Willelma, daughter of Robert and Maud, the wife of Sir John Roches of Bromham (Wilts.).[42] The latter died in 1400 and Willelma in 1411, when the family estates in Wiltshire passed to her elder daughter Joan, the wife of Nicholas Baynton, and Heyford to the younger daughter Elizabeth, wife of Sir Walter Beauchamp.[43] Sir Walter was closely connected with the royal household, being a king's esquire in 1403,[44] one of the retinue of Henry V at Agincourt and an executor of Henry's will.[45] He died in 1430[46] and was succeeded by his son William, who married Elizabeth, daughter of Gerard de Braybrook, in whose right he became Lord St. Amand.[47] In 1448 the manor was settled on William, his wife and his heirs in tail male,[48] and when he died in 1457 it was held under the settlement by his wife for life.[49] In 1458 Elizabeth married as her second husband Roger

[6] Farrer, *Honors*, ii. 211; *V.C.H. Northants.* i. 287–8.
[7] *Cal. Inq. p.m.* i, p. 157; *Close R.* 1261–4, 284.
[8] *Cal. Inq. p.m.* v, pp. 327, 344.
[9] *Complete Peerage*, v. 719.
[10] Ibid. xii (1), 174 sqq.; cf. C 136/85; *Cal. Close*, 1402–5, 235.
[11] C 139/180.
[12] *Cal. Inq. p.m.* i, p. 157.
[13] In 1166 Jordan de Champernowne held 2 fees in Glos. of the Earl of Gloucester: *Red Bk. Exch.* (Rolls Ser.), 291. Jordan's mother was Mabira, daughter of Robert, Earl of Gloucester: *Cal. Doc. France*, ed. Round, 192.
[14] *Oseney Cart.* ii. 434; v. 388; vi. 51, 59. William was Jordan's grandson.
[15] *Cal. Inq. p.m.* i, pp. 157, 159.
[16] Ibid. ii, p. 95; *Feud. Aids*, iv. 157.
[17] *Cal. Inq. p.m.* vi, p. 344; cf. *Oseney Cart.* vi. 51.
[18] J. L. Vivian, *Visit. Devon* (1889), 160.
[19] *Cal. Inq. p.m.* iv, p. 48; *Cal. Pat.* 1317–21, 260; *Cal. Close*, 1339–41, 57.
[20] *Cal. Close*, 1339–41, 57.
[21] *Cal. Inq. p.m.* ix, pp. 90, 197, 199.
[22] Ibid. xi, p. 124.
[23] C 136/23; ibid. 85.
[24] *V.C.H. Oxon.* i. 427. Cf. *V.C.H. Northants.* i. 312b, where Round identified this Heyford as Upper Heyford.
[25] *Fines Oxon.* 51.
[26] *V.C.H. Berks.* iv. 303–4.
[27] *Facsimiles of Early Northants. Chart.* ed. F. M. Sten-

ton (Northants. Rec. Soc. iv), 94; *V.C.H. Northants.* iii. 176–7.
[28] For Richard's suits concerning property in Heyford neighbourhood see *Close R.* 1227–31, 547, 576, 582; *Fines Oxon.* 111.
[29] *Bk. of Fees*, 825; *Ex. e Rot. Fin.* (Rec. Com.), i. 371.
[30] *Close R.* 1261–4, 334.
[31] *Cal. Pat.* 1258–66, 473.
[32] *Abbrev. Plac.* (Rec. Com.), 180, 187.
[33] *Cal. Inq. p.m.* ii, p. 95.
[34] *Cal. Fine R.* 1272–1307, 63.
[35] Bridges, *Northants.* ii. 281.
[36] *Cal. Pat.* 1266–72, 423.
[37] *Cal. Inq. p.m.* ii, p. 136.
[38] *Cal. Fine R.* 1272–1307, 93. For his career see *Cal. Pat.* 1292–1301, 104, 298.
[39] Kennett, *Paroch. Antiq.* ii. 162, citing New Coll. Chart. no. 190.
[40] C.P. 25(1)/189/17/47.
[41] Ibid. 190/19/20.
[42] C.C.C. Bursary Transcripts, iv, p. 277.
[43] *Cal. Close*, 1409–13, 138, 259.
[44] *Cal. Pat.* 1401–5, 255.
[45] *Complete Peerage*, xi. 301 n.
[46] Will in *Testamenta Vetusta*, ed. N. H. Nicolas, 217–18.
[47] *Complete Peerage*, xi. 301–2.
[48] C 139/164.
[49] Ibid.; *Cal. Close*, 1454–61, 235.

Tocotes, who was knighted in 1461.[50] In 1484 he was attainted and his estates forfeited for his part in the Duke of Buckingham's rising.[51] They were granted to the royal favourite Sir Thomas Everingham,[52] but Sir Roger's attainder was reversed in 1485[53] and he continued to hold the manor until Elizabeth died in 1491. It then reverted to Richard, Lord St. Amand, the son of Elizabeth's first husband, on whom the manor had been settled in 1475.[54] Richard died in 1508 without legitimate children, and by 1511 Heyford passed to John Baynton of Fulstone (Wilts.),[55] the descendant of Nicholas Baynton and his wife Joan.[56] In 1528 John's son and heir, Sir Edward Baynton, acquired the De la Mare manor, and in 1533 sold both Heyford manors to Corpus Christi College, Oxford, for £709.[57] In 1956 they were still in the college's possession.

For the greater part of the 16th and 17th centuries Corpus Christi's demesne lands in Heyford were mostly divided into two estates held by the yeoman families of Bruce and Merry. John Bruce was 'farmer and receiver' of Heyford in 1535,[58] and was followed by Richard Bruce,[59] and William, who died at the Black Assizes in Oxford in 1577.[60] Another descendant, a William Bruce, rebuilt the manor-house before his death in 1683.[61] In 1685 his son William settled the estate upon his only daughter Elizabeth and her husband Robert Kenricke of Oxford.[62] In 1737 after Elizabeth's death her son James Kenricke sold the estate, by then mortgaged, to William Leigh,[63] who was succeeded as the college's lessee by his brother, the Revd. Thomas Leigh (d. 1744). In 1765 his widow[64] assigned the remainder of her lease to Sir Charles Cottrell-Dormer of Rousham.[65]

Simon Merry was farmer of the other part of the demesne by 1548 and died in 1588.[66] A Mrs. Merry was farmer in 1598, and she was succeeded by the long-lived Gabriel Merry (1591–1684).[67] The last of the family to be a lessee of the college seems to have been John Merry. His farm was leased by Corpus Christi to John Macock in 1740.[68] Macock's son Richard was the lessee[69] until 1787, when he sold the remainder of his current least to Sir Clement Cottrell-Dormer of Rousham.[70] The Cottrell-Dormers had acquired a leasehold estate of some 310 acres in all,[71] and this they held until the early 20th century.[72]

LESSER ESTATE. One large freehold estate in Caulcott did not belong to Corpus Christi's manor, and was reputed to be a separate manor in the 18th century.[73] At the beginning of the 17th century it was held by Bartholomew Tipping of Stokenchurch:[74] its earlier history is unknown, though it may be conjectured to have originated in the lands held direct of the manor of Wallingford by Geoffrey de Browman in 1279.[75] In 1605 Tipping conveyed it to Richard Brangwyn of Kingsey (Bucks.),[76] whose descendants held it until 1795,[77] when John Brangwyn, son of John Brangwyn of Middle Barton, sold it to John Churchill of Woodstock.[78] The latter's son Benjamin succeeded him about 1797, and in 1809 conveyed his Caulcott estate to George Villiers, Earl of Jersey.[79] About the time of the inclosure of Lower Heyford in 1802 the Churchill family acquired a number of copyhold estates in the parish.[80] These were also purchased by Lord Jersey, who thereby obtained an estate of 191 acres freehold and 131 acres copyhold.[81] The earls of Jersey held these lands throughout the 19th century and in 1871 the 7th earl bought the freehold of the 131 acres from Corpus Christi.[82]

ECONOMIC AND SOCIAL HISTORY. The evidence found in excavating Harborough Bank,[83] a Saxon burial mound to the south-east of the village, and other nearby graves makes it probable that Heyford has been continuously settled since the 6th century. Its name probably means 'the ford used at hay harvest'.[84] Linguistic reasons are strengthened by the fact that much of the meadow-land lay on the far side of a loop of the Cherwell.[85] The river was presumably fordable somewhere near Heyford Bridge, while farther downstream another ford gave access to the island meadow of Cotmeadham.[86] While these fords probably led the Saxons to settle at Lower Heyford, the siting of the village and, at a later date, of its hamlet of Caulcott, was clearly influenced by the necessity of securing a good water-supply. Heyford village, unlike the rest of the parish, lies on the Marlstone with impervious Lower Lias Clay beneath, and Caulcott lies by a stream in a depression in the Oolitic Limestone. Even when the stream dries up water can be reached by wells near its course.[87]

Heyford was the only recorded settlement in 1086

[50] Cal. Pat. 1452–61, 420; Complete Peerage, xi. 302.
[51] Rot. Parl. vi. 245.
[52] Cal. Pat. 1476–85, 429; Hist. MSS. Com. 9th Rep. i. 213.
[53] Rot. Parl. vi. 273.
[54] Cal. Inq. p.m. Hen. VII, i, p. 306.
[55] Complete Peerage, xi. 303.
[56] L. & P. Hen. VIII, i (1), p. 474.
[57] C.C.C. Bursary Transcripts, iv, no. 16/73, 79–84.
[58] C.C.C. Mun. Ao 5.
[59] Ibid.; Blo. L. Heyf. 12.
[60] C.C.C. Mun. Mb 2; Wing, Annals, 79.
[61] Blo. L. Heyf. 12–13.
[62] Heyford deeds penes Mr. T. Cottrell-Dormer, Rousham Park (cited below as Dormer D.) F 1. For renewals of lease see ibid. F 19, F 4, F 8, 9.
[63] Ibid. F 9.
[64] Ibid. F 10; C.C.C. Mun. Mc 13.
[65] Dormer D. F 11; for the Cottrell-Dormers see Burke, Land. Gent. (1937).
[66] C.C.C. Mun. Ao 5; Blo. L. Heyf. 13.
[67] C.C.C. Mun. Ao 9; Mc 13; Blo. L. Heyf. 13; Par. Coll. ii. 174.
[68] Dormer D. F 30.
[69] C.C.C. Mun. Ao 9; Dormer D. F 31–34.

[70] Dormer D. F 36.
[71] C.C.C. Mun. Ao 8.
[72] Dormer D. F 37 sqq.
[73] e.g. O.R.O. J IX e/23.
[74] Cf. C.C.C. Mun. Langdon's Map; ibid. Ao 10.
[75] Rot. Hund. (Rec. Com.), ii. 826–7.
[76] O.R.O. J IX e/1, 5.
[77] Ibid. e/9, 10, 12, 13; Blo. L. Heyf. 17–18; Hearth Tax Oxon. 192.
[78] O.R.O. J IX e/23, 24.
[79] Ibid. e/28, 56–59.
[80] Ibid. J IX f, g, h, i passim; O.R.O. Incl. award; C.C.C. Mun. Ao 9.
[81] C.C.C. Mun. Ao 8: survey 1832.
[82] O.R.O. J IX f/12.
[83] V.C.H. Oxon. i. 354–5.
[84] P.N. Oxon. (E.P.N.S.), i. 219; cf. Alexander, P.N. Oxon. 125–6.
[85] See below, p. 189.
[86] C.C.C. Mun. Ao 2: Ct. R. 1589; ford shown on Langdon's Map (see above, p. 182, n. 14).
[87] C. V. Butler, Village Survey Making, 17 and Map I: there were 14 wells (average depth 25 ft.) in use in Heyford in 1926.

and all its available arable was not under cultivation. The two estates there held by Ralph and Robert each had land for 6 ploughs, but on Ralph's estate there were 2 ploughs in demesne and the peasants had 3, while on Robert's there were 3 ploughs in demesne and the peasants had two. Each estate had 30 acres of meadow and a mill, the one worth 10s., the other 20s. The total value of each estate was £6, as it had been before the Conquest. In all there were 11 villeins (*villani*), 12 bordars, and 5 serfs.[88]

The survey of 1279 records considerable development.[89] There were still two principal estates in Heyford. Roger de Lisle held 1½ carucates in demesne, with 9 cottars each holding a cotland for 2s. 6d. a year and working at his will; Peter de la Mare held 1½ carucates in demesne and 10 cottars with cotlands of 11 acres each paid 2s. 6d. a year and worked at Peter's will. A free tenant held a messuage and 2 acres of Roger de Lisle for 1d., as well as 3 acres and a park of Geoffrey de Browman for 3s. In the new hamlet of Caulcott, Roger had 8 villein virgaters, who each paid 5s. a year and worked at his will. Peter de la Mare held 17 virgates, of which 15 were held by 16 villeins who owed only labour services. Hugh de Broke, whose father Lawrence had acquired lands in Caulcott in the 1240's,[90] had an estate of 12 virgates, which was held of him by a free tenant, who held 3 virgates for 19s. 6d. a year, and 9 villein virgaters, who owed 5s. 6d. a year and labour services. Another free tenant held 2 virgates of Geoffrey de Bromwam for 15s. a year. Both the Heyford rectors held 2 virgates each. As in 1086 two water-mills were recorded—one held by the rector of the Eynsham moiety of the church[91] and the other by Roger de Lisle, who also had the fishery in the Cherwell.

The most notable changes recorded in this survey were the new settlement at Caulcott, the extended cultivation, and the increased population. Whereas Heyford was a riverside village, the new hamlet (if indeed it was new and not merely accounted for in Domesday as part of Heyford) was an upland one. Its name 'the cold cottages' (OE *ceald cote*) was no doubt a reference to its comparatively exposed position.[92] The names of many of its late-13th-century inhabitants suggest that it had been colonized by men from the neighbouring villages— Rousham, Middleton, Souldern, Northbrook, Fencott, and Murcott,[93] and since its lands mostly belonged to the two Heyford manors the De la Mares and the predecessors of the De Lisles may have either taken the initiative in its foundation or at least encouraged its growth. As for the area of cultivation, rather less than 22 virgates of arable[94] were recorded in Heyford and 39 in Caulcott, making, with 4½ virgates for the rectory lands, a total of 65½ virgates, compared with a possible 48 virgates (i.e. land for 12 ploughs) in 1086. The Heyford virgate was 20 'field acres',[95] so in 1279 the fields of Heyford and Caulcott may have covered an area of at least 1,300

field acres or about 850 statute acres.[96] In population Caulcott had outgrown Heyford, having 33 villeins to the 19 cottars recorded in the mother village. A possible connexion between the early 13th-century field name Coldhememere, 'boundary of the people of Caulcott', and the modern Cold Harbour farm, which lies on the boundary of Heyford with Kirtlington, suggests that by the early 13th century cultivation had here reached the frontier of the parish.[97]

In 1292 the De la Mare manor was worth £19 0s. 7d. a year. There were 80 acres of arable, worth 4d. an acre, in the demesne, with pasture worth 8d. an acre, meadow, and a dovecote. The water-mill and the fishery brought in 16s. a year.[98] In 1308 the manor comprised a capital messuage with dovecote worth 6s. 8d. a year, 200 acres of arable worth 33s. 4d. at 2d. an acre, 20 acres of meadow worth 40s. at 2s. an acre, a separate pasture worth 10s., a water-mill worth 13s. 4d., and a fishery worth 12d. The whole was valued at £5 4s. 4d. a year. The rents of 6 free tenants amounted to 42s. 8d. There were 14 virgaters and 8 half-virgaters, whose rents amounted to 47s. and dayworks and other customary payments to 68s. 0½d. Thirteen of the virgaters each owed 2s. rent, 3 hens and a cock worth 6d. at the feast of St. Martin, and works at the time of hoeing, mowing, and reaping worth 3s. 2d. Seven half-virgaters made payments for brewing in addition to their rent of money and poultry. There were 3 cottars, of which 2 held for a rent of 2s. and a hen and a cock worth 2½d. The third paid 6d.[99] By 1349 the customary works of the unfree tenants were said to have been commuted.[1] In the 1420's, however, a half-virgater still owed two autumn works with two men besides a rent of 8s. a year.[2]

Fourteenth-century tax lists suggest that Caulcott maintained its lead in population and show it to have been the wealthier of the settlements. In 1316 it had 28 contributors compared with Heyford's 13, and an assessment of £3 16s. 9d. as against Heyford's £2 0s. 9d.; in 1327 it had 28 contributors compared with Heyford's twenty.[3] The parish as a whole was evidently one of the most prosperous in Ploughley hundred, for its assessment of £5 13s. 4d. from 1334 onwards was the seventh highest in the hundred.[4] The joint return for the two villages for the poll tax of 1377[5] shows a total of 84 contributors, a comparatively high number for the hundred. There may, however, have been a fall in the number of inhabitants about this time, as later evidence points to a decline in the area of arable land.

Much of the land brought under cultivation between 1086 and 1279 must have formed the 'New Breach' in Caulcott, for in the late 13th century Caulcott lands were much more extensive than those of Heyford and had to support a larger population. It is probable that the Breach was maintained as arable until after the Black Death at least, when it may have fallen out of cultivation. Langdon's map

[88] *V.C.H. Oxon.* i. 418, 427.
[89] *Rot. Hund.* (Rec. Com.), ii. 826–7.
[90] *Fines Oxon.* 119, 127.
[91] See below, p. 192.
[92] *P.N. Oxon.* (E.P.N.S.), i. 219. Caulcott had certainly been settled by 1199: *Fines Oxon.* 7.
[93] *Rot. Hund.* (Rec. Com.), ii. 826–7.
[94] Assuming a cotland = c. ½ virgate.
[95] C.C.C. Mun. Ao 10: report on Caulcott farm c. 1600.

[96] Calculation based on comparison of *Langdon's Map* and O.S. Maps.
[97] *P.N. Oxon.* (E.P.N.S.), i. 219.
[98] C 133/63/1.
[99] C 134/10/5.
[1] C 135/104/1.
[2] S.C. 2/197/45.
[3] E 179/161/8, 9.
[4] Ibid. 161/17.
[5] Ibid. 161/39.

shows that in 1606 most of the Breach was rough pasture,[6] but that the two Caulcott fields were then still as large as those of Heyford. Two remaining furlongs of the Newbreach lay in Caulcott fields and rents were being paid for strips in them in the late 16th and early 17th centuries.[7] The decline of the hamlet was greater than the map alone would indicate, for its land was poorer than Heyford's.[8]

It seems likely that still more land had reverted to rough pasture by the end of the 18th century. It was then thought, for instance, that the 'Newbreach rents' had been paid for waste land.[9] If Davis's map of 1797 is sufficiently accurate to be used as evidence, there was then no arable between Caulcott closes and the parish's eastern boundary, while the Moors, immediately north-east of Heyford village, and the Cleeves, the Linches, and Briar Furlong in the west had fallen out of cultivation. Like the South Cow Pasture, which had turned into scrub land called High Bushes,[10] they may have become covered with scattered trees and undergrowth. The inclosure award of 1802 recorded 125 acres of waste ground, but there may have been a good deal more among the 1,383 acres said to be open-field arable and meadow.[11]

Judging from later evidence, Heyford and its hamlet had separate systems of two open fields each in the Middle Ages.[12] It is probable that by the 16th century these four fields had been united into one system: the agricultural ordinances of the Elizabethan courts clearly applied to the whole parish, and the majority of copyhold tenants of Corpus Christi College who appear in the court rolls held yardlands in both Heyford and Caulcott.[13] Experiments in cropping may have been started by 1600, when it was said that of the 12 yardlands of Caulcott farm—which lay entirely in the two Caulcott fields[14]—8 might be sown in a year, pointing to a three-course rotation.[15] Seventeenth- and 18th-century terriers show that a redivision of the Heyford fields took place. In a terrier of 1679 the rector's lands in Heyford were arranged in three groups—the first and second headed North Field and the third headed South Field. The first group of lands lay entirely in the furlongs north of Bicester Way.[16] Terriers of 1761 and 1775 call these furlongs 'the North side of the Field', while the remainder of the old North Field, with perhaps the northernmost furlongs of the old South Field, were called Middle Field.[17] On this evidence it can be argued that Heyford fields were being rearranged into three by 1679. At that date Caulcott still had two fields.[18]

As elsewhere, good pasture land was scarce at Heyford, and so in the late 16th century there was a lengthy controversy between Heyford and Steeple Aston over rights in Broadhead meadow. The meadow had been awarded in 1575 to Corpus Christi College, who as lords of Heyford claimed both the hay and rights of common after hay harvest. The dispute with Aston arose largely because Aston men could get their beasts into Broadhead in time of flood when Heyford men could not. Up to some 30 years before, witnesses said, Broadhead had been clearly divided from Aston mead by the old course of the Cherwell, but the main water course had been altered when the mills had been moved.[19] A compromise was eventually reached, for in the 17th century one of the farmers of the Heyford demesne had the hay, while the meadow was common to Heyford between hay harvest and 8 September, and common to Aston between 8 September and 25 March.[20]

Another indication of the shortage of pasture is the alteration in the usual stint. In 1600 the stint was 3 cattle and 30 sheep to the yardland,[21] but in 1637 this was reduced by one-fifth. The rector was allowed to graze 8 cattle and 160 sheep on the common pasture instead of 10 cattle and 200 sheep, and the stints of the farmers and customary tenants were reduced to 3 cattle and 20 sheep, and 2 cattle and 20 sheep respectively.[22]

No woods are mentioned in early records and none are shown on Langdon's map of 1606, but Heyford's timber acquired a moderate importance in the 17th century owing to the general scarcity. Small quantities were sold by the college throughout the century, increasing in the second half. It received over £25 a year from sales in 1659, 1670, 1674, and 1679, and in 1687 174 trees—57 elms and 117 ashes—on the copyhold lands were marked for sale.[23] Not until after the inclosure of 1802 was there any further felling except for repairs.[24] Some £520 worth of timber was then sold and over £400 worth in 1810.[25] The only woodland to survive was the High Bushes, but this was cut down partly in 1846–7, when the railway was being built, and partly in 1851.[26]

Copyhold was the predominant form of tenure from the 16th to the 19th century. In the 17th century copyholds, as elsewhere in Oxfordshire, were frequently granted for two lives only,[27] but by the 18th century it was the custom for each copyhold to be for three lives and a widowhood.[28] From time to time the copyholders nominated new reversioners to fill up the three lives on their copies.[29] Towards the end of the 18th century it was the custom of the college to require two years' purchase for a third life and four years' purchase for a second; and one year's value with a heriot for a change from one living person to another.[30]

In 1598 there were seventeen copyholders with holdings varying from a cottage only to two cottages and 5 yardlands. Eleven of them had an average of 4 acres in the Newbreach. Their rents, amounting to £5 2s. in all, changed little in the 17th century. By

[6] *Langdon's Map*; see sketch map opposite.
[7] C.C.C. Mun. Ao 9: rental 1598.
[8] In 1798 a yardland in Heyford was worth £14 a year, a yardland in Caulcott only £7 10s.: C.C.C. Mun. Ao 8.
[9] Ibid.
[10] Davis, *Oxon. Map*; Blo. *L. Heyf.* 34.
[11] H. L. Gray, *Eng. Field Systems*, 537.
[12] *Langdon's Map*; Blo. *L. Heyf.* 84 sqq.: rectory terrier 1679.
[13] C.C.C. Mun. Ao 9: rental 1598.
[14] *Langdon's Map*; cf. sketch map, p. 189.
[15] C.C.C. Mun. Ao 10: rep. on Caulcott.
[16] Oxf. Archd. Oxon. b 40, f. 164, printed in Blo. *L. Heyf.* 84 sqq.
[17] C.C.C. Mun. Ao 9.

[18] Blo. *L. Heyf.* 84 sqq.
[19] C.C.C. Mun. Ao 10; ibid. Bursary Transcripts, iv, p. 411. For alteration of course of river see above, p. 182.
[20] Ibid. Ao 8: sketch map with note on Broadhead.
[21] Ibid. Ao 10: rep. on Caulcott.
[22] Ibid. Ao 2; ibid. misc. correspondence about Heyf.
[23] Ibid. Ao 5: bailiffs' accts.; ibid. Ao 9: timber sales.
[24] Ibid. misc. correspondence.
[25] Ibid. Ao 6: bailiffs' accts.
[26] Ibid. misc. correspondence: letters 1846–7; Blo. *L. Heyf.* 34.
[27] C.C.C. Mun. Ao 21.
[28] Ibid. Ao 8: letters.
[29] Ibid. misc. correspondence.
[30] Ibid. Ao 8: letter 1790.

SKETCH MAP OF LOWER HEYFORD
IN THE 17th CENTURY

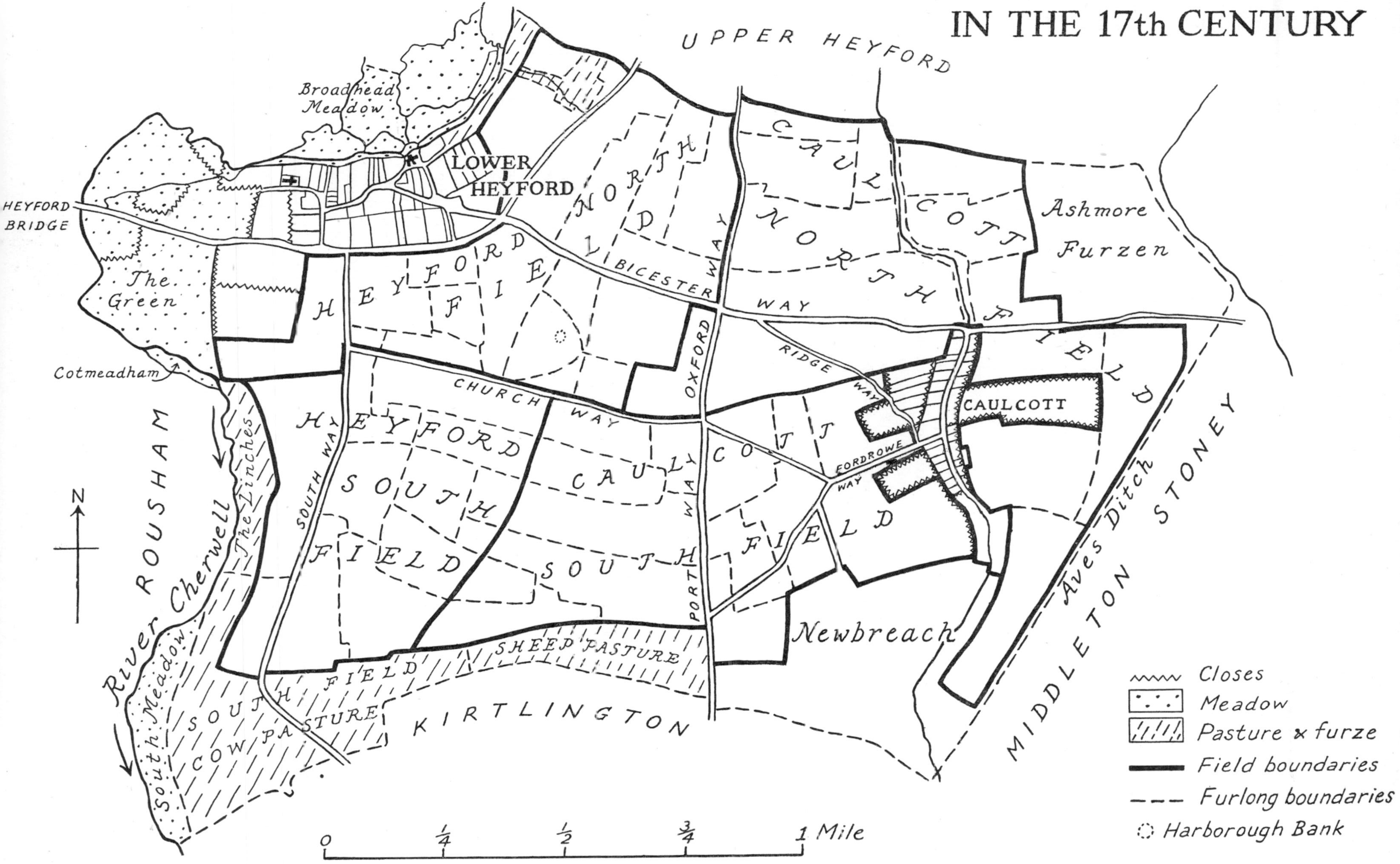

STONEY

MIDDLETON

Aves Ditch

Ashmore

Furzen

CAULCOTT

CAULCOTT

NORTH FIELD

FIELD

CAUL COTT

UPPER HEYFORD

RIDGE WAY

FORDROWE

WAY

COTT FIELD

Newbreach

NORTH WAY

BICESTER WAY

OXFORD WAY

CAULWAY

PORT WAY

SHEEP PASTURE

KIRTLINGTON

LOWER HEYFORD

HEYFORD NORTH FIELD

CHURCH WAY

HEYFORD SOUTH FIELD

CAULWAY SOUTH FIELD

Broadhead Meadow

HEYFORD BRIDGE

The Green

Cotmeadham

HEYFORD SOUTH FIELD

SOUTH WAY

The Linches

Cotwell Meadow

South Meadow

COW PASTURE

SOUTH FIELD

SOUTH FIELD

RIVER ROUSHAM CHERWELL

N

Closes

Meadow

Pasture & furze

Field boundaries

Furlong boundaries

Harborough Bank

0   ¼   ½   ¾   1 Mile

The above map is based on documents cited in the text and on Thomas Langdon's maps of 1606.

1685 24 copies were held by 22 tenants, and in 1750 26 by twenty-three. The customary lands decreased from about 36 yardlands in 1598 to 30 (21 of them in Caulcott) in 1750, when the majority of the copyholders paid rents between 10s. and £1: only two paid more than £1. Entry fines rose considerably in the 18th century and although there were still 640 acres of customary lands in 1832, Lord Jersey, who had acquired a number of copies, held 131 acres of them: only 3 out of 16 other copyholders had more than 50 acres.[31] Copyhold died out soon after 1840, when Corpus Christi began to replace copies which had fallen in by leases for 20 years.

The demesnes were held in 1598 by two farmers and the miller, who paid £4 8s. 9d., £4, and £1 6s. 8d. respectively, plus corn rents, which had been introduced soon after 1526: the miller paid a third of his total rent of £2 with 1 qr. wheat and 3 qrs. malt.[32] From about 1590 the tenants of the demesne paid a corn increment.[33] In 1717 there were still three leaseholders: the appearance of a fourth, the rector, by 1750 accounts for the decrease in the area of customary lands. By 1802 some five-sixths of the leasehold lands were held by the Cottrell-Dormers of Rousham. There were three freeholdings by 1832, of which Lord Jersey held 191 acres out of a total of 220 acres. There were then three large estates, Lord Jersey's, Lady Cottrell-Dormer's, and the rector's; the last increased to about 460 acres after the inclosure of 1802.[34]

The manorial courts, combining the business of courts leet and customary courts, were held regularly until 1712, and afterwards infrequently until 1832:[35] none was held between 1782 and 1796.[36] Tithingmen and constables were elected and 2s. 'head-silver' a year was paid at the courts.[37] In the 16th and 17th centuries business included public health, village morals, highway repairs, keeping the ditches and backwaters of the Cherwell clear, repairs to the ford at Cotmeadham, and the unsuccessful encouragement of archery; but the court's most important functions were the election of officers, the making and enforcement of agricultural by-laws, and the admission of new copyholders. Every year a hayward and three fieldmen were elected to regulate husbandry. By-laws were enrolled in English from the 1620's, whereas the formal records of the court remained in Latin except during the Commonwealth.[38] Typical of the court's orders in the 1660's was the instruction that all tenants should meet at Caulcott in mid-October to view and set out the furze of Astmore and Newbreach by lots.[39] A fine of 5s. was imposed on anyone who carried away his furze with a horse or wagon, and of 1s. a bundle for carrying furze from the wrong lot. By the early 19th century admissions were the only remaining func-

tion of the court,[40] and with the abolition of copyhold the court lost its reason for existence.

Although inclosure of Broadhead meadow had been proposed in 1575 it was not undertaken, and by the early 17th century there had been little inclosure save immediately around the two villages.[41] Inclosure was again suggested in 1734 by the rector, Thomas Leigh, on condition that his tithes and glebe were exchanged for 8 acres and £150 a year for himself and £200 a year for his successors.[42] This may have been considered too much, for nothing came of the idea. As late as 1797, apart from an apparent considerable increase in the number of small closes round Caulcott, there seems to have been little more inclosure.[43] In 1801 an inclosure act was obtained,[44] and the award was made in 1802.[45] Corpus Christi College received a little over an acre for manorial rights. The largest awards were 280 acres to Sir Clement Cottrell-Dormer, 177 acres to Benjamin Churchill, and about 90 acres to the Revd. William Filmer, not as rector but as one of the leaseholders. The Rector of Steeple Aston received an acre in exchange for the tithes from part of Broadhead meadow—a last echo of the old controversy. None of the cottagers had any stock, so that only the larger proprietors received allotments of common grazing-land. The expense of the inclosure to the proprietors was £2 an acre.[46]

Inclosure gave the experimental farmer his opportunity, and in Lower Heyford the rector, William Filmer, led the way. Arthur Young, who commented favourably on many of his innovations, noted that he used the Staffordshire two-wheeled plough and the Kentish one-row drill. Filmer introduced a six-course rotation of crops, was fully aware of the value of swedes and sainfoin, grew lentils for hay, and bred Leicester sheep and Berkshire pigs.[47] At this time agricultural labourers at Heyford were getting 9s. a week and beer in winter; 12s. a week and no beer at hay harvest; and 21s. a week and beer at corn harvest, while women's wages varied from 7d. a day for weeding to 1s. a day and beer at corn harvest—this when bread was 9d. the quartern loaf, and mutton 7d. a pound.[48]

Improved farming had been necessary to feed the increasing population. It appears to have been rising in the late 16th century, despite occasional visitations of the plague in summer and the 'blouddy flix' in winter, and the Compton Census (1676) recorded 148 adults.[49] According to 18th-century estimates the number of inhabitants rose from 220 (40 of them in Caulcott) in 1729, to 290 (63 in Caulcott) in 1760, but had declined to 247 by 1771.[50] At the official census of 1801 the combined population was 346, and by 1861 it had increased to 625;[51] while at Caulcott itself numbers rose from an estimated 57

[31] C.C.C. Mun. Ao 9: rental 1598: Mc 10, ff. 26, 67–68: rentals 1685, 1750; Ao 6: bailiffs' accts.; Ao 8: survey 1832.
[32] Ibid. Ao 9: rental 1598; Mb 2: bailiffs' accts. (general).
[33] £8 in 1590, £38 in 1649, £25 in 1715, £80 in 1800: ibid. Mb 2; Ao 5; Ao 6.
[34] Ibid. Mc 10, ff. 38, 67–68: rentals 1717, 1750; Ao 9: valuation 1802; Ao 8: survey 1832.
[35] The earliest surviving Ct. R. are for 1422–5: S.C. 2/197/45. In C.C.C. Mun. are Ct. R. (extracts) 1547–9: Ao 10; Ct. R. 1585–1832: Ao 2; Ao 4.
[36] Ibid. Ao 8: letter 1796.
[37] In 16th cent. bailiffs of Heyf. still paid 3s. 4d. a year at Wallingford castle for suit of court: ibid. Ao 5: bailiffs' accts.; cf. Rot. Hund. (Rec. Com.), ii. 826.

[38] C.C.C. Mun. Ao 2.
[39] Ibid.; ibid. misc. correspondence.
[40] Ibid. Ao 2; Ao 4.
[41] Ibid. Ao 10; Langdon's Map.
[42] MS. Top. Oxon. ff. 50, 360b.
[43] Davis, Oxon. Map.
[44] C.C.C. Mun. misc. correspondence: minutes of meeting at 'Red Lion'; 41 Geo. III, c. 71 (priv. act).
[45] O.R.O. Incl. award.
[46] Young, Oxon. Agric. 92–93.
[47] Ibid. 76, 114, 137, 165, 178, 309, 315.
[48] Ibid. 321, 323.
[49] Blo. L. Heyf. 20–21: figures from Par. Reg.
[50] Ibid. 23–25: censuses taken by rectors.
[51] V.C.H. Oxon. ii. 221.

in 1771 to 146 in 1841. The opening of the canal and the improvement of the roads evidently changed the occupational pattern of the two villages, for by 1811 27 families were engaged in trade compared with 68 in agriculture.[52] Heyford itself was becoming a local market centre, a trend confirmed by the coming of the railway. A corn market had been started in 1845, and there were six cattle and sheep fairs, and an agricultural show every year.[53] Of the nine farmers of 1851 in the parish one was also an inn-keeper, one a coal-merchant, and one the miller. There were three boatmen, a carrier, a corn-merchant, a maltster (Heyford was famous for its malting barley), a blacksmith, a mason, two carpenters, a canal porter, a timber merchant, a road contractor, and four railway workers, besides a hurdle-maker and a wheelwright.[54] In 1831 a local Fire Engine Society had been established[55] and in 1836 the Heyford and Aston Friendly Society had been founded. The latter was dissolved in 1875 but successfully revived before 1879.[56]

There were two water-mills in Heyford in the Middle Ages,[57] but only one by 1535.[58] Copyholders still had to have their corn ground at the lord's mill in 1548,[59] and when repairs were necessary the lord provided the millstones and the 'great timber'.[60] In the 18th century one wheel of the mill was used for grinding hemp.[61] New machinery had been installed by 1858, when there were four pairs of stones. The fall of water was 6 feet, but the flow was insufficient to drive more than two pairs of stones at once. By 1873 a steam-mill had been built beside the road to Upper Heyford.[62]

About 1860 Heyford's fortunes began to decline. It is significant that in 1850 three of the inhabitants were assisted to emigrate to Canada.[63] By 1864 the cattle and sheep sales were not held at regular fairs, although sheep sales certainly continued until about 1900, the number of tradesmen dwindled, and by 1887 regular markets were no longer held.[64] The canal wharf and the railway station were still busy, but the Bicester, Heyford, and Enstone Turnpike Trust had been ruined by the competition of the railways by 1870, and the Heyford turnpikes were taken down and the toll-houses sold in 1877.[65] Of the Heyford inns the 'Red Lion' and the 'Bell' survived the decline of road traffic but the 'White Horse' had closed by 1887.[66] The steam-mill appears to have stopped work in the 1890's. In 1871 there had been 131 agricultural labourers in the population: in 1926 there were only 45.[67] In 1920 there were still two coal merchants and the water-mill was still at

work, and besides a carrier the village had a haulier and a 'motor engineer, agricultural machinist and wheelwright'.[68] Population declined from the 625 of the peak years 1861 and 1871, to 494 in 1901. By 1951 it had fallen to 398.[69] In 1956 there were twelve farmers in the parish, of whom two each farmed about 300 acres, three over 170 acres each, and the rest between 70 and 15 acres.[70]

CHURCH. The church was dedicated in the mid-11th century by Wulfwig, Bishop of Dorchester (1053–67).[71] During most of the Middle Ages the living was divided into two parts and there were two rectors. This arrangement probably began in the 12th century, when Peter de la Mare and his son Robert between the years 1168 and 1173 granted half the church to Eynsham Abbey.[72] Eynsham held the advowson of its rectory until the 15th century, when the two rectories were united.

The advowson of the second rectory belonged to the lords of the Henred manor.[73] In 1251 or 1252 there was a dispute over the right to present between Lucy de Henred, who held the manor in dower, and Richard de Henred, her son. She finally admitted that the right was his.[74] From 1279 the De Lisles and from 1349 the De la Mares presented.[75] Maud de la Mare, who held both manors in dower, was patron in 1400, but after her death, when the original Henred manor passed to her daughter, the advowson followed the descent of the De la Mare manor, Robert de la Mare presenting in 1407 and Thomas de la Mare in 1450.[76]

In 1453 the Bishop of Lincoln united the two rectories,[77] and the lord of the De la Mare manor and Eynsham presented in turn. Thomas de la Mare did so in 1474, Eynsham in 1492, and Edward Baynton in 1527. When the manor was sold to Corpus Christi College in 1533, the manorial half of the advowson went with it.[78]

When Eynsham was dissolved in 1539, its half of the advowson went to the Crown, and was sold in 1543 with much other property to Richard Andrews and Nicholas Temple, two speculators in monastic lands, who immediately sold it.[79] It ultimately went to Corpus Christi College. During these transactions, James Edmund presented to the rectory in 1544, having bought the presentation for one turn.[80]

The college has held the advowson since that time, but not without friction. President Morwent considered it his private property, and on his death in 1558 he left it to the college.[81] Thomas Greenway, a later president and Rector of Heyford (1563–71),

[52] Blo. *L. Heyf.* 25, 29.
[53] Gardner, *Dir. Oxon.*
[54] Ibid.; H.O. 107/1729.
[55] C.C.C. Mun. misc. correspondence.
[56] *Heyf. and Aston Friendly Soc. Rules* (1851, 1879): Bod. G.A. Oxon. 8° 1304; Wing, *Annals*, 78.
[57] *V.C.H. Oxon.* i. 418, 427; *Rot. Hund.* (Rec. Com.), ii. 826–7.
[58] C.C.C. Mun. Ao 5: bailiffs' accts.; see above, p. 188.
[59] C.C.C. Mun. Ao 10: Ct. R. extract.
[60] Ibid. Bursary Transcripts, iv, p. 389.
[61] Blo. *L. Heyf.* 32.
[62] C.C.C. Mun. Ao 9: valuation 1858; ibid. misc. correspondence.
[63] Bicester U.D.C. Offices; Bd. of Guardians min. bk., 1848–50.
[64] *Kelly's Dir. Oxon.* (1864, 1887); inf. Mr. R. V. Lennard.
[65] Wing, *Annals*, 72–73, 165.

[66] *Kelly's Dir. Oxon.* (1887, 1895).
[67] C. V. Butler, *Village Survey Making*, 11.
[68] *Kelly's Dir. Oxon.* (1920).
[69] *Census*, 1861–1951.
[70] Inf. Miss D. B. Dew, Lower Heyford.
[71] *Eynsham Cart.* i. 109.
[72] Ibid.
[73] See above, p. 185.
[74] *Rot. Grosse.* 502.
[75] See above, pp. 184, 185.
[76] For list of medieval presentations see MS. Top. Oxon. d 460.
[77] C.C.C. Bursary Transcripts xv, no. 39.
[78] Ibid. xvi, no. 73.
[79] *L. & P. Hen. VIII*, xviii (1), pp. 530, 539.
[80] Blo. *L. Heyf.* 53; Oxf. Dioc. d 105, p. 8.
[81] T. Fowler, *Hist. of Corpus Christi College* (O.H.S. xxv), 100.

was accused of buying the advowson for £30 of college money from the rector, James Warner.[82] In the course of the legal disputes which followed Greenway's death his family alleged that he had the right of next presentation to Heyford.[83]

Since 1931, when the rectory was united to that of Rousham, the college and the Cottrell-Dormers of Rousham Park have presented in turn.[84]

The division of the rectory into two made the livings poor. In 1254 the double rectory was valued at £6 13s. 4d., and in 1291 each half was worth £5.[85] The rector of the Eynsham half had to pay a pension of £1 a year to the abbey. This payment probably began with the gift of the advowson to Eynsham, but it is first mentioned in an episcopal confirmation of 1197-8.[86]

Each rector had his own glebe. That of the Eynsham rector—said to have been given to the church at the time of its dedication in the 11th century—comprised in the 12th century a virgate, a cotland, 8 acres, and some pasture.[87] In 1279 he was said to hold 2 virgates and 2 tenements, a mill rented for 4s., some meadow-land, and a rent of 5s. The other rector, presented by the De Lisle lords, held 2 virgates in Heyford and Caulcott, besides 10 acres which had been given by Richard de Henred in 1220, when his brother William became rector.[88] The gift was to keep a lamp always burning before the high altar, and these lamplands, 'lamp litts', or 'lamplights' are marked on Langdon's map of 1606 as lying in Heyford North Field.[89] They are mentioned as late as the inclosure award of 1802.[90]

By the mid-15th century the system of having two rectors had broken down. In 1453, when the halves of the rectory were united, the De la Mare rectory had been vacant two years because of its poverty. Both rectories, in fact, had been decreasing in value, because of the poverty and small numbers of the parishioners and the infertility of the land. The revenue, it was said, was barely enough for one rector 'in these days', and because of this the church was being deprived of services.[91] After the union the rector, in addition to the pension to Eynsham, had to pay one of 2s. to the bishop and one of 1s. to the archdeacon.[92] In 1535 the value of the living was £10 13s.[93]

By this time the chapel at Caulcott had fallen into disuse. It is not clear whether it had once been a chapel of Heyford, which ceased to be used as Caulcott declined,[94] or whether it was a private chapel. The Crown considered it the latter, for about 1575 it confiscated it as a chantry.[95] After making an inquiry, the answers to which have not been found, about the existence of such a chapel, its services, its

tithes and lands, the queen sold Caulcott chapel, with Chapel Yard, a field called Church Meade, and all appurtenant buildings and tithes, for £106. 6s. 8d. to Sir John Parrott.[96] The chapel itself was later thought to have been pulled down.[97]

After the Reformation Heyford was a well-endowed living, said in the 18th century to be worth £110.[98] Its income came partly from all the tithes in the parish, which at the inclosure award in 1802 were commuted for 269 acres,[99] and from the unusually large glebe,[1] including commons for 8 beasts and 160 sheep, which was exchanged at the same time for 91 acres. In addition, the rector of the day, William Filmer, received personally about 90 acres for leasehold lands, which he added to the rectory lands.[2] In 1831 the rectory, valued at £496, was one of the richest in the deanery.[3] The Caulcott part of the glebe was sold in 1926 and the rest in 1949.[4]

In the 13th century the rectors of both halves of the living were sworn to personal residence.[5] It is not clear how they divided the services, but one may have served the main church and the other the chapel at Caulcott. Some of them are worthy of note: Master Robert Bacon (1218/19–27) was a distinguished Dominican scholar and a close friend of St. Edmund; Sampson Brassard (1240–52) was a physician,[6] and Simon de Welles (1290–1) became a Dominican.[7] Master Alexander de Wheplade, another graduate, was excommunicated and suspended for granting the king the large tax he had demanded without papal consent.[8]

Fourteenth-century rectors were not at all notable, except for the short periods during which they held the living. Between 1292 and 1369 there were ten known incumbents.[9] One was accused of neglecting to keep the chancel in repair.[10] His successors, however, must have had the necessary work carried out, for much of the present work in the church is of 14th-century date. A clerk instituted in 1349, the year of the plague, had resigned by 1350. The evidence for the state of the church in the 15th and 16th centuries is scanty. At the visitation of 1530 there were minor complaints. The rector, Master William Man (1527–44), who had been an Augustinian canon,[11] was non-resident and had a curate, The lessees of the rectory aired their grain in the church-yard, the walls of which were dilapidated, and Richard de Henred's lamp was not kept burning in the church.[12] Man's successor, John Warner (1544–63), was presumably also non-resident for at least part of the year, for he was the first Regius Professor of Physic at Oxford, was for many years Warden of All Souls College,[13] and moreover, according to Anthony

[82] T. Fowler, *Hist. Corpus*, 115.
[83] Req. 2/37/40.
[84] *Kelly's Dir. Oxon.* (1939), under Rousham.
[85] Lunt, *Val. Norw.* 312; *Tax. Eccl.* (Rec. Com.), 31.
[86] *Eynsham Cart.* i. 46.
[87] Ibid. 109.
[88] *Rot. Hund.* (Rec. Com.), ii. 827; Blo. *L. Heyf.* 39–40 quoting will at C.C.C.; *Rot. Welles*, ii. 3.
[89] C.C.C. Mun.
[90] O.R.O. Incl. award.
[91] C.C.C. Bursary Transcripts xv, no. 39.
[92] Ibid.
[93] *Valor Eccl.* (Rec. Com.), ii. 162.
[94] See above, p. 187.
[95] C.C.C. Bursary Transcripts xvi, no. 99.
[96] Ibid. no. 98. This was done by the law of 1 Ed. VI, c. 14.

[97] Oxf. Dioc. d 553.
[98] *Par. Coll.* ii. 174.
[99] O.R.O. Incl. award.
[1] Blo. *L. Heyf.* 84–88: 1679 terrier.
[2] Ibid. 89; Oxf. Dioc. c 448, f. 71; O.R.O. Incl. award.
[3] *Rep. of Comm. on Eccl. Revenues*, H.C. 54 (1835), xxii.
[4] Inf. Miss D. B. Dew, Lower Heyford.
[5] *Rot. Welles*, i. 170; *Rot. Grosse*, 443.
[6] *Rot. Grosse.* 502; Emden, *Biog. Dict.*
[7] Linc. Reg. i, Sutton, f. 337b.
[8] Blo. *L. Heyf.* 50, citing Linc. Reg.
[9] For list of medieval incumbents see MS. Top. Oxon. d 460.
[10] See below, p. 193.
[11] *Reg. Univ.* i. 80.
[12] *Visit. Dioc. Linc. 1517-31*, ii. 35.
[13] *Reg. Univ.* i. 111.

Wood, was 'a great intruder into ecclesiastical benefices and dignities'.[14]

After the acquisition of the advowson by Corpus Christi College, the rectors were appointed from among its Fellows, and in the latter half of the 16th century two presidents held the living. Thomas Greenway (1563–71) built a rectory house at Heyford and resided there after his resignation from the presidency in 1568 until his death in 1571.[15] Though the charges that Greenway had embezzled college money and consorted with 'infamous women', two of them Heyford villagers,[16] may not have been true, he cannot be regarded as a model rector. William Cole, on the other hand, at one time a Protestant exile at Zürich and made President of Corpus Christi by Elizabeth I,[17] seems to have been so. From 1572 until 1598 he spent a part of his year at Heyford, where he was responsible for opening a market or shop.[18] His family appears to have lived at the parsonage all the year; his children were baptized and married in the church;[19] and his son Thomas Cole succeeded him as incumbent in 1600.[20] 'Blameless' and 'very diligent in ye discharge of his duty' though Thomas may have been,[21] he appears to have suffered from melancholia, for he several times entered his own burial in the parish register. He became unpopular in the village for failing to keep up the ancient custom of giving all his parishioners bread, cheese, and beer at his house on Christmas Day, and of providing a Christmas dinner to all householders. He was presented in the bishop's court in 1621 for his neglect and ordered to restore the custom, and furthermore to continue the provision of straw for the seats in the church on St. Thomas's Day from the grass in Church Mead.[22] He was ejected by the Parliamentary Commissioners in 1646,[23] and the Christmas feast probably ended with him. When the parishioners tried to revive it in 1732 and sent someone to search the registers at Lincoln, they could find no evidence for the custom.[24]

Two of his Puritan successors are interesting examples of country clergy in this troubled time: one—Thomas Butler—an army preacher, who lived at Deddington, was alleged to keep 'strumpets' and preach in 'coat and Sworde';[25] the other, an intruded Fellow of Corpus named John Dod, resided at Heyford from 1651 to 1662, but did not once administer the sacrament to his parishioners, 'alledging that they were not fit for it'.[26] But the chief distinction of Heyford rectors both in this century and the next was that they resided in their parish for the greater part of the period.[27] Indeed of one, John Franklin, it was lamented that he had 'in a manner buried' his profound knowledge of philosophy by retiring to so lonely a place.[28] Franklin is also to be remembered for his toleration of dissent in his parish; he was one of the five ministers in the county to read in church James II's declaration about liberty of conscience in 1688.[29]

At least one of the 18th-century parsons, Thomas Leigh (1728–44), was active in good works. He began the custom of keeping a record of communicants,[30] and as he said his parish was 'one of the poorest in the diocese' and his parishioners unable to give money for church repairs, he got his church restored and had the parsonage partly rebuilt.[31]

Several of the 19th-century rectors were also notable for their work in the parish. There was William Filmer (1797–1830), the son of Sir Edmund Filmer, who was an agricultural expert.[32] He farmed the glebe himself and improved its value, notably by tree-planting.[33] He was followed by George Faithful (1830–66), 'clergyman, schoolmaster, and farmer';[34] Charles Fort (1866–8), a man of saintly character, who was responsible for the restoration of the church, the rebuilding of the rectory, and the building of the school; and Henry Furneaux (1868–92), a well-known classical scholar.[35] These men attracted congregations of as many as 300 persons, though they were still thought small in proportion to the size of the parish. Many labourers and their families were usually absent, and many who were not professed dissenters went to the chapels as a result of the 'liberalism of the age'.[36] In the 1860's, nevertheless, there were about 50 communicants—a definite improvement, even after allowing for the increased population, on the 20 to 35 communicants common in the 18th century. Seventy children attended the Sunday school, and there was an evening school for boys,[37] both of which had been closed by 1897.[38]

The church of ST. MARY is a stone building of mixed styles, comprising a chancel, clerestoried nave, two aisles, south porch, and western tower.

The only remains of 13th-century work are the built-up responds of a former south arcade, a lancet window in the north wall of the chancel, and a trefoil-headed piscina in the south wall. In 1338 the chancel was reported to be in a very dilapidated state, owing to the neglect of the last rector, William de Balleby, and the executors of his will were ordered to pay for the necessary repairs.[39] The chancel was largely rebuilt some time after this, and the present east window, the timber roof, and three remaining

[14] Wood, *Fasti*, i. 82. For his benefices see ibid. 101.

[15] T. Fowler, *Hist. Corpus* (O.H.S. xxv), 109–10; Blo. *L. Heyf.* 56.

[16] Fowler, op. cit. 115–23. He was also accused of renewing a copyhold for an excessively low fine: ibid. 120. For his successor David Evans see Blo. *L. Heyf.* 56. He may never have been instituted: *O.A.S. Rep.* 1914, 216.

[17] *D.N.B.*

[18] Fowler, op. cit. 136–7. He also held the manorial court.

[19] *V.C.H. Oxon.* iii. 222; Blo. *L. Heyf.* 58.

[20] Blo. *L. Heyf.* 59. For pedigree of Cole see Wood, *Life*, i. 180.

[21] Blo. *L. Heyf.* 60–61; Fowler, op. cit. 138.

[22] MS. Top. Oxon. c 56, f. 25.

[23] *Walker Rev.* 296.

[24] Blo. *L. Heyf.* 19.

[25] Ibid. 62; *Walker Rev.* 296; J. Walker, *Sufferings of Clergy* (1714), 224.

[26] *Calamy Rev.* 165; Blo. *L. Heyf.* 62; Walker, op. cit. 224.

[27] For full list of rectors see Blo. *L. Heyf.* 49–68.

[28] Wood, *Fasti*, ii. 283.

[29] Wood, *Life*, iii. 267. See Wood, *Fasti*, ii. 380, for his successor, Hugh Barrow (1690–1720).

[30] An 18th-cent. notebook kept by rectors giving lists of communicants, &c., is MS. Top. Oxon. f 50. Blo. *L. Heyf.* 71–82 gives extracts.

[31] Blo. *L. Heyf.* 44, 64; Oxf. Dioc. d 553.

[32] Blo. *L. Heyf.* 66. For his family see G.E.C. *Baronetage*, iv. 68; see above, p. 190.

[33] Oxf. Dioc. c 448, f. 71.

[34] Wing, *Annals*, 29.

[35] Blo. *L. Heyf.* 67–68.

[36] *Wilb. Visit.*; Oxf. Dioc. c 332, c 344.

[37] Oxf. Dioc. d 553, d 562, d 570, c 332.

[38] Inf. Mr. R. V. Lennard.

[39] Blo. *L. Heyf.* 40, quoting Linc. Reg.

windows in the north and south walls are 14th-century work.

The nave has two bays on either side, which together with the north and south aisles probably date from the 14th century. The east window of the north aisle appears to be early 14th century, so that it seems probable that the north aisle was added before the south aisle; the capitals on the south side of the nave are later than those on the north side, and the east window of the south aisle, which is similar to the east window of the chancel, probably belongs to the second half of the 14th century. On either side of it are two 14th-century niches.

The tower, which has a plain parapet, was probably completed in the late 14th century. Further work on the church was carried out in the 15th century when a nave clerestory with eight windows, a new nave roof of somewhat lower pitch than the former one,[40] and a south porch were added. At the same time the walls of the aisles were partly rebuilt and the large square-headed windows inserted. Above the south porch there is a sun-dial with the motto 'Nil nisi caelesti radio'.

When Rawlinson visited the church in the early 18th century[41] he found it in a good state of repair, but a report by Bishop Secker of 1739 shows a less satisfactory picture. The porch, he said, was in danger of falling down, the paving uneven, the pews ruinous, the walls in need of whitewashing, the west door and church gate in a bad state, and the boards supporting the leads rotten. He ordered the church-wardens to take action. In 1741 and 1742 some minor sums were spent[42] and in 1757 further repairs, including the walling-up of the northern door, were ordered.[43]

The 19th-century revival of interest in ecclesiastical buildings led to considerable repairs to the fabric. In 1848 the nave and north aisle were re-roofed at a cost of about £270 (architect H. J. Underwood). A sketch of 1867 shows a western gallery approached by a wooden staircase;[44] the date of this addition is not known. In 1867 and 1868 restoration work carried out by the architect C. Buckeridge cost £1,240 and included relaying the floor of the nave and south aisle, renewing the roof of the south aisle, and removing the plaster ceiling of the chancel. Later in the century an organ was installed and an altar reredos erected.[45] In 1922 the piscina was restored, and an altar erected in the south aisle as a memorial to the men killed in the First World War.[46]

Heating was first put in in 1868.

Part of the staircase to the rood-loft remains, and the chancel screen, although much restored, is medieval; the tracery and trail on top are exceptionally good.[47] The octagonal font is inscribed 1662, although the base is probably medieval.[48] A clock, doubtless placed in the tower in 1695 (the date on the oak frame), was removed during the 1868 restoration.[49]

Of the three medieval glass shields described in 1574, two somewhat damaged ones survive in the west window of the south aisle. The west window of the north aisle also has a quarry with the initials T.G., a pelican (the crest of Corpus Christi College) and the date [15]69, for Thomas Greenway, rector (d. 1571).[50]

There is a small brass to Elizabeth, wife of William Bruce (d. 1683); a stone cartouche with coat of arms to Gabriel Myrry (d. 1684) and his wife; and a memorial with arms to the rector William Filmer (d. 1830). Inscriptions to Castell Brangwin (d. 1710) and family; to Rachael the wife (d. 1738/9) and children of Henry Hester of Withill, Tackley; and to the rectors, Ralph Pomfret (d. 1728), William Bradley (d. 1768), William Harrison (d. 1796), and George Thorpe (d. 1784), were illegible or untraceable in 1955.[51]

In 1552 the church had a chalice, two copes, and three vestments.[52] In 1955 it owned an Elizabethan chalice and paten cover, and a chalice, paten, and flagon given by William Filmer in 1825.[53]

There were three bells and a sanctus bell in 1552. The bells were ordered to be recast into five bells, for a sum not exceeding £31, in 1766. In 1955 there were six bells, two of them of 1766,[54] and a set of hand bells.

The registers date from 1539. Those of baptisms and burials (1644–64) and of marriages (1607–64) appear to be extracts and incomplete.[55] There are churchwardens' accounts from 1763 to 1858.

NONCONFORMITY. Three infrequent attendants at church are mentioned in the recusant roll of 1577,[56] but in other returns of the late 16th and early 17th centuries there is no record of Roman Catholicism. The 18th-century episcopal returns mention one papist woman.[57]

In the 17th century there was a small Quaker community in the village. It was agreed at a Quarterly Meeting of the Friends at Oxford in February 1678 that a meeting should be held there every fortnight.[58] At the time of Bishop Fell's visitation in the 1680's about seventeen Quakers attended meeting at John Marsh's barn.[59] He and John Day were presented in 1694 for not having paid tithes.[60] According to the Quaker records Richard Day had had £6 worth of corn and grain taken from him by the rector in 1693

---

[40] The marks of an earlier and higher nave roof are visible on the eastern face of the tower.

[41] Par. Coll. ii. 174.

[42] Blo. L. Heyf. 44.

[43] Oxf. Archd. Oxon. d 13, f. 33.

[44] Blo. L. Heyf. 46. For a pre-restoration view of the interior by Joseph Wilkins see opposite.

[45] Ibid. 46–47, 48.

[46] Kelly's Dir. Oxon. (1939).

[47] Arch. Jnl. lxvii. 188, where there is a sketch. It was removed and taken to pieces at the restoration of 1868 (Blo. L. Heyf. 47), but has since been restored.

[48] See drawing by J. Buckler in MS. Top. Oxon. a 67, f. 323.

[49] Blo. L. Heyf. 43–44.

[50] Lamborn, Arm. Glass, 131–2. The two shields were

dug up in 1868 and were presented to the church by Miss D. B. Dew in about 1929. The quarry in the N. aisle came from the Old Rectory and was preserved by G. J. Dew (inf. Miss Dew).

[51] Par. Coll. ii. 174; MS. Top. Oxon. c 165, pp. 367–70; for arms on monuments, see Bod. G.A. Oxon. 16° 217, p. 160.

[52] Chant. Cert. 88.

[53] Evans, Ch. Plate.

[54] Ch. Bells Oxon. ii. 163–4; Blo. L. Heyf. 44.

[55] Blo. L. Heyf. 71.

[56] C.R.S. xxii. 114.

[57] Oxf. Dioc. d 553.

[58] Quarterly Minute Bk. (1671–1746): Berks. R.O., Reading.   [59] Oxf. Dioc. d 708, f. 144.

[60] O.R.O. Cal. Q. Sess.

Interior of the church in the mid-19th century

HEYFORD BRIDGE

South-east view of the church in the mid-19th century

HEYFORD WARREN

and £4 worth in 1694 on his refusal to pay tithes.[61] The Quaker influence was not maintained, and by 1738 there was only one left, another dissenter being a Presbyterian.[62]

In the early 19th century Methodism took root. In 1804 Joseph Hockmore's house was registered as a meeting-place.[63] It was soon superseded by a chapel built by Thomas Rose,[64] the miller, who often preached himself. Circuit preachers also came.[65] The congregation in the second half of the century belonged to the United Methodists[66] (formed in 1857 and joined to the Wesleyan Methodists in 1932). In 1906 a new chapel, still in use in 1955, was built at a cost of £700.[67] In 1954 it had six members.[68]

Another Methodist centre, which remained Wesleyan, was started in Caulcott with the registration of Thomas Gee's house in 1830.[69] A chapel was built there in 1841[70] and was in use in 1955, but since it had only four members, regular services were not held.[71] In 1878 the number of Methodists in the whole parish was estimated at nearly a hundred.[72]

SCHOOLS. In 1808 two dame schools provided instruction in reading, writing, and knitting for 60 children.[73] These schools still existed in 1819 but were inadequate for the needs of the poor.[74] In 1833 there were two fee-paying schools, one of them a 'ladies' boarding school' attended by farmers' daughters.[75] These were attended by 26 boys and 35 girls, while at a third school there were 12 children of whom 4 received free instruction out of a legacy of £50 left in 1826 by Thomas Rose.[76] There were still three schools in 1854, when the rector paid for 7 children and the Rose bequest for 3, while 38 were paid for by their parents.[77]

In 1867 a National school was opened in a house in Lower Heyford adjoining the present Church of England school, which was built in the following year. It comprised one schoolroom and one classroom. There was one teacher,[78] and the average attendance was 71 in 1871, 57 in 1889, and 84 in 1906.[79] The school was reorganized as a junior school in 1932, when the senior pupils were transferred to Steeple Aston, and it became a controlled school in 1952. The number of pupils was 28 in 1937 and 48 in 1954.[80] The Rose bequest was vested in the school at its foundation, and in 1955 was used to provide school prizes.[81]

By 1833 the Countess of Jersey was supporting a school in Caulcott for 12 children.[82] This number remained unchanged in 1871,[83] but by 1887 when it had 20 pupils it had become an infants' school.[84] The older children of Caulcott were then going to school at Middleton Stoney.[85] There were 10 pupils in 1906 and the school continued to be supported by successive earls of Jersey.[86] It had closed by the 1950's.[87]

CHARITIES. Abigail Merry or Malpas, born at Heyford in 1594, by will of unknown date left to the poor a rent-charge of £1 a year on tenements in Cripplegate, to be distributed annually at Christmas.[88] The money appears to have been first received in 1680.[89] From 1795 onwards 4s. was deducted for land tax. In the early 19th century 16s. was still being paid,[90] but the income of the charity was only 8s. 10d.[91] in 1954.

Susannah Bruce (d. 1706) by her will left £10 to the poor, the interest (10s.) to be distributed each year after Christmas. In 1797 the interest was some years in arrears, but £7 10s. was then paid, and together with money raised by subscription was added to the principal, bringing it up to £20. From 1801 this sum was held by the rector, who paid £1 a year interest. In 1824 the income from the Malpas and Bruce Charities, together with money collected at the sacrament, was distributed by the rector each sacrament day in sums of 1s. to 2s. 6d. to the most needy among the poor.[92] The income of the charity in 1954 was 12s. 4d.

In 1738 it was reported that a small charity worth 10s. a year was being distributed annually by a Mr. Macock.[93] It had been lost by 1771.[94]

The inclosure award of 1802 set aside 32 acres, Poor's Land, to be held in trust for the poor, in lieu of their right to cut furze for fuel.[95] In 1852 the land brought in £30 a year in rent[96] which was distributed to the poor in coal at Christmas.[97] In 1954 the land was let at £24 a year, and the rent, together with the income from the Malpas and Bruce Charities, was distributed in money just before Christmas. The recipients had to be old-age pensioners with at least three years' residence in the parish, and only one payment could be made to one household. Thirty-seven poor people received 11s. each.

Louisa Julia Evans (d. 1935) left £336 8s. 5d. in stock. Four-fifths of the income was to be spent on tea for the poor. The first distribution was in 1938. At Christmas 1954 58 quarter-pound packets of tea were given to old-age pensioners.[98]

[61] Quart. Min. Bk. (1671–1746).
[62] Oxf. Dioc. d 553.   [63] Ibid. c 644, f. 78.
[64] See below.
[65] Oxf. Dioc. c 327, p. 298; ibid. d 574; Blo. L. Heyf. 35. The incumbent claimed that many dissenters sometimes attended church: Oxf. Dioc. d 570.
[66] Blo. L. Heyf. 35.
[67] Kelly's Dir. Oxon. (1920).
[68] Methodist Church Oxford Circuit Plan, no. 273 (1954).
[69] Oxf. Dioc. c 645, f. 153. Another house was registered in 1834: ibid. f. 226.
[70] Ibid. c 646, f. 149.
[71] Buckingham and Brackley Methodist Circuit Plan (1955–6). By 1957 it had become a garage.
[72] Oxf. Dioc. c 344.   [73] Ibid. d 707.
[74] Educ. of Poor, 725.
[75] Blo. L. Heyf. 34; Gardner, Dir. Oxon.
[76] Educ. Enq. Abstract, 748; Blo. L. Heyf. 38; for Rose, see above.   [77] Oxf. Dioc. d 701.
[78] Blo. L. Heyf. 34.   [79] Elem. Educ. Ret.
[80] Inf. Oxon. Educ. Cttee.

[81] Inf. Miss D. B. Dew, L. Heyford.
[82] Educ. Enq. Abstract, 748.
[83] Elem. Educ. Ret.
[84] Kelly's Dir. Oxon. (1887).
[85] Blo. L. Heyf. 34.   [86] List of Sch.
[87] Inf. Mr. R. V. Lennard.
[88] 12th Rep. Com. Char. 305.
[89] Blo. L. Heyf. 36; Char. Don. ii. 989.
[90] 12th Rep. Com. Char. 305.
[91] All inf. on income and distribution of charities in 1954 from Miss D. B. Dew, churchwarden.
[92] 12th Rep. Com. Char. 305.
[93] Oxf. Dioc. d 553. The Macocks were prominent Heyford yeomen: see e.g. C.C.C. Mun. Ao 9.
[94] Oxf. Dioc. d 562.
[95] O.R.O. Incl. award.
[96] Gardner, Dir. Oxon.
[97] Kelly's Dir. Oxon. (1864–1939).
[98] Inf. Miss D. B. Dew. The Stroud, Preedy and Lennard Bequests are for upkeep of church, churchyard, &c.

UPPER HEYFORD or HEYFORD WARREN

THIS oblong-shaped parish[1] of 1,628 acres has 1½ miles of the River Cherwell for its western boundary and the Romano-British Aves Ditch for its eastern.[2] Neither its northern nor its southern boundary, separating it from Somerton and Lower Heyford respectively, follows any distinctive physical features.[3] There have been no recorded changes of boundary.[4]

The parish lies almost entirely on the Great Oolite, except for a narrow belt along the Cherwell.[5] The soil is chiefly stonebrash. From the meadowland along the river the ground rises steeply to a tableland, 400 feet above sea-level in the central and eastern part. Domesday records no woodland,[6] but Davis shows Child Grove on the Ardley boundary, and it has been suggested that this wood and Ballard's Copse in Ardley were once the 'Little Ciltene' of a 10th-century charter.[7] Today the absence of trees is a noticeable feature. There is one small coppice, Goose Covert, on the south-eastern boundary.

The pre-Roman Portway[8] runs parallel with the Somerton–Lower Heyford road, which skirts Upper Heyford village. In the north of the parish it was narrowed into a bridle track only by the inclosure act of 1842.[9] A minor road connects the village with Middleton Stoney to the east.

The Heyford section of the former G.W.R.'s main line between Oxford and Banbury was completed in 1850; its high embankment traverses the meadow-land and has rendered it more liable to flooding.[10] The Oxford–Coventry canal surveyed by James Brindley in 1768 and completed in 1790 runs parallel; it is here navigated by Allen's Lock. Part of the river near the manor-house was utilized for the canal; a fresh channel, partly outside the parish, was dug for the Cherwell, and the mill-house and mill were moved from the east bank of the old Cherwell to the west bank of the new river.[11] The mill was presumably on the site of the Domesday one.[12]

The village took its name from a ford across the river that was perhaps mainly used at the time of the hay harvest.[13] It acquired its second name of Warren from its late 12th-century lord Warin Fitzgerold. In the 15th century the alternative name of Upper Heyford began to appear.[14] The early village was almost certainly centred on the church and the manor-house, which stand just above the Cherwell, but it has developed along a couple of roads which climb the hill, and the latest houses are on the extreme eastern fringe along the Somerton road. The 17th-century village was comparatively small, with only twenty

householders listed for the hearth tax of 1662.[15] In 1665 when only sixteen were listed there were two gentlemen's houses—the Rectory and the manor-house—and six other good farm-houses, each with three or four hearths. There were said to be about 30 houses during most of the 18th century, but a big increase in population occurred at the end of the century and later: 44 dwellings were built between 1811 and 1851.[16] There has also been much new building in the 20th century: 32 council houses were built between 1919 and 1954.[17]

Today the older houses in the village are mostly two-storied cottages, built of coursed rubble; they have casement windows and Welsh slate, thatched, or tiled roofs.[18] The most interesting and the oldest building is the fine medieval barn which stands near the Manor Farm. It is constructed of coursed rubble with ashlar quoins and was probably built for New College in the early 15th century. It measures 120 by 24 feet and is comparable to the barns at Swalcliffe and Adderbury. It has two projecting gabled doorways on the east side separated by two buttresses with two other buttresses at either end, and on the west side eight buttresses and a wide doorway. There are angle buttresses at each end. The roof has tie-beams with curved braces to the lower ties.

The adjoining Manor Farm is now mainly an early 19th-century building, although part of the walls and beams may date back to the 16th or 17th century. Some panelling of that date has survived in the attics, and also a large fireplace in a ground-floor room. The medieval manor-house on the site is said to have been improved and extended by New College in the 14th century. In 1665, when Gabriel Merry was the college's tenant, he returned six hearths for the tax. Buckler's drawing of 1823 shows a very irregularly shaped house, which appears to be substantially of 16th-century date, although some of its windows are medieval.[19]

In the 14th century the college is said to have moved the parsonage house from its original site near the church to half-way up the north side of the present village street.[20] It was the largest house in the village in the 17th century: seven hearths were returned for it for the tax of 1665,[21] and in 1679 it is described as a five-bay building with kitchen and stable adjoining besides twelve bays of outbuildings and a garden.[22] A description of 1685 gives the house seven bays of building and the outhouses eighteen.[23] There are amusing contemporary accounts of visits to this house by the Wardens and Fellows of New College.[24]

---

[1] In this article extensive use has been made of material supplied by the Revd. E. P. Baker, Great Milton (formerly of Upper Heyford), and by Dr. Joycelyne Dickinson.

[2] For Aves Ditch see *V.C.H. Oxon.* i. 275; *Oxoniensia*, ii. 202.

[3] O.S. Map 6", xvi (1885); 2½", 42/42, 52 (1951).

[4] *Census*, 1881, 1951.

[5] G.S. Map 1", xlv NW.

[6] *V.C.H. Oxon.* i. 414.

[7] Davis, *Oxon. Map*; *P.N. Oxon.* (E.P.N.S.), i. 197; see above, p. 7.

[8] *V.C.H. Oxon.* i. 275.   [9] Blo. *U. Heyf.* 29.

[10] E. T. MacDermot, *Hist. G.W.R.* i. 300.

[11] Blo. *U. Heyf.* 27; cf. O.S. Map 25", xvi. 14 (1881).

[12] *V.C.H. Oxon.* i. 414.

[13] *P.N. Oxon.* (E.P.N.S.), i. 220; for position of ford see Blo. *U. Heyf.* 27; cf. above, p. 182.

[14] *Cal. Pat.* 1429–39, 394.

[15] *Hearth Tax Oxon.* 201.

[16] Oxf. Dioc. d 553, d 559; *Census*, 1811, 1851.

[17] Inf. Ploughley R.D.C.

[18] Descriptions of buildings are in part based on a survey by the Min. of Housing and Local Govt.

[19] MS. Top. Oxon. a 67, no. 326.

[20] Blo. *U. Heyf.* 61.

[21] *Hearth Tax Oxon.* 201.

[22] Oxf. Archd. Oxon. c 141, p. 365.

[23] Ibid. b 40, ff. 165–9; Blo. *U. Heyf.* 59.

[24] *Woodward's Progress*, ed. R. L. Rickard (O.R.S. xxvii), 30–44.

A 'fine' new house was built, possibly in 1696,[25] with a south gable end on the village street,[26] from which it was approached by a flight of steps.[27] In 1806 this house, standing in an acre of ground, was said to be a stone building of ten bays covered with a slate roof. It was replaced in 1865.[28]

Of the older cottages the row of stone and thatch ones in the main street probably dates from the 18th century, while opposite the Rectory a solid stone-built farm-house, once Two Tree Farm and now a private residence, bears the date 1722. The 'Three Horseshoes' is mentioned by name in 1784.[29]

Nineteenth-century expansion is represented by New College Yard with its group of brick cottages put up in the first half of the century, the school (1859) that faces the green, the Rectory (1865), the Wesleyan chapel (1867),[30] and the red-brick Reading-room (1891), erected at the expense of the Earl of Jersey on land given by New College.[31] The new Rectory cost over £2,000,[32] whereas its predecessor had cost £500.[33] Local stone was used for the walling, which was lined inside with brick, and Broseley tiling was used for the roofs.[34]

Twentieth-century developments have considerably altered the character of the village: a large number of elm trees have been felled to make room for the new council houses, built of brick or cement and not of local materials.[35]

The R.A.F. station was begun in 1925 and first occupied two years later. Until 1939 it was used for training and members of the Oxford University Air Squadron gained flying experience at it; during the war it was a Bomber Command station. Between 1946 and 1951 No. 1 Parachute Training School was stationed there. The station was leased to the United States Air Force in 1951, and has since been used as a training base. The 3918th Air Base Group of the U.S.A.F. Strategic Air Command is responsible for the operation of the base. There are 125 sets of quarters for military personnel with their families on the base, and 240 new units are being constructed under an agreement between the governments of the United States of America and Great Britain. Some 90 British civilians are employed by the U.S.A.F., and a further 70 by the Air Ministry on repair and maintenance work. The majority of the married personnel live in Oxford, Banbury, Bicester, Chipping Norton, Kidlington, and Brackley, and 350 of their children are educated at the station.[36]

The only distinguished Heyford man was John Yonge (1467–1516), Fellow of New College, Master of the Rolls, and Dean of York, who was employed by Henry VII and Henry VIII on diplomatic missions in the Low Countries. His monument by Torrigiani is in the museum of the Public Record Office.[37]

MANOR. Domesday Book records that an estate assessed at 10 hides was held in 'Haiford' by Roger of Robert d'Oilly, the first castellan of Oxford.[38] The property passed with other D'Oilly lands to the honor of Wallingford.[39] The Domesday tenant was probably Roger de Chesney. His grandson, Ralph de Chesney, was recorded in the *carta* of the honor as holding 2 knight's fees, which may be identified with *HEYFORD WARREN* and Whitchurch. Ralph probably held these fees about 1154, but it is likely that by 1166 they had passed to Maud de Chesney,[40] who was probably his sister.[41] Ralph did not die until about 1196, and the transfer of Heyford and other fees to Maud in his life-time may have been made about 1160, on her marriage to Henry Fitzgerold, chamberlain to Henry II.[42] By 1185 she was a widow in the king's gift with two sons.[43] Her eldest son Warin, who gave his name to the village, came of age in 1189 and had succeeded to the manor by 1198.[44] His patrimony had been somewhat reduced by the liberal benefactions made by his mother to religious houses—Eynsham, Bicester, and Oseney.[45] His daughter Margaret, the wife of Baldwin de Riviers, son of William, Earl of Devon, succeeded him in 1216.[46] Baldwin too died in 1216[47] and Margaret was forced by King John to marry the infamous Fawkes de Bréauté. It is recorded that in 1224, after Fawkes had been exiled, she obtained possession of Heyford Warren manor 'for her support'[48] and that she was still holding it in 1235 and 1243.[49] Her son Baldwin, Earl of Devon, predeceased her in 1245, and after her death in 1252 her grandson Baldwin consequently succeeded. On his death in 1262 his estates passed to his sister Isabel, Countess of Aumale, the widow of William de Forz, who held them until her death in 1293.[50]

There is evidence that Margaret de Riviers had a son by Fawkes de Bréauté;[51] in 1255 Heyford Warren was held of Baldwin, Margaret's grandson, by a certain Thomas de Bréauté,[52] who may well have been this child. In 1279 and 1284 a Thomas de Bréauté,[53] possibly the grandson of Fawkes, was holding the manor as $\frac{1}{5}$ knight's fee. In 1279 Eynsham Abbey held 3 virgates in Somerton of this Thomas.[54] These lands were almost certainly those

[25] *Par. Coll.* ii. 174; Blo. *U. Heyf.* 61.
[26] The framework of these windows can be seen in the garden walls of the present Rectory.
[27] Blo. *U. Heyf.* 61.
[28] Oxf. Dioc. c 440.
[29] O.R.O. Victlrs' recog.
[30] See below, p. 205.
[31] *Par. Rec.*: deed of conveyance (1894). In 1929 the room was leased to the school managers for use as a classroom: inf. Revd. E. P. Baker.
[32] W. Wilkinson, *English Country Houses* (1870), pls. xxvi, xxvii.
[33] *Par. Coll.* ii. 174.
[34] Wilkinson, op cit.
[35] Inf. Revd. E. P. Baker.
[36] Inf. Capt. Alvin J. Rosengren, Information Services Officer, U.S.A.F.
[37] *D.N.B.*; for the monument see Royal Comm. on Hist. Mon. (England), *London*, ii. 117, pl. 169.
[38] *V.C.H. Oxon.* i. 382 n., 414. Cf. *V.C.H. Northants*, i. 312*b*, where H. Round identified the Heyford recorded in the Northants Domesday as Upper Heyford.
[39] Cf. *Boarstall Cart.* 323.
[40] *Red. Bk. Exch.* (Rolls Ser.), 309; *Boarstall Cart.* 309.
[41] L. F. Salzman, 'Family of Chesney', *Suss. Arch. Collect.* lxv, 29 sqq.; cf. *Misc. Gen. et Her.* 5th ser. v. 160.
[42] *Boarstall Cart.* 309; *Eynsham Cart.* i. 422.
[43] *Rot. de Dominabus* (P.R.S. xxxv), 31.
[44] *Pipe R.* 1198 (P.R.S. n.s. ix), 195; *Boarstall Cart.* 309.
[45] *Eynsham Cart.* i. 86; *Oseney Cart.* iv. 216; Hist. MSS. Com. *Rutland IV*, 57; see below, pp. 199, 203.
[46] *Complete Peerage*, iv. 317–18.
[47] Ibid.
[48] Farrer, *Honors*, iii. 231; for Fawkes' tenure of Heyford see *Rot. Litt. Claus* (Rec. Com.), i. 611, 633.
[49] *Bk. of Fees*, 445, 825.
[50] *Complete Peerage*, i. 355–6; iv. 318–23.
[51] K. Norgate, *Minority of Henry III*, 247 n.
[52] *Rot. Hund.* (Rec. Com.), ii. 44; cf. *Oseney Cart.* iv. 215.
[53] *Rot. Hund.* (Rec. Com.), ii. 834; *Feud. Aids*, iv. 158.
[54] *Rot. Hund.* ii. 838.

given to the abbey about 1142 by Alice de Langetot, widow of Roger de Chesney,[55] and since they were held of the honor of Wallingford must have been part of Heyford Warren manor though they lay in Somerton parish. Thomas was dead by 1293, when his widow Elizabeth was receiving £15 a year from Heyford Warren as her dower.[56] There is no further record of the family's tenancy.

Isabel, Countess of Aumale, survived all her children and after her death in 1293 her inheritance was disputed by Warin de Lisle and Hugh de Courtenay.[57] Warin claimed the estate in 1294,[58] but died two years later;[59] his heir Robert eventually obtained seisin of Heyford Warren in 1310 with the exception of 2½ virgates of land which, perhaps by way of compromise, were awarded to Hugh de Courtenay.[60] Robert de Lisle held the manor until 1339, when he granted it to his daughter Alice, wife of Sir Thomas Seymour, and a group of feoffees to be held of him and his heirs for the term of their lives.[61] Robert himself had entered the Franciscan order by 1342, when most of his possessions passed to his son John, and he died two years later. John, who was overlord of Heyford under the terms of his father's grant,[62] died in 1355 and was succeeded by his son Robert. By 1359 Alice Seymour, now a widow, was in sole possession for life by agreement with the surviving feoffees. Her nephew and immediate lord Robert confirmed the arrangement in the same year, when Alice agreed to grant rents in the manor of 50s. a year to the Abbess of the Minories, London, and of 12s. 6d. to the Prioress of Chicksands (Beds.), where her sister Margaret was a nun.[63] In 1380, however, Robert de Lisle, with Alice's concurrence, sold Heyford Warren manor with the advowson and certain lands in Barford St. Michael to William of Wykeham for £1,000 for the endowment of New College.[64] The property was formally handed over to the college in 1382,[65] and it has retained it ever since. In 1392 and 1495 the property was rounded off by two purchases—2 virgates of arable and 5 acres of meadow from John Mercote of Woodstock and £24 worth of land from Thomas Somerton of Balscott.[66]

At the end of the 16th century New College began to lease its manor, and for a while tenants of some social standing held the property: Sir Francis Eure, for example, who became Chief Justice of North Wales in 1610;[67] and Edward Ashworth, tenant from about 1620 to 1648.[68] Then for a century and more the yeoman family of Merry leased the manor: Gabriel, son of Gabriel Merry of Lower Heyford, from 1649 to 1705; his son John until 1718, and his grandson John until 1754.[69] Later tenants were

Thomas Pryor and John Macock (1758–63), Francis Page (1763–1804), and the Rt. Hon. W. Sturges Bourne (1805–45),[70] the politician.[71]

ECONOMIC HISTORY. The Domesday survey[72] states that there were 10 plough-lands at Heyford in 1086; of these only 9 were cultivated, 3 in demesne and 6 by the customary tenants. There were also 18 acres of meadow and 6½ acres of pasture. The whole estate was said to have been worth £8 in 1066 and £12 at the time of the inquest. Thus, there had been very considerable development in the first twenty years after the Conquest, but the rise in value cannot entirely be attributed to agricultural expansion, as the mill worth 12s. and the two fisheries with an annual render of 900 eels may have been newly introduced. Assuming that there were 4 virgates to the plough-land and that the Domesday virgate was 20 acres as at a later date,[73] then the area of arable land cultivated was about 720 field acres. The recorded population in 1086 was 10 villeins (villani), 1 bordar, and 3 serfs.

By 1279 the village with a recorded population of 31 was considerably larger.[74] The demesne was 4 carucates instead of 3 and there were 31 virgaters, 7 of whom also held cotlands. The size of the cotland is not given, but in the neighbouring village of Lower Heyford it was 11 acres, and on this basis about 1,017 field acres were then cultivated in Upper Heyford. The extent of the arable land had evidently been increased by the late 12th century, when newly cultivated land (fruisseiz) at 'Farnhulle' and 'hitchings' (inhechinges) in the fallow field are mentioned.[75] In the 19th century, before the inclosure, Heyford Great Field contained 1,300 field acres.[76]

A fairly complete picture of the village in the 1270's can be built up, as in addition to the survey of 1279 there are some manorial account rolls. The account for 1280–1[77] gives the fixed rents as £19 18s. 1d., while the rents of the tenants as given in the Hundred Rolls (12s. for a virgate and 6s. for a cotland) totalled £19 3s. There were other rents of £1 and 10s. from the acqua de Ryvar[78] and the fishery of 'le Flodgat', and 3s. for a house and courtyard, perhaps that of the demesne. The largest single item was £38 from the sale of corn, which fetched 10s. or 11s. a quarter in this year. (The demesne farm buildings included a granary by about 1220.)[79] The sale of stock, including 4 oxen, 1 heifer, 54 sheep, and 1 sick pig, produced £5 16s. 6d. The tenants of the manor kept a considerable number of horses and geese and paid 8s. to the lord for pasturing 48 farm horses at 'Farnhulle' from Michaelmas to Martinmas,

55 Eynsham Cart. i. 104.
56 Cal. Inq. p.m. iii, p. 98.
57 Complete Peerage, viii, pedigree between pp. 48 and 49; cf. ibid. iv. 323; V.C.H. Oxon. v. 240, for the descent of the claimants.
58 Rot. Parl. i. 130.   59 Cal. Fine R. 1272–1307, 380.
60 Cal. Close, 1296–1302, 37–38; ibid. 1307–13, 273–4.
61 New Coll. Arch. Heyf. chart. 26, 28; Cal. Inq. p.m. viii, p. 257.
62 Feud. Aids, iv. 180.
63 Cal. Close, 1354–60, 630 sqq.
64 New Coll. Arch. Heyf. chart. 9, 17.
65 Ibid. 8; C.P. 25(1)/191/23/25.
66 New Coll. Arch. Heyf. chart. 6, 51; Cal. Pat. 1391–6, 62.
67 Oxon. Visit. 308, 310; Yorks. Visit. 1584–5, ed. J. Foster (priv. print. 1875), 614; Par. Reg.

68 Oxon. Visit. 307; Par. Reg.
69 For these and subsequent tenants see Blo. U. Heyf. 23–25; and see above, p. 186.
70 New Coll. Arch.: inf. Mr. R. L. Rickard, sub-librarian.
71 D.N.B.
72 V.C.H. Oxon. i. 414.
73 New Coll. Arch. In rental of 1628 ¼ yardland is said to be 5 acres.
74 Rot. Hund. (Rec. Com.), ii. 834.
75 Oseney Cart. iv. 216.
76 Dunkin MS. 438/6, f. 7b.
77 New Coll. Arch. Heyf. Compotus R. 3. The series of manorial accts. 1275–1500 in New Coll. Arch. was extensively used in J. E. Thorold Rogers, Hist. of Agric. and Prices in England.
78 New Coll. Arch. Heyf. Comp. R. 3.
79 Oseney Cart. iv. 215.

and 16s. for 32 geese in the same place from 3 May to 1 August. The perquisites of the court amounted to £3 19s. 5d. in 1280. Items of revenue fluctuated very much: in 1275–6 £20 10s. 7d. was received from the court but in the next year only £1 2s. 10d. In 1280 the total receipts were £90 13s. 3¼d. The outgoings of the manor were £80 0s. 10d. and this included £52 4s. sent to the lord. The rest was expended in payments for journeys or wages, purchase of animals and corn, and payments in connexion with the sheep, the dairy, the mill, and the carts. The rents of three tenants amounting to 10s. 5d. were not paid; £4 8s. 7d. was spent in buying corn and £6 0s. 3d. in buying stock.

The entry concerning the sale of fleeces in this account was crossed out by the bailiff and was not included in the total, but there is no doubt that the demesne did keep a flock of sheep, though sheep-breeding at this time was always subsidiary to corn-growing. The accounts mention both the buying and selling of sheep and the sale of wool; in 1276–7 188 fleeces were sold for £6, but the highest sales were made at the end of the 14th century, when in the years 1394 and 1397 the fleeces were sold for £18 and £23.[80] At this period the flock numbered about 400, but in 1410 New College[81] sold its flock and no more records of sheep appear in the accounts, the demesne being farmed out. It is probable, though, that the tenants of the demesne kept their own flocks, as the demesne had the right to 300 sheep commons in the 17th century.[82]

The Black Death caused great mortality in Heyford. In 1350 there were 22 messuages and virgates and one cottage vacant in the manor, and the court rolls for many years show a high proportion of virgates in the lord's hands. A temporary expedient for dealing with the uncultivated land was adopted in 1351, when 11 tenants took parcels of 6 acres each from vacant holdings for a period of 5 years for a rent of 1s. 11d. a year. Two years later, however, some of these holdings were included in the list of those vacant. In 1357 the situation had improved and 14 virgates were taken up for rents of 5s. for all services, and in 1361 it was recorded that 18½ virgates were let out at farm and only 3 remained in hand. It is likely that there were further outbreaks of plague, since in 1368 the court roll shows 11 virgates in the lord's hands. The fixed rents, including the mill and fisheries, are given as £11 19s. 4d.

Money rents had been customary at Heyford before the Black Death, but the serious shortage of labour which it caused made the monetary value of the virgate fall. The rent of a virgate in 1279 had been 12s., but the tenants who took up vacant holdings in 1357 paid only 5s. After this, rents rose again. The parson of Heyford received 3 virgates in 1368 for the exceptionally small rent of 3 capons, but this property was probably a freehold. More typical of the copyholders, however, was the tenant who

took up a virgate in 1375, paid 14s. yearly and owed heriot. Heriot and suit of court were usually the only services mentioned in the court roll, but in 1377 three days' work was demanded from a tenant in addition to a rent of 16s.[83] The customs of the manor in the 16th century, moreover, include the farmer's right to demand labour services at reaping time; it is stated that 'when the fermer wold have his bedrypp he shall give warnyng three days before, and that all the tenants should go together on one day or he that may not go finde a man; that they should have good bredd and good plentie and to have their brekfast in the morning and att noon biffe and moton, and worts mowe or els go home and at night rost moton plentie and good chere'.[84]

The poll-tax returns for Heyford are missing, but some indication of the comparative wealth of the village can be obtained from other tax lists. In 1316 there were 38 contributors[85] and 34 in 1327,[86] and the total assessment in 1316 was £4 10s., making Heyford a village of medium wealth compared with others in the hundred. These lists also indicate considerable disparity in wealth amongst the tenants at Heyford. In each case the lord of the manor paid the highest tax, but there was a group of tenants paying a third or half as much again as the majority. This group includes Richard the Fisherman and John Skardesbrough, a virgater, who died in the plague. It is significant that none of this group, except possibly a descendant of John Kipping, who held a virgate and a cotland in 1279, appears in the Hundred Rolls. Other evidence indicates that the tenants at Heyford held, before the Black Death, more or less equal amounts of land, and the differences in their tax assessments may perhaps be explained by the possible existence of considerable sub-leasing between the tenants. When the manor was sold to William of Wykeham in 1380[87] its annual value was estimated at about £36.[88] The change in ownership probably meant little change for the tenants, as the previous lords had also been absentees.

It is difficult to estimate the amount of freehold in the manor. The Hundred Rolls do not mention free tenants. The Abbot of Eynsham had been granted a hide of land by Maud de Chesney, but as this was held by the lord of the manor at a rent of 8s.[89] it is possible that no distinction was made between it and the demesne land proper. By another grant made before 1224, Fawkes de Bréauté gave 3 messuages, 4 virgates and a villein to John de Bolein[90] for a pair of gilt spurs and 6s. a year to the Abbot of Eynsham. Another free tenant was Hugh de Courtenay, who in 1310 after a dispute concerning the manor obtained 2½ virgates in Heyford.[91] He frequently appears in the court rolls for default of suit, and after his death his holding, consisting of two messuages, a toft and 2½ virgates, was let to sub-tenants. In the 15th century Sir John Seyton of Barford St. Michael was another absentee freeholder and

[80] New Coll. Arch. Heyf. Comp. R. 25, 28.
[81] See above, p. 198.
[82] New Coll. Arch. demesne terrier 1669.
[83] Ibid. Ct. R. 3. The court rolls (152 membranes) in New Coll. Arch. cover the period 1316–1775. There are rolls for 26 years in Edw. III, but only 19 for the rest of the medieval period. A large number of rolls exist for the period after 1508, notably for 1649–1775: inf. Mr. R. L. Rickard. A court bk. covers some years between 1776 and 1918.

[84] New Coll. Arch. Ct. R.
[85] E 179/161/8.
[86] Ibid. 161/9.
[87] New Coll. Arch. Heyf. chart. 9, 17.
[88] Ibid. Comp. R. 14 (1380–1). The manor was valued at £30 a year in 1342: C 135/66/37.
[89] Eynsham Cart. i. 86.
[90] New Coll. Arch. Heyf. ch. 68.
[91] See above, p. 198.

in 1495 his rent, a pair of gloves, was 31 years in arrears.[92] No evidence has been found to show the size of his holding.

In the medieval period the ownership of 7½ freehold virgates can be traced, but there were probably more. The Prioress of Studley, for instance, is mentioned in 1375 and 1487[93] as owing suit to the manorial court and may have held land in the manor.

It appears to have been the policy of New College to obtain freeholds in the manor whenever possible. It acquired a parcel of land (2 virgates and 5 acres of meadow) in 1392 in free alms from John Morecote of Woodstock;[94] in 1498 it purchased 2 virgates from John Below of Eynsham,[95] and in 1499 a property known as 'Aveners' and comprising a messuage and 3 virgates.[96]

It was the college's practice in the late 14th century and after to lease the demesne and sometimes the whole manor. In 1395–6 the rent of the demesne was £13 6s. 8d. and in 1400 the farm of the manor was £34.[97] The fixed rents at the beginning of the 15th century were £21 or £22, but in the period 1432–62 many tenants were unable to pay their rents and the farm of the demesne fell to £10.[98] In this period of agricultural depression the price of corn in Heyford fell to as little as 2s. 8d. a quarter.[99] The college had also suffered loss early in this period through poaching in its fisheries. In 1402 it claimed losses valued at £20 and damages of £40 for the flooding of the meadow as the result of the diversion of the stream, which fed the college mill, to Somerton.[1]

A court roll of 1484, which gives a list of the tenants, shows how far the process of consolidating holdings had gone. There were then only 15 tenants compared with the 31 of 1279, but they held between them 42 virgates. One of them held 5 virgates and several others 3 virgates, so that it is likely that there were a number of landless labourers to work the land. Most of the tenants held part of their land in 'vaccantlonde'; the rents varied considerably but that paid for the 'vacant land' seems to have been less than for the other virgates; thus one tenant who held 2 virgates paid a rent of 20s., but another who held 4, one of them being in 'vacant land', paid only 8s. more. The largest landholder, who had 5 virgates, 3 being in 'vacant land', paid 44s. rent. The meaning of 'vacant land' is obscure; it may have been land which had lain uncultivated after the Black Death and was in process of being brought back into cultivation.

The agricultural arrangements in Heyford Warren appear to have remained remarkably static until the inclosure in the 19th century.[2] As elsewhere most of the tenants had one or two small closes;[3] in the demesne in 1669 there were four small closes and one large one of 28 acres, in addition to 25 acres of inclosed meadow-land, but by far the greater part of both demesne and customary land lay in the open fields with nothing but balks and merestones to separate the strips.[4] At a court baron in 1652 it was agreed to lay down more balks throughout the field of at least 1½ foot wide 'betweene partie and partie', and the lessee of the New College farm was to leave a balk between 'every acre belonging to the farm'.[5]

The early 17th-century rentals show very little change in the pattern of landholding. In 1602 there were still fifteen tenants of land and two cottagers. The largest holding was 4 virgates and the majority of tenants held 3 virgates; the total number of virgates was 41. The rents were 38s. or 36s. for 4 virgates, 28s. for 3, and £1 for 2 virgates. Between 1611 and 1651 the fine for the copyhold of a messuage and 3 virgates rented at 30s. 6d. fluctuated between £5 and £6 13s. 4d. The total rents in 1602 were £20 3s. 1d., which is very close to the medieval figure. Families, however, had changed more; only one family name, that of Tanner, appears in both the medieval and the 17th-century lists of tenants.[6]

The 17th-century rent for the demesne had also remained constant. It was still £10 3s. 4d. in 1665,[7] when a new lease was made between New College and Gabriel Merry the younger. Of this amount, £6 15s. 5d. was to be paid in cash and the remainder in corn and malt, although in practice this seems to have been commuted for a fixed sum. A similar arrangement was made for the payment of the £4 rent for the mill, which Gabriel Merry also leased.[8] It was the college's practice to let on long leases of twenty years, the tenant being responsible for repairs. These were beneficial leases for which the tenant paid a fluctuating fine. In 1633 this was £90 for the manor and mill, in 1650 £66, and between 1693 and 1717 it remained constant at £130. The fines were divided among the Fellows and were not entered in the estates account. A terrier of the demesne was made in 1669 when it comprised 224 acres, compared with the 4 carucates or 320 acres of the survey of 1279. A rental of 1669 shows that the customary tenants held between them 40¼ yardlands, so that the cultivated area of the parish at this time may be estimated to be a little over 1,030 acres.[9]

No evidence has been found of the size of the common meadow or of the common pastures of the manor. The 'Towne sheepe common' is mentioned in the terrier of 1669 and there was also a cow pasture on the low hill in the north-west of the parish.[10] Part of the demesne meadow lay in closes and some in the 'Towne Meade'. Another part called 'Gross-more' was several each year until 1 August, when it became commonable. Shepherd's

[92] New Coll. Arch. Heyf. Ct. R.   [93] Ibid.
[94] *Cal. Pat.* 1391–6, 62.
[95] New Coll. Arch. Heyf. ch. 23. This freehold cannot be traced beyond 1388.
[96] Ibid. ch. 48.
[97] Ibid. Comp. R. 28, 34.
[98] Ibid. Comp. R. 65, 75, 85, 93.
[99] J. E. Thorold Rogers, *Hist. of Agric. and Prices in Eng.* iii. 41; iv. 235.
[1] C.P. 40/566, m. 497.
[2] O.R.O. Incl. award (1842). The act is 4 & 5 Vict. c. 11 (priv. act): copy in Bodl. L. Eng. C 13 c 1 (1841, 11).
[3] New Coll. Arch. Heyf. 17th-cent. rentals.

[4] Ibid. terrier 1669.
[5] Ibid. court rolls, 1652.
[6] Ibid. rentals.
[7] Ibid. lease.
[8] In 1673 Merry transferred his leases of manor and mill to John Cartwright. It was agreed that he should remove certain effects, including 2 furnaces and a malt mill, but he was not to break up any more land than was already due to be sown with barley or pease according to the custom of the fields of Heyford Warren: deed *penes* Mrs. R. Cartwright, Aynho Park, Northants.
[9] New Coll. Arch. Heyf. terrier 1669, rental 1669.
[10] W. Wing, *Annals of Heyford Warren* (1865), 17.

Ground was 'several every other year with the lower field'. It is not entirely clear what field system was in use at Heyford, but there are indications that it was originally a two-field system. A court roll of 1377 records that John Long received a cottage and 2 acres, one in the North Field and one in the South; and the fact that Shepherd's Ground was inclosed every other year suggests a two-year rotation of crops. In the 17th century the acres were usually identified by the furlong in which they lay and the earlier distinction between a North and South Field seems to have been lost; the demesne terriers mention the 'ffarme blacke land' and the 'farme season land', and the glebe terrier of 1685[11] gives the names of Deane Field, Standhill, Elumfield, and Flex (i.e. Flax) lands.

The earliest land-tax assessment of 1760 shows that the distribution of land had remained virtually unchanged since the early 17th century. There were, for most of the period 1760–1832, fourteen properties including the glebe and demesne, which were taxed the highest at £18 and £20 respectively.[12] It is clear from the inclosure award of 1842 that most of the people entered as proprietors in the land-tax lists were in fact copyholders of New College. Copyhold or lifehold had remained the usual form of land tenure at Heyford, the only leasehold estates being the demesne farm and a small farm of 3 yardlands. Few of the copyholders occupied and farmed their land; there were only two owner-occupiers in 1794, but two of the sub-tenants each held three small farms.

A description of the open field at Heyford in 1830 says that it 'contained 1,300 acres in different occupations and the parcels were so intermixed that it was difficult to say where one began and another ended'. A notice of sale of a lifehold farm in 1810 identifies the strips by the 'quarter' in which they lay, as for example 'the Calcote quarter, 32 lands', and shows that the common rights attached to each yardland were 20 sheep commons, ½ cow commons, and 1½ 'man's mowth' in the meadow.[13]

The parish was inclosed in 1842.[14] Three freeholders including the rector, two leaseholders, and eleven copyholders received allotments. The lessee of the Manor farm, W. Sturges Bourne, received the largest allotment of 309 acres, and the smallest went to a freeholder of ¼ yardland. One of the copyholders was the Earl of Jersey, who held two tenements of 3 and 4½ yardlands which he had purchased in 1794 and 1805.[15] In 1856 he purchased the lease of the Manor farm from New College.

In the second half of the 19th century most farms changed over to sheep farming and the cultivation of the turnip became general. In 1865 the parish was stated to be noted for its turnips, barley, and sheep.[16] Farms were increasing in size: in 1907 the largest was 419 acres, but the loss of agricultural land to the aerodrome checked the trend and in 1956 farms were mainly small or of medium size. The greater part of New College's estate, for example, was divided into four farms: Manor farm (338 a.), Rectory farm (111 a.), Mudginwell farm (120 a.), and Common farm (78 a.).[17]

Population seems to have been static in the late 17th century and for most of the 18th. In 1676 the Compton Census recorded 78 adults, while throughout the 18th century incumbents returned about 30 households. By 1811, however, there were 230 persons living in 57 houses.[18] In 1821 out of 62 families 47 were engaged in agriculture and 12 in trades and handicrafts.[19] Increasing population led to a further growth in the numbers of persons engaged in non-agricultural work, though the greater part of the men continued to be employed on the farms. In the 1850's there were a miller, two beer-retailers, a shop-keeper, and a sub-postmaster and eleven craftsmen.[20] As Heyford was a 'free' village where settlement was unrestricted, and also because of the coming of the canal and the railway, population had more than doubled by 1861. Agricultural depression, however, in the second half of the century, reduced the population by 1901 to 319, less than three-fourths of the 1861 figure.[21] In 1954 the estimated civil population was 317—the census return of 1,504 in 1951 included the personnel at the air base.[22] Modern transport and the construction of the aerodrome from 1925, which had absorbed over 300 acres of the parish by 1951,[23] have brought about equally striking changes in the occupational pattern. After 1887 there were two public houses, but by 1939 other tradesmen were represented only by a thatcher and a cycle-repairer.[24] By 1951 the old occupations were represented by 4 farmers, 8 farm labourers, 3 thatchers, and 2 publicans; the rest of the village was employed in a variety of professional and other occupations—some of them in Oxford. For example, 26 were employed at the aerodrome, 24 as labourers, others on the canal, the railway, and in shops.[25]

CHURCH. There was a church in Upper Heyford by 1074, when a grant of its tithes was made (see below). A priest is recorded in about 1180.[26]

The advowson has descended with the manor. The only 13th-century presentations recorded were in 1245–6 and 1247–8 by Margaret de Riviers, lady of the manor.[27] In 1304 and 1306, when the manor was in the king's hands, he was patron, and from 1314 the De Lisles were. John de Lisle presented in 1322, when Robert was lord of the manor, and again in 1345.[28] After John's death in 1355 the advowson went to Lady Alice Seymour, the tenant of the manor.[29] When William of Wykeham bought the advowson with the manor for New College she reserved the right of presentation during her lifetime.[30] The college has been patron since 1382.

[11] Oxf. Archd. Oxon. c 141, p. 361.
[12] O.R.O. Land tax assess.
[13] Dunkin MS. 438/5, p. 72. Two other 'quarters' are mentioned.
[14] O.R.O. Incl. award.
[15] Ibid. J IX a/1–37 for the Jersey purchases.
[16] Wing, Heyford Warren, 17.
[17] J. W. Pearson, Hist. U. Heyford (1907), 30; inf. Mr. R. L. Rickard.
[18] Oxf. Dioc. d 553, d 559; Census, 1811.
[19] Census, 1821.
[20] Gardner, Dir. Oxon.

[21] Census, 1861, 1901.
[22] Inf. Ploughley R.D.C.; Census, 1951.
[23] Inf. Mr. R. L. Rickard: see above, p. 197.
[24] Kelly's Dir. Oxon. (1939).
[25] Inf. the Revd. E. P. Baker.
[26] Eynsham Cart. i. 86.
[27] Rot. Grosse. 488, 491.
[28] For list of medieval presentations see MS. Top. Oxon. d 460.
[29] New Coll. Arch. Heyf. chart. 8, 17, 69.
[30] Ibid. 7, 9, 13.

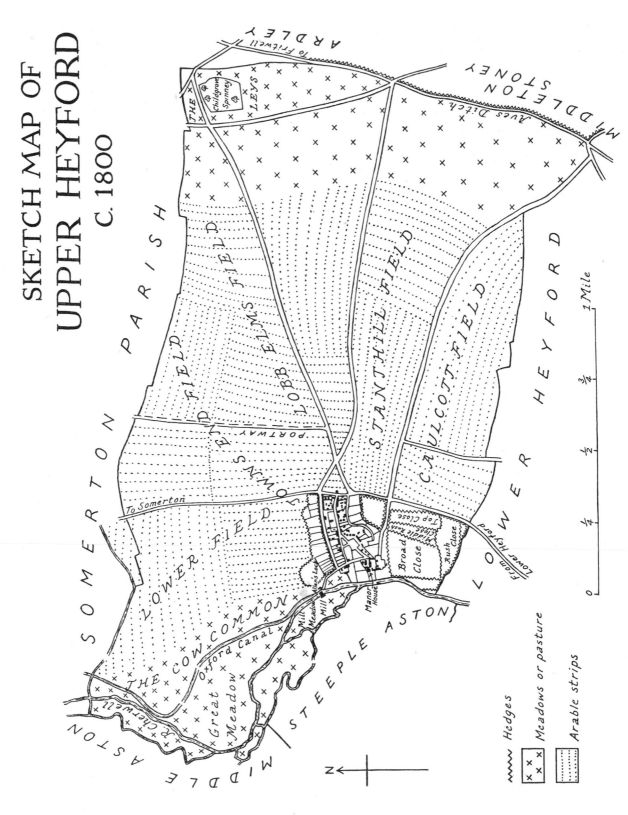

SKETCH MAP OF
UPPER HEYFORD
C. 1800

SOMERTON PARISH

ARDLEY

MIDDLETON STONEY

MIDDLETON STONEY

The Childgrove Spinney

LEYS

Aves Ditch

TOWNSEND FIELD

LOBB ELMS

STANTHILL FIELD

CAULCOTT FIELD

PORTWAY

To Fritwell

To Somerton

LOWER FIELD

LOWER HEYFORD

From Lower Heyford

Top Close

Middle Rush Close

Broad Close

Rush Close

Manor House

Mill

Meadow

Miller's Lock

THE COW COMMON

Oxford Canal

Great Meadow

R Cherwell

STEEPLE ASTON

MIDDLE ASTON

N

Hedges

Meadows or pasture

Arable strips

0   ¼   ½   ¾   1 Mile

The above map is from one of 1797 by Richard Davis and the inclosure award map of 1842 by James Saunders of Kirtlington.

Heyford Warren was rather a poor parish, valued at £3 6s. 8d. in 1254[31] and £5 13s. 4d. in 1291,[32] plus the amount paid to Oseney (see below). By 1535 its net value had risen to £13 16s.[33] The first post-Reformation valuation found dates from 1671, when the living was said to be worth less than £100;[34] by the early 18th century the value had risen to £120.[35] At the inclosure award in 1842 the tithes were commuted for £523 and the glebe for 102 acres.[36] In 1859 the net value of the living was £620.[37]

The glebe in 1634 consisted of 36 acres and 3 'lands' in the open fields, or, according to another terrier of 1679, of 91 'ridges' of arable and the meadow belonging to 2 yardlands with commons for 3 horses, 4 cows, and 60 sheep.[38] Once rated at 8 yardlands, the estate was increased to a rating of 13 yardlands in about 1670.[39] In the 18th century New College added another 3½ yardlands.[40] The glebe has been sold.[41]

Two-thirds of the demesne tithes were granted in the late 11th century by the D'Oillys to the church of St. George in Oxford castle,[42] and were transferred in 1149 to Oseney Abbey, which then collected these valuable tithes.[43] Later, additions were made to the abbey's property in Heyford: about 1180 Maud de Chesney, lady of the manor, with her son Warin's permission, granted it two-thirds of the tithes on 'inhechinges' there,[44] and in the early 13th century Margaret de Riviers gave it land for a barn in which to store its tithes.[45] Later it seems that there was trouble over the tithes, for in 1293 the lord of the manor confirmed them to Oseney,[46] and Simon the rector promised not to impede their collection.[47] They were valued at £1 10s. in 1291[48] but in 1415 Oseney leased them to the rector for an annual pension of only 13s. 4d.[49] This was being paid in 1535 and in 1542 went to Christ Church, Oxford.[50]

Maud de Chesney made an unusual grant to Bicester Priory of 5 *summae* (quarters) of wheat a year from Heyford for making bread for hosts.[51] In 1487 Bicester gave up the grain to New College in return for an annual pension of £1 6s. 8d. from the manor and a promise to provide bread for all masses in Heyford church and for the Easter communion of all parishioners.[52] This pension also was granted to Christ Church in 1542.[53]

Throughout the Middle Ages Eynsham Abbey received 8s. rent on a hide of land once held of it by Maud de Chesney.[54] After Eynsham's dissolution New College paid this rent to the Crown;[55] by the 17th century the college was under the impression that it was for tithes and wondered why it was not 'rather laid upon the parson'.[56]

Some of the medieval rectors came from the parish, such as Simon de Heyford (oc. 1293–1304) and his successor John de Heyford or de Crawell (1304–6). The latter was far from a model parish priest: he was absent from the church for more than a year while in prison as a notorious thief, and was finally deprived.[57] Other rectors were servants of the 14th-century lords of the manor. William de Boresworth (1306–14), for example, was attorney for John de Lisle, and after resigning Heyford went to Wales with Robert de Lisle.[58] Another rector, John de Wetherby (1330–45), was given permission for a year's absence while in the service of Robert de Lisle.[59] In the latter half of the century Robert Mounk (1361–?) was closely associated with Lady Alice Seymour, acting for her as a feoffee to uses and as a witness to local charters.[60] In the early 1390's he was leasing the manor from New College.[61]

In the 15th century, after New College got the advowson, the rectors were members of the college and usually Fellows.[62] One of them, Peter Maykin (1420–47), was from Heyford.[63] Of a different type were Master Thomas Wellys (1500–6), an Augustinian canon, who became Bishop of Sidon *in partibus infidelium* and Prior of St. Gregory's, Canterbury,[64] and Master Thomas Myllying (1509–35), who was chaplain to Archbishop Warham.[65] The latter had a curate in Heyford and perhaps neglected the parish, for it was during his incumbency that it was reported that several people were in debt to the church and that the windows of the church and Rectory were broken.[66]

The Fellows of New College who held the cure after the Reformation were not outstanding, but they resided for part of the year at least and were buried at Heyford.[67] John Hungerford (1645–63) was expelled as a royalist[68] and during the Commonwealth replaced by a number of ministers: one of these, John Gunter, later became chaplain to Cromwell;[69] another, John Cocke, made a Fellow by the Parliamentary Visitors, bought a copyhold in Heyford.[70]

The Rectory was at this time the largest house in

---

[31] Lunt, *Val. Norw.* 312.
[32] *Tax. Eccl.* (Rec. Com.), 31.
[33] *Valor Eccl.* (Rec. Com.), ii. 160.
[34] *Woodward's Progress*, ed. R. L. Rickard (O.R.S. xxvii), 42.
[35] *Par. Coll.* ii. 174.
[36] Blo. *U. Heyf.* 61; O.R.O. Incl. award. In 1859 the rent of the glebe was £150.
[37] New Coll. Arch. College Livings.
[38] Blo. *U. Heyf.* 59–60.
[39] *Woodward's Progress*, 32.
[40] Oxf. Dioc. d 562.
[41] Inf. Revd. E. P. Baker.
[42] *V.C.H. Oxon.* ii. 160; *Oseney Cart.* iv. 3, 25; *Oxon. Chart.* no. 58.
[43] *V.C.H. Oxon.* ii. 90.
[44] *Oseney Cart.* iv. 216.   [45] Ibid. 215.
[46] Ibid.; Kennett, *Paroch. Antiq.* i. 456, says he granted all his demesne tithes, but this is unlikely.
[47] *Oseney Cart.* iv. 216–17.
[48] *Tax. Eccl.* (Rec. Com.), 31.
[49] *Oseney Cart.* iv. 218.
[50] *Valor Eccl.* (Rec. Com.), ii. 160: *L. & P. Hen. VIII*, xvii, p. 491; C 66/715, m. 12.
[51] Hist. MSS. Com. *Rutland*, IV, 57.
[52] New Coll. Arch. Heyf. chart. 5 (transl. in Blo. *U. Heyf.* 17–18).
[53] C 66/715, m. 12.
[54] *Eynsham Cart.* i. 86.
[55] Ibid. ii. 251.
[56] *Woodward's Progress*, 30–31.
[57] Kennett, *Paroch. Antiq.* i. 505; Linc. Reg. ii, Dalderby, f. 151.
[58] *Cal. Pat.* 1307–13, 584; ibid. 1313–17, 384.
[59] Blo. *U. Heyf.* 44.
[60] e.g. New Coll. Arch. Heyf. chart. 64–65; Kennett, *Paroch. Antiq.* ii. 173.
[61] New Coll. Arch. Heyf. Comp. R. 25, 26.
[62] For their connexion with the college see Blo. *U. Heyf.* 46–47.
[63] *Reg. Chichele*, i. 181.
[64] *Reg. Univ.* i. 73; Wood, *Fasti*, i. 31; *Arch. Cantiana*, xiv. 164.
[65] *Reg. Univ.* i. 57; see Wood, *Fasti*, i. 35.
[66] *Visit. Dioc. Linc. 1517–31*, i. 124.
[67] For them see Blo. *U. Heyf.* 48–51.
[68] *Walker Rev.* 298; Hist. MSS. Com. *7th Rep. App.* 106; Blo. *U. Heyf.* 50.
[69] See *Calamy Rev.* 239–40.
[70] Wood, *Life*, i. 204; *Woodward's Progress*, 29, 30, 36.

the village,[71] and there Warden Woodward of New College dined in 1669 and received 'handsome treatment, a table set with nothing but choice dishes'.[72] About the same time the rector Thomas Fowkes (1669–94) was sued by the churchwardens for not providing a Christmas entertainment for the inhabitants, and was ordered to restore it according to custom.[73] It cost him £10 a year, or a tenth of his income.[74]

John Dalby (1695–1717), who built the new Rectory,[75] was the last resident for many years. His successor George Lavington (1717–31), later Bishop of Exeter and known as a strong opponent of Methodism,[76] was non-resident. Nevertheless, in 1738 the curate reported that the parish was 'generally well behaved', though some did not attend public service 'as might be wished'. Two services were held on Sunday and four communions a year.[77] In the second half of the century, when the church building is also known to have been much neglected, the curate lived in Oxford.[78] The rector Charles Cotton (1767–99) had a tenant in part of the Rectory, keeping part for himself.[79] Sometimes he rode over from his home at Tingewick (Bucks.), fourteen miles away, to take afternoon service.[80] There were said to be very few communicants, and the children were not catechized or instructed.[81]

In the 19th century the parish continued to be indifferently cared for. William Busby (1799–1821), a pluralist and Dean of Rochester, did not even have a resident curate: he said there was no accommodation for one, as the parish was 'chiefly inhabited by poor people'; that he planned to spend the summer in the parsonage himself and it was 'barely sufficient to hold' his own family.[82] Dissent naturally flourished when the Church was so apathetic, and the 19th-century Anglican revival did not reach Heyford until late in the century. Communicants fell from 30 in 1811[83] to about 15 in 1854, when the congregation was said to be still decreasing.[84] William Baker (1821–59), although resident, was eccentric and in his later years bed-ridden. The fact that his wife was said to attend a dissenting chapel[85] may perhaps be cited as evidence of his ineffective ministry. In the second half of the century Heyford had two rectors who left their mark on the parish: William Wetherell (1859–64), who built the school,[86] and Charles Mount (1865–78), who was largely responsible for rebuilding the church and Rectory.[87]

The church of *ST. MARY* is a 19th-century building in the style of the 15th century, comprising a chancel with vestry, nave, north aisle, west tower, and south porch.

Of the medieval building only the tower remains.

It is of three stories, with two-light belfry windows, a battlemented parapet, and a projecting staircase. The buttresses at the north-west and south-west angles bear the arms of New College and probably those of Thomas Chaundler, warden from 1455 to 1475.[88] Most of the church may have been rebuilt at that time, as before the 19th-century restoration it was largely of 15th-century date. It then had a chapel, which adjoined part of the south aisle and part of the chancel. The nave windows were square-headed,[89] and the external south wall was parapeted.

In the 17th century the south aisle caused trouble, and in 1668 a buttress was built to support the roof, 'well ramming the foundations'.[90]

In 1718 Rawlinson called the church 'good'.[91] In 1757 minor repairs were undertaken. The creed, the Lord's prayer, and 'choice sentences' were to be 'wrote upon the wall and the ten commandments to be in a frame where the king's arms are, and the king's arms put in another place. Boarded ceiling, and communion table, and pavement round same to be neatly repaired, &c.' The state of the fabric became increasingly worse in the second half of the century: in 1764 it was 'very much out of repair'[92] and in 1768 'ready to fall'.[93] Blomfield, who had access to records which have since disappeared, says that drastic repairs were made in 1769 when the south wall was rebuilt, a new nave roof put on, and the open timbers of the chancel roof covered with a coved plaster one in the 'Grecian' style, which concealed the upper part of the east window.[94]

In the 1850's the condition of the chancel caused concern[95] and by 1865 the whole building was said to be 'very much out of repair',[96] particularly the 18th-century south wall which had been badly built.[97] Restoration plans were made under the rector William Wetherell (1859–64) with Richard Hussey as architect but were apparently not carried out.[98]

On Wetherell's death the rector, C. B. Mount (1865–78), instructed the architect Talbot Bury, a pupil of Pugin, to rebuild the church. H. Cowley of Oxford was the builder. The cost was about £2,000, of which half was given equally by New College and the rector and £400 raised by a local rate.[99] The church, opened by Bishop Wilberforce in 1867, was built in imitation of the medieval one, but the nave was widened by 3 feet and a north aisle and south porch were added. The window on the north side of the chancel is original, and the east window is an exact reproduction of the original one. The chapel with its monuments on the south side of the chancel was replaced by a vestry. The clock commemorates the Diamond Jubilee of 1897.

The pulpit, dated 1618, with an hour-glass attached

[71] *Hearth Tax Oxon.* 201.
[72] *Woodward's Progress*, 39.
[73] Oxf. Archd. Oxon. c 32, f. 120; ibid. c 29, f. 231.
[74] *Woodward's Progress*, 42.
[75] *Par. Coll.* ii. 174; see above, p. 196.
[76] *D.N.B.*
[77] Oxf. Dioc. d 553.
[78] Ibid. d 559.
[79] Son of Shuckburgh Cotton, rector 1731–62; Oxf. Dioc. d 562.
[80] Blo. *U. Heyf.* 54.
[81] Oxf. Dioc. c 327, pp. 55, 297.
[82] Blo. *U. Heyf.* 55; Oxf. Dioc. c 659, ff. 33–34.
[83] Oxf. Dioc. d 572.
[84] *Wilb. Visit.*
[85] Oxf. Dioc. d 178.
[86] See below, p. 205.
[87] Blo. *U. Heyf.* 55–56; see above, p. 197.

[88] Bodl. G.A. Oxon. 4° 686, p. 174, where there is a photograph of the 2nd shield.
[89] Drawings by J. Buckler from SE. and NW. (1823) in MS. Top. Oxon. a 67, ff. 325, 326, show the old church.
[90] *Woodward's Progress*, 38. This buttress shows in the 1823 drawing.
[91] *Par. Coll.* ii. 174.
[92] Oxf. Archd. Oxon. c 75, f. 285.
[93] Oxf. Dioc. d 559.
[94] Blo. *U. Heyf.* 35–36. His description of the changes then is exaggerated.
[95] Ibid. 36; *Wilb. Visit.*
[96] MS. Top. Oxon. c 49, f. 92.
[97] W. Wing, *Annals of Heyford Warren* (1865), 20.
[98] MS. Top. Oxon. c 103, ff. 570–8.
[99] Ibid. ff. 567, 580–2; Blo. *U. Heyf.* 36–37. For a view of the old church see plates facing p. 194.

to it, was replaced. The medieval piscina remains, as does the fine recumbent effigy of a priest (probably 14th-century) under an arch in the chancel. Memorials include a stone to John Grent (rector, d. 1668/9) with his arms, and various ones to the Merry family. The majority of monumental stones have been removed.[1]

The present iron screen, formerly in Bicester church, was erected in 1916, and the organ installed in 1904. There are a 20th-century lectern, pulpit, and reredos. Electric light was installed in 1932 and electric heating in 1951.[2]

At the Reformation the church owned two chalices and several other ornaments.[3] In 1955 the only old plate was a small Elizabethan silver chalice and paten cover.[4] There were three bells, of which two were 17th-century, and a sanctus bell.[5]

The registers date from 1577.

NONCONFORMITY. No record has been found of Roman Catholicism.

Protestant dissent seems to have appeared in the 1820's and in 1829 a meeting-place was licensed,[6] which may have been the Wesleyan Methodist chapel, said to have been built in that year, and rebuilt in 1867.[7] It was still in use in 1955, but had only three members.[8]

Divisions had appeared among the Methodists, and in 1849 another meeting-place was licensed,[9] probably the Reformed Methodist chapel or meeting-house which was used until the 1880's.[10] In the 1850's and 1860's the Primitive Methodists also had a meeting-place, described by the rector as a 'nuisance and disturbance' to the parish.[11]

SCHOOLS. At the beginning of the 19th century Heyford Warren children had to go to school at Somerton or Lower Heyford.[12] By 1815 a small school had been opened, where 5 boys and 5 girls paid 3d. a week to be taught to read by a poor

widow.[13] In 1833 this school had 12 pupils, but it had closed by 1854 when the Sunday school, opened in 1828 and supported by New College, was the only school in the village.[14]

In 1859 a National school was built on land given by New College and R. Greaves, at a cost of £422, of which the college gave £150 and the rector most of the remainder.[15] The school opened in 1861 and at first had two teachers, but later only one.[16] The average attendance was 70 in 1871.[17] The original building included a teacher's house, which was converted into a new classroom in 1893. A new teacher's house was built by New College in 1904.[18] In 1906 there were 59 pupils.[19] The school became a junior school in 1925 when the senior pupils were sent to Steeple Aston, and a controlled school in 1951. There were 56 children on the roll in 1937 and 45 in 1954.[20]

CHARITIES. In 1738 6s. 6d. was distributed to the poor and 1s. 6d. used for the repair of the church way from money left by a certain Richard Dalby,[21] probably a relative of John Dalby, who built the Rectory.[22] Dalby's bequest may have been one of several small donations, the remains of which amounted to £2 4s. 4d. in 1786.[23] This sum appears to have been distributed by the churchwardens shortly afterwards.[24]

Under the inclosure award of 1842, 20 acres were set aside as Poor's Allotments in compensation for the loss of the right to cut furze on the waste for fuel.[25] The rents from the allotments, which amounted to £46 10s. 8d. in the 19th century, were distributed to the poor in coal and clothing annually on St. Thomas's day.[26] In 1891 a barn was given by Lord Jersey for the use of the allotment-holders, and the village stone-pit was later incorporated in the allotments.[27] In 1954, when not all the allotments had been taken up, the net income was £19. Owing to the expense of refencing no distribution had taken place since 1951.[28]

ISLIP

The parish of Islip is situated on both banks of the River Ray near its confluence with the Cherwell. The area of the ancient parish was 1,997 acres. Under the Divided Parishes Act of 1882 one detached part of Noke (7 a.) was added to the parish of Islip for civil purposes, and another (5 a.) was added in 1932,

giving an area in 1951 of 2,009 acres.[1] The right-angled turns of the present boundary between Islip and Hampton Poyle suggest that the line was drawn to follow the layout of arable strips already under cultivation; a date in the 12th century may be indicated. In the south-west corner of the parish the

[1] For a list see *Par. Coll.* ii. 174–5. Most were still there in 1865: MS. Top. Oxon. c 167, pp. 143–9; for arms on monuments see Bodl. G.A. Oxon. 16° 217, p. 160.
[2] Inf. Revd. E. P. Baker.
[3] *Chant. Cert.* 90.
[4] Evans, *Ch. Plate.*
[5] *Ch. Bells Oxon.* ii. 165.
[6] Oxf. Dioc. c 645, f. 135.
[7] Blo. *U. Heyf.* 31.
[8] *Buckingham and Brackley Methodist Circuit Plan,* 1955–6.
[9] Oxf. Dioc. c 647, f. 97.
[10] Ibid. c 332; *Kelly's Dir. Oxon.* (1887).
[11] *Wilb. Visit.*; *Kelly's Dir. Oxon.* (1864).
[12] Oxf. Dioc. d 707.
[13] Ibid. c 433.
[14] *Educ. Enq. Abstract,* 749; *Wilb. Visit.*
[15] MS. Top. Oxon. c 163, f. 565.

[16] Wing, *Annals,* 84; *Kelly's Dir. Oxon.* (1864, 1887).
[17] *Elem. Educ. Ret.*
[18] Inf. Revd. E. P. Baker.
[19] *Vol. Sch. Ret.*
[20] Inf. Oxon. Educ. Cttee.
[21] Oxf. Dioc. d 553.
[22] See above, p. 204.
[23] *Char. Don.* ii. 989; a bequest of £10 by Gabriel Merry in 1721 appears to have been made not to Heyford but to St. Giles-in-the-Fields (Mdx.): ibid.
[24] *12th Rep. Com. Char.* 306.
[25] O.R.O. Incl. award.
[26] *Kelly's Dir. Oxon.* (1864, 1887); Wing, *Annals,* 84.
[27] Inf. Revd. E. P. Baker.
[28] Inf. Mr. G. Brain, chairman of allotment trustees.
[1] *Census,* 1881, 1951; *Kelly's Dir. Oxon.* (1903); *Oxon. Review Order* (1932); O.S. Map 6″, xxvii, xxxiii; 2½, 42/51 (1951).

present boundary follows the line of the River Cherwell, and in the east a brook flowing into the Ray divides Islip and Oddington.

The ground in the centre of the parish rises sharply on both sides of the Ray and forms a ridge of high ground which runs the length of the parish and which rises to 330 feet in the south. This ridge is flanked on the east and west by ground which is low-lying and, in parts, liable to floods. Most of the north and west of the parish lies on either Oxford Clay or alluvium, but the village itself and the south-east of the parish are on an inlier of Cornbrash.[2] The soil is clay and stonebrash.[3]

Islip contains two stone-quarries, one north of the river and the other south of it. These pits supplied Cornbrash and Forest Marble. Both are now disused, but the former is still of scientific fame on account of its fossiliferous bed. Pratwell, or Prattle, Wood (30 a.), in the south-east of the parish, is the only survivor of the woods which covered the southern half of the parish in the early Middle Ages. Traces of their former extent were preserved until the parliamentary inclosure in the names Sart and Wood Hill and Plain, given respectively to the only open field south of the river and to the land adjoining it on the south-east; traces are still preserved in the names Upper and Lower Woods farms.[4]

The River Ray flows through the parish in an east–west direction; its bed was deepened early in the 19th century by the commissioners for the Otmoor Drainage Act.[5] A monopoly of fishing rights in Islip waters was granted by the Protector Cromwell to a local fisherman named Beckley as a reward for ferrying parliamentary troops across the Cherwell before the battle of Islip Bridge in 1645.[6] The fisheries continued to be valuable until the late 19th century and gave rise to the local industry of making osier cages or 'weels' for catching eels.

The Ray is spanned by a three-arched bridge in the village. It was formerly forded near this point. The present bridge, completed in 1878,[7] replaced an earlier, four-arched bridge of unknown date.[8] Until the 18th century Islip Bridge was used extensively only in the winter months, the customary route during the summer being that which lay over the ford.[9] In 1788, however, a turnpike was set up on the bridge and the road over the ford was closed by the Turnpike Trustees. The Dean and Chapter of Westminster, who were responsible *ratione tenure* for the upkeep of the bridge, claimed that the increased volume of traffic involved them in unprecedented expenses for repairs, and in 1816 unsuccessfully attempted to put the onus for repairs on the Turnpike Trustees or on the county.[10] Despite the allegations made by the dean and chapter it is almost certain that the total volume of traffic using the bridge declined sharply during this period.[11] Its foundations were endangered early in the 19th century by the increased volume of water passing under it as a result of the deepening of the river bed. The Otmoor Drainage Commissioners, therefore, although refusing to admit a legal obligation, contributed to the repair of two arches.[12] The construction of the present bridge necessitated widening the river. This was accomplished by the Thames Valley Drainage Commission at the expense of land belonging to the rectory. The rector was allowed £60 as compensation.[13] Part of the island opposite the Rectory was cut away at the same time.

The main road in the parish is the Wheatley road which crosses the Ray at Islip Bridge. This is a section of the old London to Worcester road on which Islip was formerly a coach and wagon station. The road was also used by traffic travelling from Buckingham and Bicester to Oxford in the winter months when the Cherwell was impassable at Gosford Bridge. Islip lost much of its traffic in the later 18th century: the wagon traffic was affected adversely by the opening of the Oxford Canal in 1790 and other traffic by the improvement of roads elsewhere in the county. In the early 19th century Vincent said that only the Bicester wagon still went regularly through the village and that most of Islip's coaches had been attracted to Oxford.[14] Islip Railway, a part of the extension of the London and Birmingham Railway from Bletchley to Oxford, was opened in 1850.[15] The extension was completed by the opening of the Islip to Oxford line in 1851. Between 1850 and 1851 passengers from Oxford wishing to connect with the Bletchley services were conveyed to Islip by horse omnibus.[16] The Dean and Chapter of Westminster, who had unsuccessfully opposed the bill sanctioning the railway,[17] received £2,310 from the company as compensation.[18]

Islip lies in the centre of the parish on the north bank of the River Ray.[19] The place-name consists of the old name of the Ray (*Ight*) and an Old English word, *slæp*, of which the precise meaning is unknown, but which may here denote a 'place where things are dragged'.[20] The date of settlement was probably Saxon: no prehistoric or Roman remains have been found here. The main village is grouped compactly on three sides of the church. The proximity of open arable fields limited expansion west of the church in the pre-inclosure village to a row of dwellings in Mill Street. This restriction no longer obtains, and the village was beginning to sprawl along the Kidlington road in the 1950's. The land immediately west of the church was acquired by the Parish Council and opened as the village playing-field in 1953.

Islip achieved importance in the 11th century

[2] G.S. Map 1″, xlv SE.; ibid. N.S. 236; *G.S. Memoir* (1946), 76, 79.
[3] *Kelly's Dir. Oxon.* (1939).
[4] See below, p. 207.
[5] Recent Chapter Office, Westminster Abbey (henceforth cited as R.C.O.), box 48.
[6] Edith Miller, *History of the Village of Islip*, 13, 16. Beckley's charter is now in the possession of the Oxford Angling Society.
[7] R.C.O. box 48.
[8] Engraving in Dunkin, *Oxon.* i, facing p. 274.
[9] *Woodward's Progress*, 42.
[10] R.C.O. box 48.
[11] See below.

[12] R.C.O. box 48.
[13] Ibid.
[14] MS. Top. Oxon. c 112, p. 65: MS. Memoranda Relative to Islip by W. Vincent; see below, p. 208.
[15] See J. E. Lloyd, 'The First Excursions by Rail from Islip and Bicester', in *Bicester Advertiser and Mid-Oxon. Chronicle*, 1 Oct. 1951.
[16] Ibid.
[17] *C.J.* ci (1), 525.
[18] R.C.O. box 48; see also Westminster Abbey muniments (henceforth cited as W.A.M.), 57776.
[19] O.S. Map 25″, xxvii. 11, 12, 15, 16.
[20] Ekwall, *Dict. Eng. P.N.* 255; *P.N. Oxon.* (E.P.N.S.), i. 222.

The chapel of Edward the Confessor in the early 18th century

South-east view of the church in about 1820

ISLIP

because of its situation on the forest bounds. Most of the present village was built in the later 17th century and in the 18th century, but mention may be made of three medieval buildings which have now vanished: the court house which grew around Ethelred's residence, the so-called Confessor's chapel which stood near it,[21] and the second court house built in the early 14th century by William de Curtlington, Abbot of Westminster 1315–33. Curtlington's house occupied a site lower in the village, near the present Manor Farm.[22] Manor Farm itself, a two-storied, L-shaped building in Upper Street, dates from the 16th century, but was much refashioned in the 19th century. Its interior contains a little reused 17th-century panelling. The oldest building in the centre of the village, with the exception of the church, is a house in High Street, formerly the King's Head Inn, a coaching-station. This dates from the mid or late 17th century; most of the wall facing the road was rebuilt in 1950, but the wooden beam over the old entrance to the inn-yard was left in position.[23]

The Old Rectory is the most pleasing building in the village. It was built in 1689–90 for Dr. Robert South, Rector of Islip 1678–1716, on the site of an older house then in disrepair.[24] The date 1689 is on a rainwater-head. According to a tradition which is still current South built his Rectory on the village waste.[25] The house is a two-storied, rectangular-shaped building of stone with attic dormers, sash windows, and two high-pitched roofs separated by a valley. The front doorway on the north elevation retains its original hood supported by carved brackets. Features of the interior of special interest are the 17th-century staircase and oak panelling of the same date in a room on the ground floor. The Rectory fell into disrepair in the 18th century, when Islip's rectors were non-resident. Dean Vincent, who secured the living in 1807 and determined to use the Rectory as his summer residence, spent over £2,000 on repairs.[26] The house was again restored in 1902.[27] Its upkeep proved a severe strain on the benefice, and in 1921 it was sold. Between 1921 and 1949 it was known as the Hall, but in the latter year it reverted to its original name. During the Second World War it was used as the sick bay for B.B.C. hostels at Weston and Bletchingdon.[28] An early engraving of the south elevation of the Rectory shows the house and gardens as they were in South's time.[29] A large tithe-barn stands in a corner of the Rectory premises. In the 19th century, and until 1952, this was used as the village hall. Its upkeep, however, remained a charge on the benefice.[30] In 1897 the rector, the

Revd. T. W. Fowle, tried to end this anomalous situation by offering the barn to the parish council. In 1952 a new village hall was opened on a site north-west of the church, purchased from the Church Commissioners. The architect was Thomas Rayson of Oxford, the builder C. E. Turner of Marston. The cost was about £4,000.[31]

Islip now possesses only three inns—the 'Red Lion', the 'Swan', and the 'Saddlers' Arms'. Five former inns are now private houses: the 'Boot', the 'Britannia', the 'Fox and Grapes', the 'King's Head' (a coaching-station known latterly as the 'Coach and Horses'), and the 'Wooster Arms'. The last named stands at the corner of Mill Street and the Walk. The 'Red Lion' was also known as the 'Worcester Arms' for a period during the 18th century.[32] Little is known about the inns which have disappeared. The 'Prince's Arms', known latterly as the 'Plume of Feathers', stood opposite the 'Red Lion'. There is a local tradition that the materials used to build it came from the Confessor's chapel, which was demolished in about the year 1780.[33] Vincent speaks of the 'Feathers' as the house for gentry and the 'Red Lion' as the house for carriers.[34] The serious decline in the late 18th century of the coach and wagon traffic was the chief cause of the closing of Islip's inns.[35] Islip mill stands on the left bank of the Cherwell, before this river meets the waters of the Ray. The present mill was last used in 1949.[36] There has been a mill at Islip since the 11th century. It was valued in Domesday Book at 20s.[37] It was given by Adeline d'Ivry to Bec Abbey in Normandy.[38] It was later secured by Westminster Abbey, almost certainly in 1203, when the manor itself was recovered.[39] Suit to the mill was obligatory for all customary tenants of the manor.[40] The rate at which molture was levied is not known. The mill was farmed after 1297.[41] A fulling mill was built at Islip in 1369;[42] it was farmed immediately.[43] In 1488 two water-mills were leased by the abbot and convent of Westminster to Nicholas Barton.[44] Sixteenth-century leases also mention two mills.[45] In 1231 licence was granted to the Abbot of Westminster to have one weaver at Islip;[46] this is the only evidence of cloth-making there. A market was granted at Islip in 1245.[47]

Of the outlying farms, Lower Woods, known locally as Leicester's, is of special interest. It dates from the 17th century, was restored in the 18th or 19th century, then became derelict, and has been rebuilt since 1946.[48] Chipping Farm derives its name from 12th-century *chypfen*, and perhaps from the O.E. *cippa fenn*, meaning 'a fen where logs are found'.[49]

[21] See below, and plate opposite.
[22] J. Flete, *Hist. of West. Abbey*, ed. J. A. Robinson, 122.
[23] Inf. the late Mrs. Douglas Roaf.
[24] For the survey of the old parsonage made by Thos. Yeomans, mason, and Ben. Beacham, carpenter, see Oxf. Dioc. c 266, f. 2b; for a certificate as to the state of the new parsonage in Dec. 1689 by Yeomans and Beacham see ibid. c 455, f. 74.
[25] MS. Top. Oxon. c 112, pp. 49–50.
[26] Dunkin, *Oxon.* i. 287 n.
[27] Miller, *Hist. Islip*, 19.
[28] Inf. the late Mrs. D. Roaf.
[29] Kennett, *Paroch. Antiq.* i, tab. ii facing p. 70.
[30] Inf. the rector.
[31] Inf. from the official programme issued on the occasion of the opening.
[32] R.C.O. box 48.
[33] J. D. Halliwell-Phillipps, *Notices of the Hist. and Antiq. of Islip*, 8.
[34] MS. Top. Oxon. c 112, p. 64.
[35] Ibid. pp. 64–65.
[36] Inf. the late Mrs. D. Roaf.
[37] *V.C.H. Oxon.* i. 422.
[38] Dug. *Mon.* vi (2), 1068.
[39] See below, p. 209.
[40] W.A.M. 14921.
[41] Ibid. 14783 b.
[42] Ibid. 14805.
[43] Ibid.
[44] Westminster Abbey Register Bk. i. 31b–32.
[45] Ibid. 136–136b; ii. 289b–290.
[46] *Memoranda Roll* 1230 (P.R.S. n.s. xi), 45; see also ibid. 89.
[47] *Cal. Chart. R.* 1226–57, 286. Grant confirmed in 1364: ibid. 1341–1417, 190.
[48] Inf. the late Mrs. D. Roaf.
[49] *P.N. Oxon.* (E.P.N.S.), i. 222.

Islip was of strategic importance in the Civil War because of its situation near the Cherwell, the outer defence line of the royalist garrison at Oxford. It was reconnoitred by a parliamentary force under Essex in 1643 and occupied by Essex in May 1644.[50] Later, the Dutch ambassadors waited on him here with proposals for mediation.[51] In 1645 royalist troops under Northampton again occupied Islip, and in April Cromwell routed Northampton in an engagement on Islip Bridge.[52] During the siege of Oxford in 1646 Islip was occupied for Parliament by Colonel Fleetwood.[53]

In July 1685, after Monmouth's rebellion, troops under Captain Finch of All Souls College, Oxford, were posted at Islip to secure the western approach to London.[54]

Edward the Confessor was born at Islip in 1004 and began the village's long connexion with Westminster Abbey.[55] Among persons having a slight connexion with the village may be mentioned Isabella, Edward II's queen, who spent some time here in 1325,[56] and John Islip, Abbot of Westminster 1500–32, who in all probability was born here.

The remaining worthies are the many men of distinction who have been presented to the living of Islip in post-Reformation times. These include Hugh Weston (rector 1554–8), a keen supporter of the Marian Reformation;[57] John Aglionby (1600–11), Principal of St. Edmund Hall, Oxford, and, according to Anthony Wood, a collaborator in the Authorized Version of the Bible;[58] Robert South (1678–1716), chaplain in ordinary to Charles II and a prolific writer in the High Church cause;[59] William Freind (1748–66), chaplain in ordinary to George II, and Dean of Canterbury;[60] three 19th-century deans of Westminster—William Vincent (1807–15), who compiled a valuable history of Islip now in the Bodleian Library;[61] John Ireland (1816–35);[62] and the eccentric William Buckland (1846–56), a pioneer geologist;[63] and Francis Chenevix Trench (1857–75), a divine and author of some note in his own day.[64]

Peter Heylyn, the partisan and biographer of Archbishop Laud, was presented to the living of Islip in 1638, but exchanged it immediately.[65] Jonathan Swift desired, but did not secure, the living.[66]

MANOR. Edward the Confessor is alleged to have given Islip to his new foundation of St. Peter at Westminster at the dedication of the church in 1065.[67] Copies are extant of two vernacular writs which notify Wulfwig, Bishop of Dorchester, Earl Gyrth and all the thegns of Oxfordshire of the king's gift of his birthplace, Islip, to Westminster, but the abbey failed to obtain possession before the Conquest.[68] Although the writs are of doubtful authenticity, their language proves that Westminster was claiming Islip very soon after the Conquest, probably before 1071.[69] The substance of the abbey's claim was probably true, for the Confessor's gift of his birthplace would have been the fitting culmination of his lavish endowments. Domesday Book records that Godric and Alwin had held Islip freely T.R.E., but makes no mention of Westminster's claim.[70] In 1086 Islip was held by Adeline, wife of Roger d'Ivry and daughter of Hugh de Grantmesnil, *in commendatione*—a phrase which may imply temporary tenure pending investigation of Westminster's case.[71] The manor had no doubt been given to Hugh by William I, and by Hugh to Adeline as part of her marriage portion.

Adeline outlived her husband and died between May 1110 and May 1111, that is within a year of giving a hide in Fencott, a member of Islip manor, to Abingdon Abbey.[72] Her gift was confirmed at her death by her daughter Adelize, who may have inherited Islip.[73] How and when Islip passed to the De Courcy family is uncertain. It is unlikely that it reverted to the Grantmesnils after Adelize's death, and eventually passed to the De Courcys as their heirs, although the families were connected by marriage.[74] The Grantmesnil lands in England descended to Ives, fourth son of Hugh, and from him passed to Robert de Beaumont, later becoming part of the honor of Leicester, with which Islip was never associated.[75]

The De Courcys of Islip belonged to the Norman branch of that family and descended from Robert, elder son of Richard de Courcy, lord of Curci-sur-Dives and Domesday tenant of Nuneham Courtenay, Sarsden, and Foscot in Idbury.[76] Robert's successor Robert, his eldest son by Rose de Grantmesnil, was probably the Robert de Courcy who was *dapifer* to Henry I and later *dapifer* and justiciar to Geoffrey of

[50] S. R. Gardiner, *History of the Great Civil War* (1901), i. 150; ibid. 351–2.
[51] *Cal. S.P. Dom.* 1644, 194–5, 199–200.
[52] Gardiner, op. cit. ii. 200–1.
[53] *Cal. S.P. Dom.* 1645–7, 251, 341, 391, 399.
[54] Dunkin, *Oxon.* i. 301.
[55] *Anglo-Saxon Writs*, ed. Florence Harmer, 368–9.
[56] *Munimenta Civitatis Oxonie*, ed. H. E. Salter (O.H.S. lxxi), 262.
[57] *D.N.B.*
[58] Ibid.
[59] Ibid.
[60] Ibid.
[61] Ibid.
[62] Ibid.
[63] Ibid.
[64] Ibid.
[65] Ibid.
[66] Letter to Halifax, 13 Jan. 1709 (quoted in *D.N.B.* liii. 276).
[67] Dugd. *Mon.* i. 293–5; R. Widmore, *Enquiry into the Time of the First Foundation of Westminster Abbey* (1743), App. 2, p. 17; H. W. C. Davis, *Reg. Regum Anglo-Normannorum*, i. App. x.
[68] *Anglo-Saxon Writs*, ed. Florence Harmer, 368–9; see also ibid. 334–7.
[69] Edwin, last of the English abbots, died in 1071.

[70] *V.C.H. Oxon.* i. 422.
[71] Ibid. 386–7, 422.
[72] *Chron. Abingdon*, ii. 72–73.
[73] Ibid. Roger d'Ivry (1) may have had a son of the same name (see *V.C.H. Oxon.* v. 60; T. Stapleton, *Hist. Notices of the House of Vernon*, 26–27). Kennett (*Paroch. Antiq.* i. 85) says that there were 3 sons of the marriage, Roger, Hugh, and Geoffrey, of whom the last eventually inherited all the Ivry estates in England. This statement seems to be without foundation. Kennett's statement that Adelize married Alberic de Vere is a mistake: Alberic married Alice daughter of Gilbert de Clare (J. H. Round, *Geoffrey de Mandeville*, 390–2). Alberic's gift of tithe at Islip to Thorney Abbey, cited by Kennett to prove the marriage, concerns Islip (Northants) (*V.C.H. Northants*, iii. 215).
[74] For this suggestion see H. Drummond, *Histories of Noble British Families* (1846), ii. Neville, 40.
[75] *Complete Peerage*, vii. 532 n., 524 and n.; L. Fox, 'Honor and Earldom of Leicester: Origin and Descent, 1066–1399', *E.H.R.* liv. 386.
[76] For the De Courcy family see *Stogursey Charters* (Som. Rec. Soc. lxi), pp. xviii–xix; Farrer, *Honors*, i. 103 sqq.; H. C. Maxwell Lyte, 'Curci', *Som. Arch. and Nat. Hist. Soc. Proc.* lxvi. 101 sqq.; *Liber de Antiquis Legibus* (Camd. Soc. xxxiv), pp. xlix sqq. These accounts, however, deal mainly with the English branch of the family.

Anjou, and may have been the Robert killed in Wales in 1157.[77] Robert's heir William, probably his son, became justiciar to Henry II and died in 1176.[78] A William de Courcy paid scutage for Islip in 1165 and held the manor at his death in 1186.[79] Later evidence shows that William had a brother Robert, *dapifer regis*,[80] and suggests that they were sons of William the justiciar, and that Robert died without issue.[81]

Beside Islip, William (d. 1186) held a group of Hampshire manors, of which Catherington and Clanfield belonged to the honor of Arundel, and Farlington and Bilsington had a tenuous connexion with that honor.[82] Warblington, which William held in chief, had been part of the honor as forfeited by Robert of Bellême in 1102, and may well have been detached from the honor while it was in the king's hands (1102–38).[83] If Henry I created in this period a small English honor for his Norman *dapifer* Robert, elder son of Robert de Courcy, it may well have included Islip as well as Warblington. William de Courcy was succeeded at Islip by his son Robert, who although not a minor was not granted his English lands until 1189.[84] Robert appears to have enfeoffed another William, probably his brother, with Islip, for in 1203 a William de Courcy took the homage of a tenant of the manor.[85] Robert, however, joined Philip Augustus of France in 1203, and the family forfeited its English lands.[86]

Copies survive of a spurious writ in which Henry I declares that he has restored to Westminster Abbey certain lands, including Islip, which [Ranulf] the chancellor held of it.[87] Westminster had a clear title to other lands mentioned in the writ, but as far as Islip is concerned it should be regarded as a clever attempt to use Ranulf's acknowledged spoliation of the church as a pretext for securing a manor to which the abbey's title was still in doubt. There is no evidence that Westminster ever held Islip in the 12th century, but in 1203 after the De Courcys' forfeiture the abbey renewed its claim with success —although the documents produced in its support were forgeries.[88] The nature of Islip's connexion

with Westminster remained obscure: in 1279 the abbot was said to hold the manor in chief in free alms 'de dono Regis Anglie, sed de quo Rege nescitur', and in 1284 he was said to hold *per baroniam*.[89] In 1446 it was established that the abbey held Islip of Edward the Confessor's gift on the condition of maintaining a chaplain to celebrate daily masses in St. Edward's chapel for the souls of King Edward, his ancestors and successors.[90]

Islip was assigned to the abbot's portion at Westminster. In May 1216 the manor was seized by King John upon a false report of the death of Abbot William de Humez. John committed the manor to Hugh de Lusignan,[91] but in December of the same year Henry III ordered its restitution to the abbot.[92]

In 1299 Islip manor, with all appurtenances except the advowson and franchisal jurisdiction, together with two liveries a year from Todenham (Glos.), was granted to William de Dernford, knight, and Cecily his wife, to hold during their lives, in exchange for the manor of Deerhurst (Glos.) and a fourth part of the hundred of Deerhurst, these properties being then held by the Dernfords of the abbot and convent in fee farm.[93] Abbot Walter de Wenlok's purpose in making this exchange was to recover a valuable manor let at fee farm by his improvident predecessor, Gervase de Blois, abbot 1137–57.[94] The Dernfords held Islip until about 1327. Cecily outlived William, remarried in or before 1316,[95] and died before 1328.[96] The series of ministers' accounts extant in the Abbey Muniment Room is resumed in 1327.

Islip was sequestrated on the surrender of Westminster Abbey in January 1540.[97] In August 1542 it was granted to the dean and chapter of the newly constituted cathedral church at Westminster.[98] In 1556 it was surrendered to the Crown and granted to the abbot and convent of the restored monastic foundation.[99] Finally, in 1560, it was again surrendered, and granted to the dean and chapter of the collegiate church constituted at Westminster by Elizabeth I.[1]

[77] Ordericus Vitalis, *Historia Ecclesiastica* (ed. A. Le Prévost 1838–55), iii. 359; *Cal. Doc. France* ed. Round, p. 213; C. H. Haskins, *Norman Institutions*, 146–7; William of Newburgh, *Historia Rerum Anglicarum*, in *Chron. of the Reigns of Stephen, Henry II and Richard I* (Rolls Ser.), i. 108. See also Round, op. cit. p. 432 (where Robert is erroneously described as the son of *Robert* de Courcy), and Ordericus, *Hist. Eccl.* iv. 363.

[78] *Red Bk. Exch.* (Rolls Ser.), 627; Hoveden, *Chronica* (Rolls Ser.), ii. 43, 82, 100. William must not be confused with a namesake, William de Courcy of Stogursey (Som.), head of the English branch of the family.

[79] *Pipe R.* 1165 (P.R.S. viii), 70; *Pipe R.* 1187 (P.R.S. xxxvii), 24–25.

[80] *Cur. Reg. R.* i. 239–40. Robert was probably the elder brother.

[81] *Magni Rot. Scacc. Normanniae*, i. 44, 267. But see Torigny, *Chronica* in *Chron. of the Reigns of Stephen*, &c. (Rolls Ser.), iv. 271.

[82] *Pipe R.* 1187 (P.R.S. xxxvii), 24–25; *V.C.H. Hants*, iii. 103. In Henry I's reign Bilsington was in the possession of William d'Aubigny, who later acquired the honor of Arundel (Round, *King's Serjeants and Officers of State*, 174). Robert de Courcy's manor, consisting of half the vill (*Bk. of Fees*, 271), was granted in 1204 to Henry of Sandwich (*Rot. Litt. Claus.* (Rec. Com.), i. 9), and in 1207 to the Earl of Arundel (ibid. 94). In 1246 it was found to be not land of the Normans (*Cal. Chart. R.* 1226–57, 292). Nothing is known about the early history of the manor of Farlington. In Henry III's reign half the vill of Drayton, one of its members, was held by Roger de Merlay of the

king's gift of the Earl of Arundel for ⅓ fee (*Cal. Inq. p.m.* i, pp. 55–56).

[83] *V.C.H. Hants*, iii. 134; *Complete Peerage*, i. 233–4.

[84] *Pipe R.* 1189 (Rec. Com.), 7; Robert was holding lands at Gefosse in 1184 (*Mémoires de la Société des Antiquaires de Normandie*, xvi [1852], 112; see also L. V. Delisle, *Recueil des Actes de Henri II*, Introduction, 440).

[85] *Cur. Reg. R.* 1201–3, 281.

[86] F. M. Powicke, *Loss of Normandy*, 493.

[87] C. Johnson and H. A. Cronne, *Regesta Regum*, ii. 1881.

[88] W.A.M. 15160; *Rot. de Ob. et Fin.* (Rec. Com.), 222; *Pipe R.* 1204 (P.R.S. n.s. xviii), 112; *Rot. Litt. Claus.* (Rec. Com.), i. 15, 32.

[89] *Rot. Hund.* (Rec. Com.), ii. 831; *Feud. Aids*, iv. 158.

[90] W.A.M. 15202.

[91] *Rot. Litt. Claus.* (Rec. Com.), i. 273, where Hugh is erroneously called Henry; cf. *Close R.* 1231–4, 345.

[92] *Rot. Litt. Claus.* i. 294.

[93] W.A.M. 32691: this refers to a third of the hundred; all other docs. concerning the exchange refer to a quarter; cf. *Cal. Pat.* 1292–1301, 429–30.

[94] W.A.M. 32668. For Gervase see Walsingham, *Gesta Abbatum* (Rolls Ser.), i. 133; J. Flete, *Hist. of Westm. Abbey*, ed. J. A. Robinson, 89; *V.C.H. Lond.* i. 436–7.

[95] *Cal. Close*, 1313–18, 281–2.

[96] *Cal. Inq. p.m.* vii, p. 88.

[97] *L. & P. Hen. VIII*, xv, p. 24.

[98] Ibid. xvii, p. 392.

[99] *Cal. Pat.* 1555–7, 349.

[1] Ibid. 1558–60, 397.

In November 1645 a committee of Lords and Commons was set up to administer the lands and revenues of the 'delinquent' Dean and Chapter of Westminster.[2] In April 1649 the lands and revenues of all deans and chapters were vested in a body of trustees appointed by the Commons.[3] Islip came under the provisions of both these acts. In September 1649, however, the manor was exempted from the operation of the latter act and assigned to the maintenance of Westminster School.[4] In December 1650 the manor was sold to Colonel Fielder and John Staunton for £4,736 5s. 2d.[5] In 1660 it was restored to the Dean and Chapter of Westminster, now reinstated. It remained in their hands until 1869, when ownership was transferred to the Ecclesiastical Commissioners.[6]

It was the policy of the Dean and Chapter of Westminster to lease the manor. The following list gives the date of each lease, the name of the lessee(s) and the term of years: the rent per annum was in all cases £54 19s. 4d. No information is available concerning fines paid:

1549, Edward, Duke of Somerset, 99 yrs.;[7] 1634, Henry Norris and George Willis, 21 yrs.;[8] 1634, George Willis and John Banks, 21 yrs.;[9] 1641, John Banks and Thomas Gilder, 21 yrs.;[10] 1660, Sir Thomas Tipping, 19 yrs.;[11] 1663, idem, 21 yrs.;[12] 1666, idem, 21 yrs.;[13] 1673, idem, 21 yrs.;[14] 1680, idem, 21 yrs.;[15] 1687, Sir John Doyley, 21 yrs.;[16] 1694, idem;[17] 1701, Revd. Timothy Halton, Provost of the Queen's College, Oxford, and Revd. Richard Davies of Sapperton (Glos.), 21 yrs.;[18] 1708, Revd. George Carter, Provost of Oriel College, Oxford, and Francis Nourse of Wood Eaton, 21 yrs.;[19] 1716, idem, 21 yrs.;[20] 1723, idem, 21 yrs.;[21] 1730, Revd. Richard Ibbetson of Lambeth, and Francis Nourse, 21 yrs.;[22] 1737, John Nourse and Thomas Trollope, 21 yrs.;[23] 1744, idem, 21 yrs.;[24] 1751, idem, 21 yrs.;[25] 1758, idem, 21 yrs.;[26] 1765, idem, 21 yrs.;[27] 1772, Harriett Browne, 21 yrs.;[28] 1779, idem, 21 yrs.;[29] 1786, idem, 21 yrs.;[30] 1793, idem, 21 yrs.;[31] 1801, Revd. George Worsley, the estate of Edward Worsley, lunatic, 21 yrs.;[32] 1808, idem,

21 yrs.;[33] 1814, idem, 21 yrs.;[34] 1823, William Worsley for Edward Worsley, 21 yrs.;[35] 1829, idem, 21 yrs.;[36] 1836, John Pinfold, assign of William and Frances Worsley, administratrix of Edward Worsley, 21 yrs.;[37] 1843, idem, 21 yrs.[38]

ECONOMIC HISTORY. No manorial extent survives. The following valuations are given in Domesday Book: T.R.E. £7; 1066, £8; 1086, £10.[39] The manor, including the mill and perquisites of the court, is valued at £17 9s. in 1291 and at £53 10s. 1d. in 1535.[40] The manor with appurtenances is valued at £40 4s. *ultra repris* in an inquisition of 1446.[41]

In 1086 there were six teamlands under cultivation at Islip.[42] In 1806 the tillage consisted of six open fields, containing about 1,200 acres.[43] The arable reached its medieval limits in the 13th century. In the 14th century the demesne began to disintegrate, and two visitations of the plague, in 1348–9 and 1361–2 respectively, caused temporary reductions in the area of tenant land under cultivation.[44] These two decades of instability were followed by 40 years during which the area under cultivation fluctuated little, only two or three small holdings being vacant each year. After 1400, however, vacant holdings greatly increased in number.[45] The rental of 1435, when compared with the custumal of 1390, shows a decrease of about 100 acres in the area of tenant land cultivated.[46] Moreover, many holdings in nominal occupation were waste, having been taken primarily for the pasture rights appurtenant to them.

In 1806, on the eve of the parliamentary inclosure, there were six open fields: the North (235 a.), East (113 a.), Lankott (156 a.), Brought (261 a.), and Mill (210 a.) Fields north of the river; Sart Field (about 200 a.) south of the river.[47] Only four of these field names occur in medieval records: North Field in 1379,[48] East Field in 1421,[49] Sart Field and Lankott repeatedly in 14th-century accounts.[50] A West Field is mentioned in a late 13th-century charter and again in 1445.[51] A terrier of the Islip glebe drawn up in 1634 mentions five arable fields: the West, West Chadgrove, Langiott, and East Fields, and Wood Eaton Field (probably Sart

[2] *Acts and Ords. of Interr.* ed. Firth and Rait, i. 803–5.
[3] Ibid. ii. 81–104.
[4] Ibid. 256–61.
[5] W.A.M. 15263. It is possible that they leased it to Edward Dewe (see below, p. 217).
[6] *Lond. Gaz.* 13 Aug. 1869. Serles Farm (88 a.) remained in the ownership of the dean and chapter.
[7] Westminster Abbey Reg. Bk. iii, f. 97b.
[8] Ibid. xiv, ff. 326b–328.
[9] Ibid. ff. 337–338b.
[10] Ibid. xv, ff. 471–2.
[11] Ibid. xvi, ff. 91–93.
[12] Ibid. xvii, ff. 44b–47.
[13] Ibid. xviii, ff. 4–7.
[14] Ibid. xix, ff. 225–227b.
[15] Ibid. xxi, ff. 113–15.
[16] Ibid. xxii, ff. 243b–245.
[17] This lease is not entered in the register, but reference to a renewal of Doyley's lease in 1694 is made in the lease of 1701: ibid. xxv, f. 240.
[18] Ibid. ff. 240–2.
[19] Ibid. xxvii, ff. 199–200b.
[20] Ibid. xxix, ff. 120–2.
[21] Ibid. xxxi, ff. 91b–94.
[22] Ibid. xxxiv, ff. 125–9.
[23] Ibid. xxxvii, f. 220.
[24] Ibid. xxxviii, ff. 219b–221b.
[25] Ibid. xxxix, ff. 134–136b.
[26] Ibid. xli, ff. 52b–54b.

[27] Ibid. xlii, ff. 165b–169.
[28] Ibid. xlv, ff. 255–9.
[29] Ibid. xlviii, ff. 169b–173b.
[30] Ibid. l, ff. 105–109b.
[31] Ibid. lii, ff. 143b–147.
[32] Ibid. lv, ff. 28–31b.
[33] Ibid. lvii, ff. 5b–8b.
[34] Ibid. lviii, ff. 186b–189.
[35] Ibid. lix, ff. 269b–272b.
[36] Ibid. lxi, ff. 139b–143.
[37] Ibid. lxii, ff. 256b–259b.
[38] Ibid. lxiv, ff. 75b–77b.
[39] *V.C.H. Oxon.* i. 422.
[40] *Tax. Eccl.* (Rec. Com.), 45; *Valor Eccl.* (Rec. Com.), i. 411.
[41] W.A.M. 5202.
[42] *V.C.H. Oxon.* i. 422.
[43] P.R.O., M.R. 249.
[44] See below, p. 215.
[45] Below, p. 214.
[46] W.A.M. 15200, 15207.
[47] P.R.O., M.R. 249. For a small-scale reproduction of the inclosure map see A. Ballard, *Domesday Inquest* (1923), facing p. 256.
[48] W.A.M. 14864.
[49] Ibid. 14899.
[50] Ibid. 14791, 14793–9.
[51] Ibid. Westm. Domesday, f. 271; W.A.M. 14918.

Field).[52] The first reference to Brought Field occurs in 1655.[53]

The field system of medieval Islip is a matter for conjecture. The original fields lay north of the river, and it seems probable that the East, North, and Lankott Fields (504 a. in all) and the Brought and Mill Fields (471 a.) represent respectively the east and west fields of the early medieval village. The evidence is scanty and inconclusive but suggests that

the Domesday pasture 3 furlongs long and 2 broad; by 1806 this pasture was about 154 acres in extent and its extreme measurements had almost doubled. Pasture in the stubble fields was stinted by common assent at 4 beasts per virgate, 2 per half-virgate, and 1 per cottage.[56] Each virgater had faldage for 80 sheep on the fallow, each half-virgater faldage for 40 sheep, and other tenants proportionately.[57] The tenants of Islip claimed common in the fields of

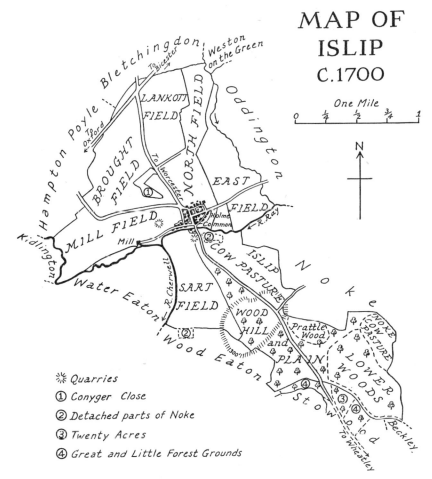

MAP OF ISLIP C.1700

The above map is based on documents cited in the text and the inclosure map of 1808.

the original east and west fields were divided in the course of the 13th century into the North, East, and West Fields and a fourth field known in the early 17th century as the West Chadgrove Field and later as Brought Field.[54] Sart Field came under cultivation in the 12th or 13th century. Lankott was a separate section of the arable by the 14th century and may represent an adjustment necessitated by assarting south of the river. Islip's six fields do not seem to be a variant of a normal three-field arrangement.[55]

The common pastures in medieval Islip were Holme Common and the Cow Pasture. The former may be identified with the meadow 30 acres in extent mentioned in Domesday Book; the latter with

Arncot in alternate years.[58] Each half-virgater had, in addition, free agistment for one pig in the abbot's wood and agistment for others on payment of pannage.[59] These facilities became inadequate in the later Middle Ages, largely as a result of the development of large-scale peasant sheep-farming By the 16th century the freeholders and copyholders of Islip had established prescriptive rights of common in Islip Wood. In 1622 they were finally allotted Wood Hill and Plain as an extra cow-pasture.[60] Part of West Field seems to have been adopted as common meadow in the 17th century. References to a west meadow occur from this date, and a reference in 1684 to a 'lay of grasse ground' in

[52] Oxf. Archd. Oxon. b 41, f. 7.
[53] W.A.M. 14966. A by-law of 1536 refers to 'the browte dytche': ibid. 14955.
[54] West Field changed its name to Mill Field in the later 17th century.
[55] See H. L. Gray, *Eng. Field Systems*, 125.

[56] W.A.M. 14898.
[57] Ibid. 14935.
[58] Ibid. 14894.
[59] Ibid. 15200.
[60] See below, p. 212.

Mill Field suggests its identity with this part of the arable.[61] Reference is made in the 18th century to a Reed Meadow.[62] In addition to these permanent meadows, Lammas lands were set apart from time to time within the different arable fields.[63]

Woods were a prominent feature of the pre-inclosure parish. Domesday Book records the existence of a wood 1 league long and ½ league in breadth.[64] That part of the parish which lies south of the Ray (997 acres), measured at its extremities, is approximately 2 miles long and 1¼ miles in breadth and is undoubtedly the site of this wood. Islip Wood was known in the Middle Ages as *Cauda Aliz*. It was affected by the struggle for disafforestment in the 13th century; in 1233 and in 1279 it was described as part of the royal forest;[65] in 1298 the wood was disafforested,[66] but here, as elsewhere, the perambulation was a dead letter.[67] The wood was finally disafforested in Edward III's reign: in 1337 it was held to be of the ancient demesne of the king and outside the forest.[68] The disafforestment deprived Islip of the common rights of a forest vill. In the 14th and 15th centuries the vill paid fines for agistment in the forest.[69] In the 17th century the Dean and Chapter of Westminster, as lords of Islip manor, were allotted 20 acres in the forest of Shotover and Stowood in satisfaction of all claims to common therein.[70]

Three processes combined to strip Islip of its woods: assarting for arable, encroachment for commons, and spoliation for timber. Assarting brought about 200 acres under tillage (i.e. Sart Field) by the 14th century. The only recorded assart was made in exceptional circumstances when, in 1233, the Abbot of Westminster obtained licence to assart 10½ acres which had been wasted by Hugh de Lusignan during his brief tenure of the manor in 1216.[71]

Encroachment on the woods for pasture began in the 14th century. Until this date the only right which customary tenants enjoyed there was that of agistment for swine.[72] Shortage of pasture led to the usurpation of more extensive rights in the later Middle Ages. By the 16th century rights of common for sheep between 29 September and 3 May had been established in Islip Wood by four vills, Islip itself, Beckley, Noke, and Wood Eaton. Tenants of Islip and Noke had common in the wood as a whole and shared the responsibility of fencing Sart on the Wood Hill side before Ascension Day each year. The vills of Beckley and Wood Eaton enjoyed limited rights between 29 September and 25 March in Hazelbed and Old Sale, two coppices which formed part of the area later known as Lower Woods.[73]

The woods were used indiscriminately, however, as pasture for all beasts. Accordingly, in or about the year 1611 the Dean and Chapter of Westminster, as lords of the manor, with Henry Norris and Thomas Gilder, their farmers, and Benedict Winchcombe, lord of Noke manor, on the one part, and the freeholders and customaries of Islip and Noke on the other part, agreed to inclose the woods and waste of Islip and apportion pasture to each party in severalty. A Chancery decision confirmed the original agreement in 1620.[74] Further representations from a few customary tenants resulted in a new settlement in Chancery in 1622.[75] The original agreement made the following allotments: to the freeholders and copyholders of Islip, Wood Hill and Leyside (about 120 a.); to the freeholders and copyholders of Noke, a portion of the soil of Islip in area five-twelfths of the allotment made to the tenants of Islip (57 a. in Lower Woods were allotted); to the lords of Islip manor, Horse Coppice and Hazelbeds, in Lower Woods; to the lord of Noke manor, Noke Wood, a parcel of ground lying between Noke Wood and Lower Woods, and that part of Prattle Wood which lay within Noke Parish. The remaining woods and waste in Islip and Noke (about 400 a. in extent) were to continue in common, saving to the farmer of Islip the right to inclose a fourth part of the woods. It appears to have been in accordance with this provision that Prattle Wood was later inclosed. The final agreement preserved these arrangements unchanged, but allowed freeholders and copyholders of Islip who so desired to inclose and hold in severalty their allotments in Wood Hill and Leyside. No provision was made for the vills of Beckley and Wood Eaton; their rights in Islip Wood were thus extinguished.

Spoliation of the woods for timber became a serious problem in the 18th century. Little is known about estovers before this date. Only two medieval customs are known: customary tenants of the manor paid 2 eggs and a hen for the right to collect dead wood;[76] the tenant of that part of Noke which was not of the Westminster fee paid 2s. 6d. a year to the Abbot of Westminster for *husbote* and *heybot* in Islip Wood.[77] In 1612 certain copyholders of Islip claimed the customary right to have the lop and top of the trees on their estates and timber for repairs.[78] Manorial customs dating from the late 17th century allow copyholders the lop and top of all timber trees and timber for repairs if any grow on their premises.[79] The latter stipulation was widely disregarded in the 18th century. In 1797 Richard Davis reported that 'sad havoc' had been wrought particularly on Wood Hill and in the plantation adjoining Wood Eaton parish.[80] Davis's estimates of the number of trees still standing show that Islip was now only thinly wooded. All traces of the Domesday extent of woodland disappeared finally in 1806, when, with the exception of Prattle Wood, most of the trees in the parish were felled as a preliminary to inclosure of the arable.[81]

In 1279 the Abbot of Westminster had at Islip

[61] W.A.M. 15092.
[62] Ibid. 15275.
[63] Ibid. 15231. For the rules concerning common pasture in the 18th cent. see R.C.O. box 47: field orders, 27 Aug. 1794.
[64] *V.C.H. Oxon.* i. 422.
[65] *Close R.* 1231–4, 345; *Rot. Hund.* (Rec. Com.), ii. 831.
[66] *Boarstall Cart.* 180.
[67] *Eynsham Cart.* ii. 211.
[68] *Boarstall Cart.* 173.
[69] Ibid. 175, 193.
[70] The grant is mentioned in a lease of 1673 as having

been made 'recently': Westminster Abbey Reg. Bk. xix, ff. 227b–228.
[71] *Close R.* 1231–4, 345–6.
[72] W.A.M. 15200.
[73] By-law, 13 Oct. 1539 (ibid. 14957).
[74] C 33/137, 755.
[75] Ibid. 141, 881–2; W.A.M. 15268 (copy).
[76] W.A.M. 15200.
[77] *Rot. Hund.* ii. 838.
[78] E 134/9 Jas. I/Hil. 23.
[79] R.C.O. box 47.
[80] Ibid. box 48: letter 19 Sept. 1797.
[81] MS. Top. Oxon. c 112, p. 109.

four carucates in demesne.[82] Estimates of demesne tillage based on information given in the ministers' accounts give a figure of about 480 acres for its extent in the late 13th century. The demesne was scattered in the open fields of Islip, Murcott, and Fencott, but most of it lay in the vill of Islip and in shots rather than in small strips. It is in this sense that the first lease of the demesne, in 1395, speaks of *omnes campos de terris dominicis*.[83] Leasing of demesne acres began in 1331.[84] By 1391 about 50 acres had been leased piecemeal.[85] Disintegration in this manner was checked in 1360 by an agreement between the Abbot of Westminster and the reeve of Islip, whereby the latter undertook the cultivation of the arable demesne and the management of the demesne pigs in return for half the yearly crop yield.[86] After a short resumption of full demesne cultivation between 1389 and 1395, a twelve years' lease of the arable demesne was made in 1395.[87] By 1400 the whole demesne, inclusive of pasture, had been leased for £15 a year.[88] By 1450 the rent had fallen to £7 3s. 4d. a year.[89] Most lessees of the demesne were half-virgaters. Joint leases by as many as ten tenants occur in the 15th century. Two phases in demesne cultivation are discernible: intensive exploitation of the arable in the 13th century, and a second phase, beginning about 1340, in which stock farming became an important, though still subsidiary, feature of manorial economy. The development of stock farming brought little change in the disposition of the demesne between arable and pasture. The emphasis was on pigs and on wool production. The former fed on the woods and waste. The latter was introduced on a modest scale: the number of sheep clipped yearly varied between 125 and 310;[90] and the estimated proceeds never rose above £13.[91] The chief interest of demesne sheep farming at Islip is its organization on an extra-manorial basis under an itinerant *supervisor bidentium*.[92] Corn sales and the provision of corn for the abbot's hospice remained the chief objects of demesne cultivation until the end. Corn sales appear to have been made locally. The demesne was cultivated by *famuli* and by customary labour. Week-work, consisting of five days' work a fortnight per half-virgate, was commuted in the 13th century by an option which demanded 3s. rent a year per half-virgate. Between 1276 and 1298 work was demanded from 20 or 30 villeins between 24 June and 29 September, and from about 10 villeins during the remainder of the year.[93] Between 1327 and 1349 it was demanded from 27 to 29 villeins (nearly all the half-virgaters in the vill) for the whole of the year.[94] Immediately after the plague of 1348–9 all week-

work was commuted, the rent per half-virgate being raised to 5s. 5d. a year.[95] By 1357 half the work due in the harvest season had been reimposed,[96] but later, probably in 1386, all week-work was permanently commuted and the rent per half-virgate was fixed at 6s. a year.[97] Boon works (demanded in full until 1349) were depleted by the farming of customary holdings after that date.[98] By 1390 225 of the 811½ boons due each year had been lost by farming. For less than half the acres sown in 1390–1 was customary labour used.[99]

In 1612 the customs of the manor were in dispute between Westminster's farmers and seven copyholders.[1] The questions in dispute were the grant of copyholds in reversion over the heads of the tenants in possession, the incidence of heriot in cases of forfeiture, the right of copyholders to grant short sub-leases, the privileges of the executors' year, and the timber rights of copyholders. Statements of manorial customs surviving from the late 17th century show that the main contentions of the defendants on this occasion were allowed. In the later 17th century and in the 18th century customs were recited at the triennial manorial courts. An executors' year was allowed on copyholds and widows' estates in the following terms: if the tenant died after Lady Day and before Michaelmas, the executor to enjoy two crops and the premises for a year and a day; if after Michaelmas and before Lady Day, the executor to enjoy a year's profits except the fallow and fallow meadow. No copyhold reversion was to be granted over the heads of the tenants in possession.[2]

Freehold tenure appeared at Islip in the period 1086–1279.[3] The only feoffment for which evidence survives is the grant of a half-virgate in fee to one William de Throp' about 1295 *pro laudabili servicio*.[4] In 1279 there were four freeholders in the vill of Islip, holding between them 3½ virgates.[5] In 1391 four freeholders held 3 virgates 2 acres and some demesne acres.[6] In 1435 three freeholders held between them little more than 2 virgates and one cottage.[7] All freehold was engrossed in the 15th century by a tenant named Wymbush.[8]

Much more is known about the development of tenure in villeinage. In 1086 there were at Islip 10 villeins (*villani*) and 5 bordars.[9] In 1279 the Hundred Rolls name two joint tenants of a virgate and 32 half-virgaters, but a near contemporary rental names 55 tenants in addition to the freeholders; seventeen of these appear to hold less than half a virgate each.[10] In 1391 there were 12 half-virgaters, 15 cottars, 9 leaseholders, and 15 tenants of composite holdings;[11] in 1435, 9 half-virgaters, 15 cottars, and 18 tenants

[82] *Rot. Hund.* ii. 831.
[83] W.A.M. 15175.
[84] Ibid. 14789.
[85] Ibid. 15200.
[86] Ibid. 14802.
[87] Ibid. 15175.
[88] Ibid. 14831.
[89] Ibid. 14923. The 'upper manor' was leased for £6 13s. 4d. a year, the 'lower manor', consisting of closes for impounding, for 10s. a year.
[90] Minimum (125) in 1352; maximum (310) in 1368 (W.A.M. 14798–9).
[91] Maximum estimate of £13 was made in 1379 (ibid. 14815).
[92] First mentioned in 1348 (ibid. 14795).
[93] Ibid. 14776–823.
[94] Ibid. 14787–97.

[95] Ibid. 14798.   [96] Ibid. 14799.
[97] Ibid. 15200.   [98] See below.
[99] W.A.M. 14828.
[1] E 134/9 Jas. I/Hil. 23.
[2] Statement of customs, 27 Aug. 1794 (R.C.O. box 47).
[3] *V.C.H. Oxon.* i. 422; *Rot. Hund.* ii. 831.
[4] Westm. Domesday, f. 273.
[5] *Rot. Hund.* ii. 831.
[6] W.A.M. 15200.
[7] Ibid. 15207.
[8] Ibid.: *modo N. Wymbussh* has been inserted in a 15th-cent. hand over the names of the 4 freeholders in the custumal.
[9] *V.C.H. Oxon.* i. 422.
[10] *Rot. Hund.* ii. 831; Gloucs. R.O. D 1099 M 37, m. 1.
[11] W.A.M. 15200; cf. ibid. 15201: abridged summary of custumal.

of composite holdings.[12] The rental of about 1540 names 8 half-virgaters, 7 cottars, and 7 tenants of composite holdings in Islip, but this document appears to be a hasty compilation, possibly incomplete:[13] the lay subsidy roll of 1524 names no less than 43 persons in Islip with goods to the value of 20s. or more,[14] and it therefore seems unlikely that only sixteen years later there were only 22 landholders in the village. By the 14th century tallage had become the only practical test of unfree tenure.[15] This it remained until 1433, when it was assimilated to the ordinary rents of assize.[16]

Three important changes occurred in the 14th century. In the first place, the half-virgater ceased to be the typical customary tenant. In the period from about 1279 to 1391, when the total number of customary tenants altered very little, the number of half-virgaters decreased from over 30 to 12. Secondly, leasehold tenure developed. The origin of leasehold —the term being used here to denote a conveyance for a term of years and exempt from entry fine—lies in the farming of villein holdings for money rents, tallage, and light services which began in the decade after the Black Death. By 1391 thirteen half-virgates were farmed.[17] Many of the farms were at first tenancies at will, granted 'quousque aliquis alius venerit qui dictum tenementum voluerit tenere secundum consuetudinem manerii'.[18] This hope was rarely fulfilled: only one of the half-virgates farmed in 1391 is known to have been taken again *ad antiqua servicia*. Some farms were later converted into leases proper. It was by the grant of farms and leaseholds that the Abbot of Westminster kept all land in Islip under cultivation in the late 14th century. Thirdly, composite holdings appeared. This development is closely connected with the appearance of leasehold: of fifteen composite holdings in 1391, eleven included lands held at farm.[19] The nucleus of nearly all these holdings was a customary half-virgate. The composite holding of the 14th century was a temporary construction liable to rapid dispersal. Only five names are common to the lists of the tenants of such holdings in 1391 and 1435, and in no instance are the holdings identical. Such holdings remained an unstable feature of the manorial structure until the development of copyhold.

The development of copyhold was the most important feature of tenurial history in the 15th century. Commutation of week work, completed about 1386,[20] had been the first step in the process. The change was completed by the acceptance of the court rolls as registers of title and by the permission of formal reversions.[21] Copies for three lives were granted occasionally. The advantage which copyhold offered was not security, but heritability. Composite holdings, consisting of tenements acquired gradually and often held by different tenures, tended to be dispersed on the death of their tenants. Copyhold made an heritable title readily available. It became common for tenants of composite holdings to surrender their lands and secure readmittance with reversion for two or three lives.

The transition to copyhold took place against a background of depopulation.[22] Vacancies became common after 1400; in 1426, for instance, eight half-virgates and ten cottages were vacant.[23] Vacancies on a disastrous scale could be prevented only by reducing or waiving the remaining incidents of customary tenure, in particular heriot and entry fine. This the Abbot of Westminster was slow to do. In the 14th century the comprehensive fine for heriot and entry in respect of a half-virgate was often 2 marks,[24] and this high level obtained in the opening decades of the 15th century. The same conservatism is shown in a reluctance to grant leases, the essence of which was immunity from heriot and entry fine. Occasional leases for varying terms were granted throughout the 15th century, but they are few in number. A change of policy began in the third decade of the century. It is interesting to speculate on its connexion with the change in the abbacy which occurred in 1420.[25] The new policy shows itself in the occasional remission of heriot, entry fine, and the first year's rent if the tenement taken by the incoming tenant was waste, and by a general reduction in the fines which were not remitted. With the exception of those paid for composite holdings, heriot and entry fines were often nominal. Only 1 capon, for instance, was taken for each of 4 tofts and half-virgates to which tenants were admitted on 20 October 1446.[26]

Despite the development of copyhold reversions, the peasant aristocracy of 15th-century Islip failed to consolidate its position. Only one of the larger holdings in existence at the beginning of the century is known to have survived for more than two or three generations. This, the holding built up by Thomas Stevens in the late 14th century, is last mentioned in 1465.[27] Only two of the persons of substance mentioned in the lay subsidy roll of 1524 or the rental of 1540 can be identified with a family mentioned in the rental of 1435. In 1524 a Thomas Cowper was assessed at £4 and a Richard Cowper at £3;[28] in 1540 Thomas Cowper held a messuage and half-virgate at will, and Richard Cowper held a messuage and virgate and half-virgate on a copy for three lives.[29] The rental of 1435 mentions an Agnes Cowper who held a messuage and half-virgate and a toft.[30] The instability of the peasant aristocracy of the later Middle Ages is reflected in the absence of an indigenous gentry at Islip in the 16th and 17th centuries, and, indeed, in the comparatively short histories of the oldest families in modern Islip. None of the names now current, Beckley, Stopp, Clarke, Neale, Miles, or Beesley, can be traced beyond the 17th century.

The medieval arable at Islip contained only one close of any importance, a plot of $3\frac{1}{2}$ to 5 acres lying

12 W.A.M. 15207.
13 Ibid. 15206 (undated).
14 E 179/161/176.
15 A freehold enfeoffment secured immediate exemption (W.A.M. 14782).
16 Ibid. 14912.
17 Ibid. 15200.   18 Ibid. 14866.
19 Ibid. 15200–1.
20 See above, p. 213.
21 This paragraph is based on the evidence of 15th-cent. Ct. R.. W.A.M. 14077 925.

22 See below, p. 215.
23 W.A.M. 14905.
24 Ibid. 14864, 14866.
25 Richard Harwden succeeded William Colchester in this year.
26 W.A.M. 14920.
27 For the descent of this holding see ibid. 15200, 14902, 14905, 15207, 14935.
28 E 179/161/176.
29 W.A.M. 15206.
30 Ibid. 15207.

in Brought Field and called *Conyger*, which was inclosed by Richard de Ware, Abbot of Westminster (1258–83).[31] In 1356 the Abbot of Westminster complained that certain persons had broken his close at Islip and felled the trees in his wood there.[32] The reference here may be to a close on a plot of 10½ acres assarted in the 13th century in *Cauda Aliz*.[33] The first large-scale inclosures took place in the early 17th century, but affected woods and pastures only.[34] Later in the century, in 1692, the dean and chapter complained of unauthorized inclosures by certain inhabitants of the parish, but no further trace of these inclosures survives.[35] The parliamentary inclosure of the open fields was authorized by an act of 1804. The inclosure award was made in 1808.[36] The principal allotments were made to the dean and chapter (376 a.) and their lessee, Edward Worsley, and to John Weyland (200 a.) of Wood Eaton. James Smith was allotted 111 acres and three others between 107 and 85 acres. Thirty-four persons had less than 30 acres. The inclosure survey resulted in the introduction of the statute acre at Islip; this replaced a customary acre equivalent to about five-sixths of the statute measure.[37]

In 1086 seventeen persons are mentioned at Islip.[38] There were about 60 landholders in the late 13th century, 55 in 1391, and 45 in 1435.[39] The proportion of the population holding land in 1391, however, was almost certainly larger than the proportion holding land in 1279. The Black Death probably provided the first check to the slow growth of population after 1086: 27 heriots were paid in the manorial year 1348–9; 11 of the 17 villeins owing chevage died, and 9 half-virgates and 7 cottages were still vacant in 1351.[40] A further spate of vacancies in the manorial year 1362–3 (five half-virgates) suggests a second visitation of the plague in 1361 or 1362.[41] There are signs of depopulation in the early 15th century, among them flight of villeins and a great increase in chevage payments.[42] In 1523 48 persons were assessed for the lay subsidy and the total assessment was £6 2s. 10d.; the figures in 1524 were 43 and £5 18s. 6d.[43] The Compton Census (1676) recorded 207 adults. Returns to episcopal visitations give the number of families or houses as about 100 in 1738, 120 in 1759, 140 in 1768, and 120 in 1771.[44] The figure returned in 1801 was 557. The population had risen to 655 by 1821 and to 744 in 1851, but declined in the later years of the century.[45] The figure returned in 1951 was 586.[46]

CHURCH. The benefice is a rectory formerly in the rural deanery of Bicester but which by 1854 had been transferred to the new deanery of Islip.[47]

According to tradition there was a church at Islip in the early 11th century in which Edward the Confessor was baptized. Gervase de Blois, Abbot of Westminster 1137–57, granted the church at Islip to Helias, *decanus*, in return for half a mark of silver a year.[48] Between 1203 and 1869 the descent of the advowson followed the descent of the manor. The advowson remained with the Dean and Chapter of Westminster after the transfer of the manor to the Ecclesiastical Commissioners in 1869. In 1531 the next presentation was granted to Nicholas Townley, clerk, and to Thomas Cromwell.[49] In 1590 the advowson was granted for 21 years to John Lloyd, advocate of the Court of Arches, to the use of Hugh Lloyd, LL.D., who was presented to the living in the same year.[50] In 1632 the next presentation was granted to William Raynton of Eaton Hastings (Berks.), to the use of Peter Heylyn.[51] Heylyn secured the living in 1638. In 1646 the committee of lords and commons for the revenues of the lands belonging to the Dean and Chapter of Westminster presented Edward Hinton to the living.[52]

The rectory was valued at £6 13s. 4d. in 1254, at £10 13s. 4d. in 1291, and at £17 4s. 2d. in 1535.[53] In 1807, at the time of the inclosure survey, it was reported that Islip contained 1,914 titheable acres, inclusive of 29 acres of glebe.[54] The tithes were valued at £449 1s. after inclosure, the glebe at £54 19s. The valuer reported that Islip could bear an increase on the existing rate (5s. 6d.), but the rector was unwilling to encounter the ill will which such a rise would cause.[55] Tithes were commuted in 1843. According to the agreement there were 1,940 titheable acres in the parish, inclusive of the glebe, of 7 acres of Noke glebe lying in the parish, and of 64 acres in Islip titheable to Noke.[56] Tithes payable to the Rector of Islip were commuted for £492 10s. a year inclusive of tithe from the Islip glebe. A rent charge of £16 a year was allotted to the Rector of Noke in lieu of his tithes in Islip. The intermixture of the tithes of Islip and Noke had long caused ill feeling between the two parishes.[57] Vincent noted that Islip had tithe in Noke to the value of about £30 'so intermingled that it can be described by the terrier only'.[58] The earliest extant terrier of glebe land, 1634, details 35 acres of glebe.[59] The decrease to 29 acres in 1807 is to be accounted for by the adoption of the larger statute acre.[60]

The living was held during the Commonwealth and Protectorate by Edward Hinton, a covenanter who, however, conformed at the Restoration.[61] Many of the post-Reformation incumbents have been men of unusual distinction.[62] Eighteenth-century rectors and parishioners were of average zeal and piety. The

[31] *Cal. Inq. Misc.* ii, p. 423; *Cal. Close*, 1339–41, 427–8.
[32] *Cal. Pat.* 1354–8, 444–5.
[33] *Close R.* 1231–4, 345–6.
[34] See above, p. 212.
[35] W.A.M. 15225.
[36] 44 Geo. III, c. 67 (priv. act); C.P. 43/901/188.
[37] MS. Top. Oxon. c 112, p. 29.
[38] *V.C.H. Oxon.* i. 422.
[39] Gloucs. R.O. D 1099 M 37, m. 1; W.A.M. 15200, 15206.
[40] W.A.M. 14796–8.   [41] Ibid. 14802.
[42] Ibid. 14883, 14887, 14893.
[43] E 179/161/204, 176.
[44] Oxf. Dioc. d 553, d 556, d 559, d 562.
[45] *V.C.H. Oxon.* ii. 221.   [46] *Census*, 1951.
[47] For the date of the formation of Islip deanery see above, p. 67, n. 97.

[48] W.A.M. 15183.
[49] Westminster Abbey Reg. Bk. ii, f. 277. For list of medieval presentations see MS. Top. Oxon. d 460.
[50] Reg. Bk. vii, ff. 85–86.
[51] Ibid. xiv, f. 142*b*.
[52] W.A.M. 15223.
[53] Lunt, *Val. Norw.* 312; *Tax. Eccl.* (Rec. Com.), 31; *Valor Eccl.* (Rec. Com.), ii. 162.
[54] MS. Top. Oxon. c 112, pp. 29–30.
[55] Ibid.
[56] Bodl. Tithe award.
[57] E 134/13 Geo. I/Mich. 5.
[58] MS. Top. Oxon. c 112, p. 60.
[59] Oxf. Archd. Oxon. b 41, f. 7.
[60] MS. Top. Oxon. c 112, p. 29.
[61] Par. Reg. i.
[62] See above, p. 208.

visitation return of 1738 records that the sacrament was administered six times a year to a 'large number' of communicants, that public service was held twice every Sunday, and that prayers were said on holy days. The rector was non-resident, but a curate was to be appointed shortly. By 1759 a curate had been appointed, but the sacrament was administered only four times a year. The number of communicants grew from 'perhaps 30' in 1759 to 'about 40' in 1771 and to '60 or 70' in 1808. Throughout the century the persistent absence from church of 'several persons of low rank' is noted, but this is attributed to ignorance or vice, not to dissent.[63] Richard Cope, rector 1767–1806, was continuously non-resident,[64] but his successor William Vincent (1807–15) resided for six months of every year, and in this he was followed by his successors.[65] In the early 19th century the living was held by the deans of Westminster, of whom Vincent was one, who used Islip as their country seat. The parish is now served by the rector.

The parish church of *ST. NICHOLAS* consists of a chancel, a nave of three bays, north and south aisles with separate pitched roofs, a western tower, and a south porch. Much of the church was rebuilt in the 14th century, but traces of the 12th-century church can be seen in the massive piers and arches which separate the north aisle from the nave, and at the west end of the south aisle, where a single round-headed window survives. The responds of the chancel arch appear to date from the 13th century, but the arch itself was rebuilt in the 14th century. The arcade on the south side of the nave was also rebuilt early in the 14th century, and most of the surviving medieval windows date from the same period. The lofty tower of three stories, with a parapet and crocketed pinnacles, is largely 15th-century work. The chancel was damaged during the fighting at Islip in 1645 and the rector, Dr. Robert South, built a large new one in 1680 at his own expense.[66] It was built in a 17th-century Gothic style by Richard Varney, a local mason.[67] All the windows, including the large east one, had round heads and simple tracery; the roof was low-pitched and the ceiling open except for the eastern bay over the altar, where there was a richly painted plaster ceiling.[68] The fittings installed by South included the oak communion table, now in the Lady Chapel, the credence table, now by the high altar, and, in the nave, a lectern and pulpit which were swept away at the 19th-century restoration.[69] South also erected a gallery in front of the tower opening.

In 1770 Gough described the church as 'a plain building of ragstone with a chancel, nave and two gabell'd aisles and a square west tower'.[70] In 1803 the artist David Cox painted the church; his picture shows no tower, but it is difficult to account for this omission except as artistic licence.[71]

The church was ruthlessly restored in 1861 by E. G. Bruton (builder G. Wyatt of Oxford), and it is Bruton's work which now dominates the whole interior. Bruton removed the gallery, threw open the tower arch, and gave the church a new roof, a new porch, and new fittings. South's chancel was reroofed, its style transformed into geometrical, and its 17th-century fittings swept away. The wall-paintings were plastered over. Bruton's restoration cost about £2,000, of which more than half was paid by John Parsons, the banker, of Oxford. Few will echo the verdict of the Revd. F. Chenevix Trench, then rector, that it had been 'a very successful undertaking'.[72] The church was restored recently (1954) at a cost of over £3,000 to save it from death-watch beetle and dry rot.

In 1824 two medieval wall-paintings were uncovered in the south aisle of the nave.[73] One depicted the adoration of the Magi, the other the Resurrection and the weighing of souls in a balance. They were plastered over at the restoration, but sketches of them made by Dean Buckland's daughter hang in the vestry.

The octagonal font, on a tall octagonal base, has a quatrefoil panel on each face.[74]

In the course of the 18th century low oak benches were provided in the chancel for the boys of Dr. South's School.[75] One of these benches is preserved in the vestry.

Part of an ancient rood screen was in the church as late as 1846.[76]

The stained glass in the east window (designed by Warrington) and that of the west window were both installed in 1861. The glass in the south chancel window was designed in 1904 by James Powell Ltd. of Whitefriars. The oak reredos was executed in 1906 by James Rogers of Oxford; it replaced a creed and ten commandments.[77] The present organ was installed in 1879 at a cost of about £180.[78]

The church contains two identical death masks, one in the north wall of the nave, and one in the vestry. The identity of these masks has never been proved, but it is possible that they are masks of Richard Busby, the famous headmaster of Westminster School, for whom Robert South, rector 1678–1716, acted as executor. Death masks of Busby are known to have been made but have never been found.[79]

The chancel contains a number of memorials, mainly of 17th-century date.[80] There are brass plates to John Aglionby, rector 1600–9/10, and his son John (d. 1610), with the Aglionby arms, and to James Harracks, rector 1610–25/6. There are tablets

[63] Oxf. Dioc. d 553, d 556, d 559, d 562, d 564, d 570.
[64] MS. Top. Oxon. c 112, p. 42.
[65] Dunkin, *Oxon.* i. 287 n.
[66] An inscription once over the east window and now over the chancel arch records this (*Par. Coll.* ii. 185). According to local tradition, Cromwell watched the battle from the church tower (Edith Miller, *Hist. Islip*, 13).
[67] Bodl. Univ. Arch. Vice-Chancellor's Ct. 1681 Mich.
[68] Described in Parker, *Guide*, 2, when it was still standing. There are early drawings (1805) in MS. Top. Oxon. b 220, f. 29, and by Buckler ibid. a 67, ff. 345–6.
[69] Miller, *Hist. Islip*, 14.
[70] Bodl. MS. Top. gen. e 23, ff. 17–18.
[71] Painting in possession of Mr. James Cannell of Morden (Surr.).
[72] R.C.O. box 48: letter of 20 Dec. 1861. For more details of restoration see *Gent. Mag.* 1861 (1), N.S. x. 285.
[73] *Archaeologia*, 1842, xxix. 420. They are reproduced in *Gent. Mag.* 1861 (1), N.S. x, opp. p. 4.
[74] Drawing in MS. Top. Oxon. b 220, f. 29b.
[75] See below, pp. 217–18.
[76] Parker, *Guide*, 3.
[77] Bodl. Par. Box (uncat.): faculties.
[78] R.C.O. box 48: letter of 17 July 1879.
[79] Inf. Mr. L. E. Tanner, Librarian and Keeper of the Muniments, Westminster Abbey.
[80] Listed in Dunkin, *Oxon.* i. 280–2.

with coats of arms commemorating Edward Dewe, gent. (a strong Puritan, possibly lessee of the manor during the Commonwealth and Protectorate,[80a] d. 1656/7), and Luke Clapham Esq. of Grays Inn (d. 1676) and Susanna his wife (d. 1669). On the north wall of the chancel is a tablet of alabaster and brass with quartered arms of Norris to Henry Norris Esq. (d. 1637/8) with one son (d. 1634), to Susanna his wife, and to her first husband, Robert Banks, gent. (d. 1605), with eighteen children, all kneeling. The east window and the communion rail are memorials to William Buckland, rector 1846–56. There is a brass to Thomas Welbank, rector (d. 1903), and a memorial to A. E. Stone, rector 1902–10. There was another brass in the south aisle which has disappeared.[81]

In 1552 the church plate consisted of one silver chalice, two candlesticks and a censer of latten, and a holy-water stoup of brass.[82] In 1955 there were a silver chalice, possibly dating from about 1635 and known as 'Dr. South's chalice',[83] a large silver paten with the hall-mark of 1713, given by Dr. South, and some 19th-century plate given by John Parsons.[84]

The five 17th-century bells formerly in the tower were cast into a set of six in 1859 at the expense of John Parsons. The sanctus bell was cast by Humphrey Keene in 1652. In 1552 there were four bells and a sanctus bell.[85]

The registers date from 1590.

A building known as the Confessor's chapel stood on the north side of the church until the 18th century. Until the beginning of the present century a plot of ground in this part of the churchyard and beyond was known as Chapel yard.[86] A sketch of the building was made by the antiquary Hearne in 1718;[87] from this it appears unlikely that the chapel was built before the 12th century. Hearne describes it as being fifteen paces in length and seven in breadth, with three small windows and a door in the north side. Richard de Ware, Abbot of Westminster 1258–83, appointed a chaplain to celebrate masses here for the soul of Edward the Confessor.[88] In the 15th century the Abbot of Westminster was held to be bound *ratione tenure* to maintain a chaplain at Islip for this purpose.[89] Monks of Westminster studying at Gloucester College, Oxford, observed the feast of St. Edward in the chapel at Islip.[90] The chapel was desecrated during the Commonwealth; when Hearne saw it the old windows and doors were blocked up and it was used as a barn. It was demolished in about 1780; some of the materials are said to have been used in additions to the 'Red Lion'.[91]

The chapel contained a font traditionally associated with Ethelred's palace and said to be the Confessor's baptismal font; it was desecrated during the Commonwealth and used at the 'Plume of Feathers' for mixing turkey food. After passing through various hands it was given to Middleton Stoney church by Lady Jersey.[92]

NONCONFORMITY. There was little Roman Catholicism in the parish: in the early 17th century there was a Catholic yeoman;[93] in 1676 there was one Catholic;[94] and in 1706 there was one Catholic family, the Palmers.[95]

Returns to episcopal visitations in the 18th century record very few Protestant nonconformists, and none of any rank. However, in 1779 the house of Edward Gulliver was registered as a meeting-house, perhaps Presbyterian,[96] and in 1791 the backhouse of Joseph Bridgewater was also registered.[97] The latter was Methodist, for early in the 19th century there were twenty Methodists in the parish who were visited by an itinerant teacher once a fortnight, but who also attended church.[98] Several dissenting meeting-places were certified between 1820 and 1843.[99]

In 1843 a Wesleyan Methodist chapel is said to have been built;[1] by this is probably meant the conversion of a carpenter's shed, which was used until the 1880's.[2] In 1851 the congregation numbered 70; the members, however, 'were by no means ill affected to the church'.[3] A new chapel and school-room were built in 1886 at a cost of £560,[4] and this chapel had a membership of about twenty in 1954.[5]

A small Baptist chapel, described as a 'poor man's house',[6] was opened in 1850, but the congregation was very small (only twelve),[7] and it did not survive until the end of the century.[8]

SCHOOLS. In 1709 the rector, Robert South, enlarged his apprenticing trust[9] to include a school for poor boys of Islip.[10] By a final revision of the trust in 1712 Dr. South's School was to take not less than 15 or more than 21 free scholars. The original endowment consisted of about 52 acres in Cutteslowe and Wolvercote, fee-farm rents of £16 14s. 8d. in Godington and Easington, and an annuity of £6 12s. The schoolmaster, who had to be a member of the Church of England, was to teach the boys to read, write, and cast accounts and to perfect them in the catechism. The teaching of French, Latin, Greek, and Hebrew was expressly forbidden. The master

[80a] See MS. Top. Oxon. c 112, p. 39.
[81] Drawing of matrix in MS. Top. Oxon. b 220, f. 30b. For blazons of arms in the church see Bodl. G.A. Oxon. 16° 217, pp. 168b, 169; ibid. 4° 686, p. 185; ibid. 4° 688, p. 185.
[82] *Chant. Cert.* 85.
[83] In the 19th cent. a churchwarden sold it to an Oxford silversmith, but it was later recovered (Miller, *Hist. Islip*, 14).
[84] Evans, *Ch. Plate.*
[85] *Ch. Bells Oxon.* ii. 180–1.
[86] Miller, *Hist. Islip*, 6.
[87] Bodl. MS. Hearne's Diaries 82, pp. 230–5; see plate facing p. 207.
[88] W.A.M. 15176.
[89] Ibid. 15202.
[90] Ibid. 15212.
[91] Halliwell-Phillipps, *Notices of Islip*, 8.
[92] Westminster Abbey Reg. Bk. lxi, ff. 86–86b; Dunkin,

Oxon. i. 277–8; see also below, p. 250.
[93] Salter, *Oxon. Recusants*, 22.
[94] Compton Census.
[95] *Oxoniensia*, xiii. 78.
[96] O.R.O. Cal. Q. Sess. viii. 810.
[97] Oxf. Dioc. c 644, f. 17.
[98] Ibid. c 327, p. 299.
[99] Ibid. c 644, f. 217 (1820); ibid. c 646, f. 25 (1835), ff. 47, 57 (1837), f. 212 (1843).
[1] Ibid. c 646, f. 198; H.O. 129/158.
[2] Inf. Chairman Oxford Meth. District.
[3] *Wilb. Visit.*; H.O. 129/158.
[4] *Oxf. Meth. Mag.*
[5] *Meth. Church Oxf. Circuit Plan* no. 273 (1954).
[6] *Wilb. Visit.*
[7] H.O. 129/158.
[8] Not mentioned in any directory after 1860.
[9] See below, p. 218.
[10] W.A.M. 15156.

received £15 a year and each boy a blue coat and cap. Scholars were nominated on Easter Tuesdays in the church chancel, and failing suitable candidates from Islip vacancies might be filled from neighbouring parishes, with a preference for Noke. The church bell was rung every school day at 6 a.m. in summer and 7 a.m. in winter; in 1955 it was being rung at 8.45. In 1812, when the annual income of the charity was about £110, 20 more free boys were admitted and the master's salary was increased.[11]

The school was built in 1710.[12] By 1815 90 to 100 boys in all were being instructed on the National Society's plan.[13] By 1833, when there were 75 pupils, girls had been admitted to the school,[14] and it subsequently appears that the 20 additional places of 1812 were given to 16 girls and 4 boys,[15] though only the 21 original scholars received clothing. In 1867 there were two teachers, neither certificated, and the only addition to the founder's curriculum was that two boys learned 'mensuration or book-keeping'.[16]

In or about 1856 an infants' school was established at Islip, under the auspices of the National Society.[17] In 1871, when there were 80 children in the school, it was enlarged. It was inadequately endowed, however, and in 1873 both it and Dr. South's School were threatened with secularization when the Education Department proposed to place the schools of Islip and Wood Eaton under a school board. A vestry committee raised subscriptions to increase the endowment of the infants' school, and both schools were thus removed beyond official criticism.[18] In the late 19th century the foundation of 1856 functioned as an infants' department of Dr. South's school. The combined average attendance was 102 in 1889,[19] and in 1893 a new school was built to replace that of 1710.[20] There were 100 pupils in 1906.[21] The school was reorganized for junior pupils in 1932, when seniors were sent to Gosford Hill, and the average attendance was only 34 in 1937. Dr. South's was the first school in Oxfordshire to acquire aided status under the 1944 Education Act—in 1950. In 1954 the junior department was housed in the buildings of 1893, and the infants' in that of 1856. There were then 84 pupils in all. The old school building was used as a parish room and for meetings of the Women's Institute.[22]

In 1771 a fund consisting of money given at the sacrament was instituted for the schooling of poor girls.[23] A school supported by the fund was opened in 1785 with a mistress and 6 pupils.[24] The latter, like the boys of Dr. South's school, were elected on Easter Tuesdays. In the early 19th century the fund paid for the education of 12 girls at two of the dame schools.[25] It was shared by 6 boys and 6 girls in 1833 and was still supporting 12 children in 1854.[26]

In the early 19th century a small boarding-school taught 8 young ladies reading, writing, English, and needlework.[27] There were also 3 dame schools in 1808 with 16 pupils who were taught reading, and 4 dame schools in 1815 and in 1818, when they had 38 pupils, all girls.[28] In 1833 three dame schools had 43 pupils, of whom 31 were paid for by their parents, and in 1854 two schools shared 60 pupils.[29] These probably did not survive long after the 1870 Education Act: there was still one 'adventure school' in 1871, but no details of it were available.[30]

CHARITIES. In 1688 William Auger gave £40 to the Islip poor: the money was used to buy land at Hampton Poyle,[31] which in 1786 was producing 19s. a year,[32] and in 1824 £1 11s. 6d. Before 1810 the income was distributed to the poor either in money or in bread and coal, but afterwards it was used for the schooling of poor girls and very young boys.[33] In 1810 the income, still unchanged, was being distributed in bread.[34] By 1939 the income was £3 4s. 4d., but by 1955 the charity had lapsed.[35]

Robert South, the rector, in 1704 set up a trust for apprenticing two poor children of Islip each year.[36] In 1712 he provided that each year part of the endowments of his school should be set aside to apprentice two or three boys, preferably scholars of his school, at fees of £7 each and at places not nearer than Oxford. The apprentice fees were increased to £15 each for two boys in 1812, and were still the same in 1870.[37] In 1955 the income received under the terms of Dr. South's will, about £240, was partly used for the apprenticing of boys.

When endowing the school in 1712, Dr. South had also stipulated that any surplus income was to be divided among those widows of Islip who were 'most noted for frequenting the church'. From 1812 onwards these widows regularly received 5s. each twice a year: £5 15s. in all was distributed to them in 1836;[38] in 1869 and 1870 £15;[39] and in the 1950's about £5 a year was distributed by the rector.

By will dated 1835 a certain person of the surname Dennett gave £300 in stock to the trustees of South's School for increasing the apprentices' fees.[40] In 1870 a dividend of £8 1s. 8d. was used for apprenticing, but in 1955 this charity could not be traced.[41]

In 1851 Martha Litchfield bequeathed about £500 in stock to augment Dr. South's charities. In 1870 an income of £16 12s. 3d. was being used for educational purposes,[42] but in 1939 the income,

---

[11] 32nd Rep. Com. Char. 691–3.
[12] For the school 1710–1837 see also V.C.H. Oxon. i. 486.
[13] Oxf. Dioc. c 433; for 1808 see ibid. d 707.
[14] Educ. Enq. Abstract, 748.
[15] Wilb. Visit.; Schools Enq. 308.
[16] Schools Enq. 308.
[17] Kelly's Dir. Oxon. (1883).
[18] R.C.O. box 48: letters of 18 Feb. 1871, 1 Feb. 1873.
[19] Ret. of Sch.
[20] Edith Miller, Hist. Islip, 19.
[21] Vol. Sch. Ret.
[22] Inf. Oxon. Educ. Cttee.; inf. Dr. D. Roaf.
[23] Par. Rec. Dr. South's register bk. containing accounts of the fund 1771–1824.
[24] Ibid.
[25] Educ. of Poor, 726.
[26] Educ. Enq. Abstract, 748; Wilb. Visit.

[27] Oxf. Dioc. d 707, c 433.
[28] Ibid.; Educ. of Poor, 726.
[29] Educ. Enq. Abstract, 748; Wilb. Visit.
[30] Elem. Educ. Ret.
[31] 12th Rep. Com. Char. 306.
[32] Char. Don. ii. 989.
[33] 12th Rep. Com. Char. 306.
[34] Gen. Digest Char.
[35] Kelly's Dir. Oxon. (1939); inf. the Revd. A. W. Blanchett.
[36] W.A.M. 15153.
[37] 32nd Rep. Com. Char. 691 sqq.; Gen. Digest Char.
[38] 32nd Rep. Com. Char. 691 sqq.
[39] Gen. Digest Char.
[40] 32nd Rep. Com. Char. 694.
[41] Gen. Digest Char.; inf. the Rector.
[42] Gen. Digest Char.

then about £12, was distributed to the poor at Christmas.[43] Mrs. Litchfield also planned to build and endow almshouses in Lower Street.[44] In 1870 £14 15s. 8d., the income from about £500 stock, was distributed to the poor in clothing,[45] and the alms-house scheme apparently never materialized. The charity could not be traced in 1955.

Under the inclosure award of 1808 about 3 acres of land on Brought Common were allotted to the churchwardens and overseers for the benefit of the poor. Another 3½ acres were awarded to them in lieu

of the former Town Lands and the Constable's Highway.[46] In 1939 the rents of the Poor's Land, £1 5s., were distributed to poor old men at Christ-mas.[47] In 1940, by agreement with the County Council, 1½ acres of the Poor's Land was taken for the Oxford–Bicester road.[48]

In 1951, after Chancery proceedings, the bequest of Miss Gertrude Mullett (d. 1947) was set up as a trust, with capital of £1,059, to be used for Dr. South's school, any surplus going towards the upkeep of the parish church.[49]

KIRTLINGTON

THE parish lies on the east bank of the River Cher-well, which divides it from the parish of Tackley.[1] The Gallows Brook forms much of its eastern boundary. The area of the ancient parish (3,582 a.) has remained unchanged.[2] The parish is mostly above the 300-foot contour, but the ground falls away slightly on the south and east and, much more markedly, on the west towards the Cherwell. The soil, primarily Cornbrash, is excellent for pasture and for barley.[3] The village, which extends for ¾ mile north and south, is in the southern half of the parish, with Kirtlington Park adjacent to it on the east. Timber is fairly plentiful, especially in and around the park. The hamlet of Northbrook lies near the river, 1½ miles north-north-west of the village. The Oxford–Banbury railway and the Rugby–Oxford canal both follow the Cherwell valley. The railway, opened in 1850, here lies mostly on the Tackley bank, but enters the parish at two points owing to bends in the river.[4] The canal, which in 1787 had just reached Northbrook, is on the Kirt-lington bank.[5]

The Inclosure Award of 1815 names six roads which shall be maintained as 40-foot public high-ways; these, with one exception, constitute the roads of the parish today.[6] The Somerton road, running north, follows the line of the pre-Roman Portway. The Bicester road was the name normally used of Akeman Street, which runs east from the Somerton road along the north edge of Kirtlington Park.[7] The

Middleton road, used as an alternative road to Bicester, runs to the north of, and roughly parallel with, Akeman Street; it was built about 1800, and is locally called New Road.[8] The Brackley road, now disused and overgrown, branched north-east from the Somerton road and ran beside the pre-Saxon Aves Ditch; reference is made to it in 1396, and it occurs earlier as Aves Ditch Way.[9] The Woodstock road, running south-west to Enslow Bridge, and the Bletchingdon (or Oxford) road are not apparently mentioned by name before the 16th century; but the Bletchingdon road at least, which was the boundary between the open fields, is much older than this. Of the existing lanes, Mill Lane is clearly medieval; Crowcastle Lane, leading from Kirtlington towards Northbrook, is part of the old Deddington Way[10] which passed to the west of Northbrook; and the seemingly ephemeral cart-tracks which lead from the village to Vicarage Farm buildings and from Crowcastle Lane to Briton Field have existed since about 1200 at least, their medieval names being Warper's Way and Plumper's Way.[11] Several roads or lanes disappeared in the 18th century. Of these the most frequently mentioned, from the 13th century, is Northbrook Church Way, an alternative track to Northbrook east of the Deddington Way.[12] In the eastern half of the parish, Weston Way, Wolwell (or Wooller's) Way, and the old Middleton Way had all vanished by 1815.[13] There were cer-tainly two fords over the Cherwell—White Hill ford

[43] Kelly's Dir. Oxon. (1939).
[44] R.C.O. box 48.
[45] Gen. Digest Char.
[46] P.R.O., L.R.R.O. I/M.R. 249: Incl. award.
[47] Kelly's Dir. Oxon. (1939).
[48] O.R.O., C.C.E. 720.
[49] Inf. the rector.

N.B. (a) Bodl. MS. D.D. Dashwood (Oxon.), a 1 and c 1, two boxes of Kirtlington manorial docs., are cited below as Dashwood (Oxon.) Dep.
(b) Kirtlington Ct. R. not in P.R.O., i.e. all later than c. 1500, are cited by date only. Ct. R. for 1757–1810 are in O.R.O., Dashwood Deeds, cited below as Dashwood D.; all others which survive are in Dashwood (Oxon.) Dep.
(c) The collection of unnumbered medieval deeds at St. John's Coll., Oxf., most of which origin-ally belonged to Aulnay Abbey, is cited as Aulnay D.
(d) New College's Kirtlington deeds, of which there are transcripts in the college's Registrum Evi-denciarum i, ff. 357–82, are cited as New Coll. D.

[1] O.S. Map 6″, xxii (4 sheets); xxvii. NE., NW. (1923); 2½″, 42/41, 42, 51, 52 (1949–51).
[2] Census, 1881, 1951.

[3] There is Forest Marble and Great Oolite on the NW. borders.
[4] J. Townsend, Oxon. Dashwoods, 42; E. T. Mac-Dermot, Hist. G.W.R. i. 300.
[5] Townsend, Oxon. Dashwoods, 37.
[6] Penes Par. Clerk, Kirtlington; copy (without map) in O.R.O. Much the best pre-inclosure map is 'Plan of Manor of Kirtlington . . . belonging to Sir Jas. Dashwood Bt.' (1750, revised 1805) at St. John's Coll., cited below as St. John's Coll. map, 1750.
[7] For Portway and Akeman St. see V.C.H. Oxon. i. 272, 275. ('Vicus qui vocatur Neuport' and 'Newporte-strete' occur, apparently used of the village main street, in New Coll. D. no. 36, no. 20.) 'Akeman Strete' occurs in rental of 1476: D.L. 43/8/17. For Roman remains found near it, see V.C.H. Oxon. i. 340.
[8] It did not exist in 1794: Davis, Oxon. Map.
[9] New Coll. D. no. 19; cf. no. 63. For Aves Ditch, see V.C.H. Oxon. ii. 342; Oxoniensia, ii. 202; xi–xii. 162.
[10] Probably 'via que ducit versus Banebery', which occurs in a 12th-cent. charter: Aulnay D.
[11] Various forms of the name Plumper's Way occur in Aulnay D. 'Warepeth' (St. Frides. Cart. ii. 218) is likely to be Warper's Way; cf. New Coll. D. no. 19.
[12] 'Via que vocatur chyrchueie de Nortbroc': Aulnay D.
[13] Of these only Middleton Way (St. Frides. Cart. ii. 215) occurs before the 16th cent.

at the mill and Catsham ford just west of Northbrook;[14] tracks from each led up to Tackley. A footbridge was built at Catsham about 1637; the present narrow stone bridge existed by 1750.[15]

Until the 15th century there was only one wood of any note; it lay in the eastern half of the parish and was called Old Wood.[16] Herons and probably also spoonbills (*volucres vocati poplers*) nested there in 1390, but had ceased to do so by 1416.[17] In an exceptional year more than £15 worth of timber was sold from it.[18] A New Wood, the present Cockshot Copse, had recently been planted in 1476.[19] These two woods are called the Great and Little Woods in some accounts of 1539,[20] and the name Great Wood is normal from this time. In 1591 the manor possessed two coppices totalling about 100 acres 'wherein are one thousand timber trees or thereabouts of all sorts'.[21] Part of the Great Wood is said to have been cut down in 1741 to clear the site for Kirtlington House.[22] Many new plantations, mostly of a few acres, were made between 1821 and 1844; in 1908 woods and plantations totalled about 219 acres.[23]

By the inclosure award Kirtlington lost its Town Green, which was allotted to Sir Henry Dashwood. It lay to the north of the present North Green, and its 10 acres had constituted a piece of common grazing.[24] There were originally gates on all roads and tracks leaving the village; 16th- and 17th-century court rolls mention at least six of these by name.[25] Apart from the inclosure of Town Green, and with the exception of the council houses built at the south end and on the west side of the village in 1948 and 1954, the general plan of Kirtlington is much as in the map of 1750. A fair number of the present houses must have been standing then. The most striking in appearance is Manor House Farm, which until recently carried a stone dated 1563. Foxtown End Farm is partly a 17th-century house, and Portway House, though much altered, has an inscription 'T.W.: A.W. 1684'.

Kirtlington House itself stands in the park, about half a mile from the village. It was built by Sir James Dashwood, who personally kept 'A general account of money expended on my new house, and the out-

works about it, begun 12th September: 1741'.[26] The first stone was laid on 22 April 1742 and the house occupied on 30 August 1746. The work was not then finished, but of the £32,388 8s. spent by 1759 the great bulk (c. £26,000) had been spent by the end of 1747, and much of the later expense was on the gardens and grounds. The architect was John Sanderson, who received £65; plans were also submitted by James Gibbs, architect of the Radcliffe Camera, at a fee of £30, and comparison of the two sets of plans suggests that Sanderson may have borrowed certain features from Gibbs. The builder was William Smith of Warwick. The house contains a room famous for its frescoed ceiling of monkeys engaged in field sports; the painter, M. Clermont, was paid £52 10s. The grounds were laid out by 'Capability' Brown, who between 1755 and 1762 received £1,574 2s. for the work. Northbrook manor-house, thought to have been built between 1579 and 1641,[27] was demolished after Kirtlington House was built. A brick dovecote and clock-tower, some of the walled gardens, and some outbuildings survive, and there are medieval fishponds in the grounds.

The names of three 17th-century inns are known. The 'Dolphin' is mentioned in 1644;[28] the 'George' and the 'Red Lion' both occur in deeds of c. 1675–1700.[29] The 'Dashwood Arms' was occupying its present site in 1815.[30] A 'Six Bells', which no longer exists, also occurs in 1815 and again in 1884,[31] when it had moved to a different site.

Domesday Book mentions two mills in Kirtlington.[32] Most, but not all, later references are to a single mill. There is evidence that in the 13th century there were two mills, close together but on opposite sides of the river.[33] In 1204 the mill was damaged.[34] The early 13th-century evidence of ownership is ample but confusing;[35] presumably various parties had different rights in the mill, or mills, simultaneously. Certainly 'the mill at Kirtlington' was sold by Ingerram de Kirtlington to John Fitzhugh, and by Fitzhugh's son-in-law, Adam Fitzhervey, to Gilbert Basset, who gave two mills to Bicester Priory c. 1240. In 1535 the priory leased the mill to John Andrewes of Kirtlington.[36] In 1568

[14] Both are mentioned in 1591: D.L. 42/117, f. 91b. White Hill *bridge* is mentioned in 1313 and 1396 (New Coll. D. no. 62, no. 19).
[15] From 1638 deeds and Ct. R. speak of Catsham 'Plank' (not 'Ford'). The bridge is marked on St. John's Coll. map, 1750, and is called 'New Bridge' in Ct. R. 1767.
[16] *Rot. Hund.* (Rec. Com.), ii. 822; *Rot. Parl.* iv. 136; D.L. 43/8/16, 17.
[17] D.L. 29/652/10541, 10559. Mins.' Accts. regularly report no profit from this source after this date.
[18] D.L. 29/652/10559.
[19] 'De exitu unius pasture voc' Cokshute . . . nihil hic de quod includitur infra boscum voc' Newewode': D.L. 43/8/17.
[20] Dashwood (Oxon.) Dep. a 1 (178).
[21] D.L. 42/117, f. 98b.
[22] Townsend, *Oxon. Dashwoods*, 26.
[23] Notes added in manuscript vol. 'Kirtlington, 1815', *penes* G. Henderson Esq., Oathill Farm, Enstone; 'Kirtlington Park and Tackley Estates': land agents' survey, 1908, *penes* G. Henderson Esq.
[24] Ct. R. 1683 and *passim*.
[25] Hatch Gate (Ct. R. 1526, 1542); Fox Gate (Ct. R. 1542); Woodstock Gate (Ct. R. 1552); Cockenbred Gate (Ct. R. 1625, 1626); Brokesgrene Gate (Ct. R. 1683; cf. New Coll. terriers, 1626, 1667); the Barrets Gate (Ct. R. 1683).
[26] This acct. and architects' and landscape gardeners' plans are *penes* Mrs. H. M. Budgett, Kirtlington House.

For Sanderson's design, see *Vitruvius Britannicus*, ed. J. Woolfe and J. Gandon, iv, pls. 32–36. See also *Country Life*, xxxi, Apr. 1912. For J. Buckler's drawing, see plate opposite.
[27] Townsend, *Oxon. Dashwoods*, 10–11. The print in Blome, *Gentleman's Recreation* (1686), ii. 94, is thought to show Northbrook House.
[28] Par. Reg.
[29] Dashwood D. box 5, bdle. 'Title deeds to the Red Lion'; box 8, bdle. 'Kirtleton Inn, 1563–1693'.
[30] O.R.O., Incl. award; incl. map *penes* Par. Clerk.
[31] O.S. Map 6", xxii (1884).
[32] *V.C.H. Oxon.* i. 400.
[33] By charter ascribed, probably incorrectly, to 1227, Walter son of Rich. de Kirtlington grants to Bicester Priory all rights 'in novo molendino super fundo meo ex alia parte de Charwelle juncto veteri molendino de Kertlinton': Kennett, *Paroch. Antiq.* i. 283. The second mill could only have been in the parish if it stood on the island made by the bifurcation of the river just above the existing mill.
[34] *Rot. Normannie* (Rec. Com.), 131.
[35] See besides previous refs. *Cat. Anct. D.* ii. A 3161–4; *Rot. Litt. Claus.* (Rec. Com.), i. 589; ii. 20; Kennett, *Paroch. Antiq.* i. 225–6. For litigation later in the 13th cent. see *Fines Oxon.* 160, 225; Kennett, *Paroch. Antiq.* i. 402; ii. 140–1; Blo. *Bic.* 143: cal. of Bicester Priory Bursar's Accts. 1301.
[36] *Valor Eccl.* (Rec. Com.), ii. 188.

North view of Kirtlington Park in 1827

South-east view of the church in 1825

KIRTLINGTON

two water-mills, with other lands formerly belonging to the priory, were bought by Anthony and John Arden from Nicholas Backhouse and Anna his wife; and this estate, including the mills, was sold to Humfrey Hide and William Keate in 1639.[37] There appears to be no later reference to two mills. By 1692 the mill had acquired its modern name of Flight's Mill;[38] in 1815 it was owned by William Enser.[39] There was also a horse-mill in the village at one time.[40]

The village, sited on a plateau of Oxford Clay capped by gravel, was settled in Saxon times: its name means the 'tun of Cyrtla's people', and a Saxon burial has been discovered there.[41] In medieval times the manor-house, it may be conjectured, stood near the centre of the village, where there is a triangular moat.[42]

The lords occasionally resided at the manor-house. Philip Basset witnessed an undated charter of one of his free tenants at Kirtlington,[43] and another, dated December 1299, was witnessed at Kirtlington by Hugh le Despenser.[44] In 1390, although the demesne was then leased out, £9 12s. 2d. was spent on building work at the manor-house, the majority of it 'in quadam capella annexa camere domini de novo construenda'.[45] In 1422 the house was certainly in good condition.[46] Later it was allowed to fall into complete decay. In 1471, for example, the hall was roofless,[47] and a lease of 1517 refers to 'the syght of the mansion of the same manor, with a barne or shepe house now thereon standing'.[48] During the baronial wars of Henry III's reign a number of houses in Kirtlington were burnt, no doubt because of the prominence in the struggle of the lord of the manor, Philip Basset.[49] The unpopularity of a later lord, Hugh Despenser the elder, led to another attack on Kirtlington.[50] Royalist troops appear to have been quartered in the village in the Civil War—one soldier was shot in the 'Dolphin' in 1644.[51] In 1646 Sir John Lenthall, who farmed the rectory, reported that he had received no money from it for five years and that 'the destruction of the houses are such that £200 will hardly repair them',[52] and St. John's College remitted him 3½ years' rent. Between April 1649 and September 1650 parliamentary soldiers were billeted in the Rectory

on eighteen occasions at a total cost of £32 2s., and there were other heavy charges upon it.[53] In 1651 it was ordered that the fee-farm of the manor should be paid to Captain Abraham Davis.[54] In 1754 Kirtlington Park was the scene of some of the preliminaries to the notorious county election in which Sir James Dashwood was a candidate.[55]

The history of the Dashwoods belongs to the county, but they naturally exercised a permeating influence, of which many visible evidences remain, on the life of the parish. All, with the apparent exception of the 3rd baronet, who became heavily encumbered with debt,[56] were active and conscientious landlords. Early in the 16th century three knightly families owned land in the parish, those of Hampden, Dormer, and Bray.[57] Of the yeoman families whose names predominate in the manorial and parish records, the most prominent is that of Hall, which first occurs in 1494[58] and disappears late in the 19th century. Over 80 Halls were born in Kirtlington, and nearly 50 died, in the period 1590–1700.[59] One of the two Kirtlington-born mayors of Oxford was Anthony Hall, vintner (mayor 1673), the other being A. J. George (mayor 1924).[60] Two more obscure individuals may be mentioned: Nicholas Jurdan of Kirtlington, a hermit (oc. 1341),[61] and Ann Thomas, who died in 1748 aged 101.[62]

MANORS. Kirtlington was a royal manor in the time of Edward the Confessor,[63] and was presumably already a hundredal manor in the 10th century. It is first mentioned in 945, when a payment was made there to the king,[64] and in 977 Edward the Martyr held a witenagemot there at which Archbishop Dunstan was present.[65] '*CHERIELINTONE*' appears in Domesday Book as an important royal manor yielding £52 yearly, and having the soke of 2½ hundreds, which are identifiable in the later hundred of Ploughley.[66] Early in Henry II's reign, however, the manor was held by Richard de Humez,[67] Constable of Normandy; and as it does not appear in the pipe rolls under *terre date* it must have already been alienated under Henry I. Richard de Humez's wife, Agnes, was a daughter of Jordan de Say and Lucy de Aulnay, by whom Kirtlington

[37] C.P. 26(1)/135/East. 10 Eliz.; C.P. 25(2)/474/Hil. 14 Chas. I.
[38] Dashwood D. box 5, bdle. 'Title deeds to Paddock near Flight's Mill'; cf. O.S. Map 6″, xxii. SW. (1923).
[39] O.R.O. Incl. award.
[40] Ct. R. 1470: D.L. 30/108/1594; Ct. R. 1597.
[41] E. Ekwall, *Dict. Eng. P.N.* For pre-Roman, Romano-British, and Anglo-Saxon remains, see *V.C.H. Oxon.* i. 264, 340, 354, 371.
[42] *V.C.H. Oxon.* ii. 329; see O.S. Map 6″, xxii. SW. (1923), for site marked 'John of Gaunt's residence, supposed site of'.
[43] Chart. of Mabel, daughter of Matthew de Launceles: Aulnay D.
[44] *Boarstall Cart.* 107.
[45] D.L. 29/652/10541.
[46] As appears from detailed description in D.L. 43/8/16: '. . . est ibidem j Manerium, in quo situantur j parva aula que nuper fuit capella manerii, cum Camera bassa et alta ad finem, uno clauso extendente ad cameram principalem, que est pulchra camera et larga cum j parva capella, una alia camera eidem annexa cum j oratorio et una latrina et cameris bassis subtus ejusdem forme, una coquina bona, una magna Grangia que quondam fuit aula, j granarium et duo stabula, que omnes [*sic*] sunt murata et cooperta cum petris et bene reparata.'
[47] D.L. 29/655/10604.
[48] Dashwood (Oxon.) Dep. a 1 (186).

[49] *Close R.* 1264–8, 411.
[50] See below, p. 222.
[51] Par. Reg.
[52] St. John's Coll. Mun. xx. 26; ibid. Coll. Reg. 7 Dec. 1646.
[53] Ibid. xx. 23.
[54] Dashwood D. box 6, bdle. 'Manor of Kirtlington, 1584–1723', order 16 Apr. 1651.
[55] Townsend, *Oxon. Dashwoods*, 27; R. J. Robson, *Oxon. Election 1754, passim*.
[56] Townsend, *Oxon. Dashwoods*, 32.
[57] All occur in Ct. R. For litigation involving the Bray property, see E. Coke, *Bk. of Entries* (1614), 625 sqq.
[58] Dashwood (Oxon.) Dep. c 1, rental of 10 Hen. VII.
[59] Par. Reg.
[60] Tablets to each on external S. wall of church. For Hall's election, see Wood, *Life*, ii. 270.
[61] Aulnay D., chart. of Nicholas Jurdan.
[62] Par. Reg. *sub anno*.
[63] *V.C.H. Oxon.* i. 375.
[64] *Cart. Sax.*, ed. Birch, ii, no. 812.
[65] *A.-S. Chron.* (Rolls Ser.), ii. 99, cited in *V.C.H. Oxon.* i. 375, 434; ii. 2.
[66] *V.C.H. Oxon.* i. 400; cf. ibid. 374; *E.H.R.* xlvii. 363.
[67] This appears from several docs. in Aulnay D. Kirtlington was presumably among the lands on which he was remitted Danegeld in *Pipe R.* 1156–8 (P.R.S. facsimile), 37.

church was given to Aulnay Abbey.[68] It seems likely, therefore, that the manor had been held by Jordan de Say, a conjecture supported by an entry in the 1130 pipe roll.[69] Richard's son, William de Humez, was holding the manor when it escheated as *terra Normannorum* in 1203.[70] By an unusual arrangement its administration was apparently placed in the hands of the reeve and four men of the village;[71] but this cannot have been for long as in 1204 it was handed over from the custody of Geoffrey le Sauvage to the royal minister, John Fitzhugh, who was to account for it at the Exchequer.[72] Fitzhugh was still in possession in November 1215, when he was ordered to hand over part of the fee to Ralph de Montibus;[73] but he deserted the king in 1216 and was deprived of the remainder of the fee in favour of John's mercenary captain William de Bréauté.[74] William held the manor until the siege of Bedford. On 11 March 1224 Thomas Basset, of Headington, was given seisin of it during pleasure; on 30 April it was restored to de Bréauté, only to be handed back to Basset three weeks later.[75] In 1227 it was formally granted by charter to Thomas Basset and his heirs.[76] In 1230 the manor passed, on Thomas's death, to his brother Gilbert Basset, of Wycombe.[77] In 1233, when Gilbert's fiefs were confiscated in consequence of his part in the rebellion of that year, Kirtlington manor was given to Henry de Trubleville during pleasure;[78] but it was shortly restored to Gilbert, who obtained a charter in 1235.[79]

William de Humez had held his Oxfordshire lands by service of $\frac{1}{2}$ knight;[80] possibly this included other lands beside Kirtlington. In the 13th century Kirtlington's assessment was for $\frac{1}{4}$ knight's fee;[81] with Nether Orton and Bignell it made up a single fee.[82]

Gilbert Basset was followed successively by his brothers, Fulk, Bishop of London 1244–59, and Philip, justiciar 1261–3. In 1255 Fulk Basset was authorized to tallage his tenants on the manor if it

was indeed ancient demesne.[83] He also had view of frankpledge.[84] On Philip's death in 1271 the manor remained as dower in the hands of his wife, Ela, dowager Countess of Warwick,[85] who in 1279 was enjoying among other rights the liberty of return of royal writs.[86]

Philip Basset's heiress, Alina, widow of Hugh Despenser who was killed at Evesham, and by her second marriage wife of Roger Bigod, Earl of Norfolk, was outlived by her mother. Kirtlington therefore passed in 1297 to Alina's son Hugh Despenser, later Earl of Winchester.[87] It was pillaged, with many other Despenser manors, when in the king's hand during Despenser's exile (1321–2).[88] On its forfeiture in 1326 it was granted (2 March 1327) with a group of Despenser's Oxfordshire manors[89] and much other property to Edward III's uncle, Thomas of Brotherton, as part of the provision intended for him by Edward I.[90] In 1332 it was among the manors which, with Thomas' acquiescence, the king granted to his kinsman, William de Bohun, later Earl of Northampton.[91] In 1360 it passed to his son, Humphrey, then a minor,[92] on whose early death in 1373 the vast Bohun inheritance was divided between his daughters, Eleanor and Mary, subsequently married to Thomas of Woodstock and Henry of Bolingbroke respectively. In 1374 Kirtlington was among the lands committed in wardship to Eleanor's future husband;[93] later it was assigned definitely to her moiety of the inheritance.[94] On her death in 1399, her daughter and heiress, Anne, Countess of Stafford, succeeded to her estates;[95] but in the repartition of the Bohun lands which took place in 1421 on the death of Humphrey de Bohun's long-lived widow,[96] Kirtlington was included in the share transferred to the king, and thus became a manor of the Duchy of Lancaster.[97]

With many other manors, Kirtlington was assigned in dower to three successive queens of England: to Katharine, the queen-mother, in 1422;[98]

---

[68] *Inspeximus* of a deed of Ric. de Humez: Aulnay D. This corroborates the statement of T. Stapleton, *Rot. Scacc. Normannie*, ii, p. clxxxvii; cf. *Cal. Doc. France*, ed. Round, 185. Dugd. *Mon.* vi (3), 1109 wrongly ascribes the foundation to Richard de Humez.

[69] Jordan de Say is remitted 23*s.* Danegeld on lands in Oxon., a sum which at 2*s.* a hide corresponds to the $11\frac{1}{2}$ hides of Kirtlington in Domesday Book; *Pipe R.* 1130 (P.R.S. facsimile), 5.

[70] *Bk. of Fees*, 614; *Rot. Hund.* (Rec. Com.), ii. 31, 45. For the de Humez family see *Reg. Antiquiss.* vi, App. II.

[71] G. C. Homans, *Eng. Villagers of 13th century*, 336, commenting on *Rot. Normannie* (Rec. Com.), i. 131.

[72] *Rot. Litt. Claus.* (Rec. Com.), i. 14.

[73] Ibid. 234.

[74] *Bk. of Fees*, 253.

[75] *Rot. Litt. Claus.* i. 587, 589, 595, 599, 612.

[76] *Cal. Chart. R.* 1226–57, 56.

[77] *Close R.* 1227–31, 378, 436, 456; *Ex. e Rot. Fin.* (Rec. Com.), i. 206. This Thomas should not be confused with Thomas of Headington, who left three coheiresses. By a charter in Aulnay D. Bicester Priory grants to Aulnay Abbey, for use as a vicarage, a house in Kirtlington which the priory had been given by one of the three, Philippa, Countess of Warwick.

[78] *Close R.* 1231–4, 235, 240, 272.

[79] *Cal. Chart. R.* 1226–57, 200.

[80] *Red Bk. Exch.* (Rolls Ser.), 83; *Pipe R.* 1201 (P.R.S. N.S. xiv), 214.

[81] *Bk. of Fees*, 588, 614, 1397; cf. *Rot. Hund.* (Rec. Com.), ii. 45 (1255). *Close R.* 1237–42, 193, shows that there had been some doubt about it. With its member Bignell it comprised $\frac{1}{2}$ knight's fee; e.g. in 1279 each was a $\frac{1}{4}$ fee: *Rot.*

[...] *Hund.* ii. 822, 839. This probably explains the assessment of $\frac{1}{2}$ fee in 1276: ibid. 31. In 1360 it is assessed at $\frac{1}{4}$ fee (*Cal. Inq. p.m.* x, p. 525), in 1397–8 at $\frac{1}{3}$ (*Cal. Close*, 1396–9, 183, 254), in 1428 at $\frac{1}{2}$ (*Feud. Aids*, iv. 191).

[82] *Bk. of Fees*, 448; but cf. ibid. 825. Other entries show there was doubt on this point. For Bignell see above, p. 23.

[83] *Close R.* 1254–6, 67.

[84] *Rot. Hund.* (Rec. Com.), ii. 45.

[85] In accordance with the explicit agreement of 1261: *Cal. Chart. R.* 1257–1300, 35; cf. *Fines Oxon.* 245.

[86] *Rot. Hund.* (Rec. Com.), ii. 822.

[87] *Cal. Pat.* 1292–1301, 206, 207; *Cat. Anct. D.* ii. A 3160.

[88] *Cal. Pat.* 1321–4, 165, 168.

[89] Deddington, Gt. Haseley, Pyrton, Ascot.

[90] *Cal. Chart. R.* 1327–41, 4; cf. *Cal. Pat.* 1330–4, 524.

[91] *Cal. Fine R.* 1327–37, 323; *Cal. Pat.* 1330–4, 322, 330, 333, 524; ibid. 1334–8, 236; cf. ibid. 1345–8, 143.

[92] *Cal. Inq. p.m.* x, p. 525; *Cal. Fine R.* 1356–68, 163; *Abbrev. Rot. Orig.* (Rec. Com.), ii. 263.

[93] *Cal. Pat.* 1370–4, 472; confirmed ibid. 1377–81, 66. Cf. ibid. 1374–7, 210.

[94] *Cal. Close*, 1377–81, 390–1. For livery to her after her husband's death in 1397, see *Cal. Close*, 1396–9, 183, 254.

[95] *Cal. Close*, 1402–5, 228.

[96] The Countess of Hereford had held Kirtlington in wardship 1400–3 during her granddaughter's minority: *Cal. Fine R.* 1399–1405, 65.

[97] *Rot. Parl.* iv. 135–40. *V.C.H. Oxon.* i. 440 states incorrectly that Kirtlington belonged to the duchy in 1399.

[98] *Rot. Parl.* iv. 188; D.L. 42/18, pt. ii, f. 49; cf. *Feud. Aids*, iv. 191.

to Margaret of Anjou in 1444;[99] and to Elizabeth Woodville in 1467–8.[1] Its stewardship was an office of profit, which was for some time held by William de la Pole, Earl of Suffolk.[2] A clerk, Richard Martyn, was granted custody of the manor for life in 1481;[3] Sir Edward Wydville was assigned a pension on it six months later.[4] In the 16th century the manor was normally farmed out. Thomas Lovett was farming it in 1517,[5] as was John Wellesborne between 1526 and 1537.[6] It was retained by the Crown 1543–55,[7] but from 1556 to 1622 it was in the hands of an Oxfordshire family, a branch of the Ardens of Cottisford.[8] In addition to farming Kirtlington manor, the Ardens were much the largest landowners in the parish. They owed their position to Anthony Arden (d. 1573), who had held some freehold land in Kirtlington since 1538;[9] later he married, as her second husband, the granddaughter and heiress of the woolman John Cockes, who had held 11¾ yardlands freehold in the manor.[10] In 1556 Anthony Arden bought from John Dormer of Steeple Aston another sizeable freehold,[11] and finally (1568) Anthony and John Arden acquired the 'manor' of Kirtlington and Tackley, which had belonged to Bicester Priory.[12] Anthony was followed by his sons John (d. 1605) and Henry (d. 1622).[13] The association of the Ardens with Kirtlington was probably more direct than that of any family which had previously held the manor. Henry Arden left no male heir, and was followed as farmer for two years by Hugh Keate.[14]

In 1604, however, the Crown had sold Kirtlington, with other manors, to Peter Vanlore, merchant, and William Blake, both of London.[15] It was to be held, in free socage, as of the manor of Enfield (Mdx.) at an annual rent of £43 6s. 8d., and the existing farmer's lease, of 41 years from 1584, was explicitly protected.[16] In 1610 Vanlore and Blake resold Kirtlington for £3,000 to Sir Thomas Chamberlayne, chief justice of Chester, who held his first court as lord of the manor in 1625,[17] in which year he died. His son Thomas bought Northbrook in 1641,[18] a step which in effect united the two manors.

In 1682 Penelope, daughter of Sir Thomas Cham-

berlayne, Bt. (grandson of the chief justice), was married to Robert Dashwood. Sir Thomas himself died in 1682. By the marriage settlement all the Chamberlayne estates in Kirtlington passed to Robert Dashwood,[19] on whom a baronetcy was conferred in 1684.[20] The Dashwoods held Northbrook and Kirtlington until 1909.[21] Although they were great landowners elsewhere in Oxfordshire, their main residence in the county was at first at Northbrook House and later at Kirtlington Park.[22] In 1909 the estate was bought by the Earl of Leven and Melville.[23] His successor sold it in 1920 to J. White Esq., who never resided in the parish. In 1921 it was bought by H. M. Budgett Esq.

Domesday Book[24] does not differentiate between Northbrook *Gaytorum* (the present *NORTHBROOK*) and Northbrook *iuxta Somerton*, once in the parish of Somerton.[25] It records 3 small fees in Northbrook; the largest of these, 2 hides held by Rainald of Robert de Stafford, is identifiable with Northbrook Gaytorum, since in 1193 Hilda de Gay held in Northbrook *de feodo Roberti de Stafford*.[26] In 1242 Northbrook *Gaytorum* was held in chief by the Abbot of Westminster as ¼ knight's fee, and in 1255 it constituted a part of the abbot's liberty of Islip, the abbot having acquired his right since 1216.[27] The heirs of Philip Basset held as sub-tenants of the abbot in 1279.[28] From the 12th century to the 16th, however, the ultimate tenants were the Gays, originally a branch of the family that held Hampton Gay.[29] The Northbrook tithing attended the two 'great courts' at Islip manor each year, and paid 3s. cert-money at least until the early 16th century.[30] After the Reformation 'the lordship and manor' of Northbrook was among the endowments of Westminster Abbey as refounded successively by Mary and Elizabeth.[31] Northbrook is mentioned as part of Islip manor in a lease of 1687, but by this date the connexion with Westminster Abbey and Islip can have been no more than a meaningless survival.[32] In practice the connexion with Kirtlington must always have been much closer, Northbrook having no separate field system. Suit was owed at Kirtlington and Adam de Gay witnessed many charters in

[99] *Rot Parl.* v. 118.
[1] Ibid. 628.
[2] *Cal. Pat.* 1436–41, 44; cf. S.C. 6/1093/11, where he is said to have held the office since Apr. 1437. Apparently it remained in his family until 1508: *Cal. Pat.* 1494–1509, 603. For other stewards see *Cal. Pat.* 1436–41, 32.
[3] D.L. 42/19, f. 18.
[4] Ibid. ff. 22, 23.
[5] Dashwood (Oxon.) Dep. a 1 (186).
[6] Ct. R. Apr. 1526; *D. of Lanc. Cal. of Pleadings* (Rec. Com.), ii. 58.
[7] As appears from headings of Ct. R.
[8] Pedigree in *Oxon. Visit.* 207, but does not show that Anthony Arden's wife, Margaret Cockes, had previously been married to John Maunde: Ct. R. May 1525.
[9] Ct. R. Oct. 1538; cf. *L. & P. Hen. VIII*, xiv (2), p. 363.
[10] Ct. R. Dec. 1518; for the Ardens see above, p. 106; for Cockes see below, p. 227.
[11] Dashwood D. box 6, bdle. 'Kirtlington 1547–1732': deed of 1 Sept. 1556.
[12] C.P. 26(1)/135, East. 10 Eliz. See below, p. 224.
[13] For Crown leases of manor to John Arden in 16 and 26 Eliz. see Dashwood D. box 6, bdle. 'Manor of Kirtlington 1584–1723'. For their Kirtlington property in general see C 142/295/82 (John Arden); ibid. 355/54 (Thos. Arden); ibid. 392/107 (Hen. Arden). Cf. C 60/477/23.
[14] Ct. R. 1622, 1623.
[15] *Cal. S.P. Dom.* 1603–10, 126; Dashwood D. box 6,

bdle. 'Manor of Kirtlington 1605–23', q.v. also for the second sale. The price of the first sale is included in that obtained for other property as well.
[16] See above, n. 13.
[17] Ct. Baron of 11 Apr. 1625 is described as his 1st: Ct. R.
[18] Dashwood D. box 4, bdle. 'Northbrook Manor or Farm': deed of 1 June 1641.
[19] Dashwood D. ibid. bdle. 'Title to the Manors, and Barford 1681–4': deed of 12 June 1682.
[20] The warrant styles him Sir Robt. Dashwood 'of Northbrooke': *Cal. S.P. Dom.* 1684–5, 123.
[21] For hist. of family see J. Townsend, *Oxon. Dashwoods*, which relates largely to Kirtlington. The six barts. who were lords of the manor were Sir Robt. Dashwood (d. 1734), Sir Jas. (d. 1779), Sir Hen. Watkin (d. 1828), Sir Geo. (d. 1861), Sir Hen. Wm. (d. 1889), and Sir Geo. J. E. Dashwood (d. 1933). Some of the documents used by Townsend are not *penes* the present bart. and have not been traced.
[22] *Oxon. Dashwoods*, 10.
[23] Ibid. 47.
[24] *V.C.H. Oxon.* i. 412, 415, 416.
[25] For Northbrook *iuxta Somerton* see p. 293.
[26] *Pipe R.* 1192 (P.R.S. n.s. ii), 273–4.
[27] *Rot. Hund.* (Rec. Com.), ii. 31, 45; cf. *Bk. of Fees*, 836.
[28] *Rot. Hund.* ii. 832.
[29] *Oseney Cart.* vi. 98.
[30] Ct. R. are in Westm. Abbey Mun.
[31] *Cal. Pat.* 1555–7, 349; cf. ibid. 1558–60, 397.
[32] Westm. Abbey Mun. 15260; cf. ibid. 15228.

the manorial court in the 13th century.[33] In 1422 the lord of Northbrook, as a tenant-at-will, owed 9s. 5d. in commuted labour services to the lord of Kirtlington,[34] while the customary tenants of Northbrook vill owed a further 4s.[35] In about 1540 the Kirtlington homage presented that John de Gay had held Northbrook of the king as of his manor of Kirtlington, owing an annual rent of 13s. 5d.[36] Between about 1570 and 1641 the manor changed hands many times. William Arscote of Holdsworthy (Devon) acquired it from the Gays after litigation arising out of non-fulfilment of a marriage agreement between the families.[37] By a marriage settlement on Arscote's daughter (1578) it passed to John Fox, yeoman, of Kirtlington.[38] By a further marriage settlement (1609) it was to pass to William Holleyman of Long Handborough; but in 1619 it was sold to John Hollins, presumably acting for John Hawley, D.C.L. of Oxford University, to whom the property was transferred almost immediately. Thomas Chamberlayne bought it from Edmund Hawley in 1641.

The *KIRTLINGTON* manor[39] of Bicester Priory was given in free alms to the priory by Gilbert Basset shortly before his death in 1241.[40] This estate, whose annual value was assessed at £5 3s. 3d. in 1291,[41] had been bought by Gilbert Basset from Baldwin de Montibus in 1239 for 100 marks.[42] It had originally been part of the main manor, having been granted by William de Humez to Baldwin's father, Ralph. Presumably it escheated with the De Humez fee in 1203, for in 1215 it was 'restored' to Ralph to be held by him in chief of the Crown. In 1222, on the death of his brother Herbert to whom he had subinfeudated it in 1217, Ralph did homage for it as for ¼ knight's fee. Shortly afterwards, however, it was in the hands of the king's uncle, William, Earl of Salisbury, on whose death it was committed to Thomas Basset during pleasure. It was again restored to Ralph de Montibus in 1227, and passed to his son Baldwin in 1234. The estate was held by Bicester Priory until the Dissolution. In 1535 the priory's lands in Kirtlington and Tackley were under one bailiff,[43] and were later sometimes called a single manor.[44] They were acquired by the Ardens in

1568[45] and thereafter followed the descent of the main manor.

The *KIRTLINGTON* manor[46] of the Abbot of Aulnay must have been larger than the 1279 survey implies. In 1341–2 his lands, apart from the glebe, comprised 3 carucates.[47] The Aulnay deeds show many instances of gifts of a few acres, or often a single acre, in free alms to the abbey by individual local freeholders. One deed mentions a tenant bringing an action for land in the abbot's court of Kirtlington *per breve regis*, and another, dated 1270, suggests that the abbot enjoyed view of frankpledge.[48]

LESSER ESTATES. Apart from the Northbrook holdings and a hide held by Osmund the priest, Domesday Book records two subsidiary fees, one of 2 hides held by Herbert of Robert d'Oilly, the other of 1 hide held by Robert d'Oilly of William Fitz-Osborn;[49] but one of the hides held by Herbert has been identified with Grove in Holton.[50] Under Henry III the tenure-in-chief of the two small D'Oilly fees in Kirtlington passed, with that of other D'Oilly lands, to the De Plessy family, which still held it in 1364.[51] In 1279 each of these fees was of 1 carucate and was assessed for scutage as ¼ knight's fee.[52] The families in possession, the De Codefords and the De Doningtons, are both prominent in local charters from before 1250.[53] The De Codeford carucate went with lands in Ducklington and Little Barford to make up 2 knight's fees held of the chief lords by the De Dives.[54] That of the De Doningtons was held by them of a mediate lord, Henry de la Grave.[55] The later history of these holdings is not known, although the carucate held by John de Croxford in 1350 is certainly one of them.[56]

Several lay tenants in the parish had their own courts in the 13th century.[57] In the 15th century one lesser holding was styled a 'manor', and in 1461 Sir Edmund Hampden was temporarily deprived, on attainder, of the 'manor of Bowelles in Kyrtlyngton', worth 60s. at that time.[58] This small fee was probably one of those held of Kirtlington manor, since in the 16th century the Hampdens owed suit there until 1554.[59]

[33] Aulnay D. *passim.*
[34] D.L. 43/8/16.
[35] S.C. 6/959/5.
[36] Dashwood (Oxon.) Dep. a 1 (60): undated Ct. R.
[37] C 3/72/36.
[38] Deeds about this and subsequent transactions in Dashwood D. box 4, bdle. 'Northbrook Manor or Farm'. There is a valuable terrier of Northbrook in this bdle.: deed of 30 Mar. 1619.
[39] So called, e.g., in S.C. 6/959/4.
[40] Kennett, *Paroch. Antiq.* i. 225–6, where the deed is wrongly ascribed to 1201.
[41] *Tax. Eccl.* (Rec. Com.), 45.
[42] *Cat. Anct. D.* ii, A 3165; iii, A 5911; *Fines Oxon.* 107. Details vary in the 3 documents. For what follows, see *Rot. Litt. Claus.* i. 234, 296, 513; ii. 103; *Bk. of Fees*, 253; *Ex. e Rot. Fin.* i. 253; *Close R.* 1231–4, 378.
[43] *Valor Eccl.* (Rec. Com.), ii. 188.
[44] e.g. C 142/355/54; ibid. 392/107.
[45] C.P. 26 (1)/135, East. 10 Eliz. For post-Reformation references to these lands see *L. & P. Hen. VIII,* xix (2), p. 77; *Cal. Pat.* 1558–60, 75; ibid. 1560–3, 402. For the Ardens see above, p. 223.
[46] The term occurs several times in 13th cent.: Aulnay D.
[47] *Inq. Non.* (Rec. Com.), 132.
[48] 'Et sciendum quod . . . pro supradictis, videlicet mesuagio et clauso, tenebuntur ad sectam curie francplegiorum in quantum tenebantur illi qui predictum mesuagium antiquitus possidebant.'
[49] *V.C.H. Oxon.* i. 415, 425.

[50] See ibid. v. 172.
[51] *Cal. Close,* 1364–8, 3; cf. *Fines Oxon.* 245.
[52] *Rot. Hund.* (Rec. Com.), ii. 823.
[53] Aulnay D.
[54] *Bk. of Fees,* 825, 837. These 2 kt's fees were held under the D'Oillys by Hugh de Chesney c. 1130: *Eynsham Cart.* i. 413. In 1279 the de Codefords held of Alex. de Archibus, who held of Robert de Grey, who held of Ralph de Dive: *Rot. Hund.* (Rec. Com.), ii. 823. Aulnay D. show that Matthew de Launceles, who held ¼ fee (the De Dive holding) of Alex. de Archibus in 1247 (*Fines Oxon.* 136; *Bk. of Fees,* 825), left 2 coheiresses who married the bros. John and Robert de Codeford.
[55] The De la Graves evidently held before 1200: *Fines Oxon.* 13; *St. Frides. Cart.* ii. 214; *Christ Ch. Arch.* 43.
[56] *Cal. Inq. p.m.* ix, p. 183; cf. 'Croxfordesplace', *Cal. Anct. D.* ii. C 524, 534, 767, 786, 1672.
[57] Thomas, son of Fulk de la Grave (holder of one of the d'Oilly fees), was said to have made a chart. 'sub medietate Curie sue de Kirliton': *Rot. Cur. Reg.* (Rec. Com.), ii. 229. Thomas le Loutre refers to 'secta curie mee': Aulnay D. In 1279 2 lay undertenants, John Fitzwilliam and Ric. de Caune, and the Prior of Bicester had free tenants owing them suit: *Rot. Hund.* (Rec. Com.), ii. 823.
[58] *Cal. Pat.* 1461–7, 473; *Rot. Parl.* v. 589; C 145/319/43. Henry de Bowelles held a messuage and 10 a. in Kirtlington of the Prior of Bicester in 1279: *Rot. Hund.* (Rec. Com.), ii. 823. For references to the family see Kennett, *Paroch. Antiq.* ii, index. It held certain lands in Kirtlington in 1422: D.L. 43/8/16.
[59] Ct. R.

ECONOMIC AND SOCIAL HISTORY. In the Middle Ages the agriculture of the whole parish was organized on a two-field economy. The fields were called the East and West Fields, or often, in early deeds, *campus versus boscum* and *campus versus aquam*: they were separated by the Somerton and Bletchingdon roads.[60] The meadow land was concentrated along Gallows Brook, on the eastern edge of the parish, and beside the Cherwell, where lay Whitmersham, Pinsey, Briton, and Northam meadows. Almost all the waste and common land lay in the northern part of the parish, either behind Northbrook and in the 'Breach Furze', east of the Somerton road, or in Roumer Leys and Grove Leys, which together covered most of the area between Akeman Street and the Middleton parish boundary.[61] In 1750 the common land amounted to 720 acres;[62] in the 16th century its extent must have been considerably greater. The court roll of October 1596, for example, records a decision to convert to tillage 1 furlong and one other parcel of land, both adjacent to Middleton Field. In 1591 a jury assessed the area in the manor 'besides wastes' as 1,086 acres, less than one-third of the area of the parish;[63] but this surprisingly low figure does not include Northbrook manor and other freeholds.

Although nearly all the early evidence indicates a completely regular two-field system, one or two deeds suggest that the two fields may not have comprised the whole of the arable;[64] and some kind of a 'hitch' evidently existed as early as 1263.[65] A 'hitche-fylde', contrasted with the 'cornefylde', occurs in 1586;[66] but it is only from 1619 that the 'pease hitch' suddenly becomes a regular feature, alternating between the two fields in a fixed four-year cycle.[67] The mention of pease, barley, and wheat crops in a single year, e.g. 1629, also suggests the introduction of a four-course rotation. In 1638, however, an agreement is recorded for the pease hitch to follow an eight-year cycle, approximately a quarter of each field to be hitched every other year. Few court rolls exist for the period 1641–1737; that of 1700 shows an eight-year cycle still in use, but the two surviving rolls of Charles II's reign indicate that a six-year cycle had been tried. How the rotation of crops was affected by these changes is not clear. Rye and oats are both mentioned in earlier rolls, and a hemp plot 'containing by estimacioun a quarter of a yard of

ground' existed at Northbrook in 1619;[68] but there is no evidence of new crops in the common fields until the 18th century. In 1738 Ramley Hill, above Northbrook, was planted with 'saint foyn' for ten years, and although the ground was reported worn out at the end of the experiment[69] some part of the fields was always under sainfoin for the rest of the century. From 1739 there was a 'horse hitch' where vetches or clover were grown for feed; grass seed was sown in 1748 and subsequent years. Between 1747 and 1757 there was regularly an area of 'three crop ground'. Turnips were grown by Sir James Dashwood in 1751[70] and in the common fields from 1764. The East and West fields were still spoken of, but they had been subdivided into various 'quarters'. In 1750 there were five quarters (in addition to the park) in the East Field and seven, or eight including Ramley Hill, in the West.[71] At least five quarters were named; others were described by their bounding roads or tracks. No definite system of crop rotation is discernible, although the court rolls show that the same ground was sown with turnips every fourth year with fair regularity.

Most of the medieval demesne of both Kirtlington and Northbrook was unconsolidated, but in 1279 Kirtlington manor is described as having a new park.[72] This park was probably inclosed from the East Field, since in 1750 the 'old park', an area of 75 acres, was taken into Sir James Dashwood's new park.[73] A few houses in the 13th century had small closes.[74] The 1476 rental mentions 6 closes of pasture and 8 of arable, totalling 39 and 60 acres respectively.[75] Sixteenth-century surveys give no estimates of acreage inclosed, but new inclosure does not appear to have been extensive. It seems unlikely to have caused the complicity of some Kirtlington men in the Oxfordshire rising of 1596.[76] In 1750 about 400 acres of inclosures were concentrated around the village and at Northbrook, of which Sir James Dashwood owned 230 acres.[77] Strip cultivation was still in full operation; John Trafford's New farm, for example, a copyhold of 245 acres, consisted of 278 pieces scattered through 115 different furlongs.[78] The new park, comprising 496 acres, reduced the size of the East Field, although the 1750 map shows many uninclosed strips inside it, a few of which still survived at the time of the award. At that date inclosures had increased to 900 acres, of

[60] For field names see D.L. 43/8/16, 17; Dashwood (Oxon.) Dep. c 1: rentals 1422, 1476, 1495.

[61] On Davis's *Oxon. Map* this whole area is simply marked 'Kirklington Leys' as opposed to 'Kirklington Fields', which covers the rest of the parish save the village and park. But several 13th-cent. Aulnay deeds relate to arable *super Roumere*. Occasionally Roumer seems to be synonymous with the E. field at that date; e.g. *Rot. Cur. Reg.* (Rec. Com.), ii. 229; cf. n. 64 below.

[62] From a survey of the parish in four MS. vols. in St. John's Coll. compiled *c.* 1750, cited below as St. John's Coll. Surv. 1750.

[63] D.L. 42/117, f. 97*b*.

[64] e.g. confirmation *c.* 1200 by Thos. *de Grava* to Aulnay of grant of 7 a. of land 'in villa de Kertlintona', of which 3 a. are 'super Roumere', 1 *iuxta crucem* and 3 *in alio campo versus aquam*: Aulnay D.

[65] Of 18 a. granted by Thos. le Loutre to Aulnay in 13th cent. ½ a. in the W. field was 'apud le Hiche': Aulnay D.; cf. in deed of 1624 'one other akere thereof lying in one furlong called Cowcrofte in the ould hich': Dashwood D. box 1, bdle. 'Northbrook . . . purchased from John Brangwin 1806'. Regular cultivation of the fallow is more certainly indicated in lease of 2 a. for 10 years from 1263 '. . . usque habeant quinque vesturas in uno campo et

quinque vesturas in alio campo insuper et omnes hechyngas infra dictum terminum': Aulnay D.; cf. in deed of similar date 'cum Hechyngis infra predictum terminum contingentibus': Aulnay D.

[66] Facts from Ct. R. unless otherwise stated.

[67] See especially Ct. R. 1631: 'there shall be a heech for four years to beginn as it hath been these twelve years past, and sowed in that order. . . .'

[68] Dashwood D. box 4, bdle. 'Northbrook Manor or Farm': deed 30 Mar. 1619.

[69] St. John's Coll. Surv. 1750.

[70] £1 9s. 10d. spent on turnip seed: entry in Sir Jas. Dashwood's 'General Account'.

[71] St. John's Coll. Surv. 1750; cf. New Coll. terrier, 1768.

[72] *Rot. Hund.* (Rec. Com.), ii. 822. Thomas Brokenton was 'parcarius parci de Curtlyngton' in 1428: New Coll. D. nos. 32, 33.

[73] St. John's Coll. Surv. 1750; cf. New Coll. terrier 1768.

[74] Aulnay D.

[75] D.L. 43/8/17.

[76] *Cal. S.P. Dom.* 1595–7, 317, 320, 343.

[77] St. John's Coll. Surv. 1750.

[78] Ibid.

which the Dashwoods' Park farm accounted for 165 acres. Under the award 2,535 acres were inclosed.

The 1279 survey shows a complicated structure of land tenure within the parish.[79] Whereas Domesday Book mentions only villeins (*villani*), bordars, and serfs,[80] a noticeable feature in 1279 is the number of small free tenants, not only in the main manor but even more markedly in the smaller fees. The more substantial of these resident free tenants, men of 3 or 4 virgates who in some cases had a few free tenants of their own, made up the class which played the leading part in village affairs.[81] The fact that there were fees independent of the main manor was, except from a legal standpoint, of much less significance than the existence of a single agricultural system, the regulation of which must always have been done in the Kirtlington manorial court. In 1279 the Prior of Bicester and Adam de Gay of Northbrook each had 9 villeins holding half-virgates or less. On the main manor, villeins held 14 virgates,[82] 9 half-virgates, and 1 quarter-virgate, figures which had changed little by 1422.[83]

The earliest surviving Ministers' Accounts (1389–90)[84] show a rent of £3 17s. 6d. (entered among the assised rents) being paid for part of the demesne arable farmed out *ex antiquo*. The rest of the demesne lands, with the labour services of free and customary tenants, were being farmed jointly by three individuals, one of them the vicar, for the term of ten years under an indenture entered into with the attorneys of the Duke of Gloucester, then lord of the manor. They paid a farm of £18 6s. 8d. In 1415[85] the position was quite different, and was substantially that depicted in a new rental compiled in 1422.[86] The demesne lands, amounting to about 233 acres of arable, 69 of pasture, and 39 of meadow, were let off piecemeal to some 20 of the manorial tenants, mostly virgaters or half-virgaters. For most of the 15th century, farm of the demesne totalled £16 17s., and assised rents £17 14s. 6½d. All labour services, which most 15th-century Ministers' Accounts set out in detail,[87] were now commuted; their value of £1 13s. 6d. compares with an estimated value of £1 17s. 6d. in 1204.[88] By custom of the manor, copyhold leases could only be granted for one life,[89] and in the 15th century, when virgate holdings seldom stayed in one family for two generations, the parcels of leased demesne did not become attached to particular holdings. In the 16th century this largely ceased to be the case. In about 1511, for example,

Peter Frankelyng's holding comprised 1 messuage and yardland; 1 toft and ½-yardland called Gyllows; a close, a 'more' and certain 'bordland' in Heryngdon; pieces of meadow in Cranmere and Pyngeye; and a piece of land in Rye Furlong. The same lands were held, at unchanged rents, by John Horne in about 1530 and by Richard Hall in 1619.[90] The more prosperous copyholders now became important men in village affairs. Whereas, of the numerous village families whose names occur in the rentals of 1422 and 1476 and the court roll of 1470–1, hardly one can be traced a hundred years later, such familes as those of Bath, Hall, Rayer, Walker, and Woodward, which originated between about 1490 and 1560, were all prominent for 200 and some for nearly 400 years.[91]

After the Dissolution, however, most freeholders were still gentry; in 1544, for example, the list comprised Sir Michael Dormer, John Gay, Owen Whitton, William Bourne, William Hampden, Anthony Arden, John Stavely (all gentry); Thomas Andrewes (not so styled); New College and Magdalen College.[92] By the end of the century the number of freeholds was increasing, and several village families were owning freehold land. Between 1684 and 1750 Sir Robert and Sir James Dashwood bought up most of the freehold farms,[93] with the result that the substantial freeholder almost disappeared from the parish. In 1750 there were only 393 acres of freehold lands, other than those of Sir James Dashwood, divided between 21 freeholders.[94] Under the inclosure award (1815) this acreage was slightly increased owing to the commutation of tithe for land. Apart from Sir Henry Dashwood, whose land amounted to 2,922 acres (including 395 held as lessee of the rector, St. John's College), the only freeholders of more than 10 acres were the vicar, 185 acres;[95] New College, 127 acres; John Hall, 114 acres. In 1908 the Kirtlington Park estate had 3,143 acres,[96] to which Vicarage farm (184 a.) was added in 1916.[97] Many properties, however, including Northbrook, were sold by the estate in the years after the First World War.

In 1591 a freeholder or copyholder might keep for each yardland he possessed 'five rother cattell and seven ploughe beastes', and might graze 50 sheep on the East Field when fallow, 40 on the West.[98] The introduction of a 4-course rotation destroyed this distinction between the fields; 36 sheep per yardland might be grazed, on either field, in 1667 and 1700, 45 in 1683.[99] After 1700 the number of

---

[79] *Rot. Hund.* (Rec. Com.), ii. 822; ibid. 832, Northbrook.

[80] For numbers see below, p. 227. Osmund the Priest is also recorded: *V.C.H. Oxon.* i. 409.

[81] This seems clear from witness lists in Aulnay D., mostly earlier than 1279. Most prominent names: Thos. de la Haye, Thos. and Ligerus le Loutre, Walter Ingerram, Adam de Marigny, Matthew de Launceles and his sons-in-law John and Robt. de Codeford, Peter de Donington, John Fitzwilliam and Adam de Gay.

[82] Virgate normally 30 a.; e.g. 3½ yardlands 'conteyning 104 Acres': Dashwood D. box 5, bdle. 'Bennet's Farm', deed 3 May 1606. A 40-acre virgate is specifically mentioned once in 1476 and twice in 1495: D.L. 43/8/17; Dashwood (Oxon.) Dep. c 1.

[83] D.L. 43/8/16.

[84] D.L. 29/652/10541.

[85] Ibid. 10559; cf. S.C. 6/959/5 (1421).

[86] D.L. 43/8/16. The 1476 rental shows little change.

[87] e.g. D.L. 29/653/10565.

[88] *Rot. Normannie* (Rec. Com.), i. 131.

[89] Customs of the manor (1591) are set out in D.L.

[ ] 42/117, ff. 98–99.

[90] See 3 rentals in Dashwood (Oxon.) Dep. c. 1.

[91] Roger Hall occurs in 1480: New Coll. D. no. 29. The last resident member of the family died in 1866: Par. Rec. Burial Register.

[92] Ct. R.

[93] Evident from Dashwood D.

[94] St. John's Coll. Surv. 1750.

[95] In addition to New Coll. D. and to New Coll. terriers, Bodl. MS. ch. Oxon. a 44 comprises deeds (1517–55) relating to this property. New College acquired it in 1495 (New Coll. D. no. 8), and sold it to Sir H. W. Dashwood in 1872: note added in MS. vol. 'Kirtlington 1815' *penes* G. Henderson Esq., Oathill Farm, Enstone.

[96] Land agents' surv. 1908: see above, p. 220, n. 23.

[97] See below, p. 229.

[98] D.L. 42/117, f. 99; cf. Ct. R. Apr. 1540, Apr. 1541. In 1619 Northbrook, with 3¾ yardlands, had common of pasture for 16 milch cattle and grazing for 218 sheep on E. field and 175 on W. field: Dashwood D. box 4, bdle. 'Northbrook Manor or Farm', deed 30 Mar. 1619.

[99] New Coll. terrier, 1667; other dates from Ct. R.

sheep per yardland declined steadily until 1761, from which year it remained at 22. The earlier figures, implying a very large total flock, suggest that wool grown by small producers and sold to middlemen buyers was the real basis of the village's prosperity. One such middleman, John Cockes (d. 1518), 'yoman, alias wolman, alias marchaunt', was himself a Kirtlington man.[1] Common meadow was allocated annually by lot; and in about 1260 a grant to Aulnay Abbey included 1 acre in the meadow called 'Brusserton' (i.e. Briton), 'in duobus locis sicut in sorte accidere consuevit'.[2] Briton is described as a 'lott meade' in 1626, and New College possessed 1½ lots in it in 1768.[3] Lots were also used for the allocation of furze and heath, e.g. in 1557 and 1700, and in 1748 the vetch crop in the horse hitch was allotted in this way.

The view of frankpledge, with court baron, was normally held once a year only, in October or early November. In the early 16th century it was being attended by three Bicester tithings, those of King's End, Bignell, and the manor of Markyate Priory. The performance of suit by Bicester King's End only lapsed in the 19th century.[4] The tithings of Kirtlington and King's End each paid 13s. 4d. at the view. The lesser court, which usually took place in March or April, and sometimes in other months, seems to have been gradually discontinued after 1600.[5]

The early surviving court rolls make no mention of elected officials other than the constable and tithingmen. The warrener,[6] later also called the woodward, was a paid officer appointed by the lord of the manor, and after 1421 by the Crown; he makes many presentments in the early rolls but disappears by 1540. A hayward first occurs c. 1522, the four fieldsmen and the common 'herd' late in Elizabeth's reign. These were the regular agricultural officials for the remainder of the period of open-field cultivation, the hayward and fieldsmen being elected and sworn annually. In 1638 and 1641 the hayward's wage was 4d. and a peck of maslin for every yardland.[7] By that date the regulation of agriculture was beginning to predominate in the court's work. Earlier the range of business, which was exceedingly various, included the hearing of cases of debt, theft, and assault.[8] In 1470 the village possessed stocks, cucking-stool, and pillory.[9] A theft was punished by pillory in 1515. The stocks were renewed in 1526 and were still in use in 1601.[10]

There is little evidence of local industries other than agriculture. Cloth was being fulled and dyed in the village in 1456; in 1543 Thomas Harres, fuller, obtained a licence to erect 'a fuller's teynter' on the green for an annual rent of 2d., and in 1619 Thomas Bull was paying 2s. 6d. annually 'for the Fuller's Racke in Oldburie', the field immediately east of the church.[11] The Prior of Bicester had a quarry which was being worked in 1425.[12] A quarry near the mill was leased in 1526 to Thomas Swetnam and in 1619 to Thomas Bull.[13] A Kirtlington lime-kiln contributed to the building of Cardinal College.[14] In 1638 Richard Hall was elected and sworn as clerk of the market and water bailiff,[15] an office which, possibly owing to the gaps in the court rolls, is not found again. Plot's map (1676)[16] shows Kirtlington as a market-town. A modern industrial undertaking was the building of the Oxford Cement Company's works beside the canal in 1905,[17] but they were abandoned after 20 years when the present works were built on the other side of the river.

The parish has always had a larger population than most others in the hundred. In Domesday Book Kirtlington, excluding Northbrook, had 71 villeins, bordars, and serfs;[18] this figure, however, probably includes Bignell. In the 1279 survey about 90 landholders, free and unfree, are named in the returns for Kirtlington and Northbrook.[19] The hearth-tax returns for 1662 and 1665 show the existence of at least 65 households;[20] then, as in 1801,[21] Kirtlington was exceeded in population only by Bicester and Islip of the parishes in the hundred. Bishop Compton's Census (1676) showed a total of 285 persons over the age of sixteen.[22] In 1738 and 1759 the number of houses was 99; in 1811, when the census showed 536 residents, there were said to be 131 families.[23] The birth rate in the early 17th century was not regularly exceeded until the sharp rise of the second decade of the 19th century. There were 167 baptisms in the decade 1623–32, 148 in 1723–32 and 236 in 1823–32.[24] The population rose to 761 in 1871, had fallen to 594 in 1901, and was 636 in 1951.[25]

Assessments to taxation in the first half of the 14th century suggest that Kirtlington, with Northbrook, was one of the wealthiest parishes in Ploughley hundred. Charlton and Islip each had a higher assessment in 1306, Chesterton and Bicester Market End in 1316; but in 1327 and 1344 only Bicester Market End exceeded the assessment of Kirtlington with

[1] For John Cockes see *Cal. Pat.* 1494–1509, 535, 569; D.L. 7/2/19; Ct. R. 1511–19 *passim*, and typical extract in *Bodl. Quart. Rec.* v (1927), 185; *B.N.C. Quatercentenary Monographs* (O.H.S. lii), no. iv, p. 9.

[2] Ch. of Thos. le Loutre: Aulnay D.

[3] New Coll. terriers.

[4] Blo. *Bic.* 74.

[5] Five rolls occur 1607–35, and none thereafter. But cf. New Coll. terrier, 1667: 'which said Court is kept in Kirtlington aforesaid once a year'.

[6] In 1279 the lord of the manor enjoyed free warren *de antiquitate*: *Rot. Hund.* (Rec. Com.), ii. 822. For the warrener see especially S.C. 6/1093/11; *Cal. Pat.* 1436–41, 141; *Rot. Parl.* vi. 373–4. He first occurs in 1389: D.L. 29/652/10541.

[7] Ct. R.

[8] *Bodl. Quart. Rec.* v (1927), 179–88: extracts from 16th cent. Ct. R.

[9] D.L. 30/108/1594.

[10] Ct. R.

[11] Bicester priory Acct. R. 34 Hen. VI, calendared in Blo. *Bic.* 188; Ct. R. 1543; Dashwood (Oxon.) Dep. c 1:

rental of 1619.

[12] Bicester priory Acct. R. 3–4 Hen. VI, calendared in N. J. Hone, *Manor and Manorial Rec.* 211.

[13] Ct. R. 1526; Dashwood (Oxon.) Dep. c 1: rental of 1619.

[14] *L. & P. Hen. VIII*, iv (3), p. 3042; H. L. Thompson, *Christ Ch.* 4.

[15] Ct. R.

[16] *Nat. Hist. Oxon.* frontispiece.

[17] Lease for 60 years from 25 Dec. 1905; see land agents' surv. 1908, above, p. 220, n. 23.

[18] *V.C.H. Oxon.* i. 400, 425.

[19] *Rot. Hund.* (Rec. Com.), ii. 822, 832. About 180 local names earlier than 1300 occur in Aulnay D. The poll-tax returns are missing.

[20] *Hearth Tax Oxon.* 199, 235.

[21] *V.C.H. Oxon.* ii. 221.

[22] Compton Census.

[23] Oxf. Dioc. d 553, d 556, d 572.

[24] Figures 1723–32 from Oxf. Dioc. c 554: par. reg. transcripts.

[25] *V.C.H. Oxon.* ii. 221; *Census*, 1951.

Northbrook.[26] Forty-eight persons, including 12 from Northbrook, contributed about £6 8s. 9d. for the 16th of 1316; 44, including 13 from Northbrook, £5 14s. 9d. for the 20th of 1327.[27] In 1523 the assessment of Kirtlington and Northbrook (£17 4s. 10d on the two payments) for the lay subsidy was exceeded by assessments of Somerton, Chesterton, and Bletchingdon.[28]

The degree of poverty existing in the parish at various times is difficult to assess. In c. 1789 many families with children were living on earnings of 6s. a week.[29] In 1802–3 the figure spent on maintenance and relief of the poor had increased steeply to £476 17s. 6d. from an average of less than £200 in the years 1783–5.[30] Of a total population of 525,[31] 75 persons, of whom 39 were adults, were permanently relieved out of the poor rate, and 13 others received occasional relief. Twenty-eight of these cases were due to old age or permanent disability. In 1840 the parish owned four cottages on the green; they were known as the College and served as an almshouse for several families of the labouring poor.[32]

In 1562 the inhabitants of Kirtlington received a royal charter exempting them from payment of toll elsewhere than in the Duchy of Lancaster.[33] It was said in 1723 that this privilege was the reason for the village's annual feast, called the Lamb Ale.[34] This was a long-established celebration in 1679. At that date it began on Trinity Monday and lasted two days; later it apparently occupied a whole week. In 1849 three persons were sworn as special constables 'for the better preservation of peace and order at the ensuing Lamb Ale Feast'.[35] The feast was discontinued in the 19th century, but has been revived in a modified form.

CHURCH. There can be little doubt that there was a Saxon church at Kirtlington, which was an important royal manor, but the earliest indication of its existence comes from Domesday Book. It records that Osmund the priest held in demesne in 1086 a hide of land worth 20s.[36] The church was conferred by Jordan and Lucy de Sai on the Norman abbey of Aulnay, a Cistercian house founded by them in

1131.[37] The appropriation to Aulnay was confirmed by Henry II in 1157,[38] by Bishop Robert de Chesney (at the petition of Richard de Humez), and by Pope Lucius III.[39] The benefice was one of the most valuable in the deanery, being assessed at £20 13s. 4d. including the vicarage, both in 1291 and in 1341–2.[40] Hostilities with France made the king take the revenues of the church into his own hand in 1324, and again in 1337.[41] In the latter year it was arranged that the abbey's proctor should have custody of its possessions in England at a farm of £46 a year; this amount was increased to £50, and the advowson of the living retained in the king's hand, in 1342.[42] In 1392 licence was given by the Crown to the new Carthusian Priory of St. Anne's, Coventry, to acquire in parcellam fundacionis the church and advowson of Kirtlington, along with Aulnay's other English property.[43] In 1535 it was being farmed under a 31-year lease, dated 1515, by John Andrews of Kirtlington for a rent of £13 13s. 4d. and the obligation to pay certain other charges totalling 50s. annually.[44] At the Dissolution, a syndicate of some 77 persons, mostly Londoners, bought the rectory and advowson,[45] but the sale was evidently not completed; and, by a deed dated 17 November 1545, the living was acquired by John Penne, armiger, and Lucia, his wife, to be held by service of $\frac{1}{40}$ knight's fee and annual payment of 26s. 8d. to the Crown.[46] A year later the Pennes sold it to Vincent Poure, armiger, of Bletchingdon Park;[47] and in April 1578 it was bought from Francis Poure by St. John's College, Oxford, for £800, its yearly value then being £46 13s. 4d.[48] In 1675 the impropriation was rented for more than £180 a year, although to the incumbent the living was worth only £22.[49] By the inclosure award of 1811 payments on the great tithes were commuted for 301 acres of land, while the glebe was exchanged for a further 93 acres.[50] The college still holds the advowson, but sold its rectorial rights to Sir Henry Dashwood in 1876.[51] A chapel existed at Northbrook in the 12th century; it belonged to the Gays, who gave the Northbrook tithes to Aulnay.[52] Oseney Abbey, however, which acquired the church of Hampton Gay c. 1185,[53] alleged that Northbrook was a part of Hampton Gay parish[54]

[26] See tax table, below, p. 359.
[27] E 179/161/8, 9.
[28] E 179/161/176, 198. Kirtlington's assessment was probably also exceeded by that of Bicester Market End, but the Bicester returns are incomplete.
[29] Surv. of labouring population of Kirtlington, compiled c. 1789, penes Miss A. Enser, Kirtlington.
[30] Poor Abstract, 404.
[31] V.C.H. Oxon. ii. 221: population in 1801.
[32] Vestry Rec. in par. chest.
[33] Text in Bodl. MS. Hearne's Diaries 131, ff. 157–9; cf. Hearne, Remarks, x. 457. The privileges of the inhabitants of the D. of Lanc. went back to 1342: Cal. Chart. R. 1341–1417, 10. The grant to Kirtlington was repeated in ch. of 1628: Dashwood D. box 6, bdle. 'Ch. granted by Chas. I'.
[34] Hearne, Remarks, viii. 68, quoting description in T. Blount, Antient Tenures (1679), 149. The Lamb Ale is also described in H. W. Taunt, Kirtlington, 36–37 and Revd. J. Deane's Log Bk. (Par. Rec.), 83 and loose enclosures.
[35] Vestry Rec.
[36] V.C.H. Oxon. i. 409.
[37] See above, p. 222.
[38] Cal. Doc. France, ed. Round, nos. 525, 526.
[39] Charter and bull in Aulnay D.
[40] Tax. Eccl. (Rec. Com.), 31b; Inq. Non. (Rec. Com.), 132.
[41] S.C. 6/1126/16, 17; Cal. Fine R. 1337–47, 35.

[42] Cal. Fine R. 1337–47, 274; ibid. 1347–56, 73–74. For Crown presentations to the living see Cal. Pat. 1348–50, 508; 1350–4, 125, 250; 1385–9, 447; 1388–92, 446. For list of medieval presentations see MS. Top. Oxon. d 460.
[43] Cal. Pat. 1391–6, 242; cf. 1381–5, 484. Other relevant documents are in Aulnay D., especially an indenture of 1393 between Aulnay Abbey and St. Anne's Priory which gives interesting details of the arrangement.
[44] Valor Eccl. (Rec. Com.), iii. 53; indenture of 1515 in Aulnay D.
[45] L. & P. Hen. VIII, xix (2), p. 311.
[46] Ibid. xx (2), pp. 449–50; St. John's Coll. Mun. xx. 6.
[47] L. & P. Hen. VIII, xxi (2), p. 245; St. John's Coll. Mun. xx. 7–9.
[48] St. John's Coll. Mun. xx. 15–19; cf. W. H. Stevenson and H. E. Salter, Early Hist. St. John's Coll. (O.H.S. N.S. i), 212, 275; C.P. 25(2)/197/Trin. 20 Eliz.
[49] Oxf. Dioc. c 155, f. 19a.
[50] O.R.O. Incl. award.
[51] J. Townsend, Oxon. Dashwoods, 45.
[52] Aulnay D.: Charter of Philip de Gay. The field name 'Chapel Piece' at Northbrook occurs in St. John's Coll. Map, 1750. The land given by 'Agnes daughter of John, son of the priest of Norbrok', to the Hospital of St. John, Oxford (Cal. Chart. R. 1226–57, 298), is the origin of the small freehold subsequently held by Magdalen College until the 19th cent.
[53] Oseney Cart. vi. 40.
[54] Ibid. 98.

and could also advance spurious evidence of its right to two-thirds of the demesne tithes of North-brook.[55] In an arbitration of July 1190 the former claim was not upheld, but Oseney's right to the tithes was substantially maintained.[56] The Oseney tithe in Northbrook was worth 13s. 4d. in 1291.[57] In 1413, after further friction, Oseney agreed to farm its share of the Northbrook tithe to St. Anne's, Coventry, in perpetuity for 16s. 8d. a year.[58]

An agreement of 1263, which cites a previous agreement of 1228, between Aulnay and Bicester Priory, shows that Bicester enjoyed tithe of hay on certain meadows of the Kirtlington demesne.[59] There was also bitter dispute between these two houses over the tithe of sheaves of Bignell, which although a 'member' of Kirtlington manor was *infra territorium de Berencestr'*. In 1304 it was agreed that Bicester should have this tithe at a perpetual farm of 40s. a year.[60] At the Dissolution St. Anne's, Coventry, was receiving 51s. yearly from Bicester, of which 11s. may have been tithe on the mill.[61]

A vicarage was ordained during the episcopate of Hugh de Welles (1209–35), by which the vicar was to receive the proceeds of the altar, rent of 23s. 4d. from land belonging to the church, and 32 sheaves of corn, valued at 15s., which the church received from the demesne of Roger Damory in Bletching-don.[62] In 1254 the vicarage was valued at 40s. and in 1291 at £4 6s. 8d.[63] The Hundred Rolls give a list of the vicar's six free tenants, holding in all 4 virgates and paying 24s. 7d. rent.[64] By 1341 it appears that there had been a change in the ordination of the vicarage, for the vicar was then receiving the small tithes, mortuaries, and oblations, valued in all at £4 3s. 8d., while the glebe, by this time worth 52s., and the great tithes belonged to Aulnay.[65] In the 16th century Kirtlington was a rich vicarage, valued at £11 9s. 4d. net.[66]

After the Reformation the value of the vicarage rose slowly, being worth £22 in 1675[67] and about £24 during Queen Anne's reign.[68] In 1731 it was given £200 from Queen Anne's Bounty,[69] with which was bought a farm of 64 acres in Eynsham parish, part of the pasture called Freeland.[70] This farm and Vicarage Farm in Kirtlington, consisting of the 179 acres awarded the vicar when the small tithes were commuted at the inclosure award in 1811,[71] formed the vicarage's only endowment in the 19th century, being worth £358 in 1831.[72] Vicarage Farm was sold to the Earl of Leven and Melville in 1916.[73]

Some of the medieval vicars had unusually long connexions with the parish. Gilbert de Wardington was vicar from 1302 until probably carried off by the Black Death in 1349;[74] Thomas de Pytchley, a lessee of the manor's demesne lands, was vicar for almost 40 years (1352–c. 1390);[75] and the 15th-century vicar, William Coston or Constantyn (c. 1422–60), also remained for about 40 years. Two of the vicars left doubtful reputations: Jordan, early in the 13th century, was defamed with a woman of Kirtlington, and threatened with deprivation if again found incontinent,[76] while in 1391 William Grene, who had goods worth £40, was outlawed for killing a man at Kirtlington.[77]

In the 13th century a house to be used as a Vicar-age was acquired by Aulnay Abbey from Bicester Priory.[78] This is, of course, to be distinguished from the Rectory House, which existed in 1665[79] and was included in the property leased to the farmers of the rectory. There was sometimes a curate in the parish in the sixteenth century.[80] Eighteenth-century vicars, who were often Fellows of St. John's College dividing their time between Oxford and Kirtling-ton, were never more than part-time residents in the parish.[81] In 1738 the vicar did not reside at all, and his curate, who was also appointed by St. John's College, usually stayed one night in each week in order to conduct the two Sunday services. Most vicars at this period, however, did not have curates, although in 1814 a licensed curate was resident in the Vicarage, the vicar being non-resident. In addi-tion to the two Sunday services, the Sacrament was administered four times annually, the number of communicants varying between 25 and 40 during the 18th and early 19th centuries. The Vicarage House was situated on the north side of the church,[82] but in 1840 St. John's College built a new Vicarage adjacent to the church on the south.[83] This was sold shortly before the Second World War, when the present Vicarage was built.

The church of *ST. MARY THE VIRGIN* com-prises a nave, chancel, north and south aisles (the south aisle prolonged to form a transept), south porch, and central tower. The tympanum now over the vestry doorway is early 12th century and the foundations of an apse were discovered beneath the chancel in 1877.[84] This was thought at the time to have been Saxon, but was more probably contem-porary with the tower-arches, which date from the early 12th century. The eastern arch has been much restored, but the western arch retains its

[55] *Osney Cart.* iv. 3, 25; cf. confirmation of the genuine deed (*Oxon. Chart.* no. 58), in which Northbrook Gay-torum is mentioned.
[56] *Oseney Cart.* vi. 99–100.
[57] *Tax. Eccl.* (Rec. Com.), 31b.
[58] *Oseney Cart.* vi. 100–1; cf. ibid. 244 and *Valor Eccl.* (Rec. Com.), ii. 221.
[59] Aulnay D.
[60] Ibid.; Dugd. *Mon.* vi (3), 1109–10, makes it appear that this rent was for the church of Kirtlington itself.
[61] *Valor Eccl.* ii. 188; Kennett, *Paroch. Antiq.* i. 226.
[62] *Lib. Ant. Welles,* 7; *Rot. Welles,* i. 148, where the rent is given as 33s. 4d. and the sheaves as 30.
[63] Lunt, *Val. Norw.* 313; *Tax. Eccl.* (Rec. Com.), 31b.
[64] *Rot. Hund.* (Rec. Com.), ii. 823.
[65] *Inq. Non.* (Rec. Com.), 132.
[66] *Valor Eccl.* (Rec. Com.), ii. 159.
[67] Oxf. Dioc. c 155, f. 19a.
[68] *Rep. of Comm. on Eccl. Revenue,* H.C. 54 (1835), xxii.
[69] *Papers Rel. to Queen Anne's Bounty 1703–1815,* H.C. 115 (1814–15), xii.

[70] E. K. Chambers, *Eynsham under the Monks* (O.R.S. xviii), 51.
[71] O.R.O. Incl. award.   [72] As n. 68 above.
[73] Par Rec. See inventory by Revd. G. C. May, 1929.
[74] See list of medieval presentations: MS. Top. Oxon. d 460.
[75] P.R.O. Mins.' Accts. Duch. of Lanc. 652/10541.
[76] *Rot. Welles,* i. 148.
[77] *Cal. Pat.* 1391–6, 381, 718.
[78] '. . . ad inhabitacionem singulorum vicariorum dicto-rum abbatis et conventus in eorum ecclesia de Curtlintona successive ministrancium': Aulnay D.
[79] *Hearth Tax Oxon.* 199. For leases of the Rectory in the 16th and 17th cents., see St. John's Coll. Mun. xx.
[80] Richard Briggs, vicar from 1558, and Adrian Whicker, vicar from 1599, had both previously been curates: *O.A.S. Rep.* 1914, 205; St. John's Coll. Reg. ii. 153b.
[81] Visitation Returns; q.v. also for what follows.
[82] O.R.O. Incl. award map.
[83] Par. Rec. docs.
[84] H. W. Taunt, *Kirtlington,* 10.

original jambs and imposts. The heads terminating the moulding on its western face are, however, later additions. The chancel was rebuilt on a rectangular plan later in the 12th century, but has been so heavily restored that none of its original features remain.

The aisled nave of three bays was built in the mid-13th century. The north aisle had a doorway, now blocked, and a 13th-century piscina shows that the chapel of St. Mary on the south side of the tower was built at the same period. Some of the capitals

in the chancel in 1691,[89] converted the south transept into a family vault and chapel in 1716, the transept then being ruinous.[90] The wrought-iron gates bearing the Dashwood arms are said to have come from Northbrook House.[91] He also constructed a gallery across the west end (1726).[92] In 1757 the church needed extensive repairs.[93] In 1761 'the parish church of Kirtlington having of late been very ruinous, as well in the body and structure, as in the pews, and other parts of the inside thereof', Sir James Dashwood 'repaired, new-pewed and

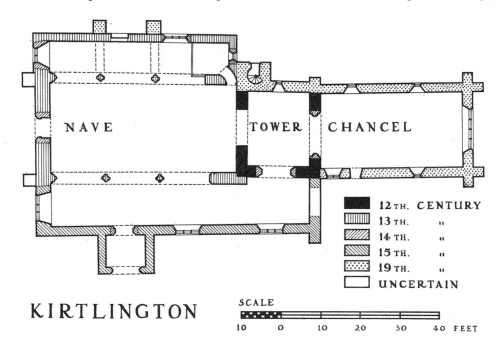

KIRTLINGTON

12TH. CENTURY
13TH. ,,
14TH. ,,
15TH. ,,
19TH. ,,
UNCERTAIN

SCALE
10   0   10   20   30   40 FEET

of the nave arcade are decorated with foliage sculpture, and one of the hood-moulds terminates in the head of a woman wearing a nose-band.[85] The east and west windows and the south and west doorways were inserted in the 14th century. The south porch and the clerestory were added in the 15th century. At the same time the wall of the south aisle, which had perhaps been pushed outwards by the original high-pitched roof, was rebuilt and given new windows.[86]

The pulpit is Jacobean. In 1661 six of the villagers were 'at the charge to beautify this church'.[87] The work perhaps included the hanging of the royal arms over the chancel arch, where they remained until 1854.[88]

Sir Robert Dashwood, whose 'black' was buried

decorated' it at his own cost.[94] In 1770, however, the tower was pulled down as unsafe.[95] Sir James Dashwood's legacy of £300 for its rebuilding was not taken up (1779),[96] and the church was without a tower for 80 years.[97] Between 1852 and 1854 the church was restored, partly at Sir George Dashwood's expense.[98] The work included the building of the present tower (architect Benjamin Ferrey), the erection of internal and external buttresses to support the wall of the north aisle, the removal of the gallery and the old square pews, paving with Minton tiles, and the installation of a new font. In 1877 the chancel was very thoroughly restored by Sir G. Gilbert Scott at Sir Henry and Lady Dashwood's expense.[99] Some further restoration was done in 1891 and 1905.[1]

[85] For other examples see R. P. Howgrave-Graham, 'Notes on some medieval European nose-bands', *Jnl. Brit. Arch. Assoc.* xvi. 87–89.
[86] Taunt, op. cit. 14.
[87] Tablet noted by Rawlinson, now removed: *Par. Coll.* ii. 197.
[88] The arms are described as 'Carolean': J. Townsend, *Oxon. Dashwoods*, 42.
[89] Tombstone against external N. wall of chancel.
[90] Oxf. Dioc. c 104, f. 112.
[91] Inf. Mr. J. Eeley, Northbrook Farm.
[92] *Oxon. Dashwoods*, 12; MS. Dunkin 439/3, f. 329.
[93] Oxf. Archd. Oxon. d 13, f. 32.
[94] Oxf. Dioc. c 455, f. 84; cf. faculty, ibid. c 434, ff. 47–48.
[95] *Oxon. Dashwoods*, 30. According to MS. Dunkin 439/3, f. 329, the dowager Lady Dashwood 'considered it dangerous and refused to go to church until her whim was com-

plied with'.
[96] *Oxon. Dashwoods*, 30.
[97] A water-colour painted in 1784 by the third Lady Dashwood hangs in the vestry. It shows that both the chancel and the stump of the tower were crenellated, as do Buckler drawings from SW. and SE. (1824–5) in MS. Top. Oxon. a 67, ff. 358–9. For a reproduction of the SE. view, see plate facing p. 220. For an account of the interior of the church before the 1852–4 restoration, see note of the fourth Lady Dashwood's description in Par. Rec. Revd. J. Deane's Log Bk. 45 and MS. Dunkin 439/3, f. 329.
[98] Faculty of 1852 in Oxf. Dioc. Reg. Bishop's Act Bk.; Par. Rec. Vestry Rec.; MS. Top. Oxon. c 105, ff. 102–3; *Oxon. Dashwoods*, 42; *Wilb. Visit.* 85.
[99] MS. Top. Oxon. c 105, ff. 102–3; *Oxon. Dashwoods*, 46; brass plate in chancel.
[1] MS. Top. Oxon. c 105, ff. 104–6; *Oxon. Dashwoods*, 46.

Wall-paintings of St. George and St. Christopher, which were rediscovered in 1905, are mainly of the late 15th century.[2]

The organ was placed in the Dashwood chapel in 1877; since about 1839, when 'the old Church band of clarinet and bassoon' had been done away with, singing had been accompanied by a barrel-organ.[3] The organ obscures a monument, made by William and Thomas Williams of Middleton Stoney in 1724, to many of the Dashwoods (including the first three baronets) on the east wall of the transept, a 13th-century piscina in the south wall, and a number of hatchments.[4]

Brass plates in the south transept and chancel commemorate the 4th and 5th baronets. The earliest monuments are of the 17th century. An undated tablet in the north aisle commemorates Rowland Bennet, who acquired Bennet's Farm at Northbrook in 1605;[5] three other 17th-century tablets to members of the Hall family are on the exterior of the south wall. The only 18th-century wall monuments, other than the Dashwood memorial, are to James Evans, described as *regius satelles* (i.e. a royal sergeant) (d. 1702), and Ralph Rawlins of Northbrook (d. 1725) and Mary his wife, who died at the age of 97. In the nave is a tablet to John David, Earl of Leven and Melville (d. 1913). There are also two tablets to 19th-century incumbents, both Fellows of St. John's: James Saunders (d. 1838) and James Guillemard (d. 1858).

In 1552 the church owned a chalice, two copes, and four vestments, and there was a light with lands worth 1s. a year.[6] A silver-gilt service, consisting of chalice, paten cover, large paten, pair of flagons, and an almsplate, were given by Sir Robert Dashwood in 1723.[7] Nearly all the bells, and also the sanctus bell, date from 1718, when the original peal of five was increased to eight at the Dashwoods' expense.[8]

The parish registers earlier than 1800 have been lost, with the exception of one for the years 1558–1699,[9] and a register of marriages for 1754–1818.

NONCONFORMITY. In the late 16th and early 17th centuries the holders of the manor, the Ardens, of the same family as the Ardens of Cottisford,[10] were Roman Catholics. Henry Arden was fined in 1592,[11] and Jane and Mary Arden some years later.[12] The latter was still a recusant in 1643, as was Margaret Arden,[13] who married George Napier (d. 1671), a prominent Oxford Catholic.[14] There

were also a number of other Catholics, including several yeomen.[15] George Napier, 'the martyr' (d. 1610), is said to have been arrested in Kirtlington.[16] In the second half of the century Roman Catholicism died out; there was only one Catholic both in 1676 and 1706.[17]

Four Protestant nonconformists were listed in 1676,[18] but otherwise dissent scarcely existed until the early 19th century. In 1821 the first meeting-house was licensed, and several others were licensed in the next ten years.[19] By 1824 Kirtlington was in the Oxford Methodist Circuit,[20] and in 1830 a Wesleyan chapel was built,[21] which was replaced in 1852 by the present chapel, 'a very neat stone building' served by local preachers.[22] At that time the congregation was said to number between 70 and 100;[23] some were described by the incumbent as 'bigoted Dissenters'. He also stated, incorrectly it seems, that there were two dissenting places of worship, a Wesleyan and a Reformed Methodist.[24] In 1867 the chapel came under the United Methodist Free Church organization.[25] There are now (1954) about six members.[26]

SCHOOLS. In 1583 John Phillips, an Oxfordshire woollen draper, bequeathed a house in Woodstock, rented at £1 a year, 'towards the finding of a School-master in Kirtlington, if it shall fortune any school to be built or erected there'.[27] A free school for 32 poor children appears to have been founded by 1603,[28] but no building had been erected by 1613, when a tenement called the Church House was being used as 'a schoolhouse, courthouse and townhouse', and when it was alleged that the Ardens[29] had failed to implement the terms of Phillips's bequest. The Commissioners for Charitable Uses appointed trustees for the Church House, which continued to serve as a school, and ordered that the endowment should be used as originally intended.[30]

In 1702 it was complained that the rents, then £6 a year, were often paid to a schoolmistress: a new master was therefore appointed.[31] By 1759 the school had closed, as the Woodstock property was too decayed to yield any rent.[32] In 1766 the property was let to the Duke of Marlborough on a repairing lease at a rent of £4 4s. a year.[33] Between 1774 and 1778 the school reopened with Sir James Dashwood and the vicar as its governors[34] and was subsequently supported by the Dashwoods as well as by the endowment. It had 30 pupils, 22 of them free scholars,

[2] O.A.S. Rep. 1933, 20; Jnl. Brit. Arch. Assoc. 3rd ser. xii. 33.
[3] Par. Rec. Deane's Log Bk. 45.
[4] For arms on the monuments and hatchments see Bodl. G.A. Oxon. 16° 217, pp. 175, 176b, 177; ibid. 4° 688, pp. 196–7.
[5] Dashwood D. box 5, bdle 'Bennet's Farm 1605–95'.
[6] Chant. Cert. 89, 31.
[7] Evans, Ch. Plate.
[8] Ch. Bells Oxon. ii. 192–4.
[9] Bodl. MS. dep. b 59 (abstract in par. chest). There are diocesan transcripts for the years 1678–79, 1720–77 (with some gaps), and 1777–1853: Oxf. Dioc. c 554. Accts. of Surveyors of Highways (1778–1818) also survive.
[10] Oxon. Visit. 207; see above, p. 223.
[11] Recusant Roll 1592–3 (C.R.S. xviii), 260.
[12] Salter, Oxon. Recusants, 16, 33, and passim.
[13] E 179/164/496A.
[14] Stapleton, Cath. Miss. 216.
[15] Recusant Roll 1592–3, 257, 259; Salter, Oxon. Recusants, passim; E 179/164/496A.
[16] A. Wood, Annals, ed. P. Bliss, 149–51.

[17] Compton Census; Oxoniensia xiii. 78.
[18] Compton Census.
[19] Oxf. Dioc. c 644, ff. 237, 241, 248 (1821); ibid. c 645, f. 138 (1829), ff. 144, 165 (1830).
[20] Circuit Plan penes Oxon. V.C.H. Cttee, New Bodleian.
[21] H.O. 129/5/158.
[22] Lascelles Oxf. Dir. (1853), 312; Cowley Rd. Methodist Church, 1852 Trust Deed: inf. Revd. H. Tomlinson.
[23] H.O. 129/5/158.
[24] Wilb. Visit.; cf. Kelly's Dir. Oxon. (1854); Oxf. Dioc. c 332 (1866).
[25] Cowley Rd. Methodist Ch. Trust deed.
[26] Methodist Ch. Oxf. Circuit Plan, no. 273 (1954).
[27] C 93/5/6.
[28] Oxf. Dioc. d 553.
[29] See above, p. 223.
[30] C 93/5/6.
[31] Ibid. 46/29.
[32] Oxf. Dioc. d 553, d 556.
[33] Ibid. d 559; 12th Rep. Com. Char. 306.
[34] Oxf. Dioc. d 564; c 327, p. 59.

in 1808, but taught only reading to the boys and reading and plain sewing to the girls.[35] Instruction in the catechism had been introduced by 1811.[36] In 1824 the £4 4s. rent was being used to pay part of the expense of teaching and clothing the free scholars, then 20 in number, Sir Henry Dashwood meeting the rest.[37] By 1833 the endowed school appears to have been virtually amalgamated with two other schools which had been founded in the village.[38]

Two 'common day schools for the poorer class', with 15 and 8 pupils respectively, had appeared by 1808.[39] One of these may have been the infants' school with 20 pupils which was supported by Sir Henry Dashwood and the parents in 1815. The other was replaced by a day school opened in 1814 which was supported by the weekly payments of the scholars, and which received the children who left the infants' school at the age of five. It was run on the National Society's plan, which was unpopular with the wealthier farmers since it put their children 'on a level with the poor', and because its methods of instruction seemed too elementary, especially when they were used to 'hear their children read, as they imagined well, in the Bible'. There were 41 children on the books, but attendance was so irregular that 'from want of practice the teachers are unequal to their office'.[40]

In 1833[41] the three schools had an attendance of 40 boys, 34 girls and 64 infants.[42] New buildings were erected in 1834 on land leased from Sir George Dashwood.[43] Evening classes in winter and a singing class for adults were held in 1854.[44] As late as 1871 there were said to be three schools,[45] but it is likely that they had long been three departments—boys, girls, and infants—of the same school. In 1867 the endowment, no doubt augmented by the Dash-

woods, amounted to £40 a year. Some pupils paid 2d. to 6d. a week, and there were three teachers, a certificated master, a sewing-mistress, and an infant-mistress. Attendance figures were 96 in 1867, 133 in 1889, and 111 in 1906.[46] Senior pupils from Bletchingdon came to Kirtlington from 1928 to 1947, when the school was reorganized for juniors and infants, and seniors were transferred to Woodstock Voluntary Secondary School. Kirtlington school was given aided status in 1951, and there were 91 pupils on the books in 1937 and 83 in 1954.[47] The endowment brought an income of £72 a year in 1955.[48]

CHARITIES. By will dated 1616 John Whicker, a London merchant, son of Adrian Whicker (vicar 1599–1616), left about 6 acres of land in Ambrosden to endow a charity for poor widows of Kirtlington.[49] In the 1820's the rent of the land, £8, was distributed annually to poor widows and widowers, each receiving from 6s. to 9s.[50] The income was £6 in 1954, when it was distributed to old people at Christmas.[51]

Robert Slatter gave £3 to the poor in 1649, and in 1664 six benefactors gave £2. These two charities, which were producing 3s. and 2s. a year respectively in 1786,[52] had been amalgamated under the name of Slatter's Charity by 1824, when 5s. was annually divided among ten poor widows.[53] Slatter's Charity was still in existence in 1852,[54] but it appears to have subsequently lapsed.

By the inclosure award of 1815 10 acres in Breach Furze were awarded to trustees for the poor in lieu of the poor's right of cutting furze for fuel on the Breach Common.[55] In 1954 this land was let at £12 10s. a year, and the rent was distributed to old people at Christmas in cash, instead of in the customary coal.[56]

LAUNTON

THIS large and very irregularly shaped parish of 2,818 acres lies between its market-town of Bicester and the Buckinghamshire border.[1] No boundary changes are recorded.[2] The Bicester–Buckingham road, which follows the line of the Roman road north from Alchester, bounds the parish on the north-west, tributary streams of the River Ray on the north and south, and the county boundary on the east. The zigzag line of the boundary with Bicester Market End and Wretchwick fields on the south-west appears to have followed the line of already existing furlongs. Geologically Launton lies mostly on the

Oxford Clay, but in the west it lies on the Cornbrash.[3] The soil is mostly clay, with some very good marl to the north-west of the village.[4]

The parish, which rises from 208 feet in the south to 270 feet in the north-east, is watered by a number of streams, feeders of the Ray, and connected by minor roads with Bicester and the surrounding villages. The Oxford and Bletchley section of the former L.M.S. Railway crosses the parish, and a station, ¾ mile north of the village, was opened in 1851.[5]

Launton lies in the south-western corner of the

35 Oxf. Dioc. d 707.
36 Ibid. c 327, p. 300.
37 12th Rep. Com. Char. 306–7.
38 Educ. Enq. Abstract, 726.
39 Oxf. Dioc. d 707.
40 Ibid. c 433.
41 In 1818 the incumbent reported that there were no schools (Educ. of Poor, 726). If this was so they cannot have been closed long: they were all in existence in 1817 (Oxf. Dioc. d 576) and the endowment school was open in 1824 (see above).
42 Educ. Enq. Abstract, 726.
43 Kelly's Dir. Oxon. (1887); Voluntary Sch. Ret.
44 Wilb. Visit.
45 Elem. Educ. Ret.
46 Schools Enq.; Schools Returns; Vol. Sch. Ret.

47 Inf. Oxon. Educ. Cttee.
48 Inf. the Revd. A. L. Gutch.
49 Will cited in Vestry Rec. minutes 1875; ibid. 1868.
50 12th Rep. Com. Char. 307.
51 Inf. the Revd. A. L. Gutch.
52 Char. Don. ii. 989.
53 12th Rep. Com. Char. 307.
54 Gardner, Dir. Oxon.
55 O.R.O. Incl. award.
56 Inf. the vicar.
1 O.S. Map 6", xvii, xxiii (1884); ibid. 2½", 42/52, 62 (1951).
2 Census, 1881, 1951.
3 G.S. Map 1", xlv SE.
4 Kelly's Dir. Oxon. (1939); local inf.
5 W. L. Steel, Hist. L.N.W.R. 185.

parish, on a low ridge between two small tributaries of the Ray. Its Saxon name means the Long Tun,[6] and the original settlement was probably along the line of Back Lanes, which ran north-east and south-west of the church. It was a large village in the Middle Ages,[7] and was relatively large in the 17th century, since as many as 46 houses appear in the hearth-tax list.[8] There was no great house but a number of comfortable gentlemen's houses and farm-houses. These included in 1665 the Rectory, 3 houses which were taxed on 4 or 5 hearths, and 7 taxed on 3 hearths each.[9] The 18th-century village as shown on Davis's map of 1797[10] lay on the south side of the Caversfield road, formerly known as Skimmingdishlane, and on a road crossing it at right angles, which ran from the town green lying to the south of the Caversfield road north-eastwards to Launton Field.[11] Eighteenth-century incumbents estimated that there were about 70 houses,[12] and in 1801 Launton was described as a village of moderate size with about 90 families.[13] In the 19th century there was a striking increase in population, and instead of the 66 village houses recorded in 1811 there were 163 in 1851. By 1901, however, there were only 129 inhabited dwellings.[14]

Chief among the new 19th-century buildings were Zion chapel near the green (1807);[15] the school, built in 1839 and enlarged in 1881, 1896, and 1946;[16] an Independent chapel with a simple classical façade dated 1850; and the reading-room, erected in 1894 and destroyed in 1919.[17] Much of the new building, which included a row of stone cottages, was on the outskirts of the village at the east end of Station Road.

Among 20th-century additions are the parish hall in Church Lane (1930) and Sherwood Close to the south-west, which has been built since 1945.[18] It contains 26 houses built by the County Council. There are also twelve other council houses.

The village still has an unusual number of well-preserved stone houses and cottages, of which many date from the 17th century. Some are in Station Road, the old way to Launton Field. There is Yew Tree farm-house, a two-storied house built on an L-shaped plan. It has a pigeon-loft built into the upper story of one wing. Laurels Farm and Grange Farm have a similar L-shaped plan. The latter is dated 1683 and has attic dormers, a hipped roof with brown tiles, which are commonly used in the village, and brick chimney-stacks. This farm and the pound opposite marked the eastern limit of the village in 1880.[19] Box Tree Farm, formerly two houses, is another building which is mainly of 17th-century date. The front has been rebuilt; it bears the inscription M:W.E. 1710 and has a simply moulded eaves cornice.

In the other of the two main village streets Manor Farm and the Rectory, standing on either side of the church, form an isolated group to the north-west over ¼ mile from the cross-roads. The farm-house is built on a long rectangular plan and probably mainly dates from the early 17th century, though one of its doorways is of 16th-century date. It has a large room with walls 2 feet thick which was formerly used as the Court Room, and at right angles to it there is a turret staircase.

The present rectory is in the main a 17th-century building, although some 16th-century work survives. Blomfield states that Henry Rowlands, rector from 1581 to 1600, enlarged the house[20] and also planted the yew hedge which is still a notable feature of the garden. Bishop Skinner was rector at the time of the fire which was mentioned in 1646.[21] It was evidently not a large house at this period as it was only taxed on six hearths in 1665.[22] In 1716 it again suffered from fire and was repaired by Thomas Goodwin (rector 1701–19).[23] In the early 19th century Dunkin describes it as 'plain and substantial' and considered it the chief mansion in the parish. It was then an L-shaped building of two stories. He admired the fine paintings in the hall, and the garden.[24] The out-buildings at about this time included two stables, a coach-house, and a large stone barn.[25]

In 1838 the house was enlarged by James Blomfield at a cost of £1,500, of which about half was borrowed from Queen Anne's Bounty.[26] The builder was John Plowman.[27] The plan of the present house is rectangular. The main building has two stories, is built of coursed rubble, and is roofed with brown tiles. The addition is built of coursed rubble and is roofed with slate. There is a fine 18th-century staircase, and some early 17th-century and early 18th-century panelling in the interior. In 1940 the rectory was used as a Missionary College, and was later requisitioned by the R.A.F. and used as a W.R.A.F. hostel. In the 1950's it was divided and only part is now used as the rectory.[28]

The village's two public houses may also date from the 17th century. The Bull Inn is a two-story house of coursed rubble with an attic dormer. It has brick chimney-stacks, casement windows, and a roof of part thatch and part tiles. The other public house, the 'Black Bull', forms part of a group of old houses which includes West End Farm and one dated 1697. It was mentioned by name in 1784, but may have been the house licensed in 1735.[29] The 'Greyhound', which closed in 1900, a two-storied house of coursed rubble, bears the inscription 1682 W.J:D. It has casement windows, tiled roofs, and brick chimney-stacks. Other public houses were the 'Pheasant' and the 'Fox and Hounds', which closed

[6] *P.N. Oxon.* (E.P.N.S.), i. 228. Roman coins found to the north of the village are the only evidence for earlier occupation (*V.C.H. Oxon.* i. 340).

[7] See below, p. 239.

[8] *Hearth Tax Oxon.* 236 for 1662 tax.

[9] Ibid. 208.

[10] Davis, *Oxon. Map.*

[11] The 'greene' is mentioned in 1601 (Oxf. Archd. Oxon. c 141, p. 385). It is not marked on 19th-cent. maps and was presumably inclosed in 1814.

[12] Oxf. Dioc. d 553, d 556.

[13] Ibid. c 327, p. 300.

[14] *Census,* 1811, 1851, 1901.

[15] Dunkin, *Oxon.* i. 304.

[16] School minute bks.

[17] Inf. Mr. F. Sharpe, Launton.

[18] Inf. Ploughley R.D.C.

[19] O.S. Map 25″, xxiii (1881).

[20] Bodl. dep. b 63.

[21] *Walker Rev.* 12.

[22] *Hearth Tax Oxon.* 208.

[23] Bodl. dep. b 63, f. 158b. The registers were lost in this fire (*Par. Coll.* ii. 197).

[24] Dunkin, *Oxon.* i. 303–4.

[25] Oxf. Dioc. c 449, f. 4. For an illustration see plate facing p. 241.

[26] Oxf. Dioc. b 70, f. 459.

[27] Details of the work done by him over and above the contract are attached to Bodl. dep. b 63.

[28] Inf. Mr. F. Sharpe.

[29] O.R.O. Victlrs.' recog.

in the second half of the 19th century and in 1930 respectively.[30]

A number of houses, such as Box Tree Farm, were modernized and there was some new building in the 18th century. Launton House in West End was the main contribution. It was probably built by John Ashby, a London haberdasher, who was living there in the early 19th century, and it is shown on Davis's map of 1797.[31] Its plan is rectangular and its three stories are built of red brick on a stone base. The stone dressings of the porch and the window surrounds came from Ambrosden Park (demolished in 1768). The tiled roof is hipped and screened by a parapet. The front door has plain stone pilasters supporting a moulded wooden pediment. The only outlying farm in the 18th century was Hareleys or 'Hoar Leys', as it was called in 1738.[32] A windmill stood in Great Stone Field in the 17th century[33] and a water-mill stood on the brook which crosses Church Lane in the 19th century. The site is still known locally as the Sluice.[34]

The village has had some eminent rectors: Bishop Skinner, rector 1632–63 and Bishop of Oxford 1641–63, was at the Rectory during the Commonwealth period and wrote in 1662 that he had secretly ordained 400–500 priests.[35] Philip Stubbs (rector 1719–38) was the author in 1704 of the first report of the Society for the Propagation of the Gospel.[36] Canon J. C. Blomfield (rector 1850–95) was the son of James Blomfield, a Launton rector, and was a local historian of some repute.[37]

The Deeley family may also be mentioned for its long connexion with Launton: two of the family are recorded as early as 1601. For the most part yeomen farmers, like John Deeley of Biggen Farm and William Deely (d. 1688), some of the family rose into the ranks of the gentry.[38] They succeeded the Oakleys, a 17th-century Shropshire family, as tenants of the manor farm.[39] There is a local tradition that the last of the Cottesford family, which leased the manor in the 15th and 16th centuries, married one of the Deeleys.[40] Mr. Deeley is the present lessee of Manor Farm.

MANOR. Edward the Confessor gave *LAUNTON* to the Abbey of St. Peter at Westminster at the dedication of the church on 28 December 1065. Three of the documents which record this gift are spurious,[41] but a fourth—a vernacular writ in the Confessor's name[42]—is genuine, and the authenticity of Edward's gift to Westminster is not in doubt.[43] Domesday Book states that Edward gave $2\frac{1}{2}$ hides in Launton, whose soke formerly belonged to Kirtlington, to St. Peter of Westminster and to

Baldwin his *filiolus*.[44] It has been suggested that Baldwin was a novice or monk of Westminster, and that the purpose of Edward's gift to the abbey was to provide for his maintenance.[45] Nothing further is known about him. Westminster's title to Launton was never disputed and the medieval descent of the manor is uneventful. Rent of £19 8s. 9d. a year in Launton was assigned to the monks' kitchen by Abbot William de Humez in the early 13th century[46] and from this date the manor formed part of the convent's lands.

Launton was sequestrated on the surrender of Westminster Abbey in January 1540.[47] In August 1542 it was granted to the Dean and Chapter of the cathedral church at Westminster.[48] In 1556 it was surrendered to the Crown and granted to the abbot and convent of the restored monastic foundation.[49] In 1557 the abbot and convent granted an annuity of £30 for life from their manors of Launton and Wheathampstead (Herts.) to Alphonso de Salynes, clerk, and an annuity of £4 for life from Launton to William Brome, gentleman.[50] Launton was again surrendered in 1560, and granted to the Dean and Chapter of the collegiate church at Westminster.[51]

In November 1645 a committee of Lords and Commons was set up to adminster the lands and revenues of the 'delinquent' Dean and Chapter of Westminster.[52] Launton came under the provisions of this act. In 1644, however, Dr. Thomas Wilson, Prebendary and Treasurer of Westminster Abbey, had obtained from the king at Oxford a warrant to collect the rents due from the abbey lands.[53] By virtue of this warrant he appears to have collected the rents due from Launton. Accordingly, in 1645, Richard Oakley, Receiver General of Westminster Abbey and lessee of Launton manor, testified that he had received no profit from Launton for over two years.[54] In April 1649 the lands and revenues of all deans and chapters were vested in a body of trustees appointed by the Commons.[55] In September 1649 Launton was exempted from the operation of this act and assigned to the maintenance of Westminster School.[56] Thus its connexion with Westminster was maintained for the greater part of the Interregnum. Finally, in 1860 the lands in Launton belonging to the Dean and Chapter of Westminster were vested in the Ecclesiastical Commissioners.[57]

The first lease of the manor was granted in 1526 (see below). A later lease was the subject of a suit in Chancery in the early 17th century. In 1600 Francis Ewer, lessee of Launton, borrowed £1,600 from his brother Edward, who at the same time was granted certain lands in the manor at reduced rents. On the death of Francis, intestate, in 1604, the lease

[30] Inf. Mr. F. Sharpe.
[31] Davis, *Oxon. Map.*   [32] Oxf. Dioc. d 553.
[33] Oxf. Archd. Oxon. c 141, p. 387.
[34] Inf. Mr. F. Sharpe.
[35] *Walker Rev.* 12. For him see also *D.N.B.*
[36] *D.N.B.*
[37] Foster, *Alumni*; for James Blomfield see below, pp. 240, 241.
[38] *Par. Coll.* ii. 198; MS. Top. Oxon. c 49, f. 107.
[39] Dunkin, *Oxon.* i. 316. The church formerly contained memorials to Samuel Oakeley, gent. (d. 1638), and Richard Oakeley, esq. (d. 1653) (*Par. Coll.* ii. 198).
[40] Dunkin, *Oxon.* i. 316.
[41] Dugd. *Mon.* i. 293–5; Westminster Domesday, ff. 43b–45b; R. Widmore, *Enq. into Time of 1st Foundation of Westm. Abbey* (1743), App. 2.
[42] *Anglo-Saxon Writs,* ed. Florence Harmer, p. 360.

[43] Ibid. pp. 323–4.
[44] *V.C.H. Oxon.* i. 400.
[45] H. Ellis, *General Introduction to Domesday Book* (1833), i. 304 n.
[46] Westm. Domesday, f. 629.
[47] *L. & P. Hen. VIII,* xv, p. 24.
[48] Ibid. xvii, p. 392.
[49] *Cal. Pat.* 1555–7, 349.
[50] Westm. Abbey Reg. Bk. iv, ff. 17–17b.
[51] *Cal. Pat.* 1558–60, 397.
[52] *Acts and Ords. of Interr.* ed. Firth and Rait, i. 803–5.
[53] Westminster Abbey Muniments (henceforth cited as W.A.M.) 15756.
[54] Ibid. 15751, 15755; see also 15753.
[55] *Acts and Ords. of Interr.* ii. 81–104.
[56] Ibid. 261.
[57] *Lond. Gaz.* 24 Feb. 1860.

passed to his widow, Joan. Edward Ewer now claimed, however, that the money lent to his brother had in fact been the purchase price of the lease of Launton. In 1604 the court decided in favour of Joan and ordered Edward to pay the arrears of rent for the lands in Launton leased to him by Francis. Further claims by Edward and counter-claims by Joan resulted in a second hearing. Finally, in 1605 it was decided that the lease should remain in Joan's hands, that Roger Mountney, her second husband, should find security for the payment of £1,200 to Joan's children by her former marriage (Edward Ewer having questioned Joan's use of moneys received on their behalf), and that Edward should pay £300 to Roger in discharge of his debts.[58] In 1608 Mountney himself was granted the lease of the manor.

The following list gives the dates of all known leases of the manor, the names of the lessees, the term for which each lease was granted, and the rent due. No information is available concerning fines paid: 1526, John Manning, yeoman of Westminster, 31 years, 6 marks;[59] 1542, Thomas Perkin, yeoman of Eynsham, 65 years, 6 marks;[60] 1576, Ralph Heydon, remaining interest in the above lease;[61] 1598, Humphrey Moore, yeoman of Bicester, 3 lives, £4, and 8 beeves and 40 muttons or £36 13s. 4d. p.a.;[62] 1600, Francis Ewer, gent. of Launton*;[63] 1608, Roger Mountney, gent. of Norfolk*;[64] 1616, Sir John Dormer, of Dorton (Bucks.)*;[65] 1620, idem*;[66] about 1630, Richard Oakley, of Oakley (Salop.), 3 lives;[67] 1663, William Oakley, of Oakley*; 1672, idem, 3 lives, £4, and 4 beeves and 20 muttons or £18 6s. 8d. p.a.; 1683, idem*; 1697, George Walcot, merchant of London, and John Crump, gent. of Barnard's Inn*; 1704, idem*; 1737, Sir Archer Croft, of Croft Castle, Hereford*; 1747, John Walcot and Andrew Hill, both of Salop.*; 1766, Earl of Jersey*; 1769, Earl of Guildford and George Grenville of Wotton (Bucks.), trustees under the will of the last lessee*; 1810, Duke of Bedford and George Bainbridge of Southampton*; 1826, idem*.[68]

ECONOMIC HISTORY. In 1291 the manor, including rents, meadows, the mill and court, was valued at £16 11s. 2d. a year, its flocks and beasts at £1.[69] In 1535 the rents and farms of Launton were valued at £17 17s. 1½d. a year, the site of the manor at £4 a year, and the perquisites of the court at £2 1s. 11d. a year.[70]

Little is known about the topography of pre-inclosure Launton. A West Field and an East Field are mentioned in the 14th century; Clay Field, Little and Great Stone Fields, Middle Field and Wake Field in 17th-century terriers.[71] There are indications that a two-field system persisted at least until the end of the 16th century.[72] From the 15th century onwards two harvest reeves were elected annually, one for the west end of the village, and the other for the east end.[73] In the 16th century the area of pasture, meadow, and waste land at Launton was estimated at 367 a. 3 r. 25¾ p., measuring 18 feet to the pole.[74] The medieval area is not known. The common meadows are named in the 17th century as Debden, Padons, Corn Slade, and Quadies.[75] The common cow pastures are named in the 18th century as Wetherell, Drannell, Peasebridge, Town Slade, and the Stone Pits.[76] Peasebridge, or Peasebreach, was 45 acres in extent, and in return for their rights of common in it the copyholders paid yearly to the Dean and Chapter of Westminster, as lords of the manor, 26s. 8d. for the provision of a boar, and £10 at Whitsuntide for the provision of 20 fat wethers.[77]

Small inclosures for pasture appear to have been allowed to the individual customary in the 14th century,[78] but the first extensive inclosure of pasture was made in 1582 by agreement between the copyholders of the manor and Ralph Heydon, farmer of the demesne.[79] Heydon was allotted 64 acres of pasture and meadow to hold in severalty, half in Stone Field and half in Broadmoor Slade, this allotment to remain to his successors as farmers of the demesne. An additional allotment of 8 acres was made to Heydon in respect of a yardland freehold in his tenure. He was to be excluded from a share in the remaining commons. The copyholders were granted permission to inclose their own share of the commons at the rate of 8 acres per yardland arable. About 150 inclosures, mainly in the south and west of the village, are said to have been made as a result of this composition.[80]

Claims to intercommoning caused some friction between Launton and neighbouring vills. In 1302 an exchange was made between the Abbot and Convent of Westminster and the Rector and College of Ashridge (Herts.) whereby the latter were to inclose 8 acres of common pasture at Blackthorn, Ambrosden, and the former were to inclose 8 acres in the common pasture at Launton lying between the vill and 'Watebrok' and between 'Bradelakestrem' and 'le Brechedech'.[81] The rights of each party in Blackthorn and Launton pastures, except in these inclosures, were to continue. A similar exchange was made in 1302 between the Abbot and Convent of Westminster and the Prior and Convent of Bicester, whereby the latter were to inclose 8 acres in the common pasture near their sheep-walk at Wretchwick in Bicester parish, and the former were to

---

[58] Reg. Bk. x, ff. 198–201; Bodl. dep. b 63, 102–4. See also Cal. Chan. Proc. (Rec. Com.), i. 279.

[59] Reg. Bk. ii, f. 225b.

[60] Ibid. iii, ff. 5–6.

[61] Ibid. vi, ff. 170b–172b.

[62] Ibid. viii, ff. 37–40. The terms of this lease are common to many of the leases. Hereafter they are indicated by an asterisk only.

[63] Ibid. ff. 101–3.

[64] Ibid. x, ff. 192–4. This lease was part of the settlement of the lawsuit arising from the previous lease.

[65] Ibid. xi, ff. 311–14.

[67] Ibid. xii, ff. 90b–94.

[67] W.A.M. 15747, 15753.

[68] Reg. Bk. xvii, ff. 59b–62b; xix, ff. 147b–150b; xxi, ff. 254–256b; xxiv, ff. 233b–236; xxvi, ff. 64b–67; xxxvi, ff. 119–121b; xxxviii, ff. 180–183b; xliii, ff. 71–76; xliv,

ff. 340–346b; lvii, ff. 212–14b; lx, ff. 179b–182b.

[69] Tax. Eccl. (Rec. Com.), 45.

[70] Valor Eccl. (Rec. Com.), i. 416.

[71] W.A.M. 15346–7; Westm. Abbey, Recent Chapter Office (henceforth cited as R.C.O.), Launton box 1.

[72] W.A.M. 15549.

[73] Ibid. 15498.

[74] Ibid. 15728.

[75] R.C.O. Launton box 1.

[76] Field orders 1726 (ibid.).

[77] W.A.M. 33246, f. 125; R.C.O. Launton box 1 (field orders 1726); ibid. box 2.

[78] W.A.M. 15345–7.

[79] Ibid. 15728.

[80] Bodl. dep. b 63, f. 101b.

[81] W.A.M. 15690; see also 15422.

inclose 8 acres in the same pasture at Launton.[82] Memory of these exchanges seems to have faded, for in 1349 the customaries of Launton alleged that the Rector of Ashridge had wrongly inclosed 8 acres of common pasture in Wretchwick and Blackthorn appurtenant to their tenements.[83] The commoners of Stratton claimed one 'hoke' of meadow every other year at 'Strethambrok' in Launton.[84] These claims were disputed. The claim of the tenants of Caversfield (Bucks.) to common at Launton was allowed in return for the performance of ploughing services and one harvest boon per tenant, but failure to perform these services caused repeated complaints.[85] The Abbot of Westminster also disposed of pasture at *Podele*.[86]

The prevalence of trespass—in many cases with large flocks of sheep—suggests a serious shortage of pasture in medieval Launton, but the stint of pasture in this period is not known. In the 16th century a cottager was allowed common for one cow and was at liberty to lease common for twenty sheep from a copyhold yardlander.[87] The inclosure agreement of 1582 allowed for the inclosure of eight acres common pasture and meadow per yardland arable.[88] In the 18th century a stint of 4 beasts, 3 horses or mares, and 40 sheep for every yardland was in force. It is interesting to note that some 18th-century orders prescribe balks at least 2 feet wide in the Stone Field between 'neighbour and neighbour' and prohibit the use of harrows on the hay growing on balks.[89]

The following medieval customs are worthy of note. Vacant lands were filled by elections in the manorial court;[90] exemption from entry fine and from heriot on surrender was sometimes granted to the tenant so chosen.[91] Widows were allowed their free bench for a year and a day; if they continued as tenants after that term they were obliged to marry or to fine to avoid marriage.[92] Husbands were elected for such widows and for unmarried female customary tenants, and fines were imposed for the refusal of either party to comply. Thus in 1326 John Alisot and John de Baynton, elected in turn to marry Agnes, widow of William King, paid 3s. 4d. and 1s. 6d. respectively to be quit. Agnes herself refused to marry the third man elected, and the seizure of her lands and chattels was ordered.[93] Dower amounting to one-third of a customary holding was allowed.[94] Heriot consisted of the best beast. It was paid at the death of the customary tenant or at the expiry of his widow's free bench. A widow holding for more than a year and a day would also pay heriot on the final surrender. In the case of a conjoint tenancy it was usual to postpone heriot until the death of the survivor.[95] A tenant in villeinage might not sell his ox or his horse without licence.[96] The reason given in 1406 for this rule is not that the sale would diminish his wainage, but that the lord must have the first refusal.[97] Two customs concerning villein tenure are

of interest because, but for evidence to the contrary, they might be considered marks only of villein status. A villein might not marry his daughter outside the manor without licence,[98] and his sons might not receive the tonsure without licence.[99] Three customs constituted the peculiar disabilities of unfree status at Launton in the later Middle Ages: a serf might not leave the manor; he might not acquire a free tenement,[1] and he must pay merchet on the marriage of his daughters. The first rule might be relaxed but, in general, was strictly enforced. Chevage, the annual fine paid by a villein living outside the manor, is significantly rare, and would still have been uncommon had the small number of fugitive serfs mentioned in the 14th- and 15th-century court rolls been brought under contribution. In 1372 one John Herberd of Brightwell, who was proved subsequently to be a serf of Launton, brought a plea against the Abbot of Westminster in the court of the steward, alleging trespass in that the abbot had arrested him within the verge and imprisoned him for three days.[2] Herberd's initiative is in no sense typical of villeinage at Launton, however: manorialism here was vigorous in its latter day.

The following customs were agreed in 1582 between the copyholders of the manor and the farmer of the demesne. Guardianship of the heir of a deceased copyholder belongs to the next of kin not in the line of inheritance to the lands, unless the heir's father or mother shall have appointed otherwise; two years' rent shall be paid as entry fine, and the best beast as heriot, when the holding is not less than a cottage or quarterland. If the beast be a horse, mare, or gelding, 40s. shall be paid instead. Heriot for a cottage or holding of less than a quarterland shall be 2s. 6d. Every copyholder may take the woods and trees growing on his land, but when a timber tree is felled two young trees shall be planted. Every copyholder may lease his land for 21 years without licence.[3]

Two conventional estimates of the area of the demesne survive. The Hundred Rolls state that the Abbot of Westminster had three hides in demesne at Launton.[4] A 16th-century inclosure agreement mentions 8 yardlands arable in demesne.[5] Estimates of demesne tillage are given in the ministers' accounts between 1328 and 1373.[6] The tillage varied between 180 and 140 acres a year, except in the last five years of the period, when it was little more than 100 acres. Earlier accounts covering the period before 1328, although omitting these estimates, state the amount of seed corn used each year.[7] Calculations using this information show that between 1267 and 1293 an average of 220 acres was sown a year. After 1293 the figure falls below 200 acres. The average annual tillage fell by about 60 acres in the course of the century 1267–1367.

Leasing of demesne acres began in 1332 but did

[82] W.A.M. 15692.
[83] Ibid. 15435.
[84] Ibid. 15441.
[85] Ibid. 15427, 15431, 15457.
[86] Ibid. 15423; see above, p. 149.
[87] W.A.M. 15533, 15548.
[88] Ibid. 15728.
[89] Field orders 1726 (R.C.O. Launton box 1).
[90] Ibid. 15428.
[91] Ibid. 15449.
[92] Ibid. 15446.
[93] Ibid. 15429. At the next court Agnes was allowed to surrender her lands to the use of her daughter.

[94] Ibid. 15421, 15428.
[95] Ibid. 15457-8.
[96] Ibid. 9287.
[97] Ibid. 15466.
[98] Ibid. 9287.
[99] Ibid. 15424.
[1] Ibid. 15448.
[2] Westm. Domesday, f. 277.
[3] Ibid. 15728.
[4] *Rot. Hund.* (Rec. Com.), ii. 832.
[5] W.A.M. 15728.
[6] Ibid. 15336-69.
[7] Ibid. 15286-335.

not become extensive. The demesne was thus virtually intact when in 1372 it was farmed for seven years at a rent of £14 a year, including labour services, the dovecot and the mill.[8] The farm was renewed in 1379 for thirteen years for £12 a year, excluding the mill.[9] The rent had been reduced to £10 a year including the mill by 1408, and to £4 a year excluding the dovecot by 1423.[10]

A demesne windmill is mentioned at Launton in 1279.[11] This was farmed after 1292.[12]

Throughout the period of demesne cultivation the following full-time servants were employed at Launton: a bailiff, a reeve, four ploughmen (two *tenores* and two *fugatores*), a woman servant, a carter, a cowherd, and a shepherd. In some years there were employed also a swineherd, a smith, and a miller. It was usual to employ an extra woman servant, an extra carter, and a harrower for six or eight weeks in the spring, and a *messor* and reep-reeve for four or eight weeks in the harvest season. A second shepherd was frequently employed in the summer, and a shepherd's boy for the lambing season. Of these servants the reeve was the tenant of a servile holding of half a virgate. The *tenores* were tenants of servile holdings of half a virgate each until 1319; between 1319 and 1351 one or both were stipendiary; after 1351 both were invariably stipendiary. In 1284 and 1285 the full-time shepherd had a service holding. It appears from the court rolls that there was a number of service holdings at Launton and that the two *tenores* were chosen from the tenants of these holdings in rotation. Thus in 1297 an inquest named five holdings whose tenants formerly held the demesne plough: 'et sic videtur quod plures alii quam illi decem qui modo ad carucam domini tenendam ordinati sunt pro voluntate domini ad illud possunt assignari'.[13] In 1325 Richard and Alice de Ambresdon, tenants of one virgate by the service of holding the plough *quando accidit*, were freed from that service,[14] and in 1335 John de Baynton, who had been elected to marry a certain widow and hold her land in villeinage, was allowed to fine in the sum of 10s. for refusing to do so, 'et non plus que est de numero tenentium qui tenent carucam domini per annum'.[15]

The stipendiary, full-time manorial servant was paid mainly in corn: the *fugatores* and the carter received one quarter every nine weeks (after 1352, every ten weeks), the shepherd, cowherd, and woman servant one quarter every twelve weeks. In addition, a common table was provided at Christmas and Easter. After 1277, however, this was replaced by a payment of 1½d. a head on both occasions. Similarly, payment of a harvest goose to the *famuli* was arrented at 1½d. a head a year. The stipendiary *famuli* also shared the produce of 3 acres and 3 roods of wheat and 3 acres 3 roods of oats a year. These sown acres are first mentioned in 1296. The bailiff received 1 mark a year and a bushel of wheat a week. The smith was paid entirely by the sown acre: he

received the produce of 1 acre of wheat and 1 acre of oats a year. Supplementary short-term labour usually received a money wage with or without a small livery of corn. The exception is the harrower, who was paid in corn only. In 1350–1 the stipendiary *tenor* received 1d. for every working day on which his services were required. (He was, in fact, paid for 129 days' work between Michaelmas and Easter.)[16] This experiment was short-lived, and after 1353 both *tenores* received the normal liveries of a stipendiary ploughman.

A common table was kept between 1 August and 29 September for the bailiff, the reeve, the women servants, the *custos animalium* and, in some years, the swineherd—that is, mainly for the supervisory servants. The full-time woman servant received no livery of corn for this period.

The *famuli* who held service holdings shared the allowances at Christmas and Easter. The reeve shared in the common table in the harvest season. Their payment does not appear to have received further supplementation. The *tenores* thus received the low remuneration of 3s. rent each a year. This low scale of payment was perhaps made possible by the system of rotation which obtained among the tenants liable to the service.

Freehold tenure does not appear at Launton until the 15th century; the only known freehold is the virgate called *Freemansland* held in 1416 by John Langeston for 6s. 4d. rent a year and suit of court, heriot and relief.[17] References to this holding—the tenant of which repeatedly failed to perform suit—occur throughout the 15th and 16th centuries until 1558, when the land was seized.[18]

In the early 13th century 35¾ virgates and 9 cotlands were occupied by customary tenants.[19] The description of Launton in the Hundred Rolls is manifestly inaccurate when compared with contemporary ministers' accounts, and must be disregarded in this connexion.[20] In 1330 35¾ virgates and 8 cottages were occupied;[21] in 1416 31¼ virgates, 4 cottages and a few miscellaneous holdings of little importance.[22] No lands were vacant for more than a few weeks at a time before 1349. In 1351 14½ virgates were vacant, only the small closes and crofts appurtenant to them having found temporary tenants.[23] Leasing began slowly about the year 1353. By this means, and through the reversion of several lands to their old services, vacancies had been reduced to 2½ virgates and 5½ cottages by 1358.[24] In 1361 they increased to nearly ten virgates.[25] Leasing now began on a larger scale, and vacancies were kept at about four virgates for the rest of the century and for the opening decades of the 15th century. Between 1421 and 1423 a determined and successful effort was made to eliminate even this deficit,[26] and vacancies were negligible for the remainder of the century.

The earliest custumal, drawn up in the early 13th century, does not list the individual tenants of the manor and their holdings. The Hundred Rolls give

8 W.A.M. 15369.
9 Ibid. 15376.
10 Ibid. 15402, 15408.
11 *Rot. Hund.* (Rec. Com.), ii. 832.
12 W.A.M. 15420.
13 Ibid. 15421.
14 Ibid. 15428.
15 Ibid. 15433.
16 Ibid. 15346.
17 Ibid. 15716.

18 Ibid. 15538.
19 Ibid. 9287.
20 *Rot. Hund.* (Rec. Com.), ii. 832. See W.A.M. 15291 sqq.
21 W.A.M. 15339.
22 Ibid. 15716.
23 Ibid. 15345.
24 Ibid. 15355.
25 Ibid. 15358.
26 Ibid. 15406–8, 15481–2.

this information but, as suggested above, probably erroneously. The first reliable picture of the tenurial structure is that provided by a custumal compiled in 1416 or 1417.[27] There were at this date 11 customary virgaters, 3 customary half-virgaters, 6 tenants of composite holdings, and 16 leaseholders. The composite holdings consisted of two or more customary holdings or of customary holdings and leaseholds combined; each such holding amounted to more than 1 virgate. The tenants of these holdings should be distinguished from the ordinary virgaters, even when both held by customary tenure, for, unlike the virgaters, they had built up their holdings gradually, as opportunity offered. The customary virgaters, however, with one exception, held lands which had never been subdivided. Of the leaseholders, 1 held 2 virgates, 3 held 1 virgate each, 7 held half-virgates, 1 held ¾ of a virgate, and the rest held cottages. Thus the peasant aristocracy at this date was to be found among the leaseholders and tenants of composite holdings. The next list of tenants was compiled in 1449 or 1450.[28] This is a rental and lists only the name of the tenants, their total holdings and the rent due. Three tenants held 2 virgates or more, 12 held between 1 and 2 virgates, 6 held 1 virgate, 5 held between ½ and 1 virgate, 1 held ½ virgate, and 7 held cottages or quarterlands. A century later, in 1561, there were at Launton 2 copyhold tenants holding 2 virgates or more, 11 holding between 1 and 2 virgates, 9 holding virgates, 6 holding between ½ and 1 virgate, and 5 holding less than ½ virgate.[29]

Of the prosperous peasant families in 15th-century Launton only one, the Cottisfords, permanently consolidated their position. Three members of this family farmed the demesne at different times in the 15th and early 16th centuries.[30] In 1448 a virgate and 2 half-virgates were granted at will to John Cottisford senior and to his son, John, and to the latter's wife, Joan.[31] In 1474 Richard and Agnes Cottisford secured copies in a messuage, curtilage and three quarterlands, a messuage and half-virgate, and a cottage, garden and 2 acres.[32] In 1561 Thomas Cottisford held copies in 3½ virgates, two cottages and a curtilage, and the freehold of another cottage.[33] In 1615 John Cottisford, *generosus*, surrendered the copy of 3 virgates, a half-acre, an orchard and some gardens.[34] The visitation of 1634 recorded the arms of John Cottisford, gentleman.[35] John left five sons and two daughters. The bequest of £300 to his second daughter, Mary, caused a protracted family dispute, settled by a Chancery decree of 1678 in favour of Mary.[36]

In the early 13th century the virgater at Launton owed 5s. rent a year, 1s. customary rent at Martinmas, and the following labour services: 9½ *opera manualia* (one day's work a month, morning to evening, from 29 September to 24 June), 3 days' ploughing without food, harrowing after the spring ploughing with fodder, 1 day's hoeing, 1 day's

mowing with food, and 1 day's mowing without food, lifting, carrying, and stacking hay without food, carrying wood at Christmas, carrying a seam of oats or half a seam of wheat to Westminster in the summer. He was bound to find three men for each of three harvest boons without food, and three men for a fourth boon with food. He and his wife and a helper received a dish of meat or pulse, and cheese and ale at Michaelmas.[37] In 1416 the virgater owed 5s. rent a year, 1s. customary rent at Martinmas, and the following services: 3 days' ploughing with his own plough without food, harrowing at the winter and spring ploughing with two beasts and two harrows, without food but with fodder in spring, 9½ *opera manualia*, 1¼ summer works between 24 June and 1 August, carriage of one quarter of oats or half a quarter of hard corn to Westminster at Whitsun, with food provided, 1 day's hoeing, 2 days' mowing, 2 days' lifting hay, ½ day carrying hay and ½ day carrying corn with his own cart, carriage of food from Oxford or elsewhere when the abbot or any monk of Westminster visited Launton (with food provided). He was bound to provide three men for four weeks at the harvest season to perform reaping when required, without food. 'Medshep' of 3s. was paid to the customaries at the hay harvest. These works were valued at 4s. 7½d. a year. A half-virgater owed exactly half these services.[38]

The services of the customary tenant who was on a labour option thus altered very little in the 13th and 14th centuries. The introduction of summer works should be noted: this took place in the 13th century. These works were always sold, never exacted. After 1358 the customaries of Launton successfully denied their liability for them.[39] One important development is not shown by the custumals: although harvest works are stated to be 12 per virgate in 1220, the accounts show that the quota was only 8 per virgate in the later 13th century and until 1362; in this year the former quota of 12 per virgate was reimposed.[40]

In the early 13th century three cottagers owed rents of 1s. and 4 hens a year; six owed rents of 6d. a year and 2 hens. By 1335 each cottar also owed 1 day's hoeing, 3 days' lifting hay and 3 harvest works.[41] A quota of 4½ harvest works per cottage was reimposed after 1342.[42]

The total number of services available for the demesne when tenant land was in full occupation was as follows: 107¼ ploughing works, 71½ harrowing works, 339½ *opera manualia*, 44½ summer works, 35¾ carrying works, 43¾ hoeing works, 71½ mowing works, 95½ works for lifting hay, 18 for carrying hay, 18 for carrying corn, and 310 (after 1342, 337, and after 1362, 465) harvest works.[43] There were no losses through vacancies before 1349, and the only works lost were those allowed to the manorial staff holding service lands. In the period between 1267 (when the accounts begin) and 1349, all works due at the hay harvest and, with a few exceptions, all hoeing works

[27] W.A.M. 15716.
[28] Ibid. 15717.
[29] Ibid. 15722.
[30] Ibid. 15410–15.
[31] Ibid. 15510.
[32] Ibid. 15523.
[33] Ibid. 15722.
[34] Ibid. 15583.
[35] *Oxon. Visit.* 284.
[36] C 78/1759/9.

[37] W.A.M. 9287.
[38] Ibid. 15716, supplemented by works accounts (ibid. 15339 sqq.).
[39] Ibid. 15359–60.
[40] Ibid. 15358.
[41] Ibid. 15340.
[42] Ibid. 15342–3.
[43] Ibid. 15340. The following paragraphs on labour services are based on ibid. 15286–369.

and works due for carrying corn were used. All ploughing and harrowing works were used until 1340, when the sale of about a quarter of the former and of nearly half the latter began. It was usual to sell the summer works, the carrying works (after 1277), and the great majority of the *opera manualia*. Harvest works were fully exacted until 1335. After that date nearly all were sold for $2\frac{1}{2}d.$ each. Three works were required to reap 1 acre; ten bushels of wheat and 10 bushels of rye were allowed to the customaries in lieu of the one meal to which they were entitled.[44] The cost of reaping an acre by task labour between 1335 and 1349 was 5*d.* or 6*d.*[45]

By 1351 vacancies had caused the following losses: $43\frac{1}{2}$ ploughing works, 29 harrowing works, $137\frac{3}{4}$ *opera manualia*, $19\frac{3}{4}$ summer works, $14\frac{1}{2}$ carrying works, 15 hoeing works, 29 mowing works, 36 works lifting and $7\frac{1}{4}$ carrying hay, $6\frac{1}{4}$ works carrying corn, and $127\frac{1}{2}$ harvest works.[46] Losses on approximately this scale were perpetuated by the terms on which leases of vacant lands were granted in the second half of the 14th century.

After 1349 the sale of summer and carrying works and the exaction of all available hoeing works and of works due at the hay harvest continued. Policy regarding the other works shows interesting changes. Sales of ploughing and harrowing works ceased in the decade after 1349, the number of defects being greater than the number of surplus works previously sold. Between 1359 and 1364 all, or the great majority, of both works were sold. By 1366 all available ploughing and harrowing works were being used again. Sales of *opera manualia* continued until 1363. For the next four years all or the great majority of these works were used for threshing corn. After 1367 sales were resumed. All harvest works were sold before 1351. After 1351 all were used. The cost of reaping an acre by task labour was now 9*d.* or 10*d.*[47]

From the point of view of the diminishing number of ordinary customary tenants at Launton the long-term effect of the Black Death was to restore the situation obtaining in the early 14th century before the sale of harvest works and of surplus ploughing works began. As far as manorial administration is concerned its main effect was to alter the proportion of the two great agricultural operations, sowing and harvest, performed respectively by customary labour and by hired labour (seasonal and permanent). Before 1349 two demesne ploughs were used and about 100 customary ploughing services each year. Between 1349 and 1352 the work was done by three demesne ploughs and about 60 services; after 1352 by two ploughs and the same number of services, except between 1359 and 1364, when all ploughing was done by the two demesne ploughs. No task labour was used for ploughing. In the decade before 1349 all reaping was done by task labour. (The *famuli* were employed for stacking and the later stages of the harvest.) For some twelve years after 1349 about half was done by customary labour and half by task

labour. After 1362 the quota of harvest services was increased and the area of the arable demesne reduced; consequently, no task labour was required between 1366 and 1372, the last years of demesne exploitation.

In the early 14th century the total assessment for the subsidies of 1316 and 1327, when 49 and 54 people respectively were assessed in Launton, show that the place enjoyed a prosperity comparable with that of Islip or Kirtlington.[48] Its fixed tax assessment after 1334 confirms this view.[49] There are suggestions of depopulation in the 14th century. The first extant presentment of a fugitive serf was made in 1330.[50] Eleven fugitives were presented in 1334, and after this date three to five persons were usually presented each year as being fugitives or lawfully outside the manor.[51] The mortality rate during the Black Death was severe: $14\frac{1}{2}$ virgates were still vacant in 1351; 10 virgates were vacant in 1361.[52] The poll-tax return of 1377 is missing. In 1416 there were 37 landholders, and in 1449, 34, compared with the unreliable list of 64 in the Hundred Rolls of 1279.[53] In the 16th century, 33 people were assessed for the subsidy of 1525, when only six other parishes in the hundred had a larger number.[54]

Small inclosures for pasture are found at Launton in the 14th century, but the first extensive inclosures were made in 1582.[55] The parliamentary inclosure, however, shows that inclosure for arable had made little progress before this date. At the inclosure in 1814 there remained about 1,650 acres of open field arable and waste, principally to the north of the village and along the Poundon road. There were about 1,080 acres of old inclosures, of which some 230 acres were redistributed under the award. The principal awards were to Lord Jersey, who received 724 acres in all for his freehold, leasehold, and copyhold estates, and to the rector, who received 312 acres apart from his 477 acres in lieu of glebe and tithes. There were five other awards of over 100 acres and five of over 30 acres. Twenty-six proprietors in all received awards; another 28—who had only cottages and small closes—received nothing.[56]

In 1760 there were two principal estates—those of Richard Oakley, lessee of the manor, assessed at £57 for the land tax, and of the rector, assessed at £26. Of the other estates, two were assessed at £16 and £14 respectively, and another nine at more than £5. In 1786 Lord Jersey's estate was assessed at £58, the rector's at £38; one other estate was assessed at more than £10 and seven were assessed at more than £5. The rector's estate was increased by the inclosure award, and was assessed at £48 in 1816. Lord Jersey's estate was assessed at £60 at this date, and six estates were assessed at £5 to £10. No significant change took place before 1832.[57]

In 1955 there were nine farms in Launton, most of them with between only 30 and 80 acres, although the largest, the Grange, comprised some 300 and Manor farm had over 200 acres. Mixed farming was practised and flocks of sheep, chiefly Border Leicesters, were kept on most of the farms. The chief

44 W.A.M. 15338.
45 Ibid. 15340–4.
46 Ibid. 15345.
47 Ibid. 15348–50.
48 E 179/161/8, 9.
49 E 164/7.
50 W.A.M. 15430.
51 Ibid. 15433.

52 Ibid. 15345, 15357.
53 Ibid. 15716–17; *Rot. Hund.* (Rec. Com.), ii. 832.
54 E 179/161/176.
55 See above, p. 235.
56 O.R.O. Incl. award and map; cf. Davis, *Oxon. Map* (1797).
57 O.R.O. Land tax assess.

crops were wheat, seeds, mangolds, kale, and potatoes. The produce was mainly sent to the markets at Banbury, Bicester, Oxford, and Thame.[58] There were about 1,730 acres of grassland and 1,123 acres of arable.[59]

In the 19th century there was a great increase in population. The Compton Census of 1676 had recorded 151 adults,[60] and by 1801 the total population had risen to 372. It was 706 in 1851,[61] and in the following year Bicester Board of Guardians sanctioned the payment of £32 for the emigration to Australia of poor persons from Launton.[62] The population continued to rise steadily until 1871, when, at 746, it was double the 1801 figure. It then declined to 458 in 1931, but by 1951 had risen to 550.[63]

CHURCH. There is documentary evidence for a church at Launton in 1157,[64] but it is probable that it existed about a hundred years earlier and that its advowson was given to Westminster Abbey with the manor by Edward the Confessor. It was certainly in the abbey's possession before 1213, by which date it had made the first known presentation.[65] The abbey retained possession of the advowson until it was dissolved in 1540. In 1534 the abbot and convent granted the next presentation to Sir Thomas Audley, the Lord Chancellor.[66] In 1542 the advowson was granted to the Abbot of Westminster,[67] and in 1554 to the Bishop of London, with whom it remained until 1852, when it was transferred to the Bishop of Oxford.[68] Throughout the Middle Ages the Abbot and Convent of Westminster claimed a pension of 2 marks a year from the Rector of Launton. The claim was allowed by the bishop in the 13th and 14th centuries,[69] but attempts to exact the pension caused much friction between the abbey and successive incumbents.[70] The pension was assigned to the almoner.[71] After the Dissolution it was separated from the advowson. In 1556 it was granted to the abbot and convent of the restored monastic foundation, and in 1560 to the dean and chapter of the collegiate church.[72]

The rectory was valued at £4 13s. 4d. in 1254, at £8 in 1291, and in 1535 its net value was £11 9s. 4d.[73] In 1601 the glebe consisted of about 200 acres, of which 18 lay in five closes allotted to the rector at the inclosure of common in 1582.[74] The living was a valuable one until the 19th century. The tithes were commuted for land, supposed to be equal to about a fifth of the arable and a ninth of the meadow and pasture, at the inclosure award of 1814.[75] The rector received 477 acres in lieu of tithes and glebe.[76]

However, tithes continued to be paid on 91 acres of early inclosures consisting of meadow, pasture, and cottages, mostly in the south-west of the parish along the Bicester boundary, until 1850, when they were commuted for a rent charge of £52.[77]

The church of Bicester claimed certain rights over the church of Launton, and until the 15th century the latter was in the position of a chapel of ease, the parishioners of Launton being obliged to take their dead to Bicester for burial. In 1435, however, an agreement was made between the Prior and Convent of Bicester and the rector and parishioners of Launton whereby the latter were granted the right of sepulture in the church and churchyard of Launton, with all oblations, on condition of paying 1s. a year to the church of Bicester.[78] The Edwardian chantry certificate for Launton mentions an obit worth 1s. 8d. given by an unknown person.[79] This may be the obit founded by Thomas Cottisford in 1522.[80]

The first recorded institution—that of Master Simon de London in 1213—was made saving the perpetual vicarage of Henry de Colewell.[81] In 1214 a dispute between Simon and Henry was settled by papal judges delegate: Henry was granted the vicarage for life, saving 2 marks a year to be paid to Simon, and 16s. 8d. a year to be paid to the almoner at Westminster in Simon's name.[82]

Continuity was preserved in the religious changes of the 17th century by the incumbencies of two men of high church sympathies: Theodore Price (1609–31), the Laudian sub-dean of Westminster, and Bishop Robert Skinner (1632–63).[83] In the 18th century the rectors were for the most part conscientious pastors. Philip Stubbs (1719–38) resided for only half the year, but employed a curate for the other half at 'the full rate of £40'.[84] Richard Browne (1750–79) was usually resident,[85] and his successor, W. F. Browne (1779–1837), prided himself on being but rarely absent.[86] Services were held twice each Sunday, but only one sermon was given. Prayers were said on Christmas Day and Good Friday, and the sacrament was administered five times a year (Christmas, the Sunday before Easter, Easter, Whitsun, and Michaelmas).[87] By 1831, however, there were only four administrations a year.[88] The number of communicants was given as 20 to 50 or more in 1759, 'decent' in 1768, 5 to 20 in 1805, and 6 to 20 in 1811.[89] With the institution of James Blomfield in 1838, the year of Queen Victoria's coronation, a 'new order of things' was begun. Sunday schools were opened; the schoolroom was built; the church repaired, and a decent order intro-

[58] Inf. Miss G. Freeman.
[59] Inf. Oxon. Agric. Executive Cttee.
[60] Compton Census.
[61] Census, 1801, 1851.
[62] Bicester U.D.C. office: Bd. of Guardians min. bk. 1851–3, pp. 138, 147.
[63] Census, 1861–1951.
[64] See below.
[65] W.A.M. 15683.
[66] Reg. Bk. ii, f. 292.
[67] L. & P. Hen. VIII, xvi, p. 244.
[68] Cal. Pat. 1553–4, 120; Lond. Gaz. 4 June 1852.
[69] Westm. Domesday, f. 646; see also ibid. ff. 644–644b.
[70] W.A.M. 15686–7, 15689, 15698, 15703.
[71] Valor Eccl. (Rec. Com.), i. 413.
[72] Cal. Pat. 1555–7, 352; 1558–60, 401.
[73] Lunt, Val. Norw. 311; Tax. Eccl. (Rec. Com.), 31; Valor Eccl. ii. 162.

[74] Oxf. Archd. Oxon. c 141, pp. 385–92.
[75] Cf. above, p. 239.
[76] 50 Geo. III, c. 89 (priv. act); O.R.O. Incl. award.
[77] Bodl. Tithe award.
[78] Kennett, Paroch. Antiq. ii. 321; Dunkin, Oxon. i. 309, citing Linc. Reg. Gray, f. 174. Cf. above, p. 40.
[79] Chant. Cert. 37.
[80] Dunkin, Oxon. i. 306.
[81] W.A.M. 15683.
[82] Ibid. 15684. The payment to the almoner was evidently part of the pension due from the rector.
[83] For Price see D.N.B.; for Skinner see above, p. 233.
[84] Oxf. Dioc. d 553.
[85] Ibid. d 556, d 559, d 562.
[86] Ibid. d 572.
[87] Ibid. d 553, d 556, d 559, d 562, d 568, d 570, d 572.
[88] Ibid. b 31.
[89] Ibid. d 556, d 559, d 568, d 572.

The Parsonage house in the 19th century

South-east view of the church in 1824

LAUNTON

duced; church services were increased; a coal and clothing club and a lending library were started; allotments of land were made to the villagers; pastoral visiting became customary. All these innovations gradually led to an improvement in parish life.[90] In 1850 the Revd. T. W. Allies, who had been rector since 1842, resigned to enter the Church of Rome.[91]

The church of *ST. MARY THE VIRGIN* consists of a nave, chancel, north and south aisles, south porch, and western tower.[92]

A chapel is mentioned in 1157.[93] Aisles and a tower were added in the late 12th and early 13th centuries. The tower and part of the south aisle survive in the present building and the foundations of a semicircular apse exist beneath the floor of the chancel. The church was enlarged in the 15th century, when the apse was replaced by a rectangular chancel. In the present building the chancel arch, the north and south walls of the chancel, the windows and the sedilia date from the 15th century, as do the north nave arcade, the east window of the south aisle, the truncated east window of the north aisle, the blocked doorway in the north aisle, and the porch. The clerestory was probably added at the same period.

The church was repaired during the incumbency of Henry Rowlands (1581–1600), afterwards Bishop of Bangor. Rowlands restored the clerestory in the nave, whitewashed the nave walls and filled the nave with open seats, put a pulpit and prayer-desk near the screen, put a new roof with a low lath and plaster roof in the chancel, destroyed the north vestry and inserted a doorway in the south side of the chancel. The clerestory, certain old timbers in the nave roof, the north and west windows of the north aisle, and the masonry of the south windows in the south aisle survive from this period. A stone on the south parapet commemorates a bequest by Rowlands of £9 6s. 8d. to the church.[94]

In the course of the 18th century a number of box pews were erected. The largest—belonging to the Ashby family—extended from the east wall of the north aisle to the first column of the nave arcade. A gallery was erected by the family in compensation for this encroachment. In the early 19th century the medieval screen was covered with lath and plaster and a doorway inserted. James Blomfield (rector 1838–42) removed the box pews from the chancel and the lath and plaster from the screen; subsequently, however, the latter was discarded. Blomfield's successor, Thomas Allies (1842–50), removed the gallery and the box pews in the nave, inserted oak pews, a prayer-desk, and a new stone altar. Major restorations were undertaken by James Charles Blomfield (1850–95) and William Miller (1895–1915). Blomfield at once restored the chancel, removed the

ceiling, reinstated the upper portion of the east window, and presented new choir stalls, altar furniture, and a reredos. He also made a three-light window in the porch and filled it with fragments of medieval glass.[95] Flying buttresses were added to the tower in 1891 (architect R. Blomfield).[96] Miller restored the nave and aisle roofs, renewed the floors, built the organ loft, and installed a new chancel screen and pulpit (architect J. O. Scott).[97] The altar stone now in the Lady Chapel was discovered under the chancel floor and put in its present position by Dr. Burton (1915–24). Electric light was installed in the church between 1931 and 1939.

The plain octagonal font is medieval.[98] Most of the many monuments and memorial tablets are of recent date, but there is an early 16th-century brass in the east wall of the nave commemorating Sir Matthew Shaw, priest, 17th-century heraldic ledgers on the nave floor to the Oakley and Deeley families, and tablets on the south wall of the nave to the Jones and Deeley families. In the churchyard is the tomb of Lancelot Jackson, Rector of Bletchingdon (d. 1750/1). There was once a brass to Thomas Cottisford (d. 1522), who founded an obit in the church, his two wives, and twenty children, among them Master John Cottisford, rector 1535–40, and a brass inscription to Richard Glasier, priest.[99]

The church possesses a Laudian chalice with paten cover dated 1633 and some 18th-century silver and pewter.[1] In 1552 the church possessed two latten crosses, one silver chalice, and three tin cruets.[2] There is a ring of six bells. Four were cast in 1701 and a fifth in 1712 by the Chandler family. In 1552 there were three bells and a sanctus bell. A sanctus bell dated 1325[3] is still in use. Notes scribbled on a custumal of the manor dated 1416–17, refer to the purchase of two bells weighing between them 12 cwt. 11 lb., and to the existence of a third bell weighing about 3½ cwt.[4]

The early parish registers were destroyed by fire in 1716, but entries of baptisms from 1648, burials from 1681, and marriages from 1671 were later compiled from other sources by Philip Stubbs (rector 1719–38).

In the churchyard is the base and broken shaft of a medieval cross.

NONCONFORMITY. There has been little Roman Catholicism. Susanna, wife of William Ewer, was fined in 1592–3,[5] and in 1676 there was one papist.[6]

Although the rectors throughout the 18th century reported no dissent, in 1772 a Presbyterian meeting-house was licensed.[7] Dissent was reported to have died out by about 1800,[8] but in 1806 another house was licensed,[9] and in 1807 a Presbyterian meeting-house called 'Zion' was built in the west end of the

[90] Bodl. dep. b 63: Blo. MS. Hist. Launton, f. 181.
[91] H. J. Buxton and F. Sharpe, *Handbook to the Church of St. Mary the Virgin, Launton* (1952), 2, 6.
[92] For accounts of the church see ibid., and Bodl. dep. b 63.
[93] Westm. Domesday, f. 5.
[94] Oxf. Dioc. d 553 and inscription on stone on outside wall of church. Dunkin (*Oxon.* i. 307) wrongly gives the bequest as £17 6s. 8d.
[95] There are drawings by J. Buckler of the church before restoration from NW. and SE. (1824) in MS. Top. Oxon. a 67, ff. 365–6. For the last see plate opposite. There is a view from NE. (1820) in MS. Top. Oxon. b 220, f. 177.
[96] Clarke MS.   [97] Ibid.

[98] Buckler drawing in MS. Top. Oxon. a 67, f. 364.
[99] For list of inscriptions once there and blazons and tricks of arms see Bodl. G.A. Oxon. 16⁰ 217, pp. 178–9; ibid. 4⁰ 686, p. 198; ibid. 4⁰ 688, p. 198; Bodl. 2194 c 15, f. 277.
[1] Evans, *Ch. Plate.*
[2] *Chant. Cert.* 83.
[3] *Ch. Bells Oxon.* ii. 195–6.
[4] Ibid. 196; W.A.M. 15716.
[5] C.R.S. xviii. 258.
[6] Compton Census.
[7] Oxf. Dioc. c 644, f. 12.
[8] Ibid. c 327, p. 300.
[9] Ibid. c 644, f. 89.

village on land given by William Freeman.[10] Richard Fletcher, a Presbyterian minister from Bicester, used to hold services there on Sunday evenings, and the greater part of the parish, as well as many from Bicester and other villages, were said to attend, but, according to the rector, mainly from curiosity.[11] The occasion for an increase of dissent is alleged by William Ferguson, the extravagant historian of dissent in this district, to have been a demand for increased tithes by the rector, W. F. Browne.[12]

In 1850 an Independent chapel, but a successor to the Presbyterian one, was built by subscription on land given by a local farmer.[13] It was located nearer the centre of the village and was called 'Bethel'.[14] Ferguson, the minister, reported in 1855 a 'large' dissenting congregation with a day school and circulating library,[15] and the chapel had its own burial ground. In 1866 the rector reported about 100 professed dissenters.[16] 'Zion', which in the later 19th century was used as a school,[17] has disappeared; 'Bethel' is now a member of the North Buckinghamshire and North Oxfordshire Congregational Union and has 25 members.[18]

There were also a few Methodists. A house was licensed for them in 1822;[19] they were connected with the Bicester Methodists and for many years were on the Brackley Circuit.[20] By 1866 they were said to be almost extinct,[21] and services ceased in about 1895.[22]

SCHOOLS. In 1738 two boys from Launton were attending what was evidently the grammar school in Bicester:[23] the rector paid £2 a year, and had been supporting pupils in this way since about 1718.[24] In Launton itself, however, there was no endowed school[25] until John Henn (d. 1803) left £50 in trust for setting one up.[26] It was reported in 1808 that two or three poor women, supported by the interest on Henn's bequest, occasionally looked after labourers' children for 2d. or 3d. a week, and taught reading, the catechism, and lace-making.[27] Soon afterwards Lady Jersey (d. 1867) took over this dame school, which became known as 'Lady Jersey's Free School', although it is said that the children who attended it had to pay 6d a week. Some pupils received clothing from Lady Jersey.[28] In 1815 the school was attended by 56 boys and girls who were instructed on Lancaster's plan.[29] About 1826, when Lord Jersey sold his property in Launton, Lady Jersey is said to have withdrawn her support, and

so caused the school to close.[30] But John Ashby, a trustee of Henn's bequest who died in 1827, left a further £50 for a school,[31] and by 1833 a day school, endowed with the £100 and further supported by £10 a year from Lady Jersey, had opened and had 15 pupils. In the same year 25 children were attending a fee-paying school.[32]

With the Henn and Ashby bequest, augmented by public subscription, a new school, Launton Church of England School, was built in 1838 at the instance of the rector, James Blomfield, and enlarged in 1846 at a total cost of about £450. The school was affiliated to the National Society in 1846;[33] had two teachers by 1852, when it was receiving an annual government grant of £15;[34] and a master and two mistresses in 1864, when there were three departments, boys, girls, and infants, in separate rooms. A master's house was built and the school improved in 1867[35] and again enlarged both in 1872[36] and 1896.[37] The number of pupils rose from 100 in 1871[38] to 118 in 1887.[39] In 1906 there were 112 pupils in two departments, mixed and infants, and a staff of three.[40] After reorganization in 1928 senior pupils were sent to Bicester, and there were henceforth two departments, junior and infants, and a staff of two. The school became controlled in 1951, and the number of pupils on the roll was 46 in 1937 and 61 in 1954.[41]

Launton Congregational Day School was established in 1845 and was held at first in the old chapel, Zion.[42] It was run on British School lines.[43] A new school, built in 1852 and enlarged in 1877, was erected on ground given by two local men, of whom one was Thomas Deeley.[44]

CHARITIES. In 1786 it was stated that £14 given to the poor by an unknown benefactor had been spent on a house producing £1 1s. a year.[45] In 1824 it was reported that a cottage and garden called the Town House had been let for the benefit of the poor at a rent of £1 1s. 'at least as far back as 1759'.[46] The charity referred to was at least as old as the 16th century, however, for in 1575 a cottage and garden called the Town House were granted to trustees for the use of the inhabitants of Launton *prout ab antiquo usitatum fuerit*, at a rent of 8d. a year. It was described as the house 'next to the stone cross'.[47] In the late 18th and early 19th centuries the rent of £1 1s. was distributed to the poor, but after 1814 the cottage was occupied rent-free by poor widows.

[10] Oxf. Dioc. c 644, f. 90; Wing, *Annals*, 93.
[11] Oxf. Dioc. d 570.
[12] W. Ferguson, *Facts Three Hundred Years Ago and Facts Now: or the Trials and Triumphs of Nonconformists* (priv. printed, Oxford 1855), 33.
[13] Gardner, *Dir. Oxon.*
[14] Wing, *Annals*, 93.
[15] Ferguson, op. cit. 35.
[16] Oxf. Dioc. c 332.
[17] Wing, *Annals*, 93.
[18] *Congregational Yearbook 1955*, 113.
[19] Oxf. Dioc. c 644, f. 262. Another house was licensed in 1832: ibid. c 645, f. 200.
[20] Brackley Circuit Plans, 1833, 1851.
[21] Oxf. Dioc. c 332.
[22] Inf. Revd. A. S. Valle, Bicester.
[23] See above, p. 51.
[24] Oxf. Dioc. d 553.
[25] e.g. ibid. d 556, d 559.
[26] Bodl. dep. b 63, f. 192b; Wing, *Annals*, 92.
[27] Oxf. Dioc. d 707.
[28] Wing, *Annals*, 92.
[29] Oxf. Dioc. c 433; cf. *Educ. of Poor*, 726.
[30] Bodl. dep. b 63, f. 201.
[31] Ibid.; Wing, *Annals*, 92.
[32] *Educ. Enq. Abstract*, 749.
[33] Bodl. dep. b 63, f. 202; Wing, *Annals*, 92; *Vol. Sch. Ret.*
[34] Gardner, *Dir. Oxon.*
[35] Bodl. dep. b 63, f. 202.
[36] Ibid.
[37] *Kelly's Dir. Oxon.* (1903).
[38] *Elem. Educ. Ret.*
[39] *Kelly's Dir. Oxon.* (1887); cf. *Ret. of Sch.*
[40] *Vol. Sch. Ret.*; *List of Sch.*
[41] Inf. Oxon. Educ. Cttee.
[42] Wing, *Annals*, 93.
[43] Gardner, *Dir. Oxon.*
[44] Wing, *Annals*, 93; see above, p. 234.
[45] *Char. Don.* ii. 990.
[46] *12th Rep. Com. Char.* 307.
[47] W.A.M. 15555; see also ibid. 15575, 15588.

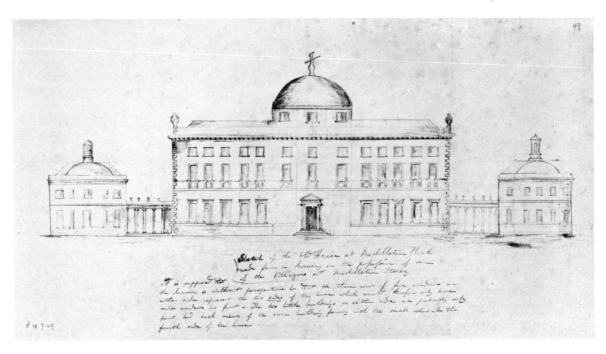

Sketch of Middleton Park in the 18th century

Middleton Park in the early 19th century

MIDDLETON STONEY

The Charity Commissioners recommended in 1824 that the rent should either be taken or paid by the parish and distributed as before,[48] but the charity had apparently lapsed by 1852.[49]

Henry Rowlands, Bishop of Bangor and some-time Rector of Launton, by will proved 1616, left £9 6s. 8d. to form a church stock for the benefit of the poor of Launton. This charity was said to have been lost in the time of the Civil War.[50]

In 1866 or 1867 Richard Wootten of Launton bequeathed £56 a year to be distributed in pensions of £14 a year for four old people.[51] Weekly payments of 8s. to seven old people were substituted about 1920, and were still being made in 1955.[52]

MIDDLETON STONEY

MIDDLETON STONEY is a parish of 1,853 acres, bounded on the west by the Aves Ditch,[1] and on the east by the Gagle Brook, a tributary of the River Ray. Geologically, most of the parish lies on an outcrop of the Cornbrash, at this point forming a plateau between 300 and 350 feet above sea-level,[2] and it is to the presence of this stone that it probably owes the second part of its name, which is first recorded in 1552.[3] There are several stone-pits from which material for dry stone walling has in the past been obtained. The parish is crossed from east to west by the road from Lower Heyford to Bicester, and from north to south by the main road from Oxford to Brackley.

Until the early 19th century the nucleus of the village lay to the south-west of the Lower Heyford–Bicester road, in the vicinity of the church and castle, although references to an 'Old Churchyard Furlong' about 1,000 yards south-west of the present churchyard suggest that there may have been an earlier church on a different site. The castle is of the motte and bailey type: it is first mentioned in 1215, after the death of Gerard de Camville, but it may well have been in existence in the time of his father Richard.[4] King John ordered its destruction in 1216, and there is no evidence that it was ever refortified. When Leland saw it in the 1530's, it was already 'over growne with bushys', but he recorded that 'sum peces of the walls of it yet a litle apcarc'.[5] There are now no signs of masonry, but the mound has been partly dug away on the west, and is covered with trees.[6] Immediately to the west of the castle stood the old manor-house of the Harmans, which survived as a farm-house until the early 19th century.[7] To the north was the Rectory, with its barn and stables,[8] and, at a point approximately half-way be-

tween the latter and the road to Heyford, the village cross, whose base is now preserved close to the churchyard.[9]

The desertion of the old manor-house in favour of an isolated mansion standing in its own grounds appears to have taken place in the time of Sir Edmund Denton (1698–1712), to whom the building of 'Middleton Park House' is attributed by Rawlinson.[10] A map of 1710 shows it in miniature as a three-storied house with a symmetrical front set in a rectangular park of 67 acres walled round and planted with trees. Soon afterwards it was considerably enlarged, for two wings flanking its southern façade are shown in plan on a map of 1736:[11] they were presumably built by Lord Carleton. The house was again enlarged by the 3rd Earl of Jersey soon after his acquisition of the estate, but was destroyed by fire in 1753.[12] A new house, described as 'a handsome brick structure', took its place. No satisfactory representation of it appears to exist, but a sketch[13] shows that it had a dome, and that the wings were connected to the body of the house by quadrant colonnades. In 1806–7 this Georgian mansion was altered and enlarged by the 5th earl to the designs of Thomas Cundy of Pimlico, who faced it with stone and added an Ionic portico forming a *porte cochère*.[14] In this form it survived until 1938, when the 9th earl demolished it in order to build a new house designed by Sir Edwin and Mr. Robert Lutyens.[15]

Until the end of the 17th century the only enclosed part of the parish was the park. Its formation was authorized by King John at the same time (May 1201) as the grant of the market to Gerard de Camville,[16] and two years later he gave Gerard 10 bucks and 40 does from Woodstock Park to stock it.[17]

[48] *12th Rep. Com. Char.* 307.
[49] Gardner, *Dir. Oxon.*
[50] Oxf. Dioc. d 553, d 556.
[51] Wing, *Annals*, 93; *Kelly's Dir. Oxon.* (1887).
[52] *Kelly's Dir. Oxon.* (1920); inf. the Revd. E. S. Tarrant.
[1] For Aves Ditch see *V.C.H. Oxon.* i. 275–6; *Oxoniensia*, ii. 202; ibid. xi. 162. It is mentioned in a charter of 995: *Cod. Dipl.* ed. Kemble, vi, no. 1289. There have been no recent boundary changes: *Census*, 1881, 1951.
[2] G.S. Map 1″, xlv SE., SW.; O.S. Map 6″, xvi, xxii (1884); ibid. 2½″, 42/52 (1951).
[3] Blo. *Mid.* 41. The derivation from *stānweg*, a 'paved road', suggested by Ekwall (*Dict. Eng. P.N.* 310), cannot be accepted; cf. *P.N. Oxon.* (E.P.N.S.), i. 229.
[4] This has been stated as a fact because Middleton is included in a list of castles and religious houses (Bodl. MS. Bodley 648, f. 30b), which has been ascribed to the 12th cent. on the ground that Bicester Priory (founded 1182–5) is omitted. But the MS. is of the late 15th cent. and is worthless as evidence of the existence of a castle in the reign of Henry II.
[5] Leland, *Itin.* ed. Toulmin Smith, ii. 35.
[6] For pottery found on the site see *Oxoniensia*, xiii. 69–70.

[7] Nicholas Harman paid tax on 7 rooms in 1665: *Hearth Tax Oxon.* 200.
[8] Cf. Oxf. Archd. Oxon. b 41, f. 32. The Revd. Timothy Neve reported that he was 'repairing or rather rebuilding' the Rectory in 1759: Oxf. Dioc. d 556.
[9] See map of 1710 by Edward Grantham in O.R.O. J IV/2 and that of 1737 hanging in the 'Jersey Arms' at Middleton. References in the terriers to 'Headless Cross furlong' adjoining the Chesterton Way suggest the former existence of a second cross.
[10] *Par. Coll.* ii. 208. It is described as 'new built' in the deed of sale to Lord Jersey of 1737: O.R.O. J 1 a/24.
[11] O.R.O. Map by Thos. Williams and Wm. Wyeth attached to J I a/24.
[12] Dunkin, *Oxon.* ii. 76.
[13] See plate opposite.
[14] Illustrated in Dunkin, *Oxon.* ii. 76, and by J. P. Neale, *Gentlemen's Seats*, ser. 2, vol. iv (1829). The wings of this house faced east, whereas those of the house burned in 1753 faced south. For a view c. 1810–20(?) see plate opposite.
[15] Described and illustrated in *Country Life*, July 5–12, 1946.
[16] D.L. 42/1, f. 439b.
[17] *Rot. Lib.* (Rec. Com.), 43.

It is described in an extent of 1328 as surrounded by a stone wall half a league in circuit,[18] and its original limits are now indicated by the bank and ditch surrounding the Home Wood. In 1280 the king gave Henry de Lacy 15 does from Woodstock in order to stock Middleton Park,[19] and in 1295, soon after the earl had obtained a grant of free warren in the demesne lands of the manor,[20] it was stocked with 36 deer from Beckley Park, Woodstock Park, and Wychwood Forest.[21] At the same time 11s. 8d. was paid to the king's huntsman for catching wolves in it. According to the extent of 1311, it was worth 10s. a year in pasture and underwood if not stocked, but nothing if it held deer.[22] The creation of the modern park which occupies nearly half the parish was the work of the 5th Earl of Jersey in the early 19th century. In 1814 he came to an agreement with the rector whereby the latter's glebe of 72 acres, valued at £106 13s. 5d. a year, was added to his park.[23] In exchange the rector received 106 acres of land between the Bicester and Oxford roads valued at £125 14s. 8d. a year, besides a new parsonage designed by Thomas Cundy in the Tudor-Gothic style.[24] This arrangement was confirmed by Act of Parliament in 1816.[25] The eastward extension of the park was completed in 1824–5, when the old manor-house and the adjoining cottages were demolished, leaving the church in isolation half-way between the mansion and the park gates.[26] New cottages were built elsewhere under Lady Jersey's personal direction, each with a rustic porch and a small flower garden, conveying to a contemporary observer 'an idea of comfort and respectability seldom enjoyed by the lower classes'.[27] It was also in the time of the Countess Sophia (who died in 1867 at the age of 82) that the 'Eagle and Child' changed its name to the 'Jersey Arms'. This inn is of some antiquity, though the existing buildings were reroofed and otherwise modernized in about 1892. It stands at the junction of the Lower Heyford–Brackley roads, in what is now the centre of the village. Few of the adjoining cottages show evidence of being of an earlier date than the 19th century, and the village as a whole, though well-built and not unpleasing in appearance, lacks architectural distinction. The former rectory on the east side of the Oxford road is now occupied as a private residence, a new and smaller rectory having been built on the Bicester road soon after 1920.

A village reading-room was built in 1884 at the expense of the 7th earl,[28] who also established a co-operative shop managed entirely by local people, and did much else to improve the conditions of his tenants. It was he who made the earliest attempts to increase the water-supply of both village and mansion by sinking new wells, who extended the schools and enlarged their scope, provided pitches for cricket and football, gave an annual harvest-home dinner to all his employees, and distributed beef and game at Christmas.[29] Allotments had already been instituted by the 5th earl in 1832,[30] and the 7th earl built a barn for the benefit of those who rented them. Few Victorian landlords, in fact, set a better example than the earls of Jersey did at Middleton, and their benevolent régime is still remembered with gratitude by those who had the good fortune to be their tenants.

MANOR. In 1086 *MIDDLETON* was held by Richard Puingiant, a Norman tenant-in-chief of whom nothing is known beyond the fact that he also held Godington and had other estates in Wiltshire, Berkshire, Hampshire, and Bedfordshire. Of his Saxon predecessor, Turi, it is recorded only that he had held Middleton freely in the time of King Edward.[31] The subsequent history of Richard's estates is obscure, but in the 12th century his Hampshire and Bedfordshire manors are found in the possession of the Chamberlain family, while those in Oxfordshire and Berkshire had passed to the Camvilles. Godington is known to have been in the hands of Richard de Camville by the middle of the century,[32] and he was evidently seised of Middleton in 1130, when he was excused the payment of 20s. danegeld in Oxfordshire,[33] for, at the rate of 2s. per hide, this implies a tenement of 10 hides, which is in fact the number of hides at which Middleton is assessed in Domesday Book. The tenure of Middleton by the De Camville family is in any case carried back to the reign of Henry I by Richard's *carta* of 1166, in which he is said to owe the king the service of one knight for the fee in Oxfordshire which he holds of him of the 'old enfeoffment'—that is, an enfeoffment made before 1135.[34] Middleton and Godington were, with Avington in Berkshire, the only manors which Richard de Camville held in chief, and the existence at Middleton of a characteristic 12th-century castle suggests that it may have been the head or *caput* of his barony, though there is no definite proof that this was the case.[35] He died in southern Italy in 1176 or 1177, while accompanying the king's daughter Joan on her journey to Palermo to be married to King William II of Sicily.[36] His manors passed to his elder son Gerard, who is recorded on the Pipe Roll for 1186–7 as owing ½ mark for waste in Middleton.[37] Gerard married Nichole, heiress of the Lincolnshire family of Hay,

[18] C 145/108/2.
[19] *Cal. Close*, 1279–88, 73.
[20] *Cal. Chart. R.* 1257–1300, 436.
[21] D.L. 29/1/1.   [22] C 134/22.
[23] O.R.O. J I t/1–3.
[24] There are designs for it in Cundy's sketch-bk. *penes* Mr. A. Andrews of Cardiff. They were, however, based on a design obtained by Lord Jersey from the architect Henry Hakewill in 1812, which was not adopted and which is now MS. Top. Oxon. a 48, ff. 43–48. The stables were added to Cundy's design under a faculty granted in 1819: Oxf. Dioc. c 435, p. 190.
[25] The glebe acquired in 1814 was sold back to Lord Jersey in 1920: O.R.O. J I af/25–26.
[26] Blo. *Mid.* 62; O.S. Map 25″, xxii. 7, 8 (1881).
[27] Dunkin, *Oxon.* ii. 57.
[28] The architect was W. D. Little. A copy of the printed catalogue of the library is in Bodl. 2590 f Middleton 1.1.

[29] R. Elkerton's MS. 'Notes on Middleton Stoney' (1951), 66–74, *penes* Col. the Hon. E. H. Wyndham, Caversfield. See also H. Wyndham, 'Middleton 60 years ago', *Oxf. Times*, 2 Jan. 1953.
[30] O.R.O. J I af/4: plan.
[31] *V.C.H. Oxon.* i. 417.
[32] Missenden Cart. (B.M. Harl. MS. 3688), f. 129b.
[33] *Pipe R.* 1130 (P.R.S. facsimile), 5.
[34] *Red Bk. Exch.* (Rolls Ser.), 304.
[35] Richard Longespée is said in 1243 to hold ¼ knight's fee in Avington 'de baronia que fuit Ricardi de Camvil' (*Bk. of Fees*, 861), and in 1216 the manor of King's Sutton (Northants) is described as 'belonging to the manor of Middleton which was Richard de Camville's' (*Rot. Litt. Claus.* (Rec. Com.), i. 252).
[36] R. W. Eyton, *Itin. of Henry II*, 204; *Eynsham Cart.* i. 399; *Rot. de Dominabus* (P.R.S. xxxv), 84 n. 4.
[37] *Pipe R.* 1187 (P.R.S. xxxvii), 48.

thus bringing into his family the castellanship of Lincoln castle which was their hereditary possession.[38] In the reign of Richard I he supported Count John in his rebellion, and Middleton was no doubt among the lands for whose restoration he paid 2,000 marks in 1194.[39] In 1201, however, his attachment to John was rewarded by the grant of a weekly market of two days at Middleton.[40] He died shortly before January 1215, when the king ordered the Sheriff of Oxford to render to his son Richard the castle of Middleton, which was of his inheritance.[41]

Richard de Camville's relations with John appear to have been less cordial than those of his father, for in December 1215 his castle of Middleton was committed to the keeping of Engelard de Cigogné, one of the king's most hated, if also most trusted, servants,[42] and in the following May a royal order was issued for its destruction.[43] Moreover Richard's daughter and heir Idoine was by now in royal custody in Corfe castle.[44] Her wardship was sold to William, Earl of Salisbury, who arranged that she should be married to his son William Longespée, then, like his fiancée, a child under age. With her he obtained the custody of all the lands which belonged to her by right of her mother Eustachia, the daughter of Gilbert Basset, lord of Bicester.[45] In view of these circumstances it has been supposed that Richard de Camville died within a few months of his father.[46] But there is evidence that he was still alive in 1217 and 1218, and the forfeiture of his castle and the granting away of his daughter's marriage in his own lifetime can only be explained on the assumption that he had taken up arms against John in 1215. In February 1217, however, protection was granted to him and to his mother Nichole de Hay,[47] and in 1218 he is recorded on the Pipe Roll for Northamptonshire and Berkshire as owing 300 marks for having the lands which belonged to his father Gerard.[48] But there is no entry to this effect under Oxfordshire, and in a list of royal escheats drawn up in 1219 it is stated that 'the heir of Richard de Camville is of the gift of the lord king and she is in the custody of the Earl of Salisbury, and her land in Middleton is worth £15'.[49] Richard de Camville's death must have taken place between 1218 and 1225, for in the latter year the Earl of Salisbury is recorded as owing 300 marks previously debited to Richard de Camville, as well as £729 3s. 4d. and 16 palfreys for having the custody of his daughter.[50] She had married his son and attained her majority before June 1226, when the king rendered to William Longespée and his wife Idoine the lands late of Richard de Camville her father.[51] Soon afterwards

the Sheriff of Oxford was ordered to desist from demanding an ox for giving them seisin.[52]

William Longespée was killed while crusading in Egypt in February 1250, and in October his widow obtained seisin of the lands which she had inherited from her Camville ancestors.[53] She died in 1251 or 1252,[54] and Middleton then descended to her son William Longespée the third, who on 19 October 1252 did homage to the king for all the lands which his mother had held in chief in Oxfordshire,[55] paying for them a relief of 50s. Two years later, however, it was decided by the barons of the Exchequer that he should pay the full baronial relief of £100 on the ground that he had inherited the barony of Richard de Camville.[56] He died early in 1257 from injuries received in a tournament at Blyth,[57] and his estates, including Middleton, passed to Henry de Lacy, Earl of Lincoln, who married his daughter and heir Margaret.[58] On the earl's death in 1311, the manor of Middleton was described as held of the king in chief as 'parcel of the honor of Pontefract', of which the Lacys were lords.[59] By the marriage of his daughter and heir Alice to Thomas, Earl of Lancaster, Middleton became part of the great accumulation of fiefs held by the house of Lancaster. After the execution of her husband in March 1322, Alice was allowed to retain her inheritance, but she sold many of her estates to Edward II for the benefit of the Despensers, and although Middleton was restored to her in July 1322, it was with remainder to Hugh Despenser the younger.[60] In 1324, however, she forfeited her lands on her marriage to Sir Ebles Lestrange without the king's licence, and although she was allowed to retain Middleton, among other manors, it was only for her lifetime, and as the tenant of Hugh Despenser.[61] Upon the fall of the Despensers in 1327 their reversionary interest in Middleton was extinguished, the situation being that on the death of the Countess Alice, the manors would come into the king's hand. But on 28 November 1328 Edward III granted several of her manors, including Middleton, to Ebles Lestrange for life,[62] and in 1331, in return for the latter's 'good service', the king settled them on Ebles and his heirs.[63] Ebles predeceased his wife, dying in 1335, and on her death in 1348 the manor passed to Roger Lestrange, lord of Knockin, in whose family it remained for over a hundred years.

To the Lestranges, whose main estates were in Shropshire, Middleton presented itself as a manor which could conveniently be assigned in dower, and it was so held, first by Joan, the widow of Roger Lestrange (d. 1349),[64] then by Alice, widow of Roger Lestrange (d. 1382),[65] and thirdly by Maud,

[38] J. W. F. Hill, *Medieval Lincoln*, 88–89.
[39] *Pipe R.* 1194 (P.R.S. n.s. v), 118. He still owed £560: cf. Hill, op. cit. 190.
[40] D.L. 42/1, f. 439b; cf. Kennett, *Paroch. Antiq.* i. 228.
[41] *Rot. Litt. Pat.* (Rec. Com.), 127.
[42] *Rot. Litt. Claus.* (Rec. Com.), i. 241; cf. ibid. 252.
[43] Ibid. 273.
[44] *Rot. Litt. Pat.* 170.
[45] Ibid. 178; *Rot. Litt. Claus.* i. 265; see above, p. 21.
[46] Kennett, *Paroch. Antiq.* i. 252–3; cf. Farrer, *Honors*, ii. 221.
[47] *Pat. R.* 1216–25, 32.
[48] E 372/62, under *nova oblata*.
[49] *Bk. of Fees*, 253.
[50] Kennett, *Paroch. Antiq.* i. 278.
[51] *Rot. Litt. Claus.* ii. 110, 123.
[52] *Ex. e Rot. Fin.* (Rec. Com.), i. 148.

[53] Kennett, *Paroch. Antiq.* i. 345.
[54] *Complete Peerage*, xi. 383.
[55] *Close R.* 1251–3, 150.
[56] Kennett, *Paroch. Antiq.* i. 347.
[57] *Complete Peerage*, xi. 384.
[58] According to the marriage contract drawn up in 1256 Middleton formed part of Margaret's marriage portion: Kennett, *Paroch. Antiq.* i. 354–5.
[59] *Cal. Inq. p.m.* v, p. 157.
[60] *Cal. Pat.* 1318–23, 575; 1321–4, 180.
[61] Ibid. 1324–7, 103.
[62] Ibid. 1327–30, 338.
[63] Ibid. 1377–81, 83.
[64] *Cal. Close*, 1349–54, 111; Kennett, *Paroch. Antiq.* ii. 103.
[65] Kennett, *Paroch. Antiq.* ii. 171; *Le Strange Records*, ed. H. Le Strange (1916), 336.

widow of John Lestrange (d. 1398).[66] In 1479 on the death of John, the grandson of John Lestrange, the manor came into the possession of the earls of Derby, by the marriage of his only daughter and heiress Joan to George Stanley, son of the 1st earl.[67] In 1597 the 6th earl sold Middleton to Richard Cox, a citizen and Merchant Taylor of London,[68] who in 1602 sold it to John Harman of Lewes for £1,100.[69] Harman died without issue in 1629, having settled the manor on his cousin Nicholas Harman of Chelsea.[70] Nicholas is said to have erected a 'commodious residence' near the site of the castle, in which he resided until his death in 1668.[71] He was High Sheriff of Oxfordshire in 1648. His only daughter Hester married in 1673 Alexander Denton of Hillesden (Bucks.), whose eldest son, Sir Edmund Denton, sold the manor to the Hon. Henry Boyle for £12,500 in February 1712.[72] Boyle was the third son of Charles Boyle, Lord Clifford of Lanesborough. He had a successful political career, holding office as Chancellor of the Exchequer and Principal Secretary of State under Queen Anne, and was created Lord Carleton in 1714 for his services to the Whig party.[73] He died unmarried in 1725, leaving his estates in Wiltshire and Oxfordshire to his nephew the 3rd Duke of Queensbury. In 1735 the duke obtained an Act of Parliament[74] permitting him to dispose of the Middleton estate in order to buy other lands adjoining his Wiltshire property. In March 1737 his trustees sold the house and park with the immediately adjoining lands to William Villiers, 3rd Earl of Jersey, for £6,000, and in June they parted with the 426 acres of Wilson's Farm to William Leigh of Southwark for £3,850. In 1740 Lord Jersey bought Abraham's Farm for £4,300, and in 1748 he acquired the manorial rights and the Duke of Queensbury's remaining lands for £2,780. In the same year he purchased the greater part of the Priory Farm from the executor of John Kinge for £1,900.[75] Finally, in 1765 he was able to buy Wilson's Farm from Thomas Leigh (brother of the original purchaser, who had died in 1740) for £5,200.[76] Thus for a total expenditure of some £20,000 Lord Jersey became the proprietor of almost the whole parish. In the time of his grandson the 5th earl (1805–59), described by 'Nimrod' as 'the hardest, boldest, most judicious, and perhaps the most elegant rider to hounds whom the world ever saw', Middleton became celebrated for its kennels and its stables, and the village gave its name to the Derby

winner of 1825. Middleton Park remained the principal seat of the Jersey family until 1946, when the 9th earl sold the house and estate to Mr. A. C. J. Wall.

LESSER ESTATE. Although the De Camvilles were considerable benefactors to Bicester Priory and other religious houses, their grants did not include any land in Middleton, nor did their successors part with any of their demesne in this way. In 1349, however, three messuages and 200 acres of land in the manor were conveyed to the Prior and Convent of Bicester under a general licence in mortmain obtained in the reign of Edward II. The nominal grantors were three chaplains, but the real donor was Thomas de Stapenhulle, who had conveyed the lands to them a few months earlier.[77] The gift was confirmed by royal letters patent on 3 October 1350.[78] After the dissolution of Bicester Priory in 1536 these lands, valued at £2 a year,[79] were among those granted by Henry VIII to Roger Moore of Bicester for £187 17s. 2d.[80] The 'Priory Farm' was subsequently acquired by Thomas Martyn from Moore's coheirs, Mary, the wife of Sir Michael Blount, and Elizabeth, the wife of Sir John Brocket of Brocket Hall (Herts.).[81] On Martyn's death it passed to his sister and heir Marian, the wife of Henry Standard, whose son Thomas is said also to have acquired a small estate in this parish formerly belonging to Oseney Abbey.[82] In the inquisition taken after the death of Thomas Standard in 1623, his estate in Middleton Stoney is described as a 'manor' comprising 3 messuages, 1 dove-house, 2 cottages, 3 tofts, 200 acres of land, and some acres of meadow.[83] It is also reputed a manor in an earlier conveyance of 1590.[84] Thomas Standard's son Henry settled at Middleton and lived at the Priory Farm during the greater part of his life. Henry's son Henry, a Fellow of All Souls, died in 1670 at the age of 23, and in the following year he sold the estate to Gabriel Merry of Heyford Warren for £800. In 1679 Merry sold it to William Kinge of Lilbourne (Northants) for the same price. After the death of William Kinge's son John in 1742, the latter's executor sold 24½ acres known as the Moor Ground to Lord Jersey for £290, and in December 1748 Lord Jersey purchased the capital messuage and 153 acres known as King's Closes for £1,900.[85] Thus the greater part of the property came into the possession of the Jersey family, and the mansion

[66] Kennett, *Paroch. Antiq.* ii. 182. For the transaction whereby, in the time of Richard Lestrange (d. 1449), the manor was granted to trustees who held it to his use, see *Cal. Pat.* 1429–36, 191; ibid. 1446–52, 62; *Cal. Close,* 1447–54, 155; *Cal. Antrobus Deeds,* ed. R. B. Pugh (Wilts. Arch. Soc. Record Branch, iii, 1947), no. 55; and C 139/134/29.
[67] *Complete Peerage,* xii. 356.
[68] C.P. 25(2)/198, East. 39 Eliz.
[69] O.R.O. J I a/1. According to Blomfield (*Mid.* 32) Harman was descended from the family of that name 'long resident at Taynton', but his will indicates that he was a native of Lewes (Suss.). He left a gilt standing cup to the town of Portsmouth 'for the love I hadd unto that place'. In legal records he is described as a merchant. For his activities as a money-lender see E 178/4132, where he is described as of Barlestone (Leics.).
[70] C 142/455/84; ibid. 462/64, 463/69; P.C.C. 50 Ridley.
[71] Dunkin, *Oxon.* ii. 75. There is a copy of Nicholas Harman's will in O.R.O. J I a/4.
[72] O.R.O. J I a/16–20.
[73] *D.N.B.*

[74] 8 Geo. II, c. 5 (priv. act).
[75] O.R.O. J I a–n.
[76] Ibid. c/8–9. A map of the land acquired by Lord Jersey in 1737 is attached to the deed of purchase. Another map, formerly at Middleton Park and now hanging in the 'Jersey Arms', marks the house and park as 'lately bought by the Rt. Honble the Earl of Jersey', and shows the lands then still in the hands of the Duke of Queensbury. A map of Wilson's Farm made in 1737 is now in O.R.O. J IV/3.
[77] Kennett, *Paroch. Antiq.* ii. 104–5; E 326/ B 2471, 2646, 3535.
[78] *Cal. Pat.* 1348–50, 576.
[79] *Valor Eccl.* (Rec. Com.), ii. 188.
[80] *L. & P. Hen. VIII,* xv, p. 408; for Moore, see above, p. 22.
[81] Dunkin, *Oxon.* ii. 79.
[82] Ibid. 80. But Middleton does not figure in the account of Oseney's property in *Valor Eccl.*
[83] C 142/397/77.
[84] C 66/1341.
[85] O.R.O. J I e/1–6, 12–13, 15–16.

house, being no longer required, was demolished or allowed to fall into decay.[86]

ECONOMIC HISTORY. In the absence of a continuous series of manorial records, the economic history of Middleton before its inclosure in the early 18th century depends almost entirely upon the meagre documentation afforded by the Hundred Rolls, two surviving account rolls, and a series of extents made in connexion with the inquisitions held after the deaths of successive lords of the manor.

In 1086[87] much of the parish was occupied by woodland (8 × 8 furlongs). There was, however, land for 16 ploughs; 3 were in demesne and 13 in the hands of 25 villeins (*villani*) with 7 bordars. There is no reference to any meadow or pasture. Its omission is significant, for in the 14th-century extents[88] there are said to be only 5 acres of meadow belonging to the manor, 3 in King's Sutton, 8 miles away in Northamptonshire, and 2 in Lower Heyford. The circumstances in which this unusual arrangement arose are not recorded, but the connexion between Middleton and King's Sutton was a feudal one, the latter manor having been granted to Richard de Camville by Henry II in or before 1155.[89] In 1241, when William Longespée, as Camville's successor, granted the manor of King's Sutton to his brother Stephen, he was careful to reserve 'a certain meadow in Sidenham which my men of Middleton were wont to mow' and to stipulate that Stephen and his heirs should provide food and drink for 25 men of Middleton on the day when they came to mow it.[90] The surviving account for 1295–6, in recording the expense of providing bread and beer for 36 villeins and cottagers raising hay for one day, duly notes that 'the lady of King's Sutton finds food for the mowers'.[91]

William Longespée's charter implies that the number of villeins was the same in 1241 as it had been in 1086. This is confirmed by the account of Middleton in the Hundred Rolls of 1279, which gives the names of 27 villein tenants, each holding a single virgate, and paying 3s. 9d. a year, besides performing unspecified 'works and customs'. There were in addition 4 free tenants holding a total of 9 virgates, and 14 burgage-holders, 10 of whom paid 1s. a year, the other 4 paid 6d.[92] The existence of these 'burgesses', coupled with the grant of a weekly market in 1202, and of a market and annual fair in 1294,[93] indicates an attempt on the part of the lords of Middleton to establish there something more than a purely agricultural community, as Robert Arsic had done at Cogges.[94] By 1295–6 the burgage rents received had risen to £1 1s. 11d., while the profits of the 'market court' amounted to 3s. 10d. The burgages are not mentioned as such in the extent of the manor drawn up after the death of Roger Lestrange in 1349.[95] But their occupants may have been among the free men formerly rendering £2 15s. 9½d. a year, whose holdings were reported to have come into the lord's hand owing to the death of the tenants, and whose lands were 'lying untilled

and uncultivated and worth nothing'. Their tenants had in fact perished in the Black Death, as had 'certain villeins who also died in the same pestilence', and whose lands and tenements were likewise lying 'uncultivated and in common'. No one, the jurors stated, would take them up, 'because almost all the men there are dead'. The perquisites of the court and view of frankpledge, valued at 24s. in 1328, were now worth only 6s. 'and not more in these days on account of the aforesaid pestilence'. Subsequent inquisitions are unfortunately not accompanied by detailed extents, so that it is impossible to say to what extent the economy of the manor may have been permanently affected by the Black Death. It is equally uncertain whether the extinction of the burgage tenements is to be attributed to the same calamity; but no further reference to them has been found, and with their disappearance Middleton became once more a normal agricultural community engaged in the cultivation of its open fields.

The history of the fields themselves is not well documented. In 1348 and 1349 it was stated that of the lord's demesne of 200 acres, half could be sown each year, that each acre when sown was worth 4d., and if not sown, nothing.[96] In 1355, however, a tenement of 1½ acres is described as lying in three different fields, one ½-acre in the field towards Chesterton, another in the 'Middelfeld', and the third in the field 'towards —'.[97] It would therefore appear that there was a change from a two- to a three-field system between 1349 and 1355, but only two fields—North and South—are described in an elaborate terrier made in 1554, and still in use in 1639.[98] According to this, 'every yardland hath 40 acres in the fields in the south field and north field, except three yards for every yardland in the north field only'. The testimony of the 17th-century glebe terriers is ambiguous, for in those of 1679 and 1701 the parson's land is said to lie partly in 'the South Fields' and partly in the North Field, while in 1697 the South Field is referred to in the singular.[99] In 1554 the total arable land amounted to some 1,986 acres. The demesne, consisting of 9 yardlands, accounted for 352 acres; 330 acres were held by freeholders, and the remaining 1,304 acres were copyhold. These 'acres' were 'not of measure, but as the acres lie, little and big'—that is, they represented the actual 'lands' or strips into which the fields were divided. The amount of grass-land is not stated in the terrier, but in October 1636 Nicholas Harman, as lord of the manor, and Edward Fitzherbert, as 'his farmer of the demesne there', agreed with the parson and the tenants 'to lay down for every yardland of the said farm and demesnes, 6 acres for grass every second year in the North field, and that every one of the said tenants shall lay down for every yardland which they hold 5 acres for grass yearly in the Cornfield'. A similar agreement was made at the court baron and court leet held on 6 October 1656, when it was 'ordered and agreed

[86] Dunkin, *Oxon*. ii. 80; Henry Standard paid tax on 10 hearths in 1665: *Hearth Tax Oxon*. 200.
[87] *V.C.H. Oxon*. i. 417.
[88] C 135/90/1; ibid. 101/6.
[89] *Pipe R.* 1156–8 (Rec. Com.), 40; cf. *Rot. Litt. Claus.* (Rec. Com.), i. 252.
[90] Kennett, *Paroch. Antiq.* i. 319; *Fines Oxon.* 236.
[91] D.L. 29/1/1.   [92] *Rot. Hund.* (Rec. Com.), ii. 833.
[93] Kennett, *Paroch. Antiq.* i. 228; *Cal. Chart. R.* 1257–

1300, 436. The grant of 1202 had evidently lapsed by 1279 as no market is mentioned in *Rot. Hund.*
[94] *Sir Chris. Hatton's Bk. of Seals*, ed. L. C. Loyd and Doris M. Stenton (Northants Rec. Soc. xv), 78.
[95] C 135/101/6.
[96] Ibid. 90/1, 101/6.
[97] S.C. 2/197/57: the last word is illegible.
[98] B.M. Add. MS. 6419, ff. 1–36.
[99] Oxf. Archd. Oxon. b 41, ff. 32–35.

that every one of the said Manor shall lay down from ploughing 4 acres of land for a yardland in each field and so after that rate for any greater or lesser quantity of land and this order shall continue for four years next ensueing the date hereof'.[1]

The inclosure of the parish began in about 1686, when part of the glebe—hitherto lying in over 50 distinct 'parcels'—was 'taken out of the common field . . . and inclos'd by a general consent of the inhabitants'.[2] In 1706 it was stated that this inclosure concerned 'part of a common field which was barren land and lay remote from the town, and is since found a very profitable improvement of the said rectory.'[3] In the following year, however, the 'three grounds then laid out for the rector' were exchanged for 'two grounds improv'd by Sanfoyn-grass' of slightly greater acreage.[4] Finally, in November 1709, Sir Edmund Denton and the other proprietors of land in the common fields 'having proposed that some considerable improvement might be made of their said lands by inclosing of some part thereof . . . came to an agreement and entered into articles', as a result of which the remainder of the parish was inclosed, the rector was freed from the obligation of keeping a bull and a boar 'for the use of the cattle . . . in the parish', and the lord was to 'hold and enjoy all the rest and residue of the said manor . . . inclosed and free and discharged of common'.[5] This agreement was confirmed by a decree in Chancery in July 1714.[6] A map of the parish made in 1710 shows it as it was 'immediately after the inclosure'.[7] There were then five principal farms, totalling 1,247 acres. By 1737, however, when another map was made for Lord Jersey,[8] three of the farms had been bought up by the Duke of Queensbury, and Lord Jersey had begun to make possible the later extension of the park by acquiring lands adjoining it on the south and east. There are now five farms in the parish: Manor (formerly Middleton Grounds) farm, Park farm, Dewar's farm, Rectory farm,[9] and Copse farm,[10] the two last being run as a single agricultural unit.

Little is known about the population before the 19th century. In 1676 the Compton census recorded 90 adults,[11] and in 1759 the rector returned that there were between 30 and 40 houses.[12] In 1801 there were 309 inhabitants. A peak of 340 was reached in 1821 and this was followed by a steady decline. The more marked fall of 1861 was due to Lord Jersey not being in residence. In 1881 the figure was 293, but this had risen to 324 by 1901. In the early 20th century there was a declining population, but between 1931 and 1951 it increased rapidly from 251 to 477.[13]

CHURCH. The remains of the existing mid-12th-century building constitute the earliest evidence for the existence of a church at Middleton. It is not known at what date the advowson was granted to the Abbot and Convent of Barlings (Lincs.), but the donor was probably Gerard de Camville, who by his marriage to Nichole de Hay had become the patron of this Premonstratensian abbey, founded by his wife's uncle Robert de Hay in 1154.[14] The gift was, however, disputed by William Longespée, Earl of Salisbury, in the time of Bishop Hugh de Welles (1209 35), whose rolls record that in view of the contention between the earl and the abbot over the advowson of Middleton, he had, at their request, presented Gervase de Pavely by authority of the Lateran Council.[15] The case was evidently decided in favour of the abbot, for he continued to present to the rectory throughout the 13th century.[16] A further dispute arose when Peter Durand, rector in the reign of Edward I, died at the Roman curia. For the Pope claimed the right to present to all benefices whose incumbents died in his court and proceeded to provide Richard de Celleseye, professor of canon law. The abbot's presentee was induced to resign, and Richard was admitted to the rectory in May 1300.[17] In 1322 Alice de Lacy, Countess of Lincoln, then lady of the manor, confirmed the gift of the advowson to the canons of Barlings,[18] but in 1334, for reasons unexplained, the abbot and convent obtained a licence to convey it to the Bishop of Lincoln.[19] During the vacancies of the see in 1342 and 1424 the king presented. The presentation remained in the hands of the bishops of Lincoln until 1856, when, by an Order in Council, it was transferred to the Bishop of Oxford in accordance with an arrangement made by the Ecclesiastical Commissioners whereby livings in episcopal patronage were transferred to the bishop in whose diocese they were locally situated.[20]

The rectory was valued at £5 in 1254,[21] at £10 in 1291,[22] and at £12 16s. in 1535.[23] Much information survives for its value in the late 17th century, for two of the rectors have left records of tithes received, ranging in value from £62 in 1666 to £116 in 1683,[24] plus the value of the glebe. At the inclosure of the parish in 1709, the tithes were commuted at the rate of £2 2s. 6d. per yardland, making a total of £100 15s.[25] In 1842 a new tithe award was made and the tithes commuted for £436 10s.,[26] thus bringing the total value of the rectory to well over £500.

The glebe, valued at 13s. 4d. in 1341,[27] was rated at 2 yardlands in the 17th century.[28] At the general inclosure of 1709 the rector received about 70 acres.[29]

[1] Antrobus Deeds (Wilts. Arch. Soc. Museum, Devizes).
[2] Oxf. Archd. Oxon. b 41, f. 36.
[3] Oxf. Dioc. (uncat.).
[4] Oxf. Archd. Oxon. b 25, ff. 251-2.
[5] O.R.O. J I ae/1: contemporary copy of agreement.
[6] Ibid. J I ae/2; Linc. Dioc. Registry, Ben. 2, 21: copies.
[7] O.R.O. J IV/2.
[8] This map now hangs in the 'Jersey Arms', Middleton Stoney.
[9] The farm buildings were erected by Lord Jersey in 1815 as part of his agreement with the rector.
[10] The present farm-house was built in 1911.
[11] Cf. the hearth tax of 1662 (the fullest for Oxon.) which lists 28 householders: Hearth Tax Oxon. 235.
[12] Oxf. Dioc. d 556.   [13] Census, 1801–1951.
[14] H.M. Colvin, White Canons in England, 76.
[15] Rot. Welles, i. 107.
[16] Rot. Grosse. 498; Rot. Graves. 227.

[17] For a list of medieval presentations see MS. Top. Oxon. d 460.
[18] B.M. Cotton. MS. Faust B. I, ff. 165b–166b: Barlings Cart.
[19] Cal. Pat. 1330–4, 522; ibid. 1334–8, 49.
[20] Blo. Mid. 83.   [21] Lunt, Val. Norw. 321.
[22] Tax. Eccl. (Rec. Com.), 31.
[23] Valor Eccl. (Rec. Com.), ii. 161.
[24] Blo. Mid. 44. There are more figures (ibid. 84) and details about different kinds of tithes (ibid. 45–52).
[25] O.R.O. J Iae/1; ibid. 2: 1714 Chancery decree confirming the arrangement; Blo. Mid. 85.
[26] Bodl. Tithe award.
[27] Inq. Non. (Rec. Com.), 132.
[28] Blo. Mid. 86.
[29] O.R.O. J I ae/1–2; terriers of 1712 in Oxf. Archd. Oxon. b 25, f. 250; of 1716 ibid. b 41, f. 37; of 1719 ibid. f. 38. See also Oxf. Dioc. c 105, ff. 7, 81b.

In 1749 he and Lord Jersey exchanged about 30 acres of land,[30] and in 1814 the rector exchanged his entire glebe, including the Rectory house, for a larger estate, which he sold in 1920.[31]

Owing to extensive alterations in the 19th century, the architectural history of the church of *ALL SAINTS* is in some respects not easy to follow, and there is little documentary evidence to supplement that afforded by the fabric itself. The earliest parts of the existing church are the chancel and the enriched south doorway, which date from the mid-12th century. The latter, however, is not in its original position, having been moved to its present setting when the south aisle was built in the 14th century. Late in the 12th century the existing chancel arch was built, and the nave was enlarged by the addition of a north aisle. The 'Transitional' arcade of three arches is supported on cylindrical columns with carved capitals. The arches are remarkable in that they are moulded on the south side only, their north face being flush with the wall above. There is a north doorway of similar date, with a hood-mould terminating in animal heads. The west tower was added early in the 13th century. Its most conspicuous feature is the arcaded upper stage of 'Early English' character, surmounted by a battlemented parapet. It was rebuilt from the ground in 1858, but the old materials were reused, and comparison with the engraving of 1846 in *A Guide to the Architectural Antiquities in the Neighbourhood of Oxford* shows that the design of the original was carefully reproduced.

The south aisle and its arcade of two arches were added early in the 14th century. The eastern bay of the aisle appears to have been separated from the nave by a solid wall, the existing plain arch being a modern insertion. The new aisle was lighted by two four-light windows with flat soffits. Similar windows were inserted in the north wall of the north aisle at the same time. Later in the 14th century two windows were inserted in the south wall of the chancel, one of two, the other of three lights. The latter survives, but the other was destroyed when the organ-chamber was built in 1868. Buckler's sketch of 1823[32] shows that there was also a 'low-side' window at the west end of the south wall of the chancel. The original high-pitched roof of the nave was replaced by the present clerestory in the 15th century, but the evidence of its former existence remained until 1858 on the east side of the tower.[33] The south porch in its present form dates from the same period, but it incorporates the moulded jambs and voussoirs of an early 13th-century arch which presumably formed part of an earlier porch.

No medieval fittings survive, but the cutting away of the 'dog-tooth' ornamentation of the chancel arch immediately above the capitals shows where the framing of the chancel screen or rood beam formerly rested.[34] A cross, two candlesticks, and a holy-water 'stoke', all of brass, are mentioned in an Edwardian inventory,[35] and in 1545 Richard Smith left 4d. towards the maintenance of the two 'standards' before the high altar.[36] In 1583 several parishioners confessed that they had portions of a cope and other church ornaments in their possession, and were ordered to restore them.[37]

Any alterations which may have been made to the fabric of the church in the 16th, 17th, or 18th centuries were obliterated in 1858, and as no churchwardens' accounts survive, no record of them has been preserved. It is known, however, that it was in the time of the Revd. William Offley, rector from 1689 to 1724, that the communion-table was first railed in, for he recorded the fact himself. In 1699 he wrote that 'There are usually five Communions in the year, 1 on Palm Sunday, Easter Day, Whitsunday, 1 after Michaelmas—Christmas Day. All the people come into the chancel, the women kneel on the north side, and the men on the south side of the chancel. I begin the sacrament to those of the north side first, and thence proceed to those on the south side, without any respect of persons, but as they kneel in order, they receive. After the bread and cup are deliver'd, the clark sings a Psalm and then I go on to conclude the office.' But in 1702 he notes that 'Since I rail'd in the Communion Table the people kneel at the rail, only the clark comes with the rector within the rail—to be ready to fetch the wine during the administration of the sacrament'.[38]

In 1805 the Jersey chapel was built on the north side of the chancel in order to contain the family monuments. It was originally Gothic in style, as can be seen from the engraving in Skelton's *Antiquities of Oxford* (1823), but at a later date it was given a 'Norman' character by rebuilding the window, archway, and pinnacles, and the interior was decorated with heraldic shields.[39] The principal monuments are to Anne, Countess of Jersey (d. 1762), George, 5th Earl of Jersey (d. 1859), and his daughters Sarah, Princess Nicolas Esterhazy (d. 1853), and Clementina (d. 1858).

The restoration of 1856–8 was carried out under the direction of S. S. Teulon.[40] It involved the rebuilding of the tower, the whole of the north aisle, and of the south aisle to the west of the porch. The roofs of both nave and chancel (previously covered by a flat plaster ceiling) were rebuilt, as also were those of the aisles. A new east window was substituted for the plain window with a central mullion shown in Buckler's drawing of 1823. In 1868 a vestry and organ-chamber were added on the south side of the chancel to the designs of G. E. Street, and the interior of the church was completely refitted with a new pulpit, lectern, altar, reredos, piscina, rails, candlesticks, and other furniture. The organ was installed in 1871, and in 1881 the last of the pre-Victorian fittings disappeared when Lord Jersey's private pew at the west end of the nave was removed.[41]

[30] O.R.O. J I e: 21 deeds 1671–1749.
[31] See above, p. 244.
[32] B.M. Add. MS. 36373, f. 193. There are also drawings by J. Buckler in MS. Top. Oxon. a 67, ff. 375–6.
[33] See Buckler drawing (f. 376) as in n. 32.
[34] The rood light is mentioned in a will of 1545: Blo. *Mid.* 67.
[35] *Chant. Cert.* 81.
[36] Blo. *Mid.* 67.
[37] Oxf. Archd. Oxon. c 5, f. 64.

[38] Par. Rec. Rector's bk. 1699 and 1702.
[39] The original designs are in MS. Top. Oxon. a 48. For blazons of arms see Bodl. G.A. Oxon. 16° 215, pp. 200 *a–d*, 202 *a–b*; Bodl. 1373 e 65.
[40] *Ecclesiologist*, 1856, xvii. 157. For a pre-restoration view see plate facing p. 267.
[41] Blo. *Mid.* 70–72. Dunkin describes the pew as 'elegantly fitted up with curtains, cushions and carpet, to which is added the singular and luxurious appendage of a grate and set of fire irons'.

The present font, which replaces a former marble one of 18th- or early 19th-century date, was presented to the church by Julia, Countess of Jersey, in about 1860. It is said to have come from the King's Chapel at Islip, but before the end of the 17th century it had passed into the possession of the Brown family of Kiddington, who believed that it was the font in which Edward the Confessor was baptized and had an inscription cut on the base to that effect.[42] Its decoration is of 14th-century character, but it is possible that this has been cut on an older tub-shaped font.

In addition to the Jersey monuments there are two late-17th-century cartouche tablets in the chancel in memory of the children of the Revd. William Offley, and there is a brass on the floor commemorating Elizabeth, wife of John Harman, 'Lord of this towne', who died in 1607.[43]

In 1552 there were three 'great bells' in the tower, one sanctus bell, and two hand bells.[44] In 1955 there were five bells, all made by Henry Bagley in 1717 and rehung in 1883, when the tenor was recast. They were again rehung in 1910.[45] Two of them bear the name of Lord Carleton, who gave a set of silver-gilt communion plate to the church in 1718. This consists of a chalice, with cover, a large paten, and a flagon. There is also a silver chalice dated 1575,[46] and a silver alms-dish given by Mrs. Susannah Harman shortly before her death in 1688.[47]

The registers begin in 1598. The parish records include constables' accounts for the years 1740–57.

NONCONFORMITY. There has been practically no nonconformity, either Roman Catholic or Protestant. In the early 18th century there was one Roman Catholic family, the Williamses.[48] In 1797 the house of Mary Benham was licensed as a dissenting meeting-place,[49] but 19th-century reports emphasize the absence of dissent.

SCHOOLS. Rawlinson mentions that the rector (William Offley, 1689–1724) had educated the poor children of the place for more than 20 years.[50] In 1724 it was stated that four children were taught at the charge of the minister.[51] The school had closed by 1738,[52] and the village was without a school until the early 19th century. By 1808 Sophia, Countess of Jersey (d. 1867), had established three schools, one an industrial school for 12 girls who were taught reading, writing, arithmetic, sewing, and housework during a three- or four-year course of training as domestic servants. In the second school 30 younger girls were taught reading and needlework, and in the third 20 or 30 younger boys were taught reading,

net-making, and 'odd jobs'. The rector ran an evening school where about 15 older boys learned the three R's. All four schools gave instruction in the catechism and all were supported by Lady Jersey, who also bore the expense of boarding and clothing the girls of the industrial school.[53] By 1815 Lady Jersey's three schools had been reorganized into a girls' school with 40 pupils, including the 12 boarders, a boys' school with 34, and an infants' with 18 children.[54] The separate infants' school was closed by 1819 and its pupils divided between the boys' and girls' schools.[55] Both schools had Sunday meetings, and in 1833 each had 36 pupils, though there were only 6 boarders. The evening school had 10 to 15 boys attending it.[56]

New school buildings for Lord Jersey's Church of England School appear to have been erected about 1837 on his land[57] and the infants became a separate department. In 1854 there were 30 boys, 20 girls, and 15 infants, but the evening school had closed.[58] By her will, proved in 1867, Lady Jersey bequeathed £4,500 for the endowment of a training school for domestic servants. Six girls chosen from Middleton, Chesterton, and Somerton schools continued to be boarded and clothed at Middleton and were placed under a matron.[59] In 1871 there were 107 pupils in all,[60] and by 1887 the departments had again been reduced to two: boys, with 35 pupils under a master; and girls and infants with 68 pupils under a mistress.[61]

The two departments which had 29 and 38 pupils respectively in 1906[62] were amalgamated in 1924, and in 1933 the school was reorganized as a junior school, senior pupils being transferred to Bicester. The school, which was controlled in 1951, had 25 pupils on its books in 1937 and 23 in 1954.[63] Lady Jersey's foundation of 1867 was regulated by a Board of Education scheme in 1931, and in 1955 when its endowments, amounting to nearly £10,000 in stock, were producing a gross yearly income of £289 6s. 6d., it was proposed that it should be amalgamated with Lady Jersey's Almshouses Charity.[64]

CHARITIES. In the early 19th century it was the custom to purchase coal for the poor out of the poor rates. As this was made illegal by the Poor Law Act of 1834, a parish meeting decided in 1835 'that a sufficient sum to purchase the usual quantity of coals should be raised by voluntary subscription'.[65] This was the beginning of the Coal Club, to which all the cottagers subscribed 6d. a week throughout the year. At Christmas, with the help of a generous subscription from Lord Jersey, a large quantity of coal was ordered from the colliery and delivered to

---

[42] The font was later bought by Sir Gregory Page-Turner, and in 1829 by Dean Ireland for Islip rectory: W.A.M. Reg. Bk. lxi, ff. 86–86b. See also Bodl. G.A. Oxon. 4° 686, p. 208; 2194 c 15, f. 158b, 169.
[43] For blazons of arms see Bodl. G.A. Oxon. 16° 217, pp. 185–7.
[44] Chant. Cert. 81.
[45] For inscriptions see Blo. Mid. 69 and Ch. Bells Oxon. ii. 171–2.
[46] In 1583 Simon Hawkins, churchwarden, confessed that he had 'chaunged the chalice of the parish into a communion cuppe of the vallewe of iii li': Oxf. Archd. Oxon. c 5, f. 64.
[47] For description of plate see Evans, Ch. Plate.
[48] Oxoniensia, xiii. 78.
[49] Oxf. Dioc. c 644, f. 32.

[50] Par. Coll. ii. 208.
[51] T. Cox, Magna Britannia, iv. 498.
[52] Oxf. Dioc. d 553.
[53] Ibid. d 707.
[54] Ibid. c 433.
[55] Educ. of Poor, 727.
[56] Educ. Enq. Abstract, 750.
[57] Vol. Sch. Ret.
[58] Wilb. Visit.
[59] Blo. Mid. 88; Wing, Annals, 109.
[60] Elem. Educ. Ret.
[61] Kelly's Dir. Oxon. (1887); cf. Ret. of Sch.
[62] List of Sch.
[63] Inf. Oxon. Educ. Cttee.
[64] Inf. Revd. W. E. Sawyer; see below.
[65] O.R.O. J VI k/3.

Heyford station, whence it was carted by the earl's teams and those of his tenant farmers to the homes of the cottagers. The average allocation was about 25 cwt. in the time of the 7th earl (1859–1915).[66] The club has since been discontinued.

By her will proved in 1867 Sophia, Countess of Jersey, left money to found a charity for the benefit of the occupants of four cottages built by Lord Jersey and known as almshouses. In 1925 the capital, consisting of £1,736 in stock, was producing an annual income of £52. The 'almshouses' were maintained by successive Lords Jersey, but were never handed over to the trustees of the charity.[67] They were sold with the rest of the Jersey estate in 1946 and were subsequently let as ordinary cottages. In 1955, when the endowment amounted to £2,045 16s. and the annual gross income to £61 7s. 6d.,

it was proposed to amalgamate the Almshouses Charity with the Countess of Jersey's Foundation. Pensions already authorized by the trustees were to continue.[68]

The scheme finally established in May 1955 provided that the trustees should apply £30 a year for the benefit of the aged poor in Middleton or its neighbourhood. They were to use the residue of the net income for the benefit of boys and girls of Bicester or the Rural District of Ploughley. First and second preference was to be given respectively to residents of Middleton and to girls. The money was to be applied in a variety of ways: for awards of scholarships, &c., tenable at an approved place of learning; for grants for foreign travel or for studying music or other arts; and for the promotion of the social and physical training of the beneficiaries.[69]

MIXBURY

THE parish lies in the north-east corner of the county with the River Ouse dividing it on the north from Buckinghamshire, and the Northamptonshire border on the west separating it from the parish of Evenley (Northants). The modern parish (2,449 a.) is smaller than the ancient one (2,972 a.),[1] which included a detached portion of 523 acres in which Willaston lay. This was transferred to Hethe parish in 1888.[2] The nearest market towns are Buckingham, 6 miles distant, and Bicester, 8 miles away.

The ground lies for the most part about 400 feet above sea-level, but in the north east it falls gradually and then more sharply to the Ouse to about 320 feet. The parish lies on the Great Oolite, but much of its eastern half is covered by flint and oolite gravel.[3] In the northern part of the parish the country is on the whole bare, although Sainfoin Corner is a fair-sized plantation. Here was the Bayard's Green of medieval and later times (see below), and the 'downs' of the Inclosure Act of 1730. The general impression, even in summer, is still of a bleak exposed plateau. The southern half of the parish is more sheltered: there are two large plantations, Mixbury Plantation and Park Thorns, in the south, and the Hulls and the Pits in the south-west. A stream flows just north of Mixbury village and joins the Ouse near Fulwell, one of the parish's two ancient hamlets.

The main road from Buckingham to Banbury, which became a turnpike in 1744,[4] bisects the parish; the village is linked to this high road and to the Oxford–Brackley road by minor roads. Other small roads and foot-paths intersect the parish and also two railways, the former London and North-Western opened in 1850 to the north and the former Great Central opened in 1899 to the east.[5] The nearest station is the former L.M.S. Fulwell and Westbury

station. Half of Fulwell Bridge is in the parish, and the other half is in Buckinghamshire. In 1877 it was reported that the road here was often flooded and that a rough causeway for foot passengers had been provided.[6]

Mixbury village is placed fairly centrally within the parish, just off the Buckingham–Banbury road. The water lies near the surface here and the many wells afford an ample supply.[7] Mixbury does not appear to have ever been a large village. In 1662 and 1665 34 and 21 householders in Mixbury and Fulwell were listed for the hearth taxes.[8] In 1665 two large houses had eight hearths each and there were only three other small farm-houses. There seem to have been about 43 dwellings in Mixbury itself, few scattered houses outside and one manor-house only at Fulwell in the mid-18th century.[9] By 1768 the house at Fulwell had been pulled down, but a farm is mentioned at Willaston, by then an almost deserted hamlet, and the total number of houses was said to be about 60.[10] The village was at its largest in the mid-19th century, but had considerably shrunk in size again by 1951, when there were only 64 houses in the whole parish.[11]

Davis's map of 1797 shows the village dwellings close to the stream and the church in a rather isolated position to the east,[12] but in 1955 the village lay on either side of the minor road which connects Mixbury with the main Banbury road. Its general appearance, which is both neat and attractive, is late-19th century, since in 1874 the thatched and dilapidated cottages, built of local stone, were replaced by order of the Court of Chancery with about 40 semi-detached houses, built of coursed rubble with red brick dressings. The twelve lime-trees, planted between the cottages, were presented by

[66] R. Elkerton's MS. notes p. 70: see above, p. 244, n. 29.
[67] Ibid.; Kelly's Dir. Oxon. (1939).
[68] Inf. Revd. W. E. Sawyer; Min. of Educ. Draft Scheme 195.
[69] Char. Com. E. 16500.
[1] O.S. Map 6″, xi (1884).
[2] Census, 1891; Local Govt. Bd. Order 21436: copy in O.R.O.
[3] G.S. Map 1″, xlv NE.
[4] 17 Geo. III, c. 43.
[5] W. L. Steel, Hist. L.N.W.R. 185; R. Bucknall, Railway Hist. 69.

[6] Oxf. County Bridges (1878), 53.
[7] Local inf.
[8] Hearth Tax Oxon. 190, 235; Willaston and outlying farms are probably included.
[9] The evidence of visitation returns is unsatisfactory: there were said to be 20 houses in 1738 (Oxf. Dioc. d 553), and 43 in 1759 (ibid. d 556).
[10] Ibid. d 559.
[11] See below, p. 257, and Census, 1951. Since 1954 two pairs of council houses have been built: local inf.
[12] Davis, Oxon. Map.

Squire Batson at the request of the rector in 1891.[13] Charles Richardson, writing about 1823, states that 'until the last twenty years many of the cottage chimneys were constructed of wood',[14] and Blomfield, writing at the end of the century, describes them as 'huts . . . with here and there an upper room reached by a ladder'.[15] Many of the cottagers had lived rent free.[16] In 1955 the church, the Rectory, Town Farm, and the village school, built in 1838,[17] all lay at the northern end of the village street.

The early 19th-century Rectory probably replaced the one which was repaired or rebuilt by Thomas Walker (rector 1630–8) and which was taxed on three hearths in 1665.[18] W. J. Palmer on his institution as rector in 1802 obtained a licence to rebuild from the Bishops of Oxford and Rochester, and was permitted to raise a loan of £390.[19] In 1805 the new house, standing in about 4 acres of ground, was stated to be stone-built. It had dormers and a roof of blue Welsh slating.[20] It was enlarged in 1855.[21] The schoolroom, approached by a flight of steps from the churchyard, is raised above stone wagon-sheds, once used by Glebe farm—an unusual and attractive arrangement. Beyond the church, on the north side of Church Lane, the impressive banks and ditches of Beaumont castle can be seen.[22] No masonry remains above the ground and the earthworks alone survive of this important early medieval fortification. This castle was probably built by Roger d'Ivry and nicknamed Beaumont because the ground north of it falls to the stream.[23] Recent excavations (1954–5) revealed a deep well or dungeon at the north-west corner of the earth ramparts with an underground passage leading out of it.[24]

Farther north are some council houses, and beyond the stream Mixbury Hall, built by Charles Kayler in about 1900, and a group of other modern houses. The village has two shops and a sub-post office, but the limekilns once in Church Lane and the smithy at the south end of the main street[25] have ceased to function. There is no public house and it is said that in the early 19th century the incumbent refused to allow one for fear of drunkenness.[26] But the 'Greyhound' throve in 1784[27] and it is possible that earlier there were two alehouses, as two different victuallers were licensed in 1732 and 1735.[28]

The parish once had two hamlets, Fulwell,[29] which lies in the extreme north-east, close to the Ouse, and Willaston. Both were largely deserted by the early 16th century. At Fulwell, Oseney Abbey had a mill[30] and a large grange, which in the 16th century became the residence of the new lord of the manor.[31] It was inhabited by the Wellesbornes, Sills, and Bathursts until the mid-18th century, but in 1738 and 1759 the incumbents noted in their

returns that the lord did not usually reside there.[32] It was 'pulled down' before 1768,[33] and the site, roughly 55 by 46 yards, can still be clearly seen. A 17th-century building adjoining the manor-house continued to be used as a farm-house;[34] it is a substantial building of two stories. The hamlet now consists of this farm-house, and a few 19th-century cottages on the road to Mixbury. It had once formed a separate manor and until 1435 was a separate parish.[35] Numerous mounds and depressions and traces of what appear to be stone paths or ruined cottages are visible in many parts of the field in front of the farm-house.

Willaston, a flourishing hamlet in the Middle Ages, was depopulated by inclosure[36] and consisted of one farm-house by the 18th century.[37] In 1955 the house was inhabited by Mr. Dewar-Harrison, owner of the ancient manor or 'lordship of Willaston' and of other neighbouring property.

There are a number of outlying farm-houses: two, Middle Farm and Cold Harbour, lie in the south of the parish and apparently date from the inclosure;[38] the other two are 17th-century houses. Monk's House, standing south of the main road and near the Northamptonshire border, bears the date 1683 on the north gable. It was, however, in existence in 1662, when the churchwardens presented that it was an encroachment on the common. They described it as 'a new erected house at the race post upon the common, built by one Monk of Evenley' (Northants).[39] It is a T-shaped building of two stories, constructed of rubble patched with brick and partly cement-faced. It has casement windows still, and a roof of red tiles and Welsh slate. The extension to the west is probably of a later date. Lawrence Broderick, rector from 1713 to 1743, lived there in the latter part of his incumbency.[40] On the other side of the parish Mixbury Lodge Farm lies just north of the main road. It consists of two portions, an early-17th-century part at the back and an incongruous 19th-century front. The original T-shaped building is constructed of coursed rubble with stone kneelers, is of two stories with attic dormers, and has a brown tile roof. It has retained its two-light windows with stone mullions and casements.

The parish is notable for a small round barrow, Barrow Hill, under half a mile west of the village, where human remains were found in the 19th century;[41] for its connexion with medieval tournaments, since in 1194 the open ground between Brackley and Mixbury was made one of the five licensed tournament grounds in England;[42] for its 'lost' hamlets of Fulwell and Willaston;[43] for horse-racing in the 17th and later centuries on the one-time tournament ground; and in the 18th and 19th

13 Blo. *Mix.* 24; Par Rec. Rector's bk.
14 MS. Top. Oxon. d 171, f. 337.
15 Blo. *Mix.* 23.
16 MS. Top. Oxon. d 171, f. 337.
17 See dated stone.
18 Par. Reg.; cf. Blo. *Mix.* 35; *Hearth Tax Oxon.* 190.
19 Oxf. Dioc. c 434, ff. 170–1.
20 Ibid. c 449; Blo. *Mix.* 52.
21 Blo. *Mix.* 41.
22 See *V.C.H. Oxon.* ii. 325–6 for fuller description.
23 Blo. *Mix.* 4.
24 Inf. Mr. P. Whiteley, Mixbury Lodge.
25 O.S. Map 25″, xi. 11 (1881).
26 MS. Top. Oxon. d 171, f. 337.
27 O.R.O. Victlrs'. recog.
28 Ibid. Cal. Q. Sess. i.

29 See below, pp. 253, 255.
30 *Oseney Cart.* vi. 229.
31 Dunkin MS. 438/7, f. 263.
32 e.g. C 142/479/112; Oxf. Dioc. d 553.
33 Ibid. d 556, d 559.
34 MS. Top. Oxon. d 171, f. 354.
35 See below, pp. 254, 255, 257.
36 Below, pp. 253, 254.
37 Oxf. Dioc. d 570.
38 Coldharbour was called Warren Farm in 1797: Davis, *Oxon. Map*, which does not show Middle Farm.
39 Blo. *Mix.* 19.
40 Ibid. 37.
41 *V.C.H. Oxon.* ii. 346.
42 Blo. *Mix.* 5; see below, p. 314.
43 See below, pp. 254, 256.

centuries for its connexion with several notable men. Benjamin Bathurst, brother to Lord Bathurst and M.P. for Gloucester, settled at Fulwell in 1738 and in 1741 married as his second wife the daughter of the rector, the Revd. Lawrence Broderick, a Prebendary of Westminster. Of his fourteen children by this marriage five were baptized at Mixbury and six buried there. His third son Henry, a future Bishop of Norwich, though born at Brackley in 1744, spent his early years at Mixbury after his family's return to Fulwell in 1747.[44] In the 19th century the Rectory was the home of the remarkable clerical family of Palmer. William Palmer, the eldest son of the Revd. W. J. Palmer, was born there in 1811. He became a leader of the Oxford Movement and a pioneer in the task of establishing friendly relations between the Greek and Anglican churches. He died in 1879 after entering the church of Rome. Palmer's second son, Roundell, became Lord Chancellor and the 1st Earl of Selborne, and another son had a distinguished academic career at Oxford, where he was Corpus Professor of Latin Literature (1870–8).[45]

MANORS. In 1086 *MIXBURY* (*Missberie*) was held by Roger d'Ivry of the king as 17 hides;[46] as part of the Ivry barony it followed roughly the same descent as the manor of Beckley and passed to the St. Valery family.[47] As Ralph Basset, the justiciar, made a grant of the advowson in about 1123 and of the tithes before 1151, it is possible that the manor passed into the hands of the Bassets for a short period after the death of Roger d'Ivry in about 1120.[48] The St. Valery family had acquired it by 1213 at the latest, for in that year Thomas de St. Valery gave Mixbury, with its appurtenances in Newton Purcell, in free alms to Oseney Abbey.[49] He reserved to himself the homage and service of his tenant of Mixbury, but acquitted the abbey of the service due to the king.[50] The grant was confirmed by King John in 1214, and by Thomas's successors as lords of the honor of St. Valery, Robert de Dreux and Richard, Earl of Cornwall, about 1225 and 1230 respectively.[51] In 1243 Oseney was said to hold 1½ knight's fee in Mixbury, but in 1292 Edmund of Cornwall agreed that in future he and his successors would claim only the service pertaining to ½ knight's fee—which was all the abbot recognized—for Mixbury and Newton Purcell.[52] The overlordship continued to follow the descent of the honor of St. Valery which was eventually merged in the Duchy of Cornwall.[53]

Roger d'Ivry held the whole of Mixbury in his own hands in 1086,[54] but in the 13th century part of

it was held under the St. Valerys by the Darreyns family, and by 1220 was called 'Muxeberi Aregnes'.[55] The first of the family, which took its name from Airaines (Somme),[56] known to be associated with Oxfordshire was Miles Darreyns, who was pardoned the payment of 10s. danegeld in the county in 1130.[57] About 1211 Bernard Darreyns held ½ knight's fee of Thomas de St. Valery in Oxfordshire,[58] and this must certainly have been in Mixbury, where he was Thomas's tenant in 1213.[59] By the end of the 12th century Bernard had acquired a considerable holding in Northumberland,[60] and c. 1240 his son Guy, who had succeeded him c. 1225,[61] gave Oseney Abbey all his land in Mixbury, i.e. 6 virgates, all held in villeinage, and the service of 4 virgates held freely.[62] The remaining knight's fee[63] in Mixbury does not appear to have been subinfeudated, and the existence of Beaumont castle, and the reference in the Oseney Cartulary to land held by the men of the castle bailiff, argue that the D'Ivrys and St. Valerys occasionally lived there.[64] The fact that Mixbury was a far more valuable estate than Beckley lends force to the suggestion that Mixbury and not Beckley may originally have been the *caput* of the honor.[65] Part of the estate acquired by Oseney in 1213 was held by free tenants. Between 1218 and 1270 the abbey gradually obtained their holdings, a virgate from William Jordan in 1218, a virgate from Alice of Mixbury in 1225, which in 1236 was confirmed to the abbey after a dispute, and other smaller grants.[66] By 1279 the whole manor, save 3 carucates of demesne, was held in villeinage under the abbey.[67] Oseney continued to hold the manor until its dissolution in 1539.[68]

The adjoining manor of *FULWELL* ('Fulewelle') was held in chief in 1086 by Robert d'Oilly as 3½ hides.[69] The overlordship followed the same descent as that of Bucknell[70] and many other manors of the honor of Hooknorton, passing in the 13th century from the D'Oillys to the De Newburghs, and from them to the De Plescys. Robert d'Oilly's tenant in 1086 was Gilbert Damory,[71] ancestor of the Damorys of Bucknell who were recognized as mesne lords of Fulwell until at least the end of the 13th century.[72] In 1205 Adelelm of Fulwell, tenant of the manor under Robert Damory, granted it for £40 down and a rent of £2 a year to Oseney Abbey. The grant was confirmed by Robert, by Adelelm's son and heir John, his daughters Agnes and Melior, who were each to receive £1 of the farm, and by their husbands Walter Buti and Adam of Balscot.[73] Oseney became responsible for the forinsec service attached to 1 knight's fee, but c. 1250 Walter Buti of Devon,

[44] *D.N.B.*
[45] Ibid.; Blo. *Mix.* 38–41.
[46] *V.C.H. Oxon.* i. 415.
[47] Ibid. v. 60 sqq.
[48] See below, p. 258.
[49] Ibid.
[50] *Oseney Cart.* v. 387–8.
[51] Ibid. 388, 389, 391.
[52] *Bk. of Fees*, 824; *Oseney Cart.* v. 398–9; cf. *Feud. Aids*, iv. 190.
[53] *Feud. Aids*, iv. 180, 190; see *V.C.H. Oxon.* v. 60 sqq. for details.
[54] *V.C.H. Oxon.* i. 415.
[55] *Bk. of Fees*, 318.
[56] *Northumb. Co. Hist.* vi. 177.
[57] *Pipe R.* 1130 (P.R.S. facsimile), 5.
[58] *Red Bk. Exch.* (Rolls Ser.), 586.
[59] *Oseney Cart.* v. 387 n. 3.

[60] *Northumb. Co. Hist.* vi. 177 sqq.; xii. 488 sqq.; xiii. 94.
[61] *Oseney Cart.* v. 389.
[62] 'Muxeberi Aregnes' was rated at only 1 carucate in 1220: *Bk. of Fees*, 318.
[63] See above.
[64] See above, p. 252; *Oseney Cart.* v. 399–402.
[65] Blo. *Mix.* 4; *V.C.H. Oxon.* i. 415.
[66] *Oseney Cart.* v. 391, 394–8; *Fines Oxon.* 102.
[67] *Rot. Hund.* (Rec. Com.), ii. 832.
[68] Ibid.; *Valor Eccl.* (Rec. Com.), ii. 216.
[69] *V.C.H. Oxon.* i. 414. Until 1435 Fulwell formed a separate parish: see below, pp. 257, 258.
[70] See above, p. 73.
[71] *V.C.H. Oxon.* i. 414.
[72] *Bk. of Fees*, 824; *Rot. Hund.* (Rec. Com.), ii. 832; for the Damory family see above, p. 73.
[73] *Oseney Cart.* v. 407–9, 411.

grandson of Agnes, and Adam of Balscot, son of Melior, quitclaimed the £2 farm to the abbey.[74] In the course of the 13th century Oseney acquired the free holdings in the manor[75] so that by 1279 there was none left.[76] The abbey held the manor until the Dissolution.[77]

In 1539 the tenant of the Oseney estates at Fulwell was Sir John Wellesborne, a gentleman of the Privy Chamber, whose mother was a Poure of Bletchingdon.[78] In 1532 Thomas Cromwell had requested the grant of the farm of Mixbury for Wellesborne, and in 1537 the latter, knowing that the Abbot of Oseney was dying, suggested to Cromwell that a new abbot might be persuaded to give Mixbury and Fulwell to the king, who could then reward Wellesborne with them.[79] In 1541 Wellesborne obtained his desire, a grant in fee of both Mixbury and Fulwell manors.[80] In 1543 he obtained further lands there by purchase.[81] Wellesborne died and was buried at Mixbury in 1548,[82] his widow Elizabeth receiving both manors for life, with reversion to his son John, then aged two, or his younger son Edward.[83] Elizabeth married as her second husband Edward Chamberlayne of Astley (Warws.), who died in 1557. In 1566 she granted to Arthur Wellesborne, her first husband's natural son, an annuity of £2 from her manors of Mixbury and Fulwell.[84] She subsequently married a third husband, Richard Hussey of Coventry (d. 1574).[85] In 1565 Mixbury and Fulwell had been included in the marriage settlement of the young John Wellesborne and Ann Greenway, step-daughter of Michael Harcourt of Leckhampstead (Bucks.), and in 1593, by which date his mother must have been dead, he settled both manors on himself and his wife for life, then on his only child Elizabeth and her husband John Sill, and finally upon their son Wellesborne Sill and his heirs male.[86] Ann Wellesborne died in 1606 and John Wellesborne in 1611, predeceased by John Sill, whose widow married Edward Mole in 1608. In 1632 the manors were settled on Wellesborne Sill and his wife Philippa: he died in 1634 and she survived until 1656.[87] Their son Wellesborne continued to live at Fulwell, but left no son although he married twice. All traces of the Sill family disappear from the records of Mixbury after his death in 1707.[88]

By 1718 the manors had passed into the possession of Benjamin Bathurst, son of Sir Benjamin Bathurst of Paulerspury (Northants) and brother of Allen, 1st Lord Bathurst.[89] Not long before his death in 1767 he sold his estates to Stanlake Batson of Horseheath (Cambs.).[90] Batson was succeeded by his son of the same name, who in 1823 sold a large part of the estate to John Harrison of Shelswell. The second Stanlake Batson was followed by his son Stanlake Ricketts Batson (d. 1871) and his grandson Stanlake Henry Batson,[91] who mortgaged the estate to Charles Edward Kayler. Between 1894 and 1903 Kayler foreclosed.[92] In 1935 Mrs. John Aldworth was lady of the manor.[93]

Of the 17 hides of Mixbury in Domesday Book, 2½ seem to have later formed part of Newton Purcell manor;[94] Oseney Abbey's manor of Mixbury was rated at 10 hides in 1255,[95] and the remainder formed *WILLASTON* manor in Mixbury parish. Like Mixbury manor it belonged to the honor of St. Valery, but it was not included in Thomas de St. Valery's gift to Oseney in 1213 and passed on his death in 1219 to Robert, Count of Dreux, and in 1227 to Richard of Cornwall with the rest of the honor.[96] Richard held Willaston in demesne as ½ knight's fee and had the view of frankpledge there, but when his successor Edmund founded Rewley Abbey *c.* 1281 he endowed it with the manor.[97] In 1303 Edmund's widow Margaret unsuccessfully claimed a third of Willaston in dower.[98] Rewley Abbey held the manor until its dissolution in 1536, and in the closing years of its ownership let it at farm to the Arden family of Cottisford.[99] The manor was granted by Henry VIII to Thomas Pope in 1537, but the Ardens continued as tenants until at least *c.* 1590.[1] Little is known of its subsequent history, but it seems to have descended in the Pope family, no doubt following the same descent as Ardley until 1655 when Thomas Pope, Earl of Downe, conveyed it to Ambrose Holbech.[2]

By 1698 Willaston was held by Sir John Holman, Bt., of Banbury and Weston Favell (Northants), and on his death in 1700 descended to his nephew William Holman of Warkworth (Northants).[3] After his death in 1740 it was held by his widow Mary (d. 1744).[4] The lands of the manor continued to be held separately until about 1815, when they were sold to John Harrison of Shelswell, who soon afterwards bought Mixbury manor.[5]

ECONOMIC AND SOCIAL HISTORY. The place-names Mixbury, Fulwell, and Willaston indicate that all were Anglo-Saxon settlements. Willaston was the *tūn* of Wiglaf, while the other two are derived from *mixen-burgh* and *fūl-welle* or *ful-welle*.

74 *Oseney Cart.* v. 410–11.
75 e.g. ibid. 412, 417; *Fines Oxon.* 86.
76 *Rot. Hund.* (Rec. Com.), ii. 832.
77 *Valor Eccl.* (Rec. Com.), ii. 216.
78 Ibid.; *L. & P. Henry VIII*, v, p. 655.
79 *L. & P. Henry VIII*, v, p. 521; xii (2), p. 343.
80 Ibid. xvi, p. 577.
81 Ibid. xviii (1), p. 402.
82 *Par. Coll.* ii. 218 for his monument (wrong dates of death are given).
83 C 142/87/56.
84 *Cat. Anct. D.* v, A 13120.
85 C 142/167/75.
86 E 41/AA 154; C 142/349/156.
87 C 142/479/112; Finmere Par. Reg.
88 Blo. *Mix.* 16.
89 *Par. Coll.* ii. 217; *Complete Peerage*, ii. 29.
90 Blo. *Mix.* 16–18.
91 Ibid. 18; Burke, *Land. Gent.* (1894).
92 Inf. Mr. Watts, Fulwell Farm; *Kelly's Dir. Oxon.* (1903).
93 Ibid. (1935).

94 *V.C.H. Oxon.* i. 415; see below, p. 263.
95 *Rot. Hund.* (Rec. Com.), ii. 832.
96 *V.C.H. Oxon.* v. 60–61; N. Denholm-Young, *Rich. of Cornwall*, 169–70.
97 *Bk. of Fees*, 613, 824; *V.C.H. Oxon.* ii. 82; *Blk. Prince's Reg.* iv. 30; *Feud. Aids*, iv. 158.
98 *Cal. Inq. p.m.* iii, pp. 482, 487, 488; *Cal. Pat.* 1301–7, 197.
99 *Cal. Pat.* 1317–21, 43; *Feud. Aids*, iv. 169; *Valor Eccl.* (Rec. Com.), ii. 254; C 1/563/5; see above, p. 106.
1 *L. & P. Hen. VIII*, xii (1), p. 252; cf. ibid. xx (1), p. 217; Oxf. Dioc. d 16, f. 160b.
2 See above, pp. 9–10; C.P. 25(2)/588/Trin. 1655. Mr. A. Wood, who kindly searched the Holbeck papers (Warws. R.O.), was unable to find any information about the family's connexion with Mixbury.
3 O.R.O. Reg. of Papists' estates, pp. 38–39. For pedigree see Baker, *Northants*, i. 741; for Sir John Holman see G. E. C. *Baronetage*, iii. 277.
4 O.R.O. Reg. of Papists' estates, pp. 209–10. Cf. C.P. 25(2)/1187/Trin. 14 & 15 Geo. II.
5 O.R.O. Land tax assess.

It may be that the 'foul stream' of the latter was the result of the 'dunghill' of the former, or Fulwell may have been named after the spring which still wells strongly up on the site of the deserted village.[6]

At Mixbury in 1086 there was land for 15 ploughs: on the demesne were 1 plough and 1 serf, while 18 villeins (*villani*) and 11 bordars had 6 ploughs. There were 50 acres of pasture, and 2 mills rendering 9s. 4d. The value of the estate, £15, was the same as at the Conquest.[7] There was evidently far more land available than was under cultivation, although Mixbury was a comparatively large community, and it was no doubt the existence of extra land which prompted the post-Conquest settlement of Newton Purcell.[8]

Willaston, although not mentioned by name in the survey, was apparently included in the account of Mixbury, being the site of one of the two mills, for there were never more than two in the parish.[9] In 1086 Fulwell was a separate manor and already almost certainly a separate parish with a church of its own.[10] There was land for 3 ploughs there, but there were only 2 in use, there being 1 plough and 1 serf on the demesne, while 3 villeins (*nativi*) and 2 bordars had another plough. There was a mill worth 10s. and 20 acres of pasture. Since 1066 the value of the estate had dropped steeply from £6 to £3.[11] Although its economic value was greatly increased after it came into the possession of Oseney Abbey in 1205, the decline of Fulwell village may well have been accelerated.[12]

The abbey added the neighbouring manor of Mixbury to its estate in 1213[13] and in about 1240 also obtained the part of Mixbury consisting of 6 virgates of villeinage and 4 free virgates which had been infeudated to the Darreyns family.[14] Thus of the land of the two parishes only Willaston manor remained outside Oseney's control.

The history of Oseney's estate is not well documented, but what evidence there is all points to an emphasis on sheep farming in Fulwell in the 13th century and to the gradual conversion of most of the hamlet's fields into a sheep farm by the end of the century. The abbey increased its demesne between 1205 and 1230 by the addition of 3 virgates in Fulwell's fields from three freeholders,[15] and in the second half of the century it acquired another acre[16] and obtained the meadow of 'Winstonelake' in the neighbouring parish of Westbury.[17] The hamlet was still in existence in the 1230's, for when Oseney appropriated Fulwell church it undertook to provide a suitable secular chaplain, and there were arable fields in the parish in the 1270's.[18] But in 1279 only the abbey's grange was recorded under Fulwell, and seven cottars (four of them women) holding lands of the 'fee' of Fulwell are listed under Mixbury: six held 2 acres and one an acre, mostly for rents of 2s.[19] It may be that Fulwell's remaining inhabitants

had been transferred to Mixbury by the abbey and that the abbey's demesne arable was cultivated by labourers resident at the grange.

Though Mixbury was predominantly an arable estate, the abbey kept a fair-sized flock there too. As early as 1216 there is evidence showing that Oseney had its separate pasture in Mixbury and a flock of at least 300 sheep.[20] Later the pasture appears not to have been fully stocked, for after a tithe dispute in 1251 the rector was allowed to pasture 150 sheep and 8 cattle there.[21] The account of 1279 reveals a flourishing community: Oseney had 3 carucates and a water-mill in demesne; 37 villeins held a virgate apiece, worked, were tallaged at their lord's will, and had to pay a fine when their sons left the manor (*redimere pueros*). Eight of them had also to contribute to the abbot's scutage when it was demanded; of eleven cottars ten held 6 acres each for works and 2s. rent, and the eleventh held 1 acre for 1s. Thus Mixbury had a total of 55 tenants, including the Fulwell tenants.

On the Willaston manor at this date the Earl of Cornwall had in demesne only a water-mill (apparently one of the two Mixbury mills recorded in Domesday) worth £1 4s., and a meadow worth £2 a year. There were 16 villeins holding virgates for 5s. a virgate and 2 holding half-virgates for 3s. each a year, while 1 cottar paid 1s.[22]

The decline of Fulwell in the 13th century is confirmed by early 14th-century tax lists. For purposes of taxation it was merged with Mixbury, and Willaston, which belonged to Rewley Abbey, was assessed separately. Willaston's lands, rents, mill, view of frankpledge, and court were valued in 1291 at £8 17s. 10d.[23] For the tax of 1306 there were 32 contributors in Mixbury and Fulwell, and 27 in 1316 and 1327, but it is significant that the grange of Fulwell, which had become the headquarters of one of Oseney's bailiwicks, accounted for nearly half the total assessment in 1306. Willaston had at least 16 contributors in 1306, 13 in 1316, and 10 in 1327.[24] At the reassessment of 1344 Mixbury's contribution was fixed at £1 13s. 8d. and Willaston's at 15s. 10d. Both figures, unlike those of other villages in the hundred, are remarkably smaller than the assessments for 1327.[25]

Both Mixbury and Willaston hamlets seem to have survived the Black Death without serious depopulation, for in 1377 Mixbury had a population of at least 80 and Willaston of 32 adults.[26] There is no record of Fulwell among the poll-tax returns nor is it listed in 1428 among the hamlets with under ten inhabitants. The reason no doubt was that it had long ceased to be regarded officially as a hamlet or a separate parish, and in 1435 only one man and his family were living in the parish.[27]

When Oseney's Fulwell estate is next recorded in 1510 its water-mill was being leased separately for

[6] *P.N. Oxon.* (E.P.N.S.), i. 230; cf. Alexander, *P.N. Oxon.* 112, 154.
[7] *V.C.H. Oxon.* i. 415.
[8] See below, pp. 263–4.
[9] See below.
[10] See above, p. 252, and below, p. 257.
[11] *V.C.H. Oxon.* i. 414.
[12] *Oseney Cart.* v. 407; see above, p. 252.
[13] *Oseney Cart.* v. 387–9.
[14] Ibid. 389–90.   [15] Ibid. 412.
[16] Ibid. 391.
[17] Ibid. 414.

[18] Ibid. 391, 413. Some arable was inclosed as late as 1510 (see below).
[19] *Rot. Hund.* (Rec. Com.), ii. 832.
[20] *Oseney Cart.* v. 401–2.   [21] Ibid. 402–5.
[22] *Rot. Hund.* ii. 824. The manor had been worth £7 in 1237: *Bk. of Fees*, 613.
[23] *Tax. Eccl.* (Rec. Com.), 45.
[24] E 179/161/8, 9, 10. The top of the Willaston entry for 1306 is missing.
[25] E 164/7.
[26] E 179/161/39.
[27] *Oseney Cart.* vi. 306.

£1 10s. and the manor was being leased for £6 13s. 4d. a year to William Councer, who was keeping in addition 400 sheep for the abbey.[28] He was among the inclosers proceeded against in 1517, when he was accused of having hedged 30 acres and converted them to pasture.[29] By 1535 the rent of the manor had been raised to £10 15s., and in the opinion of the lessee John Wellesborne the estate was worth more than £20 a year.[30] It is clear that his main interest was sheep, for the reason he put forward when negotiating for a grant of Mixbury manor was that he wanted more pasture and water for his flocks.[31] Mixbury was bringing into the abbey £22 8s. 4d. a year, £14 1s. 8d. of this sum being from the rents of customary tenants.[32] Wellesborne eventually acquired the freehold of both Fulwell with its water-mill and Mixbury with its warren,[33] and at his death in 1548 Fulwell was worth £10 15s. a year clear, and Mixbury £21 15s. 4d.[34]

For the subsidy of 1523 Mixbury, including Fulwell and Willaston, paid £2 6s. There were 27 contributors, of which Thomas Yardley, who was probably Oseney's lessee, with his payment of £1, was far the largest. Fifteen paid between 1s. and 3s., and twelve the lowest contribution of 4d.[35]

Willaston, a much larger estate than Fulwell, was being leased from Rewley Abbey in the early 16th century by John Arden, perhaps a son of John Arden of Cottisford, for £10 a year.[36] It is likely that he almost depopulated the village at a stroke by his inclosure in 1502 of 200 field acres of arable. They were converted to pasture; 7 ploughs were put down and 42 people evicted 'et otiosi lacrimose ab inde recesserunt'.[37] Nevertheless, there were still a few inhabitants in Willaston in the 17th century.[38] Six were recorded in the Overseers' Book in 1666, three of them Wellicombs, a yeoman family of standing.[39] By 1658 the Grantham family were lessees of the manor: they held 280, 62, and 12 acres respectively and paid a total rent of £235. Part of the land at this time was used for pasture and stocked with sheep and cattle, and part was sown with barley, oats, rye, and peas.[40] Wheat, the growing of which had been encouraged by the rector Thomas Russ (1667–86), was grown soon after,[41] and possibly sainfoin. It is uncertain when the latter crop was first introduced into the parish, but it must have been well established by 1740, when the Mixbury field-name Sainfoin Corner occurs.[42]

It is probable that Willaston's land was all inclosed by the time the Granthams were tenants. Field names show that besides the Cow Common and a number of closes there were an Upper Mill Field, a Nether Mill Field, and three or four other

'fields'.[43] Certainly by the early 18th century Willaston was almost all one large farm, which was rented for £200 a year. In 1698 the fine for a 21-year lease was £150 and in 1728 £630 for a 40-year lease.[44] When the property was bought by John Harrison in the early 19th century the remaining derelict cottages were pulled down.[45]

In 1699 the hamlet or 'inship' as it was called had been rated at 55 yardlands out of the 195¼ at which the whole parish was rated. Fulwell was rated at 36¼ yardlands, Monk's House at 1 yardland, Mixbury rectory at 20, the town at 51, and the lord of the manor at 32 yardlands. He was assessed on his warren, fishpond, North Heath, and castle, i.e. on the field in which the castle had once stood.[46] In 1700 a Quarter Sessions case shows that Thomas Grantham of Willaston complained that he had been overtaxed in comparison with the inhabitants of Mixbury, who were rated at £2 a yardland instead of at £4, the true value of their estates.[47]

At this time Mixbury had three open fields, Sandfield, West Field, and Middle Field. A glebe terrier of 1662 shows that the rector's acres were still divided into acre and ½-acre strips, which were said to be 'marked with the parsonage mark, which is a picked baulk betwixt the lands at each acres'.[48] In the early 18th century, when the glebe consisted of 65 field acres, they were divided between the three fields in the proportion of 26, 25½, and 9,[49] a distribution which suggests that there had been originally two fields. There were extensive common lands. Race Hill and the 'hill towards Cottisford' are mentioned in the 16th century, when it was complained that the poor of Evenley (Northants) were encroaching there.[50] At that time, and probably until the inclosure, there were still lot leys, and every landholder, including the rector, had an allotment of grass and thorns there according to his number of yardlands.[51]

A valuable part of the manor was the rabbit warren. The Abbot of Oseney had been granted free warren at Mixbury in 1268,[52] and in 1279 the 'warren' was recorded under the heading of the abbey's grange in Fulwell, but the Mixbury rabbit warren was certainly meant.[53] In 1535 it was being farmed for £8 a year, and it was probably the first large inclosure in the township.[54] The profits to be derived from rabbits may be judged from the complaint of 1662 that all the burrows on Sweetingtree Hill were an encroachment, there being no ancient burrow there but ploughed land belonging to the landholders of Mixbury and 'known and distinguished by acre and ley'.[55]

Inclosure of the open fields did not come until

[28] Oseney Cart. vi. 229, 257.
[29] Dom. of Incl. i. 366.
[30] Valor Eccl. (Rec. Com.), ii. 216; L. & P. Hen. VIII, xii (2), p. 343.
[31] L. & P. Hen. VIII, v, p. 521.
[32] Valor Eccl. ii. 216; cf. Oseney Cart. vi. 228, 257.
[33] See above, p. 254; L. & P. Hen. VIII, xvi, p. 577.
[34] C 142/87/56.
[35] E 179/161/204.
[36] Valor Eccl. (Rec. Com.), ii. 254. In the Cottisford subsidy list for 1523 John Arden is described as 'gent.' The Mixbury Arden has no rank. For the family's Cottisford estate see above, p. 106.
[37] Dom. of Incl. i. 349.
[38] E 179/161/204.
[39] Par. Rec. Overseers' bk
[40] E 134/1658/East. 16.

[41] Blo. Mix. 46.
[42] Incl. act, 3 Geo. II, c. 5 (priv. act): copy in Bodl. G.A. Oxon. c 191 and in Par. Rec.
[43] E 134/1658/East. 16.
[44] O.R.O. Reg. of Papists' estates, pp. 38–39, 209–10.
[45] Blo. Mix. 18.
[46] Ibid. 21.
[47] O.R.O. Cal. Q. Sess. iii, p. 366.
[48] Blo. Mix. 46.
[49] Incl. act (see above, n. 42).
[50] Blo. Mix. 19.
[51] Ibid. 19, 46.
[52] Cal. Chart. R. 1257–1300, 69. In 1255 he was stated to have appropriated it: Rot. Hund. (Rec. Com.), ii. 31.
[53] Rot. Hund. (Rec. Com.), ii. 832.
[54] Valor Eccl. ii. 216; cf. Oseney Cart. vi. 228, 257.
[55] Blo. Mix. 19.

1730. There were then only two proprietors in Mixbury and Fulwell, Benjamin Bathurst, the lord of the manor, and the rector, and these alone had rights of common. Agreement between the two was easily reached, and open fields, leys, Mixbury Meadow, and Warren, about 2,400 acres in all, were inclosed by private act in 1730.[56] Lands were exchanged to make a compact glebe for the rector, and Bathurst undertook to build a wall between the glebe and that part of the ancient warren which he proposed to stock with rabbits.

One immediate effect of inclosure was to double the rents. The estate had been rented for £321, but after inclosure, when it was slightly increased in size, it was proposed to raise the rents to £700 and after nine years to £900.[57] Another consequence was a decrease in the number of tenants and a probable increase in the size of farms: at the time of inclosure the manor had twenty tenants but by 1786 there were only five.[58] The only evidence found for the size of Mixbury farms before inclosure is a reference in 1703 to a small farm of 2 virgates.[59] In 1832 there were two large farms, which were rented for over £200, four of which were rented for between £90 and £160, and two smaller properties.[60] The usual tendency for farms to increase in size after this date occurred here. In the 1850's there were five farmers in the parish and though there were six farms in 1939 all were over 150 acres.[61] By 1956 there were 13 farms. Out of a total of 1,592 acres of cultivated land, 811 were grassland and 781 arable.[62]

Farming has remained the main occupation of the villagers. In about 1823 61 families were engaged in agriculture, compared with 12 engaged in trade and crafts.[63] In the 1850's the village had a blacksmith, a baker, two shopkeepers, and a carrier.[64] As late as 1903 there were a blacksmith and a shopkeeper, but by 1939 the only tradesman left was a shopkeeper.[65]

Mixbury had the usual parish officers. Some record of the 17th-century churchwardens and overseers of the poor, who presented their accounts on Rogation Monday, and of the way-ward and cowkeeper, chosen by the 'concert of the neighbourhood', have been preserved in extracts made by Blomfield.[66] He also quotes from constables' accounts, now lost.[67] Overseers' accounts for 1732 to 1755 have survived; the annual expenditure varied between £11 6s. and £34 7s. until the year 1754–5, when there was a sharp increase to £52 15s. The overseers were the leading farmers: John Westcar, tenant of Willaston, for example, or Thomas Wellicomb.[68] By 1776 the annual expenditure exceeded £73; from 1783 to 1785 there was an average of over £141 and

in 1803 over £500. The poor rate of 8s. in the pound was then the highest in the hundred.[69] The parish continued poor and neglected and in 1854 the children were still leaving school at eight or nine years of age to work in the fields or to make lace.[70] Bishop Wilberforce in 1855 noted the poverty and the poor condition of the cottages, for which he blamed the old and non-resident squire.[71] The rector, W. J. Palmer, also complained that although the squire owned the whole village and half the parish he never did anything for it. Palmer could only remedy the effects of the landlord's neglect and the continued agricultural depression by encouraging emigration.[72]

As elsewhere in the hundred population increased in the second half of the 18th century. In 1665 21 houses were listed for the hearth tax, and they did not include those worth less than 20s. of which there may have been several, and in 1676 the number of adults over sixteen was 106. In 1738 the incumbent described Mixbury as a small village with about 40 houses.[73] By 1759 this number had risen to 43 and in 1768 to about 60, almost certainly an exaggeration, as in 1771 only 40 were returned and in 1781 50 houses.[74] Official returns for 1801 and 1811 gave population figures of 304 and 336.[75] The greatest number of baptisms in the century was in the decade 1840 to 1849, and in 1851 the population reached the peak of 402. Thereafter, owing to the agricultural depression, it declined to 221 in 1901 and to the further low figure of 184 in 1951.[76]

CHURCH. As in other cases in the hundred, parish and township were not coterminous at Mixbury. The parish included Mixbury, Willaston, and after 1435 Fulwell, and a fraction of the township of Newton Purcell. Although Willaston had its own chapel, it was always dependent on Mixbury.[77] The inclusion of some of Newton Purcell probably dated from the early Middle Ages, when Mixbury manor included land in Newton Purcell,[78] and the arrangement survived into the post-Reformation period. In 1582 two houses in Newton, one with a close and 3 acres in the fields of Newton, belonged to Mixbury parish. One paid all tithes to Mixbury, the other paid a third of its tithes to Mixbury and the rest to Newton.[79] The inhabitants of these houses went to church at Newton but paid church dues to Mixbury, where they went four times a year for Communion.[80]

In the early Middle Ages Fulwell was a separate parish. In 1074 Robert d'Oilly, the lord of Fulwell, granted two-thirds of the demesne tithes to the church of St. George in Oxford castle.[81] In 1149

---

[56] Incl. act (see above, n. 42); see also Oxf. Archd. Oxon. b 25, f. 265.

[57] Gloucs. R.O. D 421/E 58. According to it, the common fields covered 2,012½ acres, and the leys apparently the remainder.

[58] Ibid.; O.R.O. Land tax assess. There were two other tenants in the parish.

[59] Gloucs. R.O. D 421/M 88.

[60] O.R.O. Land tax assess.

[61] MS. Top. Oxon. d 171, f. 337; Kelly's Dir. Oxon. (1939).

[62] Inf. Oxon. Agric. Executive Cttee.

[63] MS. Top. Oxon. d 171, f. 337.

[64] H.O. 107/1729.

[65] Kelly's Dir. Oxon. (1903, 1931).

[66] Blo. Mix. 19.

[67] Ibid. 22–23.

[68] Par. Rec. Overseers' accts.

[69] Poor Abstract.

[70] Wilb. Visit.

[71] Oxf. Dioc. d 178.

[72] Blo. Mix. 39.

[73] Hearth Tax Oxon. 190; Compton Census; Oxf. Dioc. d 553.

[74] Oxf. Dioc. d 556, d 559, d 562, b 37.

[75] V.C.H. Oxon. ii. 221.

[76] Blo. Mix. 53; V.C.H. Oxon. ii. 221; Census, 1951.

[77] Oseney Cart. vi. 131; E 134/1658/East. 16.

[78] See above, pp. 253, 255; below, p. 262.

[79] This may be connected with the grant of two-thirds of the demesne tithes of Mixbury to Oseney Abbey: see below, p. 258.

[80] Oxf. Dioc. d 15, ff. 43–45b.

[81] Oseney Cart. iv. 3.

these passed to Oseney Abbey (see below). Oseney was given the advowson of Fulwell with the manor in 1205 by Adelelm of Fulwell.[82] Shortly after 1235 the church was appropriated to the abbey on condition that 26s. 8d. was distributed annually to poor scholars at Oxford, a condition which was still being fulfilled in 1535.[83] The appropriation was confirmed in 1319/20.[84]

Fulwell church was valued at 10s. in 1254,[85] but is not mentioned in later valuations. In 1435, when Fulwell's independent parochial status ended, the church was said to be worth 40s., less the 26s. 8d. due to the Oxford scholars. In that year the bishop confirmed an arrangement between James Job, the Rector of Mixbury, and Oseney Abbey whereby, in return for certain concessions (see below), the rector agreed to minister to the spiritual needs of Fulwell's single parishioner and his household, instead of the chaplain whom Oseney had formerly maintained there.[86] The rector was to receive in Mixbury church for services and sacraments all who stayed within the parish of Fulwell's church of St. Michael the Archangel. He was to give them penance, extreme unction, and other necessary sacraments. If any person was too ill to attend Mixbury church the rector was to administer the appropriate sacrament at Fulwell, except for burial, purification of women, and baptism of children. He and his successors were to say mass in the church of Fulwell every year on the feast of St. Michael as long as there were sacred vestments and books there. The inhabitants and those staying in Fulwell, like the parishioners of Mixbury, were to give the rector their personal tithes at Easter and mortuaries when they fell due. If they failed to do so the abbey was to see to the payment under penalty of 20s. A like sum was to be paid to the abbey by the rector if he neglected to administer the sacraments.[87]

During the 13th century the ownership of the tithes of Fulwell was disputed between Oseney and successive rectors of Mixbury. The first dispute was settled in 1216, and in 1251 the tithes of sheaves in *Fullewelheth* formed one of the subjects of a composition between Oseney and John de Exeter.[88] In 1263 the abbey's right to receive these tithes was reaffirmed after further dissension.[89] One of two undated bulls of Nicholas V (1447–55), apparently confirmations of the 1435 agreement, included the Fulwell tithes amongst those granted by Oseney to the Mixbury rectors, but the other specifically reserved to the abbey all the greater and lesser tithes of *Fullewelheth*, except a few personal ones.[90] Oseney certainly retained them, for in the 16th century they were farmed out with the manor.[91] After the abbey's dissolution they were granted in 1541 to Sir John

Wellesborne.[92] The rector received a modus of £1 12s.[93]

The earliest evidence for the existence of the church at Mixbury dates from the grant of its tithes in 1074 (see below). Willaston's were granted at the same time and it may already have had its own chapel, although it is possible that its tithes still formed part of the endowment of the mother church. A chapel there was first specifically recorded in a charter of 1151 confirming a grant in about 1123 of Mixbury advowson.[94] The chapel always remained dependent on Mixbury and was still being used, at least for christenings and burials, as late as 1645.[95]

In the late 11th and early 12th centuries the advowson of Mixbury was probably held by the D'Ivrys, but after the death of Roger d'Ivry in about 1120 or possibly earlier it must have passed to the justiciar Ralph Basset.[96] In or soon after 1123 Basset gave to a clerical son all his advowsons. These, including the advowson of Mixbury and its chapel of Willaston, were granted by the latter to Oseney Abbey perhaps on its foundation in 1149, and were confirmed to the abbey in 1151 by Archbishop Theobald.[97] In the confusion of Stephen's reign the abbey perhaps lost the advowson, for by 1213 it was in the hands of Thomas de St. Valery, the lord of the manor. When he granted Mixbury to Oseney in that year he reserved the advowson to himself and his heirs.[98] Confirmations by Robert, Count of Dreux, in 1225, and Richard, Earl of Cornwall, in 1230, made the same reservation.[99] But between 1274 and 1277 Edmund, Earl of Cornwall, gave the advowson to Walter de Merton, Bishop of Rochester, and his successors, in part exchange for the advowson of St. Buryan (Cornwall).[1] Nevertheless, in 1334 John of Eltham, Earl of Cornwall, unsuccessfully attempted to claim it from Bishop Hamo Hethe as belonging by right to his honor of St. Valery.[2] Oseney Abbey also tried at this period to secure the advowson. In 1352 and 1354 Edward III granted it licences to exchange the advowsons of Bucknell and Swerford for that of Mixbury.[3] Nothing came of this, and a further attempt to exchange (the advowson of Cornwell being substituted for that of Swerford) was made in 1396, the year in which Oseney was given permission to appropriate the church.[4] The exchange did not materialize, even though Bishop Bottlesham of Rochester was apparently willing and obtained a similar licence.[5]

The advowson remained in the possession of the bishops of Rochester, the Crown presenting during vacancies of the see, until 1852, when it was transferred to the Bishop of Oxford.[6] Since the union of the benefices of Finmere and Mixbury in 1931, the

---

[82] *Oseney Cart.* v. 407.
[83] Ibid. 413; *Valor Eccl.* (Rec. Com.), ii. 216.
[84] *Oseney Cart.* iv. 48.
[85] Lunt, *Val. Norw.* 313.
[86] *Oseney Cart.* vi. 306–7.
[87] Ibid. iii. 358–61, 365–6.
[88] Ibid. v. 402–3; see below, p. 259. John de Exeter was also Chancellor of York Minster.
[89] *Oseney Cart.* v. 405: cf. ibid. iii. 359.
[90] Ibid. iii. 360, 365: see below, p. 259.
[91] *Oseney Cart.* vi. 229, 257.
[92] C 66/703, m. 10. The entry from this in *L. & P. Hen. VIII*, xvi, p. 577, does not mention tithes.
[93] Blo. *Mix.* 47.
[94] *Oseney Cart.* vi. 130–1.
[95] E 134/1658/East. 16. A bequest was made to it in 1535:

Blo. *Mix.* 14; Blo. *Cot.* 16.
[96] *Oxon. Chart.* no. 58: see above, p. 253.
[97] F. M. Stenton, *1st Century of English Feudalism*, 84 n. 1; *Oseney Cart.* vi. 130–1.
[98] *Oseney Cart.* v. 387–8; *Cat. Anct. D.* iv. A 8836.
[99] *Oseney Cart.* v. 388–9.
[1] J. Thorpe, *Registrum Roffense*, 2. The final concord is dated 1287: ibid. 201.
[2] Ibid. 502–4; Linc. Reg. iv, Burghersh, f. 270b.
[3] *Cal. Pat.* 1350–4, 227; 1354–8, 2–3.
[4] Ibid. 1396–9, 19.
[5] Ibid. For a list of medieval presentations see MS. Top. Oxon. d 460.
[6] There were royal presentations in 1559, 1667, and 1759: Blo. *Mix.* 34, 36, 37. In 1656 the Keeper of the Great Seal presented: ibid. 35.

bishop has presented for one turn and the Misses Ashwell for three turns.[7]

Mixbury rectory was valued at £8 in 1254.[8] In 1291 its net value, which included the glebe worth 13s. 4d., was £10 13s. 4d.[9] It had risen to £15 9s. 4d. by 1535.[10]

The church's endowment consisted of tithes from Mixbury, Willaston, and a portion of Newton Purcell, together with the income from its glebe land.[11] The rectors' claim to the tithes of Fulwell was abandoned finally in 1435 (see above). In 1074 Roger d'Ivry granted two-thirds of the demesne tithes of Mixbury and Willaston to the church of St. George in Oxford castle: in 1149 they passed, with the rest of that church's property, to Oseney Abbey.[12] During the 13th century there were several disputes between the rectors of Mixbury and the abbey about the tithes of Mixbury. The first, under eight headings, was settled in 1216.[13] In 1251 it was decided that Oseney among other things was to have two-thirds of the tithes of sheaves in the Earl of Cornwall's demesne in Willaston hamlet and the abbey's own demesne in Mixbury, and a tithe of the water-mill at Mixbury. The abbey was to pay the rector a pension of £2 a year and to allow him pasture for 150 sheep and 8 beasts in its special pasture, in addition to his rights in the common pasture. This arrangement was reaffirmed in 1263 after another dispute with a later rector.[14] There was further dissension in 1311 when some of the beasts of John, the parson of Mixbury, were said to have been taken and unjustly detained by the abbey.[15] Clearly the arrangement was unsatisfactory, and in 1435 a new agreement was concluded.[16] In future the Rector of Mixbury was to be responsible for the cure of souls in Fulwell (see above). He surrendered his pension of £2[17] and all rights of pasture outside the parish. In return the abbey conceded certain tithes to him and his successors. The confirmatory bulls of Nicholas V appear to be contradictory (see above), or they may refer to two distinct agreements. One of them confirmed the rectors' right to all tithes from lands within the parish of Mixbury, except those of Fulwell. The other acknowledged their right to the tithes of *Fullewelheth* alias *le Breche*, of *Brondlond*, and to two-thirds of those of *Castellond* and Willaston, though with reservation to the abbey of certain lesser tithes.[18] Despite this settlement, there were further tithe disputes in the 16th century.[19]

After the Reformation, as was often the case elsewhere, the payment of tithes caused continual trouble. The commutation of the tithes of Willaston for a modus of £4 is first recorded in the time of Ralph Pontisbury (rector 1521–59).[20] Lessees of the rectory later in the century testified that they received almost all the tithes of Willaston in kind, but William Rickard (rector 1587–99) again accepted the £4 modus from John Arden, the influential tenant of Willaston, in the hope that he would be 'better unto him, but found him otherwise'.[21] Rickard was unsuccessful in his attempt to break the modus, which with rising prices had become very prejudicial to the rector, but Thomas Walker (rector 1630–8), who was also Rector of Somerton and no doubt a richer man, after repeated legal action recovered the right to tithe in kind worth £24.[22] During the Civil War the modus was reimposed,[23] and the efforts of Timothy Hart in 1658 and 1659 to recover tithes in kind were unavailing, the inhabitants denying that such tithes had ever been paid.[24] In 1664 he made an arrangement with his parishioners by which every Good Friday 2s. should be paid for a tithe lamb, 1d. for the tithe milk of a new milch cow, and 9d. for that of an old milch cow. In lieu of the tithes of Mixbury Warren, the rector received 30 couple of rabbits yearly.[25] Later these tithes were leased, and at the inclosure in 1730 were commuted for £105.[26] At the same time the scattered glebe (65 field acres), which consisted of 2 yardlands in 1662, was exchanged for a holding of 49 acres.[27] In 1730 it included Parsonage Meadow by the river and Parsonage Quarry, which were exchanged in 1825 for Home Piece and Slade Piece.[28]

Throughout the 19th century the rent of the glebe, £105 for Mixbury's tithes, and the two small moduses for Willaston and Fulwell, made up the endowment of the rectory. In 1831 it was valued at £180, making it one of the poorer rectories in the deanery.[29] In 1955 there were 8 acres of glebe.[30]

Being a moderately rich church, Mixbury had some medieval rectors of good standing. Master William de San Maxentio in the early 13th century was a university graduate and a canon of Lincoln.[31] He had a chaplain in Mixbury, who among other things collected his tithes.[32] Another clerk of his gave a virgate of land to Oseney Abbey, and was buried there.[33] At that time there was a married clerk (*clericus conjugatus*), Thomas de Mixbury, living in the parish. He was a member of a prosperous local family, for he held 2 virgates of land, and his sister held another as her dowry.[34] Of later medieval rectors, it can be said that one 14th-century rector was responsible for alterations to the chancel, that from 1425 the living was usually held by

[7] Bodl. Finmere Par. Box (uncat.), Order in Council.
[8] Lunt, *Val. Norw.* 311.
[9] *Tax. Eccl.* (Rec. Com.), 31; *Inq. Non.* (Rec. Com.), 133.
[10] *Valor Eccl.* (Rec. Com.), ii. 161.
[11] *Oseney Cart.* v. 386–7. In 1435 the Mixbury tithes were said to be worth 20 marks or more: ibid. vi. 307.
[12] *Oxon. Chart.* no. 58; *Oseney Cart.* iv. 3, 26, &c.; *V.C.H. Oxon.* ii. 160.
[13] *Oseney Cart.* v. 399–402.
[14] Ibid. 402–5.
[15] Ibid. 406.
[16] Ibid. vi. 306–7.
[17] In 1291 and 1428 the pension was valued at 30s.: *Tax Eccl.* (Rec. Com.), 31; *Feud. Aids*, vi. 379.
[18] *Oseney Cart.* iii. 359–60, 365.
[19] *L. & P. Hen. VIII*, xiv (2), p. 188. For a dispute of 1565 about the rector's right of common see C 3/85/37.
[20] Oxf. Dioc. d 16, f. 160b.

[21] Ibid. ff. 160b, 171b–172.
[22] E 134/1658–9/Hil. 20; ibid. 1658/East. 16.
[23] Ibid.; see also ibid. 1658/Mich. 4.
[24] Blo. *Mix.* 45. A modus of £4 was paid until the late 19th century: ibid, 47.
[25] Printed ibid. 42–44.
[26] Incl. act, 3 Geo. II, c. 5 (priv. act): copy in Bodl. G.A. Oxon. c 191; cf. Oxf. Archd. Oxon. b 25, f. 265; ibid. c 141, f. 589.
[27] Incl. act; Blo. *Mix.* 46: 1662 terrier.
[28] Blo. *Mix.* 47; Oxf. Dioc. c 435, pp. 423–4, 477–87.
[29] *Rep. of Comm. on Eccl. Revenue*, H.C. 54 (1835), xxii; Blo. *Mix.* 47.
[30] Inf. the Revd. M. G. Sheldon.
[31] *Oseney Cart.* v. 397, 399.
[32] Ibid. 401.
[33] Ibid. 398.
[34] Ibid. 397–8.

university graduates, and that in 1535 James Arden, a member of a local family of gentry, was rector.[35]

The tithe dispute of 1216 between the rector and Oseney tells something of the early church customs of the parish. The canons complained that when a married man died leaving two beasts the rector took one; when a widow or unmarried person died, he took the best beast. The rector replied that this was the custom in the archdeaconry, and he seems to have won his point.[36]

Mixbury was fortunate in the 17th and 18th centuries in having mostly resident rectors, which partly made up for the disadvantage of absentee landlords in the second half of the 18th century. The first who calls for remark is Timothy Hart (1656–66). He was presented by the parliamentary government and, in spite of the fact that he conformed in 1662 and obtained a royal presentation, he remained, together with his brother, Theophilus Hart, Rector of Wappenham (Northants), an object of suspicion to Charles II's government.[37] Hart took a great interest in his rectory and parish, and was a diligent recorder of parochial matters. Among other things, he kept a list of communicants: from 1657 to 1662 they varied between 38 and 65 in number, but there were usually 45 at least.[38] He was, as his monumental inscription in the church stated, a 'godly, faithful and vigilant rector'.

Various 17th-century church customs are recorded in the parish records. The old churchwardens presented their accounts, and the new ones were chosen, on the Monday of Rogation week; it was agreed in 1695 that the parish clerk was to receive 10s. from the churchwardens at Easter, in addition to 4d. from every house in Mixbury and 2s. from Fulwell and Willaston;[39] for every parishioner who died worth £30 or more a mortuary of 10s. was paid to the rector, who also received 2d. at Easter from every family.[40]

At that time the church possessed lands assigned to its maintenance. These were carefully recorded by Hart in 1662, when £1 of the income from them was being used to augment the parish clerk's wages.[41] It was the custom to let the land from year to year to the highest bidder, the rent being received by the churchwardens. After the inclosure Benjamin Bathurst, as lord of the manor, took over these lands at an annual rent of £3.[42] In 1751 he stopped paying, and in spite of various attempts to induce payment, Bathurst and his widow remained obdurate. The matter was allowed to drop and the lands were lost to the church.[43]

Among 18th-century rectors may be mentioned Lawrence Broderick (rector 1713–43), an active magistrate in the county, whose daughter married Benjamin Bathurst;[44] and James Johnson (rector 1744–59), who became Bishop of Worcester.[45]

The benefit of a resident rector was demonstrated in this period by the greater frequency and regularity with which services were held than in some of the neighbouring parishes. In 1738 there were two services and a sermon every Sunday; Communion was celebrated three times a year, and there were about 30 communicants; the children were catechized.[46] Much the same state of affairs prevailed during the long incumbency of Just Alt (1759–1801), except that he also conducted services on the great feast and fast days.[47] He has been described as 'a proud, imperious priest', and was also a magistrate.[48] The number of communicants tended to drop (in 1781 the average number was fifteen), and in 1784 Alt reported that there were 'too many who are chiefly absent' from church.[49] With the advent of W. J. Palmer (rector 1802–51), also Rector of Finmere, who rebuilt the Rectory, built the school, and restored the church, church life began to improve. Already in 1808 there was a celebration on the first Sunday of every month as well as on the three chief festivals, though in 1831 the number of communicants at each celebration was still very small and only about two-sevenths of the population attended church.[50]

The church of *ALL SAINTS* is a stone structure comprising a nave, chancel, north aisle, western tower, and south porch.[51]

The building dates from the 12th century, but the only Romanesque feature left is the south door. Repairs in 1842 to 'one of the chancel windows' revealed the head of a circular window carved with chevrons after the style of the south doorway.[52]

There was considerable rebuilding in the early 14th century. New windows were inserted in the north, east, and south walls of the chancel. The east window of three lights with Geometrical tracery is a good example of the period, and was once decorated with medieval coats of arms in stained glass, which were noted by Rawlinson in about 1718.[53] In addition, a tower of three stages, with a battlemented parapet and gargoyles, and having a west doorway, was erected and remains unaltered; an arcade of three arches supported on octagonal pillars and an aisle were built on the north side of the nave; windows were inserted in the south wall of the nave.[54] The north wall of the aisle was decorated with a wall painting.[55] A clerestory, lighted by three two-light windows on either side, was added.[56]

In the 17th century many changes were made to the fabric. In 1630 a storm blew in one of the windows, and in the next few years repairs were executed for which a special rate was levied.[57] In 1662 another storm did further damage.[58] At some time during the century the south wall of the chancel was rebuilt,

[35] See list of medieval presentations in MS. Top. Oxon. d 460 and Emden, *O.U. Reg.* i. For the Ardens see above, p. 106.
[36] *Oseney Cart.* v. 399–402.
[37] Blo. *Mix.* 35; *Cal. S.P. Dom.* 1664–5, 143.
[38] Blo. *Mix.* 18.
[39] Ibid. 18, 20. [40] Ibid. 44.
[41] Ibid. 47–48.
[42] Oxf. Dioc. d 553.
[43] Blo. *Mix.* 48; *Char. Don.* ii. 991.
[44] Blo. *Mix.* 17, 37; see above, p. 253.
[45] For him see *D.N.B.*
[46] Oxf. Dioc. d 553.
[47] Ibid. d 559.
[48] MS. Top. Oxon. d 171, f. 345.

[49] Oxf. Dioc. b 37.
[50] Ibid. d 571, b 38. For him see above, pp. 253, 257.
[51] Accounts of the church building will be found in Blo. *Mix.* 26–30, and Parker, *Eccles. Top.*
[52] Par. Rec. Rector's bk.
[53] *Par. Coll.* ii. 217.
[54] As the nave windows have been restored their original date is uncertain.
[55] Blo. *Mix.* 27. Portions of this wall painting were preserved for some time, when it was uncovered during the restoration work in 1848.
[56] Drawing by J. C. Buckler in MS. Top. Oxon. a 67, f. 386.
[57] Blo. *Mix.* 49.
[58] Ibid. 19.

although the 14th-century windows were preserved; a roof of very low pitch was put over nave and chancel; and a large south porch was added, rising to the middle of the clerestory. At the end of the century a Latin inscription was placed in the chancel commemorating the successful struggle over poor rates with the hamlets of Willaston and Fulwell and the restoration of the church. It ran 'in memoriam . . . templi insuper primaevi redditi elegantiae utinam et pietati quarum alteram perennet alteram provehat Deus. P.W.F. 1696'.[59] Although declared to be in a state of 'sufficient repair' in 1761,[60] this was no longer the case 50 years later. The rector, W. J. Palmer, began by removing in 1807–8 the old pews and inserting new and additional oak ones, and the churchwardens reported that he was 'making alteration' to the church.[61] In 1843 he restored the chancel;[62] and it is likely that it was at this date that the Romanesque chancel arch was rebuilt.

He also proposed to make extensive repairs to the rest of the fabric, and to remove the old screen between the belfry and the nave, making it 'good in a handsome way', on certain conditions which the vestry refused to accept. In 1848, on receipt of a letter from the bishop concerning the repair of the church, the vestry at last agreed to do what was legally necessary. George Wyatt, builder, of Oxford, reported that the south wall was so much 'bulged and shaken' that it ought to be rebuilt; that the dressings of the door and windows and the string course could be mostly reused; that the upper portion of the north wall up to the clerestory windows should be rebuilt; and that the roof should be re-timbered with oak and releaded with new lead. His estimate, which included replastering the interior and renewing the roof corbels in Bath stone, amounted to £402. The rector offered to meet the bill if the vestry would agree to a repayment of £280 raised by rates levied in the years 1849–51. His offer was finally accepted and the work was put in hand.[63] At this time also the south porch was rebuilt on a smaller scale in the Romanesque style. The dates of the construction and removal of the west gallery are not known.[64]

The elaborate restoration, especially of the chancel, with the installation of a new carved altar, stained glass, tiles, panelling, the Lord's Prayer and Creed framed in Gothic stonework, and other furniture, is of interest, as it was the earliest work of the kind undertaken in the Bicester deanery. Palmer's object, in his own words, was 'to restore the older character of the church, and get rid as much as possible of that of the period of the last repair'.[65] Various other additions, including an organ, candlesticks and lamps, stained-glass windows, the gift of Lord Selborne, and an alabaster pulpit given by

Archdeacon Palmer, were made later.[66] The font also belongs to this period.

The incised slab to Sir John Wellesborne (d. 1548) and his wife, showing the full-length figures of themselves and two daughters, which Rawlinson noted in the chancel, has disappeared except for some small fragments now embedded in the floor of the nave; it was probably destroyed during the 19th-century restoration, since Skelton mentions it as greatly obliterated in 1823.[67] There is a floor slab to Wellesborne Sill (d. 1706/7), a tablet to Benjamin Bathurst (d. 1767) and his widow, and tablets commemorating the donors of charities: Stephen Painter, Simon Rogers, Anne Rogers, and the Revd. W. J. Palmer. The inscription to Timothy Hart, rector (d. 1666), and various inscriptions to 17th-century members of the Sill family, noted by Rawlinson in about 1718, cannot now be traced. Painted records of charitable gifts dating from 1639 to 1711 are on the west wall.[68]

Mixbury is unusually rich in inventories of church goods. There are lists for 1552, 1662, 1757, and 1884,[69] and W. J. Palmer noted the communion plate in 1805.[70] The plate now (1956) includes two silver chalices with paten covers, inscribed respectively with the names of Thomas Rus, rector, 1681, and W. J. P[almer], rector, 1847; and a silver alms plate, hall-marked 1682, inscribed *Ecclesia de Mixbury 1716* and bearing the Glover arms.[71] There are also a heavy pewter flagon (*c.* 1699), two pewter plates, both 18th century, and another flagon inscribed '1847, W. J. P[almer]'.[72] In 1552 there had been a parcel-gilt chalice.[73]

In 1552 there were two bells, a sanctus bell, and two hand bells. In 1956 there was a ring of three bells hanging in a 17th-century oak frame. John Wellesborne gave the tenor, inscribed 'God save King James, 1609', and his grandson gave the second, inscribed 'God save King Charles, 1627'.[74]

In addition to the goods listed in the inventories, the church owned, in the mid-16th century, two cows and some sheep, given by John Hogges and Joan Gloucester, widow, to pay a priest to keep their obits.[75]

The registers begin in 1645, and the first volume contains notes on church customs made by Timothy Hart in the 1660's. There is also a manuscript history of the parish and church compiled in 1851–2 by the rector W. J. Palmer. There are later additions ending in 1948.

NONCONFORMITY. There have occasionally been Roman Catholics in Mixbury: two were fined in 1610;[76] a poor Papist was recorded in 1706;[77] and there was one in 1738.[78] In the second half of the 18th century one of the farmers was a Roman Catholic.

[59] Blo. *Mix.* 21; *Par. Coll.* ii. 218. This Latin inscription has since disappeared. Buckler drawings from SE. and NE. (1825–6) in MS. Top. Oxon. a 67, ff. 387–8, show the high porch and low-pitched roof.
[60] Oxf. Archd. Oxon. c 84, f. 241.
[61] Ibid. ff. 343–4.
[62] Ibid. c 40, ff. 559b–560; Blo. *Mix.* 29.
[63] Par. Rec. Rector's bk.; ibid. Vestry bk.
[64] MS. Top. Oxon. d 171, f. 341.
[65] Blo. *Mix.* 29–30.   [66] Ibid. 30.
[67] Skelton, *Oxon.* (Ploughley), 6–7. His inscription, as given in *Par. Coll.* ii. 218, says he died in 1544, but in fact he died in 1548: C 142/87/56.
[68] *Par. Coll.* ii. 218–91. For arms on monuments see

Bodl. G.A. Oxon. 4° 686, pp. 217–18; ibid. 16° 217, p. 191. In 1864 Hart's inscription was covered by the encaustic tiles which formed the footstone to the altar: Par. Rec. Rector's bk.
[69] Printed in Blo. *Mix.* 28–29; Par. Rec. Vestry bk.
[70] Oxf. Dioc. c 449, f. 9.
[71] Bodl. G.A. Oxon. 4° 686, p. 217.
[72] Evans, *Ch. Plate.*
[73] *Chant. Cert.* 77.
[74] *Ch. Bells Oxon.* ii. 213; Par. Rec. Rector's bk.
[75] *Chant. Cert.* 41.
[76] Salter, *Oxon. Recusants*, 26.
[77] *Oxoniensia*, xiii. 78.
[78] Oxf. Dioc. d 553.

He and his family and servants were returned as such in 1767.[79] In 1781 there was also a Roman Catholic labouring family.[80] All had disappeared by about 1800.[81]

Protestant dissent appeared in about 1830, for in that year and in 1831 certificates for meeting-houses were granted.[82] It did not flourish: in 1854 there were two dissenters, and in 1866 none.[83]

SCHOOLS. There was no school in the 18th century,[84] but about 1803 the rector opened one which in 1808 taught reading, the catechism, and handicrafts to about 20 children.[85] In 1815 it was reported that the girls were starting lace-making at seven years of age and that the boys were leaving school at ten to work on the farms. There were then 25–30 pupils, and the parish clerk was teaching reading, writing, and the catechism to about 20 older boys at winter evening-classes.[86] In 1818 there were only 12 children at the day school,[87] and in 1833 there was no day school at all.[88]

The Revd. W. J. Palmer, the rector, built a school on part of the glebe in 1838, and in 1852 endowed it with £103 4s. 6d. and a close in Finmere, which produced an income of £16 a year. By 1853 £9 18s. had also been left by Mary George for the schooling of one or more poor children.[89] There were 60 children in the school in 1854, although they were still leaving at eight or nine years of age.[90] The rectors continued to support the school, which had one teacher and an attendance of 57 in 1889[91] and 47 in 1906.[92] It was successively reorganized as a junior school in 1928 and as an infants' school in 1948: the older children were sent to Fringford school. It was granted aided status in 1954. There were 23 pupils on the books in 1954,[93] but it was closed in 1955 as no one could be found to clean the school. The income from Palmer's endowment was then £22 11s. 4d. and £5 8s. 8d. was also received from other legacies.[94]

CHARITIES. Between 1611 and 1727 a series of small bequests amounting to £43 was made by John Wellesborne, Julian Webb, Thomas Gibbs, John Wellicome, George Gibbs, Richard Strange, Aaron Gibbs, and Moses Gibbs.[95] As early as 1738 these charities were administered as one: the money was held by the lord of the manor, and the interest he paid was distributed annually on New Year's Day, in bread to the poor and in money to widows.[96] The annual income was £2 3s. in 1786[97] and in 1824, when the distribution was in bread only.[98]

By will dated 1812 Simon Rogers (d. 1820) left £100 in trust for the poor, the interest to be distributed annually as the rector and churchwardens thought fit.[99] Stephen Painter (d. 1834) left £100, the distribution to be in bread on 1 January, and Ann Rogers (d. 1835) left £100, the interest to be applied for the benefit of the poor or their children each Christmas.[1]

All the foregoing charities were amalgamated in 1932 by a scheme of the Charity Commission, their endowment then amounting to about £360 in stock.[2] In 1955 the total annual income was £8 17s. 8d. The charity was then distributed yearly in the form of vouchers for the purchase of goods at 2s. in the £ discount. Distribution was on a three-yearly basis— to children under 7 years of age in the first year, to children between 7 and 15 in the second, and to old people in the third. Each voucher was worth about 10s.[3]

By will dated 1890 the Revd. G. H. Palmer left £100 to purchase coal for the poor. The legacy was paid in 1922 and invested in stock.[4] In 1954 the annual income of £4 6s. 6d. was distributed in coal to old people at Christmas.[5]

By will proved 1928 C. C. Barrett of Finmere left £100 for the benefit of five of the oldest and poorest parishioners who had lived good lives, the annual income to be distributed on New Year's Day.[6] In 1954 £3 9s. 2d. was distributed to five old people at Christmas.[7]

NEWTON PURCELL

THE parish lies on the Oxfordshire and Buckinghamshire border, six miles north-east of Bicester, but with Buckingham as its nearest market-town.[1] The ancient parish covered only 602 acres,[2] and was long and narrow, being 1½ miles long and ½ mile broad: it was a comparatively new unit, for at the time of Domesday Book a part of its land lay in Mixbury parish and a part in Fringford.[3] Its eastern boundary has always been the county boundary, and

since at least the end of the 12th century, when there is evidence that Newton had become an independent parish,[4] its southern boundary has been a tributary of the River Ouse which flows east from Fringford Mill. The old western bounds used to lie just east of Spilsmere Wood, but in 1932[5] Newton Purcell was amalgamated with Shelswell to form a new civil parish of 1,424 acres.[6]

The parish lies between the 300- and 325-foot

79 Oxf. Dioc. c 431, f. 9.
80 Ibid. b 37.
81 Ibid. c 327, p. 302.
82 Ibid. c 645, ff. 180–1, 196.
83 *Wilb. Visit.*; Oxf. Dioc. c 332.
84 Oxf. Dioc. d 553, d 556, d 559.
85 Ibid. d 707.
86 Ibid. c 433.
87 *Educ. of Poor*, 727.
88 *Educ. Enq. Abstract.*
89 Par. Rec. Vestry Bk. *sub anno* 1853; Blo. *Mix.* 26.
90 *Wilb. Visit.*
91 *Kelly's Dir. Oxon.* (1887); *Ret. of Sch.*
92 *Vol. Sch. Ret.*
93 Inf. Oxon. Educ. Cttee.
94 Inf. the Clerk to the Parish Council.
95 *12th Rep. Com. Char.* 308; Par. Rec. Rector's bk. p. 83; cf. *Par. Coll.* ii. 219.

96 Oxf. Dioc. d 553.
97 *Char. Don.* ii. 990.
98 *12th Rep. Com. Char.* 308.
99 Ibid.; Par. Rec. Rector's bk. p. 85.
1 Rector's bk. pp. 85–87; Blo. *Mix.* 25–26.
2 Rector's bk.: copy of Char. Com. scheme.
3 Inf. the Clerk to the Parish Council.
4 Rector's bk. pp. 86, 98–99.
5 Inf. the Revd. P. A. Parrott.
6 Rector's Bk. pp. 92, 100.
7 Inf. the Revd. P. A. Parrott.
1 O.S. Map 6", xvii (1885); ibid. 2½", 42/63 (1949).
2 *Census*, 1881.
3 See below, p. 263; *Bull. Inst. Hist. Res.* x. 167–8.
4 See below, p. 266.
5 *Census*, 1931; *Oxon. Review Order* (1932): copy in O.R.O.
6 *Census*, 1951.

contour lines: it is almost all on drift gravel over-lying the Cornbrash, which appears in a band mid-way between Newton Purcell and Newton Morrell, and which was quarried for road-stone there in the 19th century.[7] The soil is stonebrash with a clay sub-soil.[8] Much of the ancient parish was once moor-land;[9] the small Hopyard Spinney is the only wood now lying within it.

The Roman road from Bicester to Towcester traverses the parish. Near the middle of the village it now diverges as a cart-track from the modern road, which was straightened in 1939.[10] A bridle-track running south of Spilsmere Wood connects Newton Purcell with Shelswell, 1½ miles away, but it does not follow the line of the 18th-century way marked on Davis's map, nor does the road he shows to Finmere exist now.[11] The turnpike from Bicester to Buckingham, formed in 1813, made the parish more accessible, and a coach between Oxford and North-ampton ran through the village daily.[12]

A station called Finmere, less than half a mile from the village, but in Shelswell parish, was opened in 1899.[13]

The village of Newton Purcell, 'the new tun',[14] like its offshoot Newton Morrell, was originally a settlement where the Roman road crossed a spur of higher ground. It took its second name from the Purcel family, who held it in the 12th century,[15] while its hamlet may have been called after the Morrells, who held land in Addingrove (Bucks.) in the 12th and 13th centuries and at Long Crendon in Henry III's reign.[16]

Neither can have been a large settlement in the Middle Ages.[17] In 1662 and 1665 only seventeen and eleven houses were listed for the hearth tax and of these even the Rectory and the two biggest farm-houses had only three or four hearths.[18] In the 18th century there were probably about 22 houses in the two hamlets.[19] These had increased to 28 in 1851, but had dropped to 20 by 1901.[20] The village seems to have once extended farther southwards than at present, for the foundations of buildings were said to have been found there in the last quarter of the 19th century.[21]

Today (1956) Newton Purcell consists of 27 cot-tages, which mostly lie on either side of the main road. For the most part they are built of grey rubble stone and are thatched. One bears the inscription W W E 1662. Two groups of cottages at the south end were rebuilt before the Second World War with their original stone and the original type of thatched roof. Another group was similarly rebuilt except that tiles were used instead of thatch. On the east side of the main village street a mound and three sections of a moat mark the site of the medieval manor-house of the Purcels.[22] In a lane, which makes a loop to the west of the main village street, lie Elms Farm, built above the level of the road on the site of the second manor-house,[23] the red-brick 19th-century school (1872), and the church. North of the lane is the Victorian Rectory, built about 1844,[24] and near by some glebe land has been converted into allotments. Farther north still the main road dips into the valley, where the new part of the village lies, quite distinct from the old. Here is the station, the station-master's house, and three red-brick cottages, built when the railway was cut; and the Shelswell Inn (P.R.H.A.).[25]

Newton Morrell, a mile south of Newton Purcell, now consists only of a farm-house and two adjoining cottages built on rising ground.

'Griff' Lloyd (rector 1805–42)[26] was a well-known hunting parson and for several years acted as deputy to his cousin Sir Thomas Mostyn, Master of the Bicester Hunt. Both men figure in an oil-painting of the first meet of the Bicester Hounds.[27] 'Griff' Lloyd was a 'character' and stories about him can be found in the books of H. H. Dixon ('The Druid') such as *Silk and Scarlet* (1856).

MANOR. Of the 5 hides[28] of *NEWTON* manor held by the Purcel family in the 13th century, 2½ were held of the honor of St. Valery, 2 of the barony of Arsic and the remaining ½-hide, a late acquisition, of the honor of Gloucester.[29] No manor of Newton appears in the Domesday survey and it is clear that the 2½ hides of St. Valery were originally part of Mixbury, held in 1086 by Roger d'Ivry, and that the 2 hides of Arsic were part of Fringford, held by Odo, Bishop of Bayeux.[30] Roger d'Ivry's lands, in-cluding Mixbury, passed in the 12th century to the St. Valery family.[31] In 1213 Thomas de St. Valery gave to Oseney Abbey Mixbury manor, including the homage and service of Robert Purcel for his fee in Newton.[32] The overlordship of this fee continued to follow the descent of the honor of St. Valery[33], which was later merged in the honor of Wallingford. Thomas de St. Valery's grant was confirmed by successive overlords, Robert of Dreux and Richard of Cornwall,[34] and until the Dissolution Oseney Abbey as mesne lord received an annual rent of £1 4s. from the Purcels, who were also responsible for the forinsec service of half a knight.[35] Odo of Bayeux's Fringford estate passed to the Arsic family,

[7] G.S. Map 1″, xlv NE.; *G.S. Memoir* (1864), 31.
[8] *Kelly's Dir. Oxon.* (1939).
[9] Moor is mentioned in a 13th-cent. grant of Rich. Fitzniel to Bicester Priory: Blo. *Newt.* 3; and in 1601: ibid. 22.
[10] Local inf.
[11] Davis, *Oxon. Map.*
[12] Blo. *Newt.* 9.
[13] See below, p. 285.
[14] *P.N. Oxon.* (E.P.N.S.), i. 231; O.S. map 25″, xvii. 4 (1881).
[15] See below, p. 266.
[16] *V.C.H. Bucks.* iii. 443 n. 14; iv. 42, 83. *P.N. Oxon.* gives no derivation.
[17] See below, p. 359.
[18] *Hearth Tax Oxon.* 209, 236.
[19] The 12 houses reported in 1738 seem likely to have been an error (Oxf. Dioc. d 553), as in 1768 22 families were recorded: ibid. d 559.

[20] *Census*, 1851, 1901.
[21] Blo. *Newt.* 9.
[22] *V.C.H. Oxon.* ii. 329.
[23] Blo. *Newt.* 9, 20.
[24] See below, p. 267.
[25] Local inf.; O.S. Map 25″, xvii. 4; this part of the village is in the former parish of Shelswell.
[26] See below, p. 266.
[27] In the possession of Mrs. Mansfield, Hethe Brede, Stoke Lyne.
[28] *Fines Oxon.* 231.
[29] *Rot. Hund.* (Rec. Com.), ii. 834, 837; cf. O.R.O. Misc. CW I/1.
[30] *V.C.H. Oxon.* i. 404, 415.
[31] For the descent see ibid. v. 60.
[32] *Oseney Cart.* v. 387.
[33] e.g. *Bk. of Fees*, 824; *Rot. Hund.* (Rec. Com.), ii. 834.
[34] *Oseney Cart.* v. 388–9.
[35] Ibid. 419; vi. 229, 258.

who were overlords of part of Newton until the death of Robert Arsic in 1230. The overlordship then followed the descent of the Grey manor in Fringford.[36] In 1198 Ralph Purcel was said to hold by sergeanty 1 carucate in demesne in Newton.[37] The lands attached to the usher sergeanty, which the Purcels held of the king (see below), were in Wallbury (Essex),[38] and this Newton sergeanty probably represents the lands they held of the Arsics, for in 1227 Robert Purcel undertook that when on duty as an usher at the king's court he would perform certain services for Robert Arsic.[39]

The Purcels of Newton were descended from Oyn Purcel, an usher sergeant under Henry I.[40] The sergeanty and the family lands at Catteshill (Surr.) descended to Oyn's son Geoffrey, and Geoffrey's son Ralph, on whose death about 1155 they were granted to his uncle Ranulf. Ralph, however, had married a sister of Robert Burnel of Shareshull (Staffs.), another usher sergeant, and had a son Ralph, to whom in about 1155 Henry II granted the office and lands of his uncle Robert.[41] Although in 1283 it was asserted in a lawsuit that the Purcels had held in Newton of the honor of St. Valery before the elder Ralph's marriage,[42] it is more likely that their Oxfordshire lands came to them from Robert Burnel, who in 1130 had been excused payment of danegeld on some $3\frac{1}{2}$ hides in the county.[43]

Ralph Purcel the younger was still alive about 1180,[44] but the Ralph who held lands in Newton in 1198 was probably his son and successor,[45] and was dead by 1213, when his widow Sybil claimed her dower in Newton from his son Robert.[46] At some time between 1189 and 1199 Robert's father Ralph had acquired 2 virgates in Shelswell from William de Weston in exchange for 2 virgates in Colly Weston (Northants). In 1222 William's widow Alice successfully claimed the virgates in Shelswell as part of her dower, although it was agreed that they should revert to Robert Purcel on her death.[47] In 1233, however, Alice quitclaimed the virgates to Robert,[48] and they became part of Newton manor, being held of the lords of Shelswell, who in turn held of the Earl of Gloucester.[49]

Robert, who also held lands in Bainton[50] and Westcot Barton, was still alive in 1243,[51] but was succeeded soon afterwards by his brother Henry.[52] Henry was dead by 1247 and Newton passed to

Otwel Purcel, probably his son.[53] Otwel was holding Newton in 1279,[54] but was dead by the following year, when the wardship and marriage of his son Otwel was granted to William and Joan Poure of Oddington.[55] Otwel (II) became Sheriff of Oxfordshire in 1317–18[56] and was apparently alive in 1327.[57] By 1332 he had been succeeded by his son Thomas, who in that year conceded that the Abbot of Oseney might make distraint in the whole manor—not only in the St. Valery fee—for arrears of his annual rent.[58] Thomas was still lord of Newton in 1340;[59] a John Purcel was lord in 1375[60] and another John in 1425.[61] The family evidently retained the manor until the 16th century, for a Thomas Purcel of Newton is recorded in 1475,[62] and in 1521 payment of the annual rent to Oseney Abbey was made by the guardian of the Purcel heir.[63] Soon afterwards, however, the manor seems to have passed to Richard Duke, who was in residence by 1523.[64]

After the dissolution of Oseney Abbey, Sir John Wellesbourne was granted in 1541 Mixbury manor and all the Oseney lands in Newton,[65] in fact Oseney's mesne lordship in Newton, for the manor continued in the tenure of the Duke family. The John Duke who signed the inventory of church goods in 1552 may have been Richard's grandson who held Frankton manor (Warws.) and died in 1565;[66] but by 1559 Newton was probably held by Roger Duke, perhaps John's brother. His tenure lasted until 1568 at least;[67] in 1596 his successor Paul Duke and his wife Sabina conveyed the manor to John Sill,[68] husband of Elizabeth, the granddaughter of Sir John Wellesborne.[69] The conveyance was later disputed by the Frankton branch of the Duke family,[70] but the Sills retained the manor. Elizabeth's husband John was dead by 1611 and in 1615 her second husband Edward Mole was holding lands in Newton in her right.[71] In 1632 Wellesborne Sill, Elizabeth's son, and his step-father Edward Mole conveyed Newton to Richard Blower.[72] The Blowers were still lords of the manor in 1667 when Robert Blower and his wife Anne conveyed it to Ambrose Holbech,[73] who in 1677 conveyed it to Samuel Trotman of Siston (Glos.),[74] son of Samuel Trotman of Bucknell (d. 1684/5). Samuel the younger's only daughter Dorothea married her cousin Samuel, son of Lenthall Trotman of Bucknell,[75] to whom she brought Newton manor on her

[36] Cal. Chart. R. 1226–57, 285; see above, p. 127.
[37] Bk. of Fees, 11.
[38] Red Bk. Exch. (Rolls Ser.), 507.
[39] Fines Oxon. 78.
[40] For the Purcels and their usher sergeanties see E. St. John Brooks, Bull. Inst. Hist. Res. x. 161–8; cf. J. H. Round, King's Serjeants, 98–108.
[41] Brooks, op. cit. 163–4; V.C.H. Surr. iii. 32.
[42] Hist. Collect. Staffs. vi (1). 128–9.
[43] Pipe R. 1130 (P.R.S. facsimile), 5.
[44] Brooks, op. cit. 166.   [45] Bk. of Fees, 11.
[46] Fines Oxon. 231; Hist. Collect. Staffs. iii. 177.
[47] Bracton's Note Bk. ed. Maitland, ii. 128–9; Fines Oxon. 233.
[48] Bracton's Note Bk. ii. 681; Fines Oxon. 91.
[49] Rot. Hund. (Rec. Com.), ii. 837.
[50] 'Badintun Purcel' (Bk. of Fees, 319) is Bainton, not Newton as in index; cf. P.N. Oxon. (E.P.N.S.), i. 231, which repeats the error.
[51] Bk. of Fees, 824; cf. Fines Oxon. 115.
[52] Oseney Cart. v. 389 (dated too early); ibid. 467.
[53] Fines Oxon. 133; Rot. Hund. (Rec. Com.), ii. 44.
[54] Rot. Hund. (Rec. Com.), ii. 834.
[55] Oseney Cart. v. 419–20; the Purcel descent (ibid. 420 n.) is incorrect.

[56] P.R.O. L. and I. ix; cf. Blo. Newt. 6.
[57] E 179/161/9; cf. ibid. 161/8, 10; cf. Feud. Aids, iv. 169.
[58] O.R.O. Misc. CW I/1.
[59] Bodl. MS. ch. Oxon. Oseney 399.
[60] Blo. Newt. 6.
[61] Dunkin, Bic. 234.
[62] Cal. Pat. 1467–77, 500.
[63] Oseney Cart. vi. 229, 258.
[64] E 179/161/198; cf. ibid. 161/176; see Dugd. Warws. 197.
[65] L. & P. Hen. VIII, xvi, p. 577.
[66] Chant. Cert. 87; V.C.H. Warws. vi. 92.
[67] E 179/162/319, 331; C.P. 25(2)/196/Mich. 3 Eliz.
[68] C.P. 25(2)/198/Hil. 38 Eliz.
[69] V.C.H. Bucks. iv. 267.
[70] C 2 Jas. I, 27/60; cf. V.C.H. Warws. vi. 93. The Dukes retained property in Newton. Rich. Duke held land there in 1601 and 1634, Paul Duke in 1665 and 1679: Oxf. Archd. Oxon. b 41, ff. 46–48; Hearth Tax Oxon. 209.
[71] Dunkin MS. 438/2: transcript of B.M. Harl. MS. 843, f. 26.
[72] C.P. 25(2)/473/Trin. 8 Chas. I.
[73] Ibid. 707/Hil. 19 Chas. II; C 5/49/37.
[74] C.P. 25(2)/709/Mich. 29 Chas. II.
[75] Fosbrooke, Glos. ii. 56–57; Oxf. Dioc. c 155, f. 55a.

father's death in 1720. Samuel was succeeded in 1749 by his nephew Samuel, and on the latter's death in 1775 Newton passed to his nephew Fiennes, son of his brother Edward Trotman of Shelswell.[76] Thereafter Newton followed the same descent as Shelswell.

ECONOMIC HISTORY. As Newton was colonized after 1086, the first record of the community comes from the Hundred Rolls of 1279.[77] Otwel Purcel then had 18 virgates in demesne. Of his villeins (*nativi*) 8 held half-virgates for 6s. 8d. a year—3 of them owed labour services as well—and 1 held ¼ virgate for 1s. 8d. Six others, evidently cottars, held only a messuage each for 2s. a year. He had no free tenants, but there were 4 on the estate held of the lord of Shelswell by John Fitzniel. John held 3 virgates in demesne and his 4 free tenants held 4 virgates for suit at the hundred and county courts and for rents varying from 2½d. to 1s. 4d. for a half-virgate. A fifth freeholder in Newton held 3 virgates (possibly part of Mixbury manor) of Bicester Priory, which held of Oseney Abbey.[78]

There are no manorial extents or court rolls to throw light on the later agrarian history of Newton, but there is one early 13th-century charter which gives some information about the topography of the parish. There was moorland, besides pasture, meadow, and the fields. Some furlong names are recorded, e.g. 'Brocfurlong' and 'Sunistedfurlong', and it is revealed that meadow-land lay near Fringford Mill and was assigned by lot.[79]

The 14th-century tax lists show as one would expect in so small a parish that the community was neither populous nor rich. Between nine and twelve persons were taxed, of whom only three had much property. Among the three was Otwel Purcel, the lord, but he was not always the biggest contributor. Newton's total contribution in 1327 places it among the poorer parishes in the hundred. Its tax was increased at the reassessment of 1334, but this may denote earlier evasion rather than economic progress.[80] There had evidently been a decline in population before 1428, when there were fewer than ten resident householders in Newton.[81] By 1524, when seven small contributors paid to the subsidy, Newton was the lowest-taxed parish in the hundred.[82] This was in part because of its small area, but also on account of the absence of any marked concentration of wealth. By the middle of the century there are signs that this had been taking place. In 1558 the lord, Roger Duke, paid on £7 worth of land, and one other paid on goods worth £11.[83]

Little is recorded which throws light on the field system or the process of inclosure. A terrier of 1634 shows that there were three fields: the field towards Finmere, the field 'butting upon the Broad Meadowe',

and the field adjoining 'Willaston Lordship'.[84] As the meadow-land mostly lay along the river bank in the south of the parish, a glance at the map makes it clear that these fields are the North, South, and West Fields mentioned in a terrier of 1679.[85] This terrier also shows that the Cow Pasture lay south of the village, no doubt where the two present-day fields, Dairy Ground and Long Dairy Ground, lie.[86] Mowing ground in the West Field is recorded and many acres of furze. Much of the last lay in Morwell, which was close to the ford by Fringford Mill. The villagers were entitled to take furze from South and West Fields for fuel. The parson's terrier also states that besides meadow ground there were 'several hades (i.e. headlands) belonging to each land in every field either at one end of the land or at both wheresoever other neighbours have hades belonging unto theirs'.

As the land still lay dispersed in strips in 1679 inclosure must have taken place after that date, but there is no record of parliamentary inclosure. It is likely that the open and waste land was inclosed by private agreement at the end of the 17th century after Samuel Trotman became lord of Shelswell.[87]

In the period 1786–1832 there were only two estates in the parish, belonging to the lord of the manor and the rector; they were assessed for land tax at £32 and £6 6s. respectively. Both were occupied by tenant farmers.[88] In 1851 the parish was divided between three large farms of 429 acres, 317 acres, and 226 acres.[89] In 1953 there were still three farms, all belonging to Mr. Dewar-Harrison of Willaston Farm.[90]

In the absence of constables' books or overseers' accounts nothing can be said about local government in the 18th and 19th centuries. The school log book, however, attests that Shelswell Park played a vital part in village life in the last quarter of the 19th century. On 13 December 1878 it records that several children had gone to Shelswell that morning 'to fetch soup', and the villagers still remember this weekly event at the 'big house'.[91] The charity of Lady Louisa Harrison is also recorded on a tablet in the church.

Agriculture has probably been almost the sole occupation of the villagers. In 1279 one of the villeins of Newton was named William the miller,[92] but there is no certain record of a mill in the parish. When the parsonage was viewed for dilapidations in 1706 by five craftsmen, not one belonged to Newton.[93] In 1851, however, the census recorded a grocer and a lacemaker.[94] In 1953 there were three tenant farmers and the majority of the villagers lived in tied cottages and worked on the Dewar-Harrison estate.[95]

Population did not increase appreciably during the late 17th and 18th centuries. In 1676 there were 60

[76] Burke, *Land. Gent.* (1937) under Dickenson-Trotman; P.R.O. Inst. Bks.; see below, p. 287.
[77] *Rot. Hund.* (Rec. Com.), ii. 834–5.
[78] See above, p. 253.
[79] Bodl. MS. Rawlinson D 404, f. 130.
[80] E 179/161/8, 9, 10.
[81] *Feud. Aids*, iv. 201.
[82] E 179/161/176.   [83] Ibid. 161/319.
[84] Oxf. Archd. Oxon. b 41, f. 46.
[85] Ibid. f. 48; ibid. c 141, pp. 409–11.
[86] Names supplied by Miss B. Gough, Newton Purcell.
[87] Blo. *Newt.* 9. Blomfield suggests that inclosure took

place during the lifetime of Sir John Cope, but for the descent of Shelswell manor see below, p. 287.
[88] O.R.O. Land tax assess.
[89] H.O. 107/1729.
[90] Local inf.
[91] Newton School, Log bk.
[92] *Rot. Hund.* (Rec. Com.), ii. 835. A Mill Furlong is mentioned in a terrier of 1601: Oxf. Archd. Oxon. c 141, p. 401.
[93] Bodl. MS. Rawl. B 383, f. 369b.
[94] H.O. 107/1729.
[95] Local inf.

adults and in 1738 the rector returned 12 houses in the parish. At the first official census in 1801 there were 93 inhabitants and this number rose to a peak of 143 in 1821. Thereafter there was a steady decline until 1881 when there were 90 inhabitants. In 1911, when Shelswell was also included, there were 172 inhabitants: there were 103 in 1951.[96]

CHURCH. Architectural evidence shows that there was a church at Newton by at least the mid-12th century, although the first documentary evidence dates from the charter, probably c. 1200, by which Ralph Purcel granted Newton church to Bicester Priory.[97] His son Robert in 1213 claimed in the king's court that it belonged to him,[98] but nevertheless later confirmed his father's grant.[99] Bicester may have remained as patron until its dissolution, but its last presentation was in 1484. After the mid-14th century the priory found the advowson of little value, for on six occasions (1351, twice in 1353, 1492, 1513, and 1531) it allowed the right of presentation to lapse to the bishop; in 1496 Notley Abbey presented, and in 1503 and 1528 the owners of Shelswell manor.[1] In the post-Reformation period the advowson followed the descent of Shelswell manor,[2] and from 1573 the two livings were held together.[3] In 1850 the ecclesiastical parishes were united by an Order in Council,[4] which gave legal recognition to a long-standing practical arrangement. In 1955 the patron was the lord of Shelswell manor.

In the Middle Ages Newton Purcell was so poor a church that it was not included in the valuations of 1254 and 1291. In 1339 it was taxed at £2 13s. 4d.,[5] and was thus worth less than the 5 marks considered desirable for the maintenance of a parish priest. Even by 1535 it was worth no more than £3 15s. 4d.[6]

A reason for this poverty was that the parish of Newton was not coterminous with the township. Two tenements of 3½ yardlands and ½ yardland respectively with appurtenances—common and pasture—, though lying in the fields of Newton, belonged to Shelswell parish, to which they paid tithes. The furze and thorns gathered in the fields by the tenants of these holdings were also tithable to Shelswell. Their farm-houses lay in Newton village, and in 1608 the holder of the larger farm was said to be churchwarden of Shelswell 'in the right of his tenement'.[7] The origin of Shelswell's claims probably lies in the tenurial arrangements of the 13th century, when a half-fee in Newton was held of the lords of Shelswell manor.[8]

A tithe case of 1614 shows something of the tithe customs of the parish, and discloses incidentally how well each farmer knew his neighbour's business.

For every colt born the rector received 1d., for every sheep dying or sold between Candlemas and shearing time ½d., and for every sheep sheared in the parish he received the whole tithe.[9]

By 1675 the rectory was said to be worth £32,[10] and in 1716 the combined livings of Newton and Shelswell were worth £66.[11] In 1847 the tithes of Newton were commuted for £132,[12] and in 1849 those of Shelswell for £186.[13]

Part of the income of the living has always come from the glebe, valued at 13s. 4d. in the reign of Edward III.[14] Terriers of 1601, 1634, and 1679 show that it then consisted of about 35 pieces of land in the open fields,[15] which were later exchanged for 28 acres.[16] It was thus smaller in area than the glebe usually enjoyed by parsons, and was not increased after 1850 by any land from Shelswell.

Owing to the poverty of the church in the Middle Ages the living was difficult to fill and the incumbents changed frequently, especially after 1349. The only known point of interest about these incumbents is the sudden succession of eight graduates, who held office between 1462 and 1503.[17] In the century after the Reformation John Lawrence (1597 to at least 1634) was clearly resident, for he built himself a substantial new dwelling on the north side of the church. (The medieval Rectory, consisting of three bays, stood on the south side.) The new house had stables of four bays, a five-bay barn, and a cowhouse.[18] Richard Addington (rector 1662–1705), a member of the Addington family of Fringford,[19] was resident in 1665 when he paid tax on five hearths, and seems to have lived for many years in the parish.[20] But subsequent rectors did not reside: in 1768 the rector Samuel Trotman, who had been presented by his brother Fiennes Trotman of Shelswell, was reported to be living in Gloucestershire although he frequently officiated at Newton.[21] He had an unlicensed curate with a salary of 10s. 6d. a Sunday, serving another cure and living a mile away. Nevertheless, there was a service each Sunday at Newton and on other listed days, Holy Communion being celebrated four times a year. In the early 19th century the ruinous state of the parsonage made nonresidence inevitable: Griffith Lloyd, rector from 1805 until his death in 1842, was licensed by his bishop to reside at Swift's House, near Stoke Lyne, on condition that he performed his duties.[22] As a hunting parson, this arrangement suited him admirably for Swift's House was the home of his cousin Sir Thomas Mostyn, the Master of the Bicester Hunt.[23]

Of a very different type from Lloyd was his successor, John Meade (1843–83).[24] As the old Rectory

[96] Compton Census; Oxf. Dioc. d 553; *Census*, 1801–1951.　　　　　[97] E 210/D 5672.
[98] *Fines Oxon.* 231.
[99] *Cat. Anct. D.* iii, D 903.
[1] For a list of medieval presentations see MS. Top. Oxon. d 460.
[2] See below, p. 287.
[3] *Reg. Parker*, iii (Cant. and York Soc. xxxix), 1005.
[4] Bodl. Newton Par. Box (uncat.); Blo. *Newt.* 19.
[5] *Inq. Non.* (Rec. Com.), 133.
[6] *Valor Eccl.* (Rec. Com.), ii. 160.
[7] Oxf. Dioc. c 25, ff. 4–6b.
[8] See above, pp. 264, 265, and below, p. 286.
[9] Oxf. Dioc. c 25, ff. 218–219b. For other tithe customs see Blo. *Newt.* 22.
[10] Oxf. Dioc. c 155, f. 2.

[11] Ibid. f. 55Ab.
[12] Bodl. Tithe award.
[13] Ibid.
[14] *Inq. Non.* (Rec. Com.), 133.
[15] Blo. *Newt.* 20–23; Oxf. Archd. Oxon. c 141, pp. 401–11.
[16] Bodl. Tithe award.
[17] See MS. Top. Oxon. d 460.
[18] Blo. *Newt.* 23: terrier 1634.
[19] See above, p. 129.
[20] *Hearth Tax Oxon.* 209; Devon R. O. Sidmouth and Addington Trust Pps. For his will see ibid.
[21] Oxf. Dioc. d 559.
[22] Blo. *Newt.* 16–18; Oxf. Archd. Oxon. b 25, f. 268.
[23] See below, p. 313.
[24] Blo. *Newt.* 18–19.

South-east view of the church in 1825

NEWTON PURCELL

South-west view of the church in 1823

MIDDLETON STONEY

had been converted into four cottages, he at once built a new Rectory, farther to the north of the church.[25] There he resided continuously and exercised a faithful and fruitful cure of souls.[26]

The church of *ST. MICHAEL* is a small stone structure covered with pebble dash. It comprises a continuous nave and chancel with a bell-gable at the west end. Originally a Romanesque building, the church was repaired and 'beautified' in 1813 at the cost of John Harrison of Shelswell House, when most of the ancient features were destroyed.[27] A restoration by C. N. Beazley in 1875–6 at the expense of Edward Slater-Harrison and the rector, John Meade, almost amounted to a rebuilding, leaving only the foundations of the original walls.[28] A 13th-century piscina survives and the present 12th-century doorway was moved from the north, where it is shown in Skelton's illustration, to the south side;[29] it has chevron mouldings and a roughly carved tympanum of a dove and two interlocked snakes. The restoration also included the removal of the old pews and gallery, the restoration of the chancel, and the building of the bell-gable, vestry, and south porch. In 1875 a 13th-century incised stone, now on the north wall of the chancel, commemorating a heart burial and inscribed 'Hic jacet . . .' was discovered in a niche (probably the old aumbry) in the chancel wall. There are two lancet windows at the west end, and a window on the north side contains early 19th-century glass after Raphael's 'Transfiguration'. The font and pulpit are modern.

There are memorials to the Trotman, Harrison, and Slater-Harrison families, successive owners of Shelswell House. Those commemorated include Edward Trotman (d. 1743); his sons Samuel Trotman, rector (d. 1773), and Fiennes Trotman (d. 1782); Gilbert Harrison, merchant of London (d. 1790), with a marble bust and elaborate emblems of commercial enterprise; Mary, his widow (d. 1825), with a monument by P. Rouw of Regent Street; John Harrison (d. 1834); John Slater-Harrison (d. 1874); and Edward Slater-Harrison (d. 1911); and one to George Tyrwhitt-Drake (d. 1915).[30]

The church once had some medieval silver: a chalice and paten were listed in 1552.[31] The chalice was doubtless the one presented by Leonard and Margaret Verney, who mentions it in her will of 1530.[32] A pewter almsplate has disappeared since 1892, and the plate consisted in 1955 of a silver chalice and paten of 1798.[33] In 1955 there were two bells, as there were in 1552; both are 14th-century, and one is inscribed 'Ave Maria Gracia Plena'.[34]

The registers begin in 1705, but there are transcripts for 1681–1705. The churchwardens' book begins in 1759.

NONCONFORMITY. No record has been found of Roman Catholicism.

There has been little Protestant dissent. One dissenting family was reported in 1778, and in 1793 a single 'Anabaptist'.[35] In 1839 a house was licensed as a place of worship,[36] but there never seems to have been more than about one family of dissenters in the village. In 1854 one dissenter was said to attend church every Sunday morning.[37]

SCHOOLS. There was no school in Newton Purcell in the early 19th century.[38] By 1854, however, there was a dame school supported by J. H. Slater-Harrison,[39] which was attended by 20 children from Newton and Shelswell. There was also an evening writing-school for 6 boys supported by the rector.[40] Either the dame school or its successor had 18 pupils in 1871.[41]

Newton Purcell Church of England school was built in 1873 at the joint expense of the patron, the rector, the Revd. John Meade, and other residents, on ground given by J. H. Slater-Harrison.[42] It was attended by 14 children in 1889[43] and, after being enlarged in 1898,[44] by 31 children in 1906.[45] It was reorganized as a junior school in 1929, when the older children were sent to Fringford, and was given aided status in 1952. There were 10 pupils in 1937 and in 1954.[46]

CHARITIES. There are no charities older than the 19th century.[47] By deed dated 1884 the Revd. John Meade (rector 1843–83) gave £250 in stock. Of the yearly interest £1 was to be paid to the sexton and the remainder was to be distributed at Christmas to widows, the sick and aged poor of Newton Purcell and Shelswell.[48] In 1954, when the annual income was £6 15s., the charity was still distributed by the rector at Christmas.[49]

[25] Par. Rec. Plan; Gardner, *Dir. Oxon.*
[26] *Wilb. Visit.*; Oxf. Dioc. c 332, c 344.
[27] Blo. *Newt.* 12. For a drawing (1825) by J. Buckler see plate opposite. It shows the church between the two restorations. It had a small east window with a pointed head, and 3 two-light south windows of the same shape.
[28] Blo. *Newt.* 12; Bodl. Par. Box (uncat.): faculty.
[29] Skelton, *Oxon.* (Ploughley), 7.
[30] For blazons of arms see Bodl. G.A. Oxon. 4° 689, p. 228.
[31] *Chant. Cert.* 87.
[32] Blo. *Shels.* 7.
[33] Evans, *Ch. Plate.*
[34] *Ch. Bells Oxon.* ii. 218.
[35] Oxf. Dioc. c 327, p. 65.

[36] Ibid. c 646, f. 104.
[37] *Wilb. Visit.*; Oxf. Dioc. c 332, c 344.
[38] *Educ. of Poor*, 727.
[39] See below, p. 288.
[40] *Wilb. Visit.*
[41] *Elem. Educ. Ret.*
[42] Par. Rec.; *Kelly's Dir. Oxon.* (1887); Blo. *Newt.* 18.
[43] *Ret. of Sch.*
[44] *Kelly's Dir. Oxon.* (1920).
[45] *Vol. Sch. Ret.*
[46] Inf. Oxon. Educ. Cttee.
[47] e.g. Oxf. Dioc. d 553; *Char. Don.* ii. 990.
[48] Blo. *Newt.* 18; *Kelly's Dir. Oxon.* (1939).
[49] Inf. the Revd. R. C. H. Duquenoy.

NOKE

THIS small, irregularly shaped parish of 794 acres, which has the appearance of having been carved out of Islip, lies between Otmoor and the hills of Wood Eaton and Stowood.[1] It lies partly on the Islip inlier of the Cornbrash, but mostly on the Oxford Clay.[2] The only natural boundaries are those on the north and north-east which follow the River Ray and a tributary brook, which sweeps round the edge of Otmoor. Here the land is below the 200-foot contour and is subject to flooding, but in the direction of Beckley and Wood Eaton it rises sharply to over 300 feet. Noke Wood (52 a.), in the extreme south-east, alone survives of formerly extensive woodland. In the Middle Ages and later Islip woods, Prattle Wood, and Lower Woods bounded the parish on the west and south.[3]

In the late 17th century Plot found traces of what he took to be a Roman road running south from Noke to Drunshill, but this cannot now be located with certainty.[4] Today the parish's chief road is a branch of the Islip–Wheatley road. It runs steeply downhill to Noke village and then on to the edge of Otmoor. The Otmoor inclosure award of 1815 provided for roads from this point, Noke Lane end, which ran northwards to Oddington and eastwards to Moor Leys Bridge on the Roman road across the moor.[5] These new roads, however, seem to have followed the line of an old track, called the Greenway at least as early as the 13th century.[6] A small close beside the road on the Beckley boundary was called Greenway Piece in the mid-19th century.[7] In 1492 'Osyat Brugge' in Noke was said to be broken 'in uno se archs' [sic].[8] This structure may have carried the Greenway over the Ray towards Oddington. A footpath which provides a short cut to Islip from the western end of Noke village may represent the 'corpse way' which, it was alleged in 1630, had been blocked up when woodland was cleared and turned into Islip cow pasture.[9] In the early 19th century the footpath to Beckley skirted the western side of Noke Wood,[10] a narrow strip of which was called Purley Lane in 1843.[11]

Noke village lines both sides of the parish's chief road, its houses and half-dozen farms being spread out over about half a mile.[12] There were at least eighteen houses in 1665 including the manor-house and four substantial farm-houses.[13]

In 1955 there was one inn, the 'Plough', but in the 1840's there was another called the 'Marlborough Arms'.[14] Neither appears to have been in existence as an inn in the 18th century.[15] In the centre of the village lies the Old Rectory, and close by are St. Giles's church in its walled churchyard and the old thatched school, now used as a parish room. At the eastern end of the village there is a narrow strip of rough ground which with the field on the south side is called the Green, most of which, however, lies in Islip parish.[16] East of Noke Lane end is a rectangular and moated enclosure. This may have been the site of the manor-house of the Foliots or their successors in the Middle Ages.[17] In the early 19th century a water-house or pump-house stood beside Pulley's Lane.[18] This seems to have used a spring in Pulley's Close. Wells were formerly numerous in the village and did not need to be of any great depth. Frequently the parish has suffered from too much water: the local historian Dunkin noted in 1823 that its lanes were nearly impassable in winter.[19] The draining of Otmoor improved the healthiness of Noke's situation, previously said to be 'poisoned by the vapours that arise' from the moor.[20]

Manor Farm is L-shaped in plan, and has two stories, with cellar and attic, built of coursed rubble. The north wing was probably originally built in the late 16th or early 17th century, but has been much altered. It is probably a part of the 17th-century manor-house for which 24 hearths were returned in 1665.[21] The west wing may be 18th-century, but has been modernized. The tradition that the Duchess of Marlborough pulled down most of the manor-house and converted the remainder into a farm-house at the beginning of the 18th century is of doubtful validity, as the house was the property of the trustees of the Blewbury Charity.[22] A two-storied gabled projection on the east side probably once housed the staircase, which appears to have been moved southwards. Two original fireplaces and some panelling, probably early 17th century, survive. A short distance to the north-west stands a rectangular two-storied building in coursed rubble with ashlar quoins, roofed with stone slates. It has windows with stone mullions but no fireplaces, chimneys, or proper staircase. It probably dates from around 1600, and is traditionally supposed to have been the stables of the manor-house of the Bradshaws, Winchcombes, and Halls.[23]

The Old Rectory, now divided into three flats, consists of a 17th-century central block between a 19th-century extension on the east, built in 1883, and an 18th-century extension on the west. The central block is of two stories of coursed rubble, roofed with

---

[1] Detached portions of 13 acres in all were given to Islip under the Divided Parishes Act, 1882, and *Oxon. Review Order* (1932); O.S. Map 6″, xxvii, xxviii, xxxiii, xxxiv (1884); 2½″, 42/51 (1951); see *V.C.H. Oxon.* v. 2.

[2] G.S. Map 1″, xlv SE.; see above, p. 211.

[3] See map, p. 211; MS. Top. Oxon. c 56, f. 30; see below, p. 272.

[4] *V.C.H. Oxon.* i. 278–9. A few Roman coins have been found in the village: ibid. 341.

[5] O.R.O. Incl. award.

[6] *P.N. Oxon.* (E.P.N.S.), i. 233.

[7] Bodl. Tithe award map.

[8] S.C. 2/197/49: court roll, Oct. 8 Hen. VII.

[9] MS. Top. Oxon. c 56, f. 30.

[10] A. Bryant, *Oxon. Map* (1823).

[11] Bodl. Tithe award map.

[12] O.S. Map 25″, xxvii. 16 (1876). For a view see plate facing p. 276.

[13] *Hearth Tax Oxon.* 203.

[14] Bodl. Tithe award map.   [15] O.R.O. Victlrs' recog.

[16] Bodl. Tithe award map.

[17] See below, p. 269; the moat is not mentioned in *V.C.H. Oxon.* ii.

[18] A. Bryant, *Oxon. Map* (1823); O.R.O. Incl. award map (1829).

[19] Dunkin, *Oxon.* ii. 81.

[20] *Observations on the Bill . . . for Draining Otmoor* (1788).

[21] *Hearth Tax Oxon.* 203.

[22] Dunkin, *Oxon.* ii. 81; see below, p. 271.

[23] Inf. Min. of Housing and Local Govt.; personal observation; local inf.

stone slates. On the south side there are two gabled projections and one old two-light casement window. The house was extensively repaired in 1899, and was sold in 1926 for £2,000.[24] The Plough Inn, which may date from the 17th century, is a two-storied building of local stone, with a stone-slate roof and brick chimney-stacks.

In the 16th century Noke is said to have been used as a refuge for members of Oxford University in time of plague.[25] There was fighting in the neighbourhood in 1643 and early in 1645 Captain Abercromby surprised royalist forces quartered at Noke, and claimed to have carried off 50 horses and other plunder.[26] According to the royalists, however, Abercromby's attack on 'Master Irons' house' was beaten off with heavy loss.[27] In the late 18th and early 19th centuries Noke villagers contributed to the disturbances over the inclosure of Otmoor.[28]

MANORS. After the Conquest an estate of 2½ hides in *NOKE* was given to William FitzOsbern, Earl of Hereford.[29] After the rebellion and imprisonment of William's son Roger in 1075 it is probable that his lands in Noke passed like those of Fritwell to Roger de Chesney, and that Roger's granddaughter Maud brought the overlordship of the manor to the Fitzgerold family by her marriage about 1160 to Henry Fitzgerold, chamberlain to Henry II. From Maud's son Warin Fitzgerold (d. 1216) it passed to Margaret, wife of Baldwin de Reviers, and so to the earls of Devon and the Isle.[30] Margaret's son Baldwin was overlord of Noke in 1235,[31] and the overlordship followed the descent of the earldom until the death of Isabel, Countess of Aumale, Devon, and the Isle, in 1293.[32] Like the overlordship of Fritwell it then passed to the De Lisles of Rougemont, who remained overlords[33] until 1368, when Robert de Lisle surrendered Noke with many other fees to Edward III.[34] Thereafter the tenants of Noke probably held in chief, although in the reign of Richard II the manor may have been regarded as part of the Duchy of Lancaster.[35]

The tenant in 1086 of the estate which had belonged to the FitzOsberns was Rainald,[36] the ancestor of the Foliot family who in the 12th century probably held Noke—as they held part of Fritwell—under their kinsmen the Chesneys.[37] Sampson Foliot, who succeeded Henry Foliot about 1233, held ½ knight's fee in Noke of successive earls of Devon and of the Countess Isabel.[38] His lands in Noke

were seized by the Earl of Gloucester in 1265 after the battle of Evesham,[39] but were probably soon restored. Sampson's sons died during his lifetime and he had been succeeded by 1285 by Henry Tyes.[40] Henry died in possession of the manor in 1307,[41] and was succeeded by his son Henry, who was hanged in 1322 for his part in Thomas of Lancaster's rebellion.[42]

In 1326 Noke was committed to the keeping of Nicholas de la Beche,[43] but at the beginning of Edward III's reign Henry's sister and heiress Alice, widow of Warin de Lisle of Kingston Lisle, obtained posession.[44] Alice held the manor until her death in 1347.[45] She left it to her younger son Warin, who died childless in 1361,[46] and was succeeded by his nephew Warin, son of his elder brother Gerard.[47] The younger Warin was the tenant of Robert de Lisle of Rougemont in Noke when the latter surrendered his fees to the Crown.[48] In 1373, when Warin agreed that his son Gerard should marry Anne, daughter of Michael de la Pole, arrangements were made to settle Noke upon Gerard and his heirs.[49] But Gerard died in 1381, a year before his father,[50] who was succeeded by his daughter Margaret, wife of Thomas, Lord Berkeley.[51] Noke manor was delivered to Margaret and Thomas in 1382,[52] but Warin de Lisle's widow Joan may have held part of it in dower until her death ten years later as she held a third share of the advowson.[53] Margaret died in 1392, and after Thomas's death in 1417[54] Noke passed to their daughter Elizabeth, wife of Richard de Beauchamp, Earl of Warwick. Elizabeth died in 1422 leaving three daughters, Margaret, Eleanor, and Elizabeth, who succeeded to her possessions after the death of the earl in 1439.[55] Noke was in the king's hands in 1440,[56] but by a partition of the Lisle lands between the coheiresses the manor fell to the share of the youngest sister Elizabeth, wife of George Nevill, Lord Latimer. Elizabeth's husband died in 1469, a few months after his son Henry, who had been killed on the Lancastrian side at Banbury, and who left a son Richard who was only a year old. Elizabeth continued to hold Noke until her death in 1480, when her heir was her grandson Richard.[57] There is no evidence, however, that Richard or the subsequent Lords Latimer[58] held the manor, and its history is unknown until it reappears in the 16th century as part of the estate of Henry Bradshaw (see below).

Westminster Abbey's manor, the second of the

---

[24] Par. Rec. *Particulars of Sale of Noke Advowson* (1884); ibid. Vestry minute bk. (1888–1949); Bodl. Par. Box (uncat.), deed of sale.

[25] Dunkin, *Oxon.* ii. 82 n.

[26] Par. Reg.: 2 soldiers were buried at Noke in 1643; Dunkin, *Oxon.* ii. 82 n.

[27] Cf. Par. Reg. for several contemporary Ironses in Noke; Dunkin MS. 438/4, f. 63; for Abercromby see also above, p. 21.

[28] See below, p. 273.

[29] *V.C.H. Oxon.* i. 425.

[30] Farrer, *Honors*, iii. 234–5; see above, p. 136.

[31] *Bk. of Fees*, 447.

[32] Ibid. 825; *Rot. Hund.* (Rec. Com.), ii. 45, 838; *Complete Peerage*, iv. 316–23; *Feud. Aids*, iv. 157.

[33] e.g. *Cal. Inq. p.m.* vii, p. 24; xi, p. 273.

[34] *Cal. Close*, 1364–8, 496; *Cal. Fine R.* 1369–77, 3.

[35] C 136/72/7; cf. Dunkin, *Oxon.* ii. 91.

[36] *V.C.H. Oxon.* i. 425.

[37] Farrer, *Honors*, iii. 234.

[38] Ibid. 235; *Bk. of Fees*, 447, 825; *Rot. Hund.* (Rec. Com.), ii. 45, 838.

[39] *Cal. Inq. Misc.* i, p. 262.

[40] *Feud. Aids*, iv. 157; Farrer, *Honors*, iii. 236.

[41] *Cal. Inq. p.m.* v, pp. 26–27.

[42] *Complete Peerage* (orig. edn.), vii. 381; *Feud. Aids*, iv. 170.

[43] *Cal. Fine R.* 1319–27, 427.

[44] *Cal. Inq. p.m.* vii, pp. 23–24.

[45] *Feud. Aids*, iv. 180; *Cal. Inq. p.m.* ix, p. 395.

[46] *Cal. Inq. p.m.* xi, p. 273.

[47] *Complete Peerage*, viii. 50.

[48] *Cal. Close*, 1364–8, 496.

[49] Ibid. 1369–74, 557.

[50] *Complete Peerage*, viii. 53; C 136/26/7.

[51] Kennett, *Paroch. Antiq.* ii. 164–5.

[52] *Cal. Close*, 1369–74, 557.

[53] Ibid. 1389–92, 459; C 136/72/7.

[54] *Complete Peerage*, ii. 131.

[55] Ibid. viii. 54; C 139/94.

[56] *Cal. Pat.* 1436–41, 367, 434.

[57] *Complete Peerage*, vii. 480–1; I. H. Jeayes, *Berkeley Muniments*, nos. 594, 615; C 140/77.

[58] *Complete Peerage*, vii. 481 sqq.

two principal Noke estates, is not mentioned in the Domesday survey, but since its connexion with Islip was so close throughout the Middle Ages it is possible that it was included with Islip among the lands held temporarily *in commendatione* by Adeline d'Ivry. Edward the Confessor's gift of these lands to Westminster Abbey was not confirmed until 1204.[59] Like the Lisle manor the abbey's estate in *NOKE* was ½ knight's fee,[60] though in area it was a little smaller.[61] In practice it was administered like the abbey's lands in Fencott and Murcott as a member of the liberty of Islip,[62] and it was not separately listed in the accounts of the abbey's possessions made after the Dissolution.[63] When the abbey was refounded in 1556 Noke manor was restored, and four years later passed to Queen Elizabeth's foundation of the collegiate church of St. Peter.[64] Dunkin recorded that as late as about 1800 the Dean and Chapter of Westminster still claimed the overlordship of Noke, and that within living memory the villagers had been summoned to Islip church to hear certain documents read.[65]

From the 13th to the 15th century the tenants of Westminster's ½-fee at Noke were members of the Willescote or Williamscote family, who took their name from Williamscot near Cropredy. The first of the family to be definitely associated with Noke was Richard de Williamscote, who was the tenant in 1279.[66] Richard's grandfather of the same name had obtained Over Kiddington manor about 1220,[67] and the family's ½-fee in Noke followed a similar descent until the end of the 15th century. Richard the younger was Sheriff of Oxfordshire in 1290 and died soon afterwards,[68] being succeeded by Henry, probably his son, who held Kiddington in 1308.[69] Henry was dead by 1316, and his successor Richard, Sheriff of Oxfordshire in 1354,[70] lived until about 1360,[71] when he was followed by Thomas de Williamscote (d. 1373) and by Thomas, son of Thomas, who was a minor.[72] The latter was holding Kiddington and presumably Noke in 1398, and was still alive in 1424,[73] but by 1428 Elizabeth de Williamscote was holding both Williamscot and Kiddington in dower.[74] According to an inquiry made in 1497 the last of the male line to hold Kiddington and Noke was Ralph de Williamscote, possibly son of Thomas and Elizabeth. Ralph was said to have left a daughter Elizabeth, who brought the manor to her husband Robert Babington,[75] the fourth son of Sir William Babington of Chilwell (Northants).[76] Robert was certainly in possession by 1454. At his death in 1464 he left

Noke with Over Kiddington and Asterleigh to his son William,[77] who two years later settled Noke on himself and his wife Ellen, daughter of Sir Richard Illingworth, chief baron of the Exchequer.[78] William was succeeded by three sons in turn, Richard, Edward who died in 1497, and William.[79] William died about 1535, but although his successors continued to hold Kiddington until the early years of the 17th century,[80] there is nothing to show that they retained any holding in Noke, and it is possible that they lost their lands there at the Dissolution.

The steps by which all estates in Noke eventually passed into the possession of Henry Bradshaw are not clear. The Oseney lands (see below) were granted to him by the king in 1544,[81] and he and his successors paid to the Crown an annual farm of 1s. 5d.[82] While a royal grant of the manor was made to Henry within the same year, he had in fact purchased the Westminster Abbey lands from a certain Michael Ashefield in 1539.[83] Henry Bradshaw, possibly the eldest son of William Bradshaw of Wendover (Bucks.), was successively Solicitor-General (1540), Attorney-General (1545), and chief baron of the Exchequer (1552). He witnessed the will of Edward VI in favour of Lady Jane Grey, but avoided the possible consequences by dying soon after the succession of Queen Mary in 1553.[84] Henry's only surviving son Benedict, a minor, died shortly afterwards, and the family property was eventually divided between Benedict's sisters Christian and Bridget.[85] Christian married Thomas Winchcombe of Chalgrove, a descendant of the famous clothier 'Jack of Newbury',[86] and Bridget married first Henry White and second Thomas Fermor of Somerton (d. 1580).[87] Henry Bradshaw's widow Joan held Noke manor until her death in 1599,[88] when it passed to her grandson Benedict, son of Christian and Thomas Winchcombe, who in 1576 had agreed with Bridget and Thomas Fermor for the partition of the Bradshaw property.[89] Benedict Winchcombe died in 1623, having settled Noke upon his nephew Benedict, son of his sister Mary and William Hall of High Meadow (Glos.).[90]

The Halls were staunch Royalists as well as Roman Catholics.[91] Benedict garrisoned High Meadow for King Charles and took part in the siege of Gloucester in 1643.[92] In 1653 Noke was held by lease from the commissioners for sequestrations by John Harper, a member of a family of substantial yeomen of Noke,[93] but Benedict Hall recovered his

---

[59] *V.C.H. Oxon.* i. 386–7, 422; see above, p. 209.
[60] *Feud. Aids,* iv. 157.
[61] *Rot. Hund.* (Rec. Com.), ii. 836, 838.
[62] e.g. S.C. 2/197/48, 49.
[63] *Valor Eccl.* (Rec. Com.), i. 411; Dugd. *Mon.* i. 328.
[64] *Cal. Pat.* 1555–7, 349; 1558–60, 397–8.
[65] Dunkin, *Oxon.* ii. 82, 98; but see below, p. 274.
[66] *Rot. Hund.* ii. 836.
[67] Thomas Warton, *Hist. and Antiq. of Kiddington* (1815), 40.
[68] Ibid. 42; P.R.O. *L. and I.* ix.
[69] Warton, *Kiddington,* 42; *Cal. Inq. p.m.* v, p. 23.
[70] *Feud. Aids,* iv. 167; P.R.O. *L. and I.* ix.
[71] *Cal. Inq. p.m.* x, p. 537.
[72] Warton, *Kiddington,* 42; C 135/224/11.
[73] C 136/104, 105; C 139/18, 19.
[74] *Feud. Aids,* iv. 186, 189.
[75] *Cal. Inq. p.m. Hen. VII,* ii, p. 69.
[76] For the Babingtons see Nichols, *Leics.* iii (2), between pp. 954 and 955; Warton, *Kiddington,* 44 sqq.; *Topographer and Gen.* (1846), i. 254 sqq.; Dunkin MS. 438/1, pedigree 10.

[77] Warton, *Kiddington,* 45.
[78] *Cal. Close,* 1461–8, 379.
[79] *Cal. Inq. p.m. Hen. VII,* ii, pp. 30, 69.
[80] Dunkin MS. 438/1, pedigree 10; Warton, *Kiddington,* 47.
[81] *L. & P. Hen. VIII,* xix (2), p. 181.
[82] Dunkin MS. 438/3: fee-farm roll, 148.
[83] C 142/184/1; C 1/951/43.
[84] Foss, *Judges,* v. 292; *V.C.H. Bucks.* ii. 339; C 142/101/99.
[85] *V.C.H. Bucks.* ii. 339.
[86] *Visit. Glos. 1623* (Harl. Soc. xxi), 74; Elias Ashmole, *Antiq. Berks.* (1719), iii. 300.
[87] *R.C. Families,* i. 6.
[88] Ibid. 31: will of Henry Bradshaw; cf. E 179/162/33.
[89] Dunkin, *Oxon.* ii. 94; cf. *V.C.H. Bucks.* ii. 339.
[90] C 142/399/149; *Par. Coll.* iii. 229; *Visit. Glos. 1623,* (Harl. Soc. xxi), 74.
[91] Stapleton, *Cath. Miss.* 114–15.
[92] For this and other information see *Trans. Bristol and Glos. Arch. Soc.* vii. 248–9, 264–6.
[93] *Cal. Cttee. for Compounding,* 696; cf. ibid. 2200.

lands at or before the Restoration.[94] On his death in 1668 his property descended to his son, Henry Benedict Hall, who died in 1687, and to his grandson Benedict Hall. The latter sold much of his property to pay his debts and to provide a marriage portion for his only daughter and heiress Benedicta.[95] In 1707 part of the Halls' estates in Noke—about 570 acres—was purchased for £9,776 by the trustees of William Malthus. In accordance with the will he had made seven years before, the rents of these lands were henceforth applied to the maintenance of Reading Blue Coat School and a new school at Blewbury (Berks.).[96] The trustees of the Blewbury Charity remained one of the principal landowners in Noke throughout the 18th and 19th centuries.[97] The remainder of Benedict Hall's estates was sold about the same time to the 1st Duke of Marlborough,[98] whose descendants were lords of the manor[99] until 1886, when the Marlborough estates in Noke were sold to Henry Williams of Oxford by George Charles, the 8th duke. Manorial rights were not subsequently claimed.[1]

LESSER ESTATES. In 1086 ½ hide of waste land in Noke was held by Robert d'Oilly and Roger d'Ivry,[2] but its subsequent descent is unknown. In 1388 Richard II was found to hold a messuage and 80 acres of land in Noke.[3] This may have been a carucate of land once held by John Marshal, Sheriff of Bedfordshire in 1328–30, which had been seized by Edward III in satisfaction of John's debts. In 1368–9 this land had been held by John de Bekke at a farm of 20s. a year, and in 1412 it was granted for a term of 20 years to William Tristur and William Craule at an increased farm of £1 6s. 8d.[4] It is uncertain when Oseney Abbey acquired an estate in Noke. In 1509 it was receiving 16s. a year from John Toller for lands and tenements there, and was paying 2s. a year to the king, of whose lands in Noke the estate was presumably part. John Toller seems to have been an assign of Thomas Andrew of Islip, to whom the abbey had let the estate for 80 years from 1506.[5] At the Dissolution it was held for the same rent by John Andrew.[6]

ECONOMIC HISTORY. The place-name 'at the oak trees' suggests that Noke had its beginnings as a clearing in extensive woodlands.[7] It may have been a comparatively late Anglo-Saxon settlement, for there was little arable land in the eastern half of the parish—the only part surveyed—in 1086. Although there were 2 ploughs on Rainald's estate, one of them on the demesne of 5 virgates, there was land for only one. An increase in the value of Rainald's lands from 30s. to 40s. since the Conquest may indicate that

clearance of the forest was continuing. There was a wood (4×3 furls.) besides pasture (3×2 furls.). On the estate were 3 villeins (*villani*), 6 bordars, and 2 serfs. The ½ hide of waste in Noke held in 1086 by Robert d'Oilly and Roger d'Ivry may later have belonged to the Westminster Abbey manor.[8]

In 1279 Sampson Foliot, tenant of the De Lisle manor, held 4 virgates with meadow and pasture land in demesne. Under him 11 villeins—2 virgaters and 9 half-virgaters—held for rents of 5s. a year a virgate, and owed labour services and tallage at his will, and had to pay fines if their sons left the manor. Three free tenants held half-virgates, two for rents of 3s. 4d. and 6s. 8d. respectively, while the third did suit at the county and hundred court for Sampson Foliot, and a fourth held a virgate for 1d. a year. On Westminster's manor Richard de Williamscote held 3 virgates in demesne for 30s. a year. Four villein virgaters paid 1s. 6d. and 6 cottars, each with 6 acres, 3s. a year. Two free virgaters paid 6s. and 3s. a year respectively, and 2 others paid 1s. 6d.—one for a half-virgate and one for 4 acres. In the whole parish then there were about 23 virgates of arable, 8 freeholders, and 21 unfree tenants.[9]

In 1390 Thomas Berkeley held in demesne 4 virgates in the De Lisle manor and, like his predecessor Sampson Foliot, paid 2s. 6d. a year to the Abbot of Westminster for husbote and haybote in Islip Wood. On the abbot's manor Richard de Williamscote, with a demesne of 4 virgates, paid 30s. a year; while of tenants who owed rents and services direct to the abbot, one held a messuage and croft, owed boon works in the autumn, and paid 3s., a hen and 9 eggs a year, and 8 others owed 1d., a hen and 12 eggs each. The annual rents received by Richard de Williamscote amounted to about £6 16s.[10] The estate which Oseney Abbey held before the Dissolution contained about 66 acres of meadow and 55 acres of the woodland which covered most of the south-east of the parish, but no arable.[11] The abbey lands were let on long leases in the early 16th century.[12] With the total of 29 tenants in 1279 may be compared the number of contributors to taxes in the early 14th century, 22 in 1306 and 1316, and 29 in 1327,[13] figures which are not likely to represent the total number of householders in any case; and at Noke Westminster Abbey's lands were exempt from taxation. The village may not have suffered heavily from the Black Death, for in 1377 there were 43 contributors to the poll tax on the De Lisle manor alone.[14]

The population of Noke probably varied little from the mid-15th to the mid-16th century. The customary tenants on the Westminster Abbey manor, who attended the view of frankpledge at Islip, were organized in two tithings throughout the period. The

[94] *Hearth Tax Oxon.* 203.
[95] *Trans. Bristol and Glos. Arch. Soc.* vii. 235, 265, 266; S. Rudder, *Hist. Glos.* (1779), 569, 690; cf. *Complete Peerage*, v. 596.
[96] *Par. Coll.* iii. 229; *Char. Don.* i. 30; *1st Rep. Com. Char.* H.C. 83, p. 16 (1819), x (A); O.R.O. Misc. Torr. IV/9.
[97] O.R.O. Land tax assess.; *Kelly's Dir. Oxon.* (1854, &c.).
[98] *Par. Coll.* iii. 229.
[99] O.R.O. Gamekprs' deps.; *Kelly's Dir. Oxon.* (1854, 1864).
[1] *Sale cat.* 1909: Bodl. G.A. Oxon. b 91 (36); *Kelly's Dir. Oxon.* (1939).

[2] *V.C.H. Oxon.* i. 425.
[3] C 47/48/7/169.
[4] *Cal. Fine R.* 1405–13, 234.
[5] Dunkin, *Oxon.* ii. 94; *Oseney Cart.* vi. 236, 248, 267.
[6] *Valor Eccl.* (Rec. Com.), ii. 218.
[7] *P.N. Oxon.* (E.P.N.S.), i. 233.
[8] *V.C.H. Oxon.* i. 425.
[9] *Rot. Hund.* (Rec. Com.), ii. 836, 838.
[10] W.A.M. 15200.
[11] Bodl. Tithe award and map.
[12] See above.
[13] E 179/161/8, 9, 10.
[14] Ibid. 161/39.

tithings were never full, and the sums of head-silver paid annually at Islip at the rate of 1d. a head averaged 1s. 2d. In 1435, when only 9d. was paid, 5 cottages and 8 messuages were in the lord's hands.[15]

The Islip court rolls give no hint of the number of open fields in Noke in the Middle Ages: a reference in 1485 to *stadium vocatum Cammsffild*[16] probably indicates the whole of the common field arable. There appears to have been only one common field, or group of fields, in which the lands of the two Noke manors lay intermingled. The 238 common field 'lands' out of a total of 517, which in the 18th century paid tithes to Islip,[17] probably represented the share of the Westminster Abbey manor, and the remainder, save 14 glebe 'lands', the share of the De Lisle manor. The Common Field or Town Field, as it was called, lay in the north-western part of the parish—on the good Cornbrash land[18]—and in the 16th century was bounded by Islip Wood and cow pasture, by the crofts lining the village street, and by the meadows bordering the River Ray and Otmoor. Its area would have been about 240 statute acres. In the mid-18th century it was divided into 28 furlongs and butts, of which the 7 furlongs in the north-east corner were called Log Field[19]—the name survives. If, besides the 7 furlongs, Log Field once included adjoining land, called after inclosure New Ground, its area would have been about 80 acres, a third of the whole Common Field, and it may originally have been one of a group of three open fields.

The lot-meadows of the parish lined its northern and north-eastern boundaries, and Back of Town, pasture ground south-east of the common field, was still divided into leys in the 18th century. Together with their neighbours of Islip, Beckley, and Wood Eaton the tenants of Noke had common for sheep and pigs in Westminster's Islip Wood. Sheep might graze in 'Hasylbede' and 'Old Sale' from Michaelmas to Lady Day, and elsewhere in the woods in the summer. Pigs might feed in the woods but no pigstyes were to be put up there, and the tenants of Noke had to help in making a hedge between the woods and Sart Field in Islip.[20]

In 1498 a Westminster Abbey tenant was alleged to have encroached upon the lord's soil in Noke and to have inclosed it from the field,[21] while a few years before two other tenants had allowed the destruction of two cottages and may have inclosed a small area of arable.[22] Inclosure on a large scale may have begun with Henry Bradshaw's acquisition of both manors and the Oseney lands in the 1540's, but the only evidence there is suggests that inclosure took place mainly in the 17th century. In 1634 the rector had only one 2-acre close, but by 1685 he had inclosed 7 acres, Pulley's Close, from the common field.[23] The demesne lands which descended to the Hall family covered 394 acres, more than half the parish,

and it is significant that all this and all the old Oseney estate had been inclosed by the end of the 18th century. Two large pieces of the common field which had also been inclosed appear to have been demesne consolidated by an exchange of strips.[24] By 1767 New Ground had been inclosed at the south-east corner of the Common Field, and the 7 furlongs called Log Field had all been acquired and inclosed by the Blewbury Charity trustees by 1829.[25] The estate which the Charity Trustees had bought from the Halls in 1707 formed one large farm bringing in a gross annual rent of £420 until about 1791, when a second farm was created. Between 1787 and 1791 the trustees spent £600 on a new house and farm buildings, and between 1787 and 1812 they sold nearly £1,500 worth of timber, mostly ash and elm but some oak, off their Noke estate.[26] It is therefore likely that the fields immediately north of the present Noke Wood—Upper, Lower, and Great Wood Ground, Paddock Ground, and Great and Little Ash Grove—were inclosed from former woodland between 1787 and 1797, when Richard Davis showed them and 'New Farm', to which they belonged, on his map of Oxfordshire.[27] Inclosure advanced more slowly on the Duke of Marlborough's estates in the western part of the parish, but a couple of small closes had appeared by 1767[28] and all the meadows north of the common field had been inclosed by the beginning of the 19th century.

Under the Otmoor inclosure award of 1815 the Blewbury Charity Trustees and the Duke of Marlborough—the only proprietors in Noke—received 54 and 18 acres respectively, and the trustees purchased another 53 acres of the lands sold to defray the expenses of inclosure.[29] Before the inclosure award of 1829 there remained about 130 acres of common field arable in Noke. Under the award the Duke of Marlborough received 115 acres and the Charity Trustees 12 acres,[30] the latter having previously exchanged many of their strips with the duke for a compact block of meadow-land.[31] Under neither award did the cottagers of Noke receive any compensation for loss of rights of common. But as in Charlton[32] the movement in 1829–30 to reclaim Otmoor as common was not confined to the poorest class. The chief organizer of the systematic destruction of fences on Otmoor in September 1830 was John Ward of Noke, tenant of the Charity Trustees' new farm of 280 acres.[33]

In the Middle Ages the lords of Noke seem seldom to have resided in the village and it was only in the late 16th and early 17th centuries, the time of Joan Bradshaw and Benedict Winchcombe, that the parish benefited from the presence of a wealthy family. A few yeoman families, the Johnsons and Harpers in the 16th and early 17th centuries, the Tippings, Lipscombes, and Steeles in the late 17th and 18th

[15] S.C. 2/197/48, 49.
[16] Ibid. Ct. R. Apr. 2 Rich. III.
[17] Par. Rec. Tithe notebk. (1767–8).
[18] See above, p. 268.
[19] Par. Rec. Tithe notebk.
[20] Barbara Harvey, 'Islip Manor' (Bodl. MS. B. Litt. d 53), 279, citing W.A.M. 14959.
[21] S.C. 2/197/49.   [22] Dom. of Incl. 335.
[23] Oxf. Archd. Oxon. c 142, ff. 59, 63.
[24] Ibid. f. 63; Bodl. Tithe map (1849).
[25] Par. Rec. Tithe notebk.; O.R.O. Incl. award map.
[26] 1st Rep. Com. Char. H.C. 83, pp. 17–19, 21 (1819), x (A).

[27] Davis, Oxon. Map (1797).
[28] Par. Rec. Tithe notebk.: Hindes or Haines Close and Fishers, later called Hatton's Close.
[29] O.R.O. Otmoor incl. award.
[30] O.R.O. Incl. award (the priv. act is 58 Geo. III, c. 11). For map showing open-field furlongs immediately before the inclosure see Oxf. Dioc. c 436, p. 332c; cf. ibid. c 449: rectory terrier (1805).
[31] Cf. Oxf. Dioc. c 436, p. 332c and O.R.O. Incl. award map.
[32] See above, p. 86.
[33] Dunkin MS. 438/6, f. 49; 1st Rep. Com. Char. 18.

centuries,[34] enjoyed comparative prosperity, but throughout the 18th century the rectors reported that there were no families of note in the parish.[35] The poor became a serious burden in the late 18th century, when the population was probably increasing. In 1676 there had been 43 adults,[36] and incumbents reported in 1738 and 1759 that there were about 20 houses, but by 1811 there were 31.[37] The poor rate rose from 2d. in the pound in 1752 to 3d. in 1780, 6d. in 1800, and 1s. 3d. in 1806. Three levies in 1730 had raised only £10 8s. 1½d., but receipts rose to £46 in 1780, £116 in 1800, and £216 in 1815.[38] The poverty of the village naturally made the villagers strongly opposed to the proposed inclosure of Otmoor, with the consequent loss of their common rights.[39] Their rector, Alexander Litchfield, on the other hand, was on the side of the 'progressive' farmers.[40]

In the 19th century population increased from 150 in 1801 to 187 in 1831. Thereafter it dropped to 116 by 1861 and to 88 by 1901.[41]

Even before the inclosures of 1815 and 1829 most of the inhabitants must have been labourers on the half-dozen farms of the parish. In 1823, 28 out of 31 families were engaged in agriculture and only two in trade.[42] In 1850 there were only three tradesmen, the innkeeper, a blacksmith, and a carpenter.[43] There were then six farms, two of 280 acres each on the Charity estate, and four of 120, 86, 81, and 33 on the Marlborough estate.[44] The village had a carrier and a shoemaker by 1854 and a shopkeeper by 1864. A brick-kiln was built shortly before 1870.[45] Since 1880 farms have changed hands frequently, and have seldom remained in the same family for two generations. There were at least six farms in 1920, and four in 1939, the latter all of more than 150 acres.[46] As in much of central Oxfordshire arable farming has been largely abandoned in favour of dairying. Whereas in 1849 there were about 320 acres of arable to 370 acres of meadow and pasture,[47] in 1939 there were only about 90 acres of arable—Great Warren and Noke Field (part of the old common field)—and most of the parish was permanent grassland.[48] By 1955 agriculture was no longer the predominant occupation, and many of the villagers—who numbered 95 at the Census of 1951—worked in Oxford. One craft at least, thatching, was still practised by the Shirley family.[49]

CHURCH. There was a church at Noke at least by 1191, when a priest was first recorded.[50]

In the Middle Ages the advowson normally descended with the Foliot-Lisle manor. Some exceptions may be noted. In 1346 Warin de Lisle, who was to inherit the manor from his mother, recovered in the king's court his right to present against his elder brother Gerard of Kingston Lisle.[51] In 1371 Richard Mercer of Oxford, attorney of Robert de Grendon, possibly a distant relative of the De Lisles,[52] was patron. After the death of the Earl of Warwick in 1439, while the manor went to his daughter Elizabeth, the advowson went to another daughter Margaret, wife of John Talbot, 4th Earl of Shrewsbury. The king presented in 1440, and the bishop collated through lapse in 1451, but Margaret presented in 1455 and 1461. After her death in 1467[53] the descent is not clear. The next known presentation was a collation by the bishop in 1511, and in 1520 Ralph Massy was patron.

After the manors were united by Henry Bradshaw, the advowson remained in the hands of the lords of the manor, except that in 1698 Benedict Hall, who was in financial difficulties, evidently sold it for one turn to Martha May of Kidlington.[54] From the early 18th century the dukes of Marlborough were patrons until 1884, when the advowson was sold for £430 to J. C. Holder of Birmingham.[55] In 1915 it was sold by J. H. Redcliffe to the Dean and Chapter of Westminster,[56] also patrons of Islip, with which Noke is usually held.

In the Middle Ages Noke was in Bicester Deanery,[57] but its position on the boundary between Cuddesdon and Bicester deaneries later led to confusion. In 1526 there was a question of its being in Cuddesdon,[58] but in 1535 it was considered in the Deanery of Oxford.[59] By the 17th century it was in Cuddesdon Deanery,[60] and when the Deanery of Islip was formed in about 1852, Noke was placed in it.[61]

It is possible that Noke was originally a chapel of Islip, for the parishes were closely connected. Westminster Abbey's land in Noke certainly formed part of Islip parish: it paid tithes to the Rector of Islip.[62] On the other hand 63 acres in Islip, mostly consisting of Noke Cow Pasture, paid tithes to the Rector of Noke.[63] Those who paid tithes to Islip, seven or eight households in the 18th century,[64] were no doubt buried at Islip. In 1630 there was a case in the church court about Church Way from Noke to Islip, running through Lyehill Copse, along which Noke parishioners had carried their dead for burial in Islip. Witnesses stated that it had been used up to about 50 years before, but had become a cow pasture and was impassable, and in 1768 it was stated that the minister of Islip never does 'duty of

[34] E 179/161/176; ibid. 162/331; ibid. 164/476; Cal. Chan. Proc. (Rec. Com.), i. 418; Hearth Tax Oxon. 203; Par. Reg.; Dunkin, Oxon. ii. 85, 87.
[35] Oxf. Dioc. d 553, d 559.
[36] Compton Census.
[37] Oxf. Dioc. d 553, d 556; Census, 1811.
[38] Par. Rec. Overseers' accts.; Dunkin, Oxon. ii. 81.
[39] Cf. Wing, Annals, 116.
[40] Par. Rec.; for the Otmoor inclosures and the riots of 1830 see V.C.H. Oxon. v. 70–71.
[41] Census, 1901–51.
[42] Dunkin, Oxon. ii. 81.
[43] Gardner, Dir. Oxon.
[44] Bodl. Tithe award; ibid. G.A. Oxon. b 91 (46): Sale Cat.
[45] Kelly's Dir. Oxon. (1854, 1864); MS. Top. Oxon. c 104, f. 82; O.S. map 6", xxvii (1884). The brickyard was south of the village, in Islip parish.
[46] Kelly's Dir. Oxon. (1887–1939).
[47] Bodl. Tithe award.
[48] O.S. Land Utilization Map 1", sht. 94.

[49] Local inf.
[50] Eynsham Cart. i. 93.
[51] For list of medieval presentations see MS. Top. Oxon. d 460.
[52] V.C.H. Bucks. iv. 53.
[53] Complete Peerage, xi. 704.
[54] Dunkin, Oxon. ii. 86.
[55] Par. Rec.
[56] Bodl. Par. Box (uncat.), Order in Council.
[57] Lunt, Val. Norw. 312; Inq. Non. (Rec. Com.), 133.
[58] Subsidy 1526, 259, 276.
[59] Valor Eccl. (Rec. Com.), ii. 176.
[60] Oxf. Dioc. d 708, f. 30b.
[61] For date of formation of Islip deanery see above, p. 67, n. 97.
[62] Bodl. Noke tithe award. Of 517 lands in 28 furlongs, 265 paid tithes to Noke and 238 to Islip; the rest was glebe: Par. Rec. Tithe notebk.
[63] Bodl. Islip tithe award.
[64] Oxf. Dioc. d 559.

minister' to any inhabitant of Noke.[65] As late as about 1800 Noke villagers in the liberty of Islip were called on to hear the reading of documents in Islip church,[66] which probably concerned the payment of tithes.

An early 13th-century parson of Noke, Walter Foliot, was styled rector and was affluent enough to be able to appeal to the Pope.[67] On the other hand, John, who was instituted rector in 1247–8, was bound to reside in person like a vicar.[68] It seems therefore that Noke was by this time an independent parish, although its church was called a chapel until the late 13th century.[69] It was valued at 13s. 4d. in 1254[70] and was, with Stonesfield, the poorest in the county. The assessor, indeed, commented *non valet servicium*. The church was not taxed in 1291, being worth less than 5 marks, but in the 14th century it was taxed at £3.[71] By 1535 its value had greatly increased to £7 19s. 7d.[72]

In the 16th century the living of Noke was sometimes held with that of Oddington: Master Edmund Horde, who became a canon of Oseney in 1520, was Rector of Oddington, as was his successor, Master John Leicester, who had a curate at Noke, to whom he paid £2 13s. 4d.,[73] not enough for a full-time minister. At the episcopal visitations of about 1520 and 1530, apart from the usual complaints about dilapidated buildings, there were none of importance. The chancel, barn (*horreum*), and cemetery walls were in need of repair;[74] although the inhabitants were supposed to contribute to the upkeep of the church, it was said that some failed to do so.[75]

In the post-Reformation period Noke became a very poor living. The fact that the rector's house was taxed on only two hearths in 1665 is significant, and in 1707, the date of the earliest recorded valuation of the church, the value of the living was £42.[76] By 1808 the value had risen to £96,[77] but it failed thereafter to keep pace with rising costs.

In 1849 the remaining tithes were commuted. The land which had belonged to Oseney Abbey (122 a.) had always been exempt from tithe; the tithes on the 393 acres belonging to the Blewbury Charity had already long been commuted for a modus of £13; those on the 120 acres belonging to Islip were now commuted for £26, and those on the rest of the parish (138 a.), belonging to the Rector of Noke, were commuted for £57 14s.[78] The rector had already been awarded £16 a year for the tithes on 63 acres[79] in Islip, when the tithes of that parish were commuted in 1843.

The glebe was small. After inclosure in 1829 it consisted of about 14 acres,[80] half of which had been added as a result of the inclosure of Otmoor in 1815.[81] The 17th-century glebe had consisted of twelve 'lands' in the open fields.[82]

So poor a parish naturally did not attract able rectors, and its spiritual history is not inspiring. After the death in 1571 of John Daniel, who had also been Rector of Oddington, there was serious neglect. It was complained that the non-residence of his successor, Thomas Langley, was 'to the harm of the souls of his parishioners', and in 1574 the revenue of the parish was sequestrated and put into the hands of two parishioners.[83] Robert Warland, who became rector that year, was not a graduate and was only considered 'tollerable',[84] yet he remained for 62 years.[85] All that is known of his ministry is that he began the parish register, and that in 1584 he was several times summoned because his chancel was ruinous.[86] He left at his death in 1636 an estate of over £171,[87] but he was a married man with children and his neglect of the church fabric may have been due to his family obligations. Two of his successors, Hugh Holden (1636–67) and Richard Vesey (1698–1732), both Fellows of Magdalen, were noted for their strong political views rather than for their work as country parsons. Holden as a royalist was expelled from his Noke living in 1648 and restored in 1660.[88] Vesey, also Rector of Brightwell Baldwin, was a leading opponent in 1688 of the President of Magdalen chosen by James II.[89] Hearne, who was certainly prejudiced, said that he was a 'long and dull' preacher.[90] Vesey probably had a curate to serve Noke like his successor Charles Hall (1732–9), who had a curate from Oxford.[91] Gilbert Stephens (1739–73) took a more active interest in the parish. In 1745[92] he came to live in the Rectory House, described in 1635 as one of four bays,[93] but it was presumably too small for an 18th-century family and Stephens repaired and enlarged it.[94] In 1752 he protested to the bishop against the appointment of a new vicar to Beckley, which he had been serving, stating that even with the additional money he had barely enough to live on;[95] he was consequently allowed to go on serving Beckley and in 1764[96] became its vicar. It was perhaps partly for financial reasons that he complained in 1768[97] that those who paid tithes to Islip never went to church. He was also a strong anti-Romanist. In 1767 he wrote that 'if the beneficed clergy would reside in their parish, throw away their cards and forbear to act in the commission of peace', they might then be able to inspire among

65 MS. Top. Oxon. c 56, ff. 30–31.
66 Dunkin, *Oxon.* ii. 82.
67 *St. Frides. Cart.* ii. 223–4. This was a tithe case affecting Fritwell.
68 *Rot. Grosse.* 490.
69 *Rot. Graves.* 224.
70 Lunt, *Val. Norw.* 312.
71 *Inq. Non.* (Rec. Com.), 133.
72 *Valor Eccl.* (Rec. Com.), ii. 176.
73 *Subsidy 1526*, 276.
74 *Visit. Dioc. Linc.* (*1517–31*), i. 124.
75 Ibid. ii. 36.
76 Oxf. Dioc. c 155, f. 41.
77 Ibid. c 446, f. 127.
78 Bodl. Noke tithe award.
79 Ibid. Islip tithe award.
80 Ibid. Noke tithe award. The incl. award, as far as the glebe was concerned, was superseded by an exchange of 5 acres with the Duke of Marlborough: Oxf. Dioc. c 436, ff. 321–32.

81 O.R.O. Otmoor incl. award.
82 MS. Top. Oxon. c 61, ff. 36, 38.
83 *Reg. Parker*, iii (Cant. and York Soc. xxxix), 1009.
84 *O.A.S. Rep.* 1919, 251.
85 His death in 1636 is in the Par. Reg.
86 *Archd. Ct.* i. 53, 59, 65.
87 Bodl. MS. Wills Oxon. 199, f. 228.
88 *Walker Rev.* 297. His other living was Seele (Suss.). See also J. R. Bloxam, *Magd. Reg.* (*Demies*), ii. 106–7; Macray, *Magd. Reg.* iii. 158.
89 Bloxam, op. cit. iii. 26; *Magdalen and Jas. II*, ed. J. R. Bloxam (O.H.S. vi), 232–3.
90 Hearne, *Remarks*, iv. 173; v. 130, 222.
91 Oxf. Dioc. d 553.
92 Ibid. c 652, f. 73.
93 MS. Top. Oxon. c 61, f. 36.
94 Oxf. Archd. Oxon. c 86, f. 11.
95 Oxf. Dioc. c 653, f. 70.
96 Clerus Oxon.
97 Oxf. Dioc. d 559.

their parishioners 'a rational and well-grounded abhorrence of Popery'.[98] He was followed by Alexander Litchfield (1773–1804),[99] a philosopher, who divided his time between Noke and Wadham.[1]

The history of the 19th century was uneventful, except that in 1837 a Mr. Latimer, probably the curate, was accused of being a habitual drunkard.[2] In 1854 John Carlyle (1840–63), the first rector for many years to hold no second benefice, held two services on Sunday, with a sermon in the afternoon, and gave three communions a year. He reported that the number taking this was 'lamentably small', not more than seven or eight; that because of the decrease in population the congregation was also small, but that someone attended from almost every family.[3] Although his Rectory was reported on his death in 1863 to be 'in so bad a state of repair, and so ill arranged' as to be unusable,[4] he had at his own expense built and endowed a village school.[5]

The church of *ST. GILES* is a small stone building which has been much restored but dates originally from the first half of the 13th century.[6] It comprises a nave with a small bell-cote above the western gable, chancel, and south porch. Both the chancel with its double lancet window in the south wall and the chancel arch, which is of poor proportions, are probably 13th-century. On either side of the arch are two 14th- or 15th-century niches. The nave roof is well constructed and the timber beams are old. On the north side of the nave there was a mortuary chapel, built by Joan Bradshaw (d. 1598/9) for herself and members of the Winchcombe family. Her grandson Benedict Winchcombe repaired it and left money to repair the church,[7] the chancel of which had been ruinous in 1584.[8] In 1745 the Winchcombe chapel, whose upkeep had become the responsibility of the Hall family, was so dilapidated that it was endangering the chancel:[9] it was pulled down and its door in the north wall stopped up.[10] Further repairs to the church were ordered in 1758,[11] and it is thought that the square-headed east window of the chancel was inserted in the early 19th century.[12] By the middle of the century there was a western gallery, since removed, and the church was described as being 'neatly paved with extraordinary good stone'.[13] By 1870 the rector considered that it should be rebuilt, especially as it was 'deficient in design and workmanship'.[14] However, restoration was delayed until the end of the century and was then limited to removing the plaster, repointing the walls, and replacing the square wooden belfry with its tiled roof by a stone belfry (architect W. Wilkinson of Oxford).[15]

The cylindrical font is 13th-century and rests on a circular base;[16] the lead basin is marked 'Noke 1773'. There is a Jacobean pulpit and the remains of an iron hour-glass stand.

On the north wall of the chancel is a brass, decorated with coats of arms, depicting Joan Bradshaw (d. 1598/9) and her two husbands and eight children. There are also inscriptions to Benedict Winchcombe (d. 1623) and an early 17th-century mutilated stone figure of a man. There are inscriptions from a 'fair raised monument of black marble', which bore the figure of a man lying on a cushion, and was erected in the Winchcombe chapel by Benedict Winchcombe's nephew and heir, Benedict Hall.[17] The memorials to John Gilder, rector (d. 1697/8), and to Alexander Litchfield, rector (d. 1804), have been destroyed, but one to John Carlyle, rector (d. 1863), remains.

In 1552 the church owned a silver chalice, two copes, and two vestments. There was also a lamp supported by lands worth 2d. a year.[18] In 1596 John Harper of Noke was presented at the bishop's court for having lost the parish's pewter chalice, valued at 6d. or 7d.[19] In 1955 the church had a chalice (1577) and paten cover (1576), both in their original case.[20] As at the Reformation, there were two bells, but they were of 17th-century date. In the 19th century there had been a sanctus bell.[21]

In the 19th century repairs to part of the churchyard wall were the responsibility of the Blewbury Charity.[22]

The registers date from 1574. There are gaps from 1650 to 1667 in marriages and burials, and the baptisms in this period were irregularly entered.

NONCONFORMITY. In the 17th and 18th centuries there were a few Roman Catholics in the parish: in 1625 two women, a Hatton and a Day, were fined.[23] Although Benedict Winchcombe (d. 1623), the lord of the manor, was a cousin of the Fermors,[24] he does not seem to have been a recusant, but his successor, Benedict Hall, apparently was, as in 1654 his estates were sequestrated.[25] Francis Hall and his wife were also popish recusants. In 1665 it was stated that they would not conform.[26] No Roman Catholics were recorded in 1676, but by 1706 there was a small community consisting of John Palmer, gentleman, probably the lessee of the manor-house, his family, and members of two yeoman families.[27] The rector reported in 1767 that a popish priest had visited a house in the parish to baptize and 'mutter

98 Ibid. c 431, f. 18.
99 R. B. Gardiner, *Wadham Reg.* ii. 114.
1 Oxf. Dioc. d 565.
2 Ibid. c 664, f. 114.
3 *Wilb. Visit.*
4 MS. Top. Oxon. c 104, ff. 76–80.
5 See below, p. 276.
6 For a view see plate facing p. 276.
7 Inscription on Benedict Winchcombe's tomb in chancel. Cf. *Par. Coll.* iii. 229.
8 *Archd. Ct.* i. 53, 59, 65.
9 Oxf. Archd. Oxon. c 86, f. 11.
10 Dunkin, *Oxon.* ii. 84.
11 Oxf. Archd. Oxon. d 13, f. 48.
12 There are several early drawings: from SE. (1805) in MS. Top. Oxon. b 220, f. 23; drawing by J. Buckler (1823) in MS. Top. Oxon. a 67, f. 396; cf. Dunkin, *Oxon.* ii. 82. There is also a photograph (*c.* 1880) in the church.
13 Parker, *Guide*, 201–2; MS. Top. Oxon. b 220, f. 23.

14 MS. Top. Oxon. c 104, f. 87.
15 Ibid.
16 See Buckler drawing in MS. Top. Oxon. a 67, f. 395.
17 See above, p. 271. For drawing see MS. Top. Oxon. b 220, f. 23b; tricks of arms: Bodl. G.A. Oxon. 16° 217, pp. 195, 198a; ibid. 4° 687, p. 230; rubbings of shields: Bodl. G.A. Oxon. b 180, Ploughley, pp. 6a–c; Soc. 2184 d 105/21, p. 74a; G.A. Oxon. 4° 689, p. 230.
18 *Chant. Cert.* 84, 27.
19 MS. Top. Oxon. c 56, f. 19.
20 Evans, *Ch. Plate.*
21 *Ch. Bells Oxon.* ii. 220.
22 Oxf. Dioc. c 444, f. 13; Oxf. Archd. Oxon. c 41, f. 35.
23 Salter, *Oxon. Recusants*, 40, 46.
24 See above, p. 270.
25 *Cal. Cttee. for Compounding*, 696.
26 MS. Top. Oxon. c 56, f. 80.
27 Compton Census; *Oxoniensia*, xiii. 80; Stapleton, *Cath. Miss.* 114.

dirges over the dead'.[28] Otherwise no papists are recorded in the later 18th century.

Protestant dissent appeared early, for in 1739 Robert Dorman's house was registered as a meeting-place for Baptists.[29] Records of dissent are scarce: at the beginning of the 19th century there were two Methodists, in 1811 an 'Anabaptist',[30] a few dissenters in the following decades; but in 1854 the rector reported that someone attended church from every house.[31]

SCHOOLS. There was no school in Noke in the 18th century[32] but children might sometimes be admitted to Dr. South's school at Islip.[33] In 1808 there was a dame school where six or seven pupils were taught reading and needlework,[34] but it had closed by 1815.[35] The village remained without a day school until 1863, but some children attended schools in Islip[36] and by 1833 there was a Sunday school with 18 pupils.[37]

Noke Parochial School was built in 1863, on land belonging to the Duke of Marlborough, by the Revd. John Carlyle who endowed it in the same year with £200.[38] The average attendance was 18 in 1871.[39] A certificated mistress was appointed in 1880 and was provided with a cottage.[40] From 1904, when the County Council assumed responsibility for the school, the Carlyle legacy was applied to the upkeep of the building, and, from 1913 onwards, to paying half the rent of the teacher's cottage.[41] The average attendance was 29 in 1889, 25 in 1906,[42] and 15 in 1937. The school was reorganized for junior pupils only in 1931, when the seniors were transferred to Gosford Hill and Marston. In 1946 the school was closed and the pupils have since gone to Islip.[43]

CHARITIES. By deed dated 1560 Joan, widow of Henry Bradshaw,[44] gave to trustees a rent charge of £3 6s. 8d. on land called 'The Vaches' in Aston Clinton (Bucks.), of which £3 was to be distributed each year on All Saints' Day among ten of the poorest householders of Noke, the trustees receiving the remaining 6s. 8d. for their trouble. If there were not enough poor people in Noke then the number was to be made up from among the poor of Halton (Bucks.).[45] Joan Bradshaw originally also granted eleven cows to the trustees, to be hired to eleven other poor householders of Noke at 2s. a year each, the money to be distributed to the poor on Good Friday. This gift was amended to giving the trustees £22 which might be lent to eleven householders at 5 per cent. interest.[46] In 1810 it was resolved that the money should be called in and reissued, but in the following year it was declared that the £22 had been lost for more than 50 years, as the trustees had not taken care to secure repayment.[47] Despite difficulties in securing payment of the £3 6s. 8d. rent charge,[48] the £3 seems to have been regularly distributed.[49] Before 1813 the 6s. 8d. was allowed to accumulate to form a fund for the purchase of cloth for the poor and for church repairs. In 1954,[50] as in 1824, it was being used to defray expenses connected with the charity.[51]

ODDINGTON

THE parish lies some eight miles north-east of Oxford and on the western edge of Otmoor.[1] It has retained its area of 1,363 acres unchanged.[2] Its curious shape with a northern projection running up almost to a point by Weston Wood is explained by charter evidence,[3] which shows that Thame Abbey's estate here was bounded by the wood. There can be little doubt that the parish boundary in the north was drawn to follow the boundary of an already existing estate. The River Ray forms a natural boundary on the south and provides an ample water-supply, for its tributaries mark the greater part of the eastern and western boundaries and a branch flows through the centre of the parish.[4] There are a number of springs noted for their mineral properties and their supposed capacity to cure cattle of a disease known as 'the Otmoor evil'.[5]

The land is uniformly flat, never rising much above 200 feet above sea-level. Its soil is chiefly loam with clay and brash sub-soil above beds of Oxford Clay.[6] There is no woodland now to relieve the monotony of the scenery and none was recorded in Domesday, but at the end of the 12th century a wood belonging to the lord of the manor was recorded, and at the end of the 18th century there were 23 acres of woodland.[7] A plantation is shown on Davis's map of 1797 near Oddington Grange.[8] Medieval furlong names reveal the former and indeed the present nature of the ground: Morefurlong, Burnesmere, Ruthmere, Chippefen, Russfurlong, and Waterfurlong.[9]

The Islip–Charlton road, with a branch to Oddington village, follows a course defined in the Oddington inclosure award of 1791.[10] The Islip–Merton road,

[28] Oxf. Dioc. c 431.
[29] Ibid. c 644, f. 3.
[30] Ibid. c 327, p. 240; ibid. d 573.
[31] Wilb. Visit.
[32] Oxf. Dioc. d 553, d 556, d 559.
[33] See above, p. 218.
[34] Oxf. Dioc. d 707.
[35] Ibid. c 433.
[36] Wilb. Visit.
[37] Educ. Enq. Abstract, 750.
[38] Vol. Sch. Ret.; Par. Rec. Carlyle legacy bk. For a view see plate opposite.
[39] Elem. Educ. Ret.
[40] Par. Rec. Vestry minute bk.
[41] Ibid. Carlyle legacy bk.
[42] Ret. of Sch.
[43] Inf. Oxon. Educ. Cttee.
[44] See V.C.H. Bucks. ii. 315; see above, p. 270.

[45] 12th Rep. Com. Char. 308–9; cf. V.C.H. Bucks. ii. 341.
[46] Par. Rec. deeds (1676, 1738, 1776).
[47] Oxf. Dioc. d 549, p. 58.
[48] Par. Reg. note (1773); inf. the Revd. A. W. Blanchett.
[49] Par. Rec. Vestry minute bks.: charity accts.
[50] Inf. the Revd. A. W. Blanchett.
[51] 12th Rep. Com. Char. 309.
[1] O.S. Map 6", xxvii, xxviii (1884).
[2] Census, 1881, 1951.
[3] Thame Cart. i. 6, no. 9.
[4] O.S. Map 2½", 42/51 (1951).
[5] Plot, Nat. Hist. Oxon. 48.
[6] Kelly's Dir. Oxon. (1939).
[7] Thame Cart. i. 6, no. 9; O.R.O. Incl. award.
[8] Davis, Oxon. Map.
[9] Magd. Coll. Arch. 7, 13, 19–21, 25; cf. P.N. Oxon. (E.P.N.S.), i. 234.
[10] O.R.O. Incl. award.

Grantham's Wharf in the mid-19th century

HEYFORD BRIDGE

The church and school in the mid-19th century

NOKE

which was in part made into a raised causeway by Sir Edward Turner[11] in the 18th century, crosses the parish. So does the former L.M.S. railway.

There are several disused quarries south of Oddington village which once provided a good quality limestone for house-building and road-making.[12]

The village lies on the parish's eastern boundary, on the edge of Otmoor and about half a mile north of the River Ray:[13] an inlier of Cornbrash rising out of the surrounding Oxford Clay accounts for its position.[14] The New River Ray, which now flows parallel to the main village street and $\frac{1}{4}$ mile to the east, is an outcome of the inclosure of Otmoor in 1815.[15] The name Oddington indicates early settlement. It means in Old English 'Ot(t)a's hill' and the site was probably first settled by the man who gave his name to Otmoor and to Otley (O.E. Ot(t)a's lē(a)h).[16] The discovery in about 1815 of a pagan Saxon cemetery in the Rectory garden is proof that there was a settlement here in the 6th century.[17]

The earliest information about the topography of the village, however, comes from the hearth tax returns of 1662 and 1665.[18] Out of the nine householders listed in 1665 only one had a moderate-sized farm-house with three hearths, while two or one hearth were returned by the rest. In 1662 sixteen householders were listed. In 1738 the village was said to have ten farm-houses and fourteen labourers' cottages besides the Parsonage.[19]

A map of 1797 shows a circular green with some buildings on it and the church lying to the south-west.[20] Four roads radiate from the green and houses lie on three sides of it and along three of the roads: only the ground to the north was unbuilt on. In the early 19th century, when Dunkin described the village, the houses were built so as to form a square with the highway on the west side and the green at the south-west corner. At this end was the public house and the better houses. To the north were the remains of the manor-house, which had been occasionally occupied by the lord during the 18th century, but was pulled down at the end of the century.[21] The size of this house is not known, as it does not appear in the hearth tax list of 1665, presumably because it was then unoccupied. Nothing now remains above ground.[22] In 1821 a new Rectory was built at the northern end of the village, as the old one had been reported unfit to live in: it stands isolated in its own grounds.[23] The old one was alleged to have suffered serious dilapidation during the Civil War, and was taxed on only one hearth in 1665.[24] In a lawsuit of 1676 the parish clerk testified that the

Rectory then consisted of a mansion house, a barn, stable, ox-house, and a kitchen 'divided from the dwelling house by a little court'. It was revealed that the seven-bay barn and kitchen had collapsed and had been only partly rebuilt. Eight craftsmen estimated that the cost of these and other repairs would amount to about £60. It is of interest that it was thought that the kitchen roof should be tiled and not thatched and that the cost of building two bays of the barn was estimated at £31 15s.[25] Another 19th-century addition was the schoolhouse.[26] By 1955 all the old stone-built cottages with their thatched roofs were derelict, but three of the old farm-houses remained. Two, Manor Farm and Log Farm, both dating from about 1700, were still roofed with stone slates. Six council houses were built between 1946 and 1954.[27]

There are a number of outlying farm-houses in the parish: Brookfurlong, shown on a map of 1797 as Cold Harbour Farm,[28] New House Farm (formerly White House), Barndon Farm, and the Grange. The first three were probably all built in the late 18th century or in the 19th century after the inclosure of the open fields in 1791. The Grange, however, represents the medieval grange of Thame Abbey.[29] It lies just east of the moated site[30] of the first house of the Cistercian monks of Thame, close by the ancient road which skirts Weston wood and leads to Weston-on-the-Green.

The village was in the middle of the battle area before the siege of Oxford in 1645;[31] in 1845 it was involved in a minor conflict with the surveyors for the Buckinghamshire Railway. They were attacked by a tenant farmer and several others, including the village constable, and the Riot Act had to be read. Proceedings were begun by Charles Sawyer, the lord of the manor, but the affair was settled out of court[32] and the railway was eventually made across the parish.

The village has had a number of notable residents: Randall Catterall, an antiquary of repute, lived there from about 1570;[33] Gilbert Sheldon (1598–1677), the future Archbishop of Canterbury,[34] and Thomas Browne (1604–73), a noted royalist divine,[35] were two of several outstanding rectors; William Cureton (1808–64), a Syriac scholar, was a curate of Oddington.[36] Princess Maggie Papakura, a Maori of Rotorua, New Zealand, lived in the village for some years and was buried there in 1930.[37]

MANORS. In Edward the Confessor's time Oddington, assessed at 3 hides and half a virgate, was held freely by a certain Alwi,[38] but by a charter dated

[11] V.C.H. Oxon. v. 15.
[12] O.S. Map 25″, xxvii. 12 (1876).　　[13] Ibid.
[14] G.S. Map 1″, xlv SE. Forest Marble outcrops in the village.
[15] V.C.H. Oxon. v. 71. It runs just outside the parish.
[16] P.N. Oxon. (E.P.N.S.), i. 234.
[17] V.C.H. Oxon. i. 354.
[18] Hearth Tax Oxon. 201, 235.
[19] Oxf. Dioc. d 553.
[20] Davis, Oxon. Map.
[21] See Par. Reg. for Sawyer baptisms and burials; Dunkin, Oxon. ii. 99.
[22] e.g. Oxf. Dioc. d 556; ruins were visible in 1842: Lewis, Topog. Dict. Eng.
[23] Oxf. Dioc. c 435, pp. 237 sqq. The architect was Joseph Patience; the estimated cost £1,088; see also below, p. 284.
[24] MS. Top. Oxon. c 113, f. 186; Hearth Tax Oxon. 201.

[25] Lambeth Libr. Ct. of Arches B 9/79, Bbb 398 (inf. Miss D. Slatter).
[26] See below, p. 285.
[27] Inf. Ploughley R.D.C. For a criticism of the Council's failure to preserve the character of the old village see Country Life, 3 June, 1 July, 29 July 1954.
[28] See below, p. 283; Davis, Oxon. Map.
[29] For the medieval Grange see below, p. 283.
[30] V.C.H. Oxon. ii. 330.
[31] F. J. Varley, Siege of Oxf. 13.
[32] MS. diary of Chas. Sawyer, penes Mrs. E. I. Sawyer, Bicester; Wing, Annals, 119.
[33] Wood, Fasti, i. 185.
[34] D.N.B.; Oxf. Dioc. c 264, f. 127.
[35] D.N.B.
[36] Ibid.; Walker Rev. 43.
[37] See gravestone; local inf.
[38] V.C.H. Oxon. i. 422.

1065 the Confessor granted this estate together with Islip to the Abbot of Westminster. The king died before the abbey had taken possession,[39] and William the Conqueror appears to have granted *ODDING-TON* manor to Hugh de Grantmesnil, Sheriff of Leicestershire, from whom it passed to his daughter Adeline, the wife of Roger d'Ivry.[40] In 1086[41] she was holding it from the king, *in commendatione* as it was said, perhaps while the claims of Westminster Abbey were being investigated.[42] These were eventually recognized, for on Adeline's death about 1111 the manor did not descend cither to her heirs or to those of Roger d'Ivry.[43] The abbey remained overlord from the 12th century until the Dissolution:[44] it administered the manor as a part of its liberty of Islip, and Oddington's lord therefore owed suit of court twice yearly at Islip. After the Reformation the manor was granted to the Dean and Chapter of Westminster,[45] and in the early 17th century was known as 'Westminsterside'.[46]

The exact date when the Poure family, who were to be lords of the manor until the early 17th century, first became tenants of Westminster is not clear. The earliest record of the family's connexion with Oddington dates from the latter half of the 12th century, when William Poure of Oddington agreed to an exchange of land near Otley Grange with the monks of Thame.[47] It is possible that he was the son of the distinguished civil servant Roger *Pauper*, Chancellor between 1135 and 1139, and son of the famous Roger, Bishop of Salisbury, by his mistress Maud of Ramsbury.[48] Roger was styled *pauper* because of the contrast between his own poverty and his father's wealth.[49] William Poure was succeeded by his son Gentischieve some time after 1180 and certainly before 1194.[50] At about this time Gentischieve is found confirming grants of land, and himself making grants, to Thame Abbey.[51] He is known to have been alive in 1237[52] but by 1243 his grandson John, the son of Richard Poure, held the manor.[53] John was still alive in 1253 and possibly later,[54] but by 1279 his son William was lord.[55] The latter's widow Joan, the daughter of John Mulant,[56] was in possession in 1285,[57] and by 1307 her son Walter.[58] Walter had married Katherine, the sister of Sir Richard Damory of Bletchingdon, before 1312;[59]

he was still alive in 1330, when he presented to Oddington church,[60] but must have died soon after. In 1337 his son Thomas was lord;[61] he died before 1346, when his eldest son John was in possession.[62] John died childless,[63] leaving Oddington to his brother Richard, who granted it in 1376[64] to his younger brother Hugh, the lord of Bletchingdon.[65]

From this point until 1630 the descent of Oddington manor followed that of Bletchingdon.[66] In the early 17th century the two marriages[67] of Francis Poure (d. 1619) involved the family in a ruinous series of Chancery suits over the two properties.[68] In 1613 his prospective heir, Richard Poure, borrowed £3,000 from Edward Ewer, his brother-in-law,[69] to redeem the manors, which had both been mortgaged to Sir John Lenthall.[70] In 1614 it was agreed that Lenthall should sell his interest in Oddington to a fourth party and that after three years it should pass to Ewer.[71] In 1621 the Court of Chancery ordered Ewer to reconvey Oddington to Richard Poure, who had by now repaid his debt, but in 1630 Poure sold it to Edward Ewer for £4,100.[72] In the following year it was settled with Bucknell and Bainton manors on Ewer's son Francis on his marriage to Jane Savage.[73] In 1638 on his father's death Francis Ewer inherited a heavily encumbered estate and his attempts to raise money plunged him into another interminable series of Chancery suits which completed his ruin. A moiety of Oddington had been mortgaged in 1633 to Samuel Trotman, and in 1666 the interest on the mortgage of £2,660 was said to amount to over £159 a year. In 1671 Francis Ewer wrote from the Counter prison in Wood Street, saying that Lady Katherine Pasley and her brother had saved him from starvation. Lady Katherine was the daughter of Sir John Lenthall and in 1669 had redeemed the moiety of Oddington for £900.[74]

In 1673 Francis Ewer conveyed the manor and the advowson of Oddington to Dr. Edmund Dickinson for £50 and his promise to pay the mortgage to Lady Pasley and other debts. Francis was to have a cottage worth £8 a year for his life. Later in the year Lady Katherine sold her moiety of the estate to Dr. Dickinson for £2,220.[75] The doctor was the son of William Dickinson, Rector of Appleton (Berks.), and

[39] *V.C.H. Oxon.* i. 386–7.
[40] For Roger see ibid. v. 60.   [41] Ibid. i. 422.
[42] Ibid. 386–7; see above, p. 208.
[43] *V.C.H. Oxon.* i. 387 n.
[44] Barbara Harvey, 'Manor of Islip' (Bodl. MS. B.Litt. d 53).
[45] *L. & P. Hen. VIII*, xvii, p. 392.
[46] Sawyer deeds, bdle. 22, *penes* Mrs. E. I. Sawyer, Bicester. These documents are mostly unsorted, but some have been arranged in bundles.
[47] *Thame Cart.* i. 9: this charter (no. 14) is dated too late.
[48] Kennett, *Paroch. Antiq.* i. 496, suggests this relationship; for the Poure family see *Misc. Gen. et Her.* 5th ser. vi. 363.
[49] *D.N.B.*; cf. *Genealogist*, N.S. xii. 315–16, 321–3.
[50] *Thame Cart.* i. 6, 7, and n.
[51] Ibid. 6–12.
[52] Ibid. 13–14; Kennett, *Paroch. Antiq.* i. 282, mistakenly stated that Gentischieve married Emma de Poders; cf. *Misc. Gen. et Her.* 5th ser. vi. 373–4.
[53] *Bk. of Fees*, 825; *Thame Cart.* i. 21–22; Dunkin, *Oxon.* ii. 122*, wrongly includes Gentischieve as witness to a charter of 1257.
[54] *Thame Cart.* i. 20–21; cf. ibid. 21–22.
[55] *Rot. Hund.* (Rec. Com.), ii. 835.
[56] *Oxon. Visit.* 210; John was possibly a kinsman of

Roger de Meulan, Bishop of Lichfield: W.A.M. 15164, 15166–7, 15192.
[57] *Feud. Aids*, iv. 158.
[58] *Cal. Pat.* 1301–7, 527; Kennett, *Paroch. Antiq.* i. 495.
[59] C.P. 25(1)/189/14/75; see above, p. 58.
[60] Linc. Reg. iv, Burghersh, f. 261b.
[61] C.P. 25(1)/190/18/16.
[62] *Feud. Aids*, iv. 181; cf. *Cal. Close*, 1339–41, 269.
[63] *Misc. Gen. et Her.* 5th ser. vi. 364.
[64] *Cal. Close*, 1374–7, 355; Hugh may have had possession earlier, for he presented to Oddington church in 1371: Linc. Reg. x, Buckingham, f. 353b.
[65] See above, p. 58.
[66] See above, p. 58. In 1428, however, ½ fee in Oddington was held by Robert Andrew, husband of Agnes Poure of Charlton: *Feud. Aids*, iv. 191.
[67] *Oxon. Visit.* 209–11; see above, p. 59.
[68] A crucial case, Ewer *v.* Poure (C 5/604/149), is not available.
[69] C 21/20, E 2/40.
[70] C 2, Jas. I, E 2/40.
[71] C 2, Jas. I, C 21/20, E 2/40.
[72] Sawyer deeds (see above, n. 46); C 3/349/12.
[73] Sawyer deeds.
[74] Dunkin, *Oxon.* ii. 113–14; Blo. *Buck.* 15, 17, 18; *Misc. Gen. et Her.* 5th ser. i. 226.
[75] Sawyer deeds; Dunkin, *Oxon.* ii. 113–14.

physician-in-ordinary to the king from 1684 to 1688. He died in 1707,[76] leaving his estates to his daughter Elizabeth, who had married a foreigner, Charles, Baron Blomberg, for her life, and afterwards to her son Edmund Charles Blomberg. Elizabeth appears to have lived at her estate at Kirby Misperton (Yorks.), but her son lived at the manor-house at Oddington at least before 1732, when he became equerry to the king. Baroness Blomberg died in 1744 and her husband in 1745.[77] The Blomberg family probably held Oddington until 1771, when William Blomberg appears to have sold[78] the estate to Anthony Sawyer of Heywood (Berks.). Anthony died in 1784 at Heywood, where he and his successors resided. The lordship of Oddington manor descended from father to eldest son for three generations of the Sawyers of Heywood, to Anthony's son John (d. 1845), and then to Charles (d. 1876) and Lieut.-General Charles Sawyer (d. 1892). General Sawyer, who lived at Little Milton,[79] was succeeded by his nephew Edmund Charles Sawyer (d. 1920). In 1924, on the death of Edmund Sawyer's son Charles Anthony, the manor passed to his brother John Sawyer, who was lord of the manor in 1939.[80] The present (1956) lord is R. S. Hall, Esq.[81]

Only one estate in Oddington is mentioned in Domesday Book, but a second known as *OTLEY GRANGE* or *ODDINGTON GRANGE* was formed later. In the 12th century a quarter of the vill was held by the Gay family of the Earl of Gloucester and was part of one of the $\frac{1}{2}$-fees of the manor of Hampton Gay.[82] About 1137 Robert de Gay gave all his land in Oddington for the foundation of a new Cistercian abbey, but the chosen site, called Otley, was soon found to be unsuitable and the new house was established at Thame.[83] About 1138 Reginald de Gay, with the consent of his overlord the earl, confirmed his father's grant and by 1179 Otley, with the consent of Reginald's son Robert, had become the site of one of the abbey's granges.[84] Between 1243 and 1249 Oseney Abbey gave up all claims to scutage from the lands which Thame held in Oddington of Oseney's fee of Hampton Gay.[85]

Thame Abbey's estate was increased by various gifts[86] and extended into the two neighbouring parishes of Weston-on-the-Green and Charlton.[87] In 1291 it was worth £9 1s. 3d. a year in lands and rents.[88] Thame held the Grange until the Dissolution, when it was bringing in £13 6s. 8d. a year.[89]

In 1543[90] the Grange, together with many of the other manors previously held by Thame Abbey, was granted to Sir John Williams, later Lord Williams of Thame.[91] He died in 1559 leaving two daughters, Isabel and Margaret.[92] He left his Oddington estate to his wife Margaret for life, with reversion to his younger daughter Margaret.[93] The elder Margaret and her second husband Sir William Drury had alienated a part of the estate by 1561,[94] but by 1582 the remainder had apparently passed to Margaret and her husband Henry, Lord Norreys, who in that year sold property in Oddington,[95] perhaps the manor,[96] together with the manor of Sunningwell (Berks.)[97] to Margaret's sister Isabel and her second husband, Richard Huddlestone. The subsequent descent of the manor is uncertain until 1625, when Sir Thomas Chamberlayne of Wickham died in possession.[98] It may have descended to Isabel's grandson Richard Wenman, Viscount Wenman of Tuam: the latter and Sir Thomas Chamberlayne married sisters, Agnes and Elizabeth, daughters of Sir George Fermor of Easton Neston (Northants).[99] Alternatively, Chamberlayne may have acquired it from Henry Norreys' successor Francis, Earl of Berkshire.[1]

Sir Thomas's son and heir Thomas was created a baronet in 1643 and died in the same year. His son Sir Thomas died in 1682 and his lands were divided between his daughters Katherine and Penelope.[2] Oddington Grange fell to Penelope's share, and passed to the Dashwoods of Kirtlington on her marriage to Sir Robert Dashwood (d. 1734). It remained in the family for over a century,[3] but was eventually sold in 1804 by Sir Robert's great-grandson, Sir Henry Watkin Dashwood, to the Revd. William Frederick Browne, Rector of Launton.[4] The latter's daughter Anne married Moses William Staples of Broughton Gifford (Wilts.) and Norwood (Surr.) in 1811, and in 1842 her son Richard Thomas succeeded to his grandfather's entailed estate and assumed the surname of Browne.[5] He was one of the chief landowners in Oddington in 1852,[6] but by that time manorial rights had lapsed.

ECONOMIC HISTORY. The agricultural history of the parish may well go back to the 6th century.[7] The Saxon settlement there was manorialized by the time of the Domesday survey.[8] The manor then had sufficient land for 3 ploughs, but in fact possessed 4; 2 belonged to the demesne which had 2 serfs, and 2

[76] *D.N.B.*
[77] Dunkin, *Oxon.* ii. 113–14; *Par. Coll.* iii. 238.
[78] Sawyer deeds, bdle. 19; cf. Dunkin, *Oxon.* ii. 113–14.
[79] Burke, *Land. Gent.* (1879, 1937); *Kelly's Dir. Oxon.* (1854, &c.); Gardner, *Dir. Oxon.*
[80] Burke, *Land. Gent.* (1937); *Kelly's Dir. Oxon.* (1939); for the Sawyer family see also *V.C.H. Berks.* iii. 173–4; W. Berry, *Pedigrees of Berks. Families* (1837), 88, 104.
[81] Inf. Mrs. E. I. Sawyer, Bicester.
[82] *Thame Cart.* i. 2, 21 n.; *Oseney Cart.* vi. 39; cf. *Bk. of Fees*, 825.
[83] *Thame Cart.* i. 1, 2.
[84] Ibid. 4–5; *V.C.H. Oxon.* ii. 83–84.
[85] *Oseney Cart.* vi. 39, 150–1; *Thame Cart.* i. 21 and n. See above, p. 153.
[86] *Thame Cart.* i. 5, 8–21; *Rot. Hund.* (Rec. Com.), ii. 836.
[87] *Thame Cart.* i. 2–3, 6–7.
[88] *Tax. Eccl.* (Rec. Com.), 45.
[89] Dugd. *Mon.* v. 406.
[90] *L. & P. Hen. VIII*, xviii (1), p. 130; E 318/1227; cf.

E 318/1223; *L. & P. Hen. VIII*, xxi (1), p. 354, for other grants to Lord Williams in Oddington.
[91] *D.N.B.*
[92] *Complete Peerage* (orig. edn.), viii. 91, 140–1; ibid. (new edn.), ix. 643 sqq.
[93] C 142/126/150; will: P.C.C. 11 Mellershe.
[94] *Cal. Pat.* 1560–3, 142.
[95] C 66/1230.
[96] Dunkin, *Oxon.* ii. 117.
[97] *V.C.H. Berks.* iv. 424, 530.
[98] C 142/421/127; Dunkin, *Oxon.* ii. 117.
[99] Baker, *Northants*, ii. 142–3; *Oxon. Visit.* 179.
[1] C 60/434/44.
[2] G.E.C. *Baronetage*, ii. 206–7; cf. above, p. 223.
[3] C.P. 25(2)/957/Hil. 11 Anne; J. Townsend, *Oxon. Dashwoods, passim.*
[4] Dunkin, *Oxon.* ii. 117.
[5] Burke, *Land. Gent.* (1906).
[6] Gardner, *Dir. Oxon.*
[7] *V.C.H. Oxon.* i. 354; cf. ibid. 341.
[8] Ibid. 422.

to the customary tenants, 10 villeins (*villani*) and 4 bordars. There were also 40 acres of meadow and a stretch of pasture, 3 by 2 furlongs. Although the estate had risen in value very considerably since 1066, from £2 to £3, it was still a poor manor. The increase in value, together with the fact that there were more ploughs than were necessary for the amount of land under cultivation, suggests that the settlement was expanding. It must be remembered, however, that Oddington is on clay which is heavy and difficult to work. The ratio of population to land was higher than in some other places in Oxfordshire, for only about 240 or 250 acres were probably under cultivation.[9]

The survey of 1279 shows that considerable expansion had taken place.[10] Poure's manor had 3 carucates of land in demesne and also a mill worth 13s. 4d. and a wood of 3 acres. There was one free tenant, a widow who held a virgate, and thirteen customary tenants, ten of whom held ½ virgate each and three who held ⅓ virgate each. The division between villeins and bordars of 1086 had been retained, but in 1279 there was one fewer of the latter class. The demesne and the land of the customary tenants appears to have increased by 6 virgates, but the real expansion lay outside the Poure manor.

Thame Abbey's estates had been built up gradually.[11] Some of their land had come from the Poures themselves, but the major grant was that of Robert de Gay, who gave 3 carucates of land.[12] The extent of Thame's estate in Oddington, including the 95 acres which it had received from Thorold of Oddington and his son Martin, was probably about 340 acres.[13] This family held a large freehold in the parish which must be taken into account in an estimate of the amount of land cultivated at the end of the 13th century. It is known to have granted away 150 acres: only the part granted to Thame appears in the Hundred Rolls, but Martin also made a series of grants, probably in the 1230's and 1240's, to the Hospital of St. John, Oxford, whose property later passed to Magdalen College.[14] These four estates, and a small property belonging to Balliol College, which also dates from the early medieval period,[15] were still the only freehold properties at the time of the inclosure award in 1791.

Reference to North, South, and East Fields make it probable that a three-field system was worked in the early 13th century.[16] The fields were divided into strips of sometimes less than ½ acre.[17] At the end of the 13th century the manor was certainly not as large as it was in 1791, when the owner received 735 acres under the inclosure award.[18] It seems to have contained only about 400 acres in 1279.

Two detailed accounts have survived for the period from November 1296 to Michaelmas 1298.[19] The neighbouring manor of Islip was a demesne manor of Westminster Abbey and the accounts show considerable co-operation between the two. Money was transferred to Oddington from Islip; barley, beans, drage, and oats were sent for the sowing; and on one occasion men came from Islip to help with reaping. Most of the normal villein services were exacted at Oddington. The Hundred Rolls show that merchet was paid,[20] and it is known that a tallage was sometimes taken.[21] Labour services were partly performed in the two years covered by the accounts. The situation in Oddington may have been similar to that in Islip at this date, where 3s. a year was paid by the half-virgaters as commutation of week-work, but if the lord exacted the work the remission of rent was entered under expenses.[22] The ten half-virgaters at Oddington paid a rent of 3s. a year, but their land was described as *operabilis*. The total rents from the customary tenants, as set down in the Hundred Rolls, was £1 16s., but the rent received in 1296–7 was £4 0s. 11½d. The difference may lie in rents paid in commutation of week-work, but in this case the tenants must have paid more than those at Islip. In 1296–7, £1 of rent was debited as expenses; for example, for 4 virgates *terre operantis* from St. John Baptist to Michaelmas, 6s.[23]

In the account for the following year there is no mention of week-work, but in both years boon-works were done; in 1296–7 48 ploughing-works were done in Lent and in 1297–8 there were 94 men reaping at one boon. Most of the other reaping in this year was done *ad tascham*, at either 5d. or 4½d. an acre.

The chief evidence for the economic life of the community during the next few centuries comes from taxation returns. In 1377 72 adults paid the poll tax.[24] The amounts paid by Oddington in the 14th century to other levies show that the village enjoyed moderate prosperity. The lord of the manor and the Master of St. John's Hospital were assessed most highly, but there were usually two or three others who paid sums above the average. Twenty-six persons were taxed in 1316, 32 in 1327, and the village's assessment was slightly raised at the re-assessment of 1344.[25] The records of the subsidy raised in 1523 and 1524[26] are more informative. In the first year 17 persons paid the tax, and in the second, 20; of these 11 were assessed on wages and the rest on goods. William Gryden, who was probably the lessee of the manorial demesne, was assessed at three times the rate of some of the others. Thus, there were considerable differences in wealth between one farmer and another. It is worthy of note that none of the

[9] *Census*, 1951. The virgate according to later evidence = c. 20 acres.

[10] *Rot. Hund.* (Rec. Com.), ii. 835–6.

[11] *Thame Cart.* i. 2–32. A water-mill, 'Bakkesmulne', was first recorded in the late 12th cent., and gave its name to Box Mill Field; the mill stream was called 'Bakkebroc'. There was also a windmill near by: ibid. 8, 14, 16, 17; Magd. Coll. Arch. Oddington, 7, 13, 19–21, 25; cf. *Rot. Hund.* (Rec. Com.), ii. 835.

[12] *Rot. Hund.* ii. 836.

[13] The first name is illegible in *Rot. Hund.*, but the donor can be identified as the Thorold of Oddington who held land at Tackley in 1235: *Fines Oxon.* 92.

[14] Magd. Coll. Arch. Oddington, 2a, 7, 13, 19, 20, 21, 25; cf. *Cal. Chart. R.* 1226–57, 298: deed of 1246 recording grant of 55½ acres. This figure, probably a summary, does not agree with the grants in various charters in Magd.

Coll. Arch., which amount to 50 acres. Magdalen College acquired the property in 1458: *V.C.H. Oxon.* iii. 193.

[15] See Balliol Coll. Arch. A 23, nos. 1–39. The college had acquired by 1558 the property granted by William Poure to William Urlewyne between 1253 and 1273. It consisted of a house, ½ virgate of arable and 4½ a. of meadow. The college usually leased it to local yeomen.

[16] Magd. Coll. Arch. Oddington, 10a, 25a.

[17] e.g. ibid. 21a; *Thame Cart.* i. 9–11, 16.

[18] O.R.O. Incl. award.

[19] W.A.M. 14784, 14785.

[20] *Rot. Hund.* (Rec. Com.), ii. 835.

[21] W.A.M. 14783.

[22] Barbara Harvey, 'Islip Manor': Bodl. MS. B. Litt. d 53.

[23] W.A.M. 14784.

[24] E 179/161/39.

[25] Ibid. 161/8, 9; see below, p. 359.

[26] E 179/161/176, 198.

names listed appear in the hearth-tax returns of 1665.[27]

A lease of the manor-house and farm in 1578[28] shows that the farm then consisted of 135 acres and so was smaller than the demesne in 1279; it was leased for 21 years for £3 6s. 8d. a year. During the 17th century the evidence in a series of Chancery suits[29] indicates that some of the land attached to the manor may once have been part of Thame Abbey's Grange. A schedule of the manor estate, made in 1624, valued the properties said to have belonged to the Grange at £3 16s. 4d. out of a total valuation of £132 8s. 6d.[30]

The inclosure of the open fields came in 1791.[31] Certain old inclosed grounds and woods belonging to the Grange were expressly excluded from the inclosure. It is likely that Thame Abbey had made its scattered field strips into a compact estate by exchange and inclosure at an early date.[32] The abbey was amongst those accused of inclosing by the Crown in Tudor times. In 1517 it was alleged that a messuage with 80 acres of arable leased by the abbot in 1513–14 was in ruins, that four persons lacked houses, and that the land had been converted to pasture.[33] In the 18th century the Grange was reckoned as 27 yardlands and was virtually tithe-free.[34] There was also a number of old inclosures belonging to the manor, the parsonage, and other holdings. Among these possibly were the 40 acres which had been inclosed for animal pasture in the early 16th century by a freeholder, a William Aleyn.[35]

Unsuccessful attempts at inclosure in order to increase the value of the estate had been made in 1613 and 1614.[36] The question was reopened in the 1760's. The patron of the living, Trinity College, Oxford, considered in 1766 that inclosure would benefit the living and the rector agreed to it provided that he received one-fifth of the arable and one-ninth of the pasture in lieu of tithes.[37] In fact, this plan was not followed.

At the time of the award in 1791 there were four main fields, being worked on a rotation of wheat, barley, beans and fallow.[38] Their names in the award are Wood Field, Middle Field, Bandon Field, and Islip Field, but the rector used the older names of Bax Mill Field for Bandon Field and Log Field for Islip Field. Each of these fields contained a proportion of 'greenswerd', which appears to have been permanent grassland. Log Field is said to have had 159 acres of arable and 83 of grass. It is not clear whether this grassland was pasture or mowing grass. There are indications that there had long been a certain concentration on sheep-farming: besides Otmoor, where the people of Oddington had rights of common, there was the 'great common' to the north-west of the village. The pastures of the Grange

manor moreover were said to be worth £160 a year in 1624.[39]

The meadow probably lay mostly along the River Ray and its tributaries: there was meadow in North and South Fields; Wivering meadow was said to lie near the village; and 'doles' of meadow lay near the 'greteford' and beneath 'la Grave' which bordered on Otmoor.[40] One charter grants 1 acre in Oddington with the whole crop and the head of mead belonging to it.[41] With this may be compared the '2 parcels of mead called Bamstollease and Saguinne', of which one at least went with a large holding in the open fields.[42]

Out of a total acreage of 923 the award gave the rector 47 acres in Woodfield 'as near as may be to the parsonage'. Magdalen College received 99 acres in Woodfield, Middle Field, and Bandon Field; Balliol 21 acres in Woodfield; John Sawyer, the lord of the manor, 735 acres. He appears to have received all of Islip Field and some land in each of the others. The Sawyers divided their estate into six farms whose gross rental in 1824 was £1,059; three of these were under 100 acres, the others 151, 206, and 445 acres.[43] The creation of larger farms was probably responsible for the drop in the number of farm-houses in the village. Instead of the ten farm-houses of 1738 there were said to be poor cottages and only four farm-houses in 1808.[44] How far inclosure affected the rise in the poor rate from £36 in 1776 to £86 in 1803 is uncertain.[45]

In 1829 the inclosure of Otmoor, where Oddington had rights of common, took place.[46] Oddington's share of the moor was 311 acres;[47] Balliol, Magdalen, and the rector received small allotments and John Sawyer and the Revd. W. F. Browne, the proprietor of the Grange, received 189 and 44 respectively; 31 acres were sold to a Thomas Packer. Browne exchanged his part of the moor for 63 acres of land belonging to Sawyer, which adjoined Oddington Grange. Sawyer, following Arthur Young's opinion, obviously thought the moor land to be better farming land. The large allotments at Oddington are a marked contrast to the numerous small ones at Charlton and Murcott and Fencott. The loss of common rights, combined with a general agricultural depression, was probably responsible for the disturbances of 1845, when there was a riot involving more than 100 persons.[48]

Population seems to have varied during the 18th century. Although the Compton Census had recorded 105 adults in 1676, there were said to be only 25 houses in 1738, 35 in 1759, and 30 families 'all farmers' labourers or poor' in 1768.[49] At the official census of 1801 there were 158 inhabitants and there was a gradual rise to 176 in 1831. For the rest of the century the population tended to fluctuate. In

[27] *Hearth Tax Oxon.* 201.
[28] Sawyer deeds, bdle. 15 (see above, p. 278, n. 46).
[29] Ibid. bdle. 22: the deeds date from 1632 to 1652.
[30] Ibid.: 1624 schedule.
[31] O.R.O. incl. award.
[32] The only evidence for this is from the 12th cent. when William Poure and the Abbot of Thame exchanged 4 a. near the Grange for a close: *Thame Cart.* i. 9.
[33] *Dom. Incl.* i. 361–2.
[34] Oxf. Archd. Oxon. b 26, f. 27. There is a map by Wm. Grantham of Oddington Grange in 1745 among the Dashwood deeds: Bodl. dep. a 4 (R).
[35] *Dom. Incl.* i. 367.
[36] C 2/284/79.
[37] Oxf. Archd. Oxon. b 26, f. 25.

[38] Ibid.; O.R.O. Incl. award; Sawyer deeds (see above, p. 278, n. 46), bdle. 21.
[39] Sawyer deeds, bdle. 22.
[40] Magd. Coll. Arch. Oddington, 10, 10a, 25, 25a.
[41] Ibid. 20.
[42] Sawyer deeds, bdles. 15, 22.
[43] Ibid. bdle. 21; O.R.O. Incl. award.
[44] Oxf. Dioc. d 553; ibid. d 571.
[45] *Poor Abstract.*
[46] O.R.O. Otmoor incl. award.
[47] This land did not become part of the parish but was accounted part of Beckley.
[48] See above, p. 277, and Bicester magistrates' min. bk. (1843–6) *penes* Mr. E. K. Truman, Bicester.
[49] Oxf. dioc. d 553, d 556, d 559.

1861 it was 169, but by 1901 it had dropped to 109. There were further fluctuations in the 20th century. In 1911 there were 131 inhabitants; only 90 in 1921. Since 1921 there has been a steady increase, and the estimated population was 118 in 1954.[50]

The village has remained completely agricultural; in 1939 there were still no shops. The Sawyer family sold their farms, often to their tenants, and in 1899 Staples Browne, the owner of the Grange, and Magdalen College were the principal landowners.[51] In 1955 there were six farms in the parish, Log, College, Manor, Glebe, and Barndon (200 a.) farms, and the Islip Pedigree Breeding Centre at the Grange (409 a.). The last specialized in beef cattle—pedigree Aberdeen-Angus—and Manor farm in dairying, with a herd of pedigree Guernseys. The other farms practised mixed farming, and kept non-pedigree Frisians and Shorthorns. No sheep were kept, and the chief crops were grass and cereals.[52]

CHURCH. A papal bull of 1146, confirming the exemption of Thame Abbey from paying tithes on its lands, including those of its Oddington Grange, implies that there was a church at Oddington by the mid-12th century at least.[53] The church was in Bicester deanery, but by 1854 had been transferred to the new deanery of Islip.[54]

The first recorded presentation to the rectory was made in 1223,[55] and from then until the 18th century the advowson usually belonged to the lords of the manor. There were, however, a number of occasions when they did not present. In 1250 or 1251, for instance, the right of presentation was in the bishop's hands, perhaps by lapse, and as he was abroad, the Prior of Bicester presented in his place.[56]

Later in the century the advowson seems to have belonged to William Poure's wife Joan, for William was said to have presented Richard Poure in his wife's right. This late-13th-century presentation[57] figured in a long legal case in 1327, when Walter Poure, lord of the manor, and Master Walter de Islip,[58] a civil servant, who claimed that the manor had been demised to him for life, were at law over the right to present. Poure seems to have won, probably because his mother held the advowson separately from the manor, and the bishop was ordered to admit his candidate, William Poure, but in the meantime after a six months' lapse the bishop had collated.[59] In 1330 it was Walter Poure who presented. In 1361 Westminster Abbey, the overlord of the manor, was patron, perhaps during a minority.[60] Other presentations during minorities were in 1483 and probably 1487 during the minority of John Poure, and in 1532 and 1537 during that of Vincent Poure.

The descent of the advowson in the 17th century is very complicated. On the death of the rector Roger Ewer in 1614 there was a three-cornered Chancery case between Sir William Cope and others, the lessees of the manor, Lewis Proude, a claimant to the manor, and Oxford University,[61] which based its claim on the right to present when the patron—in this case Richard Poure—was a Roman Catholic.[62] The University evidently won, for Andrew Morris, who resigned in 1623, was its nominee.[63] The next presentation, in the same year, was by a group, headed by Sir Edward Frere of Water Eaton, of which Poure and Edward Ewer were members.[64]

With the division of the manor into two parts the advowson also became divided, and was the subject of many legal complications. For example, the Ewers mortgaged half of it to Samuel Trotman in 1633,[65] but it was the king who presented Gilbert Sheldon in 1636.[66] This presentation led to a Chancery suit in 1638 in which William Wyck of Mentmore (Bucks.) and William Wyck the younger of Caversfield claimed that the Ewers had fraudulently sold them the next presentation, to which they had no claim, for £150.[67] In 1639 William Moreton of Winchcombe (Glos.) presented,[68] and in 1640 Orlando Bridgeman,[69] who had bought the presentation from Francis Ewer.[70] The Ewers constantly tried to raise money from the advowson. They sold it (or rather probably only the right of next presentation) in 1664, for instance, for £30 to Samuel Baker,[71] who later presented a petition in Chancery claiming that the advowson had already been mortgaged to Samuel Trotman.[72]

In 1673 Baker sold whatever right he had to Edmund Dickinson for £50,[73] and in the same year, when Dickinson acquired the whole manor, he also tried to get all rights to the advowson.[74] He was able to present in 1674,[75] but in 1679, for an unknown reason, the king was patron.[76] In 1699 Dickinson presented again,[77] and in the same year sold the advowson for £322 to Dr. Ralph Bathurst,[78] President of Trinity College, Oxford, who in 1701 gave it to his college, 'considering that there are but few preferments in the gift of the said College for the advancement of the Fellows'. In future the rector, who was to be 'an able and pious minister', was to be chosen from among the Fellows of the college.[79] Trinity

[50] Census, 1801–1951; inf. Ploughley R.D.C.
[51] Kelly's Dir. Oxon. (1899).
[52] Local inf. Medcraft farm was a smallholding of 8 acres.
[53] Thame Cart. ii. 143–4.
[54] For the date of its formation see above, p. 67, n. 97.
[55] Rot. Welles, ii. 12. For list of medieval presentations see MS. Top. Oxon. d 460.
[56] Rot. Grosse. 497.
[57] It has not been found, but Poure was rector by 1286: Oriel Coll. Records (O.H.S. lxxxv), 259.
[58] For him see Cal. Pat. 1327–30, passim.
[59] Linc. Reg. iv, Burghersh, f. 259b; C.P. 40/270, m. 18. Walter de Islip resisted the decision then given against him: C.P. 40/273, m. 1d; 274, m. 37d; 275, m. 192d. The end of the case has not been traced.
[60] Cf. Misc. Gen. et Her. 5th ser. vi. 368.
[61] C 3/283/86.
[62] This was according to 3 Jas. I, c. 5, par. xiii, An act to prevent dangers which may grow by Popish Recusants. See also Oxf. Dioc. c 264, f. 63.

[63] Oxf. Dioc. c 264, f. 107b.
[64] Ibid. f. 108b.
[65] Sawyer deeds penes Mrs. E. I. Sawyer, Bicester.
[66] Oxf. Dioc. c 264, f. 127.
[67] C 3/419/65.
[68] Oxf. Dioc. c 264, f. 133b.
[69] Ibid. f. 134b.
[70] Sawyer deeds: 1639 Covenant.
[71] Ibid. 1664 Grant.
[72] Ibid. 1671 Bill.
[73] Ibid. 1673 Grant.
[74] Sawyer deeds. Trin. Coll. Arch. Reg. B, Deed A, pp. 19–20, mentions indentures between the Dickinsons, Lady Katherine Pasley, Francis and Jane Ewer, and Edmund Lenthall.
[75] Oxf. Archd. Oxon. d 9, f. 3.
[76] Oxf. Dioc. d 106, f. 70b.
[77] Ibid. f. 158.
[78] Trin. Coll. Arch. Reg. B, Deed A, pp. 19–20.
[79] Ibid. Deed C, pp. 22–25.

College continued as patron until about 1890,[80] when it sold the advowson.[81] Since then there has been a succession of private patrons.[82]

Oddington was a poor rectory in the early Middle Ages. In 1254 it was valued at £3 6s. 8d.,[83] in 1291 at £6 13s. 4d.,[84] and in 1535 at £12 16s.[85] A hundred years later it was valued at £100[86] and by the early 18th century at £140,[87] i.e. £110 from the lease of the great tithes and £30 from the glebe.[88] In addition, the rector seems to have had the small tithes.[89] During the century the value of the living rose rapidly[90] and by 1820 it had become a comparatively rich one and was valued at £361 16s.[91]

Before the inclosure of 1791 the glebe consisted of Home Close (9¾ a.) and of 64 arable acres[92] with rights of common for 80 sheep, 4 horses, 12 cows, and a bull.[93] At the award the rector received 47 acres. He also had right of common on Otmoor without stint,[94] and at the inclosure of Otmoor in 1829 was awarded 12 acres.[95]

By the Oddington award the rector was allotted a rent charge of £230 in lieu of tithes.[96] There had long been a composition of £2 on Oddington Grange farm (200 a.), which was confirmed by the tithe award of 1849, while Brookfurlong farm (93 a.) was tithe free.[97] This exemption must have dated from the 12th century when the Cistercians first held the land. Thame Abbey's claim to freedom from tithes for demesne lands at Otley[98] was more than once confirmed by the Pope during the 12th century,[99] probably as a consequence of counter-claims by the rectors. There was certainly constant strife with an early 13th-century rector over the payment of tithe on assarts made by the abbey.[1] He asserted that the church had lost 100 marks as the result of the abbey's failure to pay the due sums. After an appeal to the Pope, a compromise was arranged in 1231. The rector received a piece of land bordering the village street in return for giving up his claim.[2] There were further similar disputes: in 1235-6 the bishop decided that certain of the abbey's furlongs were to be tithe free; and the rector received 2 acres of land in compensation[3] and another 3 acres in 1246, when he gave up his claim to tithes on more of the abbey's assarted land.[4]

Some of the medieval rectors of Oddington are noteworthy. Roger de Turberville (1223-50), the rector who championed the church's claim to tithes, described himself as of noble birth and educated in the liberal arts and civil law.[5] In his time, in 1235-6, the bishop allowed Thame Abbey to have a chapel at its Grange and celebrate services there so long as Oddington's normal parishioners were excluded. On Sundays and feast days the abbey's labourers (*familia*) were to attend the parish church as usual; all obventions from the chapel were to go to the church, unless a bishop or nobleman staying there had services said by his own chaplain.[6] In 1246 it was decided that if a labourer at the Grange fell ill and had to be taken to Thame, the church of Oddington should still be entitled to mortuary or other dues.[7] Later in the century a member of the lord of the manor's family, Richard Poure, was rector (by 1286-1327) for over 40 years.

By the 15th century the rectors were mostly university graduates, some of them distinguished ones, which meant that the church was often held in plurality. Master John Beke (1443-7), for instance, was a pluralist and a 'very remarkable personality'.[8] At the end of the century there were Master Thomas Randolph (1487-99), a prebendary of Lincoln,[9] and Master Ralph Hamsterley (1499-1507), Principal of St. Alban Hall,[10] and later of University College. Master Edmund Horde (1516-20) was another distinguished rector connected with the University,[11] but he appears to have neglected Oddington. When he resigned in 1520,[12] it was noted that the rectory and chancel were dilapidated and the cemetery not properly inclosed.[13] During many of the changes of the 16th century the living was held by a member of a local family, Adrian Bury (1549-58), brother of James Bury of Hampton Poyle.[14]

Some post-Reformation rectors were also outstanding,[15] but the strong anti-Puritan views of one, Thomas Browne (1640-73), led to the sequestration of the living during the Civil War.[16] It was given to James Robins (d. 1659), who is described in the parish register as the 'painful minister of Oddington'.[17] After the Restoration the royalist rector Thomas Browne returned to Oddington and held the living with his Windsor canonry until his death in 1673.[18]

Close relations between church and manor were established with the presentation in 1699 of Thomas Dickinson, nephew of the lord of the manor. He lived part of the time in Islip, but came to Oddington 'as frequently as there is occasion'. He held two services and preached one sermon on Sundays, and celebrated the sacrament four times a year.[19]

After Trinity College had acquired the advowson, the living was held by its Fellows or graduates. The first of these, John Bruere (1746-76), was notable for

[80] *Kelly's Dir. Oxon.* (1891).
[81] Trin. Col. Bursary, *Reg. of Estates Belonging to Trinity Coll. 1898.*
[82] *Kelly's Dir. Oxon.* (1891 and after).
[83] Lunt, *Val. Norw.* 312.
[84] *Tax. Eccl.* (Rec. Com.), 31.
[85] *Valor Eccl.* (Rec. Com.), ii. 160.
[86] Dunkin, *Oxon.* ii. 104.
[87] *Par. Coll.* iii. 238.
[88] Oxf. Archd. Oxon. b 26, f. 43.
[89] Ibid. e.g. f. 54 and *passim.*
[90] Ibid. ff. 23-24b, 31-32.
[91] Oxf. Dioc. c 435, p. 240.
[92] Oxf. Archd. Oxon. b 26, f. 27.
[93] Ibid. f. 25.   [94] Ibid. f. 19.
[95] O.R.O. Otmoor incl. award.
[96] O.R.O. Incl. award.
[97] Bodl. Tithe award.
[98] See above, p. 279.
[99] *V.C.H. Oxon.* ii. 83-84.
[1] See below.

[2] *Thame Cart.* i. 26-30.
[3] Ibid. 24-26.   [4] Ibid. 23-24.
[5] *Rot. Welles,* ii. 325-7.
[6] *Thame Cart.* i. 24-26.
[7] Ibid. 23-24.
[8] *Cal. Papal. L.* ix. 35. For him see A. Clark, *Lincoln,* 6-8, 12-15; Emden, *O.U. Reg.* i.
[9] J. Le Neve, *Fasti,* ii. 117, 142.
[10] G. C. Brodrick, *Memorials of Merton* (O.H.S. iv), 240.
[11] *Reg. Univ.* i. 40.
[12] Kennett, *Paroch. Antiq.* i. 496.
[13] *Visit. Dioc. Linc. 1517-31,* i. 123.
[14] R. E. C. Waters, *Genealogical Memoirs of Chester,* i. 64, 66.
[15] See above, p. 277. For Richard Astlie (1623-36) see C. G. Robertson, *All Souls Coll.* 98.
[16] *D.N.B.*; *Walker Rev.* 43.
[17] Dunkin, *Oxon.* ii. 107.
[18] For the rectory in his time see above, p. 277.
[19] Oxf. Dioc. d 553.

his insistence on his church's rights. He quarrelled with the squire over the cost of repairing the church-yard wall, the payment of tithes, and over some alleged glebe land.[20] He also had a number of minor disputes with his parishioners over the matter of small tithes, which he collected with an exaggerated care.[21] Among Bruere's 'many virtues'[22] was the regularity with which he held services, increasing the celebration of sacraments from four to five a year, an unusually large number for the period. But his influence declined towards the end of his ministry. Whereas in 1759 he was satisfied with his parishioners,[23] twelve years later he complained that they neglected services because of wakes, and that the sacrament was administered to 'but few'.[24] From 1795 to 1817 the parish was served by a curate, although one of the two rectors of this period appears to have paid occasional visits, as he reserved for himself the hall, best parlour, and bedroom in the parsonage.[25] The curate was receiving £30 in 1785[26] and £40 in 1808, and lived in part of the Rectory. The bishop considered the stipend insufficient for 'so valuable a living', and advised that it should be raised to £45 clear.[27]

Philip Serle (1818–57), on the other hand, who built a new Rectory,[28] was constantly resident. He was unpopular with the parish, however, because of his support of the inclosure of Otmoor,[29] and also with Bishop Wilberforce, who considered him a sceptic.[30] The bishop persuaded his successor to have two sermons on Sunday.[31] By 1866 the 19th-century religious revival had had a modest effect. Communion was being given six times a year; there were sixteen communicants in the parish; the morning congregation numbered 40, the afternoon one 55–60, and by 1878 had 'slightly increased'.[32] In the 20th century the rectors were high churchmen and introduced much ritual into the services.

The church of *ST. ANDREW* is a plain stone building, dating mainly from the end of the 13th and beginning of the 14th centuries, but much restored. It comprises a chancel, nave, western tower, south porch, and north aisle. The nave of three bays has late 13th-century buttresses; it has been suggested that there may once have been a chapel on the northern side.[33] The tower with its two stories, steeply-pitched roof of stone slates with no parapet, and lancet windows, together with the south door, are parts of the original church. The chancel retains part of a late 14th-century window and an elegant 14th-century piscina.

Dunkin, writing before 1823, described the church as 'disguised by alterations', and Parker, writing before 1846, as 'mutilated' and 'concealed by plaster'.[34] Some of the alterations were of recent date: the south porch, once inscribed 'w.w. 1810', was added in that year; the walls of the nave were lowered, a slate roof put on, and the church paved before 1823 and possibly in 1821, when the chancel was taken down and rebuilt.[35] In 1884–6 a thorough restoration by the architect E. G. Bruton was carried out at a cost of about £1,200. The tower was rebuilt, a north aisle and chapel on the north side of the chancel were added, and some new windows inserted.[36]

The plain circular font is probably 13th-century,[37] and the pulpit is Jacobean. The chancel screen with rood-loft, described by Rawlinson as being carved with white and red roses, though still there in 1823, no longer exists.[38] Fragments of medieval glass, which in Rawlinson's time represented St. Peter, are in the east window.[39] The royal arms were formerly over the chancel arch.

There is an undated brass in the chancel to Ralph Hamsterley, Rector of Oddington and Fellow of Merton College (d. 1518); he is represented as a skeleton in a shroud, being eaten by worms.[40] There are also some 17th- and 18th-century inscriptions to other Oddington rectors:[41] James Robins, minister (d. 1659), Henry Brocker (d. 1679), Thomas Dickinson (d. 1746) and his wife Jane (d. 1733), and to John Bruere (d. 1776). There are stone slabs to Gabriel Braithwaite (d. 1686/7) and William Dickinson, brother to the lord of the manor (d. 1716).

At the west end there is a large carved pietà, supported on a plinth decorated with carved Maori totems. It is a memorial to the Maoris who fell in the First World War.

In 1552 it was recorded that the church owned a silver chalice and an ivory pyx with 'smale spanges of silver'; it was also well provided with vestments, and three bells and two handbells.[42] In 1955 the plate included an early 18th-century silver chalice and paten cover, inscribed with coats of arms, which was the gift of William Phipps, a maltster of Oxford, who leased the small Balliol property in Oddington in the late 17th century.[43] The church was very elaborately furnished in the high church manner by the rector, S. H. Scott (1915–49); it was lit by both electric light and candles in candelabra. There were three bells, two dating from the early 17th century, and a sanctus bell.[44]

---

[20] Oxf. Archd. Oxon. b 26, ff. 58–77.
[21] Ibid. e.g. ff. 7, 77b–81b.
[22] See monument in church.
[23] Oxf. Dioc. d 556. His notes are collected in Oxf. Archd. Oxon. b 26. See ibid. ff. 50–54 for his peculiar behaviour.
[24] Oxf. Dioc. d 559, d 562.
[25] Oxf. Archd. Oxon. b 26, ff. 23–25.
[26] Ibid. f. 37.
[27] Oxf. Dioc. c 658, ff. 100–3.
[28] See above, p. 277. This was done under the provisions of Gilbert's Act, 17 Geo. III, c. 53, amended by 21 Geo. III, c. 66: Oxf. Dioc. c 435, p. 237 sqq.
[29] Rosa M. Marshall, *Oxon. By-Ways*, 100.
[30] Oxf. Dioc. d 550, f. 19; d 178.
[31] Ibid. d 178, c 332.
[32] Ibid. c 344.
[33] Parker, *Guide*, 7.
[34] Dunkin, *Oxon.* ii. 100. The drawing on p. 99 shows a round-headed window on the S. side of the nave: Parker, *Guide*, 7.

[35] Dunkin, *Oxon.* ii. 100; Oxf. Archd. Oxon. c 89, ff. 93, 95, 97. A drawing of 1807 in MS. Top. Oxon. b 220, f. 75, shows the original chancel with a late 14th-century E. window. A drawing by J. Buckler (1825) in MS. Top. Oxon. a 68, f. 410, shows little but the tower.
[36] MS. Top. Oxon. d 42, f. 93; Bodl. Par. Box (uncat.), faculty.
[37] Buckler drawing in MS. Top. Oxon. a 68, f. 409.
[38] *Par. Coll.* iii. 238; *Arch. Jnl.* lxvii. 193.
[39] E. S. Bouchier, *Notes on Stained Glass of Oxford District*, 84; *Par. Coll.* iii. 239; Bodl. G.A. Oxon. 4° 689, p. 239.
[40] For this see M. Stephenson, *Monumental Brasses*, 410. He was not buried at Oddington.
[41] For inscriptions see Dunkin, *Oxon.* ii. 100–2.
[42] *Chant. Cert.* 82.
[43] Evans, *Ch. Plate*. For arms on chalice in 1712 see Bodl. G.A. Oxon. 4° 687, p. 238. See also Balliol Coll. Arch. A 23, no. 22.
[44] *Ch. Bells Oxon.* ii. 224.

The registers date from 1571. Between 1644 and 1651 no marriages are entered.[45]

In the churchyard there is the ancient base and head of a cross, raised on three steps.[46] It was restored in 1949.

NONCONFORMITY. Before 1605 Richard Poure, son of Francis Poure, the lord of the manor, was 'convicted as a Popish recusant'.[47] Early in the 17th century John Poure, another son, was fined for recusancy.[48] In the course of the next twenty years John Foxe, also a gentleman, and the members of two yeoman families were also fined.[49]

In 1796 the house of Richard Scrivener was licensed for dissenting meetings.[50] The nonconformists met on Sunday evenings and were visited by a 'teacher from a distance',[51] perhaps James Hinton

(d. 1823), who is said by the Baptists to have started village preaching in Oddington.[52] There continued to be a few dissenters throughout the 19th century; in 1866 there were about twenty, but many were said to attend church occasionally.[53]

SCHOOL. There was no school in the 18th century, but by 1808 a dame school supported by the rector and the principal landowners had been opened to teach reading and the catechism.[54] This school had 20 pupils in 1819[55] and 27 in 1834, when it was reported that children left school at ten years of age.[56] It seems to have continued in existence until 1871, when it had 12 pupils,[57] but to have closed soon afterwards. Children then went to school at Charlton.

CHARITIES. None known.

SHELSWELL

THE ancient parish covered 822 acres,[1] and there was no change in its area until its union with Newton Purcell in 1932. The joint parish now covers 1,424 acres.[2] Shelswell's boundary used to extend almost to Newton Purcell village on the east, on the north it skirted Mixbury Plantations, and on the south-west it cut through Shelswell Plantation and Shelswell Park.[3] The parish lies partly on the Great Oolite and partly on the Cornbrash, both, however, being mostly covered with drift gravel.[4] The ground rises from south to north and reaches a height of just over 400 feet on the northern boundary. No major road passes through the parish, but lanes connect Shelswell House and Home Farm with Newton Purcell, Hethe, and Cottisford. A minor road from Mixbury to Hethe runs along the western edge of Shelswell Park.[5] The north-eastern corner of the parish is crossed by the former Great Central Railway from Brackley to Quainton Road, constructed in 1899,[6] and the station called Finmere, on the outskirts of Newton Purcell village, is in the former parish of Shelswell. Between 1923 and 1947 the line was a part of the L.N.E.R., after which it was transferred to British Railways (Midland Region).

A spring which has long since disappeared probably determined the site of the medieval village: the earliest form of the place-name suggests that it meant the spring or stream of *Scield*, the personal name of some Saxon settler.[7] Near the village the

stream formed a line of wet and useless ground—there were 10 acres of marsh in 1581[8]—which was excavated, probably in the 18th century, to form the Fish Pond.[9]

The moats, shown on the ordnance map near Home Farm,[10] probably mark the site of the medieval manor-house. The site of St. Ebbe's church and the lost medieval village adjoins them. The manor-house was standing and was inhabited in 1530, when Margaret Verney referred to the 'great chamber' in it in her will.[11] Inclosure and the consequent depopulation were completed by 1601.[12] The parsonage, which lay to the north of the church, was still standing in 1634,[13] but was unoccupied. The 17th-century lords of the manor were non-resident, and the larger of the two houses of Shelswell, recorded in the hearth-tax returns of 1665,[14] may have been the Home Farm. A large house, but no village, is marked on a map of 1677.[15] The Trotmans are said to have built in the early 18th century a new manor-house, on the site of the present Shelswell House.[16] In 1875 a stone bearing the date 1699 was found. Fiennes Trotman (d. 1782) enlarged this house and greatly improved the park, with plantations.[17] In 1875 Edward Slater-Harrison pulled down nearly the whole of the house and replaced it by the present mansion, designed by William Wilkinson of Oxford.[18] It bears the date 1875 and the crests of Slater and Harrison. In 1956 it was untenanted and falling into disrepair.

[45] For description see Dunkin, *Oxon.* ii. 106–7.
[46] Drawings in Bodl. G.A. Oxon. a 117, f. 37; MS. Top. Oxon. a 68, f. 410.
[47] C 3/283/86.
[48] Salter, *Oxon. Recusants*, 22; cf. *Oxon. Visit.* 211.
[49] Salter, *Oxon. Recusants*, *passim*.
[50] Oxf. Dioc. c 644, f. 25.
[51] Ibid. c 327, p. 303.
[52] Regent's Park Coll. Libr. Oxford, W. Bottoms and W. Stevens, *New Inn Road Chapel* (pamphlet).
[53] Oxf. Dioc. c 332.
[54] Ibid. d 707.
[55] *Educ. of Poor*, 728.
[56] Oxf. Dioc. b 39; cf. *Educ. Enq. Abstract*, 751.
[57] *Wilb. Visit.*; *Kelly's Dir. Oxon.* (1864); *Elem. Educ. Ret.*
[1] O.S. Map 6″, xvii (1885).
[2] *Oxon. Review Order* (1932); *Census*, 1951.
[3] O.S. Map 6″, xi, xvii (1885); cf. Bodl. Tithe award map (1846).

[4] G.S. Map 1″, xlv, NE.
[5] Said by Blomfield (*Shel.* 15) to have been diverted in early 19th cent. but followed present course in 1797: Davis, *Oxon. Map.*
[6] R. Bucknall, *Railway Hist.* 69; *Brasenose Quatercentenary Mon.* vi (O.H.S. lii), 24.
[7] *P.N. Oxon.* (E.P.N.S.), i. 232.
[8] Dunkin MS. 438/2, f. 91.
[9] Blo. *Shel.* 2.
[10] O.S. Map 25″, xvii. 3 (1881).
[11] Blo. *Shel.* 7; for Margaret see below, p. 287.
[12] See below, p. 288.
[13] Blo. *Shel.* 11.
[14] *Hearth Tax Oxon.* 205: it returned 6 hearths.
[15] Plot, *Nat. Hist. Oxon.* frontispiece.
[16] Dunkin MS. 439/3, f. 203.
[17] Blo. *Shel.* 12–14; Dunkin MS. 439/3, f. 203. In 1939 it covered 228 a.: *Kelly's Dir. Oxon.* (1939).
[18] Blo. *Shel.* 17; ibid. 13 for illustration of house before 1875.

Flora Thompson has given a vivid description of the celebrations connected with Queen Victoria's Jubilee in 1887 in 'Skeldon' (Shelswell) Park. She has also given a glimpse in 'Lark Rise' of the excitement caused to the children by the sight of 'Squire Harrison's four-in-hand, with ladies in bright summer dresses . . . on the top of the coach', and the white-hatted squire handling his four greys.

MANOR. Before the Conquest *SHELSWELL*, assessed at 10 hides, was held by Edwin, son of Burred, and in 1086 by Geoffrey, Bishop of Coutances.[19] On the latter's death in 1093 his estates passed to his nephew Robert de Mowbray, Earl of Northumberland, who forfeited his lands to William II in 1095. Shelswell may have been subsequently granted to Robert FitzHamon and may have passed to Robert, Earl of Gloucester, who married FitzHamon's daughter,[20] or it may have been granted directly by Henry I to Robert, who was his illegitimate son. The earls of Gloucester were certainly overlords of Shelswell in the 13th century[21] and as late as 1560 the manor was said to belong to the honor of Gloucester.[22]

The tenant of Shelswell in 1086 was Herluin, who also held of the Bishop of Coutances an estate at Colly Weston (Northants), which in the 12th century passed to his son William.[23] A family deriving its name from Shelswell appears towards the end of the 12th century: a Nicholas 'de Scaldeswelle' is mentioned about 1180, and a Eustace 'de Saldeywell' in 1219.[24] The immediate lord of Shelswell in the reign of Richard I was William son of Ralph of Weston, lord of Colly Weston and possibly a descendant of William son of Herluin.[25] William of Weston's son Peter was known alternatively as 'of Weston' or 'of Shelswell',[26] so Nicholas and Eustace of Shelswell may have been kinsmen of the lord of the manor. William of Weston exchanged 2 virgates in Shelswell for two in Colly Weston with Ralph Purcel of Newton[27] and was dead by 1221, when his widow Alice de Bendinges was holding Shelswell in dower.[28] William's heir was his son Peter,[29] but Alice was still alive and in possession of Shelswell in 1243.[30] By 1255, however, the manor had passed to Nicholas of Weston, probably Peter's son. Nicholas held of a Thomas de Dunington, who held of the

Earl of Gloucester, and Thomas's heir, another Thomas, was mesne lord in 1279 and 1285.[31] The 14th-century lords of Shelswell held directly of the honor of Gloucester.

The lords of Shelswell in the 13th century held ½ knight's fee in Shelswell itself, and another ½ fee in the neighbouring parish of Newton.[32] The tenant of the latter under the Westons in the early 13th century was Niel of Newton, who was a benefactor of Bicester Priory.[33] Niel was dead by 1219, when his widow Alice was claiming her dower in Newton, and he was succeeded by his son Richard Fitzniel,[34] who was dead by 1243, and his grandson John, who was still alive in 1279.[35] By 1346, when the lord of Shelswell held 'a third of Newton', the Fitzniels' ½-fee seems to have been absorbed into Shelswell manor.[36]

Nicholas of Weston died in 1281 and was succeeded by his daughter Amice and her husband Ellis de Hauville,[37] who was granted free warren in Shelswell in 1289.[38] Amice survived her husband (d. 1297),[39] and by 1300 she appears to have married Sir Henry Maulever.[40] Walter de Langton, Bishop of Coventry and Lichfield, seems to have acted as an intermediary in a settlement made in the same year by which part of Shelswell was to be held by Sir Henry and Amice and part by Sir William Tuchet.[41] Amice alone, however, was lady of the manor in 1316.[42] Sir Henry may have died by 1313,[43] and Amice herself was dead by 1322,[44] in which year Sir William was executed for his part in the rebellion of Thomas of Lancaster.[45] Shelswell presumably fell into the king's hands, but by 1327[46] it had been granted to Richard of Cornwall (*de Cornubia*), who had owned property in the manor from 1316 onwards.[47] Richard, described as 'the king's clerk and cousin' in 1327, may have been a younger son of Sir Richard of Cornwall,[48] illegitimate son of Earl Richard of Cornwall. Richard of Cornwall of Shelswell had been knighted by 1338[49] and was still holding the manor in 1346.[50] He was succeeded by William Cornwall, who presented to Shelswell church in 1367,[51] and William Cornwall the younger, who in 1397 quitclaimed the manor to Thomas and Alice Stokes, the parents of his wife Cicely, by whom he had a son John and three daughters.[52] In 1398 the Stokeses leased Shelswell to Cornwall for

[19] *V.C.H. Oxon.* i. 427; cf. above, p. 184.
[20] *V.C.H. Northants,* i. 287–8; *Complete Peerage,* v. 683; ix. 705.
[21] *Bk. of Fees,* 824; *Feud. Aids,* iv. 157.
[22] C 142/127/39.
[23] *V.C.H. Oxon.* i. 427; *V.C.H. Northants,* i. 388; ii. 551.
[24] *Collectanea,* ii (O.H.S. xvi), 291; Blo. *Shel.* 4.
[25] *Bracton's Note Bk.* ed. Maitland, ii. 128; cf. *V.C.H. Northants,* ii. 551.
[26] Blo. *Shel.* 4.
[27] See above, p. 264, for the subsequent history of this land.
[28] *Bracton's Note Bk.* ii. 128; cf. ibid. iii. 425.
[29] *Fines Oxon.* 233.
[30] *Bk. of Fees,* 824.
[31] *Rot. Hund.* (Rec. Com.), ii. 44, 836; *Feud. Aids,* iv. 157.
[32] Cf. above, p. 264: part of Newton Purcell manor was in Shelswell.
[33] Bodl. MS. Rawlinson D 404, f. 130.
[34] *Cur. Reg. R.* viii. 126.
[35] *Bk. of Fees,* 824; *Rot. Hund.* (Rec. Com), ii. 834.
[36] *Feud. Aids,* iv. 179.
[37] *Cal. Fine R.* 1272–1307, 141; *Feud. Aids,* iv. 157; *Cal. Close,* 1296–1302, 205.
[38] *Cal. Chart. R.* 1257–1300, 339.

[39] *Cal. Inq. p.m.* iii, p. 258.
[40] C.P. 25(1)/188/12/64.
[41] *Cal. Chart. R.* 1257–1300, 481; 1300–26, 3: Langton was granted free warren in the demesne of Shelswell in Jan. 1300 and Tuchet was granted it in Feb. 1301 on the bishop's 'information'; C.P. 25(1)/188/12/64 (Langton and Sir Henry were parties to a fine of the manor in 1300); see below, p. 289.
[42] *Feud. Aids,* iv. 169.
[43] Linc. Reg. ii, Dalderby, f. 163*b*; cf. f. 150*b*.
[44] *Cal. Inq. p.m.* vi, p. 188.
[45] *Complete Peerage,* ii, App. C, 599.
[46] *Cal. Chart. R.* 1327–41, 3.
[47] E 179/161/8; *Cal. Close,* 1318–23, 308; *Cal. Pat.* 1321–4, 353.
[48] For Sir Richard see N. Denholm-Young, *Richard of Cornwall,* 112 n.; Eyton, *Salop.* iv. 244, 254; *Oxoniensia,* iii. 106.
[49] Linc. Reg. iv, Burghersh, f. 280; the Cornwalls of Shelswell are not included in accounts of the descendants of Earl Richard, e.g. Earl of Liverpool and Compton Reade, *House of Cornewall.*
[50] *Feud. Aids,* iv. 179.
[51] Linc. Reg. x, Buckingham, f. 341*b*.
[52] *Cal. Close,* 1396–9, 238, 239.

50 years, with the proviso that after the death of the lessors and lessee the manor should revert to Cornwall's heirs.[53] Presentations to Shelswell church were made between 1441 and 1466 by a John Cornwall,[54] perhaps by two Johns, father and son; it was no doubt the latter who in 1478, as John Cornwall, 'gentleman' of Shelswell, was exempted for life from being put on assizes and juries, perhaps on account of old age.[55] He was still alive in 1486, when the manor was recovered against him by John Swelyngton, in what was probably a fictitious action to establish Cornwall's title.[56]

Cornwall had two daughters, Jane, who married a man named Tomlyns, and Margaret, who married Henry Brothers.[57] Jane was given two closes in Shelswell, and Margaret seems to have come to an arrangement with Swelyngton by which she got the rest of the land.[58] In 1501 she and her husband were trying to establish their title to the manor and advowson.[59] Brothers died within a few years, and by 1508 his widow had married Leonard Verney, Esq.[60] By this time Jane was also dead, but her claim to half the manor was contested by her son, Roger Tomlyns, 'a poor man', who was unable to bear the expense of litigation. In 1507 he made an arrangement with Sir Henry Wyatt, a friend of Henry VII and Henry VIII and in the 1520's treasurer of the king's chamber, who was to help him recover his property, and in return was to receive the reversion of half of it.[61] The result of legal action and a complicated series of conveyances was that the Verneys got possession of the whole manor except for about 90 acres, which in the 1530's came to Brasenose College,[62] while Roger Tomlyns gave up his claim to half the manor and lost all his Shelswell lands.[63]

The Verneys lived at Shelswell and Margaret was buried in the church there. Although Peter Brothers, a son of her first marriage, survived her, she left Shelswell by her will, dated 1530, to her daughter Dorothy and her husband Richard Heath, who died in 1542.[64]

Heath's marriage into a county family and his acquisition of the manor is of particular interest. He was the son of Michael Heath,[65] an Oxford brewer and the holder of many civic offices, who had acted as overseer of Margaret Verney's will.[66] Richard Heath was also active in civic affairs. Various payments were made to him by the town in 1523, e.g. 20s. 'for makying of iii boks for the Kyng's subsidie',[67] and in 1541 he was made a bailiff.[68] He made provision in his will for his second wife Jane (Bush), and

admonished his eldest son Robert to 'applye his lernyng', and to allow his brother Percival and a partner temporarily to occupy his father's lands at Shelswell and elsewhere.[69] Percival Heath continued the family tradition of civic service, being admitted a hanaster of Oxford corporation in 1542–3.[70] The Shelswell estate ultimately passed to Robert, who died in 1558,[71] and to his widow Katherine, daughter of Thomas Carter of Swyncombe, who married Philip Mordaunt of Essex as her second husband and died in 1560.[72] Robert's eldest son Thomas Heath, who married Jane, a daughter of John Denton of Ambrosden, succeeded to Shelswell and was living there in the late 16th century.[73] He seems to have had no children, and in about 1595 he sold the reversion of the manor on his own death and that of his wife (probably his second wife) Elizabeth to Sir Anthony Cope of Hanwell (d. 1615).[74] After Thomas Heath's death in 1605[75] Elizabeth married Devorax Barrett, and Cope leased the manor from them for £400 a year, £100 more than it was worth, according to him. Barrett died in about 1621, but Elizabeth was still alive in 1624, when Sir Anthony's son Sir William Cope was at law with her over the terms of the lease.[76]

On her death the Copes acquired the manor, and it remained in the family until the death of Sir Anthony Cope, 4th Bt., in 1675. He left his property, including Shelswell, to his brother, Sir John, for life, but not to his brother's children.[77] Although Sir John lived until 1721, he may have sold Shelswell to the Trotmans in the 1680's. In 1686 Samuel Trotman of Siston (Gloucs.), the eldest son of Samuel Trotman (d. 1685) of Bucknell, and his brother Lenthall were parties to a fine levied on the manor,[78] and there is evidence in the early 18th century pointing to the ownership of the manor by the Trotmans. From 1705 Samuel Trotman of Siston (d. 1720) and then his nephew Samuel, son of Lenthall Trotman of Bucknell, presented to Newton Purcell church,[79] and this is significant, as since the 16th century the advowson of Newton had descended with Shelswell manor. Samuel Trotman appears to have settled Shelswell on his younger brother Edward, who was buried at Newton Purcell in 1743.[80] In 1746, when Edward's only daughter Susannah married the architect Sanderson Miller, he was described as 'Edward Trotman, Esq., of Shelswell'.[81] His son Fiennes, who succeeded him, died without issue in 1782 and was buried like his father in Newton Purcell church.[82]

The reversion belonged to Fiennes's nephew

[53] Ibid. 241.
[54] Linc. Reg. xviii, Alnwick, ff. 173, 178b, 180; ibid. xx, Chedworth, ff. 236b, 243.
[55] Cal. Pat. 1476–85, 125.
[56] B.N.C. Mun. Shels. 26; C.P. 40/898, m. 450.
[57] B.N.C. Mun. Shels. 26.
[58] Ibid.
[59] C.P. 40/958, m. 507.
[60] B.N.C. Mun. Shels. 4. It has been impossible to establish any connexion between Leonard Verney and the Verneys of Claydon (Bucks.).
[61] B.N.C. Mun. Shels. 26; for Wyatt see D.N.B. under Thos. Wyatt.
[62] See below, p. 288.
[63] B.N.C. Mun. Shels. 7, 11.
[64] Blo. Shel. 7: M. Verney's will; C 142/66/62.
[65] P.C.C. F 12 Spert.
[66] W. H. Turner, Oxf. City Rec. 1509–83, passim; Michael's will was proved 1537: P.C.C. 14 Dyngeley.
[67] Turner, Oxf. City Rec. 44.
[68] Ibid. 162.
[69] P.C.C. F 12 Spert; C 142/66/62.
[70] Turner, Oxf. City Rec. 173.
[71] C 142/115/33.
[72] Ibid. 127/39.
[73] Oxon. Visit. 208.
[74] C 2/Jas. I, C 13/83.
[75] Bodl. MS. Wills Oxon. 289 (index).
[76] C.P. 25(2)/339/East. 4 Jas. I; C 2/Jas. I, C 13/83.
[77] G.E.C. Baronetage, i. 36–37; Blo. Shel. 11–12.
[78] C.P. 25(2)/806/Hil. 1 & 2 Jas. II.
[79] Oxf. Dioc. c 266, ff. 205, 155b. For Trotman family see Fosbrooke, Glos. ii. 56.
[80] For Edward's M.I. see Blo. Shel. 12. He is said by Blomfield to have acquired the manor by his marriage to Mary Filmer, the niece of Lawrence Fiennes, 5th Vct. Saye and Sele (d. 1742), and the daughter of his sister Susannah and Thomas Filmer of Amwellbury (Herts.), but no evidence for this has been found.
[81] An 18th-cent. Correspondence, ed. L. Dickins and M. Stanton (1910), 123, 456.
[82] Oxon. Poll, 1754; Blo. Newt. 15; Blo. Shel. 14.

Samuel Trotman, but the latter sold it during the life of his uncle. The manor was purchased by Gilbert Harrison, a London merchant (d. 1790), whose son John attained his majority in 1802 and died in 1834. John Harrison was unmarried and he made his nephew John Harrison Slater, son of his sister Ann Harrison and John Slater of Margate, his heir, on condition that he assumed the surname Harrison. John Slater-Harrison died in 1874 and was succeeded by his only surviving child Edward. The latter died in 1911 and his second wife Emma Cecilia (née Cartwright) continued in possession of Shelswell until her death in 1943, when she was succeeded by John Francis Dewar-Harrison, grandson of her husband's sister Augusta, wife of William W. M. Dewar of Cotmore House, Fringford.[83]

LESSER ESTATES. An estate of 90 acres became detached from the manor in about 1500. It consisted of three closes in the eastern corner of the parish—Barley and Drake Closes (sometimes called Nast Field) and Pasture Mede. After passing through various hands including those of William Spencer of Adderbury they were bought in 1533 for £162 from William Fermor of Somerton by John Claymond, President of Corpus Christi College.[84] He gave them in the same year with other property to Brasenose College to endow scholarships.[85] The college leased the property as two estates, often to neighbouring gentry, such as Richard Heath and later Fiennes Trotman of Shelswell or the Ardens of Kirtlington.[86] Eleven acres were sold to the Great Central Railway in 1895.[87] The college held the rest of the property, called Barleyfield farm, in 1955.[88]

ECONOMIC HISTORY. Domesday Book records that in 1086 there was land for 7 ploughs, all of which was apparently being cultivated, for there were 3 ploughs on the demesne, where there were 2 serfs, and 4 ploughs worked by 7 villeins (villani) and 7 bordars. A considerable advance in prosperity since the Conquest is indicated by the increase of the value of the estate from £5 to £10.[89] In 1279 some 24½ virgates of arable appear to have been under cultivation. The demesne consisted of 8 virgates, beside meadow and pasture, and 7 villeins held 11½ virgates, working and being tallaged at the lord's will, and all paying money rents as well: the rent paid is only recorded in one instance, where a villein holding 2½ virgates paid 8s. Of the other villeins 3 held 2 virgates, and 3 held 1 virgate each. There were 3 free tenants, of whom 2 held 2 virgates each, one for 1s. rent, the other for 7d. and for per-

forming suit of hundred and county twice a year for his lord. The third, the Prior of Bicester, held 1 virgate in free alms and had a subtenant, but his rent is not recorded.[90] In 1297 the manor was worth £10 a year.[91]

The number of tenants at Shelswell had fallen between 1086 and 1279, and it is possible that the decline of the village had started comparatively early. Fourteen people were assessed for taxation in 1316, and eleven in 1327.[92] The total assessment fixed after 1334 at £1 19s. 8d. was comparatively small, but indicates that Shelswell was about as prosperous as the neighbouring villages of Cottisford, Hardwick, and Tusmore.[93] The decline of Shelswell evidently continued, for by 1428 there were less than ten resident householders.[94] By the end of the 16th century inclosure had virtually completed the destruction of the village. In 1497 Henry Brothers, husband of the lady of the manor, had destroyed 2 houses, evicted 11 people, and put down to pasture 60 acres of arable land.[95] There were 200 acres of arable in the manor in 1501 to 400 acres of pasture, and 20 acres of meadow.[96] In 1523 there were six contributors to the lay subsidy in Shelswell, only one of whom, Leonard Verney,[97] was a man of substance:[98] in 1569 Shelswell was assessed jointly with Newton Purcell and there were only five contributors in both villages.[99] William Spencer of Adderbury, who in 1528 held two closes of 60 acres in the parish, was alleged to be responsible for further evictions.[1] By 1581 the arable land of the manor had decreased to 100 acres, and the pasture showed a corresponding increase to 500 acres.[2] In 1601 inclosure was said to be complete,[3] and the first half of the 17th century probably saw the destruction of the last vestiges of the medieval village.[4]

The construction of Shelswell House and the coming of the Trotman family to live in the parish in the late 17th or early 18th century[5] must have started a modest repopulation. There were, however, still only three families in the parish in 1768 according to the incumbent's report,[6] but by 1801 the population was about forty.[7] In 1786 there were at least two farms—the Home farm, and another on the estate[8] of about 90 acres which Brasenose College had acquired in 1533, and which had then, it may be noted, consisted of three closes.[9] Division of the large closes had started by 1670, and 18th-century terriers suggest that the estate was principally used as pasture: a close of 22½ acres was called Dairy Ground in 1752, and one of the farms was let to a grazier, the son of a yeoman who had been the college's tenant.[10] By 1816 there were two farms on the college estate,[11] one of them, Barleyfield, taking

[83] Blo. Shel. 14–17; Burke, Land. Gent. (1937) under Trotman-Dickenson and Slater-Harrison; Kelly's Handbk. (1954).
[84] B.N.C. Mun. Shels. 14, 17, 27, and passim.
[85] Brasenose Quatercentenary Mon. iv. 12; vi (O.H.S. lii), 24.
[86] B.N.C. Mun. Shels. 33, 35, 66.
[87] Brasenose Quat. Mon. vi. 24; see above, p. 285.
[88] Inf. the Bursar; see below, p. 289.
[89] V.C.H. Oxon. i. 427.
[90] Rot. Hund. (Rec. Com.), ii. 836–7.
[91] C 133/78/8.
[92] E 179/161/8, 9.
[93] E 164/7; see below, p. 359.
[94] Feud. Aids, iv. 201.
[95] Dom. of Incl. 349.
[96] C.P. 40/958, m. 507.

[97] See above, p. 287.
[98] E 179/161/198.
[99] Ibid. 162/33.
[1] Sta. Cha. 2/5/126–7; see above.
[2] Dunkin MS. 438/2, f. 91.
[3] Blo. Shel. 11.
[4] See above, p. 285.
[5] Ibid.
[6] Oxf. Dioc. d 559.
[7] V.C.H. Oxon. ii. 221.
[8] O.R.O. Land tax assess. A farm-house had been built on the college estate by 1752: B.N.C. Mun. Shels. 543.
[9] Brasenose Quat. Mon. vi (O.H.S. lii), 24. For rents and heriots demanded in the 17th and 18th cents. see B.N.C. Mun. Shels. 17, 33, 38, 43.
[10] B.N.C. Mun. Shels. 543: terriers 1670, 1678, 1717, 1752; ibid. 53, 61, 63.
[11] O.R.O. Land tax assess.

its name from one of the closes of 1532.[12] In the middle of the 19th century there were four farms, two on the college estate and two on the Slater-Harrison estate, of 51, 43, 207, and 364 acres. Seventeen acres were let to a farmer outside the parish, and 124 acres were in the hands of the lord of the manor. In 1849 there were 272 acres of arable, 405 acres of meadow and pasture, and 91 acres of woodland.[13] Shelswell Plantation (26 a.), Pondhead (27 a.) at the northern end of the Fish Pond, and Spilsmere Wood (40 a.) were the largest tracts of woodland in 1952, the last two being perhaps the remains of the extensive woods in the parish mentioned in 1581.[14] During the 19th century the only occupations were agriculture and service at Shelswell House. In 1939 there were two farms—Home farm and Barleyfield[15]—and there remained only about 60 acres of arable.[16]

Shelswell has always been one of the least populous places in the hundred. In 1676 only 21 adults were recorded at the Compton Census. The estimated population was 42 in 1801 and it increased slightly during the century: it was 51 in 1901.[17]

CHURCH. The original church building at Shelswell has gone and the earliest documentary evidence for the existence of a church comes from the collation of a chaplain, Robert Basset, by the bishop in c. 1215.[18] There can be little doubt, however, that there was a church here at an early date. Between 1093 and 1095 Robert de Mowbray, Earl of Northumberland, was lord, and the church was dedicated to the Northumbrian saint St. Ebbe.

From 1250 to 1251 the advowson followed the descent of the manor. In 1306 the bishop collated because of a dispute between Sir William Tuchet and the Maulevers, who were sharing the manor.[19] The latter evidently won, for in 1313 Lady Amice Maulever presented. In 1372, on unknown grounds, Sir Robert Hotot, lord of Clopton, was patron. When in 1398 the Stokeses leased the manor to the Cornwalls, they kept the advowson, for in 1409 and 1422 Thomas Stokes presented. No patron is named in 1417, and in 1435 the bishop collated by lapse. After this the descent of the advowson followed that of the manor.

From 1573 Shelswell and Newton Purcell, which had the same patron, were held together,[20] and Shelswell was usually referred to as a chapel of Newton.[21] In 1850 the ecclesiastical parishes were united.[22]

Shelswell was a very poor parish, valued at only 15s. in 1254[23] and not included in the taxation of 1291. In the later Middle Ages it was taxed at £2 13s. 4d.[24] In the reign of Henry VIII its value had risen to £4.[25] In later valuations it was included with Newton Purcell, although the tithes were separately commuted in 1849 for £186.[26] After the Reformation the income of the parish came from tithes, for the glebe, which had been worth 6s. 8d. in the 14th century,[27] was absorbed into the lands of the manor by inclosure and had disappeared by 1601. The Rectory of two bays was still standing in 1634; next to it were Parsonage Close and Parsonage Orchard, but Parsonage Barn had by that time disappeared.[28]

The church of *ST. EBBE* has completely disappeared. It stood to the north-east of the house on the site now occupied by the stables of Home Farm. From the wills of Margaret Verney and Richard Heath, who were both buried in the church, it is known that it had at least two altars,[29] and from the Edwardian inventories of 1552 that there were two bells. The church also possessed a cope, two sets of vestments, a silver-gilt chalice and paten, and two pewter candlesticks.[30] It was standing in 1618 but was probably no longer used, as there were no 'mounds' round the churchyard.[31] In the early 18th century the church was described as a dilapidated chapel,[32] and in 1740 it was reported that no services had been held in it in 'the memory of man'.[33] The reports continue in much the same strain—in 1757 the chapel was described as decayed and gone to ruin[34]—until 1795; but in 1796 the chapel had been taken down.[35] Two stone-carved recumbent figures from the church, one male, the other female, in the dress of the late 16th century, are possibly memorials of members of the Heath family, and are in the grounds to the north-east of Shelswell House.

NONCONFORMITY. None known.

SCHOOLS. None known.

CHARITIES. None known.

[12] Cf. Bodl. Tithe award and map (1849); for Barleyfield see *P.N. Oxon.* (E.P.N.S.), i. 232, where, however, the examples of early forms of name do not appear to be Barleyfield in Shelswell.
[13] Bodl. Tithe award and map.
[14] O.S. Map 6″, xvii, NE. (1952); Dunkin MS. 438/2, f. 91.
[15] *Kelly's Dir. Oxon.* (1939).
[16] O.S. Land Utilization Map, 1″, sheet 94.
[17] *Census,* 1801–1901. During the 20th cent. the population figures have been included in those for Newton Purcell: see above, p. 266.
[18] *Rot. Welles,* i. 110; see MS. Top. Oxon. d 460 for a list of medieval presentations.
[19] See above, p. 286.   [20] Ibid. pp. 266, 287.
[21] Oxf. Dioc. d 106, f.14; ibid. c 266, f. 205.

[22] Bodl. Newton Par. Box (uncat.): Order in Council.
[23] Lunt, *Val. Norw.* 311.
[24] *Inq. Non.* (Rec. Com.), 133.
[25] *Valor Eccl.* (Rec. Com.), ii. 161.
[26] Bodl. Tithe award.
[27] *Inq. Non.* (Rec. Com.), 133.
[28] Blo. *Shel.* 11.
[29] Ibid. 7: will of Margaret Verney; P.C.C. F 12 Spert.
[30] *Chant. Cert.* 78. The bells are not mentioned here, but they are in Blo. *Shel.* 8.
[31] Oxf. Archd. Oxon. c 118, f. 260; Blo. *Shel.* 11; Oxf. Archd. Oxon. c 141, p. 403: 1601 terrier.
[32] Oxf. Dioc. d 553.
[33] Oxf. Archd. Oxon. c 98, f. 134.
[34] Ibid. d 13, f. 34.
[35] Ibid. c 98, f. 185.

SOMERTON

THE ancient parish used to cover 1,842 acres,[1] but in 1888 it was increased to 1,977 acres by the addition of a detached part of Fritwell.[2] It lies along the banks of the Cherwell about 16 miles north of Oxford with Banbury as its nearest market-town. The Cherwell forms most of the western boundary, but in the north by Aston Mill the line has been drawn east of it and in the south-west the boundary follows the western arm of the river so as to include in Somerton some meadowland on the right bank. Part of the eastern boundary is formed by the ancient dyke of Aves Ditch.[3]

The parish stands on the limestone escarpment which forms the watershed between the Thames and the Ouse.[4] Most of it is a bleak and treeless table-land, 300 feet above sea-level, but rising to 400 feet near Somerton village. Here the land falls away steeply towards the Cherwell, where the low-lying valley was once marsh and is still liable to flooding. Several springs rise on the edge of this hill and run into the Cherwell; noted for their fossilizing properties, they excited the interest of Robert Plot, the 17th-century scientist.[5]

The parish is crossed by a network of roads and by an ancient trackway, the pre-Roman Portway, which runs from north to south.[6]

The bridges over the Cherwell and its arms were numerous and were kept up by both Somerton and North Aston parishes. The bridge called 'Gambon brugge'[7] over the western arm on the road to North Aston was first mentioned in the 13th century, and although in Aston parish its upkeep led to disputes with Somerton. As late as the early 17th century it was said to be customary for the lord of Aston to assist with the maintenance of the causeway from 'Cumon's Mill to old Cherwell', and to pay a quarter of the cost of upkeep of the bridge over 'old Cherwell' and of 'six or seven' other bridges adjoining.[8] By an agreement of 1624 the lord of Aston agreed to maintain the bridge over 'Old Charwell' and the next bridge towards Somerton; the lord of Somerton was to maintain all the other bridges, and the causeway to Somerton.[9]

The Oxford canal, completed in 1790, runs parallel to the river.[10] A wharf and weighbridge, now disused, were made near the village and the Cherwell and Somerton lock on the parish's northern boundary. The Oxford–Banbury section of the G.W.R. was completed in 1850 and a station (called Fritwell and Somerton in 1955) was opened in 1855.[11] It stands on the site of the Domesday mill.[12]

The village, now without any definite pattern, lies at the north-western corner of the parish. It straggles up the slopes of the steep hill above the banks of the Cherwell: the main village street is the road from North Aston which runs past the Railway Inn to the centre of the village and on to Ardley. The church has a commanding position half-way up the hill.[13] It is possible that the medieval village lay to the south of it and not as now mainly to the north. In a field slightly north-east of the church and sloping down to the river, mounds and fishponds can still be seen marking the site of the medieval castle of the De Greys.[14] An extent of 1295 mentions its court, dove-cote, fishponds, curtilages, and gardens.[15] It was presumably uninhabited in the early 16th century, when William Fermor built a new manor-house on another site, but the chapel in the castle yard was still standing in 1580 when Thomas Fermor bequeathed it for use as a school. There is a tradition that the present school-house stands on the site of this chapel. Thirteenth-century pottery was dug up near by in 1954.[16]

The village was one of the largest and richest in Ploughley hundred in the Middle Ages and remained so until the mid-19th century.[17] In the 1660's there were at least ten substantial houses besides the manor-house,[18] of which many survive today. In the 18th century incumbents estimated that there were about 40 houses.[19] A great amount of building took place in the first half of the 19th century and the number of houses rose from 55 in 1811 to 78 in 1851. But thereafter population declined, and although there has been much new building in the 20th century, houses still numbered 64 in 1951 as they had done in 1901. The village's new council houses lie along the Ardley Road.[20]

The oldest house in Somerton is probably the present schoolroom.[21] It is thought to be a late-16th or early 17th-century building. It is L-shaped in plan, is constructed of coursed rubble, and retains part of its ancient roof of stone slates. The school-master's house was originally part of the 16th-century building, but was rebuilt in about 1750 and there have since been 19th-century additions.[22]

A wall with a two-light window and the remains of tracery in it is all that is left of the village's chief 16th-century house. This was the new manor-house, built early in the century by William Fermor on a new site south-east of the village and near the present Manor Farm.[23] In 1665 it was returned for the hearth tax as having 22 hearths.[24] It had a central

[1] O.S. Map 6″, xvi (1884).
[2] *Local Govt. Bd. Order 21435*: copy in O.R.O.; *Census*, 1891, 1951.
[3] Blo. *Som.* 90; for Aves Ditch see above, p. 7, n. 4, and map facing p. 1.
[4] Blo. *Som.* 89–90; G.S. Map 1″, xlv NW.: the Great Oolite is bounded on the W. by Northampton Sand, Upper Lias, and Marlstone.
[5] Plot, *Nat. Hist. Oxon.* 33; Blo. *Som.* 89.
[6] O.S. Map 6″, xvi; ibid. 2½″, 42/42, 52 (1951); see also map facing p. 1.
[7] *Rot. Hund.* (Rec. Com.), ii. 838; Muriel, widow of Gambon, held North Aston water-mill in 1279: ibid. 860.
[8] O.R.O. J VIII e/13.   [9] Ibid.
[10] Blo. *Som.* 157.
[11] Ibid.; E. T. MacDermot, *Hist. G.W.R.* i. 300 and n.

[12] See below, p. 296; Blo. *Som.* 91.
[13] O.S. Map 25″, xvi. 6, 10 (1881).
[14] See below, p. 291.
[15] Blo. *Som.* 97.
[16] V.C.H. *Oxon.* i. 487; *12th Rep. Com. Char.* 309; in Ashmolean Museum.
[17] See below, p. 294.
[18] *Hearth Tax Oxon.* 192.
[19] Oxf. Dioc. d 554, d 557, d 560.
[20] *Census*, 1811, 1851, 1901, 1951. Ten council houses were built between 1946 and 1954: inf. Ploughley R.D.C.
[21] Descriptions of buildings are based on inf. from Min. of Housing and Local Govt. and on personal observation.
[22] See below, p. 300.
[23] Blo. *Som.* 104.
[24] *Hearth Tax Oxon.* 192.

dining-hall with mullioned windows and 'great' parlour above and flanking wings. The windows of the
hall, chapel, and parlour were filled with coats of
arms, which Anthony Wood carefully described.[25]
This house was the home of the Fermors until 1625
when Henry Fermor moved to Tusmore.[26] It was then
owned for 30 years by Lord Arundell, and may have
been let by him.[27] The house is marked on Plot's
map of 1677,[28] but by 1738 it was 'almost ruinous'
although the chapel was still being used.[29] Later in
the century the house was partly pulled down and
stone from it was used for the new Fermor house at
Tusmore. By 1827 only a fragment of the hall remained.[30]

Among the 17th-century houses are Manor Farm,
a two-storied house with cellars and a steep-pitched
roof covered with stone slates; and Dovecote Farm
at the top of the village street. The last consists of
three buildings joined at an angle; it has two stories
and cellars; is built of coursed rubble like all the
older houses in the village and is roofed with Welsh
slate. It is named after its dovecote, dated 1719—
a square building with a four-gabled roof of stone
slates. Each gable has a window and there are 1,100
nests.

The early 17th-century Rectory which once stood
opposite the church was replaced in 1847.[31] It was
built in about 1615 by the rector, William Juxon, and
was a large stone house with a high gabled roof. The
south front had eleven windows and the entrance
doorway; dovehouse, stables, and other outhouses
adjoined it.[32] The new 19th-century Rectory cost
£2,000 and was enlarged in 1896, but was abandoned
as a Rectory for a smaller house built at the top of the
hill in 1928.[33] Other 19th-century additions to the
village are the red-brick cottages opposite the church
and the Railway Inn near the river, where the well-
known Oxfordshire surveyor for inclosure awards,
James Jennings (d. 1832), once lived.[34] A Somerton
victualler was licensed in 1735, but the name of his
premises is not known.[35]

One outlying farm—Troy Farm[36]—dates from
the 16th century. It was probably built on the site
of the manor-house known as 'Somertons', which
belonged to the 15th-century Astons,[37] and may
have been occupied in the early 17th century by
William Tempest, who had land in the parish.[38]
Today its chief interest is a well-preserved turf
maze, cut in the garden opposite the house, of which
only seven are said to survive in England. The name
Troy, used figuratively to denote a scene of confusion, was often given to mazes.[39]

Mudginwell Farm-house, a stone building on the
Middleton Stoney road, close to the Upper Heyford
boundary, is no longer in use as a farm-house. It
dates from the 17th century.

The parish is noteworthy for its long connexion
with a well-known Roman Catholic family, the
Fermors,[40] and for three eminent rectors. Master
Nicholas Hereford, rector in 1397, may have been
the well-known collaborator of Wycliffe; Robert
King (rector 1537–52), the son of a yeoman farmer
of Thame, was the first Bishop of Oxford; and
William Juxon (rector 1615–33), a noted Episcopa-
lian and President of St. John's College, Oxford,
attended Charles I on the scaffold and later became
Archbishop of Canterbury.[41]

MANORS. In 1086 Odo of Bayeux and Miles
Crispin shared the lordship of SOMERTON. Odo
held 9 hides, while Miles held two small estates of
1 hide each.[42] The latter had been held before the
Conquest by Brictric and Ketel, a Dane, but in
1086 Rainald Wadard or Waard was the under-
tenant of all three estates. Wadard was closely
associated with Odo of Bayeux—he appears in the
Bayeux tapestry—and was the latter's tenant in
several neighbouring Oxfordshire villages besides
holding lands of him in five other counties.[43] After
Odo's banishment his Somerton lands appear to
have been granted to Manasses Arsic, thus becoming
a part of the Barony of Cogges. On Miles Crispin's
death his Somerton estates were added to the Arsic
lands.[44]

Throughout the 12th century Somerton remained
united and followed the Arsic descent, until in 1230
Robert Arsic died leaving two coheiresses, Joan and
Alexandra, between whom the barony was divided.
Joan was successively wife of Eustace de Grenvile
and of Stephen Simeon, and Alexandra married
Thomas de la Haye.[45] Each held half of the manor,
which remained divided until the 16th century.

Sybil de Crevequer, Robert Arsic's widow, held
lands in Somerton in dower, but was dead by 1245,
for in that year Stephen Simeon and Joan conveyed
their share of the manor to Walter, son of Robert de
Grey, in exchange for land at Cornwell and 200
marks. Later in the year Walter obtained a charter
confirming to him these lands, as well as others
granted him by his uncle Walter de Grey, Archbishop of York.[46] His son Robert succeeded in 1268,[47]
and on his death in 1295[48] Somerton was assigned
in dower to his widow Joan. She died in 1312, leaving
as heir her grandson, John de Grey, a minor.[49] His
wardship was committed to Hugh Despenser until 1322,
when John attained his majority.[50] He was succeeded
in 1359 by his son John (III),[51] who in 1361 entailed
the manor on his son John (IV) and his intended wife
Elizabeth de Ponynges.[52] But John (IV) predeceased
his father, so in 1368 it was resettled on Elizabeth for
life, with remainder to her daughter.[53] Apparently
both Elizabeth and her daughter were dead by

[25] *Par. Coll.* iii. 268.
[26] See below, p. 293.
[27] Ibid.
[28] Plot, *Nat. Hist. Oxon.* frontispiece.
[29] Oxf. Dioc. d 554.
[30] *Gent. Mag.* 1827, xcviii (1), 115. See plate facing
p. 334.
[31] Blo. *Som.* 145.
[32] *O.A.S. Rep.* 1900, 19–20 and reproduction of water-
colour drawing.
[33] Local inf.
[34] Wing, *Annals*, 144.
[35] O.R.O. Victlrs' recog.
[36] Blo. *Som.* 101–2.   [37] See below, p. 292.
[38] *Cal. S.P. Dom.* 1638–9, 224.

[39] *P.N. Oxon.* (E.P.N.S.), i. 235; *O.E.D.*
[40] See below, p. 292.   [41] See below, p. 297.
[42] *V.C.H. Oxon.* i. 404, 418, 419.
[43] Ibid.; Sir H. Ellis, *Introd. to Domesday*, ii. 404.
[44] Blo. *Som.* 92; see above, p. 126
[45] *Ex. e Rot. Fin.* (Rec. Com.), i. 193.
[46] *Cal. Chart. R.* 1226–57, 285; *Fines Oxon.* 237.
[47] *Ex. e Rot. Fin.* ii. 464–5; for the Greys see above,
p. 127.
[48] *Cal. Inq. p.m.* iii, p. 182.
[49] Ibid. v, p. 220.
[50] *Cal. Fine R.* 1307–19, 151.
[51] *Cal. Inq. p.m.* x, p. 406.
[52] *Cal. Close*, 1360–4, 259.
[53] *Cal. Pat.* 1367–70, 81.

1375, or had surrendered their estates, since after John (III) died in that year Somerton was assigned to his widow Maud in dower.[54] In 1379 John (II)'s third son Robert, now 4th Baron Grey of Rothfield, obtained licence to settle the reversion of the manor, still held in dower by Maud, on himself and his wife Joan in tail, and did so in 1380.[55] Robert died seised of the manor in 1388,[56] leaving an infant daughter as heiress, so that the Grey manor passed into the king's custody. However, his widow Elizabeth married John de Clinton in the same year, and was assigned the manor in dower.[57] John de Clinton died in 1398 and Elizabeth married as her fourth husband Sir John Russell;[58] she continued to hold the manor until her death in 1423.[59] Robert de Grey's only daughter Joan had married John Deincourt, and in 1401, when she came of age, she and her husband were given seisin of the barony.[60] She died in 1408 and the barony eventually passed to her daughters Margaret and Alice as coheiresses.[61] Alice, the elder, was wife of William Lovel, and it was to them that the Grey moiety of Somerton reverted on Elizabeth's death. In 1435 William settled the property on himself and his wife,[62] and when he died in 1455[63] Alice married Sir Ralph Butler and continued to hold the manor until her death in 1474.[64] Her grandson Francis, Lord Lovel, succeeded, but was attainted in 1485 and was probably killed in 1487 at the battle of Stoke.[65] The manor remained in royal hands until granted in 1512 to William Fermor.[66]

The other moiety of *SOMERTON*, which passed to Alexandra Arsic and her husband Thomas de la Haye, was in 1255 held of her by the queen at fee-farm.[67] Her daughter, also Alexandra, had married William de Gardinis by 1279, when he was holding half Somerton, and in theory shared with Robert de Grey the obligation to find three knights for the garrison of Dover castle throughout the year.[68] In practice, however, Somerton was regarded as only $\frac{1}{4}$ knight's fee.[69] William died in 1287, but had already given his son Thomas an estate *pur auter vie*[70] in his lands in Somerton. Thomas's daughter Alexandra married John Giffard 'le Boef' of Twyford (Bucks.), and when Thomas died in 1328 the estate passed to their son John Giffard.[71] The Giffards held Somerton until 1437, but appear never to have lived there. John Giffard the younger and

his son played a prominent part in local government in Buckinghamshire, but scarcely at all in Oxfordshire.[72] In 1361 Sir John obtained licence to settle the manor on his son Thomas,[73] who succeeded in 1369.[74] In 1383 Thomas settled the property on his eldest son Roger and the latter's wife Joan, daughter of Baldwin de Bereford of Shotteswell (Warws.),[75] to whom it passed in 1394,[76] but in the following year Roger sold it to his mother Sybil,[77] who held it until her death in 1429.[78] In the meantime Roger had married Isabel Stretele and had died in 1419.[79] Their son Thomas succeeded to the manor.[80] He had been a ward of his mother and stepfather John Stokes, and appears to have conveyed to them part or all of his Twyford estates.[81] Some time before 1437 John Aston, Thomas Giffard's brother-in-law, acquired sole ownership of these, for he then conveyed them to Thomas and became in exchange a feoffee of Somerton.[82] The reason for this series of conveyances is obscure: it may have been necessary to solve the problem of tenure created by Thomas's minority.

The Astons had held property in Somerton since at least 1327.[83] Members of the family had been in the church and in trade in London.[84] Richard Aston was the lessee of Eynsham Abbey's estate in the early 15th century and John Aston completed the purchase of the Giffards' Somerton manor in 1438.[85] Before his death in 1459 he conveyed the manor to feoffees, no doubt for his son William and his wife Isabel, daughter of Thomas Clederow, to whom the estate passed in 1465.[86] They held it until 1504, when they conveyed their moiety of Somerton to a group of feoffees which included Richard Fermor,[87] who in turn must have conveyed it to William Fermor, his younger brother, for the Astons are said to have held it 'till they covenanted with William Fermor'.[88] The other moiety, which had been in the king's hands since the attainder of Francis, Lord Lovel,[89] was granted to William Fermor in 1512 at a yearly rent of £15 11s.[90] Thus the manor was re-united.

Richard and William Fermor were the sons of Thomas Richards *alias* Fermor of Witney, a wealthy merchant of Welsh descent who had married the widow of Henry Wenman, another wool merchant.[91] William played an active part in local government:

54 *Cal. Close*, 1374–7, 155.
55 *Cal. Pat.* 1377–81, 334; C.P. 25(1)/289/52/28.
56 C 136/52/2.
57 *Cal. Close*, 1385–9, 544.
58 *Complete Peerage*, vi. 149.
59 C 139/12.
60 *Cal. Close*, 1399–1402, 247.
61 *Complete Peerage*, iv. 124–7; vi. 150.
62 C.P. 25(1)/292/68/56.
63 C 139/158.
64 C 140/47.
65 *Complete Peerage*, viii. 225.
66 *L. & P. Hen. VIII*, i (1), p. 509.
67 *Rot. Hund.* (Rec. Com.), ii. 44.
68 Ibid. 838; cf. above, p. 128.
69 *Feud. Aids*, iv. 157.
70 C 133/50/21.
71 *Cal. Inq. p.m.* vii, p. 107; *V.C.H. Bucks.* iv. 256.
72 *V.C.H. Bucks.* iv. 256 and references cited there; *Cal. Close*, 1339–41, 436.
73 *Cal. Pat.* 1358–61, 571.
74 *Cal. Close*, 1369–74, 22; *Cal. Inq. p.m.* xii, p. 340.
75 *Cal. Pat.* 1381–5, 295; *V.C.H. Warws.* v. 148.
76 C 136/83.
77 *Cal. Pat.* 1391–6, 608.
78 C 139/45.

79 Ibid.
80 Ibid.
81 *Cal. Close*, 1429–35, 107.
82 *Cal. Pat.* 1436–41, 119.
83 See E 179/161/9 for Wm. Aston (fl. 1327).
84 For Wm. Aston, clerk (fl. 1380), see C.P. 25(1)/289/52/28; *Cal. Pat.* 1377–81, 334. For Wm. Aston of London, mercer, a mainpernor for Rich. Aston of Somerton in 1405, see *Cal. Close*, 1402–5, 522.
85 Blo. *Som.* 101. He was certainly in possession by 1452, when he presented to the church: Linc. Reg. xx, Chedworth, f. 229. For him see also *Cal. Close*, 1422–9, 119, 212, 319, 324, 403, 465; 1429–35, 488; 1435–41, 24, 101.
86 For his will (1459) see Blo. *Som.* 101: he asked to be buried at Somerton and left money for the repair of the church; *Cal. Pat.* 1461–7, 467.
87 C.P. 25(1)/191/31/31.
88 *Tusmore Papers*, ed. L. G. Wickham Legg (O.R.S. xx), 4.
89 C 142/78/40.
90 C 66/617, m. 2; *L. & P. Hen. VIII*, i (1), p. 509. The rent was later granted to Humphrey Bannister: *L. & P. Hen. VIII*, i (2), p. 1176; cf. C 54/382/24–26.
91 For Fermor pedigree see Blo. *Tus.* 64; Blo. *Som.* 122; *Oxon. Visit.* 46; *Gent. Mag.* 1827, xcvii (1), 114, 580.

in 1509 he was appointed coroner and attorney of the King's Bench, in 1511 a Justice of the Peace for Oxfordshire, and in 1533 High Sheriff of the county.[92] He died in 1552, leaving no children, and his nephew Thomas, younger son of Richard Fermor,[93] was his heir. By the terms of William's will, however, his widow Elizabeth was to hold Somerton for her life,[94] and she was still lady of the manor as late as 1568.[95] By 1573 Thomas Fermor had succeeded her.[96] It is likely that he leased part of the manor to his sister Mary and her husband Sir Richard Knightley,[97] and to Robert Austen, grocer of London and the second husband of John Aston's sister Alice.[98] Though Thomas Fermor was M.P. for High Wycombe in 1562–3,[99] he took no further part in public affairs, probably because, like his father, he was a recusant. He died in 1580, having provided that Somerton manor should be held by his executors in trust for his young son Richard.[1]

Richard came of age in 1596, and purchased Tusmore manor, which was to become the principal residence of the Fermor family.[2] His elder son John married Cicely Compton, but died without issue in 1625, leaving Somerton to his widow in dower.[3] Cicely married as her second husband Henry, Lord Arundell of Wardour, head of another leading Roman Catholic family,[4] and in 1627 leased lands at Somerton to Sir Richard Fermor.[5] When the latter died in 1643 his second son and heir, Henry Fermor, who had already moved to Tusmore, left his sister-in-law in occupation of Somerton.[6] While Henry maintained a prudent neutrality in the Civil Wars[7] his kinsmen rallied to the support of Charles I.[8] Lord Arundell's pro-royalist activities[9] led to his estates, including his wife's lands at Somerton, being sequestered in 1646. In 1653 Somerton was purchased for £1,609 15s. 10d. from the Treason Trustees on his behalf by his brother-in-law Humphrey Weld of Lulworth (Dors.), for the lives of Arundell and his wife Cicely,[10] and so Lord Arundell was in possession of Somerton manor-house in 1665.[11]

Henry Fermor died in 1673, having provided by will[12] that certain bequests in Somerton would only take effect after Cicely's death. His son Richard inherited Somerton when Cicely died in 1675.[13] The Fermors, however, continued to live at Tusmore, though they chose to be buried with their ancestors in the south aisle of Somerton church.

Richard Fermor died in 1684,[14] and was succeeded by five generations of Fermors, who continued the staunch Roman Catholic tradition of the family.[15]

William Fermor, the last of the direct male line, died in 1828, having sold Somerton in 1815 to the Earl of Jersey for £90,000.[16]

George Villiers, Earl of Jersey, who held the manor from 1815 until his death in 1859, was the principal landowner in the parish but resided at Middleton Stoney.[17] On the death of his son George Augustus Frederick Villiers, also in 1859, Somerton passed to his son Victor Albert George Villiers, the 7th earl.[18] After Lord Jersey's death in 1915 his Somerton estate was sold, much of it to Thomas Edwin Emberlin, who became lord of the manor.[19] In 1955 J. Emberlin Esq. was lord of the manor.

LESSER ESTATE. In the 1140's Alice de Langetot, widow of Roger de Chesney, lord of Heyford Warren, gave Eynsham Abbey 3 virgates in Somerton,[20] held of the honor of Wallingford.[21] In 1390 Eynsham received 10s. rent for two tenements in Somerton,[22] and about 1420 Richard Aston of Somerton held 2 virgates there of the abbey for the same rent.[23] The estate has not been traced subsequently.[24]

ECONOMIC HISTORY. The Anglo-Saxons doubtless chose to settle at Somerton largely on account of the good water-supply and the rich meadowland, which afforded pasture for cattle in the summer months when the uplands in this area were liable to drought. The old English name *Sumor-tun* means 'farm used in summer',[25] and it is possible that it was originally used for a part of the year only by the upland settlement at Fritwell and later permanently colonized from there.[26] By 1086 at all events the community at Somerton was unusually large for this neighbourhood. On the principal manor of 9 plough-lands there were 2 plough-teams and 1 serf in demesne, while 17 villeins (*villani*) and 9 bordars shared 7 plough-teams. The survey records a large extent of meadow (40 a.) and, what is more unusual in this part of the country, 156 acres of pasture. The value had risen steeply from £9 to £12 since the Conquest. On each of the smaller Somerton estates, each worth 20s., and now in the hands of one lord, there was land for 1 plough. In one case all the land was in demesne and was worked by one serf. There were 8 acres of meadow.[27] The total working population thus recorded was at least twenty-eight.

Domesday Book also records a settlement on an unidentified site at Northbrook. A certain Rainald held there of Roger d'Ivri two small holdings of 1 hide and ½ hide. On the larger estate there was

[92] *L. & P. Hen. VIII*, i (1), p. 46; i (2), p. 1542; Davenport, *Oxon. Sheriffs*.
[93] Blo. *Som.* 106.
[94] Ibid. 105.
[95] *O.A.S. Trans.* 1906, 19, 21.
[96] Ibid. 25.
[97] C.P. 40/1267, m. 339; *N. & Q.* 3rd ser. viii. 424. The Knightleys held land in Somerton from 1568: *R.C. Families*, i. 19; C.P. 40/1322, m. 518.
[98] C 3/1/14.
[99] *M.P.'s*, H.C. 69–I, p. 403 (1878), lxii (1).
[1] Blo. *Som.* 118.
[2] Davenport, *Oxon. Sheriffs*.
[3] Stapleton, *Cath. Miss.* 68.
[4] *R.C. Families*, iii. 236.
[5] Ibid. i. 35.
[6] Blo. *Som.* 121; Stapleton, *Cath. Miss.* 68; see below, p. 336.
[7] *Tusmore Papers*, ed. L. G. Wickham Legg (O.R.S. xx), p. ix.
[8] For his half-brother Col. Thomas Morgan see Blo.

Som. 120–1; *Par. Coll.* iii. 267.
[9] *R.C. Families*, iii. 236. He compounded in 1653 for some of his estates: ibid. 155.
[10] *Cal. Cttee. for Compounding*, 1223; C 54/3733/5.
[11] *Hearth Tax Oxon.* 192.
[12] *R.C. Families*, i. 27.
[13] Ibid. vi. 236; Blo. *Tus.* 64.
[14] Wood, *Life*, iii. 86.
[15] For the family succession see below, p. 336.
[16] O.R.O. J VIII e/5.
[17] Gardner, *Dir. Oxon.*
[18] *Complete Peerage*, vii. 91–93.
[19] *Kelly's Dir. Oxon.* (1920).
[20] *Eynsham Cart.* i. 104, 411.
[21] *Rot. Hund.* (Rec. Com.), ii. 838; see above, p. 198.
[22] *Eynsham Cart.* ii, p. lxxvi.
[23] Ibid. 48.
[24] Cf. ibid. p. lxviii.
[25] *P.N. Oxon.* (E.P.N.S.), i. 235; Ekwall, *Dict. E.P.N.*
[26] Suggested by Dr. W. G. Hoskins.
[27] *V.C.H. Oxon.* i. 404, 418, 419.

1 plough-team in demesne, and 5 peasants had ½ plough. Its value of 20s. remained unchanged since the Conquest. The figures given for the smaller holding are so high that it is likely that the returns from the two estates may have been partly amalgamated. Though there was only ½ plough-land, there was one plough-team on the demesne and another shared by 9 peasants. The value of the holding had risen from 10s. to 30s. The hamlet was next mentioned in 1220, when it was included in the 12 carucates of Somerton.[28] A fine of 1244 shows that land there—2 carucates in Somerton and Northbrook—belonged to the Barony of Arsic and became part of the De Grey manor of Somerton,[29] and the survey of 1279 records that Ardley manor consisted of ½ fee in Ardley and ½ fee in the part of the vill of Somerton called Northbrook.[30]

By this time Somerton itself had grown in size and its tenurial structure had become more complicated. The De Grey and the De Gardinis manors[31] held 16 virgates of arable in demesne with appurtenant meadow and pasture. On the De Grey manor 2 villeins held a virgate each for 3s. 8d. rent, owed works and tallage, and had to pay fines at the lord's will if their sons left the manor, while on the two manors 26 half-virgaters held on the same terms but in proportion to the size of their holdings.

The comparatively new class of fifteen free tenants apparently held 18½ virgates. The most important was Simon son of Master, who held a hide by the service of providing in war-time a man to guard Robert de Grey's *curia* at Somerton for 40 days. There were three other De Grey tenants who probably held about 4 virgates. Seven free tenants of the De Gardinis manor held 7½ virgates between them. Among the free tenants were two members of the De Broke family, lords of Finmere, who each held 2 virgates partly let to undertenants of De Grey and De Gardinis respectively, and had inherited the land from Lawrence de Broke, who had acquired it in the 1230's and 1240's.[32] Another important free tenant was Eynsham Abbey with 3 virgates, which it was leasing for 15s. a year.[33] Other religious houses, whose small properties were not mentioned in the survey of 1279, were Merton Priory, with rents worth £1 4s. 8d., and Cogges Priory, with a rent worth 2s.[34] Thus about 49 virgates of cultivated land are accounted for.

Extents of 1300 and 1312 for the De Grey manor and of 1267 for the De Gardinis manor add further details about the economy of Somerton in the late 13th and early 14th centuries. In 1300 there were 128 acres of arable in demesne, valued at 4d. an acre, 10 acres of meadow valued at 3s. the acre, and pasture valued at 2s. yearly. The fishery was worth 12d., the water-mill 20s., rents of freemen amounted to 13s. 2¼d. and of 20 half-virgaters to 22½d. The last

also owed works with 4 ploughs (2½d. a plough), and day-work every second day between the feasts of the Nativity of St. John the Baptist and Michaelmas, amounting to 26 works, each work being valued at 1d. The value of all works and customs was £4 3s. 4d., and the total value of the manor was £10 0s. 10¼d.[35] In the extent of 1312 there are slight variations. Pasture, for instance, was worth 10s. between Easter and Michaelmas, while free tenants paid 6s. 6d. in rents and a coulter worth 1d., and 48 villeins £3 17s. 5d. in rents. Their works between Midsummer and Michaelmas were worth £3 0s. 1d. Fixed rents were worth £4 4s.[36]

On the smaller De Gardinis manor 40 acres of arable were worth 20s., or 6d. an acre, but meadowland (8 a.) was less valuable there than on the De Grey manor, being worth only 1s. 8d. an acre. Free tenants' rents came to £1, villeins' rents to £1, and their works to £1.[37]

Early 14th-century tax returns indicate a prosperous parish: after the market-town of Bicester and Stoke Lyne, more people (i.e. 53) were taxed than in any other parish in the hundred.[38] Many of them were substantial men. The population in the late 14th century was also one of the largest in the hundred, for 108 adults were listed for the poll tax of 1377.[39]

By the 16th century the pattern of land-holding had changed still further. Of the 39 persons assessed for the subsidy of 1524 at least 11 were wage-earners.[40] Later in the century, when the greater part of the parish was owned by the Fermors, a list of the tenants of the manor in 1573 shows that there were 2 non-resident freeholders, Sir John Arundell and the heirs of Nicholas Odill,[41] and 19 other tenants, 3 of whom were cottagers. They held at will or for life. About 38 virgates were held by the 16 farmer tenants, but 2 of these, it may be noted, held properties of more than average size consisting of 7¼ and 5½ virgates respectively. The average rent was between 10s. and 15s. a virgate.[42]

Few Somerton families had a connexion of more than 100 years with the parish. The Astons, however, were an exception. William Aston, Esq., the son of John and Isabel Aston and donor of a church bell in 1635,[43] was probably a descendant of the 15th-century Aston family, members of which had once been lords of a Somerton manor[44] and later became tenants of the purchasers, the Fermors. William's mother was a lessee under the Fermors of an estate of 2 yardlands.[45] Of the sixteen tenants in 1573, not counting cottagers, two-thirds came from families which had been in the parish at least since 1530, while five were from new families.[46] But 100 years later, in 1665, only three of these families were prosperous enough to be assessed for the hearth tax.[47] By 1720 only one family, the Hores, remained

[28] *V.C.H. Oxon.* i. 415, 416; *Bk. of Fees*, 319.
[29] *Fines Oxon.* 237. For the Arsic connexion see above, p. 291.
[30] *Rot. Hund.* (Rec. Com.), ii. 838.
[31] Ibid. 838–9.
[32] *Fines Oxon.* 102, 121, 123, 128.
[33] See above, p. 293.
[34] *Tax. Eccl.* (Rec. Com.), 45. The Merton property has not been traced and it is not clear which Merton is referred to. For the connexion between Cogges and Somerton see below, p. 296.
[35] C 133/72/6. Cf. Inq. p.m. of 1295: Blo. *Som.* 97.
[36] Blo. *Som.* 97.

[37] C 132/34/9.
[38] E 179/161/8.
[39] Ibid. 161/39.
[40] Ibid. 161/176.
[41] *O.A.S Trans.* 1906, 22. For the Odills or Woodhulls of Mollington see *Oxon. Visit.* 198.
[42] *O.A.S. Trans.* 1906, 25–27: roll of Court of the Supervisor, 1573, for which see ibid. 3. For other court rolls see ibid. 10–24.
[43] *Ch. Bells Oxon.* iv. 379.
[44] See above, p. 292.
[45] *O.A.S. Trans.* 1906, 26.
[46] Ibid. 17, 25–26.
[47] *Hearth Tax Oxon.* 192.

from the tenants of 1573.[48] In the 18th century family fortunes changed even more quickly: of the tenants of 1720, only the Collingridges and Hores were assessable for land tax in 1786.[49] The Hores were thus the one yeoman family which survived as tenants from the 16th to the 19th century. In 1700 there were three branches of them, all with substantial farms, worth together between a quarter and a fifth of the value of the whole parish.[50] By the end of the century the family held one small farm.[51]

The Mynnes are of interest as a family which rose into the ranks of the gentry from small beginnings. In the 16th century they were simple husbandmen, although prosperous ones,[52] renting one farm of 3 yardlands.[53] William Mynne, on the other hand, the last of the family and a recusant who was buried in the church in 1665,[54] was a gentleman who had built up a considerable landed estate in several places.[55]

Between the 16th and the 18th centuries the Fermors got possession of the whole parish. In about 1720 the total yearly value of James Fermor's estate of 48 yardlands was £478.[56] Almost all the land was let out, the Fermors only keeping in hand Ladyham Close, some woods and several plots of furze in the common fields. There were 25 tenants, 13 of them smallholders and cottagers, and the rest substantial farmers with farms of between 2 and 5½ yardlands, who paid rents varying between £13 and £50. The hearth-tax returns of 1665 bear out this evidence of a prosperous group of yeomen. Out of 17 householders listed for the tax a high proportion had comfortable houses in the village. Five of them, however, were discharged owing to poverty,[57] and nine others listed in 1662 were not listed again. The population continued to be comparatively large: 242 adults were recorded in 1676.

Until the second half of the 18th century Somerton was an open-field parish, for an incipient movement to inclose in the 16th century had been checked. In 1512 William Fermor, who was also inclosing at Hardwick, was accused of converting 40 acres in demesne from arable to pasture.[58] There was talk in 1736 of inclosing about 20 acres of 'poorland', which had been planted with sainfoin.[59] A little later some new inclosures were made by William Fermor.[60]

The only evidence for the field system comes from 17th-century terriers. They show that there were four fields in 1634:[61] one lay north of the road to Ardley and adjoined Fritwell Moor; a second lay on the south side of the Ardley road; and the other two fields were on both sides of the Bicester road. By 1685 the field names had been altered and possibly some changes in cropping practice had been introduced;[62] by 1734 the glebe was divided among seven 'quarters'.[63]

There is no clear evidence for the area of the Somerton yardland, but in 1765, when the parish was inclosed, there were said to be 48½ yardlands or about 1,800 acres of common land.[64] This would make each yardland of arable, meadow, and pasture consist of about 37 acres. It may be noted here that although Somerton's pastures were always fairly rich and comparatively extensive, they were carefully stinted. In the 16th century the holder of each yardland was allowed to keep five horses or oxen at most and 30 sheep on the common in winter. The stint was rigorously enforced by the court, and even the lady of the manor's son was presented in the 1560's for overstocking the common with sheep.[65]

In 1765 William Fermor obtained an Act of Parliament to inclose the open fields: it was a simple matter as except for the glebe he was the sole owner. How far inclosure contributed to the increase in population which took place in the second half of the century is uncertain. According to Blomfield there was an excess of 68 deaths over births in the period 1670 to 1749, but between 1766 and 1785 there was an excess of 33 births over deaths.[66] During the Napoleonic war population continued to increase, and by 1821 had reached 400. The cost of maintaining the poor also rose steeply at this time, as elsewhere. The average sum raised between 1773 and 1775 was about £120; in 1803 it was £272.[67] Another indication of poverty in the early 19th century comes from a note in the Overseers' Book for 1819 to 1823.[68] It states that all women able to work were to go to the overseer, who would instruct them where to go on their rounds and allow them 6d. a day.

One effect of inclosure was probably to accelerate the process of increasing the size of farms, which was already under way. In 1820 the twelve farms of 1720 had been reduced to five, the largest, Troy farm, having over 600 acres.[69] This pattern of landholding continued through the 19th century. When the manor was sold in 1919 it still consisted of three large and two small farms,[70] covering the whole parish except for the glebe land. At present (1956) there are seven farms of which four are over 250 acres.[71]

The effect of inclosure on farming practice is uncertain. Judging from a map of 1797,[72] a high proportion of the land was devoted to pasture. This trend continued into the following centuries: in the second half of the 19th century two Somerton farmers were well-known sheep-breeders, and just over half the cultivated land was under grass;[73] in the 20th century Somerton has had a high reputation for its dairy products.[74] Its population in 1801 numbered only 254. It fell sharply after 1821 from 400 to 329 in 1841 as a result of the agricultural depression.

[48] O.R.O. Reg. of Papists' estates, pp. 87–90.
[49] Ibid. Land tax assess.
[50] MS. Top. Oxon. d 351, f. 32.
[51] O.R.O. Land tax assess.
[52] E 179/161/176; ibid. 162/319; Bodl. MS. Wills Oxon. 189, f. 195: will of Thos. Mynne, d. 1593; ibid. 193, f. 84: will of Wm. Mynne, d. 1604.
[53] O.A.S. Trans. 1906, 26.
[54] Stapleton, Cath. Miss. 71.
[55] P.C.C. 66 Carr.
[56] O.R.O. Reg. of Papists' estates, pp. 87–90.
[57] Hearth Tax Oxon. 192, 235.
[58] Dom. of Incl. i. 348–9, 367.
[59] Req. 2/40/102.
[60] O.R.O. Incl. act.

[61] Oxf. Archd. Oxon. b 41, ff. 101–2; cf. H. L. Gray, Eng. Field Systems, 493–4.
[62] Oxf. Archd. Oxon. b 41, f. 108.
[63] Ibid. f. 99.
[64] 5 Geo. III, c. 83 (priv. act) (copy in O.R.O. and in Bodl. G.A. Oxon. 4° 349); Incl. award in O.R.O. deals only with roads.
[65] O.A.S. Trans. 1906, 21–22.
[66] Blo. Som. 127.
[67] O.R.O. Land tax assess.
[68] Par. Rec.
[69] O.R.O. J VIII a/25.
[70] Ibid. e/29: estate map.
[71] Local inf.
[72] Davis, Oxon. Map.
[73] Wing, Annals, 133; Blo. Som. 159.
[74] J. B. Orr, Agric. in Oxon. 41.

It recovered slightly, but fell again after 1871 to 265 in 1901. In 1951 there were 220 inhabitants.[75]

Although most of the inhabitants of Somerton have always been farmers or labourers,[76] some had other occupations. Outstanding among these was milling. In 1086 the mill paid a rent of 20s. a year and 400 eels;[77] in the late 13th century, when it belonged to the De Greys, it was rented for 20s.[78] By the 15th century there were two mills: one was called Somerham mill,[79] and the other, since it belonged to John Fuller,[80] was presumably a fulling mill. In the next century three mills are recorded, Somerham mill and two others belonging to the Fermors. Both then and in the preceding century the miller at Somerham mill was presented in the court for flooding the meadow-land.[81] By the 18th century there was only one mill left to the Fermors: it was let with the mill-house and meadow for £28.[82] In the 19th century its rent varied between £90 and £145, and it gave employment to a manager and five men.[83]

Two 16th-century bakers and a butcher have left a record because they cheated their customers.[84] In the 18th century there was a shop and a bakehouse, as well as a butcher, a shoemaker, a blacksmith, and a carpenter.[85] The fuller records of the 19th century supply the names of a number of additional trades: in the first quarter there was a brickmaker;[86] in 1851 there were a stonemason and a thatcher, two dressmakers, a tailor, a lacemaker, a smockmaker, a wheelwright, an instrument-maker, and a contractor and two men employed on railway work.[87]

CHURCH. Somerton church must have been in existence by 1074, when a grant was made of the tithes of Northbrook, part of Somerton parish (see below). In 1107 the church with its tithes and the land of William the priest was given by Manasses Arsic to the alien priory of Cogges,[88] but this grant either never materialized, or the church was later lost by the priory, for in the early 13th century Robert Arsic, lord of the manor from 1205, gave the advowson to the London hospital of St. Thomas of Acon, belonging to the military order of St. Thomas the Martyr.[89] The canons of St. Thomas obtained possession, but by 1222, when they presented to the church, they were planning to transfer the advowson to a proposed convent at Medley.[90] This never came into existence, and the advowson returned to the manor.

In 1231 the two Arsic heiresses, Alexandra de la Haye and Joan de Grenvile, and their husbands were disputing about the advowson after Eustace de Grenvile, Joan's husband, had tried to present his nephew.[91] Finally an agreement was made: the first presentation was to be made together, and the following ones alternately by the two couples and their heirs.[92] This arrangement continued until the two parts of the manor were united by the Fermors.[93] Because part of the manor was often in the hands of the king, there were royal presentations in 1392, 1398, 1496, and 1504.

From 1537 the Fermors acted as patrons, but by the end of the 16th century were disqualified from doing so as Roman Catholics. Lord Arundell, who chose the rector in 1660,[94] was the only lord of the manor after the Reformation to do so, and the advowson frequently changed hands. It was common practice for the purchaser to present either himself or a member of his family. In 1719, for example, Sir Edward Cobb of Adderbury named John Cobb, his younger brother,[95] as rector;[96] Barfoot Cotton and Henry Wintle in 1769 and 1804 became rectors on their own nomination.[97] By 1875 the patron was William Barnes, a banker,[98] who presented his son, G. E. Barnes, one of the last of the hunting parsons.[99] The advowson now (1956) belongs to W. G. Barnes of Horsham (Suss.).

In the Middle Ages Somerton was a rectory of medium value. In 1254 it was valued at £5 and in 1291 at £6 13s. 4d.[1] By the 16th century the value had risen to £15 1s. 9d.[2] From at least 1291, and probably before, the rector paid a pension of 6s. 8d. to Oseney Abbey.[3] It came from the demesne tithes of Northbrook, part of Somerton parish which was held with Ardley manor;[4] two-thirds of these tithes had been granted in the late 11th century by Robert d'Oilly to his church of St. George in Oxford castle, which was given to Oseney Abbey in 1149.[5] In 1253 Oseney was still collecting these tithes in kind, for when it summoned the lord of the manor before the ecclesiastical court for non-payment he promised to follow the old custom of carrying the sheaves to his barn, having them tithed there and safely kept until the arrival of the tithe-collector.[6]

The effect of the Reformation on the financial position of the church cannot be assessed, as no valuations have been found, but it is known that in the 17th century the glebe consisted of 2½ yardlands in the common fields, with right of common for

[75] Census, 1821–1951; V.C.H. Oxon. ii. 221.
[76] e.g. Oxf. Dioc. d 554.
[77] V.C.H. Oxon. i. 404.
[78] Blo. Som. 97; Rot. Hund. (Rec. Com.), ii. 838.
[79] O.A.S. Trans. 1906, 11.
[80] Ibid.; called Scrowe's mill in 16th cent.: ibid. 22.
[81] Ibid. 11, 20.
[82] O.R.O. Reg. of Papists' estates, pp. 87–90.
[83] Ibid. J VIII e/1, 10, 16.
[84] O.A.S. Trans. 1906, 12; O.R.O. Reg. of Papists' estates, pp. 87–90; Blo. Som. 128.
[85] O.R.O. Cal. Q. Sess.
[86] Par. Rec. Overseers' accts.
[87] H.O. 107/1729.
[88] V.C.H. Oxon. ii. 161; O.A.S. Rep. 1930, 321–2. Cogges's rent of 2s. in Somerton, recorded in 1291, probably dates from a grant by Manasses Arsic of two-thirds of the demesne tithes in 1103: ibid.; Tax. Eccl. (Rec. Com.), 45.
[89] Rot. Welles, ii. 8; V.C.H. Lond. i. 491.
[90] Rot. Welles, ii. 8. The consent of the Bishop and Chapter of Lincoln and the Abbey of Fécamp (Nor-

mandy) were required for the foundation. The Medley referred to may have been an Oseney manor: Oseney Cart. iv. 86–91.
[91] See above, p. 291; Rot. Welles, ii. 35.
[92] Fines Oxon. 89.
[93] Cal. Inq. p.m. x, p. 406; Cal. Pat. 1396–9, 482. For a list of medieval presentations see MS. Top. Oxon. d 460; see above, p. 292.
[94] Blo. Som. 142.
[95] G. E. C. Baronetage, iii. 268.
[96] Blo. Som. 143.
[97] Ibid. 144.
[98] Ibid. 145.
[99] Venn, Alumni.
[1] Lunt, Val. Norw. 312; Tax. Eccl. (Rec. Com.), 31.
[2] Valor Eccl. (Rec. Com.), ii. 160.
[3] Tax. Eccl. 31. But see Valor Eccl. ii. 160 and Oseney Cart. vi. 245, where the pension is given as 7s. 6d.
[4] See above, p. 294.
[5] Oxon. Chart. no. 58; Oseney Cart. iv, 26; V.C.H. Oxon. ii. 90.
[6] Oseney Cart. vi. 28–29.

105 sheep and 8 beasts.[7] In the early 18th century the living was said to be worth about £160.[8] In 1766, at the inclosure award, the glebe was exchanged for 44 acres, and the tithes commuted for £150.[9] In the early 19th century, when the glebe and parsonage were let for £75, the rector reckoned that the exchange had not been beneficial and that the tithes on 1,800 acres of inclosed land were worth £800.[10]

The connexion between the manor and church was especially close in the 14th century, when two members of the De Gardinis family were rectors for many years. In 1323, when Richard de Gardinis was rector (1316–49), the bishop granted eleven days' indulgence to those praying for the souls of William de Gardinis (d. 1287) or his wife, and to those who had contributed to the building of the lady chapel.[11] In 1330 Richard was given permission to found a chantry in this chapel; the chaplain, who was to be supported by 5 marks' worth of land in Somerton, was to say daily service in honour of the Virgin.[12] It may also have been Richard who rebuilt the chancel. He died in 1349, probably of the plague.[13] William de Gardinis (by 1377–92) was a cousin, it seems, of the Giffards, who had become joint patrons,[14] and is alleged to have committed robbery with violence.[15]

In common with many other churches Somerton suffered in the later Middle Ages from the abuses of non-residence and pluralism. Robert Marying (by 1401–18) was allowed to be non-resident for seven years and to let his Rectory while he was at the papal court, studying at a university, or in the service of a spiritual lord.[16] His successor, Richard Compton (1418–?), 'of noble race', was allowed to be a pluralist.[17] In the early 16th century Robert Nelson though apparently resident was, it seems, otherwise undesirable: he allegedly kept three women in his house.[18] Later, the distinguished Robert King,[19] presented to the church in 1537 by William Fermor, held many other offices and had a curate, Thomas Gardiner, at Somerton, who replaced him in 1552.[20] King is of interest as a conservative reformer, who opposed those who wished to 'pull down the images of the Saints, and who denied that the Virgin and Saints are mediators'.[21]

Among the post-Reformation rectors, many of whom were above the average in ability, William Juxon probably influenced the parish most. As Vicar of St. Giles' in Oxford he had been much frequented for 'his edifying way of preaching', and after his presentation to Somerton in 1615[22] he built a new Rectory and spent six years there before he succeeded Laud in 1621 as President of St. John the Baptist's College.[23] When president he had a curate[24] at

Somerton, but spent his vacations there until he resigned the living in 1633.[25] He remembered the parish at his death, when he left £50 for the poor of Somerton.[26] His religious views were shared by his successor, Thomas Walker, presented by the king in 1633, and probably removed from his benefice in 1647, when the church registers cease.[27] Although restored later to the Mastership of University College,[28] he was never reinstated at Somerton. Two dissenting ministers followed him there after 1647: Edward Archer, a moderate, who signed a protest against the execution of the king,[29] and John Fenwick,[30] perhaps less moderate, as he was connected by marriage with Joshua and William Sprigg,[31] two active Independent preachers and pamphleteers. But the survival of the medieval reredos testifies that the sympathy of at least some of the parishioners was not with the Puritans. Influenced possibly by the strong Roman Catholic element, they are said to have concealed the reredos.[32] In the late 17th century, after 1672 when Samuel Jemmatt (1665–1713) ceased to reside,[33] the parish appears to have been left mainly in charge of a curate, and in the time of John Cobb (1719–25), Warden of New College,[34] non-residence must have been the rule for at least a part of the year.

For a good part of the 18th century the parish was fortunate in having a conscientious priest. John Watson (1729–69), still remembered by his charity, lived and worked zealously among his parishioners. Though he laboured so that 'none should be perverted to popery', he did not favour a revival of the penal laws against the large Roman Catholic community. As for his own parishioners he reported that though 'some frequent the church tolerably well',[35] too many were absent on account of the 'contemporary disregard for religion', and that there was 'too much tippling at the ale-house on Sunday'; in fact he found too many who were 'common drunkards and swearers'.[36] A persistent absentee from church was the blacksmith; between 1745 and 1760 he was reported as always absent. The miller was another backslider, but he may have been a papist.[37] The church itself was also kept in decent order: by 1766 it had been whitewashed throughout and a new pulpit set up, while orders had been given for painting the king's arms and putting up the creed and sentences.[38]

After Watson's death in 1769 there began a long period of non-residence which continued until about 1850, the parish being considered too small and poor to support a resident priest. Barfoot Cotton (1769–1804), for instance, a pluralist,[39] was in 1801

[7] Blo. *Som.* 146–7; Oxf. Arch. Oxon. b 41, ff. 100–1.
[8] Blo. *Som.* 147.
[9] O.R.O. Incl. award.
[10] Oxf. Dioc. c 658, f. 144; c 662, ff. 115–16.
[11] Blo. *Som.* 132.
[12] *Cal. Pat.* 1330–4, 18. This chantry is not mentioned in the 16th-cent. certificates.
[13] Linc. Reg. ix, Gynewell, f. 242b. His successor also died in the summer of 1349: ibid. f. 244.
[14] See above, p. 292.
[15] *Cal. Pat.* 1377–81, 91.
[16] *Cal. Papal L.* v. 500.
[17] Ibid. vii. 531.
[18] *Visit. Dioc. Linc. 1517–31*, i. 123.
[19] See above, p. 291.
[20] Blo. *Som.* 137.
[21] *V.C.H. Oxon.* ii. 28; *L. & P. Hen. VIII*, ix, p. 207.
[22] Blo. *Som.* 138.

[23] For his life see *D.N.B.*; above, p. 291.
[24] e.g. Robert Kenrick: *Walker Rev.* 364; *Cal. S.P. Dom.* 1660–1, 417.
[25] Blo. *Som.* 140.
[26] Ibid. 139.
[27] Ibid. 140.
[28] W. Carr, *Univ. Coll.* 125–6.
[29] *Calamy Rev.* 14.
[30] Ibid. 193.
[31] For them see *D.N.B.*
[32] See below, p. 298.
[33] Blo. *Som.* 142.
[34] For him see G.E.C. *Baronetage*, iii. 268 note a; Hearne, *Remarks*, iii. 331; v. 377.
[35] Oxf. Dioc. d 554, d 557.
[36] Oxf. Archd. Oxon. c 102, f. 2.
[37] Blo. *Som.* 150.   [38] Ibid.
[39] Venn, *Alumni*.

accused by the bishop of neglecting the parish by appointing a non-resident curate who was not in orders. The curate, however, supported by the churchwardens, denied the charge that the sacrament had not been administered for several years.[40] Henry Wintle (1804–31), another non-resident rector,[41] hired curates,[42] who resided in part of the Rectory, which had been repaired early in the century after long being uninhabitable.[43] But it was not until about 1850 that the parish obtained a resident rector. When Bishop Wilberforce ordered Robert Clifton, rector since 1831, to reside he pleaded the absence of a suitable house as a cause of his absence and the 17th-century parsonage was accordingly replaced by a new one.[44] In 1854 large congregations of between 140 and 190 were reported, and the sacrament was administered monthly, instead of the five times a year customary in the 18th century.[45] Though the rector later wrote of the need for social activities as a counter-attraction to the public house, drinking being the chief hindrance to his ministry, as many as 220 out of a population of 300 were said to come to church in 1869.[46]

The church of *ST. JAMES* is a fine stone building consisting of a chancel, clerestoried nave, north aisle, south chapel, north porch, and western tower.[47] All that now remains of the original 12th-century church is a blocked-up doorway in the centre of the south wall of the nave. The north aisle was added in the late 12th or early 13th century, and is separated from the nave by an arcade of four arches carried on circular columns. A single late-13th-century window indicates that the chancel was probably rebuilt at that period, but the sedilia and the other windows date from the 14th century. The east window and the chancel arch are 19th-century restorations.

On the south side of the nave are two 14th-century arches which indicate that a south aisle preceded the existing chapel. The spring of another unfinished arch shows that a third bay was intended but never built.

In the north aisle are two early 14th-century recesses: one may have been originally the tomb of Sir William de Gardinis (d. 1287), for in 1323 an indulgence was granted to all persons praying for the repose of his soul at the newly erected altar to the Virgin in this aisle.[48] Square-headed windows were inserted later in the east and west walls. The tower dates from the late 14th century, but the battlements and pinnacles were added in the 15th century. On the north side there is a shallow niche which contains a finely carved holy rood,[49] probably of late-14th-century date. The clerestory and a

battlemented parapet were added to the nave and aisles in the late 15th or early 16th century, perhaps when the Fermor chantry (see below) was built, and the tie-beam roof of the nave, supported on carved corbels, dates from about the same period. At the beginning of the 16th century the east end of the south aisle, which he probably lengthened, was converted into a chantry by William Fermor; he inserted new windows, made a new entrance, and built the present round-headed arch which gives access to the aisle from the chancel. The aisle became the burial-place of the Fermor family, which was responsible for its upkeep until the end of the 19th century.[50]

The original high-pitched chancel roof survived until the beginning of the 19th century and was replaced, probably in 1811, by a flat one;[51] about this time the east window was lowered and the 15th-century oak seats were removed except for the few that can still be seen (1956) in the north aisle. In 1825 seats were inserted under the gallery for the use of the schoolchildren;[52] in 1854 £75 was spent on repairs to the church, when the chancel arch was rebuilt and new flooring put down.[53] By 1889 the church was reported to be unsafe by the architect J. D. Sedding.[54] The building was conservatively restored in 1891 at a cost of about £2,500. In addition to repairs to the nave and roof, a buttress was added to the north wall of the chancel.[55]

The 14th-century hexagonal font is unusual. A few medieval tiles have survived. The stone reredos, perhaps of early 14th-century date, is also notable. It represents Christ with eleven of His Apostles at the Last Supper and is similar to an altar-piece at Bampton, which is made of stone from Brize Norton. In the 17th century the reredos is said to have been hidden to save it from being destroyed by the Puritans,[56] but in 1658 it was seen by Wood.[57] In 1822, after having been restored at the rector's expense, it was replaced in its original position.[58]

The chancel screen dates partly from the 15th century. The loft and vaulting have gone, and the lower panels were restored by J. D. Sedding in 1891.[59] The shield with Bishop Juxon's arms was added in 1632. Two late 15th or early 16th-century screens separate the south chapel from the nave, and a Jacobean screen completes the inclosure of the Fermor aisle.[60] The reading-desk was renewed in 1757 and the pulpit in 1764.[61] The oak screen in the tower door designed by Thomas Garner was erected in memory of the Coronation of Edward VII and the carved oak vestry screen was added in 1915.[62] Electricity was put in in 1936.[63] Two glass panels

[40] Oxf. Dioc. c 655, ff. 136–8, 142.
[41] Ibid. c 429, f. 118.
[42] Ibid. d 573; ibid. c 658, f. 144. In 1813 the curate's salary was £50: ibid. d 705, f. 243.
[43] Oxf. Archd. Oxon. c 102, f. 77.
[44] Blo. *Som.* 145; see above, p. 291.
[45] *Wilb. Visit.*
[46] Oxf. Dioc. c 332, c 335.
[47] For an early account of the building, see Blo. *Som.* 130–4.
[48] Ibid. 132, quoting Linc. Reg. For Sir William see above, p. 292.
[49] Blo. *Som.* 131; O.A.H.S. *Proc.* 1870, N.S. ii. 215.
[50] The Ramsays of Croughton (Northants) were said to be responsible for the aisle in 1889: MS. Top. Oxon. d 42, f. 166.
[51] Par. Rec. Churchwardens' accts.: £62 was spent in this year. The marks of the old roof against the nave can

be seen in a drawing in MS. Top. Oxon. a 68, f. 482.
[52] Oxf. Archd. Oxon. c 102, f. 102; Blo. *Som.* 134.
[53] Blo. *Som.* 134; Par. Rec. Churchwardens' accts.
[54] MS. Top. Oxon. d 42, f. 166.
[55] Bodl. Par. Box (uncat.), faculty; list of subscribers in MS. Top. Oxon. c 105, f. 206. There are drawings by J. Buckler (1823) of the church before restoration in MS. Top. Oxon. a 68, ff. 481–2.
[56] Blo. *Som.* 131 and n. 3.
[57] *Par. Coll.* iii. 268.
[58] Blo. *Som.* 131.
[59] O.A.S. *Rep.* 1902, 14.
[60] *Arch. Jnl.* 1910, lxvii, 196, where there are 2 photographs.
[61] Oxf. Archd. Oxon. d 13, f. 33; c 102, f. 24; Blo. *Som.* 150.
[62] Clarke MS.; *Kelly's Dir. Oxon.* (1939).
[63] Par. Rec.

with Juxon's arms were erected in the 17th century in the east window of the chancel; these were later removed to the Rectory.[64]

The church is chiefly noted for the fine 16th-century monuments in the Fermor chapel. There is a brass to William Fermor (d. 1552) and his wife Elizabeth Norreys, with figures and shields of arms. There is an alabaster monument to Thomas Fermor (d. 1580) and his wife Bridget Bradshaw, who are represented with their four children. The tomb was originally inscribed in gold lettering and embellished with painted coats of arms; traces of the original colouring can just be seen. The agreement for the making of the tomb between Thomas Fermor's executors and the masons, Richard and Gabriel Roiley of Burton-on-Trent, survives: they charged £40, and Gabriel Roiley and his man spent about six weeks in Somerton putting up the tomb.[65] There is also a large monument to Sir Richard Fermor (d. 1642/3), with an heraldic escutcheon and the figure of a recumbent man in armour. Of similar design is the tomb of Sir John Fermor (d. 1625). There is an undated wall tablet to James Smith and a floor slab to Colonel Thomas Morgan, husband of Jane Fermor, who was killed at the battle of Newbury in 1643. There are many other inscriptions to members of the Fermor family and their wives: to Henry (d. 1672/3), his son Richard (d. 1684/5), and his son Henry (d. 1702/3). Later holders of the manor buried there are James Fermor (d. 1722), Henry Fermor (d. 1746/7), William Fermor (d. 1806), Richard (d. 1817), and William Fermor of Tusmore (d. 1828), the last Fermor to be buried in Somerton. On the north side of the chancel arch there is a wall tablet to William Mynne, gentleman (d. 1665), and Mary Mynne (d. 1659/60). There is a floor slab to Richard Todkill, gentleman and school-master (d. 1656/7). A stone to James Wilmer, curate (d. 1641), mentioned by Wood, is no longer visible.[66]

In 1552 the church had three bells and a sanctus bell. It owned a silver chalice, as well as vestments.[67] In 1955 it had an inscribed silver chalice (c. 1750), which was mentioned in 1757.[68] Five of the church's ring of six bells were cast in the Chalcombe foundry between 1635 and 1707. All are inscribed, the tenor being given by William Aston, 'esquire', and the fourth by John Hore, churchwarden.[69]

The registers date from 1627, with a gap between 1647 and 1660. There are churchwardens' accounts from 1778.

The medieval cross in the churchyard has its shafts and steps still intact. It is thought there was once a Roman Catholic burial-ground under part of the school, as several skeletons and a silver cross were found under the floor in the 19th century.[70]

ROMAN CATHOLICISM. From the 16th to the 19th century, owing to the influence of its lords of the manor—the Fermor family—Somerton was one of the chief Roman Catholic centres in Oxfordshire. Unlike his elder brother, Sir Richard Fermor of Easton Neston (Northants),[71] William Fermor did not oppose Henry VIII's religious policy, but rather acted in support of the royal supremacy.[72] Sir Richard's son Thomas, who succeeded to Somerton in 1552, and his descendants, however, were all staunch adherents of the Roman faith,[73] but only one member of the family, Cornelia, wife of Sir Richard Fermor (d. 1643), seems to have been fined for recusancy.[74] In 1700 a commission, appointed to inquire into whether certain recusant estates in Oxfordshire had been used unlawfully for superstitious purposes,[75] held an inquiry at the White Hart Inn at Wheatley. Among the accused was Henry Fermor, who was said to have given his Somerton lands in trust to the Jesuits of St. Omer. Two local men, tenants of Fermor at Somerton, gave evidence regarding the value of the estate, and of popish practices in the village. The result of the inquiry does not appear, but it is probable that no penalty was imposed. In 1705 Henry Fermor's house was searched to see if he was contravening the law by keeping a horse, and the houses of two farmers, Collingridge and East, were also searched.

During Thomas Fermor's life-time there was a chapel in the courtyard of the old castle,[76] which may have been the original medieval chapel, or which may have been newly built by Thomas Fermor and used during Mary's reign for Catholic services.[77]

The chapel in the house, seen by the antiquary Rawlinson before 1718,[78] was probably built in the 16th century, when it seems to have been in regular use. In an account book of the Fermors there is an entry of 1580 for 10s. paid to the 'prest for his wages',[79] which suggests that mass was celebrated in the house. There is no other record of a resident priest, but at the inquiry of 1700 it was alleged that a Mr. Weston, who had been in the parish, was a reputed priest.[80]

Though the Fermors ceased to live at Somerton in about 1625, the chapel in the house continued in use. In 1738 the rector reported that papists met there once a month for services held by a priest from Tusmore[81] or Godington. Later, when the chapel had become a ruin with the manor-house, occasional services were held in a farm-house by a priest from Tusmore, but generally all the adults worshipped at Tusmore, though some of the younger children attended the parish church at Somerton.[82]

The Catholic community was probably always a

---

[64] In 1955 they were stored in the church. For armorial glass see Lamborn, *Arm. Glass*, 155–6. There are five small quarries, with arms or crest of Juxon, four of them dated 1630. There are also two larger and older quarries, from the Fermor chapel, with the initials w. e. for Wm. Fermor (d. 1552) and his third wife Elizabeth Norreys.

[65] The indenture of agreement and some accounts connected with the tomb are in *Arch. Jnl.* 1851, viii. 181, 185–6. The tomb was not finished until 1583.

[66] For inscriptions see *Par. Coll.* iii. 264–70, and *Gent. Mag.* 1827, xcvii (1), 115–16, reprinted in *Gent. Mag. Library*, ed. G. L. Gomme, *English Topography*, ix (1897), 207–15, where all the Fermor inscriptions and a pedigree of the family are given. For arms see Bodl. G.A. Oxon. 4° 687, pp. 264–9; 4° 689, pp. 264–8; 16° 217, p. 220.

[67] *Chant. Cert.* 86.

[68] Evans, *Ch. Plate.*

[69] *Ch. Bells Oxon.* iv. 378–9.

[70] Stapleton, *Cath. Miss.* 67 n. 1.

[71] Blo. *Som.* 105 n. 3.

[72] Ibid. 104–5.

[73] See below, p. 338.

[74] Salter, *Oxon. Recusants*, 26.

[75] MS. Top. Oxon. d 351, ff. 31–32.

[76] *12th Rep. Com. Char.* 309, citing Thomas Fermor's will.

[77] Blo. *Som.* 124; see below, p. 300.

[78] *Par. Coll.* iii. 268.

[79] *Arch. Jnl.* 1851, viii. 184.

[80] MS. Top. Oxon. d 351, f. 32.

[81] Oxf. Dioc. d 554.

[82] Ibid. c 327, pp. 68, 301.

fairly large one. The first recorded recusant was Thomas Bonde in 1577. In 1592 three persons were recorded,[83] and in 1605 nineteen were fined as recusants.[84] In 1620 Somerton was considered sufficiently important to be chosen as one of the Oxfordshire centres of the newly formed Roman Catholic Province in England.[85] Subsidy lists of 1643 and 1644 show that the community was a prosperous one: besides Sir Richard Fermor, there were fourteen Catholics, belonging to ten families, with enough property to be taxed.[86] Numbers increased: in 1676 there were 51 recorded papists and about 45 in 1706.[87] Two cases when the penal laws were enforced are evidence of the open practice of Roman Catholicism in the village.[88] In 1631 Joanna Lovell was warned that she must not teach the children of recusants, and in 1633 the churchwardens were accused of failing either to report Sir Richard Fermor and his family as recusants or to record the birth of two children, one a Fermor, neither of whom had been baptized in church. To the first charge they pleaded that Sir Richard had asked them not to report him—an incident which shows the degree to which the administration of the penal laws was governed by local goodwill or influence.

Visitation returns give some idea of the relationship between the Protestant and Roman Catholic communities in the 18th century. In 1738 the rector reported that there were 47 papists, of whom 19 were members of the Fermor household, and 48 Anglicans; he added the apparently contradictory statement that the papists had formerly formed half the parish, but were greatly diminished, and that during the last five years 10 or 12 had been converted.[89] As the same family names recur in successive returns, each religious community evidently preserved its own loyalties; intermarriage was, however, common and in 1738 the rector reported that Anglicans and Papists 'are so blended and united together' that a revival of the penal laws would be inadvisable. There is little evidence of religious friction: the Catholics are described as living in a quiet and neighbourly fashion and showing respect and civility towards the rector.[90] In 1767 among the 42 Catholics listed two were farmers, Collingridge and Jennings, and their families, the butcher's wife, 3 craftsmen, and 3 labourers.[91] The community still numbered 48 in 1811.[92]

During the 19th century, after the sale of the manor by the Fermors, there was a gradual decline in numbers. In 1834 there were still eight Roman Catholic families living in the parish;[93] in 1854 20 adherents were recorded, but at the end of the 19th century only two were left.[94]

PROTESTANT NONCONFORMITY. There is no evidence of Protestant dissent until 1834,[95] when two nonconformists were reported. In 1840 a house was licensed for Wesleyan meetings.[96] There continued to be a few Methodists, but most of them were said also to go to church.[97] By the 1870's they had joined the United Free Church Methodists.[98] In the 20th century there was a cottage meeting-place attached to the Brackley circuit of the Wesleyan Methodist Connexion. It was closed in about 1914 and pulled down in 1915.[99]

SCHOOLS. Thomas Fermor, by will proved in 1580, endowed a free school at Somerton for boys to be instructed in 'virtue and learning'.[1] His executors invested £160 in land in Milcombe in Bloxham parish; and the chapel in the castle courtyard was converted into a school building.[2] A schoolmaster's house was built in about 1750 and appears to have been maintained by the Fermors, who also appointed the master, and regularly paid his salary of £10 a year out of the Milcombe estate until the beginning of the 19th century.[3] By 1738 the old custom of the Milcombe tenants bringing the schoolmaster's money to the church porch had been dropped.[4] The names of several 17th- and 18th-century schoolmasters are known.[5]

It is possible that Fermor's original intention was to found a grammar school for the sons of neighbouring yeomen, but for part of the 18th century only reading, writing, and arithmetic were taught, and in 1738 the master teaching these was described as very 'diligent in his office'.[6] By 1787, however, most of the village children were excluded, as only children who could already read were admitted.[7] Protests by the rector to William Fermor appear to have been ineffective; the numbers declined and by 1815 the school was attended by four local boys in the summer and about a dozen in the winter. The master supplemented his income by taking in about 20 fee-paying boarders.[8]

Although in 1833 26 boys (16 of whom were free scholars) attended the school,[9] the curate found in 1837 that only 5 children were receiving free education, and that no child under 7 years old was admitted, so that the village was not profiting sufficiently by the foundation.[10] He attempted to check these abuses by instituting a system of half-yearly examinations and in 1838 examined 16 boys in the winter and 12 in the summer, when the numbers dropped because of harvest work. He found that the school was, generally speaking, in a 'very inefficient state', with 'writing tolerably good', but reading 'slovenly and defective and reli-

[83] C.R.S. xxii. 111; ibid. xviii. 256, 260.
[84] Salter, *Oxon. Recusants, passim.*
[85] Stapleton, *Cath. Miss.* 6; H. Foley, *Records of English Province*, ser. xi. 569.
[86] E 179/164/484; ibid. 496A.
[87] Compton Census; *Oxoniensia*, xiii. 79.
[88] Blo. *Som.* 148, citing churchwardens' presentments.
[89] Oxf. Dioc. d 554. Cf. churchwardens' presentment of 1736, when 25 papists were named: Blo. *Som.* 149.
[90] Oxf. Dioc. d 554.
[91] Ibid. c 431.
[92] Ibid. d 573.   [93] Ibid. b 39.
[94] *Wilb. Visit.*; Oxf. Dioc. c 344.
[95] Oxf. Dioc. b 39.
[96] Ibid. c 646, f. 126.
[97] *Wilb. Visit.*; Oxf. Dioc. c 332, c 344.
[98] Wing, *Annals*, 137.

[99] Local inf. Chas. W. King kept a record of the preachers who preached there each Sunday 1873–1910: MS. Top. Oxon. e 260.
[1] *V.C.H. Oxon.* i. 487; *12th Rep. Com. Char.* 309; P.C.C. 30 Arundell.
[2] O.R.O. J VIII d/2; *V.C.H. Oxon.* i. 487.
[3] *V.C.H. Oxon.* i. 487. From 1822, after part of the Milcombe estate had changed hands, only £1 2s. instead of £1 10s. 4d. was paid by the new tenant and the balance was never recovered: *12th Rep. Com. Char.* 310.
[4] Oxf. Dioc. d 554.   [5] Tablet in church.
[6] Oxf. Dioc. d 554, d 557.
[7] O.R.O. J VIII d/2.
[8] Ibid.; Oxf. Dioc. c 433.
[9] *Educ. Enq. Abstract*, 754; see also *12th Rep. Com. Char.* 309–11.
[10] O.R.O. J VIII d/16.

gious instruction poor'. The master responsible for these low standards was John Hore, and on his death in 1861 his son applied for the post of school-master, which had been in the family for a hundred years.[11]

In 1850 the school was repaired at a cost of £75, paid out of £200 received from the G.W.R. as compensation for the annexation of some school land; in 1864 a further £200 was spent on repairs and in 1870 £60, given by Lord Jersey.[12] There were 14 boys in the school in 1867; the master was un-certificated and there was no state inspection.[13] By 1871 the school had been amalgamated with the girls' and infants' schools and had 74 pupils. Religious instruction was then undenominational, but the school was affiliated to the National Society by 1887.[14] In 1894 it was modernized at a cost of £200.[15] Average attendance rose from 40 in 1889 to 55 in 1906.[16] Since the school's reorganization as a junior school in 1930, senior pupils have gone to Fritwell. It was controlled in 1951. There were 18 pupils in 1954.[17]

In 1815 there were two other schools, one recently opened by Lady Jersey for 12 girls, and the other for 12 children. Two boys attended the National school at Deddington, where, it was said, 9 girls from Somerton were shortly to be admitted.[18] In 1833

Lady Jersey paid for 20 children and provided clothes, and 5 others were paid for by their parents.[19] The school was regularly inspected by a panel of lady visitors.[20] By 1854 Lady Jersey was supporting two schools, one for 24 girls and one for 18 infants: some of the pupils paid small fees.[21] Between 1864 and 1871 these schools were merged in Fermor's school.[22]

CHARITIES. The rector William Juxon, by will proved 1663, gave £50 to the poor of Somerton, but there is no later record of his charity.[23] By his will, dated 1766, the Revd. John Watson left £20 in money to buy bread for poor members of the Established Church. The annual income was reported to be 16s. in 1787, when it was said that the principal was to be 'laid out in land'.[24] This charity was later neglected and lost until 1806, when the Revd. John Martin Watson of Aynho (Northants), nephew of the original benefactor, gave £62, the principal and interest, to the parish.[25] In 1824 £2 19s. 6d. was distributed to the poor in bread at Christmas.[26] Watson's charity was still distributed in bread at Christmas in 1954, when the annual income was £1 12s. 8d.[27] An unknown donor gave £43, which was producing £2 6s. a year in 1787,[28] but had evidently been lost by 1824.

SOULDERN

THE parish lies on the southern borders of Northamptonshire, mid-way between the market towns of Banbury and Bicester. The area of the ancient parish, 1,496 acres, was unchanged in 1951.[1] The county boundary which runs through the southern end of Aynho Park and follows Ockley Brook bounds the parish on the north; the Cherwell forms the western and the Aynho and Somerton roads most of the eastern and southern boundaries.[2]

The eastern edge of the parish lies on the Great Oolite, with a belt of Inferior Oolite forming a ring round the village, and the Upper Lias Clay and Marlstone appear between the latter and the alluvium of the Cherwell valley.[3] The surface soil is composed of sand and stonebrash on the high ground, clay and loam near the river; and the subsoil, which varies in different parts of the parish, consists of limestone, ironstone, clay, and gravel.[4] The white limestone has been much quarried for building purposes and road-making, but the ironstone is not known to have been worked.[5] Most of the parish lies within the 300-foot

contour, except for the river meadowland, which is liable to flooding, and the plateau on the eastern side which rises to over 400 feet above sea level. At the edge of the scarp there are a number of springs which give a good water-supply.

The pre-Roman Portway may have crossed the parish from north to south, and the important medieval highway between Bicester and Banbury was made a turnpike in 1791.[6] A toll-gate near the eastern approach to the village was removed in 1876.[7] The toll-house still remains. A number of 'private highways' were created by the inclosure decree: these included 'from the turnpike to Chadwell Gate' (i.e. Mill Road), and from the town well to the church.[8]

Sections of two former G.W.R. lines, Oxford to Banbury, completed in 1850, and the main Birmingham to London line, completed in 1910,[9] and the Oxford Canal, completed in 1790, run along the east bank of the Cherwell. The nearest station, Aynho Park, lies over the county border three miles distant.

[11] Blo. *Som.* 154–6, quoting the curate's report and entries in a school book kept by Mr. Price and formerly in parish chest.　　　　[12] Blo. *Som.* 156.
[13] *Wilb. Visit.*; *Schools Enq.* 308.
[14] *Elem. Educ. Ret.*; *Kelly's Dir. Oxon.* (1887).
[15] O.R.O. J VIII d/22.
[16] *Ret. of Sch.*; *Vol. Sch. Ret.*
[17] Inf. Oxon. Educ. Cttee.
[18] Oxf. Dioc. c 433.
[19] *Educ. Enq. Abstract*, 754.
[20] O.R.O. J VIII d/5.
[21] *Wilb. Visit.*
[22] *Kelly's Dir. Oxon.* (1864); *Elem. Educ. Ret.*
[23] Blo. *Som.* 138–9.
[24] *Char. Don.* ii. 990.
[25] *12th Rep. Com. Char.* 311; Wing, *Annals*, 142.
[26] *12th Rep. Com. Char.* 311.

[27] Inf. the Revd. W. P. Hares.
[28] *Char. Don.* ii. 990.
[1] *Census*, 1881, 1951; 506 acres of Fritwell were transferred to Souldern in 1953: *Oxon. Confirm. Order* (copy in O.R.O.).
[2] O.S. Map 6″, x, xvi (1886); 2½″, 42/43, 52, 53 (1951).
[3] G.S. Map 1″, xlv NE., NW.
[4] Blo. *Sould.* 4.
[5] J. H. and A. P. Gough, *Hist. Notices of Souldern* (O.A.S. 1887), 7; *G.S. Memoir* (1864), 16–18.
[6] *V.C.H. Oxon.* i. 275 and map between pp. 266 and 267; Blo. *Sould.* 43; 31 Geo. III, c. 103.
[7] 39–40 Vic. c. 39.
[8] For these and for a dispute over their upkeep, particularly Wharf Lane, see Cartwright Mun. Aynho Park, Northants.
[9] E. T. MacDermot, *Hist. G.W.R.* i. 300; ii. 448.

A canal wharf was built and connected to the village by Wharf Lane (originally called 'Haleway'), so that Souldern, like other parishes bordering the canal, was able to enjoy cheap coal.[10]

The village lies near the parish boundary on the southern edge of Aynho Park, well protected by trees on the north and by the high land to the east.[11] Despite its comparatively high position it appears to have been unhealthy: the death-rate among children was high; in 1855 there was a severe cholera epidemic; and later the local historian Wing noted that Souldern was liable to a sort of fever, which was never long absent.[12] The main village street runs from east to west with two roads branching off to the south, and one at the east end by the town well runs north and down the hill past the site of the one-time manor-house (see below) and the church to Ockley Brook. In the 17th century and later there was an open green and a bowling-green between Souldern Gate and the village; these were given to the use of the poor by the 1613 inclosure award.[13] A late-18th-century map shows the village as triangular in shape with three grass closes in the middle. A green is also shown in front of the church.[14] Souldern's name, meaning thorn-bush in a gully (O.E. *Sulh-þorn*), suggests that the original settlement was mainly by the church and the manor.[15] The village had an unusual number of substantial houses in the second half of the 17th century. Out of seventeen houses listed for the hearth tax in 1665 three were gentlemen's houses: the manor-house of the Weedons and Richard Kilby's were each taxed on ten hearths and a third on eleven hearths, which was probably the Rectory.[16] In addition there were three farm-houses with four hearths apiece.[17]

The village is still a beautiful and well-preserved example of building with local materials. Most of the dwellings, many of them substantial houses, are stone-built and have stone slates or thatch on their roofs. The prevailing colour is silver-grey with patches of yellow lichen. Among the many early buildings that survive, the following are the most notable. The Court was probably built about 1600. Its plan is L-shaped and it has two stories with a cellar and attic dormers. The date 1666 can be seen on the garden gateway and there have been many other alterations and additions in later periods. The Hollies is also L-shaped in plan and dates from about 1600. It has preserved its original stone-mullioned windows of three or four lights and a later stone fireplace. The Barn House, although much restored, was also originally a 16th-century or possibly an early 17th-century building. Rectangular in plan, it has two stories with a cellar and hipped dormers. The ground floor has four-light windows with stone mullions, the first floor three-light windows with stone mullions. Greystones is similar in plan, but has a steep-pitched roof of thatch. Its windows have moulded stone frames and square labels. Souldern House (formerly Souldern Lodge) is in origin another early 17th-century house of rectangular plan. It has two stories, cellar, and attic dormers. The house was for several centuries the home of the Gough family and a gazebo in the garden is dated 'R. G(ough) 1706'.[18] The Hermitage is also rectangular in plan; it has two stories and attic dormers and is of two builds, the west being of 16th-century date and the east of 18th-century date. The house is mainly built of coursed rubble but the gables are coped with dressed stone. Its 17th-century staircase is said to have come from the Court.[19]

The present manor-house, formerly called Souldern House, stands on the brow of the hill at the western end of the village street. It is built of coursed rubble and was probably erected in the second half of the 17th century, as the date 1665 appears on the stone-work of one of the rooms formerly known as the 'old vestry'. The west front has two projecting gabled wings with stone finials, and the main entrance on this side was once surmounted by a cupola. The house has been considerably altered in later periods, notably in 1850 and in 1955–6 for Lord Bicester. The Roman Catholic chapel standing in the grounds, erected in 1869, consists of an old stone outhouse and a brick extension.[20] The manor used to be approached by a fine avenue of sycamore trees, but only a few of these remained at the end of the 19th century when Blomfield described the house.[21] The history of this house is uncertain: Blomfield thought it was built by Bernard Weedon (d. 1679), who returned ten hearths for the tax of 1665, and that after the Weedons had moved to Staffordshire it was let to the Kilby family from 1679 until Robert Kilby's death in 1757.[22] The Kilbys already had one substantial house in Souldern in 1665,[23] and in 1717 Robert Kilby was reported to have a freehold estate in Souldern and 'Hyett House in his own possession'.[24] About the same time Rawlinson noted that a Mr. Cox was occupying the manor-house.[25] This must have been Samuel Cox, the husband of Alice Kilby and father of Samuel Cox, the infant lord of the manor, who finally came to reside in 1757.[26]

Mention should also be made of Manor Farm's fine stone barn, on the outskirts of the village. It is 75 feet long, has oak rafters, and had a thatched roof until about 1950.

The medieval manor-house was situated on the east side of the road leading to the church, but it seems to have become a ruin at an early date. A map of 1767 shows no house south of the church and by the 19th century only its foundations and fishponds marked its site in Great House Close.[27]

Another house which has gone is the old Rectory. This stood north of the church and was built before 1638 by the rector Thomas Harding.[28] It was repaired in 1809 by Robert Jones, whom Wordsworth

[10] Cartwright Mun. Aynho Park; Gough, *Hist. Souldern* (O.A.S.), 8.
[11] O.S. Map 25″, xvi. 3 (1881).
[12] Par. Reg.; Wing, *Annals*, 147.
[13] Traces of the bowling-green could be seen in the late 19th cent.: Gough, *Hist. Souldern* (O.A.S.), 10; see below, p. 306.   [14] Davis, *Oxon. Map.*
[15] *P.N. Oxon.* (E.P.N.S.), i. 236.
[16] The third was occupied by '— Hodges, gent.' Thomas Hodges, rector, had resigned in 1662: see below, p. 309.
[17] *Hearth Tax Oxon.* 191.
[18] Blo. *Sould.* 26–29.

[19] Local inf.
[20] Blo. *Sould.* 99–100; see below, p. 311.
[21] Blo. *Sould.* 22–23.
[22] *Hearth Tax Oxon.* 191; Blo. *Sould.* 23–24.
[23] *Hearth Tax Oxon.* 191.
[24] O.R.O. Reg. of Papists' estates, pp. 55–56.
[25] *Par. Coll.* iii. 270.
[26] Blo. *Sould.* 25; see below, p. 305.
[27] T. Jefferys, *Co. of Oxf. Survey'd*; O.S. Map 25″, xvi. 3 (1881); local inf.
[28] See below, p. 309. It was 'new built' in 1638: Blo. *Sould.* 95.

described as 'one of my earliest and dearest friends'.[29] Wordsworth stayed in the house, probably in 1820, and afterwards wrote the sonnet called 'A Parsonage in Oxfordshire'.[30] Later, in another sonnet, he described 'this humble and beautiful parsonage', and the church and churchyard.[31] The rectory had well-stocked fishponds in 1723 at least, when the rector noted that 31 brace of carp had been taken out of one.[32]

There was much modernization in the 18th and 19th centuries: for instance, the stone-mullioned windows of Souldern House, many at the Hermitage, and most of those at the manor-house were altered to sash windows. Rooms were panelled as at the Hollies, and many houses such as the manor-house and Souldern House were re-roofed with Welsh slate. But in the 19th century in particular new buildings were added to the village. By 1824 seventeen cottages for the poor had been built on the green;[33] a school and Wesleyan chapel (1869) were put up;[34] and in 1890 the old gabled Rectory, which seems to have been a house of some interest,[35] was pulled down and the present Rectory was built on a new site for £1,434 by the architect E. G. Bruton.[36]

In the 1850's there were three public houses, the 'Fox', the 'Crown',[37] and the 'Bull's Head'; the last was mentioned in 1784, when the 'Fox' was also licensed.[38] Only one licensed house is recorded in 1735[39] and in 1939 there was again only one, the 'Fox'.[40]

There are a number of outlying farms: these seem to have been built as a result of the inclosure of the fields in 1613. Five are recorded in 1774, and Chisnell Farm, Hill House Farm, and three others are marked on a map of 1797.[41] All show architectural evidences of an earlier origin. Hill House is said to have been built by the Westcars:[42] it is L-shaped and has two stories with gabled dormers. The south-west wing is earlier in date than the south-east wing, which was probably added in the late 17th century. The main entrance, through a door-frame with fluted Doric-style pilasters and a dentilled cornice, is in the north-east front of this wing, which has six first-floor windows and six dormers. There is evidence that in the 18th century it had an ornamental Queen Anne garden with two summer-houses.[43]

During the Civil War the village suffered from the quartering of troops and requisitioning of food supplies by both the contending armies: in 1643, for instance, six regiments of parliamentary troops from London were quartered there; and in 1641

Souldern was ordered to send carts and provisions to the king at Oxford.[44]

In the 19th century Souldern Gate was well known as a meet of the Bicester Hunt.[45] Besides this sport, the village still enjoyed a number of its ancient feasts and customs. Children processed on St. Valentine's day and May Day, and the village feast beginning on 18th September lasted a week. It was accompanied by a fair.[46]

Thomas Harding (d. 1648), an eminent scholar and schoolmaster, was Rector of Souldern.[47] Later in the century Mrs. Bryan Stapleton (d. 1919), author of Catholic Missions in Oxfordshire, was brought up at Souldern House, then locally important as a centre of Roman Catholicism.[48]

MANOR. No Domesday manor has yet been identified with SOULDERN,[49] but the exceptional privileges it is known to have possessed in the 13th century were said to date from the Conquest. It is not impossible that it was among the lands in divers counties that were granted to Robert de Rumilly by the Conqueror and that it was inherited by his daughter Lucy, the wife of Jordan de Say, lord of extensive estates including another Oxfordshire manor of exceptional importance, the nearby Kirtlington. He granted Souldern Church to Eynsham Abbey some time before 1161, when his son William was buried there. Another son Ranulf witnessed the grant.[50] Souldern became attached to the honor of Richard's Castle by the marriage of Eustachia de Say to Hugh FitzOsbern, who was dead by 1140.[51] Eustachia was co-foundress of Westwood Nunnery (Worcs.),[52] and was of sufficient importance for her sons Osborn and Hugh to adopt Say as their surname. Osborn died about 1185, and his brother Hugh, who succeeded him, married Lucy, daughter of Walter de Clifford, by whom he had at least three sons and a daughter Lucy. Hugh died about 1190, and his eldest son Hugh died some six years later.[53] Lucy married Thomas de Arderne,[54] a tenant of the honor of Richard's Castle at Astwood Savage (Worcs.),[55] to whom her brother Hugh gave Souldern manor in exchange for Kingston manor in Yeovil (Som.).[56]

The overlordship of Souldern continued to follow the descent of the honor of Richard's Castle.[57] Hugh de Say, Lucy's brother, was succeeded by his daughter Margaret, and Richard's Castle was held by her and her three husbands, Hugh Ferrers (d. 1204), Robert Mortimer (d. 1219), and William

[29] Oxf. Dioc. c 435, pp. 32–36. The cost was over £600 and the S. front was remodelled.
[30] H. W. Garrod, 'Wordsworth and Oxford,' Oxf. Mag. 27 Apr. 1950, 400–2; Misc. Sonnets, pt. III, vii.
[31] Note to 'Pastoral Characters', Eccl. Sonnets, pt. III, xviii.
[32] Blo. Sould. 14 n.
[33] See below, p. 312.
[34] See below, p. 311.
[35] 'An interesting specimen of an old parsonage': Gardner, Dir. Oxon.
[36] MS. Top. Oxon. c 105, f. 207; Blo. Sould. 89–90 and illustration facing p. 98.
[37] Gardner, Dir. Oxon.
[38] O.R.O. Victlrs'. recog.
[39] Ibid.
[40] Kelly's Dir. Oxon. (1939).
[41] Oxf. Dioc. d 565; Davis, Oxon. Map.
[42] Blo. Sould. 53.
[43] Ibid.
[44] Ibid. 31; Dunkin MS. 438/4, f. 45b.

[45] Blo. Sould. 43.
[46] Gough, Hist. Souldern (O.A.S.), 10–11.
[47] D.N.B.; see below, p. 309.
[48] O.A.S. Rep. 1924, 2; see below, p. 311.
[49] V.C.H. Oxon. i. 393.
[50] Eynsham Cart. i. 118. For the identification of this Jordan de Say with the Norman Jordan de Say, and for the connexion between the families of Rumilly and Say, see Early Yorkshire Charters, ed. C. T. Clay, vii. 31–33. See above, pp. 221–2.
[51] Eyton, Salop. iv. 302 sqq.
[52] V.C.H. Worcs. ii. 148: her relationship to Jordan has not been established, but it is not unlikely that she was a daughter.
[53] Eyton, Salop. iv. 502 sqq.; Complete Peerage, ix. 256.
[54] Complete Peerage, ix. 257; Montacute Cart. (Som. Rec. Soc. viii), 135–6.
[55] Feet of F. (P.R.S. xvii), 140; Red Bk. Exch. (Rolls Ser.), 605.
[56] Rot. Litt. Claus. (Rec. Com.), i. 261.
[57] Cf. Somerset Fines (Som. Rec. Soc. vi), 266.

de Stuteville. Margaret died in 1242, and William held the overlordship of Souldern[58] until his death in 1259. It then passed to Hugh Mortimer, Margaret's son by Robert, and followed the descent of the Mortimers of Richard's Castle,[59] who as the 'heirs of Say' were overlords of Souldern in 1279.[60] On the death of Hugh (II) Mortimer in 1304 Richard's Castle was inherited by one of his daughters, Joan, whose first husband Thomas de Bykenore was overlord of Souldern in 1316.[61] Thomas died without issue, and Joan's possessions eventually passed to John, her son by her second husband Richard Talbot.[62] John was overlord of Souldern in 1346, the last occasion on which the overlordship is mentioned.[63]

Thomas de Arderne was dead by 1231[64] and his widow Lucy continued to hold Souldern in free marriage.[65] By 1255 she had been succeeded by Ralph de Arderne,[66] presumably her son, who may have died by 1259 when another Thomas de Arderne was holding the family lands at Astwood Savage (Worcs.).[67] By 1278[68] Souldern was held of Thomas by Lucy—a granddaughter of the first Lucy de Arderne[69] and therefore probably his sister—and her husband Thomas de Lewknor of Greatworth (Northants).[70] The hundredal inquisitions of 1279 show that Souldern was an especially privileged manor, 'manerium liberum in se', whose lords had enjoyed free warren, waifs, view of frankpledge and freedom from suit of hundred ever since the Conquest. Thomas de Lewknor owed a pound of cumin every year to Thomas de Arderne, the mesne lord,[71] but neither of them seems to have owed any military service for the manor, although it was described as $\frac{1}{2}$ knight's fee in 1255 and as a whole fee in 1285.[72] In 1243 Lucy de Arderne had been said to owe no scutage for Souldern.[73] In 1285 Thomas de Arderne conveyed his annual rent of a pound of cumin to John de Lovetot,[74] who may be identified as the Justice of the Common Pleas who was removed on charges of extortion in 1289.[75] He died in 1294 and the mesne lordship of Souldern[76] passed to his son John.[77] By 1316, however, the manor was said to be held directly of the honor of Richard's Castle.[78]

Thomas de Lewknor was dead by 1305,[79] and by 1307 his widow Lucy had apparently conveyed the manor to Master Thomas de Abberbury, who died

in possession in that year.[80] The Abberbury family took its name from Adderbury, but was subsequently most closely connected with Donnington (Berks.), another of Thomas's acquisitions. Thomas was succeeded in turn by his brother Walter and by his nephew Richard.[81] John de Lewknor, possibly a son of Lucy and Thomas, and a certain William de Tingewike entered the manor by force. Later William obtained a formal grant of it from John and died in possession in 1316.[82] Richard de Abberbury had regained Souldern by 1323,[83] and held it at his death in 1333, when it passed to his son John.[84] John died without issue in 1346, and Souldern passed to his uncle Thomas,[85] perhaps the Thomas de Abberbury who held lands in Wootton in 1316.[86] Thomas was succeeded by his son Richard, the most distinguished member of the family, by 1362.[87] Richard was a knight of the shire for Oxfordshire in 1373 and 1387, and a royal servant. He is best known for his rebuilding of Donnington castle and his endowment of Donnington Hospital.[88] Both the hospital and the Crutched Friars of Donnington received grants of lands and rents in Souldern from Sir Richard.[89] The latter was dead by 1401[90] and was probably succeeded first by his brother Thomas, who had lands in Souldern in 1399,[91] and then by Thomas's son Richard.[92]

The younger Richard married Alice, widow of Edmund Danvers of Chilton (Berks.),[93] but had no children. By 1415 his heir presumptive was probably Sir Richard Arches, the son of his sister Lucy,[94] to whom with other feoffees he conveyed Souldern manor in that year.[95] Richard Abberbury, on the grounds of a defect in his uncle's grant, seized the Crutched Friars' Souldern lands and in 1448 granted them to William de la Pole, Duke of Suffolk,[96] on whose death in 1450 they were put in custody of his widow Alice.[97] Sir Richard Arches, whose father was perhaps Simon Arches of Waddesdon (Bucks.),[98] died in 1417. His only son John died without issue, and Souldern manor descended to his daughter Joan and her husband Sir John Dynham.[99] Sir John died in 1458[1] and Joan retained the manor[2] as her own inheritance until her death in 1497, when she was succeeded by her son, another Sir John Dynham, who died in 1501.[3]

The Dynham estates were then divided among

[58] Rot. Hund. (Rec. Com.), ii. 44.
[59] Complete Peerage, ix. 258–65; Eyton, Salop. iv. 302 sqq.
[60] Rot. Hund. ii. 823.
[61] Cal. Inq. p.m. v, pp. 414–15.
[62] Complete Peerage, xii (1), 630–1.
[63] Cal. Inq. p.m. viii, p. 470.
[64] Fines Oxon. 89.
[65] Ibid. 101; Bk. of Fees, 831.
[66] Rot. Hund. (Rec. Com.), ii. 44.
[67] Cal. Inq. p.m. i, p. 135.
[68] Fines Oxon. 209.
[69] Eynsham Cart. i. 349 sqq.
[70] Baker, Northants, i. 508.
[71] Rot. Hund. (Rec. Com.), ii. 823.
[72] Ibid. 44; Feud. Aids, iv. 158.
[73] Bk. of Fees, 831; cf. Cal. Inq. p.m. iii, p. 134.
[74] Fines Oxon. 222.
[75] Foss, Judges, iii. 123; Cambs. Antiq. Soc. l (1926), 37–38; Thoroton, Notts. i. 63.
[76] Cal. Inq. p.m. iii, p. 134.
[77] Ibid. iv, p. 288.
[78] Ibid. v, pp. 414–15.
[79] Eynsham Cart. i. 349.
[80] Cal. Inq. p.m. iv, p. 288.

[81] For the Abberburys see C. C. Brookes, Hist. of Steeple Aston (1929), 51 sqq.; Berks. Arch. Jnl. iv. 52 sqq.
[82] Cal. Inq. p.m. v, pp. 414–15; cf. Feud. Aids, iv. 169.
[83] Cal. Inq. Misc. ii, p. 209.
[84] Cal. Inq. p.m. vii, p. 390.
[85] Ibid. viii, p. 470.
[86] Berks. Arch. Jnl. iv. 55.
[87] Inq. a.q.d. (P.R.O. L. and I. xxii), ii. 525.
[88] Brookes, Steeple Aston, 57–63; V.C.H. Berks. ii. 93; iv. 91.
[89] Cal. Pat. 1391–6, 369; 1396–9, 469; Inq. a.q.d. (P.R.O. L. and I.), ii. 706.
[90] Cal. Pat. 1399–1401, 486.
[91] Ibid. 1396–9, 469.   [92] Ibid. 1446–52, 169.
[93] F. N. Macnamara, Memorials of Danvers Family, 495, 509.
[94] Brookes, Steeple Aston, 68, citing C 1/29/62–63.
[95] C.P. 25(1)/191/26/6, 7; cf. C 1/29/62–63.
[96] Cal. Pat. 1446–52, 169.
[97] H. A. Napier, Swyncombe and Ewelme, 90, 104.
[98] V.C.H. Bucks. iv. 86.
[99] Complete Peerage, iv. 377.
[1] C 139/170.
[2] e.g. Cal. Pat. 1485–94, 3.
[3] Complete Peerage, iv. 378.

four coheirs, Sir John's two surviving sisters Elizabeth and Joan, and his nephews, Sir Edmund Carew, son of Margery Dynham and Sir John Carew, and Sir John Arundell of Lanherne, son of Katherine Dynham and Sir Thomas Arundell.[4] Souldern manor was divided into four parts, each of which pursued a separate descent throughout the 16th century. Shortly before his death in 1513 Sir Edmund Carew conveyed his quarter-share of another Dynham manor, Oving (Bucks.), to feoffees of Sir William Compton,[5] and it is likely that he conveyed his share of Souldern about the same time, for Sir William held a quarter of that manor at his death in 1528.[6] Under Sir William's grandson, Henry, Lord Compton, a quarter of Souldern appears to have been held by Anker Brente[7] of Little Wolford (Warws.), which was one of the Comptons' manors.[8] Sir John Arundell held a quarter of Souldern at his death in 1545,[9] and his share descended through his son Sir John (d. 1557) to his grandson,[10] a third Sir John, who died in 1590.[11] Elizabeth Dynham married three times: her first husband Fulk Bourchier, Lord Fitzwarine, died in 1479; her second, Sir John Sapcotes of Elton (Hunts.), in 1501; and her third, Sir Thomas Brandon, in 1510.[12] In 1509 Elizabeth settled her lands on herself and Sir Thomas for life, with reversion to Richard Sapcotes, her son by her second husband.[13] Richard duly succeeded her in 1516, and it is probable that he conveyed his share of Souldern as well as his share of Steeple Aston to Sir Michael Dormer of Ascot in 1539, for in 1547, two years after Sir Michael's death, three of his sons, Thomas, William, and Geoffrey, conveyed a quarter of Souldern manor to their brother John.[14] From John it appears to have descended to his third son John (see below), and in 1604 his niece Elizabeth, daughter of Thomas Dormer of Yarnton,[15] and her husband John Stampe of Compton (Berks.) quitclaimed a quarter of Souldern to John Weedon.[16] The fourth share of Souldern passed from Joan Dynham to her son John, Lord Zouche,[17] but is lost to view from 1533[18] until 1579, when it appears in the possession of Paul Tracy of Stanway (Glos.), who with his wife Anne and son Sir Richard conveyed it to John Weedon in 1604.[19]

It has been stated that the four quarters of the manor were sold to John Stutsbury of Souldern,[20] Robert Weedon and his son John by Henry, Lord Compton, Sir John Arundell of Lanherne, Paul Tracy, and John Dormer. Robert Weedon married John Stutsbury's daughter,[21] and at his death in 1598 held three-quarters of Souldern manor.[22] Robert must have acquired two quarters by 1590, Sir John Arundell having died in that year and Henry, Lord Compton, in 1589. John Dormer still held his quarter of Steeple Aston in 1592.[23] The completion of the purchase of the manor seems to have been John Weedon's acquisition of Paul Tracy's quarter in 1604, and John certainly held the whole manor in 1615.[24]

The Weedons were Roman Catholics and in the Civil War their estates were sequestrated. Although it was alleged in 1646 that John Weedon had aided the rebels in Ireland before the war and the king throughout the war, he was permitted in 1653 to receive a third of the rents of his estates.[25] The family recovered their lands at the Restoration, and John seems to have died before 1665, when his son Bernard was living at Souldern.[26] Bernard died in 1679, and his son John in 1702. The last of the family to hold Souldern manor was another John, who died in 1710 and devised all his property there to Samuel Cox, the infant son of Samuel Cox of Farningham (Kent) and his wife Alice, daughter of Richard Kilby of Souldern.[27] John Weedon's brother William claimed, unsuccessfully, that John's will had been obtained by fraud,[28] but in 1718 he gave up his claim to the manor.[29] Samuel Cox was succeeded at his death in 1781 by his nephew Robert Kilby Cox. The latter resided occasionally at Souldern and died in 1828. His son and successor Samuel died childless in 1851, and the manor passed to Lt.-Col. Richard Snead Cox, a great-nephew of Robert Kilby Cox.[30] Lt.-Col. Snead Cox resided at Broxwood (Herefs.), and although called lord of Souldern manor in the 1860's was not subsequently given that title, and manorial rights may be said to have lapsed.[31]

ECONOMIC HISTORY. Souldern cannot be identified with any Domesday village and it may have been omitted as it was so highly privileged a manor.[32] It is known to have belonged in the early 12th century to the important Say family,[33] but the earliest evidence for its economic history comes from the hundred rolls of 1279. The manor then had 41 virgates of arable land, almost the same number as in the 17th century. Twelve were in demesne, $17\frac{1}{2}$ were held in villeinage and $11\frac{1}{2}$ freely. Besides its arable land, the large demesne had adjacent meadow and pasture, including Goldenham Meadow, along the Cherwell bank, and free fishing from this meadow to Fritwell Meadow.[34] There was a group of 7 free tenants, holding $11\frac{1}{2}$ virgates. The most prosperous was Thomas Silvester, who had the water-mill and 3 virgates, while 4 others had $5\frac{1}{2}$ virgates between them, paying a rent of about 2s. a virgate, and Ralph de Arderne, no doubt a relative of the lord of the

[4] Ibid. 381; Brookes, *Steeple Aston*, 72 sqq.
[5] *V.C.H. Bucks.* iv. 86.
[6] C 142/48/111.
[7] Bodl. MS. ch. Oxon. 3749.
[8] *V.C.H. Warws.* v. 216.
[9] C 142/86/11.
[10] Bodl. MS. ch. Oxon. 3748.
[11] *R.C. Families*, iii. 226–8.
[12] *Complete Peerage*, v. 508–9.
[13] Brookes, *Steeple Aston*, 73.
[14] Ibid. 74–75.
[15] Lipscomb, *Bucks.* i. 118.
[16] C.P. 25(2)/339/Mich. 2 Jas. I.
[17] *Complete Peerage* (orig. edn.), viii. 224.
[18] C.P. 25(2)/34/227/Trin. 25 Hen. VIII.
[19] Ibid. 197/Hil. 21 Eliz.; ibid. 198/Mich. 44–45 Eliz.; ibid. 339/Mich. 2 Jas. I; W. A. Shaw, *Knights of Eng.* ii. 133.

[20] Blo. *Sould.* 15–16, citing document in Par. Rec.; see *Oxon. Visit.* 206.
[21] Blo. *Sould.* 16.
[22] C 142/291/15; ibid. 295/15.
[23] Brookes, *Steeple Aston*, 74, 76.
[24] C.P. 25(2)/340/Mich. 13 Jas. I.
[25] Stapleton, *Cath. Miss.* 100–1.
[26] *Hearth Tax Oxon.* 191.
[27] Blo. *Sould.* 19–24.
[28] C 5/637/29.
[29] C.P. 25(2)/1049/Mich. 5 Geo. I.
[30] Blo. *Sould.* 25; Burke, *Land. Gent.* (1937).
[31] *Kelly's Dir. Oxon.* (1864, 1887).
[32] See above, p. 4.
[33] See above, p. 303.
[34] *Rot. Hund.* (Rec. Com.), ii. 823–4; Goldenham meadow recurs in the tithe award.

manor, held 2 virgates for 1*d.* Another virgate was held in free alms by the Prior of Banbury.[35] There were 10 villein virgaters and 15 half-virgaters. The rent paid by the Souldern villein was unusually small—19*d.* for a virgate, which may have meant that he had to perform unusually heavy services. All owed tallage and had to pay fines when their sons left the manor (*redimere pueros*).

No cottagers are mentioned in the Hundred Rolls, but an early 14th-century inquisition[36] lists sixteen besides about the same number of free tenants and villeins as that recorded in 1279. Thus the total number of landholders was about fifty. The tax lists of this period show a comparatively prosperous population, with between 30 and 35 people assessed, many of them relatively highly. The parish's total assessment ranks high among the medium group of contributors in the hundred.[37]

The next detailed information dates from the time of the early 17th-century inclosure. Before this 150 acres near Somerton Hedge had been inclosed, but the occasion for general inclosure was a dispute between the lord of the manor, who was bent on inclosing his demesne and extinguishing all right of common, and the freeholders. When the case was taken to law the judge advised the parties to accept the arbitration of Sir Thomas Chamberlayne of Wickham, and he ruled that the lands should be 'measured, divided and inclosed'. The parish was surveyed by William Jourden and the award ratified by Chancery in 1613.[38]

Out of 46 yardlands in the open fields, 12 belonged to the manor. There were 9 substantial freeholders with 2 or more yardlands, 5 with between 1 and 2 yardlands, and 8 with less than a yardland. There were also 12 cottages for the poor, each with common.[39] The largest allotment (350 acres) went to the lord of the manor, Edward Love of Aynho received 106 acres, and there were 6 allotments of between 50 and 100 acres, 9 of between 20 and 50 acres, and 6 smaller ones.[40] The 12 cottagers were given 8 acres and the herbage along Haleway and Chadwell, enough for a beast each; 13 acres were set aside for the poor at Cole's Cross, on the Green, and the 'Pitt and adjacent bowling place'; and the town meadow, which later lay along the west bank of the canal, seems to have continued as common land for the freeholders. It is mentioned at various times; in 1669, for example, the parishioners sold its second crop for £30.[41] This meadow and the common, 65 acres in all, were inclosed in 1856.[42]

At the end of the 17th century it was reckoned that there were 45½ yardlands instead of the 46 of 1613, probably because of the many acres lost through the making of hedges and ditches. The yardland usually contained 30 or 32 acres, though some contained as many as 40 acres.[43] A common fraction, an eighth of a quarter, was equal to an acre.[44] All yardlands were rated equally, except the seventeen belonging to the Weedons. Their land, as they were so 'powerful', was subject to a lower rate.[45] There was also other land in the parish which was not rated at all and therefore not reckoned among the yardlands.

There were various changes after inclosure, some immediate and others gradual. A list of landowners in 1676 shows that there had been little change in the system of landholding since 1613:[46] the demesne had somewhat increased in size, and the size of the average estate had slightly decreased, but the parish still consisted largely of freeholders. Eight came from families which had been in the parish since the early 16th century.[47] By the mid-18th century the number of non-resident owners had probably increased, seven of the eighteen 40-shilling freeholders not living in the parish.[48] By 1842, when there is another complete survey,[49] freeholders farming their own land had almost disappeared. With one exception, all the farms were let to tenants; the few owner-occupiers with 10 acres or less depended on some trade for their living, two having bakeries, one a grocery, and one a smith's shop.

While some of the 17th-century yeoman families (e.g. Dodwell, Bower, Bignell, King) had disappeared, two prominent families of that period continued as landowners. One was the Cartwrights of Aynho (Northants), who from about 1660 owned the mill and 4 yardlands,[50] and by the 19th century nearly 300 acres. The other was the Gough family, who owned about 3 yardlands in the 17th century.[51] They had bought some of the manor lands,[52] probably Chisnell Farm, by the 18th century, and in the 19th century owned some 200 acres.[53]

The effect of inclosure on the land was immediate. First, large tracts of land were divided into smaller ones and hedged and ditched.[54] (These hedges, it was said, took up 60 acres of land.) Secondly, the amount of land used for meadow and pasture greatly increased. A possible reason for this may have been the scarcity of grass in neighbouring parishes and another the desire to keep tithes as low as possible.[55] While 16 or 18 teams were said to have been kept before inclosure, by 1676 it was alleged that there were not more than five or six. It was alleged that 'quantities' of land had been converted to pasture, traces of ridge and furrow showing where this had been done, and that by then no more than a third or a quarter of the land was being ploughed.[56] The principal method of conversion seems to have been the sowing of sain-

---

[35] This must have been one of the two Banbury hospitals: D. M. Knowles and R. N. Hadcock, *Medieval Religious Houses*, 252.

[36] Blo. *Sould.* ii, citing inquest post mortem of Thos. de Abberbury (d. 1307).

[37] e.g. E 179/161/8.

[38] C 78/381/10. No copy could be found in the parish at the end of the 17th cent., and the rector paid £2 12*s.* to have a copy from London. The Cartwrights of Aynho Park, Northants, have a copy; there is no map.

[39] Cf. C 5/575/87. These were the ones who were probably later exempted from tithe in 1676: Par. Rec. Bk. i, p. 40.

[40] Cartwright Mun. Aynho Park: Incl. decree.

[41] Ibid. leasebook, f. 27*b*.

[42] O.R.O. Incl. award.

[43] Par. Rec. Bk. i, pp. 1, 6, 7, 9, 11.

[44] Ibid. p. 6; 1676 award.

[45] Blo. *Sould.* 19.

[46] Par. Rec. 1676 award.

[47] E 179/161/176. Dodwell (3), Bowers (2), Bignell, Owen, King.

[48] *Oxon. Poll, 1754.*

[49] Bodl. Tithe award.

[50] Par. Rec. 1676 award; Cartwright Mun. Aynho Park. For the Cartwrights see *V.C.H. Northants. Families.*

[51] C 78/381/10.

[52] Blo. *Sould.* 21.

[53] For the family see ibid. 26–29; J. H. and A. P. Gough, *Notes on Souldern* (Bicester, 1882), 59–60.

[54] E 134, 27 Chas. II, Trin. 3.

[55] Blo. *Sould.* 30; see below, p. 309.

[56] E 134, 27 Chas. II, Trin. 3.

foin, which by about 1700 had at least doubled the value of the land since inclosure,[57] making it far more valuable than the open fields of Fritwell.[58]

Another change was that fattening stock had been substituted for breeding stock, and that the proportion of sheep to cattle in the parish in the late 17th century had been increased.[59] It continued largely as a grazing parish, in 1842 being a third arable and two-thirds meadow and pasture,[60] the same proportion as in the early 20th century.[61] The size of farms, however, changed little. In 1842 there were still as many as thirteen farms. They were mostly of 30 to 100 acres, only three being more than 100 acres.[62]

In the 17th century there is mention of an unusual number of trades. Of the four Dodwells in the village, one was a tailor and one a mercer;[63] there were also a smith, another tailor, a carpenter, a mason,[64] and a weaver. As at Banbury, cheese-making was an important farm-house industry.[65] In the early 20th century it is said that as many as fifteen cheese-makers were employed at Manor Farm.[66] Souldern still had a large number of craftsmen and small traders in the mid-19th century. In addition to three public houses (the 'Bull', the 'Crown', and the 'Fox'), there were two bakehouses, a brewhouse, a beer-house, a shoemaker's shop, a wheelwright's shop, a carpenter's shop, two smith's shops, and a limekiln.[67] The village had three tailors and a milliner and, being in the stone country, eight masons amongst its craftsmen. Furthermore, the cottage industry of lace-making flourished, having over 30 lacemakers in 1851.[68] At one time there were three lacemaking schools, but towards the end of the century the industry declined.[69] Millers have always been among the village's chief tradesmen. The mill, on Ockley Brook opposite Aynho, is first mentioned in 1279, when it was rented together with 3 virgates by a freeholder for 18s.[70] Unlike most mills, it became detached from the manor, and by the early 17th century belonged to Edward Love of Aynho.[71] It passed to the Cartwrights, and later in the century, when two mills are mentioned, they were being let for £20 with a ½ yardland,[72] consisting of Floodgate Mead, Miller's Lam, Miller's Little Close, Mill Lane and Garden, Miller's Great Close, and Miller's Mead.[73] The second mill was not permanent, but one mill, which may have served Aynho as well as Souldern, being called Aynho mill in 1797,[74] was still being driven by water in 1920.[75] In 1939 there

were still eight private tradesmen and the Banbury Co-operative store.[76]

The Compton census of 1676 provides the first clue to the number of villagers: it recorded 130 adults.[77] In the first half of the 18th century the incumbent noted that there were about 50 houses; he particularly noted that his figure included the houses of the poor which 'are many in proportion to the rest'.[78] Numbers rose in the second half of the century: about 60 houses are recorded in 1768 and in 1811 there were 93 houses for 96 families.[79] This overcrowding was partly remedied by 1851 in spite of the great increase in the number of inhabitants to 619, 225 more than there had been in 1801. They occupied 132 houses. By 1901 the agricultural depression had reduced the population to 406, and it has since dropped to 371 in 1951.[80]

CHURCH. The church was given before 1161 to Eynsham Abbey by Jordan de Say to commemorate the burial of his son William in the abbey.[81] The gift was confirmed by Archbishop Theobald (1139–61), and several times later.[82] Nevertheless Eynsham had often to defend its right to present; between 1209 and 1219, for instance, Robert Mortimer claimed the advowson, and the abbey, doubtless under compulsion, presented his nominee, but appealed to the bishop.[83] He evidently upheld Eynsham's right, for the abbey continued to present. In 1236, probably to avoid further question, the lady of the manor quitclaimed the advowson to the abbot for 12 marks.[84] During the vacancy of Eynsham in 1264 Bishop Gravesend, because of his unusual position as patron of the abbey,[85] collated,[86] although this privilege was usually reserved to the king during the vacancy of religious houses. In 1305, when litigation arose over the patronage between the abbot and the lady of the manor, the king's court decided in favour of Eynsham,[87] which remained patron until its dissolution in 1539, although in 1505 the abbey sold one presentation to John Lihinde of Fifield.

In 1544 the king sold the advowson to Sir Ralph Sadler, Master of the Great Wardrobe;[88] in 1551 John Hales of Coventry granted it to his brother Stephen;[89] but by 1562 William Holt of Stoke Lyne was patron.[90] From Hugh Throckmorton, patron in 1571,[91] who lived at Souldern and was lessee of the rectory as late as 1590,[92] descended for the next hundred years two rival claims to the advowson. The Catholic conspirator Francis Throckmorton[93]

[57] Par. Rec. Bk. i, p. 7; ibid. loose papers c. 1700.
[58] Blo. Sould. 92.
[59] C 5/575/87; Par. Rec. 17th-cent. tithe bk.
[60] Bodl. Tithe award.
[61] J. B. Orr, Agric. in Oxon., maps facing pp. 161, 201.
[62] Bodl. Tithe award.
[63] Cf. Hearth Tax Oxon. 191; see below, p. 312.
[64] Cartwright Mun., Aynho Park: Leasebook, ff. 34b–35.
[65] E 134, 27 Chas. II, Trin. 3.
[66] Local inf.
[67] Bodl. Tithe award.
[68] H.O. 107/1729.
[69] Gough, Notes on Souldern, 13.
[70] Rot. Hund. (Rec. Com.), ii. 823.
[71] C 78/381/10.
[72] Cartwright Mun. (Aynho Park): Leasebook, f. 80: lease 1681.
[73] Ibid. lease 1738.
[74] Davis, Oxon. Map.
[75] Kelly's Dir. Oxon. (1920)
[76] Ibid. (1939).
[77] Compton Census. The hearth-tax return of 1662 (the

fullest) gives only 25 householders: Hearth Tax Oxon. 235.
[78] Oxf. Dioc. d 554, d 557.
[79] Ibid. d 560; Census, 1811; cf. Oxf. Dioc. d 565: 68 houses in 1774.
[80] Census, 1801, 1851, 1901, 1951; cf. Gough, Hist. Souldern (O.A.S.), 8, for influx of poor in early 19th cent.
[81] Eynsham Cart. i. 118.
[82] Ibid. 57; e.g. ibid. 45.
[83] Rot. Welles, i. 20.
[84] Eynsham Cart. ii. 168; Fines Oxon. 101.
[85] V.C.H. Oxon. ii. 65.
[86] Rot. Graves. 218. For list of medieval presentations see MS. Top. Oxon. d 460.
[87] Eynsham Cart. i. 349–52; Linc. Reg. ii, Dalderby, f. 149.
[88] L. & P. Hen. VIII, xix (2), p. 83.
[89] Warw. R.O. DR 127.
[90] Blo. Sould. 68.
[91] Ibid. 69; O.A.S. Rep. 1914, 222.
[92] Oxf. Dioc. d 16, f. 149b. The relationship of Hugh Throckmorton to the rest of the family has not been traced,
[93] For him see D.N.B.

claimed to hold it by grant from Sir Hugh, and on his attainder in 1584 it was argued that the advowson had lapsed to the Crown. It presented in 1621 and 1622[94] and in 1623 granted the advowson to John Williams, Bishop of Lincoln,[95] who in turn gave it with three other advowsons to St. John's College, Cambridge, of which he was a Fellow.[96] The second claim was based on a sale of the advowson in 1572 by Hugh Throckmorton to George Throckmorton of Fulbrook (Bucks.)[97] for £100 and 100 sheep. The latter presented Thomas Norbury in 1592 and sold the advowson to him. A Chancery case of 1619 shows that Throckmorton's right to present had been challenged and that although his nominee was allowed to remain in possession the advowson had been awarded to the Crown.[98] By the 1650's William Norbury of Hanwell was in possession of the second claim. He sold it to the rector Thomas Hodges for £40 and the latter in 1662 granted it to St. John's College, which thus became the possessor of both claims to the advowson. The title to the second claim, which had never been legally confirmed, was causing trouble to the college as late as 1704.[99] The college was still patron in 1955, when the living was held with Fritwell.

Eynsham Abbey never appropriated Souldern, although in about 1200, when the abbot's nephew was made vicar,[1] it was probably planning to do so. By 1197–8 the abbey was receiving from the church the large pension of £5, allocated to its kitchen.[2] In the mid-14th century the rector Thomas Solers (1350–61) withheld payment of this pension, but was finally condemned in 1361 by the king's court to pay arrears of £52 10s. plus damages of £10.[3] His successor, Master Simon of Lambourne, continued the suit, but unsuccessfully,[4] as the pension was still being paid in the early 15th century.[5] By 1535 it had been reduced to £2 13s. 4d.,[6] a sum which the Crown continued to receive until the 18th century.[7]

Had it not been for this medieval pension to Eynsham, worth originally about a half and later a third of the living, Souldern would have been one of the richest rectories in the deanery. Even so it was a moderately good one, valued at £6 13s. 4d. in 1254[8] and £10 in 1291,[9] a value which by 1535 had declined to £8 14s.[10] During the 17th and 18th centuries, according to the two tithe agreements of 1613 and 1676 (see below), it was worth about £100 and then £150. After the tithe agreement of 1808 its value was increased to about £500.[11]

Souldern in common with other churches was often involved in litigation. One dispute, of unexplained origin, was with Oseney Abbey. Robert de la Haye (rector 1231–44) claimed by the 'custom of churchscot' an acre of grain from the abbey's demesne in Mixbury and 4d. from Fulwell, claims which he ultimately gave up for a composition of £5.[12]

More serious trouble was caused by the glebe of Souldern, which mainly consisted of a hide in the fields of Fritwell. Known as the 'Chercheyde de Souldern,' this land was once held by William the clerk, who presumably served the church of Souldern, but in 1199 was given by Eynsham Abbey to Miles and Millicent of Fritwell, to be held of the church of Souldern for a pound of pepper, in exchange for a ¼ knight's fee in Wood Eaton.[13] The exchange was probably made at the time that the abbey was planning to appropriate the church, but the appropriation did not take place, and a few years later the rector demanded the return of his glebe. After at least two years' litigation, in the course of which Stephen of Fritwell, Miles's son, was excommunicated, papal judges ordered the return of the land to the church.[14]

Further litigation occurred when the Rector of Souldern refused to pay tithes on it to St. Frideswide's Priory, the appropriator of Fritwell. In 1229, before papal commissioners, one rector promised to cause no further trouble about these tithes,[15] but his successor Robert de la Haye refused to pay them. A multitude of people from both parishes attended the hearing of the case; many gave evidence, and it was again decided that the land lay in Fritwell.[16] Finally in 1237, before papal commissioners, a compromise was made: the rector was to collect the tithes but was to pay 2s. pension to St. Frideswide's.[17] After the Reformation the land was exempt from all tithes.[18]

Another part of the glebe consisted of a few acres in Souldern, part at least of which had been granted to the church in about 1200.[19] In 1291 the rector was at law over his land with the lord and lady of the manor.[20]

At least one early rector, John Barnewell (d. 1305), resided in Souldern, for he was allowed to divert the stream so that it ran through the court of his house.[21] He was accused of having abducted the daughter of the lord of the manor.[22]

Several later rectors came from distinguished clerical families. From 1317 to 1349, for instance, the living was held by three members of the family of John Dalderby, Bishop of Lincoln, one of whom, Master Peter de Dalderby, later became Precentor of Lincoln.[23] Two others, Master Simon of Wells

---

[94] Oxf. Dioc. c 264, ff. 100, 106b.
[95] For him see *D.N.B.*
[96] Blo. *Sould.* 71; *Statutes for the Coll. of St. John* (Cambridge, 1885), 113–14; Bodl. MS. Rawl. Lett. 112, f. 4.
[97] For family see *V.C.H. Bucks.* iv. 55; Lipscomb, *Bucks.* i. 271.
[98] Blo. *Sould.* 69–70.
[99] Much of the account comes from Blo. *Sould.* 72–75, quoting a letter of 1704 from the rector; C.P. 25(2)/340/Hil. 9 Jas. I.
[1] *Eynsham Cart.* i. 135.
[2] Ibid. 57, 307.
[3] Ibid. ii. 89–90.
[4] *Cal. Papal Pet.* i. 404.
[5] *Eynsham Cart.* ii, pp. lxviii, 48.
[6] Ibid. 251.
[7] Par. Rec. For a detailed history of this pension see Blo. *Sould.* 90 n. 1.
[8] Lunt, *Val. Norw.* 312.
[9] *Tax. Eccl.* (Rec. Com.), 31.
[10] *Valor Eccl.* (Rec. Com.), ii. 161.
[11] Oxf. Dioc. c 658, f. 62.
[12] *Oseney Cart.* v. 393.
[13] *Eynsham Cart.* i. 132–3.
[14] Ibid. 399–400.
[15] *St. Frides. Cart.* ii. 226.
[16] Ibid. 253–5. The document is dated 1271, but the archbishop named in it is Robert (i.e. Robert Kilwardby 1273–9). Robert de la Haye, however, was rector 1231–44, and it seems that the case may have been heard in 1231, when Richard le Grant was archbishop.
[17] Ibid. 226–7, 389. The pension was granted in 1532 to Christ Church: *L. & P. Hen. VIII*, v, p. 587.
[18] Oxf. Archd. Oxon. b 24, f. 94; O.R.O. Fritwell incl. award.
[19] *Eynsham Cart.* i. 401.
[20] *Abbrev. Rot. Orig.* (Rec. Com.), i. 69, 80.
[21] *Inq. a.q.d.* (P.R.O. L. and I. xvii), 36.
[22] *Abbrev. Plac.* (Rec. Com.), 291.
[23] *Cal. Papal L.* ii. 187; iii. 318; J. Le Neve, *Fasti*, ii. 83.

and Master Simon of Lambourne, who was also a Fellow of Merton College and a University proctor,[24] were probably relatives of two 14th-century abbots of Eynsham.[25] Early 15th-century rectors were not graduates and the church was the subject of frequent exchanges. Later, graduate rectors were again instituted: they included Master Robert Darcy (1462–6), Master Walter Bate (1466–79), a benefactor of Lincoln College,[26] Master Thomas Warner (d. 1514)[27] and his successor. The last was studying in Oxford in about 1520, with the result that the episcopal visitors found the church defective, the rectory farmed, and the walls of the cemetery broken, so that cattle wandered in.[28]

The state of confusion in the church during the religious changes of the 16th century is illustrated by a case in the archdeacon's court in 1584–5. John Hale, once churchwarden, admitted having sold the chalice to buy a communion cup; the cross, crucifix, and altar cloths were in the hands of three parishioners; another parishioner, shortly afterwards returned as a recusant, had bought the chalice for 40s.; and another admitted to having a sepulchre which was used as a cupboard.[29]

Seventeenth-century rectors were above the average in competence and were resident. Norbury (see above), a 'preaching minister' and a married man,[30] brought much trouble on the church by agreeing to the terms of the inclosure award of 1613, whereby the tithes were commuted for 40s. a yardland.[31] This agreement was to prove increasingly disadvantageous, and in 1638, on the petition of Norbury's successor Thomas Harding (1622–c. 1645), was reversed by a decree of Chancery.[32] Harding, who was removed from his living, was a characteristic 17th-century divine of the Laudian school,[33] and was long remembered at Souldern for his rebuilding of the parsonage[34] and for his 'hospitality and charity to the poor'.[35] Thomas Hodges (1647–62)[36] and William Twine (1663–6),[37] on the other hand, were Low Church sympathizers. In the time of Bryan Turner (1666–98), a well-known preacher,[38] the tithe dispute again flared up. The farmers wanted another money settlement in lieu of tithes,[39] while the rector protested against various practices of tithe-evasion, comparing Souldern with the neighbouring parish of Fritwell, where the great tithes were worth £120, while at Souldern, where the land was much more

valuable, the tithes could only be let for £90.[40] The dispute was eventually referred to the Bishop of London, who in 1676 made an award, which was to stand until the early 19th century, commuting the tithes for £2 12s. 6d. a yardland.[41]

With one exception 18th-century rectors were resident. One, John Russell (1735–72), is memorable for beginning the unusual practice of holding services on Wednesdays and Fridays, as well as for having two services on Sundays. He administered the sacrament four times a year, catechized the children in summer, and was able to report 20 to 30 communicants and a parish 'very regular about going to church'.[42] The same number of services were continued by his successor, John Horseman[43] (1772–1806), well known in the neighbourhood as an inclosure commissioner.[44] He continued, however, to accept the tithe agreement, by this time very disadvantageous to the church, as he preferred to remain on good terms with his parishioners.[45] His successor Robert Jones (1806–35)[46] was determined to overthrow the composition, which brought in about £120 for all tithes, instead of their estimated value of over £300.[47] In 1808, backed by St. John's College, Cambridge, he made a settlement with the landowners for £435 a year,[48] and in 1842 the tithes were commuted for £431.[49] The rectory thus became a very comfortable one, for the rector in addition to the tithes had his glebe: a few acres in Souldern, and about 55 acres in Fritwell[50] with commons for 8 beasts and 62 sheep,[51] which were exchanged in 1808 for Inland farm (123 a.).[52]

Because of the bitterness of the tithe dispute and the dilapidated state of the Rectory, Jones did not come to Souldern until the bishop forced him to do so in 1809.[53] His expenditure on the repair of the Rectory[54] and farm buildings,[55] on top of expenses for inclosure in Fritwell, so crippled him financially that from 1822 he was allowed to be non-resident and to hire a resident curate.[56]

The religious revival of the mid-19th century was covered by the long incumbency of Lawrence Stephenson (1835–89), considered an Evangelical Anglican[57] and rather conservative. In 1854, when there were between 30 and 40 communicants and a congregation of 150, he said he made no effort to fill his church, as the Wesleyans did theirs.[58]

The church of *ST. MARY THE VIRGIN* is a

[24] G. C. Brodrick, *Mem. of Merton* (O.H.S. iv), 208; *Cal. Papal Pet.* i. 390.
[25] *V.C.H. Oxon.* ii. 67.
[26] A. Clark, *Lincoln Coll.* 30; Emden, *O.U. Reg.* i.
[27] See below, p. 310.
[28] *Visit. Dioc. Linc. 1517–31*, i. 123.
[29] Blo. *Sould.* 58–59; *Archd. Ct.* ii. 209, 242, 247.
[30] Blo. *Sould.* 69.
[31] Blo. *Sould.* 90; C 78/381/10: Incl. decree. The principal materials for the tithe dispute are the parish records and records at St. John's Coll., Camb., both cited in Blo. *Sould.* 91–94.
[32] *Cal. S.P. Dom.* 1637–8, 342, 405; Par. Rec. Bishop of London's 1676 award, notes at back.
[33] C 5/575/87, where he is said to have been imprisoned for his loyalty.   [34] See above, p. 305.
[35] Tablet in church. See also *D.N.B.* and *Walker Rev.* 297.
[36] For him see Hist. MSS. Com. *6th Rep. App.* 203; *Calamy Rev.* 270; and Venn, *Alumni.* He was the first of a long line of Fellows of St. John's Coll., Camb., to be rector.
[37] Blo. *Sould.* 75.
[38] Ibid. 76.   [39] C 5/575/87.
[40] E 134/27 Chas. II/Trin. 3; Blo. *Sould.* 92–93; H. Gwillim, *Coll. re Tithes*, ii. 524–6.

[41] Blo. *Sould.* 92; Par. Rec. Bishop of London's 1676 award.
[42] Oxf. Dioc. d 554.
[43] Ibid. d 565.
[44] Blo. *Sould.* 81–82. See also the unflattering broadside *Who was the Revd. John Horseman?*, Bodl. G.A. Oxon. 16° 33(18).
[45] Blo. *Sould.* 94.
[46] See above, p. 302.
[47] Blo. *Sould.* 94.
[48] Oxf. Dioc. c 658, f. 62.
[49] Bodl. Tithe award.
[50] See above, p. 142.
[51] Blo. *Sould.* 93.
[52] O.R.O. Fritwell incl. award; Wing, *Annals*, 65. Before inclosure this land had been rented for £55, but later greatly increased in value: Blo. *Sould.* 94, 98. Inland farm and other land, 130 a. in all, still belonged to the living in 1955: inf. the Revd. H. G. Benson.
[53] Oxf. Dioc. c 658, f. 62.
[54] See above, p. 302.
[55] Blo. *Sould.* 95–96.
[56] Oxf. Dioc. c 429, f. 130.
[57] Blo. *Sould.* 84.
[58] *Wilb. Visit.*

stone building consisting of a chancel, clerestoried nave, south aisle and porch, and a western tower.[59]

The earliest parts of the church are the tower and the north wall of the nave, which, together with the north doorway, date from the second half of the 12th century. The foundations of an eastern apse are said to have been discovered when the chancel was rebuilt in 1896, and the original Romanesque church probably consisted of an aisleless nave with apsidal chancel and western tower. The presence of a 12th-century capital reused as the base of one of the columns of the arcade on the south side of the nave may, however, indicate that a south aisle was added

described this building as a 'low-roofed, room-like, mean erection'.[65] In 1815 a western gallery was erected and in 1855 the original carved seats were removed from the nave and replaced by pews.[66] In 1877 the church was again in urgent need of repair: the architect A. Hodgson of Bloxham proposed that the chancel should be rebuilt[67] by the lay rectors and in 1878 restoration work was started by J. Cox of Souldern, who removed the gallery and the plaster in the nave. A new chancel and organ-chamber were built in 1896–7 to the designs of Bucknall and J. N. Comper, and in 1906 the tower was taken down and rebuilt by G. F. Bodley.[68]

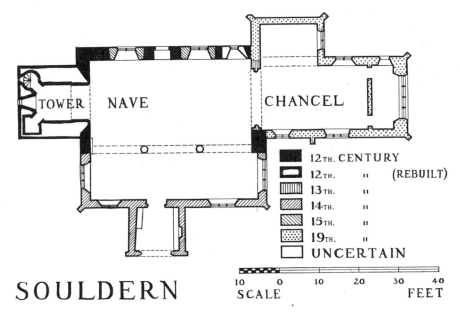

TOWER NAVE CHANCEL

■ 12TH. CENTURY
□ 12TH.   "   (REBUILT)
▤ 13TH.   "
▨ 14TH.   "
▧ 15TH.   "
▦ 19TH.   "
□ UNCERTAIN

SOULDERN

10   0   10   20   30   40
SCALE   FEET

before the end of the 12th century. Early in the 13th century the chancel was rebuilt on a rectangular plan and given a new chancel arch with sculptured capitals. During the first half of the 14th century the south aisle was rebuilt on a larger scale, and the spacious south porch with stone benches was added. The existing arcade was reconstructed with new arches, but the old circular pillars were reused. Late in the 15th or early in the 16th century the high-pitched roof of the nave was replaced by a flat roof and clerestory of small rectangular windows.[59] In 1698 nearly £100 was spent on repairs,[60] and about twenty years later Rawlinson found the church neat and well kept.[61] Repairs were ordered in 1757 and in 1758 the church was painted.[62] In 1775 the condition of the chancel was serious: the roof had fallen in and the walls were crumbling. The medieval chancel was pulled down by the rector and a much smaller one erected in its place.[63] This filled only about half of the chancel arch, the top part of which was blocked up and three lancet windows inserted.[64] Blomfield

The 12th-century stone font is plain and circular.[69] The wooden pulpit is 19th century and the organ was built by Jackson of Oxford. Nothing remains of the coats of arms seen by Rawlinson in the chancel windows.[70] There are the remains of a wall-painting —probably St. Christopher—on the north wall.

Among the memorials in the church is a restored heart brass of c. 1460. The commemorative inscription has been lost, and its place is now occupied by a modern restoration of a 16th-century inscription in memory of John Throckmorton.[71] There are also brasses to Thomas Warner, parson (d. 1514), and to an unknown female of the 16th century. There is a tablet in the nave to F. and A. G. dated 1664 and many other 18th- and 19th-century inscriptions to the Gough family. Inscriptions to other prominent Souldern families, Kilby, Dodwell, and Weedon,[72] which were recorded in 1882, are now nearly illegible.

In 1552 the church was furnished with a silver-gilt chalice, two brass candlesticks, some vestments,

[59] Cf. Gough, *Hist. Souldern* (O.A.S.), 19 sq., for an account of 1887.
[60] Blo. *Sould.* 57 quoting churchwardens' accts.
[61] *Par. Coll.* iii. 270.
[62] Oxf. Archd. Oxon. d 13, f. 33; Blo. *Sould.* 57.
[63] Oxf. Archd. Oxon. b 26, f. 392; ibid. c 122, f. 70; Oxf. Dioc. c 434, f. 73*b*.
[64] See plate opposite. It shows the drawing by J. Buckler (1823) in MS .Top. Oxon. a 68, f. 484, showing 18th-cent. chancel. It had a square-headed three-light east window. See opposite for a pre-restoration view of the interior by Joseph Wilkins.

[65] Blo. *Sould.* 57.
[66] Ibid.
[67] J. H. and A. P. Gough, *Notes on Souldern* (Bicester, 1882), 26.
[68] Bodl. Par. Box (uncat.): faculties.
[69] There is a Buckler drawing in MS. Top. Oxon. a 68, f. 483.
[70] *Par. Coll.* iii. 270; Bodl. G.A. Oxon. 4° 687, p. 270.
[71] *Trans. Monumental Brass Soc.* viii (vi). 227–30.
[72] For complete list see *Par. Coll.* iii. 271–2, and Gough, *Notes on Souldern*, 29–38; for arms see Bodl. G.A. Oxon. 16° 217, pp. 221–2.

Interior of the church from the west in the mid-19th century

South-east view of the church in 1823

SOULDERN

transferred to Fritwell in 1930, and the school was controlled in 1951. The number of pupils was 47 in 1937, but only 17 in 1954.[15]

St. Joseph's Roman Catholic School was built in 1879 on a site given by Lt.-Col. R. S. Cox.[16] There were one mistress and 18 pupils in 1887, but only 8 pupils in 1903.[17] The school was closed in 1904.[18]

CHARITIES. The inclosure award of 1613 assigned to the poor 13 acres of land[19] and a rent of 5s. a year paid by the rector for waste ground by the parsonage. Up to 1814 the allotment was used as common pasture by the inhabitants, and was the subject of frequent disputes. Responsible trustees were only appointed in 1815. By 1824 seventeen cottages, with gardens, had been built on the allotment either by the parish or the poor themselves, and there were 40 other gardens. Poor families paid the trustees 1s. 6d. a year for a cottage and garden or 1s. for a garden only. Vacancies were filled from the oldest poor inhabitants. The remainder of the allotment was let, and the annual income of the whole including the rector's 5s. was about £5, which was distributed to the poor by the vestry, those without cottages or gardens getting 5s. each, and those with them 1s. A small surplus was reserved for poor widows and old men.[20] In 1948 sixteen cottages brought in £108 13s. 6d. and 48 gardens £4 7s.; land was rented for £6 6s. and with the rector's 5s. and a rent charge of £7 on part of the Souldern manor estate the total income was £126 11s. 6d.[21]

Thomas Dodwell, by deed dated 1694, gave a rent charge of £1 10s. a year to buy clothing for two poor people to be chosen by those Protestant parishioners who held ¼ yardland or more. In the 1820's five or six poor Protestants received cloth to make jackets or petticoats, the oldest married parishioners not receiving relief benefiting in turn.

By other deeds, dated 1694 and 1699, Dodwell conveyed about 20 acres of land on trust that its successive owners should distribute threepenny loaves to four poor people every Sunday morning in the parish church. Recipients were to be chosen in the same way as for the clothing charity. In 1824, however, four poor widows were nominated by the vestry.

Richard Cartwright of Aynho, by will dated 1634, left a rent charge of £9 19s. 4d. to provide bread for the poor of Aynho, Croughton (Northants), and Souldern. In 1824 £2 3s. 4d. charged on lands in Aynho was spent on eightpenny loaves for five poor widows chosen by the vestry.[22]

Elizabeth Westcar of Hill House, by will dated 1820, left property in trust to raise £600, of which £400 was to be invested and the income used to purchase bread and clothing. These were to be distributed to the poor on Christmas day.[23]

In 1832 John Westcar bequeathed £506 6s. 7d. in stock to provide clothing for the poor. The income of the charity was £15 3s. 9d. in 1870.[24]

The Souldern charities were regulated by a scheme of the Charity Commissioners made in 1891, but in the early 20th century their administration and distribution were irregular and caused many disputes.[25] Under a new scheme all the charities were amalgamated in 1949, and the income was to be used to buy medicine and appliances for the sick, to help young people to enter trades, to supply food, fuel, and clothes for the needy, and to make loans of money in cases of special distress.[26] Many of the cottages on the poor's allotment were condemned after 1948, and charity funds had temporarily to be employed to repair others. In 1955 the total income was £89 16s. 4d. and was made up of poor's allotment: £57 11s.; Westcar charities: £26; Dodwell charities: £4 2s., and Cartwright charity: £2 3s. 4d.[27]

STOKE LYNE

THIS large parish, said to be ten miles in circumference in the 18th century,[1] once stretched right from Fritwell on the west to Fringford on the east, with Bicester four miles to the south-east as its nearest market-town, but in 1948 it lost to Ardley 685 acres, including its hamlet of Fewcot, and has since comprised 3,216 acres.[2] The parish is well watered by a number of streams: one, the Ockley Brook, forms the boundary with Northamptonshire in the north; a small stream divides Stoke Lyne from Tusmore Park; another stream, the Bure,[3] flowing south-east from Bainton Spinney, marks the southern boundary for a short way; while the Birne,[4] a small tributary of the Great Ouse, demarcates the parish for a stretch on the north-east. Round Hill, a tumulus, stands on the northern boundary.[5]

The parish lies mostly on the Great Oolite belt which crosses the county,[6] but there are small areas of Cornbrash. On the eastern boundary the land is low-lying and liable to flooding, but the rest of the parish is upland, nearly 400 feet above sea-level. In Domesday Book woodland (3 × 2 furlongs) is recorded;[7] in 1279 12 acres of wood and 4 of spinney are mentioned;[8] and in the late 18th and 19th centuries it was the coverts in the parish which helped to make it a well-known hunting district. Stoke and Little Stoke Woods lie on either side of Swift's House (see below), and Sycamore Grove, Stoke

15 Inf. Oxon. Educ. Cttee.
16 Blo. *Sould.* 100; see above, p. 305.
17 *Kelly's Dir. Oxon.* (1887, 1903).
18 Inf. Oxon. Educ. Cttee.
19 Cole's Cross (7 a.), the Green (5 a.), the Pits and the Bowling Green (1 a.); see above, p. 306.
20 *12th Rep. Com. Char.* 311–12.
21 Par. Rec. copy of Char. Com. scheme (1948).
22 *Char. Don.* ii. 990; *12th Rep. Com. Char.* 312–13.
23 *12th Rep. Com. Char.* 313–14.
24 *Gen. Digest Char.*
25 Inf. the Revd. H. G. Benson.
26 Par. Rec. Char. Com. scheme.

27 Inf. the Revd. H. G. Benson.
1 Blo. *Stoke,* 31, citing Bodl. MS. Rawl. B 400 f, f. 53.
2 O.S. Map 6″, xvi, xvii (1885); ibid. 2½″, 42/52, 53 (1951); *Census,* 1951. For Fewcot ecclesiastical parish, see below, p. 321.
3 Blo. *Stoke,* 2 n.
4 Called the Claydon Brook farther east. In the Middle Ages its name was the Bune: *P.N. Bucks.* (E.P.N.S.), 2; E. Ekwall, *Eng. River Names,* 56.
5 *V.C.H. Oxon.* ii. 347.
6 G.S. Map 1″, xlv NE.
7 *V.C.H. Oxon.* i. 411.
8 *Rot. Hund.* (Rec. Com.), ii. 825.

Bushes, and Bainton Copse are others. Three hundred oaks, felled in the First World War, were planted in this last copse in 1792 by Joseph Bullock of Caversfield.[9]

The parish is crossed by the main roads from Oxford to Brackley and from Bicester to Banbury. They intersect at Baynard's Green, the modern name for the historic Bayard's Green (see below). The nearest railway stations lie over the borders at Somerton, 4½ miles distant, and at Bicester.[10]

The mother village of Stoke Lyne is centrally placed and lies in the valley of the Bure stream, but at an early date colonizing settlements were made at Bainton, or 'Bada's farm', on the southern boundary, and at Fewcot, close to two springs in the extreme west of the parish. Its name means 'few cottages' (O.E. *fēawe cotu*).[11] The name Stoke was derived from the Old English *stoc* meaning 'cattle-farm'.[12] It was once called Stoke Insula or Stoke de Lisle after the medieval lords of the manor; but after it passed into the Lynde or Lyne family in the 15th century the suffix Lyne came into use.[13]

Both Stoke and Bainton must have been fair-sized villages in the 14th century.[14] Indeed Stoke may have been once larger than it was in the 17th century, when traces of decayed houses gave rise to the erroneous belief that the place had once been a market-town.[15] As the number of houses listed for the hearth tax and by 18th-century vicars may relate to the hamlets as well as to Stoke Lyne, it is impossible to be precise about its size or the number of its substantial houses. Altogether, besides the manor-house of Stoke, there were 2 large houses of 7 and 8 hearths and 5 small farm-houses besides one-hearth dwellings listed in 1665.[16] In the mid-18th century some 40 or so houses were recorded.[17]

In 1797 Davis's map shows that most of the village of Stoke lay north of the church on what once may have been an open green.[18] In 1881 the stocks were still standing there, with the public house to the south; Church Farm, the smithy, the post office, and the school, built in 1858 at the expense of Sir Henry Peyton, lay south of the church.[19] Much of the village had already been rebuilt in consequence of a fire in 1851 which destroyed about 25 thatched cottages.[20] Some of those who were rendered homeless built themselves cottages in Stratton Lane, and in 1860 the lord of the manor, on whose land they had squatted, went to law. The 'Stoke Lyne Ejectment Trials' resulted in a verdict in the lord's favour, but with damages of 1s.[21] The 'Royal George' was opened between 1851 and 1864 and was later named the

'Peyton Arms'.[22] A large vicarage was built in 1872.[23]

The manor-house, the home of the Lynes, Holts, and Pettys, had become a ruin by 1808[24] and was pulled down. In Ralph Holt's day in the 1660's it was a substantial house which was taxed on ten hearths.[25] It is thought to have been built by William Lyne in the 15th century; traces of its site could still be seen south of the church at the end of the 19th century.[26] It is memorable as the home of Charnel Petty, a cousin of Anthony Wood, who was a frequent visitor. The antiquary was there for a week in 1658, when he rode about the country making notes on monuments and arms, and again in 1659.[27]

The only trace today of the former hamlet of Bainton is four farm-houses and a cottage.[28] The sometime manor house is the present Bainton Manor Farm, a late 16th-century or early 17th-century house.[29] It is built of coursed rubble, with ashlar quoins, on a double rectangular plan; it has a valley roof covered in stone slates. At the end of the 19th century Blomfield noted the remains of a fine avenue of elm trees which had once led up to it.[30] It is likely that John Marsh of Bainton lived there in the early 16th century. He is known to have been a man of means, who willed that there should be six priests at his burial in Stoke Lyne church and that each should have 6d. apiece and the poor 40s.[31] In the 18th century the Pettys of Bainton may have occupied it. In 1783 John Warde, a celebrated rider to hounds, was using it as a hunting-box, and he and Joseph Bullock of Caversfield, who had bought the manor, co-operated in building stables and kennels. In 1800 Sir Thomas Mostyn, who later built Swift's House, was living there.[32] An obelisk erected in the early 19th century over the burial-place of a noted fox-hound commemorates the days when the Bicester kennels were at Bainton.[33]

Fewcot, on the other hand, still flourished in 1955, and retained a number of its 17th-century houses and cottages of coursed rubble. Fewcot Farm is built on a T-shaped plan and has contemporary chimney shafts of brick set diagonally. A cottage has similar chimneys, a thatched roof, and staircase projection. Manor Farm is also rubble-built, but on a rectangular plan. Its roof is of stone and Welsh slate. It has casement windows.[34] The 'White Lion', which was not used as an inn until about 1891, is a similar house. The vicarage, first used as such in the early 20th century,[35] was once two ancient cottages which have been modernized and partly rebuilt.

The chief mansion in the parish is now Swift's

[9] Joseph Bullock's diary *penes* Col. the Hon. E. H. Wyndham, Caversfield.
[10] *Kelly's Dir. Oxon.* (1939).
[11] *P.N. Oxon.* (E.P.N.S.), i. 239.
[12] Ekwall, *Dict. Eng. P.N.*
[13] See below, p. 316. The Lyndes were commonly called Lyne: Blo. *Buck.* 26; Blo. *Stoke*, 11. There seems no need for the explanation of the name given in *P.N. Oxon.* (E.P.N.S.), i. 237.
[14] See below, p. 319.
[15] Wood, *Life*, i. 264 n. 1.
[16] *Hearth Tax Oxon.* 207: 5 small farms listed, some perhaps in Bainton and Fewcot.
[17] Oxf. Dioc. d 554, d 557, d 560.
[18] Davis, *Oxon. Map.*
[19] O.S. Map 25″, xvii. 9 (1881).
[20] Blo. *Stoke*, 32–33.
[21] Ibid. 34.
[22] *Kelly's Dir. Oxon.* (1864); Gardner, *Dir. Oxon.* (1851)

does not mention it. In 1784 there were 3 inns: O.R.O. Victlrs'. recog.
[23] See below, p. 322.
[24] Blo. *Stoke*, 22.
[25] *Hearth Tax Oxon.* 207.
[26] Blo. *Stoke*, 22.
[27] Wood, *Life*, i. 184, 263, 276–7. Stoke Lyne is omitted from *Par. Coll.* See, however, Bodl. MS. Rawl. B 400 c, ff. 179–86.
[28] O.S. Map 25″, xvii, 14 (1881); see below, p. 319.
[29] H. Wyndham, *A Backward Glance*, 55–58, where there is a photograph of the manor house.
[30] Blo. *Stoke*, 22.   [31] Ibid.
[32] Joseph Bullock's diary: see above, n. 9. The house was repaired in 1775 and 1783.
[33] Blo. *Stoke*, 22–23. For further information about the Bicester Hunt see above, p. 35, and below, p. 325.
[34] *Kelly's Dir. Oxon.* (1887).
[35] See below, p. 322.

House, the home since 1830 of the Peyton family.[36] The present house was built in about 1800 by Sir Thomas Mostyn on the site of an inn owned by one Swift on the Bicester–Aynho turnpike.[37] It is a three-story house of stucco with a Welsh slate roof; there is a contemporary plaster frieze of some distinction in the drawing-room.[38] It is possible that Swift's Inn is to be identified with a 17th-century inn, described in 1634–5 as a messuage in Bainton. It was bought in about 1616 by a certain John Manning. It was then called the 'Woolsack' and had long been used as an inn, but the new owner renamed it the 'White Horse'.[39]

The parish may have been the scene of a 6th-century battle. It has been suggested that an unidentified wood in Stoke Lyne, called 'Fethelee' in 1198, gave its name to the battle of Fethanleag, fought in 584 between Ceawlin, king of the West Saxons, and the Britons.[40] On the other hand this region seems to have been already sparsely settled by the Saxons and it has been argued that Ceawlin's campaign was more likely to have been fought in the Severn valley.[41]

The open character of the country also seems to have led to its use for tournaments in the Middle Ages. Davis's map of 1797 marks the high ground in the north of the parish on the Northamptonshire border and the western boundary of Tusmore as Bayard's Green (i.e. horse's green).[42] The green is traditionally supposed to have been the site of the tournaments ordered to be held at Brackley in the 13th century.[43] It begins about six miles to the south-west of Brackley and it may be that all this area, if not used for the actual tournament, served as a camping-ground for horses and men. The green seems to have been well known in the 17th century and to have covered a larger area.[44] Richard Symonds speaks of it as if it partly lay east of Brackley: in 1644, he says, Charles I's army en route for Brackley from Buckingham came to a 'large greene or downe called Bayard's Greene, where often is horse-race-ing, six myle long'.[45] There are 18th-century references to it as lying on the northern boundary of Cottisford and Mixbury.[46] It therefore seems as if it once lay on both sides of the Brackley road and extended from Brackley southwards towards Stoke Lyne.

In view of the extent of the former Bayard's Green it is impossible to say with certainty how much of the Civil War took place in Stoke Lyne parish. There are references to a military rendezvous on the green in 1644[47] and to the king's engineers and horse being encamped there before the Battle of Naseby.[48]

In the 19th century the parish was a noted hunting centre. John Warde of Bainton was the founder in the late 18th century of the celebrated Bicester pack,[49] and in about 1800 Sir Thomas Mostyn established himself and his hounds at Swift's House.[50] He was later followed by the Peytons, another noted hunting family.[51] Sir Henry Peyton (d. 1854), his son Sir Henry, and Major-General Sir Thomas Peyton, the 5th baronet, were also well known in the parish and outside as gentlemen coach-drivers. The elder Sir Henry and his four-in-hand coach were described by Thackeray in *The Four Georges*. He kept an average of ten greys in his stables at Swift's House and was a familiar figure on the Oxfordshire roads.[52]

The villagers also had their amusements and Stoke Lyne men had a morris-dancing team in the 19th century, which was well known locally.[53]

MANORS. Before the Conquest Stoke Lyne was one of the two Oxfordshire manors held by Tostig, Earl of Northumbria,[54] who was killed at Stamford Bridge in 1066. By 1086, assessed at 10½ hides, it was held by Walter Giffard,[55] a cousin of William I and shortly to become Earl of Buckingham. With his nine other Oxfordshire manors, Stoke Lyne formed part of his honor of Giffard, of which the *caput* was Long Crendon (Bucks.). On Walter's death in 1102 his property descended to his son Walter Giffard, with whom the male line of the Giffards ended in 1164.[56] The Giffard lands were inherited by Richard de Clare, Earl of Pembroke, the conqueror of Ireland, who was descended from a sister of the first Walter Giffard. His lands followed the descent of the earldom of Pembroke until the death of the last Marshal earl in 1245.[57] The Pembroke lands were divided among five coheiresses, and the overlordship of Stoke Lyne went to the earls of Gloucester, descended from Gilbert de Clare (d. 1230), the husband of Isabel Marshal.[58] When the last Clare earl was killed at Bannockburn in 1314, and his estate divided among his three sisters, Stoke Lyne was not mentioned.[59] From then it was held directly of the king by the earls of Oxford, as part of their honor of Whitchurch (Bucks.), until at least the 16th century.[60]

In 1086 the under-tenant was Hugh de Bolebec,

---

[36] See below, p. 316.

[37] Blo. *Stoke*, 23, records the tradition that it was a coaching inn, but this is not confirmed by coach time-tables. A Jonathan Swift was an inn-keeper in Stoke parish in 1753: O.R.O. Victlrs'. recog.

[38] See photo., Nat. Buildings Record.

[39] C 78/1199/8.

[40] F. M. Stenton, *Anglo-Saxon Eng.* 29; cf. *P.N. Oxon.* (E.P.N.S.), i. 238; *Anglo-Saxon Chron.* ed. G. N. Garmonsway (1953), 20–21.

[41] See E. T. Leeds, 'The Growth of Wessex', *Oxoniensia*, xix. 57–58.

[42] Described in the 19th cent. as an elevated table-land on the S. bank of the Ouse near Evenley Mill: Baker, *Northants*, i. 573.

[43] N. Denholm-Young, 'The Tournament in the 13th century', *Studies presented to F. M. Powicke*, 240 sqq.

[44] No record of the name Bayard's Green has been found earlier than the 17th cent.

[45] R. Symonds, *Diary of Civil War*, ed. C. E. Long (Camd. Soc. 1st ser. lxxiv), 22; Kennett, *Paroch. Antiq.* i. 212–13, takes the Brackley tournament to have been on

Bayard's Green. See above, p. 252.

[46] *P.N. Oxon.* (E.P.N.S.), i. 238.

[47] Luke, *Jnl.* 230.

[48] Letter from Luke cited in A. Beesley, *Hist. Banbury*, 408.

[49] *V.C.H. Oxon.* ii. 356; H. Wyndham, *A Backward Glance*, 21.

[50] Blo. *Stoke*, 23.

[51] Ibid. 25–26; *V.C.H. Oxon.* ii. 357.

[52] Blo. *Stoke*, 24–25.

[53] Clare Coll. Libr., Cambridge, MS. Sharp, Folk Dance Notes, 4, 91.

[54] *V.C.H. Oxon.* i. 411, 426.

[55] Ibid. i. 411. For Giffard's estate of 6 virgates, half in Stoke and half in Tusmore, see below, p. 335.

[56] *Complete Peerage*, ii. 836–7.

[57] Ibid. vi. 501, note f; x. 358–77.

[58] Ibid. v. 695; *Rot. Hund.* (Rec. Com.), ii. 825; *Cal. Inq. p.m.* i, pp. 157, 159.

[59] *Complete Peerage*, v. 714; *Cal. Inq. p.m.* v, pp. 325–54.

[60] *Cal. Inq. p.m.* x, p. 519; C 142/35/93; for the honor's history see *V.C.H. Bucks.* iii. 443.

who probably came from Bolbec in Normandy, where he was also a tenant of Walter Giffard.[61] He held seven of Walter Giffard's ten Oxfordshire manors, and was himself tenant-in-chief of another Oxfordshire manor, Rycote in Great Haseley.[62] About 1166 his grandson Hugh de Bolebec, the son of Walter de Bolebec, owed the service of 20 knights to the honor of Giffard, in which Stoke Lyne was included.[63] The male line of the family ended with Hugh's son Walter; and half of the family estates, including Stoke Lyne, descended through Isabel de Bolebec, Walter's sister and coheiress, who had married Robert de Vere, 3rd Earl of Oxford, to the earls of Oxford.[64] They were thus mesne tenants throughout the 13th century, and became tenants-in-chief only in the 14th century.

By the end of the 12th century Stoke Lyne had been divided into two manors. One, later known as *COKEFELDISPLACE*, was held as $\frac{1}{2}$ knight's fee by Robert de Tinchebray, who took his name from Tinchebrai in Normandy. He was of the Norman family of Peverel, and may have been a knight of Hugh de Bolebec.[65] He was apparently alive during Stephen's reign, but was dead by 1191,[66] and Lucy his daughter[67] inherited Stoke Lyne and other lands. In 1194 her cousin Robert Peverel of Sampford Peverel (Devon), the son of William Peverel, her father's first cousin, claimed she was illegitimate and tried to get possession of her property.[68]

Lucy, who kept Stoke Lyne, was by this time the widow of Adam de Cokefield of Feltwell (Norf.), an important East Anglian landowner. Their son Adam was dead by 1212, leaving his son a minor.[69] After this there was further subinfeudation of the manor, and by 1255 it was being held of Robert de Coke-field, who was probably Adam's son.[70] Robert was himself holding of the Earl of Oxford, who held of the Earl of Gloucester, the tenant-in-chief. Robert's heir was probably another Adam de Cokefield, but it is not known if he succeeded. Adam's son was Robert (II) de Cokefield of Feltwell, who was holding in 1279.[71] He died in 1297, leaving as heiress his sister Joan.[72] She was married three times and it was she who was lady of Stoke Lyne in 1316.[73] In 1346 a $\frac{1}{2}$-fee was said to be held of a Robert de Coke-

field,[74] but the branch of the family in Stoke Lyne seems to have died out.

In the early 13th century the Cokefields' under-tenants at Stoke Lyne were a family of Eyville, which held land in several counties.[75] In 1243 Robert d'Eyville was tenant, in 1255 Denise d'Eyville held it of Robert de Cokefield in dower, and in 1262 Thomas d'Eyville (*de Everus*) was tenant.[76] In 1265 the under-tenant was John de Cokefield, member of another branch of the De Cokefield family.[77] He was one of Edward I's knights, a cousin of Robert de Cokefield, and a prominent landowner with land in Nottinghamshire and Suffolk.[78] The manor was seized after the Barons' War by the Earl of Gloucester, but as John de Cokefield had not opposed the king it was soon restored.[79] He died in 1310 or 1311.[80] His widow continued to hold land in Stoke Lyne on which she was assessed in 1327, but her son Sir John de Cokefield, who had been in debt for £60 to Sir Richard Damory,[81] had already sold him the manor in 1321. Into the 15th century it retained the name 'Cokefeldisplace'.[82]

Unlike the Cokefields, the De Lisles, who held the other manor, known as *STOKE INSULA* or *STOKE DE LISLE*, were primarily an Oxfordshire family. They first appear in Stoke round 1185, when Otwel de Lisle granted land to the Templars.[83] In 1198 he was at law with Lucy de Cokefield about lands in Stoke, and his name frequently occurs as a witness to local charters until as late as 1216.[84] By his wife Adelize he had two sons, and after his death one, Robert, appears to have held of the other, Otwel.[85] It may have been Otwel's son Robert who was mesne tenant in the 1250's, and whose land was temporarily seized by the Earl of Gloucester in 1265.[86] Robert was mesne tenant in 1279 and 1285.[87]

The under-tenants probably descended from the first Otwel's younger son Robert, who held the manor in 1236, and who was dead by 1241, when his son Giles was a minor in the custody of Walter de Raleigh, Bishop of Norwich.[88] Giles was in posses-sion by 1253, when he made an agreement with Robert de Lisle as to their tenurial relationship with the Earl of Oxford,[89] but seems to have been dead by 1260.[90] His son and heir, a minor, later became

---

[61] *V.C.H. Oxon.* i. 411; L. C. Loyd, *Anglo-Norman Families* (Harl. Soc. ciii), 17.

[62] *V.C.H. Oxon.* i. 410–12.

[63] *Red Bk. Exch.* (Rolls Ser.), 312. For the pedigree of the De Bolebecs see *Rot. de Dominabus*, ed. J. H. Round (P.R.S. xxxv), pp. xxxix–xli. Their home was at Whit-church (Bucks.): *V.C.H. Bucks.* iii. 443.

[64] For the complicated descent see *Rot. de Dom.* ed. Round, pp. xxxix–xli.

[65] *V.C.H. Bucks.* iii. 443 n. 14.

[66] *Cal. Chart. R.* 1327–41, 103; see also Dugd. *Mon.* v. 212; *V.C.H. Bucks.* iii. 429.

[67] She may have been the wife of Richard Fitzniel of Bletchingdon: *Eynsham Cart.* i. 97.

[68] *Rot. Cur. Reg.* (Rec. Com.), i. 46. The relationship of these Peverels to the famous William Peverel (d. 1114) has not been found. They are not mentioned in the pedi-gree of his family: *Complete Peerage*, iv. 771. Possibly they were descended from his brother Robert: ibid 761, note b.

[69] Farrer, *Honors*, iii. 365; *Rot. Litt. Claus.* Rec. Com.), i. 140, 159, 272.

[70] *Rot. Hund.* (Rec. Com.), ii. 44.

[71] Farrer, *Honors*, iii. 366; *Cal. Chart. R*, 1257–1300, 265; *Rot. Hund.* (Rec. Com.), ii. 825; *Cal. Inq. p.m.* iii, p. 256.

[72] *Cal. Inq. p.m.* iii, p. 256, C. Moor, *Knights of Edw. I*, i (Harl. Soc. lxxx), 221. For the family see F. Blomefield, *Norfolk*, ii. 190 and *passim;* Thoroton, *Notts.* ii. 253.

[73] Farrer, *Honors*, iii. 366–7; *Feud. Aids*, iv. 169.

[74] *Feud. Aids*, iv. 181. This Robert does not fit in with any genealogy of the family.

[75] *Bk. of Fees*, index.

[76] Ibid. 824, 833; *Rot. Hund.* (Rec. Com.), ii. 44; *Cal. Inq. p.m.* i, pp. 157, 159.

[77] *Cal. Inq. Misc.* i, p. 261.

[78] Thoroton, *Notts.* ii. 253, makes him a second cousin. Their mothers also were related: Blomefield, *Norfolk*, ix. 361; Moor, *Knights of Edw. I*, i. 221, where he is incorrectly said to have died in 1304.

[79] *Cal. Inq. Misc.* i, p. 261.

[80] Blomefield, *Norfolk*, ix. 376, 410.

[81] E 179/161/9; *Cal. Close*, 1318–23, 231.

[82] C.P. 25(1)/189/16/12; ibid. 191/25/23–24.

[83] *Sandford Cart.* 302; see also *St. Frides. Cart.* ii. 149. 151.

[84] *Fines Oxon.* 4; *Cur. Reg. R.* i. 60; Kennett, *Paroch. Antiq.* i. 255.

[85] *Sandford Cart.* 302; *Eynsham Cart.* i. 133; *Fines Oxon.* 113.

[86] *Fines Oxon.* 168; *Rot. Hund.* (Rec. Com.), ii. 44; *Cal. Inq. Misc.* i, p. 261.

[87] *Rot. Hund.* (Rec. Com.), ii. 826; *Feud. Aids*, iv. 157.

[88] *Sandford Cart.* 302; *Fines Oxon.* 70; *Bk. of Fees*, 557, 833; *Fines Oxon.* 113.

[89] *Fines Oxon.* 168.

[90] Kennett, *Paroch. Antiq.* i. 361.

Sir Giles de Lisle, a prominent local knight, who held Stoke in 1279 and 1285.[91] He seems to have had only three daughters,[92] and to have granted his Stoke manor during his lifetime to Richard Damory,[93] who was soon also to acquire the De Cokefield manor.

The Damorys were an important Oxfordshire family, who lived at Bucknell.[94] Sir Richard died in 1330 and his widow held at least part of Stoke until her death in 1354.[95] Their son Richard, who was heavily in debt to the king, then enfeoffed Sir John Chandos with his Oxfordshire lands in payment of a debt of £2,000 to the king, and was granted them back for life.[96] He died in 1375, his heirs being the sisters of Sir John Chandos.[97] Stoke is not mentioned in his inquisition post mortem, and it is uncertain when it passed to Sir Robert Bardolf of Mapledurham, who was in possession at his death in 1395.[98] He too was the last of a prominent Oxfordshire family.[99] His wife Amice, the daughter of Sir Alan de Buxhull, was the widow of Sir John Beverley, who had been granted the Damory manor of Bucknell by the king,[1] and Stoke may have come to Sir Robert Bardolf in the same way. Amice Bardolf, who lived at Mapledurham, held Stoke Lyne for life;[2] she died in 1416, leaving £5 to be distributed to her poor tenants of Stoke and Mapledurham.[3] Stoke manor then passed with Mapledurham to her nephew William Lynde, the son of Roger Lynde (d. 1407), her sister's husband.[4]

The Lyndes were to hold Stoke Lyne for 100 years. William Lynde died in 1438,[5] and his son Thomas in 1485.[6] In the time of Thomas's son John (d. 1519), the last member of the family, much of the family property was dispersed.[7] He left five daughters and Stoke Lyne went to the second daughter, Elizabeth, the wife of Robert Holt.[8] Robert Holt was probably dead by 1558,[9] and his son William, who married Catherine Dormer of Olney (Bucks.), died in 1583.[10] He was succeeded by his son Thomas (probably died 1608), and by his grandson Ralph (d. 1634),[11] who married Helen, the daughter of Walter Jones of Chastleton. Soon after his father's death Ralph was involved in financial difficulties and

borrowed £925 from his wife's family. Later, in 1617, he sold his growing timber, said to be worth at least £2,000, and demised the manor and rectory to the Joneses for a term of years to pay off his debts. The deed was to be annulled if Holt managed to pay his debts otherwise. In 1620 he was at law with his father-in-law, who he claimed had only lent him money to get possession of the estate.[12] Ralph Holt died in 1633 leaving a son Thomas,[13] who married Susan, a daughter of Charnell Petty of Tetsworth, and died young in 1644, leaving a son Ralph, then aged six.[14] On the death of Ralph Holt, senior, Charnell Petty came to live in Stoke, and later acted as guardian to his grandson and was buried in the church in 1662.[15] Ralph Holt, junior, became High Sheriff of Oxfordshire in 1678, and held the manor until his death in 1702.[16] He was succeeded by his son Charles, the last of the male line of the family, who probably held the manor until his death in 1731.[17] His daughter Susannah was his heir. She married Lt.-Col. Newsham Peers of Alveston (Warws.),[18] who was holding the manor in the 1730's.[19] He was killed in 1743 at the Battle of Dettingen.[20] He and his wife left no children, and for the next few years the descent of the manor cannot be traced.

By 1756 George Vernon, who in 1777 was created Earl of Shipbrook, had an interest in Stoke Lyne, for he was one of the patrons of the vicarage.[21] He held the whole manor by 1774,[22] and on his death without children in 1783 his widow continued to hold it until her death in 1808.[23] The manor descended to her cousin's husband, Major Thomas Rea Cole of Twickenham (Mdx.), and his grandson sold it in the 1850's to Sir Henry Peyton, Bt.[24] The Peytons, who earlier in the century had bought Swift's House, were a prominent Cambridgeshire family.[25] In 1955 Sir Algernon Peyton, 7th Bt., was lord.

The small manor of *BAINTON* has always been closely connected with land in Buckinghamshire. In 1086 it was rated at 2½ hides and held by Ghilo, the brother of Anscul de Picquigny, a former sheriff of

[91] See C. Moor, *Knights of Edw. I*, iii (Harl. Soc. lxxxii), 43; *Rot. Hund.* (Rec. Com.), ii. 825; *Feud. Aids*, iv. 157, for him.
[92] *Cal. Close*, 1323–7, 168.
[93] *Feud. Aids*, iv. 169; *Cal. Fine R.* 1307–19, 317.
[94] *Complete Peerage*, iv. 46–48; see above, p. 73.
[95] *Cal. Inq. p.m.* x, p. 145.
[96] *Cal. Close*, 1354–60, 56.
[97] *Complete Peerage*, iv. 48; *Cal. Inq. p.m.* xiv, p. 115.
[98] C 136/83: his wife is wrongly said to be Agnes, daughter of Michael, Lord Poynings.
[99] A. H. Cooke, *Hist. of Mapledurham* (O.R.S. vii), 31–34.
[1] *Cal. Pat.* 1364–7, 225; see above, p. 73.
[2] C 136/83; *Cal. Close*, 1413–9, 326.
[3] Cooke, op. cit. 41–42; *Cal. Inq. p.m.* (Rec. Com.), iv, p. 23.
[4] Cooke, op. cit. 34–35.
[5] Ibid. 44; 45 for pedigree; *Cal. Inq. p.m.* (Rec. Com.), iv, p. 181.
[6] *Cal. Inq. p.m. Hen. VII*, i, p. 80; Stoke Lyne is not mentioned. For Thomas's younger brother William, the best-known member of the family, see Cooke, op. cit. 46–47.
[7] *Cal. Inq. p.m. Hen. VII*, i, p. 80; *V.C.H. Bucks.* iii. 210; Cooke, op. cit. 58.
[8] C 142/35/93; *L. & P. Hen. VIII*, iii (1), p. 460; Blo. *Stoke*, 18. John Lynde left Stoke to his wife Mary for life unless she remarried. A few years later her second husband John Fettiplace was at law with the Lynde sisters about the profits: C 1/586/39.

[9] E 179/162/319.
[10] C 142/200/58. His brass is in the church. A pedigree is in Blo. *Stoke*, 18.
[11] C 142/470/50.
[12] Ibid.; C 3/311/18. The estate may have been mortgaged in Elizabeth's reign: C.P. 43/1385/429.
[13] C 142/470/50.
[14] Blo. *Stoke*, 16, 18.
[15] *Oxon. Visit.* 286; Wood, *Life*, i. 184.
[16] Blo. *Stoke*, 16–17; tablet in church.
[17] The manor may have been mortgaged in 1703: C.P. 25(2)/956/ Trin. 2 Anne; see also C.P. 43/433/26. Holt presented to the church in 1706 and was buried there: Oxf. Dioc. c 266, f. 204b; Blo. *Stoke*, 34.
[18] *Misc. Gen. et Her.* 4th ser. ii. 87–88. Blomfield (*Stoke*, 17) states that Holt died without children, but had a niece Susannah. Peers had his tablet placed in Stoke church: MS. Top. Oxon. c 61, f. 6.
[19] Oxf. Dioc. c 266, f. 138b; C.P. 25(2)/1186/East. 5 Geo. II.
[20] *V.C.H. Warws.* iii. 286.
[21] Oxf. Dioc. b 21, f. 45b.
[22] C.P. 25(2)/1389/Trin. 14 Geo. III. For him see *Complete Peerage*, iii. 644; xi. 681–2.
[23] Blo. *Stoke*, 22; O.R.O. Incl. award.
[24] Burke, *Land. Gent.* (1846) under Cole. Since Thos. Cole died in 1807, it was probably his son Stephen who inherited: Blo. *Stoke*, 22.
[25] Burke, *Peerage*; Blo. *Stoke*, 23–27, for personal recollections; see above, p. 314.

Buckinghamshire, whose son William held Great Hampden (Bucks.).[26] Bainton followed the descent of Great Hampden and not that of Ghilo's other lands, and during the 13th century was held in chief by the De Hamden or De Hameldon family, ancestors of the 17th-century John Hampden.[27] In 1255 Bainton was held of Alexander de Hameldon (d. 1264); in 1279 of another Alexander de Hameldon; and in 1329 of Edmund de Hameldon, a member of a younger branch of the family,[28] and the last recorded overlord.

In 1086 the tenant of Bainton was Erchenbald,[29] and by the end of the 12th century the Carbonel family, which also held Addington and Beachampton (Bucks.). The first Carbonel known to be connected with Bainton was Richard, who was dead by 1198, when his widow Maud, remarried to Geoffrey de Upton, claimed her property against her brother-in-law, Hamon Carbonel.[30] As lord of Beachampton Hamon was a knight of the honor of Wallingford, and evidently Richard's brother and heir. Among other things, he granted Maud a third of Bainton, including the capital messuage.

Hamon Carbonel was alive in 1210, but dead by 1212, having left as his heir a minor.[31] His son Peter had succeeded by 1236 and was holding Bainton in 1255.[32] John Carbonel, a minor in 1265, held Bainton in 1279 from Alexander de Hameldon by the service of castle guard at Windsor.[33] It is not clear where he lived, but he was evidently a prominent man in the region—a knight and a frequent witness to charters.[34] His name is found as late as 1287, but he may have died in that year, when the manor was in the hands of Philip de Willoughby, a king's clerk,[35] probably on account of the minority of the heir. The latter, Peter Carbonel, seems to have still been a minor in 1300.[36] He was lord of Bainton in 1316 and is known to have added to his Buckinghamshire property[37] and to have died in 1329.[38] His wife Isabel was still alive in 1346,[39] but by 1353 she and her son John were both dead,[40] and with him the male line of the Carbonels came to an end.

From this point the descent of Bainton is confused. In 1364 it was held for their lives by John Kentwood and Alice his wife;[41] she may have been the widow of John Carbonel and Kentwood her second husband. By a series of transactions the Kentwoods acquired the whole manor, perhaps from three Carbonel heiresses: a half from Nicholas Baron and Alice his

wife in 1364, a quarter from Roger Smale and Joan his wife in 1368, and a quarter from Henry de Merston and Isabel his wife in 1376.[42] John Kentwood died around 1392, but Alice was still alive in 1404.[43]

On the death of the Kentwoods, half of Bainton was to go to William de Barton, probably owner of the property in Buckingham called Bartons.[44] He died in 1389, and his right descended to his younger son, John de Barton (d. 1434).[45] At his death John held all Bainton, which he had settled on his wife Isabel with provision that on her death half was to go to his sister and heiress, Isabel Ampcotes, and half to Thomas Dodds, clerk, John Arderne, and Thomas More.[46] John de Barton's widow was not given possession until 1439.[47] At this time Isabel Ampcotes was suing Dodds and More for her property,[48] and for the next twenty years Bainton was the subject of a series of legal transactions, especially between John Wellysbourne and Thomas More, both knights of the shire for Buckinghamshire, and Thomas Fowler, fishmonger of London.[49] In 1471 it came into the hands of Sir Edmund Rede of Boarstall and Checkendon,[50] who had acquired much property in Oxfordshire and held an important position in the county.[51] He died in 1489, leaving Bainton by his will to a younger son Alan.[52] Alan Rede's son Kenelm was holding Bainton in 1517 and in 1525, when he was leasing it to John Marshe.[53] He may have been dead by 1530, when Leonard Rede sold it to two land speculators—Edmund Peckham, cofferer to the king, and John Williams, later Lord Williams of Thame.[54]

The next notice of the manor occurs in 1562, when John Denton of Ambrosden and Bicester settled it on his eldest son John on his marriage to Theodora Blundell, the daughter of a London merchant. This son died young and his wife, who later married a Champneys, held the manor for life. After John Denton's death in 1576, Bainton was inherited by his son and heir Edward, who in 1586 settled it on his son-in-law Edward Smythe of Stoke Prior (Worcs.).[55]

The Smythes, whose interests were in Worcestershire, soon sold Bainton, which was the subject of complicated legal and financial transactions during the 17th century. In 1613 Edward Ewer of Bucknell sold Bainton to Sir William Cope of Hanwell for £5,300, but leased it back from him for a term of

[26] V.C.H. Oxon. i. 419; V.C.H. Bucks. i. 209, 254.
[27] V.C.H. Bucks. i. 215; pedigree in Lipscomb, Bucks. ii. 302, corrected in V.C.H. Bucks. ii. 287–8.
[28] Rot. Hund. (Rec. Com.), ii. 44, 825; Lipscomb, Bucks. ii. 302; Cal. Inq. p.m. vii, p. 111.
[29] V.C.H. Oxon. i. 419.
[30] Feet of F. (P.R.S. xxiii), 130.
[31] Fines Oxon. 43; Bk. of Fees, 119.
[32] Bk. of Fees, 119; Rot. Hund. (Rec. Com.), ii. 44.
[33] V.C.H. Bucks. iv. 139; Rot. Hund. (Rec. Com.), ii. 829.
[34] Boarstall Cart. 100; Kennett, Paroch. Antiq. passim.
[35] Kennett, Paroch. Antiq. i. 437; Cal. Inq. Misc. i, p. 404.
[36] Boarstall Cart. 299.
[37] Feud. Aids, iv. 169; V.C.H. Bucks. iv. 19–20. There are many references to this in the later patent rolls: e.g. Cal. Pat. 1327–30, 382.
[38] Cal. Inq. p.m. vii, p. 111.
[39] Feud. Aids, iv. 169.
[40] Cal. Pat. 1350–4, 437.
[41] C.P. 25(1)/190/21/73.
[42] Ibid.; 190/22/25; 288/50/765. John Carbonel had 2

daughters, one of whom was Alice Baron; Joan Smale and Isabel Merston were daughters of Alice's sister: V.C.H. Bucks. iv. 329.
[43] V.C.H. Bucks. iv. 329.
[44] Hants. R.O. Cope deed 218; V.C.H. Bucks. iii. 484.
[45] V.C.H. Bucks. iv. 242; ibid. ii. 145; iv. 247.
[46] Hants. R.O. Cope deed 223.
[47] Ibid. 221, 223.
[48] C 1/9/137.
[49] Hants. R.O. Cope deeds 219, 220, 225; C.P. 25(1)/191/29/2; Cat. Anct. D. iii, A 5711; Cal. Close, 1454–61, 221. For Wellysborne and More see J. C. Wedgwood, Hist. Parl.: Biogs.
[50] Hants. R.O. Cope deed 228.
[51] Wedgwood, op. cit.; Boarstall Cart. pp. ix–x.
[52] Boarstall Cart. 273.
[53] Dom. of Incl. i. 331; Hants. R.O. Cope deed 214.
[54] Hants, R.O. Cope deed 216. For Rede see also Compton Reade, Record of the Redes (Hereford, 1899), 120.
[55] C 142/178/61; C.P. 25(2)/197/Trin. 28 Eliz.; Oxon. Visit. 229. It had been mortgaged in 1584 to Sir John Brocket of Hatfield: Hants, R.O. Cope deed 213.

years for £400 a year. In 1619 he was suing Cope in Chancery for part of the purchase price.[56] In 1628 there was a further series of transactions between the two families by which the Ewers recovered Bainton.[57] In that year Edward Ewer alleged that he paid Sir William Cope £2,150 for a part of the manor (he had already paid £1,200 for another part) and Francis Ewer paid £350 to Richard and John Cope for that part of the manor which Sir William had leased to his son John in 1616.[58] In 1632 it was settled on Francis Ewer on his marriage to Jane Savage.[59] The family was, however, in serious financial difficulties, and in 1637 Bainton was sold to George Shiers,[60] a Londoner and since 1614 lord of Slyfield manor in Great Bookham (Surr.).[61] He died in 1642, leaving Bainton to his son Edward Shiers of Hadham (Herts.).[62] Bainton passed in 1683 to his nephew Sir George Shiers, Bt.,[63] who died childless in 1685, leaving his property to his mother Elizabeth Shiers, well known as a benefactress of Exeter College.[64] Bainton, however, seems to have been sold in 1690, before her death in 1700.[65] The manor is mentioned in 18th-century fines,[66] and in 1775 was bought from a Miss Hervey by Joseph Bullock, the lord of Caversfield manor.[67] In the 19th century it descended in the Bullock-Marsham family,[68] but the manor did not consist of the whole township, and manorial rights probably lapsed.

LESSER ESTATES. In addition to Notley Abbey, the appropriator of the church, three religious houses held estates in Fewcot. The largest estate belonged to the Cistercian Abbey of Woburn (Beds.) and consisted of 2 carucates given by Hugh de Bolebec.[69] In the 13th century the abbey held at least part of this land in demesne: its sheep are mentioned in 1224;[70] in 1279 the names of two tenants are given;[71] and in 1291 the land was valued at £1 15s. 6d., which came from rents and sheep and cattle.[72] In 1535 the value of the grange, which was partly rented and partly farmed, was £2 13s. 8d., from which a payment of 6s. 8d. was made to Oxford castle.[73]

The Preceptory of Sandford, belonging first to the Templars and then to the Hospitallers, held a virgate, given in the late 12th century by Otwel de Lisle.[74] In 1185 this was held freely for 4s. a year,[75] and in 1279 Agnes le Templer held it in the same way.[76] The tenant of 1513 held a toft, a small close, and a virgate of customary land with appurtenances, for a rent of 4s., and did suit of court at the Hospitallers' manor of Merton.[77]

Yet another estate was recorded in 1279, when the Templar Commandery of Hogshaw (Bucks.)[78] had 2 virgates and 6 acres, rented by 2 free tenants.[79] No later record of this land has been found.

ECONOMIC HISTORY. At the time of Domesday Book, although Stoke manor was stated to have land for 14 ploughs, it had 17 teams at work, 4 of them in demesne and 13 outside. There were also 12 acres of meadow, 10 of pasture, and a wood (2× 3 furls.). The estate was valued as before the Conquest at £12.[80] Three virgates in Stoke belonged to the Tusmore estate.[81] A second estate at Bainton was valued at £2. It had 3 plough-lands, but only 2 plough-teams, one of which was in demesne. There were 4 acres of meadow.[82]

The population was relatively large: in Stoke there were 34 villeins (villani) and 9 bordars, with 2 serfs in demesne,[83] and in Bainton there were 1 villein and 2 bordars.[84] By 1279 there had been some notable changes:[85] population had increased, the tenurial pattern had become more complex, and a new hamlet had been colonized. There were now 3 manors, 4 lesser estates, and about 35 recorded households in Stoke, 17 in Bainton, and 9 in Fewcot, the new settlement. The De Lisles had 14 villein (nativi) tenants, of which 6 held a virgate each and one a half-virgate. They paid 5s. a virgate rent, worked at will, and paid fines when their sons left the manor. There were 6 cotlanders, who each paid 2s. 6d. rent, and owed works and other services at will. A smith held 2 acres for 14d.

The De Cokefield tenants were mostly designated as servi; 2 virgaters and 2 half-virgaters each owed 5s. and 4s. rent a year respectively, and 9 cotlanders each paid 2s. 6d. rent. Both classes owed works and tallage and had to pay fines at will if their sons left the manor. There were also 2 cottagers in Stoke, each holding 2 acres for 1s. a year.

Among the new class of free tenants in Stoke, six in all, some owed special services: one held a cotland of Giles de Lisle for rent and suit of court every three weeks; another held a water-mill for 10s.; a third, a tenant of the De Cokefields, held 2 acres for 2s. rent and suit of court.

On the small Carbonel manor in Bainton a carucate was held in demesne by John Carbonel, who had 8 villein virgaters, each owing 4s. 4d. a year rent, works, and tallage, and owed fines at will if their sons left the manor. A further 3½ virgates were held of John de Cokefield's 'fee of Stoke'. The next most im-

[56] C 3/307/1. For litigation of 1623 between William Anderson of Broughton (Lincs.) and Cope over several manors, including Bainton and Shelswell, see C 2/Jas. I, A5/30.
[57] C 5/94/14.
[58] Ibid.; C 5/1/40.
[59] Sawyer deeds penes Mrs. E. I. Sawyer, Bicester: settlement; C 5/94/14, a case of 1683 where some of the earlier documents are listed.
[60] Ibid.; C.P. 25(2)/473/Trin. 13 Chas. I; ibid. 585/East. 1652.
[61] V.C.H. Surr. iii. 329.
[62] C 142/621/23.
[63] C 5/94/14; see also C.P. 25(2)/710/East. 35 Chas. II.
[64] G. E. C. Baronetage, iv. 134; O. Manning and W. Bray, Surr. ii. 692; Mrs. R. L. Poole, Cat. of Oxf. Portraits (O.H.S. lxxxi), ii. 70.
[65] C.P. 25(2)/863/Mich. 2 Wm. & Mary.
[66] Ibid. 865/Trin. 12 Wm. III; ibid. 1187/Trin. 13 Geo. II.
[67] H. Wyndham, A Backward Glance, 55.

[68] Bodl. Tithe award; for family see V.C.H. Bucks. iv. 160.
[69] Rot. Hund. (Rec. Com.), ii. 826; see above, p. 315.
[70] Fines Oxon. 70–71; see below, p. 319.
[71] Rot. Hund. (Rec. Com.), ii. 826.
[72] Tax. Eccl. (Rec. Com.), 45.
[73] Valor Eccl. (Rec. Com.), iv. 212, 213.
[74] Sandford Cart. ii. 302; see above, p. 315.
[75] Beatrice A. Lees, Records of the Templars (Brit. Acad. 1935), 45.
[76] Rot. Hund. (Rec. Com.), ii. 826.
[77] Bodl. MS. C.C.C. 320, f. 15.
[78] V.C.H. Bucks. i. 390.
[79] Rot. Hund. (Rec. Com.), ii. 826.
[80] V.C.H. Oxon. i. 411.
[81] See below, p. 336.
[82] V.C.H. Oxon. i. 419.
[83] Ibid. 411.
[84] Ibid. 419.
[85] Rot. Hund. (Rec. Com.), ii. 826.

portant landowner in Bainton was Otwel Purcel with 9 virgates. He was a free tenant of Giles de Lisle, and his lands were leased to 2 free tenants and to 3 women members of the Purcel family, perhaps Otwel's daughters, who leased their land to others.[86]

In Fewcot the De Lisles had two virgaters and the De Cokefields four. It is noteworthy that in this comparatively recently developed land four religious houses held small properties.

Early 14th-century tax assessments show that the parish was taxed at £6 15s. 7d. in 1316,[87] the highest rate for any rural parish in the hundred. Thirty people were assessed in Stoke, 18 in Bainton, and 8 in Fewcot. The last was clearly relatively poor, even in proportion to its numbers, and Stoke and Bainton paid by far the highest contributions. The tenants of the three manors were assessed most highly, but there were a number of others assessed at relatively large sums—an indication of a thriving community.

Fewcot, which never formed a separate manor, but appears to have had its own field system, is mentioned first in the late 12th century, when Otwel de Lisle gave a virgate there to the Templars.[88] It is probable that Fewcot land in the west of the parish was being cleared during the earlier part of the century or in the late 11th century. Early 13th-century field names such as 'Levrichesbreche', 'Pesebreche', and 'Alfledesbreche' are suggestive of the work of colonization and reclamation of uncultivated land.[89] A grant of 40½ acres at this date by a Fewcot tenant throws some light on the layout of these fields.[90] Eighteen acres lay in East Field, which abutted on Buckingham Way (the modern road to Caversham) to the east of the hamlet, and 22½ in North Field. From references to Croughton Way, Brackley Way, and Souldern Way as boundaries of furlongs in the North Field, it seems evident that by this time the field stretched up to the parish's northern boundary. With a few exceptions all the land granted lay in ½-acre strips. The charter also indicates that separate meadowland existed, that there was a mill, and that sheepfarming was practised.[91] For the last the undrained upland nature of the country, continually emphasized in the field names (e.g. Wellmore, Westmore, Labrodemore, Turresmore), was more suited than for arable farming. Indeed, in 1224 the Abbot of Woburn was accused by Robert de Lisle of overburdening the common pasture of Fewcot and Stoke with his animals. It was agreed that the abbot should have pasture for 180 sheep only, unless he acquired further tenements with appurtenant pasture rights in the townships.[92]

In the early 16th century Stoke, Bainton, and Fewcot were still assessed separately for the subsidy, but since the 14th century, wealth had become concentrated in fewer hands. In 1524 there were 8 persons assessed at Stoke, 5 at Bainton, and 3 at Fewcot.[93] There is evidence too that all three places were affected by other changes common to the age: by the change from arable to pasture, and by the movement towards the accumulation or consolidation of farms. A tenant of the Lyndes in Fewcot had, for instance, converted 20 acres of arable into pasture;[94] in Stoke two farms, one of 60 and one of 36 acres, had been consolidated;[95] and John Marsh, the richest Bainton inhabitant,[96] also had a farm in Stratton Audley.[97]

The extensive common pasture known as Bayard's Green was still probably largely devoted to sheep. Early in the 17th century, when the boundary between Stoke Lyne and Tusmore was in dispute, Thomas Pigot of Tusmore claimed the right to keep 400 sheep there.[98] A lawsuit of 1616 shows that Bayard's Green also supported another profitable animal, the rabbit, besides being a source of turf. The lord of the manor was accused of encroaching on the green by digging turf and building a house there with a rabbit 'warren and 300 burrows'.[99]

The timber here and elsewhere in the parish was also valuable, particularly at this period, when there was a scarcity in the county. In 1620 it was alleged in a Chancery suit that Ralph Holt had growing timber worth at least £2,000 on his Stoke Lyne manor.[1]

The conversion from arable to pasture proceeded so rapidly in Bainton manor that by the mid-17th century all its land had been turned into meadow and pasture and the village had been depopulated.[2] Apart from three small closes (30 a.) next to Hethe Brede the 1,000 acres of the manor were divided into large fields ranging from 50 acres (Crabtree Close) to 300 acres (Great Dry Leyes and also 'the grounds up to London Highway'). The whole manor was let for over £300. It would be tempting to attribute the very small numbers of 20 and 12 householders listed in 1662 and 1665 to this depopulation were it not for the fact that the 166 adults recorded in 1676 in the Compton Census make it probable that the hearthtax returns are an unreliable guide for the population of a village.[3]

By 1775 the lands of Bainton manor had been partly sold. The estate which Joseph Bullock of Caversfield bought consisted of one large farm.[4] In the next few years he 'laid out a great sum of money' on improving the land and buildings, and he at once raised the rent from £105 to £140. Among other things, he planted the 'great heath' with sainfoin seed;[5] he 'quicked', ditched, and fenced the field next to Bucknell; he divided the 'moor' with a ditch, making one side into a meadow and planting the other side with trees; he cleaned out the two fishponds and stocked them with carp and tench.[6] His was probably not the only inclosure, for Davis's

---

[86] Ibid. 829.
[87] E 179/161/8.
[88] Sandford Cart. ii. 302.
[89] E 40/A 353.
[90] Ibid.
[91] e.g. pratum Wydonis de Tursmere, 'mullows', 'mullbroke', bercaria grangie.
[92] Fines Oxon. 70–71.
[93] E 179/161/176.
[94] Dom. of Incl. i. 362.
[95] Ibid.
[96] E 179/161/176.
[97] Dom. of Incl. i. 331.
[98] C 3/96/58.

[99] C 2, Jas. I, F 12/23; see also ibid. F 3/62.
[1] C 3/2/311/18.
[2] S.P. 16/408/141.
[3] Hearth Tax Oxon. 207, 235; E 179/164/514, a second roll for 1665, records the same number of hearths; Compton Census.
[4] O.R.O. Land tax assess.
[5] Rawlinson noted in about 1718 that the soil of the parish was stony, but that it had been improved by growing 'cinquefoil': Bodl. MS. Rawl. B 400 f, f. 53.
[6] H. Wyndham, A Backward Glance (1950), 55–58; Joseph Bullock's diary for 1775, 1779, penes Col. the Hon. E. H. Wyndham, Caversfield.

map of 1797 shows that the great open spaces of the 17th century had been replaced by moderately small fields of arable and pasture.[7] By 1850 there were only about 350 acres, divided into two farms, still belonging to the manor. Of the two other large farms, one was owned by William Mansfield, the tenant of one of the manor farms. By this time the land was mostly arable, there being 537 acres of arable, 188 acres of pasture, and 15 acres of wood.[8]

Fewcot, on the other hand, remained primarily an open-field township until the parliamentary inclosure of 1794.[9] Some 1,711 acres, or about half the land in the two townships of Stoke and Fewcot, was then uninclosed. Of this about 900 acres was taken up by the common pasture of Bayard's Green, part belonging to Fewcot and part to Stoke; there were about 100 acres of cow-pasture, the Stoke one considerably larger than the Fewcot one; and nearly 700 acres of arable. Almost all of it, 26 yardlands, was in Fewcot. The Fewcot field system, in the absence of maps, cannot be worked out, but field names indicate that the medieval fields had been subdivided and replaced by Home Field, Bonners Field, Hill Field, Middle Quarter, and Fewcot Clay Field. The award records old inclosures in the north-west of the parish.

Of the 1,700 approximate acres inclosed in 1794, the main allotments were 491 acres in lieu of tithes;[10] over 400 acres to the Countess of Shipbrook for the manor and nearly 300 acres to William Fermor of Tusmore; 200 acres to William Ellis; and about 100 acres to Thomas Stuchbury and William Hopcraft, two local freeholders.

The effect of inclosure is not easy to define. Arthur Young stated about fifteen years later that the value of the land had trebled in rent and produce, and noted the absence of dairies.[11] In 1786, before inclosure, the manor, which included slightly over half the parish, was divided into five farms, and there were ten or eleven others of about 100 acres or more in size. In 1816 the manor still consisted of five farms, but by 1832 there were only two,[12] and there was a tendency in the 19th century for farms in the rest of the parish to increase in size. In 1850, for example, one consisted of 850 acres, there were four of 300 acres and over, and four more of 150 and over.[13] In the 18th century the owners of several of the freehold properties lived in the parish: of the seven 40-shilling freeholders of 1754 (excluding the vicar), four were resident.[14] In 1832, to take one 19th-century example, eight freeholders lived on their own land.[15] Of these, only two had holdings of more than a few acres: William Mansfield, who owned land himself and was also the tenant of Hethe Brede

farm in Bainton,[16] and the Stuchbury family, who had been in the parish since the 17th century.[17]

Before the 19th century there is little record of village crafts. In 1811 there were only two out of 77 families not engaged in agriculture.[18] By 1831 there were nine in retail trade,[19] and in 1851 there were two carpenters, a smith,[20] a wheelwright, a grocer, and a baker in Stoke, and a blacksmith and a maltster in Fewcot.[21] There were also many cottage lace-makers—32 in Stoke and two in Fewcot.

During the first half of the 19th century there was a rapid increase in the parish's population. The upward trend may have already begun in the late 18th century. Incumbents had returned 40 or so houses in the mid-18th century,[22] but in 1801 the population was officially returned as 334. It rose to 593 in 1831 and to 631 in 1851. Thereafter, as a result of the agricultural depression, it declined to 409 in 1901, and 20th-century mechanization and the boundary changes of 1948, when Fewcot hamlet was transferred to Ardley, were responsible for the low figure of 124 in 1951.[23] Evidence for the relative size of Stoke and its hamlets is unsatisfactory in the modern period before 1821, the first year in which their inhabitants were listed separately. Stoke then remained the largest settlement, with 303 persons, but Bainton, which had been larger than Fewcot in the Middle Ages, was now far outdistanced by it. The latter had 148 inhabitants compared with Bainton's 58, and increased rapidly to 220 in the next two decades.[24]

CHURCHES. The earliest reference to Stoke church occurs in the mid-12th century, when it was granted to Notley Abbey (Bucks.) by Walter Giffard, the overlord of the manor, and his wife.[25] He founded this abbey—one of the few houses of Arrouasian canons in England—some time before 1164, the year of his death.[26]

By the Giffards' charter, Notley was granted not only the advowson but the demesne tithes of Stoke Lyne and its chapel of Hardwick;[27] it was after this that Hardwick became a separate parish. By the early 13th century the abbey had appropriated Stoke church.[28] The living was one of the richest in Bicester deanery: in 1254 it was valued at £10 13s. 4d., in 1291 at £13 6s. 8d., and in 1535 it was let for £12 0s. 8d.[29]

Notley Abbey surrendered to the Crown in 1538.[30] In 1542 much of its property, including the rectories of Stoke Lyne and Caversham, was among the extensive grants of monastic lands made to Christ Church, the cathedral church of the new see of

---

[7] Davis, *Oxon. Map.* A 1745 map of Bainton Farm (219 a.) by Wm. Grantham among the Dashwood deeds (Bodl. dep. a 5(R)) shows that it consisted of about 10 fields of from 10 to 30 acres. In 1850 this farm belonged to J. H. Slater-Harrison: Bodl. Tithe award.

[8] Bodl. Tithe award.

[9] O.R.O. Incl. award. There is no map. The act is 32 Geo. III, c. 27 (priv. act) (copy in Bodl. L. Eng. C 13 c 1 (1793, i)).

[10] See below, p. 321.

[11] Young, *Oxon. Agric.* 91.

[12] O.R.O. Land tax assess.

[13] H.O. 107/1729.

[14] *Oxon. Poll, 1754.*

[15] O.R.O. Land tax assess.

[16] Bodl. Bainton tithe award.

[17] *Hearth Tax Oxon.* 207.

[18] *Census*, 1811.

[19] Ibid. 1831.

[20] There is evidence for a smith in 1279 (*Rot. Hund.* (Rec. Com.), ii. 826), and for a blacksmith's shop in the late 18th cent., belonging to the family which owned the business in 1955.

[21] H.O. 107/1729.

[22] Oxf. Dioc. d 554, d 557, d 560.

[23] *V.C.H. Oxon.* ii. 221; *Census*, 1951.

[24] Blo. *Stoke*, 31–32.

[25] Dugd. *Mon.* vi (1), 278.

[26] *V.C.H. Bucks.* i. 377.

[27] Dugd. *Mon.* vi (1), 278; see above, p. 171.

[28] *Rot. Welles*, i. 182.

[29] *Tax. Eccl.* (Rec. Com.), 31; Lunt, *Val. Norw.* 312; *Valor Eccl.* (Rec. Com.), iv. 233.

[30] *V.C.H. Bucks.* i. 378.

Oxford.[31] When the college was refounded in 1547, the rectory was not among its endowments. By 1552 it was in the hands of Sir John Williams of Thame, who had already acquired Bainton manor, and Sir Richard Lee. These two profiteers in monastic lands sold it to Edward Love,[32] who had been Notley Abbey's tenant, and was the richest man in the parish.[33] He died in 1557 and is commemorated by a brass in the church.[34] In 1566–7 Edward Love of Aynho (Northants) sold the rectory to William Holt, the lord of Stoke Lyne manor,[35] perhaps as part of the marriage settlement between his daughter Ann and Thomas Holt.[36]

From then the advowson and rectory descended with the manor until 1796, when Joseph Bullock, lord of the manor and patron of Caversfield (Bucks.), bought the advowson from the Countess of Shipbrook for £700.[37] The lay rectory continued to follow the descent of Stoke Lyne manor,[38] but the advowson followed that of Caversfield.[39] About 1870 the livings of Caversfield and Stoke Lyne were united; in 1902 they were separated,[40] but the advowson of Stoke remained with the Wyndhams, patrons of Caversfield. In 1933 the livings of Stoke Lyne and Ardley were united.[41] Since then Col. the Hon. E. H. Wyndham has had the right to present for two turns, and the patron of Ardley for one.

In the Middle Ages the rectory's endowment consisted of the great tithes;[42] but the small tithes and 2 virgates in Fewcot,[43] which belonged to the vicarage, were also held by Notley Abbey (see below). The tithes of Fewcot and Stoke Lyne were commuted at the inclosure award in 1794 for 491 acres of land.[44] The Countess of Shipbrook received 264 acres, mostly in Bayard's Green, for rectorial tithes. In 1850 the tithes of Bainton were commuted for £290, £233 of which went to the lay rector.[45]

The history of Bainton's tithes goes back to the late 12th century, when St. Frideswide's had a claim to part of the tithes on the Carbonel demesne.[46] This led to a dispute with Notley Abbey, which collected the tithes on the rest of the parish. Around 1200 a composition was made: St. Frideswide's gave up its claim in return for a pension of 2s. a year from Notley.[47] This sum was confirmed in 1344, but by 1480 St. Frideswide's was receiving 4s. a year from Notley.[48] Later this pension went to Wolsey's college in Oxford and in 1532 was granted to Henry VIII's college.[49]

Chancery cases in the 1620's show how complicated the administration of tithes could be.[50] Ralph Holt, the lay rector, who seems to have

wanted to regain possession, was said to have leased them in 1614 to Sir William Cope for 80 years at £20 a year. In 1619 Cope leased part of them for three years to Nathaniel Palmer and Richard Marrott for £90. They in turn sublet them to Edward Ewer, the tenant of Bainton manor, while a certain Mr. Nayler was the actual occupier.

In the early 13th century a vicarage in Stoke Lyne said to be worth 5 marks was ordained by the bishop.[51] The vicar was to have the altar offerings and the small tithes from the whole parish, plus all tithes from 6 virgates in Fewcot; he was also to have a house and ½ hide of land. There is no record of the abbey ever presenting a vicar. The Notley canons probably either served the church themselves—their power to do so was confirmed by the pope in 1402[52] —or hired a curate. They had a poor reputation as patrons: in 1345, for example, an inquiry was made by the Bishop of Lincoln as to the rights by which the canons held so many churches *in proprios usus* and omitted to provide them with vicars; in 1493 their churches were found to be ruinous and badly served; in 1530 the chancel and roof at Stoke Lyne were found to be dilapidated.[53] At that time the curate was being hired by the lessee of the rectory and was receiving £5 6s. 8d.[54] The practice of having curates continued until the end of the 16th century.[55]

When in the early 17th century the vicarage was revived, there was trouble between the lay rector and the vicar. There is a reference in a Chancery suit, which Thomas Dennis (vicar 1622–42) brought against Ralph Holt, to the original ordination of the vicarage and the vicar's right to have part of the great tithes of Fewcot, which were being refused him.[56] Dennis probably won his case, for when the tithes of Stoke Lyne and Fewcot were commuted in 1793, the vicar was stated to be entitled to all the small tithes and to the great tithes on six closes in Fewcot (18 acres in all) and on 6 yardlands in the common fields of Fewcot.[57] Before inclosure he seems to have had no glebe, but he was then awarded 227 acres of land, which have been sold, and a rent-charge of £3 13s. 9d.;[58] in 1850 he was awarded £57 a year in place of the small tithes at Bainton.[59] In 1707 the living was valued at £37 8s. 10d. and by 1809 was worth at least £150.[60]

The 17th-century vicars seem to have lived in the parish, but George Fletcher (1706–34), a pluralist, was the last to do so.[61] At about this time the dilapidated vicarage, which probably stood on the north side of the churchyard, was pulled down.[62] From this time the church was either served by a curate,[63]

[31] *L. & P. Hen. VIII*, xvii, p. 491.
[32] *Cal. Pat.* 1550–3, 273; for Williams and Lee see *D.N.B.*
[33] Bodl. MS. ch. Bucks. 38b; E 179/161/204.
[34] C 142/112/140.
[35] C.P. 25(2)/196/East. 9 Eliz.
[36] Blo. *Stoke*, 14; C 142/200/58.
[37] Joseph Bullock's Diary *penes* Col. the Hon. E. H. Wyndham, Caversfield.
[38] E. H. Cole, the impropriator, was neglecting the chancel in 1854: Blo. *Stoke*, 36.
[39] For that see *V.C.H. Bucks.* iv. 160.
[40] Oxf. Dioc. c 344; *Kelly's Dir. Oxon.* (1920), under Caversfield.
[41] Bodl. Par. Box (uncat.), Order in Council.
[42] *Rot. Welles*, i. 182.
[43] *Rot. Hund.* (Rec. Com.), ii. 826.
[44] O.R.O. Incl. award.
[45] Bodl. Bainton tithe award.   [46] See above, p. 317.

[47] *St. Frides. Cart.* ii. 198.
[48] Ibid. i. 76, 484.
[49] *L. & P. Hen. VIII*, v, p. 587.
[50] C 3/360/75; C 2, Jas. I, H5/24.
[51] *Rot. Welles*, i. 182.
[52] *Cal. Papal L.* v. 508.
[53] *V.C.H. Bucks.* i. 377; *Visit. Dioc. Linc. 1517–31*, ii. 36.
[54] Bodl. MS. ch. Bucks. 38b; *Subsidy 1526*. 274.
[55] *O.A.S. Rep.* 1914, 234.
[56] C 2, Jas. I, D3/27.
[57] Blo. *Stoke*, 27.
[58] O.R.O. Incl. award; MS. Top. Oxon. c 61, f. 91: 1805 terrier, which says 215 a.
[59] Bodl. Tithe award.
[60] Bacon, *Lib. Reg.* 793; Oxf. Dioc. c 446, f. 26.
[61] Blo. *Stoke*, 42–43.
[62] Ibid. 43–44.
[63] Oxf. Dioc. d 554.

or by the vicar, who lived in the neighbourhood and always held another cure.[64] The curate received £25 a year. Two services were held and one sermon preached on Sundays, and the sacrament was administered four times a year.[65] During most of the 19th century the living was held with Caversfield by members of the Marsham family, the patrons, Charles Marsham being vicar from 1812 to 1867.[66]

In the middle of the century Stoke Lyne was known as a 'bad' parish.[67] Marsham, though kindly and constant in visiting his parishes, was inefficient and incapable of keeping abreast of the times. He did

ever, the Rector of Ardley's sister-in-law, Miss Anne Hind (d. 1870), determined that Fewcot should be better served, and left £2,000 for the curacy of Fewcot as well as £1,000 for the vicarage house of Stoke Lyne.[74] A church built at Fewcot was consecrated in 1871, but continued as a chapel of Stoke Lyne. In 1907 Fewcot was formed into a separate ecclesiastical parish, and the living became a perpetual curacy in the gift of the Vicar of Stoke Lyne.[75] In 1921 it was united to Ardley.[76]

The church of *ST. PETER* comprises a chancel, nave, and north and south transepts, with a tower

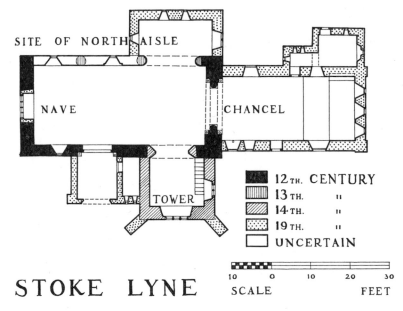

SITE OF NORTH AISLE

NAVE

CHANCEL

TOWER

■ 12 TH. CENTURY
▥ 13 TH. "
▨ 14 TH. "
▦ 19 TH. "
□ UNCERTAIN

STOKE LYNE

SCALE   FEET

10   0   10   20   30

not see the necessity of a day school; he only held one service on Sundays, alternatively in the morning and afternoon; nor would he hire a curate until he was an old man. Services then became more frequent, and music was introduced.[68] During the century the number of communicants rose from about 20 to 50 in 1878;[69] there was then a steady congregation of 130 to 150, while some parishioners went to church at Ardley.[70]

In about 1870 the parish was united with Caversfield, Bishop Wilberforce consenting reluctantly on condition that a vicarage was built in Stoke Lyne. It was built in 1872 at a cost of £2,500.[71]

For most of the century Fewcot people had a bad reputation as churchgoers: Bishop Wilberforce (1845–69) considered the hamlet 'quite heathen'.[72] Its distance from the parish church was in part responsible and had always been a problem. In the 16th century many had gone to Ardley church, which was nearer. One parishioner who was cited to the archdeacon's court for doing so was told to go to Stoke Lyne at least once a month.[73] In 1846 the Rector of Ardley offered to make it part of his parish if £10 were paid to him from the vicarage of Stoke Lyne, but the patron Dr. Marsham refused the offer. How-

over the south transept. The nave and chancel were built in the 12th century, and both the chancel arch and the fine south doorway are Romanesque work of this period. Over the doorway there is a niche containing a contemporary statue of a seated figure, probably St. Peter. There is a 19th-century porch.

The south transept was added early in the 14th century and forms the lower stage of the tower. This is lighted by a three-light window with reticulated tracery, and has an embattled parapet and a pyramidal roof. Its repair or alteration in 1658 is recorded by an inscription on the exterior.

The church once had a northern aisle. Christopher Pettie is said to have been buried in it in 1651,[77] but it had been destroyed by the early 19th century with the exception of the eastern bay, which was reconstructed to form a quasi-transept. The blocked-up arches of the arcade can still be seen in the north wall of the nave.

Repairs in 1757 included repointing the tower, plastering the roof, and walling up one of the doors.[78] By the mid-19th century the church was in a dilapidated condition: the chancel walls and roof were in need of repair, the floors were uneven, and the walls green with damp.[79] In 1868–9 the church was re-

64 Ox. Dioc. c 327, p. 70; Blo. *Stoke*, 44.
65 Oxf. Dioc. d 554, d 557, d 560.
66 Blo. *Cav.* 42. He was also Vicar of Ilsington (Devon).
67 Oxf. Dioc. d 178.
68 Blo. *Cav.* 43; Blo. *Stoke*, 44.
69 Oxf. Dioc. c 327, p. 305; ibid. c 344.
70 Ibid. c 332, b 39.
71 Ibid. d 178; Blo. *Stoke*, 44–45.

72 Oxf. Dioc. d 178.
73 Blo. *Stoke*, 38.
74 Ibid. 38–39.
75 *Kelly's Dir. Oxon.* (1920).
76 Bodl. Par. Box (uncat.), Order in Council.
77 Blo. *Stoke*, 34.
78 Oxf. Archd. Oxon. d 13, f. 33.
79 Blo. *Stoke*, 55.

stored at a cost of £2,130; the architect was H. Woodyer, the builder C. Chappel.[80] The chancel was rebuilt on the old foundations: the three Romanesque windows at the east end were copied from the originals, but the circular window above them was a new feature. The stained glass was given by Lady (Algernon) Peyton in 1873. The walls of the nave were repaired and a new west window built. The tower was raised and buttressed and battlements were added. The porch was rebuilt, a vestry added, and the church reseated.[81]

In 1951 the chancel was again restored and re-furnished by Sir Algernon and Lady Peyton. The Victorian reredos was removed, and a new altar and altar rails of unstained oak installed. The whole effect of the white-washed interior is one of extreme simplicity and beauty.

The round font is medieval. Ten pews were installed in 1654, but the other existing ones are modern.[82] In 1873 Lady Peyton also gave an organ, and electric light was installed in 1949, the brackets being made at the local forge.

There is a fine brass to Edward Love (d. 1557) and his wife Alice (d. 1535/6);[83] and an altar-tomb with brass to William Holt (d. 1582/3) and his wife Katherine Dormer. There is a monument to Ralph Holt (d. 1702) and his two wives; and inscriptions to Charnell Pettie (d. 1661/2) and to Susanna Holt (d. 1704), wife of the Revd. Edmund Major. There are two Peyton tablets. Those to Elinor Pettie (d. 1662/3), Christopher Pettie (d. 1651), Charles Holt (d. 1731), Eustace Pettie (d. 1735), George Fletcher, vicar (d. 1734), could not be traced in 1956.[84] The coats of arms seen by Rawlinson in a window in about 1718 were also no longer there.[85]

Stoke Lyne is not included on the chantry commissioners' usual list, but there was a light at the Reformation which was supported by land worth 1s. 6d. a year and three animals, given by Thomas Grevell, gent.[86]

In 1955 the only valuable pieces of plate were a silver chalice and paten cover of 1637.[87] There were three bells, none earlier than 1812.[88]

The registers date from 1665, but the volume for 1753–1813 is missing; Rawlinson mentioned an earlier one which was already lost.[89]

The church of *ALL SAINTS* at Fewcot was built in 1870 at a cost of about £900, and consecrated in 1871; the architect was H. Woodyer.[90] It is a simple building consisting of a nave and apsidal chancel, and an open west turret containing a bell. The register dates from 1908.

NONCONFORMITY. A few Roman Catholics have been recorded in the parish since the Reformation: one in 1676, two (a yeoman and his son) in 1706,[91] and in 1738 a tradesman.[92] A few Roman Catholics continued in the parish through the late 18th and most of the 19th centuries.[93]

No record of Protestant dissent in the 17th and 18th centuries has been found. In 1838 the Methodists opened a meeting-place in a labourer's house. Although a congregation of about 70 was reported in 1851,[94] when it belonged to the Brackley Circuit, the incumbent stated in the 1860's that there were not more than fifteen 'thorough-going' dissenters.[95]

SCHOOLS. In 1815 31 children were taught at two small schools at their parents' expense, but a free school was much needed for the remaining 74 children. One of these schools was said to have existed for 25 years, but no schools had been recorded by the incumbent in 1808.[96] In 1819 there were three schools for 18 children; in 1833 one day school with 20 pupils supported by the vicar and the parents; and in 1850 a school kept by an old blind man, and two dame schools.[97] It was probably these last three schools which were said in 1854 to be supported by Lady Peyton and the vicar and to have a total attendance of 40.[98]

A Church of England School was built in 1864 by Sir Henry Peyton, and was subsequently largely supported by the Peyton family.[99] The average attendance was 28 in 1871 and 50 in 1889 and 1906.[1] After the school's reorganization as a junior school in 1930, the senior pupils were transferred to Fritwell. It was given aided status in 1952, and the number of pupils was 24 in 1954.[2]

In 1854 Fewcot children were attending Ardley school, to which the Vicar of Stoke Lyne subscribed £2 a year.[3] Miss Anne Hind[4] is said to have founded a school in Fewcot, apparently in the 1870's,[5] but it was not until 1886 that a National school with accommodation for 50 children was opened.[6] The average attendance was 33 in 1889, but the school appears to have closed by 1903.[7]

CHARITIES. None known.

[80] MS. Top. Oxon. c 104, ff. 335–9. A drawing by J. Buckler (1825) in MS. Top. Oxon. a 68, f. 517, shows medieval chancel. It had 3-light square-headed E. window.
[81] Blo. *Stoke*, 36–37, where a list of contributors is given.
[82] The date 1654 is inscribed on one.
[83] M. Stephenson, *Monumental Brasses*, 421. The brass was evidently made at the time of his wife's death, although he lived 20 years longer. For rubbings of shields see Bodl. G.A. Oxon. b 180, Ploughley, 8a–e.
[84] Blo. *Stoke*, 34.
[85] Bodl. G.A. Oxon. 4° 689, p. 290; G.A. Oxon. 16° 217, pp. 229, 270a.
[86] *Chant. Cert.* 35.
[87] Evans, *Ch. Plate.*
[88] *Ch. Bells Oxon.* iv. 389.   [89] Blo. *Stoke*, 31.
[90] Ibid. 39; inf. the Revd. B. F. L. Clarke, Knowl Hill Vicarage, Reading.
[91] Compton Census; *Oxoniensia*, xiii. 79.

[92] Oxf. Dioc. d 554, d 557.
[93] Ibid. c 431; ibid. c 327, p. 70; ibid. b 39; ibid. c 344.
[94] H.O. 129/158.
[95] *Brackley Circuit Plan*, 1851; Oxf. Dioc. c 332.
[96] Oxf. Dioc. c 433; ibid. d 707.
[97] *Educ. of Poor*, 730; *Educ. Enq. Abstract.* 755; Blo. *Stoke*, 33.
[98] *Wilb. Visit.*
[99] *Kelly's Dir. Oxon.* (1887); Blo. *Stoke*, 33.
[1] *Elem. Educ. Ret.*; *Ret. of Sch.*; *Vol. Sch. Ret.*
[2] Inf. Oxon. Educ. Cttee.
[3] *Wilb. Visit.*
[4] See above, p. 322.
[5] Wing, *Annals*, 126; not included in *Elem. Educ. Ret.* (1871).
[6] *Kelly's Dir. Oxon.* (1887).
[7] *Ret. of Sch.*; *Kelly's Dir. Oxon.* (1903); inf. Oxon. Educ. Cttee.

STRATTON AUDLEY

THIS long and narrow parish of 2,308 acres lies two miles north-east of Bicester.[1] The old parish, which does not appear to have been created until the mid-15th century,[2] probably only covered a little over 2,000 acres, as a part of Stratton village and its open fields belonged to Caversfield parish, and so to the county of Buckinghamshire.[3] At the inclosure of 1780, as compensation for the loss of its scattered strips, Caversfield was assigned two pieces of ground covering 220 acres on the southern boundary of Stratton.[4] In 1844 these two enclaves were transferred to Oxfordshire[5] and they were added to the civil parish of Stratton Audley, increasing its area to 2,308 acres.[6]

The Roman road from Alchester to Towcester[7] bounds the parish on the north-west; the Birne, a tributary of the Ouse, on the north-east, while in the south much of the ancient and modern boundaries follow small feeders of the River Ray. The ground rises northwards from about 250 feet to its highest point of 378 feet on Fringford Hill and then falls to 300 feet on the northern boundary.

There was no woodland in 1797 and only some small plantations in 1951.[8] The village and most of the parish lie on the Cornbrash, bounded on the east by the Oxford Clay.[9] There have been stone-pits on the Cornbrash since the 14th century at least.[10]

Before the inclosure of 1780 there were only two roads in the parish: the main road from Bicester to Buckingham along the western boundary of the parish, and the road through the village and past the mill to Buckingham, which was only a 'field road'.[11] The inclosure act ordered the latter to be improved and two new roads to be staked out: one to Bicester and one to Launton Gate.[12]

The village lies close to the western boundary of the parish, half a mile from the Roman 'street' which gave it its first name.[13] In the 13th century Stratton acquired the suffix Audley after the family that held the manor.[14] Until the 19th century the village was remarkable for being divided between two counties: in the Middle Ages the part of it which belonged to the Gargate manor of Caversfield had been attached to Caversfield parish.[15] Hence in 1242 six inhabitants of Stratton were parishioners of Caversfield,[16] and

in 1755 fourteen houses were said to be in the Caversfield part of Stratton.[17] Nineteenth-century evidence shows that these lay on the east side of the main village street and included the Plough Inn.[18]

The village was a comparatively large one in the Middle Ages[19] and 17th-century evidence indicates that it was still well populated. It had 41 houses listed for the hearth tax of 1662 and there was an unusual number of substantial gentlemen's or farmers' houses. In 1665 three were taxed on 5 to 7 hearths each, and five on 3 or 4 hearths. The Rectory with 12 hearths was the largest house in the village; the Vicarage with 2 was a comparatively mean house.[20] In the 18th century there were said to be 50 to 60 houses, of which 5 in 1774 were noted as farmhouses.[21] This estimate is surprisingly close to the official return of 1811 with its 60 houses. There was much building after 1851, and although the population had declined by 1901, there were still 80 inhabited houses.[22] The village has increased little in size in the 20th century: only six council houses were built between 1945 and 1954.[23]

Stratton is shaped like the letter H with most of its houses scattered along two parallel streets, connected by a road that passes the church and manor-house, lying on either side and forming the village's natural centre. South-east of the church in a meadow called Court Close, which lies in the bend of a stream, is the site of the Audleys' medieval castle,[24] now destroyed. It was to repair this building that James Audley was granted oak from Brill forest in 1263, and it was here that his widow was living in 1274.[25] The castle was inclosed by a rectangular moat which may be on the site of an earlier Romano-British inclosure.[26] The angles of the castle's foundations were excavated about 1870.[27] Near by on the village street were the stocks and the pound.[28] The Plough Inn, which still survives, was recorded in 1784 and may well be one of the two alehouses licensed in 1735.[29] The 'Red Lion', now at the west end of the village, was in existence in 1851, but the name at least is comparatively new as in 1784 Stratton's second inn was called the 'Mill Stone'.[30] Several important additions were made to the village in the 19th century: the school had been built by 1837;[31] a new 'handsome white brick' parsonage had been

---

[1] O.S. Map 6″, xvii, xxiii (1885); ibid. 2½″, 42/52, 62 (1951).

[2] See below, p. 330.

[3] See below.

[4] O.S. Map 25″, xvii. 14, 15; xxiii. 2, 3 (1881).

[5] V.C.H. Bucks. iv. 157; cf. Davis, Oxon. Map.

[6] Local Govt. Bd. Order 21435 (copy in O.R.O.): 12 houses and 59 people were transferred.

[7] V.C.H. Oxon. i. 277; cf. P.N. Oxon. (E.P.N.S.), i. 241–2.

[8] Davis, Oxon. Map; O.S. Map 2½″, 42/62 (1951).

[9] G.S. Map 1″, xlv NE.: there is drift clay and gravel on the higher land in the N.

[10] G.S. Memoir (1864), 31; see below, p. 330.

[11] O.R.O. Misc. Ey. IV/1.

[12] 20 Geo. III, c. 50 (priv. act).

[13] P.N. Oxon. (E.P.N.S.), i. 240; a branch of Akeman Street was once erroneously thought to pass through the village: V.C.H. Oxon. i. 275. Finds of Roman coins have been recorded from the 17th cent. on: ibid. 343.

[14] See below, p. 326.

[15] Below, pp. 327, 328. Part of Stratton field was also in

Caversfield: see Joseph Bullock's diary (p. 181) penes Col. the Hon. E. H. Wyndham, Caversfield.

[16] MS. Top. Oxon. c 398, ff. 98–99: transcript of E 326/ B 8646.

[17] Browne Willis, Hist. and Antiq. of Buck. (1755), 167.

[18] O.S. Map 25″, xvii. 15 (1881).

[19] See below, p. 328.

[20] Hearth Tax Oxon. 205–6, 235. For the Rectory and 'Parsonage' see below.

[21] Oxf. Dioc. d 554, d 565.

[22] Census, 1811, 1901.

[23] Inf. Ploughley R.D.C.

[24] V.C.H. Oxon. ii. 330; Dunkin, Oxon. ii. 149 n.; it gave its name to John ad Castellum (1279): Rot. Hund. (Rec. Com.), ii. 829.

[25] Cal. Pat. 1258–66, 293; Kennett, Paroch. Antiq. i. 396.

[26] V.C.H. Oxon. ii. 330.

[27] Kelly's Dir. Oxon. (1887).

[28] O.S. Map 25″, xvii. 15 (1881).

[29] O.R.O. Victlrs'. recog.

[30] Ibid.; Gardner, Dir. Oxon.

[31] See below, p. 333.

Stratton Audley Park in about 1870

STRATTON AUDLEY

Bignell House in 1866

BICESTER

recently erected in 1852; the old rectory had been converted into a hunting-box by T. Tyrwhitt-Drake,[32] and by 1880 the house and stables had been still further enlarged. It was known as Stratton Audley Hall.[33] To the south of it were and still are (1956) the kennels and exercising-grounds of the Bicester and Warden Hill Pack. The village has a shop and post office.

In the north of Stratton are two large fishponds connected by sluices; near them are traces of excavations made early in the 19th century by Sir John Borlase Warren, Bt., in the vain hope of finding coal.[34]

The oldest house in the village is the manor-house. It retains a 16th-century block on the west corner, the rest of the house having been repaired and enlarged in 1878 and again modernized and rebuilt early in the present century. The ancient west range is known as the 'Court Room' and was probably built by John Borlase in about 1545.[35] It has walls of coursed rubble (2 ft. 3 in. thick). The first-floor room is lined with early 17th-century panelling and has a contemporary plaster cornice of enriched vine-leaf design. The moulded 16th-century ceiling beams remain but the plaster ceiling is modern. In this room was found a stone achievement of the Royal Stuart arms probably inserted by Sir John Borlase on his return to the house in 1672; it is now set in the east wall of the room below. Reset in the modern north porch is a shield of carved stone bearing the arms of Audley. In the 18th century the mansion-house and gardens covered 52½ acres.[36]

The houses of West farm, Elms farm, and Manor farm lie in the village, but those of Oldfields farm and Pool farm, built in 1871, are outside. So also is Stratton Audley Park, built in 1860 for the banking family of Glen.[37] The mill lies in the extreme north of the parish on the Buckinghamshire border: there is no mention of a mill in Domesday Book, but there was probably one on this site by 1279 at least, when a miller was recorded among the tenants of the manor.[38]

The parish is notable for various incidents which occurred during the Civil War in the 17th century; for its association with fox-hunting in the 19th and 20th centuries; and for the modern R.A.F. dormitory site, a dependant of the R.A.F. station at Bicester.[39]

During the Civil War Mainwaring's Red Regiment was quartered at Stratton in 1643;[40] troop movements were recorded in the parish in the following year when the king's forces were quartered in the village,[41] and in 1645 the parliamentarian Captain Abercromby was defeated and fatally wounded in a skirmish near it.[42] It is possible that the small circular earthwork lying north-east of the village and known as 'Stuttle's Bank', which has been thought to be some kind of military or defensive work, belongs to this period.[43]

Stratton became the centre of the Bicester and Warden Hill Hunt when T. Tyrhwitt-Drake lived there and built the Stratton Audley kennels. He was Master for most of the period 1851 to 1866, and between 1872 and 1893 two other well-known Masters, Viscount Valentia and Lord Chesham, successively rented Stratton Audley Hall.[44]

Like many other Oxfordshire villages, Stratton had its team of Morris dancers until at least 1860.[45]

MANORS. Robert d'Oilly held 5 hides in *STRATTON* at the time of the Domesday survey,[46] possibly, as in many other estates, as the successor of Wigod of Wallingford. Stratton was among those fees of D'Oilly which later formed part of the honor of Wallingford, perhaps passing to Miles Crispin on his marriage to Robert d'Oilly's daughter.[47] The overlordship of the manor followed the descent of the honor of Wallingford and was in turn merged in the Earldom and the Royal Duchy of Cornwall,[48] and later in the honor of Ewelme.[49]

In 1086 Robert d'Oilly's tenant at Stratton was Alward,[50] who was succeeded by Gilbert Basset, possibly the brother of Ralph Basset the justiciar.[51] Gilbert, who held 7 fees of the honor of Wallingford, was in possession of Stratton by 1109.[52] On his death in about 1154 his son Thomas succeeded. Thomas was Sheriff of Oxfordshire in 1163–4 and died in 1180, when Stratton passed to his eldest son Gilbert,[53] the founder of Bicester Priory.[54] Gilbert's only daughter Eustachia married firstly Thomas de Verdun, lord of Hethe,[55] and secondly Richard, son of Gerard de Camville of Middleton Stoney and Godington.[56] Gilbert Basset died in 1205, and in the following year Richard succeeded to his wife's considerable inheritance, including Stratton.[57] In 1215 he succeeded to his father's estates,[58] but died in 1216 or soon afterwards.[59] William, Earl of Salisbury, had obtained from the king the wardship of Richard's daughter and heiress Idoine,[60] and she was subsequently married to his son William, who received her inheritance in 1226.[61]

In 1244 William and Idoine gave the manor in

[32] Gardner, *Dir. Oxon.*
[33] O.S. Map 25″, xvii. 15 (1881). The Hall is not mentioned in Gardner, but was so named on the O.S. map. The old part of the present building bears the date 1676.
[34] Dunkin, *Oxon.* ii. 149; a bore 240 ft. deep was made: *G.S. Memoir* (1864), 23; see below, p. 327.
[35] See below, p. 326.
[36] O.R.O. Misc. Ey. IV/1. In 1956 work began on converting the house into 3 flats: inf. Mr. C. Farthing, National Buildings Record.
[37] Wing, *Annals*, 130. For an engraving see plate opposite.
[38] *Rot. Hund.* (Rec. Com.), ii. 828.
[39] Inf. Wing-Commander R. C. Rotheram, R.A.F. Bicester.
[40] Dunkin MS. 438/4, f. 45*b*.
[41] Luke, *Jnl.* 243.
[42] Dunkin MS. 438/4, f. 64; Wood, *Life* i. 118.
[43] *V.C.H. Oxon.* ii. 334.
[44] *Kelly's Dir. Oxon.* (1864); *V.C.H. Oxon.* ii. 356–8; Wing, *Annals*, 177–82.

[45] Clare College Libr. (Cambridge), Sharp MS. Folk Dance Notes, iv. 90.
[46] *V.C.H. Oxon.* i. 414.
[47] *Boarstall Cart.* 323.
[48] *Red Bk. Exch.* (Rolls Ser.), 597; *Rot. Hund.* (Rec. Com.), ii. 828; *Cal. Inq. p.m.* iii, p. 428; S.C. 2/212/2.
[49] S.C. 2/212/20.
[50] *V.C.H. Oxon.* i. 414.
[51] *Boarstall Cart.* 324. [52] *Eynsham Cart.* i. 36.
[53] *Boarstall Cart.* 324; P.R.O. *L. and I.* ix; for the Basset family see *D.N.B.*
[54] *V.C.H. Oxon.* ii. 94; B.M. Add. Ch. 10593, 10595, 10616, 10617.
[55] See above, p. 175.
[56] *Boarstall Cart.* 324; *Rot. de Ob. et Fin.* (Rec. Com.), 64.
[57] *Rot. de Ob. et Fin.* 348; Kennett, *Paroch. Antiq.* i. 240; *Red Bk. Exch.* (Rolls Ser.), 597.
[58] *Rot. Litt. Pat.* (Rec. Com.), i. 127.
[59] See above, p. 245.
[60] *Rot. Litt. Pat.* i. 178; see also ibid. 170.
[61] *Rot. Litt. Claus.* (Rec. Com.), ii. 110, 123.

marriage to their daughter Ela and her husband James Audley.[62] A mesne lordship was thus created which descended after William's death in 1250 to his son William (d. 1257) and then to his grand-daughter Margaret and her husband Henry de Lacy, Earl of Lincoln.[63] On Henry's death in 1311 it passed to his daughter Alice, Countess of Lincoln and Salisbury.[64] Stratton Audley was then accounted to be $\frac{1}{3}$ knight's fee, the whole fee being made up by Bicester and Wretchwick.[65] Alice de Lacy died in 1348 leaving part of her possessions, including Bicester, to Roger Lestrange, Lord Strange, nephew and heir of her second husband Sir Ebles Lestrange,[66] and Roger's descendants claimed that Stratton was held of them as of their manor of Bicester.[67] In 1460, however, Stratton was said to be held of the king in chief.[68]

James Audley received a grant of free warren in Stratton in 1252[69] and held the manor until his death in 1272.[70] In 1273 his widow Ela settled Stratton upon her fifth and youngest son Hugh Audley, who was lord of the manor in 1279.[71] He later took part in the Scottish and French wars of Edward I,[72] was summoned to Parliament in 1321, joined in Thomas of Lancaster's rebellion in 1322, but surrendered before the battle of Boroughbridge. He died while a prisoner in Wallingford castle,[73] probably early in 1326.[74] Stratton Audley, as the manor was now called, was then in the king's hands, but was restored to James, son of Hugh Audley, in 1327.[75] In 1330 James Audley with Eva, described as his wife, made a settlement of the manor by fine.[76] Eva was mistress of James Audley, having been already twice married, firstly to Thomas Audley, James's first cousin, and secondly to Sir Thomas de Ufford, who died in 1314. The irregularity of their union may have been due to some difficulty in obtaining a dispensation on account of their blood relationship, or to a wish to avoid the heavy fine Eva would have to pay on marriage.[77] The settlement of the manor in 1330 mentions James and Peter their sons, and Katherine, Anne, and Hawise their daughters. James Audley died without legitimate issue in 1334,[78] and Stratton did not descend to either of his sons but passed to his younger brother and legal heir Hugh Audley, who certainly held the manor in 1335, when various persons were accused of breaking into his house at Stratton Audley, assaulting his servants and carrying away his goods there.[79] In 1337 he was created Earl of Gloucester.[80] Two

years later Stratton Audley manor was the security for a debt of 1,000 marks, which Hugh owed a London vintner.[81] On Hugh's death in 1347 the Audley lands passed to his daughter Margaret, wife of Ralph, Lord Stafford, but she was dead by 1351. Her husband, who was created Earl of Stafford in 1351, survived until 1372, but it is likely that Stratton had already passed to his son Hugh as Margaret's heir.[82] Hugh married Philippa, daughter of Thomas de Beauchamp, Earl of Warwick, and died in 1386, leaving at least four surviving sons, all under age. In 1387 a number of trustees, headed by the Earl of Warwick, was granted the issues of Stratton,[83] which later seems to have been settled upon Hugh's youngest son[84] Hugh, who died in possession in 1420, and was succeeded by his nephew Humphrey, Earl of Stafford.[85]

In 1426 Humphrey granted the manor to a group of no less than sixteen feoffees,[86] but he evidently retained at his death in 1460 rights of overlordship,[87] which descended to his great-grandson Edward Stafford, Duke of Buckingham, who was executed for high treason in 1521,[88] and to Edward's son Henry, Lord Stafford.[89] By 1460 only two of the original feoffees of the manor were still alive,[90] one of whom was Henry Bourchier, the cousin and heir of Elizabeth, Lady Bourchier, widow of Hugh Stafford (d. 1420).[91] Though the history of the manor is uncertain during the period of the Wars of the Roses, it clearly remained in the Bourchier family, for in 1517 the lord or perhaps the lessee of the manor was a great-nephew of Henry Bourchier,[92] John Bourchier, Lord Berners,[93] who received a formal grant of Stratton from Henry VIII in 1528. Four years later Henry, Lord Stafford, made over his interest in the manor.[94] Lord Berners died in 1533, and by 1542 Stratton had been alienated by his daughter Jane and was in the possession of Sir John Baldwin.[95]

Sir John died in 1545 leaving as coheirs his grandsons John Borlase and Sir Thomas Pakington.[96] The latter gave up his half-share of the manor to John Borlase in 1551,[97] and the Borlase family continued to hold Stratton for more than two centuries. They were, however, more intimately concerned with Buckinghamshire than with Oxfordshire affairs.[98] John Borlase died in 1593, having settled Stratton upon his wife Anne, and was succeeded by his son William,[99] to whom the manor had reverted by 1616.[1] William died in 1629,[2] and his son William

[62] *Fines Oxon.* 129; *Complete Peerage,* i. 338.
[63] *Rot. Hund.* (Rec. Com.), ii. 828; *Boarstall Cart.* 301.
[64] *Cal. Inq. p.m.* vi, p. 410; *Feud. Aids,* iv. 180.
[65] *Feud. Aids,* iv. 158.
[66] Blo. *Mid.* 26–27; *Complete Peerage,* vii. 687–8; xii (1), 353.
[67] C 139/4; *Feud. Aids,* iv. 190 (1428).
[68] C 139/180.
[69] *Cal. Chart. R.* 1226–57, 409.
[70] *Ex. e Rot. Fin.* (Rec. Com.), ii. 574.
[71] *Cal. Inq. p.m.* vi, p. 410; *Rot. Hund.* (Rec. Com.), ii. 828.
[72] *Complete Peerage,* i. 347.   [73] Ibid.
[74] *Cal. Inq. p.m.* vi, p. 410.
[75] *Cal. Close,* 1327–30, 23.
[76] C.P. 25(1)/189/17/41.
[77] *Complete Peerage,* i. 339, 348.
[78] Ibid. 348.
[79] *Cal. Pat.* 1334–8, 214.
[80] *Complete Peerage,* i. 346–7.
[81] *Cal. Close,* 1339–41, 241.
[82] *Complete Peerage,* i. 347; xii (1), 176–7; C 135/230/1.

[83] *Complete Peerage,* xii (1), 178–9; *Cal. Pat.* 1385–9, 365.
[84] Dunkin, *Oxon.* ii. 166; cf. N. H. Nicolas, *Testamenta Vetusta,* 119.   [85] C 139/4.
[86] Ibid. 180; *Cal. Close,* 1422–9, 318.
[87] C 139/180.   [88] E 150/798/7.
[89] C 54/399/28.
[90] C 139/180; cf. Hist. MSS. Com. *4th Rep. App.* 176.
[91] *Complete Peerage,* ii. 247–8.
[92] Ibid. 153–4.
[93] *Dom. of Incl.* i. 331; he may have held the manor since 1514: *L. & P. Hen. VIII,* v, p. 406.
[94] *L. & P. Hen. VIII,* iv (2), p. 1774; C.P. 25(2)/34/227/East. 23 Hen. VIII.
[95] *Complete Peerage,* ii. 154–5; C.P. 40/1109, m. 14d.
[96] C 142/73/7.
[97] C.P. 25(2)/66/548/East. 5 Edw. VI.
[98] Dunkin, *Oxon.* ii. 169–70; *V.C.H. Bucks.* iii. 80–81.
[99] C 142/237/121.
[1] Ibid. 459/48; C.P. 43/148/17; cf. Kennett, *Paroch. Antiq.* ii. 427.
[2] C 142/451/107.

in 1630.[3] The younger William's son John came of age in 1640, and was created a baronet in 1642.[4] He was one of those Members of Parliament who joined the king at Oxford in 1643. All his estates, presumably including Stratton Audley, were sequestrated by the Parliament, but by the end of 1645 he had taken the Covenant, and he finally compounded for his delinquency in 1647.[5] His son, another Sir John, lived at Stratton Audley and was buried there in 1689.[6]

The Borlase estates then passed to Sir John's sister Anne, wife of Arthur Warren of Stapleton (Notts.). She died in 1703, but her son Borlase Warren seems to have held Stratton by 1701.[7] Borlase Warren (d. 1747) was succeeded by John Borlase Warren (d. 1763) and Admiral Sir John Borlase Warren,[8] the distinguished naval officer.[9] Sir John died at Stratton Audley in 1822,[10] and his estates passed to his surviving daughter Frances Maria, wife of George Sedley Vernon.[11] Stratton, however, remained in the hands of the trustees of Sir John's will until at least 1850.[12] It was purchased by 1864 by George Glen, and after his death in 1885 it again passed to trustees.[13] Colonel George Gosling, who purchased Stratton Audley Park in 1889, had acquired the manorial rights by 1903. He was succeeded in 1915 by his son Major George Edward Gosling, who died in 1938.[14] In 1939 Major Gosling's widow was lady of the manor.[15]

Part of Stratton Audley was held with the neighbouring manor of Caversfield of the honor of Warenne, and like Caversfield was probably held after the Conquest by Brien or Brienz, who was also William de Warenne's tenant at Gatehampton.[16] Until the early 14th century the overlordship of this estate followed the descent of the Earldom of Surrey, but by 1317 it had passed to Aymer de Valence, Earl of Pembroke. After the earl's death in 1324 it first passed to his niece Joan, Countess of Athol, and her descendants, and then after 1357 to the heirs of his eldest sister Isabel.[17]

In the 12th century the tenants of the earls of Surrey were the Gargates, whose pedigree has not been completely worked out, although it is clear that they were the same family that held Warmington (Northants). Robert Gargate occurs about 1160, and he was probably succeeded by his elder son Roger. Roger's son Hugh succeeded by about 1189, and died between 1216 and 1220.[18] Hugh's widow

Sybil was said in 1243 to hold ¼ fee in Stratton,[19] but the estate had already been alienated by Hugh's daughters and coheiresses, Muriel, widow of William de Ros, and Isabel, wife of Gerard de Munbury, who in about 1233 gave their shares of Stratton (described in 1279 as 1½ virgate, enough for the maintenance of three canons) together with half of Caversfield to Bicester Priory.[20] Another virgate appears to have been given by Robert Gargate,[21] probably the younger brother of Roger.

Bicester already had an estate in Stratton, given it by Gilbert Basset, the founder of the priory. When he gave the chapel in the 1180's[22] it was already endowed with a virgate of land and he added another.[23] By 1279 the priory held 8½ virgates in Stratton, including the chapel's 2 virgates and the 2½ of the Gargates.[24] The land formed one estate known as the RECTORY MANOR. Sometimes the priory leased it; sometimes it administered it directly.[25] In 1536 the priory was suppressed, and in 1542 the manor was granted to Christ Church, Oxford.[26]

Christ Church leased the estate along with the tithes. After 1555–6, when the rectory estate was reconstituted, it consisted of 5½ yardlands or 314 acres, and was the only land in the parish not belonging to the manor.[27] It was known as Manor farm, and with it went the house called the Parsonage House. The property was usually leased by the same family for many years. The original 16th-century rent of £17 6s. 8d. remained unchanged until the late 19th century, but the great rise in land values in the 18th century is reflected in the size of the fine paid on the renewal of the lease. It was £130 in 1765, £250 in 1779, £517 in 1807, £1,519 in 1815, and £1,025 in 1835.[28]

In 1535 the lease was held by Thomas Denton of Hillesden (Bucks.), a prominent Buckinghamshire man, and it continued in his family at least until 1596, when Margaret Denton, a widow, left it to her nephew Thomas.[29] In the first half of the 17th century it was held by the Chamberlayne family, who probably rented the manor-house.[30] Edward Chamberlayne's estate was sequestered around 1650. In 1661 a new lease was given to Edward Bush.[31] He was to pay the curate, give him a room, repair the chancel, give the inhabitants such entertainment as had been usual, and entertain the chapter of Christ Church, if it did not exceed ten persons with ten horses, once a year for two days and three nights.[32]

[3] Ibid. 459/48.

[4] Dunkin, *Oxon.* ii. 170; G.E.C. *Baronetage*, ii. 169.

[5] G.E.C. *Baronetage*, ii. 169; *V.C.H. Bucks.* iii. 80; *Cal. Cttee. for Compounding*, 27, 66, 800, 919.

[6] Dunkin, *Oxon.* ii. 170–1; G.E.C. *Baronetage*, ii. 169–70; for the Borlase family see W. C. Copeland Borlase, *Borlase of Borlase* and pedigree in *Genealogist*, N.S. ii. 288–9.

[7] Dunkin, *Oxon.* ii. 171; *V.C.H. Bucks.* iii. 81; C.P. 43/475/54.

[8] Dunkin, *Oxon.* ii. 171–3; C.P. 43/660/28; 685/355; 769/288.

[9] *D. N. B.*; G. E. C. *Baronetage*, v. 183–4.

[10] W. C. C. Borlase, *Borlase of Borlase*, 67.

[11] C.P. 43/973/242; *Genealogist*, N.S. ii. 289.

[12] O.R.O. Land tax assess.; ibid. Gamekprs' deps.; Gardner, *Dir. Oxon.*

[13] *Kelly's Dir. Oxon.* (1864); ibid. (1887).

[14] Ibid. (1891–1939); Burke, *Land. Gent.* (1937); *Who Was Who* (1928–40).

[15] *Kelly's Dir. Oxon.* (1939).

[16] *V.C.H. Oxon.* i. 411, 426; Farrer, *Honors*, iii. 410.

[17] *V.C.H. Bucks.* iv. 157–8; *Cal. Pat.* 1317–21, 150.

[18] *V.C.H. Bucks.* iv. 158; *V.C.H. Northants.* iii. 115; Farrer, *Honors*, iii. 411.

[19] *Bk. of Fees*, 826.

[20] Farrer, *Honors*, iii. 411–12; *V.C.H. Bucks.* iv. 158; *Cat. Anct. D.* i, B 946; E 210/D 3456; Kennett, *Paroch. Antiq.* i. 188, 265–6.

[21] S.C. 11/551.

[22] See below, p. 330.

[23] Kennett, *Paroch. Antiq.* i. 188; *Cal. Pat.* 1313–17, 359; *Rot. Hund.* (Rec. Com.), ii. 828.

[24] *Rot. Hund.* ii. 828–9.

[25] See below, p. 328.

[26] *L. & P. Hen. VIII*, xvii, p. 491; xxi(2), p. 334.

[27] Dunkin, *Oxon.* ii. 150: extract from incl. act.

[28] Ch. Ch. Arch. leases.

[29] *Valor Eccl.* (Rec. Com.), ii. 188; *V.C.H. Bucks.* iv. 175, 180; P.C.C. Drake 34–35. For pedigree see Lipscomb, *Bucks.* iii. 17.

[30] Dunkin, *Oxon.* ii. 170.

[31] *Cal. Cttee. for Compounding*, 2523; Ch. Ch. Arch. 1661 lease.

[32] Ibid. 1669 lease.

Later, in 1673, he mortgaged the estate for £1,300 to Jasper Scoles of Wroughton (Wilts.), who took possession.[33] Twenty years later the mortgagee was involved in a long Chancery suit with Bush's son Edmund, one of his complaints being that the Bushes had pulled down part of the Rectory House and used the material to build another house outside the college property.[34] The Bush family held the rectory intermittently for a hundred years.[35] In 1779 Richard Arnold, the steward of Sir John Borlase Warren, took the lease, and he also heavily mortgaged the property.[36] From 1815 it was held by John Perry, a London builder, and his family.[37]

In 1780, by the inclosure award, Christ Church was allotted 217 acres for its 5½ yardlands,[38] and in 1865 the estate, which had been increased by 251 acres, awarded for tithes at inclosure, was divided into two farms: West farm (223 a.) and East or Manor farm (249 a.). They were sold in 1939 and 1952 respectively.[39]

LESSER ESTATE. By 1279 Cirencester Abbey had obtained a small estate of 1½ virgate.[40] It still held it at the Dissolution, when it was receiving 14s. 6d. a year rent from Stratton.[41] The estate was granted by the Crown in 1544 to Thomas Denton,[42] then a lessee of the rectory estate.

ECONOMIC AND SOCIAL HISTORY. Because part of the ancient township of Stratton formed part of Caversfield manor there is no full Domesday entry for the later parish of Stratton. A part of it was included in the entry for Caversfield, which had 8 plough-lands, of which 3 were in demesne.[43] This manor had 21 villeins (villani) and bordars with 5 plough-teams, and some of these with their land must, it seems, have been in Stratton. Stratton's principal manor had 6 plough-lands; in demesne there was 1 plough-team and 1 serf, while 8 villeins and 2 bordars shared 2 other plough-teams. There were 25 acres of meadow, a comparatively large amount. Since the Conquest the value of the Stratton estate had risen from £2 to £3, in spite of the fact that it was apparently not fully worked.[44]

There is an exceptionally full account of the parish in the Hundred Rolls.[45] The 55 tenants recorded, almost all villeins, indicate a comparatively large population for a rural village in this hundred. The principal manor had 2½ carucates in demesne; its tenants included 6 villein virgaters, 4 holding ¾ virgate each, and 28 half-virgaters.[46] All worked at the lord's will. Besides the villeins there were 8 cottagers, who each had 5 acres at a rent of 2s. Of the 6 free tenants, 3 held some 4 virgates, while the Augustinian Abbey of Cirencester had 1¼ virgate leased to 3 tenants. The total number of virgates recorded was about 46, 9 more than in an 18th-century survey.

Two unusual features were the large number of half-virgaters and the comparatively high rent of 8s. a virgate or 4s. a half-virgate.

The Prior of Bicester's small manor consisted of 8½ virgates, of which 4½ were in demesne. The manor's six villeins held between them 4 virgates and paid rent at the rate of 6s. a virgate.[47]

At this date and in the early 14th century Stratton seems to have been at the height of its prosperity, perhaps largely because the Audleys were resident there.[48] The fact that Hugh Audley was granted in 1318 the privilege of a weekly market in Stratton and a yearly fair for three days at the feast of the Exaltation of the Holy Cross (Sept. 14th) shows that it was hoped that the village might develop as a trading centre. There is no later reference to this market, but in spite of its lying within five miles of the market-town of Bicester, it may have prospered temporarily. Unfortunately the early 14th-century tax returns for Stratton are either missing or incomplete. The village's total payment, though not the total number of contributors, has, however, survived for 1306. It was the sixth highest contributor in the hundred and there were at least 45 contributors.[49] The evidence of the poll tax of 1377 with 144 adults taxed also supports the indications of a comparatively large medieval population. In spite of the heavy death-rate suffered by the neighbourhood in 1349, this figure was one of the highest in the hundred.[50] A survey of Bicester's small manor made in 1412–13 mentions that before the 'magna mors' it had been leased on account of the increase of villein holdings, and at the date of the survey the number of customary tenants was still higher than in 1279.[51]

Early 16th-century subsidy lists indicate that Stratton compared with other parishes in the hundred was still a fairly populous and prosperous community: 35 persons were taxed in 1524 and in 1542 there were 56 contributors.[52] From 17th-century evidence it appears that there were 30 taxable houses in 1665 and 126 adults in 1676.[53]

The survey of 1412–13 shows that since 1279 villein rents had about doubled on the Bicester manor, the rate for a half-virgate now being between 6s. and 7s. Services had been commuted. In addition to the customary tenants, some 35 tenants rented smallholdings of various sizes on eight-year leases. The priory still kept some demesne, however, and an account of 1409–10 records that its total receipts were £20 16s. 3½d. and that about half its income came from its Stratton grange from the sale of hay and grain. Peas, barley, and wheat were grown.[54] In 1433–4 the priory received £17 6s. 9d. from the grange, a smaller amount than usual because grain, &c., was sent to the canons; in 1447 it received £20 0s. 9d. and 57 lambs delivered to the priory for stock; in 1452 £15 0s. 7½d.[55]

[33] Cal. Cttee. for Compounding, 2523; Ch. Ch. Arch. 1669 lease.
[34] C 5/107/56, 204/10 (1693, 1699). For a later suit brought by Wm. Gibbons see ibid. 607/87 (1710).
[35] See below, p. 331.
[36] Dunkin, Oxon. ii. 161; Ch. Ch. Arch. lease.
[37] Ch. Ch. Arch. lease.
[38] 20 Geo. III, c. 50 (priv. act).
[39] Ch. Ch. Arch.
[40] Rot. Hund. (Rec. Com.), ii. 828.
[41] Dugd. Mon. vi (1), 179.
[42] L. & P. Hen. VIII, xix (1), p. 373.
[43] See above, p. 324; V.C.H. Oxon. i. 426.
[44] Ibid. 414.   [45] Rot. Hund. (Rec. Com.), ii. 828–9.

[46] See above, p. 326.
[47] See above, p. 327.
[48] See above, p. 326; Cal. Chart. R. 1300–26, 389.
[49] E 179/161/10.   [50] E 179/161/39.
[51] S.C. 11/551; cf. Rot. Hund. (Rec. Com.), ii. 829.
[52] E 179/161/176; 162/222; see below, p. 359.
[53] Hearth Tax Oxon. 205; Compton Census.
[54] Dunkin, Oxon. ii. 157–8.
[55] Blo. Bic. ii. 172, 182, 185. For bailiffs' accounts relating to the priory's possessions in Stratton from the time of Ed. I to Ed. IV see S.C. 6/961/21–29; 956/3; 1117/11; 1146/15. Extracts have been printed in Dunkin, Oxon. ii. 220–48, and in Blo. Bic. ii. 133–205, where there is a detailed list. Other accounts are in Trin. Coll. Arch.

The survey further supplies the earliest evidence for the field system. It shows that the early two- or three-field system had broken down, and mentions at least five—Bradenhull, Blakedon, Lantehull, and Langdon Fields and *Campus Petri*, among which each tenant's land was divided.[56] A later survey of 1710 records a more complicated division of the fields.[57] Only two of the 15th-century field names survived: Langdon Field, which lay in the south next to Launton, and Lower, Middle, and Upper Stone Fields (the former *Campus Petri*), in the west along the Fringford boundary. Other fields were Grislow, Stubb, and Home Fields, and in the north-east next to Godington was Old Field, entirely furze, from which before inclosure the villagers cut furze for fuel.[58]

There is no evidence about the inclosure of land before the 16th century. In 1517 John Marche was accused of amalgamating two farms, each worth £7 6s. 8d., one in Bainton and the other in Stratton.[59] In 1542 a copyhold close called Madcrofts is mentioned[60] and in the 1550's the lord of the manor was allowed to inclose a ground called Manmore south of Fringford Field.[61] All the early inclosure was meadow, for a record of 1779 shows that at least 300 acres of meadow, but no arable, had been inclosed.[62] In 1780 the open fields were inclosed. At that time all the land was divided between the manor (31¼ yardlands) and Christ Church, the lay rector, and its lessee (6 yardlands). Of some 2,000 acres belonging to the manor, 919 were arable strips in the open fields, thus making the yardland equal about 29 acres; 740 were common pasture; 50 were common meadow; and 300 were inclosed meadow.[63] The pasture consisted of the Cow Common (343 a.), the Horse Common (207 a.), and the Sheep Common (188 a.). The Town Meadow was 50 acres, and there was a large inclosed meadow of 217½ acres and a smaller one called the Mill Closes of 74 acres. The inclosure act[64] awarded 217 acres to Christ Church in place of its 5½ yardlands and 251 acres in lieu of all tithes; 23 acres to Richard Arnold, its lessee, for a ½ yardland; 32 acres to the Vicar of Caversfield in lieu of tithes on 4 yardlands; and almost all the rest to the lord of the manor. The poor, with rents of 40s. or below, were allotted four acres for fuel in place of the privilege of gathering fuel from the common lands, and Christ Church was freed from the responsibility of keeping a bull and a boar for the use of the inhabitants.

The effect of inclosure seems to have been to increase the amount of dairy farming, for which the soil, 'rich and well watered', was particularly well suited. In 1780 about half the parish had been arable, but a map of 1797 shows almost all the land south of the village as pasture, while to the north arable and pasture were mixed.[65] The best meadow-land

lay along the Birne and near the mill (see below). Even before inclosure the number of cattle and sheep allowed for every yardland was unusually large owing to the richness of the grazing-land:[66] 4 cows, 3 horses, 40 sheep, and 22 lambs. The total for the manor was 156 cows, 90¼ horses, 1,250 sheep, and 687½ lambs. In the early 19th century Arthur Young noted that much of the land was under dairies and that 'great tracts have been laid down for cows'. He also noted that rents had quintupled since inclosure, although this seems to have been an exaggeration.[67] Later in the century Stratton was considered an agriculturally progressive parish, largely on account of a rich and 'spirited resident landed proprietor', George Glen.[68] It has continued primarily as a grazing parish. In 1891, for example, out of 1,049 acres for sale, 839 were pasture and only 152 arable,[69] and in 1901 four-fifths of the parish was grazing-land.[70] War conditions naturally led to an increase in arable in the early 20th century, but in 1939 the land was still chiefly pasture.[71] In 1956 there were 1,616½ acres of grassland compared with 722⅔ acres of arable.

It is impossible to be precise about the effect of inclosure on the position of the small landowner as no pre-inclosure list of tenants has been found. In 1851 there were eight farms of over 100 acres, five of them being between 200 and 300 acres,[72] and in 1891 there were seven large farms.[73]

Few local government records have survived. The Surveyors' accounts (1719–1811) show that a rise in expenditure had occurred early in the second half of the 18th century. During most of the first half expenditure had averaged about £3 a year, but by 1765 it had risen to £18. For the rest of the century about £15 a year was spent, and it does not appear that inclosure had any marked effect on the problem of pauperism. At the beginning of the 19th century in common with other parishes in the hundred expenditure rose steeply: £25 to £30 was expended annually except for the peak years 1801 to 1802 and 1810 to 1811, when £40 and £50 respectively were spent.

Administration was tightened up in 1797. The surveyor was to state in his book the duty which each person was bound to do and the days on which he performed his duty. The fine for failure to do this was £5. From 1798 until 1809 the amount of duty is duly entered.[74]

Besides having the usual craftsmen and traders, such as a baker, a blacksmith, a shoemaker, and a bricklayer, in the mid-19th century Stratton was a centre of lace-making, a home industry which was particularly flourishing in Buckinghamshire. Twenty-seven lacemakers were counted in 1851.[75] Since medieval times the parish had its miller. The water-mill is first recorded in the early 15th century when

[56] S.C. 11/551; *P.N. Oxon.* (E.P.N.S.), i. 240–1, gives many furlong names from this survey.
[57] Christ Ch. Arch. terrier of 1710.
[58] Cf. 20 Geo. III, c. 50 (priv. act): incl. act.
[59] *Dom. of Incl.* i. 331.
[60] C.P. 40/1109, m. 14d.
[61] Christ Ch. Arch. lease of 2 & 3 Phil. & Mary.
[62] O.R.O. Misc. Ey. IV/1.
[63] Ibid.
[64] 20 Geo. III, c. 50 (priv. act); copy in Bodl. L. Eng. C 13 c 1 (1780). There is no separate award.
[65] Davis, *Oxon. Map.*
[66] O.R.O. Misc. Ey. IV/1.

[67] Young, *Oxon. Agric.* 91. He said rents had increased from £500 to £2,500, but in 1779 a fair rent was said to be £1,343: O.R.O. Misc. Ey. IV/1.
[68] Wing, *Annals*, 127.
[69] Bodl. G.A. Oxon. b 92* (2): *Sale Cat.*
[70] Bd. of Agric. Returns 1901.
[71] *Kelly's Dir. Oxon.* (1939); inf. Oxon. Agric. Executive Cttee.
[72] H.O. 107/1727.
[73] Bodl. G.A. Oxon. b 92* (2).
[74] Par. Rec. Surveyors' accts. 1719–1811.
[75] H.O. 107/1727; Gardner, *Dir. Oxon.*

it formed part of the manor,[76] as it continued to do. In 1891 it was let, with 32 acres, for £75,[77] and was driven by steam and water.[78] Another mill, perhaps a windmill, was recorded on the Bicester manor in the early 15th century.[79] Another of Stratton's most important occupations apart from husbandry was quarrying. Field names indicate the prevalence of stone in the parish,[80] and in the 14th century 'Helmendene' quarry is mentioned.[81] The quarry lay in the south-west corner of the parish; its stone was used to build Stratton Audley Park in 1860,[82] and when it was sold at the same time as the manor in 1891, it and a neighbouring limekiln were let for £47.[83] In 1939 the quarry was being worked by the Bicester Stone Company.[84]

In the 18th century the parish—which did not include that part of the village which lay in Caversfield—was well populated. In 1738 the curate estimated that there were between 50 and 60 houses and by 1801 there were 379 inhabitants. The population fluctuated until 1861 when it was 378. During the remaining decades of the century it declined and by 1901 it was 263. There were 305 inhabitants in 1911 and there were estimated to be 304 in 1954.[85]

CHURCH. A grant of tithes before 1109 (see below) may indicate the existence of an 11th-century church in Stratton, but not necessarily, as at that time Stratton was in the parish of Bicester. The church is first specifically mentioned when it was granted with the church of Bicester, of which it was a dependent chapel, by Gilbert Basset, lord of the manors of Bicester and Stratton, to the Augustinian Priory of Bicester at its foundation between 1182 and 1185.[86] The priory had appropriated the church and chapel by 1220 at the latest,[87] and it retained them until its dissolution in 1536.

At the ordination of Bicester vicarage in 1226 no mention is made of the chapel at Stratton, but reference to the vicar's chaplain and clerks combined with later evidence (see below) suggests that the vicar was made responsible for Stratton at that date.[88] In 1455 he was relieved of the duty of supplying a chaplain for Stratton and the burden was undertaken by the prior and convent.[89] This agreement probably marks the creation of a separate parish of Stratton. After the Reformation it was certainly independent of Bicester, and by 1665 all ties with the mother church had been severed. The Bicester churchwardens then presented those of Stratton for not paying a pension of 15d. to Bicester church, 'the same having been formerly, usually and accustomarily paid', probably as a sign of subjection to the mother church. But the warden of Stratton testified in the bishop's court that during 40 years in the parish he had never heard of any such pension.[90] In the early 18th century it is stated that Stratton was 'taken out of Bicester parish'.[91]

In 1542 Henry VIII granted Stratton to the Dean and Chapter of Christ Church.[92] After the Reformation the living remained a perpetual curacy until 1868, when it became a vicarage.[93] Christ Church continued as patron until 1928, when the living was changed to a rectory and combined with that of Godington.[94] Since then Christ Church and Corpus Christi College have presented alternately.

Before 1109 Gilbert Basset had given to Eynsham Abbey two-thirds of his demesne tithes in Stratton.[95] When Stratton chapel was given to Bicester Priory, controversy arose between the two religious houses over these tithes. In 1188 an agreement was reached before episcopal judges sitting in Stanton church (probably Stanton St. John). Bicester was to collect all the tithes, and in return was to give Eynsham a pension of 12s. a year.[96] This arrangement was soon confirmed by Gilbert Basset, and the pension continued to be paid until the Dissolution.[97]

It thus appears as if by 1188 Bicester Priory was already collecting the tithes of the parish. If this was so the charter of 1208–9, by which Richard de Camville and Eustachia his wife gave the priory the whole tithe of hay from their demesne in Bicester, Wretchwick, and Stratton, was probably a confirmation.[98]

Caversfield church from the early Middle Ages had a claim to some of the tithes of Stratton. When Caversfield was appropriated to Missenden Abbey (Bucks.) between 1209 and 1235, these tithes were divided between the abbey and the vicar, each taking half of the tithes of 6 virgates.[99] A few years later Bicester Priory was resisting this claim, and in 1242 papal judges delegate made a compromise: Caversfield was allowed to continue collecting tithes on $4\frac{1}{2}$ virgates and their holders as well, while the tithes on the rest were given to Bicester.[1] This arrangement continued until the inclosure of Stratton fields in 1780, when the tithes on 4 yardlands, to which the Vicar of Caversfield was entitled, were commuted for 32 acres. This ancient connexion between Stratton and Caversfield church was not broken until 1928, when the 220 acres in Stratton field which had been assigned to Caversfield at the inclosure of 1780 were added to the ecclesiastical parish of Stratton.[2] The tithes of Stratton were commuted at the inclosure for 251 acres.[3]

The tradition that Master William of Drogheda, an eminent Oxford lecturer in canon law in the first half of the 13th century, was Rector of Stratton is ill founded.[4] The parish was in fact probably partly

[76] C 139/4.
[77] Bodl. G.A. Oxon. b 92* (2).
[78] Kelly's Dir. Oxon. (1891).
[79] Dunkin, Oxon. ii. 158 n.
[80] e.g. Stratton Stones: S.C. 11/551.
[81] S.C. 6/961/25.
[82] Wing, Annals, 130.
[83] Bodl. G.A. Oxon. b 92* (2), lot 5.
[84] Kelly's Dir. Oxon. (1939).
[85] Oxf. Dioc. d 554; Census, 1801–1951; inf. Ploughley R.D.C.
[86] V.C.H. Oxon. ii. 94; Kennett, Paroch. Antiq. i. 188.
[87] V.C.H. Oxon. ii. 94.   [88] See above, p. 43.
[89] Kennett, Paroch. Antiq. ii. 393–5.
[90] MS. Top. Oxon. c 56, f. 80. The churchyard recorded in 1584 may have been a burial-ground: Archd. Ct. i. 97.

[91] Bacon, Lib. Reg. 793.
[92] L. & P. Hen. VIII, xvii, p. 491; ibid. xxi (2), p. 334; St. Frides. Cart. i. 96.
[93] By 31 & 32 Vict. c. 117.
[94] Par. Rec. Deed of union.
[95] Eynsham Cart. i. 36.   [96] Ibid. 71, 121, 72.
[97] Valor. Eccl. (Rec. Com.), ii. 210. The 16s. given ibid. 188 is a mistake.
[98] Kennett, Paroch. Antiq. i. 240. For rectory estate see above, p. 327.   [99] Rot. Welles, i. 196.
[1] MS. Top. Oxon. c 398, ff. 98–99: transcript of E 326/B 8646.   [2] See above, p. 324.
[3] 20 Geo. III, c. 50 (priv. act).
[4] D.N.B. The mistake arises from a misreading of the papal letters. In Cal. Papal L. i. 214, 'Stratsun', taken by the editors as Stratton Audley, should be Grafton Underwood (Northants): Rot. Grosse. 213.

served by the Vicar of Bicester, who may have come out to say mass, while 14th-century accounts show that there was a deacon at the chapel. His stipend in 1340 seems to have been 15s. 2d.; by 1360 this had been raised to £1. For marriages and purifications Stratton people had to come to Bicester church and they were buried in Bicester churchyard. Fees for marriages ranged from 7½d. to 15d., for purifications from ½d. to 2d., and for burials from 1d., according to the family's wealth. The offerings at the various festivals also formed part of the revenue of Bicester vicarage: in 1340–1, 3s. was collected at Christmas and 4s. 9d. at Easter.[5]

In 1423 two people were buried in Stratton chapel. This was an infringement of the rights of the mother church, and the Prior of Bicester brought a suit against the parishioners of Stratton. Proceedings were opened in Stratton church by the Bishop of Worcester as judge delegate, who listened to the 'evidences of old men in divers towns' as to whether 'at any time in their day they saw, or in the days of their fathers heard of, any burial made there'. The eventual judgement was that the two bodies buried in the chapel were to be exhumed and reburied at Bicester. Stratton had to pay various costs.[6]

The costs of this suit, amounting to £22 16s. in 1423–4 and £16 15s. 9d. in 1424–5, show how expensive litigation was; each year's expenses averaged about a year's income from all priory lands and tithes in Stratton. The largest payment was one of £6 13s. 4d. to the episcopal judge, while his officers received gifts and his servants 24 pairs of gloves. Among the many other expenses were those for entertainment on the first day of the trial, when a sumptuous dinner was given at the Rectory.

In 1455, when a new ordination was made of Bicester vicarage, it was agreed that the priory was to take all tithes and other revenue belonging to Stratton, and was to bear the burden of keeping a chaplain there and of administering the rites and sacraments to the parishioners.[7] Early 16th-century visitations showed certain neglect and irregularities. In about 1520 there were no distributions to the poor, the mass and other services were not celebrated at regular hours, and the *sedilia* in the choir were broken. The chapel had been served by a canon from Bicester Priory, but he was removed for ill conduct with women.[8] About ten years later the curate, whose stipend was £5 6s. 8d., did not know how to sing or hold a service with song.[9]

The income of the living came from a stipend from Christ Church or its lessee and from the glebe, called Parson's Ground (c. 18 a.), in Caversfield.[10] In 1762 the income was augmented by a £400 benefaction, half from Queen Anne's Bounty and half from Christ Church.[11] The living, however, was still a poor one, worth only £58 10s. in 1809, £30

of which was paid by Christ Church.[12] In the 1830's it was again augmented by £1,000, half given by Christ Church.[13]

From 1542 the curate was normally appointed and paid by the Christ Church lessee.[14] A tithe case of 1663 between Edward Bush, the new lessee of the rectory, who had the right to nominate, and John Bedwyn, a churchwarden, reveals that there might be friction in the parish over the nomination of curates. It appears that the college's nominee had been threatened in 1660 'by those which kept possession of the parsonage house' (i.e. the wardens) so that he 'did not dare to come to the church'.[15] Bush presently allowed the churchwardens to select a curate, whom he paid. In 1669, when the lease of the rectory was renewed, Christ Church retained the nomination of the incumbent and raised his salary from £11 to £20. A room in the parsonage house, described as a wainscot chamber over the brewhouse with a cockloft above, was to be reserved for his use by the lessee of the rectory.[16] Henceforth, the incumbents were graduates of Christ Church.

It is probable that the poverty of the living forced the curates to be pluralists, while residence was certainly made difficult by there being no house. In 1738, for instance, Fielder Hammond (1736–45) reported that he could find no one with whom to board in the summer, and that in winter he lived in one room.[17] After this, conditions were somewhat improved, for in 1768 William Ellis (1761–95), who was also Vicar of Stoke Lyne, had a house in Stratton belonging to the living.[18] His successor, Edward Houlditch (1795–1814), nevertheless, was forced to add to his income by holding another living at Speen (Berks.). He lived there and paid a curate £25 a year to serve Stratton, with the result that the parish was neglected. Houlditch's curate said he was underpaid and so too poor to attend the bishop's visitation;[19] the bishop complained that only one Sunday service was held and that at 2 o'clock in the afternoon.[20] The vicar's excuse was that this was the custom in many parishes. It was not until after 1834 that there were any marked signs of religious revival. There was then a resident curate who was paid £70 a year. Congregations of 300 to 350 were reported, and two services were held on Sundays;[21] by 1851 a parsonage house had been built and by 1854 there were daily prayers, two sermons on Sundays, and communion once a month.[22]

Despite this progress, when John Tweed (1857–98) came to the parish, Bishop Wilberforce found him dejected about it, and it was admitted that it was a difficult one.[23] The living was still so poor that Tweed had to augment his salary by taking other kinds of work. However, he had the church building restored and was able to report that the congregation was at least 'not decreasing', and that in winter he

[5] Blo. *Bic.* ii. 98–101. Christenings were probably also held at Bicester, but they were not entered in the accounts since they were not supposed to be charged for.

[6] Dunkin, *Oxon.* ii. 155–7, where the accounts are printed.

[7] Kennett, *Paroch. Antiq.* ii. 393.

[8] *Visit. Dioc. Linc. 1517–31*, i. 125.

[9] Ibid. ii. 38; *Subsidy 1526*, 276.

[10] *Ch. Ch. Arch.* 187; Oxf. Dioc. c 449, f. 45.

[11] Oxf. Dioc. c 446, f. 174; *Papers Rel. to Queen Anne's Bounty, 1703–1815*, H.C. 115 (1814–15), xii.

[12] Oxf. Dioc. c 660, ff. 171–2.

[13] C. Hodgson, *Account of Queen Anne's Bounty* (1845), pp. 217, 222, 324.

[14] *Ch. Ch. Arch.* lease 11 Eliz.

[15] Oxf. Archd. Oxon. c 33, ff. 280–8; cf. *Hearth Tax Oxon.* 205.

[16] *Ch. Ch. Arch.* 1669 lease. The curate's stipend had been £9 in 1660 and £11 in 1661: ibid. 1661 lease. In 1665 the curate was living in a house with 2 hearths: *Hearth Tax Oxon.* 205.

[17] Oxf. Dioc. d 554.

[18] Ibid. d 560.

[19] Ibid. c 655, ff. 106, 190.

[20] Ibid. c 661, f. 43.

[21] Ibid. b 39.

[22] Gardner, *Dir. Oxon.*; *Wilb. Visit.*

[23] Oxf. Dioc. d 178.

held an evening school with 'success as great as could be expected here'.[24]

The church of *ST. MARY AND ST. EDBURGA* is a stone building comprising a chancel, clerestoried nave, north and south aisles, north porch, and west tower. There is a sanctus bell-cote above the chancel arch.[25]

The church was largely rebuilt in the 13th and 14th centuries, but a 12th-century doorway (now disused) remains in the south wall of the south aisle. It is probably not in its original position. The north aisle was added early in the 13th century, and the

The church has electric light.

When the church was visited by Wood in the second half of the 17th century the windows of the north and south aisles contained armorial glass.[28] There are still early 14th-century shields in the west window of the south aisle (Clare) and the east window of the north aisle (Segrave and Sandford or Fiennes).[29] There is also some medieval glass in one of the chancel windows.[30]

The ancient octagonal font is of uncertain date;[31] the pulpit is Jacobean; an elm table given by the churchwardens is dated 1636, and a tower screen

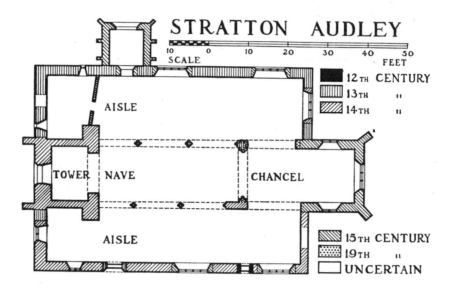

STRATTON AUDLEY

SCALE 10 0 10 20 30 40 50 FEET

12TH CENTURY
13TH ,,
14TH ,,

15TH CENTURY
19TH ,,
UNCERTAIN

AISLE

TOWER NAVE CHANCEL

AISLE

clustered columns which separate it from the nave are of this period. The remains of a blocked-up lancet at the west end of the south aisle imply that this, too, was added or rebuilt during the 13th century, but it was widened in the 14th century, and its arcade is of later date than that on the north side. Early in the 14th century the east window of the north aisle was rebuilt, and towards the end of the century a battlemented west tower was erected within the west wall of the nave.

In the 15th century the chancel was rebuilt and the nave clerestory added. Several additional windows were inserted in the aisles in the course of this century, and the ornate battlemented porch is of the same period.

Few records of repairs to the church have survived. They were ordered in 1757, when a new font-cover was provided, again in 1804, and in 1853 the roof was repaired and the floor relaid.[26] In 1861 the church was fully restored by the architect Roger Smith. The restoration, which cost about £800, included rebuilding the chancel arch, putting on a new chancel roof, releading the nave roof, removing the chancel screen, and reseating both nave and aisles.[27]

of carved oak designed by T. Lawrence Dale was erected in the 20th century.

There is a fine marble tomb to Sir John Borlase (d. 1688/9), represented as a Roman in recumbent position with two weeping figures on either side. There are also tablets to Sir John's brother Baldwin (d. 1678) and to Sir John Borlase Warren (d. 1822). There are inscriptions to Edmund Woodward (d. 1713/14) and family, and to the 18th-century Bush family.[32] Later memorial tablets are to George Glen (d. 1885), Major-Gen. Charles Cavendish, 3rd Baron Chesham (d. 1907), Lt.-Col. George Gosling (d. 1915), Major-Gen. Merton Beckwith-Smith (d.1942), and Norman Joseph Goss (d. 1944).

In 1552 the church was richly furnished with a silver chalice gilded within, a silver paten, a number of vestments of velvet and silk, and two copes.[33] In 1805 it owned a pewter tankard and cup.[34] The present plate is notable for its fine Restoration pewter service, which is unique of its kind and includes a chalice made by Richard Mastead in about 1665–75, a small flagon (c. 1700), and two plates dating from the late 17th century.[35] There is also a large silver paten (1777), a chalice (1836), and a silver flagon,

[24] Oxf. Dioc. c 332.
[25] For an early account of the building, see Dunkin, *Oxon.* ii. 150–3.
[26] Oxf. Archd. Oxon. d 13, f. 35; ibid. c 106, f. 200; ibid. c 43, f. 401.
[27] MS. Top. Oxon. c 104, ff. 359–62. Drawings by J. Buckler (1824) in MS. Top. Oxon. a 68, f. 524, and another (ibid. b 220, f. 16) show the church before restoration.
[28] *Par. Coll.* iii. 291.
[29] Lamborn, *Arm. Glass*, 160–1, and pl. 58.

[30] E. S. Bouchier, *Notes on Stained Glass of Oxford District*, 88.
[31] There is a drawing by J. C. Buckler in MS. Top. Oxon. a 68, f. 523.
[32] See above, p. 328. The floor slabs have illegible inscriptions. For blazons of arms on monuments see Bodl. G.A. Oxon. 4° 687, p. 291; ibid. 16° 217, pp. 231–2.
[33] *Chant. Cert.* 74.
[34] Oxf. Dioc. c 449, f. 45.
[35] The initials R.K. and E.B. on one are no doubt those of the 18th-cent. churchwardens R. King and E. Bush.

all given to the church in 1842 by the curate and churchwardens.[36]

The tower has a ring of five bells: the second, third, and fourth are late 17th-century; the treble and tenor 18th-century and inscribed with the names of the churchwardens. The bells were rehung in 1902 and part of the original frame, dated 1636, is preserved in the church. In 1552 there were three bells and a sanctus bell. The last was recast in the 17th century and in 1955 was in the tower.[37]

The church did not acquire a churchyard until after 1455 at the earliest, when the villagers acquired parochial independence of Bicester.[38] The remains of the medieval cross can still be seen, and there is a cross by W. R. Lethaby to members of the armed services who died in the First World War.[39]

The register for marriages begins in 1755 and for baptisms and burials in 1813. The earlier ones, which began in 1696 and were there in 1823,[40] have probably been destroyed. Some of the remaining books have been damaged by fire and water.

NONCONFORMITY. Except for a recusant woman in 1643,[41] there is no record of Roman Catholicism until the second half of the 18th century. In 1768 there was one papist family. Throughout most of the 19th century there were two: early in the century they worshipped at the chapel at Hethe,[42] and when the chapel at Bicester was built in 1883, they went there.[43] In 1866 they were said to oppose the payment of church rates.[44]

There is little record of Protestant nonconformity. In 1759 the incumbent recorded one Presbyterian woman.[45] Early in the 19th century the Methodists held cottage services; and there were about ten dissenters,[46] who were described as Presbyterians. But dissent did not flourish; in 1854 there was only one dissenting family, which went to services at Bicester,[47] and by 1878 there were said to be no dissenters.

SCHOOLS. In 1802 the parishioners were paying a teacher to instruct their children in reading and the catechism.[48] A school which opened in 1808 had 20 boys and 20 girls and was supported by Sir John Borlase Warren, who provided a free cottage for the master and paid him £5 5s. a year.[49] In 1815 this school had 40 day-boys and 6 boarders, of whom 12 were paid for by Thomas Fitzhugh, and there was a dame school with 4 boys and 9 girls.[50] In 1819 the two schools had 50 pupils in all, but by 1833 only the larger survived with 43 pupils.[51] A new school with accommodation for 80 pupils was built in 1837[52] and was principally supported by the lord of the manor. An infants' school supported by the parents had 15 pupils in 1854.[53] The average attendance at the new school, which was affiliated to the National Society, was 68 in 1871 and 66 in 1906.[54] It had one master, and was attended by children from neighbouring parishes.[55] In 1929 it was reorganized as a junior school and the senior pupils then went to Fringford. It became a controlled school in 1951. The number of pupils on the books was 22 in 1937 and 24 in 1954.[56]

CHARITY. By a codicil to her will dated 1879 Elizabeth Coles bequeathed £100, the interest to be used each year to buy coal for the poor, preference being given to widows and large families. The principal was invested in stock which in 1955 produced an annual dividend of £2 13s. 8d. Coal was bought and distributed about February each year.[57]

TUSMORE

THE 19th-century parish covered 735 acres,[1] but since 1932 it has been united with Hardwick to form the parish of Hardwick with Tusmore.[2] The Ockley Brook formed a natural boundary in the north, and on the south Buckingham Lane marked most of the boundary with Hardwick, and Sheep Walk and the stream draining Tusmore Lake much of that with Stoke Lyne. Hardwick Heath lay on the eastern boundary.[3] Tusmore lies on the Great Oolite, which is covered by fine flint gravel along the Hardwick boundary.[4] The soil is mostly stonebrash. Most of the parish lies just below the 400-foot contour line, but it rises to 412 feet in the north. The park is intersected now, as in the 18th century,[5] by several bridle roads and footpaths which link it with the Oxford–Brackley road, which crosses the west of the parish, and also with Cottisford and Hardwick. A lime and yew avenue runs from Tusmore House to Hardwick. The central and eastern parts of the parish have many trees; the remaining portion, except for occasional clumps, is bare.[6]

The village, which was the poorest in the hundred in the early 14th century[7] and probably the smallest, was depopulated by the Black Death.[8] Tusmore, with its church and a parsonage house, is thought to have been situated to the north of the present Tusmore

36 Evans, *Ch. Plate*.
37 *Ch. Bells Oxon.* iv. 396–7.
38 See above, p. 330.
39 *Kelly's Dir. Oxon.* (1939).
40 Dunkin, *Oxon.* ii. 153.
41 E 179/164/484.
42 Oxf. Dioc. d 560.
43 Ibid. b 39; Stapleton, *Cath. Miss.* 94.
44 Oxf. Dioc. c 332.
45 Ibid. d 554.
46 Ibid. d 571; c 327, p. 306.
47 *Wilb. Visit.*; Oxf. Dioc. c 344.
48 Oxf. Dioc. c 327, p. 306.
49 Ibid. d 707.
50 Ibid. c 433.
51 *Educ. of Poor*, 731; *Educ. Enq. Abstract*, 755.

52 *Kelly's Dir. Oxon.* (1887).
53 *Wilb. Visit.*
54 *Elem. Educ. Ret.*; *Vol. Sch. Ret.*
55 Wing, *Annals*, 130.
56 Inf. Oxon. Educ. Cttee.
57 Inf. the Revd. D. G. Peek.
1 O.S. Map 6", xvii (1884); 2½", 42/52 (1951), 42/53 (1949).
2 *Census*, 1931; *Oxon. Review Order*, 1932 (copy in O.R.O.).
3 O.S. Map 25", xvii. 1, 5 (1881).
4 G.S. Map 1", xlv NE.
5 Davis, *Oxon. Map*.
6 Personal observation.
7 See below, p. 337.
8 Ibid.

House.[9] The 'chapel' was 'quite gone' when Rawlinson visited Tusmore in 1718,[10] though the field names 'Church yard' and 'Churchyard close' have preserved its memory.[11] The parson's house was uninhabited at the date of the hearth tax of 1665, when the only taxable house was Henry Fermor's mansion.[12] There is no visible trace of the hamlet today, and though there were thought to be signs of the site of the church in the late 19th century, it is not visible on the modern air map.[13] When the Tusmore estate was sold in 1857, besides the big house there were just two farm-houses in the parish.[14] Both are stone-built and slated, one, Chase Barn, lying a short distance to the north-east of Tusmore House, the other, Pimlico Farm, in the north-west of the parish.[15]

When Sir Roger de Cotesford obtained his licence to enclose the village in 1358 it was probably with the intention of building a house at Tusmore and enclosing it in a park.[16] It is not known if any of this medieval building was still standing when Sir Richard Fermor came to live at Tusmore in about 1625.[17] He or his son Henry may have rebuilt and enlarged it and added the domestic chapel, or possibly it was the already existing medieval chapel which attracted them to the house. At all events it is known that the 17th-century house for which Henry Fermor returned nineteen hearths for the tax of 1665 was built of local stone and rough-cast.[18] It had casement windows, a chapel and garden (probably a kitchen garden) walled with red brick,[19] and pleasure-gardens of an outstanding character. After mentioning the famous garden walks at Aston Rowant and Rowsham, Robert Plot says that of all walks the Tusmore one with its fish-pond and hedges was 'the most wonderfully pleasant'. He describes in detail the curious optical illusion it produced.[20] From a description of the house in James Fermor's time (1703–22) it is known to have had dove-house, malt-house, orchards, gardens, and other appurtenances.[21] The tradition that it had a priest's hiding-hole is more credible than many such traditions.[22]

In 1758 William Fermor visited Rome and there sought instruction in architecture from Robert Mylne (1734–1811), the Scottish architect and engineer, who is best known for his construction of Blackfriars Bridge.[23] At Fermor's request Mylne went to Tusmore and later submitted plans for a new house. The shell of the new building was completed by 1770, the date which appears on the frieze of the east portico. Another nine years were occupied in the work of interior decoration, in the laying out of the gardens, which included a lake, a Temple of Peace, dedicated to Pope, and the 'landscaping' of

the park. Little was left of the old house except the chapel (which was redecorated), and this remnant was burned down in 1837.[24]

Mylne's design, though perhaps 'rather stark', possessed balance and dignity.[25] Views of the east and principal front and of the south elevation are given in George Richardson's *New Vitruvius Britannicus* published in 1810.[26] The house was of the Italian villa type with the main suite of rooms placed on the first floor in order to command some prospect in a flat country. A double flight of steps led up to the main entrance, which opened on to a hall and saloon, with the 'best' staircase lying beyond. A plan in the *New Vitruvius* shows the layout of the *piano nobile*, the old chapel left standing to the north-east and connected with the parlour and breakfast-room. A basement, a second story of bedrooms, and an attic floor, completed this well-proportioned, unpretentious house.[27]

Local stone from a nearby quarry at Fritwell was largely used. It contains the russet tint of iron which gives it a warm appearance. Freestone from Tottenhoe, near Dunstable, and from Glympton were used for the columns and pilasters of the east and west fronts. Taynton stone and common stone from Headington were also employed. Bricks were made on the estate, and its oaks were felled for timber.[28] The total cost of the building, including the architect's expenses, amounted to £11,305.

Tusmore House as created by Mylne and William Fermor lasted for less than a century. After 1857 when Henry Howard, 2nd Earl of Effingham, bought the estate, the symmetry of the original design was spoilt by the addition of a barrack-like office wing to the north on the site of the chapel, and the main entrance was lowered to the basement story, an interior staircase being substituted for the exterior flight of steps. These alterations were carried out by William Burn in 1858. In 1929, however, Tusmore was bought by the late Vivian Hugh Smith, afterwards Lord Bicester. Assisted by his architects, Messrs. Imrie and Angell, he was responsible for a thorough restoration. The Victorian wing disappeared from sight, only the screened base being retained, and extending screen-walls terminating in four pyramidal-roofed pavilions at the corners were added in order to relate the house to its surroundings. The basement entrance was retained, but the arcade that once supported the steps was kept in the form of a *porte cochère*. The floor of the original entrance hall was removed, and a large staircase hall of two stories, with a double flight, was constructed. Nevertheless, in spite of its maltreatment in the Victorian period and the subsequent extensive 20th-century

[9] Blo. *Tus.* 88, 93; masonry and bones have been found near by. No site is marked on O.S. maps or the air photo. mosaic 6″, 42/53 SE.

[10] *Par. Coll.* iii. 164.

[11] O.R.O. Reg. of Papists' estates, p. 86.

[12] *Hearth Tax Oxon.* 207; cf. Blo. *Tus.* 93.

[13] Blo. *Tus.* 93.

[14] Bodl. G.A. Oxon. b 85*b* (57): *Sale Cat.* 1857.

[15] A barn and stables called Pimlico occur in the early 18th cent.: O.R.O. Reg. of Papists' estates, p. 86.

[16] See below, p. 337.

[17] A large number of coins of Jas. I's reign were found in the old house in the 1760's: Blo. *Tus.* 74.

[18] *Hearth Tax Oxon.* 297.

[19] Blo. *Tus.* 65.

[20] Plot, *Nat. Hist. Oxon.* 261–2.

[21] O.R.O. Reg. of Papists' estates, p. 86.

[22] Blo. *Tus.* 68.

[23] A. E. Richardson, *Robert Mylne* (1955), 72, 74, 76, 79, 82, 85, 89, 93–94.

[24] Blo. *Tus.* 84.

[25] *Country Life*, 30 July and 6 Aug. 1938: two illustrated articles on the house by Arthur Oswald.

[26] G. Richardson, *New Vitruvius Britannicus*, ii, pl. iv, v; two lithograph views of the SW. and SE. aspects attached to the sale cat. of 1857 are also of value: Bodl. G.A. Oxon. b 85*b* (57).

[27] Richardson, op. cit., pl. iii. For another view see plate opposite.

[28] For extracts from the Fermor accts. see Blo. *Tus.* 73–74. The originals cannot now be traced. It has been suggested that Robert Adam designed the ceilings for the drawing- and dining-rooms, but there are no designs in the Soane Museum (London) or at Tusmore.

Tusmore House in the early 19th century

TUSMORE

Ruins of the manor-house in 1823

SOMERTON

alterations, enough remains of the 18th-century conception for the elegance of the original design to be appreciated.

Smith also made drastic changes to the grounds, and nothing now remains of Mylne's landscape gardening except the lake, already mentioned, and a temple at its northern end. The park of over 150 acres in extent is entered from the Brackley approach through a triumphal arch of free-stone, erected in 1906 by the 4th Earl of Effingham.

During the Howard ownership, a fine collection of portraits, chiefly of members of the Howard family, was housed at Tusmore.[29]

The half-timbered granary and dovecote stood in the farmyard to the north of the old manor-house and was incorporated within the area north of the new house, which contained the offices and stables. Judging by the mouldings of the bressumers and the brackets and shafts supporting the overhang, the granary cannot be later than the beginning of the 16th century.[30] The building is formed of oak posts, studs, and panels, and formerly rested on rude stone supports which have now been replaced by concrete blocks. It is rectangular in plan and has an overhang and entrance at the west side. There are three floors, of which the two lower ones are used as a granary and the top as a dovecote: the stone-slate roof contains a louvre. This is an unusual construction to find surviving in stone country.

Apart from its architectural interest, Tusmore House is noted for its connexion with the Fermors, a Roman Catholic family. One of them, Ursula the daughter of Richard Fermor, was the mother of two well-known Jacobites, John and Francis Towneley,[31] although otherwise the Oxfordshire branch of the family seems to have played no active part in the movement. Arabella, the daughter of Henry (II) Fermor, achieved some distinction as the heroine of Pope's *Rape of the Lock*. William Fermor, the builder of the new house, was a keen huntsman, and this side of his activities is commemorated in an oil painting at Aynho Park (Northants). Furthermore, he was frequently the host of Mrs. Fitzherbert in the 1790's, and tradition has it that she married George IV at Tusmore House.[32] After William Fermor's death in 1806, his eldest son left Tusmore and the house was let to a succession of tenants for most of the period from 1810 until 1857, when it became the home of the earls of Effingham and later of Lord Bicester, who for more than half a century was one of the outstanding business men in the City of London. He played an active part in Oxfordshire, being Lord Lieutenant from 1934 until his death in 1956, chairman of the Bicester Hunt Committee, and a well-known race-horse owner.[33]

MANOR. In 1086 3 virgates in *TUSMORE* and 3 in Stoke Lyne were held by a certain Turald of Walter Giffard, later Earl of Buckingham, who was lord of the remainder of Stoke Lyne.[34] The overlordship and mesne lordship of Turald's estate seem to have followed the same descent as Stoke Lyne,[35] and its division into two parts in Domesday Book is reflected by the attachment in the 13th century of a part of Tusmore to each of the two manors in Stoke Lyne. In 1199 Guy of Tusmore held 6 virgates of Otwel de Lisle,[36] and it was probably this estate, then rated as 1 hide, which was held of Giles de Lisle by Richard, son of Guy, in 1279. At the latter date another hide in Tusmore was held of John de Cokefield, tenant of the smaller Stoke Lyne manor, by Morand de Pichelesthorn, and of him by Alan of Tusmore,[37] who appears as a witness to deeds in the neighbourhood from about 1250.[38] The descent of these properties after 1279 is not known, but the connexion with Stoke Lyne was maintained into the 14th century, for in 1327 part of Tusmore was grouped with the hamlets of Bainton and Fewcot in Stoke Lyne for the assessment of a 20th.[39]

It is reasonably certain that $2\frac{1}{2}$ hides of the $7\frac{1}{2}$ hides in Hardwick held by Robert d'Oilly in 1086,[40] and which Robert had obtained by an exchange of lands with Walter Giffard,[41] subsequently became part of Tusmore.[42] In 1242–3 $\frac{1}{2}$ knight's fee in Tusmore was held of the honor of D'Oilly by Guy son of Robert, lord of the manor of Ardley and the descendant of Drew d'Aundeley who had been Robert d'Oilly's tenant of Hardwick in 1086.[43] The lords of Ardley[44] may well have held this half-fee since the Domesday Survey, and they continued to be recognized as mesne lords until the mid-14th century.[45] In the 13th century they were also mesne lords of a manor in Cranford St. Andrew (Northants), where their tenants were the D'Aundeleys, descendants of Maurice d'Aundeley who had held it early in the 12th century[46] and who was no doubt a kinsman of Drew d'Aundeley. Maurice had been succeeded at Cranford by Ralph (living 1189), Maurice, Ralph (living 1228), and a third Maurice, the first of the family to be definitely associated with Tusmore, where he was Guy son of Robert's tenant in 1243.[47] In 1265, after the battle of Evesham, Maurice's lands in Tusmore were seized by the royalists, but either he or his son Hugh recovered them, for the latter was holding the half-fee in Tusmore in 1279 and 1284–5.[48] By 1316 it had passed to Hugh's son John,[49] perhaps the same John who was holding in Tusmore in 1346 and who was dead by 1349.[50] Although John's grandson William may have brought some claim to the Tusmore estate[51] it is likely that the former was the last of the D'Aundeleys to hold it.

[29] Blo. *Tus.* 86–87.
[30] *Country Life*, 30 July 1938. A sketch made in 1845 and measured details made in 1887 are illustrated in Blo. *Tus.* 64–65.
[31] *D.N.B.*
[32] Blo. *Tus.* 83.
[33] *The Times*, 18 Feb. 1956, and see below, p. 336.
[34] *V.C.H. Oxon.* i. 411.
[35] See above, p. 314; *Rot. Hund.* (Rec. Com.), ii. 825.
[36] *Fines Oxon.* 6.
[37] *Rot. Hund.* ii. 825.
[38] E.C.R. nos. 30, 33–36, 38–39; *Oseney Cart.* ii. 401.
[39] E 179/161/9: the remainder of Tusmore was assessed separately.   [40] *V.C.H. Oxon.* i. 414.

[41] Ibid.
[42] Cf. *Oseney Cart.* v. 431.
[43] *Bk. of Fees*, 824; *V.C.H. Oxon.* i. 414.
[44] For their descent see above, p. 8.
[45] *Feud. Aids*, iv. 158, 180; *Rot. Hund.* (Rec. Com.), ii. 825.
[46] *V.C.H. Northants.* i. 389; iii. 187.
[47] Ibid. iii. 187; *Bk. of Fees*, 824. For Guy son of Robert in 1255 see *Rot. Hund.* (Rec. Com.), ii. 44.
[48] *Cal. Inq. Misc.* i, p. 261; *Rot. Hund.* ii. 825; *Feud. Aids*, iv. 158.
[49] *Feud. Aids*, iv. 169.
[50] Ibid. 180; *Cal. Inq. p.m.* ix, p. 183.
[51] *Feud. Aids*, iv. 190; cf. *V.C.H. Northants*, iii. 187.

Another hide in Tusmore, also held of the honor of D'Oilly, appears in the 13th century as part of the manor of Bucknell,[52] held by Guy of Tusmore of Simon de Turvill, who held it of Roger Damory. In 1236 Simon conveyed the rent and homage owed by Guy to Hugh Pateshull, while Guy became responsible for the service owed to Roger.[53] Hugh Pateshull, Treasurer of the Exchequer and later Bishop of Coventry and Lichfield, died in 1241 and was succeeded by his nephew Sir Simon, son of Walter Pateshull (d. 1232). Sir Simon died in 1274 and in 1279 the hide in Tusmore was held of his successor Sir John (d. 1290) by Richard, son of Guy.[54] It is uncertain when the Pateshull connexion with Tusmore ended: no estate there is included in the inquisitions post mortem of Sir John's successors Simon (d. 1295), Sir John (d. 1349), or Sir William (d. 1359),[55] and no lands in Tusmore were included in the partition of the Pateshull inheritance between William's sisters and coheiresses,[56] although the advowson was.[57]

In the mid-14th century a single manor of Tusmore appears in the possession of Sir Roger de Cotesford, who seems to have acquired the D'Aundeley half-fee between 1346[58] and 1357, and possibly before 1349.[59] In all probability Sir Roger acquired the Pateshull estates and the lands of the manor of Giffard in Tusmore about the same time: his successors certainly held a manor which was said to include lands in Stoke Lyne and Fewcot.[60] Sir Roger died in 1375[61] and was succeeded by Sir Thomas de Cotesford.[62] By 1417 the latter had conveyed the manor to John Ralegh of Wardington, who in that year conveyed it in turn to John Danvers of Calthorpe.[63] In 1418 Sir Thomas quitclaimed the manor to Danvers,[64] but shortly afterwards[65] it passed from the latter to John Langston of Caversfield, whose son John married Danvers's daughter Amice. John Langston the elder died in 1435, and his son in 1506,[66] the latter being succeeded at Tusmore by his younger son Thomas. By Thomas's will made in 1525 the manor passed to his niece Catherine, daughter of Christopher Langston, and her husband Thomas Pigott of Doddershall (Bucks.). Catherine died in 1557 and Thomas, who was Sheriff of Buckinghamshire in 1552 and 1557, in 1559.[67] Their son Thomas Pigott the younger conveyed Tusmore in 1572 to Sir John Spencer of Althorp (Northants),[68] who in 1574 conveyed it to Thomas Williamson and his wife Bridget,[69] who became resident at Tusmore that year.[70]

In 1606 Thomas and Bridget Williamson conveyed the manor to Sir Richard Fermor of Somerton.[71]

Fermor probably moved into his new possession not later than 1625, as in that year Somerton Place was settled for life upon Cecily Compton, the widow of his eldest son, Sir John Fermor.[72]

For seven generations[73] the Fermors continued as lords of the manor. They were Henry Fermor (1642–73), son of Sir Richard; Richard Fermor (1673–84); Henry Fermor (1684–1703); James Fermor (1703–22); Henry Fermor (1722–47); William Fermor (1747–1806); and William Fermor (1806–28). The last-named died without male heirs, and through the marriage of his adopted daughter, Maria, with Captain John Turner Ramsay (d. 1840), of Croughton (Northants), the property passed to the latter. In 1857 the Tusmore estate was sold by the Ramsays to Henry Howard, 2nd Earl of Effingham (1806–89).[74] The property was subsequently held by his son, Henry Howard, 3rd Earl of Effingham (1837–98), and his grandson, Henry Alexander Gordon Howard, 4th Earl of Effingham (1866–1927).[75] The estate was bought from Lord Effingham's heir in 1929 by the late Vivian Hugh Smith (d. 1956), who was created Baron Bicester of Tusmore in 1938.[76]

ECONOMIC HISTORY. The name Tusmore means 'Thur's pool' (O.E. *Thures-mere*), or possibly 'a lake haunted by a giant or demon' (O.E. *pyrs-mere*).[77] Even by the time of Domesday much of its land may have been uncultivated. Turald's holding of 6 virgates, half in Tusmore and half in Stoke Lyne, was certainly undercultivated: there was land for 2 plough-teams, but only one was in use. Although it is probable that part of Tusmore's land was included in the Domesday account of Hardwick, there is no direct reference to Tusmore apart from Turald's 3 virgates. The estate was still worth 20s. as it had been in 1066. Nothing can be said about the numbers working on it owing to the intermixture of holdings between the three parishes.[78] The survey of 1279 records considerable advance: of the three lords, Hugh d'Aundeley and Richard son of Guy each held 2 virgates in demesne; none is recorded for Alan of Tusmore. On D'Aundeley's holding there were seven villein (*servi*) virgaters each paying 6s. a year rent, paying tallage, working and paying fines if their sons left the manor at the lord's will. Two cottagers each held half a virgate for an annual rent of 3s. and owed the same services as the virgaters. On Richard's estate there was one virgater and two half-virgaters paying rent at the rate of 6s. the virgate and owing the same services as D'Aundeley's villeins. Four cottars each held 3 acres at a rent of 2s. 6d. a year. The rector with a half-virgate

[52] *Rot. Hund.* ii. 45.
[53] *Fines Oxon.* 77, 103, 104.
[54] *Rot. Hund.* ii. 825; for the Pateshulls of Pattishall (Northants) see *D.N.B.*; Baker, *Northants*, ii. 297; *Complete Peerage*, x. 311 sqq.
[55] *Cal. Inq. p.m.* iii, p. 232; ix, pp. 288, 422; x, p. 410.
[56] *Cal. Close, 1364–8,* 435.
[57] See below, p. 337.
[58] *Feud. Aids,* iv. 180; for Sir Roger, see above, p. 60.
[59] *Cal. Inq. Misc.* iii, p. 93; cf. *Cal. Pat. 1358–61,* 4.
[60] *Cal. Close, 1413–19,* 446, 499.
[61] *Cal. Fine R. 1369–77,* 327.
[62] *Cal. Pat. 1385–9,* 384; C.P. 25(1)/191/24/50.
[63] *Cal. Close, 1413–19,* 446; C.P. 25(1)/191/26/25.
[64] *Cal. Close, 1413–19,* 499.
[65] Langston held the advowson in 1419: MS. Top. Oxon. d 460.
[66] *V.C.H. Bucks.* iv. 158; see above, p. 74.

[67] C 142/124/154. For the Pigotts see *Papers from an Iron Chest at Doddershall*, ed. G. Eland (Aylesbury, 1937).
[68] C.P. 40/1299, mm. 315, 316.
[69] *Tusmore Papers*, ed. L. G. Wickham Legg (O.R.S. xx), 4.
[70] *Oxon. Visit.* 328.
[71] C.P. 25(2)/339/East. 4 Jas. I.
[72] Stapleton, *Cath. Miss.* 68.
[73] For the Fermors see above, pp. 293, 299.
[74] Blo. *Tus.* 84–85; Bodl. G.A. Oxon. b 85*b* (57).
[75] For earls of Effingham see *Complete Peerage*, v. 14–16; Burke, *Peerage*.
[76] *Country Life,* 6 Aug. 1938, 136. For Lord Bicester see above, p. 335.
[77] *P.N. Oxon.* (E.P.N.S.), i. 216; Ekwall, *Dict. Eng. P.N.*
[78] *V.C.H. Oxon.* i. 411.

was the only freeholder. Alan of Tusmore had 3 cottar tenants holding a half-virgate, 3 acres and a messuage, and 1½ acre respectively for rents of 3s., 1s., and 2s.[79] Fourteenth-century tax lists confirm the above picture of a small community: in 1327 only seven persons contributed to the tax.[80] The village's normal tax after 1334 was 21s. 6d.,[81] but in 1354 it received an abatement of the whole sum.[82] The Black Death struck the village with particular severity. A writ of 1358 refers to the death from the pestilence of the bondmen on Roger de Cotesford's fee and implies that the whole village had become deserted. He was licensed to inclose it.[83] It never seems to have been resettled: it paid no tax in 1428 since there were fewer than ten householders,[84] and it does not appear on the 16th-century subsidy rolls or in the return for the Compton census of 1676.[85] Division of the parish into inclosures may have soon followed the depopulation and imparking of the 14th century: Barley Close, Townsend Close, and North Close are mentioned in a deed of 1629.[86]

In the Middle Ages there may have been a two-field system, for the North Field is mentioned in a charter of 1374.[87] Field names used in the 18th and 19th centuries[88] perhaps preserved a little of the topography of the open-field parish—Ox Pasture on the eastern boundary, Barley Field in the south, and Stoney Field in the north-east corner. About 1717 the greater part of the parish was in the occupation of James Fermor, and the remainder was let to two farmers.[89] In 1857 there were two large farms, Pimlico (155 a.) and Chase Barn (382 a.); another 30 acres were let to a Stoke Lyne farmer; Tusmore House and the grounds immediately surrounding it (21 a.) had been let in recent years, and the woods and plantations, which were now numerous, amounted to 139 acres.[90]

The life of the small community at Tusmore has for some centuries revolved around and been dependent on the House, whose inhabitants have made up the majority of the population, which has varied from 16 in 1831 to 51 in 1901.[91]

CHURCH. The first evidence for the possible existence of a church at Tusmore dates from 1074, when a grant (confirmed c. 1127) was made of a part of its tithes (see below). As the early manorial history of Tusmore was so closely interrelated with that of Hardwick and Stoke Lyne, it may be that the township's tithes belonged to one of these churches, but there is no evidence that this was so. No church

building has survived at Tusmore and even its dedication is unknown, so neither can provide any clue to the early history of the church.

The advowson is first mentioned in 1236, when it was granted by Simon de Turville to Hugh Pateshull, who soon afterwards presented to the church.[92] During the 13th century it followed the descent of the hide in Tusmore held by the Pateshull family.[93] In 1301, during the minority of John Pateshull, his stepfather, Walter Lord Teyes,[94] was patron. Sir John presented to the church in 1338, and although in 1354 the bishop collated by lapse, Sir William Pateshull must have held the advowson at his death in 1359, for in 1368 it was awarded to one of his sisters and coheiresses, Catherine, the widow of Sir Robert de Tudenham,[95] and their son Sir John presented to the church in 1391. The bishop again collated in 1403, but from 1419, when John Langston presented, the advowson followed the descent of the united manor.

After the Reformation, although the church disappeared, presentations continued to be made to the living, and from 1612 the Fermors, who were the patrons, presented on at least two occasions, although Roman Catholics.[96] In about 1840 the rectory was united to that of Hardwick, and since 1867 it has been held with Cottisford.[97] The patron in 1956 was Lord Bicester.

The value of the rectory in 1254 was £2, which by 1291 had increased to £6.[98] By the 16th century it had sharply declined, being worth only £3 5s. in 1535.[99] At some time between then and the early 18th century the tithes, and whatever glebe there was,[1] were commuted for a modus of £15, which the rector received from the lord of the manor.[2] Later, when the tithes had increased in value, the rector could not 'gain information' as to the origin of this arrangement,[3] which was confirmed by the tithe award of 1852.[4]

In 1074 Robert d'Oilly granted two-thirds of the demesne tithes of Tusmore, with those of many other manors, to the church of St. George in Oxford castle, and these in 1149 passed, with St. George's, to Oseney Abbey.[5] They are mentioned in 1374, when an agreement was made between the abbot and Sir Roger de Cotesford whereby the latter acknowledged the justice of the abbot's claim to these tithes, and in particular to those from certain furze lands.[6] In 1436 they were leased for 20 years to the rector, Nicholas Ridell, for 20d. This arrangement continued, for early in the 16th century the abbey

[79] Rot. Hund. (Rec. Com.), ii. 825.

[80] E 179/161/8, 9, 10: the list for 1307 is incomplete, but Tusmore appears to have been joined with another village, as it was in 1316.

[81] e.g. E 164/7.

[82] E 179/161/30.

[83] Cal. Pat. 1358–61, 4. Cf. M. Beresford, Lost Villages of Eng. 382.

[84] Feud. Aids, vi. 379.

[85] See below, pp. 359, 361.

[86] O.R.O. Misc. Ey 1/6.

[87] Bodl. MS. ch. Oxon. 442. The word campo is nearly illegible.

[88] O.R.O. Reg. of Papists' estates, pp. 86, 93–94; Bodl. G.A. Oxon. b 85b (57).

[89] O.R.O. Reg. of Papists' estates, p. 86.

[90] Bodl. G.A. Oxon. b 85b (57). For 1807 timber accounts on Fermor estates in Tusmore, Cottisford, Hardwick, and Fritwell see MS. Top. Oxon. e 259.

[91] V.C.H. Oxon. ii. 221. In the 1951 Census it was combined with Hardwick.

[92] Fines Oxon. 103; Rot. Grosse. 450. For list of medieval presentations see MS. Top. Oxon. d 460.

[93] For the Pateshulls, see above, p. 336.

[94] Complete Peerage, x. 315.

[95] Cal. Close, 1364–8, 435. For family see Cal. inq. p.m. x, p. 410; Baker, Northants, i. 186; ii. 197.

[96] Richard Fermor presented in 1612 and Helen Fermor in 1704: Oxf. Dioc. c 264, f. 56b; P.R.O. Inst. Bks.

[97] Gardner, Dir. Oxon.; Clerus Oxon.

[98] Lunt, Val. Norw. 312; Tax. Eccl. (Rec. Com.), 31.

[99] Val. Eccl. (Rec. Com.), ii. 161.

[1] There is no certain record of glebe; the rector held ½ virgate in 1279 of Richard son of Guy, but this may not have belonged to the church: Rot. Hund. (Rec. Com.), ii. 825.

[2] Bacon, Lib. Reg. 793; Par. Coll. ii. 164.

[3] Oxf. Dioc. c 446, ff. 188–9.

[4] Bodl. Tithe award.

[5] Oseney Cart. iv. 3, 26, &c.; V.C.H. Oxon. ii. 90.

[6] Oseney Cart. v. 433; Bodl. MS. ch. Oxon. Oseney 442.

successfully sued the rector for 47 years of arrears.[7] In 1542 this part of the tithes, now called a pension, was granted to Christ Church.[8]

Probably from the time of the depopulation of the village in the 14th century[9] Tusmore ceased to be an ordinary parish church. In the 15th century it is called a chapel or free chapel.[10] The Fermors did not need it as a place of worship; they, and often their dependants, were buried in the Fermor chapel at Somerton.[11] The Tusmore chapel probably ceased to be used in the 16th century.[12]

A church of unknown dedication existed by 1236.[13] It was at least partly rebuilt at a later date as fragments of 15th-century masonry have been found on the site.[14] It was probably no longer in use in the 16th century as it was not included in either of the two early 16th-century episcopal visitations,[15] or in the Edwardian inventories of church goods.[16] The building had certainly disappeared by 1718,[17] when Rawlinson visited the village.

NONCONFORMITY. From the 17th to the 19th centuries Tusmore was one of the two centres in the hundred of the Oxfordshire Roman Catholic Mission.[18] The Catholic connexion probably began when the Fermors started to live there in about 1625. They were a strongly Roman Catholic family.[19]

Several of their members entered religious orders,[20] and in 1693 the Society of Jesus granted Henry Fermor and his family a letter of confraternity.[21]

The family kept a resident chaplain, often a Jesuit but sometimes a member of another order or a secular priest,[22] and the domestic chapel[23] served as the Catholic church for the surrounding parishes. With a few years' exception in about 1770, when Tusmore House was being rebuilt,[24] this was the case until 1810, when William Fermor left Tusmore and leased the house. Although the chapel was excepted from the lease,[25] the priest moved to Hardwick.

The inhabitants of Tusmore, consisting of servants and dependants of the Fermors, were probably until then mostly Papists. For the subsidy of 1644, besides Henry Fermor and his wife, six Papists are listed, including a chambermaid, a cook, and a dairymaid.[26] In 1706 there were six Papist servants;[27] in the 1767 return of Papists, seven names come from Tusmore;[28] and in 1808 all the parishioners were said to be Roman Catholics.[29]

No record of Protestant dissent has been found.

SCHOOLS. None known.

CHARITIES. None known.

WENDLEBURY

THE parish (1,154 a.) lies along the road from Oxford to Bicester,[1] which is three miles distant and its nearest market-town. The parish boundaries are mostly very irregular and were no doubt drawn along the limits of already existing fields; the northern boundary follows for part of its course the northern edge of the site of the Roman town of Alchester.[2] On the east Wendlebury is divided from Merton by the Bure, a tributary stream of the River Ray. No boundary changes have been recorded.[3]

Wendlebury lies in the area of the Oxford Clay; its soil is chiefly clay, overlaid in places with gravel.[4] Plot maintained that objects buried in the ground at certain places were petrified and preserved.[5] The main road from Oxford to Bicester, made a turnpike in 1793, crosses the parish and once ran through the village:[6] in 1938 it was widened and straightened so as to leave the village to the east of it. The Roman

road leading south from Alchester, called 'Buggestret' in the 13th century, crosses the north-east corner of the parish.[7] A network of footpaths connecting Wendlebury with all the neighbouring villages was confirmed by the inclosure award of 1801.[8]

The Bletchley–Oxford section of the former L.N.W.R. passes through the parish. In 1851 three railway labourers were returned in the census as lodging in the village, presumably when the railway was being constructed.[9]

The site of the Roman town was peculiarly damp[10] and the Saxon settlers, for this and superstitious reasons perhaps, made their settlement to the south-west, close to the western boundary of the later parish, with all their fields lying to the east. A feeder of the Ray runs southwards along the village street and provided an ample water-supply. The Saxon

---

[7] *Oseney Cart.* v. 432–3; vi. 245.
[8] *L. & P. Hen. VIII*, xvii, p. 491. For later history of this pension see C.P. 25(2)/863/Hil. 1 Wm. & Mary.
[9] See above, p. 336.
[10] e.g. Linc. Reg. xx, Chedworth, ff. 231*b*, 239.
[11] See above, p. 299.
[12] See below.
[13] See above, p. 337.
[14] Blo. *Tus.* 88.
[15] *Visit. Dioc. Linc. 1517–31*, i. 121 n. 18; ii. 32 n. 5.
[16] *Chant. Cert.*
[17] *Par. Coll.* ii. 164; cf. Bacon, *Lib. Reg.* 793, where the church is described as *ecclesia destructa.*
[18] H. Foley, *Records of English Province*, ser. xi. 569; Stapleton, *Cath. Miss.* 6. Somerton was the other.
[19] See above, p. 299.
[20] Stapleton, *Cath. Miss.* 70–71, 72.
[21] Blo. *Tus.* 67–68.
[22] For these chaplains see Stapleton, *Cath. Miss.* 90–93, and T. B. Trappes-Lomax, MS. Historical Introduction

to the Registers of Holy Trinity Chapel, Hethe, *penes* Catholic Record Society.
[23] See above, p. 334.
[24] Ibid.
[25] Stapleton, *Cath. Miss.* 79.
[26] E 179/164/496A.
[27] *Oxoniensia*, xiii. 79.
[28] Oxf. Dioc. c 431, f. 12*b*.
[29] Ibid. d 549, p. 209; ibid. c 327, p. 306.
[1] O.S. Map 6″, xxiii (1885); 2½″, 42/51, 52 (1951).
[2] *V.C.H. Oxon.* i. 281 sqq.; see below.
[3] *Census*, 1881, 1951.
[4] G.S. Map 1″, xlv SE.
[5] Plot, *Nat. Hist. Oxon.* 64, 213.
[6] 33 Geo. III, c. 180; O.S. Map 25″, xxiii. 13.
[7] *P.N. Oxon.* (E.P.N.S.), i. 241–2; *V.C.H. Oxon.* i, map between pp. 266a–7.
[8] O.R.O. Incl. award.
[9] *Census*, 1851; W. L. Steel, *Hist. of L.N.W.R.* 185.
[10] *V.C.H. Oxon.* i. 281.

Wændel had his *burh* or fortified house here and gave the village its name.[11] Its position on an important highway did not compensate for its small amount of land and the medieval village never became large.[12] In the 17th century it had two gentlemen's residences: the rector's with its six taxable hearths and Henry Trafford's with seven. There were also two substantial farm-houses, for each of which four hearths were returned for the tax of 1665, and ten other smaller dwellings were listed.[13] But there were evidently many more which were not taxed.[14] In the early 18th century 32 houses were recorded, 49 in 1851, and 67 in 1901.[15] By 1951 these had been reduced to 50. Six council houses were built between 1918 and 1954.[16]

The appearance of the present village (1955) with its dwellings mainly built of the local rubble stone or mellowed red brick of local manufacture is harmonious and, on account of its open stream, unusual. A few of the cottages and probably the core of the Manor House date from the 17th century. The last was modernized in the 18th century. The present house is of two builds, consisting of a west and an east block with a continuous roof over both. The east block is built of coursed rubble, the west has been faced with ashlar. At the back there are some mutilated rough-cut battlements which are said to date from the early 20th century.[17] The chief interior feature is an 18th-century staircase in pinewood.

The old Rectory, standing to the east of the manor-house, was rebuilt in 1840 for £1,150.[18] It is a two-storied house, built of coursed rubble with ashlar quoins. The 17th-century parsonage was described in 1634 as a house of six bays of building with extensive outhouses; in 1679 it consisted of seven bays including its kitchen and dairy and was flanked by three gardens.[19]

The 'Red Lion' is an 18th-century building of coursed rubble. It is of two stories with three hipped dormer windows in a slate roof. A 19th-century drawing shows it with an outside flight of steps.[20] The house was sold in 1732 to Elizabeth Jarvis of Chesterton, and the terms of the sale imply that it had become an inn during the ownership of the seller.[21] Manorial courts were held there in the 19th century.[22] Two licences were issued in 1735,[23] one perhaps to the 'Plough', the 19th-century name of the village's second public house.[24]

The parish's only outlying farm-house, Starveall, formerly Lone Farm, lies in the extreme south.[25]

Alchester, excavated by Francis Penrose of Chesterton in 1766, was one of the earliest Roman settlements in Britain, and was a commercial centre rather than a military post.[26]

Wendlebury's only inhabitant of note was George Dupuis (d. 1839), rector and progressive farmer.[27]

MANORS. Before the Conquest *WENDLEBURY* was held by 'Asgar', who is to be identified with Esegar the staller, Sheriff of Middlesex,[28] rather than with Ælfgar, Earl of Mercia.[29] The Conqueror granted the village to Geoffrey de Mandeville,[30] whose grandson of the same name was created Earl of Essex by King Stephen. The overlordship of Wendlebury followed the descent of the earldom in the Mandeville family, and in 1236 passed with it to Humphrey de Bohun, Earl of Hereford.[31] It then followed the descent of the De Bohun earls of Hereford and Essex until the death of Humphrey de Bohun in 1373. Eleanor, his elder daughter and coheiress, brought one of the 2 knight's fees of Wendlebury to her husband, Thomas of Woodstock, youngest son of Edward III, who held the overlordship of this fee until his death in 1397, when it reverted to his widow.[32] Eleanor, together with a son and daughter, died in 1399.[33] The overlordship of 1 fee in Wendlebury reverted to the Crown, which granted it probably in 1400 to Eleanor's daughter Anne and her husband Edmund, Earl of Stafford, with the rest of her mother's lands.[34] Edmund possessed the overlordship at his death in 1403,[35] but there is no later mention of it and it may be assumed to have lapsed. Of the overlordship of the other knight's fee in Wendlebury nothing is recorded after 1373. If it passed to Mary de Bohun, the younger coheiress, it would have been merged in the Crown after the accession of her husband, Henry, Earl of Derby, as King Henry IV.

In 1086 Wendlebury was held of Geoffrey de Mandeville by 'Sasualo',[36] who was doubtless the Norman ancestor[37] of the Oseville family, who were mesne tenants of Wendlebury until the mid-13th century, and who commonly bore the name 'Saswallus' or Sewel. A Sewel de Oseville made a grant to the Templars of a stream in Wendlebury between 1156 and 1166[38] and was probably already holding 2 knight's fees there of the Earl of Essex.[39] Another Sewel, perhaps his son, was lord of Wendlebury in 1196,[40] and a third of the same name, who appears to have been a minor in 1220,[41] was in possession of the 2 fees in Wendlebury between 1236 and 1255.[42] This last Sewel is said to have enfeoffed Ralph de St. Amand with his property in Oxfordshire and Berkshire, but Ralph died in 1245, and Sewel was the lord of Wendlebury as late as 1255. In 1256,

[11] *P.N. Oxon.* (E.P.N.S.), i. 241.
[12] See below, p. 359.
[13] *Hearth Tax Oxon.* 189–90.
[14] Cf. 25 householders listed in 1662: ibid. 235.
[15] Oxf. Dioc. d 554; H.O. 107/1729; *Census*, 1901.
[16] Inf. Ploughley R.D.C.
[17] Inf. the owner, Brig. B. C. Lake.
[18] Oxf. Dioc. b 70, f. 811.
[19] Oxf. Archd. Oxon. b 41, ff. 139, 141.
[20] Bodl. G.A. Oxon. a 39, f. 150.
[21] Bodl. MS. ch. Oxon. 4405.
[22] Dunkin, *Oxon.* ii. 197 n.
[23] O.R.O. Cal. Quart. Sess.
[24] O.S. Map 25″, xxiii. 13 (1875).
[25] Ibid. 2½″, 42/51 (1951); ibid. 6″, xxiii (1885).
[26] *V.C.H. Oxon.* i. 281–8.
[27] See below, pp. 343, 344.
[28] *V.C.H. Oxon.* i. 420 and n.

[29] Dunkin, *Oxon.* ii. 186–7: Dunkin followed Kennett's misreading of the name as 'Algar'.
[30] *V.C.H. Oxon.* i. 420.
[31] *Complete Peerage*, v, between pp. 116–17: Mandeville pedigree; ibid. 134–5; *Bk. of Fees*, 831.
[32] *Complete Peerage*, vi. 474; *Cal. Close*, 1377–81, 392; C 136/99.
[33] *Complete Peerage*, vi. 475.
[34] C 137/12; *Complete Peerage*, vi. 475.
[35] C 137/38, 39.
[36] *V.C.H. Oxon.* i. 420.
[37] Dunkin, *Oxon.* ii. 189.
[38] *Sandford Cart.* ii. 285.
[39] *Red Bk. Exch.* (Rolls Ser.), 345.
[40] *Thame Cart.* i. 133.
[41] *Bk. of Fees*, 298.
[42] Ibid. 449, 826; *Rot. Hund.* (Rec. Com.), ii. 45.

however, Aymer de St. Amand, Ralph's son, came of age and obtained possession of the Oseville manor of East Ilsley (Berks.),[43] so that it is likely that he received Wendlebury about the same time by virtue of some agreement between his father and the former lord. In 1279 Aymer was mesne tenant of Wendlebury.[44] Guy, Aymer's son, succeeded him in 1285, but died only two years afterwards, and was followed by his brother Aymer. The mesne lordship of Wendlebury then followed the descent of the barony of St. Amand until the early 15th century.[45]

Thomas Poure, who died in 1407, was stated to hold his lands in Wendlebury of the heirs of Aymer de St. Amand, the last of the direct male line, who had died in 1402. Thomas was a minor, and in 1406 Aymer's widow Eleanor had claimed his wardship, since his father Sir Thomas Poure (see below) had held Wendlebury manor of Aymer's manor of East Ilsley. Thomas had in fact been in Aymer's custody for a short while in 1400, but had been abducted, so Eleanor claimed, by William Gernon of whom the Poures held in Black Bourton.[46] The successors of the St. Amands do not appear to have maintained their claim to mesne lordship, and in 1428 the immediate lords of the tenants to Wendlebury manor were not known.[47]

By the end of the 12th century the St. Fey family were tenants of one of the 2 knight's fees of Wendlebury. Walter de St. Fey gave land in Wendlebury to Thame Abbey in 1196 and his son Hamon added to his gift in 1202.[48] The Hamon who held the fee in 1243[49] was probably the latter's son, and he appears to have died by 1255,[50] leaving his daughters, Isabel, wife of William de Grenevile,[51] and Eleanor, wife of Geoffrey de Lucy, who divided his lands. Eleanor held the fee in 1279[52] and she was still alive in 1285.[53] The descent of the St. Fey fee in the 14th century is obscure: in 1316 it was held by a certain John son of Peter,[54] and in 1428 by William Pepyr,[55] perhaps a kinsman of the John Pepar of Wendlebury who was receiving an annual pension from Bicester Priory in the early years of Henry VI's reign.[56]

The de Pavely family of Paulerspury (Northants)[57] appear to have been the tenants of the second knight's fee in WENDLEBURY at the beginning of the 13th century. According to later evidence it was granted by Geoffrey de Pavely (d. 1217) to William de Stanford on his marriage to Geoffrey's sister Maud.[58] William was probably the William son of Aumary who held 1 fee in Wendlebury in 1243.[59] William's daughter and heiress Alice de Stanford held the fee in 1255,[60]

but in 1258 she conveyed it to Nicholas de Sifrewast and his wife Anne.[61] They in turn enfeoffed Richard Poure of Charlton-on-Otmoor before 1279.[62] Another mesne lordship was thus created and was claimed by Nicholas and his descendants at least until 1346.[63] Richard Poure was dead by 1283[64] and was succeeded by his son William[65] and eventually by Sir Thomas, who died about 1398, leaving a son Thomas and a daughter Agnes.[66] Thomas, a minor at his father's death (see above), died in 1407,[67] and his estates passed to his sister. She married, firstly, William Winslow, who died in 1414, and secondly Robert Andrew, who was said to hold only ½ knight's fee in Wendlebury in 1428.[68] Robert died in 1437, and Agnes, who was still alive in 1441, was succeeded by Thomas Winslow, her son by her first husband. In 1458 Thomas and his wife Agnes granted the manor to their daughter Elizabeth and her husband John, son of James Terumbere or Towker.[69] John and Elizabeth seem to have died without issue, for the manor passed to Isabel, one of Elizabeth's four sisters and coheiresses, and her husband Humphrey Seymour. From Humphrey it descended to his son Simon or Symond, who died about 1524,[70] and to Simon's son Alexander. Alexander was dead by 1556 when his widow Isabel was claiming her dower in Wendlebury.[71] Isabel and Alexander's second son and heir was John Seymour, but what happened to the manor is not clear.[72]

According to Dunkin it was the Pavely-Seymour manor which was purchased by Lord Williams of Thame,[73] but the later descent of the advowson, which had followed this manor since the 13th century, suggests that it came into the possession of the Dormers. In 1560/1 John and William Dormer sold it, with the advowson, to William Smyth (or Haddon), a yeoman of Cottisford. The manor passed to Richard Stanley, and later to Thomas, son of Roger Hitch of Kempston (Beds.), who was living in Wendlebury in 1574.[74] In 1618 he leased 4½ yardlands, 3 of which were accounted part of the ancient demesne land of the manor, to his son John,[75] and in 1621 John sold it to William Payne.[76] The manor seems to have been breaking up, for in 1653 1½ yard land demised to Philip Holman for 99 years were said to have been formerly part of it and to have been sold by Thomas Hitch.[77] In 1656 Philip Holman held the manor, a manor-house, and 4½ yardlands.[78] In 1717 it was assigned in trust to William Dyer and leased to Toby Chancy.[79]

The manor held by Lord Williams of Thame

[43] V.C.H. Berks. iv. 26; Rot. Hund. ii. 45; Complete Peerage, xi. 296–7.
[44] Rot. Hund. ii. 834.
[45] Complete Peerage, xi. 297–300.
[46] Misc. Gen. et Her. 5th ser. vi. 369–70.
[47] Feud. Aids, iv. 191.
[48] Thame Cart. i. 132–3.
[49] Bk. of Fees, 826.
[50] Rot. Hund. (Rec. Com.), ii. 45.
[51] Cat. Anct. D. vi. C 5889.
[52] Rot. Hund. ii. 834.
[53] Feud. Aids, iv. 157, where she is called Eleanor de St. Fey.
[54] Ibid. 169.   [55] Ibid. 191.
[56] Kennett, Paroch. Antiq. ii. 252.
[57] See Baker, Northants, ii. 200–1; cf. W. J. Watney, Wallop Family, 612.
[58] C.P. 40/428, m. 241: suit of 1367; Farrer, Honors, i. 193.   [59] Bk. of Fees, 826.
[60] Rot. Hund. (Rec. Com.), ii. 45.
[61] Fines Oxon. 178.

[62] Rot. Hund. ii. 834.
[63] Feud. Aids, iv. 157, 180, where Nicholas and his heirs are given as mesne lords of the St. Fey fee also, but on what grounds is not known.
[64] For the Poures see G. A. Moriarty, 'Poure Family of Oxon.', Misc. Gen. et Her. 5th ser. vi. 363–4 (pedigree), 365 sqq.
[65] Moriarty, op. cit. 364; Feud. Aids, iv. 180.
[66] Moriarty, op. cit. 364.
[67] C 137/59; Cal. Close, 1405–9, 299.
[68] Moriarty, op. cit. 364; Feud. Aids, iv. 191.
[69] Cal. Close, 1454–61, 285, 296; Oxon. Visit. 177–8.
[70] C 142/40/26; Oxon. Visit. 162.
[71] C 1/1470/15, 16; ibid. 1423/37.
[72] Oxon. Visit. 162.
[73] Dunkin, Oxon. ii. 194.
[74] C.P. 25(2)/196/Mich. 3 Eliz.; Bodl. MS. ch. Oxon. 4088; Oxon. Visit. 233.
[75] Bodl. MS. ch. Oxon. 4088.   [76] Ibid. 4087.
[77] O.R.O. Misc. Gr. I au/2.
[78] Queen's Coll. Mun. E 11.   [79] Ibid.

passed, on his death in 1559, to his daughter Margaret and her husband Henry, later Lord Norreys of Rycote.[80] Henry died in 1601 and was succeeded by his grandson Francis, later Earl of Berkshire, the son of William Norreys, who had died in 1579.[81] From Francis, Earl of Berkshire, the manor descended through his daughter Elizabeth to the Bertie earls of Abingdon,[82] who held it until 1764. In that year the manorial estate was purchased by Sir Edward Turner of Ambrosden from the trustees of Willoughby, 3rd Earl of Abingdon, for £3,350.[83] The manor was again sold by Sir Edward Turner's heir Sir Gregory in 1771 to John Pardoe, who had been Sir Edward's steward, for £3,150,[84] and in 1799 it was purchased by John Coker of Bicester from Pardoe's executors.[85] It remained in the Coker family until 1856, when it was sold by Lewis Coker to John Leman,[86] from whom it was purchased in 1862 by the Queen's College, Oxford,[87] which is at present the chief landowner. Manorial rights have lapsed.

In the 17th century the 'overlordship' of the manor was said to have been held by the Spencers of Yarnton.[88] This is presumably a reference to the right of the Spencers as lords of Ploughley hundred to receive 2 quarters of oats from Wendlebury.[89] The 'overlordship' probably followed the same descent as Ploughley hundred and Hampton Poyle manor and passed to the Tilsons and from them, in 1795, to the Annesleys.[90] In the 1820's Arthur Annesley of Bletchingdon was actually holding the court leet and view of frankpledge of Wendlebury manor,[91] although the Cokers were lords of the manor. This situation may have been a consequence of the death of John Coker in 1819 and the succession to the property of an absentee nephew. Statements that the dukes of Marlborough were lords of the manor appear to have arisen from the fact that they held the early title-deeds of the manor after 1765, when the custody of the deeds was delivered to George, Duke of Marlborough, by Sir Edward Turner on condition that they should be produced if required to defend the Turner family's title.[92]

LESSER ESTATES. In 1279 Thame Abbey held 5 virgates in Wendlebury,[93] but in 1317, when Edward II confirmed the abbey's possessions, this estate was not included,[94] and the abbey held nothing in Wendlebury at the Dissolution. In 1293 Rewley Abbey held 8 virgates and 20 acres of meadow in Wendlebury,[95] and at the Dissolution it had an estate there worth £1 14s. 6d. in rents.[96] In all

probability Rewley had acquired the Thame estate between its foundation in 1281 and 1293. A sale or exchange between the two houses is the more likely because Thame was closely concerned with the foundation of Rewley and supplied its first abbot and monks.[97] After the Dissolution Rewley's estate was granted to Thomas Pope of Wroxton.[98]

Notley Abbey, Bicester Priory, and Studley Priory also held small estates in Wendlebury in 1279,[99] and retained them until the Dissolution, when Notley's lands appear to have been merged in the manor which Sir John Williams acquired.[1] In 1540 Thomas Pope was granted the former Bicester and Studley properties.[2] The latter was subsequently granted to John Croke,[3] and the former to Roger Moore of Bicester.[4] Moore sold the estate to John Waterhouse of Bignell in 1542; in 1547 Waterhouse sold it to John Denton of Blackthorn;[5] and in 1556 Denton sold it to John Marten of Rousham,[6] after which it cannot be traced. A house in Wendlebury was known in the early 18th century as Prior's House,[7] and had perhaps belonged to Bicester.

ECONOMIC AND SOCIAL HISTORY. Sewel de Oseville's manor[8] seems to have suffered from the Conquest, for although there was land for 8 ploughs in 1086, there were only 2 worked by 3 serfs in demesne and a further 3 shared by 4 villeins (*villani*) and 5 bordars. There was meadow (8×2 furls.), and pasture (15×2 furls.) in addition, which may account for the fact that the holding was then worth £5 as before the Conquest.[9]

By the end of the 13th century there had been considerable changes. The demesne land had increased: in 1279 Richard Poure held a virgate, Eleanor de Lucy 4 virgates, and the Abbot of Thame 5 virgates—of which the last holding passed to Rewley Abbey soon afterwards.[10] There had been some sub-infeudation: eight free tenants, six of them virgaters and two half-virgaters, now held of different lords for rents varying from 1s. to 13s. 4d. a year for a virgate. The serfs had been succeeded by villeins; there were 13 altogether, of whom 5 held a virgate or more, and the rest half-virgates, the most usual rent being 6s. 8d. the virgate. Labour services are not recorded and had no doubt been commuted. In all, 27 virgates, including the rector's land (i.e. 6¾ carucates), appear to have been under cultivation compared with a recorded 5 carucates two centuries earlier.[11]

Early 14th-century tax assessments show that the community was fairly prosperous: there were 24

[80] C 142/126/150; *Complete Peerage* (orig. edn.), viii. 140.
[81] *Complete Peerage*, ix. 645.
[82] Ibid. i. 45 sqq.; O.R.O. J II a/1–26.
[83] Queen's Coll. Mun. E 19–20; Bodl. MS. ch. Oxon. 4178.
[84] Queen's Coll. Mun. E 22; Dunkin, *Oxon.* ii. 194.
[85] Queen's Coll. Mun. E 1, i–iii.
[86] Ibid. E 5, iv; for the Cokers see above, p. 24.
[87] Queen's Coll. Mun. E 5, vi.
[88] In 1625 the heir of Sir Thomas Spencer (d. 1622) was overlord of Hampton Poyle manor 'held of his manor of Wendlebury': MS. Top. Oxon. b 87, f. 217. For the Spencers see Mrs. B. Stapleton, *Three Oxon. Parishes* (O.H.S. xxiv), 285–303.
[89] See above, p. 5.
[90] Ibid.; Bodl. MS. D.D. Valentia a 1, Abstract of Title.
[91] Dunkin, *Oxon.* ii. 197.
[92] Queen's Coll. Mun. E 20, iii. According to *P.O. Dir.*

Oxon. (1854) and *Kelly's Dir. Oxon.* (1939), for example, he was lord of the manor.
[93] *Rot. Hund.* (Rec. Com.), ii. 834.
[94] Dugd. *Mon.* v. 415; *Cal. Pat.* 1313–17, 633.
[95] Dugd. *Mon.* v. 700; C 145/53/5.
[96] *Valor Eccl.* (Rec. Com.), ii. 254.
[97] *V.C.H. Oxon.* ii. 81–82.
[98] *L. & P. Hen. VIII*, xii (2), p. 350.
[99] *Rot. Hund.* (Rec. Com.), ii. 834.
[1] Dunkin, *Oxon.* ii. 195.
[2] *L. & P. Hen. VIII*, xv, p. 169.
[3] Ibid. p. 116; see *V.C.H. Oxon.* v. 63.
[4] *L. & P. Hen. VIII*, xvii, p. 259.
[5] *Cal. Pat.* 1547–8, 226.
[6] Ibid. 1555–7, 129.
[7] Bodl. MS. ch. Oxon. 3863.
[8] See above, p. 339.
[9] *V.C.H. Oxon.* i. 420.
[10] See above.
[11] *Rot. Hund.* (Rec. Com.), ii. 834.

contributors in 1316 and 23 in 1327. The total assessment of £4 8s. 9d. in 1316 and the later assessment to the 15th fixed in 1334 at £5 2s. 8d. place Wendlebury among the more flourishing villages of Ploughley Hundred.[12] If it suffered from the Black Death as severely as some of its neighbours, it would appear to have recovered by 1377, when there were 60 contributors to the poll tax.[13] The relative prosperity of the village may be attributed to its good arable land, and it is significant that in the 18th century the virgate or yardland in the parish was estimated to contain only 15 statute acres.[14]

At the beginning of the 13th century the arable was divided into two open fields, East Field and West Field, and a virgate given to Thame Abbey in 1202 consisted of 9 acres in the one field, 13½ acres in the other, 4½ acres of meadow, and 2 butts for a messuage and curtilage.[15] Two late 13th-century charters[16] give extensive lists of field-names, including those of Alchester (Alcestre), Cattesbrein, Gurefen, and La Hardelonde. Many survived for centuries: by 1666 Gurefen, for instance, had become Garfine or Garven, and by 1801, Carvens;[17] while Hardelonde is found in the 17th and 18th centuries as Ardland. Many also throw light on the original character of the land—names such as Longmerse, Wythybedde (willow bed), Rediforlong, and Fernforlong.

There is no record of the date of the change to three fields: in the early 17th century they were called North, South, and West Fields; and later in the century they were described as the fields 'towards Bicester', 'towards Charlton', and 'towards Weston'.[18] The last-named lay in the angle of the Oxford road and a brook running southwards from Wendlebury village, and appears from Davis's map (1797) to have been divided from South Field by a strip of meadow or pasture. South Field and most of North Field lay between this strip and another brook running south-east from Alchester. A detached part of North Field, called 'old Chester' in the 17th century, lay immediately east of the site of the Roman town beyond a second belt of meadow, and a long narrow strip of pasture lay on the right of the Oxford road, going south-west from the village.[19]

A three-course rotation was followed in the 17th century: every year one field was sown with wheat and barley, and another with pulse, while the third lay fallow. In 1615 it was estimated that an acre of corn was worth 10s. in an average year, while pulse was worth 6d. a cock. To every yardland there belonged 4 acres of meadow, and each acre usually produced ten cocks of hay worth 6d. a cock.[20] By 1636 it had been found that the common pasture was seriously overburdened with stock, and a new body of regulations was drawn up which imposed a stint of

6 cattle, 1 calf, and 1 horse to the yardland in the moors, 2 more cattle or horses being allowed after 1 August. Twelve sheep to the yardland could be put on the fallow field and commons between 24 August and 18 October, and 20 between then and 26 April.[21] The strips in the open fields were called lands in the 17th century, but by the 18th century the term 'ridgers' was the one most commonly used,[22] perhaps because on the wetter lands of Wendlebury the ridges were very high.[23] Three 'ridgers' were equal to 1 acre.

Stukeley's account of the site of Alchester throws some light on farming methods in the early 18th century. The site of the city was a common belonging to the inhabitants and everyone had a portion to plough up. 'Whence,' he wrote, 'the land is racked to the last extremity and no great care taken in the management.' Because of the 'prodigious blackness and richness of the earth', however, it bore very good wheat crops.[24]

Records of population at this period give 101 adults in 1676, and '160 souls including children and hired servants' in 1774. A report of an early 18th-century incumbent described the village as consisting of two small streets with 32 contiguous houses.[25]

Two substantial families can definitely be said to have lived in the village over a long period—the Traffords and Vennimores. Henry Trafford inhabited the largest house in 1665[26] and his successors continued to be freeholders under the earls of Abingdon throughout the 18th century.[27] By 1801 the family was clearly much reduced, but it continued to live in the parish until at least 1832.[28] A Vennimore held property as early as 1558[29] and the family only sold its land shortly before 1774.[30] Another family, the Bees, who were mercers and hosiers of Oxford and London, held property from the mid-17th century well into the 18th century.[31]

In the 18th century, according to one account, the parish consisted of 32 yardlands; according to another, there were 34 yardlands or about 1,200 acres of arable and pasture.[32] A late 18th-century list of the farmers in the parish gives nine, with farms ranging from 2 to 5½ yardlands.[33] Ten or 10½ yardlands, or about a third of the parish, belonged to the Abingdon manor.[34] When the manor was sold in 1764 it consisted of eight farms, the largest of 3 yardlands or 52½ acres of arable, the smallest of ½ yardland or 9¼ acres of arable.[35] Rentals for 1753–4 and 1761–2 show that the annual value of the rents collected in this period varied between £133 and £165, the greatest part of which came from rack rents.[36] Early in the century copyholding was the normal method of tenure. In 1728 there were nine tenants, all copyholders except for one leaseholder

12 E 179/161/8, 9, 17.
13 Ibid. 161/39.
14 Bodl. MS. ch. Oxon. 4178: particulars of manor.
15 Thame Cart. ii. 132–3.
16 Cat. Anct. D. iii, C 3646, 3733. See also P.N. Oxon. (E.P.N.S.), i. 241–2.
17 Bodl. MS. ch. Oxon. 302, 637; O.R.O. Incl. award.
18 Oxf. Archd. Oxon. b 41, f. 140.
19 Ibid.; Davis, Oxon. Map.
20 Oxf. Dioc. c 25, f. 236.
21 See C 78/499/4 for these and many more regulations.
22 MS. Top. Oxon. e 302, f. 4.
23 Young, Oxon. Agric. 103.
24 W. Stukeley, Itinerarium Curiosum (1724), 39.
25 Compton Census: Oxf. Dioc. d 565; ibid. d 554. Cf. the

small number of 25 houses listed for the hearth tax of 1662: Hearth Tax Oxon. 235.
26 Hearth Tax Oxon. 189.
27 MS. Top. Oxon. b 178–89.
28 O.R.O. Incl. award; ibid. Land tax assess. 1832.
29 E 179/161/319.
30 Queen's Coll. Mun. X 4a.
31 Hearth Tax Oxon. 189; MS. Top. Oxon. b 178–89; ibid. c 167, pp. 301–2; see below, p. 344.
32 Bodl. MS. ch. Oxon. 4178; O.R.O. Misc. Wo. 1/5.
33 O.R.O. Misc. Wo. 1/5.
34 MS. Top. Oxon. c 381, ff. 103–5; Bodl. MS. ch. Oxon. 4178.
35 Bodl. MS. ch. Oxon. 4178.
36 MS. Top. Oxon. b 178, b 186.

for lives.[37] By the 1750's leaseholding had increased and rack-renting had begun. In 1753–4, for example, there were four tenants at a rack-rent, and the nine other tenants, three of whom were smallholders or cottagers, were copyholders or leaseholders for lives. By 1761–2 there were only two rack-renters.[38] At this time there were four freeholders, of whom the Queen's College was probably the largest, compared with 36 in 1636.[39]

By the custom of the manor, as stated in 1764,[40] copyholds were to run for two lives, but it was provided that if the first party died in possession of the land, his widow should 'enjoy the estate for her life, provided she live chaste and sole'. Both parties paid heriot on taking up the estate.

There were two major changes in the 19th century: the open-field husbandry was superseded by modern farming methods and population increased considerably. Comparatively little land had been inclosed before the general inclosure of 1801. The 'Great Close' is mentioned in 1764,[41] and there are references to Shenstone Close and Little Close, but the suggestion made earlier in the century to turn the 200 acres of common pasture (excellent land) into meadow, and the poor meadow-land into common, came to nothing.[42] The late inclosure is partly to be explained by the good quality of the arable ground of which the manor chiefly consisted. On this account it was thought in 1764 that the advantage to be derived from its inclosure would fall far short of that to be expected from inclosing Chesterton.[43] In fact, although the land was valued at 24s. an acre after inclosure compared with 10s. before, the increase in value was not as great as in some of the neighbouring villages.[44]

Eleven persons received allotments by the award;[45] there were also allotments for glebe, tithes, and church land, and the poor. John Coker, the lord of the manor, got about 500 acres of the 1,160 inclosed; William Tanner and Richard Curtis, tenants of the Queen's College, received over 100 acres each; four others round about 20 acres and the rest even smaller holdings. Inclosure does not seem to have led to a loss of population, though it may have caused poverty, for in 1811 it was estimated that there were between 30 and 40 families, composed of 'farmers and paupers' and the total population had risen from 146 in 1801 to 181 persons.[46] The change did not affect the old rotation of fallow–wheat–beans–barley, which continued to be practised by most farmers. Only the Revd. George Dupuis, while cautious in ploughing down the old high ridges, introduced a seven-course rotation: fallow–wheat–beans–barley–clover–vetches–wheat.[47] In common with the rest of the Bicester area much of the arable land of Wendlebury was converted to pasture in the late 19th century—a trend which continued in the

20th century except during the abnormal conditions of the two World Wars. In 1939 most of the parish was permanent grass;[48] today (1956) out of 977½ acres of cultivated land 837½ are grassland and the rest arable.[49]

The character of the village has always been rural and agricultural. An attempt was made in 1790 to set up a brewery, but after being for some years in the hands of William Hartin, a yeoman farmer of Merton, the business failed and was put up for auction in 1809.[50] In 1820 it was purchased by a Bicester brewer.[51] The census of 1841 records that out of 241 persons living in the village, 203 had been born there; that the rector took pupils, that a local auctioneer lived in the village, and that there were a village baker, shoemaker, farrier, carpenter, and wheelwright.[52] In 1851, of 54 agricultural labourers, six were women and two were children under fourteen. Eight girls were described as general servants; they probably worked at either the Rectory or Wendlebury House (the home of a solicitor), the only two large establishments in the parish, or with the two substantial farmers.[53] The population reached its peak in 1861, when there were 257 inhabitants. Thereafter there was on the whole a steady decline in the number of villagers and by 1901 there were 196 and 67 inhabited houses. The decline continued in the early years of the 20th century, but in 1951 there were 178 inhabitants compared with 148 in 1931.[54] During this century many of the villagers have found work in Oxford, and at the nearby military depot at Arncot.

CHURCH. It is probable that the church of Wendlebury was originally a chapel of ease to the neighbouring church of Chesterton, to which it paid a pension throughout the Middle Ages.[55] By the early 13th century, when Wendlebury church is first recorded, Wendlebury was a separate parish.[56] The advowson in the 13th and 14th centuries belonged to the Pavely family. They were a prominent Northamptonshire family, who also held land in other counties, and seem to have died out in the late 14th century.[57] They held the advowson because of their rights in the manor. In 1279 the Hundred jurors expressly said they held only the advowson and no land.[58] The first recorded presentation was made in about 1215 by Walter de Godarville, guardian of Robert de Pavely.[59] Sir Robert de Pavely presented in 1340, and the next known presentation was in 1402 by Joan Chetwind, perhaps an heiress, who presented again in 1414.

In 1418 Robert Andrew, the second husband of Agnes Poure, who was also connected with one of the Pavelys' Northamptonshire manors,[60] was patron. When the manor was settled on John and Elizabeth Terumbere in 1458 the advowson was

[37] Ibid. e 381, ff. 103–4.
[38] Ibid. b 178, b 186.
[39] Bodl. MS. ch. Oxon. 4178; C 78/499/4.
[40] Bodl. MS. ch. Oxon. 4178.
[41] Queen's Coll. Mun. E 12.
[42] MS. Top. Oxon. c 381, f. 105.
[43] Bodl. MS. ch. Oxon. 4178.
[44] Young, Oxon. Agric. 37, 91.
[45] O.R.O. Incl. award.
[46] Oxf. Dioc. d 573; V.C.H. Oxon. ii. 221.
[47] Young, Oxon. Agric. 127.
[48] O.S. Map 1″, land utilization, sht. 94 (1939).
[49] Inf. Oxon. Agric. Executive Cttee.
[50] Dunkin MS. 438/3, pp. 210, 356–7; 438/5, p. 48.

[51] Dunkin, Oxon. ii. 175.
[52] H.O. 107/887.
[53] Ibid. 1729.
[54] V.C.H. Oxon. ii. 221; Census, 1931, 1951.
[55] 13s. 4d. and later 6s. 8d.: Rot. Welles, i. 151; Kennett, Paroch. Antiq. ii. 203.
[56] Rot. Welles, i. 151.
[57] For them see V.C.H. Northants, iv. 263; Bridges, Northants, i. 311, 597; Thoroton, Notts. i. 124.
[58] Rot. Hund. (Rec. Com.), ii. 834.
[59] Rot. Welles, i. 151. For a list of medieval presentations see MS. Top. Oxon. d 460.
[60] V.C.H. Northants, iv. 263.

granted to John's father James Terumbere,[61] who presented in 1461 and 1473. In 1485 Humphrey Seymour was patron, and the advowson passed with the manor to William Haddon (or Smythe), who sold the presentation in 1578.[62] In 1605 Thomas Hitch, who had bought the manor, presented; and Thomas Aldrich, who held the presentation for that turn, presented John Bird in 1614.[63] Bird (d. 1653) seems to have bought the advowson, and may have sold it to the Bee family, for Matthew Bee (d. 1674) was the next rector and Thomas Bee was then three times patron.[64] In 1700 John Bee sold the advowson, and eventually it was bought in 1708 by the Dean and Chapter of Christ Church.[65] They were patrons until 1923, when the living was united with that of Chesterton.[66] New College and Christ Church, therefore, now (1956) present alternately.

In 1254 the value of the living was £5 6s. 8d., in 1291 £7, and in 1535 £11 9s. 4d.[67] At the beginning of the 17th century it was reckoned to be worth £80.[68] When George Dupuis became rector in 1789, the nine principal farmers in the parish met at the 'Red Lion' and decided to offer him 200 guineas a year for the lease of the tithes and glebe. The rector accepted the offer, as it was ever his 'wish to live upon the best of terms' with his parishioners.[69] At the inclosure award of 1801 the tithes were commuted for 189 acres and the glebe, which in the 18th century consisted of 1 yardland,[70] was exchanged for 25 acres, 19 of which lay in Bicester Field.[71] Dupuis farmed the land himself,[72] and in 1831 the rectory was valued at £210.[73]

In the 13th and 14th centuries the living, which was of moderate value, was treated as a family living by the patrons, the Pavely family, three of its members becoming rectors.[74] The Rectory house, however, was ruinous in about 1518 and the incumbent was non-resident.[75] He was David Griffith Bye, apparently one of the many men of Welsh descent in this part of Oxfordshire.[76] But 17th-century parsons appear to have resided, for the Rectory had been rebuilt by 1634 and was occupied by Matthew Bee in 1665.[77] Many of his family were buried in the church and his youngest son bought the neighbouring rectory of Beckley.[78] Bee, or his successor Stephen Cupper, bought an additional small house at the other end of the village. It was first recorded in 1679.[79]

The parish continued to benefit from a resident parson. During the first half of the 18th century it was fortunate in having Robert Welborne (1730–64).[80] In 1738 and 1759 he reported that he resided

constantly; preached each Sunday, held prayers on all festivals and fasts; administered the sacrament four times a year (sometimes to as many as 43 communicants); and catechized the children.[81] He was active in raising money for the rebuilding of the church and in making plans for the new building.[82] In the second half of the century there was some falling off in the amount of duty performed by the rector. Joshua Kyte (1764–88), a tutor at Westminster School, said in 1767 and 1768 that he had not hitherto resided above two months in the year, though he intended to in future. A curate, a student of Christ Church, was paid £36 a year to minister to the parishioners —'industrious farmers and labourious cottagers'.[83] Communion was now administered on two festivals only, and there was no catechism as the children could not read. Communicants numbered about 20. In 1774, however, the rector was again resident. He once stated that he often held prayers on saints' days and festivals for his family only, as his parishioners, 'whose support depends on unremitting labour, are seldom able to attend these days'.[84] By 1793 communicants were down to seven or eight,[85] a state of affairs which may be partly explained by the report of 1808 that except for the farmers the 30 or 40 families in the village were 'paupers'. At this date the rector, George Dupuis (1789–1839), who had had a curate paid £30 a year in 1789, was again resident.[86] His successor, W. L. Brown, also resided and in 1854 was catechizing adults every Sunday, and the children were being catechized at school by the schoolmistress. Monthly communion had been introduced and communicants had risen to 30; his congregation numbered 80 to 100 persons out of 240 inhabitants; he had a Sunday school and held evening classes during the winter months, but lamented that too few came.[87] A similar picture of hard work and moderate success is found in 1866, when the congregation had increased to about 150 and there were about 50 children in the Sunday school. The choir had improved and the rector had plans for evening classes for the elder children.[88]

The church of *ST. GILES* is an 18th-century building of stone, comprising a chancel, nave, and north transept. It replaces a medieval church of 13th-century date which was cruciform in shape with two transepts and a western tower. The medieval church had an altar dedicated to the Virgin[89] and a rood-loft approached by a staircase from the north transept.[90] The structure gave continual trouble, as the church was built on clay, and in 1639 the south transept was demolished as dangerous.[91]

[61] *Cal. Close*, 1454–61, 285.
[62] C.P. 25(2)/197/Trin. 24 Eliz.; Dunkin, *Oxon.* ii. 182.
[63] Dunkin, *Oxon.* ii. 182; see above, p. 43.
[64] Dunkin, *Oxon.* ii. 182 n. citing B.M. Harl. MS. 843; ibid. 183; see above, p. 342.
[65] C.P. 25(2)/865/Mich. 12 Wm. III; C.P. 43/470/187; ibid. 502/211; C.P. 25(2)/957/Hil. 7 Anne. Dr. Henry Smith, a canon, left by will of 1700 £500 for the purchase of an advowson: Ch. Ch. Arch. 'Livings'.
[66] Bodl. Par. Box (uncat.), Order in Council.
[67] Lunt, *Val. Norw.* 312; *Tax. Eccl.* (Rec. Com.), 31; *Valor Eccl.* (Rec. Com.), ii. 160.
[68] Dunkin MS. 438/2, f. 173.
[69] O.R.O. Misc. Wo. 1/3, 4.
[70] Ibid. 5; Christ Ch. Arch. Bk. of Livings. For terriers of 1634 and 1679 see Oxf. Archd. Oxon. b 41, ff. 139–41.
[71] O.R.O. Incl. award.
[72] See above, p. 343.
[73] *Rep. of Commissioners on Eccl. Revenue*, H.C. 54 (1835), xxii.

[74] Henry de Pavely, 1275–98; Walter de Pavely, 1315–40; Geoffrey de Pavely, 1340–(?). For list of medieval rectors see MS. Top. Oxon. d 460.
[75] *Visit. Dioc. Linc. 1517–31*, i. 123.
[76] Cf. above, pp. 76, 101.
[77] *Hearth Tax Oxon.* 189; see above, p. 339.
[78] See *V.C.H. Oxon.* v. 72.
[79] Oxf. Archd. Oxon. b 41, f. 141. It was ruinous by 1770 and pulled down: Oxf. Dioc. b 20, f. 58.
[80] For notes from his alphabetical arrangement of the registers see MS. Top. Oxon. c 167, pp 301–5.
[81] Oxf. Dioc. d 554, d 557.
[82] See below.
[83] Oxf. Dioc. c 431, d 560.   [84] Ibid. d 565.
[85] Ibid. b 18.   [86] Ibid. d 571.
[87] *Wilb. Visit.*   [88] Oxf. Dioc. c 332.
[89] *Cat. Anct. D.* ii. C 3733.
[90] Par. rec. account of former church made in 1761 by Robert Welborne, rector.
[91] Dunkin, *Oxon.* ii. 176–7.

By 1757 the whole building was considered to be beyond repair[92] and a brief was issued authorizing the collection of money for a new church.[93] In March 1761 the old church was demolished and by September the exterior of the new one was completed.[94] The medieval tower was kept, as well as some early decorated windows and a doorway. Part of the old materials were also used.

The foundations of the original church can still be traced at the east end, as the new church is 10 feet shorter than the old.

The new church had a gallery at the back of the north transept which was designed for use as a choir and parochial library, while the ground floor of the tower was to be used as a porch and place for parish meetings. The south transept was reserved for landowners and their sons, with the servants in front. The wives and maid-servants and all children sat in the north transept; labourers and tradesmen sat on the south side of the nave and their wives on the north side.[95]

Plans were made in 1863 by G. E. Street for the partial rebuilding of what was then considered 'a modern and extremely unsightly church',[96] but they did not materialize. In 1866 the rector repaired the chancel.[97]

The foundations of the new church were as troublesome as those of the old one and the cracked and leaning tower was reported unsafe;[98] it was demolished between 1901 and 1902 together with the south transept. Neither has been rebuilt. At the same time the roof was renewed and new seating installed (architect J. O. Scott).[99]

There is a plain circular font[1] and good wooden altar railings.

When Rawlinson visited the original church in the early 18th century he found a stone in the chancel with a poem to John Birde (d. 1653), vicar of Bicester and rector of Wendlebury, and some armorial glass.[2] The present church has inscriptions to several rectors: Matthew Bee (d. 1674), Stephen Cupper (d. 1676), John Bond (d. 1692/3), and Zachary Hussey (d. 1719); an urn-shaped marble plaque to Robert Welborne (d. 1764), a tablet to Thomas Edgerton (d. 1785), and a marble plaque by Bossom of Oxford[3] to George Dupuis (d. 1839).[4] There are also inscriptions to other members of the Bee family,[5] and one to Mrs. Rachel Stevens, daughter of Zachary Hussey, who died at 94, beloved for her 'charity and benevolence'.

Two coffins, one a rector's, were found when the south transept was demolished in 1639.[6]

In 1552 the church was poorly furnished with a chalice, two copes, and a vestment. There were three bells and a sanctus bell.[7] The plate now includes a small Elizabethan chalice and paten cover and a huge bell-shaped chalice and paten of 1730, the gift of Thomas Turner, rector.[8] Since the destruction of the tower the three bells, two of the 16th century and one of 1695, have been standing at the west end of the nave.[9]

The registers date from 1579. Robert Welborne, an 18th-century rector, made an alphabetical index to them with comments from 1579 to 1738.[10] He notes that the earliest gravestone in the churchyard was dated 1667/8.

NONCONFORMITY. A number of Roman Catholics were recorded in the late 16th century. In the 1570's Richard Davey, gentleman, and his wife, members of a prominent Roman Catholic family who were patrons of the mission at Overy near Dorchester, were living in the parish.[11] In 1592 William Bourne of Wendlebury, the brother of John Bourne of Chesterton,[12] was one of the recusants at liberty in the county,[13] and in the same year four others, including Bourne's sister, were fined.[14] Some of the names recur in 17th-century lists until 1612.[15] Except for a family living in the parish in about 1800,[16] there seems to have been no later Roman Catholicism.

No record has been found of Protestant dissent until the late 19th century, when there was a small Methodist meeting-place, closed in about 1897.[17]

SCHOOLS. In 1808 there was a dame school where children paid 3d. each a week.[18] This was probably the same school as the one mentioned in 1815, when about a dozen children were being taught to read and write. It was said to be difficult to support a teacher in so small a village, and that parents needed to send their children to work.[19] Nevertheless, a private school opened in 1826,[20] and in 1833 there was a school with 10 pupils supported by a private donation.[21] In 1838 there were about 25 children receiving no schooling at all.[22] A National school was opened in 1850[23] for children aged three and upwards; there were 40 pupils in 1854,[24] and new school buildings were erected in 1863.[25] Average attendance rose from 23 in 1871 to 52 in 1906.[26] The school was reorganized as a junior school in 1927, when senior pupils were transferred to Bicester, and it became controlled in 1952. In 1954 there were 18 pupils, 6 more than in 1937.[27]

[92] Oxf. Dioc. c 654, f. 27; Oxf. Archd. Oxon. d 13, f. 36b.
[93] B.M. AV 8. The provisions of the brief included a house-to-house collection in Oxon., Bucks., and Northants.
[94] Dunkin, Oxon. ii. 178–9, where there is an account of the rebuilding; Oxf. Dioc. c 654, f. 29. The total cost was about £275 to the end of Nov. 1761.
[95] Oxf. Dioc. c 654, f. 31 (plan).
[96] MS. Top. Oxon. c 104, f. 432.
[97] Oxf. Dioc. c 332.
[98] Obadiah Scott, Memoranda on State of Church, in Oxf. Dioc. Registry; Dunkin, Oxon. ii. 179.
[99] Bodl. Par. Box (uncat.): faculty. There are early 19th-century drawings of the church in MS. Top. Oxon. b 220, f. 95, and a 69, f. 577. For a view of 1820 see below, plate facing p. 352.
[1] Buckler drawing: MS. Top. Oxon. a 69, f. 576.
[2] Par. Coll. iii. 335.
[3] This is probably the son of Charles Bossom (d. 1830).
[4] For Dupuis see above, pp. 343–4.
[5] For list see Dunkin, Oxon. ii. 179–80.

[6] Plot, Nat. Hist. Oxon. 213; Dunkin, Oxon. ii. 177.
[7] Chant. Cert. 84.
[8] Evans, Ch. Plate.
[9] Ch. Bells Oxon. iv. 436, including photographs.
[10] Dunkin, Oxon. ii. 183–5, gives extracts.
[11] C.R.S. xxii. 109 and n. 2.
[12] See above, p. 103; for family see Oxon. Visit. 316.
[13] Hist. MSS. Com. Salisbury MSS. IV, 270.
[14] C.R.S. xviii. 260.
[15] Salter, Oxon. Recusants, passim.
[16] Oxf. Dioc. c 327, p. 307.
[17] Inf. Methodist Minister, Bicester.
[18] Oxf. Dioc. d 707.   [19] Ibid. c 433.
[20] Dunkin MS. 438/5, p. 264.
[21] Educ. Enq. Abstract, 757.
[22] Oxf. Dioc. b 41.
[23] Kelly's Dir. Oxon. (1887).
[24] Wilb. Visit.   [25] Wing, Annals, 155.
[26] Elem. Educ. Ret.; Vol. Sch. Ret.
[27] Inf. Oxon. Educ. Cttee.

CHARITIES. In the reign of Edward VI certain arable lands which had been given in the Middle Ages to maintain a light in the church were confiscated by the Crown.[28] In 1549 they were granted to a Londoner,[29] but in 1573 they were bought by the rector, William Brownrig, who gave them to trustees for the benefit of the poor. The income, 3s. 4d. a year, was distributed at Easter and All Saints' Day.[30] In 1738 the income was £1 15s. and in 1790 the poor received £1 in bread at Easter.[31] After the inclosure of 1801, when the trustees received an allotment of 2½ acres, the income rose to £6 6s. a year in 1824. At Christmas 1823 123 poor people received 9d. each.[32] The rent of the allotment was £4 16s. in 1870.[33]

By will dated 1626 William Eberton left lands to the poor which in 1786 were producing £1 15s. a year.[34] There is no further mention of this charity.

Wendlebury shared the Bowell apprenticing charity with Bicester and Chesterton,[35] but it was reported 'long unused' in 1738. By that date three donations amounting to £20 were held by the churchwardens,[36] but both their origin and their subsequent history are unknown. John Coker (d. 1819), lord of the manor, left £40 for blankets and clothing for the poor.[37]

The Revd. G. D. Bowles, rector 1865–1902, left £100, the interest to be spent on bread for the poor.[38] In 1931 T. Holton, who had lived in Wendlebury as a boy, left property to be sold for the benefit of the poor.[39]

WESTON-ON-THE-GREEN

IN the 19th century the parish covered an area of 2,295 acres, but in 1932 a detached portion of Chesterton in which lay Weston Park farm was added to it, increasing its area to 2,483 acres. The parish measures some four miles from north to south, and two miles from east to west at the widest point. Akeman Street forms the northern boundary and Gallows Brook most of the western boundary. Two other streams rising near Akeman Street bound the parish on the east.[1]

The northern third of the parish lies on the Cornbrash, and the Forest Marble is exposed in the valley of the Gallows Brook in the north-west, but most of the parish lies in the area of the Oxford Clay;[2] its soil is clay and stonebrash. The ground slopes slightly from north to south, being about 275 feet above sea-level in the north and 200 feet in the south, with a slight rise called Sandhill or Sainthill to the south of the village. It is a well-watered area; besides the streams on the boundaries others run south through the parish. No woodland is recorded in Domesday, but there was some in the 18th century, and Great Spinney and Middleleys Spinney are noted in 1848.[3] In 1955 there were several woods, the largest being Weston Wood (48 a.) and Mead Copse.

Two main roads cross the parish: the main road from Oxford to Brackley, a busy highway from medieval times, and the road from Oxford to Bicester. The minor road to Bletchingdon was mentioned in 1766 when it was being repaired.[4]

It is possible that the original settlement at Weston was named 'West tun', as it lay on the west side of an ancient trackway and in the extreme west of the parish.[5] It still lies on one side only of the Oxford–Brackley road. Throughout its recorded history it appears to have been a fair-sized village. There were 37 taxable houses listed for the hearth tax of 1665: besides the big manor-house, the village had 13 substantial farm-houses with 4 or 3 hearths apiece.[6] For the greater part of the 18th century there were 50 or so houses, including 8 farm-houses.[7] By 1811 there were 82 dwellings in the village, and by 1851 25 more had been built. Owing to the considerable fall in population there were only 67 inhabited houses in 1901, but the number had increased to 97 by 1951.[8] Much new building took place between 1951 and 1955.[9] Many of the new concrete council houses are near the church; others have been built near the Roman Akeman Street, where there were already a few houses which had been built during the First World War. Here too is a large building occupied by the Danish Bacon Company. During the Second World War, the airfield (285 a.), built in 1915 by Canadians and by German prisoners of war, was a satellite of the Bomber Command station at Upper Heyford. Since 1946—except for a short period—it has been used as a dropping zone for the R.A.F. Parachute Training School.[10]

Despite these changes the appearance of the old village has altered little since the mid-19th century.[11] Many of the cottages, built of stone from local quarries, are still thatched, although slate roofs are gradually replacing the thatch. Some like Manor Cottage, once the dower house of the manor,[12] and the 'general store' (dated 1617) are of 17th-century origin. A few houses and cottages lie scattered along the Brackley road from the 'Chequers'[13] at the south

[28] 12th Rep. Com. Char. 314.
[29] Cal. Pat. 1549–51, 85.
[30] 12th Rep. Com. Char. 314.
[31] Oxf. Dioc. d 554; ibid. c 327, p. 73.
[32] 12th Rep. Com. Char. 314.
[33] Gen. Digest Char.
[34] Char. Don. ii. 990.
[35] See above, pp. 55, 103.
[36] Oxf. Dioc. d 554.
[37] Dunkin, Oxon. ii. 194 n.
[38] Oxf. Dioc. d 560.
[39] Kelly's Dir. Oxon. (1939). It has not been possible to obtain information about the state of the charities in 1956.
[1] O.S. Map 6", xxii, xxvii (1885); ibid. 2½", 42/51, 52 (1951); Oxon. Review Order (1932): copy in O.R.O.
[2] G.S. Map 1", xlv SE.

[3] V.C.H. Oxon. i. 414; Davis, Oxon. Map; Bodl. Tithe award map.
[4] MS. Top. Oxon. d 266.
[5] P.N. Oxon. (E.P.N.S.), i. 243.
[6] Hearth Tax Oxon. 197–8.
[7] e.g. Oxf. Dioc. d 554, d 557, d 560.
[8] Census, 1811, 1851, 1901, 1951.
[9] Inf. Ploughley R.D.C.: estimated popn. 1954 was 636.
[10] Inf. R.A.F. It is also the H.Q. of the Oxford Gliding Club.
[11] See Gardner, Dir. Oxon.; cf. Kelly's Dir. Oxon. (1939); O.S. Map 25", xxii. 16, xxvii. 4 (1875); cf. ibid. 2½", 42/51 (1951).
[12] Bodl. G.A. Oxon. b 92* (16): Sale Cat. 1918.
[13] Mentioned in 1852: Gardner, Dir. Oxon.

end of the village as far as the entrance to the manor-house, but the main village street branches off the main road and runs on into Church Lane. The church and Vicarage lie to the north of the road and farther north and west is the water-mill, probably on the site of one of the two medieval mills.[14] Windmill Clump to the north of the village perhaps marks the position of a third mill, mentioned as late as 1808.[15] Beyond the turn to Church Lane is the 'Ben Jonson's Head', mentioned by name in 1784,[16] but possibly in existence as early as 1735 at least, when two Weston victuallers were licensed.[17] A second but shorter village street called North Lane branches off the main road beyond the public house. Here are the 19th-century nonconformist chapel and the school.[18] Between these two streets probably lay the ancient village green which gave the place its name of Weston-on-the-Green. As late as the end of the 19th century there was a small triangular green on which the stocks stood near the 'Ben Jonson's Head'.

Apart from the manor-house, one of the best houses in the village is the Vicarage. It is a handsome stone building, roofed with blue slate and containing seventeen rooms. Dunkin described it in 1823 as a 'neat and commodious mansion' which had been occupied for many years by the vicar James Yalden (d. 1822).[19] It had replaced a 'mean' house, which in 1635 and 1685 was described as having only three bays of building.[20] The house was enlarged in 1823 by the architect S. H. Benham of Oxford at a cost of some £300.[21]

There was a medieval manor-house which was probably of some size, as it was the seat of Oseney Abbey's bailiff for the bailiwick of Weston.[22] Two sides of its 13th-century rectangular moat were existing, and a third side could be traced, before they were largely filled in in 1908.[23] The present house, however, was probably mainly built in the mid-16th century by Lord Williams of Thame or his widow.[24] The main survival of the earlier building is the great hall (19 × 42 ft.), very probably the court room of the manor. Its walls date from the early 16th century. An entry into the hall from the corridor between the great hall and the buttery and kitchen quarters is called the Monk's Hole or Hall, but as it now stands it appears to be of a later period and probably dates from about 1851, when the Hon. the Revd. F. A. Bertie was rebuilding and making extensive alterations to the house.

On the outside of the south wall is a staircase turret, bearing the arms of the Bertie family,[25] and leading up to a minstrels' gallery, perhaps adapted from the solar of the older hall. Inside, the hall has oak linen-fold panelling and above a carved frieze of foliage and mermaids, and a head probably representing that of St. John the Baptist on a charger. A legend 'Time Deum et recede a malo. Principium

sapiencie timor est Dei' runs round the frieze, with the name of Richard Rydge, the last Abbot of Notley (Bucks.), between the two sentences. Peregrine Bertie (1741–90) moved this panelling from Notley in about 1780 and put it up in the hall at Weston;[26] the open timber roof now in the hall also came from Notley, but was first used to roof a barn in Chesterton and was not placed in the hall of Weston Manor until between 1840 and 1850. The plaster corbel angels supporting the roof were probably a part of F. A. Bertie's restoration.

The main block of the 16th-century house is rectangular: with its two small projections at the back it encloses a courtyard (45 × 30 ft.). The stables and outbuildings lie to the right of the house across a paved stable-yard, through which may once have been the main approach. The size of the house before the 19th-century alterations may be gauged from its 20 hearths returned for the hearth tax of 1665.[27] It was among the county's larger mansions, although not in the same class as Lord Anglesey's house with its 30 hearths at nearby Bletchingdon.[28] An etching of about 1823 shows it as it was before its original 16th-century frontage was replaced by a Gothic-revival façade in the 1820's. The front of the main building has a gable at either end and the central porch is flanked by bay windows, extending the whole height of the building, which was of two stories with attics. An unpretentious low wall or paling separates the house from an open field, and farm outhouses lie on both sides.[29]

The principal other points of interest in the present building are the William and Mary panelling in the drawing-room; the bow window of this room, which extends to the top of the first floor; the Tudor fireplace in the entrance hall; and the adornments of the central courtyard. This last has a central well surrounded by a low wall bearing the arms of the Bertie family, and against its west wall two doors from the Jacobean chapel of Exeter College. They bear the arms of George Hakewill, a Fellow and Rector of the college, at whose cost the chapel had been built; and were probably acquired by the Berties when Exeter chapel was rebuilt in 1856.[30]

The gardens have an avenue of deciduous trees, called the Monks' Walk, but undoubtedly planted by the Berties. The last of the elm trees, planted in 1672 and 1682 and noted in the parish register by Edward Norreys himself,[31] was struck by lightning in 1952 and removed. The house has been used as an hotel since 1949.

The parish has played a small part in national affairs. In the Civil War royalist troops were quartered in the village in 1643 and 1644[32] and parliamentary troops under Colonel Fleetwood were stationed there before the siege of Oxford in 1646.[33] The manor-house was the home for over two centuries of

[14] See below, p. 349.
[15] C.P. 43/902/258; O.S. Map 25″, xxii. 16.
[16] O.R.O. Victlrs' recog.
[17] Ibid.
[18] See below, p. 352.
[19] Dunkin, Oxon. ii. 199.
[20] Oxf. Archd. Oxon. c 141, p. 133; MS. Top. Oxon. c 55, f. 252. It cannot be identified with any house in Hearth Tax Oxon. (1665) as the vicar's name is unknown.
[21] Oxf. Dioc. c 435, pp. 414–19.
[22] See below, p. 348.
[23] V.C.H. Oxon. ii. 330.
[24] The following account of the manor-house is based on a survey by Mr. P. S. Spokes; see also Hamilton Carr,

Country Life, 25 Aug. 1928, 268–74.
[25] Bodl. G.A. Oxon. 8° 1262, p. 166; G.A. Oxon. b 180, Ploughley, pp. 8f–8h.
[26] Cf. Dunkin, who says Norreys Bertie did this: Oxon. ii. 214–15.
[27] Hearth Tax Oxon. 197.
[28] Ibid. 196.
[29] Dunkin, Oxon. ii, facing p. 198.
[30] V.C.H. Oxon. iii. 116; Bodl. G.A. Oxon. 4° 692, pp. 56a–d; ibid. 691, p. 67; ibid. 8° 1262, p. 134; N. & Q. 1944, clxxxvii. 137–9.
[31] Par. Reg.
[32] Luke, Jnl. 101, 109, 253.
[33] Dunkin MS. 438/4, f. 77.

the Bertie family.[34] John Warde, 'the father of fox-hunting', established kennels at Weston in 1778.[35]

MANOR. At the time of the Conquest *WESTON* was one of the possessions of the Saxon lord Wigod of Wallingford. On Wigod's death shortly afterwards many of his lands including Weston passed to Robert d'Oilly, the first Norman castellan of Oxford, who is said to have married Wigod's daughter. Robert held Weston rated at 10 hides in 1086[36] and on his death in 1094[37] it passed to his brother and successor Nigel.[38] Nigel lived until about 1115[39] and was succeeded by his son Robert (II) d'Oilly, who married Edith, daughter of Forne, to whom he gave Weston as part of her dower.[40] It is likely that Robert's gift about 1130 to his new foundation of Oseney Abbey of the church of Weston[41] was accompanied or followed by a grant of lands in the manor; Henry (II) d'Oilly confirmed to the abbey 6 virgates which were the gift of his grandmother Edith and his father Henry (I).[42] In 1137 Edith, with Robert's consent, gave 35 acres of land in Weston to the new foundation of Otley Abbey in Oddington, later removed to Thame.[43] Robert died in 1142,[44] and was succeeded by his son Henry (I), who confirmed his mother's gift to Thame[45] and confirmed or augmented her gift to Oseney. Edith presumably held Weston until her death between 1151 and 1154.[46] Her son Henry (I) died in 1163 and was succeeded by his son Henry (II), a minor who came of age about 1175.[47] In 1213 Henry granted Weston in marriage with his daughter Maud to Maurice de Gaunt, who undertook to discharge a debt of 1,200 marks owed by Henry to the king. Maud had died without issue by 1220 when Henry sought to recover the manor from Maurice. The king's court eventually decided that, since Maurice had been given twelve years in which to pay Henry's debt by annual instalments, he should hold Weston until 1225, when Henry should recover possession.[48] Oseney Abbey had meanwhile increased its estate in Weston by a number of small gifts from tenants of the manor.[49] In 1227 Henry d'Oilly sold to Oseney the whole manor with the exception of the manor-house, the mill, and certain demesne lands for 300 marks, which the abbey paid to a creditor of Henry, David the Jew of Oxford.[50] Soon afterwards, probably in 1228, Henry gave the remainder of the manor to Oseney Abbey.[51]

Henry d'Oilly died in 1232,[52] and the overlordship of Weston passed to his nephew Thomas de Newburgh, Earl of Warwick, and followed the same descent as the overlordship of Bucknell.[53] In practice

the overlordship soon lapsed, and the Abbot of Oseney virtually held the manor in chief.[54] About 1260, however, the manor was claimed against the abbot by Roger Damory of Bucknell. At the time of the Domesday survey Robert (I) d'Oilly's tenant at Weston had been Gilbert,[55] probably the ancestor of the Damory family, who also held of Robert at Bucknell, Bletchingdon, and Fulwell. Gilbert's descendants[56] may have held lands at Weston as tenants under the D'Oillys, but although Robert Damory (d. 1236) witnessed grants of land in the manor about 1220,[57] it does not appear that either he or his son Roger held lands there themselves: they were certainly not among the numerous tenants of the manor who granted their lands to Oseney between 1230 and 1270.[58] Roger nevertheless brought his suit, but in 1260 at Beckley, before Richard of Cornwall, he agreed to quitclaim the manor to the abbot for 300 marks.[59] From 1260 until the Dissolution[60] Oseney Abbey remained in undisputed possession of the whole manor with the exception of the 35 acres given to Thame in 1137 and quitclaimed to that abbey by Roger Damory in 1257.[61]

As a reward for his services to Henry VIII, notably as surveyor of monastic lands in Oxfordshire, Sir John Williams of Thame obtained Weston manor in 1540, and in 1546 he purchased certain lands and rents reserved in his original grant.[62] Sir John, later Lord Williams of Thame, died in 1559 leaving Weston to his second wife Margery Wentworth.[63] Margery married secondly Sir William Drury (d. 1579) and thirdly James Croft. On her death in about 1588 Weston passed by the terms of Lord Williams's will to Henry, Lord Norreys, husband of Margery, Lord Williams's younger daughter by his first wife.[64] Lord Norreys, however, allowed James Croft to retain Weston as his tenant. Sir William Norreys, Lord Norreys's eldest son, had died in 1579, and in 1586 his widow Elizabeth married Henry Clinton, Earl of Lincoln.[65] The earl claimed Weston manor as part of his wife's jointure, turned Croft out of the manor-house by force and occupied it himself. Lord Norreys brought an armed band from Rycote to his tenant's help, and after some fighting with the earl's servants Croft was reinstalled. The earl, however, continued his fight in the Star Chamber court from 1590 to 1597. Judgement was finally given in Lord Norreys's favour.[66]

On the latter's death in 1601 Weston passed to his grandson Francis Norreys, later created Earl of Berkshire. Francis married Bridget, daughter of Edward de Vere, Earl of Oxford, by whom he had a

[34] *D.N.B.* under Francis Norreys; Oxf. Dioc. d 557, d 560; Par. Reg.
[35] *V.C.H. Oxon.* ii. 356.   [36] Ibid. i. 414.
[37] *Oxon. Chart.* no. 102.
[38] For the D'Oilly descent see *Oseney Cart.* refs. cited below; W. D. Bayly, *House of D'Oyly* (1845), is inaccurate.
[39] *Oseney Cart.* iv. 416; cf. *Eynsham Cart.* i. 411.
[40] *Thame Cart.* 2.
[41] *Oseney Cart.* i. 1.
[42] *Cal. Chart. R.* 1300–26, 420.
[43] *Thame Cart.* 2.
[44] *Oseney Cart.* i, p. xxv.
[45] *Thame Cart.* 3.
[46] *Oseney Cart.* i. 74.
[47] *Eynsham Cart.* i. 78; cf. *Pipe R.* 1175 (P.R.S. xxii), 12.
[48] *Cur. Reg. R.* viii. 296; ix. 144, 334–6.
[49] *Oseney Cart.* vi. 18–20.
[50] Ibid. 6–10; *Cal. Chart. R.* 1226–57, 48; for David see C. Roth, *Jews of Med. Oxf.* (O.H.S. n.s. ix), 46 sqq.

[51] *Oseney Cart.* vi. 2; *Cal. Chart. R.* 1226–57, 165.
[52] *Oseney Cart.* i, p. xxvi.
[53] *Bk. of Fees*, 831; *Feud. Aids*, iv. 158; see above, p. 73.
[54] *Rot. Hund.* (Rec. Com.), ii. 830.
[55] *V.C.H. Oxon.* i. 414.
[56] See above, p. 58, for details.
[57] *Oseney Cart.* vi. 18.
[58] Ibid. 5, 10–18, 21–26.
[59] Ibid. 3; *Fines Oxon.* 186.
[60] e.g. *Tax. Eccl.* (Rec. Com.), 45; *Valor Eccl.* (Rec. Com.), ii. 216.
[61] *Thame Cart.* 22.
[62] *L. & P. Hen. VIII*, xv, p. 169; xxi (1), p. 354; Dunkin MS. 438/1, f. 178.
[63] N. J. O'Conor, *Godes Peace and the Queenes* (1934), 17.
[64] Ibid.; *Complete Peerage*, ix. 645.
[65] O'Conor, op. cit. 37, 41; *Complete Peerage*, vii. 694.
[66] O'Conor, op. cit. 81; *Acts of P.C.* 1589, 194; ibid. 1597–8, 506.

daughter Elizabeth, who inherited most of his lands on his death in 1624. Weston, however, by virtue of a settlement made in 1619 passed to Francis's illegitimate son Francis Rose, who assumed the name of Norreys after his father's death.[67] Sir Francis, as he became in 1633, was Sheriff of Oxfordshire in 1635 and later M.P. for the county under the Commonwealth. He married Hester, daughter of Sir John Rouse, and was succeeded by his eldest son Sir Edward Norreys on his death in 1669.[68] Sir Edward, many times M.P. for either the county or city of Oxford, died in 1713, when Weston was inherited by his eldest daughter Philadelphia and her husband Captain Henry Bertie, a younger son of James, Earl of Abingdon.[69] In 1734 Captain Bertie was succeeded by his grandson Norreys Bertie, who died unmarried in 1766 and who bequeathed Weston to his greatnephew Peregrine Bertie. Peregrine also left no children, and on his death in 1790 Weston passed to his elder brother Willoughby, Earl of Abingdon, who entailed the manor so that it should only be held by his successors in the earldom if there were no younger brother to hold it. Willoughby was succeeded as Earl of Abingdon in 1799 by his third and eldest surviving son Montague, but Weston under the entail was inherited by his fourth son, the Hon. the Revd. Frederick Arthur Bertie, when the latter came of age. He married Georgina, daughter of Admiral Lord Mark Ker, and was succeeded in 1868 by his son Captain Frederick Arthur Bertie.[70] Captain Bertie's widow, Rose Emily Bertie, sold the manor by auction in 1918 after the death of her only son in action in Palestine in the previous year. The estate has been split up and manorial rights have lapsed.[71]

ECONOMIC AND SOCIAL HISTORY. In 1086 there was land for 12 ploughs in Weston-on-the-Green, all under cultivation. On the demesne were 4 ploughs and 5 serfs, while 17 villeins (*villani*) and 11 bordars had 8 ploughs. There were two mills worth 4s. and the value of the estate had increased £8 to £12 since 1065.[72] In c. 1228 Oseney Abbey acquired the manor from Henry (II) d'Oilly, the latter's grant including the manor-house, a wood and one of the mills, presumably in the north-west of the parish, since meadowland near it was described as 'towards Kirtlington'.[73] In the course of the 13th century Oseney gradually accumulated lands from the freeholders of the manor,[74] and in about 1270 obtained the second mill, a water-mill.[75] Only one mill, however, was recorded among the abbey's possessions in 1279. The demesne then included 5 carucates of land, a park of 4 acres, and a warren. There were only 5 free tenants, including the Abbot of Thame and 3 socagers, holding a little over 10 virgates in all. Nineteen villeins held a virgate each, paid 5s. a year, and worked and were tallaged at their lord's will. They had to pay fines if their sons left the manor,

pay for the right to brew ale and to pasture their swine, and could not sell horses or oxen without licence. Sixteen half-virgaters held by the same services and paid rent at the same rate. Between them they provided 6 labourers all the year round for the abbot, and another 6, who worked every day from Midsummer to Michaelmas except Saturdays. At Christmas they paid their lord half a quarter of oats, and another half-quarter if they did not harrow, and at Candlemas they paid 3d. for being excused carrying services outside the shire. Ten cottars held between them about 5½ virgates. One of them, the miller, paid £1 4s. 3d., and the others paid up to 8s. 3d. a year. Three of them worked at the lord's will, but five of them owed only one autumn boonwork.[76] The population had evidently increased since 1086, and by 1279 there appear to have been about 64 virgates under cultivation.[77]

The rents received by Oseney Abbey in the year 1279–80 amounted to £13 18s. 10d.[78] In 1291 the manor brought in an estimated income of £16 6s. 10½d., while the produce and stock were worth another £5.[79] Like other Oseney manors Weston and its dependent estates at Chesterton and Ardley sent considerable quantities of produce to the abbey—wheat and oats, cattle, pigs and poultry, cheese, butter and eggs, and notably in 1279–80 314 fleeces, 223 sheepskins and 47 lambskins. At Michaelmas 1280 the stock remaining in the bailiwick of Weston, of which the manor was the administrative centre with a canon in residence as bailiff, amounted to 25 horses, 86 cattle, 422 sheep, and 64 pigs.[80] Weston was a two-field village in the 13th century: in a number of grants of land to Oseney the acres were equally divided between the two fields, the South Field and the East Field, the latter called in one grant 'the field towards Chesterton'.[81] There is no indication whether a fixed amount of meadow went with every virgate of arable, but meadow or mowing ground in the headlands of the arable are frequently mentioned,[82] and there were certain lot-meadows.[83] Three crofts were included in Henry d'Oilly's grant in 1228, and others are mentioned later, some of them inclosures of arable.[84] The taxation assessments of the early 14th century show that Weston was among the more prosperous villages in Ploughley hundred: 36 inhabitants were assessed in 1316 and 37 in 1327,[85] and from 1334 onwards the village's assessment was fixed at £3 10s.[86]

At the end of the 15th century the demesne lands were let, but by 1509 they had been taken back into the abbey's hands 'pro husbondria ibidem manutenenda'. The former farmer of the demesne, John Cocks, still held two pastures, 'Roundehill' and 'Churchwestmorelese', for £13 6s. 8d. a year, and had held Sevenacre, a pasture close which had been an arable furlong in the 13th century.[87] It is possible that at Weston Oseney Abbey had resumed control

[67] D.N.B.; P.C.C. 2 Byrde: Earl of Berks.'s will.
[68] D.N.B.; C.P. 25(2)/587/Mich. 1649; C.P. 43/267/52; ibid. 319/210; Hearth Tax Oxon. 197.
[69] D.N.B.; Dunkin, Oxon. ii. 211 sqq.; Complete Peerage, i. 45.
[70] Burke, Land. Gent. (1914); O.R.O. Land tax assess.
[71] Bodl. G.A. Oxon. b 92* (16): Sale Cat.; Kelly's Dir. Oxon. (1920, 1939).
[72] V.C.H. Oxon. i. 414.
[73] Oseney Cart. vi. 2, 6.
[74] Ibid. 5–25 passim.
[75] Ibid. 12.
[76] Rot. Hund. (Rec. Com.), ii. 830–1.

[77] Including 35 a. held by the Abbot of Thame recorded under Oddington: ibid. 836; cf. Thame Cart. i. 22.
[78] Oseney Cart. vi. 192.
[79] Tax. Eccl. (Rec. Com.), 45.
[80] Oseney Cart. vi. 192–3.
[81] Ibid. 14, 16, 17.
[82] Ibid. 14, 17, 21.
[83] Ibid. 12 and n.
[84] Ibid. 2, 11.
[85] E 179/161/8, 9.
[86] E 164/7; see below, p. 359.
[87] Oseney Cart. vi. 229; cf. ibid. 21.

of its demesnes as a check on the activities of an inclosing grazier. In 1521 the demesnes were still in the abbey's hands; and so were the two pastures, where the abbey's own sheep and cattle now grazed.[88] Before 1535, however, the demesnes were again farmed, first to a single tenant and later to a number of tenants. The abbey's gross income from the estate in 1535 was £55 8s. 11d.—£18 15s. 7d. from the rents of customary tenants and £36 13s. 4d. from the farm of the manor, rectory, vicarage, and tithes.[89]

The progress of inclosure at Weston is not documented. Since the Norreys and Bertie lords of the manor owned very nearly the whole parish[90] the decision to inclose must have depended on them. There is no inclosure act, and both open fields and commons appear to have been inclosed about the middle of the 18th century, certainly before 1773.[91] In 1774 the Bertie estate was charged with the payment of annuities to three people 'in lieu of lifehold estates of land in the Common Field granted on inclosing the commons and wastes of Weston'.[92] In 1783 the two surviving annuitants were both about 60 years of age.[93] The number of common fields before inclosure is not known, but a deed of 1803 records that South Field Mead had been inclosed in three parts, 48 acres in all, and there were six inclosures, 107 acres in all, in what was 'formerly the Common South Field'. 'Southill fields' are mentioned as formerly part of the common fields, and Green Close (28 a.) had been part of Weston Green before inclosure.[94]

In 1773 the Bertie estate at Weston was producing £1,941 a year in rents. There were 11 leaseholders, 9 of them paying over £40 a year, 17 cottagers, and 17 tenants of small plots and cottages for one, two, or three lives.[95] There were nine 'farms and grazing land', and two of the leaseholders held the mill and the stone-pits.[96] The total area of the estate was estimated at 2,371 acres in 1783, when there were still nine farms—one called a dairy farm and one a grazing farm—held, however, by seven farmers. The smallest farm was 92 acres, the largest 343 acres, and all the rest were around 200 acres. There were 18 cottagers, and 26 tenants for life, with 3 houses and 21 cottages.[97] There were still nine farms in 1848, some of them with increased area, since the lord of the manor had only 69 acres in hand compared with 602 in 1783.[98] In 1918 there were eight farms—including Weston Park, then in Chesterton parish, and the mill, which had 66 acres attached to it, on the Bertie estate; and another farm on the Valentia estate purchased in 1803.[99] In 1848 there were 1,215 acres of arable to 1,089 acres of meadow and pasture,[1] but by 1867 two-thirds of the parish was said to be arable,[2] a proportion which held good in the 20th century.[3]

In 1801 the population of Weston was 350; by 1851 this had risen to a peak figure of 517. A high proportion of the inhabitants was employed in agriculture during this period, 74 families out of 90 in 1821, and 86 out of 102 in 1831, when there were 99 farm labourers.[4] Many of these were employed outside the parish: in 1867 there were about 40 working on farms in Bletchingdon, Oddington, and Chesterton but living in Weston.[5] Lack of cottages in neighbouring parishes appears to have been the main reason. One serious consequence earlier in the 19th century had been the liability of Weston parish to relieve sick, poor, and aged labourers whose work had been outside. Sums raised by poor rates had risen from £112 in 1776 to about £635 in 1813.[6] Although the cottages of Weston were overcrowded in 1867 they were reported to be 'good and commodious', with good gardens, while all had allotments. Many cottages had outhouses, and all had privies; rents ranged from 3d. to 1s. 3d. a week.[7]

In the 18th century, building-stone, paving- and flooring-stone were quarried in the stone-pits; the Peat Pits, on the western boundary stream, north of the village, were then worth between £40 and £80 a year; and marl was dug for use on the land.[8] In the early 19th century there were fifteen families engaged in trade or handicrafts:[9] of the latter lace-making was the most important and there were 22 women and girls employed in it in 1851.[10] At that date there were also 4 railway navvies, probably employed on the construction of the Bletchley–Oxford line, 3 bricklayers, a 'stoneman', 2 tailors, a shoemaker and a cordwainer, a carpenter, a wagoner, a toll-collector, and the miller, who was also the baker.[11] The number of agricultural labourers declined later in the century when the population dropped steadily from 517 in 1851 to 263 in 1901 and many young men left the village.[12] In 1903 the village had a blacksmith, a carrier, and a wheelwright, and one shopkeeper.[13] There were still a wheelwright and a blacksmith in 1939, when there were two shops, a café, a coal merchant, and a drainage contractor.[14] The population has increased rapidly from 256 in 1921 to 353 in 1931 and 522 in 1951.[15]

CHURCH. There was probably an 11th-century church at Weston. Wigod of Wallingford was followed as lord by Robert d'Oilly, who in 1074 granted two-thirds of his demesne tithes there to his foundation of the church of St. George in Oxford castle.[16]

[88] Oseney Cart. vi. 258–9.
[89] Valor Eccl. (Rec. Com.), ii, 216; see below, p. 351; cf. Oseney Cart. vi. 229, 258–9, for receipts in 1510 and 1521.
[90] The vicarage glebe was very small: Oxf. Archd. Oxon. b 41, f. 142; there was only one freeholder besides the lord of the manor in 1783: MS. Top. Oxon. b 121, f. 157.
[91] MS. Top. Oxon. b 121, ff. 137–8. The court rolls (1606–1768) among the Chancery Masters' exhibits at Ashridge (Herts.) may throw light on this point. They have been extracted from C 103/156, their former reference number.
[92] MS. Top. Oxon. b 121, f. 141.
[93] Ibid. f. 158.
[94] Bodl. MS. D.D. Valentia c 13.
[95] MS. Top. Oxon. b 121, ff. 137–8.
[96] Ibid. ff. 140–1.
[97] Ibid. ff. 157–8; cf. ibid. b 197–9, a 46–47: accounts of bailiff of Weston.

[98] Bodl. Tithe award; cf. O.R.O. Land tax assess.
[99] Bodl. G.A. Oxon. b 92* (16): Sale Cat.
[1] Bodl. Tithe award.
[2] Agric. Rep. 352.
[3] Local inf.
[4] Census, 1801–51.
[5] Agric. Rep. 335, 352.
[6] Dunkin, Oxon. ii. 200.
[7] Agric. Rep. 352.
[8] MS. Top. Oxon. b 121, f. 158.
[9] Census, 1821, 1831.
[10] H.O. 107/1727.
[11] Ibid.
[12] Local inf.; Census, 1851–1901.
[13] Kelly's Dir. Oxon. (1903).
[14] Ibid. (1939).
[15] Census, 1921–51.
[16] V.C.H. Oxon. ii. 160; Oxon. Chart. no. 58.

St. George's church passed in 1149 with all its possessions to Oseney Abbey. Weston church was part of Robert d'Oilly the younger's foundation grant to Oseney Abbey in about 1130,[17] a gift which was soon afterwards several times confirmed.[18] By at least the early 13th century the abbey had appropriated Weston;[19] it retained it until its dissolution in 1539. In 1540 the rectory and advowson were granted with the manor to Sir John Williams of Thame,[20] and followed the manor's descent until its sale in 1918. Since then William Parlour Esq. of Darlington has been patron. An exception to the normal rule of presentation by the lord of the manor occurred in 1601 when the queen presented.[21]

The value of the rectory rose from £8 in 1254[22] to £9 6s. 8d. in 1291.[23] No later valuation has been found, as in 1535 it was valued with the vicarage and manor.[24]

When the vicarage was formed Oseney took almost all the glebe. Two early 13th-century vicars, John and Henry, who possessed some land and a rent of 6s., granted them to Oseney, in return for which the latter was to have his *obit* said in the abbey.[25] The land once belonging to the church evidently became amalgamated with the manor land, and no separate record has been found of it. Before the Reformation Oseney seems to have collected all the tithes; afterwards the lay rector was entitled only to the great tithes, which were commuted in 1848. Peregrine Bertie received a rent-charge of £270 for tithes on 2,226 acres, and Lord Valentia £34 for the tithes on 236 acres belonging to him.[26]

No medieval valuation of the vicarage has been found, showing that in 1291 it must have been worth less than 5 marks.

A vicarage was ordained during the episcopate of Hugh de Welles (1209–35) on the same conditions as Oseney's other vicarages,[27] an arrangement confirmed in 1284 by Bishop Sutton.[28] The vicar was to receive 2 marks a year for his vestment and a certain share of mortuaries and oblations. Otherwise his support was to fall on the abbey: the canons were to provide him with food from their grange in Weston, and he was privileged to eat with the canons when any were present in the parish. They were to provide him with a clerk and a boy, and a horse when he needed to travel on church business; they were to meet all expenses of the church.

This ordination implied a close connexion between the vicar and the abbey, and may have proved unsatisfactory. After 1451 institutions to the vicarage cease, and in the 16th century the church was served by a curate who received a fixed stipend of £5 6s. 8d.,[29]

while Oseney kept the endowment of the vicarage.[30] At an episcopal visitation of this period, the most important complaint was that no distributions were made to the poor,[31] the abbey's responsibility, while nothing was said against the curate. One mid-16th-century curate, frequently mentioned in local wills,[32] remained in the parish for 30 years.[33]

By the 17th century the ordination of the vicarage had been changed. In addition to about an acre of land, the vicar was to have the small tithes and a pension of 6s. 8d. from the Rector of Bletchingdon.[34] In the mid-18th century the vicarage was valued at £34,[35] and in 1808 at £125, a sum derived almost entirely from the small tithes,[36] which were commuted in 1848 for £232.[37]

The history of the church seems to have been uneventful: few records of it survive and even the names of some of the vicars have not been found. By the 18th century the vicars were usually non-resident, perhaps partly because the Vicarage house[38] was considered inadequate. In 1738 John Bertie, a member of the Bertie family of Rycote, was a Student of Christ Church, where he lived, and he served the church himself. He held two services on Sundays, and said that about 50 people took the sacrament given four times a year.[39] His successors were pluralists: James Hakewill, for example, vicar for over fifty years (c. 1746–98), had a curate at Weston while he himself held two other Oxfordshire churches, 'by which means' his income was 'more comfortable' to him.[40]

After 1823 when the Vicarage was enlarged the vicars began to live in the parish.[41] Attendance at church increased during the century, the number of communicants having risen considerably by 1834.[42] In the middle of the century, in spite of the growth of dissent, congregations were good, numbering about 150, but many, it was said, attended both church and chapel.[43]

The church is dedicated to *ST. MARY*,[44] although in the 19th century there was a tradition that it had once been dedicated to St. Bartholomew.[45] The present church is a plain rectangular building dating from the 18th century except for the western tower, which is probably 13th-century and belongs to an earlier medieval church. The tower has a later parapet and has been buttressed at the south-west corner. The original medieval church had three altars, dedicated by the bishop in 1273 to the Virgin, to St. James the Apostle, and to St. Nicholas the Confessor; twenty days' indulgence was granted to all those who gave to these altars.[46] In 1564 the church, 'being in great decay', was reroofed and the seats were

[17] V.C.H. Oxon. ii. 90; Oseney Cart. i. 1.
[18] e.g. Oseney Cart. i. 3, 4.
[19] Lib. Antiq. Welles, 7. For references to medieval presentations see MS. Top. Oxon. d 460.
[20] L. & P. Hen. VIII, xv, p. 169.
[21] Dunkin MS. 438/2, f. 284b, citing Cant. Reg. Whitgift, f. 67.
[22] Lunt, Val. Norw. 313, 508.
[23] Tax. Eccl. (Rec. Com.), 31.
[24] Valor Eccl. (Rec. Com.), ii. 216.
[25] Oseney Cart. vi. 18–21.
[26] Bodl. Tithe award.
[27] Lib. Antiq. Welles, 1–2, 7.
[28] Oseney Cart. vi. 126–7.
[29] Subsidy 1526, 275; Valor Eccl. (Rec. Com.), ii. 223.
[30] Valor Eccl. ii. 216.
[31] Visit. Dioc. Linc. 1517–31, i. 122.
[32] O.A.S. Rep. 1914, 233.

[33] MS. Top. Oxon. c 56, f. 215.
[34] Ibid. c 55, f. 252.
[35] Oxf. Dioc. d 557.
[36] Ibid. c 446, ff. 198–9.
[37] Bodl. Tithe award.
[38] See above, p. 347.
[39] Oxf. Dioc. d 554.
[40] Ibid. d 557.
[41] Ibid. c 435, pp. 414–19; and see above, p. 347. £300 towards the cost was borrowed under Gilbert's Act, 17 Geo. III, c. 53: Oxf. Dioc. c 435, pp. 414–19.
[42] Oxf. Dioc. b 39.
[43] Ibid. c 332, c 344, d 179.
[44] Oseney Cart. vi. 1.
[45] Vicar's letter (1882): MS. Top. Oxon. d 90, ff. 126b–127; Gardner, Dir. Oxon.
[46] Oseney Cart. vi. 1.

renewed.[47] By 1741 it was falling down, and in 1743 and 1744 was rebuilt by Norreys Bertie,[48] whose initials and arms and the date 1743 can be seen on the rainwater heads. The present church has a pedimented south door, built in the classical style with an elaborately carved architrave and frieze on the outside; on the inside, stonework contemporary with the original building still surrounds it. The round-headed windows, four on the north and three on the south side, of the 18th-century church remain.[49] In 1810 extensive repairs were made to the roof, and the original heavily ornamented ceiling fell down and was replaced by the present plain one.[50]

The church was restored in the 1870's by the architect R. P. Spiers for about £500; a plan for building an apse 'to make the building more church-like' was never executed, and the actual work only included repairs to the tower, the addition of the south porch, reseating, and the addition of Gothic tracery and glass to the windows.[51] An organ was bought in 1885[52] and in 1923 the north and south walls were panelled.

The 12th-century font is circular, with interlacing arcading on a moulded circular base of later date.

Above the altar there is a large 18th-century canvas of the Ten Commandments surrounded by cherubs and symbols of the Crucifixion.[53] Other decorations include a Russian triptych of the Virgin and two saints, the Assumption of the Virgin copied from an Italian original, and over the vestry arch an 18th-century Royal Arms in raised and painted plaster. The church also contains a medieval iron cross, given by Lady Greville, and a plaster statue of the Virgin given in 1929.[54] The iron gates at the eastern end of the churchyard were erected in 1951 as a war memorial.

There are a number of monuments to the Norreys family, including those to Sir Francis Norreys (d. 1669); to Sir Edward Norreys (d. 1713), his wife Jane (d. 1722) and their children, to his second son Francis and his wife Jane; and to Norreys Bertie (d. 1766). There are also 19th-century memorials to the Bertie family. In the old church was a monument to Richard Chamberlaine (d. 1624/5), and a brass to Alise Saxeye (d. 1581).[55]

In 1552 the plate consisted of a silver and gilt chalice.[56] In 1955 it included a silver chalice and paten cover of 1751, the gift of Mary Norreys.[57] There were five bells, all 19th-century. Formerly there were three bells, dating from the 15th, 16th, and 17th centuries.[58]

The registers date from 1591, with a gap from 1672 to 1695. There is a churchwardens' book covering the years 1767 to 1917.

NONCONFORMITY. The only early recusant recorded was Joan, the wife of Richard Poure,[59] who was fined in 1603. In the late 18th and early 19th centuries there were a few Roman Catholics, probably not more than one family, who went to chapel at Tusmore.[60]

Protestant dissent appeared soon after this, when in 1818 the first house was licensed for worship.[61] From 1829 the meetings were held in the village shop.[62] The owner, George White, sold the garden to the Methodists for £20, and in 1838 the present chapel was built by the labour of the members themselves.[63] By the middle of the century congregations were large—over 100 in 1851.[64] In 1878 there were said to be 60 professed dissenters, but many people attended both church and chapel.[65] The chapel had eighteen members in 1955.[66]

SCHOOLS. In 1808 there was a small school for 12 to 20 children, who were paid for by their parents.[67] It had apparently closed by 1819,[68] but in 1833 there was a fee-paying school for about 20 children.[69] A Church of England school was opened in 1855;[70] its average attendance was 48 by 1890,[71] and 42 in 1906.[72] The school was taken over by the County Council in 1920 and was reorganized as a junior school in 1937. There were 22 children in the school in 1954 compared with 39 in 1937.[73]

CHARITIES. Sums of money, amounting to £30, were left to the poor of the parish at unknown dates by William and Francis Drake, William Webb, Thomas Croxton, and Hannah Maunde.[74] The interest was distributed to the poor in bread in 1759.[75] The principal, however, was held by Norreys Bertie, who died bankrupt in Ghent in 1766. Peregrine Bertie, his successor as lord of the manor, nevertheless paid £1 10s. a year, which was distributed in meat and bread, until 1772. Only two other payments, in 1781 and 1788, were made before his death in 1790.[76] Although he left £5 for a sermon on 30 January and for prayers on Ash Wednesday and Good Friday,[77] Peregrine Bertie appears to have allowed the charity for the poor to lapse, and although a yearly payment of £1 laid out on bread was recorded in 1805[78] the charity was regarded as lost in 1824.[79]

[47] Oxf. Dioc. c 22, f. 76; MS. Top. Oxon. c 56, f. 227.
[48] Oxf. Archd. Oxon. c 111, f. 7; Oxf. Dioc. c 651, ff. 113–16; see above, p. 349.
[49] A drawing (1820) by J. Buckler (MS. Top. Oxon. a 69, f. 581) shows the unaltered windows. For a view from SE. see plate opposite.
[50] Oxf. Archd. Oxon. c 111, ff. 82, 85–86; Par. Reg.
[51] MS. Top. Oxon. c 104, ff. 451–60; ibid. d 90, f. 128.
[52] Par. Reg.
[53] Par. Rec. terrier (1934).   [54] Par. Reg.
[55] For list see Dunkin, Oxon. ii. 200–3; for arms, transcripts of inscriptions, and plans of ledgers in church see Bodl. G.A. Oxon 4° 689, p. 335; ibid. 16° 217, p. 251; Bodl. 17031 e 17, pp. 185–96.
[56] Chant. Cert. 77–78.
[57] Evans, Ch. Plate.
[58] Ch. Bells Oxon. iv. 437.
[59] Salter, Oxon. Recusants, 16.
[60] Oxf. Dioc. d 560, d 575, d 577; ibid. c 327, p. 307.
[61] Ibid. c 644, f. 198. Another house was licensed in 1819: ibid. f. 203. Neither of the petitioners could write.

[62] Ibid. c 645, f. 142.
[63] For account of building of church see Weston on the Green, Methodist Church Centenary (1938).
[64] H.O. 129/158.
[65] Oxf. Dioc. c 332, c 344.
[66] Buckingham and Brackley Methodist Circuit Plan, 1955–6.
[67] Oxf. Dioc. d 707.
[68] Educ. of Poor, 732.
[69] Educ. Enq. Abstract, 757.
[70] Vol. Sch. Ret.
[71] Ret. of Sch.
[72] Vol. Sch. Ret.
[73] Inf. Oxon. Educ. Cttee.
[74] 12th Rep. Com. Char. 315; Char. Don. ii. 990. For Croxton see MS. Top. Oxon. c 55, f. 252.
[75] Oxf. Dioc. d 557.
[76] 12th Rep. Com. Char. 315; Char. Don. ii. 990.
[77] Oxf. Dioc. c 327, p. 74.
[78] Ibid. p. 363.
[79] 12th Rep. Com. Char. 315.

South-east view of the church in the mid-19th century

WESTON-ON-THE-GREEN

South-east view of the church in 1820

WENDLEBURY

STATISTICAL MATERIAL
FOR PLOUGHLEY HUNDRED

STATISTICAL MATERIAL FOR THE VILLAGES AND HAMLETS OF PLOUGHLEY HUNDRED 1086-1768

ESTATES AND TENANTS IN 1086 AND 1279

THE following table shows the number of Domesday estates and the number of recorded persons working on them in 1086; and the number of manors and lesser estates in 1279 with the numbers of free and unfree tenants attached to them.

	DOMESDAY SURVEY 1086[a]					HUNDRED ROLLS SURVEY 1279[b]						
	No. of estates	Villani	Bordars	Serfs	Total no. of tenants	No. of manors	No. of lesser estates	Free tenants	Nativi	Servi	Cottars	Total no. of tenants
Ardley	1	8	15	..	23	1	..	5	9	..	..	14
Bicester	1	28	14	5	[c]	1	..	3	14	..	..	17
Bignell	..	..	..	..		2	..	7	23	..	..	30
Wretchwick	1	..	..	..	[d]	1	..	..	25	..	7	32
TOTAL	2	28	14	5	47	4	..	10	62	..	7	79
Bletchingdon	2	9	7	7	23	2	1	18	20	..	..	38
Boycott (Bucks.)[e]	1	1	..	..	1	1	..	..	13	..	6	19
Bucknell	1	6	3	3	12	1	2	2	13	..	4	19
Saxenton	2	9	4	..	13	..	..	2	9	..	..	11
TOTAL	3	15	7	3	25	1	2	4	22	..	4	30
Charlton	1	..	..	..	..	1	1	5	26	..	2	33
Fencott	..	..	..	..	..	..	..	2	30	..	8	40
Murcott	..	..	..	..	..	..	..	1	..	..	..	1
TOTAL	1	15	11	6	32	1	1	8	56	..	10	74
Chesterton, Great	1	..	..	..	..	1	..	3	24	..	28	55[f]
„ , Little	..	..	..	..	..	..	..	2	8	..	..	10
TOTAL	1	22	10	2	34	1	..	5	32	..	28	65
Cottisford	1	10	5	..	15	1	1	5	15	..	1	21
Finmere	2	10	5	4	19	1	..	4	29	..	..	33
Fringford	2	18	8	4	30	2	..	4	19	..	8	31
Fritwell	2	12	7	3	22	2	..	11	14	14	5	44
Godington	1	16	2	1	19	1	2	7	21	..	6	34
Hampton Gay	2	1	..	..	1	1	..	8	2	..	..	10
Hampton Poyle	1	7	2	2	11	1	..	6	15	..	7	28
Hardwick	1[g]	5	2	..	7	1	2	2	8	..	..	10
Hethe	1	8	5	1	14	1	1	1	..	26	2	29
Heyford, Lower	2	..	..	..	..	2	..	1	..	..	19	20
Caulcott	..	..	..	..	..	..	1	6	33	..	..	39
TOTAL	2	11	12	5	28	2	1	7	33	..	19	59
Heyford, Upper	1	10	1	3	14	1	..	..	31[h]	..	7	38
Islip	1	10	5	2	17	1	..	6	..	34	..	40
Kirtlington	4	42	25	4	71	1	4	36	40	..	2	78
Northbrook	1	2	..	1	3	1	..	6	9	..	1	16
TOTAL	5	44	25	5	74	2	4	42	49	..	3	94

[a] *V.C.H. Oxon.* i. 400–28.
[b] *Rot. Hund.* (Rec. Com.), ii. 822–38.
[c] Probably included in Kirtlington.
[d] Included in Bicester.
[e] See above, p. 3.
[f] Represents probable minimum; see above, p. 96.
[g] By 1279 Tusmore included 2½ hides of Hardwick.
[h] Seven of the 31 also held cottages and are listed twice.

	DOMESDAY SURVEY 1086[a]					HUNDRED ROLLS SURVEY 1279[b]						
	No. of estates	Villani	Bordars	Serfs	Total no. of tenants	No. of manors	No. of lesser estates	Free tenants	Nativi	Servi	Cottars	Total no. of tenants
Launton . .	1	..	..	..	..	1	..	..	64	..	..	64
Lillingstone Lovell (Bucks.)[c] . .	2	8	2	1	11	3	..	16	10	..	15	41
Middleton Stoney	1	25	7	5	37	1	..	18[d]	27	..	..	45
Mixbury . .	1	18	11	1	30	1	..	..	37	..	11	48
Fulwell . .	1	3	2	1	6	1	..	..	..	..	7	7
Willaston . .	..	..	..	..	..	1	..	..	18	..	1	19
TOTAL	2	21	13	2	36	3	..	..	55	..	19	74
Newton Purcell .	..	..	..	..	..	1	..	7	9	..	6	22
Noke . . .	2[e]	3	6	2	11	2	..	8	15	..	6	29
Oddington . .	1	10	4	2	16	2	2	1	13	..	..	14
Shelswell . .	1	7	7	2	16	1	..	3	7	..	..	10
Somerton . .	3	17	9	2	28	2	..	15	28	..	..	43
Northbrook .	2	9	5	..	14	..	2	..	..	..	..	..
TOTAL	5	26	14	2	42	2	2	15	28	..	..	43
Souldern . .	..	..	..	..	..	1	..	7	25	..	..	32
Stoke Lyne .	1[f]	34	9	2	45	2	..	6	14	13	2	35
Bainton . .	1	1	2	..	3	1	..	5	11	..	..	16
Fewcot . .	..	..	..	..	..	..	4	4	..	6	..	10
TOTAL	2	35	11	2	48	3	4	15	25	19	2	61
Stratton Audley .	1	8	2	1	11	2	1	6	44	..	8	58
Tusmore .	1[f]	..	..	..	..	2	3	1	..	10	9	20
Wendlebury .	1	4	5	3	12	2	2	9	13	..	..	22
Weston . .	1	17	11	5	33	1	..	5	35	..	10	50
TOTAL	54	424	225	80	729	55	29	264	820	103	188	1,375

Holders of *burgagii* are recorded only at Middleton Stoney, and the men known to have been 'living on the market' at Bicester were not recorded.[g] The villein tenants included *nativi*, *servi*, *cottagarii*, *cottarii*, and *coterelli*. Generally speaking *nativi* and *servi* appear to be alternative words for the class of villeins who held a virgate or half-virgate. At Stoke Lyne, for instance, where there were two manors, the virgaters were listed as *nativi* on one and as *servi* on the other, and their recorded services were the same in each case.[h] The other three classes of tenants have all been tabulated as cottars. Though there may have been some differences in status, the survey makes no clear distinction between them. At Wretchwick the list of those holding either cotlands or cottages is headed *coterelli*: the cotlander owes services and a higher rent than the cottager, who has no recorded services.[i] At Stoke those described as *cottagarii* are distinguished from the holders of cotlands, who mostly owed the same services as the half-virgaters, but paid 6s. rent instead of 5s. At Heyford the *nativi* all held cotlands.[j] In other places where tenants of cotlands are listed with the *nativi* or *servi* it appears to be merely a case of the lack of precision which often characterizes the survey.[k] Lillingstone Lovell and a few other villages had free cottars.[l]

The survey of 1279 for this hundred gives a very detailed tenurial picture compared with that of many other hundreds, but evidence from other sources shows that in at least some cases it is unreliable.[m] It contains also a number of scribal errors, such as omissions and duplications of names, which make any accurate reconstruction of the system of tenure difficult.[n]

As a basis for the assessment of population in 1086 or 1279 the preceding figures are unsatisfactory. The difficulties with regard to the interpretation of the Domesday figures are well known and there is no reason to suppose that they were any more accurate than those of 1279. Both surveys recorded only a few of the existing priests, and even if it is assumed that most tenants were heads of families, the size of the average family can only be conjectured and there is no clue to the number of

[a] *V.C.H. Oxon.* i. 400–28.
[b] *Rot. Hund.* (Rec. Com.), ii. 822–38.
[c] See above, p. 3.
[d] Fourteen held *burgagii*.
[e] The Westminster estate of Noke is not recorded.
[f] Three virgates in Stoke Lyne formed half of the Tusmore estate.
[g] See above, p. 25.   [h] *Rot. Hund.* (Rec. Com.), ii. 825.

[i] Ibid. 828.   [j] Ibid. 825, 826.
[k] Holders of a few acres only or of messuages are often classed as cottars, e.g. at Stratton: ibid. 828.
[l] Ibid. 826, 834, 835.   [m] See above, pp. 149, 213.
[n] e.g. Hethe: *Rot. Hund.* (Rec. Com.), ii. 837; Hampton Gay: ibid. 836; Tusmore: ibid. 825. For total numbers cf. E. A. Kosminsky, *Studies in the Agrarian Hist. of England in the 13th Century*, 205.

household servants, which other medieval sources indicate to have been generally numerous. Moreover, in the preceding table a few free tenants are duplicated, as they held more than one holding, either in the same or in different parishes, and there are a few villeins who also held cottages and have therefore been reckoned twice over in the list of tenants.[a]

HONORS AND KNIGHTS' FEES (MID-13TH CENTURY)

Honor and overlord	Manors	Fees	Mesne lords	Tenants
WALLING-FORD EARL OF CORNWALL	Bicester Wretchwick Stratton Audley Chesterton Lower Heyford Upper Heyford	.. 2 .. 2 1 1	.. Longespée	Longespée Audley Audley De Chesterton De La Mare Redvers
D'OILLY EARL OF WARWICK	Bletchingdon Bucknell and part of Tusmore Fulwell Hardwick Kirtlington Tusmore Weston-on-the-Green	1 1 1 1 ½ ½ 2	.. Damory Damory Fitz Wyth .. Fitz Wyth ? Damory	Damory { Damory { Pateshull Oseney Abbey Aundeley { Dives { De La Grave Aundeley Oseney Abbey
ARSIC	Fringford Fritwell Newton Purcell Somerton	.. .. Sergeanty ..	.. .. Grey ..	{ Grey { Gardiner Grey Purcel { Grey { Gardiner
CHESTER EARL OF ARUNDEL	Ardley with Northbrook in Somerton	1	Earl of Warwick	Fitz Wyth
RICHARD'S CASTLE MORTIMER	Souldern	..	..	De Arderne
GIFFARD	Stoke Lyne with lands in Tusmore	{ 1 ½ }	Earl of Oxford	{ De Lisle { De Cokefield
HONOR OF GLOUCESTER	Finmere Hampton Gay with Otley in Oddington Hethe Lower Heyford Newton Purcel Shelswell	1 ½ ½ .. 1	 Champernoun .. Champernoun ..	De Turri—De Broke { De Gay—Oseney { Thame Abbey De Verdun Henred { Purcel { De Weston { De Newton
HONOR OF ST. VALERY	Hampton Gay Mixbury Newton Purcell Willaston	½ 1½ ½ ½	.. ..	De Gay—Oseney Abbey Oseney Abbey Purcel (demesne manor)
ISLIP LIBERTY	Islip with Fencott and Murcott Launton Northbrook in Kirtlington Noke Oddington	.. .. ¼ ½ ½	.. ..	.. .. De Gay De Williamscote Le Poure

[a] e.g. Kirtlington: *Rot. Hund.* (Rec. Com.), ii. 822–3.

Honor and overlord	Manors	Fees	Mesne lords	Tenants
DEVON AND THE ISLE	Fritwell Noke	.. ½	.. ..	Foliot Foliot
HONOR OF WARENNE	Stratton Audley	¼	..	Gargate—Bicester Priory
STAFFORD DE STAFFORD	Bletchingdon	½ (Mortain)	Grenvile	Prescote
MANDEVILLE EARL OF HEREFORD	Wendlebury	2	De Oseville	{ St. Fey { Fitz Aumary
ANCIENT DEMESNE	Kirtlington ⎫ Bignell ⎭	½	Tenants in chief	{ Basset { Le Bret—De Langley

LESSER TENANTS IN CHIEF	Godington
	Middleton Stoney
	Bainton
	Cottisford
	Charlton
	
	Hampton Poyle
	
	Bletchingdon
	
	'Saxinton'
		..
		..
		..
		free alms
		free alms
		
		1
		
		Sergeanty
		
		..
			Longespée
			Longespée
			De Hampden
			Abbey of Bec
			Abbey of St. Évroul—
			   Priory of Ware
			De Hampton—De la
			   Poyle
			Grenevile—Prescote
			
			Boffin
				Camville
				..
				Carbonel
				Priory of Ogbourne
				Le Poure
				
				..
				
				De Blakeville

VILLAGE TAX ASSESSMENTS AND NUMBERS OF CONTRIBUTORS 1306–1523

	1306[a] a 30th		1316[b] a 16th		1327[c] a 20th		1377[d] Poll Tax	1415[e] a 15th	1523 Lay Subsidy 1st payment[f]		1523 Lay Subsidy 2nd payment[g]	
	£ s. d.	Contributors	£ s. d.	Contributors	£ s. d.	Contributors	Contributors	£ s. d.	£ s. d.	Contributors	£ s. d.	Contributors
Ardley	1 19 10½	25	7 1 2	53[h]	2 0 8	20	..	2 12 5	8 8	10	6 6	7
Bicester, Market End	1 15 0¾	21	9 1 7	122	7 6 10	106	140	10 19 10	9 15 11	84	8 3 4	53
King's End	..	..	4 18 10	35	3 18 5	28	73	5 5 2	1 0 10	21	18 0	15
Bignell	*1 2 6½*	*23+*	2 0 11	11	1 13 5	9	19	2 3 11	3 0 8	3	3 0 4	2
Wretchwick	(10 9½)	5+	..	..	..	..	..	..	..	..	..	..
Total	(3 8 4¾)	49+	16 1 4	168	12 18 5	144	232	18 8 11	13 17 5	108	12 1 8	70
Bletchingdon	2 14 10	13+	3 9 1	35	4 4 10	26	100	6 7 8[i]	9 4 6	37	8 11 2	40
Boycott (Bucks.)[j]	12 10¾	11	1 6 4	13	3 12 5	35[k]	24	1 12 4	..	..	..	..
Bucknell and Saxenton	*2 5 8*	*27*	3 0 3	26	3 10 7	37	92	5 0 6	4 1 8	15	3 17 10	12
Charlton	3 19 6¼	31	4 13 1	28	4 10 8	25	..	6 10 7	10 6	17	10 10	14
Fencott	2 0 11	17	1 15 9	16	2 3 4	16	40	} 5 7 2	11 8	11	10 10	12
Murcott	(1 1 5¾)	8+	1 15 10	15	2 11 4	17	..		11 2	15	10 0	13
Total	(7 1 11)	56+	8 4 8	59	9 5 4	58	..	11 17 9	1 13 4	43	1 10 10	39
Chesterton, Great	*1 10 11½*	*11+*	..	..	..	..	..	..	..	..	..	..
Little	(1 5 10¼)	17+	..	..	..	..	..	..	..	..	..	..
Total	(2 16 9¾)	28+	6 10 5	44	5 10 6	45	79	6 6 2	9 5 6	22	9 3 0	20
Cottisford	1 10 7¼	15	2 0 5	16	1 5 2	15	27	1 16 0	7 5 8	10	6 0 8	4
Finmere	(16 0½)	12+	3 17 6	29	4 4 7	32	..	5 3 0	15 4	21	15 8	21
Fringford	(15 0¼)	13+	3 15 7	31	2 10 0	22	..	3 5 4	1 9 4	25	1 10 2	25
Fritwell	*2 14 6½*	*22+*	6 2 5	34	3 10 10	32	60	5 6 6	5 3 2	17	4 0 6	21
Godington	1 19 5	19	2 8 4	16	2 1 5	23	43	2 17 4	1 14 10	8	1 16 2	10
Hampton Gay	1 1 4½	9	1 0 9	12	19 10	12	..	6 7 8[i]	4 6 0	7	4 3 8	6
Hampton Poyle	1 8 8¼	22	2 12 0	25	2 13 6	25	67	5 2 8[l]	2 17 8	13	2 15 8	13
Hardwick	18 5¼	10+	7 1 2	53[h]	2 0 8	17	37	2 9 10	1 13 4	7	1 13 4	7
Hethe	..	..	2 18 6	29	2 7 0	16	..	3 6 0	9 2	11	9 8	13
Heyford, Lower	*1 9 9¼*	*19+*	2 0 9	13	1 12 8	20	..	..	..	..	..	..
Caulcott	(11 8½)	14+	3 16 9	28	2 13 7	28	..	..	..	..	..	..
Total	(2 1 5¾)	33+	5 17 6	41	4 6 3	48	84	5 13 4	3 5 6	23	2 17 8	17

Heyford, Upper	1 16 10	28	4 10 10	38	3 0 4	34	56[m]	4 15 4	1 8 4	25	1 6 10	23
Islip	*4 6 10¼*	*26+*	5 8 6	39	4 14 2	44	..	6 2 8	6 2 10	49	5 18 6	41
Kirtlington	..	41+	5 8 9	36	4 8 3	31	..	5 18 8	..	..	..	..
Northbrook	(9 8)	11	(1 4 9)	12	1 6 1	13	..	1 4 2	..	..	..	..
Total	3 18 0	52+	(6 13 6)	48	5 14 9	44	..	7 2 10	9 7 10	53	7 17 0	57
Launton	*3 18 8¾*	*24+*	5 5 1	49	4 17 0	54	..	6 2 1	2 18 8	34	3 0 10	33
Lillingstone Lovell (Bucks.)[j]	(18 1½)	21+	2 9 4	21	3 12 5	35	..	3 13 5	7 16 0	24	8 0 2	25
Middleton Stoney	2 6 10¼	29	2 6 4	31	2 10 6	35	..	4 15 8	15 4	11	1 2 4	25
Mixbury and Fulwell	*3 17 5¾*	*32+*	3 9 6	27	2 0 9	24	80	1 13 8	..	..	..	..
Willaston	*1 0 0½*	*16+*	1 10 3	13	1 1 0	10	32	15 0	..	..	..	..
Total	*4 17 6¼*	*47+*	4 19 9	40	3 1 9	34	112	2 8 8	2 6 0	27	2 5 0	25
Newton Purcell	17 11¼	12	1 2 4	9	1 1 6	11	..	1 14 10	6 10	7	8 2	7
Noke	2 11 2½	22	3 2 5	22	3 3 6	29	43	1 19 9[l]	17 0	18	12 0	15
Oddington	(1 11 1½)	22+	3 2 8	26	2 15 0	32	72	3 10 0	17 10	17	18 2	20
Shelswell	12 0¼	10	1 6 0	14	1 2 8	11	10	1 9 8	2 4 10	6	1 17 4	6
Somerton	(1 8 11¼)	31+	6 3 0	53	3 17 0	29	108	5 12 0	13 15 8	36	13 5 8	39
Souldern	(1 14 3½)	22+	4 7 0	34	3 7 6	31	92	5 2 7	3 3 0	26	3 4 4	26
Stoke Lyne	1 18 3	12	3 11 5	30	1 15 5	23	..	3 16 1	13 0	9	15 4	8
Bainton	1 5 10½	18	2 10 3	18	} 4 1 10[n]	31	..	{ 2 15 9	1 16 0	6	1 12 8	5
Fewcot	5 7¾	5	13 11	8				{ 1 0 6	11 2	3	10 8	3
Total	4 5 9¼	35	6 15 7	56	5 17 3[n]	54	69	7 12 4	3 0 2	18	2 18 8	16
Stratton Audley	*3 1 7½*	*45+*	..	..	..	..	144	..	2 11 9	33	2 10 10	35
Tusmore	(5 0½)	5+	7 1 2	53[h]	12 8	7	..	1 1 6	..	..	..	..
Wendlebury	..	..	4 8 9	24	3 12 4	23	59	5 2 8	1 0 10	18	19 4	17
Weston-on-the-Green	(1 11 0¾)	15+	5 3 0	36	3 17 6	37	..	3 10 10	1 18 6	34	1 15 10	25

\+ Mutilated: number of names incomplete
Italics. Rubric missing, village identified by the names of contributors.
( ) Mutilated. The total given is the sum of the surviving payments.

[a] E 179/161/10.
[b] E 179/161/8.
[c] E 179/161/9. For these Edwardian taxes, see J. F. Willard, *E.H.R.* xviii. 517–21; xxix. 317–21; xxx. 69–74.
[d] E 179/161/39; E 179/161/40. The receipts for the hundred are incomplete: some are missing and others are illegible or partly destroyed. No lists of contributors have survived.
[e] E 164/7: an example of the assessments fixed in 1334. Cf. E 179/161/17.
[f] E 179/161/204. Cf. E 179/161/198.
[g] E 179/161/176. See *V.C.H. Oxon.* v. 319.
[h] Total for Ardley, Hardwick, and Tusmore.
[i] Total for Bletchingdon and Hampton Gay.
[j] See above, p. 3.
[k] Total for Lillingstone Lovell and Boycott.
[l] Includes the 'non geldable' half of Noke (i.e. Westminster's manor).
[m] The name of the village on the receipt is partly illegible, but 'constable de —ford et John Heyford' can be read.
[n] Part of Tusmore included with Bainton and Fewcot.

CLERICAL AND SECULAR RETURNS
FROM 1662 TO 1811

In the following table the first column shows the total number of householders (including those exempted) returned for each village and hamlet in Ploughley hundred in accordance with the Act of 1662 for establishing an additional revenue.[a] These returns are the fullest of any made for the Oxfordshire hearth taxes. In spite of intervening attempts to tighten up the administration, the figures returned in 1665 show a decline of from 30 to 50 per cent.[b] The second column gives the number of conformists, papists, and non-conformists of sixteen years and over returned by the incumbents in 1676 in response to Archbishop Compton's request.[c] The third and fourth columns contain the clerical answers made in 1738 and 1768 to the bishop's question 'What number of houses doth it [i.e. the parish] comprehend?' The numbers of houses and families recorded in the official census of 1811 are listed in the fifth and sixth columns.

	HEARTH[d] TAX 1662	COMPTON[e] CENSUS 1676	DIOCESAN RETURNS[f] 1738		1768		CENSUS RETURNS 1811	
	Householders	Adults	Houses	Inhabitants	Houses	Inhabitants	Inhabited houses	Families
Ardley	11	51	19[g]	..	c. 20	..	28	30
Bicester, Market End .	112	..	..	..	305	..	377	438
King's End .	12	..	..	..	..	..	47	60
Bignell . .	..	..	..	..	2	..	..	..
Wretchwick .	..	..	..	..	5	..	..	..
Total	124	844	c. 400[g]	..	400–500[h]	..	424	498
Bletchingdon . . .	31	160	c. 60[i]	..	42[j]	..	109	116
Boycott (Bucks.)[k] . .	6	..	..	..	..	..	5	5
Bucknell . . .	23	78	28	..	18[l]	..	43	45
Charlton . . .	24	..	..	..	..	..	61	75
Fencott . . .	29	..	..	..	..	..	57	59
Murcott . . .								
Total	53	228	95	450	c. 80	..	118	134
Chesterton, Great . .	..	..	32	..	..	..	..	..
Little . .	..	..	11	..	..	..	..	..
Total	28	82	43	..	c. 50	..	73	85
Cottisford . . .	9	46	13	..	c. 18	99	32	33
Finmere . . .	28	81	34	..	c. 40	219	54	72
Fringford . . .	35	105	34	..	42	223	52	57
Fritwell . . .	40	252	66	..	c. 66	..	85	85
Godington . . .	9	65	16	..	c. 13[m]	..	22	22
Hampton Gay . . .	10	28	..	..	..	..	13	17
Hampton Poyle . .	17	63	..	..	c. 21	..	22	24
Hardwick . . .	2	23	5	..	11[h]	..	14[n]	16[n]
Hethe . . .	25	203	c. 49	..	c. 25[h]	200	67	59
Heyford, Lower . .	..	..	41	..	..	..	..	..
Caulcott . .	..	..	12	..	..	..	..	..
Total	39	148	53	240	70[o]	360[o]	71	71
Heyford, Upper . .	20	78	32	..	c. 30	..	55	56
Islip	65	207	c. 100[g]	..	c. 140	..	137	139

[a] *Statutes of the Realm*, v. 390–3.
[b] Ibid. 493–5. For a comparative table of figures for 1662 and 1665 see *Hearth Tax Oxon.* 235.
[c] For a discussion about the use of the Census for estimating population see D. V. Glass, 'Greg. King's Estimates of the Pop. of Engl. and Wales,' *Pop. Studies,* iii (4), 338–74.
[d] E 179/255/4 (constables' returns). Cf. *Hearth Tax Oxon.* 235.
[e] Compton Census.
[f] Oxf. Dioc. d 552–4, d 558–60.

[g] Number of families.
[h] Oxf. Dioc. d 561–3: 1771 return as no figure given in 1768.
[i] Some of which were stated to be empty.
[j] Cf. 60 houses returned in 1771: Oxf. Dioc. d 561.
[k] See above, p. 3.
[l] Cf. 35 houses given in 1771: Oxf. Dioc. d 561.
[m] Inf. given in return for Middleton Stoney.
[n] Hardwick and Tusmore are combined.
[o] Oxf. Dioc. d 564: 1774 return as no figure given in 1768.

	HEARTH[a] TAX 1662	COMPTON[b] CENSUS 1676	DIOCESAN RETURNS[c] 1738		1768		CENSUS RETURNS 1811	
	Householders	Adults	Houses	Inhabitants	Houses	Inhabitants	Inhabited houses	Families
Kirtlington	..	..	92	..	c. 90[d]	..	..	..
Northbrook	..	..	7	..	..	..	..	..
Total	65	285	99	..	c. 90	..	115	131
Launton	46	151	70	..	..	..	66	86
Lillingstone Lovell (Bucks.)[e]	27	64	c. 22	..	32[f]	..	31	31
Middleton Stoney	28	90	c. 40	..	40–50[f]	..	70	73
Mixbury	..	..	40	..	c. 60	..	..	..
Fulwell	..	..	2	..	..	..	..	..
Willaston	..	..	2	..	1	..	..	..
Total	34	106	44	..	c. 61	..	74	73
Newton Purcell	17	60	12	..	22[g]	..	24	24
Noke	25	43	c. 20	..	c. 30	..	31	31
Oddington	16	105	25	..	30[h]	..	34	34
Shelswell	2	21	4	..	3[g]	..	7	7
Somerton	26	242	c. 40	..	c. 40	..	55	55
Souldern	25	130	c. 50	..	60	..	93	96
Stoke Lyne	20	166	37	..	40[f]	..	71	77
Bainton	..	..	..	..	..	..	..	..
Fewcot	..	..	..	..	..	..	..	..
Stratton Audley	41	126	50–60	..	..	..	60	63
Tusmore	1	..	..	..	..	..	i	i
Wendlebury	25	101	32	..	35	..	36	43
Weston-on-the-Green	51	125	50	..	50	..	82	85
Total	1,024	4,557	j	j	..	..	2,273	2,473

In cases where there is other contemporary evidence for assessing the number of families in a village, it has been found that the Oxfordshire hearth-tax figures give far fewer.[k] This is not surprising as the tax is known to have been very unpopular, to have been 'much obstructed for want of true and just accounts' from the occupiers of houses, and by the 'negligence' of the constables.[l]

The accuracy of the clerical returns was likely to vary in proportion to the degree of conscientiousness possessed by the various incumbents. In the 18th-century returns the frequency of the appearance of round numbers and the use of terms such as 'about' or 'upwards of' certainly suggests that the returns were only approximately accurate.

[a] E 179/255/4 (constables' returns). Cf. *Hearth Tax Oxon.* 235.
[b] Compton Census.
[c] Oxf. Dioc. d 552–4, d 558–60.
[d] Oxf. Dioc. d 561–3: 1771 return as no figure given in 1768.
[e] See above, p. 3.
[f] Oxf. Dioc. d 555–7: 1759 return as no figure given in 1768.

[g] Number of families.
[h] Number of houses and families.
[i] Hardwick and Tusmore are combined.
[j] No total given as parish returns are incomplete.
[k] See above, pp. 34, 113, and *Hearth Tax Oxon.* pp. xvii, 256–9.
[l] *Statutes of the Realm*, v. 493–5.

INDEX

NOTE. The following abbreviations have been used: abp., archbishop; Abr., Abraham; acct., account; admin., administration; adv. (advs.), advowson(s); Alex., Alexander; Alf., Alfred; And., Andrew; Ant., Anthony; archd., archdeacon; Art., Arthur; b., born; Baldw., Baldwin; Bart., Bartholomew; Ben., Benjamin; Bern., Bernard; bldg., building; bnss., baroness; bp., bishop; Brig.-Gen., Brigadier-General; bro., brother; bt., baronet; c., circa; Cath., Catherine; cent., century; ch. (chs.), church(es); ch. bldg., church building; ch. hist., church history; chap. (chaps.), chapel(s); char. (chars.), charity (charities); Chas., Charles; chpl., chaplain; civ. par., civil parish; civ. war, civil war; clk., clerk; coll., college; Compt. cens., Compton census; const., constable; ct. (cts.), court(s); ctss., countess; cttee., committee; d., died; Dan., Daniel; dau., daughter; Dav., David; dchss., duchess; depop., depopulation; dom. arch., domestic architecture; Dot., Dorothy; ec. hist., economic history; Edm., Edmund; Edw., Edward; Eliz., Elizabeth; est. (ests.), estate(s); f., father; fl., flourished; Fr., Father; Fred., Frederick; Gab., Gabriel; Geo., George; Geof., Geoffrey; geol., geology; Gil., Gilbert; grddau., granddaughter; grds., grandson; Greg., Gregory; Hen., Henry; Herb., Herbert; ho. (hos.), house(s); hon., honor; hosp., hospital; How., Howard; Humph., Humphrey; hund. (hunds.), hundred(s); incl., inclosure; Jas., James; Jon., Jonathan; Jos., Joseph; jr., junior; jurisd., jurisdiction; Kath., Katharine; Laur., Laurence; Lawr., Lawrence; ld., lord; Len., Lennard; Leon., Leonard; Lew., Lewis; m., married; Magd., Magdalen; Maj., Major; Maj.-Gen., Major-General; man., manor; man. ho., manor house; Marg., Margaret; Mat., Matthew; Max., Maximilian; mchss., marchioness; med., medieval; Mic., Michael; mkt., market; mod., modern; mqss., marquess; Nat., Nathaniel; Nic., Nicholas; noncf., nonconformity; occs., occupations; Osw., Oswald; Oxf., Oxford; P.N., Place Names; par. (pars.), parish(es); par. govt., parish government; Pet., Peter; Phil., Philip; pk., park; pncss., princess; poor rel., poor relief; pop., population; preb., prebendary; pres., president; princ., principal; profssns., professions; prop., property; Prot. noncf., Protestant nonconformity; prov., provost; prss. (prsses.), prioress(es); quad., quadrangle; r., rector; R.C., Roman Catholic; rcty., rectory; Rcty. (Recties.), Rectory (Rectories) (building); rds., roads; Reg., Reginald; Revd., Reverend; Reyn., Reynold; Ric., Richard; riv., river; rlwy., railway; Rob., Robert; Rog., Roger; Rom. Cathm., Roman Catholicism; s., son; Sam., Samuel; sch. (schs.), school(s); Seb., Sebastian; Sim., Simon; sis., sister; soc., society; soc. conds., social conditions; Sol., Solomon; sr., senior; st., street; Steph., Stephen; Theoph., Theophilus; Thos., Thomas; Tim., Timothy; top., topography; v., vicar; vct., viscount; vctss., viscountess; Vic., Vicarage (building); vics., vicars; vill. (vills.), village(s); Vinc., Vincent; w., wife; Wal., Walter; ward. (wards.), warden(s); wd. (wds.), wood(s); wid., widow; Wm., William; yeo. fam., yeoman family.

ADDENDA AND CORRIGENDA TO VOLUME V

Page xv, line 2 from end, *for* Mis *read* Miss

  ,,   4, line 8, *for* 1492 *read* 1592

  ,,   11*a*, lines 9–12, *for* He was dead by 1566 . . . was in possession.[1] *read* In 1566 he and his mother are found dealing with the manor of Tiddington.[99] In 1580 he was still in possession[1]

  ,,   11*a*, line 15, *for* presumably *read* later

  ,,   33*b*, line 8 from end, *for* Sir Beauchamp *read* Sir John Beauchamp

  ,,   55*a*, line 5, *delete* the vicar of Great Milton,

  ,,   55*a*, line 6, *after* walked over *add* from Stadhampton, where he lived,

  ,,   100*b*, line 2 from end, *for* Only a fireplace *read* Nothing

  ,,   104*b*, line 19 from end, *for* vice-principal *read* principal

  ,,   106*a*, note 2, *for* Snerd *read* Sneyd

  ,,   109*a*, line 16 from end, *for* in High Street *read* on Vicarage Hill

  ,,   109*a*, line 12 from end, *for* Moreland *read* Morland

  ,,   115*a*, line 15, *for* Archibald *read* Abraham

  ,,   115*b*, line 18 from end, *after* all *add* but this

  ,,   118*b*, line 23 from end, *for* Lord North *read* Col. North, the husband of Susan Lady North,

  ,,   120*b*, line 16, *for* Lord North *read* Col. North

  ,,   170*a*, line 7, *for* 1805 *read* 1808

  ,,   171*a*, line 24, *after* her death *add* in 1505

  ,,   171*a*, lines 27–31, *for* and probably died in 1502 . . . presumably this Richard whom Leland calls *read* and Leland calls him

  ,,   171*a*, note 71, *add* Cal. Inq. p.m. Hen. VII, iii, pp. 306–7

  ,,   171*a*, *delete* note 72

  ,,   176*b*, line 11, *for* Lady Pusey *read* Lady Lucy Pusey

  ,,   193*b*, line 3 from end, *after* In *add* 1787

  ,,   221*b*, note 7, *for* p. 222 *read* p. 15

  ,,   246*b*, lines 14 and 15 from end, *omit* In 1759

  ,,   277*b*, note 67, *for* Fenealogy *read* Genealogy

  ,,   284*b*, line 14, *for* hous *read* house

  ,,   289*b*, line 20 from end, *for* Pontefact *read* Pontefract

  ,,   325*a*, *s.v.* Cave, *delete* (d. by 1566) *and* Edw. (fl. 1580), 11;

  ,,   325*b*, *s.v.* Chilworth, *add* 116

  ,,   326*a*, *s.v.* Coombe, *add* 116

  ,,   329*b*, line 2, *delete* Sir Ric. (d. *c.* 1502), 171;

  ,,   335*c*, *s.v.* North, *add* Lady Susan, 118; Col., 118, 120;

  ,,   340*b*, *add* Stadhampton, 55

PRINTED IN GREAT BRITAIN
AT THE UNIVERSITY PRESS, OXFORD
BY VIVIAN RIDLER
PRINTER TO THE UNIVERSITY